SPECIAL EDITION
USING
Microsoft®
Office Access 2007

Roger Jennings

800 East 96th Street
Indianapolis, Indiana 46240

CONTENTS AT A GLANCE

P9-DTG-922

SPECIAL EDITION USING MICROSOFT® OFFICE ACCESS 2007

Trademarks

All terms mentioned in this book that are known to be trademarks or service marks have been appropriately capitalized. Que Publishing cannot attest to the accuracy of this information. Use of a term in this book should not be regarded as affecting the validity of any trademark or service mark.

Warning and Disclaimer

Every effort has been made to make this book as complete and as accurate as possible, but no warranty or fitness is implied. The information provided is on an "as is" basis. The author and the publisher shall have neither liability nor responsibility to any person or entity with respect to any loss or damages arising from the information contained in this book or from the use of the CD or programs accompanying it.

Bulk Sales

Que Publishing offers excellent discounts on this book when ordered in quantity for bulk purchases or special sales. For more information, please contact

U.S. Corporate and Government Sales
1-800-382-3419
corpsales@pearsontechgroup.com

For sales outside of the U.S., please contact

International Sales
international@pearsoned.com

Safari This Book Is Safari Enabled

The Safari® Enabled icon on the cover of your favorite technology book means the book is available through Safari Bookshelf. When you buy this book, you get free access to the online edition for 45 days. Safari Bookshelf is an electronic reference library that lets you easily search thousands of technical books, find code samples, download chapters, and access technical information whenever and wherever you need it.

To gain 45-day Safari Enabled access to this book

- Go to http://www.quepublishing.com/safarienabled
- Complete the brief registration form
- Enter the coupon code YIGA-QDSF-4N9H-RGFU-RENH. If you have difficulty registering on Safari Bookshelf or accessing the online edition, please email customer-service@safaribooksonline.com.

Associate Publisher
Greg Wiegand

Acquisitions Editor
Loretta Yates

Development Editor
Kevin Howard

Managing Editor
Gina Kanouse

Project Editor
George E. Nedeff

Copy Editor
Bart Reed

Senior Indexer
Cheryl Lenser

Proofreader
Leslie Joseph

Technical Editor
Scott Diamond

Publishing Coordinator
Cindy Teeters

Multimedia Developer
Dan Scherf

Book Designer
Anne Jones

Composition
Bronkella Publishing LLC

CONTENTS

I   Getting Acquainted with Access 2007

IV   Designing Forms and Reports

About the Author

Roger Jennings is an author and consultant specializing in Windows database applications. He was a technical beta tester for all nine editions of Microsoft Access, SQL Server 6.5, 7.0, 2000, and 2005, every release of Visual Basic since version 2.0, as well as Windows 3.1 and all subsequent Microsoft Windows operating systems. He also was one of the founding members of Microsoft's former Access Insiders group.

Roger's books have more than 1.25 million English copies in print and have been translated into more than 20 languages. He is the author of Que's *Special Edition Using Microsoft Access* titles for Access versions 1.0, 1.1, 2.0, 95, 97 (first and second editions), 2000, 2002, and 2003, and *Platinum Edition Using Access 97*. He also wrote Que's *Special Edition Using Windows NT Server 4*, *Special Edition Using Windows 2000 Server*, *Unveiling Windows 95*, *Access Hot Tips*, and *Discover Windows 3.1 Multimedia*. For Pearson Education's Sams imprint, he has written two editions of *Access Developer's Guide* and three editions of *Database Developers Guide with Visual Basic*. Additionally, he was the series editor for the *Roger Jennings' Database Workshop* titles.

Roger is a contributing editor for the Redmond Media Group's *Visual Studio Magazine* and a columnist for the group's .NET*Insight* newsletter. Roger co-authored with Microsoft's Greg Nelson "A Client/Server Application: From Concept to Reality," a Tech*Ed presentation and white paper on Access 2.0 that was featured in the *Microsoft Developer Network News*. An Access 2007 version of the application described in the white paper is located in the \SEUA12\Chaptr15 folder of the accompanying CD-ROM.

Roger has more than 25 years of computer-related experience, beginning with his work on the Wang 700 desktop calculator/computer. He is a principal of OakLeaf Systems, a Northern California software consulting firm, and is the author of the OakLeaf Systems blog (http://oakleafblog.blogspot.com). His OakLeaf U.S. Code of Federal Regulations (CFR) XML Web services demonstration project won the 2001 Microsoft .NET Best Award for horizontal solutions. You can contact Roger at Roger_Jennings@compuserve.com.

Dedication

This book is dedicated to my wife, Alexandra.

ACKNOWLEDGMENTS

Loretta Yates, senior acquisitions editor, made sure that I didn't fall too far behind the manuscript submission and author review schedule. Bart Reed, copy editor, fixed my typos and grammatical errors. Kevin Howard was this edition's development editor. Dan Knott and George Nedeff, project editors, worked hard to make sure that all of the components of this edition flowed through the editing process and got to their final destination on time. Media developer Dan Scherf handled production of the accompanying CD-ROM.

Technical Editor Scott B. Diamond is a seasoned database designer. During the last 20+ years, he has designed databases on a wide range of platforms, including dBASE, FoxPro, SQL/DS, Lotus Approach, Lotus Notes and, for the past 10 years, Microsoft Access. Scott has worked as an in-house and freelance consultant and support professional at firms who are among the leaders of their industries. Scott spends some of his free time answering questions at the premier site for Access support: http://www.utteraccess.com. Scott's sharp eyes alerted me to technical issues and inconsistencies in my manuscript. However, any technical errors that remain are entirely my responsibility.

Steven Gray and Rick Lievano, authors of *Roger Jennings' Database Workshop: Microsoft Transaction Server 2.0*, created the original version of the CD-ROM's Oakmont.accdb Access and Oakmont.mdf SQL Server database.

WE WANT TO HEAR FROM YOU!

As the reader of this book, *you* are our most important critic and commentator. We value your opinion and want to know what we're doing right, what we could do better, what areas you'd like to see us publish in, and any other words of wisdom you're willing to pass our way.

As an associate publisher for Que Publishing, I welcome your comments. You can email or write me directly to let me know what you did or didn't like about this book—as well as what we can do to make our books better.

Please note that I cannot help you with technical problems related to the topic of this book. We do have a User Services group, however, where I will forward specific technical questions related to the book.

When you write, please be sure to include this book's title and author as well as your name, email address, and phone number. I will carefully review your comments and share them with the author and editors who worked on the book.

Email: feedback@quepublishing.com

Mail: Greg Wiegand
Associate Publisher
Que Publishing
800 East 96th Street
Indianapolis, IN 46240 USA

READER SERVICES

Visit our website and register this book at www.quepublishing.com/register for convenient access to any updates, downloads, or errata that might be available for this book.

INTRODUCTION

In this chapter

Microsoft Office Access 2007 (version 12, called *Access 2007* in this book) is a powerful, robust, and mature 32-bit relational database management system (RDBMS) for creating desktop and client/server database applications that run under Windows Vista/XP/2000+. As a component of the Professional and higher editions of the 2007 Microsoft Office System, Access 2007 has a totally revamped user interface that's consistent with the other members of the Office 2007 suite.

Access has vanquished all desktop RDBMS rivals except Visual FoxPro and FileMaker Pro. The primary reasons for Access's success are its inclusion in Microsoft's productivity suite and its prowess as a rapid application development (RAD) environment for creating industrial-strength database applications. Another contributor to Access's market share is the capability to duplicate on the PC desktop the features of client/server relational database systems, also called *SQL databases*. Client/server RDBMSs have led the way in transferring database applications from costly mainframes and Unix servers to modestly priced networked PCs and mobile devices. Despite Access's power—and the claims of its erstwhile competitors—this desktop RDBMS is easy for nonprogrammers to use.

Microsoft's top priority for Access 2007 was to broaden the base of new users by focusing on typical tracking applications generated by a bevy of out-of-the box templates and more templates from Office Online that take maximum advantage of Access 2007's new navigation features and tabbed document presentation. Many potential Access customers view Access as difficult to master. The new Access templates enable information workers to create and begin using simple database applications in a few minutes.

The Access team devoted substantial resources to integrating Access 2007 with Windows SharePoint Services (WSS) 3.0 and Microsoft Office SharePoint Server (MOSS) 2007. WSS 3.0 is a no-charge add-on to Windows Server 2003 that lets you share Access 2007 applications from document libraries and use Access to create or edit SharePoint lists. WSS 3.0 ease of use lets workgroup members manage their own SharePoint website. MOSS 2007 builds on WSS 3.0 to create complete document management systems. WSS 3.0 and MOSS 2007 (collectively called *SharePoint* in this book) are Microsoft's primary workgroup and enterprise-level collaboration tools for knowledge workers.

Near the top of the feature list is support for Microsoft SQL Server 2005 and its freely distributable Express Edition (SSX). SSX Graphic table and query designers make creating and modifying SQL Server tables, views, functions, and stored procedures almost as easy as working with Access tables and queries. Extended properties add lookup fields, subdatasheets, input masks, and other Access accouterments to SQL Server databases. Access data projects (ADP) take advantage of Access's well-deserved reputation for rapid application development (RAD) to develop robust, production-quality multiuser database programs.

Microsoft's rallying cry for Windows Vista/XP/2003+ Server and Office 2007 is total cost of ownership (TCO). Ease of use is one of the primary requisites for reducing TCO; Access 2007 includes many wizards and other aids designed for first-time database users. If you're still using Access 97 or 2000, Access 2007 and SQLX alone justify the cost of upgrading to Office 2007. If your team has a SharePoint site, make upgrading from Access 2000 your first priority.

WHO SHOULD READ THIS BOOK

Special Edition Using Microsoft Office Access 2007 takes an approach that's different from most books about database management applications. This book doesn't begin with the creation of a database for Widgets, Inc., nor does it require you to type a list of fictional customers for the company's new WidgetPlus product line to learn the basics of Access. Instead, this book makes the following basic assumptions about your interest in Microsoft's relational database management system:

- You aren't starting from "ground zero." You now have or will have access via your computer, network, the Internet (or all three) to much of the data that you want to process with a Windows database manager. You've acquired Access and want to learn to use it more quickly and effectively. Or, you might be considering using Access as the database manager for yourself, your department or division, or your entire organization.

- Your existing data is in the form of databases, spreadsheets, mailing lists, web pages, or even plain-text files that you want to manipulate with a relational database management system. Access 2007 can process the most common varieties of these file types, as well as HTML tables, element-centric XML files, Outlook contact lists, WSS lists, and other tabular data sources.

- If you're planning to use Access 2007 as a front end to a client/server RDBMS, you'll use SQL Server 2005 Express Edition (SSX) or SQL Server 2005 as the back-end database. Access 2007 lets you replicate data between a local or workgroup copy of SSX and SQL Server 2005 on a network server.

- If your data is on a mainframe computer, you're connected to that computer by a local area network and a database gateway, or through terminal-emulation software and an adapter card. Alternatively, you download text files from the mainframe to create Access or SQL Server tables.

If some or all of your data is in the form of ASCII/ANSI text files, or files from a spreadsheet application, you need to know how to create an Access database from the beginning and import the data into Access's new .accdb file structure. If your data is in the form of dBASE, FoxPro, or Paradox files, you can import it directly to Access tables. Access 2007 also lets you link Excel workbook and conventional text files, as well as Outlook and SharePoint lists to Access databases. The capability to link files in their native format lets you synchronize the contents of your database tables with the original source documents. All these subjects receive thorough coverage in this book.

Learning relational database design and management with Access 2007 as the training tool is the quickest and easiest way to upgrade your professional skills. If you're a web designer, the expertise in client/server database techniques that you gain by working with Access data projects, SQL Server, and Data Access Pages greatly enhances your future employment prospects. Despite the prolonged downturn in the dot-com sector, there's no slack in the demand for unlocking islands of data stored in client/server databases and making the data available as usable business information on corporate intranets.

Access 2007 is a great first step in gaining XML, XML schema (XSD), and XSL transform (XSLT) skills. Most XML-related books and other training materials use trivial examples to illustrate XML and XSL(T) methodology. Access 2007 lets you dynamically generate real-world XML data, and provides a standard transform to render data in HTML format. Working with the resulting .xsl files and their embedded VBScript is the fastest way to learn practical XSLT techniques for delivering XML data as fully formatted web pages.

How This Book Is Organized

Special Edition Using Microsoft Office Access 2007 is divided into seven parts arranged in increasing levels of detail and complexity. Each division after Part I, "Getting Acquainted with Access 2007," follows the normal course of database application design, which involves the following initial steps:

- **Create tables to hold the data and establish relationships between the tables**— Once you've defined the purpose of your database application and have found and organized the data it will process, you design a table for each *entity* (also called an *object* or *subject*). For example, contacts, tasks, orders, line items, and invoices are entities. In many cases, table data will be available in files that have another format. Part II, "Learning the Fundamentals of Access Databases," covers table design and importing or linking data to tables.

- **Design queries to filter, format, sort, and display data contained in one or more tables**—Relational databases use queries for turning raw data into useful information. Part III, "Transforming Data with Queries and PivotTables," shows you how to master Access's graphic query designer and generate PivotCharts and PivotTables.

- **Prepare forms for data entry and visualization**—Although you can enter data into tables directly, providing one or more forms simplifies data entry and minimizes the potential for entering bad data. Forms with graphs, PivotTables, and PivotCharts make data understandable to your supervisors and managers. Three of the chapters in Part IV, "Designing Forms and Reports," cover this topic.

- **Lay out reports to summarize data**—Access is famous for its report designer, which lets you quickly design fully formatted reports with group subtotals and grand totals, or generate mailing labels. Part IV's remaining two chapters show you how to take best advantage of Access reports.

Parts II, III, and IV draw on the knowledge and experience that you've gained in the previous parts, so use of the book in a linear, front-to-back manner through Part IV, "Designing Forms and Reports," is recommended during the initial learning process. After you absorb the basics of working with Access databases, you progress through changing from single-user to multiuser database applications and upsizing databases to SSX or SQL Server 2005. Chapters on Access's HTML, XML, and SharePoint features follow the SQL Server chapters. Finally, you learn how to automate your applications with Access macros and Visual Basic for Applications (VBA) code.

As you progress through the chapters in this book, you create a model of an Access application called Human Resources Actions. In Chapter 5, "Working with Access Databases and Tables," you create the HR Actions table. In the following chapters, you add new features to the HR Actions application. Be sure to perform the sample exercises for the HR Actions application each time you encounter them because succeeding examples build on your previous work. (The accompanying CD-ROM contains sample databases at each stage of the process).

The seven parts of *Special Edition Using Microsoft Office Access 2007* and the topics that they cover are described in the following sections.

PART I: GETTING ACQUAINTED WITH ACCESS 2007

The chapters in Part I introduce you to Access and many of the unique features that make Access 2007 the premier desktop database management system.

- Chapter 1, "Access 2007 for Access 200x Users: What's New," provides a summary of the most important new features of Access 2007 and a detailed description of each addition and improvement. Much of this chapter's content is of interest primarily to readers who now use Access 2000, 2002, or 2003 because there are major changes between these versions and Access 2007. Readers new to Access, however, benefit from the explanations of why many of these new features are significant in everyday Access 2007 use. Chapter 1 includes detailed instructions for installing SQL Server 2005 Express.

- In Chapter 2, "Building Simple Tracking Applications," you create a database from an out-of-the-box database template included with Access 2007. You gain a basic understanding of the standard data-related objects of Access, including tables, queries, forms, reports, and macros. Chapter 2 also introduces you to automating Access operations with Access macros.

- Chapter 3, "Navigating the New Access User Interface," shows you how to take best advantage of Access 2007's revolutionary ribbon user interface by explaining its command button, menu, and context menu choices and then showing how they relate to the structure of the Access object model. Chapter 3 also shows you how to use Access 2007's new and improved online help system.

PART II: LEARNING THE FUNDAMENTALS OF ACCESS DATABASES

Part II is devoted to understanding the design principles of relational databases, creating new Access tables, adding and editing table data, and integrating Access tables with other sources of data. Most of the techniques that you learn in Part II also apply to SQL Server tables.

- Chapter 4, "Exploring Relational Database Theory and Practice," describes the process that you use to create relational database tables from real-world data—a technique called *normalizing the database structure*. The chapter also introduces you to the concepts of key fields, primary keys, data integrity, and views of tables that contain related data.

- Chapter 5, "Working with Access Databases and Tables," delves into the details of Access desktop database tables, shows you how to create tables, and explains how to choose the optimum data types from the many new types that Access offers. Chapter 5 explains how to use subdatasheets and lookup tables to display and edit records in related tables. The chapter also explains how to use the Database Documentor tool included with Access 2007 to create a data dictionary that fully identifies each object in your database.

- Chapter 6, "Entering, Editing, and Validating Access Table Data," describes how to add new records to tables, enter data in the new records, and edit data in existing records. Using keyboard shortcuts instead of the mouse for editing speeds manual data entry. Adding input masks and data validation rules minimizes the chance for typographic errors when entering new data.

- Chapter 7, "Sorting, Finding, and Filtering Data," shows you how to arrange the data in tables to suit your needs and to limit the data displayed to only that information you want. You learn how to use Find and Replace to search for and alter multiple instances of data in the fields of tables. Chapter 7 further describes how to make best use of the Filter by Form and Filter by Selection features of Access 2007.

- Chapter 8, "Linking, Importing, and Exporting Tables," explains how to import and export files of other database managers, spreadsheet applications, and text files downloaded from mainframe or Unix database servers or the Internet. You also learn how to use the Access Mail Merge Wizard to create form letters from data stored in Access tables.

PART III: TRANSFORMING DATA WITH QUERIES AND PIVOTTABLES

The chapters in Part III explain how to create Access queries to select the way that you view data contained in tables and how to take advantage of Access's relational database structure to link multiple tables with joins. Part III also covers Access 2007's PivotTable and PivotChart views of query result sets.

- Chapter 9, "Designing Queries for Access Databases," starts with simple queries you create with Access's graphical Query Design window. You learn how to choose the fields of the tables included in your query and return query result sets from these tables. Examples of Access SQL generated by the queries you design let you learn SQL "by osmosis." Chapter 9 shows you how to use the Simple Query Wizard to simplify the design process.

- Chapter 10, "Understanding Access Operators and Expressions," introduces you to the operators and expressions that you need to create queries that provide a meaningful result. Most Access operators and expressions are the same as those that you use in VBA programs. You use the Immediate window of the Office 2007 VBA editor to evaluate the expressions you write.

- In Chapter 11, "Creating Multitable and Crosstab Queries," you create relations between tables, called *joins*, and learn how to add criteria to queries so that the query result set includes only records that you want. Chapter 11 also takes you through the process of designing powerful crosstab queries to summarize data and to present information in a format similar to that of worksheets.

■ Chapter 12, "Working with PivotTable and PivotChart Views," shows you how to manipulate data from multitable queries in the OWC's PivotTable control and then display the results in PivotChart controls. The query design and PivotTable/PivotChart techniques that you learn here also apply to PivotTables and PivotCharts that you embed in Access forms and Data Access Pages.

■ Chapter 13, "Creating and Updating Access Tables with Action Queries," shows you how to develop action queries that update the tables underlying append, delete, update, and make-table queries. Chapter 13 also covers Access 2007's advanced referential integrity features, including cascading updates and cascading deletions.

Part IV: Designing Forms and Reports

The chapters in Part IV introduce you to the primary application objects of Access. (Tables and queries are considered database objects.) Forms make your Access applications come alive with the control objects that you add from the Form Tools, Design ribbon, and Report Tools. Access's full-featured report generator lets you print fully formatted reports, export or mail reports as PDF or XPS (XML Paper Specification) files, and save reports to files that you can process in Excel 2007 or Word 2007.

■ Chapter 14, "Creating and Using Basic Access Forms," shows you how to use Access's Form Wizards to create simple forms and subforms that you can modify to suit your particular needs. Chapter 14 introduces you to the Subform Builder Wizard that uses drag-and-drop techniques to automatically create subforms for you.

■ Chapter 15, "Designing Custom Multitable Forms," shows you how to design custom forms for viewing and entering your own data with Access's advanced form design tools.

■ Chapter 16, "Working with Simple Reports and Mailing Labels," describes how to design and print basic reports with Access's Report Wizard, and how to print preformatted mailing labels by using the Mailing Label Wizard.

■ Chapter 17, "Preparing Advanced Reports," describes how to use more sophisticated sorting and grouping techniques, as well as subreports, to obtain a result that exactly meets your detail and summary data-reporting requirements. Chapter 17 also covers the technology that lets you distribute Access reports as Outlook email attachments.

■ In Chapter 18, "Adding Graphs, PivotCharts, and PivotTables," you first learn to use the OLE-based Chart Wizard to create data-bound graphs and charts based on Access crosstab queries. PivotCharts are destined to replace conventional Access Charts, so Chapter 18 builds on Chapter 12 by showing you how to add bound PivotTables and PivotCharts whose data is supplied by the form's data source.

PART V: MOVING TO NETWORKED MULTIUSER APPLICATIONS

From Access 2000 on, SQL Server has been the preferred back-end data source for secure, robust, and reliable Access multiuser applications. You can link SQL Server tables to a conventional Access .accdb front-end file, but a direct connection to an Access data project (.adp) front end is the better approach. This is especially true because Access 2007 no longer supports user-level (also called *workgroup*) security. If you're new to client/server RDBMSs, Access 2007 is the ideal learning tool for upgrading your database design and management skills to the requirements of today's job market.

- Chapter 19, "Linking Access Front Ends to Access and Client/Server Tables," explains how to use the Upsizing Wizard to migrate from single-file or split (front-end/back-end) Access applications to SQL Server back-end databases. Retaining the front-end queries and application objects in an Access (.accdb) file, and using the SQL Server ODBC driver to connect to the server database, minimizes application changes required to take advantage of client/server technology. This chapter also explains how to secure Access databases with file system Access Control Lists (ACLs), because Access 2007 supports workgroup information (.mdw) files only for earlier version's .mdb files.

- Chapter 20, "Exploring Access Data Projects and SQL Server 2005," introduces you to Access data projects and SSX. The chapter shows you how to use Access 2007's built-in project designer to create and modify SQL Server tables, views, functions, and stored procedures. Backing up, restoring, copying, and moving SQL Server databases is covered in detail. You also learn how to link other databases, including Access .accdb files, with OLE DB data providers and how to secure ADP front ends as .ade files.

- Chapter 21, "Moving from Access Queries to Transact-SQL," provides a formal introduction to ANSI-92 SQL and explains how the Access and Transact-SQL dialects differ. Special emphasis is given to queries that you can't create in the graphical project designer—such as UNION queries and subqueries—and enabling transactions in stored procedures that update two or more tables.

- Chapter 22, "Upsizing Access Applications to Access Data Projects," explains how to use the Upsizing Wizard to convert existing Access applications directly to Access data project front ends and SQL Server tables, views, functions, and stored procedures. The wizard can't upsize Access crosstab queries, so the chapter explains how to write T-SQL PIVOT queries to emulate Access crosstab queries.

PART VI: COLLABORATING WITH ACCESS DATA

The chapters in Part VI explain how to take advantage of Access's new XML features and the upgraded Data Access Pages technology of Access 2002.

- Chapter 23, "Importing and Exporting Web Pages," shows you how to generate Access tables from HTML tables and lists in web pages, optimize HTML files to ensure proper importation, and export static or dynamic HTML pages. The chapter also explains how to gather data by email with Outlook 2007 HTML forms and automatically add the data acquired to the appropriate table.

- Chapter 24, "Integrating with XML and InfoPath 2007," explains the role of XML in database applications and how Access 2007's ReportML XML schema describes Access objects as an XML data document. The chapter shows you how to take advantage of the Report2HTML4.xsl XML transform to generate HTML pages from tables and queries with the Save As XML option. You learn how to modify Access's standard XSLT files to format the resulting tables and add images to the tables. Exporting conventional Access reports as fully formatted static and live web reports also receives detailed coverage. The chapter also explains the role of InfoPath 2007 as an alternative to Outlook 2007 HTML forms for gathering data.

- Chapter 25, "Collaborating with Windows SharePoint Services," introduces you to WSS 3.0 and its data-related features. You learn to export Access or SQL Server tables to WSS 3.0 lists, and how to link the lists to Access tables (and vice versa). You also learn to take linked SharePoint lists offline, modify them while disconnected, reconnect to SharePoint, and synchronize your's and others' changes. Finally, the chapter shows you how to publish Access applications to SharePoint document libraries and share the published .accdb files with multiple collaborators.

Part VII: Programming and Converting Access Applications

The chapters in Part VII assume that you have no programming experience in any language. These chapters explain the principles of writing Access macros and VBA programming code. They also show you how to apply these principles to automate Access applications and use VBA to work directly with ADO `Recordset` objects. Part VII also supplies tips for converting Access 97 and 200x applications to Access 2007.

- Chapter 26, "Automating Access Applications with Macros 2007," is an introduction to Access macros, which Microsoft resurrected from their previously deprecated status in Access 97 and later. You learn how to write simple standalone or embedded macros to run a query and open a form or report when you click a button on a form.

- Chapter 27, "Learning Visual Basic for Applications," introduces you to the VBA language with emphasis on using VBA to automate your Access front ends. The chapter describes how to write VBA code to create user-defined functions stored in modules and to write simple procedures that you activate directly from events.

- Chapter 28, "Handling Events with VBA and Macros," describes how to use embedded macros and VBA event-handling subprocedures in class modules. This chapter explains the events triggered by Access form, report, and control objects, and tells you how to use macro actions or methods of the `DoCmd` object to respond to events, such as loading or activating a form.

- Chapter 29, "Programming Combo and List Boxes," shows you how to take maximum advantage of Access 2007's unique combo and list boxes in decision-support applications. This chapter explains the VBA coding techniques for loading combo box lists and populating text and list boxes based on your combo box selections.

- Chapter 30, "Understanding Data Access Objects, OLE DB, and ADO," explains Microsoft's approach to Access and SQL Server data connectivity in Office applications, and describes how to program Data Access Objects (DAO) and ActiveX Data Objects (DAO), as well as tells how to decide on DAO or ADO for your new Access 2007 projects.

- Chapter 31, "Upgrading 2000X Applications to Access 2007," tells you what changes you need to make when you convert your current 32-bit Access database applications and data access pages to Access 2007.

GLOSSARY

The glossary presents a descriptive list of the terms, abbreviations, and acronyms used in this book that you might not be familiar with and that can't be found in commonly used dictionaries.

THE ACCOMPANYING CD-ROM

 The CD-ROM that accompanies this book includes Access database files containing tables, queries, forms, reports, HTML pages, VBA, and special files to complement design examples, and it shows you the expected result. An icon identifies sections that point to chapter files included on the accompanying CD-ROM.

A very large (20MB) database named Oakmont.accdb is included for optional use with some of the examples in this book. Oakmont University is a fictional institution in Texas with 30,000 students and 2,300 employees. Databases with a large number of records in their tables are useful when designing applications to optimize performance, so the CD-ROM also includes a version of the Northwind.accdb database, NwindXL19.accdb, that has 21,096 records in the Orders table and 193,280 Order Details records.

Installing the sample files on the accompanying CD-ROM to your \SEUA12 folder requires about 200MB of free disk space.

HOW THIS BOOK IS DESIGNED

The following special features are included in this book to assist readers.

 If you've never used a database management application, you're provided with quick-start examples to gain confidence and experience while using Access with the Northwind Traders sample database. Like Access, this book uses the *tabula rasa* approach: Each major topic begins with the assumption that you have no prior experience with the subject. Therefore, when a command button on a ribbon, such as Design view, is used, its icon is displayed in the margin.

TIP

Tips describe shortcuts and alternative approaches to gaining an objective. These tips are based on the experience the author has gained during more than seven years of testing successive alpha and beta versions of Access and Microsoft Office Developer (MOD).

NOTE

Notes offer advice to help you use Access, describe differences between various versions of Access, and explain the few remaining anomalies that you find in Access 2007.

Access SQL

The book provides numerous examples of Access SQL statements for queries and Transact-SQL statements for views, functions, and stored procedures.

XML

Part VI of this book includes sample XML, XSL, and XML Schema documents (XSD) and examples of altering XSL Transforms (XSLT) to modify the presentation of HTML documents.

CAUTION

Cautions are provided when an action can lead to an unexpected or unpredictable result, including loss of data; the text provides an explanation of how you can avoid such a result.

 Features that are new or that have been modified in Access 2007 are indicated by the 2007 icon in the margin, unless the change is only cosmetic. Where the changes are extensive and apply to an entire section of a chapter, the icon appears to the left or right of the section head.

 References to resources available on the Internet—such as World Wide Web Consortium (W3C) Recommendations—are identified by the Web icon.

Cross-references to specific sections in other chapters follow the material that they pertain to, as in the following sample reference:

→ For more information, **see** "A Section in Another Chapter," **p. XXX**.

Most chapters include a "Troubleshooting" section at the end of the tutorial and reference contents. The elements of this section help you solve specific problems—common and uncommon—that you might run into when creating applications that use specific Access features or techniques.

At the end of each chapter is an "In the Real World" section that discusses the relevance of the chapter's content to the realm of production databases, the Internet, and other current computer-related topics that affect Access users and developers. The opinion-editorial (op-ed) style of many of the "In the Real World" sections reflects the author's view of the benefits—or drawbacks—of new Access features and related Microsoft technologies, based on experience with production Access applications installed by several Fortune 500 corporations.

TYPOGRAPHIC CONVENTIONS USED IN THIS BOOK

This book uses various typesetting styles to distinguish between explanatory and instructional text, text that you enter in dialogs (set in **bold**), and text that you enter in code-editing windows (set in `monospace` type).

KEY COMBINATIONS, MENU CHOICES, AND FILENAMES

Key combinations that you use to perform Windows operations are indicated by joining the keys with a plus sign: Alt+F4, for example. In cases when you must press and release a key, and then press another key, such as Alt to activate KeyTips, the keys are separated by a comma without an intervening space: Alt,H. Conventional shortcut key combinations appear as Ctrl+*Key*.

Sequences of individual menu items are separated by a comma: Edit, Cut.

Most file and folder names are initial-letter-capitalized in the text and headings of this book to conform with 32-bit Windows filenaming conventions and the appearance of filenames in Windows Explorer.

SQL STATEMENTS AND KEYWORDS IN OTHER LANGUAGES

SQL statements and code examples are set in a special `monospace` font. Keywords of SQL statements, such as `SELECT`, are set in all uppercase. Ellipses (…) indicate intervening programming code that isn't shown in the text or examples.

Square brackets in `monospace` type (`[ ]`) that appear within Access SQL statements don't indicate optional items, as they do in syntax descriptions. In this case, the square brackets are used instead of quotation marks to frame a literal string or to allow use of a table and field names, such as `[Order Details]`, that include embedded spaces or special punctuation, or field names that are identical to reserved words in VBA.

TYPOGRAPHIC CONVENTIONS USED FOR VBA

This book uses a special set of typographic conventions for references to Visual Basic for Applications keywords in the presentation of VBA examples:

- Monospace type is used for all examples of VBA code, as in the following statement:

```
Dim NewArray ( ) As Long
ReDim NewArray (9, 9, 9)
```

- `Monospace` type also is used when referring to names of properties of Access database objects, such as `FormName.Width`. The captions for text boxes and drop-down lists in which you enter values of properties, such as Source Connect String, are set in this book's regular textual font.

- **`Bold monospace`** type is used for all VBA reserved words and type-declaration symbols, as shown in the preceding example. Standard function names in VBA also are set in **`bold monospace`** type so that reserved words, standard function names, and reserved symbols stand out from variable and function names and values that you assign to variables.

- *`Italic monospace`* type indicates a replaceable item, as in
  `Dim` *`DataItem`* **`As String`**

- ***`Bold italic monospace`*** type indicates a replaceable reserved word, such as a data type, as in
  `Dim` *`DataItem`* **`As`** ***`DataType`***

  `DataItem` is replaced by a keyword corresponding to the desired VBA data type, such as **`String`** or **`Variant`**.

- An ellipsis (…) substitutes for code not shown in syntax and code examples, as in
  `If…Then…Else…End If`

- Braces ({}) enclosing two or more identifiers separated by the pipe symbol (¦) indicate that you must choose one of these identifiers, as in
  `Do {While¦Until}…Loop`

  In this case, you must use the **`While`** or **`Until`** reserved word in your statement, but not the braces or the pipe character.

- Three-letter prefixes to variable names indicate the VBA data type of the variable, such as `bln` for **`Boolean`**, `str` for **`String`**, and `lng` for **`Long`** (integer).

- Square brackets (`[]`) enclosing an identifier indicate that the identifier is optional, as in
  `Set` `tblName` = `dbName`**`.OpenTable(`**`strTableName`**`[, `**`blnExclusive`**`])`**

  Here, the `blnExclusive` flag, if set to **`True`**, opens the table specified by `strTableName` for exclusive use. `blnExclusive` is an optional argument. Don't include the brackets in any code that you type.

TYPOGRAPHIC CONVENTIONS USED FOR VBSCRIPT

The few Visual Basic Scripting Edition (VBScript) examples in this book use lowercase `monospace` type for reserved words, a practice that originated in ECMAScript (JavaScript or Microsoft JScript). Variables are in mixed case with a data type prefix, despite the lack of VBScript support for data types other than **`Variant`**. Object, property, and method names included in the World Wide Web Consortium (W3C) Document Object Model (DOM) standard also are in lowercase.

SYSTEM REQUIREMENTS FOR ACCESS 2007

Access 2007 is a very resource-intensive application, as are all other Office 2007 members, including InfoPath 2007. You'll find execution of Access applications on Pentium PCs slower than 500MHz running Windows XP SP2 to be impaired, at best. A 667+ MHz Pentium III delivers acceptable performance, but a 1GHz x86 or similar AMD-powered machine is a more realistic minimum. The Windows Vista Capable PC minimum—"A modern processor (at least 800MHz)"—isn't likely to provide generally accepted performance standards.

Microsoft's somewhat optimistic minimum RAM recommendations for Microsoft Office Professional 2007 running under Windows XP (SP2) or Windows 2000 Professional (SP3) is 256MB. However, the Windows Vista Capable PC minimum is 512MB.

The preceding recommendations don't take into account the RAM required to run SQL Server 2005. Double the realistic RAM recommendations to 1GB to achieve acceptable performance with SSX. All the examples of this book were created and tested under Windows XP Professional (SP2) or Windows Vista, or Windows Server 2003 running on a 2.3GHz Intel x86 computer with 2GB RAM.

Standard installation of Office Professional 2007—without SSX, SQL Server Management Studio, or SQL Server Books Online—requires 1GB of free disk space. Add another 100MB for SQL Server, and 50MB each for InfoPath and Windows SharePoint Services. From a practical standpoint, you need 1.5GB or more of free disk space to use Office 2007 effectively. Add another 200MB for the sample files on the accompanying CD-ROM.

OTHER SOURCES OF INFORMATION FOR ACCESS

Relational database design and SQL, discussed in Chapters 4 and 21, are the subject of myriad guides and texts covering one or both of these topics. Articles in database-related periodicals in print form or on the Internet provide up-to-date assistance in using Access 2007. The following sections provide a bibliography of database-related books and periodicals, as well as a brief description of websites and newsgroups of interest to Access users.

BOOKS

The following books complement the content of this book by providing detailed coverage of database design techniques, Structured Query Language, VBA database programming, SQL Server 2000, XML, and HTML:

- *Database Design for Mere Mortals, Second Edition*, by Michael J. Hernandez (Addison-Wesley, ISBN 0-201-75284-0), is a comprehensive guide to sound relational database design techniques for developing productive desktop and client/server databases. The book is platform-agnostic, but the methods that you learn are especially effective for Access and SQL Server database design.

■ *Understanding the New SQL: A Complete Guide*, by Jim Melton and Alan R. Simpson (Morgan Kaufmann Publishers, ISBN 1-55860-245-3), describes the history and implementation of the American National Standards Institute's X3.135.1-1992 standard for Structured Query Language, SQL-92, on which Access SQL is based. Melton was the editor of the ANSI SQL-92 standard, which consists of more than 500 pages of fine print.

NOTE

> *SQL: 1999 – Understanding Relational Language Components*, by Jim Melton and Alan R. Simpson (Morgan Kaufmann Publishers, ISBN 1-55860-456-1, 2001), is a newer book that covers SQL-99. However, neither Access nor SQLX supports the elements added to SQL-92 by SQL-99.

■ *SQL Queries for Mere Mortals*, by Michael J. Hernandez and John L. Viescas (Addison-Wesley, ISBN 0-201-43336-2), is your best source for learning to write effective SELECT queries in any SQL dialect. The book includes detailed coverage of JOIN, UNION, GROUP BY, HAVING, and subquery syntax.

■ *Special Edition Using XML, Second Edition*, by David Gulbrandsen, et al. (Que, ISBN 0-7897-2748-X), describes the technologies and standards that make up XML. It includes chapters that cover modeling with XML Schema, managing namespaces, using XSL transformations, and applying styles with XSL Formatting Objects and Cascading Style Sheets.

■ *Special Edition Using HTML and XHTML*, by Molly E. Holzschlag (Que, ISBN 0-7897-2713-5), is an indispensable tutorial and reference for learning the basics of HTML and gaining a full understanding of Dynamic HTML (DHTML), Cascading Style Sheets (CSS), and XHTML.

PERIODICALS

The following magazine and newsletter cover Access topics:

■ *Advisor Guide to Microsoft Access*, published by Advisor Media, Inc., is a magazine intended to serve Access users and developers and is published several times a year. Online sample databases, utilities, and other software tools for Access supplement your subscription (http://msaccess.advisorguide.com/).

■ *Smart Access* is a monthly newsletter of Pinnacle Publishing, Inc., which publishes several other database-related newsletters. *Smart Access* is directed primarily to developers and Access power users. This newsletter tends toward advanced topics, such as creating libraries and using the Windows API with VBA (http://www.pinpub.com/spec_access.htm).

INTERNET

Microsoft's Office Online and Access Developer Portal websites now are the primary source of new and updated information for Access users and developers. Following are the primary websites and newsgroups for Access 2007 users and developers:

- Microsoft's Access page, http://office.microsoft.com/en-us/access/default.aspx, is the jumping-off point for U.S. Access users. It includes links to all related Access 2007 and earlier pages on the Microsoft website.

- Microsoft's Access Developer Portal page, http://msdn2.microsoft.com/en-us/office/aa905400.aspx, provides links to information of particular interest to the Access developer community.

- The Access Team blog (http://blogs.msdn.com/access/), subtitled "A discussion of what's new in Access 2007," is a running source of information on the new features in Access 2007.

- Microsoft's online support page for 2007 Microsoft Office Suites, http://support.microsoft.com/ph/8753, provides links to Microsoft Knowledge Base pages for all its products. For other support options, go to http://www.microsoft.com/support/.

- Office Watch has an Access page at http://office-watch.com/access/index.asp. Peter Deegan and Helen Feddema offer the *Access Watch (AW)* newsletter.

- Microsoft's msnews.microsoft.com news server offers various Access-related newsgroups at microsoft.public.access.*subject*. When this book was written, there were 28 Access subject areas.

- The Usenet comp.databases.ms-access newsgroup is an active community of Access users and developers.

GETTING ACQUAINTED WITH ACCESS 2007

CHAPTER 1

ACCESS 2007 FOR ACCESS 200x USERS: WHAT'S NEW

In this chapter

Access 1.0, 1.1, and 2.0 were very successful standalone desktop database platforms. The first Access team consisted of highly skilled development, marketing, and management personnel who were devoted entirely to making Access the premier desktop relational database management system (RDBMS) for Windows. Access, which reports say cost $60 million to develop, sold for US$99 and, according to Jim Gray of Microsoft Research, was generating revenue of about US$300 million per year by February 1994 or earlier.

Microsoft created Office 95 Professional by adding Access to Office 95 Standard's Word, Excel, PowerPoint, and Schedule+ applications, and adding US$100 to the retail price. Access gained a few new features with each subsequent release, but generally suffered from not-so-benign neglect by Office management. Access 2003, for example, delivered only minor, incremental improvements over Access 2002.

The ninth iteration of Microsoft Access finally has received the resources it deserves from the Microsoft Office 2007 System organization. According to Erik Rucker, Group Program Manager for Access, the development team for Access 2007 was about seven times as large as that for Access 2003. The overwhelming changes to its user interface represent only a fraction of the new and improved features of Access 2007.

NOTE

> Access 2007 no longer supports many less widely used Access features, such as Data Access Pages and user-level security for the new .accdb and .accde file formats.

→ To learn what elements of earlier versions Access 2007 drops, **see** "Features Missing from Access 2007," **p. 59**.

WHAT'S NEW IN MICROSOFT OFFICE ACCESS 2007: AN OVERVIEW

Microsoft's primary goals for Access 2007 are to improve usability for new users and increase productivity for experienced users and developers. Following are brief descriptions of the new features of Access 2007:

- **The Office 2007 ribbon user interface**—The objective of the new ribbon UI is to make features previously hidden in toolbars or hierarchical menus more discoverable by users (see Figure 1.1). On the other hand, customizing the ribbon is a much more challenging process than that for toolbars and menu bars. Whether the new Office user interface truly contributes to Microsoft's usability and productivity goals for Access 2007 remains to be seen. Chapter 3, "Navigating the New Access User Interface," covers the ribbon UI in detail.

Figure 1.1
The ribbon UI occupies a substantial amount of space at the top of Access's main window, but you can hide or show it by pressing Ctrl+F1.

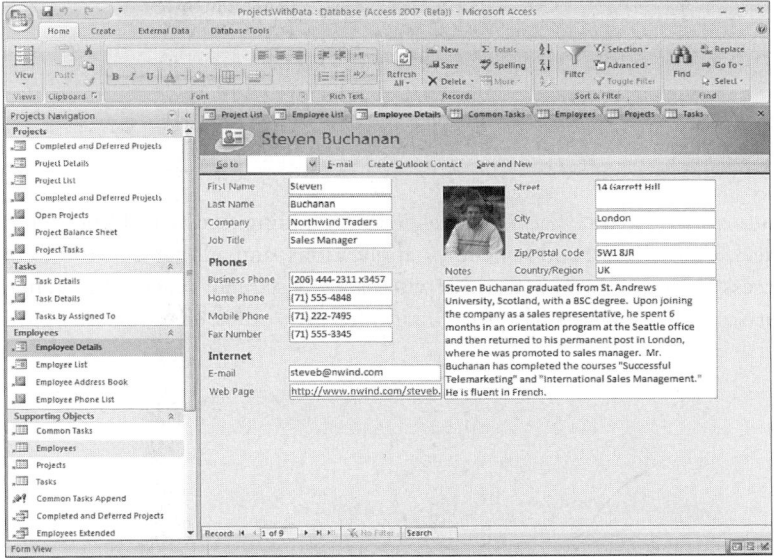

- **Security, trusted locations, packages, and certificates**—Access 2003 required signed VBA code to avoid security warnings when opening an Access database or data project. Access 2007 lets users avoid security warnings by specifying *trusted locations* (folders) for .accdb and .adp files. Developers can package and sign .accdb (but not .adp) files with a code-signing certificate to eliminate security warnings in nontrusted locations.

- **Tabbed documents and modal dialogs**—Access traditionally has used the Multiple Document Interface (MDI, or overlapping windows). Access 2007 implements an optional Single Document Interface (SDI) with a main tabbed document window (refer to Figure 1.1). Access 2007 templates use tabbed documents for lists and modal dialogs (pop-up forms) for details (data entry), as shown in Figure 1.2. Tabbed documents are likely to be the favorite new feature for users *and* developers. In Chapter 2, "Building Simple Tracking Applications," you create tabbed documents and modal dialogs from Access templates downloaded from Microsoft Office Online.

- **The Navigation pane**—You can customize the retractable Outlook 2007–style Navigation pane at the left of Access's main window to group Access database objects by function (refer to Figure 1.1), object type, creation date, or modified date. The combination of tabbed documents and the Navigation pane makes the Switchboard Manager obsolete for most applications.

- **Changes to tables and the Access Database Engine**—Access has used the Jet (Joint Engine Technology) database engine since version 1.1. Access 2007 has its own version of Jet called the *Microsoft Office Access 2007 database engine*, which supports the new Attachment data type, multivalued lookup fields (MVLFs), and HTML formatting of Memo fields (refer to Figure 1.2). Access databases use .accdb or .accde instead of .mdb or .mde as their file extension.

Figure 1.2
Access 2007 templates create modal dialogs for detailed data entry and editing tasks. Memo fields support basic HTML (rich text) formatting with a pop-up floating menu called a *mini toolbar*.

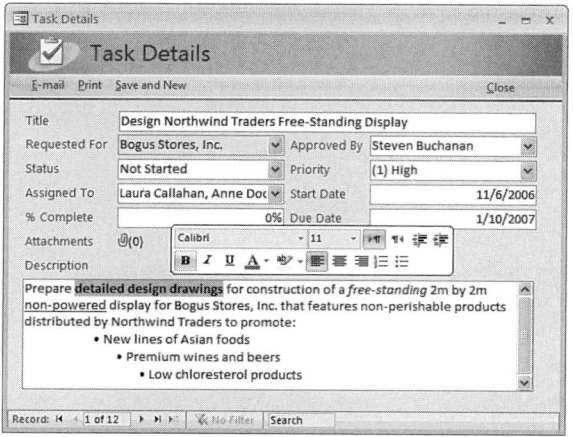

- **Application development by templates**—Microsoft encourages users to customize starter templates for tracking applications. Access 2007 comes with 10 "out-of-the-box" templates for tracking assets, contacts, events, faculties, issues, projects, sales, students, and tasks. Microsoft Office Online offers several more specialized templates. Templates are great for familiarizing new users with the look and feel of basic Access applications (see Figure 1.3). Chapter 2 shows you how to customize templates to your tracking needs.

Figure 1.3
The default Getting Started with Microsoft Office Access dialog opens with an illustrated list of featured templates and links to Office Online's Template pages for additional selections. Alternatively, you can create a new empty database or Access project.

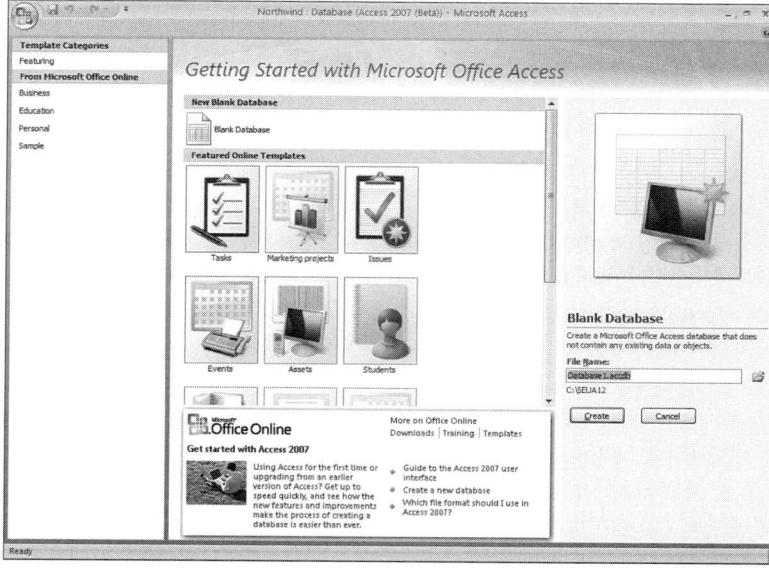

■ **New form and report features**—The Create ribbon lets you auto-generate new stacked layout, split, or multiple-items (list) forms based on the table or query you select. Layout view for forms and reports lets you arrange and size controls containing live data. Stacked and tabular layouts let you move multiple controls as a group (see Figure 1.4). You also can anchor controls for resizable forms. The chapters of Section IV, "Designing Forms and Reports," deliver detailed instructions for modifying standard form and report types as well as customizing them for specific applications.

Figure 1.4
Clicking the Split Form button with a table or query selected generates a form with the Datasheet on the top, bottom, or either side. Selecting a Datasheet row displays columns in the stacked layout shown below. This figure illustrates Layout view with a single stack selected for moving.

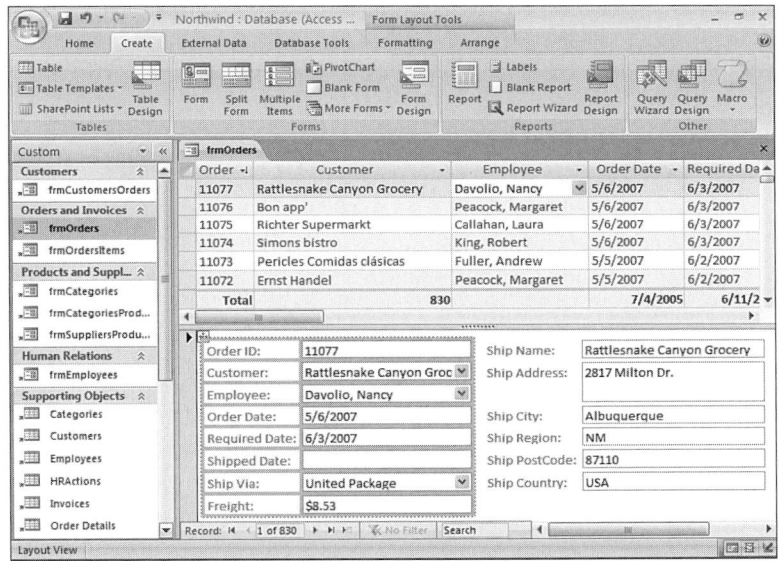

■ **Access macros redux**—Access macros have been deprecated in favor of VBA programming code since Access 97. Now Microsoft is encouraging use of macros by letting you embed macro sheets in forms and reports. Embedded macros follow the same pattern as code in Class Modules behind forms. Macros now respond to an On Error event for limited error-handling capability. Macros enable simple application automation without requiring the .accdb file to be placed in a trusted location or having a signed .accde file from a package. Chapter 26, "Automating Access Applications with Macros 2007," shows you how to respond to events with macros.

■ **Collaboration with SharePoint**—Microsoft downplays Access 2007/SQL Server projects for client/server applications in favor of linking Access tables to or from SharePoint lists and sharing .accdb files from SharePoint Document Libraries. Interest in manipulating relational data in a nonrelational, Web-based environment probably will interest only organizations that have a substantial commitment to a Windows SharePoint Services (WSS) 3.0 or Microsoft Office SharePoint Server (MOSS) 2007 infrastructure. Chapter 25, "Collaborating with Windows SharePoint Services," introduces you to linking or moving tables to WSS 3.0 or MOSS 2007.

The sections that follow expand on the brief descriptions in the preceding list and provide cross-references to detailed coverage of new features in later chapters.

TIP

> The remainder of this chapter assumes familiarity with Access 2000, 2002, or 2003. If you haven't used an earlier Access version, you might want to skip to the "SQL Server 2005 Express Edition SP2 Setup" section near the end of this chapter. The succeeding chapters of this book cover in detail all the material presented in this chapter, with the exception of initial SQL Server 2005 Express Edition setup.

THE OFFICE 2007 RIBBON USER INTERFACE

Microsoft developed the ribbon UI to make features in Office System applications easier for users to discover. It's a common estimate that Word and Excel customers use only 10% or so of the applications' available features. Microsoft's assumption—warranted or not—is that disuse is due to difficulty of discovery with toolbars, hierarchical menus, or task panes and that customers would take advantage of more arcane features if they knew the features were present and could find commands to use them.

It's doubtful if Access customers and developers incurred this problem because there is no way that one can create a usable Access application without taking advantage of a substantially larger percentage of Access's available features. Like it or not, the ribbon UI and its hierarchy of grouped buttons replace toolbar buttons, task panes, and the one or two upper levels of hierarchical menus. Many multilevel galleries open from buttons (see Figure 1.5). Hierarchical context menus remain essential to accomplish common tasks efficiently (see Figure 1.6).

Figure 1.5
Hierarchical menus still have their place with ribbons. Subdatasheet is a two-level hierarchy at full 1024×768 resolution, but increases to a three-level hierarchy as you decrease Access's window width.

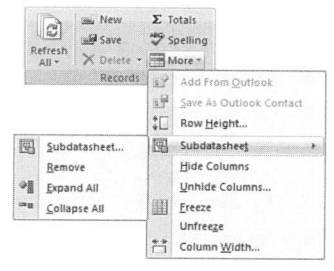
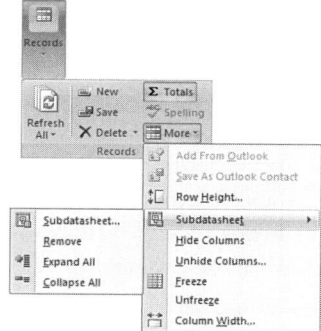

TIP

> Press Ctrl+F1 to toggle visibility of the ribbon body but not the tabs. When you hide the body, clicking a tab overlays the main window with the ribbon body.

Figure 1.6
Access context menus emulate ribbon galleries, as demonstrated by the context menu for a form item in the Navigation Pane.

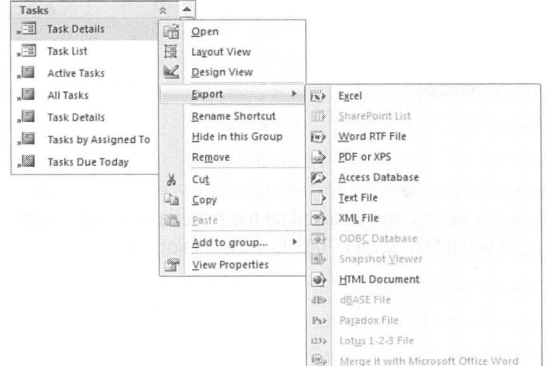

Access 2007's Main Ribbons

Access has four main ribbons, which Microsoft refers to as *command tabs*. Press Alt to display the shortcut keys (called *KeyTips*) for each main ribbon, the Office button, and Quick Access Toolbar (1...*n*), as shown in Figure 1.7 (top). Pressing Alt+*Key* has the same effect as clicking the button or tab. Pressing Alt again displays the second-level shortcut keys (see Figure 1.7 center and bottom). Access 2007 preserves most shortcut-key sequences of Access 2003 and earlier.

Figure 1.7
The top Home half-ribbon shows shortcut-key combinations to activate one of the four main ribbons, the Office button, or the Quick Access Toolbar.

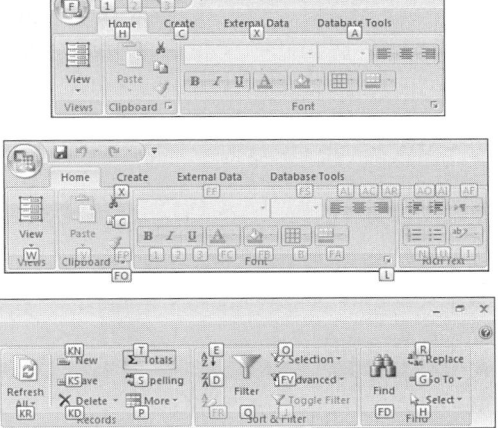

Following are brief descriptions of the primary purposes of each main ribbon:

- **Home**—Lets you select Datasheet, Form, Report, Layout, or Design view; perform Clipboard operations; specify font properties; format memo fields with HTML; and refresh, add, delete, save, sort, filter, find and spell-check records (see Figure 1.8).

Figure 1.8
Drop-down galleries let you choose extended options for Views, Clipboard, Font, Rich Text, Sort & Filter, and Find groups.

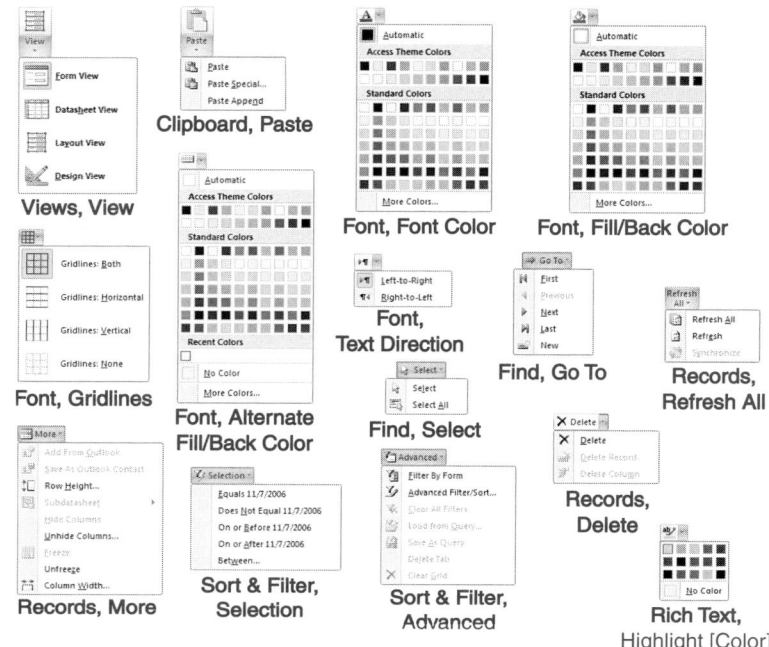

- **Create**—Lets you create a new empty table or a table from a template in Datasheet view, or an empty table in Design view; create a SharePoint list and a table that links to the list; create a form or report bound to a table or query that's selected in the Navigation pane; and create a new query, macro, module, or class module (see Figure 1.9).

Figure 1.9
The Create ribbon's buttons and drop-down galleries enable adding new Access objects to your database.

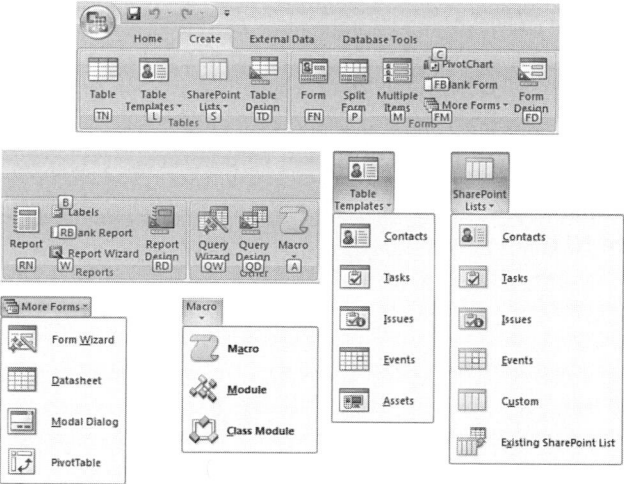

- **External Data**—Lets you import, link, or export external data in a wide variety of formats; collect or update data via emailed HTML forms; save import or export specifications; work with SharePoint lists while offline; and move select objects or the entire database to a SharePoint site (see Figure 1.10).

Figure 1.10
The External Data ribbon has galleries for choosing the Import and Export data types.

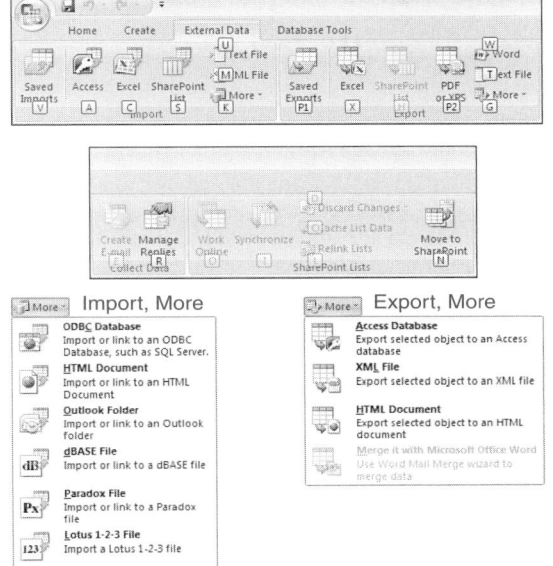

- **Database Tools**—Lets you open the VBA editor for a module or Class Module; run a macro, create a shortcut menu from a macro, or convert a macro to VBA; open the Relationships window to create or edit table relationships; show or hide the Object Dependencies pane, property sheet for an object, or message bar; run the Database Documenter, Performance Analyzer, or Table Analyzer Wizard; move tables to a back-end Access database or upsize tables and queries to SQL Server 2005 Express; run the Linked Table Manager for linked Access tables; create or edit a switchboard with the Switchboard Manager; encrypt the database and set a database password; manage Access add-ins; and make an execute-only database by stripping out VBA source code (see Figure 1.11).

Figure 1.11
The Database Tools ribbon's buttons perform their actions without the need for gallery choices.

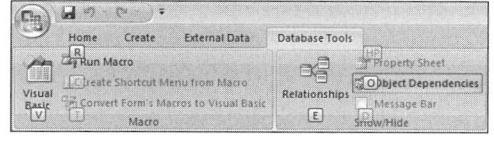

CONTEXTUAL RIBBONS FOR ACCESS DATABASES

Access 2007 has 16 different contextual ribbons, which contain buttons for commands that are appropriate to specific Access object contexts. With the exception of the Print Preview ribbon, all contextual ribbon tabs appear to the right of the Database Tools tab. Chapter 3 provides detailed descriptions of these ribbons and illustrates galleries, when applicable.

Following is a list of contextual ribbons for conventional (.accdb) applications:

- **Print Preview**—Replaces all other ribbons when you choose Office, Print, Print Preview (see Figure 1.12).

Figure 1.12
The Print Preview ribbon and its galleries let you select page size, orientation, margins, and display parameters, as well as export data in all formats that Access supports.

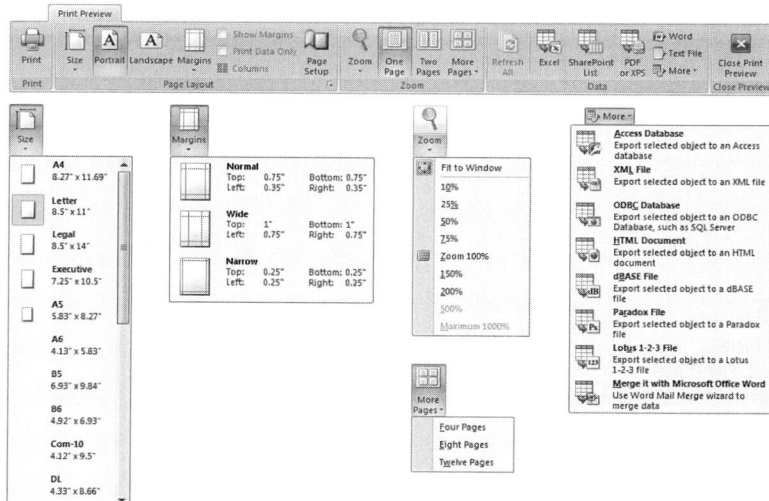

- **Table Tools, Datasheet**—Opens when you select the Datasheet view of a table and enables modifying table design in Datasheet view (see Figure 1.13, top)

Figure 1.13
Each view of a table—Datasheet, Design, PivotTable, and PivotChart—has its own Tools context menu.

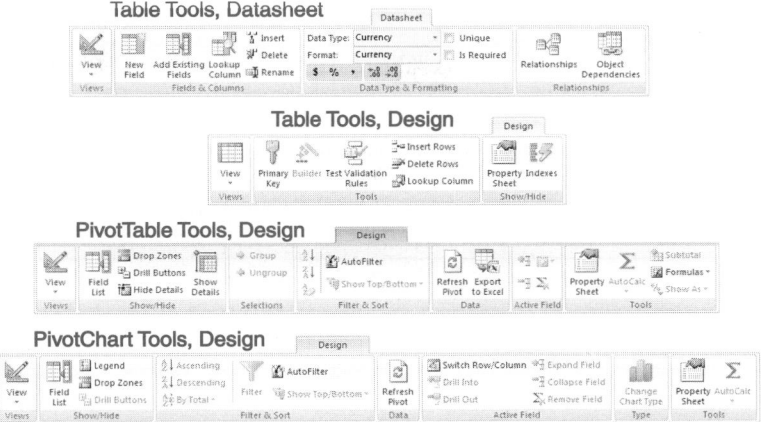

- **Table Tools, Design**—Opens when you select the Design view of a table (see Figure 1.13, second from top)

- **PivotTable Tools, Design**—Opens when you select the PivotTable view of a table or query (see Figure 1.13, third from top)

- **PivotChart Tools, Design**—Opens when you select the PivotChart view of a table or query (see Figure 1.13 bottom)

- **Relationship Tools, Design**—Opens when you click the Database Tool ribbon's Relations button (see Figure 1.14 top)

Figure 1.14
The Relationship Tools, Design ribbon (top) and the Query Tools, Design ribbon (bottom, split horizontally) have the expected buttons. Queries have Datasheet, PivotTable, PivotChart, SQL, and Design views.

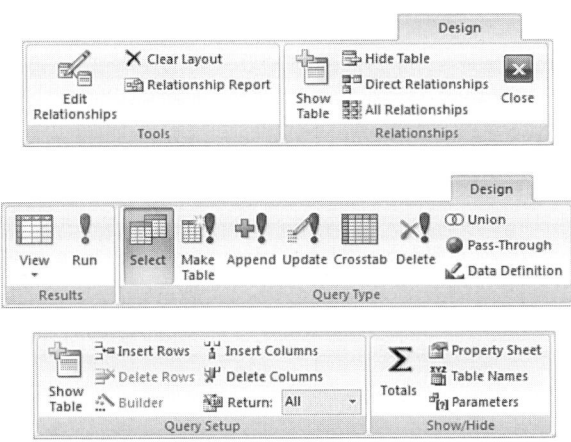

- **Query Tools, Design**—Opens when you create a new query or edit a query in Design view (see Figure 1.14 bottom)

- **Form Layout Tools, Formatting**—Opens with the following ribbon when you open a form in Layout view (see Figure 1.15 top)

Figure 1.15
Form Layout view has its own pair of Formatting (top, split horizontally) and Arrange (bottom) ribbons.

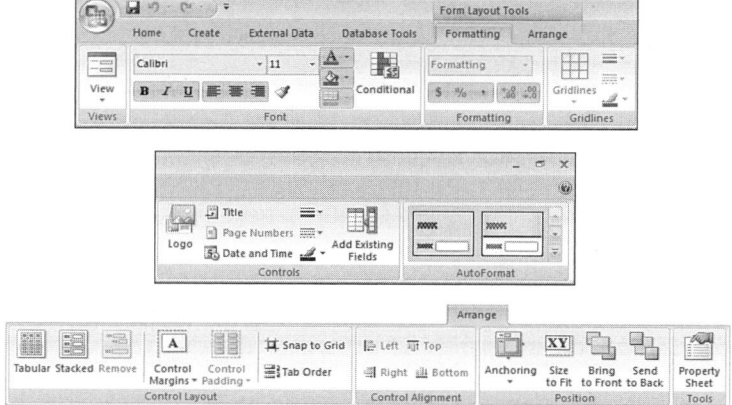

- **Form Layout Tools, Arrange**—Opens to the right of the preceding ribbon when you open a form in Layout view (see Figure 1.15 bottom)
- **Form Design Tools, Design**—Opens with the following ribbon when you open a form in Layout view (see Figure 1.16 top, split horizontally)

Figure 1.16
Form Design view also has pair of Formatting (top, split horizontally) and Arrange (bottom) ribbons. The Formatting ribbon contains the contents of prior versions' Toolbox.

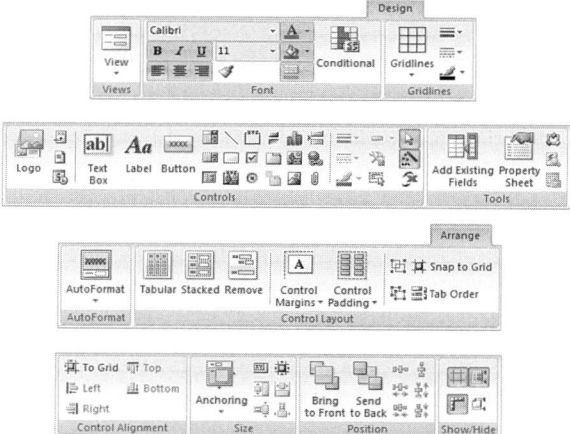

- **Form Design Tools, Arrange**—Opens to the right of the preceding ribbon when you open a form in Layout view (see Figure 1.16 bottom, split horizontally)
- **Report Layout Tools, Formatting**—Opens with the following ribbon when you open a report in Layout view (see Figure 1.17 top, split horizontally)

Figure 1.17
Opening a report in Layout view displays three Report Layout Tools tabs: Formatting (top, split horizontally), Arrange (center), and Page Setup (bottom).

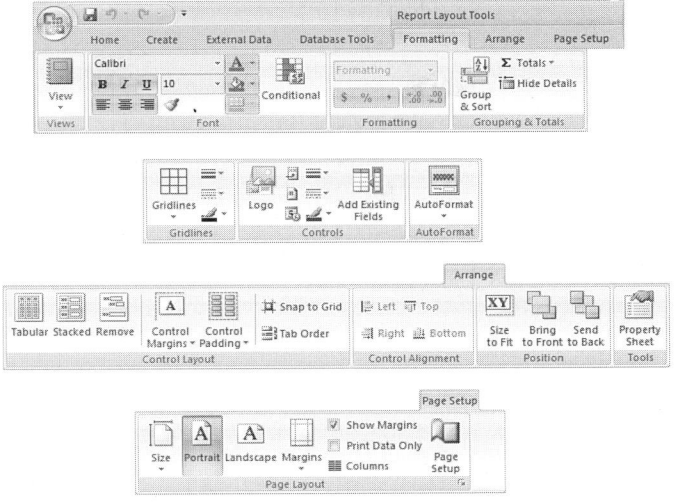

- **Report Layout Tools, Arrange**—Opens to the right of the preceding ribbon when you open a report in Layout view (see Figure 1.17 center)
- **Report Layout Tools, Page Setup**—Opens to the right of the preceding ribbon when you open a report in Layout view (see Figure 1.17 bottom)
- **Report Design Tools, Design**—Opens with the following ribbon when you open a report in Design view (see Figure 1.18 top, split horizontally)

Figure 1.18
Opening a report in Design view displays three Report Design Tools tabs—Formatting (top, split horizontally), Arrange (center), and Page Setup (bottom, split horizontally)—similar to the corresponding Layout tabs.

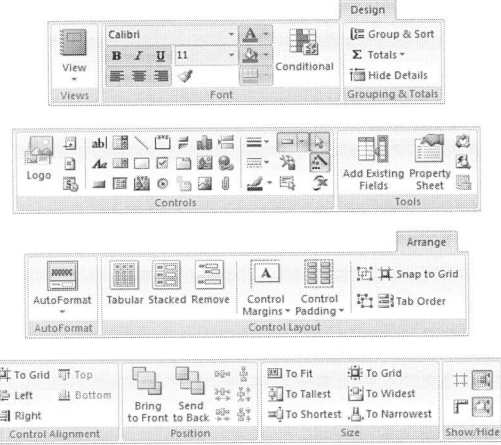

- **Report Design Tools, Arrange**—Opens to the right of the preceding ribbon when you open a report in Design view (see Figure 1.18 bottom, split horizontally)
- **Report Design Tools, Page Setup**—Opens to the right of the preceding ribbon when you open a report in Design view (same as the Report Layout Tools, Page Setup ribbon)

CONTEXTUAL RIBBONS FOR ACCESS DATA PROJECTS

Four contextual ribbons are specific to Access data projects (.adp and .ade) and the da Vinci design tools for SQL Server 2000 and 2005, including MSDE and SQL Server Express. Table, form, report, and macro ribbons are the same (with very minor exceptions) as those for .accdb databases.

Following are the ADP-specific ribbons:

- **Diagram Tools, Design**—Corresponds to Access's Relationships Tools ribbon and opens when you select a Database Diagram from the Navigation pane (see Figure 1.19 top, split horizontally)

Figure 1.19
The Diagram Tools, Design ribbon (top, split horizontally) lets you edit SQL Server 2000 and 2005 Database Diagrams. The Function and View Tools, Design ribbon (bottom) enables the creating and editing of inline functions and views.

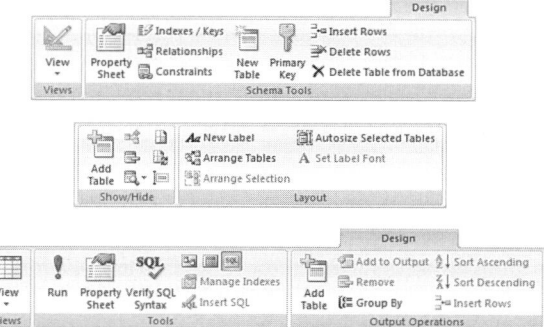

- **Function & View Tools, Design**—Corresponds to Access's Query Tools, Design window and opens when you select Design In-Line Function or Design View in the New Query dialog, which you open by clicking the Query Wizard button in the Create ribbon's Other group or open a function or view from the Navigation pane's Queries group (see Figure 1.19 bottom)

- **Stored Procedure Tools, Design**—Opens when you select Design Stored Procedure in the New Query dialog or open a stored procedure from the Navigation pane's Queries group (see Figure 1.20 top, split horizontally)

Figure 1.20
The Stored Procedure Tools, Design ribbon (top, split horizontally) lets you use the da Vinci graphic designer to create or edit stored procedures. The SQL Statement Tools, Design ribbon (bottom) aids in writing Transact-SQL (T-SQL) statements.

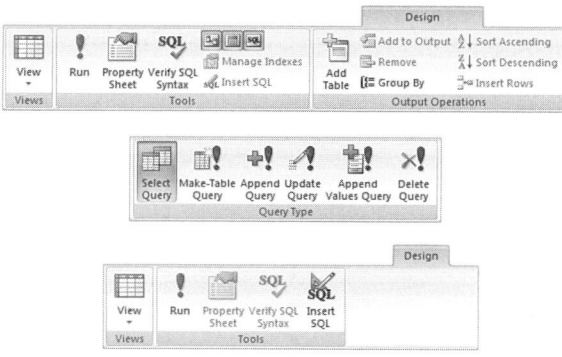

- **SQL Statement Tools, Design**—Opens when you select Create Text Stored Procedure, Create Text Scalar Function, or Create Text Table-Valued Function in the New Query dialog or open one of these objects from the Navigation pane's Queries group (see Figure 1.20, bottom)

Chapter 20, "Exploring Access Data Projects and SQL Server 2005," Chapter 21, "Moving from Access Queries to Transact-SQL," and Chapter 22, "Upsizing Access Applications to Access Data Projects" make extensive use of the preceding four ribbons.

CUSTOMIZING RIBBONS FOR SPECIFIC APPLICATIONS

Customizing ribbons by adding or removing command buttons or command groups, hiding or replacing complete ribbons, and the like involves a much more complex process than customizing Access 2003 and earlier command bars. The new Access Options dialog's Current Database page lets you select a custom ribbon from the Ribbon and Toolbar Options' Ribbon Name list. Entries in the Ribbon Name list come from the RibbonName field of the USysRibbons system table.

You define a custom ribbon with a Ribbon Extensibility (RibbonX) XML document that you save in the USysRibbon's RibbonXML field. Following is the Orders document that defines a relatively simple ribbon:

```
<customUI xmlns="http://schemas.microsoft.com/office/2006/01/customui">
  <ribbon startFromScratch="false">
    <tabs>
      <tab id="tabOrders" label="Orders">
        <group id="grpHome" label="Home">
          <button id="cmdHome" label="Home" imageMso="MeetingsWorkspace"
            size="large" onAction="onOpenFormEdit" tag="frmMain"/>
        </group>
        <group id="grpOrders" label="Orders">
          <button id="cmdAddOrder" size="large" label="Add Order"
            imageMso="FormatPainter" onAction="nyi"/>
          <button id="cmdPay" size="large" label="Mark Paid"
            imageMso="MarkTaskComplete" onAction="nyi"/>
        </group>
        <group idMso="GroupClipboard"></group>
        <group idMso="GroupRecords"></group>
      </tab>
    </tabs>
  </ribbon>
</customUI>
```

The `<tab id="tabOrders" label="Orders">` element adds the Orders tab to the ribbons. `<group id="grpHome" label="Home">` and `<group id="grpOrders" label="Orders">` create two custom groups that contain button(s) defined by `<button id="cmdName" …>` elements. `<group idMso="GroupClipboard">` and `<group idMso="GroupRecords">` add two standard groups to the ribbon.

Figure 1.21 shows the custom ribbon created by the preceding XML document.

Figure 1.21
A 20-line RibbonX XML document creates this custom ribbon whose tab is visible when an Orders form is open. The first set of two groups (Home and Orders) is custom; the second set (Clipboard and Records) are standard groups from the Home ribbon.

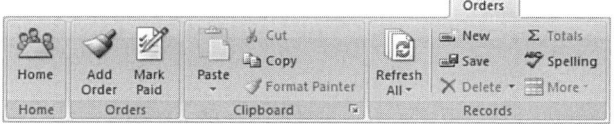

Custom ribbons require VBA callback routines to act as event handlers for button actions specified by the onAction attribute value. Here's the callback event handler routine for the nyi (not yet implemented) event:

```
Public Sub nyi(control As IRibbonControl)
    MsgBox "The callback for the control '" & control.Id & _
        "' has not been implemented", vbExclamation, "NYI"
End Sub
```

→ For more information on programming your own ribbons, **see** "Customizing Applications with Ribbon Objects," **p. 1226**.

THE QUICK ACCESS TOOLBAR

The Quick Access Toolbar (QAT) lets you create custom shortcuts to frequently used commands. By default, the QAT has three command buttons: Save, Undo, and Redo. The Undo and Redo buttons usually are disabled and sport Can't Undo and Can't Redo ToolTips.

Clicking the drop-down button to the right of the Can't Redo button opens a gallery of popular command buttons that you can add to the QAT (see Figure 1.22).

Figure 1.22
You can add popular command buttons to the QAT and specify its location—above or below the ribbon—from its drop-down gallery.

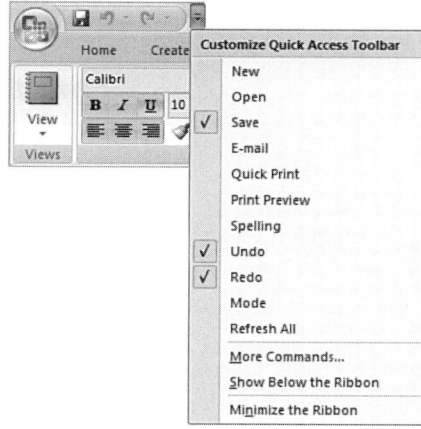

Figure 1.23 shows the QAT with all buttons added from the standard list and compares locating the QAT above or below the ribbons.

Figure 1.23
This double exposure compares locating a QAT—with all popular buttons added—above or below the ribbons.

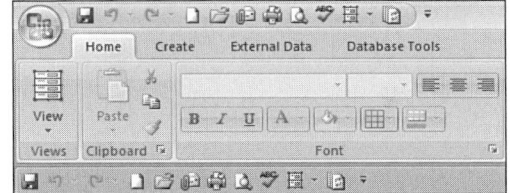

Clicking the More Commands button opens the Access Options dialog with the Customize page active. You can add more command buttons and group them with separators, as shown in Figure 1.24. The Customize Quick Access Toolbar drop-down list lets you apply the customized QAT list to all documents (databases) or to the current database.

Figure 1.24
The Access Options dialog's Customize page lets you choose additional commands to add to the QAT and specify if your customization applies to all databases or only the current database.

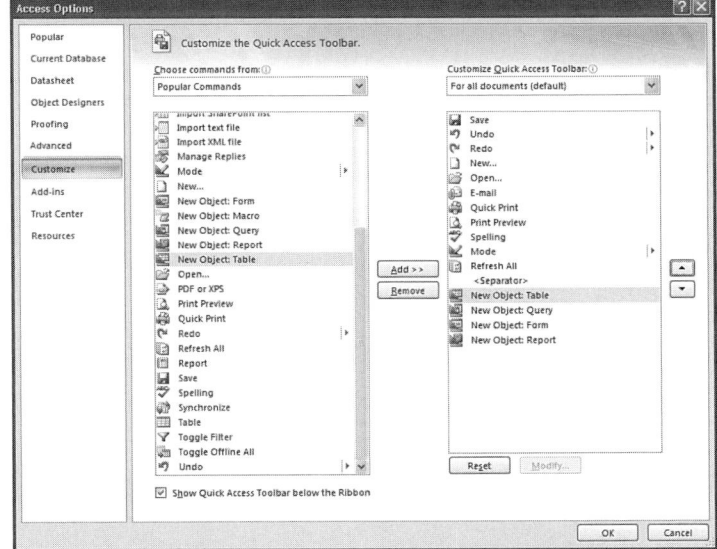

Access 2007's ribbons and galleries contain about 500 unique command buttons and icons. You can increase the scope of search for useful custom command buttons for the QAT by opening the Choose Commands From list and selecting one of the main or context ribbons, the Office gallery, or other tabs not discussed previously, such as Add-ins and Source Control (see Figure 1.25).

Figure 1.25
Opening the Choose Commands From list lets you select commands for the QAT from the about 500 unique buttons in the 21 ribbons and the Office gallery.

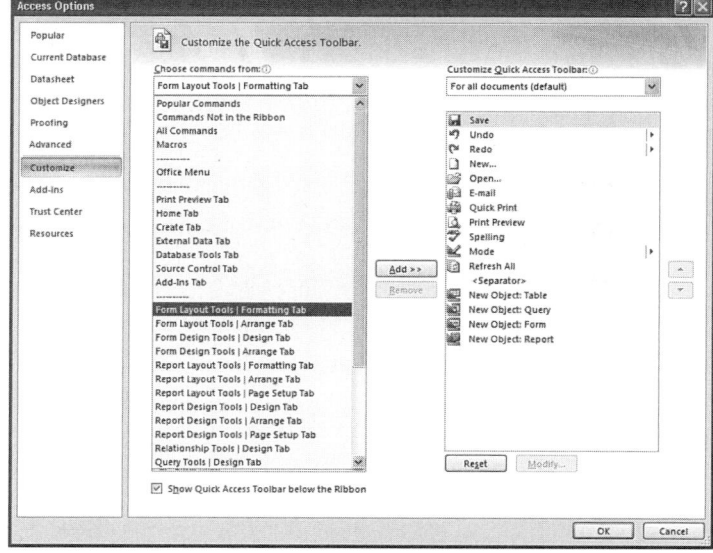

NOTE

Availability of commands from main and context ribbons is one of the reasons for including figures for *all* ribbons in the preceding sections.

THE OFFICE BUTTON AND ITS GALLERY

There's no conventional File or Tools menu, so the Office gallery that opens when you click the Office button handles many of those two menu's former tasks. The gallery opens with a most frequently used (MRU) file list (see Figure 1.26).

Here's what happens when you click one of the gallery's following nine command buttons with an .accdb file open:

- **New**—Opens the Getting Started with Microsoft Office Access dialog, which lets you create a database from a local or downloaded template, open and empty database, or open a new ADP (refer to Figure 1.3).

- **Open**—Opens the Open File dialog, which lets you browse for new and old Access files (*.accdb, *.mdb, *.adp, *.mda, *.accda, *.mde, *.accde, *.ade).

- **Save**—Saves the currently open file with its current filename and extension.

- **Save As**—Opens a second-tier gallery with options to save the current object as a new object, publish to PDF or XPS, and save the database file in Access 2007, 2002-3, or 2000 format (see Figure 1.27).

Figure 1.26
The Office gallery's default view is a most recently used file list.

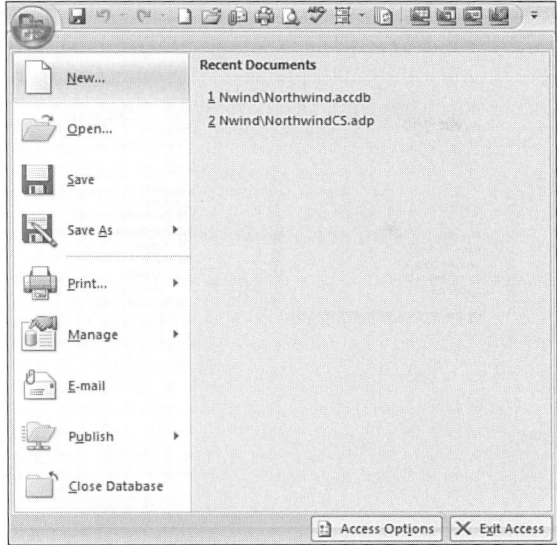

Figure 1.27
The Save As gallery offers the option to save or publish the current object or save the file in one of the three latest Access formats.

■ **Print**—Opens a second-tier gallery with options to print with the Windows Print dialog, quick print to the default printer, and open the Print Preview ribbon and page (see Figure 1.28).

Figure 1.28
The Print gallery offers three print options. Quick Print, which prints immediately to the default printer, is new.

■ **Manage**—Opens a second-tier gallery with options that apply to the current database: Compact and Repair Database, Back Up Database by creating a copy named *DatabaseName_YYYY-MM-DD.ext*, and Database Properties to open the DatabaseName Properties dialog (see Figure 1.29).

Figure 1.29
Choosing Database Properties opens the *DatabaseName* Properties dialog for Office DocFiles.

- **E-mail**—Opens the Send Object As dialog to send the currently selected object (the Task List form) by Outlook in one of the nine supported Multipurpose Internet Mail Extensions (MIME) types (see Figure 1.30). PDF, XML Paper Specification (XPS), Excel Binary Workbook (*.xlsb), and Excel Workbook (*.xlsx) are new Office 2007 export formats. When you click OK, an Outlook message dialog opens with an enclosure created from the selected object (see Figure 1.31).

Figure 1.30
Choosing E-mail opens the Send Object As dialog. Selecting a MIME type and clicking OK opens the Outlook 2007 Message dialog.

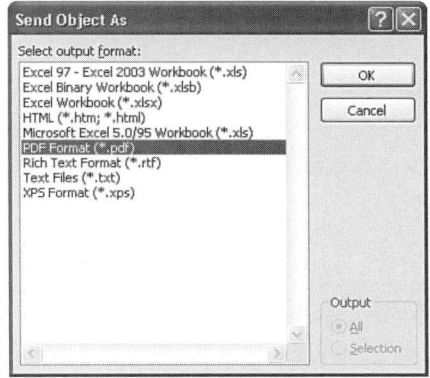

Figure 1.31
The currently selected object becomes a message attachment of the selected MIME type. The new Outlook Message dialog has a ribbon UI, but the main Outlook window doesn't.

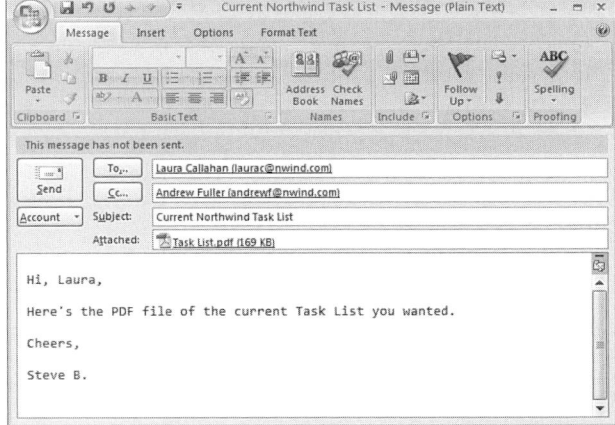

- **Publish**—Opens a second-tier gallery with two choices (see Figure 1.32). Choosing Document Management Server from the Publish gallery lets you export an .accdb database to a WSS 3.0 or MOSS 2007 Document Library and share the database with authorized SharePoint users. The Package and Sign choice lets you create an Access Signed Package (.accdc file), as described in the following section.

Figure 1.32
Choosing Document Management Server from the Publish gallery moves the database file to a WSS 3.0 or MOSS 2007 Document Library. The Package and Sign choice enables creating an Access Signed Package (.accdc file).

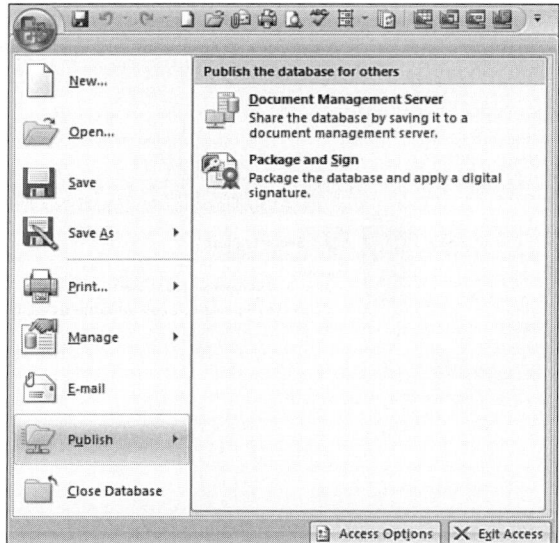

- **Close Database**—Closes the current database and opens the Getting Started with Microsoft Office Access dialog.

> **TIP**
>
> You can quickly exit any Office 2007 application by double-clicking the Office button.

SECURITY, TRUSTED LOCATIONS, PACKAGES, AND CERTIFICATES

Access 2007's approach to system and database security is significantly different from its predecessors. System security attempts to prevent—or at least dissuade—users from opening database or project files that might contain *harmful code* in macros or VBA modules. The term *harmful code* generally means code that can access local computer or network resources and (potentially) install malware, bots, or viruses.

When you open any database from a location that you haven't designated as trusted or that hasn't been signed with a digital signature from a publisher you trust, Access opens with a Security Warning bar and, when you click the Options button, opens a Security Alert dialog (see Figure 1.33).

Figure 1.33
The Security Warning bar and Security Alert dialog appear for empty Access databases that aren't in a trusted location or signed with a digital signature.

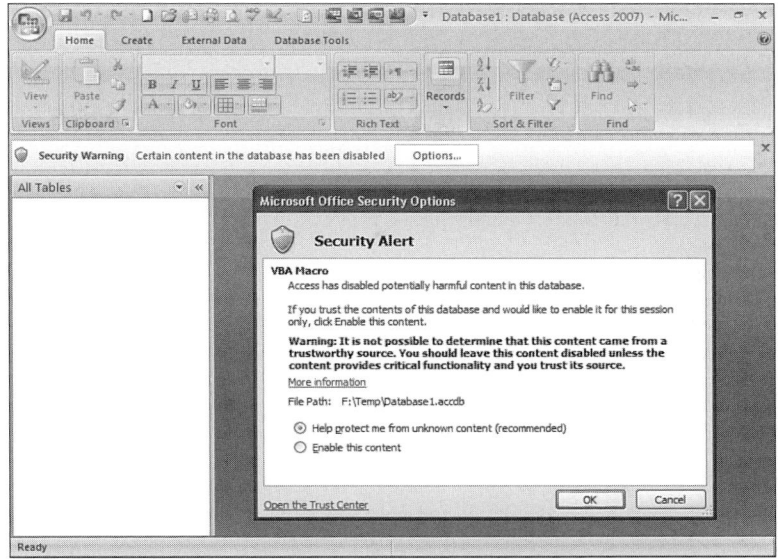

NOTE

The Database1.accdb database shown in Figure 1.33 contains no objects other than a few system tables, which means that the Security Warning bar's "Certain content in this database has been disabled" message is incorrect. The same is true for the Security Alert's "Access has disabled potentially harmful content in this database" admonition. There is nothing in the database to be disabled.

When you create a new empty (blank) database in the Getting Started with Microsoft Office Access dialog, the Security Warning bar doesn't appear until you reopen the database.

SPECIFYING TRUSTED LOCATIONS

You can prevent the Security Warning bar and the Security Alert dialog from appearing by storing the .accdb or .adp file in a *trusted location* (folder). You specify trusted location(s) in the Trusted Locations dialog of the Access Options dialog's Trust Center page.

→ For an example of creating a trusted location, **see** "Designating the Default Database Folder as a Trusted Location," **p. 78**.

PACKAGING AND CODE-SIGNING DATABASES

An alternative to requiring users of your Access application to create a trusted location for the database is to create a Microsoft Office Access Signed Package (.accdc file) from the .accdb file. Creating a Signed Package code-signs all objects in the database and compresses the file by a factor of about five to reduce download time.

To sign a package, you must have a code-signing (Class 3) certificate from a commercial certificate authority (CA), such as Comodo, Thawte, or Verisign, or create a self-signed certificate with Office 2007's Digital Certificate for VBA Projects application (SelfCert.exe). Code-signing certificates from a commercial CA cost from $99 to $199 per year.

Self-signed certificates usually are limited to personal or small workgroup use. By default, self-signed certificates work only for packages you extract on the same machine that created and signed them. Use trusted locations to avoid security warnings unless you have a compelling reason to do otherwise.

ENABLING NONTRUSTED APPLICATION AUTOMATION WITH MACROS

 Access 2007 users in organizations with highly secure computer operations might be prevented from enabling "potentially harmful content" by a group policy setting. In this case, you can take advantage of the default "safe" subset of Access macro actions that will run without enabling VBA code by trusting the database. To enable unsafe macro actions, you must click the Macro Tools, Design ribbon's Show All Actions button, which toggles between displaying a list of all and safe-only actions.

> NOTE
>
> Microsoft touts the capability of macro actions to execute in nontrusted applications as one of the reasons for the resurrection of Access macros as a recommended programming technology.

→ For more information on Access macros, **see** "Access Macros Redux," **p. 56**.

THE NAVIGATION PANE

The Navigation Pane (NavPane) replaces the Database Window and, for most Access applications, switchboards that you design with the Switchboard manager. The retractable Access NavPane is based on Outlook 2007's design, as is that of Microsoft Office Accounting Express 2007. (Accounting Express's NavPane isn't retractable.) Figure 1.34 compares the three applications' NavPanes.

The Access NavPane consists of a hierarchical list of categories, groups, and items. Items are shortcuts to your application's objects. The NavPane for a new empty database contains default Custom, Tables and Related Views, Object Type, Created Date, and Modified Date categories, and an empty Custom Group 1. The NavPane opens the Tables and Related Views (All Tables) category with a Table1 group and Table1: Table item.

You can populate Access's Custom category by renaming Custom Group 1 and adding groups, such as Tasks, Contacts, Employees, and Supporting Objects (refer to Figure 1.34). New objects you create fall into a default Unassigned Object group. This group remains visible until you drag-and-drop or cut-and-paste all items in the Unassigned Object to a custom group.

Figure 1.34
Navigation Panes of Office Access (left), Outlook (center), and Accounting Express 2007 (right) are similar, but only Access lets you customize its NavPane extensively.

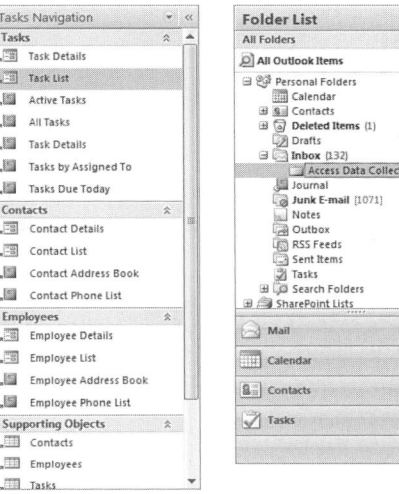

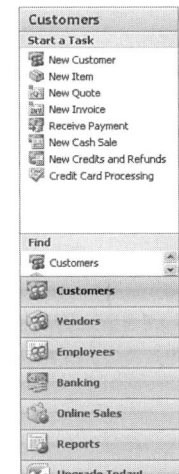

> **NOTE**
>
> It's a common practice to place table, query, macro, and module objects in a hidden group to discourage ordinary users from opening tables or queries directly, rather than reviewing or entering data with forms, and modifying macros or VBA code. Applications you create from Access templates store these objects in a Supporting Objects group that you can hide with an embedded macro or VBA code.

→ For an example of an Access 2007 application created from a template, **see** "Creating Access Applications from Downloaded Templates," **p. 73**.

Figure 1.35 illustrates the initial appearance of the five NavPane categories of a simple application after adding three simple tables, queries, forms, and reports, plus a single stand-alone macrosheet and module. The categories are (from left to right): Tables and Related Views (All Tables), Object Type (All Access Objects), Created Date and Modified Date (All Dates, identical), and Custom. Access creates these NavPane layouts for you.

> **NOTE**
>
> The \SEUA12\Chaptr01\NavPane.accdb database includes the starter objects shown in Figure 1.35.

CUSTOMIZING THE CUSTOM CATEGORY

Most Access power users and developers probably will customize the default Custom category and Custom Group 1 group, and then add new groups to suit their application design. For this example, the *ObjectName*1 objects will track customers, *ObjectName*2 objects will track orders, and *ObjectName*3 will track products. The following steps create an Order Tracking category with Customers, Orders, Products, and Supporting Objects groups:

Figure 1.35
The NavPane offers four different categorized views of Access application objects: All Tables (Tables and Related Views), All Access Objects (Object Type), All Dates (Created Date and Modified Date), and Custom (before customization).

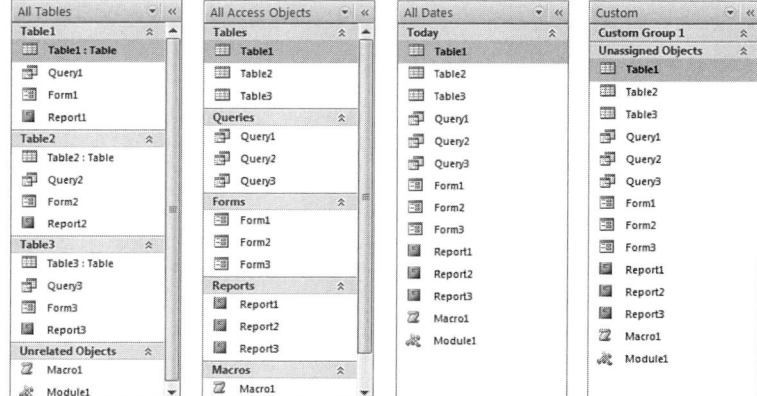

1. Open \SEUA12\Chapter01\NavPane.accdb, expand the NavPane, if necessary, right-click the All Tables NavPane header, and choose <u>N</u>avigation Options to open the dialog of the same name.

2. Select the Custom category, click the R<u>e</u>name Item button, and change Custom to **Order Tracking** (see Figure 1.36).

Figure 1.36
The Navigation Options dialog lets you customize the Custom category and its groups. You also can change the order of items you add to the Tables and Related Views category.

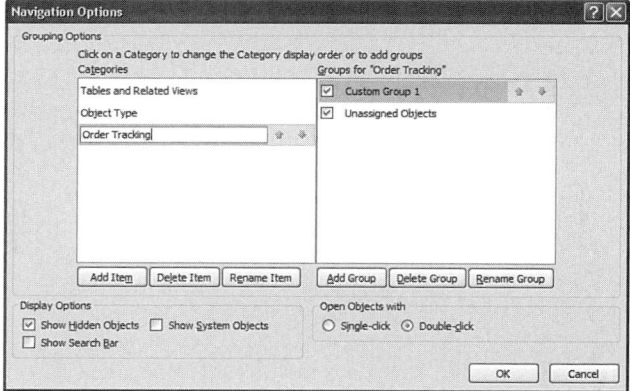

3. Select the Custom Group 1 group, press F2, and change its name to **Customers**.

4. Click <u>A</u>dd Group and change the new group's name from Custom Group 1 to **Orders**.

5. Repeat step 4 and change the new group's name to **Products**.

6. Create another group named **Supporting Objects** to hold tables, queries, macros, and modules. The dialog appears as shown in Figure 1.37.

Figure 1.37
The Navigation Options dialog lets you customize the Custom category and its groups. You also can change the order of items you add to the Tables and Related Views category.

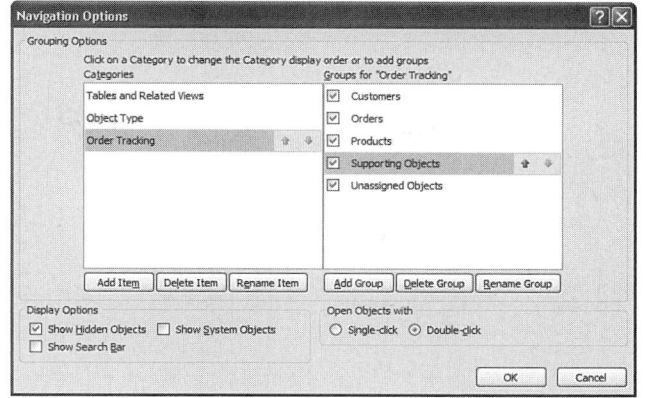

> **NOTE**
>
> Arrows for selected custom categories and groups let you specify their sequence in the NavPane. You can't change the relative position of prebuilt categories or groups.

7. Clear the Show Hidden Objects check box and click OK to apply your changes to the NavPane (see Figure 1.38, far left).

Figure 1.38
The four stages of customizing the NavPane for a sample order-tracking application.

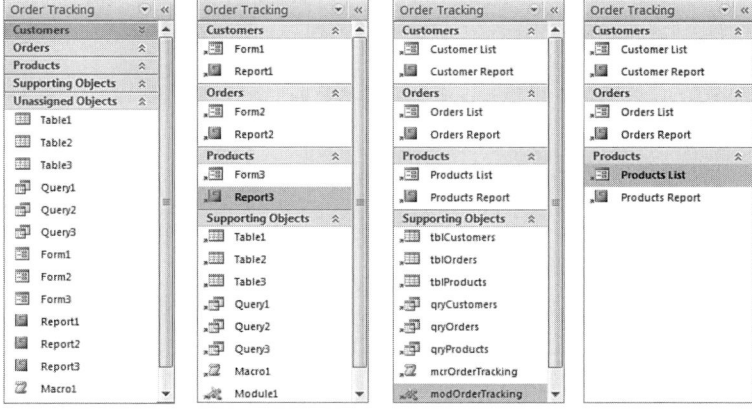

8. Drag the three table items, three query items, Macro1, and Module1 from the Unassigned Objects group to the Supporting Objects group. Alternatively, Ctrl+click the objects and drag the multiple selection to the Supporting Objects group.

9. Drag Form1 and Report1 to the Customers group, Form2 and Report2 to the Orders group, and Form3 and Report3 to the Products group. The Unassigned Objects group is now empty (refer to Figure 1.38, left-center).

10. Optionally, change the names of the items by right-clicking them and selecting <u>R</u>ename Shortcut or pressing F2 to make them more understandable by users (refer to Figure 1.38, right-center).

> **N O T E**
>
> The capability to rename NavPane items lets you continue to use standard prefixes for Access object names, such as `frm` for forms and `rpt` for reports.

11. Right-click the Supporting Objects group header and choose <u>H</u>ide to make the group disappear (refer to Figure 1.38, far right).

> **N O T E**
>
> If a "ghost image" of the Supporting Objects group remains, you didn't clear the Show Hidden Objects check box in step 7.

Access 2007 doesn't support user-level security, so determined users can thwart your attempt to prevent them from accessing Supporting Objects by opening one of the prebuilt categories or opening the Navigation Options dialog, marking the Show Hidden Objects check box, and then right-clicking the ghost image and choosing <u>U</u>nhide.

HIDING PREBUILT CATEGORIES AND LOCKING THE NAVIGATION PANE

 Access 2007 has SetDisplayedCategories and LockNavigationPane macro actions that solve problems with inquisitive or hostile users attempting to open Supporting Objects. The later "Access Macros Redux" section describes how to write a macro to defeat attempts by users to open tables or queries.

> **N O T E**
>
> You must distribute to users the Access 2007 equivalent of an Access MDE file (an .accde file) to prevent them from modifying the design of forms and reports.

> **C A U T I O N**
>
> Hiding prebuilt categories, locking the Navigation Pane, and distributing .accde files to users doesn't secure the database. Users must have a copy of Access 2007 to open the .accde file; this means they can import or link to tables and queries. (Forms, reports, macros, and modules are protected.)
>
> If database security is important to your application, consider using an Access data project (ADP) or linking to an SQL Server 2005 Express Edition (SSX) SP2 database. Alternatively, you can link to tables in an .accdb file on a server share and manage access by user permissions for the share and file. The chapters of Part V, "Moving to Networked Multiuser Applications," cover both alternatives.

→ To learn more about SSX SP2, **see** "SQL Server 2005 Express Edition SP2 Setup," **p. 59**.

SEARCHING, FILTERING, AND SORTING THE NAVIGATION PANE

A large, production Access application can include hundreds of objects. Thus, the NavPane provides an optional search bar that restricts visible items to those that match the search term. To toggle the adding and removing of the search box on the NavPane, right-click the NavPane header and choose Search Bar (see Figure 1.39, far left, top).

Figure 1.39
The NavPane offers a search box and filters for built-in groups (top); the filter for the Order Tracking category is similar to that for Tables and Related Views. The sort menu lets you specify a sort by property followed by ascending or descending sorts on object names (bottom).

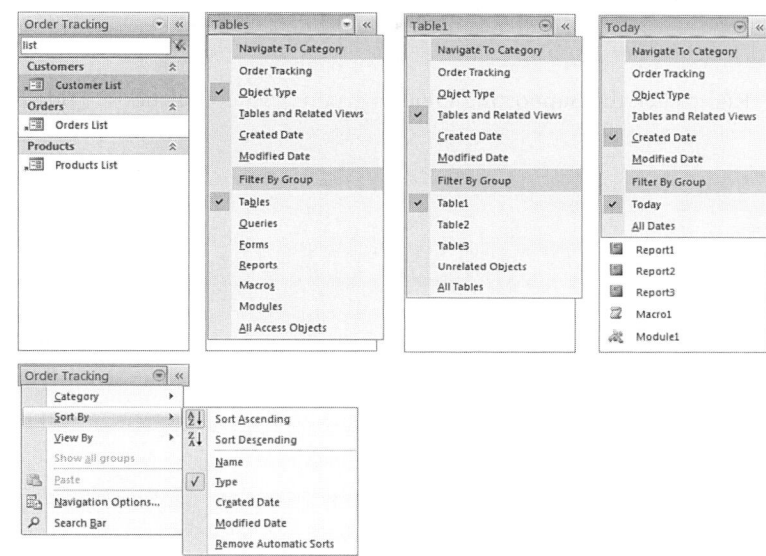

You can filter built-in categories by object type, table name, or created or modified date (see Figure 1.39, left-center to far right, top). You also can sort items by name, object type, and created or modified date (see Figure 1.39, bottom).

CHANGES TO TABLES AND THE ACCESS DATABASE ENGINE

Compared with the UI, Access 2007's changes to tables and the Access database engine are relatively minor, unless you're a WSS 3.0 or MOSS 2007 developer. As noted in the next section, the most significant changes are to enhance Access's support for SharePoint lists. Whether the Access team's promotion of nonrelational (SharePoint list) back-end storage for a relational database management platform will gather many adherents remains to be seen.

TAKING ADVANTAGE OF NEW OR UPGRADED DATA TYPES

Access 2007 adds the Attachment field data type, an Allow Multiple Values property to the Lookup pane for fields, and two enhancements to the Memo data type. Following are brief descriptions of the new data types and cross-references to topics in other chapters that explain how to use them:

- **Attachment**—A new field data type that supplements the OLE Object data type. Attachment fields usually store images, but can store any MIME type or binary file. Right-clicking an Image control bound to an Attachment field and choosing Manage Attachments opens a dialog of the same name (see Figure 1.40). Attachment fields compress binary data in uncompressed file formats, such as .bmp, and can embed multiple attachments in a single table cell.

Figure 1.40
The Attachments dialog lets you view, add, delete, and save multiple binary or text documents in a single table cell.

→ For an example of adding an image to an Attachment field, **see** "Opening Forms from the Navigation Pane and Adding Records," **p. 87**.

- **Multivalued Lookup Field**—An MVLF "field" lets you select multiple values in a lookup combo box's list and display the multiple lookup values in a comma-separated list in the combo's text box (see Figure 1.41). MVLFs generate a many-to-many relationship between the host and lookup tables by creating a hidden relation table. Technically, an MVLF is a property (Enable Multiple Values) in the Table Design view's Lookup pane, not a field data type.

→ For instructions on adding MVLFs to forms, **see** "Conform MVLF Combo Boxes of List and Details Forms," **p. 107**.

→ To learn more about MVLFs, **see** "Creating Multivalued Lookup Fields," **p. 474**.

- **"Rich Text" Memo Fields**—Changing the new Text Format property value from Plain Text to Rich Text enables limited HTML text formatting of Memo fields (refer to Figure 1.2). You can change font family and size; apply bold, italic, underline, color, and highlight attributes; specify alignment, direction, indent, and outdent; and add bulleted or numbered lists.

→ For general information on Access field properties, **see** "Field Properties," **p. 209**.

Figure 1.41
Designating a field as a lookup field and setting the Allow Multiple Values property value to Yes lets users mark check boxes to add more than one lookup value to a comma-separated list.

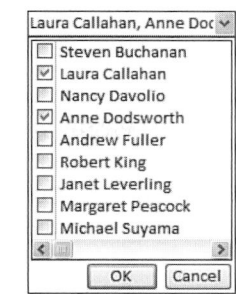

- **Append-Only Memo Fields**—Setting the Append Only property value to Yes prevents users from deleting or editing previously entered content in Memo fields. The purpose of append-only memo fields is for change tracking.

Microsoft added the Attachment data type, MVLFs, and the Rich Text and Append-Only property values to support similar data types and properties of WSS 3.0 and MOSS 2007 lists. SQL Server doesn't support data types or features.

ENHANCING DATASHEET VIEW

Tables and queries get a facelift with tabbed documents for Datasheet and Design view. Both views feature a "Web 2.0"–style blue, orange, and gray color scheme, and Datasheet view replaces previous versions' 10-pt Arial font with 11-pt Calibri. Calibri is the new default ClearType font for all Office 2007 applications and supports.

The following are the more significant new features of Datasheet view:

- **Enhanced filtering and sorting**—Clicking the Home ribbon's Filter button opens the Quick Filter tools for the selected Datasheet field. Quick Filter options change by data type: Figure 1.42 (left) shows Text Filters, Figure 1.42 (right) illustrates Number Filters, and Figure 1.43 displays the extraordinary number of Date Filters.

Figure 1.42
Quick Filter options are data type–sensitive. The left Quick Filter tool is for Text fields; the right for Number fields.

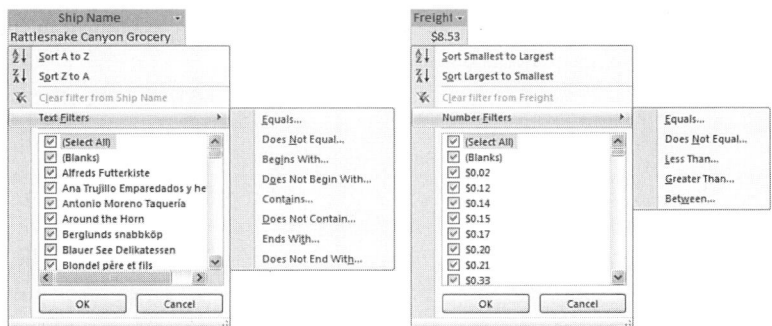

Figure 1.43
Quick Filter includes Date Filters for almost any condition you can imagine.

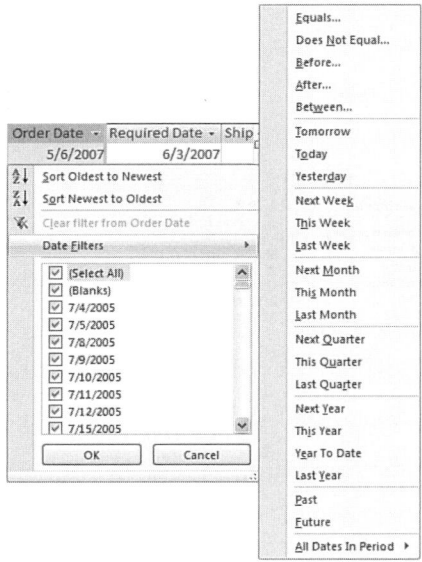

■ **Totals row**—Clicking the Home ribbon's Totals button toggles the visibility of a Totals row immediately below the last Datasheet row. Columns with numeric data types let you choose None, Sum, Average, Count, Minimum, Maximum, Standard Deviation, or Variance (see Figure 1.44).

Figure 1.44
This totals row contains (left to right) count, average, sum, and standard deviation values for numeric columns of the Northwind sample database's Order Details table. The Add New Field column appears in all Access 2007 tables.

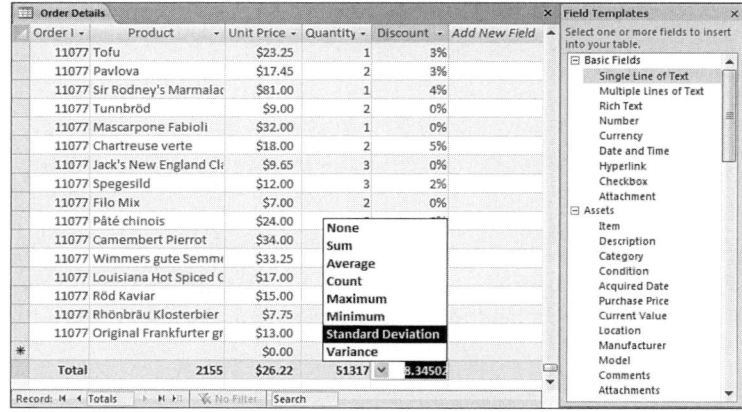

■ **Alternate background color**—Datasheets now have an Alternate Background Color property to emulate striped printer paper intended for dot matrix and chain printers. You set the alternate background color—as well as other Datasheet properties—on the Access Options dialog's Datasheet page (see Figure 1.45). The default color is very light gray (refer to Figure 1.44).

Figure 1.45
You set the Alternate Background Color, as well as other Datasheet properties for all datasheets, on the Access Options dialog's Datasheet page.

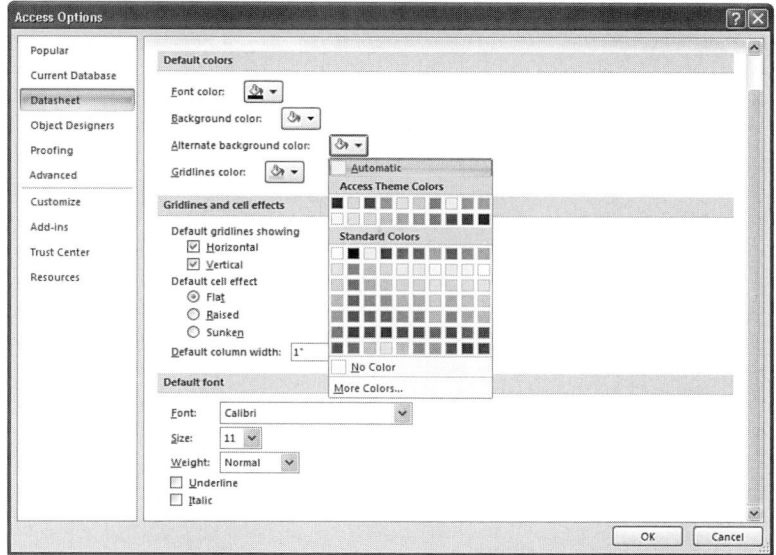

- **Add New Field column**—This column appears by default in Datasheet view of all tables (refer to Figure 1.44). Like in earlier Access versions, you can type values in Datasheet view to create the column. What's new is that Access 2007 infers the column's data type from the entries you make. If you make a subsequent entry that Access infers as a different data type, you receive a warning and an opportunity to change the data type or abandon the entry.

- **Field Templates pane**—Clicking the Table Tools, Datasheet's New Field button opens the Field Templates pane to the right of Datasheet view. This pane contains links to commonly used (Basic) fields, as well as fields from the Assets, Contacts, Events, Issues, Projects, and Tasks tables from Access 2007 templates of the same name. Drag the description or *FieldName* item from the pane to the position you want in the table (see Figure 1.46).

- **Field List pane**—Clicking the Table Tools, Datasheet's Existing Field button opens the Field List pane, which displays related and unrelated tables and their fields (see Figure 1.47). If you drag a field to a table that's open in Datasheet view, the Lookup Wizard starts.

Figure 1.46
The new Field Templates pane lets you drag predesigned fields to the currently open table and drop them in the relative position you specify.

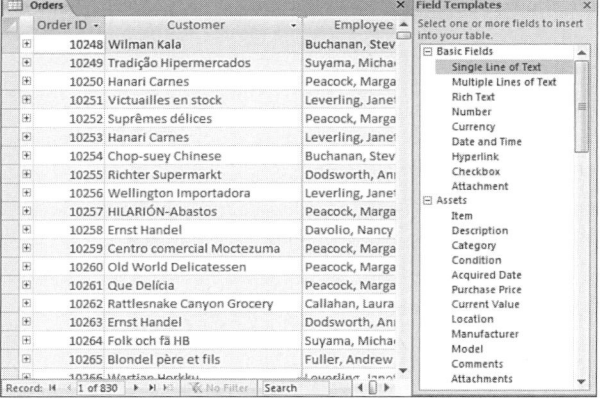

Figure 1.47
Dragging a field item from the Field List pane to the Datasheet starts the Lookup Wizard.

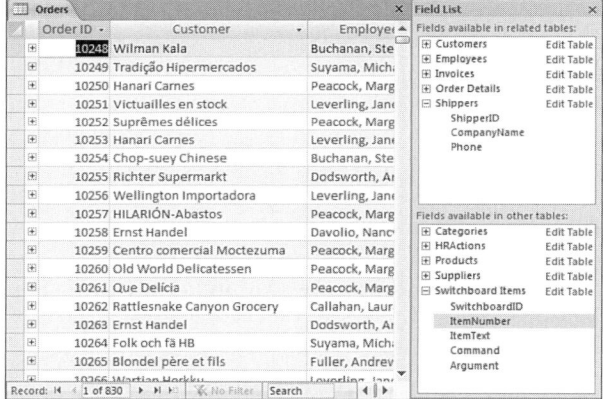

APPLICATION DEVELOPMENT BY TEMPLATES

Microsoft's Access 2007 marketing propaganda touts prebuilt application templates as the first or second most important new feature of the latest version of Access. For example, Office Online's Microsoft Office Access 2007 Top 10 Benefits page (http://office.microsoft.com/en-us/access/HA101650211033.aspx) lists "Get better results faster with a new user interface" and "Get started quickly using prebuilt solutions" as the number one and two top benefits, respectively.

Similarly, Access 2007's online help's "Quickly get started tracking information" section of the "What's New in Microsoft Office Access 2007" topic points to "New, improved user interface" and "Great templates to get you started" captions. The problem is that the out-of-the-box and Office Online templates seldom—if ever—represent the design of a full-featured, production-quality database application. As an example, the Contacts template has only a single table, which makes it only slightly more useful than a spreadsheet for tracking contacts.

→ For an overview of Access 2007 templates, **see** "Reviewing Featured Templates," **p. 75**.

The Access team commissioned a complete makeover of the 25 Access 2003 templates available from Office Online at http://office.microsoft.com/en-us/templates/CT101426031033. aspx. These templates were popular; for example, the Contact Management template had close to 600,000 downloads when this book was written. This template has four related tables and manages detailed contact information *and* call history. Another benefit of Access 2003 and earlier templates is that most have a few rows of sample data.

→ To learn how to create an Access 2007 application from earlier versions' templates, **see** "Creating a Database from Any Access Template on Microsoft Office Online," **p. 81**.

NEW FORM AND REPORT FEATURES

Access 2007 has made more changes to form and report design and development than versions 1.1 through 2003 combined. The following sections describe the most significant upgrades to forms and reports.

TABBED DOCUMENTS AND MODAL DIALOGS

The most obvious change to the Access 2007 UI is the move from the MDI's overlapping windows to an SDI with tabbed documents for Design, Layout, and Form or Report views. Unlike earlier Access versions, which commonly used non-modal pop-up switchboards to open forms and print reports, the Navigation Pane is always accessible. Hiding the ribbon UI gives Access 2007 applications about the same or slightly more screen real estate as previous versions that use conventional toolbars and menu bars.

Microsoft released Access 1.0 when most data entry occurred in 640×480 mode and only developers had "high-end" 800×600 monitors. The default 8-pt MS Sans Serif font for forms and reports was fine for low-resolution displays, but is too small for 1,024×768 or 1,280×1,024 mode. The new 11-pt Calibri default is much better suited to today's high-resolution, 17-inch or larger LCD monitors with operating systems and applications using ClearType. However, 11-pt fonts are generally too large for use in reports (other than for headers).

Access 2007 templates use modal, pop-up dialogs for *TableName* Details forms. Most of these forms use much more screen area than necessary, and aren't an appropriate design exemplar for general use. Chapter 2 provides examples of putting obese Details forms on a space-saving diet.

FORM AND REPORT LAYOUT VIEW

Sizing controls in Design view involves guessing the required width of text boxes to make all or most data in a cell visible. Access's new Layout view for forms and reports lets you arrange and size controls with live data visible. You can open the property sheets for forms, reports, and controls in Design and Layout views (see Figure 1.48).

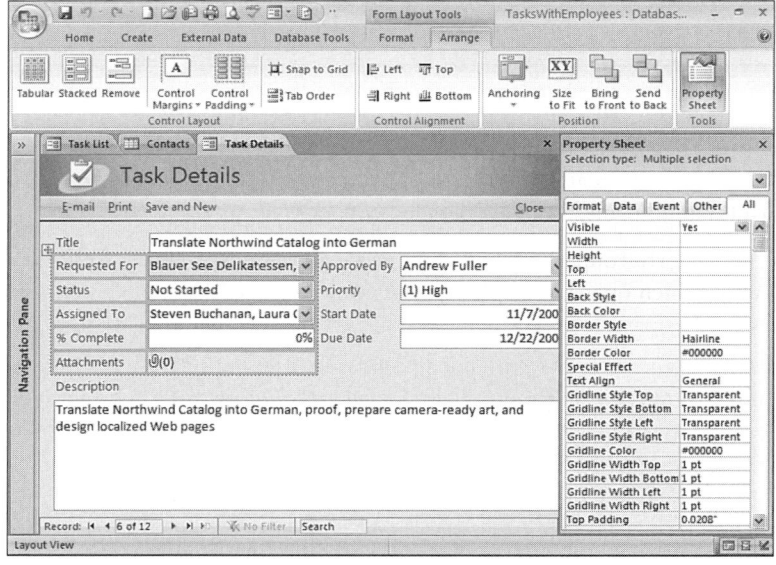

Figure 1.48
This modified Task Details form from a database generated from the Task template is open in Layout view with the Form Layout Tools, Arrange ribbon active.

DEFAULT FORM AND REPORT LAYOUTS

The Create ribbon's Forms section has buttons to auto-generate the following three types of forms from a table or query item selected in the NavPane:

- **Form**—Creates a form with Access 2007's default format that has one or two columns of stacked controls, depending on the number of table fields or query columns. If the selected object is a table that has a one-to-many relationship with another table in the database, an auto-generated Datasheet subform appears below the controls for the selected (parent) form (see Figure 1.49).

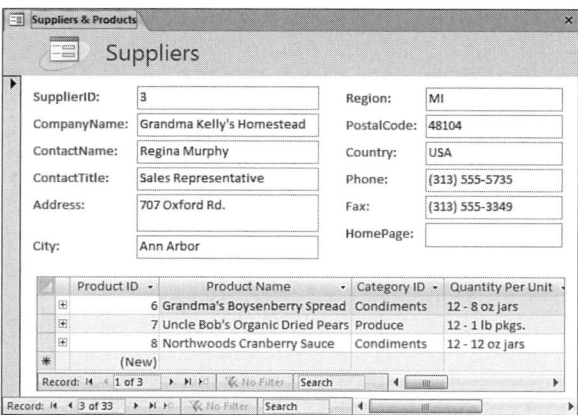

Figure 1.49
Clicking the Create ribbon's Form button generates a form-subform (master-child) form from tables that have an unambiguous one-to-many relationship with another table in the database. In this case the Northwind database's Suppliers table is the master (parent) and the Products table is the child.

■ **Split Form**—Creates a form with Access 2007's default format that has one or two columns of stacked controls (refer to Figure 1.4).

 ■ **Multiple Items**—Creates a tabular form with Access 2007's default format (refer to Figure 1.48).

Chapter 14, "Creating and Using Basic Access Forms," and Chapter 15, "Designing Custom Multitable Forms," provide detailed coverage of Access forms.

The Report group's Report button generates a tabular report from the selected table or query, which opens in Report Layout view. Access 2007 supplements the Print Preview view with a Report view that's better suited to display as a tabbed document (see Figure 1.50). As mentioned earlier, the default 11-point font size is attractive in Design and Layout views but causes forms to consume an excessive amount of paper and toner or ink.

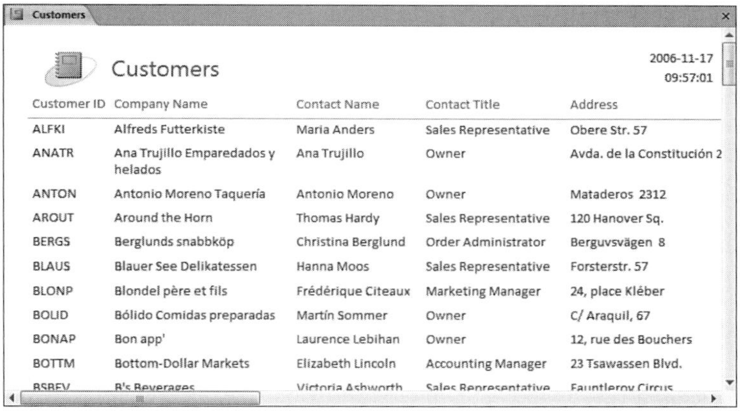

Figure 1.50
This Northwind Customers report is shown in Access 2007's new Report view, which supplements Print Preview view. Reports have the same default font size as forms, which is larger than necessary for reports.

Customers				2006-11-17 09:57:01
Customer ID	Company Name	Contact Name	Contact Title	Address
ALFKI	Alfreds Futterkiste	Maria Anders	Sales Representative	Obere Str. 57
ANATR	Ana Trujillo Emparedados y helados	Ana Trujillo	Owner	Avda. de la Constitución 2
ANTON	Antonio Moreno Taquería	Antonio Moreno	Owner	Mataderos 2312
AROUT	Around the Horn	Thomas Hardy	Sales Representative	120 Hanover Sq.
BERGS	Berglunds snabbköp	Christina Berglund	Order Administrator	Berguvsvägen 8
BLAUS	Blauer See Delikatessen	Hanna Moos	Sales Representative	Forsterstr. 57
BLONP	Blondel père et fils	Frédérique Citeaux	Marketing Manager	24, place Kléber
BOLID	Bólido Comidas preparadas	Martín Sommer	Owner	C/ Araquil, 67
BONAP	Bon app'	Laurence Lebihan	Owner	12, rue des Bouchers
BOTTM	Bottom-Dollar Markets	Elizabeth Lincoln	Accounting Manager	23 Tsawassen Blvd.
BSBEV	B's Beverages	Victoria Ashworth	Sales Representative	Fauntleroy Circus

CONTROL GROUPING, ANCHORING, MARGINS, AND PADDING

 You can group or ungroup a set of selected controls in tabular or stacked format by clicking the Form Layout Tools, Arrange ribbon's Tabular, Stacked, or Remove button. Stacked format is the default for Access forms. Tabular format is better suited for reports and forms with a few fields. You can move grouped controls as a unit; changes made to the width or height of labels or text boxes apply to all members of the group. Controls added by the Form, Split Form, and Multiple Items buttons are grouped by default. To ungroup a control, select it and click the Remove button. Alternatively, right-click the control and choose Layout, Remove.

 Anchoring lets you specify how a control behaves as users resize a form. By default, controls anchor to the top-left corner of the form. Clicking the Form Layout Tools, Arrange ribbon's Anchoring button opens a gallery that offers the nine anchoring options shown in Figure 1.51. Previously, relocating and resizing controls when resizing forms required writing a substantial amount of VBA code.

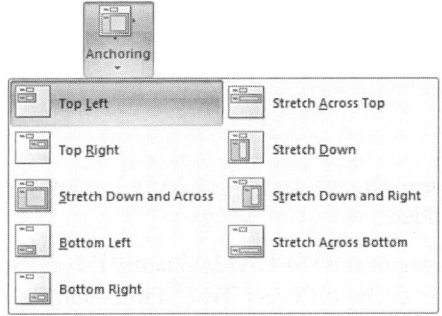

Figure 1.51
Apply one of these Anchoring options to controls to relocate or resize them when users change the size of the form.

Control margins specify the amount of space between the content of the control (usually characters) and the four edges of the control. The options are <u>N</u>one (0"), <u>Na</u>rrow (0.0153"), <u>M</u>edium (0.0313"), and <u>W</u>ide (0.0625").

Control padding specifies the space between grouped controls. The options are <u>N</u>one (0"), <u>Na</u>rrow (0.0208"), <u>M</u>edium (0.0625"), or <u>W</u>ide (0.125").

PUBLISH TO PDF OR XPS DOCUMENTS

 You can publish most Access objects as static Adobe PDF or Microsoft XML Paper Specification (XPS) documents by clicking the External Data ribbon's PDF or XPS button in the Export group.

> **NOTE**
>
> You must download and install the 2007 Microsoft Office Add-in: Microsoft Save as PDF or XPS from the Microsoft website before you can save copies of objects in PDF or XPS format. The first time you use the PDF or XPS feature, you're prompted to download the add-in.

ACCESS MACROS REDUX

 Access 2007 treats macros as full-fledged objects, and the Access team encourages their use by new users and seasoned developers alike. As of Office 97, which replaced Access Basic with VBA, macros were deprecated. VBA was designated the strategic programming language for automating Access applications, and Office 97 included a macro-to-VBA converter to ease the upgrade effort. (The Database Tools ribbon's Macro group includes a Convert Form's Macros to Visual Basic button.)

Original Access macros had two basic defects: no error-handling capability and the lack of an equivalent to form and report Class Modules (also called *code behind forms*, or CBF). Access 2007 overcomes the first limitation with the new On Error macro action, which lets you specify how errors are handled with one of the following values of the Go To argument:

- **Next** disregards the error, and execution proceeds to the next macro action.
- **MacroName** stops executing the current macro and jumps to the named macro.
- **Fail** stops execution and displays an error message.

Embedded macros handle the missing CBF equivalent. Each form or report event has a builder button that opens a Choose Builder dialog that lets you select a Macro Builder, Expression Builder, or Code Builder.

As an example, an embedded macro in the \SEUA12\Chaptr01\NavPane.accdb database's Form1 (Customers List) hides the prebuilt Object Type, Tables and Related Views, Modified Date, and Created Date categories and locks the NavPane when you open the form (see Figure 1.52). Ordinarily, the AutoExec macro would execute these actions.

Figure 1.52
This embedded macro prevents users from seeing tables and queries in the NavPane, which otherwise might tempt them to explore or enter data directly instead of with forms.

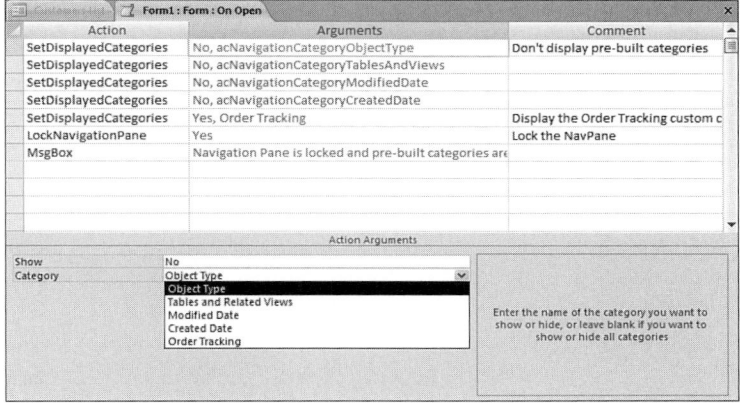

A similar macro that enables the prebuilt categories and unlocks the NavPane executes when you open Form2 (Orders List).

Chapter 26, "Automating Access Applications with Macros 2007," and Chapter 28, "Handling Events with Macros and VBA," show you how to write Access macros to handle simple tasks. VBA is better used for complex application automation chores.

COLLABORATION WITH SHAREPOINT

WSS 3.0 is a do-it-yourself intranet portal for facilitating collaboration between members of an organization's teams, workgroups, and small departments. WSS 3.0's primary claims to fame are easy installation, management by users, and no per-seat licensing fees. WSS 3.0 is a no-charge add-on to all versions of Windows Server 2003 and later. Microsoft promotes WSS 3.0 and MOSS 2007 as the linchpin for cooperative interaction between users of Office 2007.

WSS 3.0 components aren't included with Windows Server 2003, so system administrators must download and install the product from the Windows Update site. Once provisioned by the IT department, WSS 3.0 users often manage their own WSS sites.

If you have a WSS site on your intranet or a subscription to an Internet-hosted WSS site, you can export Jet or SQL Server tables as shared WSS lists. You can then connect the list to a linked Jet table and synchronize the list's contents between Access applications and WSS. (You can't link SQL Server tables to WSS lists.) Figure 1.53 shows in WSS list view a list imported from Northwind.mdb's Products table and linked to a table named Northwind Suppliers in the same database. Changes made to the table in Access or the list in WSS replicate automatically.

Figure 1.53
The shared Products list is linked to an Access Northwind Products table in Northwind.accdb. Updates propagate from Access to WSS, and vice versa.

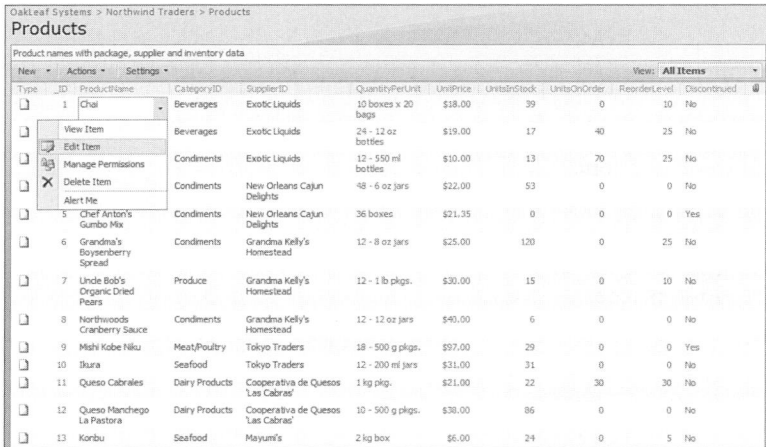

Access 2007 and WSS 3.0 enable taking an application offline, modifying data in local copies of linked data, reconnecting with WSS 3.0, and then synchronizing changes to the content made while offline in Access and SharePoint. You also can share .accdb or .accde files from WSS 3.0 document libraries.

Chapter 25, "Collaborating with Windows SharePoint Services" describes how to take full advantage of SharePoint lists.

NOTE

> MOSS 2007 is a greatly extended version of WSS 3.0 that replaces Microsoft SharePoint Portal Server and Content Management Server. There is no significant difference between the Access-related features of MOSS 2007 and WSS 3.0.

FEATURES MISSING FROM ACCESS 2007

Access 2007 no longer supports the following capabilities of Access 2003 and earlier versions:

- **User-level security**—Also known as object or workgroup security, user-level security uses workgroup files to grant very granular permissions on Access objects to users and groups of users. If you want truly secure applications, use client/server architecture with an ADP front-end and an SQL Server 2005 Express (SSX) SP2 or later back-end. Alternatively, link to SharePoint lists if you're willing to sacrifice performance, especially with large tables.

> **NOTE**
>
> Access 2007 is compatible with workgroup security for Access 2003 and earlier .mdb and .mdw files. Access doesn't support workgroup security for .accdb or .accde files.

- **Database replication**—Access replication enables users to synchronize multiple replicas of an Access database with a common replication master version. Access 2007 doesn't support replication of .accdb files but you can replicate an .mdb database. SSX can replicate SQL Server 2005 Workgroup edition or higher tables but can't be a replication partner with another SSX instance.
- **Data access pages (DAP)**—Access 2007 can't open or edit DAP. Access 2003 was the end of the line for Microsoft's attempt to add intranet connectivity to Access forms.
- **ODBCDirect workspaces**—Access 2007 no longer supports ODBCDirect workspaces to connect to external data sources without using the Access database engine. Microsoft recommends substituting ActiveX Data Objects (ADO).
- **Standard menus and toolbars**—The UI for earlier version's menu and toolbar customization isn't present, so you can't return to "classic mode."
- **Snapshot Viewer**—The Snapshot Viewer isn't included but you can export objects in PDF or XPS format. You can download the Snapshot Viewer from Office Online.

The only unsupported feature that has distressed long-time Access developers is user-level security. Access's 2007 workarounds to emulate revoking user permissions for viewing and editing objects are clumsy, at best.

SQL SERVER 2005 EXPRESS EDITION SP2 SETUP

SQL Server 2005 Express replaces Access 2000's Microsoft Data Engine (MSDE) 1.0 (based on SQL Server 7.0) and Access 2002 and 2003's Microsoft SQL Server Desktop Engine (MSDE) 2000 (based on SQL Server 2000). SSX is a major upgrade to MSDE 2000 and took Microsoft almost five years to complete the latest SQL Server version. Unlike MSDE, SSX includes a management tool—SQL Server Management Studio Express (SSMS). SSX removes MSDE's performance throttle, which limited query execution to five simultaneously running queries.

> **TIP**
>
> If you're creating multiuser database applications for an organization or team and loss or corruption of data would have serious economic or social consequences, consider substituting Access data projects and SSX for .accdb databases. SSX is a much more robust, secure, and reliable data engine than Access's. The only downside of moving to SSX is loss of new SharePoint-specific features, such as the Attachment field data type, MVLFs, and append-only Memo fields.

Office 2000–2003 included installation code for MSDE 1.0 and 2000; the Office 2007 CD-ROM doesn't include SQL Server 2005 Express Edition with Advanced Services (SSX-AS) Service Pack 2, which is the recommended version for Access users who don't have a network connection to SQL Server 2000 Standard or 2005 Workgroup Edition or higher.

> **NOTE**
>
> SSX-AS SP1 or later is required to work through the client/server examples of this book's Part V under Windows XP or Windows Server 2003. SP2 or later is required for Windows Vista or "Longhorn" Server.

DOWNLOADING AND INSTALLING SSX

If you intend to develop or just explore Access 2007 data projects (ADP) or Access front-ends linked to SQL Server 2005 tables, do the following to install SSX-AS SP2 on your client PC or a network server:

1. Download the SQL Server 2005 Express Edition with Advanced Services Service Pack 2 installer (SQLExpr_Adv.exe, 256.1MB) from the location specified at http://www.microsoft.com/sql/.

2. Run SQLExpr_Adv.exe with an administrative account, accept the End User License Agreement, click Next, and then click Install to install the prerequisite SQL Server Native Client and Setup Support files.

3. After the prerequisites install, click Next to perform a system configuration check and display the Microsoft SQL Server 2005 Setup dialog. Click Next to perform another System Configuration Check, and click Next to start the installation.

4. In the Registration Information dialog, type your name, if necessary, clear the Hide Advanced Configuration Options check box, and click Next.

5. In the Feature Selection dialog, open and select Entire Feature Will Be Installed on Local Hard Drive for Database Services, Reporting Services, and Client Components (see Figure 1.54). The disk space requirement is about 370MB. Click Next.

Figure 1.54
The Feature Selection dialog lets you choose the features to install. For this example, select Entire Feature Will Be Installed on Local Hard Drive for the three main features.

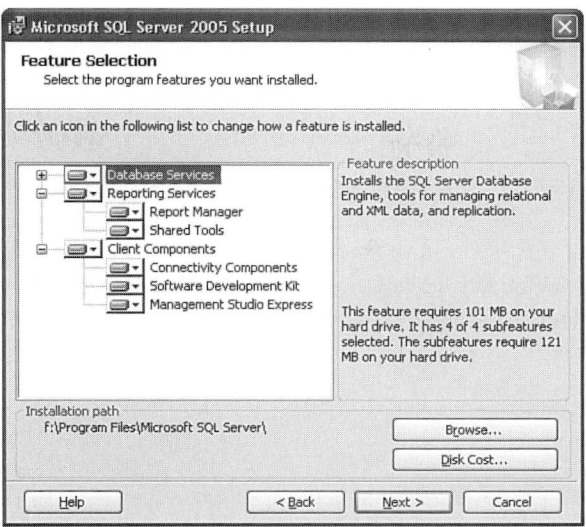

TIP

> If you don't plan on exploring SQL Server Reporting Services or testing SQL Server Full-Text Search features, you can accept the default Not Available choices.

6. By default, SSX installs as a named instance (*COMPUTERNAME*\SQLEXPRESS), so accept the Instance Name dialog's Named Instance option (see Figure 1.55). ADPs use the complete name of the instance, such as OAKLEAF-MS16\SQLEXPRESS, to connect to SSX. Click Next.

Figure 1.55
Accept the Named Instance option and the default SQLEXPRESS instance name unless you have a good reason for doing otherwise.

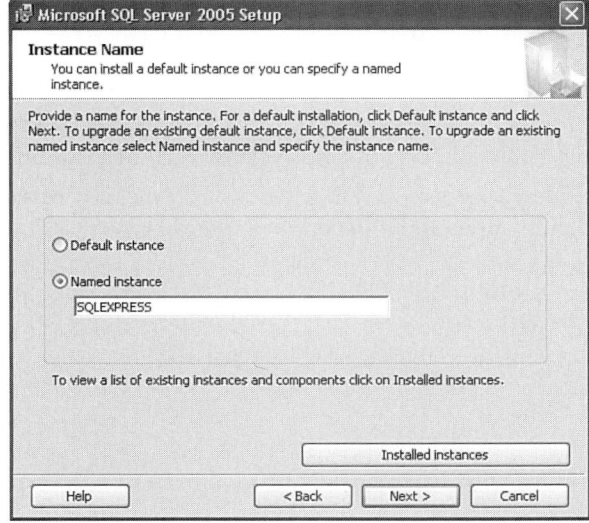

7. If the Existing Components dialog appears, mark the check boxes to upgrade them and then click Next.

8. In the Service Account dialog, accept the defaults unless you want to run SSX under an account other than the Network Service account (see Figure 1.56). Click Next.

Figure 1.56
Network Service is the default for SSX's service account because it has a relatively low security level.

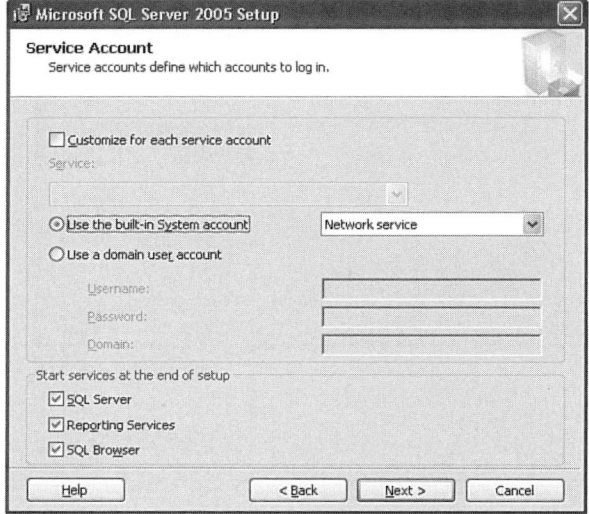

9. The Authentication Mode dialog lets you enable SQL Server Security by selecting the Mixed Mode option and then typing and confirming a strong password for the sa (system administrator) account (see Figure 1.57). Enabling the sa account is good insurance if you don't have a Domain Admins or higher Active Directory account or your computer isn't a member of an Active Directory domain. Click Next.

10. In the Configuration Options dialog, mark the Add User to the SQL Server Administrator Role check box. This is a very important option when running SSX under Windows Vista (see Figure 1.58). Click Next.

11. Accept the default Report Server Installation Options and click Next.

12. Optionally, mark the Automatically Send Error Reports and Automatically Send Feature Usage Data check boxes if you want to send this information to Microsoft. Click Next.

13. Review the Ready to Install dialog. If the dialog warns that components installed are at a different service pack level, follow the instructions to upgrade those components after completing the main upgrade.

Figure 1.57
Specifying Mixed Mode security and adding a strong password for the sa account gives you insurance that you won't lose system administrator rights to SSX as the result of an Active Directory problem.

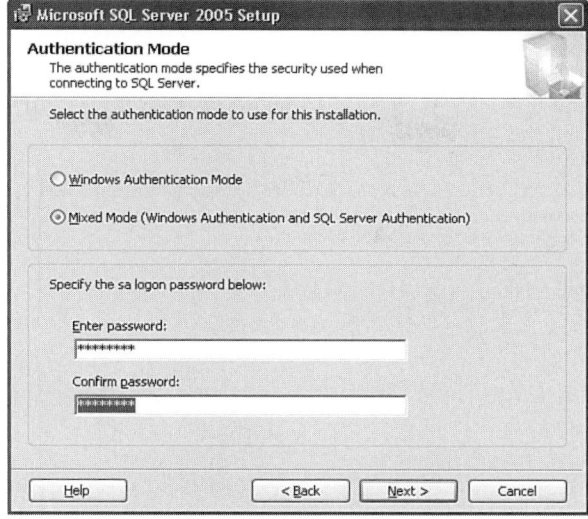

Figure 1.58
Windows Vista discourages users from logging on with administrative rights, so mark the Add User to the SQL Server Administrator Role check box.

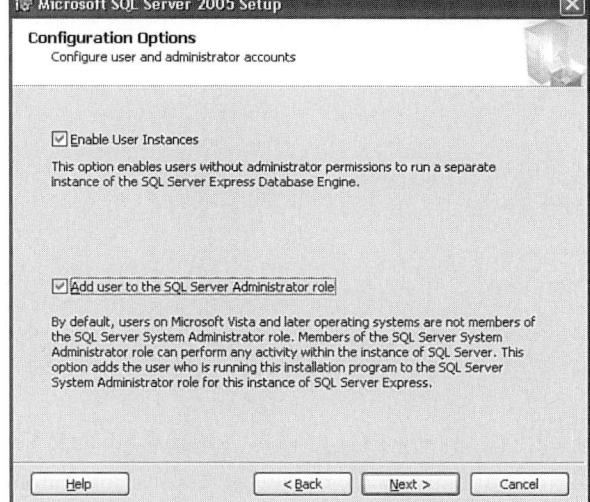

14. Click Install to start the final installation process, which takes 20–30 minutes on a moderately fast computer. The installation progress dialog monitors the process (see Figure 1.59).

Figure 1.59
The installation progress dialog follows the setup operations for the three major components you selected in step 5.

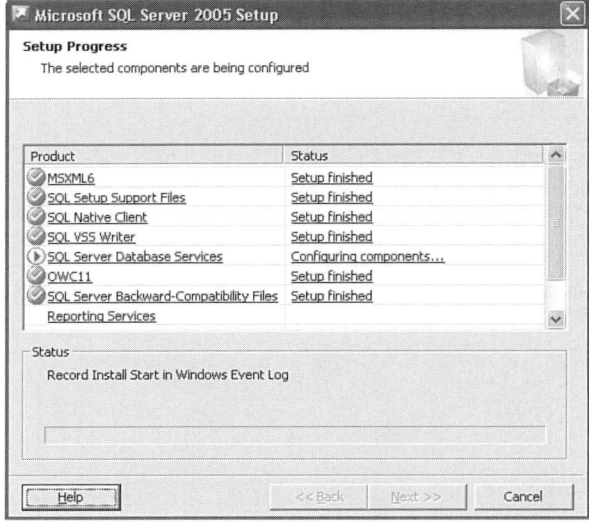

NOTE

Users with SSX already installed might need to upgrade Microsoft SQL Server 2005 Tools (SQL_Expr_Toolkit.exe) in a later operation.

15. Review the Completing Microsoft SQL Server 2005 Setup dialog for additional steps you need to perform, such as downloading the latest version of SQL Server Books Online (about 130MB), the online help file for SSX (see Figure 1.60). Click Finish to complete the first phase of the installation.

16. Complete the additional installations or upgrades identified in steps 14 and 15.

Setup installs a Programs, Microsoft SQL Server 2005 submenu. If you selected all available SSX-AS SP2 features in preceding step 5, the submenu has Configuration Tools, SQL Server Management Studio Express, and Documentation and Tutorials. Installing the Microsoft SQL Server 2005 Toolkit adds a Business Intelligence Development Studio menu choice if you install Reporting Services. Installing Books Online adds its choice to the Documentation and Tutorials submenu.

→ To learn more about SQL Server Management Studio Express (SSMSX), **see** "Moving from MSDE to the SQL Server 2005 Express Edition," **p. 1346**.

Figure 1.60
Completing the
Microsoft SQL Server
2005 Setup dialog
summarizes addi-
tional setup steps that
follow the main
installation operation.

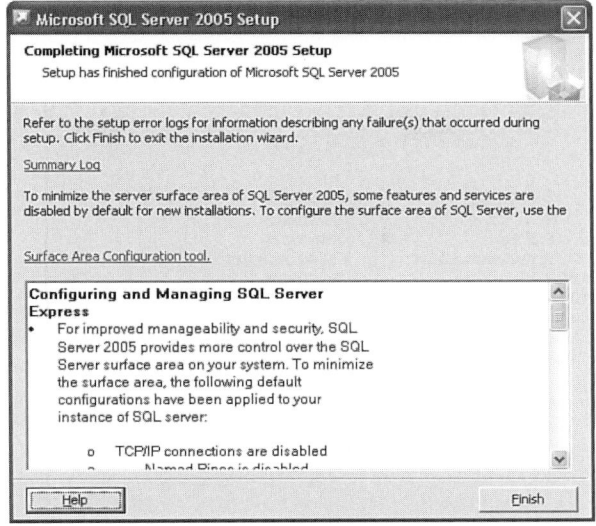

MANAGING SSX

If you run SSX on the same machine as your Access front end, you don't need to do anything after installation. SSX will start as a service automatically when you boot your com-
puter. If you want to make the instance of SSX you install accessible to remote networked
users, you must perform some minimal management tasks. You must set the SQL Server
Browser Service to start automatically and enable at least the TCP/IP protocol for SSX. The
Browser Service enables clients to locate SQL Server 2005 instances on remote computers.
If you're running the Windows Firewall and Install doesn't establish exceptions for SQL
Server and SQL Server Browser, you must create an exception for SQL Server and Browser
connections also.

MAKING SSX ACCESSIBLE TO REMOTE USERS

To make a local SSX instance accessible to other networked computers, do the following:

1. Choose Programs, Microsoft SQL Server 2005, Configuration Tools, SQL Server
   Configuration Manager to open the dialog of the same name.

2. Double-click the SQL Server Configuration Manager (Local) node to display the nodes
   SQL Server 2005 Services, SQL Server 2005 Network Configuration, and SQL Native
   Client Configuration.

3. Double-click the SQL Server 2005 Services node to display the SQL Server Browser
   and SQL Server (SQLEXPRESS) service items in the right pane (see Figure 1.61). If
   you installed other services, they will appear also.

Figure 1.61
Installing the SSX database engine installs but doesn't start the SQL Server Browser service automatically.

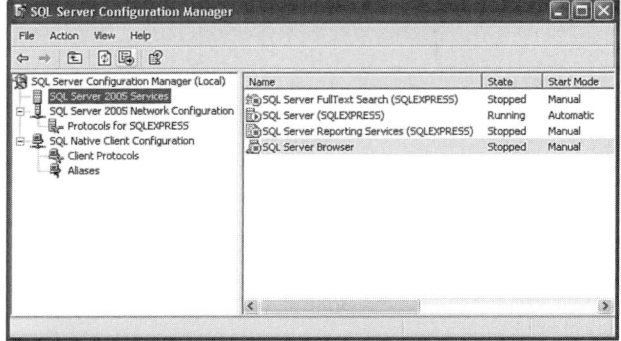

4. Right-click the SQL Server Browser item and choose Properties to open the SQL Server Browser Properties dialog. Click the Service tab, open the Start Mode list box, and choose Automatic (see Figure 1.62). Click OK to close the Properties dialog.

Figure 1.62
Change the SQL Server Browser's Start Mode setting to Automatic.

5. Right-click the SQL Server Browser item and choose Start to start the service for the first time.

6. Double-click to expand the SQL Server 2005 Network Configuration item, select the Protocols for SQL Express node, right-click the TCP/IP item in the right pane's Protocol Name list, and choose Enabled (see Figure 1.63). Acknowledge the message that states you must stop and restart SSX for the change to become effective.

Figure 1.63
Enable the TCP/IP protocol for SSX to communicate with remote clients.

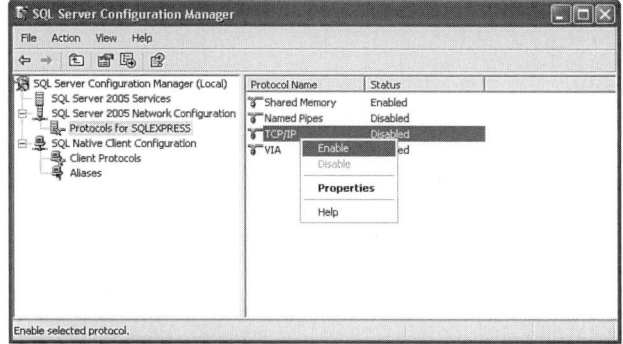

7. If you want to communicate with remote SSX or SQL Server instances, expand the SQL Native Client Configuration node, select Client Protocols, and enable the TCP/IP protocol.

8. Select SQL 2005 Services, right-click SQL Server (SQLEXPRESS), choose Stop, wait for the service to stop, and then choose Start. If SQL Server Reporting Services or FullText Search are started, stop them to conserve resources.

9. Close SQL Server Configuration Manager.

Alternatively, you can access SQL Server Configuration manager from the Computer Management dialog's Services and Applications node.

VERIFYING OR ENABLING SSX CONNECTIONS THROUGH THE WINDOWS FIREWALL

If the computer from which you want to share access to SSX runs Windows Firewall, then follow these steps:

1. Open Windows Firewall by clicking Start, Run, typing **firewall.cpl** in the text box, and clicking OK.

> **TIP**
>
> If you receive a message asking if you want to start the Windows Firewall/Internet Connection Sharing service or the Off option is selected in the Windows Firewall dialog, you're not running Windows Firewall, so you can quit at this point.

2. Click the Windows Firewall dialog's Exceptions tab and look for the SQL Server and SQL Server Browser check boxes in the Programs and Services list (see Figure 1.64). If they're present and checked, close the dialog; otherwise, check them and close the dialog.

Figure 1.64
SSX setup has added Windows Firewall exceptions for SQL Server and SQL Server Browser.

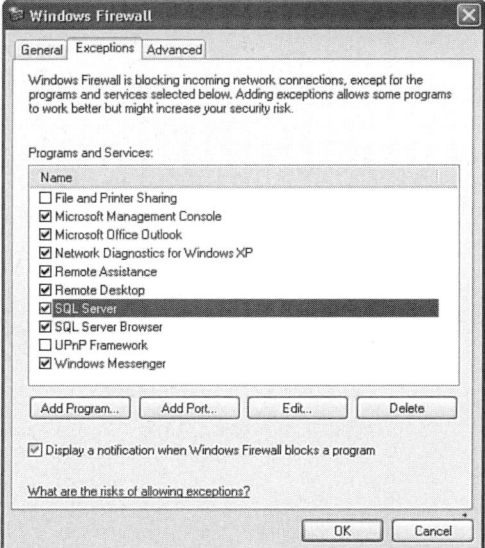

3. If the two check boxes weren't present, click Add Programs and then click Browse.

4. Navigate to and select the C:\Program Files\Microsoft SQL Server\MSSQL.1\MSSQL\Binn\sqlservr.exe file, click Open, and click OK.

5. Repeat steps 2 and 3, but open the C:\Program Files\Microsoft SQL Server\90\Shared\sqlbrowser.exe executable program, click Open, and click OK.

6. Close Windows Firewall.

ACCESS RUNTIME AND DEVELOPER EXTENSIONS

Microsoft announced on January 30, 2007—Microsoft Office 2007's retail release date—that the Access 2007 Runtime Edition and Developer Extensions will be available for download from the Microsoft Office Online site at no charge. Previously, the Runtime and Developer Extensions were components of Visual Studio Tools for Office (VSTO), which cost about $800 for new users and $550 for upgrades.

Access 2007 Runtime is an executable file that enables developers to provide Access applications that don't require users to have their own Microsoft Office or Access 2007 license. (Access is the only Office member that has a runtime edition.)

Access 2007 Developer Extensions include the following three components:

- **Package Solution** is a wizard that creates a Windows Installer Package (MSI file) to install an Access database and its supporting files. You can include the Access 2007 Runtime Edition in the package or specify a prompt for the user to download the Runtime.

- **Save As Template** lets you create database templates (.accdt files) that can be included on the Access 2007 Getting Started page.
- **Source Code Control** provides integration with Microsoft Visual Source Safe or other source code control systems.

The Access 2007 Developer Extensions don't include the Property Scanner and Customer Startup Wizard components that were included in previous versions.

IN THE REAL WORLD—MAKING ACCESS EASIER TO USE

Microsoft Access was just turning 14 when Access 2007 released to manufacturing on November 6, 2006. (Microsoft introduced Access 1.0 on November 16, 1992, at Fall Comdex.) Although the Access team added many features to the seven subsequent versions (1.1, 2.0, 95, 97, 2000, 2002, and 2003), Access's basic approach to database application creation, data and application object set, and user interface changed very little over the years. Creating a production database application with any desktop relational database management system (RDBMS) of the era was more complex than most other PC activities, so power users and database developers became Access's target market. Access was Microsoft's first productivity application to offer a runtime version—the Access Distribution Kit (ADK) for version 1.1 and Access Developer's Toolkit (ADT) for Access 2.0 and 95.

The inclusion of Access 97 and later with the Professional and higher editions of the Microsoft Office suite expanded Access's target audience greatly. Knowledge workers began to replace spreadsheets with relational tables to make data entry more efficient and reliable, data presentation more flexible and attractive, and data reporting more versatile. Wizards, which Access introduced, simplified many individual tasks, but creating a production-grade database application was beyond the skill level of most PC users at the time.

Access has by far the largest share of the desktop RDBMS market, but longtime competitors, such as FileMaker Pro, Alpha Five, and even Microsoft's own Visual FoxPro (VFP), continue to attract new users. Alpha Five and VFP usually are classified as developer tools, while Access and FileMaker Pro are targeted at both end users and developers. Web-based database managers, typified by Intuit Corp.'s QuickBooks, compete for end-users' attention. A recent surge of new entrants at the low end of the Web database management spectrum offer free or low-cost subscriptions to forms-based data entry and sharing applications. Microsoft's Web-based Office Live Premium competes in the small-office, home-office (SOHO) database market segment with Office Live Business Contact Manager and pre-built SharePoint templates for about 30 business applications. Office Live Premium costs $39.95 per month and includes website hosting, 50 email accounts, and 4GB of storage.

FileMaker, Inc., which is a head-on Access competitor, claims to have shipped 10 million copies of FileMaker Pro during the two decades from 1984 to 2004. Apple Computer spun off FileMaker, Inc., from its Claris subsidiary as a wholly owned subsidiary in 1998. By 2000, according to analysts Aberdeen Group, FileMaker, Inc., had hit U.S.$100 million in sales for its Windows and Macintosh versions. While other desktop RDBMS competitors, such as Lotus Approach (part of IBM's Lotus SmartSuite) and Paradox (part of Corel's WordPerfect Office suite), have stagnated, by 2004 FileMaker Pro claimed to have garnered an estimated 25% share of the Windows and 90% of the Macintosh desktop database platform market.

NOTE

> OpenOffice.org 2.0's Base database application has gained some adherents of "open source" software and Sun Microsystems includes its proprietary StarBase in StarOffice 8, but Base isn't a significant contender in the desktop RDBMS market. StarOffice also includes a copy of SAP's Adabas D 13 Personal Edition, which is limited to three concurrent users and 100MB of data. SAP offers an AccessPlus migration tool for Access users.

The most probable reason for FileMaker Pro's success is ease of use. Access has what many users contend is an undeserved reputation for being difficult for new users to fathom. A Google search on "I hate Access" returned 723 hits when this book was written, but "I hate FileMaker" returned only 47.

As noted near the beginning of this chapter, Microsoft's stated goal for Access 2007 is to improve usability for new users and increase productivity for experienced users and developers. Moving from the traditional Database Window to the new ribbon UI, Navigation Pane and tabbed documents probably makes creating a simple single-table application easier for database neophytes. But the new tracking templates probably will contribute the most to ease of use by new Access customers.

Third parties sell FileMaker templates, but FileMaker, Inc., offers single-purpose tracking applications—Donations, Meetings, Tasks, and Work Requests—at prices ranging from US$69 to $129, as well as the $299 Recruiter for tracking job candidates. The individual applications don't include the FileMaker Pro 8.5 RDBMS, which sells for $299, or the $499 Advanced version.

QuickBase claims to have "more than 200 ready-made applications to help corporate workgroups better manage their business workflows" and "almost half of the Fortune 100" as users. Many of these "ready-made applications" are more sophisticated versions of Access 2007 templates. Despite the fact that QuickBase's lowest-priced subscription is $249 per month for 10 users, QuickBase has taken significant market share from Access.

Hopefully, the initial Access 2007 tracking templates will be supplemented by increasingly specialized versions with more related tables and sophisticated navigation techniques, forms, and reports. Templates to create Access applications that emulate and are compatible with Office Live Essentials' business applications might be a good start. In the meantime, give today's templates described in the next chapter a try to see if they make Access easier to use and more fathomable for you or your colleagues.

CHAPTER 2

BUILDING SIMPLE TRACKING APPLICATIONS

In this chapter

UNDERSTANDING ACCESS'S APPROACH TO APPLICATION DESIGN

Unlike other members of 2007 Microsoft Office System, Access 2007 requires that you build an application to take advantage of the product's power as a database development platform. It's up to you to design and implement the Access applications you need for most database projects.

A full-scale Access application involves at least the following four basic Access object types:

- *Tables* that store the data you or others add to the database

- *Queries* to filter and sort table data as well as to combine data in related tables

- *Forms* for displaying and entering data, controlling the opening and closing of other forms, and printing reports

- *Reports* to print detail data, summary information, or both in tables

Many Access applications include *modules* to store Visual Basic for Applications (VBA) code. Word 2007 and Excel 2007 let you automate simple repetitive operations by recording VBA macros. Access 2007 also supports a set of *macro commands* (also called *macro actions*) primarily for compatibility with previous versions, but Access macros don't use VBA. Access doesn't capture your mouse clicks or keystrokes and turn them into a series of macro commands or VBA code. You define Access macros by selecting the macro command you want from a list and customizing its action.

Access forms can (and often do) contain VBA code in a special type of module, called a *Class Module*. Access 2007 forms also can contain a new type of macro, called an *embedded macro*, which corresponds to a Class Module. Bear in mind that you can create many useful Access applications without writing a single macro or a line of VBA code.

TIP

> All versions of Access have offered macros as an alternative to writing programming code. Starting with Access 97, Microsoft recommended abandoning the use of macros in favor of VBA code in modules and Class Modules. Access 97 and later include a Macro to Module Converter that automates replacing macro commands with VBA code. The implication was that macros would disappear in future Access versions.
>
> Now Microsoft is resurrecting macros in the belief that writing macros presents a lesser challenge for new Access users than writing VBA code. The downside of adopting macros is that eventually you'll find that you need VBA code to accomplish many tasks for which there are no macro commands. In this case, you would need to learn *two* programming methodologies and languages.

All objects that make up your application are stored in a container called a *Database object*, which is a single file with an .accdb extension, such as the Northwind.accdb sample database that the CD-ROM stores in your \SEUA12\Nwind folder. Access is unique in that it can store an entire database application in a single file. Other desktop databases, such as Microsoft FoxPro, require multiple files to store their objects.

CREATING ACCESS APPLICATIONS FROM DOWNLOADED TEMPLATES

New Access users often find it difficult to "get a grip" on how to start developing a self-contained database application. Dealing with an unfamiliar set of objects tends to intimidate first-time database developers. Fortunately, Microsoft Office Online offers a set of templates that create typical Access 2007 "starter" applications automatically.

 In this chapter, you download templates to create a relatively simple but useful data compilation and tracking application. Then you explore the objects generated by the templates to gain perspective on the relationship of Access objects and learn how they're integrated within a typical Access database application.

USING THE GETTING STARTED WINDOW TO DOWNLOAD TEMPLATES

When you launch Access 2007 from the Start, Programs menu, the Getting Started with Microsoft Office Access window opens by default (see Figure 2.1).

Figure 2.1
The Getting Started with Microsoft Office Access window is the entry point to creating a new Access database application.

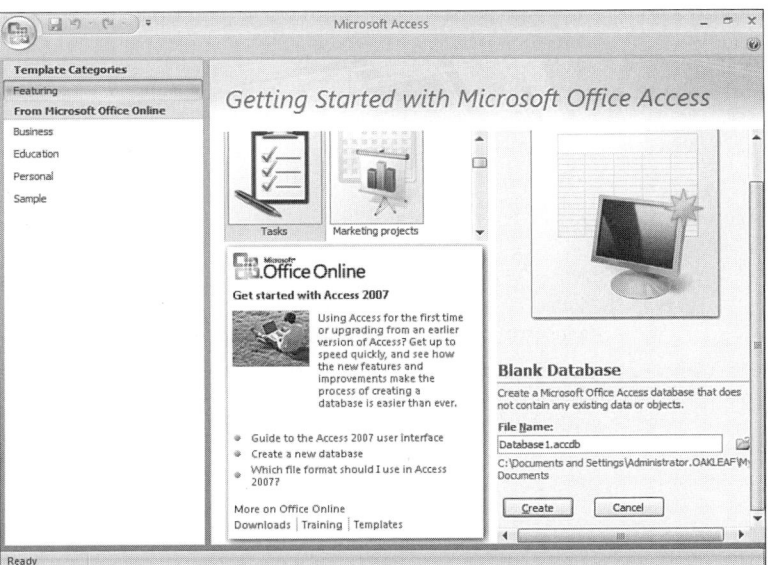

The Getting Started window offers the following options:

- Open a blank (empty) database with no Access objects other than a starter table. You can type data into the starter table's initial column and as many more columns as you need. (The starter table disappears if you don't modify its design and save your changes.) You then add table, query, form, and report objects with the Create ribbon's button.

- Open a blank Access data project (ADP or project). A project substitutes an SQL Server database for Access's built-in table and query objects. Chapter 20, "Exploring Access Data Projects and SQL Server 2005," through Chapter 22, "Upsizing Access Applications to Access Data Projects," cover projects.

- Select one of about 10 popular Access 2007 templates to download from the Microsoft Office Online website at http://office.microsoft.com/en-us/templates/default.aspx.

- Open the Templates home page of the Microsoft Office Online website, where you can search for and then browse a collection of templates for Access 2000 and later.

- Move the tables to a Windows SharePoint Services (WSS 3.0) or Microsoft Office SharePoint Server (MOSS) 2007 site and then link them to the database by checking the Create and Link Your Database to a Windows SharePoint Services Site check box. Chapter 25, "Collaborating with Windows SharePoint Services," covers interacting with WSS 3.0 and MOSS 2007.

To open the Getting Started window if you have a database open, click the Office button in the upper-left corner of Access's main window to open the File gallery and then click the New link (see Figure 2.2).

Figure 2.2
Click the Office button to open the File gallery and click the New link to open the Getting Started window.

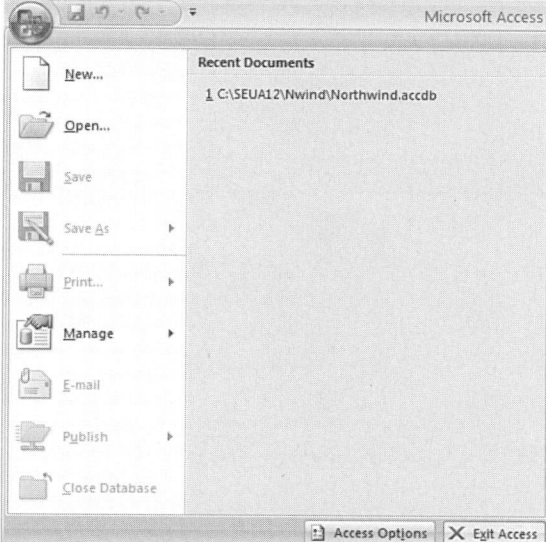

CHANGING THE DEFAULT FOLDER FOR NEW DATABASES AND PROJECTS

Access stores all new databases and projects that you create in the C:\Documents and Settings*UserName*\My Documents folder (Windows XP and Server 2003) or C:\Users\ *UserName*\Documents folder (Windows Vista) by default.

You can change the default database location by doing the following:

1. Click the Office button in the upper-left corner of Access's main window to open the File gallery (refer to Figure 2.2).
2. Click the Access Options button to open the Access Options dialog.
3. On the default Popular page's Default Database Folder text box, type or browse to the path to the new default database location (see Figure 2.3).
4. Click OK to close the Access Options dialog and File gallery and to set the new default file location.

Figure 2.3
Specify the default database folder in the default page of the Access Options dialog.

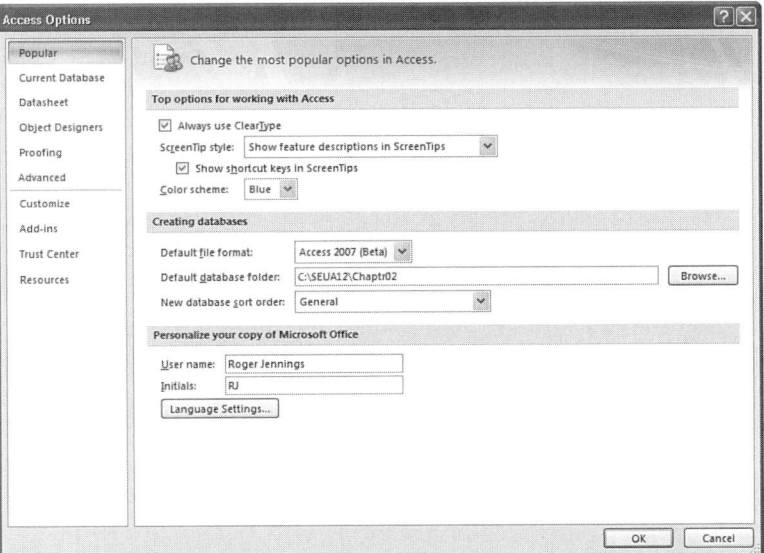

CREATING A DATABASE FROM A GETTING STARTED WINDOW TEMPLATE

The scrolling list in the top center of the Getting Started window contains icons for templates that are designed specifically for Access 2007's new user interface (UI).

REVIEWING FEATURED TEMPLATES

Following are the names and brief descriptions of featured templates whose icons appear in the list when you click the Featuring link:

- **Assets**—Contains the Assets and Contacts tables, Assets Extended and Contacts Extended queries, seven forms, and eight reports that relate to tracking and valuing business assets.

- **Contacts**—Contains a Contacts table, Contacts Extended query, Contact List and Contact Details forms, and Contact Address Book and Contact Phone List reports. A button that executes an embedded macro lets you populate the Contact List table from an Outlook contacts list.

- **Events**—Contains an Events table, Current Events query, Event Details and Event List forms, and five reports classified by date and time.

- **Faculty**—Contains a modified version of Contacts that includes the capability to classify a faculty member by selections from Faculty Type and Department combo boxes. Although you can edit the combo box lists, it's a better database design technique to populate combo and list boxes from entries in tables.

NOTE

> Faculty also has Emergency Contact and Medical Information incorporated as fields of the Faculty table, which violates relational database design rules. As you'll learn in Chapter 4, "Exploring Relational Database Theory and Practice," Emergency Contact and Medical Information should be contained in separate, related tables.

- **Issues**—Contains the Issues and Contacts tables, Contacts Extended and Open Issues queries, seven forms, and eight reports. Issues is a starting point for a help desk, customer service, or bug reports database.

- **Marketing Projects**—An expanded version of Projects that contains Projects, Deliverables, Common Deliverables, Employees, and Vendors tables, 9 queries, 16 forms (one of which is a PivotChart form for budgets), and 10 reports. Marketing Projects is the most complex of the databases generated from featured templates.

- **Projects**—A basic project management database with Projects, Tasks, Common Tasks, and Employees tables, 7 queries, 11 forms, and nine reports.

- **Students**—A simplification of the Faculty database that shares its defective table design.

- **Sales Pipeline**—A mini customer relationship management (CRM) application with Customers, Opportunities, and Employees tables, 5 queries, 13 forms, 9 reports, and a standalone macro group. Sales Pipeline offers PivotChart and PivotTable forms for forecasting.

- **Tasks**—A variation on the Issues theme with Contacts and Tasks tables, Contacts Extended and Open Tasks queries, five forms, and seven reports.

The Assets, Contacts, Events, Issues, and Tasks templates create database tables that have the same structure as the same-named WSS 3.0 and MOSS 2007 lists.

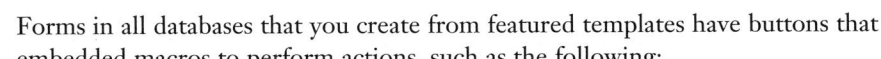

NOTE

Databases with single tables—such as Contacts, Events, Faculty, and Students—offer few, if any, advantages compared with an Excel worksheet containing the same information. The capability to quickly generate nicely formatted reports might be a plus for Access, but data entry probably would be faster in Excel.

EMBEDDING MACROS IN FEATURED TEMPLATES

Forms in all databases that you create from featured templates have buttons that execute embedded macros to perform actions, such as the following:

- **New Item**—Opens the *Item* Details form for the item type, such as Contact or Event, to add a new row to the table. *Item* Details forms are unnecessarily obese modal dialogs, not tabbed documents.

- **Collect Data via E-Mail**—Opens a multistep Collect Data Through E-Mail Messages Wizard that uses Outlook 2007 and an HTML form to update existing or add new rows to the form's underlying table.

- **E-Mail List**—Lets you send the content of the *Item* table as an email enclosure in one of nine standard or proprietary formats.

- **Reports List**—Lets you open each of the databases reports in Access 2007's new Report view, which complements Print Preview view.

Some templates, such as Marketing Projects, include standalone macro groups also. Standalone macro groups aren't limited to execution from a particular form.

SPELUNKING SPECIALIZED TEMPLATES FOR BUSINESS AND PERSONAL USE

The following are additional templates for more specialized use in the Business and Personal categories

- **Business Account Ledger (Business)**—A simple, single-entry application that can generate a profit and loss statement. A Categories table represents a simple chart of accounts for income and expenses.

- **Customer Service (Business)**—Contains Customers, Cases, Calls, Employees, and Knowledge Base tables, 7 queries, 16 forms, 11 reports, and a standalone Report Center macro group. The most interesting feature of this database is the Report Center form with a Tab control to display Overdue, Days Active, Status, and Category PivotCharts.

- **Lending Library (Business)**—Intended for a book or equipment rental service with Assets (for rent), Contacts (customers), and Transactions tables, 3 queries, 8 forms (including Check Out and Check In), 13 reports, and a standalone Transactions macro group.

- **Home Inventory (Personal)**—A single-table database for creating a home inventory list, presumably for insurance purposes.

- **Nutrition (Personal)**—A very complex application with 8 tables, 9 queries, a start-up screen, 18 other forms, and 8 standalone macro groups.

- **Personal Account Ledger (Personal)**—A version of the Business Account Leger with a Categories table that has accounts more suited to personal income and expenses.

NOTE

Copies of all the preceding template-generated databases are in the C:\SEUA12\Chaptr02 folder, if you transferred the sample files from the CD-ROM to your C:\ drive.

DOWNLOADING TEMPLATES TO GENERATE SAMPLE DATABASES

To download a template and create the corresponding *TemplateName*.accdb database, do the following:

1. Select the template category in the Getting Started window's left pane.
2. Select the template to download in the scrolling list.
3. Click the Download button (refer to Figure 2.1) to open the Microsoft Office Genuine Advantage message box.
4. Mark the Don't Show This Message Again check box and click Continue to perform the authenticity test, download the template, create the database, and open its default form in Access 2007's new tabbed window.
5. If the Navigation Pane isn't open, click the Open Shutter Bar button to display it.
6. If all the Navigation Pane's headers don't display items below them, click their Category Items Show buttons to expand them.
7. Click Ctrl+F1 to hide the ribbon, if necessary, to add depth to the Navigation Pane so it shows all or most items.

Figure 2.4 shows the Tasks.accdb database's empty Tasks List form open in Form view. The default Tasks Navigation, Show All navigation options are selected in the Navigation Pane at the left of the Contact List. This chapter's later "Understanding the Role of the Navigation Pane" section describes Navigation Pane options.

DESIGNATING THE DEFAULT DATABASE FOLDER AS A TRUSTED LOCATION

Figure 2.4 illustrates the Message Bar for the Contacts database displaying a Security Warning: "Certain content in the database has been disabled." Clicking the Options button opens a Security Alert – VBA Macro dialog that claims "Access has disabled potentially harmful content in this database" (see Figure 2.5). This statement is bogus. There is no VBA code in the Contacts database, and Access did not disable anything; the message appears for databases without VBA code or macros.

Figure 2.4
The Tasks template creates the Tasks.accdb database with table, query, form, and report objects and opens its default Tasks List form. Tables don't appear by default in the Navigation Pane.

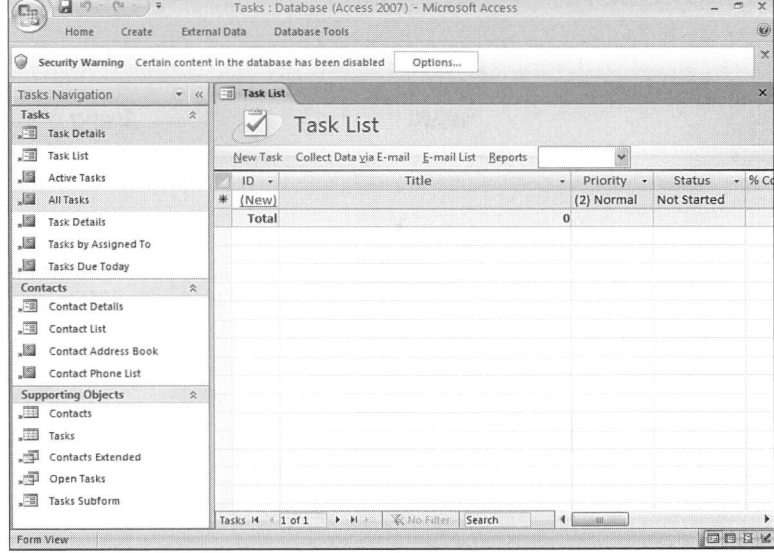

Figure 2.5
Clicking the Message Bar's Options button opens the Security Alert dialog that claims the database has "potentially harmful content" and offers an Enable This Content option for this session only.

VBA code and certain Access macro commands (actions) can access your computer's resources, such as disk drives or, for VBA, network interface cards. This means that a database with malicious code or macros could plant a virus or worm on your disk that might infect your network.

You can click the Options button and select the Enable This Content option each time you open any Access database, or specify one or more folders on your local machine or networked computers as *trusted locations*. Databases opened from trusted locations don't display the Message Bar.

To specify a folder—C:\SEUA12 for this example—and its subfolders as trusted locations, do the following:

1. Click the Office button to open the File gallery, and click the Access Options button to open the Access Options dialog.

2. Click the Trust Center button to open the Trust Center page, and click the Trust Center Settings button to open the Trusted Locations page, which has by default a single trusted C:\Program Files\Microsoft Office\Office 12\ACCWIZ\ folder for Access's wizards.

3. Click the Add New Location button to open the Microsoft Office Trusted Location dialog. Then type the folder's path in the Path text box, mark the Subfolders of This Location Are Also Trusted check box, and type a brief description of the folder in the Description text box (see Figure 2.6).

Figure 2.6
The Microsoft Office Trusted Location dialog lets you specify that Access is to trust any databases stored in the specified location and, optionally, its subfolders.

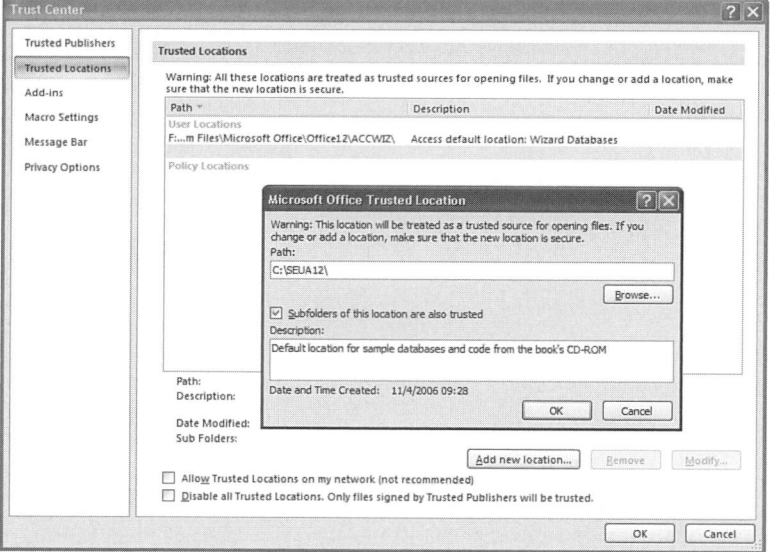

4. Click OK to add the location to the User Locations list (see Figure 2.7). Mark the Allow Trusted Locations on My Network check box if you want. Click OK twice to close the dialogs and gallery, and trust the new location.

Figure 2.7
The User Locations list has an item for each location on your local computer and, optionally, your intranet.

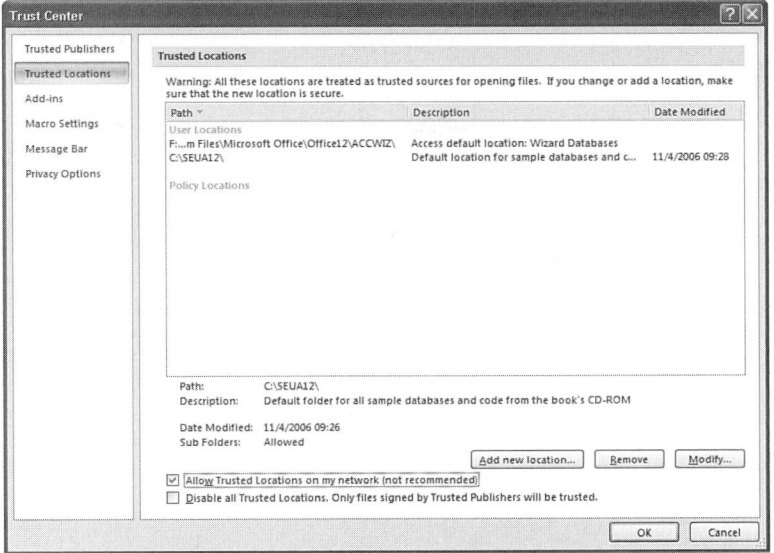

The next time you open a database from the C:\SEUA12 folder or its subfolders, the Security Warning message box won't appear.

CREATING A DATABASE FROM ANY ACCESS TEMPLATE ON MICROSOFT OFFICE ONLINE

The Microsoft Office Online Website's Templates page offers many Access templates for versions 2000, 2002, and 2003. You can generate Access 2007 databases from these templates, but you might need to modify their forms somewhat to accommodate Access 2007's new UI. Many Access 2007 templates have roots in those earlier Access versions.

To view the full list of Access templates and give one of the templates a test drive, open the File gallery and click Close to close any open database, and then follow these steps:

1. In the Office Online box, click the Templates link to open the Office Online Website's Templates page.

2. Type **Access** in the Search Templates text box, and click Search to display a list of available templates in the Search Result page.

3. Click one of the template names, such as Contact Management, to open a template preview dialog (see Figure 2.8).

4. Click the Download Now button to retrieve the template file and open a message about the visibility of "Favorites" in earlier versions of Access (see Figure 2.9). You can disregard the warning if you don't plan to open the database in earlier Access versions.

Figure 2.8
Each online Access template has a Preview dialog that displays the application's primary form.

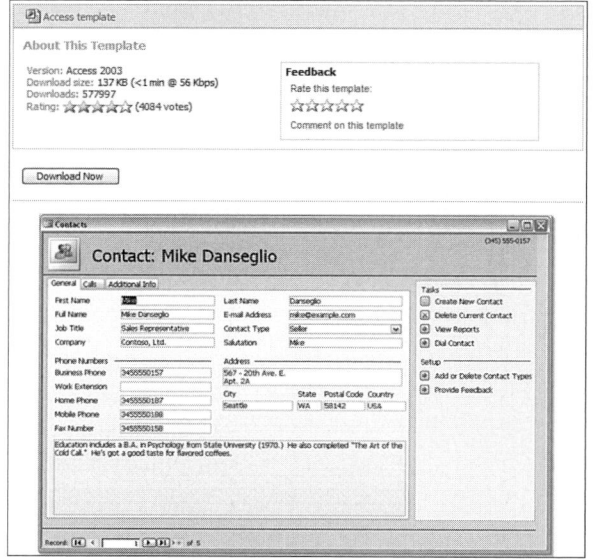

Figure 2.9
This warning appears when you open in Access 2007 a template intended to create an Access 2003 or earlier database.

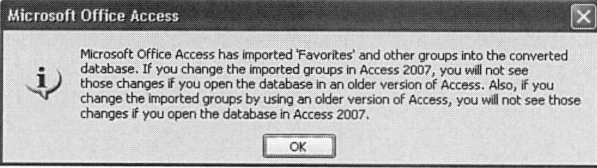

5. Click OK to open the Contacts form as an overlapping window and then click the form's maximize button (see Figure 2.10).

CHANGING FORMS FROM OVERLAPPING WINDOWS TO TABBED DOCUMENTS

Tabbed Documents is most users' preferred display format option. To change from Overlapping Windows to Tabbed Document, do the following:

1. Click the Office and Access Options buttons to open the Access Options dialog.

2. Click the Current Database button to open the page of the same name.

3. In the Document Window Options group, select the Tabbed Documents option (see Figure 2.11).

Figure 2.10
Access 2007's default document window display option is Overlapping Windows, which is equivalent to the multiple document interface (MDI) of Access 2003 and earlier.

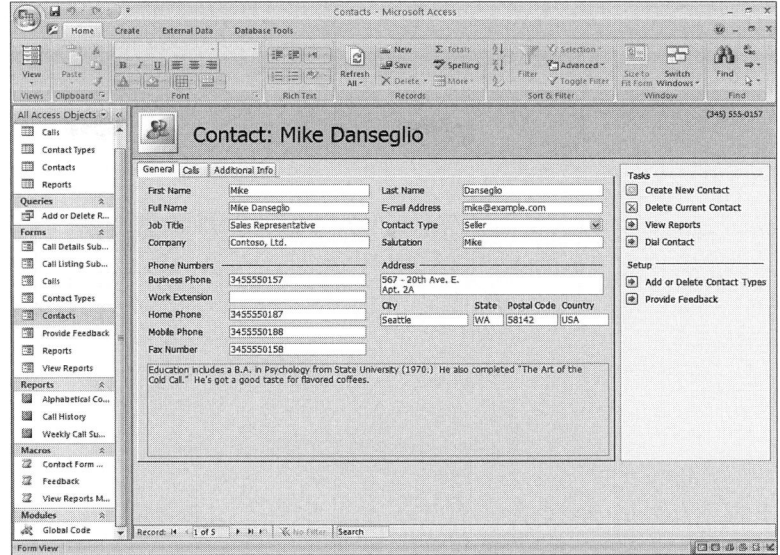

Figure 2.11
Change the display mode of the current database from Overlapping Windows to Tabbed Documents on the Access Options dialog's Current Database page.

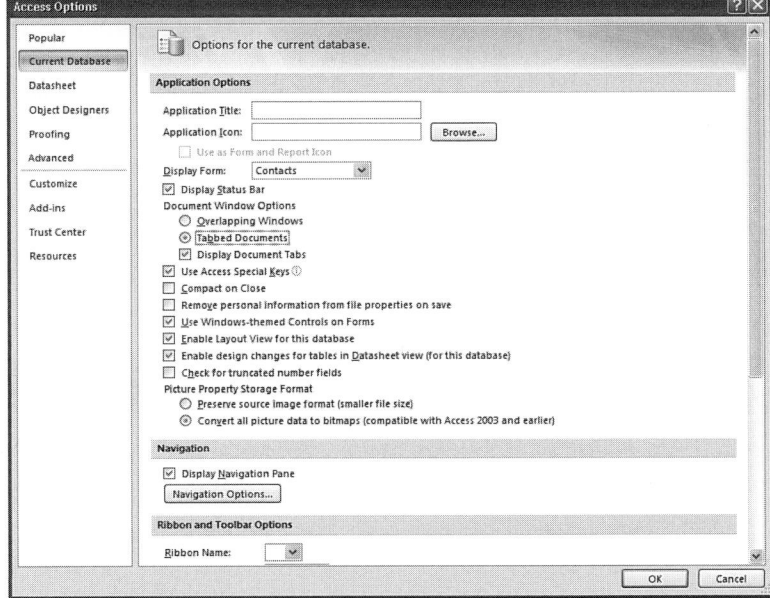

4. Click OK to accept the change. Then click OK to acknowledge the message that the change won't take place until you close and reopen the database.

5. Close and reopen the database to display the default form in its new display format (see Figure 2.12).

Figure 2.12
Tabbed Documents is the preferred default display option of most Access 2007 users and developers.

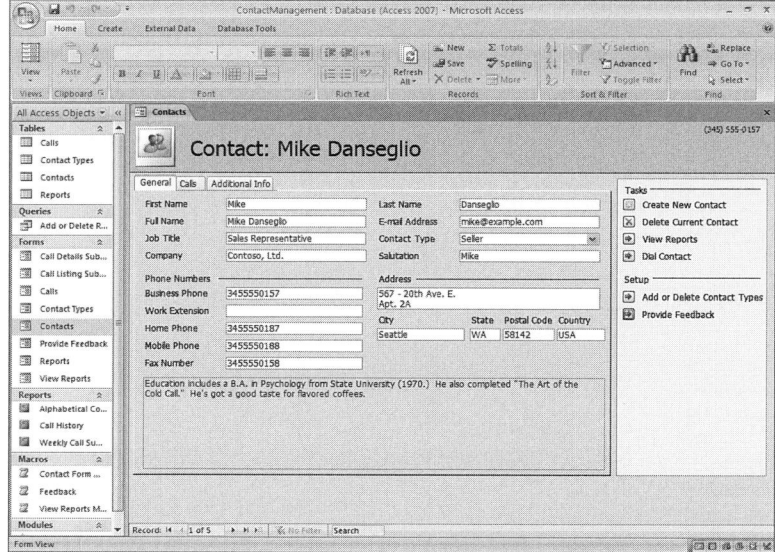

NOTE

A copy of the ContactManagement.accdb database with the Tabbed Documents option selected is in the C:\SEUA12\Chaptr02 folder, if you transferred the sample files from the CD-ROM to your C:\ drive.

Forms generated by many Access 2003 sample templates have a Tasks pane on the right. The Tasks pane buttons execute macro commands from macro groups instead of Access 2007's embedded macros. Clicking the Dial Contacts button opens the Access Autodialer accessory that uses a modem to dial the contact's number.

One of the useful features of earlier templates is the provision of sample data with the templates. The ContactManagement application's Contacts table has six sample records, and the Calls table has 16 records that are related to Contacts records.

TOURING THE MODIFIED TASKS APPLICATION

Most databases generated from Access 2007 templates use *pop-up modal dialogs* instead of tabbed documents for *Items* Details data entry forms. Pop-up modal dialogs are forms that overlay all other open windows, can't be minimized, and must be closed before the application's user can proceed to other tasks. The \SEUA12\Chaptr02\Tasks.accdb database's Contact Details form's default view has been changed from a modal dialog to a tabbed document. This form also is reduced in size so as to display fully in the 800×600 format used for most of this book's figures. The remainder of this chapter's examples assume use of the \SEUA12\Chaptr02\Tasks.accdb database.

UNDERSTANDING THE ROLE OF THE NAVIGATION PANE

The Outlook-like Navigation Pane at the left of the main window is Access 2007's most important new feature. The Navigation Pane—called *NavPane* from this point for brevity—replaces the Database Window of Access 2003 and earlier. The primary purpose of the NavPane is to let you select, open, lay out, design, export copy, classify, and delete Access objects. Figure 2.13 shows the context menu that opens when you right-click a table object.

Figure 2.13
The context menu for a NavPane's table item in the NavPane requires only one or two mouse clicks to perform the most common operations for the selected object type (tables in this case).

Template-generated databases default the NavPane's navigation category to *Items* Navigation, Show All, where *Items* represents the database name, such as Tasks, or the name of the main table, such as Projects for Marketing Projects.

CHOOSING THE OBJECT CLASSIFICATION METHOD

You can select the NavPane's object classification method (Navigate To category) by clicking the Navigation Options button and selecting one of the five Navigate To options and one of the two to five Filter By Group options shown in Figure 2.14.

Figure 2.15 shows the Tasks database's NavPane for Figure 2.14's four Navigate To selections.

Figure 2.14
Each Navigate To category you choose has a set of Filter By Group options. For this example, the application was created and modified the same day this figure was captured, so the Created Data and Modified Date categories have only Today and All Dates options under Filter By Group.

Figure 2.15
This is the appearance of the Tasks application NavPane for the four object classification methods shown in Figure 2.14.

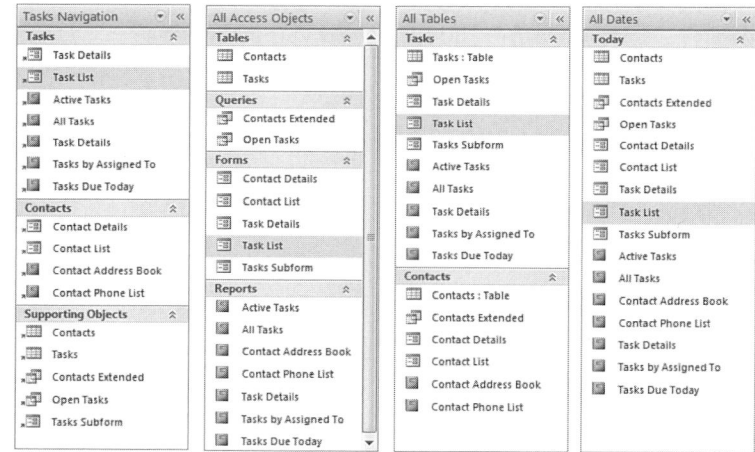

> **NOTE**
>
> Access 2007 creates the NavPane's Supporting Objects, Unclassified Objects, Tables, Queries, Forms, Reports, Macros, and Modules categories and Filter By Group options. (Macros and Modules appear if the database contains these objects). Tasks and Contacts are custom (user-created) groups.

Large-scale Access applications can involve hundreds or even thousands of objects, which require assignment to many custom groups to make navigation manageable. Access assigns each new object you create to the Unclassified Object category. Items in this category have an Add to Group context menu choice with custom categories, Supporting Objects, and New Group submenu choices.

OPENING FORMS FROM THE NAVIGATION PANE AND ADDING RECORDS

It's a generally accepted database application design practice (GADBADP) to require ordinary users to use forms to add or edit records in tables. The alternative—entering data directly in a table—is prone to typographic and other data entry errors.

To open—and add an entry to—the Contacts table, do the following:

1. Double-click a NavPane form item (Contact Details for this example) to open the form as a tabbed document in Form view. If the Home ribbon isn't visible, toggle it with Ctrl+F1.

2. Type an entry for a first fictitious customer as the first contact. (Look ahead to Figure 2.18 for a suggestion).

3. If you have a photo of the customer in a file format that's supported by Access 2007's new Attachment data type, right-click the temporary image, and choose <u>M</u>anage Attachments to open the Attachments dialog. (If you don't have a photo, skip to step 7.)

> **NOTE**
>
> The Attachment data type supports .bmp, .gif, .jpg, .png, .tif, and other image formats. You also can attach Word, Excel, or PDF files, as well as other common Multipurpose Internet Mail Extensions (MIME) documents.

4. Click the Add button to open the Choose File dialog and select the image file to add (see Figure 2.16).

Figure 2.16
Select the image file(s) for a field of the Attachments data type in the Choose File dialog.

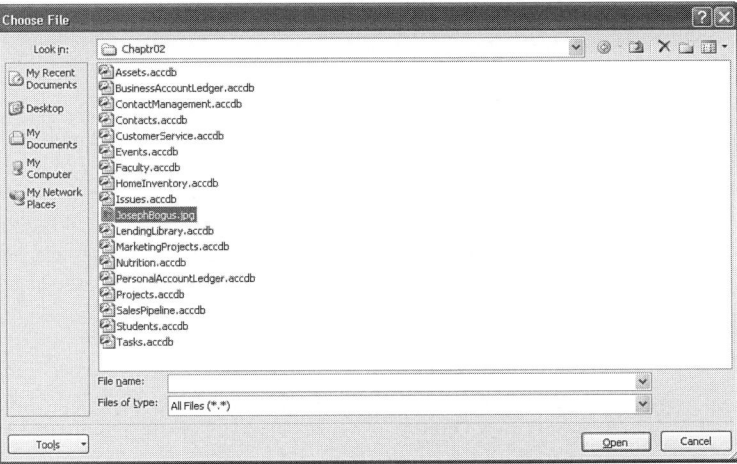

5. Click OK to close the dialog and add the filename to the Attachments dialog (see Figure 2.17).

Figure 2.17
The Attachments dialog lets you add multiple MIME attachments to a single record.

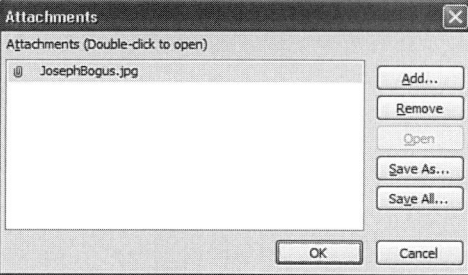

6. Click OK to close the Attachments dialog and return to the Contact Details form (see Figure 2.18).

Figure 2.18
The completed Contract Details form for the first contact is ready for addition to the Contacts table.

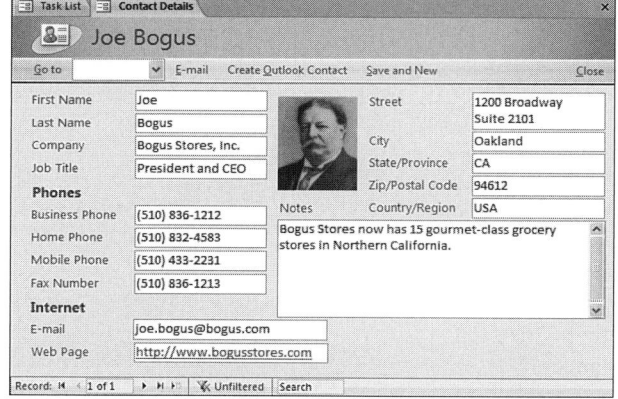

7. When you're satisfied with the entry, click the Save and New link button to add the record to the Contacts table and open a new empty form.

8. Double-click the NavPane's Contact List item to open the Contact List form, which displays the newly added record with an ID value of 1 and a second record with an ID value of (New).

NOTE

This book calls the empty (New) record the *tentative append record*, because this record isn't saved in the table until you take a deliberate action to save the record, such as adding another record or clicking the …Details form's Save and New button. Until you save the record, you can return the tentative row to its original empty condition by closing the form or, in the …List form, pressing Esc twice.

9. Click the Shutter Bar Close button to devote more room to the Contact List (see Figure 2.19). Notice that the Contact List is missing 10 of the 17 fields for which you entered data in the Contact Details form.

Figure 2.19
The Contact List form has only seven data columns. Access generates the numeric ID column's incremental value automatically.

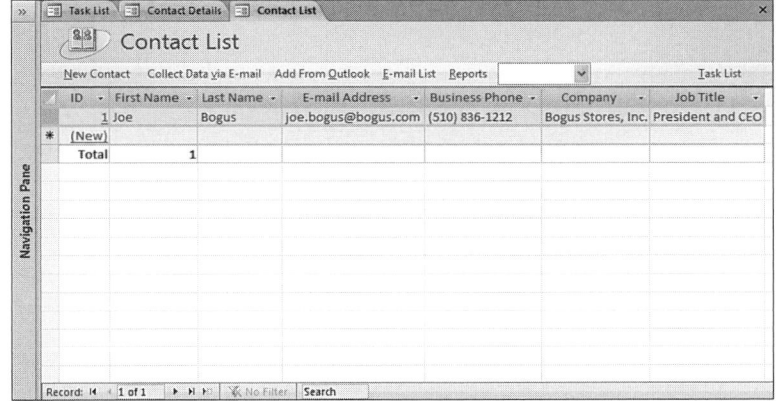

 The type of the Contact Details and Contacts List's forms is a *split form*, which is one of Access 2007's three new form types. A split form lets you display multiple records in row/column (Datasheet) format above the split. You also can type data for the selected record in the text boxes of a panel below the split. The Contacts List's panel below the split is hidden, so only the Datasheet panel is visible. The Contact Details' panel above the split is hidden, so only the data entry form is visible. You can select other orientations, such as the Datasheet panel below the data entry panel.

> **NOTE**
>
> Chapter 14, "Creating and Using Basic Access Forms," provides examples of Access 2007's conventional data entry and editing forms.
>
> Chapter 18, "Adding Graphs, PivotCharts, and PivotTables," describes how to take advantage of special-purpose, read-only forms.

ADDING A TASK RECORD

The Task Details form also is modified to open as a tabbed document from the Navigation Pane instead of a pop-up modal dialog. To create an initial task, do the following:

1. Double-click the NavPane's Task Details item to open an empty form as a tabbed document.

2. Type a task title, select a contact from the Assigned To combo box (Joe Bogus is the only choice at this point), select Not Started from the Status combo box, accept 0% as % Complete, select a Priority value, and accept today's date as the Start date.

3. Tab to the Due Date text box to activate the Date Picker icon, and click it to open the new Date Picker control (see Figure 2.20). Scroll to a later month and click a day of the month to set the Due Date value and close the Date Picker.

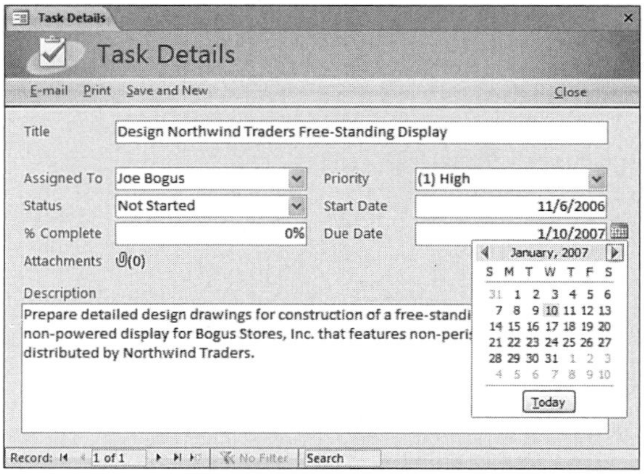

Figure 2.20
The new Date Picker control lets you select a date by scrolling months and clicking a day of the month.

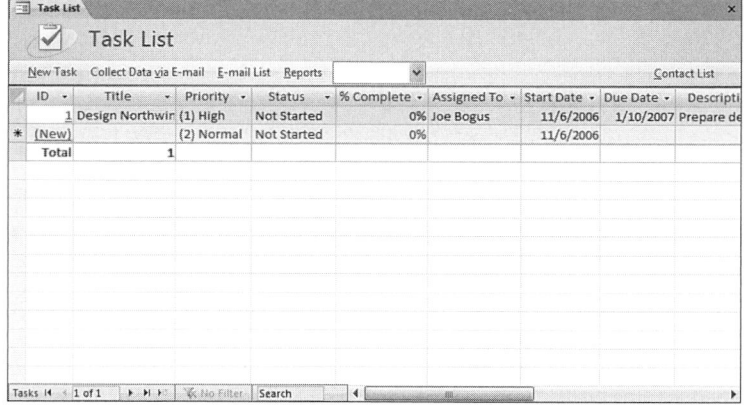

4. Type a description of the task in the Description text box, click the <u>S</u>ave and New link button to save the first Tasks record, and click Close.

5. Double-click the NavPane's Task List item to verify the presence of the new record in the Task List form (see Figure 2.21).

Figure 2.21
The Task List displays all Task table columns (including the Attachments column to the right of the Description column).

Unlike the Contact List, the Task List includes all columns (fields) of the Tasks table.

NOTE

> The Tasks application is designed to track tasks assigned to contacts. This design assumes that contacts are employees or independent contractors. An application that tracks supplier marketing tasks performed for specific customers and assigned to particular employees might be more useful in the real world. In an example of customizing a template-generated database, you modify the Tasks application to that design later in the chapter.

OPENING FORMS AND REPORTS WITH MACROS

The Contact List and Task List forms' ID field is formatted as a hyperlink. Clicking the (New) or serially numbered ID cell of a particular row or clicking the New *Item* link button opens the corresponding Contact or Task table record in the dialog version of the Details form (see Figure 20.22).

Figure 2.22
Clicking a …List form's (New) cell, an ID column number, or the New *Item* button opens a …Details dialog instead of a tabbed document, unless the …Details form is open. If the …Details form is open, Access activates the form.

Clicking a text box or a link button fires an On Click event. You can select Event Procedure (VBA code) or Embedded Macro as the *event handler* to respond to the event. All template-generated Access 2007 applications use embedded macro event handlers.

To inspect the macro that handles the ID column's OnClick event, do the following:

1. Right-click the Contact List or Task List form's NavPane item and choose Layout View to open the form in Access 2007's new Layout view.

2. Right-click the Contact List label, choose Properties to open the Property Sheet, click the ID column header or open the drop-down list and choose ID, and click the Event tab to display the On Click event in the first row (see Figure 2.23).

Figure 2.23
All template-based applications handle On Click and other events with Embedded Macros.

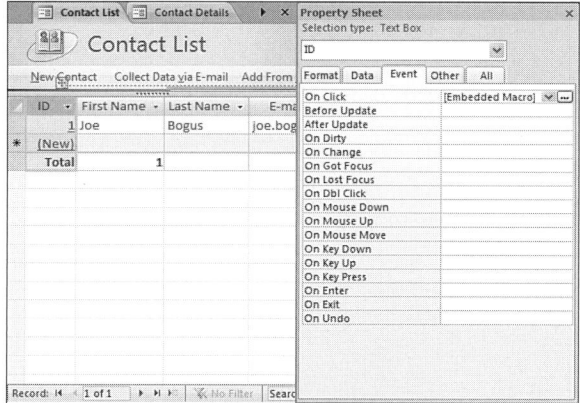

3. Click the builder button to the right of the drop-down list arrow to open the embedded macro in Design view with the Macro Tools, Design ribbon activated (see Figure 2.24). The selected OpenForm macro action opens the …Details form in Dialog mode.

Figure 2.24
Macro Design view displays the set of sequential actions to take when responding to an event—in this case the …List ID column's On Click event.

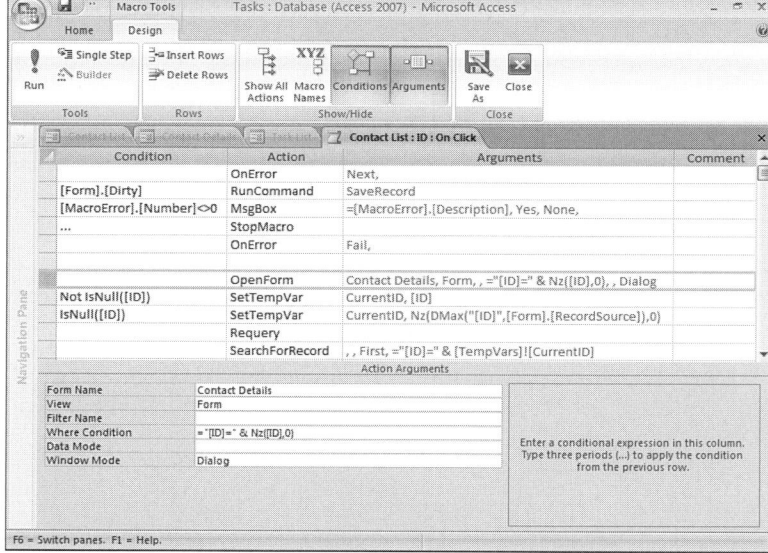

4. Click the Close box to close the macro design window (also called *macrosheet*).

The Task Details form has a <u>P</u>rint link button whose On Click event runs an embedded macro to open the Windows Print dialog over a Report view tabbed document (see Figure 2.25). Report view is a new Access 2007 alternative to Print Preview for reports.

Figure 2.25
Substituting the OpenReport and Print actions for the OpenForm action prints a report from the ...Details data and displays it in Report view.

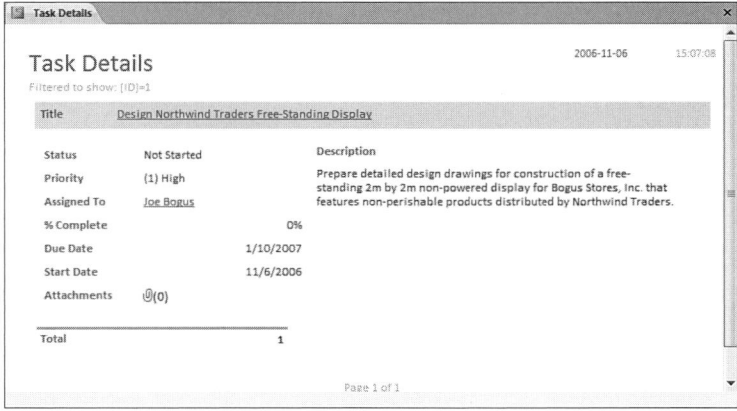

Condition	Action	Arguments	Comment
...	StopMacro		
	OnError	Next,	
[Form].[Dirty]	RunCommand	SaveRecord	
[MacroError].[Number]<>0	MsgBox	=[MacroError].[Description], Yes, None,	
...	StopMacro		
	OnError	Fail,	
	Close	, , Prompt	
	OpenReport	Task Details, Report, , ="[ID]=" & [ID], Normal	
	RunCommand	Print	

Action Arguments

Report Name	Task Details
View	Report
Filter Name	
Where Condition	="[ID]=" & [ID]
Window Mode	Normal

Enter a conditional expression in this column. Type three periods (...) to apply the condition from the previous row.

NOTE

A detailed description of macro programming techniques is beyond the scope of this chapter. Chapter 26, "Automating Access Applications with Macros 2007," and Chapter 28, "Handling Events with VBA and Macros," cover macro programming in detail.

Figure 2.26 shows the Task Details report in Report view. The Title text box and Assigned To combo box links have On Click embedded macros that open the Task Details and Contact Details forms as dialogs.

Figure 2.26
Access 2007's new Report view shows details for the first added task.

Task Details
2006-11-06   15:07:08
Filtered to show: [ID]=1

Title	Design Northwind Traders Free-Standing Display

Status	Not Started
Priority	(1) High
Assigned To	Joe Bogus
% Complete	0%
Due Date	1/10/2007
Start Date	11/6/2006
Attachments	(0)

Description
Prepare detailed design drawings for construction of a free-standing 2m by 2m non-powered display for Bogus Stores, Inc. that features non-perishable products distributed by Northwind Traders.

| Total | 1 |

Page 1 of 1

The Tasks application has seven prebuilt reports, but reports other than Task Details are of little interest without more task or contact entries.

IMPORTING AND EXPORTING DATA FROM AND TO OUTLOOK 2007

One of Microsoft's primary sales pitches for Office 2007 is application interaction and Office server integration. The primary integration points for Access are SharePoint, Outlook, Excel, and Word. Template-generated Access 2007 applications include forms that import and export contact data from and to Outlook Contact folders, collect data with Outlook-generated forms, as well as send lists as email attachments and detail items as messages.

> **TIP**
>
> Making Access tables compatible with Outlook contact items requires that table column (field) names match Outlook contact field names. Outlook field names contain spaces, virgules (/), and other punctuation characters that are permissible in—but not recommended for—Access and SQL Server field names.
>
> When you start designing your own Access tables, avoid using spaces or any punctuation characters other than the hyphen (-) or underscore (_) in table and field names. It's also a good practice to do the same with query, form, and report objects.

IMPORTING CONTACTS FROM AN OUTLOOK CONTACTS FOLDER

The Contact List form has an Add From Outlook link button that executes the AddFromOutlook macro action. This feature lets you search for and import Contact items from Outlook Contacts folders into the Contacts table. The Contacts table and Contact List form have fields whose contents correspond to fields of the same name in Outlook contact records.

> **NOTE**
>
> If you have Outlook contacts that are suited to the role of customers in the Tasks application, you can add them to the \SEUA12\Chaptr02\Tasks.accdb application. Otherwise, open the \SEUA12\Chaptr02\TasksWithData.accdb database, which has contacts added from the \SEUA12\Nwind\Northwind.accdb sample database's Customers table.

To add contacts from an Outlook Customers contacts folder, do the following:

1. Open the Contact List form and click the Add from Outlook link button to open the Select Names to Add dialog.

2. Open the Address List drop-down list, and select the Contacts folder to open (Customers for this example; see Figure 2.27).

3. Select as many contacts as you want in the list, and click Add to add their names to the text box below the list (see Figure 2.28).

Select Names to Add: Customers
Search: Name only More columns
Address Book
Go
Customers
Advanced Find
Name
Display Name
E-mail Address
Alejandra Camino
Ana Trujillo
Anabela Domingues
Ann Devon
Annette Roulet
Art Braunschweiger
Bernardo Batista
Carine Schmitt
Carlos González
Carlos Hernández
Catherine Dewey
Christina Berglund
Daniel Tonini
Diego Roel
Add ->
OK
Cancel

Figure 2.27
For this example, the Select Names to Add: Customers dialog lists Outlook contacts that are contained in a Customers folder.

Select Names to Add: Customers
Search: Name only More columns
Address Book
Go
Customers
Advanced Find
Name
Display Name
E-mail Address
Peter Franken
Pirkko Koskitalo
Renate Messner
Rene Phillips
Rita Müller
Roland Mendel
Sergio Gutiérrez
Simon Crowther
Sven Ottlieb
Thomas Hardy
Yoshi Latimer
Yoshi Tannamuri
Add ->
Simon Crowther (Business Fax); Sven Ottlieb (Business Fax); Thomas Hardy (Business Fax); Yoshi Latimer (Business Fax); Yoshi Tannamuri (Business Fax); Yvonne Moncada (Business Fax); Zbyszek Piestrzeniewicz (Business Fax)
OK
Cancel

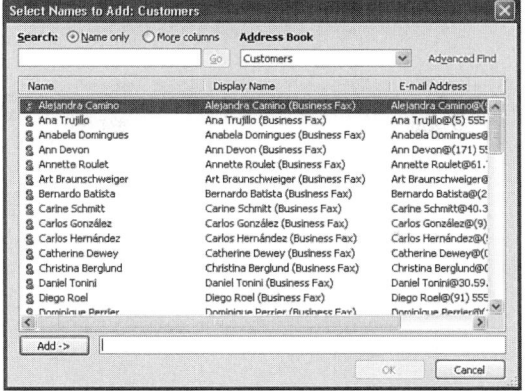

Figure 2.28
Clicking the Add button copies the selected names to a text box for addition. The purpose of the (Business Fax) suffix isn't known.

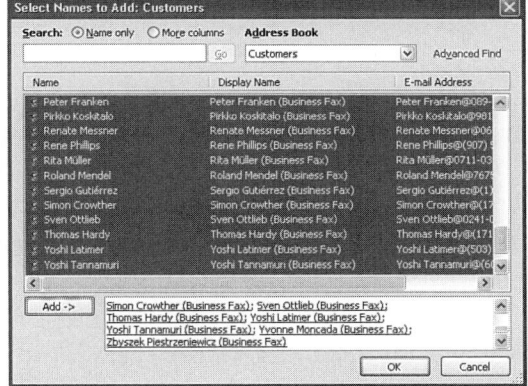

4. Click OK, wait for a few seconds, and then verify that the number of names that you specified have been added to the Contacts list (see Figure 2.29).

Contact List
Contact List
New Contact
Collect Data via E-mail
Add From Outlook
E-mail List
Reports
Task List
Navigation Pane
ID
First Name
Last Name
E-mail Address
Business Phone
Company
Job Title
60 Renate Messner 069-0245984 Lehmanns Markts Sales Representat
70 Yvonne Moncada (1) 135-5333 Océano Atlántico Sales Agent
28 Hanna Moos 0621-08460 Blauer See Delika Sales Representat
50 Maurizio Moroni 0522-556721 Reggiani Caseifici Sales Associate
62 Rita Müller 0711-020361 Die Wandernde K Sales Representat
30 Helvetius Nagy (206) 555-8257 Trail's Head Gourr Sales Associate
66 Sven Ottlieb 0241-039123 Drachenblut Delik Order Administrat
42 Manuel Pereira (2) 283-2951 GROSELLA-Restau Owner
17 Dominique Perrier (1) 47.55.60.10 Spécialités du mo Marketing Manag
36 Jytte Petersen 31 12 34 56 Simons bistro Owner
31 Henriette Pfalzheim 0221-0644327 Ottilies Käseladei Owner
61 Rene Phillips (907) 555-7584 Old World Delicat Sales Representat
71 Zbyszek Piestrzeniewi (26) 642-7012 Wolski Zajazd Owner
25 Georg Pipps 6562-9722 Piccolo und mehr Sales Manager
Total 70
Record: 51 of 70
No Filter
Search

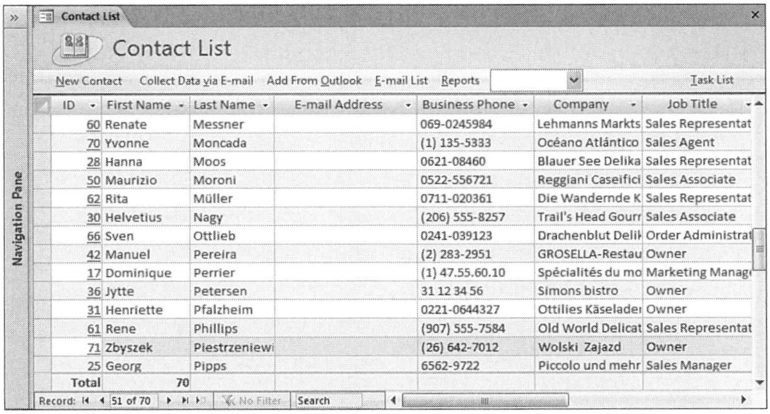

Figure 2.29
The 69 contacts from the Outlook Customers folder are added to the Contact List, which contained one earlier contact (Joe Bogus).

NEW
Σ The built-in Totals row at the bottom of a form's Datasheet is a new Access 2007 feature. Record count is your only choice for columns containing ID (Autonumber) or text values. Numeric columns can display total, count, sum, average, maximum, minimum, standard deviation, and variance. Date/Time columns can have count, average, maximum, and minimum values. Click the Home ribbon's Records button and select Totals to toggle the visibility of the Total row.

TIP
> An alternative to importing Contact items from Outlook is to substitute an Access table that's linked to a Contacts folder. This permits users of multiple application copies to share a common Outlook Contacts list. In this case, it isn't necessary to import or export Contact items.

→ To learn more about creating an Access table linked to an Outlook Contacts folder, **see** "Linking with the Exchange/Outlook Wizard," **p. 335**.

EXPORTING CONTACTS TO OUTLOOK

The Contact Details form has a Create Outlook Contact link button that exports a Contacts table record to Outlook by executing the SaveAsOutlookContact macro action. To test-drive this new Access 2007 feature, do the following:

1. Open the Contact List form, select the contact to export, and click its ID column link to open the Contact Details form for the selected contact.
2. Click the Create Outlook Contact link button to open Outlook's Contact entry form.
3. If you have a photo file, click the Add Contact Picture button, navigate to the picture's folder, and double-click the file item to add it to the contact (see Figure 2.30). Outlook doesn't add images from Attachments fields. The storage format of Access and Outlook images differs.
4. Click the Save & Close button to add the contact to Outlook's default Contacts folder. There's no option to select an alternate folder.
5. Drag the added contact from the Contacts folder to another folder of your choice (Customers for this example; see Figure 2.31).

→ For a different approach to exporting and importing Access data to and from Outlook folders, **see** "Importing and Exporting Access Tables with Outlook 2007," **p. 331**.

USING OUTLOOK TO EMAIL LISTS AND DETAIL ITEMS

Automating communication between participants in a process, such as tracking tasks for customers, is an important element of all tracking applications. Integration with WSS 3.0 or MOSS 2007 on an intranet is one approach to facilitating collaboration, but email is a much more universal communication method than SharePoint.

Figure 2.30
Access can export a fully compatible Outlook contact to Outlook's Contacts folder.

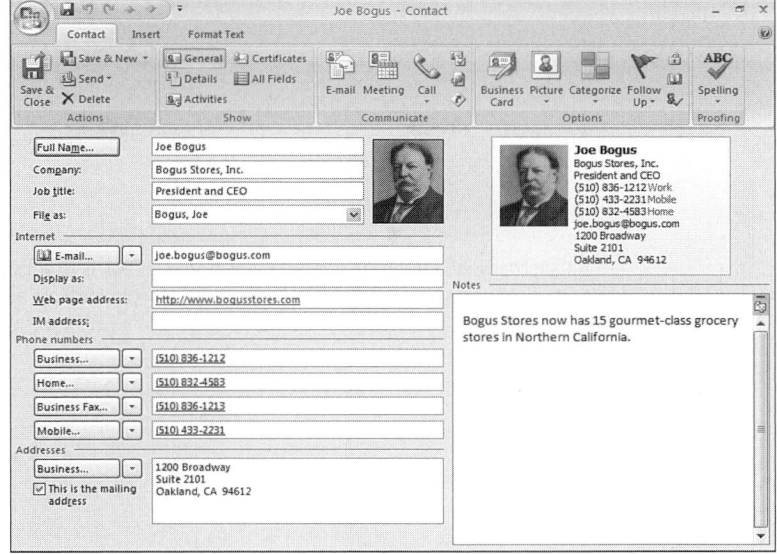

Figure 2.31
Use drag-and-drop or cut-and-paste to move the added contact from the Contacts folder to the Customers folder.

The Contact List and Task List forms have E-mail List buttons that execute the SendObject macro action to create a message with the Contact List or Task List as an attachment. Figure 2.32 shows the Contact List's Send macro sheet with added argument values. (The original macro version had only Form and Yes argument values.)

Figure 2.32
The SendObject macro action's arguments let you specify the list attachment's format, recipients, subject line, and message. Setting the Edit Message argument to Yes lets the sender edit a message before processing it.

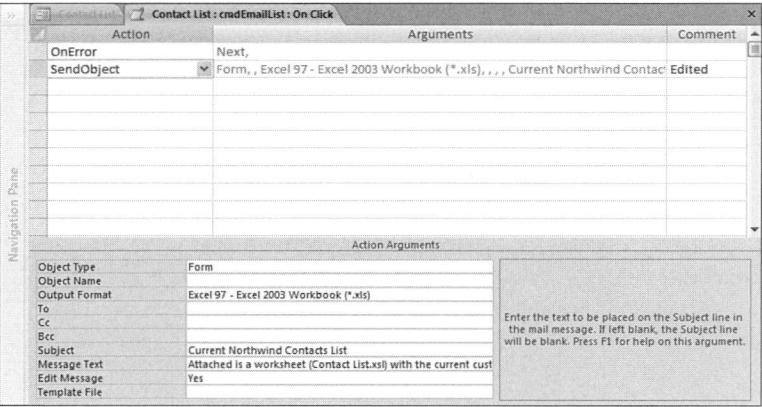

NOTE

You can format list attachments as Excel 97 – Excel 2003 Workbook (*.xls), Excel Binary Workbook (*.xlsb), Excel Workbook (*.xlsx), HTML (*.htm; *.html), Microsoft Excel 5.0/95 Workbook (*.xls), PDF Format (*.pdf), Rich Text Format (*.rtf), Text Files (*.txt), or XPS Format (*.xps).

When you click the Contact List's <u>E</u>-mail List button, the Outlook message window appears, as shown in Figure 2.33, after adding a pair of recipients.

Figure 2.33
Figure 2.32's SendObject macro action creates this message and Contact List.xls attachment.

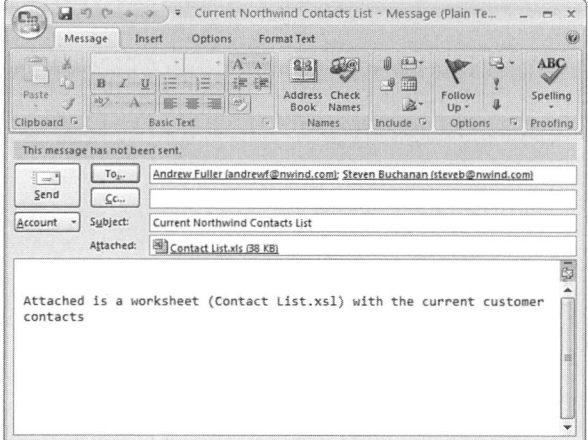

The worksheet generated by the Send action includes an empty cboReport column (A) that you can delete before sending the message (see Figure 2.34).

Figure 2.34
The list worksheet attachment might need editing before sending. The worksheet shown here has auto-adjusted column height and width, and has an empty cboReport column that you can delete.

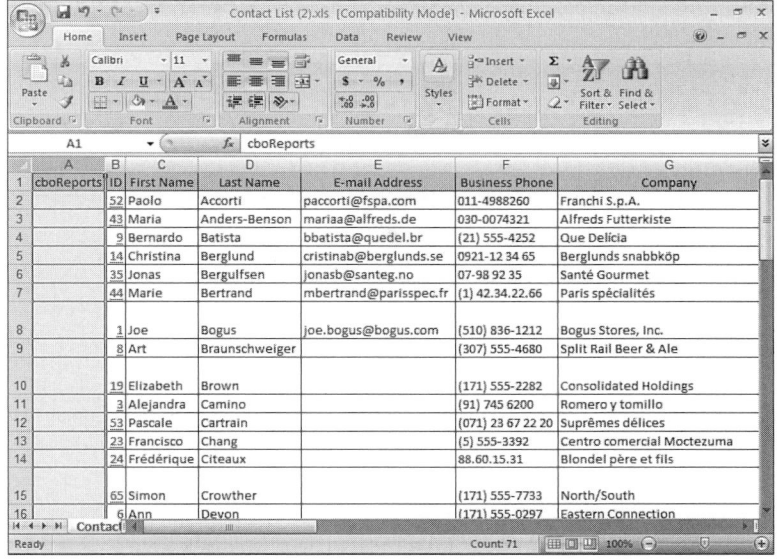

Confirming task creation and sending periodic task status information is an important tracking application capability. The Task Details and Contact Details forms have E-mail buttons that execute the SendObject macro action with complex functions to provide the email address, subject line, and, for Task Details, description. Figure 2.35 shows the macro sheet for the On Click event of the Task Details form's E-mail button.

Figure 2.35
Argument values for a SendObject macro action that handles the On Click event of the E-mail button uses functions to supply argument values.

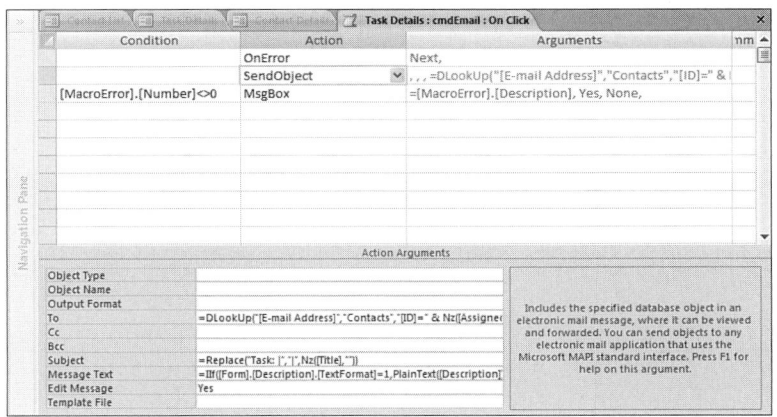

Following are the complete function text values for the SendObject macro's To, Subject, and Message Text arguments:

- To =DLookUp("[E-mail Address]", "Contacts", "[ID]=" & Nz([Assigned To], 0)) looks up the email address of the selected contact.

- Subject =Replace("Task: ¦", "¦", Nz([Title],"")) prefixes the form title with "Task: "

 - Message Text =IIf([Form].[Description].[TextFormat]=1, PlainText([Description]), [Description]) converts HTML-formatted text in Memo fields to plain ASCII text.

> **NOTE**
>
> The ability to include HTML-formatted text in table Memo fields is a new Access 2007 feature. Memo fields can store up to 65,535 characters when you enter them from a text box or one billion characters if you create the text with VBA code.

Figure 2.36 is the starting text of a message to Joe Bogus that his requested task has been initiated.

Figure 2.36
The default message for a Task Details email needs editing to be meaningful to the recipient.

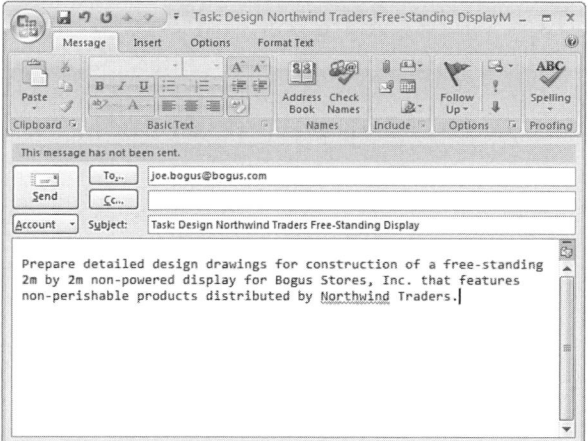

It's obvious from the preceding function list that writing macros isn't always a piece of cake. In fact, VBA code to supply argument values to and execute the SendObject macro action is probably simpler to write and certainly much easier to debug than an embedded macro. VBA code also lets you add other field values to and format the default message.

TIP

Template-based databases are an excellent source of special-purpose embedded macros that you can copy and paste into empty macro sheets in the application that you're developing.

COLLECTING DATA BY EMAIL WITH OUTLOOK HTML FORMS

NEW Access 2007 introduces the capability to auto-generate Outlook 2007 HTML forms that enable message recipients to edit existing data in or add new records to Access tables. You click the Collect Data via E-mail button to start a wizard-like process that defines the fields to edit, specifies the recipients, and determines how replies are handled.

→ For an example of collecting data with an Outlook HTML form, **see** "Gathering Data by Email with HTML Forms," **p. 1043**.

The process for creating the HTML form is complex and beyond the scope of this chapter. Figure 2.37 shows the upper 10% of the HTML form for editing Joe Bogus's contact data.

Figure 2.37
The recipient can edit and submit the HTML data collection form sent by Outlook.

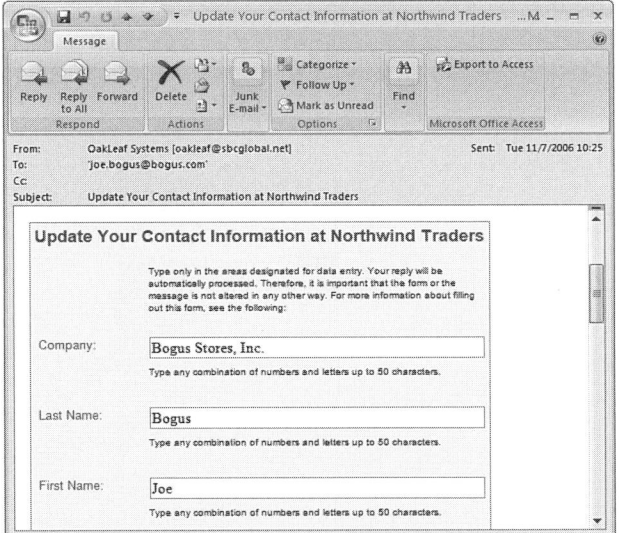

INTEGRATING OBJECTS FROM OTHER TEMPLATE DATABASES

As mentioned earlier in the chapter, template-based applications are "starter kits" for real-world tracking applications. The Tasks application for a marketing team, as an example, would involve customer-related tasks that are assigned to an employee to perform or manage. A task might benefit a few or many customers (contacts).

TIP

> The following sections cover advanced Access topics and introduce many new terms. If you don't feel up to performing the steps of this example, scan the instructions with the \SEUA12\Chaptr02\TasksWithEmployees.accdb database open. This database has all objects from the \SEUA12\Chaptr02\ProductsWithData.accdb database fully integrated.

IMPORT MISSING OBJECTS

For this example, the Tasks application needs a set of employee-related objects similar to that for contacts: Employees table, Employees Extended query, Employee List and Employee Details forms, and Employee Address Book and Employee Phone List reports. These objects are available from the Project.accdb database, but for this example, you import the objects from the \SEUA12\Chaptr02\ProjectsWithData.accdb database. That database has an Employee Details form that's similar to the Contact Details form (see Figure 2.38) and data imported from the Northwind.accdb sample database's Employees table (see Figure 2.39).

Figure 2.38
The ProjectWithData application's Employee Details form is modeled on the TasksWithData database's modified Contact Details form.

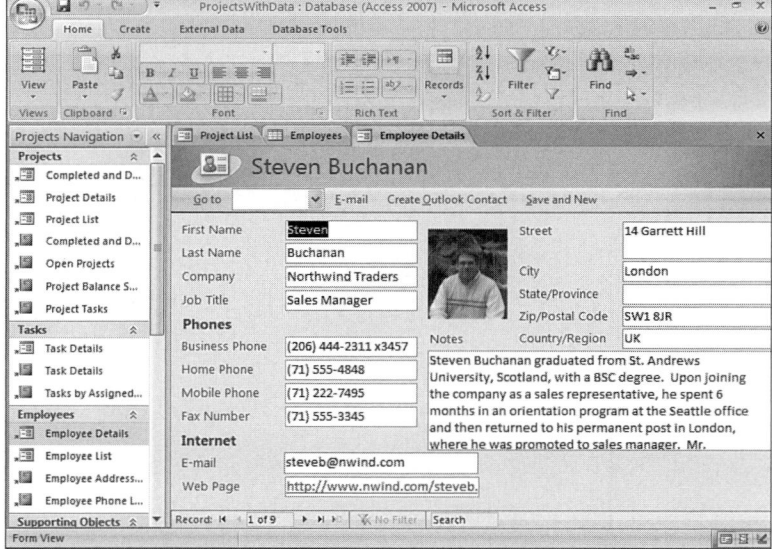

To import the preceding objects into the \SEUA12\Chaptr02\TasksWithData.accdb database, which has 70 Contacts List items and 12 Tasks List items, do the following:

1. Open \SEUA12\Chaptr02\TasksWithData.accdb, if it isn't already open, click the External Data tab, and click the Import group's Access button to open the Get External Data – Access Database dialog.

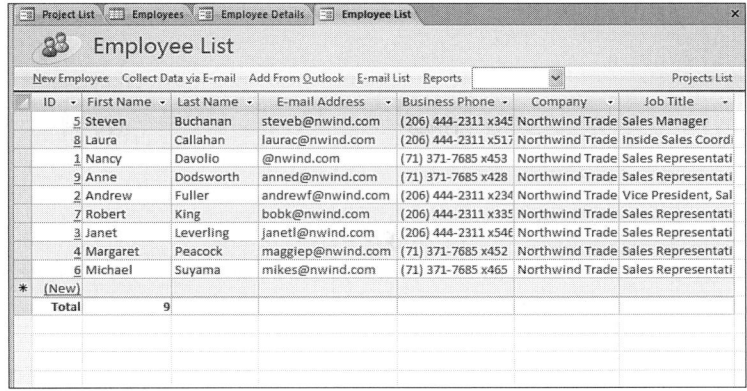

Figure 2.39
The layout of the ProjectWithData application's Employee List form is very similar to that of the Contact List.

2. Click Browse to open the File Open dialog, navigate to the \SEUA12\Chaptr02 folder, double-click the ProjectsWithData.accdb file to return to the Get External Data dialog, and click OK to open the Import Objects dialog.

3. On the default Tables page, select Employees (see Figure 2.40), click the Queries tab, and select Employees Extended.

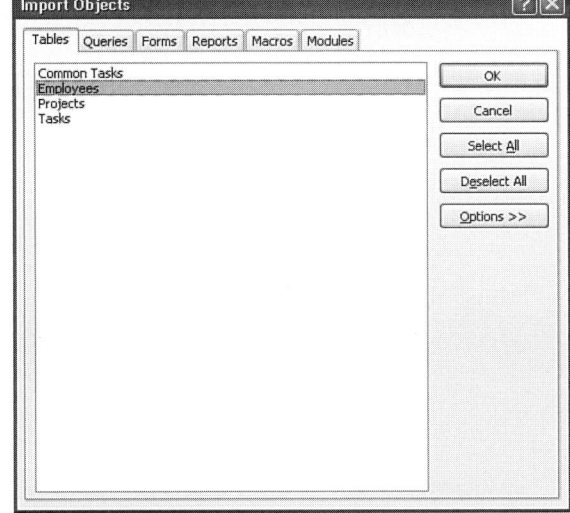

Figure 2.40
The Import Objects dialog lets you import all the objects you select on its six pages in a single operation. In case of duplicate names, the import object names gain a 1 suffix.

4. Click the Forms tab, select Employee Details and Employee List, click the Reports tab, and select Employee Address Book and Employee Phone List.

5. Click OK to import all objects to the TasksWithEmployees database and close the dialog.

The Access objects you import into a database create items in the NavPane's Unassigned Objects group. To assign these objects to a new Employees navigation group, do the following:

1. Right-click the Employee Details form item, and choose Add to Group, New Group to add a new Custom Group 1 bar to the NavPane.

2. Rename the Custom Group 1 bar to Employees.

3. Right-click the Employee List form item, and choose Add to Group, Employees. Repeat this step for the Employee Address Book and Employee Phone list reports.

4. Right-click the Employee table, and choose Add to Group, Supporting Objects.

Refer to Figure 2.38 for an example of the correct contents of the Employees group.

ALTER INAPPROPRIATE FIELD NAMES

The Task table's Assigned To field, which you'll change shortly to Requested For, has a combo box with a *lookup list* that displays values from the Contact Name field and sets values from the ID field of the Contacts table. Doing this requires a query with the following Row Source property, which is an SQL query statement:

```
SELECT [Contacts Extended].ID, [Contacts Extended].[Contact Name]
FROM [Contacts Extended]
ORDER BY [Contacts Extended].[Contact Name];
```

When you change the name of the Assigned To field to Requested For, displaying the company name before the contact name and sorting the combo box list by company name, it makes choosing the right contact easier for users. Here's the revised version of the Row Source SQL statement to create the example that follows:

```
SELECT [Contacts Extended].ID, [Contacts Extended].[Company],
    [Contacts Extended].[Contact Name]
FROM [Contacts Extended]
ORDER BY [Contacts Extended].[Company];
```

Here's a simpler version that accomplishes the same result:

```
SELECT ID, Company, [Contact Name]
FROM [Contacts Extended]
ORDER BY Company;
```

Chapter 9, "Designing Queries for Access Databases," shows you how to create queries graphically and with Access SQL statements.

NOTE

A lookup field is a new Access 2007 convenience for creating many-to-many relationships between tables. As an example, many tasks can be requested for different contacts. Relational database purists consider lookup fields and, especially, multivalued lookup fields (MVLFs) for creating many-to-many relationships to be an abomination.

→ To learn more about MVLFs, **see** "Creating Multivalued Lookup Fields," **p. 474**.

To change the name of the Assigned To field to Requested For, and establish a many-to-many relationship between the Contacts and Tasks tables with an MVLF, do the following:

 1. Click the Database Tools tab and click the Relationships button to open the Relationships window. Select the line between the Contacts and Tasks field lists (see Figure 2.41), press Delete, and click Yes to confirm that you want to remove the relationship. You can't create an MVLF until you remove all relationships that rely on the field. Close the Relationships window.

Figure 2.41
Selecting the relationship line with the mouse thickens it. You must select the relationship line to delete the relationship between the Contacts and Tasks tables.

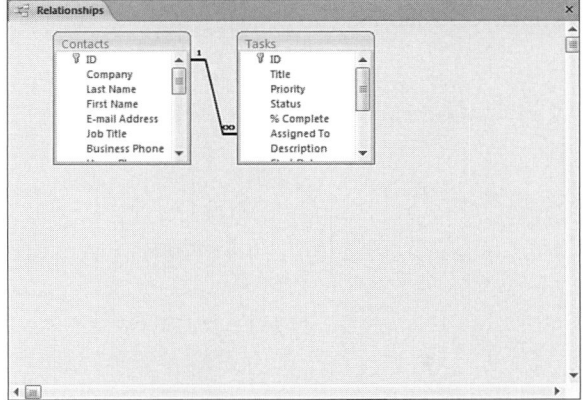

2. Close all open forms, right-click the Tasks table item in the NavPane's Supporting Objects group, and choose Design View.

3. Scroll down, if necessary, to the Assigned To field and change its Field Name to **Requested For**.

4. A task can be requested for multiple customers, so click the Lookup tab and change the Allow Multiple Values property from No to Yes. Click Yes to acknowledge the message that warns you can't undo this change and set the Yes property value (see Figure 2.42).

5. Place the cursor in the Row Source text box, and press Ctrl+F2 to open the Zoom dialog with the Row Source's SQL statement. (Click the Font button to increase the font size, if necessary.)

6. Type **[Contacts Extended].[Company]**, after ….ID, to add the company name prefix to the combo box list and change ORDER BY [Contacts Extended].[Contact Name]; to ORDER BY [Contacts Extended].[Company]; to sort the list by company name (see Figure 2.43).

Figure 2.42
Setting the Multiple Values for a lookup field to Yes opens a message box that warns you that Undo can't reverse this operation.

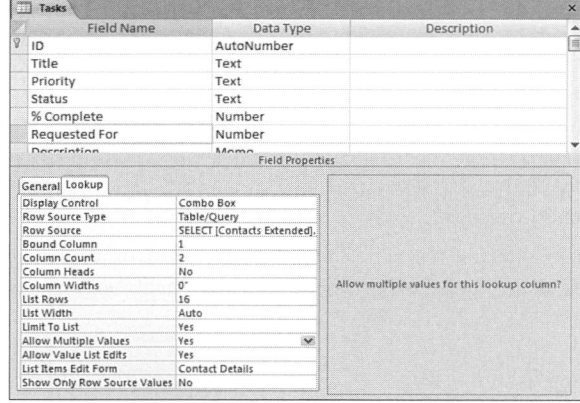

Figure 2.43
This SQL statement for the Row Source property delivers a two-column list of Company and Contact Name values.

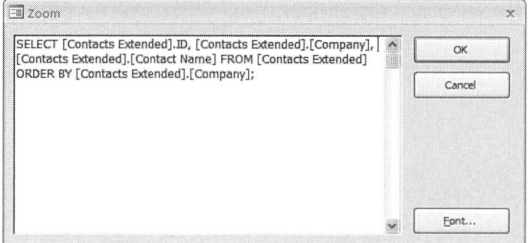

7. Change the Column Count property value from 2 to **3**, change the Allow Value List Edits from Yes to No, delete Contact Details from the List Items Edit Form property, and change Show Only Row Source Values from No to Yes (see Figure 2.44).

Figure 2.44
The Lookup page's property values reflect the changes in the preceding steps and prevent users from editing the combo box list. (The change to the Row Source property isn't visible).

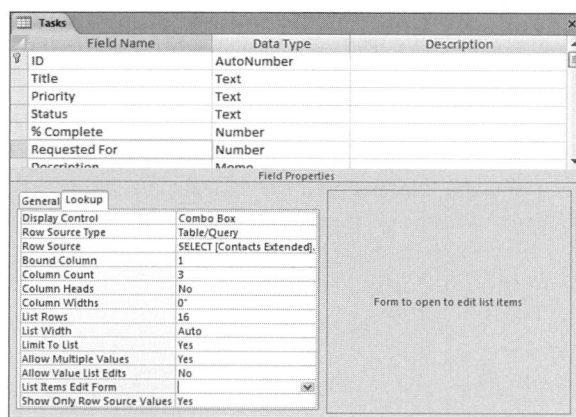

8. Click the Datasheet View button and click Yes to save your changes.

Test the MVLF's Requested For combo box list and verify that the Task Details form's Assigned To combo box needs fixing by doing the following:

1. In the Task List table's Datasheet view, scroll to the right until the Requested For column is visible and then expand the width of the column by dragging the right-hand column head border to the right.

2. Place the cursor in the first row, and click the arrow button to display the combo list with check boxes (see Figure 2.45). Notice that the check box adjacent to Bogus Stores, Inc. | Joe Bogus is marked.

Figure 2.45
The list element of a combo box for an MVLF has a column of list boxes to make the multiple selections required by a many-to-many relationship (in this case between Contacts and Tasks).

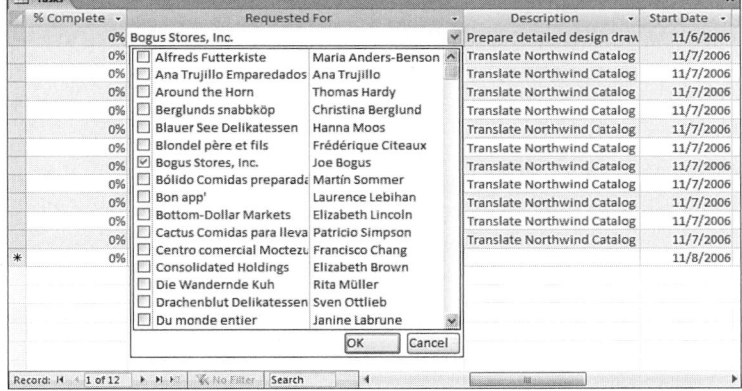

3. Close the Tasks table's window and save your layout changes.

4. Open the Task Details form in Form view and open the Assigned To combo box. The list is unchanged by the modifications to the underlying table.

CONFORM MVLF COMBO BOXES OF LIST AND DETAILS FORMS

The Task List and Task Details forms aren't modified by the changes you made to the former Assigned To table field, so you must create the Requested For combo box on both forms.

To create the Task List form's Requested For combo box, do the following:

1. Right-click the Task List form item in the NavPane and choose Design View to open the form in Design view.

2. Click the Add Existing Fields button to open the Field List pane.

3. Drag the Requested Field item from the Field List and drop it immediately below the Assigned To field, as shown in Figure 2.46.

Figure 2.46
Dragging a field from the Field List to the Design view of a form adds a label and combo box for a single-valued or mul-tivalued table lookup field.

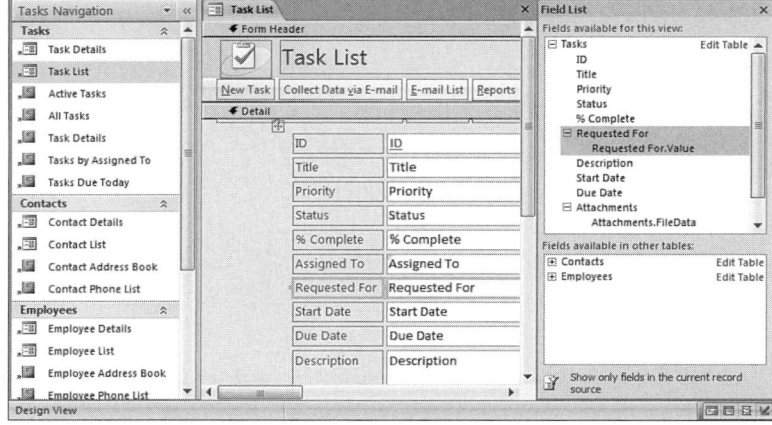

4. There's no longer an Assigned To field, so select and delete the Assigned To label and combo box.

5. Place the cursor in a Requested For cell, press F4 to open the Property Sheet, click the Data tab, and then change the value of the Allow Value List Edits property from Yes to No, delete the Contact Form from the List Items Edit Form property, and change Show Only Row Source Values from No to Yes.

6. Click the Form View button and scroll to the right to expose the Requested For field. Select the field header, drag the field to the right of the Title field, and open the combo box list (see Figure 2.47).

Figure 2.47
Combo box lists for MVLFs contained in forms open to the right of the associated column. The TasksWithData.accdb database has 11 translation tasks added to make the application more interesting.

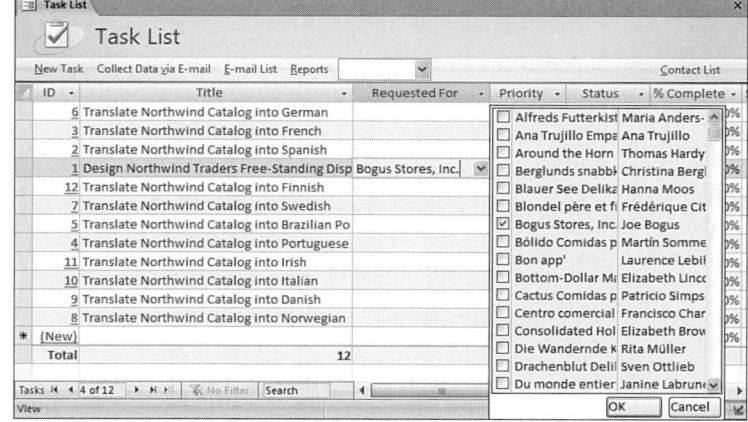

7. Close the Task List form and save your design changes.

To create the Task Details form's Requested For combo box, do the following:

1. Open the Task Details form in Design view and click the Add Existing Fields button.

2. Delete the Assigned To label and the adjacent combo box, and drag the Requested For field from the Field List to the location of the deleted controls.

3. Select the new Requested For combo box, open the Property Sheet, and click the Format tab. Then change the Border Style property value from Transparent to Solid, change Column Widths from 0" to **0";2";2"**, and change List Width from Auto to **4"**.

4. Click the Data tab and make the same changes as you did in step 5 of the preceding example.

5. Click the Form View button and test the combo list (see Figure 2.48).

Figure 2.48
The Task Details form's Requested For combo box emulates that of the Task List form.

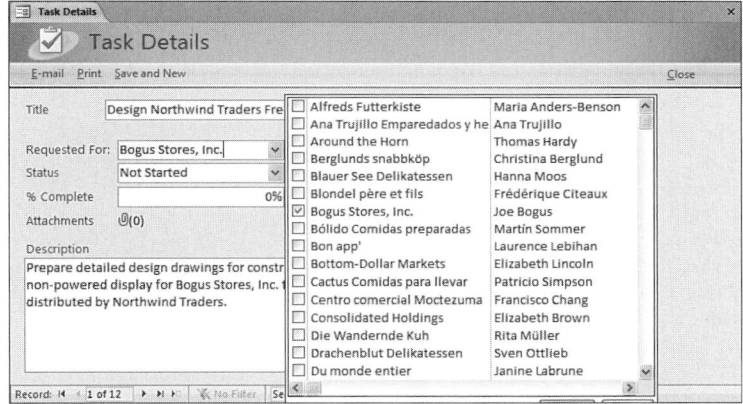

ADD APPROVED BY AND ASSIGNED TO EMPLOYEE LOOKUP FIELDS

Customers can make requests to any marketing department employee to initiate a task on their behalf. However, an employee with a title of Manager or higher must approve the task and then assign one or more employees to complete the task. This business rule means you must add, for starters, an Approved By single-valued lookup field and an Assigned To MVLF to the Tasks table.

To add the Approved By field to the Tasks table, do this:

1. Close all forms and open the Tasks table in Design view.

2. Select the Description field and press Insert to add an empty field above.

3. Type **Approved By** as the field name, tab to the Data Type column, and select Number from the list. The Field Size property value is Long Integer by default, which matches the field size of the Employees table's ID field.

4. Click the Lookup tab and change the Display Control property value from the default Text Box to Combo Box.

5. Type **SELECT ID, [First Name] & " " & [Last Name] FROM Employees WHERE [Job Title] IN("Sales Manager", "Vice President, Sales", "President") ORDER BY [Last Name];** as the Row Source property value. Press Shift+F2 to use the Zoom box if you want.

Access SQL

SELECT ID, [First Name] & " " & [Last Name] returns the employee ID number and first and last names separated by a space. The WHERE [Job Title] IN("Sales Manager", "Vice President, Sales", "President") SQL clause limits the list to employees with those titles.

→ To learn more about lookup fields in general, **see** "Using Lookup Fields in Tables," **p. XXX** *(Ch 11)*.

6. Change the Column Count property value from 1 to **2**, Column Widths from empty to **0";2.0"**, Limit to List from No to Yes, Value List Edits from Yes to No, and Show Only Row Source Values from No to Yes (see Figure 2.49).

Figure 2.49
Design view of the Approved By single-valued lookup field is identical to that of the Requested For MVLF except for the Row Source, Column Count, Column Widths, and Allow Multiple Values property values.

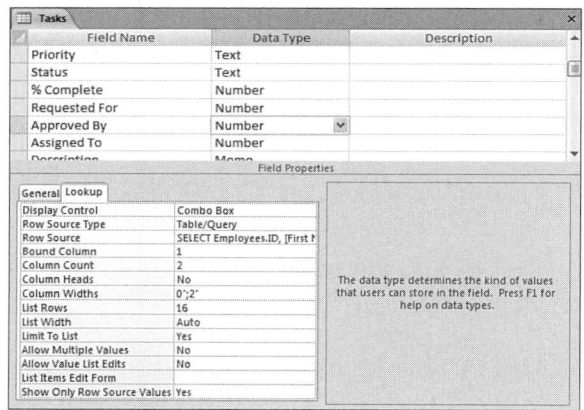

7. Change to Form view, save your changes, scroll to the Approved By field, and test your work so far (see Figure 2.50).

To add an Assigned To MVLF to the Tasks table, repeat the preceding steps, except:

1. In step 3, type **Assigned To** as the field name.

2. In step 5, omit the WHERE [Job Title] IN("Sales Manager", "Vice President, Sales", "President") clause.

3. In step 6, change the Allow Multiple Values property value from No to Yes.

Figure 2.50
Only Andrew Fuller, Vice President, Sales, and Stephen Buchanan, Sales Manager, can approve requests for marketing tasks.

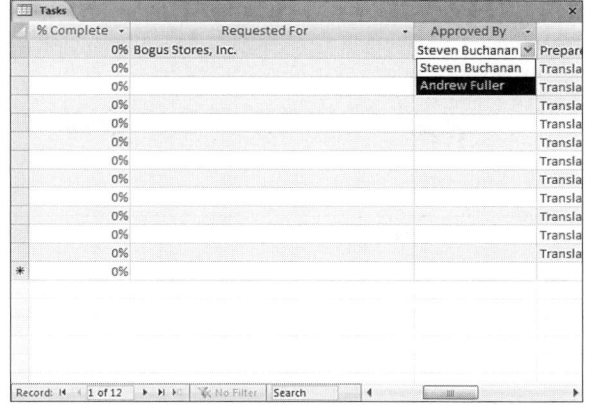

When you change to Form view, the Assigned To combo box appears as shown in Figure 2.51.

Figure 2.51
This combo box for an MVLF has only a single column for the full employee name.

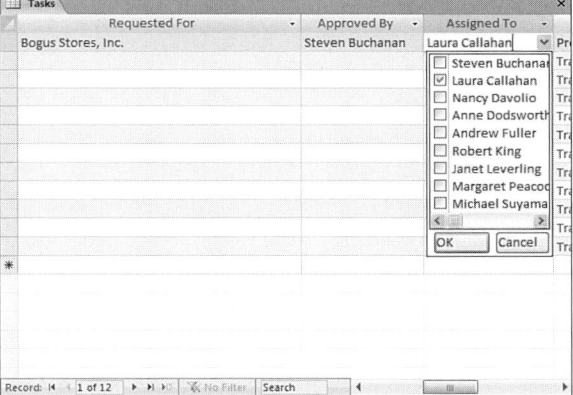

ADD APPROVED BY AND ASSIGNED TO COMBO BOXES TO LISTS AND DETAILS FORMS

The final step in the initial application modification is to add the Approved By and Assigned To fields' combo boxes to the Task List and Task Details form by the same technique that you used to add the Requested For combo boxes. Figure 22.52 shows the Task Details form with the two added combo boxes. Note that when you add multiple values, the values appear (separated by commas) in the combo box's text box.

Figure 2.52
The Approved By and Assigned To combo boxes have been added to the Task Details form.

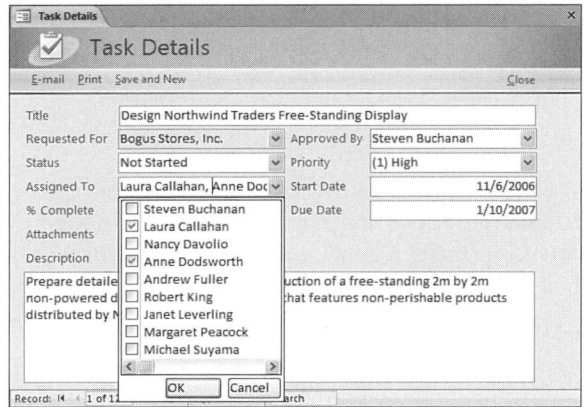

At this point you've created a working three-table application that has a many-to-many relationship between customer contacts and marketing tasks. Many tasks can be requested for a specific contact, and the result of a specific task, such as the translation of a catalog, can be useful to multiple contacts or companies.

You've also added a one-to-many relationship between employees who have approval authority and tasks. Only one manager is needed to approve a task, and a manager can approve many tasks.

Finally, you added another many-to-many relationship between tasks and the employees whom management assigns to complete them. It might take a team of employees to complete a task, and one employee might be assigned to several tasks simultaneously.

NOTE

> The completed version of the TasksWithData.accdb project is \SEUA12\Chaptr02\ TasksWithEmployees.accdb, which is used for examples in other chapters also.

IN THE REAL WORLD—MAKING ACCESS EASIER TO USE

If you're new to Access, many terms used in this chapter might sound like ancient Aramaic. The objective was to give you an overview of some of the most important objects that make up an Access application, the relationships between these objects, and how you assemble the objects you create into self-contained, easily navigable database applications.

Chapter 1, "Access 2007 for Access 200x Users: What's New?" includes the observation that Access 2007 has experienced its first complete overhaul in its 14-year history. (Microsoft released Access 1.0 in November 1992.) The Office team's objective for replacing command bars, buttons, and hierarchical menus with the new Office ribbon UI is to make taking full advantage of the entire Office suite easier for new users. Similarly, Access's new features, such as the Navigation Pane, tabbed document window, Attachment data type, MVLFs, and online tracking application templates are intended to flatten the learning curve for database neophytes. Using templates helps you quickly understand the components and comprehend the behavior of a completed Access application.

If you didn't perform the step-by-step tutorial to create the sample application and web page of this chapter, not to worry. The completed TasksWithEmployees.accdb database is in the \SEUA12\Chaptr02 folder of the accompanying CD-ROM. Sample databases and related files for most of this book's chapters are included in corresponding \SEUA12\ Chaptr## folders, which you can copy to your fixed disk.

The remainder of this book covers each category of Access objects in detail, beginning with table and query objects and then progressing to form and report objects. By the time you get about halfway through this book, you gain the experience necessary to design your own versions of these objects. The last half of this book deals with advanced topics, such as exporting Access forms and reports to XML-based web pages, using InfoPath to collect data and update tables, generating SharePoint lists from tables and queries, working with Access macros, and writing professional-quality VBA code.

2

CHAPTER 3

NAVIGATING THE NEW ACCESS USER INTERFACE

In this chapter

UNDERSTANDING ACCESS FUNCTIONS AND MODES

Access, unlike word processing and spreadsheet applications, is a truly multifunctional program. Although word processing applications, for example, have many sophisticated capabilities, their basic purpose is to support text entry, page layout, and formatted printing. The primary functions and supporting features of all word processing applications are directed to these ends. You perform all word processing operations with views that represent a sheet of paper. Most spreadsheet applications use the row-column metaphor for all their functions. In contrast, Access consists of a multitude of related tools for generating, organizing, segregating, displaying, printing, and publishing data. The following sections describe Access's basic functions and operating modes.

DEFINING ACCESS FUNCTIONS

To qualify as a full-fledged relational database management system (RDBMS), an application must perform the following four basic but distinct functions, each with its own presentation to the user:

- *Data organization* involves creating and manipulating tables that contain data in conventional tabular (row-column or spreadsheet) format, called *Datasheet view* by Access.

- *List management* substitutes Access tables linked to SharePoint lists. SharePoint lists behave similarly to Access tables, but don't maintain referential integrity with foreign key constraints.

→ For an explanation of the benefits of referential integrity, **see** "Maintaining Data Integrity and Accuracy," **p. 192**.

- *Table joining and data extraction* use queries to connect multiple tables by data relationships and create virtual (temporary) tables, called *Recordsets*, stored in your computer's RAM or temporary disk files. Expressions are used to calculate values from data (for example, you can calculate an extended amount by multiplying unit price and quantity) and to display the calculated values as though they were a field in one of the tables.

- *Data entry and editing* require design and implementation of data viewing, entry, and editing forms as an alternative to tabular presentation. A form lets you, rather than the application, control how the data is presented. Most users find forms much easier to use for data entry than tabular format, especially when many fields are involved.

- *Data presentation* requires the creation of reports that you can view, print, or publish on the Internet or an intranet (the last step in the process). Charts and graphs summarize the data for those officials who take the "broad brush" approach.

The basic functions of Access are organized into the application structure shown in Figure 3.1. If you're creating a new database, you use the basic functions of Access in the top-down sequence shown in Figure 3.1.

Figure 3.1
This diagram shows the relationship of the basic and supporting functions of Access. Reports have a one-way relationship with other functions, because you can't use a report to modify data.

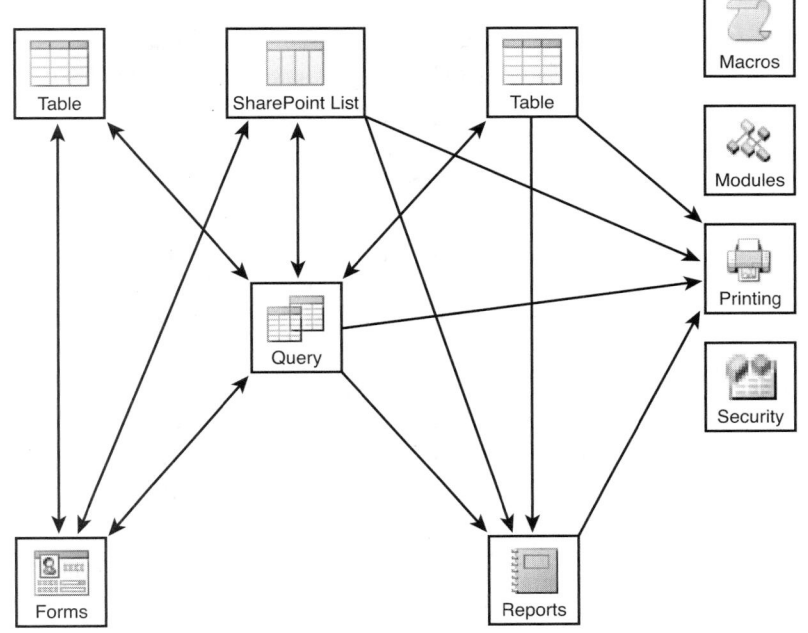

> **NOTE**
>
> You can base forms and reports on data from Access or SQL Server tables, or linked SharePoint Lists, but it's more common to use a query as the data source for forms and reports. An SQL Server view is the direct counterpart of an Access SELECT query. You also can use SQL Server inline functions and stored procedures as data sources for forms and reports.

Four supporting functions apply to all basic functions of Access:

- *Macros* are sequences of actions that automate repetitive database operations. In Access 97 and earlier versions, macros were the most common means of automating database operations. In versions 2000 through 2003, macros were supported for backward compatibility only and Microsoft recommended Visual Basic for Applications (VBA) to automate Access applications.

> **TIP**
>
> Microsoft now recommends using macros wherever possible because macros will run under more restrictive security settings than VBA. Microsoft also raises the dubious contention that macros are simpler for new users to write than VBA code. In an attempt to make macros more palatable to application developers, the Access team created a new class of embedded macros and added event-handling actions.

continues

continued

> Only Access uses these macros, so learning to construct them gains you no leverage with the many other applications that use VBA. What's worse, macros have a very limited programming repertoire. If you intend to create Access applications for others to use, learning to write VBA code is highly recommended.

→ For a brief introduction to embedded macros, **see** "Access Macros Redux," **p. 56**.

- *Modules* are containers for functions and procedures written in the VBA programming language. You use VBA functions to make calculations that are more complex than those that can be expressed easily by a series of conventional mathematical symbols. You run a VBA subprocedure by attaching it to particular event, such as clicking a command button with the mouse when a form or page is the active object.

- *Security* features for Access 2007 applications have been downgraded dramatically. You no longer can grant access to user groups and individuals with user-level security. Nor can you restrict users' ability to view or modify objects in the database except by creating an encrypted .accde file, which corresponds to earlier versions' .mde file.

> **NOTE**
>
> Access 2007 supports user-level (also called *workgroup*) security for Access 2000 through 2003 .mdb files and Access 2000 through 2007 .adp (data project) files. However, using older file formats disables new Access 2007 features, such as the Attachment data type, multivalued lookup columns, and append-only memo fields. Access data projects (ADPs) don't support new Access 2007 features.

- *Printing* lets you print virtually anything you can view in Access's run mode. Printing is the most common form of distributing reports, but you also can export reports to web pages or to Portable Document Format (Adobe .pdf), Microsoft XML Paper Specification (.xps), or Report Snapshot (.snp) files.

The terms *open* and *close* have the same basic usage in Access as in other Windows applications but usually involve more than one basic function:

- Opening a database makes its content available to the application through the Navigation Pane, which replaces earlier versions' Database window. You can open only one database at a time in the Access user interface, but you can link tables from Access, client/server, and other desktop databases, as well as Windows SharePoint Services (WSS) 3.0 or Microsoft Office SharePoint Services (MOSS) 2007 lists. You also can open multiple databases with VBA code.

- Opening a table displays a *Datasheet view* of its contents. Access automatically creates the first table of a new database and defines its structure by the data you enter in it.

- Opening a SELECT query, the most common query type, opens one or more tables and displays the data specified by the query in Datasheet view. You can change data in the tables associated with the query if the query's *Recordset* is *updatable* (write-enabled).

- Opening a form or report automatically opens the table or query that's associated with it. As mentioned earlier, forms and reports usually are associated with (called *bound to*) queries rather than tables.

- Closing a query closes the associated tables.

- Closing a form or report closes the associated query and its tables or the table to which it's bound.

You open existing database objects by double-clicking the corresponding item in the Navigation pane. Closing a query, form, or report doesn't close its associated objects (table, query, or both) if you've opened them independently.

DEFINING ACCESS OPERATING MODES

Access has four basic operating modes:

- *Startup* mode occurs after you launch Access 2007 but before you open an existing database or create a new one. By default, Startup mode displays the Getting Started with Microsoft Office Access window, which gives you the options of creating a new blank (empty) database, or creating an Access application from one of 10 local (also called *out-of-the-box*) template files or online templates in one of three categories (see Figure 3.2). Sample isn't a template category.

Figure 3.2
When you launch Access 2007 for the first time, the Getting Started with Microsoft Access window opens and lets you create a new blank database or generate a database from one of the 10 local templates or more online templates in three categories.

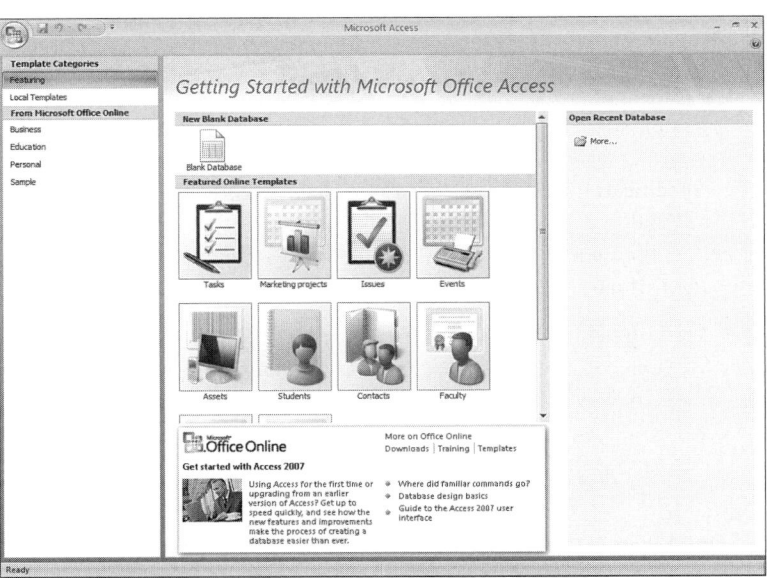

NOTE

> Chapter 2, "Building Simple Tracking Applications," shows you how to create a complete Access database application from the Tasks online template in a few minutes.

After you've opened one or more databases, the last one opens automatically when you launch Access. You must click the Office button and choose <u>C</u>lose Database or <u>N</u>ew from the gallery to return to the Getting Started with Microsoft Access window.

- *Run* mode displays your table, form, and report designs as tabbed documents in a single window (the default display type). Run mode displays tables and queries in Datasheet view, forms in *Form view*, and reports in *Report view* or *Print Preview* for reports. Report view is new in Access 2007.

NOTE

> Earlier Access versions' .mdb files open by default as conventional overlapping (non-modal) windows.

- *Design* mode lets you create and modify the structure of tables and queries; develop forms to display and edit your data; format reports for printing; design macros; or write VBA code in the separate VBA Editor application. Access calls design mode *Design view*.

- *Layout* mode lets you alter the layout of the forms and reports that you created in Design mode or generated from a template. The primary advantage of layout mode is that you can adjust the size and location of controls (typically text boxes) with live data visible. Data sources (tables or queries) for your forms or reports have content to gain the most out of layout mode. Layout mode, which Access calls *Layout view*, is new in Access 2007.

→ For more information on Layout view, **see** "Form and Report Layout View," **p. 53**.

You can choose Data<u>s</u>heet, <u>F</u>orm, <u>R</u>eport, La<u>y</u>out, or <u>D</u>esign view from the Home ribbon's Views group or you can press Alt and the appropriate shortcut key. Access's shortcut keys are the same as Access 200x's, despite the dramatic change to Office 2007's user interface.

OPENING THE NORTHWIND.ACCDB SAMPLE DATABASE

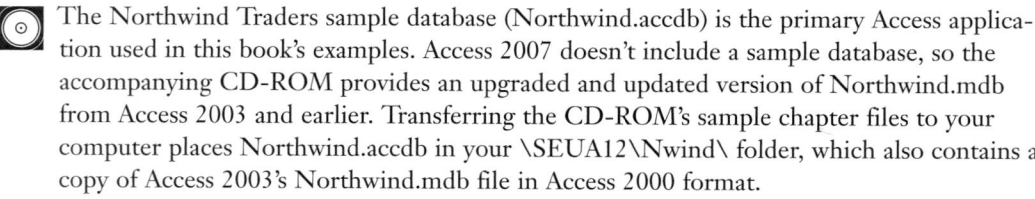

The Northwind Traders sample database (Northwind.accdb) is the primary Access application used in this book's examples. Access 2007 doesn't include a sample database, so the accompanying CD-ROM provides an upgraded and updated version of Northwind.mdb from Access 2003 and earlier. Transferring the CD-ROM's sample chapter files to your computer places Northwind.accdb in your \SEUA12\Nwind\ folder, which also contains a copy of Access 2003's Northwind.mdb file in Access 2000 format.

N O T E

The default location for Access databases and other application-related files, such as graphics files for images, is Windows XP's My Documents folder or Windows Vista's Documents folder. The \Program Files\Microsoft Office\Office12\Samples folder, formerly used to hold the Access sample files, contains only the venerable SOLVSAMP.XLS file.

After installing the sample files from the CD-ROM, open Northwind.accdb and display its Home ribbon and default Navigation Pane by doing the following:

1. Launch Microsoft Office Access 2007, if it isn't running.

2. Click the Office button to open the gallery (menu) and choose Open to launch the Open dialog. Navigate to your \SEUA12\Nwind folder, which contains three sample files (see Figure 3.3).

Figure 3.3
The Open dialog lets you open almost all varieties of Access 2000 through 2007 database files.

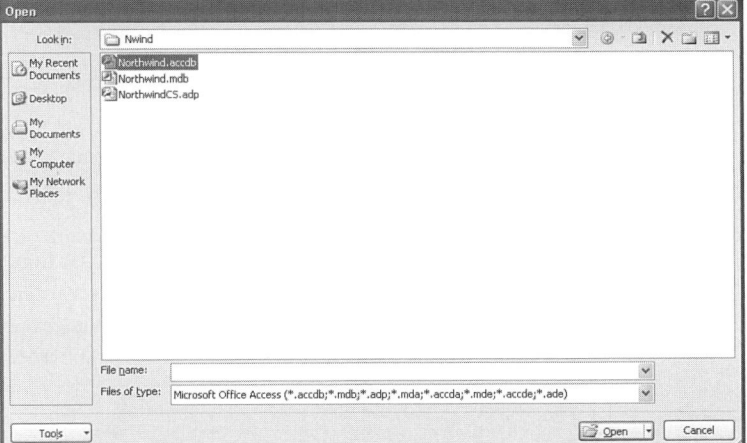

3. Select Northwind.accdb, and click Open to open the Switchboard form as a tabbed document (see Figure 3.4). The message bar displays a security warning with an Options button. The content that's been disabled is the VBA code in the Utility Functions module.

4. Optionally, click the Products and Suppliers button and then click a button to open one of the sample forms or reports. Figure 3.5 shows the Suppliers and Products List in Form view.

Figure 3.4
The Switchboard form's default page lets you select one of four categories of sample forms and sales reports to open. The Navigation pane displays all database objects in an Outlook-style sidebar.

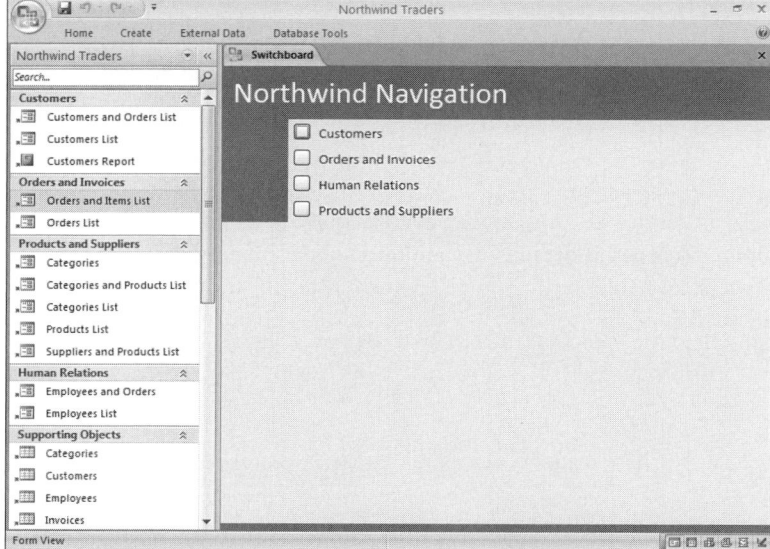

Figure 3.5
The Suppliers and Products form displays values from the Suppliers table's record for the selected supplier above a datasheet view containing related products' records from the Order Details table.

NOTE

NEW

Access 2007's Switchboard Manager differs from earlier versions by substituting Access macros for VBA code to open forms or reports and perform other actions. VBA code won't run when the Security Warning message is present, but most macro actions aren't embargoed.

→ To learn more about enabling VBA code to run, **see** "Security, Trusted Locations, Packages and Certificates," **p. 40**.

After you open Northwind.accdb for the first time, it opens automatically when you launch Access, and an entry for the database appears in the Office gallery's Recent Documents pane. It's quicker to open Northwind.accdb or any other recently used databases from the Recent Documents pane.

TIP

To prevent the Switchboard form from appearing each time you open Northwind.accdb, click the Office and Access Options buttons to open the Access Options dialog, and then click the Current Database button to open the Options for the Current Database page. Open the Display Form list, select (None), click OK to close the dialog, and click OK again to dismiss the message that you must close and restart Access for the change to take effect.

→ For the details of setting all Access options for the current and new databases, **see** "Setting Default Options," **p. 143**.

3

UNDERSTANDING ACCESS'S TABLE WINDOWS

You're probably familiar with the terms for and behavior of many new components that comprise the basic window in which all Office 2007 applications run. Ribbons, groups, command buttons, and the Quick Access Toolbar (QAT) replace conventional hierarchical menus and toolbars. As with other Office 2007 applications, the presentation of Access windows varies with each basic function that Access performs. Because tables are the basic component of relational databases, the examples that follow use Table Datasheet view. Figure 3.6 shows Access 2007's display for run-mode operations with tables; Table 3.1 describes the window's Access-related components.

TIP

Press Ctrl+F1 to toggle the ribbon's visibility. Hiding the ribbon adds a substantial amount of workspace.

Figure 3.6
Access uses the default document interface (MDI) to display all database objects except code in modules and scripts for pages. The VBA editor and Microsoft Script editor are separate applications.

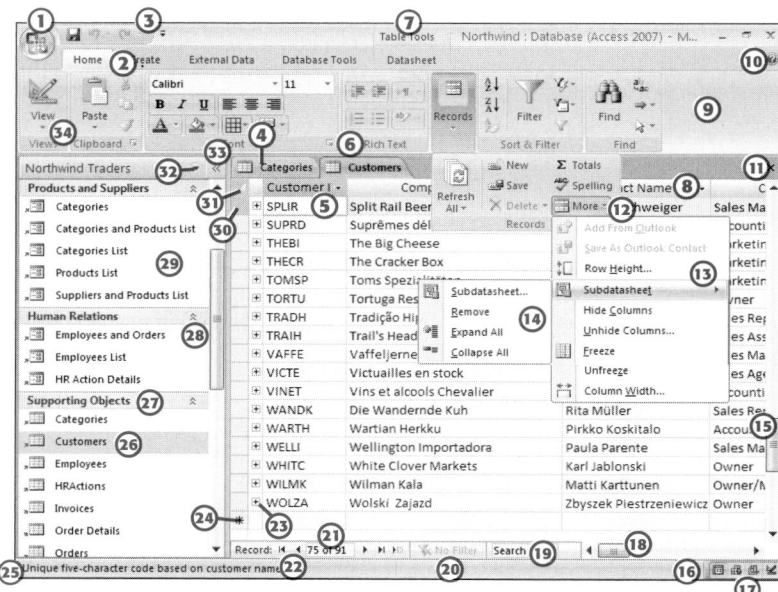

1. Office button
2. Ribbon tab
3. Quick-Access toolbar
4. Tabbed document
5. Selected cell
6. Button group
7. Contextual ribbon
8. Field headers
9. Ribbon
10. Online/Offline help
11. Document Close button
12. Gallery
13. Context menu
14. Context submenu
15. Record scrollbar
16. Status bar
17. View shortcuts
18. Field scrollbar
19. Quick Search textbox
20. Filter status
21. Record indicator
22. Record Navigation bar
23. Open subdatasheet
24. New Record
25. Status message
26. Navigation item
27. Navigation group
28. Show/Hide Navigation items
29. Navigation pane
30. Row Selection button
31. Select All button
32. Show Navigation gallery
33. Navigation pane expand/retract
34. Open View or Gallery button

TABLE 3.1 COMPONENTS OF THE ACCESS DISPLAY FOR TABLES

Term	Description
Office Button	Opens the Office gallery (menu) with New, Open, Save, Save As, Print, Manage, E-Mail, Publish, and Close Database choices, as well as an Access Options button to open the Access Options dialog and an Exit Access button.
Ribbon Tab	Selects the active ribbon from the four standard ribbons—Home, Create, External Data, Database Tools—and one or two contextual (Tools) ribbons, such as Table Tools, Datasheet(w) or Table Tools, Design.

Term	Description
Quick Access Toolbar	Lets you add icons that act as shortcuts to command buttons on all ribbons and most galleries. The default choices are Save, Undo, and Redo.
Tabbed Document	Access 2007's default window for displaying all database objects in any view.
Selected Cell	The currently selected cell into which you can type data.
Button Group	A collection of a ribbon's command buttons that perform related tasks.
Contextual Ribbon	A ribbon that appears in response to the selected object type (table, query, form, or report) and mode (run or design).
Field Headers	Displays the name of the field and, when clicked, selects all cells of the column. Right-clicking opens a context menu with choices similar to those of the context submenu shown in Figure 3.6.
Ribbon	The standard navigation window for Office 2007 that's customized for each Office application.
Online/Offline Help	Opens Access's help window, which draws from help content on Office Online as well as local help files.
Document Close Button	Closes the active tabbed document.
Gallery	A graphic menu with command button icons that represent choices. Access uses galleries to display buttons that aren't visible in a group.
Context Menu	An extension to a gallery or a floating right-click menu that offers choices that depend on the selected button or object type.
Context Submenu	A second or third menu hierarchy.
Record Scroll Bar	Scrolls table records or query rows.
Status Bar	Displays context information or user-specified text.
View Shortcuts	Provides a context-based alternative to selection from the Views group's gallery: Datasheet, PivotChart, PivotTable, Form, Report, Design.
Field Scroll Bar	Scrolls table fields or query columns.

continues

TABLE 3.1   CONTINUED

	Term	Description
	Quick Search Text Box	Typing text searches for the first instance of the characters in any field. If a match is found, pressing Enter finds the next occurrence.
	Filter Status	Advises the user if all records are visible (No Filter) or a filter has been applied (Filtered).
	Record Indicator	Displays the number of the current record and the total number of records displayed.
◀◀ ◀ ▶ ▶▶ ▶*	Record Navigation Bar	Provides VCR-like buttons (First, Previous, Next, and Last) for selecting the current table record or query row and a New Row button to navigate to the tentative append record, if the table or query is updatable.
⊞	Open Subdatasheet	Opens a table's subdatasheet that displays records in a related table, if a subdatasheet has been defined.
✳	New Record	The tentative append record that becomes a new record when you type in at least one field.
	Status Message	Context information or user-specified text.
	Navigation Item	A shortcut to a database object; double-clicking the item opens it in a tabbed document (the default) or a modal dialog form.
	Navigation Group	A named collection of related navigation items.
	Show/Hide Navigation Items	Expands or collapses the list of a navigation group's items.
	Navigation Pane	An Outlook-style, customizable, shutter-bar list of all database objects, except those that are hidden deliberately.
	Row Selection Button	Click to make the row the current row.
	Select All Button	Click to select all rows and columns (the equivalent of pressing Ctrl+A).
▾	Show Navigation Gallery	Click to open or close the Navigation gallery; right-click to open a context menu with Category, Sort By, View By, Show All Groups, Paste, Navigation Options, and Search Bar choices.

	Term	Description
» «	Navigation Pane Expand/Retract	Expand or retract the Navigation Pane. The default state is expanded.
◣	Open View or Gallery Button	Clicking the icon displays the specified view; clicking View opens a gallery of the available views for the object.

→ For a detailed overview of the ribbon UI, Quick Access Toolbar, and Office gallery, **see** "The Office 2007 Ribbon User Interface," **p. 24**.

→ To learn how to customize the Navigation pane, **see** "The Navigation Pane," **p. 42**.

→ For a brief explanation of Access 2007's new tabbed documents and modal dialogs that replace conventional modeless forms, **see** "Tabbed Documents and Modal Dialogs," **p. 53**.

NAVIGATING THE HOME AND CREATE RIBBONS

The Home, Create, External Data, and Database Tools ribbons vary only slightly as you change objects, operating modes, screen resolution, or window width. Access enables or disables a few command buttons and gallery items in response to changes of object type and view. Familiarity with the Home and Create ribbons is required to get up to speed with Access 2007, so this chapter covers these ribbons in detail.

→ For a brief overview of all four primary Access ribbons, **see** "Access 2007's Main Ribbons," **p. 25**.

N O T E

This chapter concentrates on the ribbons that apply to Table Datasheet and Table Design views. Chapter 14, "Creating and Using Basic Access Forms," describes the context-specific ribbons for Form Layout and Form Design views. Chapter 16, "Working with Simple Reports and Mailing Labels," explains the elements of the Report Layout Tools, Format, Arrange, and Page Setup; Report Design Tools, Design, Arrange, and Page Setup; and Print Preview ribbons.

THE HOME RIBBON

Figure 3.7 is a multiple-exposure, split view of the Home ribbon for table Datasheet view in 1,024×768 resolution. The View, Font Color, Text Highlight Color, Refresh All, Advanced Filter Options, and Go To galleries are open.

Figure 3.7
Control buttons on ribbons haven't replaced all hierarchical Office menus. Drop-down galleries and context menus substitute icons, lists, or both for earlier Access versions' conventional Windows menu choices.

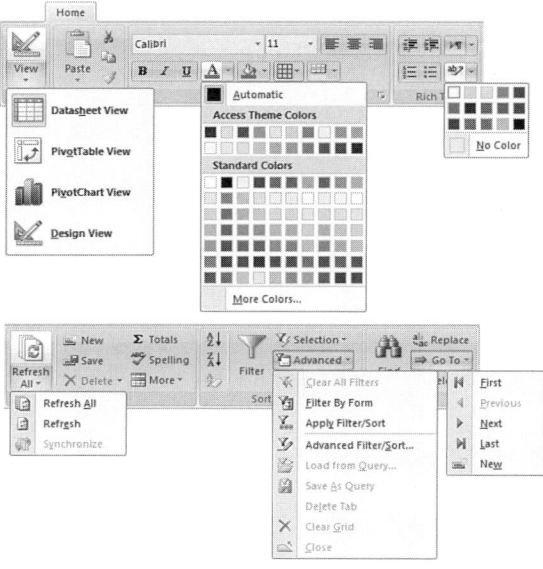

Table 3.2 lists the Home ribbon's command buttons, keyboard shortcuts (also called *KeyTips*), and actions. Press Alt+H to activate the KeyTips, release the Alt key, and then sequentially press the keys shown in the Shortcut column.

TABLE 3.2   THE HOME RIBBON'S COMMAND BUTTONS AND THEIR ACTIONS IN TABLE DATASHEET VIEW

Icon	Command Button	Shortcut Alt+H, …	Command Action
Views Group			
📄	Datasheet View	W, H	Changes to Datasheet view
📊	PivotChart View	W, O	Changes to PivotChart view
📋	PivotTable View	W, V	Changes to PivotTable view
✎	Design View	W, D	Changes to Design view
Clipboard Group			
📋	Paste	V, P (Ctrl+V)	Pastes Clipboard content
📋	Paste, Special	V, S	Pastes Clipboard content in selected format
None	Paste, Append	V, N	Inserts records copied to the Clipboard

Icon	Command Button	Shortcut Alt+H, …	Command Action
✂	Cut	X (Ctrl+X)	Cuts selected content to the Clipboard
📋	Copy	C (Ctrl+C)	Copies selected content to the Clipboard
None	Office Clipboard	F, O	Opens the Office Clipboard task pane

Font Group

Icon	Command Button	Shortcut Alt+H, …	Command Action
🖌	Format Painter	F, P	Copies the format from one object to another
None	Font, Face	F, F	Sets the focus to the Font Face list box
None	Font, Size	F, S	Sets the focus to the Font Size list box
B	Bold	1 Ctrl+B	Applies bold attribute to selected text
I	Italic	2 Ctrl+I	Applies italic attribute to selected text
U̲	Underline	3 Ctrl+U	Applies underline attribute to selected text
≡	Align Left	A, L	Aligns selected text left
≡	Align Center	A, C	Centers selected text
≡	Align Right	A, R	Aligns selected text right
A	Font Color	F, C	Opens font color picker
🪣	Fill/Back Color	F, B	Opens fill/background color picker
▦	Gridlines	B	Opens gridlines gallery
▦	Alternate Fill/Back Color	F, A	Opens fill/background color picker for alternate rows
None	Datasheet Formatting	L	Opens the Datasheet Formatting dialog (see Figure 3.8)

Rich Text Group (for rich-text-enabled Memo fields only)

Icon	Command Button	Shortcut Alt+H, …	Command Action
🔽	Decrease List Level	A, O	Decreases rich-text indent level
🔼	Increase List Level	A, I	Increases rich-text indent level
▶¶	Left-to-Right	A, F	Enables changing rich-text entry direction

continues

TABLE 3.2   CONTINUED

Icon	Command Button	Shortcut Alt+H, …	Command Action
	Numbering	N	Starts a rich-text numbered list
	Bullets	U	Starts a rich-text unordered list
	Text Highlight Color I		Opens a color picker to highlight selected rich text

Records Group (see Chapter 6)

Icon	Command Button	Shortcut Alt+H, …	Command Action
	Refresh All	K, R	Regenerates the Recordset and repaints the Datasheet
	New Record	K, N Ctrl++	Moves to the tentative append record
	Save	K, S Shift+Enter	Saves changes to a record
	Delete	K, D (Del)	Deletes the selected (current) record
	Totals	T	Toggles the appearance of a totals row below the tentative append record
	Spelling	S (F7)	Starts the spelling checker for the selected object and opens the Spelling: *Language* dialog (see Figure 3.9)
	More choices	P	Opens a context menu with Datasheet formatting

Sort & Filter Group (see Chapter 7)

Icon	Command Button	Shortcut Alt+H, …	Command Action
	Sort Ascending	E	Sorts the selected field/column in ascending (A–Z) order
	Sort Descending	D	Sorts the selected field/column in descending (Z–A) order
	Clear All Sorts	F, R	Removes sorts from all fields/columns
	Filter	Q	Opens the filter context menu for the selected field/column
	Selection	O	Opens a context menu that lets you filter records by selection
	Advanced Filter/Sort FV		Opens a context menu that lets you choose advanced filter/sort features
	Toggle Filter	J	Alternately applies and removes the current filter

Icon	Command Button	Shortcut Alt+H, …	Command Action
Find Group (see Chapter 7)			
	<u>F</u>ind	F, D Ctrl+F	Opens the Find and Replace dialog with the Find page active
	<u>R</u>eplace	R Ctrl+H	Opens the Find dialog with the Replace page active
	<u>G</u>o To	G	Opens a context menu with <u>F</u>irst, <u>P</u>revious, <u>N</u>ext, <u>L</u>ast, and Ne<u>w</u> choices
	Select	H	Opens a context menu with Se<u>l</u>ect and Select <u>A</u>ll choices

Figure 3.8
The Datasheet Formatting dialog consolidates most Datasheet appearance settings in a single location.

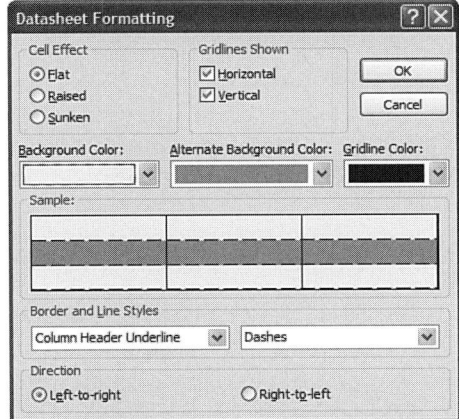

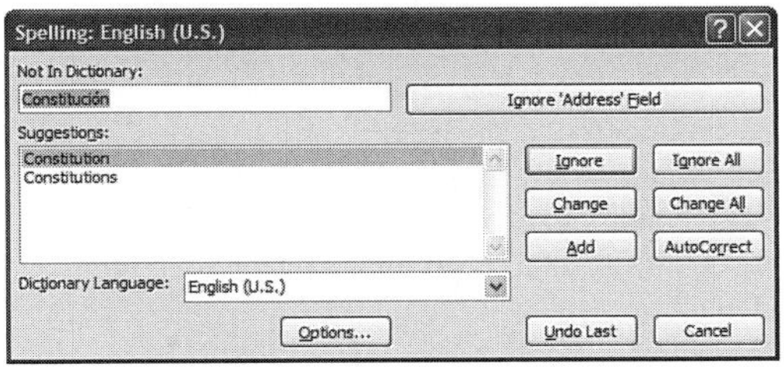

Figure 3.9
Access's Spelling: *Language* dialog is common to all Office 2007 applications.

NOTE

> The QAT and ribbon UI comprise a window that's independent of the Access window that contains the Navigation pane and tabbed documents. When you press Alt once or twice to set focus to the ribbon window and display the KeyTips, pressing the left or right arrow key cycles focus through the primary and context-specific ribbons, QAT, and Office button. Pressing Tab or an arrow key cycles the focus through the selected ribbon's command buttons. You move between ribbon and command button selection with the up- and down-arrow keys. Pressing Enter with a command button selected executes its action.

CONTEXT-SPECIFIC TABLE TOOLS RIBBONS

Opening any Access object except a module in Design view adds one or more context-specific *ObjectType* Design Tools ribbons. Similarly, opening a form or report in Layout view adds *ObjectType* Layout Tools ribbons. Opening a table in Datasheet or Design view adds a Table Tools, Datasheet ribbon. Changing to Design view substitutes a Table Tools, Design ribbon. The following sections describe these two context-sensitive ribbons briefly.

NOTE

> PivotChart and PivotTable views of tables and queries also have context menus, but these views are beyond this chapter's scope. Chapter 12, "Working with PivotTable and PivotChart Views," describes how to design these objects.

THE TABLE TOOLS, DATASHEET RIBBON

Microsoft encourages Access users to create tables in Datasheet view, type data in the default empty column provided, add new columns as needed, and populate the new columns. As mentioned earlier, opening a new empty database creates an empty starter table. Alternatively, you can add a starter table by clicking the Create ribbon's Table button. In either case, the Table Tools, Datasheet ribbon opens by default.

NOTE

> Microsoft promotes ad-hoc table design by emulating spreadsheet methodology so Access appears easier for neophytes to use. A substantial part of the market for desktop database platforms is *replacing* spreadsheets that should have been databases from the start. New users' impromptu table structures often don't abide by basic rules for relational database design. This is one of the primary reasons that RDBMSs such as Access have acquired a bad reputation.

TIP

> You can discourage users from making table design changes in Datasheet view by clearing the Enable Design Changes for Tables in Datasheet View check box in the Application Options group of the Access Options dialog's Current Database page, as described in the later section "The Current Database Page."

> To prevent users from changing options, you must split the database and secure the front end, as described in Chapter 19, "Linking Access Front Ends to Access and Client/Server Tables."

Figure 3.10 is a split view of the Table Tools, Datasheet ribbon for a database (in 1,024×768 resolution) that includes tables linked from SharePoint lists. The term *SharePoint* refers to Windows SharePoint Services (WSS) 3.0 or Microsoft Office SharePoint Server (MOSS) 2007.

Figure 3.10
The Table Tools, Datasheet ribbon for a database with tables linked to SharePoint adds a SharePoint Lists group with command buttons for common operational and maintenance duties for a site.

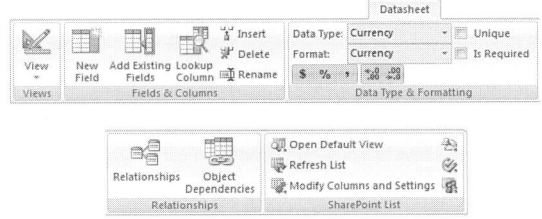

Table 3.3 lists the Table Tools, Datasheet ribbon's command buttons, shortcut keystrokes, and command actions. Like primary ribbons, you press Alt+H, release the Alt key, and then press the shortcut key. The Views button behaves identically to the same button on the Home ribbon. This ribbon doesn't have galleries, but three buttons open task panes, one button opens the Relationships window, and all buttons in the SharePoint Lists group open SharePoint pages.

> **NOTE**
>
> Chapter 25, "Collaborating with Windows SharePoint Services," provides detailed instruction for integrating Access 2007 and WSS 3.0 or MOSS 2007.

TABLE 3.3   THE TABLE TOOLS, DATASHEET RIBBON'S COMMAND BUTTONS AND THEIR ACTIONS IN TABLE DATASHEET VIEW

Icon	Command Button	Shortcut Alt+W, ...	Command Action
Fields & Columns Group (disabled for SharePoint lists)			
	New Fie<u>l</u>d	D	Opens the Field Templates task pane (see Figure 3.11, left) to select a data type and adds a field
	Add E<u>x</u>isting Fields	X	Opens the Field List task pane (see Figure 3.11, center) to clone a field from any database table

continues

TABLE 3.3 CONTINUED

Icon	Command Button	Shortcut Alt+W, ...	Command Action
	Lookup Column	L	Starts the Lookup Wizard to add lookup properties to a field
	Insert Column	I	Inserts a field to the left of existing columns
	Delete Column	T	Deletes the selected column
	Rename Column	N	Enables renaming the column, usually from Field1

Data Type and Formatting Group

Icon	Command Button	Shortcut Alt+W, ...	Command Action
None	Data Type	J	Lets you select one of Access's nine data types: Text, Memo, Number, Date/Time, Currency, Yes/No, OLE Object, Hyperlink, or Attachment (disabled for SharePoint lists)
None	Format	F	Lets you select one of Access's seven Number or seven Date/Time formats
✓	Unique	U	Adds a no-duplicates index to the selected field, which requires each cell value to be unique
✓	Is Required	Q	Prevents users from leaving empty cells in the selected field
$	Apply Currency Format	A, N	Formats the Number data with the Windows default currency format
%	Apply Percentage Format	P	Multiplies the Number data by 100 and adds two decimal digits (does not affect the cell value)
,	Apply Comma Number Format	K	Adds comma (or dot) thousands separators and two decimal digits
.00→.0	Decrease Decimals	0	Reduces the number of decimal digits
←.0.00	Increase Decimals	9	Increases the number of decimal digits

Relationships Group

Icon	Command Button	Shortcut Alt+W, ...	Command Action
	Relationships	E	Opens the Relationships window to enable establishing or editing relationships between tables
	Object Dependencies	O	Opens the Object Dependencies task pane (see Figure 3.11, right)

Icon	Command Button	Shortcut Alt+W, …	Command Action
SharePoint List Group (visible only when a table linked to a SharePoint list is selected)			
	Default View	S, V	Opens the selected linked SharePoint list's default view page in an Access Web Datasheet ActiveX control (see Figure 3.12)
	Refresh List	S, R	Causes the table to rewrite the selected linked SharePoint list data to the local Datasheet
	Modify Columns and Settings	S, M	Opens SharePoint's Customize *ListName* page on which you can change the design of the selected list
	Alert Me	S, A	Sends you an email message when users make specific types of changes to the selected list
	Modify Workflow	S, W	Opens SharePoint's Change Workflow Settings: *ListName* page for the selected linked list
	Permissions	S, P	Opens the Permissions: *ListName* page for the selected linked list

Figure 3.11
Access 2007 relies on task panes for operations that are more complex than galleries can handle.

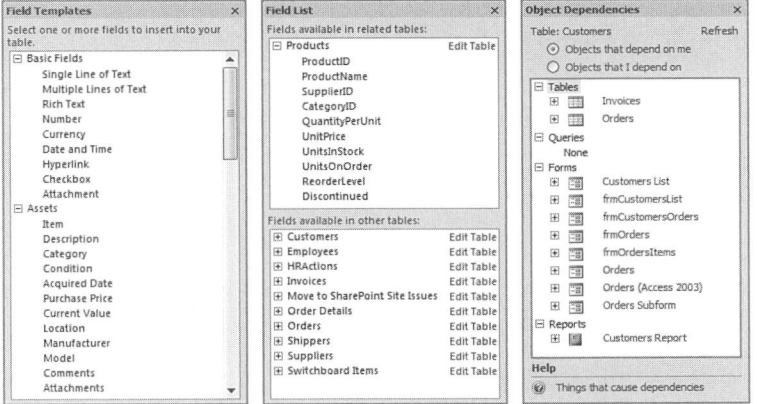

THE TABLE TOOLS, DESIGN RIBBON

Changing to table Design view replaces the Table Tools, Datasheet ribbon with the Table Tools, Design ribbon shown in Figure 3.13. Table Design view is the better choice for designing tables than typing data items to generate an ad-hoc table structure. Design view and the Table Tools, Design ribbon expose many more field and table properties than Datasheet view and the Table Tools, Datasheet ribbon.

Figure 3.12
An Access database has a Categories table linked to this SharePoint Categories list. Paperclip icons in a column indicate that the column uses the SharePoint (or Access) Attachment data type.

Figure 3.13
The simpler Table Tools, Design ribbon replaces the Datasheet version in table Design view. The field design grid and the Field Properties pane set values for individual fields. Property Sheet settings apply to the entire table.

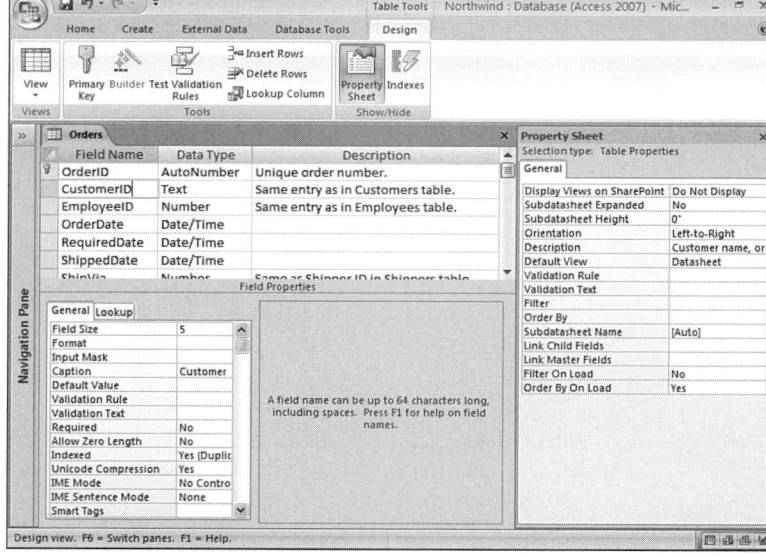

Table 3.4 lists the Table Tools, Design ribbon's command buttons, shortcut keystrokes, and command actions.

TABLE 3.4   THE TABLE TOOLS, DESIGN RIBBON'S COMMAND BUTTONS AND THEIR ACTIONS IN TABLE DESIGN VIEW

Icon	Command Button	Shortcut Alt+D, …	Command Action
Tools Group			
	Primary Key	P	Toggles the status of the selected column(s) as the primary key for the table
	Builder	B	Opens the Expression Builder dialog when entering Default Value or Validation Rule property values
	Test Validation Rules	V	Tests new or modified validation rules with existing data
	Insert Rows	I	Inserts a new field grid row above the current row
	Delete Rows	R	Deletes the selected field grid row(s)
	Lookup Column	L	Inserts a new field grid row and starts the Lookup Wizard
Show/Hide Group			
	Property Sheet	H, P	Toggles visibility of the Property Sheet pane
	Indexes	X	Opens the Indexes: *TableName* dialog to add indexes on fields other than the primary key field

→ For a brief description of primary keys, **see** "Selecting a Primary Key," **p. 241**.

→ For more information about the Expression Builder and validation rules, **see** "Adding Table-Level Validation Rules with the Expression Builder," **p. 278**.

→ To learn more about the Indexes: *TableName* dialog, **see** "Adding Indexes to Tables," **p. 242**.

TIP

Almost all nontrivial databases contain more than one table because a single-table database is the functional equivalent of a spreadsheet or a SharePoint list. Before you design a table for a production database that requires two or more related tables, read—or at least skim—Chapter 4, "Exploring Relational Database Theory and Practice," and Chapter 5, "Working with Access Databases and Tables."

Many novice database designers find the usability or performance of their application deteriorates greatly as the number of table rows increases. Changing table design to overcome deficiencies after users enter large amounts of data is time-consuming, frustrating, and prone to errors. Starting your first database project with one of the many Access database templates, even if you must modify it to suit your application, provides a reasonable degree of assurance that you won't "design yourself into a nonrelational corner."

THE CREATE RIBBON

You use the Create ribbon to add new table, query, form, report, macro, and module objects to Access databases (see Figure 3.14).

Figure 3.14
The Create ribbon lets you add new Access objects to your database and take advantage of table and field templates, when applicable.

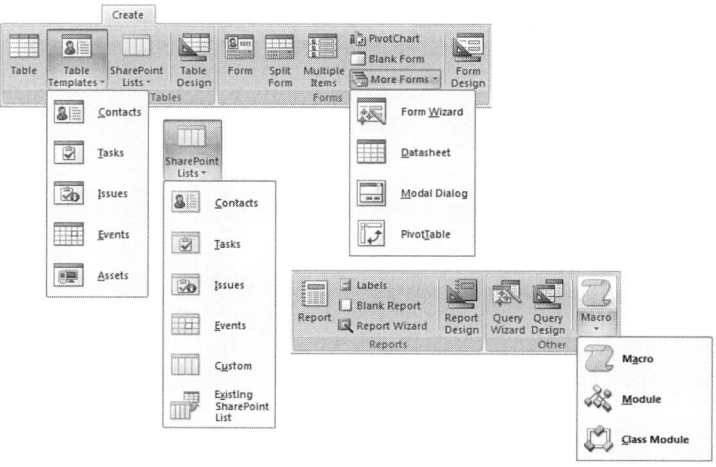

> **NOTE**
>
> Microsoft organized the Create ribbon's groups from left to right into the normal sequence of database development with one exception: A Query group is missing between the Tables and Forms groups. Placing Query Wizards and Query Design buttons in the Other group demeans the importance of queries to Access applications.

Table 3.5 lists the Create ribbon's command buttons, shortcut keystrokes, and command actions.

TABLE 3.5   THE CREATE RIBBON'S COMMAND BUTTONS AND THEIR ACTIONS IN TABLE DATASHEET VIEW

Icon	Command Button	Shortcut Alt+C, …	Command Action
Tables Group (see Part II of this book)			
	Table	T, N	Adds a new table with a single field in Datasheet view
	Table Templates	L	Opens a gallery that contains the following five command buttons
	Contacts	L, C	Adds an Outlook-compatible list for individuals from the Contacts and other application templates

Icon	Command Button	Shortcut Alt+C, ...	Command Action
	Tasks	L, T	Adds a task list that's suitable for managing a group's activities (from the Tasks application template)
	Issues	L, I	Adds an issue list that might be used for bug reporting and the like (from the Issues application template)
	Events	L, E	Adds a date-based list for scheduling events (from the Events application template)
	Assets	L, A	Adds a list that's designed specifically for tracking fixed assets (from the Assets application template)
	SharePoint Lists	S	Opens a gallery that contains the following six command buttons
	Contacts	S, C	Generates a Contacts list in the designated SharePoint site and links it and a User Information List to an Access table
	Tasks	S, T	Does the same for a Tasks list and table
	Issues	S, I	Does the same for an Issues list and table
	Events	S, E	Does the same for an Events list and table
	Custom	S, U	Generates a basic SharePoint list with visible ID (AutoNumber), Title (Text), and Attachments (Attachment) fields, as well as 11 hidden SharePoint-specific fields and links it to an Access table
	Existing SharePoint List	S, X	Lets you import or link the data from a SharePoint list you specify to an Access table
	Table Design	T, D	Adds a new Access table in Design view
Forms Group (see Chapters 14 and 15)			
	Form	F, M	Generates a formatted columnar form from the selected table or query and adds a Datasheet subform bound to a related form, if present
	Split Form	P	Generates a formatted columnar form and a Datasheet from the selected table or query
	Multiple Items	M	Generates a formatted tabular list from the selected table or query

continues

TABLE 3.5 CONTINUED

Icon	Command Button	Shortcut Alt+C, …	Command Action
	PivotChart	C	Creates a form that contains a PivotChart control (see Chapter 18, "Adding Graphs, PivotCharts, and PivotTables")
	Blank Form	F, B	Creates an empty (blank) form in Layout view and opens the Field List pane
	More Forms	F, M	Opens a gallery with the following four command buttons
	Form Wizard	F, M, W	Starts the Form Wizard, which lets you create a columnar, tabular, Datasheet, or justified form from table fields or query columns you select with a format from one of 25 predesigned styles
	Datasheet	F, M, D	Creates a form that's indistinguishable from table Datasheet view
	Modal Dialog	F, M, M	Creates an empty modal dialog (overlapping window) in Layout view and opens the Field List pane
	PivotTable	F, M, T	Creates a form that contains a PivotTable control (see Chapter 18)
	Form Design	F, D	Opens a new blank form in Design view
Reports Group (see Chapters 16 and 17)			
	Report	R, N	Generates a simple formatted list from the selected table or query with the same font size as forms and opens it in Report view
	Labels	B	Starts the Mailing Label Wizard to print mailing labels standard label sheets you specify
	Blank Report	R, B	Opens a blank report in Layout view for the selected table or query and opens the Field List pane
	Report Wizard	W	Starts the Report Wizard, which lets you base the report on a table or query you select, and add grouping, sort order, and format
	Report Design	R, D	Opens a new blank report for the selected table or query in Design view

Icon	Command Button	Shortcut Alt+C, ...	Command Action
Other Group (see Parts III and VII of this book)			
	Query Wizard	Q, W	Opens the New Query dialog, which lets you select the Simple Query, Crosstab Query, Find Duplicates, or Find Unmatched Query Wizard to help you design a query from one or more tables
	Query Design	Q, D	Opens a new query in Design view and displays the Show Table dialog
	Macro	A	Opens a gallery with the following three command buttons
	Macro	A, A	Opens an empty standalone macro object for a nonembedded Access macro
	Module	A, M	Opens an empty VBA module in the VBA Editor application
	Class Module	A, C	Opens an empty VBA Class Module in the VBA Editor application

NOTE

> Chapter 8, "Linking, Importing, and Exporting Data" covers use of the External Data ribbon, and Chapter 5, "Working with Access Databases and Tables" explains the Database Tools ribbon's command button actions.

USING THE FUNCTION KEYS

Access assigns specific purposes to all 12 function keys of the 101-key extended keyboard. Some function-key combinations, such as Shift+F4 (which you press to find the next occurrence of a match with the Find dialog), derive from other Microsoft applications—in this case, Word.

GLOBAL FUNCTION KEYS

Windows, rather than Access, uses global function-key assignments, except for F11, Ctrl+F1, and Alt+F1, to perform identical functions in all Windows applications. Table 3.6 lists the global function-key assignments.

TABLE 3.6   GLOBAL FUNCTION-KEY ASSIGNMENTS

Key	Function
F1	Displays context-sensitive help related to the present basic function and status of Access. If a context-sensitive help topic isn't available, F1 opens the Microsoft Access Help task pane page, which lets you search online help for a keyword or open its table of contents.
[NEW] Ctrl+F1	Toggles (alternates) visibility of the ribbon window in all Office 2007 members.
Ctrl+F4	Closes the active window.
Alt+F4	Exits Access or closes a dialog if one is open.
Ctrl+F6	Selects each open window in sequence as the active window.
[NEW] F11	Toggles Navigation Pane visibility.
F12	Opens the selected object's Save As dialog.
Shift+F12	Saves your open database; the equivalent of the File menu's Save command.

FUNCTION-KEY ASSIGNMENTS AND SHORTCUT KEYS FOR FIELDS, GRIDS, AND TEXT BOXES

Access assigns function-key combinations that aren't reserved for global operations to actions specific to the basic function you're performing at the moment. Table 3.7 lists the function-key combinations that apply to fields, grids, and text boxes. (To present complete information, this table repeats some information that appears in the previous tables.)

→ For an extensive list of Access shortcut key assignments, **see** "Using Keyboard Operations for Entering and Editing Data," **p. 266**.

TABLE 3.7   FUNCTION KEYS FOR FIELDS, GRIDS, AND TEXT BOXES

Key	Function
F2	Toggles between displaying the caret for editing and selecting the entire field.
Shift+F2	Opens the Zoom box to make typing expressions and other text easier.
F4	Opens a drop-down combo list or list box.
Shift+F4	Finds the next occurrence of a match of the text typed in the Find or Replace dialog, if the dialog is closed.
F5	Moves the caret to the record-number box. Type the number of the record that you want to display.
F6	In Table Design view, cycles between upper and lower parts of the window. In Form Design view, cycles through the header, body (detail section), and footer.
F7	Starts the spelling checker.
F8	Turns on extend mode. Press F8 again to extend the selection to a word, the entire field, the whole record, and then all records.

Key	Function
Shift+F8	Reverses the F8 selection process.
Ctrl+F	Opens the Find and Replace dialog with the Find page active.
Ctrl+H	Opens the Find and Replace dialog with the Replace page active.
Ctrl++ (plus sign)	Adds a new record to the current table or query, if the table or query is updatable.
Shift+Enter	Saves changes to the active record in the table.
Esc	Undoes changes in the current record or field. By pressing Esc twice, you can undo changes in the current field and record. Also cancels extend mode.

NOTE

Ctrl+G opens the VBA editor and sets the focus to the Immediate window (formerly the Debug window), and Ctrl+Break halts execution of VBA code.

SETTING DEFAULT OPTIONS

You can set about 100 options that establish the default settings for Access. (But you aren't likely to want to change default options until you're more familiar with Access 2007.) This book is a reference as well as a tutorial guide, and options are a basic element of Access's overall structure, so this section explains how to change these settings.

NOTE

The Access Options dialog discussed in this chapter corresponds to the options available using Access databases and not the Microsoft SQL Server 2005 Express Edition (SQLX), which Access data projects (ADPs) use. See Chapter 20, "Exploring Access Data Projects and SQL Server 2005," for more information on ADPs.

You set defaults by clicking the Office button to open the gallery and then clicking the Access Options button to open the Access Options dialog's default Popular page (see Figure 3.15). The options you set on the Popular, Datasheet, Object Designers, Proofing, Advanced, Customize, and Add-Ins pages apply to the system as a whole. Settings on the Current Database page apply only to the database that's open when you change the settings.

NOTE

If you're familiar with earlier Access versions, you'll notice that the Access Options dialog is a dramatic departure from the tabbed dialog that opened from the Tools, Options menu choice. Most of the individual settings are common to earlier versions, but their organization into pages differs.

Figure 3.15
The default Popular page of the Access Options properties dialog sets global option values that apply to all databases you open in Access 2007, as do all other pages except Current Database.

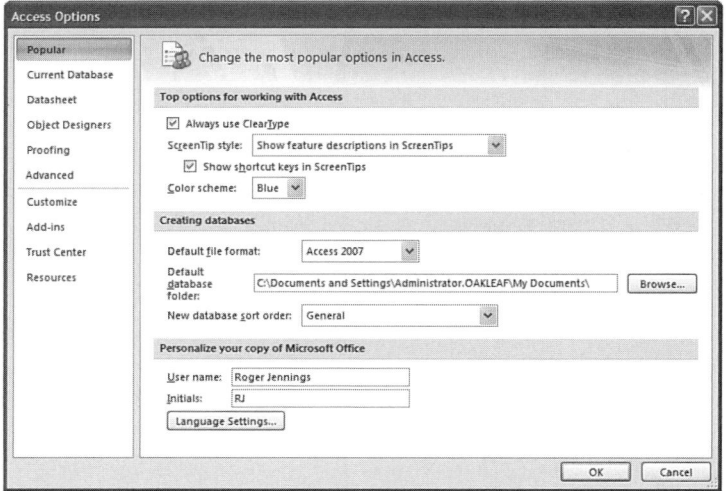

Most settings are option buttons and check boxes, although many other items require multiple-choice entries that you select from drop-down lists. In some cases, you must type a specific value in a text box. After you complete your changes, click OK to close the dialog to save your changes. If you decide not to implement your changes, click Cancel to exit without making any changes. The next few sections and their tables summarize options that affect Access as a whole and those options that affect viewing and printing data in Datasheet view.

THE POPULAR PAGE

The Popular page (refer to Figure 3.15) contains the following control groups to set the most common default option for all Access databases and projects you create:

- **Top Options for Working with Access**—Enables ClearType for LCD monitors. Also sets the ScreenTip style and default color scheme: Blue, Silver, or Black. (*ScreenTips* are the formatted ToolTips for ribbon command buttons.)

- **Creating Databases**—Sets the default file format for new database files (Access 2007 .accdb, Access 2002–2003 .mdb, or Access 2000 .mdb). Also specifies the default .accdb or .mdb file location (My Documents for Windows XP; Documents for Windows Vista) and database sort order (General to use the Windows language's sort order).

- **Personalize Your Copy of Microsoft Office**—Lets you change the default username and add or edit initials. The Language Settings button opens the Microsoft Office Language Settings 2007 dialog that's common to all Office 2007 applications (see Figure 3.16). This dialog lets you add additional editing languages and change the default editing language. However, languages other than that of your version of Office 2007 might require additional features, such as a Language Pack, to fully enable editing in those languages.

Figure 3.16
The Microsoft Office Language Settings 2007 dialog lets you make other editing languages available, but you might need additional resources to make full use of those languages.

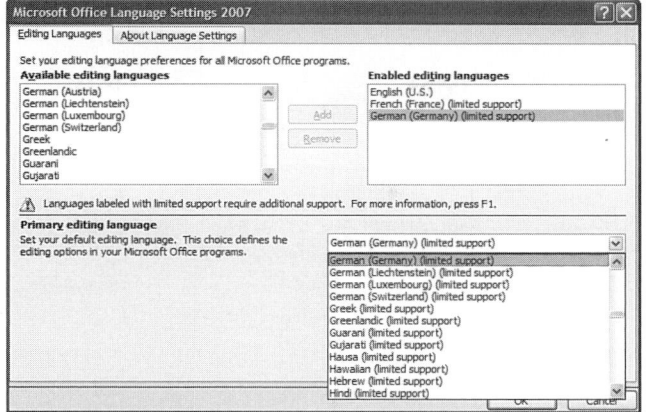

NOTE

> You also can open the Microsoft Office Language Settings 2007 dialog from the Start, Programs, Microsoft Office, Microsoft Office Tools, Microsoft Office 2007 Language Settings menu choice.

THE CURRENT DATABASE PAGE

The Current Database Page lets you change default properties of the currently open database or project with controls in the following groups:

- **Application Options**—Lets you specify a custom application title and icon; substitute the custom icon for standard form and report icons; name a startup form to open when Access loads; hide the status bar at the bottom of the Access window; replace tabbed documents with nonmodal (overlapping) windows; disable special access keys (F11 for the Navigation Pane, Ctrl+G for the VBA Editor's Immediate window, and Ctrl+Break to halt VBA code execution); and automatically compact the database after closing the file (see Figure 3.17).

  You also can remove personally identifiable information from the .accdb or .mdb file; disable Windows XP or Windows Vista themed controls; disable Layout view; disable making design changes in table Database view; disable testing for truncated numbers when changing number format; and convert all image files to Windows bitmap (.bmp) format for backward compatibility.

- **Navigation**—The Display Navigation Pane check box enables hiding the Navigation Pane (see Figure 3.18). The Navigation Options button opens the Navigation Options dialog.

Figure 3.17
The Current Database page's Application Options group includes new option settings for tabbed documents, Layout view, designing tables in Datasheet view, and the Attachments field data type.

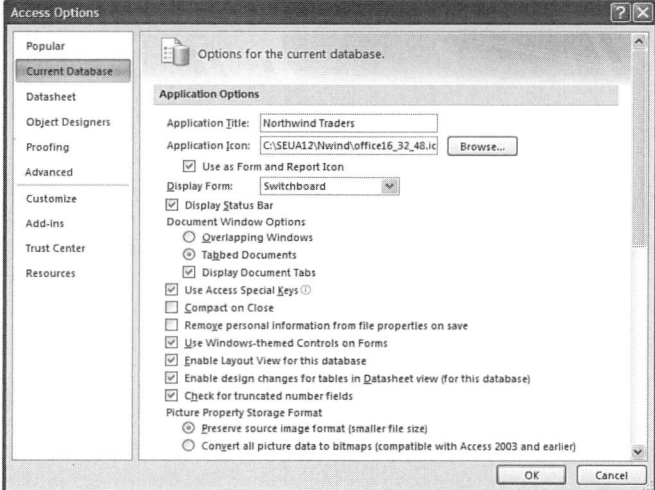

Figure 3.18
The Current Database page's remaining groups are more specialized than Application Options.

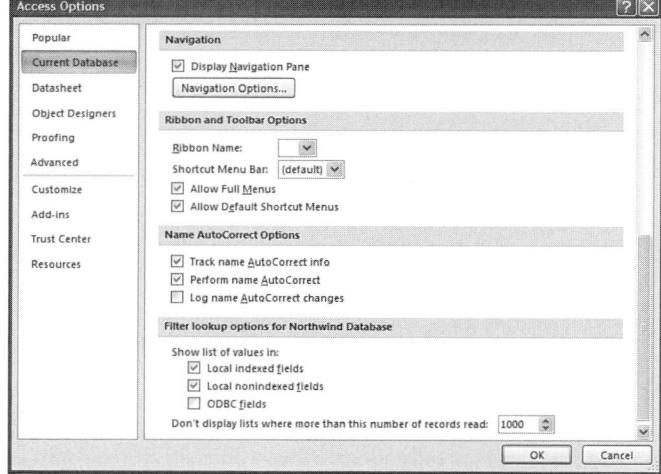

➔ To find out how to use the Navigation Options dialog, **see** "Customizing the Custom Category," **p. 43**.

■ **Ribbon and Toolbar Options**—Lets you replace all ribbons, add groups and command buttons to existing ribbons by selecting a stored RibbonX (XML) document, or discourage users from editing objects. For example, you can specify a custom shortcut (context) menu bar; clear the Allow Full Menus check box to hide all ribbons except Home; and clear the Allow Default Shortcut Menu check box to hide noncustom context menus.

➔ For an introduction to RibbonX documents, **see** "Customizing Ribbons for Specific Applications," **p. 33**.
➔ To learn how to program custom ribbons, **see** "Customizing Applications with Ribbon Objects," **p. 1226**.

- **Name AutoCorrect Options**—Enables a controversial process for conforming references to renamed Access objects. If you'd rather do the job yourself, clear the Track Name AutoCorrect Info and Perform Name AutoCorrect check boxes. (Don't bother trying Alt+A; all the check boxes have the same shortcut key combination.)

TIP

> The Name AutoCorrect feature is controversial because of its history of serious problems that occurred with the initial Access 2000 version and several issues that you might encounter with Access 2007. Most Access developers recommend that you disable this feature. To learn more about the feature's problematic history, perform a Google search on **"Name AutoCorrect" problem**.

→ To learn more about Name AutoCorrect, **see** "Altering Fields and Relationships," **p. 244**.

- **Filter Lookup Options**—Lets you disable displaying lookup field lists from indexed, non-indexed, or ODBC fields in linked or client/server tables, or where the lists would have more than a specified number of items. As an example, a lookup list of customers in an orders table might have 10,000 or more items from which to choose, which could cause a substantial performance hit.

→ For more information about lookup fields, **see** "Using Lookup Fields in Tables," **p. 466**.

THE DATASHEET PAGE

The Datasheet page (see Figure 3.19) sets the defaults for table, query, and form Datasheets.

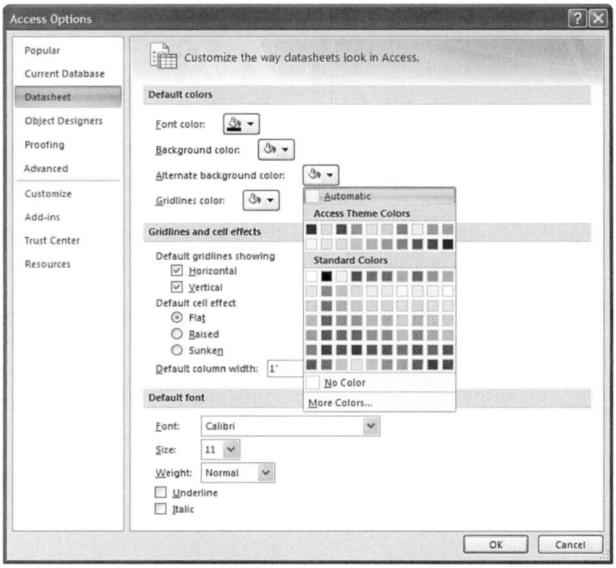

Figure 3.19
The Datasheet page sets design defaults for Datasheet views in new databases.

Following are descriptions of the page's three groups:

- **Default Colors**—Provides color pickers for Font, Background, Alternate Background, and Gridlines colors.

- **Gridlines and Cell Effects**—Enables customizing visibility of horizontal and vertical gridlines, as well as cell special effects and default column width.

- **Default Font**—Lets you change the default 11-point Calibri font to any other Windows TrueType or OpenType font.

THE OBJECT DESIGNERS PAGE

The Object Designers page (see Figure 3.20) sets the defaults for table, query, form, and report Design view.

Figure 3.20
The Object Designers page's first two groups set design defaults for table Design view, query Design view, and SQL view.

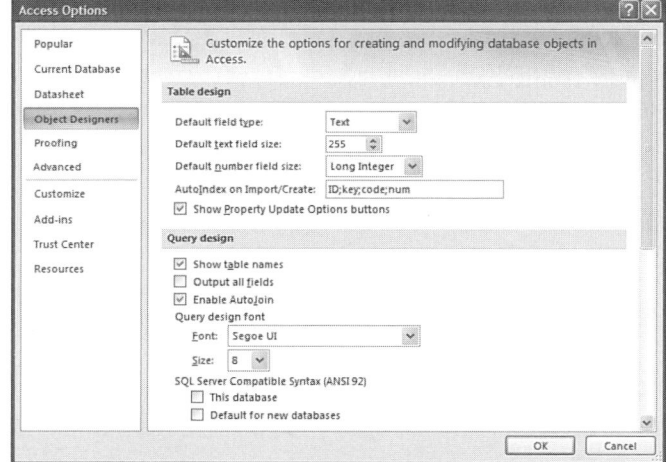

Following are descriptions of the page's four groups:

- **Table Design**—Sets the defaults for new field data types (Text) and default Text field size (255 characters, the maximum) and Number field size (Long Integer). By default, Access will add an index to any field that contains the characters "ID", "key", "code", or "num". You might want to remove the semicolon-separated string from the text box so that you, not Access, determines when to add indexes fields. Clearing the Show Property Update Options Buttons check box hides the drop-down lists for properties (such as Format) on the General page of table Design view's lower pane, which is not a recommended practice.

- **Query Design**—Lets you disable auto-addition of table names to all query SQL statements, add an all-fields asterisk (*) to all query field lists, or disable automatically creating join lines between related tables or fields with the same name. You also can change the default design font from Segoe UI to a different family and larger size, and specify SQL Server–compatible syntax based on the ANSI SQL-92 standard. With the exception of font size, departing from the default query Design settings isn't recommended.

- **Forms/Reports**—Enables changing how controls on forms and reports are selected (partial or full enclosure) and the names of form and report templates (see Figure 3.21). You can use an existing form or report as a template or create a form or report specifically as a template for the new objects you create. This book uses forms and reports generated from the default Normal templates. Marking the Always Use Event Procedures check box doesn't force Access 2007's Control and other wizards autogenerating VBA code; doing this only prevents wizards from generating embedded macro code.

Figure 3.21
The Object Designers page's last two groups specify design defaults for form and report Design view, and control design error checking.

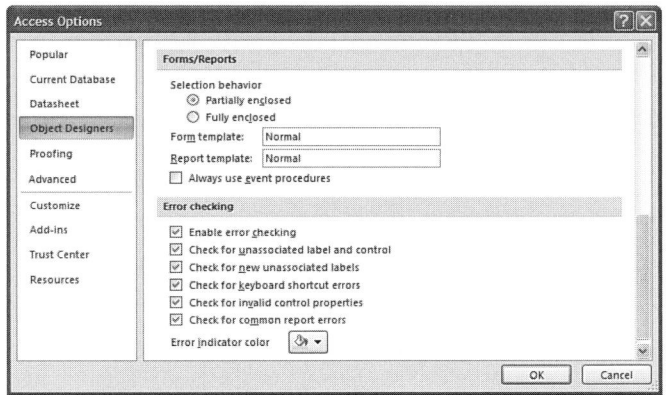

- **Error Checking**—Enables or disables Design-mode error checking and uses a color picker to select the error indicator smart tag's color.

THE PROOFING PAGE

The Proofing page enables customizing the AutoCorrect feature and Office spelling checker for all Access applications (see Figure 3.22).

The Proofing page has these two groups:

- **AutoCorrect Options**—Provides an AutoCorrect Options button to open the Office AutoCorrect dialog.
- **When Correcting Spelling in Microsoft Office Programs**—Lets you set spell-checking options, including custom dictionaries in the Custom Dictionaries dialog, and specify a main dictionary language other than the default English (U.S.).

Figure 3.22
The brief Proofing page lets you modify default AutoCorrect and spelling checker settings.

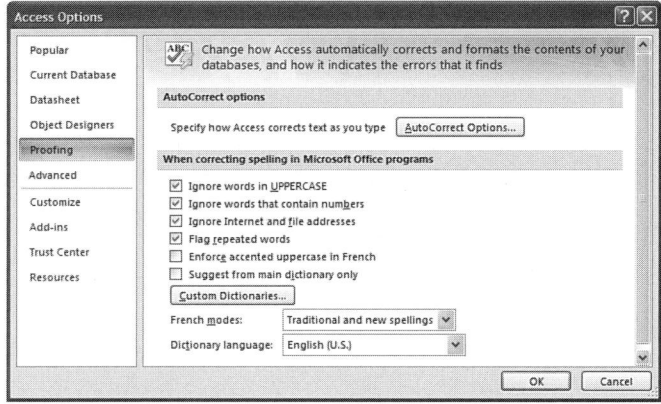

THE ADVANCED PAGE

The Advanced page (see Figure 3.23) contains the following five groups:

- **Editing**—Lets you customize the default cursor, arrow key, find/replace, confirmations, Datasheet IME (Input Method Editor) control, and Hijiri (Islamic or Arabic) lunar calendar options. (Saudi Arabia, Kuwait, and Yemen use the Hijiri calendar officially).

→ For detailed explanations of cursor and arrow-key options, **see** "Setting Data Entry Options," **p. 267**.

Figure 3.23
The Advanced page's Editing group enables customizing data entry defaults and use of the Hijiri calendar.

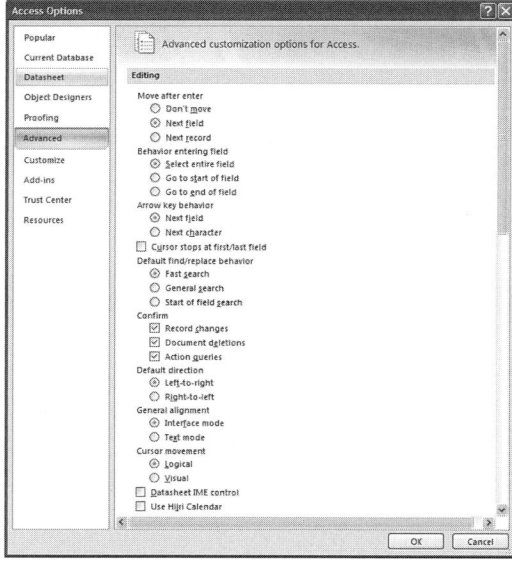

- **Display**—Enables changing the number of most recently used (MRU) databases displayed in the Office button's gallery; hiding the status bar, animations, smart tags on Datasheets, and Smart Tags on form and reports; and showing the Names and Conditions columns when editing standalone or embedded macros (see Figure 3.24).

Figure 3.24
The Advanced page's Display, Printing, and General groups let you customize 17 more properties.

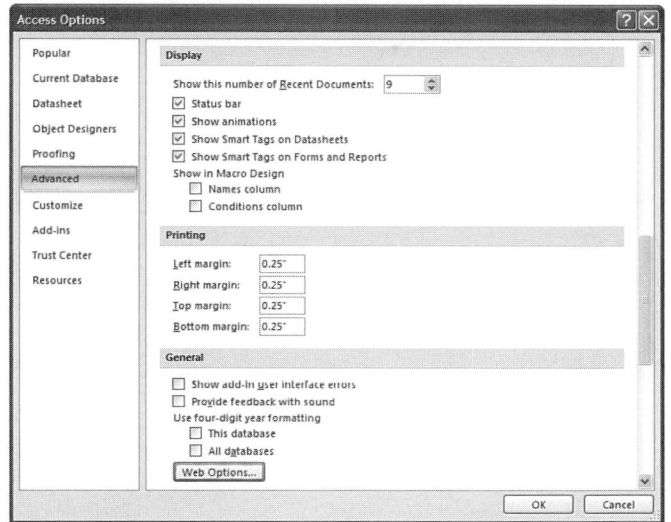

- **Printing**—Lets you change the default printing margins (0.25 inch).

NOTE

> Default printing margins in earlier Access versions were 1 inch. The new Print Preview ribbon lets you select Narrow (0.5 inch), Normal (0.75 inch), and Wide (1.0 inch) margins.

→ For a brief description and screen capture of the Print Preview ribbon, **see** "Contextual Ribbons for Access Databases," **p. 28**.

- **General**—Lets Access raise an error if a RibbonX document for a customized ribbon is incorrect, add audio cues to keyboard and other actions, animate cursors for several operations, and require four-character year formatting for the current database, all databases, or both. The Web Options button opens a dialog of the same name for setting the style of hyperlinks.

TIP

> Always mark the Show Add-in User Interface Errors check box when testing the RibbonX XML documents you author to customize ribbons. If you don't, bugs in your RibbonX documents go undetected.

■ **Advanced**—Enables specifying the last-opened database as the default when opening Access, changing the default open and record-locking mode, setting OLE/DDE and ODBC properties, and specifying command arguments to be used when starting Access (see Figure 3.25).

Figure 3.25
The Advanced page's Advanced group contains controls to set orphaned properties' default values.

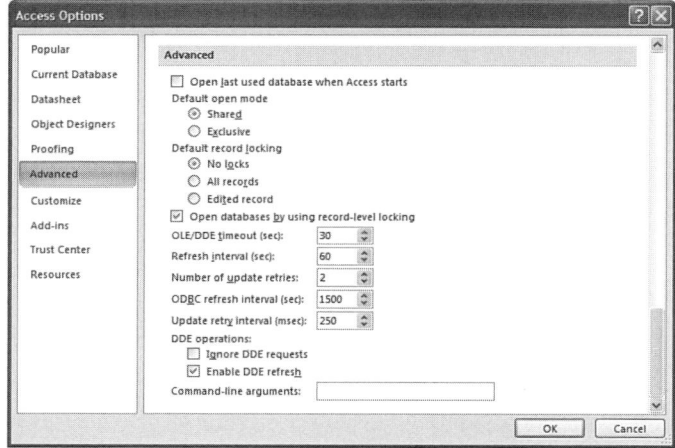

NOTE

> The only Advanced group change you'll probably want to make is to mark the Open Last Used Database When Access Starts check box.

THE CUSTOMIZE PAGE

The Customize page lets you add command buttons—represented by 16×16-pixel icons—from any standard ribbon to the Quick Access Toolbar. The Customize page opens with a list of popular commands and their icons in the left list box and an Add button to move selected commands to the right list box, which contains the default Save, Undo, and Redo commands (see Figure 3.26). Access 2007 has more than 1,000 unique icons; this book uses about 200 different icons to identify commonly used command buttons.

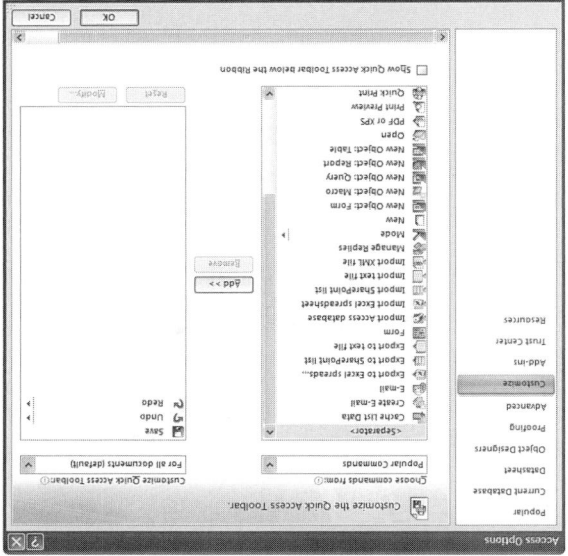

Figure 3.26
The Customize page opens with the three default commands for the QAT and the Popular Commands list for adding QAT commands.

The Choose Commands From list lets you select commands from Access's 28 ribbons (tabs) or five other categories.

You can add the most popular commands to the QAT by clicking the arrow button to the right of the QAT to open the menu shown in Figure 3.27 and clicking the commands to add. Alternatively, right-click any command button in the selected ribbon and choose Add to Quick Access Toolbar from the context menu.

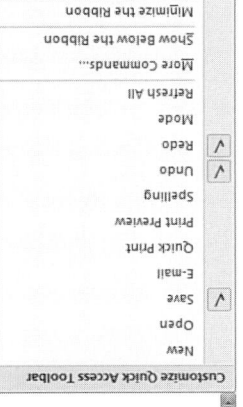

Figure 3.27
Clicking the arrow to the right of the QAT opens this menu, which lets you add the most popular commands quickly.

The Add-Ins Page

The Add-Ins page lets you manage Microsoft and third-party COM (Component Object Model) and Access add-in applications (see Figure 3.28). Microsoft includes a single COM add-in for managing replication conflicts, which is enabled only when necessary and isn't applicable to Access 2007 applications.

Figure 3.28
The Add-Ins page displays a single disabled COM add-in for resolving replication problems with earlier database versions.

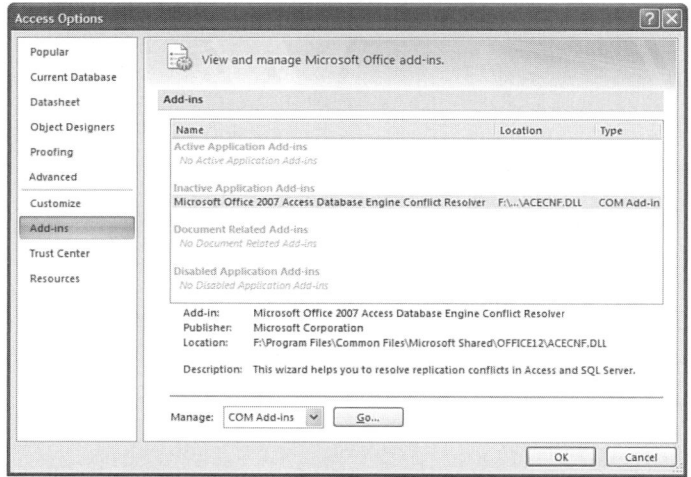

> **NOTE**
>
> Access 2007 doesn't support replication, and SQL Server 2005 Express only replicates with SQL Server 2005 Standard Edition or higher.

Selecting COM Add-Ins in the Manage list and clicking Go opens the COM Add-Ins dialog, which lets you enable, add, or remove COM add-ins. Selecting Access Add-Ins and clicking Go opens the Access Add-In manager dialog, which lets you Add New or UnInstall Access add-in libraries (.accda, .accde, .mda, or .mde files). Third-party add-in suppliers usually include detailed instructions for installing and using their add-ins.

> **NOTE**
>
> The preferred add-in architecture for Access 2007 is managed COM add-ins created with Visual Studio 2005 or later. Visual Studio 2005 Tools for Office, Second Edition doesn't support Access 2007, so you must use Visual Studio's Shared Add-In Template to create them. Writing Access 2007 add-ins is beyond the scope of this book, but you can find more details on the process in Microsoft's "Creating Managed Add-Ins for Access 2007" white paper at http://msdn2.microsoft.com/en-us/library/aa902693.aspx.

THE TRUST CENTER PAGES

The opening Trust Center page consists of links to Microsoft privacy statements and Microsoft Trustworthy Computing propaganda. The only feature of interest on this page is the Trust Center Settings button, which opens a second Trust Center page to establish Access-wide security settings.

NOTE

> As mentioned throughout this book, Access 2007 has abandoned previous versions' *user-level security* (also called *workgroup security*) features in favor of database password security combined with file- and folder-level security. User-level security, which Access 2007 supports for Access 2000 and 2002/2003 .mdb files, provides very granular access conditions to all database objects for individual user and group accounts. Access 2007's security features are rudimentary, at best.

→ For a brief overview of new Access 2007 security features, **see** "Security, Trusted Locations, Packages, and Certificates," **p. 40**.

The second Trust Center page offers the following subpages.

TRUSTED PUBLISHERS

Trusted Publishers can apply digital signatures from a code-signing certificate to Access packages or VBA code and class modules. Signing an Access package certifies that all database objects, not just code, have not been modified since being signed. If the certificate is valid, the database (and its code) is considered trusted when the user extracts it.

→ To learn how to create and sign Access packages, **see** "Packaging, Signing, and Distributing an Access 2007 Database," **p. 166**.

→ For more information on code-signing certificates, **see** "Security Issues with VBA Code," **p. 117**.

If you want to test code-signed packages without spending U.S.$99 to U.S.$199 per year, you can create a self-signed certificate with the SelfCert.exe application available at the \Programs\Microsoft Office\Microsoft Office Tools\Digital Certificate for VBA Projects. Figure 3.29 shows the Trusted Publishers page displaying a self-signed certificate for OakLeaf Systems.

TRUSTED LOCATIONS

Placing .accdb files in a trusted location (folder) is the most practical method to eliminate the need to enable VBA code and potentially dangerous macro actions for each Access 2007 session. By default, Access trusts the \Program Files\Microsoft Office\Office12\ACCWIZ folder that holds all Access wizard files, as shown in Figure 3.30.

Figure 3.29
A self-signed certificate, such as the OakLeafCodeSigning-Certificate, can be used to create a package that doesn't generate a security warning upon extracting the database.

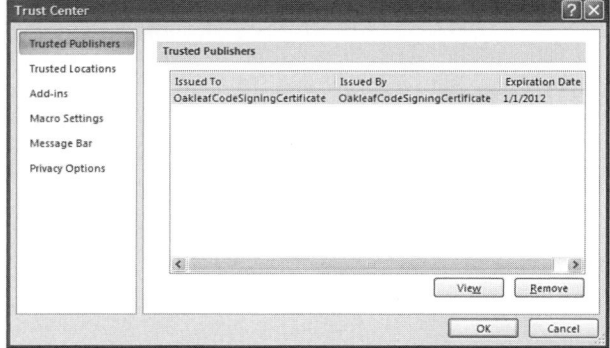

Figure 3.30
Access automatically trusts the \Program Files\Microsoft Office\Office12\ ACCWIZ folder so that Wizards will run without generating a security warning.

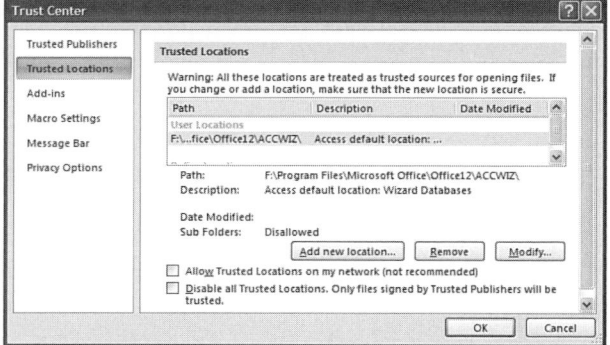

You add other folders and their subfolders as trusted documents by clicking the Add New Location button to open the Microsoft Office Trusted Location dialog, browsing to the folder you want to trust, marking the Subfolders of This Location Are Also Trusted check box (if applicable), adding an optional description, and clicking OK. You no longer see the security warning in the message bar when you open the database from the trusted location.

→ For an example of creating a trusted location, **see** "Designating the Default Database Folder as a Trusted Location," **p. 78**.

ADD-INS, MACRO SETTINGS, MESSAGE BAR, AND PRIVACY OPTIONS

The remaining Trust Center pages resemble groups of other Access Options pages (see Figure 3.31). The options names are sufficiently self-describing as to not warrant relisting here. The default selections shown in Figure 3.31 should be satisfactory for most applications.

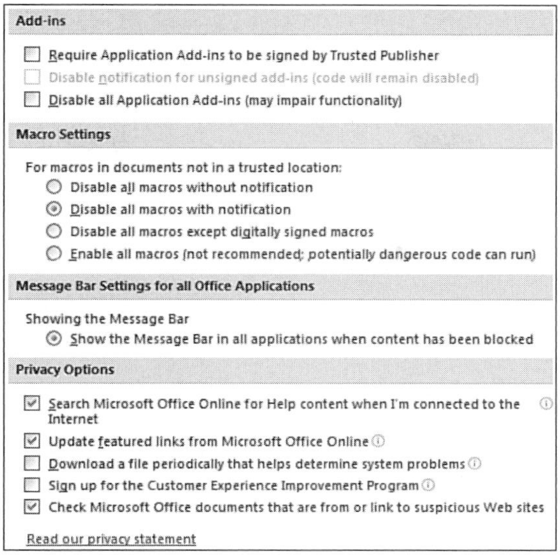

Figure 3.31
The Add-Ins, Macro Settings, Message Bar, and Privacy Options pages might better have been grouped on a single page.

Add-ins

☐ Require Application Add-ins to be signed by Trusted Publisher
☐ Disable notification for unsigned add-ins (code will remain disabled)
☐ Disable all Application Add-ins (may impair functionality)

Macro Settings

For macros in documents not in a trusted location:
○ Disable all macros without notification
◉ Disable all macros with notification
○ Disable all macros except digitally signed macros
○ Enable all macros (not recommended; potentially dangerous code can run)

Message Bar Settings for all Office Applications

Showing the Message Bar
◉ Show the Message Bar in all applications when content has been blocked

Privacy Options

☑ Search Microsoft Office Online for Help content when I'm connected to the Internet ⓘ
☑ Update featured links from Microsoft Office Online ⓘ
☐ Download a file periodically that helps determine system problems ⓘ
☐ Sign up for the Customer Experience Improvement Program ⓘ
☑ Check Microsoft Office documents that are from or link to suspicious Web sites

Read our privacy statement

THE RESOURCES PAGE

The Resources page has the following buttons, many of which were choices of earlier versions' Help menu:

- **Check for Updates**—Launches Internet Explorer (IE) 7 and runs Windows Update to check for operating system and Office 2007 updates.

- **Diagnose**—Runs the Microsoft Office Diagnostics application to test for known solutions, check memory, verify other programs' compatibility with Office 2007, verify fixed disk(s), and validate Office 2007 setup programs.

- **Contact Us**—Opens Office Online's Contact Us page, which has links to support sources, the international support website, customized Office support for developers and IT professionals, and Office Live support.

- **Activate**—Starts the Activation Wizard or opens a "This product has already been activated" message box.

- **Go Online**—Opens Office Online's default Office 2007 welcome page where you can register with a Windows Live ID (formerly Microsoft Passport account) for additional online services.

- **About**—Opens the About Microsoft Office Access dialog, which has System Info and Tech Support buttons. Clicking System Info opens the System Information dialog shown in Figure 3.32. Clicking Tech Support opens a dialog with vague recommendations for obtaining support.

Figure 3.32
The System Information window, shown here running under Windows XP Professional, displays information on your hardware, system settings, and the applications you've opened.

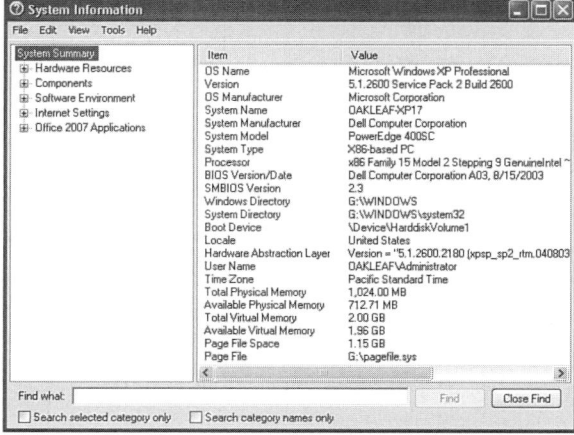

TIP

> If you have a serious problem with Access 2007 or other Office 2007 applications, a Microsoft Technical Support representative might request that you send a System Info (MSInfo, .nfo) file for inspection. To create an .nfo file in Windows XP, choose File, Save and supply a filename.
>
> The .nfo file contains a substantial amount of information about your PC and the programs you've installed, which is needed to troubleshoot major problems, but .nfo files don't include confidential personal or corporate information, such as usernames and passwords.

CREATING A CUSTOMIZED TEMPLATE FILE

Once you've set the options for all databases and the current database, you might want to use the database as a template for all new databases you create. You can specify the database to use as the template for all new databases you create by saving it as \Program Files\Microsoft Office\Templates\1033\Access\Blank.accdb. This location is called the *System Template Folder*.

Alternatively, you can save it under Windows XP as \Documents and Settings\Application Data\Microsoft\Templates\Blank.accdb or under Windows Vista as \Users*UserName*\Documents.

USING ACCESS ONLINE HELP

Access 2007 and other Office 2007 members share a common online help system that differs markedly from that of earlier releases. Access 2007's sizable Access Help window consists of a Table of Contents pane with a treeview list and, when you first click the Help button, the default Browse Access Help list in the right (content) pane (see Figure 3.33).

Figure 3.33
The Access Help window opens in normal (resizable) window mode and occupies the entire display by default. The Search menu lets you select the scope of a keyword search.

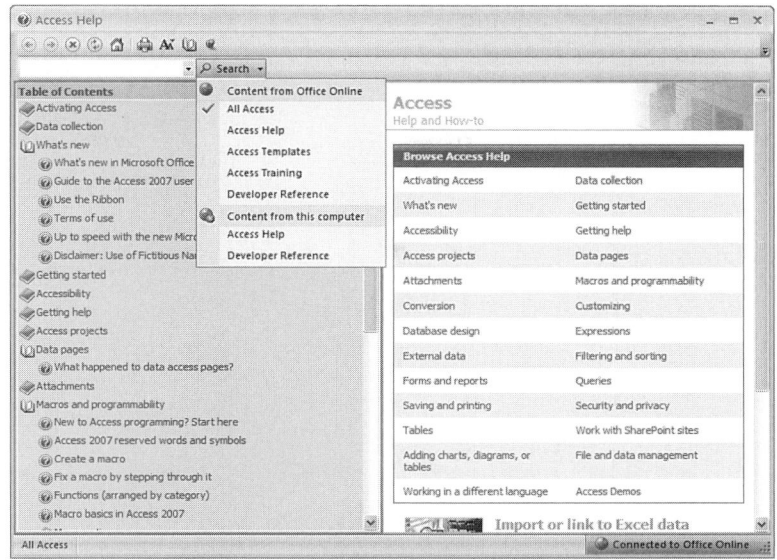

Unless you clear the Search Microsoft Office Online for Help Content When I'm Connected to the Internet check box on the Trust Center's Privacy Options page, help content from Office Online supplements the local computer's help files.

SEARCHING FOR A PHRASE

Typing a phrase without enclosing it between double quotes causes the help system to return topics with any of the words present. For example, typing **Attachment data type** in the Search text box and clicking the Search button returns more than 100 topics (see Figure 3.34). Many are obviously unrelated topics, such as "Enter or edit data in a control or column that supports rich text" and "Type ¢, £, ¥, ®, and other characters not on the keyboard." Clicking the link to open the topic in the right pane, pressing Ctrl+F to open IE 7's Find dialog, typing **Attachment** in the Find text box, and clicking Next or Previous returns no hits. Figure 3.34's Searched for: "Attachment data type" header incorrectly indicates that the search was for an exact phrase, despite missing quotes in the search expression.

Enclosing the search term in double quotes returns the four topics shown in Figure 3.35, which contain the exact phrase, as shown for the "Which file format should I use in Access 2007?" topic in Figure 3.36.

Figure 3.34
Searching for multiple words quotes the Searched For expression, which erroneously indicates searches for a phrase.

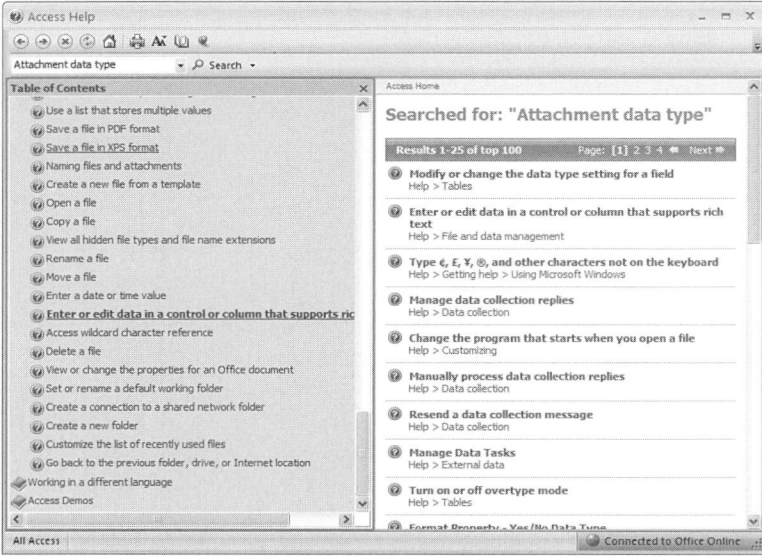

Figure 3.35
Searching for a quoted phrase in the text box wraps the Searched For expression in pairs of double quotes.

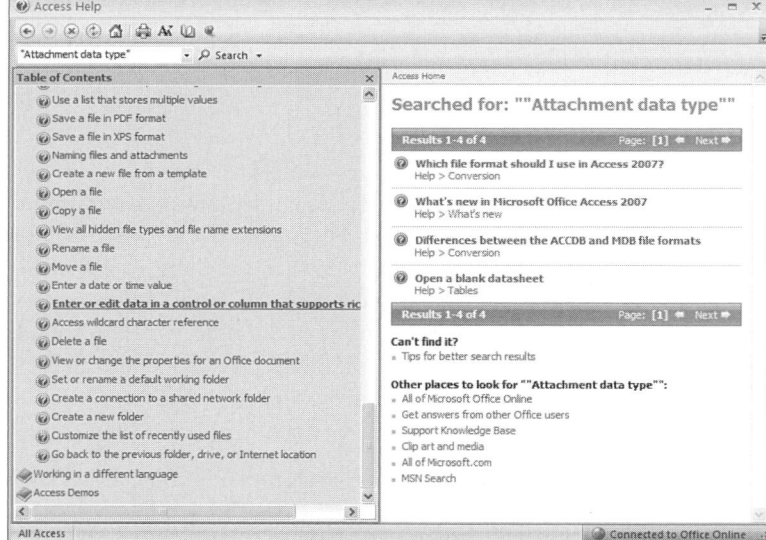

SEARCHING OTHER SOURCES

Clicking the All of Microsoft Office Online link in the results page (refer to Figure 3.35) returns a web page with five topics; the additional topic is for InfoPath's "Insert a file attachment control" topic. An All of Office Online search doesn't restrict the scope to Access 2007 or any Access version.

Figure 3.36
The text of the first topic shown in Figure 3.35 contains the expected "Attachment data type" phrase.

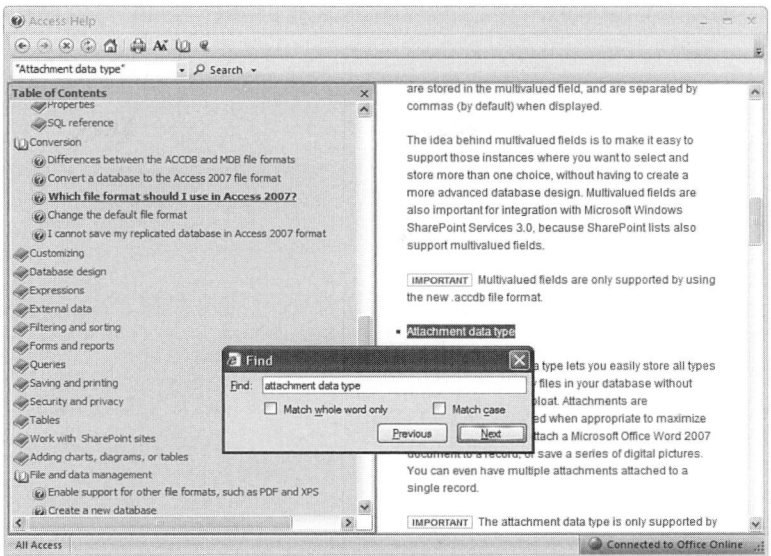

Clicking the Get Answers from Other Access Users link opens a web form that requests you to type a question of 4 to 10 words. Typing **How do I use Access's Attachment data type?** in the text box and clicking Go returned the thread from the microsoft.public.access. modulesdaovba newsgroup whose header is shown in Figure 3.37. The thread contains very detailed answers to the question.

Figure 3.37
Microsoft newsgroups, such as microsoft. public.access. modulesdaovba and its siblings, supplement local help files and online help.

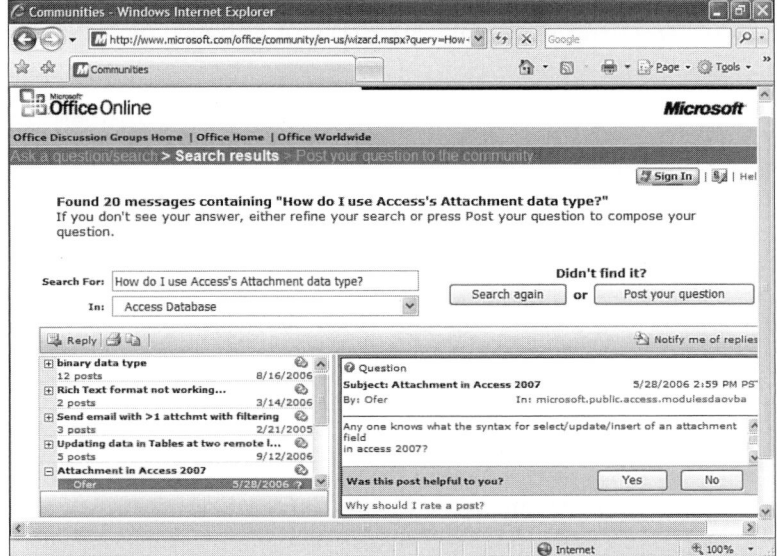

Clicking the Support Knowledge Base link executes a Knowledge Base search with Access 2007 as the search product and the quoted phrase as the search term. The first search results page contains Show Me links for Access 2007 and Access. Clicking Access 2007 opens the page shown in Figure 3.38, which adds Need More Help? and Recent KB Articles links.

Figure 3.38
Microsoft Knowledge Base (KB) articles are another good source of information on Access bugs, issues, and anomalies.

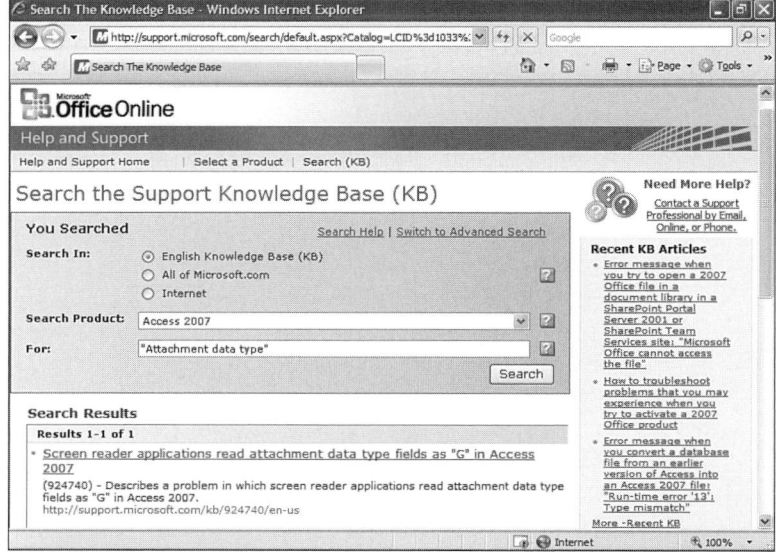

SPELUNKING THE DATABASE UTILITIES

Access 200x offered eight utility functions that you could access by choosing Tools, Database Utilities. Following are the locations of these tools in Access 2007:

- *Convert Database* becomes Office, Save As, Access 2000 Database, Access 2002 - 2003 Database, or Access 2007 Database.

- *Compact and Repair Database* moves to Office, Manage, Compact and Repair Database, which checks the database for consistency, repairs problems found, and then compacts it to save disk space. Access automatically replaces the existing database with the compacted or repaired version.

- *Back Up Database* moves to Office, Manage, Back Up Database and opens the Save Backup As dialog and proposes to save your current database file as *FileName_YYYY-MM-DD*.accdb. Using the backup feature is a bit faster than making a copy with Windows Explorer.

- *Linked Table Manager* moves to the Linked Table Manager command in the Database Tools ribbon's Database Tools group. It tests for the existence of linked .accdb or other types of data files and, if the links aren't valid, lets you change the path to the linked files. This choice is disabled if you don't have a database with linked tables open.

■ *Database Splitter* becomes the Access Database command in the Database Tools ribbon's Move Data group. It divides a single-file Access .accdb application with application and data objects into a front-end .accdb file and a back-end Access database. This choice is disabled if you don't have a database open. Chapter 19, "Linking Access Front Ends to Access and Client/Server Tables" covers linking to tables in an Access back-end database.

 ■ *Switchboard Manager* moves to a Switchboard Manager command in the Database Tools ribbon's Database Tools group. It creates a new Switchboard form if one isn't present in the current database and lets you edit the new or an existing Switchboard form. This choice is also disabled if you don't have a database open.

> **NOTE**
>
> Access 2007's Switchboard Manager generates Access macro code for switchboards in .accdb files and VBA code for switchboards in .mdb files.

 ■ *Upsizing Wizard* becomes the SQL Server (w) command in the Database Tools ribbon's Move Data group. It lets you move tables and queries from the current Access database to SQL Server 2005 [Express] and, optionally, change the .accdb file containing application objects to an Access Data Project (.adp) file. Chapter 19 describes how to use the Upsizing Wizard to link an .adddb front end to SQL Server tables. Chapter 22, "Upsizing Access Applications to Access Data Projects," covers creating ADPs.

 ■ *Make MDE File* moves to the Make ACCDE command of the Database Tools ribbon's Database Tools Group. It creates a secure copy of the file, which prevents users from opening objects in Design view and viewing or changing VBA code.

COMPACTING AND REPAIRING DATABASES

After you make numerous additions and changes to objects within a database file—especially deletions of large amounts of data in tables—the database file can become disorganized. When you delete a record, you don't automatically regain the space in the file that the deleted data occupied. You must compact the database to optimize its file size and the organization of data within the tables that the file contains. When you compact an Access file, you regain space only in 32KB increments.

To compact the current database, do the following:

1. Open the database you want to compact.
2. Choose Office, Manage, Compact and Repair Database. Access immediately closes the database and begins compacting it.

When Access finishes compacting the database, it opens the database and returns you to where you were in the application before. Your compacted database is stored with the same name it had before you compacted it.

A database can become corrupted as the result of the following problems:

- Hardware problems that occur when writing to your database file, either locally or on a network server
- Accidentally restarting the computer while Access databases are open
- A power failure that occurs after you make modifications to an Access object but before you save the object

Occasionally, a file might become corrupted without Access detecting the problem. This lack of detection occurs most frequently with corrupted indexes. If Access or your application behaves strangely when you open an existing database and display its contents, try compacting and repairing the database.

Periodically compacting and repairing production database files usually is the duty of the database administrator in a multiuser environment, typically in relation to backup operations. You should back up your existing file on disk or tape before creating a compacted version. When you're developing an Access 2007 database, you should compact and repair the database frequently. Access 2007 databases that are not compacted grow in size much more rapidly during modification than earlier versions.

> **TIP**
>
> To compact the current database automatically each time you close it, choose Office, click Access Options, click Current Database, and mark the Application Group's Compact on Close check box.

CONVERTING EARLIER DATABASE FORMATS TO ACCESS 2007 FORMAT

To convert earlier Access version .mdb database or .mda library files created with Access 95 through Access 2003 to the new database format of Access 2007, open the file in Access 2007 and click Office, Save As, Access 2007 Database. Chapter 31, "Upgrading Access 200X Applications to Access 2007," covers this conversion process in detail.

 If you encounter error messages when converting your Access 97 or 95 .mdb file to .accdb format, see the "Compile Errors in the Convert Database Process" topic of the "Troubleshooting" section near the end of the chapter.

CREATING .ACCDE FILES

An .accde file is a special version of an Access .accdb file. In an .accde file, all VBA code is stored only in compiled format, and the program source code for that database is unavailable. Also, users can no longer modify forms, reports, queries, or tables stored in that database, although those objects can be exported to other databases. Typically, .accde databases are used to create libraries of add-in wizards, deliver custom database applications intended for commercial or in-house distribution, and provide templates for forms, reports, queries, and other objects for use in other databases.

You can convert any Access 2007 .accdb database to an .accde file by opening the file, clicking the Database Tools tab, and clicking the Make <u>A</u>CCDE button to open the Save As dialog. Navigate to the location for the .accde file and click Save to create and save the file. Then close the dialog.

TIP

> Be sure to save an archive copy of any .accdb file you convert to .accde format on a removable disk, CD-ROM, or DVD-ROM and store the archive copy in a safe place. The copy you make in .accde format is permanently altered; you can't restore an .accdb from an .accde file.

CREATING .ACCDR RUNTIME FILES

 An .accdr file is called a *runtime Access file*. You create a runtime file simply by changing *FileName*.accde to *FileName*.accdr. The .accdr version hides the ribbon and Navigation Pane, so you must provide a switchboard or equivalent to open forms and reports. The QAT is disabled and the Office button's gallery offers <u>P</u>rint, <u>C</u>lose Database, and E<u>x</u>it buttons only. Runtime Access files provide a minimalist UI, as illustrated by Figure 3.39.

Figure 3.39
Access Runtime (.accdr) files open with the ribbon and Navigation Pane hidden and disabled.

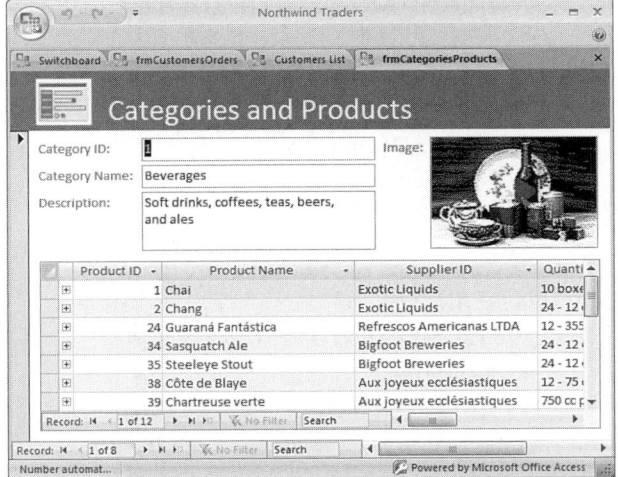

The problem with .accdr files is that users quickly discover they can simply change the file extension from .accdr to .accdb to regain lost design and navigation features.

PACKAGING, SIGNING, AND DISTRIBUTING AN ACCESS 2007 DATABASE

 The Publish menu of Office button's gallery offers the following two choices:

- **Document Management Server**—Publishes the database to a WSS 3.0 or MOSS 2007 site and enables users to open a read-only or read-write copy, depending on their group membership. Chapter 25 shows you how to share databases from a SharePoint document library.

- **Package and Sign**—Creates an Access Deployment file (.accdc) whose origin and integrity is certified by a digital signature. You can deploy database copies from an .accdc file published to a SharePoint document library. The sections that follow describe how to generate a self-signed digital certificate and then use the certificate to sign an Access Deployment file.

GENERATE AND INSTALL A SELF-CERTIFIED DIGITAL CERTIFICATE

To create a self-signed certificate, do the following:

1. Choose Start, Programs, Microsoft Office, Microsoft Office Tools, Digital Certificate for VBA Projects to open the Create Digital Certificate dialog. Type the name for the certificate in the text box (see Figure 3.40).

Figure 3.40
Type a certificate name in the text box and click OK to add the certificate to Windows' Personal certificate store.

NOTE

The dialog's boilerplate warns that Office only trusts the certificate on the machine on which you create it. Tests indicate that you can copy the certificate (.cer) file to another machine, then add the certificate to the Trusted Root Certification Authorities, Trusted Publishers, and Persons categories, and achieve the same result as if the certificate was created on the local computer.

2. Click OK to add the certificate to the Personal category of the Windows certificate store, which is managed by IE.

3. Launch IE. Click IE 7's Tools button or choose Tools, Internet Options in earlier versions to open the paged Internet Options dialog. Click the Content tab and Certificates button to open the Certificates dialog, and click the Personal tab to display the certificate you created in step 2 (see Figure 3.41).

Figure 3.41
IE's Certificates dialog displays the new self-signed certificate on the Personal page.

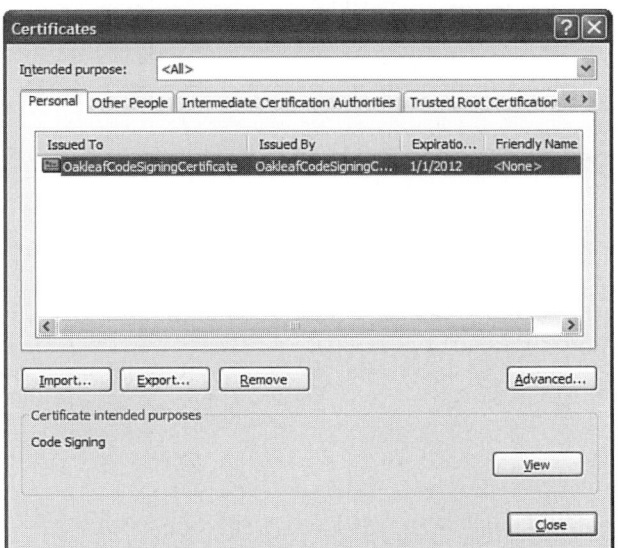

> **NOTE**
>
> The certificate isn't valid at this point because you aren't a trusted root certification authority. You must export the certificate to a file and then import it to the Trusted Root Certification Authority page to enable trust. If you double-click the entry for the certificate, a "This CA Root certificate is not trusted" warning appears on the Certificate dialog's general page.

4. Select the certificate, click Export to start the Export Certificate Wizard, and click Next to open the Export Private Key dialog. This option isn't available for self-signed certificates, so click Next to open the Export File Format dialog.

5. Accept the default DER-Encoded Binary X.509 (.CER) option, and click Next to open File to Export dialog.

6. Click Browse to open the Save As dialog, navigate to a folder in which to save the certificate, type a filename (**OakLeafCodeSigningCertificate** for this example), and click Save to save the file with a .cer extension. Click Finish to dismiss the Wizard and acknowledge the "Certificate export was successful" message.

7. Click the Certificates dialog's Trusted Root Certificate Authorities tab, click the Import button to start the Certificate Import Wizard, and click Next to open the File to Import dialog.

8. Click Browse to open the Open dialog, navigate to the location you specified in step 6, and double-click the certificate file. Click Next to open the Certificate Store dialog.

9. Accept the default Place All Certificates in the Following Store option, verify that the Certificate Store is Trusted Root Certificate Authorities, and click Next and then Finish to display a security warning (see Figure 3.42).

Figure 3.42
This security warning appears for any certificate you add to the Trusted Root Certificate Authorities list. The default list contains most generally accepted certificate authorities (CAs).

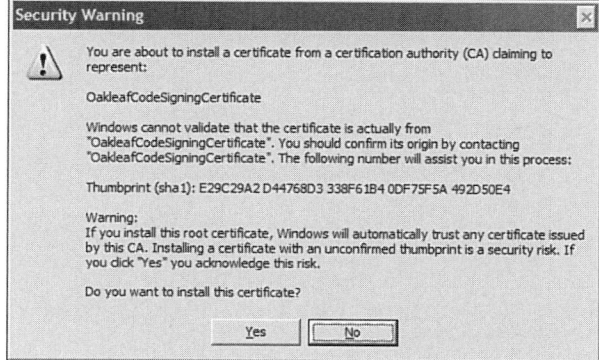

10. Click Yes to add the certificate to the Trusted Root Certificate Authorities group. Double-click the item to verify the certificate (see Figure 3.43).

Figure 3.43
A certificate with the purposes "Ensures software came from software publisher" and "Protects software from alteration after publication" is a code-signing certificate.

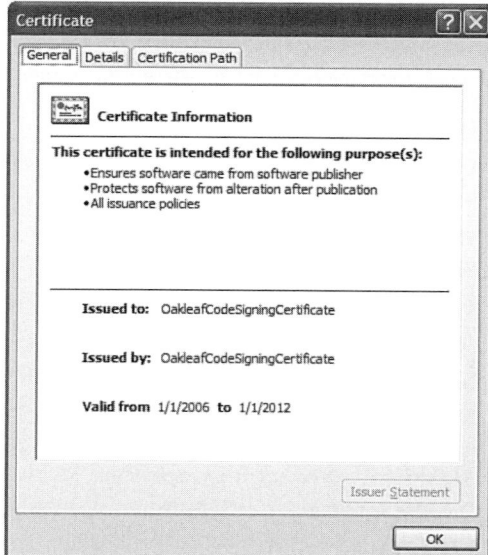

11. Repeat steps 7 to 9, except substitute Trusted Publishers for Trusted Root Certificate Authorities in each step. In this case, you don't receive the security warning described in step 9.

12. Click Office, Access Options, Trust Center, Trust Center Settings, Trusted Publishers and then verify that your certificate appears in the Trusted Publishers list (refer to Figure 3.29).

13. Click Macro Settings, and select the Disable All Macros Except Digitally Signed Macros option (refer to Figure 3.31). Click OK twice to save your changes and return to your source database.

NOTE

> If you don't make the change in step 13, you'll see a security warning in the message bar when you test the extracted file in the next section.

CREATING, SIGNING, AND TESTING THE PACKAGE

To create, sign, and test the package file, do the following:

1. Open the .accdb file to package (preferably a database with VBA code in a class module or standalone module), and choose Office, Publish, Package and Sign to open the Select Certificate dialog.

2. Select the certificate you created in the preceding section (see Figure 3.44), and click OK to open the Create Microsoft Office Access Signed Package dialog.

Figure 3.44
You must specify a valid code-signing certificate before creating the package.

3. Set the distribution location, accept the filename and .accdc extension, and click Create to sign and compress the .accdb file to the .accdc file.

4. Navigate to the distribution location, and double-click the .accdc file to open the Extract Database To dialog.

5. Navigate to the location in which to save the .accdb file (not a trusted location), and click OK to extract the signed database file.

6. Open the extracted .accdb file.

TROUBLESHOOTING

INVALID DATABASE LOCKED MESSAGES WHEN COMPACTING IN PLACE

You receive the "database that is already opened" message shown in Figure 3.21 when you attempt to compact and repair the currently open database in place.

Figure 3.45
This message indicates that the operation you're attempting can't be completed because another instance of the database is running or an exclusive lock on the database file hasn't been released.

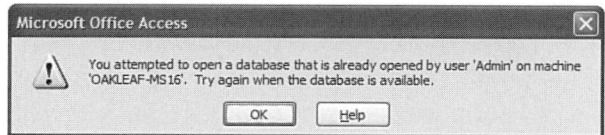

This message occurs if you—or you and another user—have two copies of Access running with the same database open. If you know that you have only a single instance of the database open, the message is the result of a locking bug. In most cases, closing and reopening Access solves the locking problem. If not, you need to reboot Windows and try again.

COMPILE ERRORS IN THE CONVERT DATABASE PROCESS

Error messages appear when converting to Access 200x from early Access versions.

Access 2.0 and earlier were 16-bit applications. The first error message you might receive is "There are calls to 16-bit dynamic-link libraries (.dll) in this application." In this case, you must alter the code of Declare statements to call the current 32-bit equivalents of the 16-bit DLLs. For example, you must change calls to functions in User.dll, Kernel.dll, and Gdi.dll to User32.dll, Kernel32.dll, and Gdi32.dll.

A more common error message when converting Access 2.0, 95, and 97 applications is "There were compilation errors during the enabling or conversion of this database." If you're converting from Access 2.0, many of these errors are likely to arise from Access Basic reserved words and symbol usage that VBA 6.0 doesn't support. Similar problems occur with applications that originated in Access 2.0 or earlier and were converted to Access 9x. In some cases, conversion of earlier application versions to Access 97, and then to Access 2007 format is easier than attempting direct conversion. See Chapter 31 for additional information on conversion issues.

IN THE REAL WORLD—READING THE RIBBON UI'S TEALEAVES

Most computer analysts and pundits have given 2007 Microsoft Office System's new Ribbon UI one or two thumbs up. The general consensus appears to be that replacing hierarchical menus and toolbar buttons with ribbons containing command buttons and galleries aids users in discovering application features. But comparative usability studies might have been skewed by the use of *IntelliMenus* and rafted toolbars in Office 2000 and later.

IntelliMenus, also called *personalized* or *adaptive menus*, attempted to cause usage patterns to determine which menu choices should appear by default. The most popular choices appeared first in a "short menu." After a few seconds (or if you clicked a chevron icon at the bottom of the menu list), the hidden choices expanded the list to a "long menu." After a few hours or days of work, users saw only short menus with the choices that they used frequently.

Jensen Harris, Group Program Manager of the Microsoft Office User Experience Team, made these basic observations about IntelliMenus in his Office User Interface Blog (http://blogs.msdn.com/jensenh/):

- "There was no way to get the default 'short' menu right."
- "Once the default short menu was wrong, the user was forced to scan the menu."
- "Auto-customization, unless it does a perfect job, is usually worse than no customization at all."

Office versions also adopted "rafted toolbars," which enabled more than one toolbar to occupy the same vertical display space by exiling lesser-used buttons to an overflow (more buttons) area. According to Harris, rafted toolbars had the same deficiencies as IntelliMenus—just replace "menu" with "toolbar" in the preceding list. Another "feature" of rafted toolbars was the ability to drag and anchor them to any side of an Office application's window or allow them to float in its workspace.

The Ribbon UI eliminates the use of adaptive menus and rafted toolbars problems, but these miscreant approaches were wrong from the git-go. However, the new face on Access 2007 doesn't get rid of all hierarchical menus. Most galleries and many context menus have one or more levels of additional choices.

Jensen said in a December 2005 presentation to the BayCHI, the San Francisco Bay Area chapter of the Association for Computer Machinery (ACM) Special Interest Group on Computer-Human Interaction (SIGCHI), that fewer than 2% of Microsoft Word users customize it intentionally. However, the percentage of Access 2003 and earlier users and developers who customized Access toolbars and menus is probably closer to 20%. The arcane RibbonX approach to modifying or extending ribbons, groups, or galleries is far more complex than customizing toolbars and menu bars with Access macros or VBA.

NOTE

> Rumors of the imminent arrival of a Microsoft graphic editor for generating RibbonX XML documents appears to have been greatly exaggerated as of the retail release of Office 2007.

When this book was written, the jury was out on the extent to which the new Ribbon UI increases the efficiency of Access users and developers, if at all. Forrester Research has determined that workers migrating to Microsoft Office 2007 will require "more intense" training than expected. This factor contributes to Forrester's estimate that most organizations won't upgrade to Office 2007 for three to five years. At the risk of damnation by faint praise, there's no question that the ribbon is a far better UI metaphor than Microsoft Bob.

P.S.: If you've never seen Microsoft Bob, the 1995 GUI shell intended to overlay and simplify the Windows 3.1 and 95 UI for new users, check out http://toastytech.com/guis/bob.html.

LEARNING THE FUNDAMENTALS OF ACCESS DATABASES

CHAPTER 4

Exploring Relational Database Theory and Practice

In this chapter

MOVING FROM SPREADSHEETS TO DATABASES

Word processing and spreadsheet applications were the engines that drove the fledgling personal computer market. In the early PC days, WordPerfect and Lotus 1-2-3 dominated the productivity software business. Today, most office workers use Microsoft Word and Excel on a daily basis. It's probably a safe bet that there's more data stored in Excel spreadsheets than in all the world's databases. It's an equally good wager that most new Access users have at least intermediate-level spreadsheet skills, and many qualify as Excel power users.

Excel's 2007 Data ribbon offers elementary database features, such as sorting, filtering, validation, and data entry forms. You can quickly import and export data in a variety of formats, including those of database management applications, such as Access. Excel's limitations become apparent as your needs for entering, manipulating, and reporting data grow beyond the spreadsheet's basic row-column metaphor. Spreadsheets basically are list managers; it's easy to generate a simple name and address list with Excel. If your needs expand to contact management and integrating the contact data with other information generated by your organization, a spreadsheet isn't the optimal approach.

The first problem arises when your contacts list needs additional rows for multiple persons from a single company. You must copy or retype all the company information, which generates redundant data. If the company moves, you must search and replace every entry for your contacts at the firm with the new address. If you want to record a history of dealings with a particular individual, you add pairs of date and text columns for each important contact with the person. Eventually, you find yourself spending more time navigating the spreadsheet's rows and columns than using the data they contain.

Contact lists are only one example of problems that arise when attempting to make spreadsheets do the work of databases. Tracking medical or biological research data, managing consulting time and billings, organizing concert tours, booking artist engagements, and a myriad of other complex processes are far better suited to database than spreadsheet applications.

Moving to a relational database management system (RDBMS), such as Access, solves data redundancy and navigation problems, and greatly simplifies updating existing information. After you understand the basic rules of relational database design, Access makes creating highly efficient databases quick and easy. Access 2007 has a collection of wizards to lead you step-by-step through each process involved in developing and using a production-grade database application. Unfortunately, there's no "Relational Wizard" to design the underlying database structure for you.

TIP

> If your goal is learning relational database fundamentals, start with Access 2007. Access is by far the first choice of universities, colleges, trade schools, and computer-training firms for courses ranging from introductory data management to advanced client/server database programming. The reason for Access's popularity as a training platform is its unique combination of initial ease of use and support for advanced database application development techniques.

RELIVING DATABASE HISTORY

Databases form the foundation of world commerce and knowledge distribution. Without databases, there would be no World Wide Web, automatic teller machines, credit/debit cards, or online airline reservation systems. Newsgathering organizations, research institutions, universities, and libraries would be unable to categorize and selectively disseminate their vast store of current and historical information. It's difficult to imagine today a world without a network of enormous databases, many of which probably contain a substantial amount of your personal data that you don't want to be easily available to others.

THE EARLY HISTORY OF DATABASES

The forerunner of today's databases consisted of stacks of machine-readable punched cards, which Herman Hollerith used to record the 1890 U.S. census. Hollerith formed the Computing-Tabulating-Recording Company, which later became International Business Machines. From 1900 to the mid-1950s, punched cards were the primary form of business data storage and retrieval, and IBM was the primary supplier of equipment to combine and sort (collate) punched cards, and print reports based on punched-card data.

NOTE

> Jim Gray's article "Data Management: Past, Present, and Future," which is available as a Microsoft Word document at http://research.microsoft.com/~gray/DB_History.doc, offers a more detailed history of data processing systems. Dr. Gray is a senior researcher and the manager of Microsoft's Bay Area Research Center (BARC).

The development of large computer-maintained databases—originally called *databanks*—is a post–World War II phenomenon. Mainframes replaced punched cards with high-capacity magnetic tape drives to store large amounts of data. The first databases were built on the hierarchical and network models, which were well suited to the mainframe computers of the 1950s. Hierarchical databases use parent-child relationships to define data structures, whose diagrams resemble business organization charts or an inverted tree with its root at the top of the hierarchy. Network databases allow relaxation of the rules of hierarchical data structures by defining additional relationships between data items. Hierarchical and network databases ordinarily are self-contained and aren't easy to link with other external databases over a network.

NOTE

> Hierarchical databases remain alive and well in the twenty-first century. For example, data storage for Windows 2000's Active Directory and Microsoft Exchange Server is derived from the hierarchical version of Access's original relational Jet databases. The name Jet comes from the original Access database engine called *Joint Engine Technology*.
>
> The Internet's Domain Name System (DNS) is a collection of hierarchical databases for translating character-based Internet domain names into numerical Internet Protocol (IP) addresses. The DNS database is called a *distributed database*, because its data is held by a global network of thousands of computers.

Early databases used batch processing for data entry and retrieval. Keypunch operators typed data from documents, such as incoming orders. At night, other operators collated the day's batch of punched cards, updated the information stored on magnetic tape, and produced reports. Many smaller merchants continue to use batch processing of customer's credit-card purchases, despite the availability of terminals that permit almost instantaneous processing of credit- and debit-card transactions.

THE RELATIONAL DATABASE MODEL

 Dr. E. F. Codd, an employee of IBM Corporation, published "A Relational Model of Data for Large Shared Databanks" in a journal of the Association for Computing Machinery (ACM) in June 1970. A partial copy of the paper is available at http://www.acm.org/classics/nov95/. Dr. Codd's specialty was a branch of mathematics called set theory, which includes the concept of *relations*. He defined a relation as a named set of *tuples* (records or rows) that have *attributes* (fields or columns). One of the attributes must contain a unique value to identify each tuple. The common term for relation is a *table* whose presentation to the user is similar to that of a spreadsheet.

> **NOTE**
>
> This book uses the terms *field* and *record* when referring to tables, and *columns* and *rows* when discussing data derived from tables, such as the views and query result sets described later in this chapter.

Relational databases solve a serious problem associated with earlier database types. Hierarchical and network databases define sets of data and explicit links between each data set as parent-child and owner-member, respectively. To extract information from these databases, programmers had to know the structure of the entire database. Complex programs in COBOL or other mainframe computer languages are needed to navigate through the hierarchy or network and extract information into a format understandable by users.

Dr. Codd's objective was to simplify the process of extracting formatted information and make adding or altering data easier by eliminating complex navigational programming. During the 1970s, Dr. Codd and others developed a comparatively simple language, Structured Query Language (SQL), for creating, manipulating, and retrieving relational data. With a few hours of training, ordinary database users could write SQL statements to define simple information needs and bypass the delays inherent in the database programming process. SQL, which was first standardized in 1985, now is the *lingua franca* of database programming, and all commercial database products support SQL.

> **NOTE**
>
> The most widely used SQL standard, SQL-92, was published by the American National Standards Institute (ANSI) in 1992. Few, if any, commercial relational database management systems (RDBMSs) today fully conform to the entire SQL-92 standard. The later SQL-99 (also called SQL3) and SQL-200n specifications add new features that aren't germane to Access databases.

> RDBMS competitors have erected an SQL Tower of Babel by adding nonstandard extensions to the language. For example, Microsoft's Transact-SQL (T-SQL) for SQL Server, which is the subject of Chapter 21, "Moving from Access Queries to Transact-SQL," has many proprietary keywords and features. Oracle Corporation's Oracle:SQL and PL/SQL dialects also have proprietary SQL extensions.

CLIENT/SERVER AND DESKTOP RDBMSS

In the early database era, the most common presentation of data took the form of lengthy reports processed by centralized, high-speed impact printers on fan-folded paper. The next step was to present data to the user on green-screen video terminals, often having small printers attached, which were connected to mainframe databases. As use of personal computers gained momentum, terminal emulator cards enabled PCs to substitute for mainframe terminals. Mainframe-scale relational databases, such as IBM's DB2, began to supplement and later replace hierarchical and network databases, but terminals continued to be the primary means of data entry and retrieval.

Oracle, Ingres, Informix, Sybase, and other software firms developed relational databases for lower-cost minicomputers, most of which ran various flavors of the Unix operating system. Terminals continued to be the primary data entry and display systems for multiuser Unix databases.

The next step was the advent of early PC-based flat-file managers and relational database management systems. Early flat-file database managers, typified by Jim Button's PCFile for DOS (1981) and Claris FileMaker for Macintosh (1988) and Windows (1992), used a single table to store data and offered few advantages over storing data in a spreadsheet. The early desktop RDBMSs—such as dBASE, Clipper, FoxBase, and Paradox—ran under DOS and didn't support SQL. These products later became available in multiuser versions, adopted SQL features, and eventually migrated to Windows. Access 1.0, which Microsoft introduced in November 1992, rapidly eclipsed its DOS and Windows competitors by virtue of Access's combination of graphical SQL support, versatility, and overall ease of use.

PC-based desktop RDBMSs are classified as shared-file systems, because they store their data in conventional files that multiple users can share on a network. One of Access's initial attractions for users and developers was its capability to store all application objects—forms, reports, and programming code—and tables for a database application in a single .mdb file. FoxPro, dBASE, Clipper, and Paradox require a multitude of individual files to store application and data objects. Today, almost every multiuser Access application is divided (split) into a front-end .accdb file, which contains application objects and links to a back-end database .accdb file that holds the data. Each user has a copy of the front-end .accdb file and shares connections to a single back-end .accdb file on a peer Windows workstation or server.

Client/server RDBMSs have an architecture similar to Access's front-end/back-end shared-file multiuser configuration. What differentiates client/server from shared-file architecture is that the RDBMS on the server handles most of the data-processing activity. The client front

4

end provides a graphical user interface (GUI) for data entry, display, and reporting. Only SQL statements and the specific data requested by the user pass over the network. Client/server databases traditionally run on network operating systems, such as Windows and Unix, and are much more robust than shared-file databases, especially for applications in which many users make simultaneous additions, changes, and deletions to the database. All commercial data-driven Web applications use client/server databases.

Since version 1.0, Access has had the capability to connect to client/server databases by linking their tables to an Access database. Linking lets you treat client/server tables almost as if they were native Access tables. Linking uses Microsoft's widely accepted Open Database Connectivity (ODBC) standard, and Access 2007 includes an ODBC driver for SQL Server and Oracle databases. You can purchase licenses for ODBC drivers that support other Unix or Windows RDBMSs, such as Sybase or Informix, from the database supplier or third parties. Chapter 19, "Linking Access Front-Ends to Access and Client/Server Tables," describes the process of linking Access and Microsoft SQL Server 2005 databases. Although Chapter 19 uses SQL Server for its examples, the linking procedure is the same for—or at least similar to—other client/server RDBMSs.

NOTE

Prior to Access 2000, Jet was Access's standard database engine, so the terms *Access database* and *Jet database* were interchangeable. Microsoft considered SQL Server to be its *strategic* RDBMS for Access 2000 and 2003. *Strategic* means that SQL Server gets continuing development funds and Jet doesn't. Jet 4.0, which was included with Access 2003 and is a part of the Windows XP and later operating systems, is the final version and is headed toward retirement.

Microsoft's Access team decided to enhance Jet 4.0 with the new features described in Chapter 1, "Access 2007 for Access 200x Users: What's New," change the file extension from .mdb to .accdb, and drop all references to Jet. To reflect this change, this edition uses the terms *Access database* and *SQL Server database*. Unless otherwise noted, *SQL Server* refers to all SQL Server 2005 editions except the Compact Edition 3.1.

Access data projects (ADP) and the Microsoft SQL Server 2005 Express Edition combine to make Access 2007 a versatile tool for designing and testing client/server databases, and creating advanced data entry and reporting applications. You can start with a conventional Access database and later use Access's Upsizing Wizard to convert the .mdb file(s) to an .adp file that holds application objects and an SQL Server 2005 back-end database. Access 2007's Upsizing Wizard has incorporated many improvements to the Access 2000 and earlier Wizard versions, but Access 2007's Wizard is the same as 2002's. Despite the upgraded wizardry, you're likely to need to make changes to queries to accommodate differences between Access and SQL Server's SQL dialects.

→ For an example of differences between Access and SQL Server SQL syntax that affects the upsizing process, **see** "Displaying Data with Queries and Views," **p. 195**.

DEFINING THE STRUCTURE OF RELATIONAL DATABASES

Relational databases consist of a collection of self-contained, related tables. Tables typically represent classes of physical objects, such as customers, sales orders, invoices, checks, products for sale, or employees. Each member object, such as an invoice, has its own record in the invoices table. For invoices, the field that uniquely identifies a record, called a *primary key* [*field*], is a serial invoice number.

Figure 4.1 shows Access's Datasheet view of an Invoices table, which is based on the Northwind.mdb sample database's Orders table. The InvoiceNo field is the primary key. Values in the OrderID, CustomerID, EmployeeID, and ShipperID fields relate to primary key values in Northwind's Orders, Customers, Employees, and Shippers tables. A field that contains values equal to those of primary key values in other tables is called a *foreign key* [*field*].

Figure 4.1
This simple Invoices table was created from the Northwind Orders table and doesn't take advantage of Access's extended properties, such as the field captions, lookup fields, and subdatasheets in the Datasheet view of the Orders table.

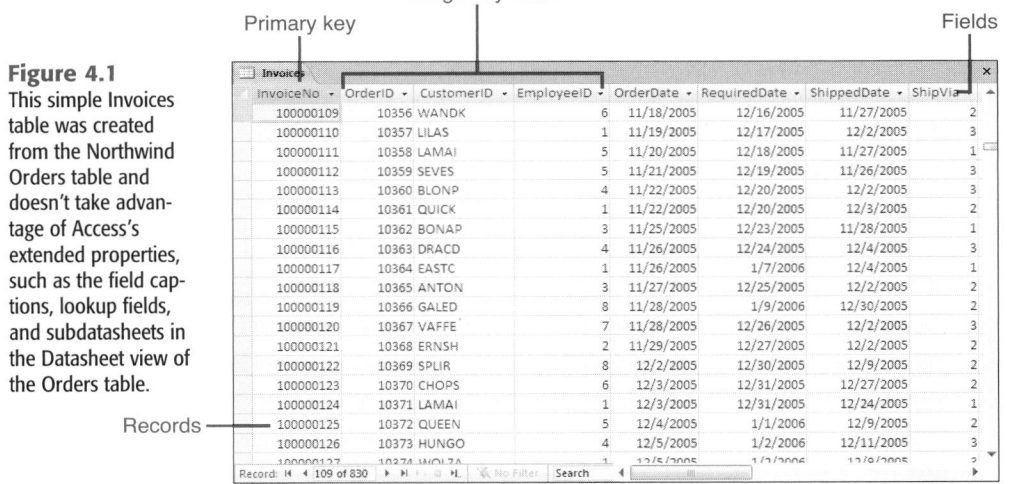

→ To learn more about primary keys in Access tables, **see** "Selecting a Primary Key," **p. 241**.

If you need information about a particular invoice or set of invoices, you open the Invoices table and search for the invoice(s) by number (InvoiceNo) or another attribute, such as a customer code (CustomerID), date (ShippedDate), or range of dates. Unlike earlier database models, the user can access the Invoices table independently of its related tables. No database navigation programming is needed. A simple, intuitive SQL statement, SELECT * FROM Invoices, returns all the data in the table. The asterisk (*) represents a request to display the contents of all fields of the table.

REMOVING DATA REDUNDANCY WITH RELATIONSHIPS

The Invoices table of Figure 4.1 is similar to a spreadsheet containing customer billing information. What's missing is the customer name and address information. A five-character customer code (CustomerID) identifies each customer to whom the invoice is directed. The CustomerID values in the Invoices table match CustomerID values in a modified version of Northwind's Customers table (see Figure 4.2). Matching a foreign key with a primary key value often is called a *lookup operation*. Using a key-based lookup operation eliminates the need to repeatedly enter name, address, and other customer-specific data in the Invoices table. In addition, if you change the customer's address, the change applies to all past and future invoices.

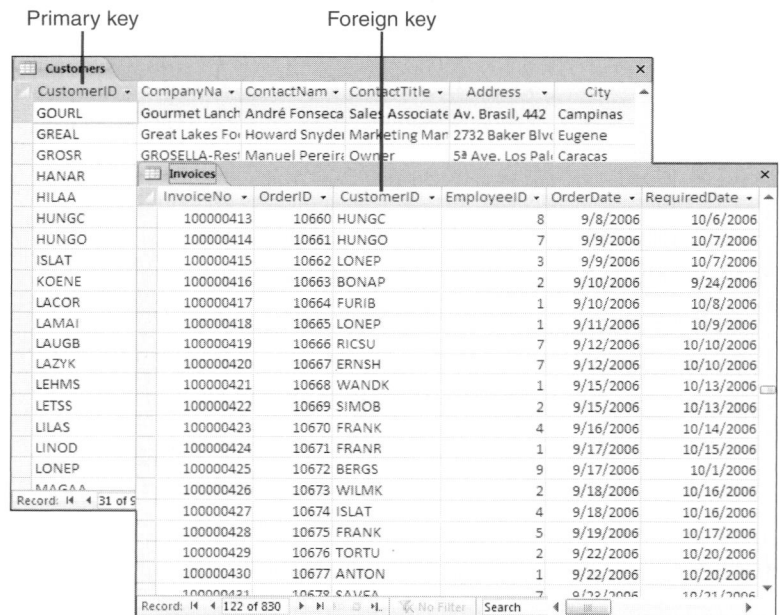

Figure 4.2
Foreign key values in the Invoices table must match primary key values in the Customers table.

Using derived key values, such as alphabetic codes for Customary, is no longer in favor among database designers. Most designers now use automatically generated numerical key values—called Access AutoNumber or SQL Server `identity` fields. The Northwind Orders and Products tables, among others, have primary keys that use the AutoNumber data type. The Employees, Shippers, Products, and Suppliers tables use AutoNumber keys to identify the persons or objects to which the table's records refer. Objects that are inherently sequentially numbered, such as checks, are ideal candidates for an AutoNumber key that corresponds to the check number, as mentioned in "Choosing Primary Key Codes" later in this chapter.

Another method of generating unique keys is by use of Globally Unique Identifiers (GUIDs), which also are called Universally Unique Identifiers (UUIDs). GUIDs are 16-byte computed binary numbers that are guaranteed to be unique locally and universally; no other computer in the world will duplicate a GUID. SQL Server's `uniqueidentifier` data type is a GUID. Because GUIDs can't represent a property of an object, such as a check number, GUID keys are called *surrogate keys*. You can't select a GUID data type in Access's Table Design mode.

The Invoices table also connects with other tables, which contain information on orders, sales department employees, and the products ordered. Connections between fields of related tables having common values are called *relationships* (not relations). Figure 4.3 shows Access's Relationships window displaying the relationships between the Invoices table and the other tables of the Northwind sample database.

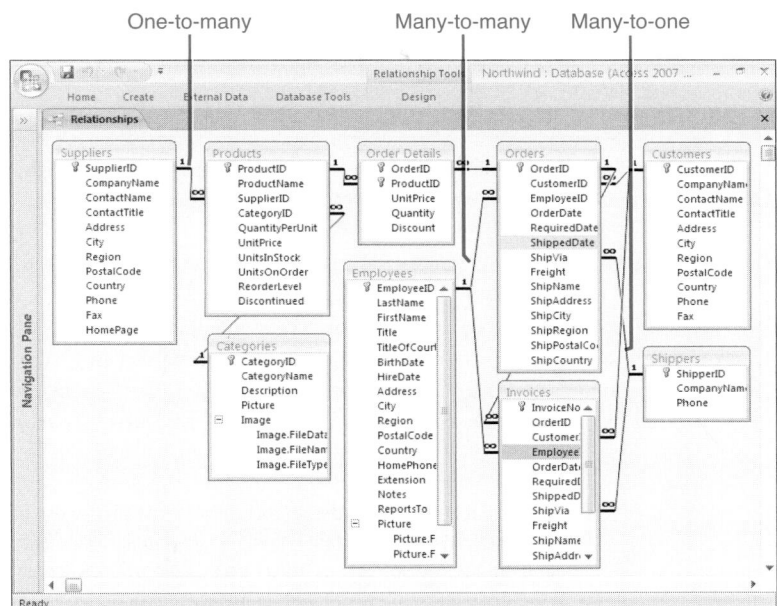

Figure 4.3
Access's Relationships window displays the relationships between the tables of the Northwind sample database, plus the added Invoices table. Every relationship between these tables is one-to-many. The many-to-many relationship between Products and Orders is an indirect relationship.

Relationships come in the following three flavors:

- *One-to-many* relationships represent connections between a single primary key value (the "one" side) and multiple instances of the same value in the foreign key field (the "many" side). One-to-many relationships commonly are identified by the number one and the infinity (∞) symbol, as in Figure 4.3. All the direct relationships between the tables in Figure 4.3 are one-to-many. One-to-many—also called many-to-one—relationships are by far the most common.

- *One-to-one* relationships connect primary key values in two tables. You might think that the relationship between the Orders and Invoices tables could be one-to-one, but an order requires more than one invoice if one or more items are backordered and then shipped later. One-to-one relationships are uncommon.

- *Many-to-many* relationships require three tables, one of which is called a *linking table*. The linking table must have two foreign keys, each of which has a many-to-one relationship with a primary key in two related tables. In the example of Figure 4.3, the Order Details table is the linking table for the many-to-many relationship between the Orders and Products tables. Many-to-many relationships also are called indirect relationships.

There are many other indirect relationships between the tables shown in Figure 4.3. For example, there is a many-to-many relationship between the Suppliers and Orders tables. In this case, Products and Order Details act as linking tables between the Suppliers and Orders tables.

> **NOTE**
>
> Access 2007's new multivalue field feature automatically generates a hidden linking table "under the covers."

> **TIP**
>
> Don't add multivalued fields to tables of databases that you might want to upsize to SQL Server some day. SQL Server doesn't support the Allow Multiple Values option that enables or disables the feature.

The OrderID and ProductID fields comprise a *composite primary key*, which uniquely identifies an order line item. You can't repeat the same combination of OrderID and ProductID; this precaution makes sense for products that have only one stock-keeping unit (SKU), such as for Aniseed Syrup, which comes only in a carton of 12 550-ml bottles.

> **NOTE**
>
> The one-product-entry-per-order restriction prevents shared use of the Order Details table as an invoice line items table. If you short-ship an order item on one invoice, you can't add another record to the Order Details table when you ship the remaining quantity of the item. Microsoft didn't add an Invoices table for Northwind Traders, probably because of the complexity of dealing with backorders and drop-shipments.

The Oakmont.accdb sample database file in the \Seua2007\Oakmont folder of the accompanying CD-ROM has a structure that differs from that of Northwind.accdb, but the design principles of the two databases are similar. OakmontSQL.mdf is an SQL Server 2005 database for use with ADP. ADP uses a special set of tools—called the *project designer* or *da Vinci toolset* in this book—for designing and managing SQL Server databases. The Oakmont files are course enrollment databases for a college. Figure 4.4 shows the Database Diagram window for the OakmontSQL database. The SQL Server Diagram window is similar to the Relationships window for Access's traditional Access databases. The key and infinity symbols at the ends of each line represent the one and many sides, respectively, of the one-to-many relationships between the tables. Access and SQL Server databases store information on table relationships as an object within the database file.

Figure 4.4
The SQL Server Database Diagram window for the OakmontSQL database shows one-to-many relationships between primary key fields (identified by key symbols) and foreign key fields (infinity symbols).

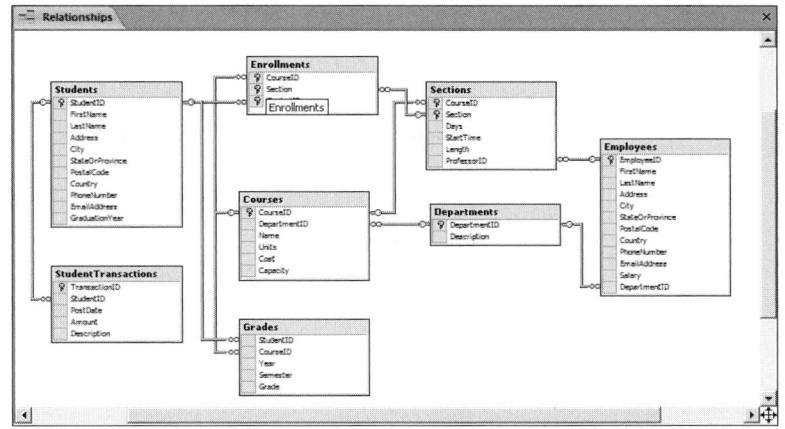

This book uses the Access 2007 and SQL Server 2005 versions of the Northwind and Oakmont sample databases in almost all examples. The tables of the Oakmont database have many more records than the Northwind tables. The large number of records in the Oakmont database makes it better suited than Northwind for predicting the performance of production Access and SQL Server database applications.

CONFORMING TO TABLE DESIGN RULES

Designing tables for relational databases follows a formalized procedure called *normalization*. Dr. Codd described the complete normalization process in his 1972 paper "Further Normalization of the Data Base Relational Model." This paper isn't an easy read; it's steeped in the language of set theory and relational algebra. The sections that follow explain in common English the application of the normalization process to Access's Northwind database.

You normalize tables in a series of steps called *normal forms*. Applying the normalization process is necessary to move spreadsheet-style data to relational tables. You also employ the normalization rules when designing a new database or analyzing existing databases. In specific cases, however, you might need to depart from strict adherence to normalization rules to retain a history of data values that change over time or to improve performance of a large database.

FIRST NORMAL FORM

First normal form requires tables to be flat and have no repeating or potentially repeating fields or groups of fields. A flat table is one in which every record has the same number of fields. In addition, a single field cannot contain multiple data values. Repeating fields must be moved to a related table. The first normal form is the most important of the normalization steps. If all your tables don't meet the rules of first normal form, you are in *big* trouble.

Northwind's Customers and Suppliers tables violate the no repeating fields rule. If a customer or supplier has more than one person involved in the ordering process, which is likely, the table would need repeating pairs of fields with different names, such as ContactName2 and ContactTitle2 or the like. To conform the Customers and Suppliers tables to first normal form, you must create two new tables—CustPers(sonel) and SuppPers(sonel), for example—to hold contact records. Including contact names in the Customers and Suppliers tables also violates third normal form, which is the subject of the later "Third Normal Form" section.

The ContactName field also violates the rule against multiple data values in a single field by combining given and family names. This isn't a serious violation of first normal form, but it's a good database design practice always to identify persons by given and family names in separate fields. When you create the new CustPers and SuppPers tables, separate the ContactName field into two fields, such as LastName and GivenName, which can include initials. You can then use a code similar to that for CustomerID for the ContactID field. For this example, the ContactID code is the first character of GivenName and the first four characters of LastName. Alternatively, you could assign an AutoNumber value to ContactID.

Figure 4.5 shows the first 19 of the 91 records of the CustPers table generated from the Customers table. The CustomerID field is required for a many-to-one relationship with the Customers table. Additional fields, such as Suffix, TitleOfCourtesy, Email(Address), Phone, and Fax, make the individual contact records more useful for creating mailing lists and integration with other applications, such as Microsoft Outlook.

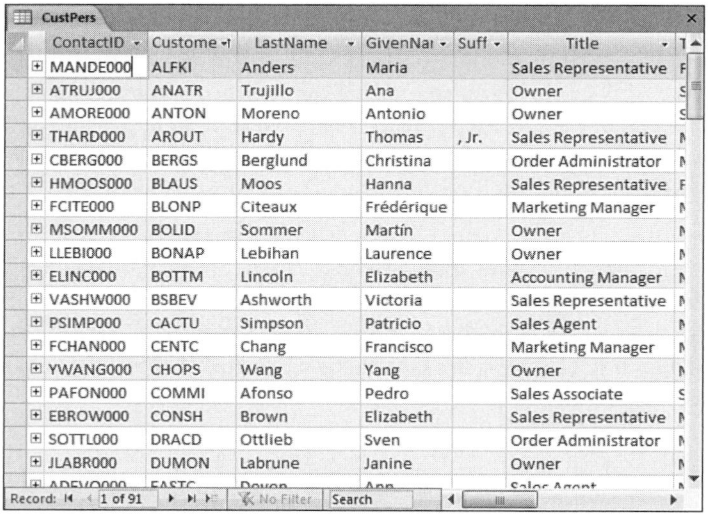

Figure 4.5
You extract data for records of the CustPers table from the ContactName and ContactTitle fields of the Customers table. Separating given and last names simplifies generating a ContactID code to identify each record.

ContactID	Custome	LastName	GivenNar	Suff	Title	T
⊞ MANDE000	ALFKI	Anders	Maria		Sales Representative	F
⊞ ATRUJ000	ANATR	Trujillo	Ana		Owner	S
⊞ AMORE000	ANTON	Moreno	Antonio		Owner	S
⊞ THARD000	AROUT	Hardy	Thomas	, Jr.	Sales Representative	N
⊞ CBERG000	BERGS	Berglund	Christina		Order Administrator	N
⊞ HMOOS000	BLAUS	Moos	Hanna		Sales Representative	F
⊞ FCITE000	BLONP	Citeaux	Frédérique		Marketing Manager	N
⊞ MSOMM000	BOLID	Sommer	Martín		Owner	N
⊞ LLEBI000	BONAP	Lebihan	Laurence		Owner	N
⊞ ELINC000	BOTTM	Lincoln	Elizabeth		Accounting Manager	N
⊞ VASHW000	BSBEV	Ashworth	Victoria		Sales Representative	N
⊞ PSIMP000	CACTU	Simpson	Patricio		Sales Agent	N
⊞ FCHAN000	CENTC	Chang	Francisco		Marketing Manager	N
⊞ YWANG000	CHOPS	Wang	Yang		Owner	N
⊞ PAFON000	COMMI	Afonso	Pedro		Sales Associate	S
⊞ EBROW000	CONSH	Brown	Elizabeth		Sales Representative	N
⊞ SOTTL000	DRACD	Ottlieb	Sven		Order Administrator	N
⊞ JLABR000	DUMON	Labrune	Janine		Owner	N
⊞ ADEVO000	EASTC	Devon	Ann		Sales Agent	N

Record: 14 ◄ 1 of 91 ► ►I ►* No Filter Search

> You don't need to retype the data to populate the CustPers and SuppPers tables. You can use Access to import the data from an Excel worksheet or text file, or use Access action queries (append and update) to handle this chore.

→ For more information on importing from Excel, **see** "Importing and Linking Spreadsheet Files," **p. 321**.

→ To learn how to use Access action queries, **see** "Creating Action Queries to Append Records to a Table," **p. 557**.

Figure 4.6 shows the Relationships window with the CustPers and SuppPers tables added to the Northwind database and their many-to-one relationships with the Customers and Suppliers tables, respectively.

Figure 4.6
The Relationships window displays the many-to-one relationships between the Customers and CustPers tables and the Suppliers and SuppPers tables.

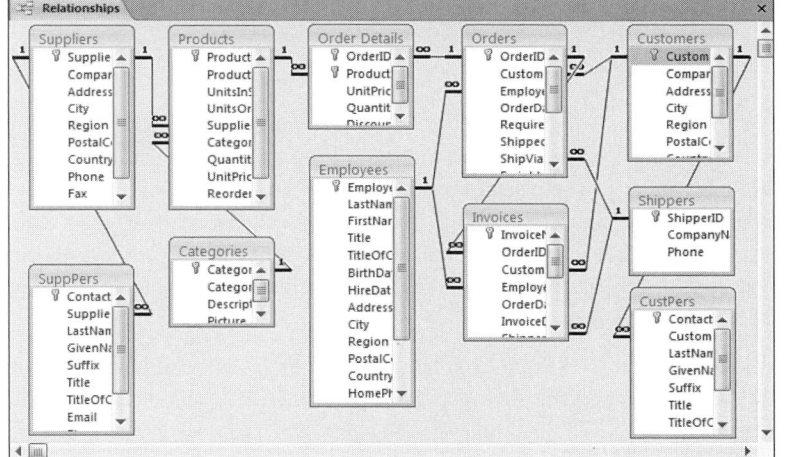

SECOND NORMAL FORM

Second normal form requires that data in all nonkey fields be fully dependent on the value of a primary key. The objective of second normal form is to avoid data redundancy in your tables.

Only Northwind's Order Details linking table (see Figure 4.7) has a composite primary key (OrderID + ProductID). The UnitPrice field appears to violate the second normal form, because UnitPrice is a field of the Products table. UnitPrice values added to the Order Details table are dependent on the ProductID component of the composite primary key and not the OrderID component, so UnitPrice data is not *fully dependent* on the primary key. On first glance, the UnitPrice field appears to be redundant data. If you change the unit price of a product, it would appear that you would need to alter the UnitPrice value in every Order Details record for the product.

Figure 4.7
The Order Details linking table has a composite primary key consisting of the OrderID and ProductID fields.

Order Details

Orde	ProductID	UnitPrice	Quantity	Discount	Add New Field
10248	11	$14.00	12	0%	
10248	42	$9.80	10	0%	
10248	72	$34.80	5	0%	
10249	14	$18.60	9	0%	
10249	51	$42.40	40	0%	
10250	41	$7.70	10	0%	
10250	51	$42.40	35	15%	
10250	65	$16.80	15	15%	
10251	22	$16.80	6	5%	
10251	57	$15.60	15	5%	
10251	65	$16.80	20	0%	
10252	20	$64.80	40	5%	
10252	33	$2.00	25	5%	
10252	60	$27.20	40	0%	
10253	31	$10.00	20	0%	
10253	39	$14.40	42	0%	
10253	49	$16.00	40	0%	
10254	24	$3.60	15	15%	

Record: 1 of 2155 No Filter Search

The Order Details table is an example of a situation in which you *must* retain what appears to be redundant information to maintain the integrity of historical data. Prices of products vary over time, so the price of a particular product is likely to change for orders placed on different dates. If the price of a product changes between the order and shipping (invoice) dates, the invoice reflects a different amount than the order. Despite the "Prices are subject to change without notice" boilerplate, customers become incensed if the invoice price is greater than the order price.

Eliminating the UnitPrice field from the Order Details table and looking up its value from the current price in the Products table also can cause accounting errors and distortion of historical reports based on bookings and sales data. Removing the UnitPrice data also violates the rules for the fifth normal form, explained later in this chapter.

Third Normal Form

Third normal form requires that data in all nonkey fields of the table be fully dependent on the value of the primary key and describe only the object that the table represents. In other words, make sure that the table doesn't include nonkey fields that relate to some other object or process and includes nonkey fields for descriptive data that isn't contained in another related table.

As mentioned in the "First Normal Form" section, including contact information in the Customers and Products table violates third normal form rules. Contacts are persons, not customer or supplier organizations, and deserve their own related table that has attributes related to individuals.

Other examples of a common third normal form violation are the UnitsInStock and UnitsOnOrder fields of the Products table (see Figure 4.8). These fields aren't fully dependent on the primary key value, nor do they describe the object; they describe how many of the product you have now and how many you might have if the supplier decides to ship your latest order. In a production order entry database, these values vary over time and must be updated for each sale of the product, each purchase order issued to the product's supplier, and each receipt of the product. Purchases, receipts, and invoices tables are the most common source of the data on which the calculations are based.

Figure 4.8
The Products table's UnitsInStock and UnitsOnOrder values must be calculated from data in tables that record purchases, receipts, and shipments of products.

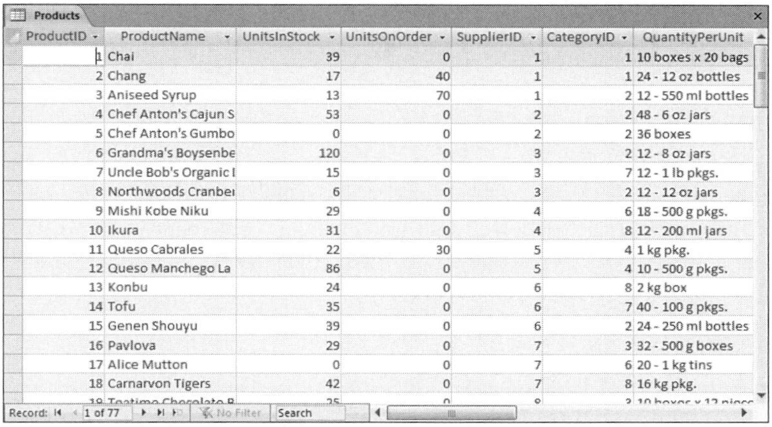

Products						
ProductID	ProductName	UnitsInStock	UnitsOnOrder	SupplierID	CategoryID	QuantityPerUnit
1	Chai	39	0	1	1	10 boxes x 20 bags
2	Chang	17	40	1	1	24 - 12 oz bottles
3	Aniseed Syrup	13	70	1	2	12 - 550 ml bottles
4	Chef Anton's Cajun S	53	0	2	2	48 - 6 oz jars
5	Chef Anton's Gumbo	0	0	2	2	36 boxes
6	Grandma's Boysenbe	120	0	3	2	12 - 8 oz jars
7	Uncle Bob's Organic I	15	0	3	7	12 - 1 lb pkgs.
8	Northwoods Cranber	6	0	3	2	12 - 12 oz jars
9	Mishi Kobe Niku	29	0	4	6	18 - 500 g pkgs.
10	Ikura	31	0	4	8	12 - 200 ml jars
11	Queso Cabrales	22	30	5	4	1 kg pkg.
12	Queso Manchego La	86	0	5	4	10 - 500 g pkgs.
13	Konbu	24	0	6	8	2 kg box
14	Tofu	35	0	6	7	40 - 100 g pkgs.
15	Genen Shouyu	39	0	6	2	24 - 250 ml bottles
16	Pavlova	29	0	7	3	32 - 500 g boxes
17	Alice Mutton	0	0	7	6	20 - 1 kg tins
18	Carnarvon Tigers	42	0	7	8	16 kg pkg.
19	Teatime Chocolate B	25	0	8	3	10 boxes x 12 pieces

Record: 14 ◀ 1 of 77 ▶ ▶I ▶* No Filter Search

Including UnitsInStock and UnitsOnOrder fields isn't a serious violation of the normalization rules, and it's not uncommon for product-based tables of order entry databases to include calculated values. The problem with calculated inventory values is the need to process a potentially large number of records in other tables to obtain an accurate current value.

TIP

> If you're designing an order entry database, make sure to take into account committed inventory. Committed inventory consists of products in stock or en route from suppliers for which you have unfulfilled orders. If you decide to include inventory information in a products table, add a UnitsCommitted field.

FOURTH NORMAL FORM

Fourth normal form requires that tables not contain fields for two or more independent, multivalued facts. Loosely translated, this rule requires splitting tables that consist of lists of independent attributes. The Northwind and Oakmont databases don't have an example of a fourth normal form violation, so the following is a fabricated example.

One of the objectives of Human Resources departments is to match employee job skills with job openings. A multinational organization is likely to require a combination of specific job skills and language fluency for a particular assignment. A table of job skill types and levels exists with entries such as JP3 for Java Programmer–Intermediate, as well as language/ fluency with entries such as TE5 for Telugu–Very Fluent. Therefore, the HR department constructs an EmplSkillLang linking table with the following foreign key fields: EmployeeID, SkillID, and LanguageID.

The problem with the linking table is that job skills and language fluency are independent facts about an employee. The ability to speak French has nothing to do with an employee's ability to write Java code. Therefore, the HR department must split (decompose) the three-field table into two two-field linking tables: EmplSkills and EmplLangs.

FIFTH NORMAL FORM

Fifth normal form involves further reducing redundancy by creating multiple two-field tables from tables that have more than two foreign keys. The classic example is identifying independent sales agents who sell multiple products or categories of products for different companies. In this case, you have a table with AgentID, CompanyID, and ProductID or CategoryID. You can reduce redundancy—at the risk of making the database design overly complex—by creating three two-field tables: AgentCompany, CompanyProduct (or CompanyCategory), and AgentProduct (or AgentCategory). Database developers seldom attempt to normalize designs to fifth normal form because doing so requires adding many additional small tables to the database.

CHOOSING PRIMARY KEY CODES

 All Northwind and Oakmont tables use codes for primary key values, as do almost all production databases. The critical requirement is that the primary key value is unique to each record in the table. Following are some tips, many with online resources, to aid in establishing primary key codes:

- Many types of tables—such as those for storing information on sales orders, invoices, purchase orders, and checks—are based on documents that have consecutive serial numbers, which are obvious choices for unique primary key values. In fact, most database designs begin with collecting and analyzing the paper forms used by an organization. If the table itself or programming code generates the consecutive number, make sure that every serial number is present in the table, even if an order is canceled or voided. Auditors are *very* suspicious of invoice and purchase order registers that skip serial numbers.

TIP

> AutoNumber primary key values work well for serially numbered documents if you don't allow records to be deleted. Adding a true-false (Boolean) field named Deleted and setting the value to true is one approach. This technique complicates queries against the tables, so you might consider moving deleted records to another table. Doing this lets you write a query to reconstruct all records for audit purposes.

- Packaged retail products sold in the United States have a globally unique 10-digit or longer Uniform Product Code (UPC). The UPC identifies both the supplier and the product's SKU. The Uniform Code Council, Inc., (http://www.uc-council.org/) assigns supplier and product ID values, which are combined into linear bar codes for automated identification and data capture (AIDC). The European Article Number (EAN) is coordinated with the UPC to prevent duplication. The UPC/EAN code is a much better choice than Microsoft's serially assigned number for the ProductID field.

- Books have a 10-digit International Standard Book Number (ISBN) code that's unique throughout the world and, in North America, a UPC. ISBNs include a publisher prefix and book number, assigned to U.S. publishers by the U.S. ISBN Agency (http://www.bowker.com/standards/home/isbn/us/isbnus.html). ISBN Group Agencies assign codes for other countries. Canada has separate agencies for English- and French-language books. Either a UPC or ISBN field is suitable for the primary key of a North American books database, but ISBN is preferred if the code is for books only.

- The North American Industry Classification System (NAICS, pronounced *nakes*) is replacing the U.S. Standard Industrial Classification (SIC) for categorizing organizations by their type of business. A six-digit primary key code for 18,000 classifications replaces the four-digit SIC code. Five of the six digits represent codes for classifications common to the United States, Canada, and Mexico. You can view a text file or purchase a CD-ROM of the NAICS codes and their SIC counterparts at http://www.naics.com/.

- The U.S. Postal Service offers Address Information Systems (AIS) files for verifying addresses and corresponding ZIP/ZIP+4 codes. For more information on these files, go to http://www.usps.com and click the Address Quality link.

- Social Security Numbers (SSNs) for U.S. residents are a possible choice for a primary key of an Employees table, but their disclosure compromises employee's privacy. Large numbers of counterfeit Social Security cards having identical numbers circulate in the United States, making SSN even less attractive as a primary key field. The Oakmont database uses fictitious nine-digit SSNs for EmployeeID and StudentID fields. Most organizations assign each employee a sequential serial number. Sequential EmployeeID numbers can do double-duty as seniority-level indicators.

Specifying a primary key for tables such as CustPers isn't easy. If you use the five-character code based on first and last names for the primary key, you encounter the problem with potential duplication of CustomerID codes discussed earlier. In this case, however, common last names—Jones, Smith, and Anderson, for example—quickly result in duplicate values. Creating a composite primary key from CustomerID and ContactID is a potential solution; doing this increases the number of new contacts you can add for a company before inevitable duplicates occur. In most cases, it's easier to use an AutoNumber key for all ID values.

 Figure 4.9 shows the final design of the modified Northwind database with the added contact details tables. The tables of this database are included on the accompanying CD-ROM as Nwind04.mdb in the \Seua2007\Chaptr04 folder.

Figure 4.9
The final design of the expanded Northwind database with customer and supplier contact details tables added.

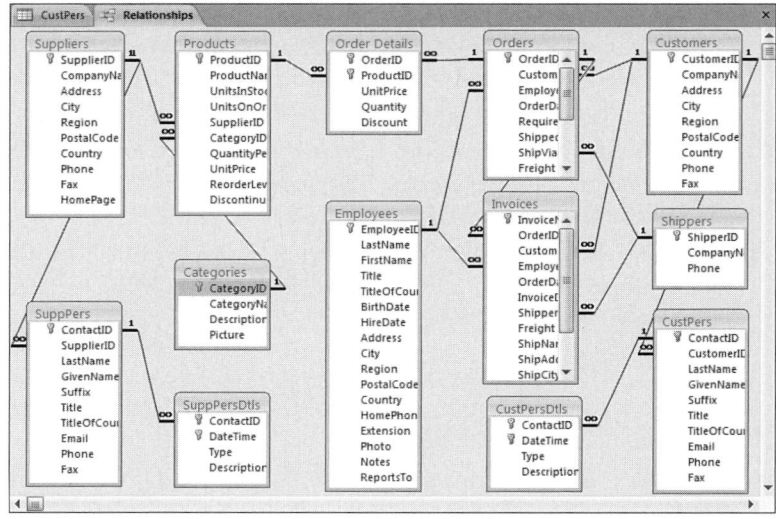

The modified Northwind database doesn't qualify as a full-fledged customer relationship management (CRM) system, but the design is sufficiently flexible to serve as the model for a sales and purchasing database for a small-sized wholesale or retail concern.

MAINTAINING DATA INTEGRITY AND ACCURACY

When you add, modify, or delete table data, it's important that the additions and changes you make to the data don't conflict with the normalization rules that you used to create the database. One of the most vexing problems facing users of large RDBMs is "unclean data." Over time, data entry errors and stray records accumulate to the point where obtaining accurate historical information from the database becomes difficult or impossible. Software vendors and database consultants have created a major-scale "data cleansing" business to solve the problem. You can avoid the time and expense of retroactive corrections to your data by taking advantage of Access and SQL Server features that aid in preventing errors during the data entry process.

REFERENTIAL INTEGRITY

Maintaining referential integrity requires strict adherence to a single rule: *Each foreign key value in a related table must correspond with a primary key value in a base (primary) table.* This rule requires that the following types of modifications to data be prevented:

- Adding a record on the many side of a one-to-many relationship without the existence of a related record on the one side of the relationship (for example, adding a record to the Orders table with a CustomerID value of BOGUS when no such customer record exists in the Customers table)

- Deleting a record on the one side of a one-to-many relationship without first deleting all corresponding records on the many side of the relationship (for example, deleting Around the Horn's Customers record when the Orders table contains records with AROUT as the CustomerID value)

- Changing the value of a primary key field of a base table on which records in a related base or linking table depend, such as changing AROUT to ABOUT in the CustomerID field of the Customers table

- Changing the value of a foreign key field in a linking table to a value that doesn't exist in the primary key field of a base table (for example, changing AROUT to ABOUT in the CustomerID field for OrderID 10355)

> **NOTE**
>
> You also must avoid changing the primary keys of or deleting one of two tables in a one-to-one relationship.

A record in a related table that doesn't have a corresponding foreign key value in the primary key of a base table is called an *orphan record*. For example, if the CustomerID value of a record in the Orders table is ABCDE and there's no ABCDE value in the CustomerID primary key field of the Customers table, there's no way to determine which customer placed the order.

Access and SQL Server databases offer the option of automatically enforcing referential integrity when adding or updating data. Cascading updates and deletions are optional. If you specify cascading updates, changing the value of a primary key of a table makes the identical change to the foreign key value in related tables. Cascading deletions delete all related records with a foreign key that corresponds to the primary key of a record in a base table that you want to delete.

→ To learn more about enforcing referential integrity in Access databases, **see** "Establishing Relationships Between Tables," **p. 237** and "Cascading Updates and Deletions," **p. 241**.

Entity Integrity and Indexes

When you add new records to a base table, entity integrity assures that each primary key value is unique. Access and SQL Server ensure entity integrity by adding a no-duplicates index to the field you specify for the primary key. If duplicate values exist when you attempt to designate a field as the primary key, you receive an error message. You receive a similar error message if you enter a duplicate primary key value in the table.

→ For more information on Access indexes, **see** "Adding Indexes to Tables," **p. 242**.

Indexes also speed searches of tables and improve performance when executing SQL statements that return data from fields of base and related tables.

DATA VALIDATION RULES AND CHECK CONSTRAINTS

Data entry errors are another major source of "unclean data." In the days of punched-card data entry, keypunch operators typed the data, and verifiers, who usually worked during the succeeding shift, inserted the cards in a punched-card reader and repeated the keystrokes from the same source document. This process detected typographical errors, which the verifier corrected. Keypunch operators had no visual feedback during data entry, so typos were inevitable; video display terminals didn't arrive until the mainframe era.

> **NOTE**
>
> Keypunch operators kept their eyes on the source documents, which gave rise to the term *heads-down data entry.* The term continues in common use to describe any data entry process in which the operator's entire working day is spent adding or editing database records as quickly as possible.

Rekeying data leads to low productivity, so most data entry applications support data validation rules designed to detect attempts to enter illegal or unreasonable values in fields. An example of a validation rule is preventing entry of a shipping date that's earlier than the order date. The rule is expressed as an inequality: ShipDate >= OrderDate, which returns False if the rule is violated. Similarly, UnitPrice > 0 prevents accidentally giving away a line item of an order.

Access tables and fields have a Validation Rule property that you set to the inequality expression. SQL Server calls validation rules *check constraints.* Both Access and SQL Server have a Validation Text property for which you specify the text to appear in an error message box when the entry violates the rule or constraint. It's a more common practice when working with client/server databases to validate data in the front-end application before sending the entry to the back-end server. Detecting the error on the server and returning an error message requires a *roundtrip* from the client to the server. Server roundtrips generate quite a bit of network traffic and reduce data entry efficiency. One of the objectives of client/server front-end design is to minimize server roundtripping.

→ To learn more about Access's validation methods, **see** "Validating Data Entry," **p. 275**.

TRANSACTIONS

A database transaction occurs when multiple records in one or more tables must be added, deleted, or modified to complete a data entry operation. Adding an order or invoice that has multiple line items is an example of a transaction. If an order or invoice has five line items, but a network or database problem prevents adding one or more item records, the entire order or invoice is invalid. Maintaining referential integrity prevents adding line item records without a corresponding order or invoice record, but missing item records don't violate integrity rules.

Transaction processing (TP), also called *online transaction processing (OLTP)*, solves the missing line item problem. Requiring TP for order entry, invoice processing, and similar multi-record operations enforces an all-or-nothing rule. If every individual update to the tables' records occurs, the transaction succeeds (*commits*); if any update fails, changes made before the failure occurs are reversed (*rolled back*). Transaction processing isn't limited to RDBMSs. Early mainframe databases offered TP and transaction monitors. IBM's Customer Information and Control System (CICS, pronounced *kicks*) was one of the first transaction processing and monitoring systems and remains in widespread use today.

Access and SQL Server databases offer built-in TP features. Access has a Use Transactions property that you set to Yes to require TP for updates. SQL Server traditionally requires writing T-SQL statements—BEGIN TRANS, COMMIT TRANS, and ROLLBACK TRANS—to manage transactions, but Access 2007's ADP forms have a new Batch Updates property that lets you enforce transactions without writing complex T-SQL statements.

DISPLAYING DATA WITH QUERIES AND VIEWS

So far, this chapter has concentrated on designing relational databases and their tables, and adding or altering data. SQL SELECT queries return data to Access, but you don't need to write SQL statements to display data in forms or print reports from the data. Access has built-in graphical tools to automatically write Access SQL for Access databases and T-SQL for SQL Server databases. Access's query tools use a modern implementation of *query-by-example (QBE)*, an IBM trademark. QBE is a simple method of specifying the tables and columns to view, how the data is sorted, and rows to include or exclude.

NOTE

> As mentioned earlier in the chapter, *fields* become *columns* and *records* become *rows* in a query. This terminology is an arbitrary convention of this book and not related to relational database design theory. The reason for the change in terminology is that a query's rows and columns need not—and often do not—represent data values stored in the underlying tables. Queries can have columns whose values are calculated from multiple fields and rows with aggregated data, such as subtotals and totals.

Linking related tables by their primary and foreign keys is called *joining* the tables. Early QBE programs required defining joins between tables; specifying table relationships automatically defines joins when you add records from two or more related Access or SQL Server tables.

Figure 4.10 is an example of Access's QBE implementation for Access databases, called Query Design View. You add tables to the query—in this case, Northwind's Customers, Orders, and Employees tables. As you add the tables, join lines indicate the relationships between them. You drag the field names for the query columns from the table lists in the upper pane to the Field row of the lower pane. You also can specify the name of a calculated column (Salesperson) and the expression to create the column values ([FirstName] & " " & [LastName]) in the Field row. The brackets surrounding FirstName and LastName designate that the values are field names.

Figure 4.10
Access's Query Design View for Access databases uses graphical QBE to create queries you can store in the database.

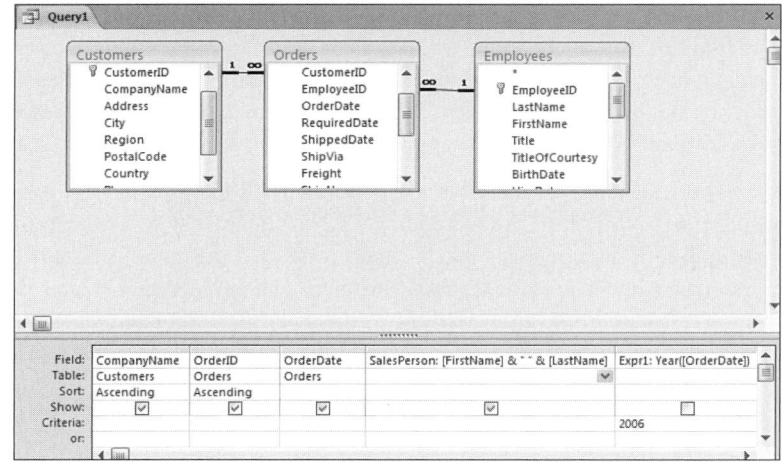

Selecting Ascending or Descending in the Sort column orders the rows in left-to-right column priority. You can restrict the display to a particular set of values by adding an expression in the Criteria column.

Running the query returns the result set, part of which is shown in Figure 4.11. You can save the query for later reuse as a named Access QueryDef(inition) object in the database.

Figure 4.11
These are the first 16 of the 408 rows of the query result set returned by executing the query design of Figure 4.10.

CompanyName	Order ID	Order Date	SalesPerson
Alfreds Futterkiste	10643	8/25/2006	Michael Suyama
Alfreds Futterkiste	10692	10/3/2006	Margaret Peacock
Alfreds Futterkiste	10702	10/13/2006	Margaret Peacock
Ana Trujillo Emparedados y helado	10625	8/8/2006	Janet Leverling
Ana Trujillo Emparedados y helado	10759	11/28/2006	Janet Leverling
Antonio Moreno Taquería	10507	4/15/2006	Robert King
Antonio Moreno Taquería	10535	5/13/2006	Margaret Peacock
Antonio Moreno Taquería	10573	6/19/2006	Robert King
Antonio Moreno Taquería	10677	9/22/2006	Nancy Davolio
Antonio Moreno Taquería	10682	9/25/2006	Janet Leverling
Around the Horn	10453	2/21/2006	Nancy Davolio
Around the Horn	10558	6/4/2006	Nancy Davolio
Around the Horn	10707	10/16/2006	Margaret Peacock
Around the Horn	10741	11/14/2006	Margaret Peacock
Around the Horn	10743	11/17/2006	Nancy Davolio
Around the Horn	10768	12/8/2006	Janet Leverling
Around the Horn	10793	12/24/2006	Janet Leverling
Berglunds snabbköp	10444	2/12/2006	Janet Leverling
Berglunds snabbköp	10445	2/13/2006	Janet Leverling

Record: 1 of 408 No Filter Search

Access SQL

Access QBE automatically converts the query design of Figure 4.10 into the following Access SQL statement:

```
SELECT Customers.CompanyName, Orders.OrderID, Orders.OrderDate,
       [FirstName] & " " & [LastName] AS Salesperson
    FROM Employees
       INNER JOIN (Customers
          INNER JOIN Orders
          ON Customers.CustomerID = Orders.CustomerID)
       ON Employees.EmployeeID = Orders.EmployeeID
    WHERE ((Year([OrderDate])=2006))
    ORDER BY Customers.CompanyName, Orders.OrderID;
```

It's obvious that using QBE is much simpler than writing SELECT queries to concatenate field values, join tables, establish row selection criteria, and specify sort order. Access's QBE features are powerful; many developers use Access to generate the SQL statements needed by Visual Basic, C++, and Java programs.

 The da Vinci QBE tool for creating T-SQL views is similar to the Access Query Design view, but has an additional pane to display the T-SQL statement as you generate it. You add tables to the upper pane and drag field names to the Column cells of the middle pane. An SQL Server view is the client/server equivalent of an Access QueryDef. As with Access QueryDefs, you can execute a query on an SQL Server view.

Despite their common ANSI SQL-92 heritage, SQL Server won't execute most Access SQL statements, and vice versa. Copying the preceding Access SQL statement to the Clipboard and pasting it into the SQL pane of the query designer for the NorthwindCS sample database doesn't work. The da Vinci designer does its best to translate the Access SQL flavor into T-SQL when you paste, but you receive errors when you try to run the query.

T-SQL

T-SQL uses + rather than & to concatenate strings, uses a single quote (') as the string delimiter, and requires a numerical instead of a string criterion for the YEAR function. Here's the T-SQL version of the preceding Access SQL statement after the SELECT and WHERE clauses have been tweaked:

```
SELECT TOP (2147483647) dbo.Customers.CompanyName,
       dbo.Orders.OrderID, dbo.Orders.OrderDate,
       dbo.Employees.FirstName + ' ' +
       dbo.Employees.LastName AS Salesperson
    FROM dbo.Employees
       INNER JOIN dbo.Customers
          INNER JOIN dbo.Orders
          ON dbo.Customers.CustomerID = dbo.Orders.CustomerID
       ON dbo.Employees.EmployeeID = dbo.Orders.EmployeeID
    WHERE (YEAR(dbo.Orders.OrderDate) = 2006)
    ORDER BY dbo.Customers.CompanyName, dbo.Orders.OrderID
```

The TOP modifier is needed to permit an ORDER BY clause in a view; prior to the addition of the TOP keyword in SQL Server 7.0, creating sorted views wasn't possible. The da Vinci query parser adds the TOP 100 PERCENT modifier if an ORDER BY clause is present. However, TOP 100 PERCENT ... ORDER BY doesn't sort SQL Server 2005 views. Replacing 100 PERCENT with a large integer (<= 2147483647) sorts the view.

The dbo. prefix to table and field names is an abbreviation for *database owner*, the default owner for all SQL Server databases you create as a system administrator. Figure 4.12 shows the design of the T-SQL query generated by pasting the preceding statement into the da Vinci query pane.

→ For more information on the da Vinci toolset, **see** "Exploring SQL Server Views," **p. 884**.

Figure 4.12
Pasting an Access SQL statement into Access's version of the da Vinci query design tool and making a few minor changes to the T-SQL statement results in an SQL Server view equivalent to the Access query of Figure 4.10.

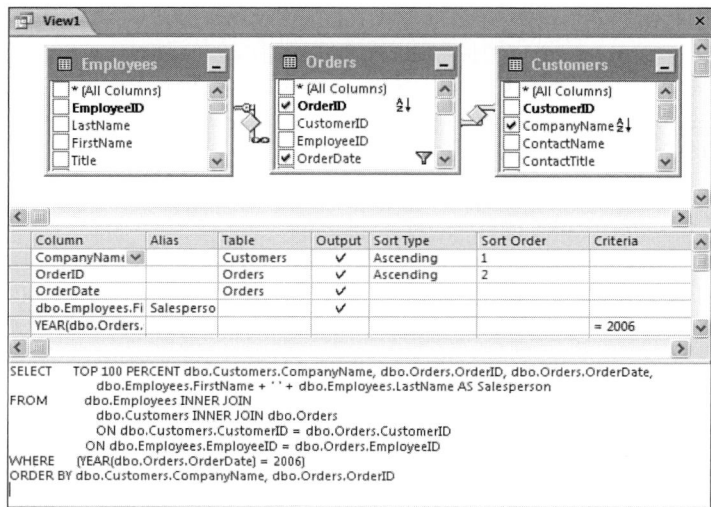

NOTE

> Access 2007 automatically creates the NorthwindCS database the first time you open the NorthwindCS.adp file after installing SSX from the distribution CD-ROM.

→ For detailed instructions on installing SQL Server Express and NorthwindCS.adp, **see** "SQL Server 2005 Express Edition SP2 Setup," **p. 59** and "Exploring the NorthwindSQL Sample Project," **p. 872**.

The Datasheet View of the SQL Server view generated by the preceding SQL statement is identical to the Access query's Datasheet View shown in Figure 4.11.

IN THE REAL WORLD—WHEN AND WHY LEARN RELATIONAL THEORY?

A corollary of the Law of Preservation of Matter is, "Everything has to be somewhere." Most books about Microsoft Access deal with relational database design theory in the first few chapters, and this latest of the 11 editions of *Special Edition Using Access* is no exception. Most previous editions categorized this subject as an "Advanced Access Technique" that appeared toward the end of the book.

Understanding relational database design requires familiarity not only with the objects that make up the database, but with the use of these objects. After you're comfortable with table and query basics, have a feeling for form and report design, and gained an introduction to Web-based database applications, you're probably better prepared to delve into the arcana of relational algebra, such as normalization rules. That's why the previous editions didn't include this chapter in the first part of the book.

After you've gained experience working with the sample relational databases in Access and this book, their design appears intuitive and entirely logical. Experienced database designers envision even the most complex business processes as collections of related tables. So, it's somewhat surprising to many that Dr. Codd's relational database theory originated in 1970, well after the development of complex network and hierarchical architectures. If you're embarking on the road to relational database development, however, you're not likely to find database design topics at all intuitive.

An argument in favor of moving the relational database design topic to the beginning of the book is that many readers decide to use Access to accomplish a specific task that involves creating a special-purpose database. In this case, you advance through the book's chapters using the sample databases as examples rather than learning models. If you're using Access as a learning tool, starting with database design and implementation also makes the structure and relationships of the tables in the sample databases of the book more meaningful.

Increasing sales of desktop and client/server RDBMSs has spawned a multitude of books—ranging from introductory tutorials to graduate-level texts—on relational database design theory and practice. Michael J. Hernandez's *Database Design for Mere Mortals* (Addison-Wesley Developers Press, ISBN 0-201-75284-0, 2003), subtitled "A Hands-On Guide to Relational Database Design, Second Edition," is an excellent resource for folks who want more than this chapter offers in the way of database design guidance. Mike and John L. Viescas, a well-known Access writer and developer, are co-authors of *SQL Queries for Mere Mortals* (Addison-Wesley, ISBN 0-201-143336-2), which delivers thorough coverage of SQL SELECT queries for Access and SQL Server users.

If you're serious about getting the most out of Access 2007, consider purchasing a copy of Mike's book or browse the bookstore shelves for titles on relational database design. Your investment will pay handsome dividends when you're able to create the optimum design to start, instead of attempting to restructure a badly designed database after it's grown to 20 or 30 tables containing thousands—or millions—of rows.

WORKING WITH ACCESS DATABASES AND TABLES

In this chapter

UNDERSTANDING ACCESS DATABASE FILES

Before the arrival of Microsoft Office Access 2007, there was only one extension for Access database files: .mdb. The traditional name for an .mdb file that stores Access application, data objects, or both, has been *Access database* since Microsoft released Access 1.0 in November 1993. As other database programming tools and technologies, such as Visual Basic and ADO.NET, began using .mdb files, *Jet database* became the preferred designation for Access files containing only tables and query definitions. Later versions of Access were only one of many Microsoft applications and programming tools to take advantage of the Jet database engine.

The use of Jet databases in Microsoft products became so widespread that the Windows development group incorporated Jet/Access dynamic link libraries (DLLs) as part of the Windows 2000, XP, 2003, and Vista operating systems. When the Windows team decided to make Jet part of Windows 2000 Professional and Server editions, the SQL Server team took ownership of Jet.

UPGRADING FROM JET .MDB TO ACCESS .ACCDB DATABASE FILES

Jet 4.0, which Access 2000, 2002, and 2003 use, is the latest *and last* Jet version. The SQL Server team considers its flagship product to be the "strategic database" for Windows applications and is unwilling to invest resources in adding new features to or otherwise improving Jet.

The Access team wanted to increase the compatibility of its database tables with Windows SharePoint Services 3.0 lists. This required new multivalued lookup fields and the Attachment data type. Therefore, the Access team created a new Access-only version of Jet—the *Access Database Engine* (sometimes called the *Access Connectivity Engine*, or *ACE*)—for Access 2007 and later. The upgraded engine requires database files to replace .mdb with an .accdb extension to gain access to the new features. However, Access 2007 also can open, edit, and save .mdb files in Access 2000 and 2002/2003 formats. Access 2007 also lets developers create compiled .accde files that don't allow users to read or modify VBA source code. (Access 2007's .accde files correspond to earlier versions' .mde files.)

→ For more information about multivalued lookup fields, **see** "Creating Multivalued Lookup Fields," **p. 474**, and for the Attachment data type, see "Choosing Field Data Types, Sizes, and Formats," **p. 213**.

TIP

> You don't need to upgrade your Access 95–2003 .mdb files to Access 2007 .accdb files unless you require the new SharePoint-specific capabilities or new macro features, such as embedded macros.

→ For more information about embedded macros, **see** "Generating Embedded Macros with Command Button Wizard," **p. 1155**.

MIGRATING FROM ACCESS APPLICATIONS TO SQL SERVER DATA PROJECTS

 Microsoft's determination to make SQL Server the database engine of choice for Access 2003 and later versions is another reason for changing from Jet to Access terminology for applications that use .accdb and related files. Access 2000 and later store application objects—forms, reports, macros, and modules—in a new compound file format called a *DocFile*. Conventional Access applications store the application object DocFile within the .accdb or .mdb file. Access Data Projects (ADP), which now represent the preferred approach to designing Access applications that connect to SQL Server databases, store the DocFile directly on disk as an .adp file. Combining ADP front ends with SQL Server back-end databases eliminates the need to periodically compact .accdb files and occasionally repair corrupted Access databases. The chapters of Part V, "Moving to Networked Multiuser Applications," cover designing ADP and SQL Server databases.

> **TIP**
>
> Using ADP and SQL Server databases for simple, single-user Access applications is overkill. You don't need the power of SQL Server 2005 for mailing list, contact management, or similar projects. Creating applications that use Access to store your data is easier than designing and managing SQL Server databases. Therefore, the beginning chapters of this book deal exclusively with Access databases.
>
> If you intend to create multiuser applications, which let several users update the database simultaneously, seriously consider using Access's no-charge version of SQL Server 2005 Express Edition (SSX) to store the data. Consider using SQL Server for any databases whose content is vital to the continued success—or existence—of an organization, such as sales orders, invoices, and accounts receivable. Access 2007 includes an Upsizing Wizard that greatly simplifies moving from Access to SQL Server databases. So, you can start with Access and then move to SQL Server as you become proficient in database application design.
>
> Another reason for migrating your data to SQL Server 2005 is the lack of support for user-level security by the .accdb or .accde file format. Access 2007 does let you edit workgroup files (System.mdw) for changing user-level security settings in existing .mdb or .mde files. The .accdb format offers more secure database password protection than earlier versions, but all users of .accdb or .accde files have Administrator permissions and, as a result, can alter any data and change the design of or delete any object in the database.

→ For more information on how to use the Upsizing Wizard, **see** "Preparing to Upsize Your Access Applications," **p. 949**.

ACCESS RECORD-LOCKING INFORMATION FILES

 When you open an .accdb or .mdb file, Access automatically creates a record-locking file having the same name as the database but with an .laccdb or .ldb extension. The purpose of the .laccdb or .ldb file is to maintain for multiuser applications a list of records that each user currently is updating. The record-locking file prevents data corruption when two or more users simultaneously attempt to change data in the same record. The presence of a record-locking file also prevents two or more users from saving design changes to the same database. If you open a database that another user has open with an object in design mode, you receive a message that you can't save any changes you make. The same restriction applies if you have the same database open in two instances of Access. When all users or instances of Access close the .accdb or .mdb file, Access deletes the .laccdb or .ldb file.

ACCESS ADD-IN (LIBRARY) DATABASES

Another category of Access database files is *add-ins*, also called *libraries*. Add-ins are Access databases—usually with an .accda, .accde, or .accdu (.mda or .mde for earlier versions) extension to distinguish them from user databases—that you can link to Access by choosing Tools, References in the VBA editor's menu. Alternatively, you can do this through the Add-In Manager, by opening the Add-Ins page of the Access Options dialog. The Add-In Manager also lets you add another class of extensions to Access called *COM Add-ins*, which have a .dll extension, such as Acecnf.dll for the Access Database Engine Conflict Resolver.

When you link an Access add-in, all elements of the library database are available to you after you open Access. The Access 2007 wizards that you use to create forms, reports, graphs, and other application objects are stored in a series of Access add-in database files: Acwzlib.accde, Acwztool.accde, Acwzmain.accde, Utility.accda, Acwzdat12.accdu, and Acwzusr12.accdu. The standard Access wizards don't appear in the Add-In Manager's dialog. Add-in databases are an important and unique feature of Access; third-party firms provide useful libraries to add new features and capabilities to Access.

CREATING A NEW ACCESS DATABASE FROM SCRATCH

If you have experience with relational database management systems, you might want to start building your own database as you progress through this book. In this case, you need to create a new database file at this point. If database management systems are new to you, however, you should instead explore the sample databases supplied with Access or that you create with templates from the Office Online site and on the accompanying CD-ROM as you progress through the chapters of this book. Before you design your first database, review the principles outlined in Chapter 4, "Exploring Relational Database Theory and Practice." Then return to this section and create your new database file.

→ For more information about creating databases from Office Online templates, **see** "Creating Databases from Downloaded Templates," **p. XXX** (Ch 02).

To create a new Access database in Access 2007's .accdb format, follow these steps:

1. If you aren't already running Access, launch it.

2. If Access doesn't open with the Getting Started with Microsoft Access dialog, click the New button of the Quick-Access Toolbar or press Ctrl+N to display the dialog.

3. Click the folder icon to the right of the File Name text box to open the File New Database dialog (see Figure 5.1).

Figure 5.1
Clicking the folder icon of the Getting Started dialog opens the File New Database dialog with Database1.accdb as the default database name and My Documents as its location.

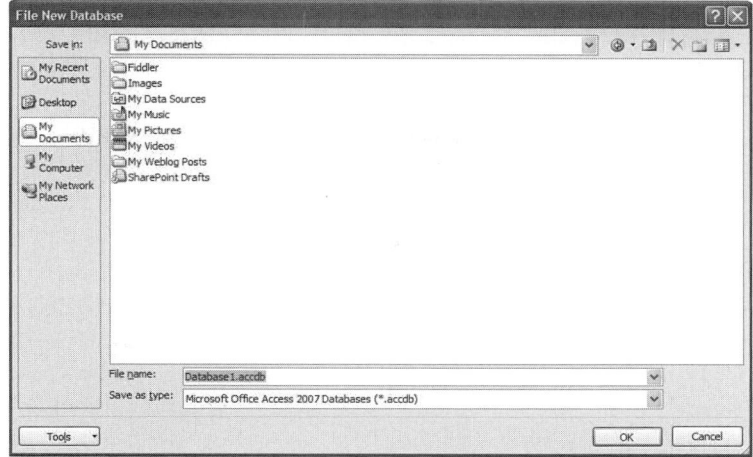

NOTE

Access supplies the default filename Database1.accdb for new databases, and proposes to save the database in your My Documents folder. If you've previously saved a database file as Database1.accdb in the current folder, Access supplies Database2.accdb as the default.

4. In the File Name text box, type a filename for the new database. Use conventional file-naming rules; you can use spaces and punctuation in the name, but doing so isn't a recommended practice. You don't need to include an extension in the filename; Access automatically supplies the .accdb extension.

5. Click OK or press Enter to close the File New Database dialog, and click Create to close the Getting Started dialog and create the new Access database file (Test.accdb for this example).

→ For more about file and object naming conventions, **see** "In the Real World—Database Strategy and Table Tactics," **p. 263**.

If a database was open when you created the new database, Access closes open windows displaying database objects. Then the Navigation Pane for the new database opens with a default empty table named Table1.

All Office 2007 applications use DocFiles to store their data and share a similar *FileName* Properties dialog, which opens when you click the Office button and choose Manage, Database Properties (see Figure 5.2). Each new .accdb database occupies 284KB of disk space when you create it. Most of the 284KB is space consumed by hidden system tables for adding the information necessary to specify the names and locations of other database elements that the database file contains.

5

Figure 5.2
The *FileName* Properties dialog for .accdb files has five tabbed pages that contain properties similar to the DocFiles and XML files created by other Office 2007 applications.

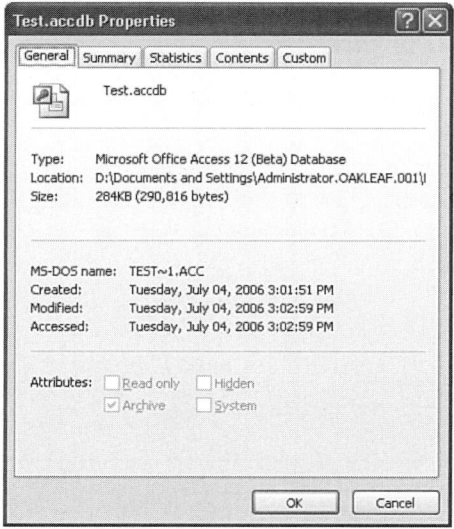

EXPLORING THE PROPERTIES OF TABLES AND FIELDS

 Before you add a table to a database that you've created or to one of the sample databases supplied with Access, you need to know the terms and conventions that Access uses to describe the structure of a table and the fields that contain the table's data items. With Access, you specify property values for tables and fields.

 Properties of Access tables apply to the table as a whole. You enter properties of tables in text boxes of the Table Properties sheet (see Figure 5.3), which you display by clicking Table Design View, saving Table1, and clicking the Properties button. Setting table property values is optional unless you have a specific reason to override the default values.

Figure 5.3
The Table Properties dialog for Northwind.accdb's Orders table uses default values for all but the Description property.

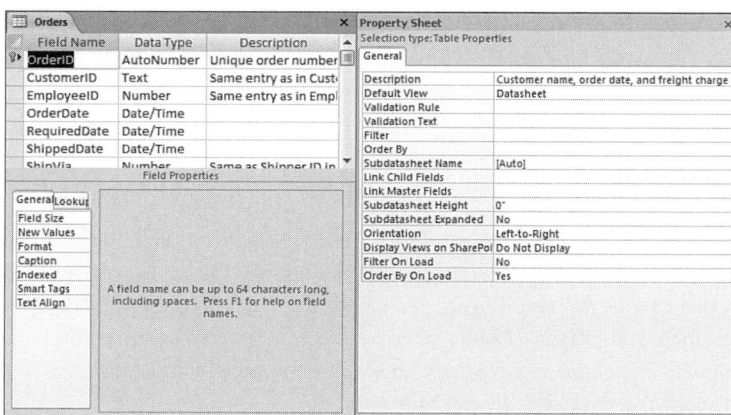

Following are brief descriptions of some of the 15 table properties of .accdb databases. The next section details properties related to subdatasheets.

- *Description* is a text explanation of the table's purpose. This description also is useful with a data dictionary, which you use to document databases and database applications.

- *Default View* lets you select from Datasheet, PivotTable, and PivotChart views of a table. The default selection is Datasheet view. PivotTable and PivotChart views of tables seldom are meaningful. Chapter 12, "Working with PivotTable and PivotChart Views," describes how to design queries that optimize the usefulness of these two views.

- *Validation Rule* is an expression (formula) that's used to establish domain integrity rules for more than one field of the table. The Validation Rule expression that you enter here applies to the table as a whole, instead of to a single field. Validation rules and domain integrity are two of the subjects of Chapter 6, "Entering, Editing, and Validating Access Table Data."

→ For more information on validation rules for tables, **see** "Adding Table-Level Validation Rules with the Expression Builder," **p. 278**.

- *Validation Text* specifies the text of the message box that opens if you violate a table's Validation Rule expression.

- *Filter* specifies a constraint to apply to the table whenever it's applied. Filters restrict the number of records that appear, based on selection criteria you supply. Chapter 7, "Sorting, Finding, and Filtering Data," discusses filters.

→ To learn more about filters, **see** "Filtering Table Data," **p. 297**.

- *Order By* specifies a sort(ing) order to apply to the table, by default whenever the table's opened in Datasheet view. Chapter 7 also explains sort orders. If you don't specify a sort order, records display in the order of the primary key, if a primary key exists. (Table1 has a default primary key field named ID.) Otherwise, the records appear in the order in which you enter them. The "Working with Relations, Key Fields, and Indexes" section, later in this chapter, discusses primary key fields.

→ For the details of applying sort order to a table, **see** "Sorting Table Data," **p. 290**.

- *Orientation*, another Access 2002 property, lets you specify right-to-left display of data in languages such as Hebrew and Arabic. Orientation is an Access-only data display property, and doesn't affect how Access stores the data. The default value for European languages is Left-to-Right.

N O T E

> SQL Server 2000 and later have an *extended properties* feature to support special Access and Access table and field properties, such as subdatasheets and lookup fields. The Table Properties dialog differs greatly from Access's version, but Table Design view of SQL Server's da Vinci toolset—also called the *project designer*—is similar to Access Table Design view.

5

- *Display Views on SharePoint* determines if forms and reports based on this table should appear in the SharePoint View menu if you publish the database to a SharePoint site. The default value is Do Not Display.

- *Filter On Load* specifies whether the filter criterion of the Filter property is applied automatically when the table is in use. The default value is No.

- *Order By On Load* specifies whether the sort order of the Sort property is applied automatically when the table is in use. The default value is Yes.

Table Properties for Subdatasheets

Access 2000 introduced subdatasheets to display sets of records of related tables in nested datasheets. You can use subdatasheets in the Datasheet view of tables and queries, and also in forms and subforms. Figure 5.4 illustrates Northwind.accdb's Orders table in Datasheet view with a subdatasheet opened to display related records from the Order Details table. The Orders Details (child) table has a many-to-one relationship with the Orders (master) table. To open a subdatasheet, click the + symbol adjacent to a record selection button.

Figure 5.4
Opening a sub-datasheet displays records of the child table (Order Details) that are related to the selected record in the master table (Orders).

→ If you're not familiar with relationships between tables, **see** "Removing Data Redundancy with Relationships," **p. 181**.

The following table properties apply to subdatasheets:

- *Subdatasheet Name* determines whether and how subdatasheets display data in related records. The default value is [Auto], which automatically adds subdatasheets for records linked from a related table that has a many-to-one relationship with the open table. You also can select a name from a list of the database's tables and queries. A value of [None] turns off subdatasheets in the master table.

- *Link Child Fields* specifies the name of the linked field of the related (subordinate) table whose records appear in the subdatasheet. You don't need to specify a value if the Subdatasheet Name property value is [Auto] and a many-to-one relationship exists with the master table.

- *Link Master Fields* specifies the name of the linking field of the master table, if you specify a Subdatasheet Name value.

- *Subdatasheet Height*, if supplied, specifies the maximum height of the subdatasheet. A value of 0 (the default) allows the subdatasheet to display all related records, limited only by the size of the master datasheet or subdatasheet.

- *Subdatasheet Expanded* controls the initial display of the subdatasheet. Setting the value to Yes causes the datasheet to open with all subdatasheets expanded (open).

> **NOTE**
>
> You can nest subdatasheets within other subdatasheets. For example, the Northwind database's Customers table has an Order table subdatasheet that, in turn, has an Order Details table subdatasheet.

➜ For information on how to create a subdatasheet for a table, **see** "Adding Subdatasheets to a Table or Query," **p. 478**.

FIELD PROPERTIES

You assign each field of an Access table a set of properties. You specify values for the first three field properties—Field Name, Data Type, and Description—in the Table Design grid, the upper pane of the Table Design window shown in Figure 5.5. As an example, the primary key of the Customers table is the CustomerID field, indicated by a small key symbol in the field selection button. You set the remaining property values in the Table Design window's lower pane, Field Properties.

Figure 5.5
Northwind.accdb's Customers table's CustomerID field is designated the primary key field. All fields of the Customer table are of the Text data type.

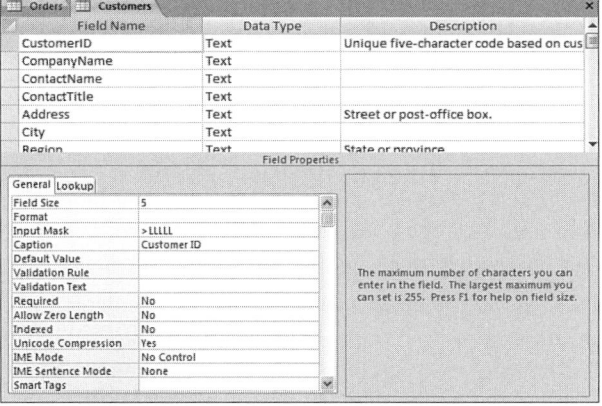

➜ If you're not familiar with the term *primary key*, **see** "Defining the Structure of Relational Databases," **p. 181**.

The following list summarizes the properties you set in the Table Design grid:

- *Field Name*—You type the name of the field in the Table Design grid's first column. Field names can be as long as 64 characters and can include embedded (but not leading) spaces and punctuation—except periods (.), exclamation marks (!), and square brackets ([]). Field names are mandatory, and you can't assign the same field name to more than one field in the same table. It's good database programming practice not to include spaces or punctuation characters in field names. [Substitute an underscore (_) for spaces or use uppercase and lowercase letters to improve the readability of field names.] Minimizing the length of field names conserves resources.

- *Data Type*—You select data types from a drop-down list in the Table Design grid's second column. Data types include Text, Memo, Number, Date/Time, Currency, AutoNumber, Yes/No, OLE Object, Hyperlink, Attachment, and Lookup Wizard. (The Lookup Wizard is an Access feature, not a data type.) Choosing a data type is the subject of the next section.

- *Description*—You can enter an optional description of the field in the text box in the Table Design grid's third column. If you add a description, it appears in the status bar at the lower left of Access's window when you select the field for data entry or editing. Description is a special property of Access and SQL Server 2005 databases and is for informative purposes only.

- *Primary Key*—To choose a field as the primary key field, select the field by clicking the field-selection button to the left of the Field Name column, and then click the Primary Key button on the Table Tools, Design ribbon.

Depending on the specific data type that you choose for a field, you can set additional properties for a table field. You set these additional properties on the General page of the Table Design window's Field Properties pane by selecting from drop-down or combo lists or by typing values in text boxes. You use the Field Properties pane's Lookup page to set the control type for lookup fields on forms—list box, combo list, and so on. Chapter 15, "Designing Custom Multitable Forms," describes how to use lookup fields.

The following list summarizes the General field properties of Access tables:

- *Field Size*—You enter the field size for the Text data type in this text box. (See the "Fixed-Width Text Fields" section later in this chapter to learn how to select a text field size.) For most Numeric data types, you determine the field size by selecting from a drop-down list. The Decimal data type requires that you type values for Precision and Scale. Field size doesn't apply to the Date/Time, Yes/No, Currency, Memo, Hyperlink, or OLE Object data type.

- *Format*—You can select a standard, predefined format in which to display the values in the field from the drop-down combo list that's applicable to the data type you selected (except Text). Alternatively, you can enter a custom format in the text box (see "Custom Display Formats" later in this chapter). The Format property doesn't affect the data values; it affects only how these values are displayed. The Format property doesn't apply to OLE Object fields.

- *Precision*—This property appears only when you select Decimal as the data size of the Number data type. Precision defines the total number of digits to represent a numeric value. The default is 18, and the maximum value is 28 for Access .accdb files.

- *Scale*—Like Precision, this property appears only for the Decimal data size selection. Scale determines the number of decimal digits to the right of the decimal point. The value of Scale must be less than or equal to the Precision value.

- *Decimal Places*—You can select Auto or a specific number of decimal places from the drop-down combo list, or you can enter a number in the text box. The Decimal Places property applies only to Number and Currency fields. Like the Format property, the Decimal Places property affects only the display, not the data values, of the field.

- *Input Mask*—Input masks are character strings, similar to the character strings used for the Format property, that determine how to display data during data entry and editing. If you click the Builder button for a field of the Text, Currency, Number, or Date/Time field data type, Access starts the Input Mask Wizard to provide you with a predetermined selection of standard input masks, such as telephone numbers with optional area codes.

- *Caption*—If you want a name (other than the field name) to appear in the field name header button in Table Datasheet view, you can enter an alias for the field name in the Caption list box. The restrictions on field name punctuation symbols don't apply to the Caption property. (You can use periods, exclamation points, and square brackets, if you want.)

- *Default Value*—By entering a value in the Default Value text box, you specify a value that Access automatically enters in the field when you add a new record to the table. The current date is a common default value for a Date/Time field. (See "Setting Default Values of Fields" later in this chapter for more information.) Default values don't apply to fields with the AutoNumber, OLE Object, or Attachment field data type.

- *Validation Rule*—Validation rules test the value entered in a field against criteria that you supply in the form of an Access expression. Unlike table-level validation rules, the field validation expression operates only on a single field. The Validation Rule property isn't available for fields with the AutoNumber, Memo, OLE Object, or Attachment field data type.

→ For an example of applying field-level validation rules, **see** "Adding Field-Level Validation Rules," **p. 276**.

- *Validation Text*—You enter the text that is to appear in the status bar if the value entered does not meet the Validation Rule criteria.

- *Required*—If you set the value of the Required property to Yes, you must enter a value in the field. Setting the Required property to Yes is the equivalent of typing **Is Not Null** as a field validation rule. (You don't need to set the value of the Required property to Yes for fields included in the primary key because Access doesn't permit Null values in primary key fields.)

- *Allow Zero Length*—If you set the value of the Allow Zero Length property to No and the Required property to Yes, the field must contain at least one character. The Allow Zero Length property applies to the Text, Memo, and Hyperlink field data types only. A zero-length string ("") and the Null value aren't the same.

5

- *Indexed*—From the drop-down list, you can select between an index that allows duplicate values and one that requires each value of the field to be unique. You remove an existing index (except from a field that is a single primary key field) by selecting No. The Indexed property is not available for Memo, OLE Object, and Hyperlink fields. (See "Adding Indexes to Tables" later in this chapter for more information on indexes.)

- *New Values*—This property applies only to AutoNumber fields. You select either Increment or Random from a drop-down list. If you set the New Values property to Increment, Access generates new values for the AutoNumber field by adding 1 to the highest existing AutoNumber field value. If you set the property to Random, Access generates new values for the AutoNumber field by producing a pseudo-random long integer.

 The "Gaps in AutoNumber Field Values" element of the "Troubleshooting" section near the end of the chapter discusses issues when you delete records from a table that has an AutoNumber field.

- *Unicode Compression*—Unicode is a method of encoding characters in multiple alphabets with two bytes, instead of the conventional single-byte ASCII or ANSI representation. Ordinarily, the use of two-byte encoding doubles the space occupied by values typed in Text, Memo, and Hyperlink fields. The first Unicode character of languages using the Latin alphabet is 0. If Unicode compression is set to Yes, the default value, Access stores all Unicode characters with a first-byte value of 0 in a single byte.

- *IME Mode* and *IME Sentence Mode*—These two properties apply only to fields having the Text, Memo, or Hyperlink data type. IME is an abbreviation for Office 2007's Input Method Editor, which governs the method of inputting characters of East Asian languages. IME Sentence Mode is applicable only to the Japanese language. A discussion of IME features is beyond the scope of this book.

- *Smart Tags*—You can add smart tags, which usually link Internet resources to a specific field. For example, you can add a Financial Symbol smart tag to an Access table field containing New York Stock Exchange or NASDAQ stock symbols to let users select from stock quotes, company reports, and recent company news from the MSN Money Central Website. Access 2007 also uses a smart tag to apply changes in a property value to dependent database objects.

- **NEW** *Text Align*—You can specify the alignment of Text and Memo fields as General, Left, Center, or Distributed (justified). General applies right alignment for numeric values; otherwise, left alignment. The default value is General.

- **NEW** *Text Format*—Specifying Rich Text enables HTML formatting of Memo fields with text formatting by selections from the Font and Rich Text groups of the Datasheet and Form views. The default value is Plain Text (no formatting).

- **NEW** *Append Only*—Prevents users from modifying existing text of a Memo field but allows adding new text. This property is useful for version control and change tracking. The default value is No.

→ For details on Access 2007's use of smart tags to propagate field property value changes to other database objects, **see** "Working with Object Dependencies and Access Smart Tags," **p. 248**.

As illustrated later in this chapter, adding the first sample table, HRActions, to the Northwind.accdb database requires you to specify appropriate data types, sizes, and formats for the table's fields.

CHOOSING FIELD DATA TYPES, SIZES, AND FORMATS

You must assign a field data type to each field of a table, unless you want to use the Text data type that Access assigns by default. One principle of relational database design is that all data in a single field consists of one data type. Access provides a much wider variety of data types and formats from which to choose than most other PC database managers. In addition to setting the data type, you can set other field properties that determine the format, size, and other characteristics of the data that affect its appearance and the accuracy with which numerical values are stored. Table 5.1 describes the field data types that you can select for data contained in Access tables.

TABLE 5.1   FIELD DATA TYPES AVAILABLE IN ACCESS 2007

Information	Data Type	Description of Data Type
Characters	Text	Text fields are most common, so Access assigns Text as the default data type. A Text field can contain as many as 255 characters, and you can designate a maximum length less than or equal to 255. Access assigns a default length of 50 characters.
Characters	Memo	Memo fields ordinarily can contain as many as 65,535 characters. You use them to provide descriptive comments. Access displays the contents of Memo fields in Datasheet view. A Memo field can't be a key field.
Numeric Values	Number	Several numeric data subtypes are available. You choose the appropriate data subtype by selecting one of the Field Size property settings listed in Table 5.2. You specify how to display the number by setting its Format property to one of the formats listed in Table 5.3.
	AutoNumber	An AutoNumber field is a numeric (Long Integer) value that Access automatically fills in for each new record you add to a table. Access can increment the AutoNumber field by 1 for each new record, or fill in the field with a randomly generated number, depending on the New Values property setting that you choose. The maximum number of records in a table that can use the AutoNumber field with the Long Integer size is slightly more than two billion.

continues

5

TABLE 5.1   CONTINUED

Information	Data Type	Description of Data Type
	Yes/No	Logical (Boolean) fields in Access use numeric values: −1 for Yes (True) and 0 for No (False). You use the Format property to display Yes/No fields as Yes or No, True or False, On or Off, or −1 or 0. (You can also use any nonzero number to represent True.) Logical fields can't be key fields but can be indexed.
	Currency	Currency is a special fixed format with four decimal places designed to prevent rounding errors that would affect accounting operations in which the value must match to the penny.
Dates and Times	Date/Time	Dates and times are stored in a special fixed format. The date is represented by the whole number part of the Date/Time value, which is the number of days from December 30, 1899. Time of day is represendt by the decimal fraction. For example, 2.25 is 1/1/1900 6:00 AM. You control how Access displays dates by selecting one of the Date/Time Format properties listed in Table 5.3.
Large Objects	OLE Object	Includes bitmapped and vector-type (Binary Data) graphics, and other BLOBs (binary large objects), such as waveform audio files and video files. You can't assign an OLE Object field as a key field, nor can you include an OLE Object field in an index. Clicking an OLE Object in Datasheet view opens the object in its editing application.
	Attachment **NEW**	An alternative to OLE Object for storing multiple large objects in a format compatible with SharePoint lists. Access compresses the attachments for more efficient storage. You can't assign an Attachment field as a key field, nor can it be indexed.
Web Addresses	Hyperlink	Hyperlink fields store Web page document addresses. A Web address stored in the Hyperlink field can refer to a Web page on the Internet or one stored locally on your computer or network. Clicking a Hyperlink field in Datasheet view causes Access to start your Web browser and display the referenced Web page. Choose Insert, Hyperlink to add a new hyperlink address to a Hyperlink field.
Related Data	Lookup Wizard	Lookup Wizard isn't a legitimate data type; it's a property of a field. Selecting Lookup Wizard starts the Lookup Wizard to add a lookup feature to the table. Most lookup operations execute a query to obtain data from a field of a related table.

→ To learn how to use the Lookup Wizard, **see** "Using Lookup Fields in Tables," **p. 466**.

5

NOTE

> The OLE Object field data type is unique to Access; other applications that use Access or Jet databases designate the OLE Object field data type as *Binary* or *Long Binary*. When you add an OLE object, such as a bitmapped graphic from Windows Paint or a Word document, Access adds a special header, which identifies the source application, to the binary graphics data. Other applications can't read data from OLE Object fields you create in Access. OLE Object fields won't upsize to SQL Server 2005, because SQL Server's `varbinary(max)` and image fields don't support the OLE Object data type.
>
> The Attachment field data type is similar to the OLE Object data type, but it stores any type of data that you can attach to an email message and doesn't depend on a local OLE server to display the attachment's contents. Each Attachment cell can contain any number of attachments, limited only by the 1GB maximum storage capacity of an Access field.

CHOOSING FIELD SIZES FOR NUMERIC AND TEXT DATA

The Field Size property of a field determines which data type a Number field uses or how many characters fixed-length text fields can accept. Field Size properties are called *subtypes* to distinguish them from the data types listed in Table 5.1. For numbers, you select a Field Size property value from the Field Size drop-down list in the Table Design window's Field Properties pane (see Figure 5.6).

Figure 5.6
You can select one of seven Field Size (data subtype) property values for fields having a Number data type from the drop-down list.

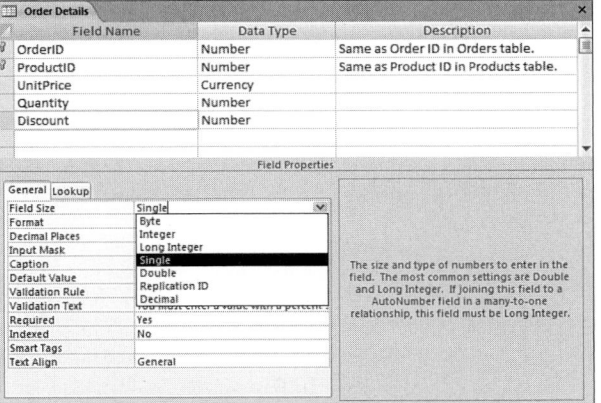

NOTE

> Access's default field type is Text with 255 characters as the default Size property value. Long Integer is the default numeric subtype. You can change these defaults in the Tables section of the Access Options dialog's Object Designers page.

SUBTYPES FOR NUMERIC DATA

The Number data type of the previously shown Table 5.1 isn't a fully specified data type. You must accept the default subtype (Long Integer) or select one of the subtypes from those listed in Table 5.2 for the Field Size property to define the numeric data type properly. To select a data subtype for a Number field, follow these steps:

1. Select the Data Type cell of the Number field for which you want to select the subtype.

2. Click the Field Size text box in the Field Properties window. You also can press F6 to switch windows, and then use the arrow keys to position the caret within the Field Size text box.

3. Click the drop-down arrow to open the list of choices shown previously in Figure 5.6.

4. Select the data subtype. (Table 5.2 describes data subtypes.) When you make a selection, the list closes.

After you select a Field Size property, you select a Format property from those listed in Table 5.3 (later in this chapter) to determine how to display the data. Table 5.2 includes the Currency data type because it also can be considered a subtype of the Number data type.

Regardless of how you format your data for display, the number of decimal digits, the range, and the storage requirements remain those specified by the Field Size property.

> **NOTE**
>
> These data types are available in Visual Basic for Applications (VBA) 6.0. VBA includes all the data types listed in Table 5.2 as reserved words. You can't use a reserved data type word for any purpose in VBA functions and procedures other than to specify a data type.

TABLE 5.2 SUBTYPES OF THE NUMBER DATA TYPE DETERMINED BY THE FIELD SIZE PROPERTY

Field Size	Decimals	Range of Values	Bytes
Decimal	28 places	-10^{-28} to $10^{28} - 1$	14
Double	15 places	$-1.797 * 10^{308}$ to $+1.797 * 10^{308}$	8
Single	7 places	$-3.4 * 10^{38}$ to $+3.4 * 10^{38}$	4
Long Integer	None	$-2,147,483,648$ to $+2,147,483,647$	4
Integer	None	$-32,768$ to $32,767$	2
Byte	None	0 to 255	1
Replication ID	None	Not applicable	16
Currency	4 places	-922337203685477.5808 to $+922337203685477.5808$	8

→ For more information on VBA reserved words for data types, **see** "Data Types and Database Objects in VBA," **p. 1180**.

As a rule, you select the Field Size property that results in the smallest number of bytes that encompasses the range of values you expect and that expresses the value in sufficient precision for your needs. Mathematical operations with Integer and Long Integer proceed more quickly than those with Single and Double data types (called floating-point numbers) or the Currency and Date/Time data types (fixed-point numbers). Microsoft added the Decimal data subtype for conformance with the SQL Server `decimal` data type.

TIP

> Always use the Decimal data type for fractional values—such as percentages—that you intend to use for calculating Currency or other Decimal values. The Order Details table's Discount field uses the Access Single data type, which is notorious for causing rounding errors in decimal calculations.

NOTE

> You can apply the Replication ID field size to Number or AutoNumber fields. A replication ID is a specially formatted 32-character (16-byte) hexadecimal number (values 0 through 9 and A through F) surrounded by French braces. The more common name for a replication ID is *globally unique identifier* (*GUID*, pronounced "goo id" or "gwid"). A typical GUID looks like {8AA5F467-3AF5-4669-B4CB-5207CDC79EF4}. GUID values, which Windows calculates for you, supposedly are unique throughout the world. If you apply the Replication ID field size to an AutoNumber field, Access automatically adds a GUID value for each row of the table.

FIXED-WIDTH TEXT FIELDS

You can create a fixed-width Text field by setting the value of the Field Size property, which limits the number of characters the field will store. By default, Access creates a 255-character-wide Text field. Enter the number, from 1 to 255, in the Field Size cell corresponding to the maximum length that you want. Datasheets will not let you enter more than the maximum nuber of characters. If the data you import to the field is longer than the selected field size, Access truncates the data, so you lose the far-right characters that exceed your specified limit. You should enter a field length value that accommodates the maximum number of characters you expect to enter in the field.

NOTE

> The terms *fixed width* and *fixed length* have two different meanings in Access. Even if you specify a fixed width for a field of the Text field data type, Access stores the data in the field in variable-length format. Therefore, setting the Length value to 255 for all Text fields has no effect on the ultimate size of the database file.

5

SELECTING A DISPLAY FORMAT

You establish the Format property for the data types you select so that Access displays them appropriately for your application. You select a format by selecting the field and then clicking the Format text box in the Field Properties window. Figure 5.7 shows the choices that Access offers for formatting the Long Integer data type. You format Number, Date/Time, and Yes/No data types by selecting a standard format or creating your own custom format. The following sections describe these two methods.

Figure 5.7
You can apply one of seven numeric display formats to fields of the Number data type and the Long Integer subtype. Access 2000 added the Euro format.

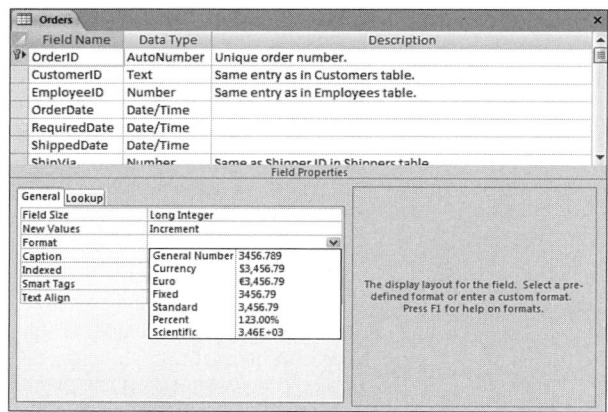

STANDARD FORMATS FOR NUMBER, DATE/TIME, AND YES/NO DATA TYPES

Access provides 18 standard formats that apply to the numeric values in fields of the Number, Date/Time, and Yes/No data types. The standard formats shown in Table 5.3 should meet most of your needs.

TABLE 5.3 STANDARD DISPLAY FORMATS FOR ACCESS'S NUMBER, DATE/TIME, AND YES/NO DATA TYPES

Data Type	Format	Appearance
Number	General Number	1234.5
	Currency	$1,234.50
	Euro	€1,234.50
	Fixed	12345 or 12345.00, depending on Decimal Places setting
	Standard	1,234.50
	Percent	0.1234 = 12.34%
	Scientific	1.23E+03
Date/Time	General Date	3/1/99 4:00:00 PM
	Long Date	Thursday, March 1, 2003
	Medium Date	1-Mar-2003

Data Type	Format	Appearance
	Short Date	3/1/2003
	Long Time	4:00:00 PM
	Medium Time	04:00 PM
	Short Time	16:00
Yes/No	Yes/No	Yes or No
	True/False	True or False
	On/Off	On or Off
	None	–1 or 0

Microsoft's Year 2000 (Y2K) compliance features include the General section of the Advanced page of the Access Options dialog. The Use Four-Digit Year Formatting group has two check boxes: This Database and All Databases. Marking either check box changes Date/Time field formatting as shown in Table 5.4. Long Date and Time formats don't change; the formatting shown in the Access 2007 Default column is based on the standard Windows Short Date format, m/d/yy.

TABLE 5.4   A COMPARISON OF ACCESS 2007 DEFAULT AND FOUR-DIGIT YEAR FORMATTING

Date/Time Format	Access 2007 Default	With Four-Digit Year
General Date (default)	1/15/03 10:10 AM	1/15/2003 10:10 AM
Short Date	1/15/03	1/15/2003
Long Date	Friday January 15, 2003	Friday January 15, 2003
Medium Date	15-Jan-03	15-Jan-2003
Medium Time	10:10 AM	10:10 AM
mm/dd/yy	01/15/03	01/15/2003

Marking the This Database check box sets a flag in the current database, so the formatting changes apply only to the current database. Marking the All Databases check box adds a Registry entry to your PC, so opening any Access database in Access forces four-digit year formatting.

TIP

> Access's Short Date (m/d/yy and mm/dd/yy) formats for the English (United States) locale default to two-digit years unless you change the default date format of Windows or set the Four-Digit Year Formatting option(s). Two-digit year presentation isn't Y2K compliant. To make the Windows short date format Y2K compliant for most applications, open Control Panel's Regional and Language Options tool, click the Customize button, select the Date tab, and check the Short Date setting. If the Short Date style is m/d/yy, change it to m/d/yyyy.

THE NULL VALUE IN ACCESS TABLES

Fields in Access tables can have a special value, Null, which is a new term for most spreadsheet users. The Null value indicates that the field contains no data at all. Null is similar but not equivalent to an empty string (a string of zero length, "", often called a *null string*). For now, the best synonym for Null is *no entry* or *unknown*.

The Null value is useful for determining whether a value has been entered in a field, especially a numeric field in which zero values are valid. The next section and the later "Setting Default Values of Fields" section use the Null value.

CUSTOM DISPLAY FORMATS

To display a format that's not a standard format in Access, you must create a custom format. You can set a custom display format for any field type, except OLE Object, by creating an image of the format with combinations of a special set of characters called *placeholders* (see Table 5.5). Figure 5.8 shows an example of a custom format for date and time. If you type **mmmm dd, yyyy - hh:nn** as the format, the date 03/01/07 displays as March 1, 2007 - 00:00. Access automatically adds double quotes around the comma when you save the table.

Figure 5.8
If one of the standard Format property values doesn't meet your needs, you can type a string to represent a custom format in the Format text box. This format string (dd-mmm-yyyy) substitutes four-digit years for the Medium Date format's two-digit years.

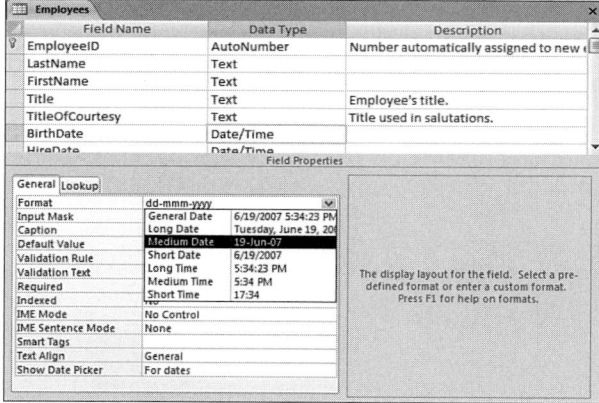

Except as noted, the sample numeric value that Table 5.4 uses is 1234.5. Bold type distinguishes the placeholders that you type from the surrounding text. The resulting display is shown in monospace type.

TABLE 5.5 PLACEHOLDERS FOR CREATING CUSTOM DISPLAY FORMATS

Placeholder	Function
Empty string	Displays the number with no formatting. Enter an empty string by deleting the value in the Format field of the Field Properties pane.
0	Displays a digit, if one exists in the position, or a zero if not. You can use the **0** placeholder to display leading zeros for whole numbers and trailing zeros in decimal fractions. **00000.000** displays 01234.500.

Placeholder	Function
#	Displays a digit, if one exists in the position. The # placeholder is similar to **0**, except that leading and trailing zeros aren't displayed. **#####.###** displays 1234.5.
$	Displays a dollar sign in the position. **$###,###.00** displays $1,234.50.
.	Displays a decimal point at the indicated position in a string of **0** and **#** placeholders. **##.##** displays 1234.5.
%	Multiplies the value by 100 and adds a percent sign in the position shown with **0** and **#** placeholders. **#0.00%** displays 0.12345 as 12.35% (12.345 is rounded to 12.35).
,	Adds commas as thousands separators in strings of **0** and **#** placeholders. **###,###,###.00** displays 1,234.50.
E- e-	Displays values in scientific format with the sign of exponent for negative values only. **#.####E-00** displays 1.2345E03. 0.12345 is displayed as 1.2345E-01.
E+ e+	Displays values in scientific format with the sign of exponent for positive and negative values. **#.####E+00** displays 1.2345E+03.
/	Separates the day, month, and year to format date values. Typing **mm/dd/yyyy** displays 03/06/2003. (You can substitute hyphens for virgules to display 03-06-2003.)
m	Specifies how to display months for dates. **m** displays 1, **mm** displays 01, **mmm** displays Jan, and **mmmm** displays January.
d	Specifies how to display days for dates. **d** displays 1, **dd** displays 01, **ddd** displays Mon, and **dddd** displays Monday.
y	Specifies how to display years for dates. **yy** displays 07; **yyyy** displays 2007.
:	Separates hours, minutes, and seconds in format time values. **hh:mm:ss** displays 02:02:02.
h	Specifies how to display hours for time. **h** displays 2; **hh** displays 02. If you use an **AM/PM** placeholder, **h** or **hh** displays 4 PM for 16:00 hours.
n	Minutes placeholder for time. **n** displays 1; **nn** displays 01. **hhnn** "hours" displays 1600 hours.
s	Seconds placeholder for time. **s** displays 1; **ss** displays 01.
AM/PM	Displays time in 12-hour time with AM or PM appended. **h:nn AM/PM** displays 4:00 PM. Alternative formats include **am/pm**, **A/P**, and **a/p**.
@	Indicates that a character is required in the position in a Text or Memo field. You can use @ to format telephone numbers in a Text field, as in **@@@-@@@-@@@@** or **(@@@) @@@-@@@@**.
&	Indicates that a character in a Text or Memo field is optional.
>	Changes all text characters in the field to uppercase.
<	Changes all text characters in the field to lowercase.
*	Displays the character following the asterisk as a fill character for empty spaces in a field. **"ABCD"*x** in an eight-character field appears as ABCDxxxx.

5

The Format property is one of the few examples in Access in which you can select from a list of options or type your own entry. Format uses a true drop-down combo list; lists that enable you to select only from the listed options are drop-down lists with the Limit To List property value set to No. The comma is a nonstandard formatting symbol for dates (but is standard for number fields). When you create nonstandard formatting characters in the Field Properties window, Access automatically encloses them in double quotation marks.

When you change Format or any other field property value, and then change to Datasheet view to see the result of your work, you must first save the updated table design. The confirmation dialog shown at the top of Figure 5.9 asks you to confirm any design changes. Clicking No returns you to Table Design view. If you want to discard your changes, close Table Design view and click No when asked if you want to save your changes (see Figure 5.9, bottom).

Figure 5.9
Changing from Table Design to Datasheet view after making changes to the table's design displays the upper message box. If you close the table in Design view, the lower message box gives you the option of saving or discarding changes, or returning to Table Design view.

If you apply the custom format string **mmmm dd", "yyyy** (refer to Figure 5.8) to the BirthDate field of the Employees table, the BirthDate field entries appear as shown in Figure 5.10. For example, Nancy Davolio's birth date appears as December 08, 1968. The original format of the BirthDate field was dd-mmm-yyyy (medium date), the format also used for the HireDate field. The Birth Date caption property value appears in the heading row.

You must expand the width of the BirthDate field to accommodate the additional characters in the Long Date format. You increase the field's width by dragging the field name header's right vertical bar to the right to display the entire field.

CONDITIONAL FORMATTING

Conditional formatting enables applying formatting that depends on the value of numeric data: greater than zero (>0); less than zero (<0); zero (=0); Null. Semicolons separate the format strings for the four value conditions.

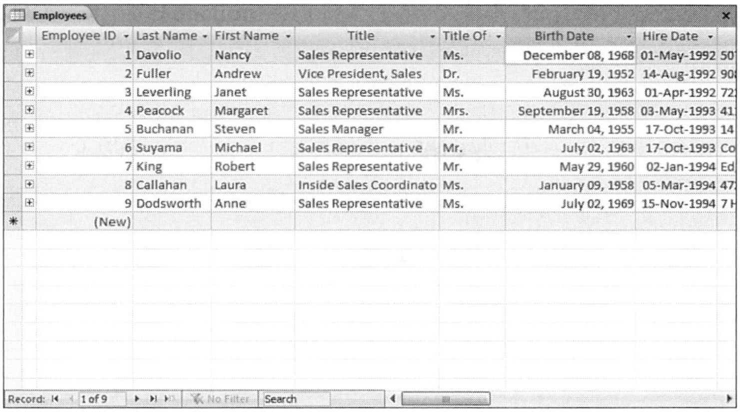

Figure 5.10
The BirthDate field of the modified employees table displays the effect of applying **mmmm dd", "yyyy** as the custom date/time format. The popup calendar for entering or editing data in Date fields is a new Access 2007 feature.

Employee ID	Last Name	First Name	Title	Title Of	Birth Date	Hire Date	
1	Davolio	Nancy	Sales Representative	Ms.	December 08, 1968	01-May-1992	50
2	Fuller	Andrew	Vice President, Sales	Dr.	February 19, 1952	14-Aug-1992	90
3	Leverling	Janet	Sales Representative	Ms.	August 30, 1963	01-Apr-1992	72
4	Peacock	Margaret	Sales Representative	Mrs.	September 19, 1958	03-May-1993	41
5	Buchanan	Steven	Sales Manager	Mr.	March 04, 1955	17-Oct-1993	14
6	Suyama	Michael	Sales Representative	Mr.	July 02, 1963	17-Oct-1993	Co
7	King	Robert	Sales Representative	Mr.	May 29, 1960	02-Jan-1994	Ed
8	Callahan	Laura	Inside Sales Coordinato	Ms.	January 09, 1958	05-Mar-1994	47
9	Dodsworth	Anne	Sales Representative	Ms.	July 02, 1969	15-Nov-1994	7 H
(New)							

Record: 1 of 9 — No Filter — Search

The following is an example that formats negative numbers enclosed in parentheses and replaces a Null entry with text:

```
$###,###,##0.00;$(###,###,##0.00);0.00;"No Entry Here"
```

The entries 1234567.89, −1234567.89, 0, and a Null default value appear as follows:

```
$1,234,567.89
$(1,234,567.89)
0.00
No Entry Here
```

USING INPUT MASKS

Access 2007 lets you restrict entries in Text fields to numbers or to otherwise control the formatting of entered data. Access's Input Mask property is used to format telephone numbers, Social Security numbers, ZIP Codes, and similar data. Table 5.6 lists the placeholders that you can use in character strings for input masks in fields of the Text field data type.

TABLE 5.6   PLACEHOLDERS FOR CREATING INPUT MASKS

Placeholder	Function
Empty string	No input mask.
0	Number (0–9) required; sign (+/–) not allowed.
9	Number (0–9) or space optional; sign (+/-) not allowed.
#	Number (0–9) or space optional (a space if nothing is entered).
L	Letter (A–Z) required.
?	Letter (A–Z) not required (a space if nothing is entered).
A	Letter (A–Z) or number (0–9) required.
a	Letter (A–Z) or number (0–9) optional.

continues

TABLE 5.6   CONTINUED

Placeholder	Function
&	Any character or a space required.
C	Any character or a space optional.
Password	Displays the characters you type as asterisks (***...) to prevent others from viewing the entry.
. , : ; / ( )	Literal decimal, thousands, date, time, and special separators.
>	All characters to the right are converted to uppercase.
<	All characters to the right are converted to lowercase.
!	Fills the mask from right to left.
\	Precedes the other placeholders to include the literal character in a format string.

For example, typing **\(000") "000\-0000** as the value of the Input Mask property results in the appearance of (___) ___-____ for a blank telephone number cell of a table. Typing **000\-00\-0000** creates a mask for Social Security numbers, ___-__-____. When you type the telephone number or Social Security number, the digits that you type replace the underscores.

> **NOTE**
>
> The \ characters (often called *escape characters*) that precede parentheses and hyphens specify that the character that follows is a literal, not a formatting character. If the format includes spaces, enclose the spaces and adjacent literal characters in double quotation marks, as shown for the telephone number format.

Access includes an Input Mask Wizard that opens when you move to the Input Mask field for the Text or Date/Time field data type and click the Builder (...) button at the extreme right of the text box. Figure 5.11 shows the opening dialog of the Input Mask Wizard for Text fields, which lets you select from 10 common input mask formats. The Input Mask Wizard offers only Long Time, Short Date, Short Time, Medium Time, and Medium Date masks for Date/Time fields. The Wizard only works with Text and Date/Time field data types.

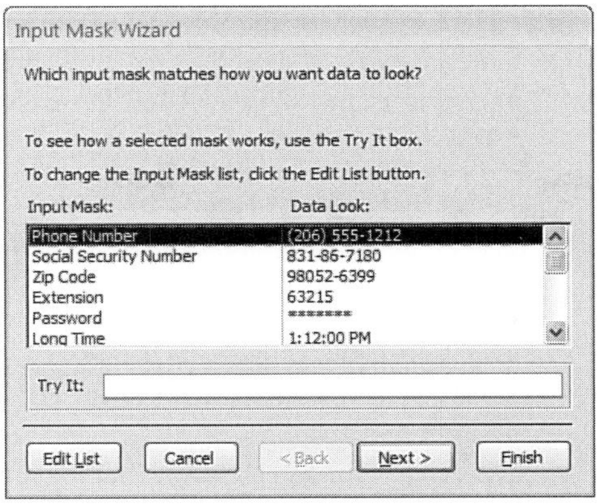

Figure 5.11
The Input Mask Wizard lets you select one of 10 preset formats to specify a fixed data entry pattern for the selected field. In the second wizard dialog, you can add a custom format.

ADDING A TABLE TO THE NORTHWIND TRADERS SAMPLE DATABASE

One fundamental problem with books about database management applications is the usual method of demonstrating how to create a "typical" database. You are asked to type fictitious names, addresses, and telephone numbers into a Customers table. Next, you must create additional tables that relate these fictitious customers to their purchases of various widgets in assorted sizes and quantities. This process is unrewarding for readers and authors, and few readers ever complete the exercises.

Therefore, this book takes a different tack. Earlier Access versions included a comprehensive—but outdated—sample order entry database, Northwind Traders (Northwind.mdb). The Microsoft Office 2007 Professional and higher editions don't include a sample database in the setup program's options. The CD-ROM that accompanies this book includes several updated versions of the Northwind database in the \SEUA12\Nwind folder. If you installed the sample code from the CD-ROM to the default \SEUA12 folder, the \SEUA12\Chaptr05 folder holds a Northwind.accdb starter version that contains only updated tables.

Rather than create a new database at this point, you create a new table as an addition to the \SEUA12\Chaptr05\Northwind.accdb table. Adding a new table minimizes the amount of typing required and requires just a few entries to make the table functional. The HRActions table you add demonstrates many elements of relational database design.

PREPARING TO ADD A TABLE RELATED TO THE EMPLOYEES TABLE

Northwind.accdb in your \SEUA12\Chaptr05 folder includes the Employees table that provides information typical of personnel tables maintained by Human Resources departments 10 or more years ago. The following sections explain how to add a new table to the Northwind database that is related to the Employees table and called HRActions. The HRActions table is a record of hire date, salary, commission rate, bonuses, performance reviews, and other compensation-related events for employees. Because HRActions is based on information in the Employees table, the first step is to review the Employees table's structure. In Chapter 6, you add validation rules to the HRActions table and enter records in the table.

Figure 5.12 shows the Employees table in Design view. The fields grid in the figure shows property values for only 6 of the 18 fields of the table. Scroll down to display the properties of the remaining 12 fields.

Figure 5.12
Design view of the Employees table displays most of the table's fields in the upper grid pane. The most important field is the primary key, EmployeeID, on which the new table's relationship depends.

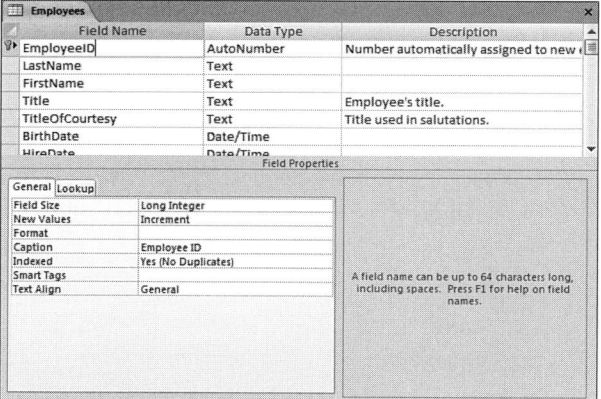

NOTE

Northwind.accdb's Employees table has an added Picture field of the new Attachments data type. Otherwise, this table is identical to the Employees table of earlier Access version.

DESIGNING THE HRACTIONS TABLE

Designing the HRActions table is typical of the process you go through when you create a set of relational tables for almost any purpose. Rather than add fields for entries—such as salary, commission rate, and bonuses—to the Employees table, you should place employee performance and remuneration data in a table of its own, for the following reasons:

- Multiple HRActions are taken for individual employees over time. If you add these actions to records in the Employees table, you would need to create many additional fields to hold an arbitrary number of HRActions. If, for example, quarterly performance reviews are entered, you would need to add a new field for every quarter to hold the review information. In this situation, which is an example of a repeating group, spreadsheet applications and flat-file managers encounter serious difficulties. Relational databases use related tables to handle the repeating group problem.

- HRActions usually are considered confidential information and are made accessible only to a limited number of people. Although you can design forms that don't display confidential information, restricting permission to view an entire table is a more secure approach.

- You can identify employees uniquely by their EmployeeID numbers. Therefore, records for entries of HRActions can be related to the Employees table by an EmployeeID field. This feature eliminates the necessity of adding employee names and other constants or slowly-changing information to the records in the HRActions table. You link the Employees table to the HRActions table by the EmployeeID field, and the two tables are joined; they act as though they are a single table. Minimizing information duplication to only what is required to link the tables is your reward for choosing a relational, rather than a flat-file, database management system.

- You can categorize HRActions by type so that any action taken can use a common set of field names and field data types. This feature simplifies the design of the HRActions table.

The next step is to start the design of the HRActions table. Chapter 4 discusses the theory of database design and the tables that make up databases. Because the HRActions table has an easily discernible relationship to the Employees table, the theoretical background isn't necessary for this example.

DETERMINING WHAT INFORMATION THE TABLE SHOULD INCLUDE

Designing a table requires that you identify the type of information the table should contain. Information associated with typical Human Resources department actions might consist of the following items:

- *Important dates*—The date of hire and termination, if applicable, are important dates, but so are the dates when the employer adjusts salaries, changes commission rates, and grants bonuses. You should accompany each action with the date when it was scheduled to occur and the date when it actually occurred.

- *Types of actions*—Less typing is required if HRActions are identified by a code character rather than a full-text description of the action. This feature saves valuable disk space, too. First-letter abbreviations used as codes, such as H for hired, T for terminated, and Q for quarterly review, are easy to remember.

- *Initiation and approval of actions*—As a rule, the employee's supervisor initiates a personnel action, and the supervisor's manager approves it. Therefore, the table should include the supervisor's and manager's EmployeeID number.

- *Amounts involved*—Salaries are assumed to be bimonthly based on a monthly amount, hourly employees are paid weekly, bonuses are quarterly with quarterly performance reviews, and commissions are paid on a percentage of sales made by the employee.

- *Performance rating*—Rating employee performance by a numerical value is a universal, but somewhat arbitrary, practice. Scales of 1 to 9 are common, with exceptional performance ranked as 9 and candidacy for termination as 1.

5

■ *Summaries and comments*—The table should provide for a summary of performance, an explanation of exceptionally high or low ratings, and reasons for adjusting salaries or bonuses.

NOTE

Fields containing a code for pay type—salary, hourly, commission—and bonus eligibility would be useful additions to the Employees table. You could use such codes to validate amount entries in the HRActions table.

If you're involved in personnel management, you probably can think of additional information that the table might include, such as accruable sick leave and vacation hours per pay period. The HRActions table is just an example; it isn't meant to add full-scale Human Resources application capabilities to the database. The limited amount of data described so far serves to demonstrate several uses of the new table in this and subsequent chapters.

ASSIGNING INFORMATION TO FIELDS

After you determine the types of information—called *data attributes* or just *attributes*—to include in the table, you must assign each data entity to a field of the table. This process involves specifying a field name that must be unique within the table. Table 5.7 lists the candidate fields for the HRActions table. Candidate fields are written descriptions of the fields proposed for the table. Data types are logically derived from the type of value described. Table 5.8 adds specifics for the data types.

TABLE 5.7   CANDIDATE FIELDS FOR THE HRACTIONS TABLE

Field Name	Data Type	Description
EmployeeID	Number	The employee to whom the action applies. EmployeeID numbers are assigned based on the EmployeeID field of the Employee table (to which the HRActions table is related).
ActionType	Text	Code for the type of action taken: H is for hired; Q, quarterly review; Y, yearly review; S, salary adjustment; R, hourly rate adjustment; B, bonus adjustment; C, commission rate adjustment; and T, terminated.
InitiatedBy	Number	The EmployeeID number of the supervisor who initiates or is responsible for recommending the action.
ScheduledDate	Date/Time	The date when the action is scheduled to occur.
ApprovedBy	Number	The EmployeeID number of the manager who approves the action proposed by the supervisor.
EffectiveDate	Date/Time	The date when the action occurred. The effective date remains blank (Null value) if the action has not occurred.

Field Name	Data Type	Description
HRRating	Number	Performance on a scale of 1–9, with higher numbers indicating better performance. A blank (Null value) indicates no rating; 0 is reserved for terminated employees.
NewSalary	Currency	The new salary per month, as of the effective date, for salaried employees.
NewRate	Currency	The new hourly rate for hourly employees.
NewBonus	Currency	The new quarterly bonus amount for eligible employees.
NewCommission	Percent	The new commission rate for commissioned salespersons, some of whom might also receive a salary.
HRComments	Memo	Abstracts of performance reviews and comments on actions proposed or taken. The comments can be of unlimited length. The supervisor and manager can contribute to the comments.

TIP

> Use distinctive names (without spaces or punctuation characters) for each field. This example precedes some field names with the abbreviation HR to associate—or establish relations with—field names in other tables that might be used by the Human Resources department.

CREATING THE HRACTIONS TABLE IN DESIGN VIEW

Now you can put to work what you've learned about field names, data types, and formats by adding the HRActions table to the Northwind Traders database. Table 5.8 shows the field names, taken from Table 5.7, and the set of properties that you assign to the fields. Fields with values required in a new record have an asterisk (*) following the field name. The text in the Caption column substitutes for the Field Name property that is otherwise displayed in the field header buttons.

TABLE 5.8   FIELD PROPERTIES FOR THE HRACTIONS TABLE

Field Name	Caption	Data Type	Field Size	Format
EmployeeID*	ID	Number	Long Integer	General Number
ActionType*	Type	Text	1	>@ (all uppercase)
InitiatedBy*	Initiated By	Number	Long Integer	General Number
ScheduledDate*	Scheduled	Date/Time	N/A	mm/dd/yyyy
ApprovedBy	Approved By	Number	Long Integer	General Number
EffectiveDate	Effective	Date/Time	N/A	Short Date
HRRating	Rating	Number	Byte	General Number

continues

TABLE 5.8   CONTINUED

Field Name	Caption	Data Type	Field Size	Format
NewSalary	Salary	Currency	N/A	Standard
NewRate	Rate	Currency	N/A	Standard
NewBonus	Bonus	Currency	N/A	Standard
NewCommission	% Comm	Number	Single	#0.0
HRComments	Comments	Memo	N/A	(None)

> **NOTE**
>
> You must set the EmployeeID field's Field Size property to the Long Integer data type, although you might not expect Northwind Traders to have more than the 32,767 employees that an integer allows. The Long Integer data type is required because the AutoNumber field data type of the Employees table's EmployeeID field is a Long Integer. Later in this chapter, the "Working with Relations, Key Fields, and Indexes" section explains why EmployeeID's data type must match that of the Employees table's EmployeeID number field.

To add the new HRActions table to the Northwind database, complete the following steps:

1. Close the Employees table, if it's open.

 2. Click the Create tab and then click the Table Design button. Access enters design mode, opens a blank grid, and selects the grid's first cell. The General page of the lower properties pane is empty for a new table with no fields.

3. Type **EmployeeID** as the first field name, and press Tab to accept the field name and move to the Data Type column. Access adds the default field type, Text.

4. Click to open the Data Type list (see Figure 5.13) and select Number. Alternatively, type **N[umber]** in the list. Typing characters that unambiguously match an item in the drop-down list selects the item.

> **NOTE**
>
> Another selection alternative in drop-down lists is to use Alt+down arrow to open the list, press the up- or down-arrow key to make the selection, and then press Enter.

5. Press F6 to move to or click the Field Size text box in the Field Properties window. Access has already entered Long Integer as the value of the default Field Size property for a Number field.

Figure 5.13
The Data Type list lets you select from one of the nine Access data types or the Lookup Wizard. If you type a text value in a Data Type cell, the value must match the first character or two of one of the entries in the drop-down list.

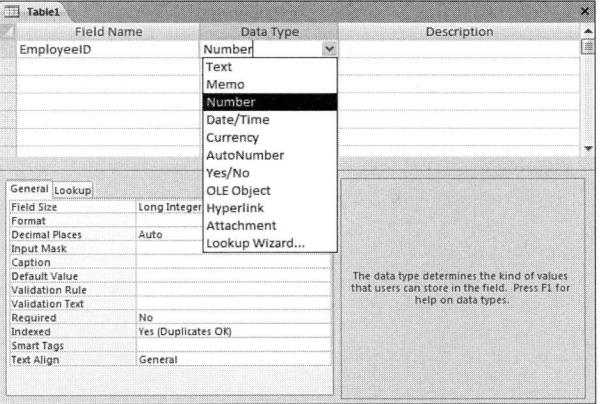

> **NOTE**
>
> Whenever you create a new Number type field, Access enters Long Integer in the Field Size property as the default. Because the EmployeeID field should be a Long Integer, you don't need to set the Field Size property for this field and can skip to step 8; continue with steps 6 and 7 when you enter the other fields from Table 5.8.

6. For Number data types other than Long Integer, select from the list the appropriate Field Size value from Table 5.8, or type the first letter of one of the values of the list, such as **B[yte]** or **S[ingle]**. For Text fields, type the maximum number of characters.

7. Press the down-arrow key or click to select the Format text box, and type **G[eneral]** or select General Number from the list (see Figure 5.14).

Figure 5.14
Select one of the seven standard number formats from the list or type a format string in the Format text box. The General Number format applies if you don't set the Format property value.

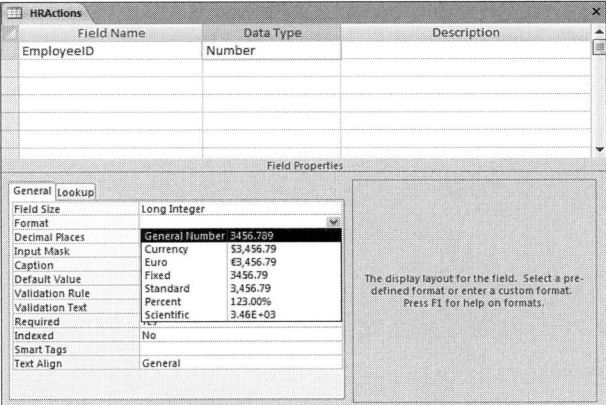

8. Press the down-arrow key, or select the Caption text box, and type **ID** as the caption. ID is used as the Caption property to minimize the column width necessary to display the EmployeeID number.

9. Press the down-arrow key four times, bypassing the Default Value, Validation Rule, and Validation Text properties, and type **Y** in the Required text box. Typing **Y[es]** or **N[o]** is an alternative to selecting Yes or No in the drop-down list.

NOTE

> When entering a Text field with the Required property set to Yes, set the Allow Zero Length property value to No.

10. Press F6 to return to the Table Design grid.

TIP

> Add descriptions to create prompts that appear in the status bar when you are adding or editing records in Run mode's Datasheet view. Although descriptions are optional, it's good database design practice to enter the field's purpose if its use isn't obvious from its Field Name or Caption property.

11. Press Enter to move the caret to the first cell of the next row of the grid.
12. Repeat steps 3 through 11, entering the values shown in Table 5.8 for each of the 11 remaining fields of the HRActions table. N/A (not applicable) means that the entry in Table 5.8 doesn't apply to the field's data type.

Your Table Design grid should now look similar to the one shown in Figure 5.15, with the exception of the optional Description property values. You can double-check your properties' entries by selecting each field name with the arrow keys and reading the values shown in the property text boxes of the Field Properties window.

Figure 5.15
The 12 fields of the new HRActions table fully describe any of the eight types of personnel actions defined by the ActionType codes. Adding the Description property, which can be up to 255 characters long, is optional but recommended.

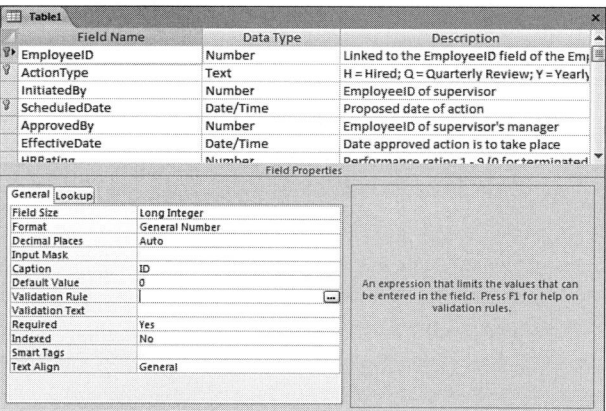

Click the Datasheet View button to view the results of your work. Click Yes when the "Do you want to save the table now?" message opens (see Figure 5.16, top). The Save As dialog opens, requesting that you give your table a name and suggesting the default table name, Table1. Type **HRActions**, as shown in Figure 5.16 (middle), and press Enter or click OK.

At this point, Access displays a message informing you that the new table does not have a primary key (see Figure 5.16, bottom). You add primary keys to the HRActions table later in this chapter, so click No in this message box.

Figure 5.16
When you change the view of a new table that doesn't have a primary key to Datasheet, these three messages appear in sequence.

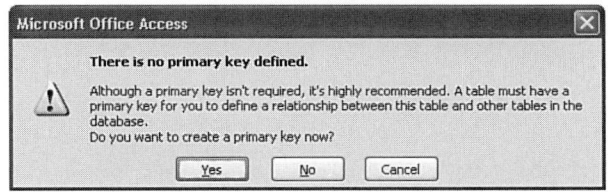

Your table opens in Datasheet view, with its first default record. To view all the fields of your new table, narrow the field name header buttons by dragging to the left the right vertical bar that separates each header. When you finish adjusting your fields' display widths, the HRActions table appears in Datasheet view (see Figure 5.17). Only the tentative append record (a new record that Access adds to your table only if you enter values in the cells) is present. You have more property values to add to your HRActions table, so don't enter data in the tentative append record at this point. If you close the table, a message asks if you want to save your table layout changes. Click Yes.

CREATING TABLES FROM TEMPLATES

The Create ribbon's Tables group has a Table Templates button that opens a gallery of five table designs for tracking applications: Contacts, Tasks, Issues, Events, and Assets. The templates duplicate the primary table of the corresponding database template. Clicking a gallery button adds the table to your database.

Figure 5.17
Adjust the display width of the fields in Datasheet view so all fields appear without scrolling the window. Specifying a Decimal Places property value of 1 results in the 0.0% default entry in the % Comm field.

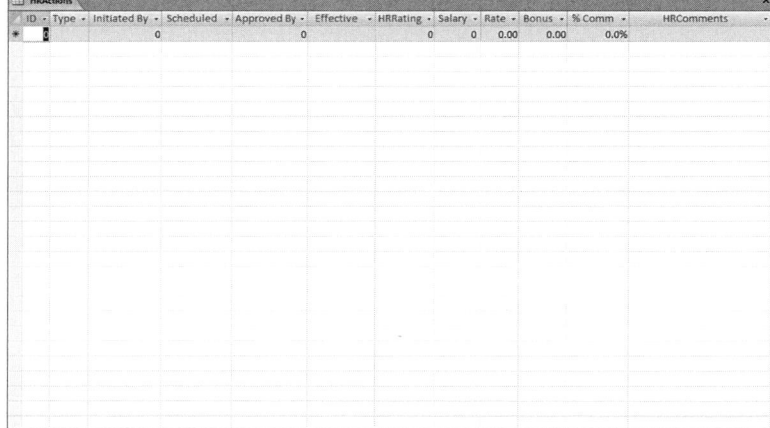

Microsoft offers Table Templates as the replacement for earlier Access versions' Table Wizard. However, the Table Wizard offered a wider variety of table types, enabled users to select desired fields, and included the capability to easily establish relationships with existing database tables. Users of earlier Access version probably will miss the Table Wizard.

CREATING A TABLE DIRECTLY IN DATASHEET VIEW

If you're under pressure to create a set of database tables immediately, Access lets you create tables directly in Datasheet view. Clicking the Table button in the Create ribbon's Tables group adds a sequentially numbered Table# starter table with an autoincrementing ID column for the primary key and an empty Add New Field column. The starter table is the same as that described in the "Creating a New Access Database from Scratch" section near the beginning of this chapter.

You can then enter data directly into the Add New Field column, which becomes a sequentially numbered Field# column when you add the first value. As you enter data, Access analyzes the data you entered and attempts to select a data type for each field that matches the entries. If you add an entry that doesn't match the initially determined data type, a smart tag opens and offers you the option to change the data type, cancel the entry, or seek help on data types (see Figure 5.18). You can edit the field names in the header row by double-clicking Field#. Thus, it's possible to create and populate a table without entering Table Design view.

Creating tables in Datasheet view is an ad hoc shortcut that seldom produces a satisfactory result. Adding tables to a database requires advance planning to ensure that the design follows Chapter 4's normalization rules, employs appropriate data types, and establishes specific relationships to existing tables.

Figure 5.18
Access 2007 lets you create new tables in Datasheet view by typing values in cells of the default table design.

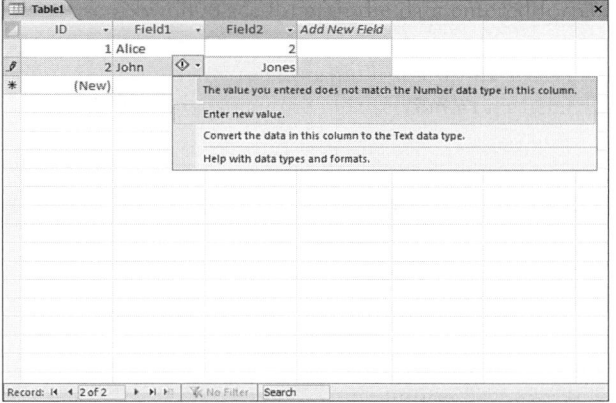

SETTING DEFAULT VALUES OF FIELDS

Access assigns Number and Currency fields a default value of 0; all other field types are empty by default. (Notice that the tentative append record in Figure 5.17 has zeros entered in all the Number and Currency fields.) You can save data entry time by establishing default values for fields; in some cases, Access's default values for Number and Currency fields might be inappropriate, and you must change them. Table 5.9 lists the default values you should enter for the HRActions table's fields.

TABLE 5.9   DEFAULT FIELD VALUES FOR THE HRACTIONS TABLE

Field Name	Default Value	Comments
EmployeeID	**Null**	0 is not a valid Employee ID number, so you should remove Access's default.
ActionType	**Q**	Quarterly performance reviews are the most common personnel action.
InitiatedBy	**Null**	0 is not a valid Employee ID number.
ScheduledDate	**=Date()**	This expression enters today's date from the computer system's clock.
ApprovedBy	**Null**	0 is not a valid Employee ID.
EffectiveDate	**=Date()+28**	This expression enters today's date plus four weeks.
HRRating	**Null**	In many cases, a rating doesn't apply. A 0 rating is reserved for terminated employees.
NewSalary	**Null**	Null represents no change.
NewRate	**Null**	Null represents no change.
NewBonus	**Null**	Null represents no change.

continues

TABLE 5.9 CONTINUED

Field Name	Default Value	Comments
NewCommission	**Null**	Null represents no change.
HRComments	No Entry	Access's default is adequate.

If you don't enter anything in the Default Value text box, you create a Null default value. It's a better database design practice to be explicit when overriding default values, so you replace 0 values with **Null**. You can use Null values for testing whether a value has been entered into a field. Such a test can ensure that users have entered required data.

You use expressions, such as `=Date()+28`, to enter values in fields, make calculations, and perform other useful duties, such as validating data entries. Expressions are discussed briefly in the next section and in much greater detail in Chapter 10, "Understanding Access Operators and Expressions." An equal sign must precede expressions that establish default values.

To assign the new default values from those of Table 5.9 to the fields of the HRActions table, complete these steps:

1. Click the Home ribbon's Datasheet View button. Access selects the first field of the table.

2. Press F6 to switch to the Field Properties window, move the caret to the Default Value text box, and type **Null** for the default value of the EmployeeID field.

3. Press F6 to switch back to the Table Design grid. Move to the next field and press F6 again.

4. Add the default values for the 10 remaining fields having the default entries shown in Table 5.9, repeating steps 1 through 3. For example, after selecting the Default Value text box for the ActionType field, type **Q** to set the default value; Access automatically surrounds Q with double quotes.

5. After completing your default entries, click the View button of the Table Design toolbar, and click Yes when asked if you want to save the table. The HRActions table appears in Datasheet view with the new default entries you assigned (see Figure 5.19).

The Nwind05.accdb database in the \SEUA12\Chaptr05 folder of the accompanying CD-ROM includes the HRActions table, which you can import into Northwind.accdb.

Figure 5.19
Datasheet view of the HRActions table confirms the changes you make to the Default Value property of the fields.

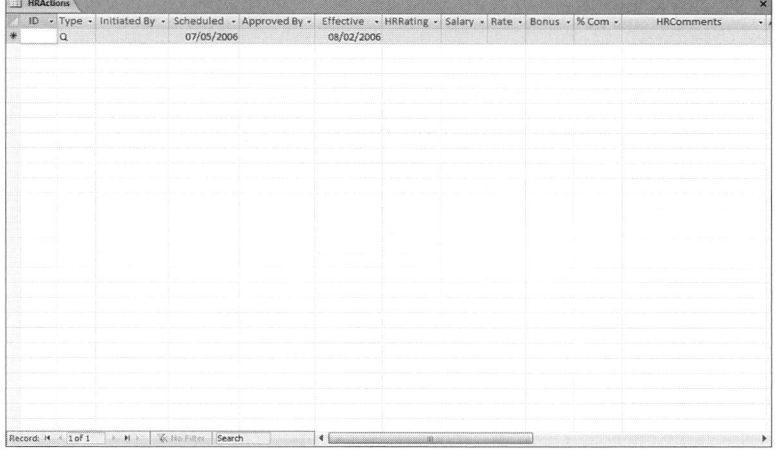

WORKING WITH RELATIONS, KEY FIELDS, AND INDEXES

Your final tasks before adding records to the HRActions table are to determine the relationship between HRActions and an existing table in the database, assign a primary key field, and add indexes to your table.

ESTABLISHING RELATIONSHIPS BETWEEN TABLES

Many records in the HRActions table apply to a single employee whose record appears in the Employees table. The HR department adds a record in HRActions when the employee is hired, and for each quarterly and yearly performance review. Also, any changes made to bonuses or commissions other than as the result of a performance review are added, and employees might be terminated. Over time, the number of records in the HRActions table is likely to be greater by a factor of 10 or more than the number of records in the Employees table. Therefore, the records in the new Personnel table have a many-to-one relationship with the records in the Employees table. Establishing the relationships between new and existing tables when you create a new table enables Access to enforce the relationship when you use the tables in queries, forms, pages, and reports.

→ For a description of the three types of relationships between tables, **see** "Removing Data Redundancy with Relationships," **p. 181**.

Access requires that the two fields participating in the relationship have exactly the same data type. In the case of the Number field data type, the Field Size property of the two fields must be identical. You cannot, for example, create a relationship between an AutoNumber type field (which uses a Long Integer data type) and a field containing Byte, Integer, Single, Double, or Currency data. (You *can* create a relationship between fields having AutoNumber and Long Integer data types.) On the other hand, Access lets you relate two tables by text fields of different lengths. Such a relationship, if created, can lead to strange behavior when you create queries, which is the subject of Part III, "Transforming Data with Queries and PivotTables." As a rule, the relationships between text fields should use fields of the same length.

Access uses a graphical Relationships window to display and create the relationships among tables in a database. To establish the relationships between two tables with Access's Relationships window, using the Employees and HRActions tables as an example, follow these steps:

1. Close the Employees and HRActions tables, and click the Relationships button of the Database Tools ribbon to open the Relationships window (see Figure 5.20).

Figure 5.20
The Relationships window for the Northwind.accdb database displays lines representing the one-to-many relationships between the original sample tables. The 1 symbol indicates the "one" side and the infinity (∞) symbol indicates the "many" side of one-to-many relationships. Bold type identifies primary key fields.

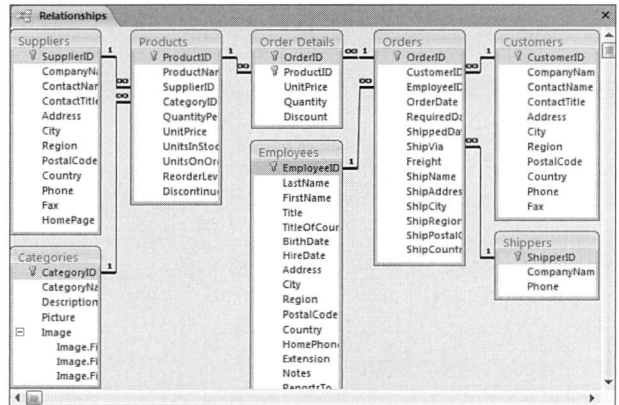

2. Click the Show Table button of the Relationship Tools, Design ribbon to open the Show Table dialog (see Figure 5.21).

Figure 5.21
The Tables page of the Show Table dialog displays a list of all tables in the database.

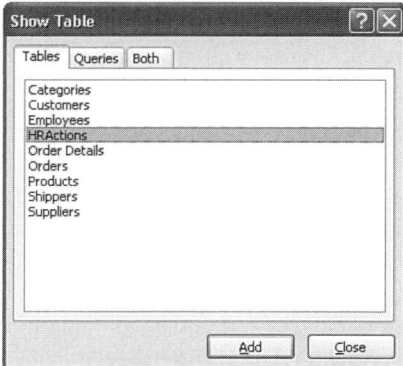

3. For this example, add the HRActions table to the Relationships window by double-clicking the HRActions entry in the Tables list, or by clicking the entry to select it and then clicking the Add button. Click the Close button.

4. Move the HRActions table object under the Products table object, and drag the bottom of the HRActions table object to expose all its fields.

5. The relationship of the HRActions table to the Employees table is based on the HRActions table's EmployeeID field (the foreign key) and the Employees table's EmployeeID field (the primary key). Click the Employees table's EmployeeID field and, holding the left mouse button down, drag it to the HRActions table's EmployeeID field. Release the mouse button to drop the field symbol on the EmployeeID field. The Edit Relationships dialog opens (see Figure 5.22).

Figure 5.22
Establishing a relationship by dragging a field symbol from one table object to another opens the Edit Relationships dialog. By default, the name of the table with a primary key field appears in the Table/Query list and the other table appears in the Related Table/Query list. In this case, Access automatically detects a one-to-many relationship.

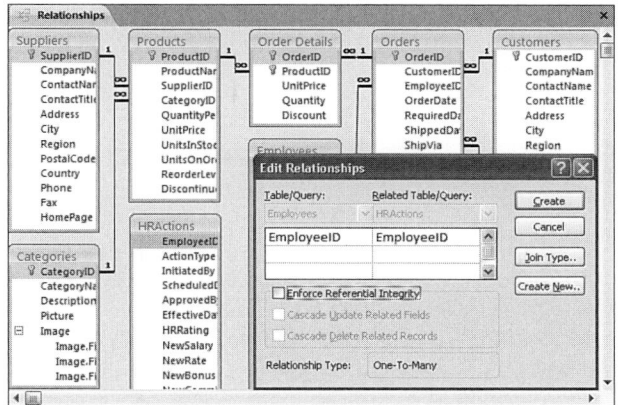

6. Click the Join Type button to display the Join Properties dialog shown in Figure 5.23. You are creating a one-to-many join between the Employees table's EmployeeID field (the one side) and the HRActions table's EmployeeID field (the many side). You want to display all Employee records, even if one or more of these records don't have a corresponding record in HRActions. To do so, select option 2 in the Join Properties dialog. Click OK to close the dialog and return to the Edit Relationships dialog.

Figure 5.23
The Join Properties dialog lets you specify one of three types of one-to-many joins for the relationship. Option 1 is called an *INNER JOIN* by SQL, 2 is a *LEFT OUTER JOIN*, and 3 is a *RIGHT OUTER JOIN*.

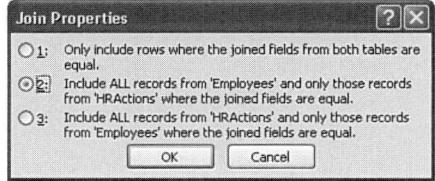

7. The Edit Relationships dialog offers the Enforce Referential Integrity check box so that you can specify that Access perform validation testing and accept entries in the EmployeeID field that correspond only to values present in the Employees table's EmployeeID field. This process is called *enforcing (or maintaining) referential integrity*. (The following section discusses referential integrity.) The relationship between these two tables requires enforcing referential integrity, so make sure to select this check box (see Figure 5.24).

Figure 5.24
Marking the Enforce Referential Integrity check box ensures that values you enter in the HRActions table's EmployeeID field have corresponding values in the EmployeeID field of the Employees table.

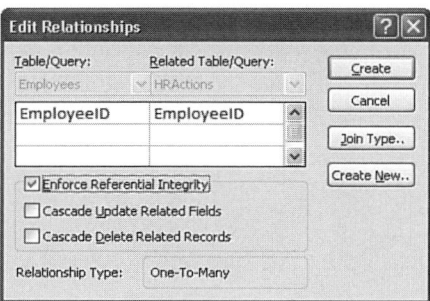

NOTE

Access automatically maintains referential integrity of tables by providing check boxes you can mark to cause cascading updates to, and cascade deletions of, related records when the primary table changes. The following section discusses cascading updates and deletions. Access enables the cascade check boxes only if you elect to enforce referential integrity.

8. Click the Create button to accept the new relationship and display it in the Relationships window (see Figure 5.25).

Figure 5.25
The Relationships window displays the newly added one-to-many relationship between the Employees and HRActions table.

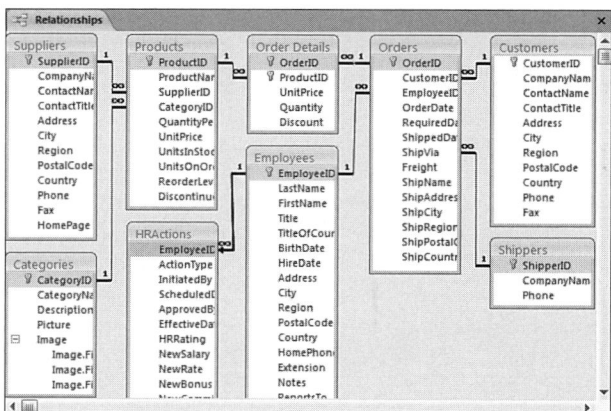

9. Close the Relationships window, and click Yes when asked to confirm that you want to save the layout changes to the Relationships diagram.

 Access uses the relationship that you've created when you design queries and design forms, pages, and reports that use data in the HRActions table. You can print the contents of the Relationships window as a report by clicking the Relationship Tools Design ribbon's Relationship Report button.

CASCADING UPDATES AND DELETIONS

Access's cascading deletion and cascading update options for tables with enforced referential integrity makes maintaining referential integrity easy: Just mark the Cascade Update Related Fields and Cascade Delete Related Records check boxes. In this case, marking the Cascade Update Related Fields check box is unnecessary, because you can't change the value of the AutoNumber EmployeeID field of the Employees table. You can delete records in the Employees table, so marking the Cascade Delete Related Records check box prevents orphan records—records without a corresponding record in the Employees table—from appearing in the HRActions table.

NOTE

> Automatically enforcing referential integrity is usually, but not always, good database design practice. An example of where you would not want to employ cascade deletions is between the EmployeeID fields of the Orders and Employee tables. If you terminate an employee and then attempt to delete the employee's record, you might accidentally choose to delete the dependent records in the Orders table. Deleting records in the Orders table could have serious consequences from a marketing and accounting standpoint. (In practice, however, you probably wouldn't delete a terminated employee's record. Instead, you'd change a Status field value to Terminated or the equivalent.)

5

SELECTING A PRIMARY KEY

Using a primary key field is a simple method of preventing the duplication of records in a table. Access requires that you specify a primary key if you want to create a one-to-one relationship or to update records from two or more tables in the same datasheet or form. (Chapter 11, "Creating Multitable and Crosstab Queries," covers this subject.)

Technically, assigning a primary key field to each table isn't an absolute requirement. The ANSI SQL specification doesn't define the term *primary key*; however, relational theory requires that one or more field values identify each record uniquely. Access considers a table without a primary key field an oddity; therefore, when you make changes to the table and return to Design view, you might see a message stating that you haven't created a key field. (Access 2000 and later ask only once whether you want to add a primary key field.) Related tables can have primary key fields and usually do. A primary key field based on field values is useful for preventing the accidental addition of duplicate records.

You can create primary keys on more than one field. In the case of the HRActions table, a primary key that prevents duplicate records *must* consist of more than one field. If you establish the rule that no more than one personnel action of a given type for a particular employee can be scheduled for the same date, you can create a primary key that consists of the EmployeeID, ActionType, and ScheduledDate fields. When you create a primary key, Access creates a no-duplicates index based on the primary key.

To create a multiple-field primary key, called a *composite primary key*, and a primary key index for the HRActions table, follow these steps:

1. Open the HRActions table in Design view.
2. Click the selection button for the EmployeeID field.
3. Ctrl+click the selection button for the ActionType field. In most instances, when you Ctrl+click a selection button, you can make multiple selections.
4. Ctrl+click the selection button for the ScheduledDate field.
5. Click the Table Tools Design ribbon's Primary Key button. Symbols of keys appear in each previously selected field, indicating their inclusion in the primary key.
6. To verify the sequence of the fields in the primary key, click the Show/Hide group's Indexes button to display the Indexes dialog, shown in Figure 5.26.

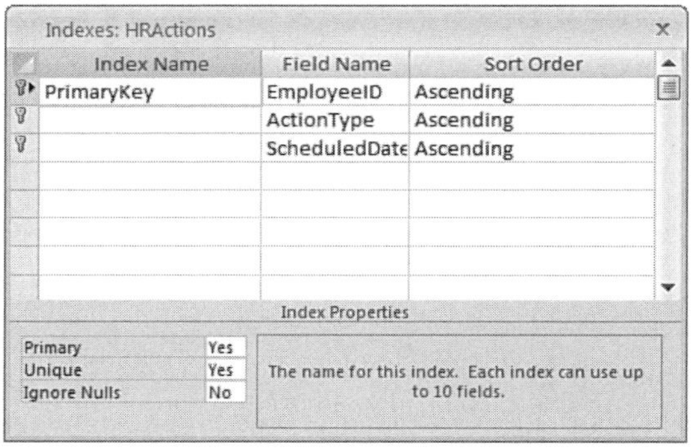

Figure 5.26
The three fields of the HRActions table's composite primary key have indexes.

Index Name	Field Name	Sort Order
PrimaryKey	EmployeeID	Ascending
	ActionType	Ascending
	ScheduledDate	Ascending

Index Properties

Primary	Yes	
Unique	Yes	The name for this index. Each index can use up
Ignore Nulls	No	to 10 fields.

7. Close the Indexes dialog, and press Ctrl+S to save your table design changes.

You now have a multiple-field primary key and a corresponding index on the HRActions table that precludes the addition of records that duplicate records with the same primary key value.

ADDING INDEXES TO TABLES

Although Access creates one or more indexes on the primary key, you might want to create an index on some other field or fields in the table. Indexes speed searches for records that contain specific types of data. For example, you might want to find all HRActions that occurred in a given period and all quarterly reviews for all employees in ScheduledDate sequence. If you have many records in the table, an index speeds up the searching process. A disadvantage of multiple indexes is that data entry operations are slowed by the time it takes to update the additional indexes. You can create as many as 32 indexes for each Access table, and five of those can be of the multiple-field type. Each multiple-field index can include as many as 10 fields.

TIP

> You should add only indexes you need to improve search performance. Each index you add slows the addition of new records, because adding a new record requires an addition to each index. Similarly, editing indexed fields is slower, because the edit updates the record and the index. When you create relationships between tables, Access automatically creates a hidden index on the related fields, if the index doesn't already exist. Hidden indexes count against the 32-index limit of each table. If an extra index appears in the Indexes dialog, see the "Extra Indexes Added by Access" item in the "Troubleshooting" section near the end of this chapter.

To create a single-field index for the HRActions table based on the EffectiveDate field, and a multiple-field index based on the ActionType and the ScheduledDate fields, follow these steps:

1. Select the EffectiveDate field by clicking its selection button.

2. Select the Indexed text box in the Field Properties window.

3. Open the Indexed drop-down list by clicking the arrow button or pressing Alt+down arrow (see Figure 5.27).

Figure 5.27
You can add an index on a single field by setting the value of the Indexed property to Yes (Duplicates OK) or Yes (No Duplicates).

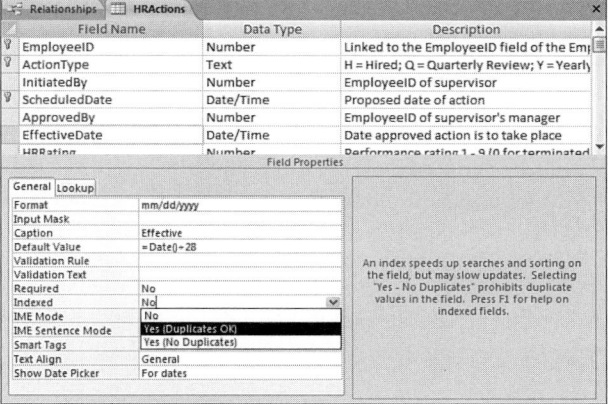

4. In this case, duplicate entries on the same date are likely, so select Yes (Duplicates OK) and close the list. You can create only a single-field index with this method.

5. Click the Indexes button. The Primary Key and EffectiveDate indexes already created appear in the list boxes. Type **ActionTypeEffectiveDate** as the name of the composite

index, and then select ActionType in the Field Name drop-down list. Move the caret to the next row of the Field Name column and select ScheduledDate to create a multiple-field index on these two fields (see Figure 5.28).

Figure 5.28
You add multiple-field indexes in the Indexes dialog.

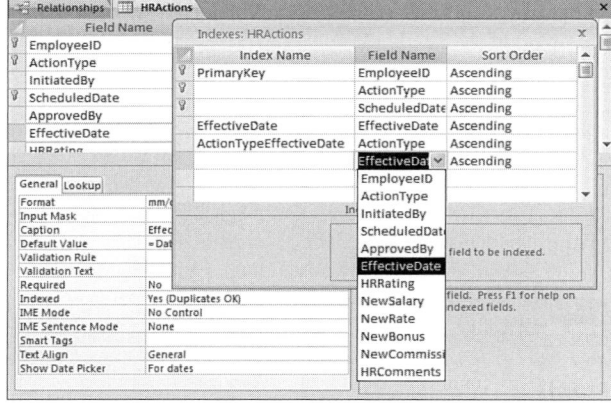

6. In the Ignore Nulls row of the Index Properties pane for the EffectiveDate field, select Yes so that records without an EffectiveDate value aren't included in the index.

7. Click the Datasheet View button, and click Yes to save your design changes.

You now have three indexes for the Primary Key table: the index automatically created for the primary key, the single-key index on EffectiveDate, and the multiple-key index on ActionType and ScheduledDate.

ALTERING FIELDS AND RELATIONSHIPS

When you're designing a database, you often discover that you must alter the original choices you made for the sequence of fields in a table, data types, or relationships between tables. One reason for adding substantial numbers of records to tables during the testing process is to discover any necessary changes before putting the database into daily use.

You can change formats, validation rules and text, lengths of Text fields, and other minor items in the table by changing to Design mode, selecting the field to modify, and making the changes in the property boxes. Changing data types can cause a loss of data, however, so be sure to read the later "Changing Field Data Types and Sizes" section before you attempt to make such changes. Changing the data type of a field that participates in a relationship with another table requires that you delete and, if possible, re-create the relationship. Changing relationships between tables is considered a drastic action if you have entered a substantial amount of data, so this subject is also covered later in "Changing Relationships Between Tables," also later in this chapter.

NOTE

> Access 2000 introduced the Name AutoCorrect feature. Renaming a database object in earlier versions required you to search manually through all objects of your database and change all references to the renamed objects. The Name AutoCorrect feature handles the corrections for you; when you open a database object, Access scans and fixes discrepancies.
>
> New databases you create in Access 2007, whether in 2000 or 2002/2003 file format, have this feature turned on by default. Databases you open as .mdb files or convert from previous versions require you to turn on Name AutoCorrect by opening the Access Options dialog's Current Database page, and then marking the Track Name AutoCorrect Info and Perform Name AutoCorrect check boxes in the Name Autocorrect Options group. Marking the Log Name Autocorrect Changes check box creates a Name AutoCorrect Log table in the database that maintains a record of all changes made by the Perform Name Autocorrect feature.
>
> Track Name AutoCorrect must be enabled to view object dependencies and enable table field property change propagation, but Perform Name AutoCorrect isn't required.

→ To learn how field property value changes propagate to dependent database objects, **see** "Working with Object Dependencies and Access Smart Tags," **p. 248**.

REARRANGING THE SEQUENCE OF FIELDS IN A TABLE

If you're typing historical data in Datasheet view, you might find that the sequence of entries isn't optimum. You might, for example, be entering data from a printed form with a top-to-bottom, left-to-right sequence that doesn't correspond to the left-to-right sequence of the corresponding fields in your table. Access makes rearranging the order of fields in tables a matter of dragging and dropping fields where you want them. You can decide whether to make the revised layout temporary or permanent when you close the table.

To rearrange the fields of the HRActions table, follow these steps:

1. Click the Datasheet View button. Rearranging the sequence of fields is the only table design change you can implement in Access's Datasheet view.

2. Click the field name button of the field you want to move. This action selects the field name button and all the field's data cells.

3. Hold down the left mouse button while over the field name button. The mouse pointer turns into the drag-and-drop symbol, and a heavy vertical bar marks the field's leftmost position.

4. Move the vertical bar to the new position for the selected field and release the mouse button. The field assumes the new position.

5. When you close the HRActions table, you see the familiar Save Changes message box. To make the field location modification permanent, click Yes; otherwise, click No.

Rearranging the field sequence in Datasheet view doesn't change the order in Design view's fields grid. To reposition fields in Design view, click the select button of the row of the field you want to move and then drag the row vertically to a new location. Changing the position of a table's field doesn't change any of the field's other properties.

CHANGING FIELD DATA TYPES AND SIZES

You might have to change a field data type as the design of your database develops or if you import tables from another database, a spreadsheet, or a text file. If you import tables, the data type automatically chosen by Access during the importation process probably won't be what you want, especially with Number fields. Chapter 8, "Linking, Importing, and Exporting Data," discusses importing and exporting tables and data from other applications. Another example of altering field properties is changing the number of characters in fixed-length Text fields to accommodate entries that are longer than expected, or converting Text to Memo fields.

CAUTION

Before making changes to the field data types of a table that contains a substantial amount of data, back up the table by copying or exporting it to a backup Access database. If you accidentally lose parts of the data contained in the table (such as decimal fractions) while changing the field data type, you can import the backup table to your current database. Chapter 8 covers the simple and quick process of exporting Access tables. After creating a backup database file, you can copy a table to Windows Clipboard and then paste the table to the backup database. The later section "Copying and Pasting Tables" discusses Clipboard operations.

→ For details on propagating field property value changes to dependent database objects, **see** "Working with Object Dependencies and Access Smart Tags," **p. 248**.

NUMERIC FIELDS

Changing a data type to one that requires more bytes of storage is, in almost all circumstances, safe; you don't sacrifice your data's accuracy. Changing a numeric data type from Byte to Integer to Long Integer to Single and, finally, to Double doesn't affect your data's value because each change, except for Long Integer to Single, requires more bytes of storage for a data value. Changing from Long Integer to Single and Single to Currency involves the same number of bytes and decreases the accuracy of the data only in exceptional circumstances. The exceptions can occur when you are using very high numbers or extremely small decimal fractions, such as in some scientific and engineering calculations.

On the other hand, if you change to a data type with fewer data bytes required to store it, Access might truncate your data. If you change from a fixed-point format (Currency) or floating-point format (Single or Double) to Byte, Integer, or Long Integer, any decimal fractions in your data are truncated. Truncation means reducing the number of digits in a number to fit the new Field Size property that you choose. If you change a numeric data type from Single to Currency, for example, you might lose your Single data in the fifth, sixth, and seventh decimal places (if any exists) because Single provides as many as seven decimal places and Currency provides only four.

You can't convert any field type to an AutoNumber-type field. You can use the AutoNumber field only as a unique record identifier; the only way you can enter a new value in an AutoNumber field is by appending new records. You can't edit an AutoNumber field. When you delete a record in Access, the AutoNumber values of the higher-numbered records are not reduced by 1.

TEXT FIELDS

You can convert Text fields to Memo fields without Access truncating your text. You can't add indexes to Memo fields, so any index(es) on the converted Text field disappear. Access won't let Memo fields participate in relationships.

Converting a Memo field to a Text field truncates characters beyond the 255-character limit of Text fields. Similarly, if you convert a variable-length Text field to a fixed-length field, and some records contain character strings that exceed the length you chose, Access truncates these strings.

CONVERSION BETWEEN NUMBER, DATE, AND TEXT FIELD DATA TYPES

Access makes many conversions between Number, Date, and Text field data types for you. Conversion from Number or Date to Text field data types does not follow the Format property that you assigned to the original data type. Numbers are converted with the General Number format, and dates use the Short Date format. Access is intelligent in the methods it uses to convert suitable Text fields to Number data types. For example, it accepts dollar signs, commas, and decimals during the conversion, but ignores trailing spaces. Access converts dates and times in the following Text formats to internal Date/Time values that you then can format the way you want:

```
1/4/2007 10:00 AM
04-Jan-07
January 4
10:00
10:00:00
```

NOTE

> Access adds the current year when converting January 4 from text to a DateTime value. Converting text time values without a date to a DateTime value sets the date to December 30, 1899.

CHANGING RELATIONSHIPS BETWEEN TABLES

Adding new relationships between tables is a straightforward process, but changing relationships might require you to change data types so that the related fields have the same data type. To change a relationship between two tables, complete the following steps:

1. Close the tables involved in the relationship.

 2. Display the Relationships window by clicking the Database Tools ribbon's Relationships button.

3. Click the join line that connects to the field whose data type you want to change. When you select the join line, the line becomes darker (wider).

4. Press Delete to clear the existing relationship. Click Yes when the message box asks you to confirm your deletion.

5. If you intend to change the data type of a field that constitutes or is a member field of the primary table's primary key, delete all other relationships that exist between the primary table and every other table to which it is related.

6. Change the data types of the fields in the tables so that the data types match in the new relationships.

7. Re-create the relationships by using the procedure described earlier in the section "Establishing Relationships Between Tables."

WORKING WITH OBJECT DEPENDENCIES AND ACCESS SMART TAGS

In versions of Access earlier than 2003, changing a table field's property value—such as the Format or Input Mask specification—often wreaked havoc on other Access form and report objects that were dependent on the field. Typically, you bind form and report control objects, such as text boxes, to fields of a table or query. In Access terminology, the control objects *inherit* the properties of the underlying table fields.

NOTE

Technically, control objects don't support inheritance as defined by standards for object-oriented programming. Instead, control objects contain a copy of the property values of the source field. The copied properties aren't automatically updated when you change the source field's property values.

ENABLING AND VIEWING OBJECT DEPENDENCIES

Access 2007 offers a feature called *object dependencies*, which enables field property change propagation to dependent objects, such as queries, forms, and reports. Before you can use change propagation, you must generate dependency data for your database. The version of Northwind.mdb included on the CD-ROM doesn't have the required hidden object dependency table. To enable the object dependency feature of the Northwind.mdb file in the \SEUA12\Nwind folder, do this:

1. Open \SEUA12\Nwind\Northwind.mdb and close all open Northwind objects except the Navigation Pane.

2. Select a table, such as HRActions, in the Navigation Pane, and mark the Database Tools' Object Dependencies check box in the Show/Hide group. If the Name AutoCorrect feature isn't turned on, a message box opens; click OK to enable Name AutoCorrect.

3. Click OK in the message box that asks if you want to update object dependencies (see Figure 5.29).

Figure 5.29
Before you can display object dependencies, you must generate a hidden dependency table for the current database.

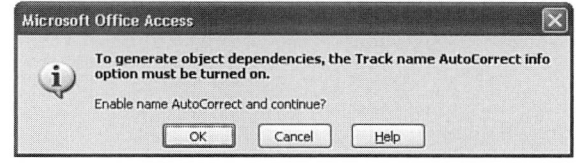

After a few seconds, the Object Dependencies properties sheet displays the dependencies for the selected table (HRActions for this example). The Employees table depends on the HRActions table because of the relationship you created in the earlier "Establishing Relationships Between Tables" section (see Figure 5.30). Some types of objects, such as union queries (Query: Customers and Suppliers by City) and SQL-specific queries (Query: Products Above Average Price) don't support dependency tracking, so they are ignored. When you select the option Objects That I Depend On, the Employees table appears, but the Ignored Objects node disappears from the list.

Figure 5.30
The Employees table depends on the HRActions table, and vice versa, because of the one-to-many relationship between the EmployeeID fields of the two tables.

NOTE

> Field property change propagation doesn't apply to changing the Name property of a field. Access's Name AutoCorrect feature propagates field name changes. As mentioned earlier in the "Altering Fields and Relationships" section, Track Name AutoCorrect must be enabled to generate object dependency data and enable viewing of dependencies in the Object Dependencies properties sheet.

At this point, no queries, forms, or reports depend on the HRActions table. To view multiple object dependencies, select the Customers table and mark the Object Dependencies check box. One table, three queries, five forms, and a report depend on the Customers table (see Figure 5.31). Click the + symbol for a dependent object to display that object's dependencies in a tree view.

Figure 5.31
Multiple Access objects depend on the Northwind 2003.accdb database's Customers table. The Orders table has even more dependencies than the Customers table.

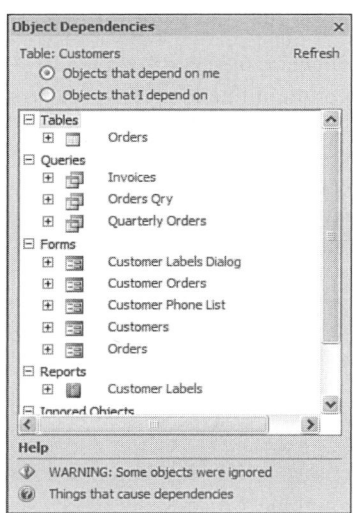

ACTIVATING THE ACCESS PROPERTY OPTIONS SMART TAG

Access uses a special-purpose Property Options smart tag to propagate altered field property values. To activate this smart tag, open the Customers table in Design view, temporarily change the CustomerID field's Input Mask property value from >LLLLL to **>LLLL**. When you move the cursor to the Caption field, the smart tag icon appears to the left of the property value text box (see Figure 5.32). Moving the mouse pointer over the icon changes its color, exposes a drop-down arrow, and adds a Property Update Options screen tip. Clicking the arrow opens the single active option—Update Input Mask Everywhere CustomerID Is Used. Don't click the option in this case; return the Input Mask property to its original value, which causes the smart tag option to disappear. Close the table without saving your changes.

Figure 5.32
Opening the Property Options drop-down list displays the single option that updates dependent objects with the altered property value. The alternative is to get help for the field properties propagation feature.

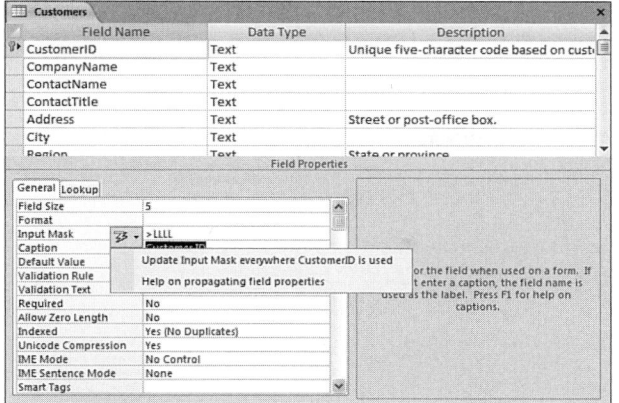

> **TIP**
>
> If you click the option, you must repeat the process with **>LLLLL** as the Input Mask value to return the objects to their original condition.

> **NOTE**
>
> The object dependencies feature and Property Options smart tags aren't available in Access data projects (ADP).

ADDING AN INTERNET-BASED SMART TAG TO A FIELD

 Access 2007 also supports smart tags linked to Web pages. The only Web-based smart tag included with the product is Financial Symbol, which links to stock quotes, company reports, and recent company news from MSN MoneyCentral. To give this smart tag a test drive, do the following:

1. Create a new table with a field named Symbol and, optionally, another field named Company.

2. Select the Symbol field, move the cursor to the Smart Tags property's text box, and click the builder button to open the Smart Tags dialog.

3. Mark the Financial Symbol check box (see Figure 5.33), and click OK to add "urn:schemas-microsoft-com:office:smarttags#stockticker" as the SmartTags property's value.

4. Change to Datasheet view, and add a few NASDAQ and New York Stock Exchange stock symbols to the Symbols field. As you add symbols, a triangular marker is present at the bottom right of the cell and a smart tag information icon appears adjacent to the cell.

5

Figure 5.33
Records in a table with a Smart Tag property value specified for a field have an identifier in the lower-right corner of the field and display a smart tag icon when selected.

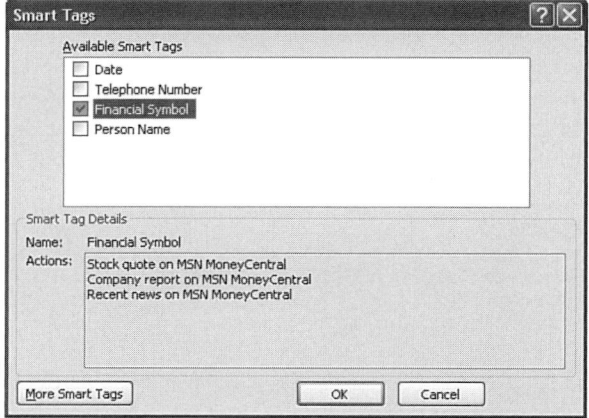

5. Move the mouse pointer over the icon, and click the arrow to open the Smart Tag Options list (see Figure 5.34).

Figure 5.34
Selecting the smart tag icon and opening its drop-down list displays the available smart tag actions.

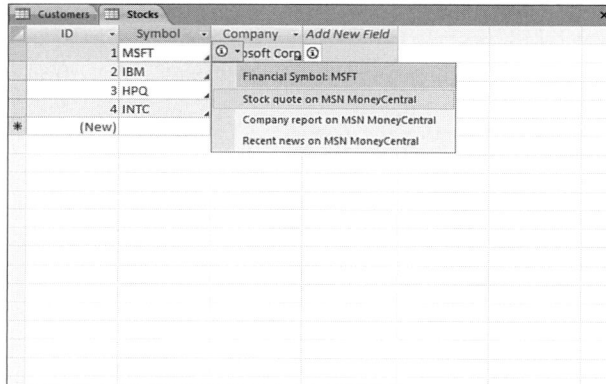

6. Select one of the options—Stock Quote on MSN MoneyCentral for this example—to open the specified Web page (see Figure 5.35).

Custom smart tags, such as Financial Symbol, are defined by XML documents. The `urn:schemas-microsoft-com:office:smarttags#stockticker` property value is the Universal Resource Name (URN) for the custom smart tag `type` attribute value. The corresponding custom smart tag is defined by the Stocks.xml document in Windows XP's or Vista's \Program Files\Common Files\Microsoft Shared\Smart Tag\Lists\1033\ folder (for the U.S. English locale). Navigate to and double-click Stocks.xml to open the document in Internet Explorer (see Figure 5.36). The three `<FL:action>` elements define the action options you see when opening the list (refer to Figure 5.36).

Figure 5.35
The MSN Money site displays the current Microsoft (MSFT) stock quotation.

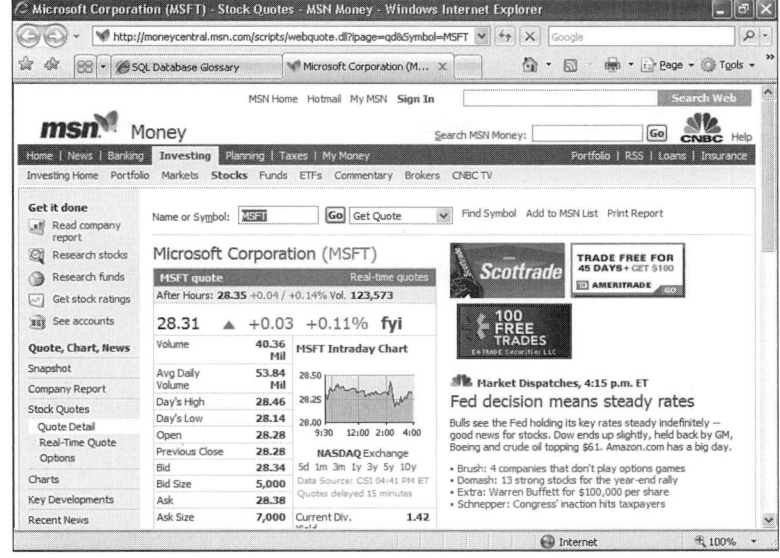

Figure 5.36
These *<FL:action>* elements of the Stocks.xml document generate two of the three fixed list *(FL)* items for the MSN Money Financial Symbols smart tag.

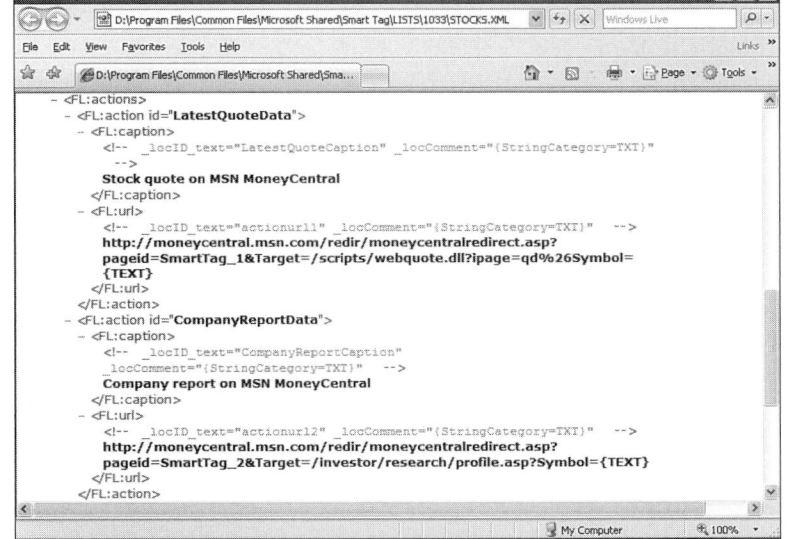

5

NOTE

Creating custom smart tags is beyond the scope of this book. If you want to learn more about Microsoft smart tag technology, go to http://msdn.microsoft.com and search for "smart tag" with the double-quotes included in the search term.

COPYING AND PASTING TABLES

To copy a complete table or the records of a table to the Windows Clipboard, use the same methods that apply to most other Windows applications. (Using the Clipboard to paste individual records or sets of records into a table is one of the subjects of the next chapter.) You can copy tables into other databases, such as a general-purpose backup database, by using the Clipboard.

To copy a table to another Access database, a destination database must exist. To create a backup database and copy the contents of the HRActions table to the database, follow these steps:

1. Expand the Navigation Pane, if necessary.
2. Click the Tables bar, if necessary, to display the list of tables.
3. Select the table that you want to copy to the new database.
4. Click the Copy button on the Home ribbon or press Ctrl+C.

   If you plan to copy the table to your current database, skip to step 7.
5. If you've created a destination backup database, click the Office button and click its link in the Recent Documents link or click Open to open the database; then skip to step 7.
6. To create a backup database, click the Office, Manage, and Back Up Database buttons to open the Save As dialog. Accept the default filename, which appends the current date in YYYY-MM-DD format, or name the new database Backup.accdb or another appropriate filename.
7. Click the Home ribbon's Paste button, press Ctrl+V, or choose Edit, Paste to open the Paste Table As dialog (see Figure 5.37).

Figure 5.37
The Paste Table As dialog lets you paste a backup copy of a table into the current or another database.

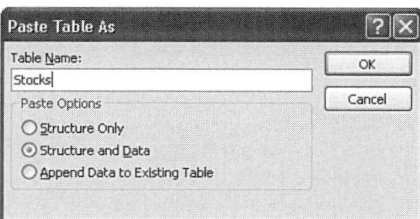

8. You have three options for pasting the backup table to the destination database. The most common choice is Structure and Data, with which you can create a new table or replace the data in a table with the name you enter in the Table Name text box. You can also paste only the structure and then append data to the table later by selecting Structure Only, or append the records to an existing table of the name that you enter. For this example, accept the default: Structure and Data.
9. Your current or backup database now has a copy of the table that you selected, and the name you entered appears in the Navigation Pane. You can save multiple copies of the

same table under different names if you're making a series of changes to the table that might affect the integrity of the data that it contains.

To delete a table from a database, select the table name in the Navigation Pane and then press Delete. A confirmation message appears. Click Yes to delete the table forever. You can't undo deleting a table.

USING THE TABLE ANALYZER WIZARD

Access 2007's Table Analyzer Wizard detects cells containing repeated data in table columns and proposes to create two new related tables to eliminate the repetition. This wizard uses the Lookup Wizard—described in Chapter 11—to create the relationship between the two new tables. After the Wizard creates the new related tables, *NewName* and *Lookup*, your original table is renamed to *TableName*_OLD, and the Wizard creates a one-to-many INNER JOIN query named *TableName* to return a result set that duplicates the Datasheet view of the original table. So, you need not change the references to *TableName* in your Access application objects.

The *Lookup* table must have a valid primary key field to provide unambiguous association of a single record in the lookup table with a foreign key field in the *NewName* table. One of the problems associated with repetitious data is data entry errors, such as occasional misspelling of a company name or an address element in *Lookup*. The Table Analyzer Wizard detects and displays instances of minor mismatches in repeated cell values, such as a missing apostrophe, for correction. If such errors aren't corrected, the *Lookup* table includes spurious, almost-duplicate entries that violate the rules of table normalization.

Northwind.accdb's Orders table has a set of fields for shipping addresses. The data in these fields is the same for every order placed by each customer with three exceptions: order numbers 10248, 10249, and 10260. Shipping addresses comprise the bulk of the data in the Orders table, so removal of duplicate shipping information greatly reduces the size of the Orders table. Placing shipping addresses in a lookup table also offers the opportunity to streamline the data entry process.

> **NOTE**
>
> The Access 97 and 2000 versions of the Table Analyzer Wizard had several bugs that resulted in error messages or spurious typographical error entries. The Access 2007 version corrects these problems.

To demonstrate the use of the Table Analyzer Wizard to eliminate duplicate shipping address information in the Orders table of Northwind.accdb, follow these steps:

1. Use the Clipboard method—described in the preceding section—to create a copy of the Orders table named SalesOrders in the Northwind.accdb database. Working with a copy prevents making changes to Northwind.accdb's sample tables that would affect later examples in this book.

5

2. Launch the Table Analyzer Wizard by clicking the Analyze Tables button in the Database Tools ribbon's Analyze group.

3. Skip the two introductory dialogs by clicking the Next button twice to reach the Table Selection dialog shown in Figure 5.38.

Figure 5.38
Select the table to analyze in the third Table Analyzer Wizard dialog.

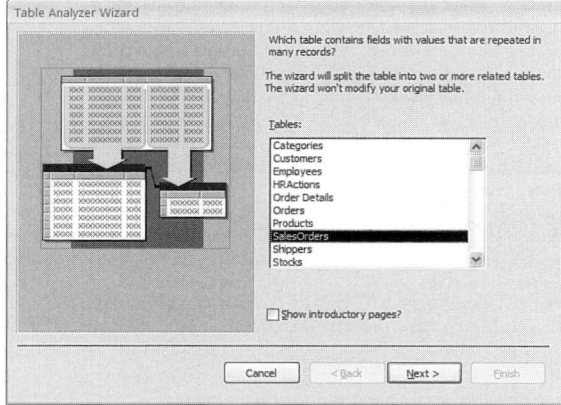

4. Select the table with the duplicated data in the Tables list box (the SalesOrders table for this example) and clear the Show Introductory Pages? check box. Click Next to continue.

5. You want to choose the fields for the *Lookup* table, so select the No, I Want To Decide option, and click Next. The wizard displays a list of fields in the SalesOrders table renamed to Table1.

6. Click to select in the Table1 field list the first of the fields with duplicated information, ShipName; then press Shift and click the last of the fields to move, ShipCountry (see Figure 5.39).

Figure 5.39
Select the fields with the duplicate data to move to a new lookup table. For this example, the fields to select begin with "Ship."

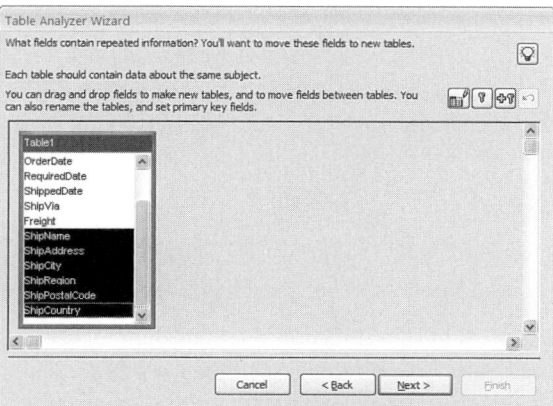

7. Holding the left mouse button down, drag the selected fields from the field list to an empty area to the right of the Table1 list. When you release the mouse button, the wizard creates a new field list for proposed Table1 with a many-to-one relationship between Table1 and Table2. The relationship is based on a lookup field in Table1 and a Generated Unique ID (AutoNumber) field in Table2. An input box opens to rename Table1; type **ShipAddresses** in the Table Name text box (see Figure 5.40). Click OK to close the input box.

Figure 5.40
The Wizard designs a lookup table to contain the fields moved from the source table, and opens an input box in which you assign a name to the lookup table.

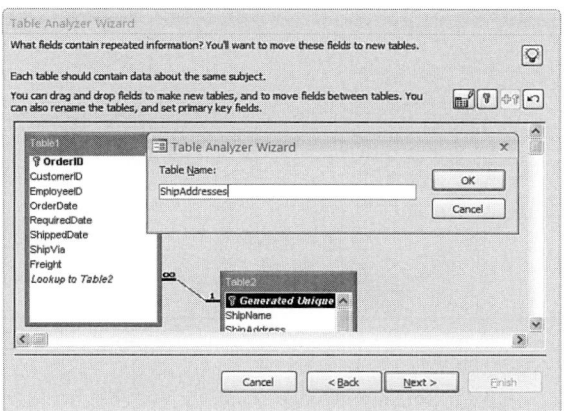

8. CustomerID is a better choice than an AutoNumber field for the initial primary key field of ShipAddresses, because there's currently only one correct ShipAddress per customer in the Orders table. Click and drag the CustomerID field from the Table1 field list to the ShipAddresses field list. With the CustomerID field selected in the ShipAddresses field list, click the Set Unique Identifier button (the one with the key icon only). The Generated Unique ID field disappears and the CustomerID field becomes the primary key for the proposed ShipAddress table (see Figure 5.41). Click Next to continue.

Figure 5.41
Specify the CustomerID field as the primary key for the ShipAddresses lookup table.

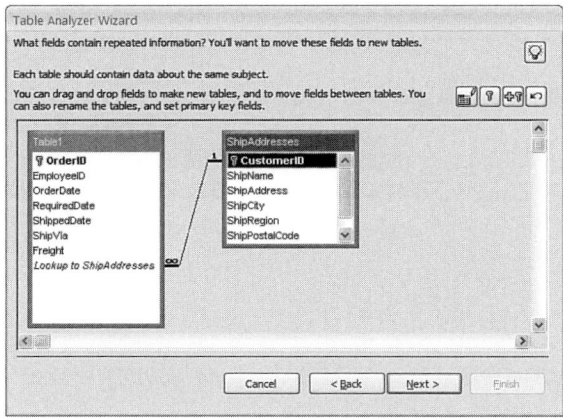

5

9. If the Wizard detects a misspelling of an entry in the lookup table, it opens a Correcting Typographical Errors… dialog. The wizard bases the value in the Correction column on the frequency of exact duplication of records. In this case, the wizard has detected two ShipAddress values for Old World Delicatessen (see Figure 5.42). Click the Next Key >>> button.

Figure 5.42
The Wizard detects and proposes to correct a misspelled shipping address, which actually reflects a second shipping address. Two additional records have different shipping addresses, which call for shipment to a destination other than the customer's billing address.

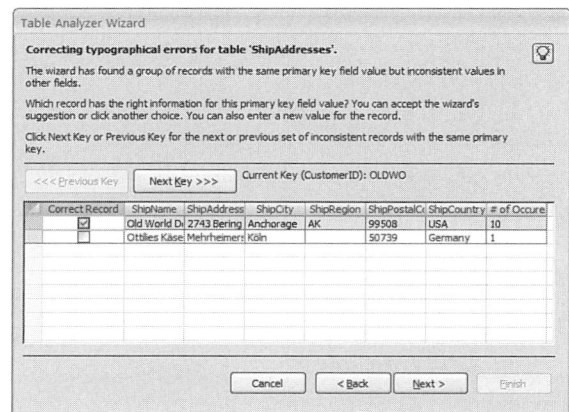

10. Click the Next Key >>> button three times to view the three additional records (10260 for OLDWO, 10249 for TRADH, and 10248 for WILMK) with different shipping addresses. Shipping information in the three records later reverts to the values selected in the check boxes, because the Wizard can't handle multiple shipping addresses for a single primary key value.

11. Click Next, and the Wizard proposes to create a query, in this case named SalesOrders, that substitutes for the original SalesOrders table. Accept the default option, Yes, Create the Query. Clear the Display Help check box to prevent two wizard Help screens from appearing when you complete the operation.

12. Click Finish to create the SalesOrders query, and then open the SalesOrders query.

13. Select the Lookup to ShipAddresses field and click the down-arrow button to open the lookup list, which displays the shipping addresses extracted from the SalesOrders table (see Figure 5.43). Notice that the list has only one entry for ALKFI, proving that the wizard corrected the spelling error.

The wizard has renamed the original SalesOrders table as SalesOrders_OLD, and substituted the SalesOrders query for the SalesOrders table. The Nwind05.accdb database in the \SEUA12\Chaptr05 folder of the accompanying CD-ROM includes the tables and query created in the preceding steps.

Figure 5.43
The SalesOrders query, which replaces the SalesOrders table, has a lookup field from which you can select a shipping address for the order.

TIP

Extracting the duplicate shipping address information from the copy of the Orders table to a new ShipAddresses table is helpful to demonstrate the use of the Table Analyzer Wizard. But the preceding example isn't practical in the real world, where individual customers might have several shipping addresses. You're likely to find this wizard better suited for extracting duplicate information from spreadsheets you import into Access tables than from existing relational tables.

To make the ShipAddresses table useful, you must add a field, such as ShipToID, to identify multiple shipping addresses for a single customer. Assign a value of 0 for the ShipToID field for the default shipping information created by the wizard. Additional shipping addresses for a particular CustomerID are numbered 1, 2, 3, ... You need to redesign forms that specify shipping addresses to allow adding new ShipAddresses records for customers. You must change the primary key to a composite primary key consisting of CustomerID + ShipToID, and you must use VBA code to create successive ShipToID values automatically for a particular CustomerID.

NOTE

If you want to return Northwind.accdb to its original state, delete the SalesOrders query plus the SalesOrders_OLD, Table1, and ShipAddress tables from the Navigation Pane.

GENERATING A DATA DICTIONARY WITH THE DATABASE DOCUMENTER

After you've determined the individual data entities that make up the tables of your database and have established the relationships between them, the next step is to prepare a preliminary written description of the database, called a *data dictionary*. Data dictionaries are indispensable to database systems; an undocumented database system is almost impossible to administer and maintain properly. Errors and omissions in database design often are uncovered when you prepare the preliminary data dictionary.

When you've completed and tested your database design, you prepare the final detailed version of the data dictionary. As you add new forms and reports to applications or modify existing forms and reports, update the data dictionary to keep it current. Even if you're making a database for your personal use, a simplified version of a data dictionary pays many dividends on the time invested.

 Access 2007's Database Documenter creates a report that details the objects and values of the properties of the objects in the current database. You can also export the report as a rich-text format (.rtf) file to Word or as an .xls file to Excel.

In many cases, Documenter tells you more than you would ever want to know about your database; the full report for all objects in Northwind.accdb, for example, requires about 400 printed pages. Most often, you only want to document your tables and, perhaps, your queries to create a complete data dictionary. The following steps show you how to create a data dictionary for the table objects (only) of Nwind05.accdb:

1. Open the database you want to document, \SEUA12\Chaptr05\Nwind05.accdb for this example, and choose Tools, Analyze, Documenter to open Documenter's tabbed dialog.

2. Click the tab for the type of database object(s) you want to document. Current Database and Tables are the most common data dictionary objects, so click the Current Database tab.

3. Mark the Properties and Relationships check boxes, or click Select All (see Figure 5.44), and then click the Tables tab.

Figure 5.44
Mark both the Properties and Relationships check boxes to list database properties and generate simple diagrams of table relationships.

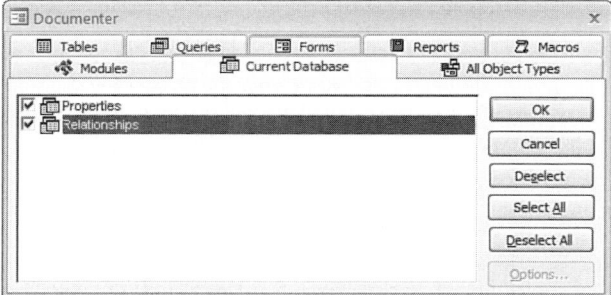

4. Mark the check boxes of the tables to analyze, Employees and HRActions for this example (see Figure 5.45), and click the Options button to open the Print Table Definition dialog.

5. Northwind.accdb isn't a secure database, so clear the Permissions by User and Group check box. The default options for fields and indexes specify the full gamut of information on these objects (see Figure 5.46). Click OK to close the dialog.

6. Click OK to close the Documenter dialog and start the report generation process. After a few seconds, page 1 of a 22-page report opens in Print Preview mode.

Figure 5.45
Select a couple of tables to give the Documenter a test run.

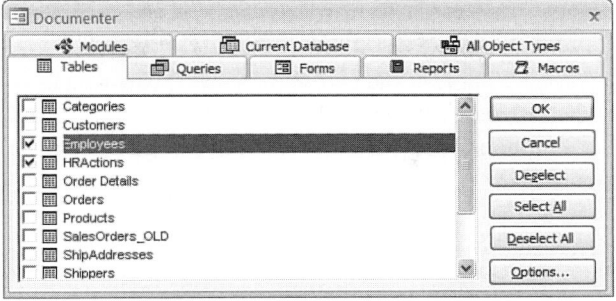

Figure 5.46
The Print Table Definition dialog lets you specify the amount of detail the report contains for tables.

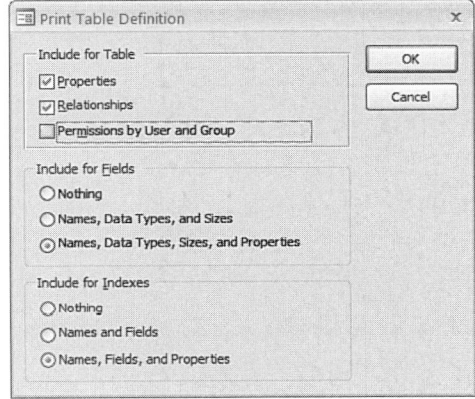

7. Click the Print Preview window to display the report at 100% scale and expand the size of the window to display the full width of the report (see Figure 5.47). For this example, the Employees table is the report's first object.

5

Figure 5.47
Properties of tables and their fields appear at the beginning of Documenter's report.

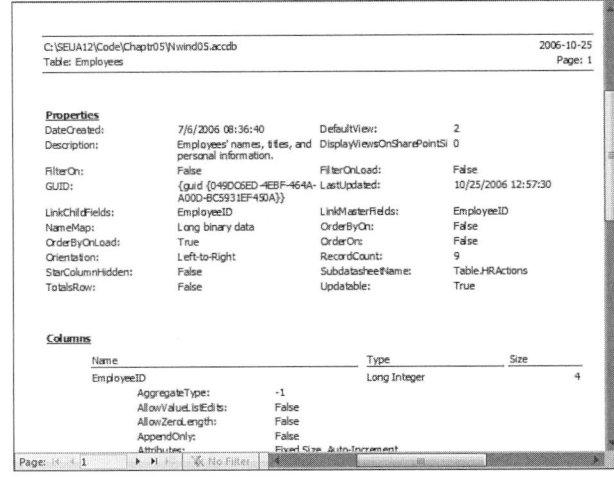

8. Scroll the report to review the remainder of page 1, and then click the next page button to display additional fields of the Employees table and the HRActions table.

9. Database properties appear at the end of the report. Navigate to page 15 to view the first page of the Database section of the report. Pages 18 through 22 of the sample report display simplified entity-relationship (E-R) diagrams for the database's relationships (see Figure 5.48).

Figure 5.48
Documenter's Current Database, Relationships option generates Spartan entity-relationship diagrams for all tables in the database, regardless of the tables you select to document.

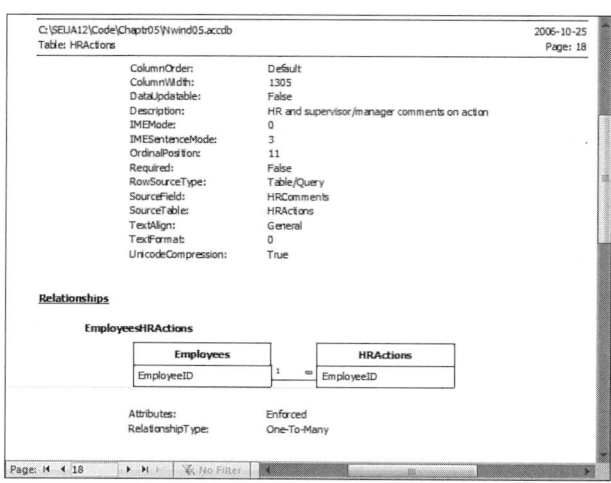

10. Click the Print button on the Quick-Access Toolbar to print the report, or right-click the report and choose Print Preview or Print.

11. Right-click the report and choose Send To, Mail Recipient (as Attachment) to open the Send dialog, where you can choose one of six formats, including HTML, Report Snapshot, and XML. Alternatively, choose Export, to open the Export Report dialog, and save the file in one of the eight supported formats.

NOTE

> To email or export Database Documenter reports in Adobe Portable Document Format (PDF) or Microsoft XML Paper Specification (XPS) format, you must download the PDF and XPS converter from the Office Live Web site, if you haven't done this previously.

Documenting other types of objects in your database follows the same method outlined in the preceding steps. The ability to send Documenter reports by email simplifies keeping others involved in the database design project up to date on changes.

TROUBLESHOOTING

GAPS IN AUTONUMBER FIELD VALUES

When I accidentally add a new record to a table with an AutoNumber field and then delete it, the next record I add has the wrong AutoNumber value—increment of 2 instead of 1.

That's the major drawback of AutoNumber fields, especially when the AutoNumber field value corresponds to a physical record, such as an invoice or check number. The AutoNumber feature offers no simple method of replacing an incorrect record that you delete from the table. The best approach, which ensures that your table is auditable, is to never delete a record from a table with an AutoNumber field. Instead, type **VOID** in a Status field, and add an explanation (if there's a field available to do so).

EXTRA INDEXES ADDED BY ACCESS

After I specified a primary key on a field containing the characters "ID", an additional index appeared for the field.

In many cases, Access automatically specifies a primary key and index on fields whose names contain the characters "ID", "key", "code", and "num" when you create or import tables. This behavior is controlled by the contents of the AutoIndex on Import/Create text box of the Tables/Queries page of the Options dialog (from the Tools menu). When you change the primary key field(s), the old index remains. You can safely delete the automatically added index.

IN THE REAL WORLD—DATABASE STRATEGY AND TABLE TACTICS

In warfare, strategy defines the objective; tactics specify the battlefield methods to achieve the strategic objective. Carl von Clauswitz's *On War* is the seminal nineteenth-century study of strategy and tactics of modern warfare. Niccolo Machiavelli's *The Art of War* and Che Guevara's *On Guerilla Warfare* provide earlier and later takes, respectively, on the subject. Designing strategic databases and laying out the tables that comprise the database shouldn't—but often does—involve open or guerilla hostilities between the participants.

As a database and table designer, try to remain on the side of your product's consumers; you might win a battle or two, but the consumers (users) ultimately will win the war. This is especially true when the consumers control your database implementation budget. Interview database users to determine their workflow and what information is important to the activities for which they're responsible. Keep your consumers in the loop as you develop the database structure. Provide users with periodic copies of the data dictionary or a printed copy of the Relationships table as you make database and table design changes. It's a good idea, however, to minimize the amount of detail in the Documenter reports you send to others involved in the database design process. As the database developer, you are responsible for the final design of the individual tables and assignment of relationships between them.

Table and field naming is an important database design tactic. There are several schools of thought on naming conventions for tables and fields, but most Access developers agree on one rule: Don't add spaces to table or field names. Northwind.accdb contains only one table, Order Details, with a space in its name, and none of the current Northwind.accdb tables have spaces in field names. Despite the fact that SQL Server 7.0 and later accommodate this dubious feature introduced by Access 1.0, don't use spaces or symbols in database, table, or field names. When you export tables or queries to XML documents, spaces in field or table names result in ugly element names, such as `<Order_x0020_Details>`, in which `_x0020_` replaces the space. Use a mixture of upper- and lowercase letters to make names more readable.

Many developers use "tbl" as a table name prefix for consistency with other Access object type identification prefixes, such as "frm" for forms and "rpt" for reports. Using a table object identifier prefix is uncommon in real-world production databases, because tables are the core objects of a database. Using table names that identify the source document or object of the table, such as "Orders," "Invoices," "Products," and the like is a good database design practice. Use plural nouns when naming tables, because tables contain multiple instances of the objects they represent.

Some database administrators (DBAs) use a short prefix for field names that identify the table that contains the fields. A field name prefix indicates to developers the source of the field without the necessity of having to refer to a database diagram or a table field list. Another benefit of adding a prefix based on a table name is avoidance of duplicate names in primary key and foreign key pairs. If you choose this approach, a logical prefix for the fields of the HRActions table would be "hra."

Some Access developers add a prefix to field names—such as "dat" (for Date/Time) or "txt" (for Text)—that specifies the Access data type, following the generally accepted convention for adding a data type prefix to VBA variable and constant names. This practice is becoming less common as more developers work interchangeably with Access and SQL Server databases. Corresponding Access and SQL Server data type names aren't necessarily the same; conflicts between Access-based prefixes and SQL Server prefixes can cause confusion when upsizing Access databases to SQL Server 2005.

CHAPTER 6

ENTERING, EDITING, AND VALIDATING ACCESS TABLE DATA

In this chapter

ENTERING DATA IN ACCESS TABLES

Ease of data entry is a primary criterion for an effective database development environment. Most of your Access database applications probably will use forms for data entry. In many instances, however, entering data in Table Datasheet view is quicker than using a form, especially during the database development cycle. For example, it's a good idea to test your proposed database structure before you commit to designing the forms and reports. Although the Name AutoCorrect feature reduces object name discrepancies, changing table and field names or altering relationships between tables after you create a collection of forms and reports can involve a substantial amount of work.

To test the database design, you must enter test data. In this instance, using Table Datasheet view to enter data makes more sense than using a form. Even if you import data from another database type or from a spreadsheet, you probably need to edit the data to make it compatible with your new application. The first part of this chapter concentrates on data entry and editing methods in datasheets.

Another important factor in a database development environment is maintaining the integrity of your data. Entity integrity rules limit the data you enter in fields to a particular range or set of valid values.

Like earlier versions, Access 2007 lets you enforce entity integrity rules (often called *business rules*) at the field and table levels. You enforce entity integrity (also called *domain integrity*) by entering expressions as the value of the Validation Rule property of fields and tables. This chapter shows you how to use simple expressions for domain integrity validation rules. After you master Access/VBA operators and expressions in Chapter 10, "Understanding Access Operators and Expressions," you'll be able to write complex validation rules that minimize the possibility of data entry errors in your Access tables.

USING KEYBOARD OPERATIONS FOR ENTERING AND EDITING DATA

Access 2007 is more mouse-oriented that its predecessors, as are the other members of the Office 2007 suite, but keyboard equivalents are available for the most common actions. One reason for providing keyboard commands is that constantly shifting the hand from a keyboard to a mouse and back can reduce data entry rates by more than half. Shifting between a keyboard and mouse can also lead to or aggravate repetitive stress injury (RSI), of which the most common type is carpal tunnel syndrome (CTS).

Keyboard operations are as important or more important in a data entry environment than they are in word processing applications. Consequently, the information concerning key combinations for data entry appears here instead of being relegated to fine print in an appendix. The data entry procedures you learn in the following sections prove useful when you come to the "Testing Field and Table Validation Rules" section near the end of the chapter.

Creating a Working Copy of Northwind.accdb

If you want to experiment with the keyboard operations described in the following sections, work with a copy of the Northwind.accdb sample database. By using a copy, you don't need to worry about making changes that affect the sample database.

TIP

This chapter uses the HRActions table for data entry and validation examples. If you didn't create the HRActions table in the preceding chapter, click the External Data tab, click the Access button, and import the HRActions table from Nwind05.accdb in the location where you saved the CD-ROM files, typically C:\SEUA12\Chaptr05. After you import the table, open the Relationships window, add the HRActions table, and create a one-to-many relationship between the EmployeeID fields of the Employees and HRActions tables. Nwind05.accdb only contains tables and a single query.

Setting Data Entry Options

Most keyboard operations described in the following sections apply to tables and updatable queries in Datasheet view, text boxes on forms, and text boxes used for entering property values in Properties windows and in the Field Properties grid of Table Design view. In the examples, the Arrow Key Behavior property is set to Next Character rather than the default Next Field value. When the Arrow Key Behavior property is set to Next Field, the arrow keys move the cursor from field to field. Data entry operators accustomed to mainframe terminals or DOS applications probably prefer to use the Next Character setting.

TIP

If you set the Arrow Key Behavior property value to Next Field, you won't be able to select a block of cells in Datasheet View in the later "Using Key Combinations for Windows Clipboard Operations" section. Data entry operators ordinarily don't need to select blocks of cells in the normal course of their work.

6

To modify the behavior of the arrow keys and the Tab and Enter keys, click the Office button to open the gallery, and click Access Options to open the Access Options dialog. Click the Advanced list item to display the Editing options settings (see Figure 6.1). Table 6.1 lists the available options with the default values. These keyboard options let you emulate the behavior of the data entry keys of mainframe and other data entry terminals.

Figure 6.1
The settings you specify on the Advanced page of the Access Options dialog apply to all databases you open, because they're stored in your computer's Registry.

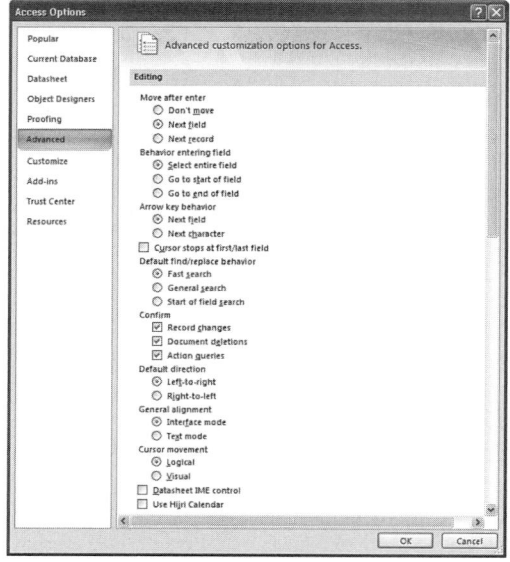

TABLE 6.1 KEYBOARD OPTIONS FOR ALL ACCESS DATABASES

Option	Function
Move After Enter Group	
Don't Move	When this option is selected, the cursor remains in the current field when you press Enter.
Next Field (default)	When this option is selected, the cursor moves to the next field when you press Enter. Use this setting to duplicate dBASE and its clones' behavior.
Next Record	When this option is selected, the cursor moves down the column to the next record when you press Enter.
Behavior Entering Field Group	
Select Entire Field (default)	When this option is selected, the entire field's contents are selected when you use the arrow keys to move the cursor into the field.
Go to Start of Field	Selecting this option causes the cursor to move to the beginning of the field when you use the arrow keys to move the cursor into the field.
Go to End of Field	Selecting this option causes the cursor to move to the end of the field when you use the arrow keys to move the cursor into the field. Use this setting to duplicate mainframe terminal and xBase behavior.

Option	Function
Arrow Key Behavior Group	
Next Field (default)	If this option is selected, pressing the right- or left-arrow key moves the cursor to the next field.
Next Character	If this option is selected, pressing the right- or left-arrow key moves the cursor to the previous or next character in the same field. Use this setting if you want to duplicate the behavior of mainframe terminal or xBase applications.
Cursor Movement Group	
Logical (default) **NEW**	If this option is selected, cursor movement progresses within bidirectional text according to the direction of the language encountered.
Visual **NEW**	If this option is selected, cursor movement progresses within bidirectional text by moving to the next visually adjacent character.
Individual Settings	
Cursor Stops at First/Last Field	Marking this check box keeps the cursor from moving to another record when the left or right arrow key is pressed and the cursor is in the first or last field of the record.
Use Hijri Calendar **NEW**	Marking this check box substitutes the Hijri lunar (Islamic) calendar for the Gregorian calendar.
Datasheet IME Control	Marking this check box enables the Input Method Editor (IME) for entering data in East Asian languages (Windows Vista, XP, and 2003 only).

Using Data Entry and Editing Keys

Arrow keys and key combinations in Access are, for the most part, identical to those used in other Windows applications. The F2 key, used for editing cell contents in Excel, has a different function in Access—F2 toggles between editing and select mode. (*Toggle* means to alternate between two states.) In the editing state, the cursor indicates the insertion point in the field; the key combinations shown in Table 6.2 are active. If the field or any character in the field is selected (indicated by a black background with white type), the editing keys behave as indicated in Table 6.3.

6

TABLE 6.2   KEYS FOR EDITING FIELDS, GRIDS, AND TEXT BOXES

Key	Function
F2	Toggles between displaying the cursor for editing and selecting the entire field. The field must be deselected (black text on a white background) and the cursor must be visible for the keys in this table to operate as described.
End	Moves the cursor to the end of the field in a single-line field or the end of the line in a multiple-line field.
Ctrl+End	Moves the cursor to the end of a multiple-line field.
←	Moves the cursor one character to the left until you reach the first character in the line.
Ctrl+←	Moves the cursor one word to the left until you reach the first word in the line.
Home	Moves the cursor to the beginning of the line.
Ctrl+Home	Moves the cursor to the beginning of the field in multiple-line fields.
Backspace	Deletes the entire selection or the character to the left of the cursor.
Delete	Deletes the entire selection or the character to the right of the cursor.
Ctrl+Z or Alt+Backspace	Undoes typing, a replace operation, or any other change to the record since the last time it was saved. An edited record is saved to the database when you move to a new record or close the editing window.
Esc	Undoes changes to the current field. Press Esc twice to undo changes to the current field and to the entire current record, if you edited other fields.

TABLE 6.3   KEYS FOR SELECTING TEXT IN FIELDS, GRIDS, AND TEXT BOXES

Key	Function
Text Within a Field	
F2	Toggles between displaying the cursor for editing and selecting the entire field. The field must be selected (white type on a black background) for the keys in this table to operate as described.
Shift+→	Selects or deselects one character to the right.
Ctrl+Shift+→	Selects or deselects one word to the right. Includes trailing spaces.
Shift+←	Selects or deselects one character to the left.
Ctrl+Shift+←	Selects or deselects one word to the left.
Next Field	
Tab or Enter	Selects the next field if the default Next Field option is selected.

Key	Function
Record	
Shift+spacebar	Selects or deselects the entire current record.
↑	Selects the first field in the preceding record when a record is selected.
↓	Selects the first field in the next record when a record is selected.
Column	
Ctrl+spacebar	Toggles selection of the current column.
←	Selects the first field in the column to the left (if a column is selected and a column is to the left).
Fields and Records	
F8	Turns on Extend mode. You see "EXT" in the status bar. In Extend mode, pressing F8 extends the selection to the word, then the field, then the record, and then all the records.
Shift+F8	Reverses the last F8.
Esc	Cancels Extend mode.

Operations that select the entire field or a portion of the field, as listed in Table 6.3, generally are used with Windows Clipboard operations.

TIP

Selecting an entire field and then pressing Delete or typing a character is a quick way to rid the field of its original contents.

USING KEY COMBINATIONS FOR WINDOWS CLIPBOARD OPERATIONS

In Table Datasheet view, the Clipboard is used primarily for transferring Access data between applications, such as copying data to an Excel worksheet or a Word table. However, you can also use the Clipboard for repetitive data entry. Access lets you select a rectangular block of data cells in a table and copy the block to the Clipboard. To select a block of cells, follow these steps:

1. Position the mouse pointer at the left edge of the top-left cell of the block you want to select. The cursor (a mouse pointer shaped like an I-beam until this point) turns into a cross similar to the mouse pointer for Excel worksheets.

2. Drag the mouse pointer to the right edge of the bottom-right cell of the desired block.

3. The selected block appears in reverse type (white on black, also called *reverse video*). Release the mouse button when the selection meets your requirement.

4. Press Ctrl+C to copy the selected block to the Clipboard.

Figure 6.2 shows a selected block of data in the Customers table. You can copy data blocks but can't cut them.

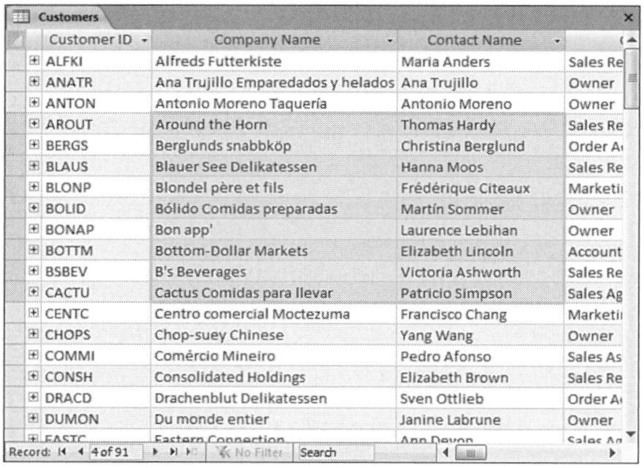

Figure 6.2
You can select a rectangular block of data to copy to the Clipboard, and paste the block to cells of an Excel worksheet or Word table.

Table 6.4 lists the key combinations for copying or cutting data to and pasting data from the Clipboard.

TABLE 6.4   KEY COMBINATIONS FOR WINDOWS CLIPBOARD OPERATIONS

Key	Function
Ctrl+C or Ctrl+Insert	Copies the selection to the Clipboard.
Ctrl+V or Shift+Insert	Pastes the Clipboard's contents at the cursor's location.
Ctrl+X or Shift+Delete	Copies the selection to the Clipboard and then deletes it. This operation also is called a cut. You can cut only the content of a single cell you select with the cursor.
Ctrl+Z or Alt+Backspace	Undoes your last Cut, Delete, or Paste operation.

TIP

To create a new, empty table from the copied block, click the Table button of the Create ribbon's Tables group. With the second column selected, click the Home tab and then click the Paste, Paste Append button to add the block to the table. Pasting the records to the table adds the field names. If you don't want the default AutoNumber primary key, delete the ID column in Table Design view.

USING SHORTCUT KEYS FOR FIELDS AND TEXT BOXES

Shortcut keys minimize the number of keystrokes required to accomplish common data entry tasks. Most shortcut key combinations use the Ctrl key with other keys. Ctrl+C, Ctrl+V, and Ctrl+X for Clipboard operations are examples of global shortcut keys in Windows. Table 6.5 lists shortcut keys for field and text box entries.

TIP

Ctrl+' or Ctrl+" are the most important of the shortcut keys for entering table data. The ability to copy data from a field of the preceding record into the same field of a new record is a welcome timesaver.

TABLE 6.5   SHORTCUT KEYS FOR TEXT BOXES AND FIELDS IN TABLES

Key	Function
Ctrl+; (semicolon)	Inserts the current date
Ctrl+: (colon)	Inserts the current time
Ctrl+' (apostrophe) or Ctrl+" (double quote)	Inserts the value from the same field in the preceding record
Ctrl+Enter	Inserts a newline character (carriage return plus line feed, or CRLF) in a text box
Ctrl++ (plus)	Adds a new record to the table
Ctrl+– (minus)	Deletes the current record from the table
Shift+Enter	Saves all changes to the current record

TIP

Emulating the data entry key behavior of a mainframe terminal or DOS database application can make a major difference in the acceptance of your database applications by data entry operators with years of experience with mainframe and DOS database applications.

ADDING RECORDS TO A TABLE

When you open an updatable table in Datasheet view, the last row is an empty placeholder for a new record, called the *tentative append record* in this book. (An *updatable table* is one whose data you can add to or edit.) An asterisk in the last record selection button in the datasheet indicates the tentative append record. Record selection buttons are the gray buttons in the leftmost column of Table Datasheet view. If you open a database for read-only access, the tentative append record doesn't appear. Tables attached from other databases can also be read-only. The updatability of attached tables is discussed in Chapter 8, "Linking, Importing, and Exporting Data."

6

TIP

To go to the tentative append record of a table quickly, press Ctrl++ (plus).

When you press Ctrl++ or place the cursor in a field of the tentative append record, the record selection button's asterisk symbol turns into the selected (current) record symbol. When you add data to a field of the selected tentative append record, the selected record symbol changes to the edit symbol (a pencil), and a new tentative append record appears in the row after your addition. Figure 6.3 shows a new record in the process of being added to the Customers table. The CustomerID field has an Input Mask property value (>LLLLL) that requires you to enter five letters, which are capitalized automatically as you enter them. The input mask changes the cursor from an I-beam to a reverse-video block.

Figure 6.3
The CustomerID field of Northwind's Customers table has an input mask that requires exactly five letters and automatically capitalizes the letters as you enter them.

→ To review how input masks work, **see** "Using Input Masks," **p. 223**.

To cancel the addition of a new record, press the Esc key twice. Pressing Esc once cancels the changes you made to the current field. You might not need to press Esc twice, but doing so guarantees canceling the record addition.

SELECTING, APPENDING, REPLACING, AND DELETING TABLE RECORDS

You can select a single record or a group of records to copy or cut to the Clipboard, or to delete from the table, by the following methods:

- To select a single record, click its record selection button.
- To select a contiguous group of records, click the first record's selection button and then drag the mouse pointer along the record selection buttons to the last record of the group.
- Alternatively, to select a group of records, click the first record's selection button and then Shift+click the last record to include in the group. You can also press Shift+↓ to select a group of records.

You can't use Ctrl+click to select noncontiguous records.

NOTE

You can cut groups of records to the Clipboard, deleting them from the table, but you can't cut data blocks. A group of records includes all fields of one or more selected records. A data block consists of a selection in a table datasheet that doesn't include all fields of the selected rows. The Edit, Cut command is enabled for groups of records and disabled for data blocks.

You can cut or copy and append duplicate records to the same table (if appending the duplicate records doesn't cause a primary key violation) or to another table. You can't cut records from a primary table that has dependent records in a related table if you enforce referential integrity. The following methods apply to appending or replacing the content of records with records stored in the Clipboard:

- To append records from the Clipboard to a table, click Paste, Paste Append.
- To replace the content of a record(s) with data from the Clipboard, select the record(s) whose content you want to replace and then press Ctrl+V. Only the number of records you select or the number of records stored in the Clipboard (whichever is fewer) is replaced.

To delete one or more records, select those records and press Delete. If deletion is allowed, a message box asks you to confirm your deletion, if you haven't cleared the Confirm Record Changes text box on the Edit/Find page of the Options dialog. You can't undo deletions of records.

VALIDATING DATA ENTRY

The data entered in tables must be accurate if the database is to be valuable to you or your organization. Even the most experienced data entry operators occasionally enter incorrect information. To add simple tests for the reasonableness of entries, add short expressions as a Validation Rule in the General page of Table Design view's Field Properties pane. If the entered data fails to pass your validation rule, a message box informs the operator that a violation occurred. You can customize the error message by adding the text as the value of the Validation Text property. Validating data maintains the entity integrity of your tables.

Expressions are a core element of computer programming. Access lets you create expressions without requiring that you be a programmer, although some familiarity with a programming language is helpful. Expressions use the familiar arithmetic symbols +, -, * (multiply), and / (divide). These symbols are called operators because they operate on (use) the values that precede and follow them. These operators are reserved symbols in VBA. The values operated on by operators are called *operands*.

You can also use operators to compare two values; the < (less than) and > (greater than) symbols are examples of comparison operators. **And**, **Or**, **Is**, **Not**, Between, and Like are called logical operators. (Between and Like are Access, not VBA, operators, so they don't appear in bold type). Comparison and logical operators return only **True**, **False**, and no value (the

6

Null value). The **&** operator combines two text entries (character strings or just strings) into a single string. To qualify as an expression, at least one operator must be included. You can construct complex expressions by combining the different operators according to rules that apply to each operator involved. The collection of these rules is called *operator syntax*.

→ To learn more about Access operators, **see** "Understanding the Elements in Expressions," **p. 413**.

Data validation rules use expressions that result in one of two values: **True** or **False**. Entries in a data cell are accepted if the result of the validation is true and rejected if it's false. If the data is rejected by the validation rule, the text you enter as the Validation Text property value appears in a message box. Chapter 10 explains the syntax of Access validation expressions.

> **NOTE**
> SQL Server substitutes CHECK constraints for the Validation Rule property. As with Access, CHECK constraints can apply at the table or field level. The Access Expression Service lets you use VBA functions, such as **UCase()**, in validation rules. SQL Server requires use of Transact-SQL (T-SQL) functions for CHECK constraints. Chapter 21, "Moving from Access Queries to Transact-SQL," explains how to translate Access/VBA functions into T-SQL functions.

Adding Field-Level Validation Rules

Validation rules that restrict the values entered in a field and are based on only one field are called *field-level validation rules*. Table 6.6 lists the simple field-level validation rules used for some fields in the HRActions table you created in Chapter 5, "Working with Access Databases and Tables."

TABLE 6.6   Validation Criteria for the Fields of the HRActions Table

Field Name	Validation Rule	Validation Text
EmployeeID	>0	Please enter a valid employee ID number.
ActionType	In("H","Q","Y","S","R","B","C","T")	Only H, Q, Y, S, R, B, C, and T codes are valid.
Initiated By	>0	Please enter a valid supervisor ID number.
ScheduledDate	Between Date()-5475 And Date()+365	Scheduled dates can't be more than 15 years ago or more than 1 year from now.
ApprovedBy	>0 Or Is Null	Enter a valid manager ID number or leave blank if not approved.
EffectiveDate	None	
HRRating	Between 0 And 9 Or Is Null	Rating range is 0 for terminated employees, 1 to 9, or blank.
NewSalary	None	None.

Field Name	Validation Rule	Validation Text
NewRate	>7.63 Or Is Null	Hourly rate must be more than the prevailing minimum wage ($7.63 per hour for the state of Washington).
NewBonus	None	None.
NewCommission	<=0.1 or Is Null	Commission rate can't exceed 10%.
HRComments	None	None.

NOTE

You must allow ScheduledDate values as early as 2000 to accommodate the hire dates in the first two records of the Employees table. This book's Northwind.accdb sample database has more recent dates than Microsoft's Northwind.mdb in the Employees and Orders tables.

TIP

The In operator simplifies expressions that otherwise would require multiple Or operators. For example, using the Or operator for the Validation Rule property value of the ActionType field requires typing **"H" Or "Q" Or "Y" Or "S" Or "R" Or "B" Or "C" Or "T"**, which has many more characters.

In their present form, the validation rules for fields that require employee ID numbers can't ensure that a valid ID number is entered. You could enter an employee ID number that isn't present in the Employees table. A validation rule for the EmployeeID field could test the EmployeeID number field of the Employees table to determine whether the employee ID number is present. You don't need to create this test because the rules of referential integrity perform this validation for you automatically. However, validation rules for InitiatedBy and ApprovedBy require tests based on entries in the Employees table.

→ To review referential integrity rules, **see** "Working with Relations, Key Fields, and Indexes," **p. 237**.

To add the validation rules of Table 6.6 to the HRActions table, follow these steps:

1. From the Navigation Pane, open the HRActions table in Design view, if it isn't already open, by right-clicking the table name and choosing <u>D</u>esign View.

2. Press F6 to switch to the Field Properties window, and then move to the Validation Rule text box.

3. Type **>0** and move to the text box labeled Validation Text.

4. Type **Please enter a valid employee ID number.** The text scrolls to the left when it becomes longer than can be displayed in the text box. To display the beginning of the text, press Home. Press End to position the cursor at the last character. Figure 6.4 shows your entries in the Field Properties text boxes.

6

Figure 6.4
The Field Properties pane displays the first Validation Rule and Validation Text property values entered from the data in Table 6.6.

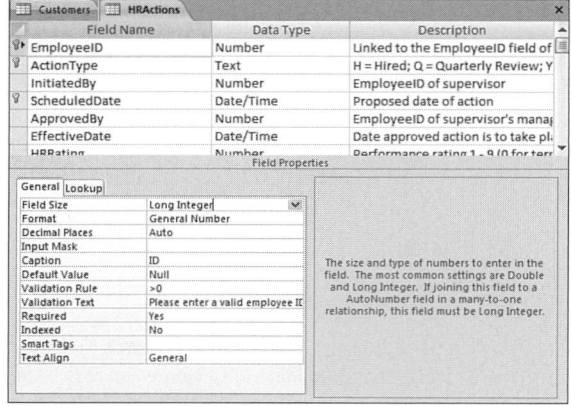

5. Enter the validation rule and validation text for the seven remaining fields listed in Table 6.6 that use data entry validation.

You test your validation rule entries later in the "Testing Field and Table Validation Rules" section.

ADDING TABLE-LEVEL VALIDATION RULES WITH THE EXPRESSION BUILDER

One field, EffectiveDate, requires a validation rule that depends on ScheduledDate's value. The effective date of the personnel department's action shouldn't be before the scheduled date for the review that results in the action. You can't refer to other field names in a Access validation rule expression; instead, you add such validation rules in the Table Properties window. Validation rules in which the value of one field depends on a previously entered value in another field of the current record are called *table-level validation rules*.

The following steps add a table description and create a table-level validation rule for the EffectiveDate field:

1. Right-click the upper pane of Table Design view to open the Table Properties sheet.

2. Type **Human Resources Department Actions** in the Description text box (see Figure 6.5).

3. In the Validation Rule text box, click the ellipsis (Builder) button to display the Expression Builder dialog. The current table, HRActions, is selected in the left list, and the fields of the table appear in the center list.

4. Double-click EffectiveDate in the center list to place [EffectiveDate] in the Expression Builder's text box at the top of the dialog. Square brackets surround field names to distinguish them from literal (string) values.

5. Type **>=** in the text box and double-click ScheduledDate in the center list to add [ScheduledDate] to the expression.

Figure 6.5
When you move the cursor to the Validation Rule row of the Table Properties Sheet, the ellipsis button appears so you can open the Access Expression Builder.

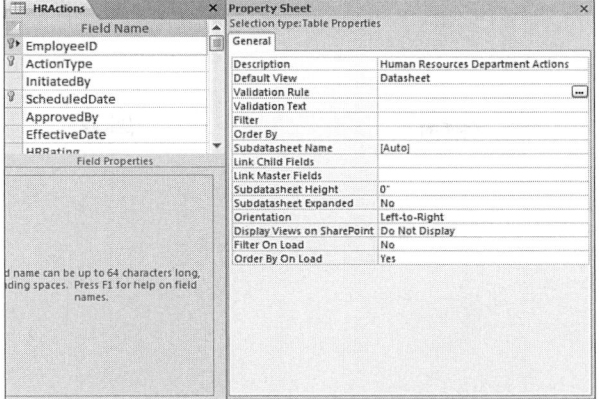

6. To accept a blank entry if the effective date of the personnel action isn't scheduled, add **Or [EffectiveDate] Is Null** to the expression, which appears as shown in Figure 6.6.

Figure 6.6
You can use the Access Expression Builder to generate more complex expressions for use as table-level validation rules.

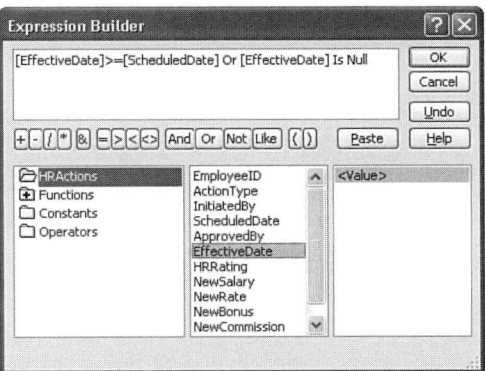

7. Click OK to add the table-level validation rule and close the Expression Builder dialog.

8. In the Validation Text text box, type **Effective date must be on or after the scheduled date**. Your Table Properties sheet appears as shown in Figure 6.7.

9. Close the Table Properties sheet.

ADDING A SIMPLE LOOKUP LIST TO THE ACTIONTYPE FIELD

Lookup tables require queries, which are the subject of this book's Part III, "Transforming Data with Queries and PivotTables." However, you can add a lookup list to the table by adding a set of values that's similar to a validation expression. You create a lookup list by selecting the field the list applies to in Table Design view, and specifying property values in the Lookup page of the Field Properties pane.

Figure 6.7
Closing the Expression Builder adds the expression of Figure 6.6 as the Validation Rule property value of the table.

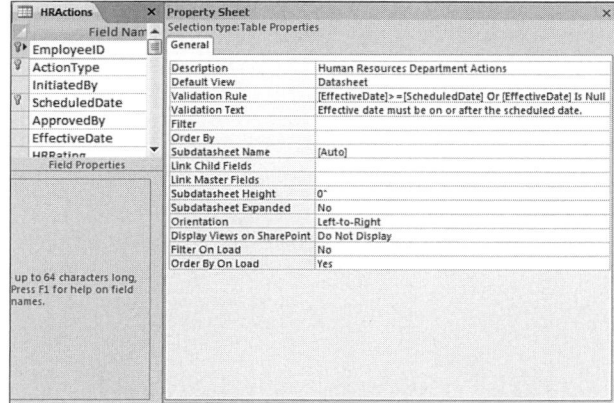

To add a combo box lookup list to the ActionType field of the HRActions table, do this:

1. In Design view, select the ActionType field and click the Lookup tab in the Field Properties pane.

2. Open the Display Control list and select Combo Box or List Box. This example uses a combo box.

3. Open the Row Source Type list and select Value List.

4. Accept the first column (1) default in the Bound Column list, and type **2** in the Column Count text box. The value list needs code and description columns.

5. In the Column Widths text box type **0.3";1.2"**, and in the List Width text box type **1.5"**.

6. Type **Y**(es) in the Limit to List text box. Limiting entries to the list's items is equivalent to the validation rule you added for this field.

7. Return to the Row Source property and type **H;Hired;Q;Quarterly Review;Y;Yearly Review;S;Salary Adj.;R;Hourly Rate Adj.;B;Bonus Adj.;C;Commission Adj.;T;Terminated** in the text box. The semicolons separate the entries that add in pairs to create the list. Your lookup list design appears as shown in Figure 6.8.

8. Return to Datasheet view and save your design changes.

9. Press Tab to move to the ActionType field and press F4 to open the lookup list (see Figure 6.9).

Lookup lists are handy for adding codes and other field values that seldom, if ever, change. When entering data, you can use the lookup list or type the code letter; the latter is considerably faster. You must keep lookup lists up to date. Also, if multiple tables use the same list, you must update each table's list manually. Lookups from tables or queries are one of the topics of Chapter 11, "Creating Multitable and Crosstab Queries," and are preferable to lookup lists. You can use a single lookup table or query for all fields that need the lookup values.

Figure 6.8
You create a lookup list by specifying a combo box or list box and setting its properties in the Lookup page of the Field Properties pane.

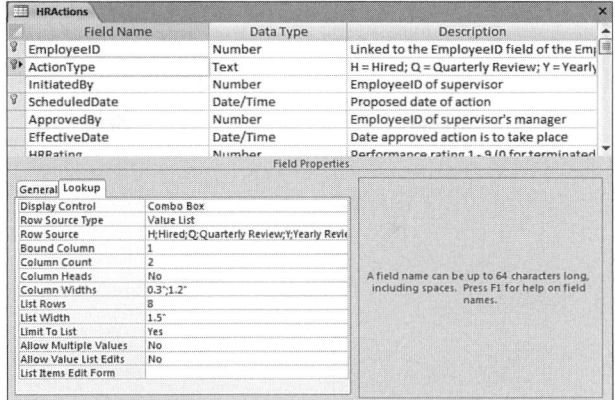

Figure 6.9
The lookup list for ActionType codes has a description for each of the eight valid codes.

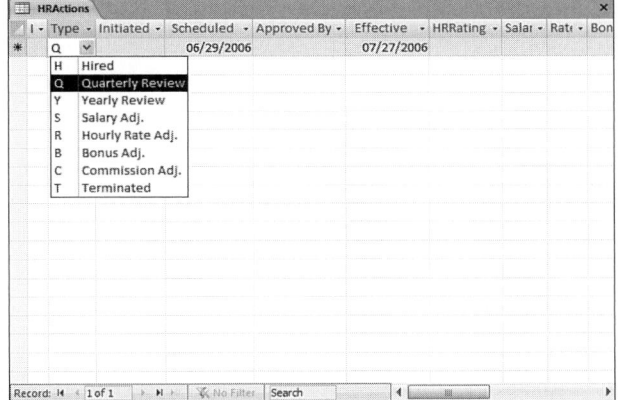

ADDING RECORDS TO THE HRACTIONS TABLE

Now you can test your work in creating the HRActions table and check whether Access is enforcing domain integrity. Table 6.7 shows the initial entries for each employee of Northwind Traders. The dates are based on values in the Employees table's HireDate field. No Rating entries appear in Table 6.7 because ratings don't apply to newly hired employees.

6

TABLE 6.7	FIRST NINE ENTRIES FOR THE HRACTIONS TABLE						
EMPLOYEE ID	ACTION TYPE	INITIATED BY	SCHEDULED DATE	APPROVED BY	EFFECTIVE DATE	NEW SALARY	HR COMMENT
1	H	1	05/01/2000	1	05/01/2000	2,000	Hired
2	H	1	08/14/2000	1	08/14/2000	3,500	Hired

continues

TABLE 6.7 CONTINUED

EMPLOYEE ID	ACTION TYPE	INITIATED BY	SCHEDULED DATE	APPROVED BY	EFFECTIVE DATE	NEW SALARY	HR COMMENT
3	H	1	04/01/2000	1	04/01/2000	2,250	Hired
4	H	2	05/03/2001	2	05/03/2001	2,250	Hired
5	H	2	10/17/2001	2	10/17/2001	2,500	Hired
6	H	5	10/17/2001	2	10/17/2001	4,000	Hired
7	H	5	01/02/2002	2	01/02/2002	3,000	Hired
8	H	2	05/05/2002	2	05/05/2002	2,500	Hired
9	H	5	11/15/2002	2	11/15/2002	3,000	Hired

Entering historical information in a table in Datasheet view is a relatively fast process for experienced data entry operators. This process also gives you a chance to test your default entries and Format properties for each field. You can enter bogus values that don't comply with your validation rules to verify that your rules are operational.

To add the first nine historical records to the HRActions table with the data from Table 6.7, follow these steps:

1. Click the Datasheet View button to return to Datasheet view, if necessary. The cursor is positioned in the EmployeeID field of the default first record.

2. Enter the EmployeeID of the employee. Press Enter, Tab, or the right-arrow key to move to the next field and to add a new default blank record to the view but not to the table's content.

3. Type **H** in the Type field or select H from the lookup list, and move to the next field.

4. Type the numeric value of 1 or greater for the InitiatedBy field. (You need a value in this field for each employee because of the field's validation rule.) Move to the next field.

5. Type the ScheduledDate entry. You don't need to delete the default date value; typing a new date replaces the default value. Then press Enter, Tab, or the right-arrow key.

6. Type the ApprovedBy value and move to the next field.

7. Type the EffectiveDate entry, and skip the HRRating field.

8. Type the NewSalary of the monthly salary at the time of hiring, and skip the NewRate, NewBonus, and NewCommission fields.

9. Type **Hired** or any other comment you care to make in the HRComments field. Move to the EmployeeID field of the next default blank record.

10. Repeat steps 2 through 9 for eight more employees in Table 6.7.

When you complete your entries, the HRActions table appears as shown in Figure 6.10. If you skipped any of the sample procedures in this chapter, an updated version of the

Nwind05.accdb database (Nwind06.accdb) with the data entered for you is in your \\SEUA12\Chaptr06 folder. As mentioned early in the chapter, importing the HRActions table requires adding a one-to-many relationship to the Employees table. If you don't add the relationship, some validation tests in the next section won't behave as expected.

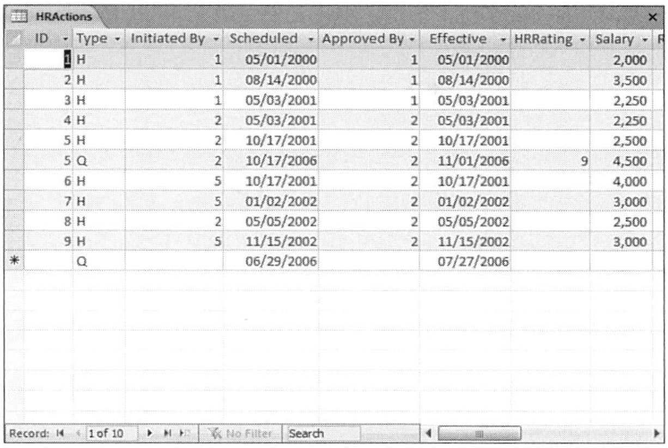

Figure 6.10
The HRActions tables contain initial entries for the nine employees of Northwind Traders.

ID	Type	Initiated By	Scheduled	Approved By	Effective	HRRating	Salary
1	H	1	05/01/2000	1	05/01/2000		2,000
2	H	1	08/14/2000	1	08/14/2000		3,500
3	H	1	05/03/2001	1	05/03/2001		2,250
4	H	2	05/03/2001	2	05/03/2001		2,250
5	H	2	10/17/2001	2	10/17/2001		2,500
5	Q	2	10/17/2006	2	11/01/2006	9	4,500
6	H	5	10/17/2001	2	10/17/2001		4,000
7	H	5	01/02/2002	2	01/02/2002		3,000
8	H	2	05/05/2002	2	05/05/2002		2,500
9	H	5	11/15/2002	2	11/15/2002		3,000
*	Q		06/29/2006		07/27/2006		

Record: 1 of 10   No Filter   Search

If you're not sure how to respond to data input error messages on validated fields, see "Error Messages from Validation Enforcement" in the "Troubleshooting" section near the end of this chapter.

TESTING FIELD AND TABLE VALIDATION RULES

You can experiment with entering table data and testing your validation rules at the same time. Testing database applications often requires much more time and effort than creating them. The following basic tests are required to confirm your validation rules:

- *Referential integrity*—Type **25** in the EmployeeID field and **2** in the InitiatedBy field of the default blank record (number 10) and then press the up-arrow key. Pressing the up-arrow key tells Access that you're finished with the current record and to move up to the preceding record with the cursor in the same field. Access then tests the primary key integrity before enabling you to leave the current record, and the message box shown in Figure 6.11 appears. Click OK and press Esc to abandon the entry.

Figure 6.11
If you violate referential integrity rules by typing an EmployeeID value without a corresponding record in the Employees table, this message appears.

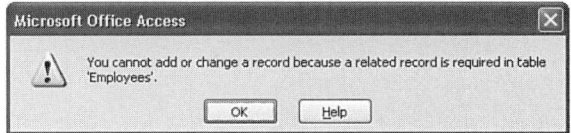

Microsoft Office Access

You cannot add or change a record because a related record is required in table 'Employees'.

OK   Help

6

- *No duplicates restriction for primary key*—In the tentative append record, attempt to duplicate exactly the entries for the first four fields of record 9, and then press the up-arrow key. You see the message box shown in Figure 6.12. Click OK, but in this case pressing Esc doesn't cancel the entry.

Figure 6.12
If you duplicate the values of another record in the EmployeeID, ActionType, and ScheduledDate fields, you receive an error message because a primary key duplication occurs.

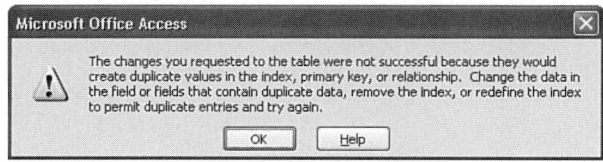

- *ActionType validation*—Type **x** in the ActionType field and press the right-arrow key to display the message that appears if you added the lookup list and set the Limit To List property value to Yes (see Figure 6.13, top). Otherwise, the message box with the validation text you entered for the ActionType field appears (see Figure 6.13, bottom). Click OK and press Esc to abandon the entry.

Figure 6.13
The error message for a lookup list with the Limit To List restriction set responds to an entry error with the upper message. If the Limit To List restriction is missing or you didn't add a lookup list, the Validation Text message appears.

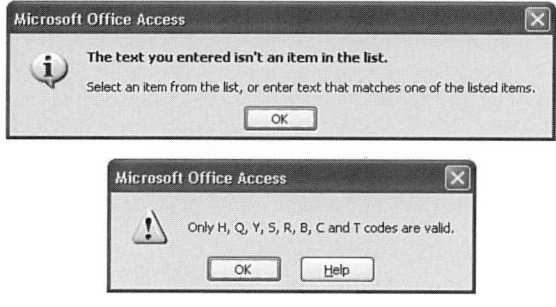

- *Employee ID validation in the InitiatedBy field*—Type **q** and move to the InitiatedBy field. When the cursor leaves the ActionType field, the q changes to Q because of the > format character used. Type **0** (an invalid employee ID number), and press the right-arrow key to display the message box shown in Figure 6.14. Click OK or press Enter.

Figure 6.14
Typing **0** in the InitiatedBy field violates the >0 validation rule and displays the validation text.

Continue with the testing. Type a date, such as **1/31/2001**, for the ScheduledDate, and type a date one day earlier (such as **1/30/2001**) for the EffectiveDate to display the error message boxes with the validation text you entered. (You must move the cursor to a different record to cause the table-level validation rule to be applied.) Enter a valid date after the test. To edit a field, rather than retype it, press F2 to deselect the entire field and display the cursor for editing. F2 toggles selection and editing operations.

When you finish your testing, click the selection button of the last record you added, and then press Delete. The confirmation message shown in Figure 6.15 appears. You can turn off record deletion confirmation messages by clearing the Record Changes text box in the Confirm group of the Access Options dialog's Advanced page.

Figure 6.15
Unless you turn off confirmation of record changes, this message appears when you delete a record.

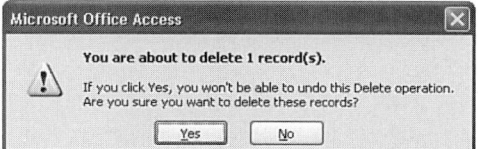

TROUBLESHOOTING

FIELD PROPERTY VALUES CAUSE PASTE FAILURES

Access beeps when I attempt to paste data into a cell.

The Paste operation would violate a domain or referential integrity rule, usually the Field Size property value. For instance, if you attempt to paste more than five characters into the CustomerID field of the Customers table, the Paste operation fails without an error message. Make sure that the cells or blocks of cells you paste conform to Field Size and other data validation rules.

MULTIPLE RECORD SELECTION CAUSES SILENT PASTE FAILURES

Nothing happens when I try to paste data into a cell.

Selecting multiple records, then attempting to paste the records into a single cell, even the first cell of the tentative append record, results in a silent paste failure. Access limits multiple-record insert operations to the <u>E</u>dit, Paste Appe<u>n</u>d command.

ERROR MESSAGES FROM VALIDATION ENFORCEMENT

Error messages appear when I enter data in fields with validation rules.

Edit or reenter the data to conform to the data types and validation rules for the field. Error messages that appear when you enter the data correctly indicate that something is amiss with your validation rules. In this case, change to Design mode and review your validation rules for the offending fields against those listed in Table 6.6. You might want to remove the validation rule temporarily by selecting the entire expression and cutting it to the Clipboard. (You can paste the expression back into the text box later.) Return to Run mode to continue with your entries.

IN THE REAL WORLD—HEADS-DOWN DATA ENTRY

This chapter's tables that list key combinations to expedite data entry make dull reading, at best. *Special Edition Using Microsoft Office Access 2007* serves as both a tutorial and a reference, and references must be comprehensive. Detailed lists of Access 2007 features and their functions, no matter how tedious the list or the features and functions, are unavoidable. There have been no significant changes to data entry key definitions since Access 2.0.

You probably won't appreciate the benefits of Access's data entry shortcut keys until you must type a large amount of table data in a Datasheet view. Clearly, it's preferable to import existing data, taking advantage of Access's flexible data import features described in Chapter 8. Almost everyone, however, faces the inevitable chore of typing table data, such as testing entries for a new database.

COMPARING HEADS-DOWN KEYPUNCH DATA ENTRY WITH ACCESS'S DATASHEET VIEW

In the days of supremacy of mainframe computers, most of which were less powerful than today's PCs, IBM 026 or 029 keypunch operators generated decks of 80-column punched cards from stacks of source documents. Keypunch operators often received piecework wages, based on the number of cards they produced; salaried operators usually had to fill a daily quota. The eyes of keypunch operators were focused eight hours per day on the top document of a stack, giving rise to the term "heads-down data entry."

N O T E

If you've never seen a punched card machine, there's a picture of an IBM 029 keypunch at `http://info.ox.ac.uk/ctitext/history/keypnch.html`. Ed Thelen, a computer historian, has posted a 34-page history of punched card computing at `http://ed-thelen.org/comp-hist/CBC-Ch-04.pdf`.

Datasheet view of a table or updatable query is the simplest and quickest means for heads-down addition of large numbers of records to tables. The need to scroll horizontally to expose more than the first few columns of a wide table, such as that for a customer name and address list, makes Datasheet entry a bit more cumbersome. If you're a good typist, using shortcut keys for column navigation quickly becomes second nature.

Datasheet view for adding related records was cumbersome in previous versions of Access, so most developers are accustomed to creating data entry form-subform pairs, described in Chapter 15, "Designing Custom Multitable Forms." Access 2007, however, offers sub-datasheets that let you add multiple related records almost as effortlessly as adding single records to base tables. The major shortcoming of subdatasheets is that expanding the sub-datasheet requires a mouse click on the + symbol. Moving between heads-down keyboard data entry and mouse operations greatly reduces data entry operator productivity.

Replacing the Punched Card Verifying Step

Verifying data to preserve domain integrity was a critical step in the keypunch process. The most common method of data verification, sometimes called validation, was retyping the original data to determine if the second typing pass matched the first. Clearly, this approach isn't practical in Datasheet view, although you could implement punched-card verification with a simple form and some VBA code to compare the two sets of entries.

Data verification and validation aren't synonymous. *Verification* attempts to eliminate typographic errors by duplication, whereas *validation* primarily tests data entry conformance to a fixed set of rules. The more clever you become in writing well-defined Access validation rules, the better the overall accuracy of the input data. Although form-level validation is more flexible, field- and table-level validation applies to data you enter with any form that's bound to the table. So, you avoid having to re-create validation operations in each of the multiple forms that permit table data entry. The most annoying thing about field- and table-level validation is having to repeatedly close Validation Text message boxes that describe data entry errors.

Where Not to Use Datasheet Entry

Datasheet entry works well for "punching" standard documents on a routine basis. Datasheet entry isn't suited to ad hoc situations, such as taking telephone orders or reservations, or other activities that involve lookup operations on related tables. The "In the Real World—The Art of Form Design" section of Chapter 14, "Creating and Using Basic Access Forms," describes some of the features of a typical Access data entry form designed for heads-down telephone order taking. A single form with list and text boxes, and a subform that appears and disappears in concert with the current operating mode, lets the operator quickly find an existing customer's record, list the customer's past and current orders, and add a new order with multiple line items. The form is designed expressly for keyboard-only operations to eliminate the transition to and from a mouse or trackball. Fortunately, data entry forms inherit the validation rules you establish for your tables.

6

CHAPTER 7 ▶

SORTING, FINDING, AND FILTERING DATA

In this chapter

Understanding the Role of Sorting and Filtering

Microsoft Office Access 2007 provides a variety of sorting and filtering features that make customizing the display data in Table Datasheet view a quick and simple process. Sorting and filtering records in tables is especially useful when you use the data to create a mailing list or print a particular set of records.

Access also includes versatile search-and-replace facilities that let you locate every record that matches a value you specify and then, optionally, change that value. Using the Search features, you can quickly locate values even in large tables. Search and replace often is needed when you import data from another database or a worksheet, which is the primary subject of the next chapter.

Access's sorting, filtering, searching, and replacing features actually are implemented "behind the scenes" by queries that Access creates for you. When you reach Part III, "Transforming Data with Queries and PivotTables," you'll probably choose to implement these features in Access's graphical Query Design window. Learning the fundamentals of these operations with tables, however, makes queries easier to understand. You also can apply filters to query result sets, use the Find feature with queries in Datasheet view, and use search and replace on the result sets of updatable queries.

Sorting Table Data

By default, Access displays records in the order of the primary key. If your table doesn't have a primary key, the records display in the order in which you enter them. Access uses sorting methods to display records in the desired order. If an index exists on the field in which you sort the records, the sorting process for large tables is quicker. Access automatically uses indexes, if indexes exist, to speed the sort in a process called *query optimization*.

The following sections show how to use Access's sorting methods to display records in the sequence you want. The Customers table of Northwind.accdb is used for most examples in this chapter because it's typical of a table whose data you might want to sort.

NOTE

You can use the \SEUA12\Nwind07.accdb database that you install from the CD-ROM as the working file for this database.

You also can use the 15MB Oakmont.accdb database, which has a 30,000-record Students table, to evaluate sorting operations on large tables. If you haven't installed all the sample files from the accompanying CD-ROM, copy Oakmont.accdb from the \SEUA12\Oakmont folder to your working folder. Right-click the Explorer entry for the copy of Oakmont.accdb, choose Properties, and clear the Read-Only check box in the Attributes group.

FREEZING DISPLAY OF A TABLE FIELD

If the table you're sorting contains more fields than you can display in Access's Table Datasheet view, you can freeze one or more fields to make viewing the sorted data easier. Freezing a field makes the field visible at all times, regardless of which other fields you display by manipulating the horizontal scroll bar.

NOTE

> This example and those that follow use field names, rather than column header names (captions). The Microsoft developers added spaces to the table's caption property when two nouns make up a field name, such as Company and Name. Caption is an extended—and, in this case, superficial—property of fields.

To freeze the CustomerID and CompanyName fields of the Customers table, follow these steps:

1. Open the Customers table in Datasheet view.
2. Click the field header button of the CustomerID field to select the first field.
3. Shift+click the CompanyName field header button. Alternatively, you can drag the mouse from the CustomerID field header to the CompanyName field header to select the first and second fields.
4. Right-click the Datasheet and choose Free<u>z</u>e Columns.

When you scroll to fields to the right of the frozen columns, your Datasheet view of the Customers table appears as shown in Figure 7.1. There are no visual elements to indicate that columns are frozen.

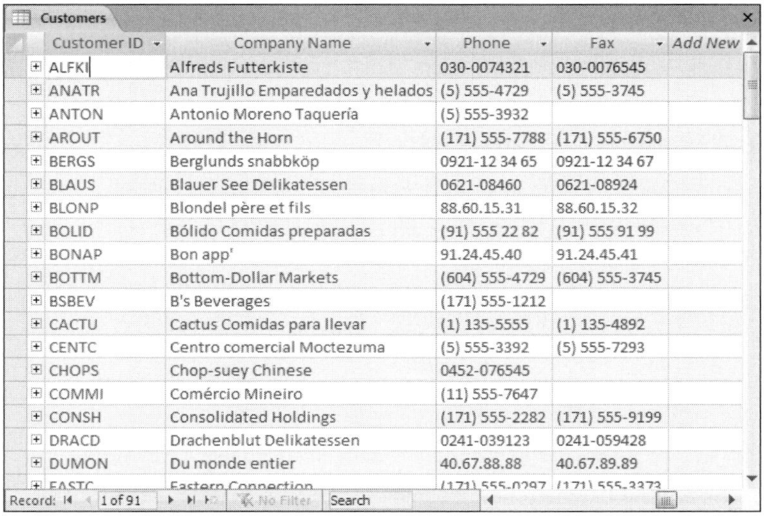

Figure 7.1
The CustomerID and CompanyName fields of this Datasheet view of the Customers table are frozen.

Customer ID	Company Name	Phone	Fax	Add New
ALFKI	Alfreds Futterkiste	030-0074321	030-0076545	
ANATR	Ana Trujillo Emparedados y helados	(5) 555-4729	(5) 555-3745	
ANTON	Antonio Moreno Taquería	(5) 555-3932		
AROUT	Around the Horn	(171) 555-7788	(171) 555-6750	
BERGS	Berglunds snabbköp	0921-12 34 65	0921-12 34 67	
BLAUS	Blauer See Delikatessen	0621-08460	0621-08924	
BLONP	Blondel père et fils	88.60.15.31	88.60.15.32	
BOLID	Bólido Comidas preparadas	(91) 555 22 82	(91) 555 91 99	
BONAP	Bon app'	91.24.45.40	91.24.45.41	
BOTTM	Bottom-Dollar Markets	(604) 555-4729	(604) 555-3745	
BSBEV	B's Beverages	(171) 555-1212		
CACTU	Cactus Comidas para llevar	(1) 135-5555	(1) 135-4892	
CENTC	Centro comercial Moctezuma	(5) 555-3392	(5) 555-7293	
CHOPS	Chop-suey Chinese	0452-076545		
COMMI	Comércio Mineiro	(11) 555-7647		
CONSH	Consolidated Holdings	(171) 555-2282	(171) 555-9199	
DRACD	Drachenblut Delikatessen	0241-039123	0241-059428	
DUMON	Du monde entier	40.67.88.88	40.67.89.89	
EASTC	Eastern Connection	(171) 555-0297	(171) 555-3373	

Record: 1 of 91   No Filter   Search

7

SORTING DATA ON A SINGLE FIELD

Access provides an easy way to sort data in the Datasheet view. Simply right-click the field you want to use to sort the table's data to open the context menu, and click either the Sort A to Z or the Sort Z to A icon of the context menu. In mailing lists, a standard practice in the United States is to sort the records in ascending ZIP Code order. This practice often is observed in other countries that use postal codes. To quickly sort the Customers table in the order of the Postal Code field, follow these steps:

1. Open the PostalCode field's context menu by right-clicking anywhere in the field's column.

2. Click the context menu's Sort A to Z button.

Your Customers table quickly is sorted into the order shown in Figure 7.2.

Figure 7.2
Access's Sort feature works on a single field or multiple fields in left-to-right sequence. This Datasheet is sorted on the PostalCode field.

SORTING DATA ON MULTIPLE FIELDS

Although the sort operation in the preceding section accomplishes exactly what you specify, the result is less than useful because of the variants of postal code formats used in different countries. What's needed here is a multiple-field sort: first on the Country field and then on the PostalCode field. You can select the Country and the PostalCode fields to perform the multicolumn sort. The Quick Sort technique, however, automatically applies the sorting priority to the leftmost field you select, PostalCode. Access offers two methods of handling this problem: reorder the field display or specify the sort order in a Filter window. Follow these steps to use the reordering process:

→ Filters are discussed later in this chapter; **see** "Filtering Table Data", **p. 297**.

1. Select the Country field by clicking its field header button.

2. Hold down the left mouse button and drag the Country field to the left of the PostalCode field. Release the left mouse button to drop the field in its new location.

3. Shift+click the header button of the PostalCode field to select the Country and PostalCode fields.

4. Right-click in either selected column and then click the context menu's Sort A to Z button.

The sorted table, shown in Figure 7.3, now makes much more sense. A multiple-field sort on a table sometimes is called a *composite sort*.

Figure 7.3
Rearrange the fields to sort on multiple fields in left-to-right sequence. Changing the sequence of fields in Datasheet view affects the display– but not the design–of the table.

REMOVING A TABLE SORT ORDER AND THAWING COLUMNS

After you freeze columns and apply sort orders to a table, you might want to return the table to its original condition. To do so, Access offers you the following choices:

- To return the Datasheet view of an Access table with a primary key to its original sort order, select the field(s) that comprise the primary key (in the order of the primary key fields), and click the Sort Ascending button.

- To return to the original order when the table has no primary key field, close the table without saving the changes and then reopen the table.

- To thaw your frozen columns, right-click the datasheet and choose Unfreeze All Columns.

- To return the sequence of fields to its original state, drag the fields you moved back to their prior positions or close the table without saving your changes.

If you make substantial changes to the layout of the table and apply a sort order, it's usually quicker to close and reopen the table. (Don't save your changes to the table layout.)

7

FINDING MATCHING RECORDS IN A TABLE

To search for and select records with field values that match (or partially match) a particular value, use Access's Find feature. To find Luleå (a relatively large city in northern Sweden close to the Arctic Circle) in the City field, follow these steps:

1. In the Customers table, select the field (City) you want to search for by clicking its header button or by placing the cursor in that field.

2. Click the Home ribbon's primary and secondary Find buttons or press Ctrl+F to display the Find and Replace dialog (see Figure 7.4). The dialog opens with the Find page active and the Search Fields As Formatted check box marked by default.

Figure 7.4
The Find and Replace dialog opens with the name of the selected field in the Look In list of the Find page. The Find Next button is disabled until you type an entry in the Find What text box.

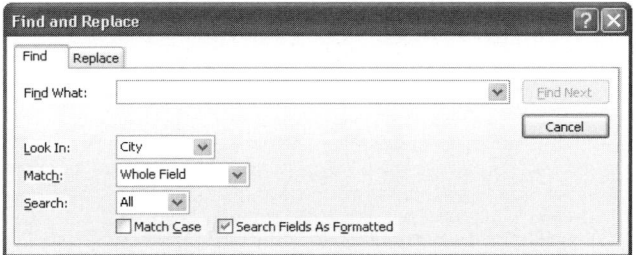

> **NOTE**
> If you select the field by clicking the field header button rather than by selecting all characters of a value in the field, the Find What value defaults to the datasheet's first cell value in the field or the last find criterion you chose.

3. Type the name of the city (**Lulea**) in the Find What text box (see Figure 7.5). The Find Next command button is enabled. The default values of the Match and Search lists are satisfactory at this point. Matching case or format isn't important here, so clear the Search Fields As Formatted check box.

Figure 7.5
A Whole Field match is selected by default, so type the entire value (Lulea for this example) to find in the Find What text box.

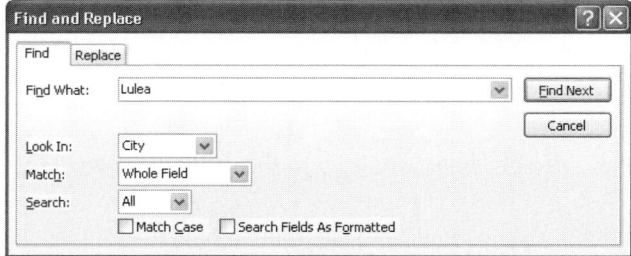

4. Click the Find Next button. If you don't have a Scandinavian keyboard, Access displays the message box shown in Figure 7.6. Click OK to dismiss the message box.

Figure 7.6
If the Find feature doesn't find a match for your entry, you receive a "not found" message.

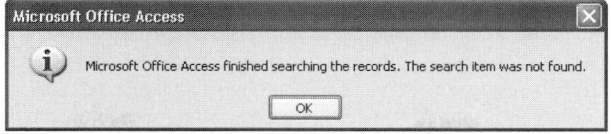

The "not found" message indicates that the Find feature didn't locate a match in the City field of the entire table. Access missed your entry because the Scandinavian diacritical ¯ is missing over the letter *a* in Lulea. In the ANSI character set, "a" has a value of 97, and "ā" has a value of 229.

TIP

> To enter international (extended) characters in the Find What text box, type the English letters and then use the Windows XP or Windows Vista Character Map (Charmap.exe) applet to find and copy the extended character to the Clipboard. (Don't worry about choosing the correct font.) Paste the character into the Find What text box at the appropriate location.

If the letters preceding an extended character are sufficient to define your search parameter, follow these steps to find Luleā:

1. Type **Lule**, omitting the *a*, in the Find What text box.
2. Select Start of Field from the Match drop-down list.
3. Click the Find Next button. Access finds and highlights Luleā in the City field (see Figure 7.7).

Figure 7.7
Omitting the special Scandinavian character from the search and using the Start of Field search option finds Luleā.

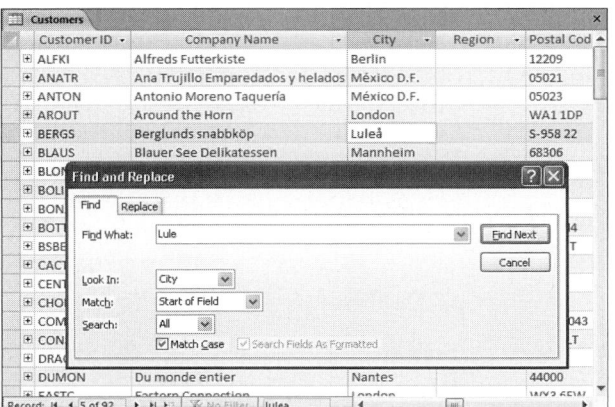

N O T E

[NEW]

You can do a quick search for the first instance of Luleå by typing **lule**, **ule**, or **lulea** into the small Search Box at the bottom of the Datasheet to the left of the horizontal scrollbar (refer to Figure 7.7). As you type characters into the Search Box, focus moves to the first cell of any field that contains the characters. After you locate the first instance of the value you want, press Enter to move to subsequent instances, if any. Ctrl+Shift+F sets the focus to the Search Box and Esc sets the focus to the found instance.

You also can find entries in any part of the field. If you type **ule** in the Find What text box and choose Any Part of Field from the Match drop-down list, you get a match on Luleå. However, you could also match Thule, the location of the Bluie West One airfield (also known as Thule Air Force Base) in Greenland. (There's no actual entry for Thule in the Customers table.)

T I P

You can search all fields of the table for a match by opening the Look In list and selecting *Tablename*: Table. Searching all fields in a table for a matching entry is usually much slower than searching a single field, especially if you have an index on the field being searched. Unless you specify the Any Part of Field Match option, Access uses the index to speed the searching operation.

Following is a list of the options available in the Find dialog:

- To specify a case-sensitive search, mark the Match Case check box.
- To search by using the field's format, mark the Search Fields as Formatted check box. This way you can enter a search term that matches the formatted appearance of the field, such as (510) 555-1212, rather than the native (unformatted) value (5105551212), if you applied a Format property value to the field. Using the Search Fields as Formatted option slows the search operation because indexes aren't used.
- To find additional matches, if any, click the Find Next button. If the Search option is set to Down, clicking the Find Next button starts the search at the current position of the record pointer and searches to the end of the table.
- To start the search at the last record of the table, select Up in the Search drop-down list.

REPLACING MATCHED FIELD VALUES AUTOMATICALLY

The Find and Replace dialog's Replace page lets you replace values selectively in fields that match the entry in the Find What text box. To open the dialog with the Replace page active, click the Home ribbon's Find button, then the Replace button, or press Ctrl+H. The shortcut key combination for the Edit menu's Replace command is Ctrl+H, which is the same for Microsoft Word and most other Office members.

The entries to search for Luleå and replace with Lulea appear in Figure 7.8. If you performed the search in the preceding section, select Customers:Table from the Look In drop-down list, click the Find Next button and then click the Replace button for those records in which you want to replace the value. You can do a bulk replace in all matching records by clicking the Replace All button. Unlike in Word and Excel, you can't undo search-and-replace operations in Access (or SQL Server) tables. Before replacements are made, a message box opens to request that you confirm the pending changes.

Figure 7.8
Click the Replace tab, if necessary, type a replacement value in the Replace With text box, and then click Find Next and Replace for each match or click Replace All for all occurrences of the Find What value.

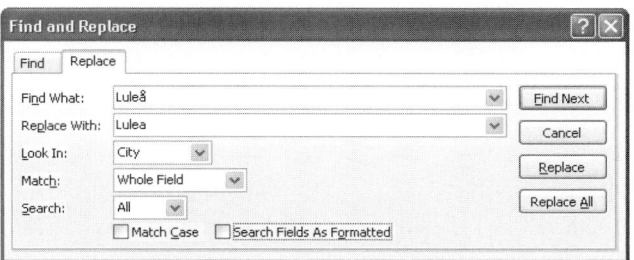

FILTERING TABLE DATA

Access lets you apply a filter to specify the records that appear in the Datasheet view of a table or a query result set. For example, if you want to view only those customers located in Germany, you use a filter to limit the displayed records to only those whose Country field contains the text Germany. Access gives you four different ways to apply filters to the data in a table:

 ■ *Filter by Selection* is the fastest and simplest way to apply a filter. You establish the filter criteria by selecting all or part of the data in one of the table's fields; Access displays only records that match the selected sample. With Filter by Selection, you can filter records based only on criteria in a single field of the table.

 ■ *Filter by Form* is the second fastest way to apply a filter. You enter the filter criteria into a blank datasheet form of the table; Access displays records that match the combined criteria in each field. Use Filter by Form to quickly filter records based on criteria in more than one field.

 ■ *Menu-based Filter/Sort* uses a context menu to apply ascending or descending sorts, a Text Filters choice that, for Text fields, lets you select Equals, Does Not Equal, Begins With, Does Not Begin With, Contains, Does Not Contain, Ends With, or Does Not End With comparison operators against characters you type in a Custom Filter input box. You also can filter for individual values by clearing or marking check boxes; this option is similar to Excel 2007's Filter menu.

NOTE

> For Number and Currency fields, the comparison operators are Equals, Less Than, Greater Than, and Between.
>
> The comparison operators for Date/Time fields are more interesting: the preceding numeric operators as well as Tomorrow, Today, Yesterday, {Next | This | Last}{Week | Month | Quarter | Year}, Past, and Future. Date Filters have a total of 24 operators, including All Dates in Period.

- *Advanced Filter/Sort* is the most powerful—but least speedy—type of filter. With an advanced filter/sort, you can make an Access filter do double duty because you also can add a sort order on one or more fields.

FILTERING BY SELECTION

Creating a Filter by Selection is as easy as selecting text in a field. When you apply the filter, Access uses the selected text to determine which records to display. Table 7.1 summarizes which records are displayed, depending on how you select text in the field. In all cases, Access applies the filter criteria only to the field in which you have selected text. Filter by selection lets you establish filter criteria for only a single field at one time.

TABLE 7.1 HOW SELECTED TEXT AFFECTS FILTER BY SELECTION

Selected Text	Filter Effect
Entire field	Displays only records whose fields contain exactly matching values
Beginning of field	Displays records in which the text at the beginning of the field matches the selected text
End of field	Displays records in which the text at the end of the field matches the selected text
Characters anywhere in field	Displays records in which any part of the field matches the selected text

To create a Filter by Selection on the Customers table (displaying only those customers located in Germany), follow these steps:

1. If necessary, open the Customers table in Datasheet view and use the scroll bars to make the Country field visible in the Table window.

2. Place the cursor in the Country field of the first record in the Customers table and, optionally, select all the text. (This entry should be Germany.)

3. Click the Home ribbon's Selection button in the Sort & Filter group, and choose Equals "Germany." Access applies the filter as shown in Figure 7.9.

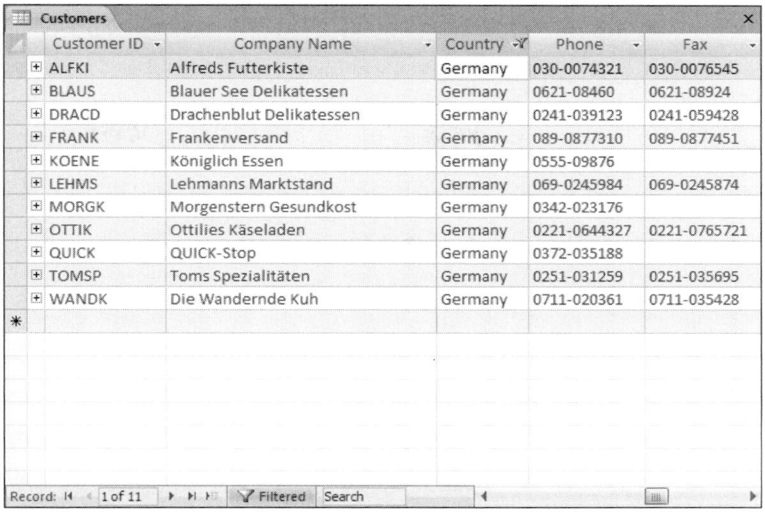

Figure 7.9
Applying "Germany" as a selection filter results in the filtered Datasheet view shown here. Notice the highlighted Filtered button to the left of the Search Box at the bottom of the Datasheet.

Customer ID	Company Name	Country	Phone	Fax
⊞ ALFKI	Alfreds Futterkiste	Germany	030-0074321	030-0076545
⊞ BLAUS	Blauer See Delikatessen	Germany	0621-08460	0621-08924
⊞ DRACD	Drachenblut Delikatessen	Germany	0241-039123	0241-059428
⊞ FRANK	Frankenversand	Germany	089-0877310	089-0877451
⊞ KOENE	Königlich Essen	Germany	0555-09876	
⊞ LEHMS	Lehmanns Marktstand	Germany	069-0245984	069-0245874
⊞ MORGK	Morgenstern Gesundkost	Germany	0342-023176	
⊞ OTTIK	Ottilies Käseladen	Germany	0221-0644327	0221-0765721
⊞ QUICK	QUICK-Stop	Germany	0372-035188	
⊞ TOMSP	Toms Spezialitäten	Germany	0251-031259	0251-035695
⊞ WANDK	Die Wandernde Kuh	Germany	0711-020361	0711-035428

Record: 1 of 11 ▸ Filtered Search

Notice that the Selection button is now displayed in active status (a contrasting background color), indicating that a filter is being applied to the table, and its ToolTip changes to Remove Filter. The legend (Filtered) also is added to the record selection and status bar at the bottom of the Table window. A small filter icon appears to the right of the field name and the Filtered button at the bottom of the Datasheet is highlighted. (The Filtered button is new in Access 2007). To remove the filter, click the activated Apply Filter button or the Filtered button.

> **TIP**
>
> Use the Search Box or Find and Replace dialog to quickly locate the first record of a group you're interested in filtering and then apply a Filter by Selection.

As mentioned previously, you can also apply a Filter by Selection based on partially selected text in a field. Figure 7.10 shows the Customers table with a different Filter by Selection applied—this time, only the letters "er" in the Country field and Equals "er" were selected. You must remove the previous filter before applying a new filter to the entire table, rather than the filtered records.

> **TIP**
>
> You can apply a Filter by Selection to more than one field at a time. For example, after applying a Filter by Selection to display only those customers in Germany, you could then move to the City field and apply a second Filter by Selection for Berlin. The resulting table would include only those customers in Berlin, Germany. An easier way to apply filters based on more than one field value is to use a Filter by Form, described in the "Filter by Form" section coming up.

7

Figure 7.10
Selecting only a part of the field–in this case the letters "er"–displays records containing the partial selection in any part of the field.

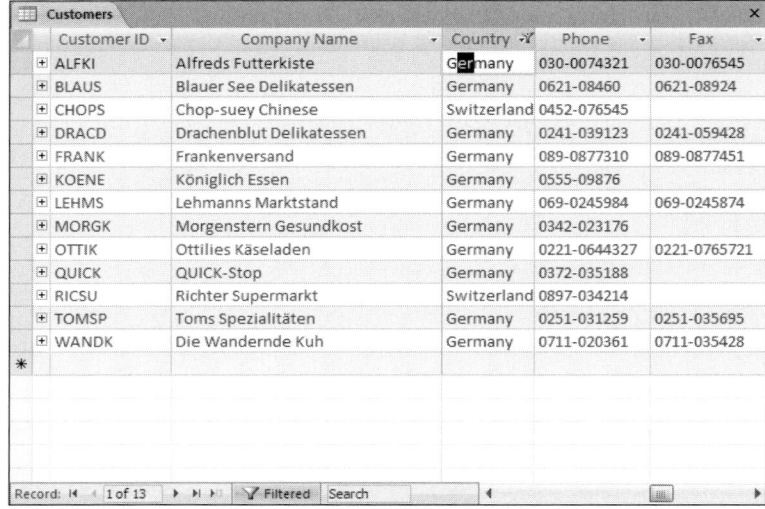

Customer ID	Company Name	Country	Phone	Fax
⊞ ALFKI	Alfreds Futterkiste	Germany	030-0074321	030-0076545
⊞ BLAUS	Blauer See Delikatessen	Germany	0621-08460	0621-08924
⊞ CHOPS	Chop-suey Chinese	Switzerland	0452-076545	
⊞ DRACD	Drachenblut Delikatessen	Germany	0241-039123	0241-059428
⊞ FRANK	Frankenversand	Germany	089-0877310	089-0877451
⊞ KOENE	Königlich Essen	Germany	0555-09876	
⊞ LEHMS	Lehmanns Marktstand	Germany	069-0245984	069-0245874
⊞ MORGK	Morgenstern Gesundkost	Germany	0342-023176	
⊞ OTTIK	Ottilies Käseladen	Germany	0221-0644327	0221-0765721
⊞ QUICK	QUICK-Stop	Germany	0372-035188	
⊞ RICSU	Richter Supermarkt	Switzerland	0897-034214	
⊞ TOMSP	Toms Spezialitäten	Germany	0251-031259	0251-035695
⊞ WANDK	Die Wandernde Kuh	Germany	0711-020361	0711-035428

Record: I◀ ◀ 1 of 13 ▶ ▶I ▶⁕ ▼ Filtered Search

USING THE TEXT FILTERS OPTION

The Text Filters option is a quick method for applying a filter to a single field. To use the Text Filters feature, do this:

1. Right-click the field on which you want to filter the table, and choose Text Filters, Equals in the context menu to open the Custom Filter input box.

2. In the text box, type the value you want to filter on, such as **USA** for the Country field of the Customers table, and press Enter to apply the filter.

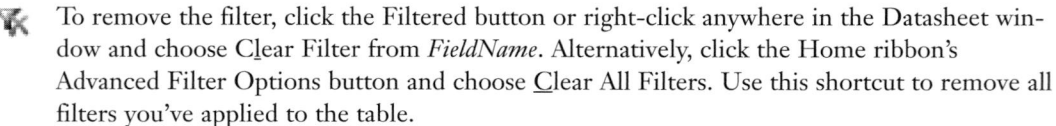 To remove the filter, click the Filtered button or right-click anywhere in the Datasheet window and choose Clear Filter from *FieldName*. Alternatively, click the Home ribbon's Advanced Filter Options button and choose Clear All Filters. Use this shortcut to remove all filters you've applied to the table.

FILTERING BY FORM

Filtering by form is slightly more complex than filtering by selection because it lets you filter records based on criteria in more than one field at a time. For example, you saw in the preceding section how to use a Filter by Selection to view only those customers in Germany. To further limit the displayed records to those customers located in Berlin, Germany (and not Berlin, New Hampshire), use a Filter by Form.

In a Filter by Form, Access displays a blank form for the table (see Figure 7.11). This window is called a form to distinguish it from the Table Datasheet window, although it's not the same as the data entry forms discussed later in this book. You can combine criteria in a Filter by Form with a logical **Or** operator or a logical **And** operator. For example, you can filter the Customers table to display only those customers in the United States or Canada. As another example, you could filter the Customers table to display only those customers in the United States with ZIP Codes beginning with the digit 9 (such as 94609 or 90807).

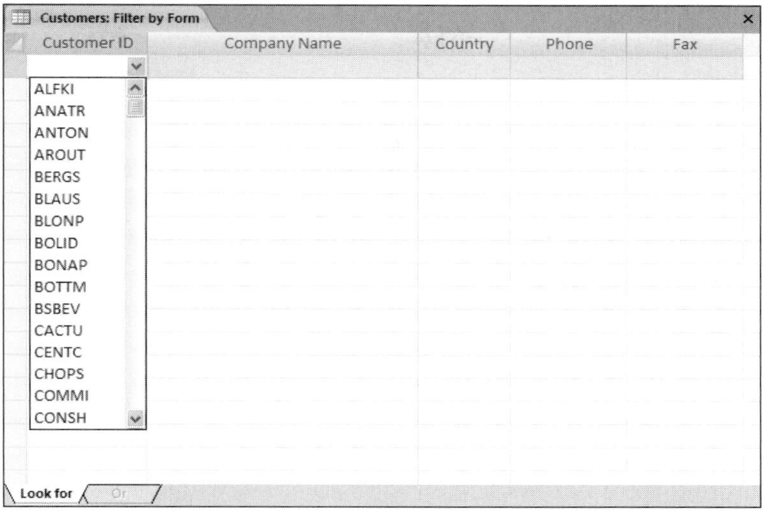

Figure 7.11
The Filter by Form variation of Datasheet view has a single row in which you add filter criteria. Each field has a drop-down list of values you can choose for the filter.

Customer ID	Company Name	Country	Phone	Fax
ALFKI				
ANATR				
ANTON				
AROUT				
BERGS				
BLAUS				
BLONP				
BOLID				
BONAP				
BOTTM				
BSBEV				
CACTU				
CENTC				
CHOPS				
COMMI				
CONSH				

Customers: Filter by Form

Look for / Or /

TIP

Verify that all the fields of the filter form are empty before designing a new filter. The last filter expression you apply appears in the filter form when you open it if the Filter on Load property value is Yes. For instance, the Country field contains `Like "*er*"` if you tested the partial selection example in the preceding section and set Filter on Load to Yes.

To create a Filter by Form on the Customers table to display only those customers in the United States or Canada, follow these steps:

1. If necessary, open the Customers table in Datasheet view.

2. Click the Home ribbon's Advanced Filter Options button and choose Filter by Form to display the Filter by Form window (refer to Figure 7.11).

3. Make the Country field visible in the Filter by Form window if necessary. (The CustomerID and CompanyName fields in the figures have been frozen, as described previously in this chapter.)

4. Click inside the Country field and open the Country list box, or press F4. The drop-down list contains all the unique values in the Country field.

5. Select Canada in the list box, as shown in Figure 7.12. Access automatically adds the quotation marks around the value you select and enters it into the Country field form box.

7

Figure 7.12
The drop-down list in the Filter by Form datasheet lets you select a single criterion on which to filter the field.

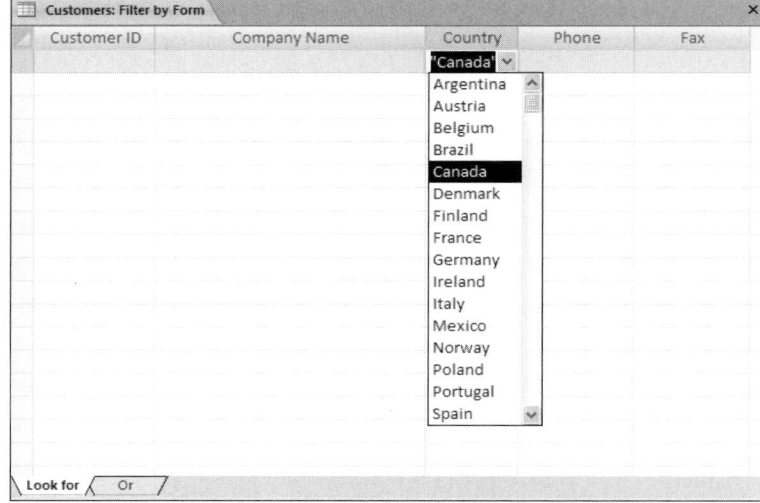

6. Click the Or tab at the bottom of the Filter by Form window. Access combines criteria that you enter on separate tabs in the Filter by Form window with a logical **Or** operator. When you add an **Or** operator, a tab for another **Or** operator appears.

7. Click the arrow to open the Country list box or press F4. Select USA from the drop-down list (see Figure 7.13).

Figure 7.13
Clicking the Or tab of the Filter by Form window opens another empty row in which you can select another criterion. Each time you add an Or criterion, an additional disabled Or tab appears at the bottom of the window.

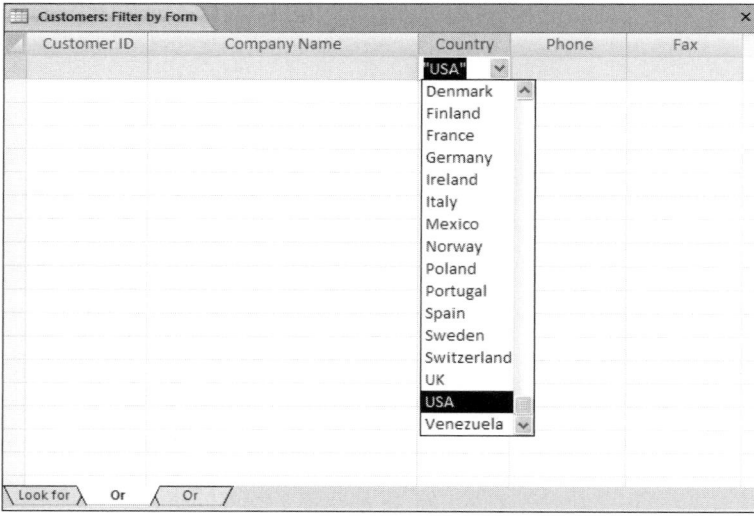

8. Click the Apply Filter button. Access applies the new filter to the table, displaying the records shown in Figure 7.14.

Figure 7.14
The Customers table in Datasheet view displays the result of applying the "Canada" Or "USA" filter.

Customer ID	Company Name	Country	Phone	Fax
⊞ BOTTM	Bottom-Dollar Markets	Canada	(604) 555-4729	(604) 555-3745
⊞ GREAL	Great Lakes Food Market	USA	(503) 555-7555	
⊞ HUNGC	Hungry Coyote Import Store	USA	(503) 555-6874	(503) 555-2376
⊞ LAUGB	Laughing Bacchus Wine Cellars	Canada	(604) 555-3392	(604) 555-7293
⊞ LAZYK	Lazy K Kountry Store	USA	(509) 555-7969	(509) 555-6221
⊞ LETSS	Let's Stop N Shop	USA	(415) 555-5938	
⊞ LONEP	Lonesome Pine Restaurant	USA	(503) 555-9573	(503) 555-9646
⊞ MEREP	Mère Paillarde	Canada	(514) 555-8054	(514) 555-8055
⊞ OLDWO	Old World Delicatessen	USA	(907) 555-7584	(907) 555-2880
⊞ RATTC	Rattlesnake Canyon Grocery	USA	(505) 555-5939	(505) 555-3620
⊞ SAVEA	Save-a-lot Markets	USA	(208) 555-8097	
⊞ SPLIR	Split Rail Beer & Ale	USA	(307) 555-4680	(307) 555-6525
⊞ THEBI	The Big Cheese	USA	(503) 555-3612	
⊞ THECR	The Cracker Box	USA	(406) 555-5834	(406) 555-8083
⊞ TRAIH	Trail's Head Gourmet Provisioners	USA	(206) 555-8257	(206) 555-2174
⊞ WHITC	White Clover Markets	USA	(206) 555-4112	(206) 555-4115

Record: 1 of 16 ▶ Filtered Search

NOTE

Access stores the last filter you applied as the value of the table's Filter property. To view the filter value, change to Table Design view and click the Property Sheet button to open the Property Sheet for the table. For the preceding example, the filter value is ((Customers.Country="Canada")) OR ((Customers.Country="USA")). The parenthesis pairs are superfluous for this filter.

You can also combine filter criteria in a logical **And** operator by entering criteria in more than one field on the same tab of the Form window. For example, you want to filter the Orders table to find all orders handled by Nancy Davolio and shipped to France. You easily can use a Filter by Form to do so, as the following example shows:

1. Open the Orders table and freeze the OrderID, Customer, and Employee fields. Then position the ShipCountry field so that it's visible (see Figure 7.15). Freezing the fields isn't an essential step, but it makes setting up the filter and viewing the filtered data easier.

2. Click the Advanced Filter Options button and choose <u>F</u>ilter by Form to display the Filter by Form window.

3. Click the Advanced Filter Options button again and choose <u>C</u>lear All Filters to clear any previous filter criteria from the Filter by Form grid. (This choice is disabled if no filters are applied.)

4. Use the drop-down list in the EmployeeID field to select Davolio, Nancy, and then use the drop-down list in the ShipCountry field to select France. You must manually add quotes around a text criterion that includes a comma (see Figure 7.16).

7

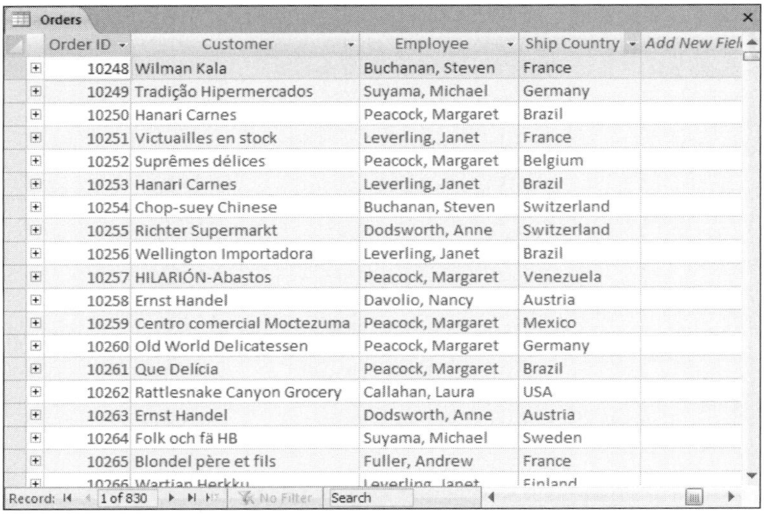

Figure 7.15
Simplify the filtering process by freezing the first three fields of the Orders table.

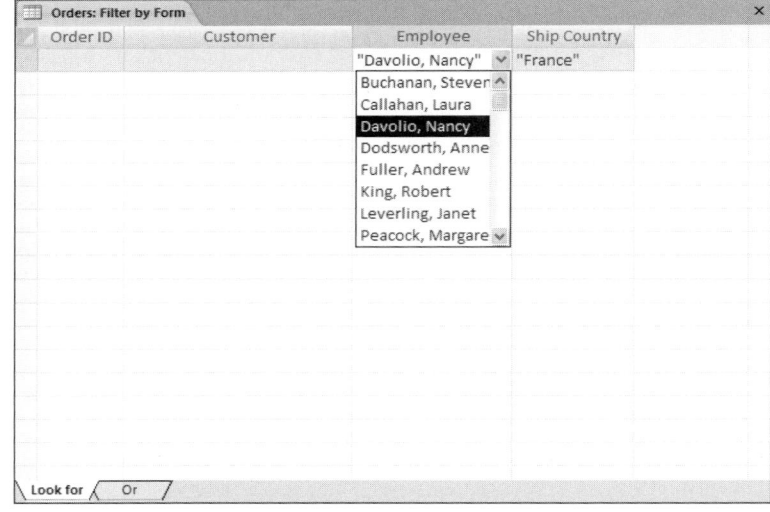

Figure 7.16
The criterion in the EmployeeID field is based on the lookup field that displays the LastName and FirstName values from the Employees tables, separated by a comma and space. Matching a composite criterion requires surrounding the value with quotes.

5. Click the Apply Filter button. Access applies the new filter to the table, displaying the records shown in Figure 7.17. This filter shows only those records for orders that were handled by Nancy Davolio and shipped to France.

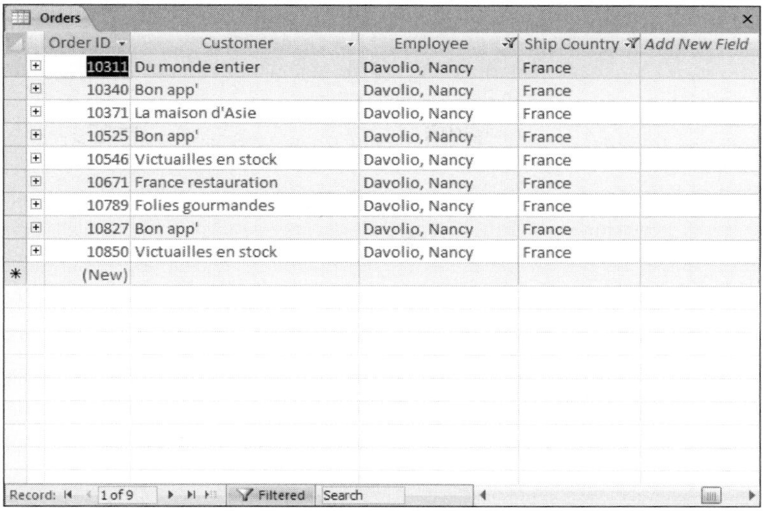

Figure 7.17
The EmployeeID and Country filter criteria shown in Figure 7.16 result in the following Datasheet view of the Orders table.

Order ID	Customer	Employee	Ship Country	Add New Field
10311	Du monde entier	Davolio, Nancy	France	
10340	Bon app'	Davolio, Nancy	France	
10371	La maison d'Asie	Davolio, Nancy	France	
10525	Bon app'	Davolio, Nancy	France	
10546	Victuailles en stock	Davolio, Nancy	France	
10671	France restauration	Davolio, Nancy	France	
10789	Folies gourmandes	Davolio, Nancy	France	
10827	Bon app'	Davolio, Nancy	France	
10850	Victuailles en stock	Davolio, Nancy	France	
(New)				

Record: 1 of 9 — Filtered — Search

NOTE

For this example, the value of the table's Filter property is ((Lookup_EmployeeID.Name= "Davolio, Nancy") AND (Orders.ShipCountry="France")), because the Lookup Row Source property for EmployeeID is SELECT DISTINCTROW Employees.EmployeeID, [LastName] & ", " & [FirstName] AS Name FROM Employees ORDER BY Employees. LastName, Employees.FirstName;.

The Lookup_FieldName.Alias expression enables comparison with the lookup value instead of the numeric EmployeeID value.

TIP

You also can apply the Filter by Form feature to Access forms that are bound to tables or queries. With forms that display field values in text boxes, clicking the Filter by Form button clears the text boxes and adds the Look For and Or tabs to the bottom of the form. You type search value(s) in the appropriate text box(es) for the **And** operator, **Or** operator, or both.

 If Access doesn't return the records you expected, try the solution in the "Troubleshooting" section near the end of the chapter.

APPLYING MENU-BASED FILTERS AND SORT ORDERS

Access 2007's new menu-based filter and sort order feature emulates Excel's approach to the process but isn't very efficient, especially for fields that store a large number of different values. To display the menu, select the field to filter, sort, or both, and then click the Home ribbon's large Filter button. Alternatively, click the small arrow to the right of the field name to open the menu.

NOTE

The Access development team appears to consider this option the default for filtering and sorting because its Filter button is much larger than the (Filter by) Selection and Advanced Filter Options buttons.

Working with menu-based filters is easy, if the feature is capable of accomplishing your task. To apply a menu-based filter for orders received in 2006 and a descending (newest to oldest) sort order to the OrderDate field of the orders table, do the following:

1. Open the Orders table, if necessary, and click the Filter button to open the filter and sort context menu.

2. Choose Date Filters to open the Date Filters context menu (see Figure 7.18).

Figure 7.18
The menu-based Date Filters for the Orders table's OrderDate field provide a range of dynamic date and date range choices.

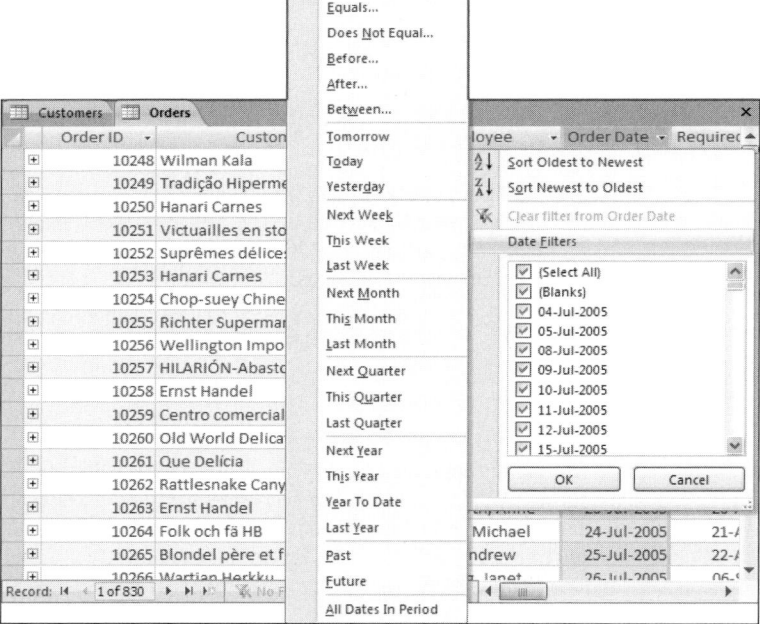

3. Select Between to open the Between Dates dialog. Type **1/1/2006** in the Oldest and **12/31/2006** in the Newest text box (see Figure 7.19) and then click OK to apply the filter.

4. Reopen the filter and sort context menu and select Sort Newest to Oldest. The Orders table window appears, as shown in Figure 7.20.

Figure 7.19
The Between Dates dialog offers Date Pickers for Oldest and Newest values, but typing the dates usually is faster than navigating the Date Pickers.

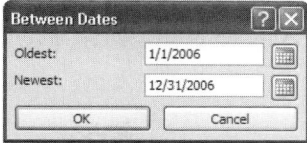

Figure 7.20
Orders rows for the year 2006 are sorted in reverse chronological order.

 5. Click the Home ribbon's Toggle Filter button to clear the filter and sort order you applied.

APPLYING ADVANCED FILTERS AND SORT ORDERS

Filters in Access, as mentioned previously, are queries in disguise, and they provide a useful introduction to single-table Access queries, the subject of Chapter 9, "Designing Queries for Access Databases." Creating an advanced filter/sort is much like creating a query, with some basic differences, as follows:

- The Show Table dialog doesn't appear.
- The Views group's View button is disabled.
- The Show row is missing from the Filter Design grid.

Filters are limited to using one table or query that Access automatically specifies when you enter Filter Design view. You can save a filter you create as a query or load a filter from a

7

query, but Access has no provision for saving a filter as a separate filter object. The table saves (persists) the filter and sort order you add if you save your changes when closing the table. The following sections describe how to add criteria to filter records and to add a sort order in the Filter Design window.

NOTE

SQL Server tables opened in ADP don't support Access's advanced filter/sort function.

ADDING MULTIFIELD SORT AND COMPOUND FILTER CRITERIA

In its default configuration, the Datasheet toolbar doesn't have an Advanced Filter/Sort button. Instead, you start the advanced filter/sort operation by choosing <u>R</u>ecords, <u>F</u>ilter, <u>A</u>dvanced Filter/Sort. To create a filter on the Orders table (which provides more records to filter than the Customers table), follow these steps:

 1. Open the Orders table, if necessary. Click the Toggle Filter button to clear filter or sort criteria, if you applied either or both previously.

 2. Click the Advanced Filter Options button and choose <u>A</u>dvanced Filter/Sort to display the Filter window (see Figure 7.21). The default filter name, Filter1, is concatenated with the table name to create the default name of the first filter, OrdersFilter1. The Field List window for the Orders table appears in the upper pane of the Filter window.

Figure 7.21
The Filter window is similar to the Query Design window, but doesn't have Table or Show rows in the lower pane's grid.

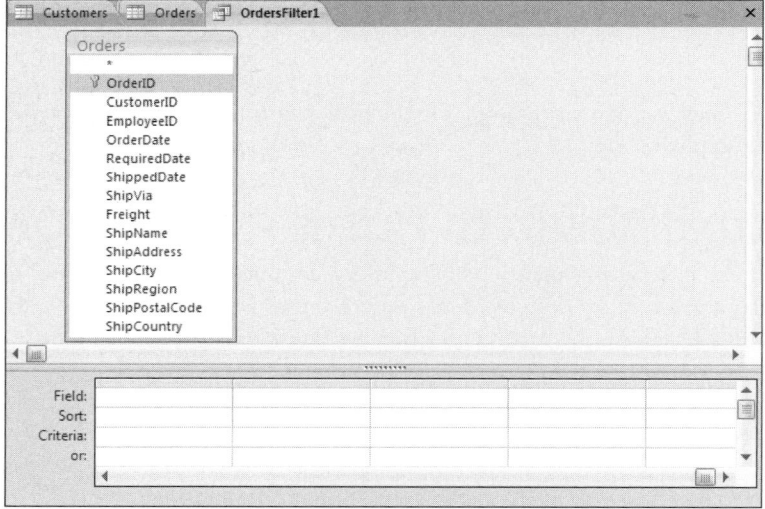

3. One field that you might want to use to sort or limit displayed records is OrderID. Click it in the field list in the upper pane and drag it to the first column of the Field row of the Filter Design grid in the lower pane. (When your mouse pointer reaches the

lower pane, the pointer turns into a field symbol.) Alternatively, double-click the OrderID field to add it to the grid.

4. Repeat step 3 for other fields on which you might want to sort or establish criteria. Candidates are CustomerID, ShipCountry, ShipPostalCode, OrderDate, and ShippedDate.

5. To check the sorting capabilities of your first advanced filter, add an ascending sort to the ShipCountry and ShipPostalCode fields by selecting Ascending from those fields' Sort cell. Your Filter Design window appears as shown in Figure 7.22.

Figure 7.22
The grid of the Filter Design window has ascending sorts specified for the ShipCountry and ShipPostalCode fields.

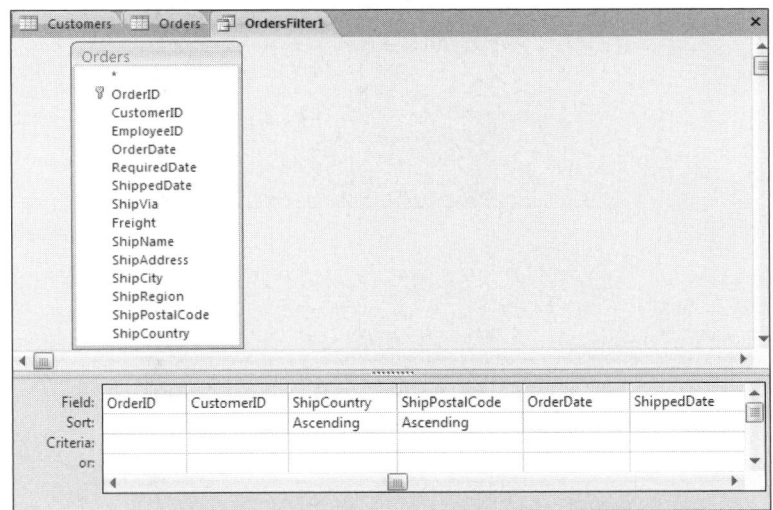

6. Click the Toggle Filter toolbar button or choose Filter, Apply Filter/Sort.

7. Freeze the OrderID and CompanyName columns and use the horizontal scroll bar of the datasheet to reveal the ShipCountry and ShipPostalCode fields. Your sorted table appears as shown in Figure 7.23.

8. Click the Advanced Filter Options button and choose Advanced Filter/Sort to edit the filter criteria.

9. Type **USA** in the Criteria row of the ShipCountry field to limit records to those orders shipped to an address in the United States. Access automatically adds quotes around "USA".

10. Click the Toggle Filter button and scroll to display the sorted fields. Only records with destinations in the United States appear, as shown in Figure 7.24.

Order ID	Customer	Ship Postal Code	Ship Country	Add Ne
10898	Océano Atlántico Ltda.	1010	Argentina	
11019	Rancho grande	1010	Argentina	
10986	Océano Atlántico Ltda.	1010	Argentina	
10958	Océano Atlántico Ltda.	1010	Argentina	
10937	Cactus Comidas para llevar	1010	Argentina	
10716	Rancho grande	1010	Argentina	
10409	Océano Atlántico Ltda.	1010	Argentina	
10916	Rancho grande	1010	Argentina	
11054	Cactus Comidas para llevar	1010	Argentina	
10881	Cactus Comidas para llevar	1010	Argentina	
10448	Rancho grande	1010	Argentina	
10828	Rancho grande	1010	Argentina	
10782	Cactus Comidas para llevar	1010	Argentina	
10819	Cactus Comidas para llevar	1010	Argentina	
10521	Cactus Comidas para llevar	1010	Argentina	
10531	Océano Atlántico Ltda.	1010	Argentina	
10686	Piccolo und mehr	5020	Austria	
10353	Piccolo und mehr	5020	Austria	
10597	Piccolo und mehr	5020	Austria	

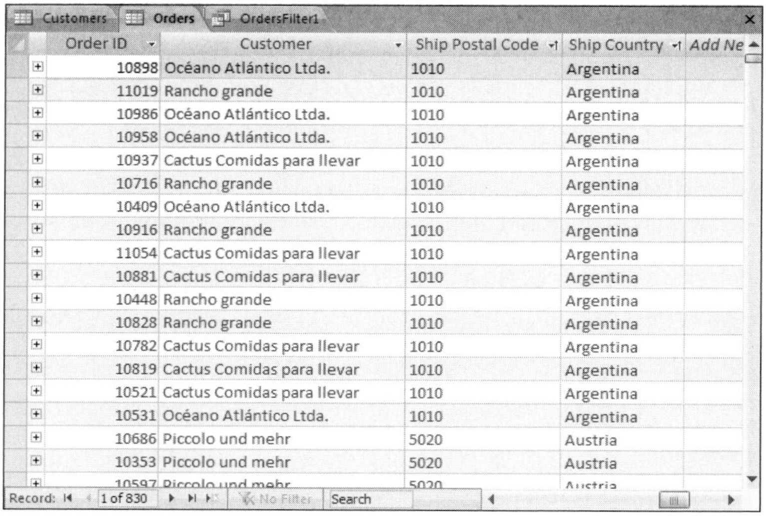

Figure 7.23
The sorted ShipCountry field is to the left of the sorted ShipPostalCode field in Query Design view (refer to Figure 7.22). Therefore, the table is sorted first by country and then by postal code. Applying an Advanced Filter/Sort doesn't require repositioning the fields in Datasheet view.

Order ID	Customer	Ship Postal Code	Ship Country
10624	The Cracker Box	59801	USA
10775	The Cracker Box	59801	USA
11003	The Cracker Box	59801	USA
10271	Split Rail Beer & Ale	82520	USA
10385	Split Rail Beer & Ale	82520	USA
10369	Split Rail Beer & Ale	82520	USA
10349	Split Rail Beer & Ale	82520	USA
10821	Split Rail Beer & Ale	82520	USA
10432	Split Rail Beer & Ale	82520	USA
10974	Split Rail Beer & Ale	82520	USA
10329	Split Rail Beer & Ale	82520	USA
10756	Split Rail Beer & Ale	82520	USA
10678	Save-a-lot Markets	83720	USA
10748	Save-a-lot Markets	83720	USA
10757	Save-a-lot Markets	83720	USA
10815	Save-a-lot Markets	83720	USA
10607	Save-a-lot Markets	83720	USA
10393	Save-a-lot Markets	83720	USA
10722	Save-a-lot Markets	83720	USA

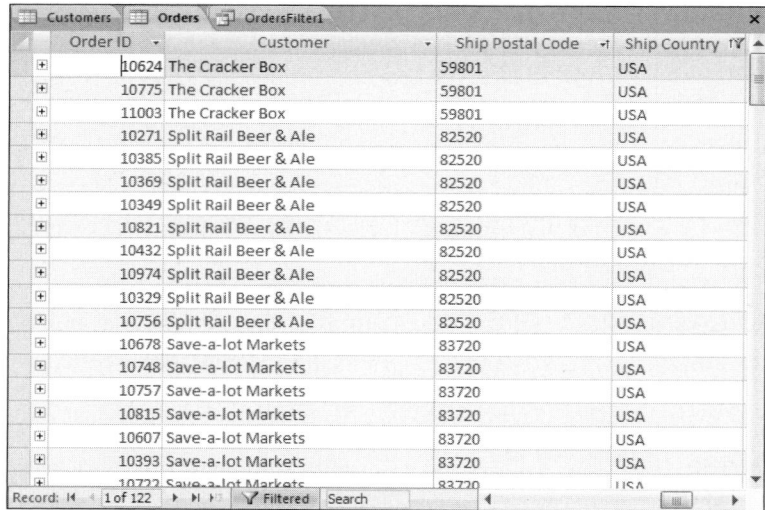

Figure 7.24
Adding "USA" in the Criteria row under the ShipCountry field filters the Datasheet view to display orders destined for the United States only.

Using Composite Criteria

You can apply composite criteria to expand or further limit the records that Access displays. Composite criteria are applied to more than one field. To display all orders from the Orders table that were received on or after 1/1/2006 with destinations in North America, extend the exercise in the preceding section and try the following:

1. Click Advanced Filter Options and choose Advanced Filter/Sort to display the Filter Design window.

2. Type **Canada** in the second criteria row of the ShipCountry field and **Mexico** in the third row; then move the cursor to a different cell. When you add criteria under one another, the effect is to make the criteria alternative—that is, combined by a logical **Or** operator.

3. Open the Sort list for the PostalCode field and select (not sorted) to remove the sort. Open the Sort list for the OrderDate field and select Ascending.

4. Type **>=#1/1/2006#** in the first criteria line of the OrderDate field. When you add criteria on the same line as another criterion, the criteria is additive (a logical **And** operator)—that is, orders placed on or after 1/1/2006. The # symbols indicate to Access that the enclosed value is of the Date/Time data type; Access adds the symbols if you don't.

5. Press F2 to select the date entry you made in step 3 and then press Ctrl+C to copy the expression to the Clipboard. Position the cursor in the second row of the OrderDate field and press Ctrl+V to add the same expression for Canada. Repeat this process to add the date criterion for Mexican orders. Your Filter Design grid now appears as shown in Figure 7.25.

Figure 7.25
The design of this composite filter restricts the display to orders received in 2006 and later destined for North America.

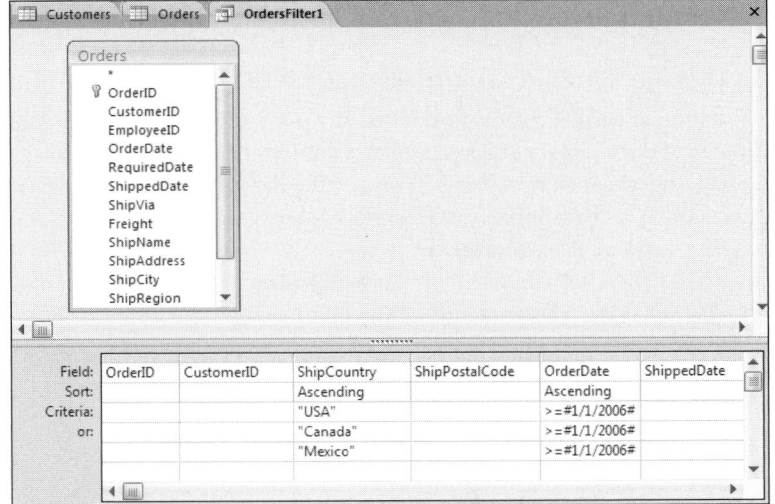

 6. Click the Toggle Filter button to display your newly filtered datasheet (see Figure 7.26, which has the field sequence rearranged and is scrolled to show the three countries).

Figure 7.26
This Datasheet view of the Orders table has the filter of Figure 7.25 applied. The field sequence has been rearranged to permit viewing the OrderDate and ShipCountry fields.

Order ID	Customer	Ship Postal Code	Ship Country	Order Date
10410	Bottom-Dollar Markets	T2F 8M4	Canada	10-Jan-2006
10411	Bottom-Dollar Markets	T2F 8M4	Canada	10-Jan-2006
10424	Mère Paillarde	H1J 1C3	Canada	23-Jan-2006
10431	Bottom-Dollar Markets	T2F 8M4	Canada	30-Jan-2006
10439	Mère Paillarde	H1J 1C3	Canada	07-Feb-2006
10492	Bottom-Dollar Markets	T2F 8M4	Canada	01-Apr-2006
10495	Laughing Bacchus Wine Cellar	V3F 2K1	Canada	03-Apr-2006
10505	Mère Paillarde	H1J 1C3	Canada	14-Apr-2006
10565	Mère Paillarde	H1J 1C3	Canada	11-Jun-2006
10570	Mère Paillarde	H1J 1C3	Canada	17-Jun-2006
10590	Mère Paillarde	H1J 1C3	Canada	07-Jul-2006
10605	Mère Paillarde	H1J 1C3	Canada	21-Jul-2006
10618	Mère Paillarde	H1J 1C3	Canada	01-Aug-2006
10619	Mère Paillarde	H1J 1C3	Canada	04-Aug-2006
10620	Laughing Bacchus Wine Cellar	V3F 2K1	Canada	05-Aug-2006
10724	Mère Paillarde	H1J 1C3	Canada	30-Oct-2006
10742	Bottom-Dollar Markets	T2F 8M4	Canada	14-Nov-2006
10810	Laughing Bacchus Wine Cellar	V3F 2K1	Canada	01-Jan-2007

Record: 1 of 144 | Filtered | Search

→ To become more familiar with the power of selecting data with criteria, **see** "Using the Query Design Window," **p. XXX** *(Ch 09)*.

SAVING YOUR FILTER AS A QUERY AND LOADING A FILTER

As mentioned earlier, Access doesn't have a persistent Filter object. A persistent database object is one you create that's stored as a component of your database's .accdb file. Persistent database objects appear as items in one of the list views of the Navigation Pane. A filter is equivalent to a single-table query, so Access lets you save your filter as a QueryDef (query definition) object. Access saves the names of the filters associated with each table in the system tables of your database when you save a filter as a query. This feature is the principal advantage of using a filter rather than a query when only a single table is involved.

To save your filter and remove the filter from the Orders table, follow these steps:

1. Click the Advanced Filter Options button and choose <u>A</u>dvanced Filter/Sort to display the Filter Design window if it isn't already displayed.

2. Right-click the upper pane and choose Save As Query to display the Save as Query input box.

3. Enter a descriptive name—such as **fltOrdersNorthAmerica2006**—for your filter in the Query Name text box. Using the flt prefix distinguishes the filters you save from conventional queries (see Figure 7.27).

Figure 7.27
Use a descriptive name when saving the filter as a *QueryDef* object.

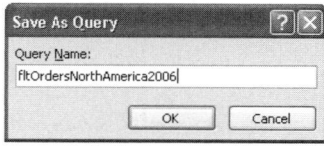

Save As Query

Query Name:
fltOrdersNorthAmerica2006

OK   Cancel

4. Click OK to save the filter, close the Filter window, add a Queries category to the Navigation Pane, and add fltOrdersNorthAmerica2006 as a member of the Queries category.

 5. Click the Advanced Filter Options button and choose Clear All Filters to remove the filter from the Orders datasheet.

6. Close the Orders table, and save the changes.

Re-applying a filter from the filter you saved as a query requires the following steps:

1. Reopen the Orders table in Datasheet view.

 2. Click the Advanced Filter Options button and choose Advanced Filter/Sort to open the Filter Design window with the default OrdersFilter1 filter.

 3. Click the Advanced Filter/Sort button again and choose Load from Query to open the Applicable Filter dialog (see Figure 7.28). You use the Applicable Filter dialog to select the filter you want if you've saved more than one filter for the table.

Figure 7.28
Clicking the Load from Query toolbar button opens the Applicable Filter dialog from which you can select the filter to apply to the table.

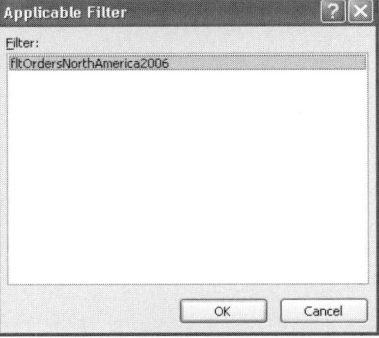

4. Double-click the fltOrdersNorthAmerica2006 filter item to load the saved query into the Filter window.

 5. Click the Toggle Filter button to display the resulting filtered set in the Orders datasheet.

> **TIP**
>
> To remove a filter saved as a query so it doesn't appear in the Applicable Filters list, delete the query from the Navigation Pane's Queries group.

7

APPLYING A SAVED QUERY AS A FILTER

An alternative to the preceding steps is to execute the saved filter as query. You execute a query the same way you open a table:

1. Close the Orders table.

2. Double-click the fltOrdersNorthAmerica2006 item under the Queries category. The Datasheet of the fltOrdersNorthAmerica window that opens is similar to the datasheet you created in step 5 of the preceding operation, except that the fields appear in the original order of the table design.

 3. Click the Design View button to display the query design (see Figure 7.29). Fields in which no selection criteria or sort order are entered don't appear in the Query Design grid.

Figure 7.29
The Query Design view of a filter is similar to the Filter Design view, but adds Table and Show rows to the grid.

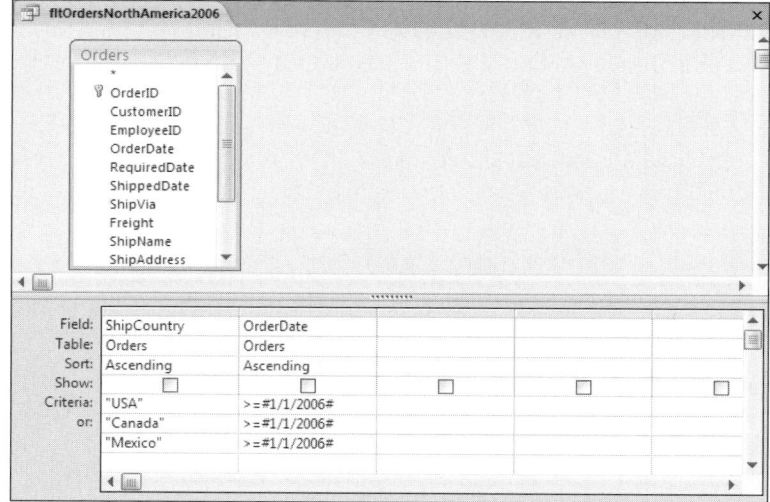

CUSTOMIZING TABLE DATASHEET VIEW

To customize the appearance of Table Datasheet view, you can hide the fields you don't want to appear in your datasheet, change the height of the record rows, eliminate the gridlines, and select a different font for your display. The following list describes each option for customizing Table and Query Datasheet views:

- To hide a field, select it by clicking its header or placing the cursor in the column for the field. Then choose Format, Hide Columns.

- To show a hidden field, choose Format, Unhide Columns to display the Unhide Columns dialog (see Figure 7.30). A mark next to the field name in the Column list indicates fields appearing in Datasheet view. Click the check box to the left of the field name to toggle between hiding and showing the field.

 - To change the font used to display and print the datasheet, use the Font drop-down list in the Home ribbon's Font group.

Figure 7.30
The Unhide Columns dialog lets you specify the fields that appear in Table Datasheet view.

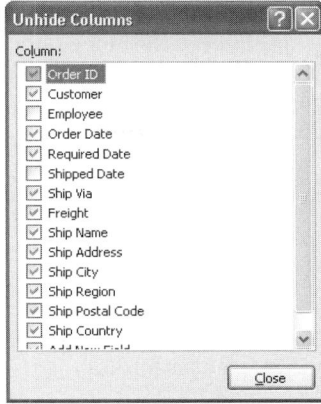

■ To remove gridlines from the display and printed versions of the datasheet, open the Font group's Gridlines drop-down list. Access displays a gallery of four gridline display choices: Both, Horizontal, Vertical, and None; click the button corresponding to the gridline display you want.

■ To change the height of the rows as displayed and printed, position the mouse pointer at the bottom edge of one of the record selector buttons. The pointer turns into a double-headed arrow (see Figure 7.31). Drag the bottom edge of the button to adjust the height of all the rows. Alternatively, choose Format, Row Height and set the height in points in the Row Height dialog. (Multiply the size of your font by about 1.25 to obtain normal row spacing; printers call 10-point type with 12-point spacing "10 on 12.")

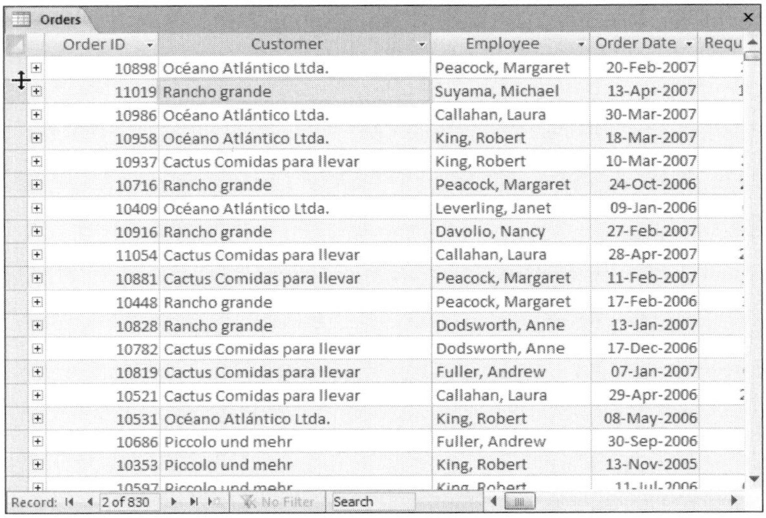

Figure 7.31
This customized Datasheet view uses a 9-point Verdana type and no gridlines. You adjust line spacing, shown here between the second and third record selection buttons, by dragging the double-headed arrow up or down.

Order ID	Customer	Employee	Order Date	Requ
10898	Océano Atlántico Ltda.	Peacock, Margaret	20-Feb-2007	
11019	Rancho grande	Suyama, Michael	13-Apr-2007	1
10986	Océano Atlántico Ltda.	Callahan, Laura	30-Mar-2007	
10958	Océano Atlántico Ltda.	King, Robert	18-Mar-2007	
10937	Cactus Comidas para llevar	King, Robert	10-Mar-2007	
10716	Rancho grande	Peacock, Margaret	24-Oct-2006	
10409	Océano Atlántico Ltda.	Leverling, Janet	09-Jan-2006	
10916	Rancho grande	Davolio, Nancy	27-Feb-2007	
11054	Cactus Comidas para llevar	Callahan, Laura	28-Apr-2007	
10881	Cactus Comidas para llevar	Peacock, Margaret	11-Feb-2007	
10448	Rancho grande	Peacock, Margaret	17-Feb-2006	
10828	Rancho grande	Dodsworth, Anne	13-Jan-2007	
10782	Cactus Comidas para llevar	Dodsworth, Anne	17-Dec-2006	
10819	Cactus Comidas para llevar	Fuller, Andrew	07-Jan-2007	
10521	Cactus Comidas para llevar	Callahan, Laura	29-Apr-2006	
10531	Océano Atlántico Ltda.	King, Robert	08-May-2006	
10686	Piccolo und mehr	Fuller, Andrew	30-Sep-2006	
10353	Piccolo und mehr	King, Robert	13-Nov-2005	
10597	Piccolo und mehr	King, Robert	11-Jul-2006	

Record: 2 of 830 — No Filter — Search

7

- To change the width of the field columns to accommodate a larger font, choose Format, Column Width and then click the Best Fit button to let Access determine the size of your columns. You might need to adjust individual column widths by dragging the right edge of the field header with the mouse.

COPYING, EXPORTING, AND MAILING SORTED AND FILTERED DATA

A common use for filters and customized datasheets is to export the filtered and sorted records to another application, such as Microsoft Excel or Word. Several methods for exporting filtered and custom-formatted records are available on the External Data ribbon.

The next chapter provides complete descriptions of Access's traditional data export features, including exporting filtered and sorted tables to Microsoft Excel workbooks and Word mail-merge documents. Chapter 24, "Integrating with XML and InfoPath 2007," and Chapter 25, "Collaborating with Windows SharePoint Services," describe other Access 2007 data export/import features.

TROUBLESHOOTING

FILTER BY FORM DOESN'T FIND THE EXPECTED RECORDS

Either too few records or records extraneous to the filter appear when using Filter by Form.

Access keeps your last filter settings for a table until you close the table. If you've applied a different filter—whether through Filter by Selection or Filter by Form earlier in your current work session—Access might be applying additional filter criteria that you're not expecting. Right-click the datasheet, and choose Remove Filter/Sort to clear all previous filter criteria and ensure that the new filter criteria you enter are the only ones in effect. Alternatively, choose Records, Remove Filter/Sort from the main Access menu.

IN THE REAL WORLD—COMPUTER-BASED SORTING AND SEARCHING

Donald E. Knuth's *Sorting and Searching, Volume 3* of his *The Art of Computer Programming* series is the seminal work on computer algorithms (programs) to perform sorts and searches. Dr. Knuth is Professor Emeritus of The Art of Computer Programming at Stanford University. Addison-Wesley published the first edition of *Sorting and Searching* in 1973. There's a good probability that every student who was granted a computer science degree during and after the mid-1970s has a well-worn copy of Knuth's classic text. Knuth updated *Sorting and Searching* with a second edition in mid-1998; the book remains required reading for assembly language programmers, but you need a good foundation in combinatorial mathematics and set theory to fully understand the contents.

THE INFLUENCE OF COMPUTER POWER ON KNUTH'S APPROACH

As Knuth points out in the first page of the chapter on sorting, a better term to describe the process is "ordering." (The 724-page book has only two chapters: Chapter 6, "Sorting," and Chapter 7, "Searching."). Structured Query Language (SQL) takes Knuth's advice and uses ORDER BY clauses to define sort sequences. One of the dictionary definitions of the verb *to sort* is "to arrange according to characteristics," and the definition of *order* includes "arrange" as a synonym.

Both sort and order infer that the process physically moves records; this was the case in the 1970s, a period when punched cards were the dominant means of computer data entry and storage. The advent of magnetic tape drives eliminated the need for punched card sorting and collating machines, but sorting still required individual records be rewritten to tape in the chosen order. Decks of punched cards and magnetic tape use sequential access, so sorting by merging expedites searching—assuming that records matching your search criteria appear early in the deck or tape. Therefore, the "Sorting" chapter precedes "Searching," as it does in this chapter. Searching is the foundation for all filtering operations.

NOTE

> SQL Server's clustered indexes physically order records in the order of the primary key to speed execution of multitable queries. When you export Access tables to SQL Server 2005 [Express] with Access 2007's Upsizing Wizard, the wizard automatically creates a clustered index on the primary key field.

Today's PCs are far more powerful than the largest mainframe computers of the 1970s. Multi-gigabyte fixed disk drives in PC clients dwarf the storage capabilities of tape and multispindle disk drives of the 1970s and early 1980s. When you apply a sort order to an Access table or query, records don't change position; Access displays the table records in the desired sequence. If you have plenty of RAM, all the record resequencing occurs in memory because Access picks those records needed to populate the visible rows of the datasheet, plus some additional records to make page down operations go faster. When Access runs out of RAM, temporary disk files store the overflow. It's no longer necessary to optimize searching by prior sorting; the brute-force approach (searching a random-order file) usually is fast enough for files of moderate (10,000 records) to even large size (1 million or more records).

KNUTH AND INDEXES

Two Russian mathematicians, G. M. Adelson-Velski and E. M. Landis, proposed a balanced binary tree indexing structure in 1963. In a balanced binary tree structure, the length of the search path to any ordered record is never more than 45% longer than the optimum. Access, like most other desktop RDBMSs, has a balanced binary tree (B-tree) structure; an Access primary key index orders the records.

One of Knuth's other contributions to computer science is his analysis of binary tree searching on ordered tables. An ordered table's records are physically or logically organized in alphabetic or numeric order by the key field being searched. Binary tree searches optimize

7

the searching process by minimizing the number of comparisons required to zero in on the record(s) with the desired value. Knuth went into great detail on "hashing" algorithms that create a set of unique values to identify each record. Hashing greatly speeds searching on the key field of tables when the key field comprises more than a few characters. The "hash tables" of early databases are called indexes today. SQL Server 2000 still generates temporary hash tables when needed to speed query processing.

When you search on a field that isn't ordered, called a *secondary key*, search efficiency drops rapidly for large tables. The early approaches used in the 1970s, including a process called *combinatorial hashing*, have given way to secondary indexes on unordered keys, such as postal codes in a table in which the primary key is a customer name or code. Each secondary key you add decreases the speed at which you can insert new records because of the need to maintain and rebalance the trees of the indexes. Despite the performance of today's PC clients and servers, it's still a good idea to minimize the number of secondary indexes on tables used for online transaction processing (OLTP).

It isn't necessary to understand the underlying details of hashing and balanced B-tree indexes to take full advantage of Access's searching and sorting features. Familiarity with the surprisingly efficient methods used in the early days of computing, however, offers a useful perspective on the dramatic improvements in database design and implementation that has occurred in the 30 years since Knuth published the first edition of his *Sorting and Searching*.

7

CHAPTER 8

LINKING, IMPORTING, AND EXPORTING TABLES

In this chapter

MOVING DATA FROM AND TO OTHER APPLICATIONS

Undoubtedly, every personal computer user has data that can be processed through database-management techniques. Any data that a computer can arrange in tabular form—even tables in word processing files—can be converted to database tables. The strength of a relational database management system (RDBMS) lies in its capability to handle large numbers of individual pieces of data stored in tables and to relate the pieces of data in a meaningful way.

PC users turn to RDBMSs when the amount of data created exceeds a conventional productivity application's capability to manipulate the data effectively. A common example is a large mailing list created in Microsoft Excel or Word. As the number of names in the list increases, using Excel or Word to make selective mailings and maintain histories of responses to mailings becomes increasingly difficult. An RDBMS is the most effective type of application for manipulating large lists.

One strong point of Access is its capability to transform existing spreadsheets, database tables, and text files created by other Windows and even DOS applications into the Access .accdb format—a process known as importing a file. Access can export (create) table files in any format in which it can import the files, including HTML and Extensible Markup Language (XML) documents. You also can import/export Windows SharePoint Services (WSS) or Microsoft Office SharePoint Services (MOSS) lists.

NOTE

> This chapter doesn't include use of Access 2007's HTML, XML, and SharePoint import/export features for intranet- and Internet-based database applications. The chapters of Part VI, "Collaborating with Access Data," cover these topics.

Access can link a database table file created by Access or another RDBMS, an Excel worksheet, or a SharePoint list to your current Access database. Access then acts as a data-entry front end for the linked object. This capability is far less common in other desktop and client/server RDBMSs. When you link a table from a different RDBMS, spreadsheet, or list, you can display and, in many cases, update the linked table as though it were an Access table contained in your .accdb file. If the file containing the table is shared on a network, in some cases others can use the file with their applications while it's linked to your database.

The capability to link files is important for two reasons: It lets you connect to multiple Access databases, and you can create new applications in Access that can coexist with applications created by other database managers and applications. Access 2007 also can link Outlook contacts, tasks, and calendar folders, as well as Outlook Express mail. Outlook 2007 also lets you import and export folders to and from Access 2007 tables.

The External Data ribbon displays Access, Excel, SharePoint List, Text File, XML File, and More buttons in the Import group. Clicking the More button opens a rogue's gallery of buttons for the aging Open Database Connectivity (ODBC) application programming interface (API), and less popular formats—HTML Document, Outlook Folder, dBASE File, Paradox File, and Lotus 1-2-3 File (see Figure 8.1).

Figure 8.1
The External Data ribbon's Import group, which would be better named the Import or Link group, has a button for each database or file type that Access can import or link.

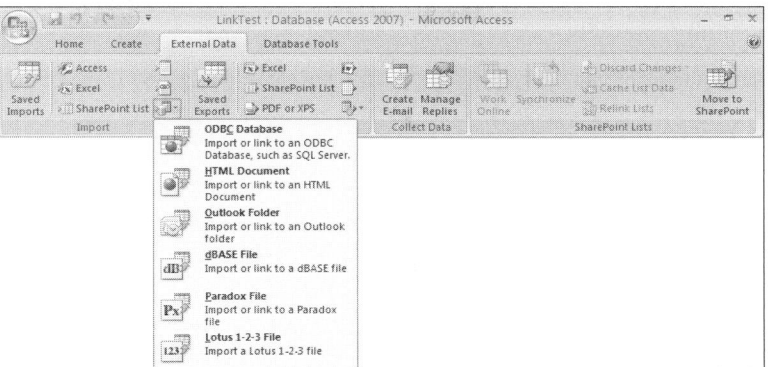

IMPORTING AND LINKING SPREADSHEET FILES

Moving spreadsheets to relational database tables is one of the more common applications for Microsoft Access. Access 2007 can import files created by spreadsheet and related applications, such as project management systems, in the following formats:

- Excel 3, 4, 5, 7, 9x, and 200x .xls files as well as task and resource files created by Microsoft Project in .xls format. You also can import Excel 2007 .xlsb, .xlsm, and .xlsx Open XML Format files. A single code library handles the import of all Excel formats.

- Lotus 1-2-3 .wks and .wj* files created by the DOS version of Lotus.

NOTE

You can use OLE to embed or link charts created by Microsoft Excel and stored in files with an .xlc extension. Copy the contents of the file to the Windows Clipboard from Excel. Choose Edit, Paste to embed or link (via OLE) the chart in a field of the OLE Object type; then display the chart on a form or print it on a report as an unbound object. Similarly, you can embed or link most views displayed in Microsoft Project, which also uses the Microsoft Graph applet; the exceptions are task and resource forms and the Task PERT chart.

CREATING A TABLE BY IMPORTING AN EXCEL WORKSHEET

Figure 8.2 illustrates the preferred format for Excel and other spreadsheet applications for importing to Access and other RDBMS tables. The names of the fields are typed in the first row and the remainder of the database range consists of data. The type of data in each column must be consistent within the database range you select.

8

Figure 8.2
This Excel 2007 worksheet was created by exporting the Orders table to a workbook file. The worksheet serves as an example for importing a worksheet to an Access table.

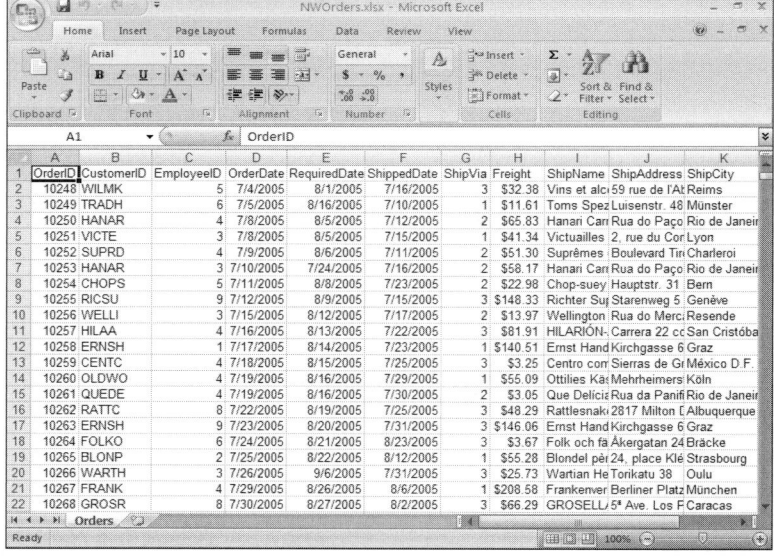

TIP

> You get an opportunity to assign field names to the columns in the worksheet during the importation process, although the process is easier if you add field names as column headings first.

To prepare the data in an Excel spreadsheet for importation into an Access table, follow these steps:

1. Launch Excel and then open the .xls, .xlsx, .xlsb, or .xlsm file that contains the data you want to import.

2. Add field names above the first row of the data you plan to export (if you haven't done so). Field names can't include periods (.), exclamation points (!), or square brackets ([]). You can't have duplicate field names. If you include improper characters in field names or use duplicate field names, you see an error message when you attempt to import the worksheet.

3. If your worksheet contains cells with data you don't want to include in the imported table, select the range that contains the field names row and all the rows of data needed for the table. In Excel, choose Insert, Name, Define and then name the range.

4. Save the Excel file (use a different filename if you froze values) and exit Excel.

Now you're ready to import worksheets from the Excel workbook file, NWOrders.xlsx for this example. (NWOrders.xls is located in the \SEUA12\Chaptr08\Excel2007 folder of the accompanying CD-ROM). To import the prepared data from an Excel spreadsheet into an Access table, follow these steps:

1. Open the database you want to add the new table to.

2. Click the External Data tab and the Import group's Excel button to open the Get External Data – Excel Data dialog, click the Browse button to open the File Open dialog, and navigate to the folder that contains the .xlsx, .xlsb, or .xlsm file with the worksheet to import (NWOrders.xlsx for this example; see Figure 8.3).

Figure 8.3
Navigate to the folder, select Microsoft Excel (*.xls; *.xlsb; *.xlsm, *.xlsx) in the Files of Type list, and select the worksheet to import.

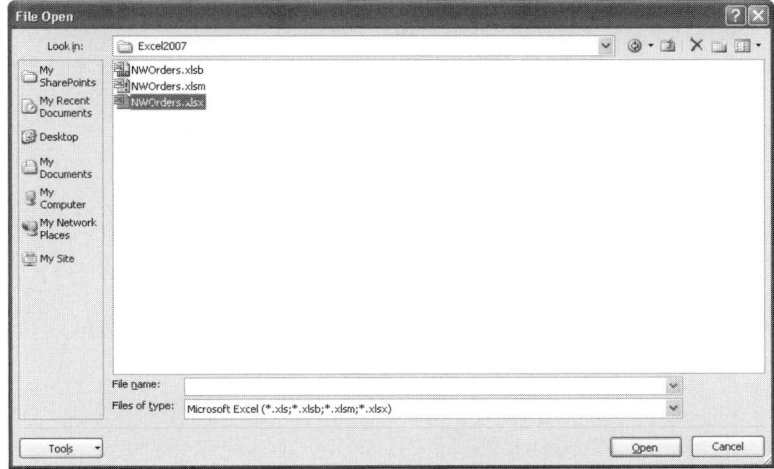

3. Double-click the name of the Excel workbook that contains the spreadsheet you want to import to return to the Get External Data – Excel Spreadsheet dialog. Alternatively, click the filename to select it and then click Open (see Figure 8.4). If you want to append rows to an existing table having the same structure and data types as the spreadsheet, select the Append a Copy of the Records to the Table option and select the table from the adjacent list. Otherwise, accept the default Import the Source Data into a New Table in the Current Database option.

4. Click OK to close the Get External Data – Excel Spreadsheet dialog and invoke the Import Spreadsheet Wizard (see Figure 8.5).

5. If you're importing an entire worksheet, select the Show Worksheets option; if you're importing a named range, select the Show Named Ranges option. The Import Spreadsheet Wizard lists the worksheets or named data ranges, depending on the option you select in the list box in the upper-right corner of the WizardWizard's opening dialog.

6. Select the worksheet or the named data range that you want to import in the list box. The Import Spreadsheet Wizard shows a sample view of the data in the worksheet (Orders in the NWOrders.xlsx workbook for this example) or the named range at the bottom of the dialog.

Figure 8.4
Accept the default Import the Source Data… option to create an Access table from the worksheet you specify in the File Name text box.

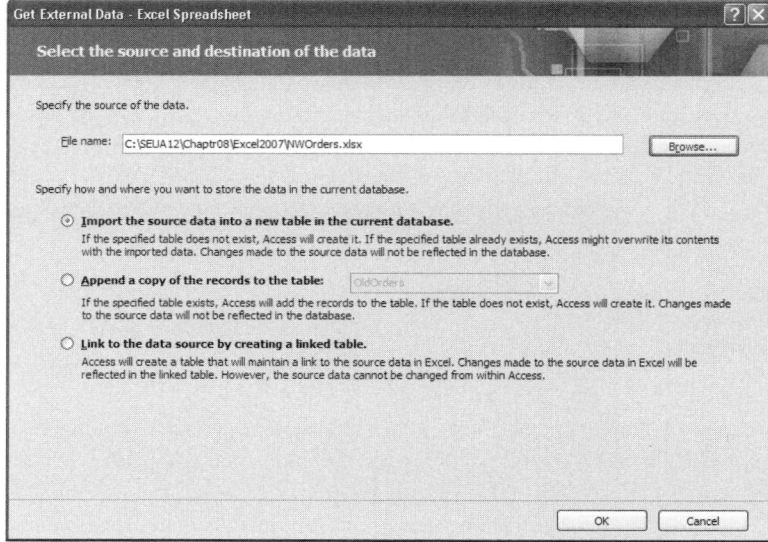

Figure 8.5
The first dialog of the Import Spreadsheet Wizard lets you select a specific worksheet or named range to import as a table.

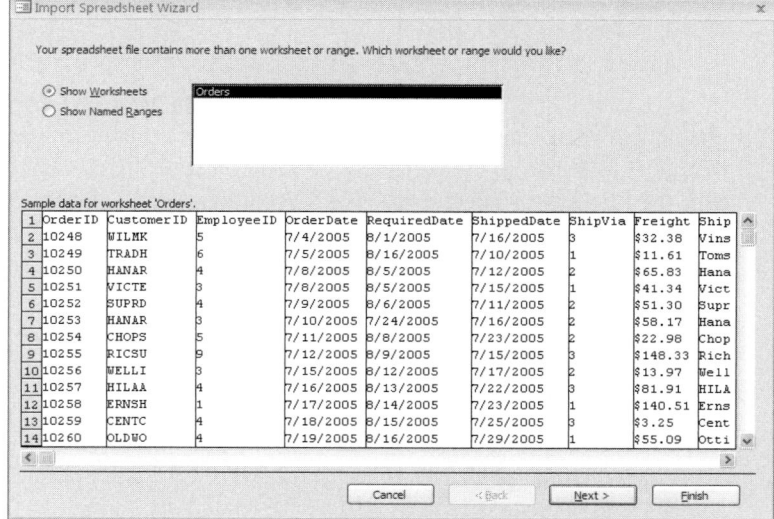

7. Click Next to move to the second dialog of the Spreadsheet Import Wizard, shown in Figure 8.6.

8. If the first row of your spreadsheet data contains the field names for the imported table, select the First Row Contains Column Headings check box. Click Next to continue with the third step; the Import Spreadsheet Wizard displays the dialog shown in Figure 8.7.

8

Figure 8.6
The WizardWizard's second dialog lets you specify whether the first row of the worksheet or named range contains column headings.

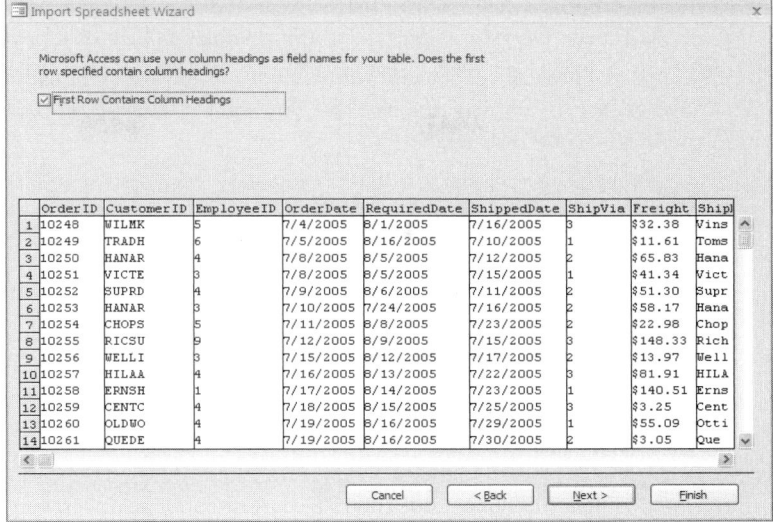

Figure 8.7
The third WizardWizard dialog lets you edit the field name, specify an index, or skip a field.

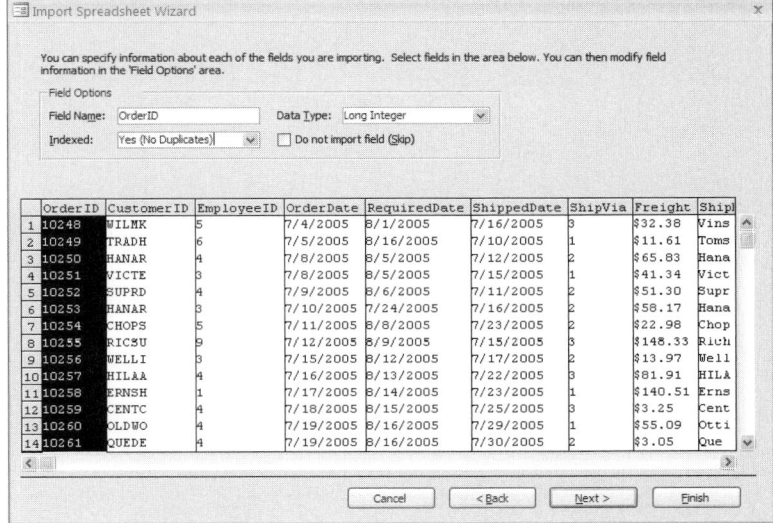

NOTE

If you elect to add the imported data to an existing table, the Import Spreadsheet Wizard skips over all intervening steps and goes immediately to its final dialog, described in step 14.

9. If you want to exclude a column from the imported database, select the column by clicking it, select the Do Not Import Field (Skip) check box, and skip to step 12.

10. The Import Spreadsheet Wizard lets you edit or add the field names for the spreadsheet columns; click the column whose name you want to edit or add and then type the name in the Field Name text box.

11. If you want Access to index this field, choose the appropriate index type in the Indexed list box; you can choose No, Yes (Duplicates OK), or Yes (No Duplicates).

12. Repeat steps 9, 10, and 11 for each column in the worksheet or data range that you import. When you're satisfied with your options for each column, click Next to move to the fifth dialog.

13. Select the Let Access Add Primary Key option to have Access add an AutoNumber field to the imported table; Access fills in a unique number for each existing row in the worksheet that you're importing. Select the Choose My Own Primary Key option and select the primary key field in the drop-down list if you know you can use a column in the worksheet or data range as a primary key for the imported table. The OrderID column is the primary key field for this example (see Figure 8.8). If this imported table doesn't need a primary key, select the No Primary Key option.

Figure 8.8
If the data you're importing contains a column with a unique value to identify each row, select the Choose My Own Primary Key option and the column name with the unique data.

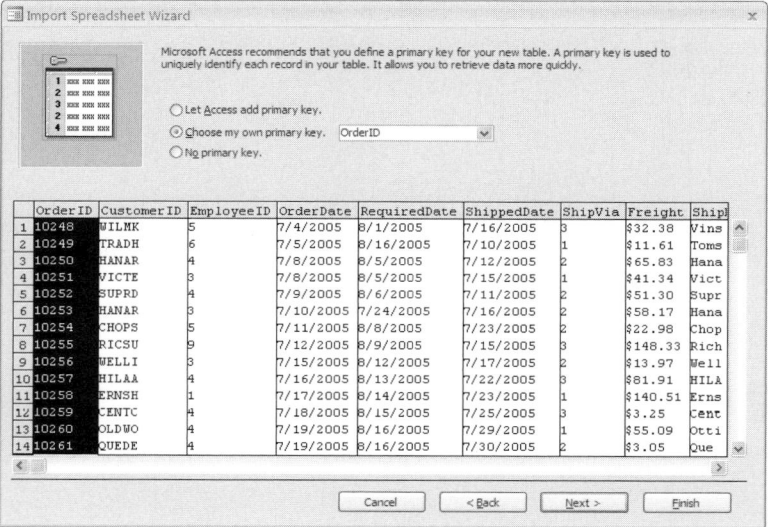

14. Click Next to move to the final dialog of the Import Spreadsheet Wizard (see Figure 8.9). Type the name of the new table (Orders for this example) in the Import to Table text box; Access uses the name of the worksheet or data range as the default table name. If you want to use the Table Analyzer Wizard to split the imported table into two or more related tables, select the I Would Like a Wizard to Analyze My Table After Importing the Data check box. You also can display the help window by marking the Display Help After the Wizard Is Finished check box.

Figure 8.9
The final
WizardWizard dialog
lets you rename the
table and, optionally,
run the Table
Analyzer Wizard on
the table data after
the import operation
completes, open the
help window, or both.

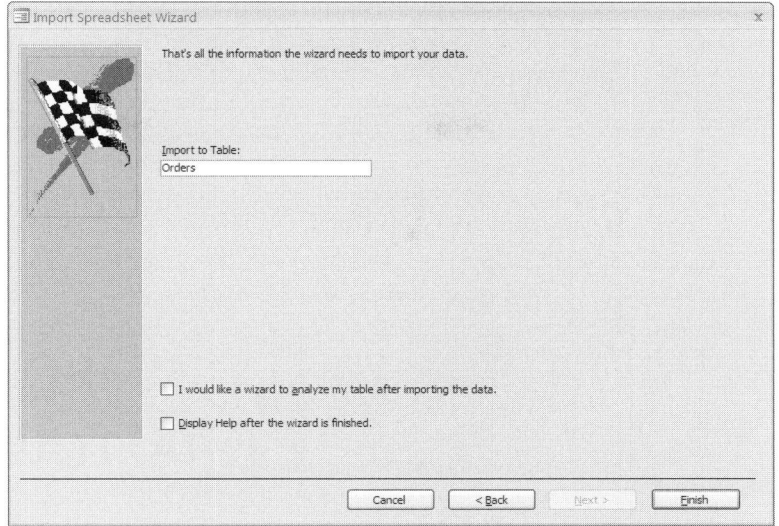

15. Click Finish to dismiss the Wizard and open the Save Import Steps dialog. If you want to save the preceding steps in an import workflow specification, mark the Save Import Steps check box and, optionally, add a description, mark the Create Outlook Task for repetitive operations, or both (see Figure 8.10).

16. Click the Save Import or Cancel button to complete the importing process. Access closes the Import Spreadsheet Wizard and imports the data. If you mark the Create Outlook Task check box, it displays the Outlook message shown in Figure 8.11. Set the recurrence parameters, if you want, and then click the Save & Close button.

> **TIP**
>
> You can use the Table Analyzer Wizard at any time on any table by clicking the Analyze Tables button of the Database Tools ribbon's Analyze group.

→ To review use of the Table Analyzer Wizard to move duplicate data to a related table, **see** "Using the Table Analyzer Wizard," **p. 255**.

> **TIP**
>
> Use scheduled repetitive import operations only for appending data to an existing table. If the import operation creates a new table, manual intervention is required to enable overwriting the existing table.

Figure 8.10
You can automate repeated spreadsheet importation by saving the import steps.

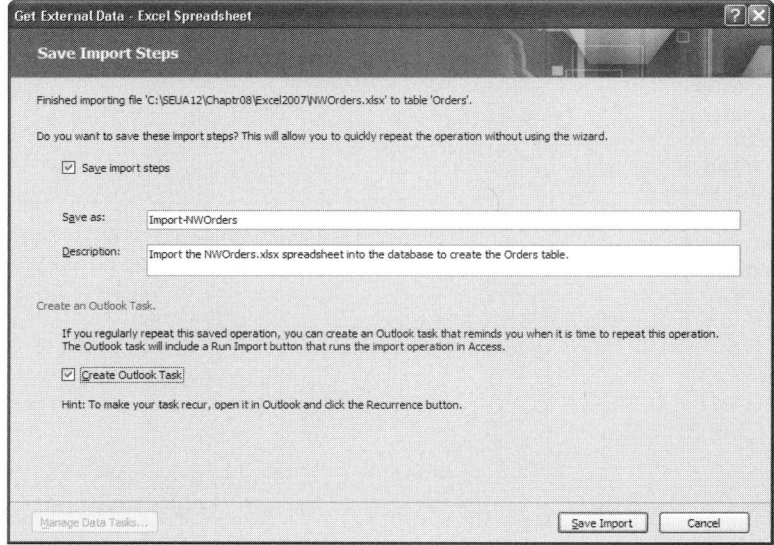

Figure 8.11
This Outlook message enables the establishing of a schedule for repetitive import operations.

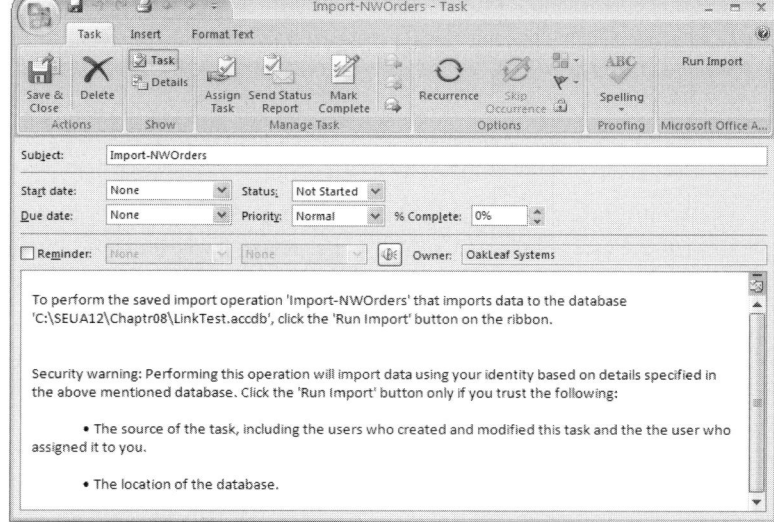

The Import Spreadsheet Wizard analyzes approximately the first 20 rows of the spreadsheet you are importing and assigns data types to the imported fields based on this analysis. If every cell in a column has a numeric or date value, the columns convert to the Number or Date/Time field data type, respectively. If a column contains mixed text and numbers, the WizardWizard converts the column as a text field. If, however, a column contains numeric data in the first 20 or so rows (the rows that the WizardWizard analyzes) and then has one or more text entries, the WizardWizard doesn't convert these rows.

If the Wizard encounters cell values that it can't convert to the data type that it assigned to the imported field, Access creates an Import Errors table with one record for each error. You can review this table, select the records in which the errors are reported, and fix them. A better approach, however, is to correct the cells in the spreadsheet, resave the file, and import the corrected data.

> **TIP**
>
> The Import Spreadsheet Wizard doesn't display an error message when it encounters inconsistent field data types; it just creates the Import Errors table. You must look in the Navigation Pane to see whether the Import Errors table is present. After you resolve the import errors, make sure that you delete the Import Errors table so that you can more easily detect errors the next time you import a spreadsheet or other external file.

The Navigation Pane now contains a new table with the name you accepted or edited in the final dialog of the Import Spreadsheet Wizard. If you import another file with the same name as your worksheet or named range, the WizardWizard asks if you want to overwrite the existing table.

The Wizard will apply the Access Double data type to all numeric fields (this includes the OrderID, EmployeeID, and ShipVia fields of the Order table), which you should change to the Long Integer data type. The Wizard will correctly detect the Date/Time data type for the OrderDate, RequiredDate, and ShippedDate fields, and the Currency data type for the Freight field (because a dollar sign prefixes data in the worksheet column).

> **TIP**
>
> Don't use the Double (or Single) data type for primary key fields. These data types require floating-point arithmetic to determine their values, which is subject to rounding errors. Relationships based on floating-point values might fail because of these rounding errors. In addition, multitable queries having relationships based on Double (or Single) fields usually exhibit very poor performance.

Linking Excel Worksheets

The advantages of linking an Excel worksheet are that you always work with the latest version of the worksheet; changes made to the Excel data appear in the linked table. However, you can't alter worksheet cell values from within Access nor can you change field data types. You can assign a primary key but Access doesn't enforce unique values in the key field(s).

> **NOTE**
>
>
>
> According to Microsoft Knowledge Base article 904953 (http://support.microsoft.com/kb/904953/), "legal issues" were responsible for making linked worksheets read-only for Access 2002 and later. The "legal issue" was an $8.9-million award in 2005 to the holder of a patent on the software to create a read/write link between Excel and Access.

Linking an Excel spreadsheet uses a truncated version of the Import Spreadsheet Wizard renamed to the Link Spreadsheet Wizard. To link an Excel worksheet to an Access 2007 table, do the following:

1. Follow the first three steps of the preceding Excel import process, but select the Link to the Data Source by Creating a Linked Table option in the Get External Data – Excel Spreadsheet dialog.

2. Click OK to start the Link Spreadsheet Wizard.

3. Select the worksheet or named range to link (the Orders sample worksheet in NWOrdersLink.xls for this example) and then click the Next button.

4. Mark the First Row Contains Column Headings check box, if applicable. Click Next to continue.

5. The Wizard proposes the name of the worksheet as the table name. Change the table name if you want, click Finish, and then click OK to link the table. The linked table is identified in the Navigation pane by an Excel icon and an arrow.

6. Open the linked table in Design view, clicking OK to acknowledge that you can't change the design of a linked table. Unfortunately, the Wizard again makes the wrong data type choice (Double) for the OrderID, EmployeeID, and ShipVia columns.

> **TIP**
>
> Excel users must save their worksheet to the .xls* file, and Access users must close and reopen the table to see changes to the linked data.

The Linked Table Manager, which is the subject of the "Using the Linked Table Manager Add-in to Relink Tables" section later in the chapter, lets you fix broken links to worksheets.

WORKING WITH MICROSOFT OUTLOOK AND EXCHANGE FOLDERS

Microsoft Outlook 2007 lets you import data from and export data to a wide range of file types, including Access 2007 databases. For example, you can export data to a variety of file types and import OPML, vCard, iCalendar, or vCalendar files. Outlook's import capability is far more eclectic than that of Access; you can import from the ACT! 3.x, 4.x, and 2000 Contact Manager and Lotus Organizer 4.x and 5.x files.

> **TIP**
>
> If you want to put data from vCard, ACT! or Lotus Organizer into Access 2007, importing to Outlook and exporting to Access is the best alternative unless you have versions of these applications that handle exporting to Access databases.

Access 2000 added the Exchange/Outlook Wizard for linking to the contents of Outlook's private and Exchange's public folders. The following two sections show you how to export, import, and link Contacts folders. The Contacts folder is most commonly used with databases; working with other folders follows a similar course.

NOTE

You must have the Outlook Import/Export engine installed to try the examples in the following two sections. If you haven't installed the engine, you receive a "Would you like to install it now?" message after you specify the action you want to take.

The following Outlook 2007 examples use personal folders. If you have Microsoft Exchange 2000+ running under Windows Server 200x, your results might differ, depending on your Outlook settings, Exchange Server configuration, or both.

IMPORTING AND EXPORTING ACCESS TABLES WITH OUTLOOK 2007

To use Outlook to import an Access table to an Outlook 2007 Contacts folder, do the following:

 1. Open Outlook and select the folder you want to import to. (Create a new empty Contacts subfolder, Northwind for this example, when you're testing import and export operations.)

2. Choose File, Import and Export to start the Import and Export Wizard. Select Import from Another Program or File in the Choose an Action to Perform list shown in Figure 8.12, and click Next.

Figure 8.12
Select Import from Another Program or File in the first dialog of Outlook's Import and Export Wizard.

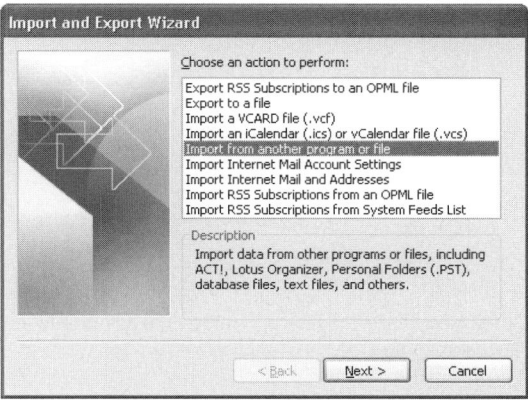

3. Select Microsoft Access in the Import a File dialog shown in Figure 8.13, and click Next.

Figure 8.13
Select Microsoft
Access in the second
Wizard dialog.

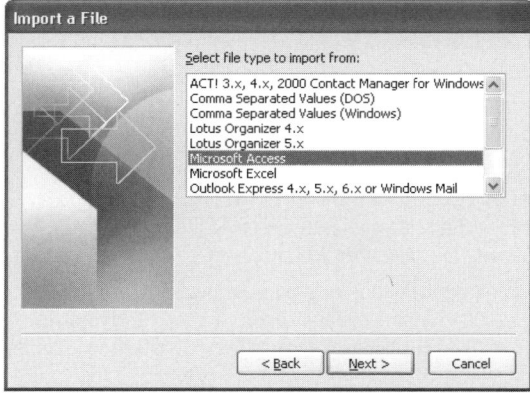

4. In the second Import a File dialog, click Browse to open the Browse dialog, and then navigate to and select the .accdb file that contains the table you want to import. This example uses Northwind.accdb's Customers table. Select an option for handling duplicates, and then click Next (see Figure 8.14).

Figure 8.14
Navigate to the database you want to import the contact data from, and select Replace Duplicates with Items Imported to ensure your Outlook contact information is up to date.

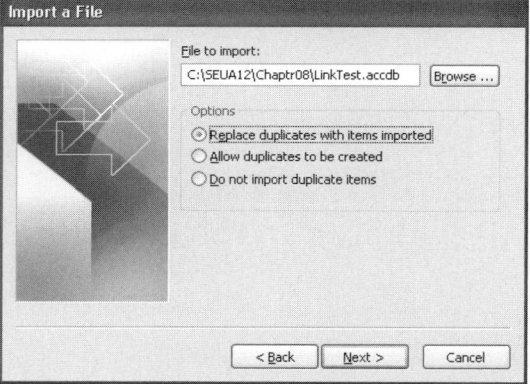

TIP

Make sure the .accdb file you intend to import the data from is closed at this point. If the .accdb file is open, you might receive an error message when you attempt to complete the next step.

5. The destination folder you specified in step 1 is selected in the Import a File dialog (see Figure 8.15). If you didn't select a folder, you must do so at this point. Click Next.

Figure 8.15
Verify the destination folder in the fourth Wizard dialog. In this case, the folder is created in the Contacts folder of your Personal Folders.

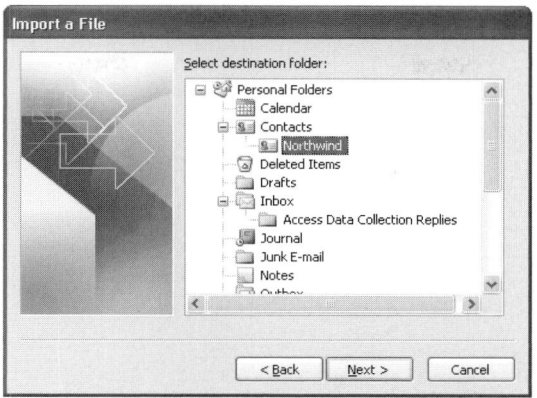

6. Mark the Import *TableName* into the *FolderName* option for the table to import (Customers into Northwind, for this example).

7. Click Map Custom Fields to open the Map Custom Fields dialog, and drag the fields you want to include in the Northwind list from the left list (the From category) to the appropriate Outlook field name in the right list (the To category), as shown in Figure 8.16. Fields that you don't drag to the right list aren't included in the new Contacts folder.

Figure 8.16
Drag field names from the Access source table to the corresponding Outlook fields.

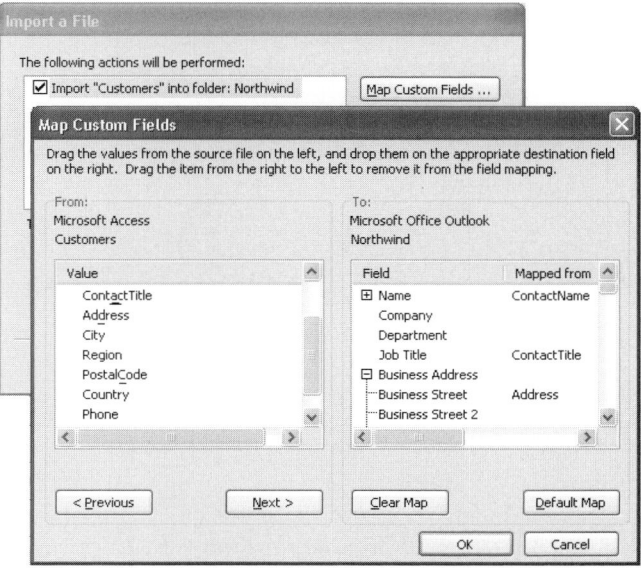

8. Click OK to close the Map Custom Fields dialog; then click Finish to close the Import File dialog and complete the import process. When the records are imported, Outlook automatically displays them (see Figure 8.17).

Figure 8.17
Outlook's Contacts folder by default displays the contact name and company address, but not the company name.

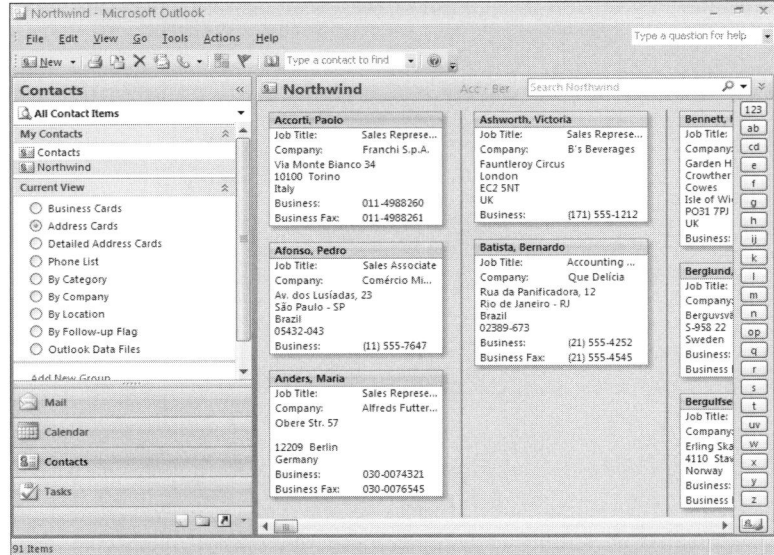

9. To add the company name to the contacts list, right-click an empty area of the contacts list and choose Show Fields to open the Show Fields dialog. Drag the Company item from the Available Fields list to the Show These Fields in This Order list below the File As item (see Figure 8.18). Click OK to complete the addition.

Figure 8.18
Use the Show Fields dialog to add additional fields to the contact list's display.

> **TIP**
>
> Alternatively, select Detailed Address Cards in the Navigation pane's Current View list to display the contact items with field name prefixes (such as Full Name:) for each field.

Exporting Contacts or other Outlook records to an Access table with the Outlook Import and Export Wizard follows the pattern of the preceding steps. Select the folder to export, choose File, Import and Export, select Export to a File, Microsoft Access, and confirm the folder selection. Then specify the destination .accdb file, and export the records to a table with the name of the folder or a name you specify.

> **TIP**
>
> The better approach is to use Access's Import Exchange/Outlook version of Outlook's Export Wizard. The Access Wizard's method of selecting the fields to import is simpler than Outlook's Export Wizard.

LINKING WITH THE EXCHANGE/OUTLOOK WIZARD

The Exchange/Outlook Wizard provides the capability of linking records in Outlook or Exchange folders to an Access table (or tables). Linking is a better option than importing because your Access table is always up to date with information entered in Outlook, and vice versa. Unlike with linked Excel worksheets, Access can update data linked to Outlook folders.

To link a Contacts folder to an Access table, follow these steps:

1. Open the database to which you want to link the Outlook folder, click the External Data tab, click the Import section's More button to open the gallery, and click the Outlook Folder button to open the Get External Data – Outlook Folder dialog.

2. Select the Link to the Data Source by Creating a Linked Table option, and click OK to open the Link Exchange/Outlook Wizard. This example uses Outlook.

3. Expand the nodes as necessary to open the folder to link. This example uses the Contacts subfolder (Northwind) you created in the preceding section (see Figure 8.19).

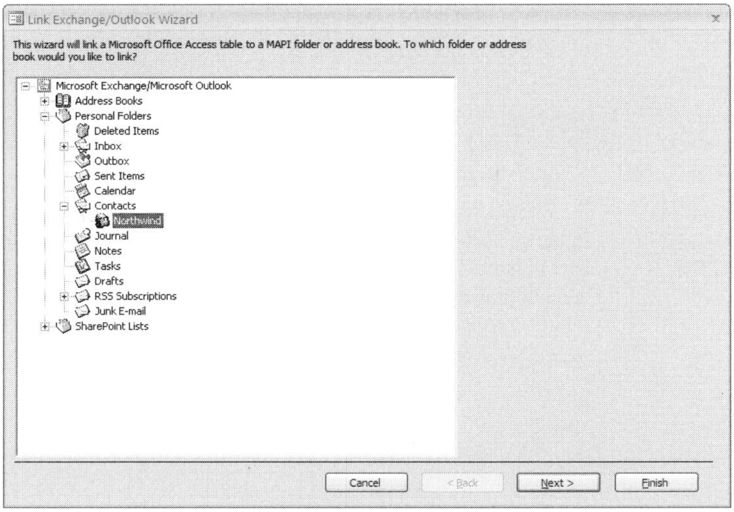

Figure 8.19
Select the folder to link in the Link Exchange/Outlook Wizard's first dialog.

8

4. Click Next to open the second (and last) Wizard dialog, in which you accept the folder name as the table name, or change it to your liking (NorthwindContacts for this example). Accept the default "I would like the Wizard to store my MAPI profile with my linked table" option if Outlook is using Exchange rather than Outlook to store contact data.

5. Click Finish to link the table, and acknowledge the "Finished linking" message. Your linked table appears in the Navigation Pane, identified by an envelope icon with an adjacent arrow.

6. Open the linked table in Datasheet view. The rows appear in company name order, and many contacts fields are empty. Right-click each empty column and choose <u>H</u>ide Columns, and rearrange the field's sequence to improve readability (see Figure 8.20). Tables linked to Exchange address lists aren't updatable. Tables linked to personal and public folders are updatable, even without a primary key field, but your account must have permissions to make changes to Exchange public folders.

Figure 8.20
The linked Oakmont table contains fields whose data is stored in an Outlook Contacts folder. Empty fields are hidden, and the Job Title field is relocated from near the end of the field list.

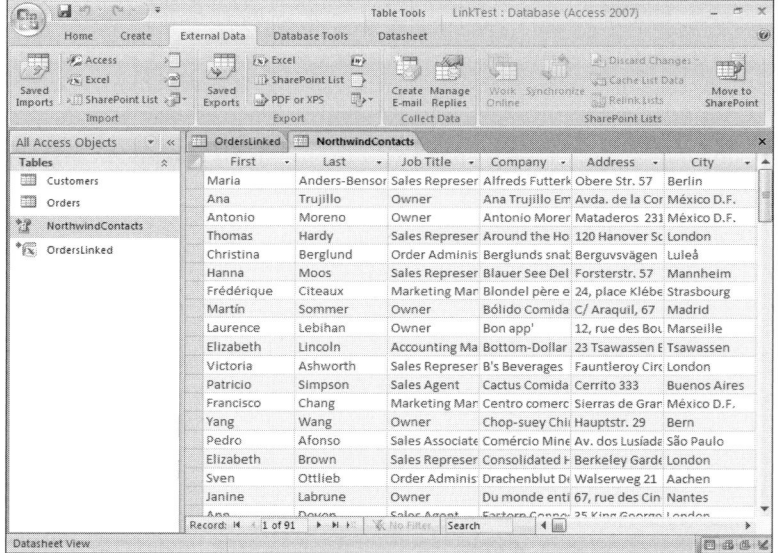

TIP

> Exchange 2000+ uses Active Directory to store recipient data, so you can link to the Global Address List. If all users on a Windows 200x Server network are mailbox-enabled (not just mail-enabled), a link to the Global Address List provides a link to information about every network user.

The response of linked Exchange public folders to changes, sorts, and other operations is slower than linked Access database tables because a local temporary link table (ACCESS*xxxx*.tmp) acts as an intermediary between Access and Exchange.

IMPORTING TEXT FILES

If the data you want to import into an Access table was developed in a database management system, word processor, or other application that can't export the data as a .dbf, .wk?, or .xls file, you need to create a text file in one of the text formats supported by Access. Most DOS- and Windows-compatible data files created from data stored by mainframes and mini-computers, as well as files generated from nine-track magnetic tapes, are text files.

Access refers to the characters that separate fields as *delimiters* or *separators*. In this book, the term *delimiter* refers to characters that identify the end of a field; the term *text identifiers* refers to the single or double quotation marks that you can use to distinguish text from numeric data.

Table 8.1 details the text formats that Access supports for import and export operations.

TABLE 8.1   TEXT FILE FORMATS SUPPORTED BY ACCESS 2007

Format	Description
Comma-delimited text files (also called CSV files)	Commas separate (delimit) fields. The newline pair, carriage-return (ASCII character 13), and line feed (ASCII character 10) separate records. Some applications enclose all values within double quotation marks, a format often called *mail merge*, to prevent commas in a field value from erroneously specifying the end of the field. Other applications enclose only text (strings) in quotation marks to differentiate between text and numeric values, the standard format for files created by the xBase command COPY TO *FILENAME* DELIMITED.
Tab-delimited text files (also called TAB files)	These files treat all values as text and separate fields with tabs. Records are separated by newline pairs. Most word processing applications use this format to export tabular text.
Space-delimited files	Some text files use spaces to separate fields in a line of text. The use of spaces as delimiter characters is uncommon because it can cause what should be single fields, such as street addresses, to be divided inconsistently into different fields.
Fixed-width text files (usually called TXT or ASCII files)	Access separates (parses) the individual records into fields based on the position of the data items in a line of text. Newline pairs separate records, and every record must have exactly the same length. Spaces pad the fields to a specified fixed width. Fixed width is the most common format for data exported by mainframes and mini-computers on nine-track tape.

N O T E

Text files in three of these formats (CSV, TAB, and TXT) derived from Northwind.accdb's Orders table are located in the \SEUA12\Chaptr08\TextFile folder of the accompanying CD-ROM.

USING THE IMPORT TEXT WIZARD

To import any of the text file types listed in Table 8.1, you follow a procedure similar to the procedure for importing any external data into Access. To import a text file, follow these steps:

1. Open the database you want to import the text file into, click the External Data tab, and click the Text File button to open the External Data – Text File dialog.

2. Accept the default Import the Source Data into a New Table in the Current Database option, and click Browse to open the File Open dialog with Text Files (*.txt; *.csv; *.tab; *.asc) selected in the Files of Type list.

3. Navigate to the folder that contains the text file you want to import (\SEUA12\Chaptr08\TextFiles\Orders.csv for the initial example) and double-click the text file's name. Access starts the Import Text Wizard, shown in Figure 8.21, which is similar to Excel's Wizard of the same name.

Figure 8.21
The first dialog of the Import Text Wizard lets you select between delimited (the default) or fixed-width files, and displays sample data from the file.

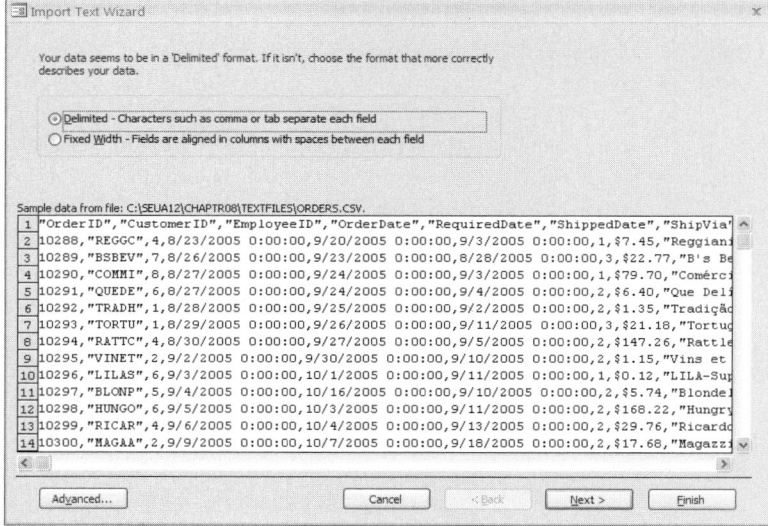

4. Select the Delimited option to import a delimited text file or select Fixed Width to import a fixed-width text file. The Import Text Wizard displays a sample of the text file's contents in the lower portion of the dialog to help you determine the correct file type. Figure 8.21 shows a comma-delimited text file (\SEUA12\Chaptr08\Orders.csv) being imported. Click Next to proceed to the next step in the Import Text Wizard.

If you selected Delimited as the file type for the Orders.csv file, the Import Text Wizard displays the dialog shown in Figure 8.22; if you selected the Fixed Width option for the Orders.txt file, the Wizard displays the dialog in Figure 8.23.

Figure 8.22
The Wizard's second dialog gives a preview of the table to be created upon importing the Orders.csv text file.

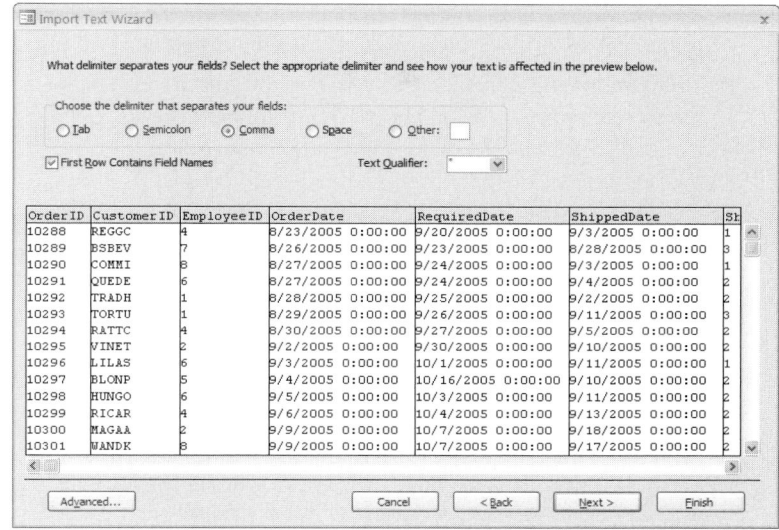

Figure 8.23
If you import from the fixed-width Orders.txt, the second dialog lets you define field boundaries.

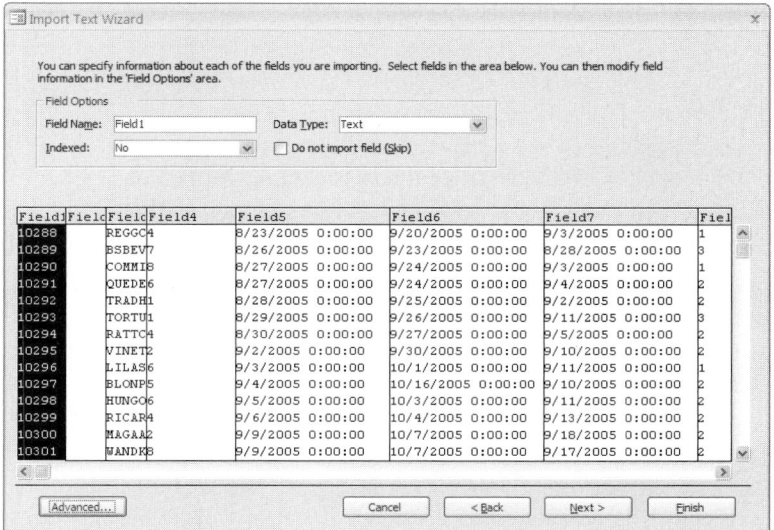

NOTE

The Wizard doesn't detect the EmployeeID field, so you must add a break after the five-character CustomerID field. You also must add a break before the RequiredDate and ShipVia fields and remove two breaks from the ShipAddress field.

8

5. If you're importing a delimited text file, accept the default or select the delimiter character that separates fields in the table (most delimited files use the tab separator). If the text file you're importing uses a text qualifier other than double quotation marks, type it in the Text Qualifier text box. If the first line in the text file contains field names (such as the column headings in a spreadsheet file), select the First Row Contains Field Names check box. Click Next to move to the next step of the Import Text Wizard.

6. If you're importing a fixed-width text file, the Import Text Wizard analyzes the columns and makes an approximation about where the field breaks lie. Scan through the sample data at the bottom of the dialog; if the field breaks aren't in the right place, there are too many field breaks, or there aren't enough field breaks, you can add, delete, or move the field breaks that the Import Text Wizard suggests. To move a field break, drag it with the mouse. To remove a field break, double-click it. To add a field break, click at the desired location. When you're satisfied with the field break arrangement, click Next to continue.

CAUTION

> The Wizard matches fields from left to right when you import a text file into an existing table. You must make sure that the data types of the fields in the imported text file match those in the Access table; otherwise, the added data values aren't inserted into the correct fields. In most cases, you end up with many import errors in the Import Errors table. If you're not certain that the format of your input data exactly matches the format of the desired table, you can choose the In a New Table option and then place your data in the existing table with an append query, as discussed in Chapter 13, "Creating and Updating Access Tables with Action Queries."

7. The third Wizard dialog lets you edit field names, choose whether to use an index and what kind to use for each field, and set each field's data type (see Figure 8.24). To set the options for a field, click the field column at the bottom of the dialog to select it; you then can edit the field name, select an index method in the Indexed drop-down list, and select the data type for the field in the Data Type drop-down list. Select the Do Not Import Field (Skip) check box if you don't want to import the selected field column.

    The OrderID, EmployeeID, and ShipVia columns require the Long Integer data type to conform to the original table design, and a No Duplicates index selection is appropriate for the OrderID primary key field. When you're satisfied with your field settings, click Next.

8. The Wizard displays the dialog in Figure 8.25. Choose the appropriate option for the primary key: Allow Access to add a new field with an automatically generated primary key, select an existing field to use as a primary key yourself, or import the table without a primary key. For this example, OrderID is the primary key. Click Next.

Figure 8.24
The third dialog lets you change or assign field names, alter data types, specify indexes, and skip fields.

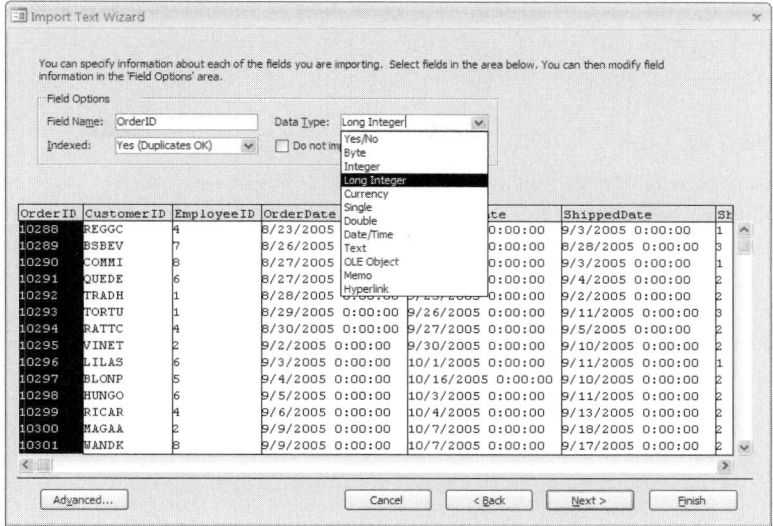

Figure 8.25
The fourth dialog offers three primary key choices. For the Orders table, select Choose My Own Primary Key option and the OrderID field as the primary key.

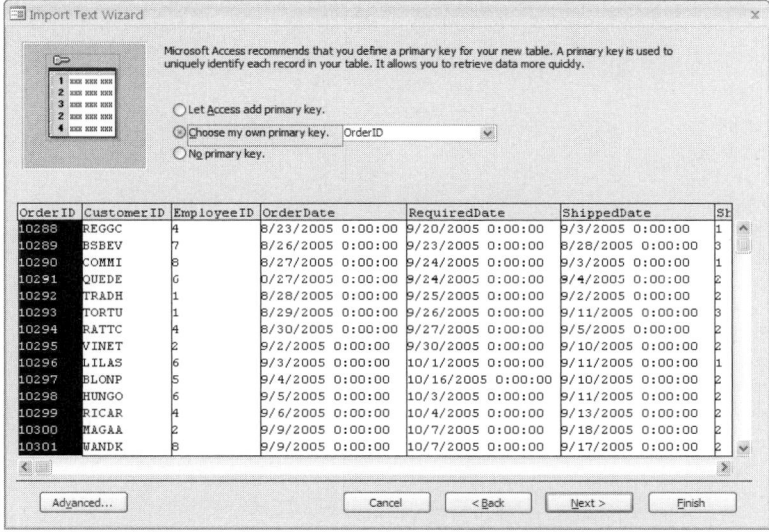

9. The Wizard displays its final dialog with the filename of the text file or the existing table you specified in step 7 as the default table name. Edit the table name, or type a different table name, if you want. Click Finish to open the Get External Data – Text dialog.

10. If you want to save an import specification, mark the Save Import Steps check box, specify the name and a description, and, optionally, mark the Create Outlook Task check box. Click OK to close the dialog, and then open the new table.

As with other import operations, Access creates an Import Errors table to document any errors that occurred during the import process and displays a message informing you that errors occurred.

SETTING THE IMPORT TEXT WIZARD'S ADVANCED OPTIONS

You're likely to find that you import text data from the same text file more than once or that you have several text files with the same format. A typical situation in many corporations is that data from the company's mainframe computer system is provided to desktop computer users in the form of a text file report. Frequently, reports are delivered over the network in a text file, using the same name for the text file each time. You can use the Import Text Wizard's advanced options to configure Access to import a text file with a specific set of options and save the option values so that you don't have to go through every step in the Wizard every time you import the text file.

Every dialog of the Import Text Wizard has an Advanced button. Clicking this button displays the *TableName* Import Specification dialog that shows all the Import Text Wizard settings in a single dialog and allows you to select a few options, such as date formatting, that don't appear in the regular Import Text Wizard dialogs. If you select the Delimited option and the text file includes field names, the Customers Import Specification dialog has the options and field grid shown in Figure 8.26. Settings in the Data Type and Indexed columns reflect the changes suggested in Figure 8.24.

Figure 8.26
The Orders Import Specification dialog for the sample Orders.csv text file lets you fine-tune field properties and indexes, as well as create a template for future import of text files in the same format.

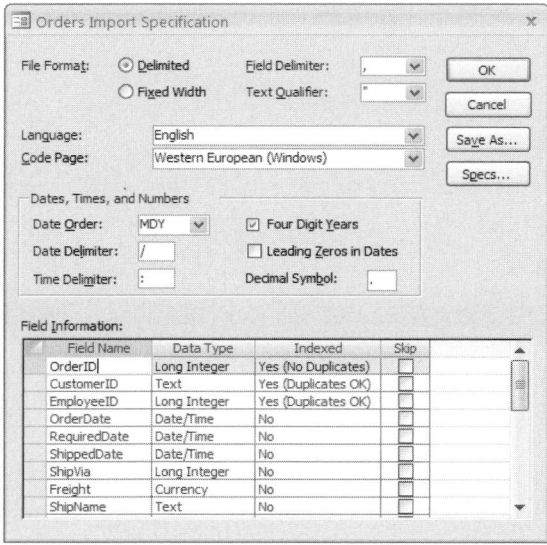

If you select the Fixed-Width option for a file without field names in the first record, the dialog has the options and field grid shown in Figure 8.27. For the Orders.txt sample file, type the field names, specify the data types, and set the indexes.

Figure 8.27
The Orders Import Specification dialog for a fixed-width table without field names in the first row assigns default Field# field names.

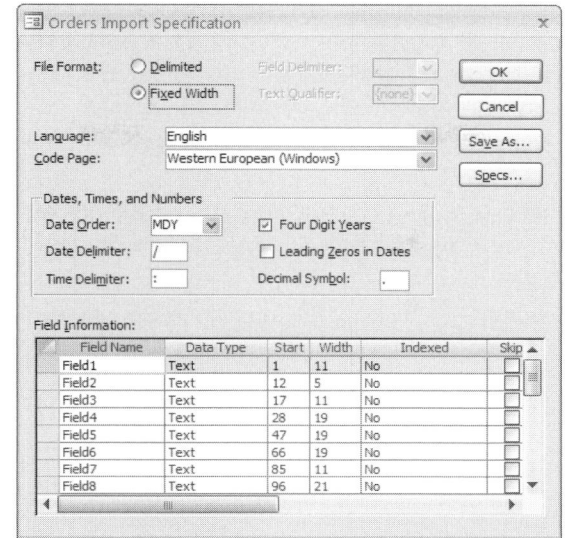

You can select the following options in the *TableName* Import Specification dialog:

- **File Format**—Use these option buttons to choose which type of text file format you're importing: delimited or fixed width. The file format you select determines which additional options are available.

- **Field Delimiter**—Use this drop-down list to select the symbol that delimits fields in the text file. This option is disabled for fixed-width text files.

- **Text Qualifier**—Use this drop-down list to select the symbol that marks the beginning and end of text strings in the text file. This option is disabled for fixed-width text files.

- **Language and Code Page**—Use these lists to handle localized text files.

- **Date Order**—If the data in the text file uses a European or other date format that varies from the month-day-year format typical in the United States, select the appropriate date order in the Date Order drop-down list.

- **Date Delimiter and Time Delimiter**—Type the symbol used to separate the month, day, and year in a date in the Date Delimiter text box; type the symbol used to separate hours, minutes, and seconds in the Time Delimiter text box. For example, in the United States, the date delimiter is the virgule (/) character, and the time delimiter is the colon (:).

- **Four Digit Years**—Mark this check box if the dates in the text file use four digits for the year, such as 8/28/2006.

- **Leading Zeros in Dates**—Mark this check box if the dates in the text file have leading zeros, such as 08/09/2006.

- **Decimal Symbol**—Type the symbol used for the decimal separator in numeric values in the text box. In the United States, the decimal symbol is the period (.), but many European nations use a comma (,).

- **Field Information**—The appearance of this grid depends on the file format you select. For a delimited text file, the Field Information grid lets you edit field names, select the field's data type and indexing, and specify whether to skip the field in importing (refer to Figure 8.26). For a fixed-width text file, the Field Information grid lets you perform the same operations but adds specifications for the starting column and width of each field (refer to Figure 8.27).

- **Save As**—Click this button to display the Save Import/Export Specification dialog. By typing a name for the specification and clicking OK, you can save the file import settings for later use (see Figure 8.28).

- **Specs**—Click this button to display the Import/Export Specifications dialog. Select a previously saved specification and click OK to use import settings that you defined previously.

Figure 8.28
The Save Import/ Export Specification dialog lets you save or select a set of saved import specifications to apply when importing a text file. This figure illustrates saving the import specification for the sample Orders.csv comma-separated-values file.

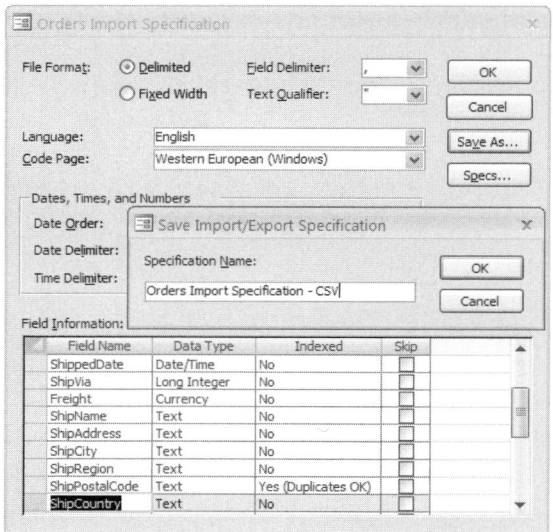

Saving the export specification from the Wizard's Orders Import Specification dialog accomplishes the same objective as marking the Save Import Steps check box in the External Data – Text File dialog. To use a saved import specification created by marking the Save Import Steps check box, click the External Data ribbon's Saved Imports button to open the Manage Data Tasks dialog's Imports page (see Figure 8.29).

 The LinkTest.accdb sample database in the \SEUA12\Chaptr08 folder of the accompanying CD-ROM includes several import and export specifications.

TIP

> If you even suspect that you'll need to import the same or a similar text file, save the import specification in your database by marking the Save Export Steps check box and adding a descriptive name and detailed description. You can edit the specification in the Wizard and resave it with the Save Export Steps check box, if necessary.

Figure 8.29
The Manage Data Tasks dialog's Imports page lists the import specifications you save by marking the Save Import Steps check box. The list does not include specifications you save with the Wizard's *FileName* Import Specification dialog's Save As input box.

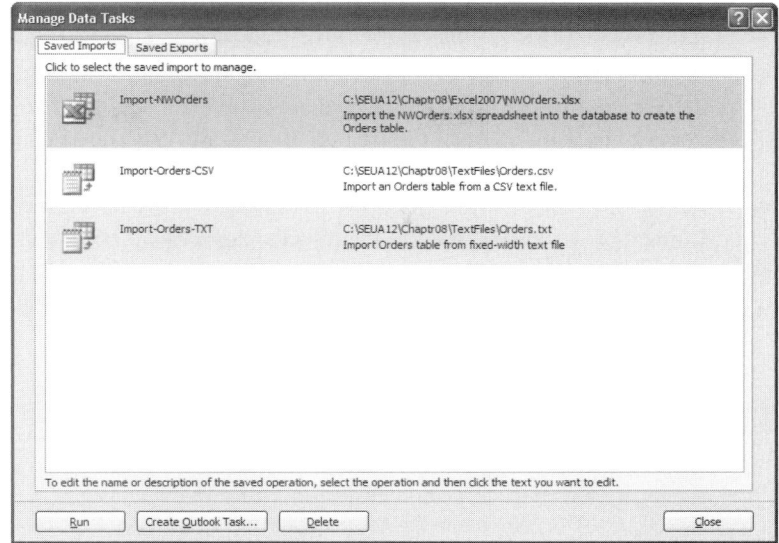

WORKING WITH TABLES IN OTHER DATABASE FILE FORMATS

Access and other Microsoft programming platforms, such as Visual Studio 2005 and later, dominate today's database front-end development market. Thus, the importance of Access's import/link support for legacy desktop database files has decreased as use of Paradox, dBASE, and FoxPro have declined, especially for new projects. Paradox, dBASE, Clipper, and FoxPro now qualify as *legacy* data formats, although today's diehard Visual FoxPro programmers certainly would argue this point.

Conventional desktop database development applications maintain each table in an individual file. Each file contains a header followed by the data. A *header* is a group of bytes that provides information on the file's structure, such as the names and types of fields, number of records in the table, and file length. This information usually is called *metadata* (data about data). When you create a table file in dBASE, Visual FoxPro, or Paradox, for example, the file contains only a header. As you add records to the file, the file size increases by the number of bytes required for one record, and the header is updated to reflect the new file size and record count.

Desktop RDBMSs create a variety of supplemental files, some of which are required to import, link, or export RDBMSs:

- Visual FoxPro and dBASE .dbf files store memo-type data in a separate .dbt file. If a FoxPro or dBASE table file contains a memo field, the .dbt file must be available. If the .dbt file is missing, you can't import or link dBASE or Visual FoxPro tables that contain a memo field.

- Use of .ndx (dBASE III), .mdx (dBASE IV+), or .idx or .cdx (FoxPro) index files is optional. You always should use index files when you have them. If you don't link the index files when you link an indexed .dbf table file, modifications you make to the linked tables aren't reflected in the index, which causes errors to occur when you try to use the indexed tables with dBASE. Linking an indexed dBASE table requires the Borland Database Engine (BDE) described in the following Note.

- Paradox stores information about the primary key index file (.px) in the associated table (.db) file; the .px file for the .db file must be available for Access to open a Paradox .db file for updating. Access links the .px file automatically if it exists. Like dBASE, Paradox stores memo-type data in a separate file with an .mb extension. Linking an indexed Paradox table also requires the BDE.

TIP

You must have exclusive access to the dBASE file when you first create the link; multiuser (shared) access is supported thereafter. For more information see the "Using dBASE Data with Access and Jet" Knowledge Base topic at http://support.microsoft.com/kb/230125/.

Office 2007 installs the Access version of Jet 4.0 Service Pack 7, which doesn't support multiuser access to Paradox files; you must have exclusive access to the Paradox file whenever you have the linked file open. See the "Using Paradox Data with Access and Jet " topic at http://support.microsoft.com/kb/230126/.

NOTE

You can't attach dBASE 7-8 or Paradox indexes to linked .dbf or .db files unless you have the Borland Database Engine (BDE) from Borland Software Corporation installed on your computer. The inability to attach indexes means that any records you add or in which you change values of indexed fields no longer are accessible from dBASE 7-8 or Paradox applications that rely on table indexes. (Almost all commercial dBASE and Paradox applications use indexes.)

You need the BDE to export or create read or write links to Paradox 7-8 and dBASE 7-8 files. You can obtain more information on the BDE, which is included with the Delphi development platform, at http://info.borland.com/devsupport/bde/. If you have a BDE version earlier than 5.01, you can obtain a no-charge upgrade to version 5.1.1 at http://info.borland.com/devsupport/bde/bdeupdate.html.

All supplemental files must be in the same folder as the related database file to be used by Access.

TIP

Create a new folder to store the tables you import or export. The default folder for exporting and importing files is \My Documents in all current Windows operating systems. If you intend to import or export a large number of files, change the Default Database Folder entry in the Personalize page of the Access Options dialog (click the Office and Access Options buttons).

DEALING WITH PC DATABASE FILES

Access can import and export, subject to the preceding limitations, the following types of database table files used by the most common PC database managers:

- **dBASE .dbf table and .dbt memo files as well as dBASE III .ndx and dBASE IV, 5.0, and 7.0 .mdx index files**—dBASE III+ files are a common denominator of the PC RDBMS industry. Most PC RDBMSs and all common spreadsheet applications can import and export .dbf files; the most popular formats are dBASE III and IV. Some of these RDBMSs can update existing .ndx and .mdx index files, and a few RDBMSs can create these index files. Access 2007 links and exports .ndx and .mdx indexes only if you have the BDE installed. You must have version 5.01+ of the BDE to import, export, or link dBASE 7.0/8.0 tables. When this book was written, the current version was 5.1.1.

- **Visual FoxPro .dbf table and .dbc database container files**—Access 2007 requires the Microsoft Visual FoxPro ODBC driver (VFPODBC.dll) for import and link operations. Prior to OLE DB and ActiveX Data Objects (ADO), Open Database Connectivity (ODBC) was Microsoft's preferred technology for connecting to client/ server databases and other data sources.

NOTE

> Windows 2000 installed VFPODBC.dll as a component of Microsoft Data Access Components (MDAC) 2.5, but Windows XP and .NET Server install MDAC 2.6, which doesn't include the Visual FoxPro driver. You can download and run version 6.01.8629.1 of the FoxPro ODBC driver installer (Vfpodbc.msi) from http://msdn.microsoft.com/ vfoxpro/downloads/updates/odbc/default.aspx. This version, which is the latest (and final) FoxPro ODBC driver that Microsoft offers, has serious limitations when exporting Access tables to FoxPro .dbf or .dbc files. You receive an "Error -7778" message if you attempt to use a file data source. The Microsoft Knowledge Base article at http:// support.microsoft.com/kb/q212886/ confirms the problem.
>
> If you use a Machine data source, the filename and all field names must be eight characters or less, and field names can't contain spaces. The Knowledge Base article at http://support.microsoft.com/kb/287674/EN-US/ has more information on this issue.

- **Paradox 3.x, 4.x, 5.x, 7.x, and 8.x .db table, .mb memo, and .px primary key files**—Access 2007 supports importing and exporting Paradox 3.x, 4.x, and 5.x .db and .mb files. Access doesn't generate .px files when you export a .db file. You can link Paradox 3-5 files with or without .px indexes, but if you don't have a .px index, the linked table won't open in Datasheet view.

NOTE

> If you work in a multiuser environment, you must have exclusive access to the file you intend to import. No one else can have this file open when you initiate the importing process, and everyone else is denied access to the file until you close the Import dialog.

CAUTION

Make sure that you work on a backup, not on the original copy of the linked file, until you're certain that your updates to the data in the linked table are valid for the existing database application.

LINKING AND IMPORTING EXTERNAL ISAM TABLES

ISAM is an acronym for indexed sequential access method, the architecture used for all desktop RDBMS tables. To link or import a dBASE or Paradox file as a table in Access 2007 (.accdb) file format, follow these steps:

1. If you have a test database that you can use for this procedure, open it, and skip to step 4.

2. If you don't have a test database, create a sample to use throughout this chapter. Click the Quick Access Toolbar's (QAT) New button to display the Getting Started with Microsoft Office Access dialog.

3. Navigate to the folder in which to store the new database, type a name (such as LinkTest.accdb) in the File Name text box, and click Create. Access creates and tests the new database. Delete the default Table1.

4. In this example, you link an external table to the database. Click the ribbon's External Data tab, and click the Import group's More button to open the secondary file-type gallery.

5. If you have a Paradox table with a primary key index to link, click the Paradox File button. Otherwise, click the dBASE File or another file type button as appropriate to the format of your table file to open the Get External Data – *File Type* dialog (see Figure 8.30).

Figure 8.30
Each file type has its own Get External Data dialog that lets you choose between importing data from or linking to the file you select in the File Name text box.

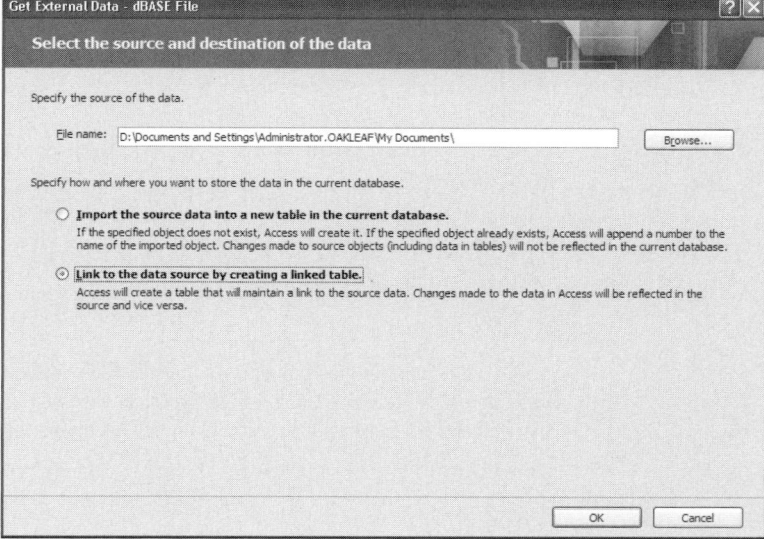

6. Click Browse to open the File Open dialog, navigate to the location of the file to link, and open the Files of Type drop-down list to select the file version, as shown in Figure 8.31.

Figure 8.31
Navigate to the folder that holds the database file to link and select the type of database file in the drop-down list.

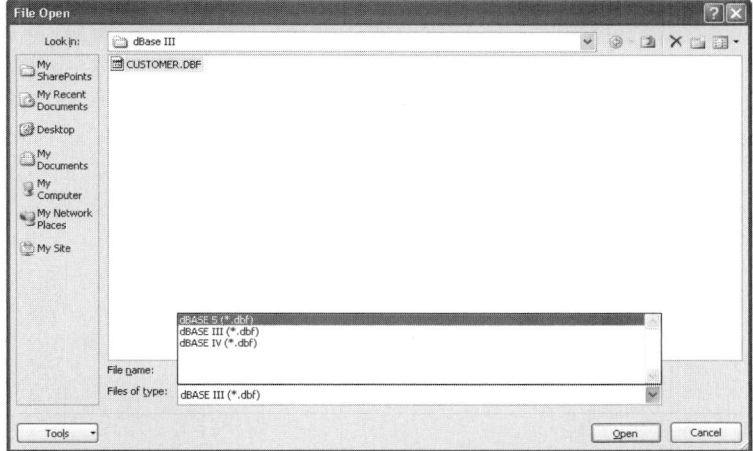

NOTE

The \SEUA12\Chaptr08 folder of the accompanying CD-ROM has subfolders that contain sample dBASE III and IV, FoxPro 6, Paradox, and text files that you can import or link to your test database.

7. Double-click the name of the table you want to link or import (or click the name to select it and then click the Link button). Access supplies the standard extensions for dBASE and Paradox table files.

8. If the Paradox file you choose is encrypted and requires a password to decrypt it, the Password Required dialog opens. Type the password and press Enter.

9. Verify that you've selected the Link to the Data Source by Creating a Linked Table option, and click OK to close the Get Extended Data – *DBType* File dialog. If a memo or other related file is missing, you receive an error message at this point.

The table(s) you linked or imported now are listed in the Navigation pane. If you linked a file, Access adds an icon that shows the type of database table and an arrow to indicate the table is linked. Figure 8.32 illustrates linked dBASE CUSTOMER, Paradox Employee, and dBASE EMPLOYEE1 tables. Access added the "1" suffix, because the Paradox Employee table was present before adding the dBASE EMPLOYEE table.

Figure 8.32
Linked tables are identified in the Navigation pane by an icon for the file type (dB for dBASE and Px for Paradox) with an arrow to represent the link. The EMPLOYEE1 table is linked from a pair of dBASE III tables—EMPLOYEE.DBF and EMPLPLOYEE.DBT. The EMPLOYEE.DBT file contains the data for the Notes field and doesn't appear in the Navigation Pane.

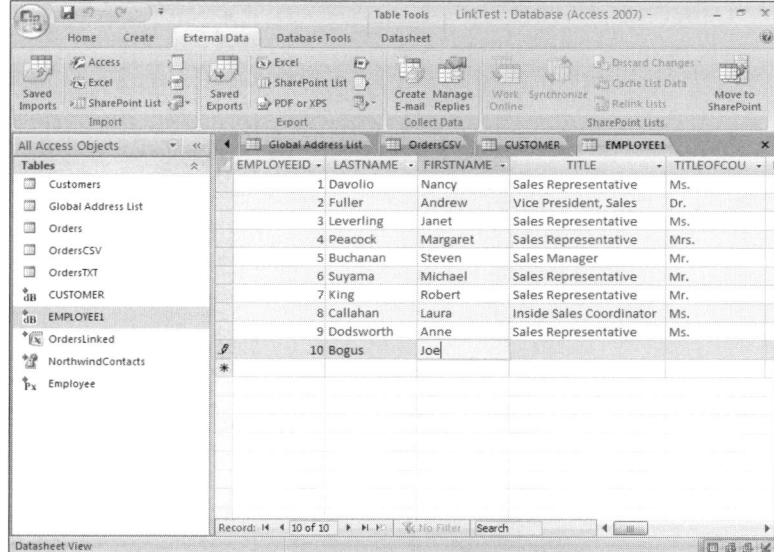

After you link an external file as a table, you can use it almost as though it were a table in your own database. If you don't have the BDE installed, linked dBASE 5 and later and all Paradox tables are read-only. A general limitation is that you can't change the structure of a linked table: field names, field data types, and the Field Size properties. There is no limitation on changing the structure or properties of an imported table.

NOTE

Although you can't change field properties for linked tables, you can change the name of the attached table within this database only. Select the link, press F2, and type the new name for the table. The name for the table (called an *alias*) is changed only in the current Access database and not in the native database.

LINKING VISUAL FOXPRO TABLES WITH ODBC

You can use the ODBC drivers provided with Office 2007 to link Visual FoxPro databases or tables to Access databases. *Data source* is a synonym for database when you use the ODBC API to link tables.

Follow these steps to link Visual FoxPro 6.0 table(s) to an Access database via ODBC:

1. With an Access database open, click the External Data tab, click the Imports group's More button, and click the gallery's ODBC Databases button to open the Get External Data – ODBC Database dialog.

2. Select the Link to the Data Source by Creating a Linked Table option and click OK to display the Select Data Source dialog. This example uses a Machine Data Source installed by the Visual FoxPro ODBC driver, so click the Machine Data Source tab.

3. Select Microsoft Visual FoxPro Tables (for a .dbf file) in the Data Source Name (DSN) list, and click OK to open the Configure Connection dialog. If you want to link tables from a .dbc file, select the Visual FoxPro Database DSN, as shown in Figure 8.33, and click OK to close the dialog.

Figure 8.33
Select the ODBC dri-ver for the type of database to link from the list of drivers installed on your machine.

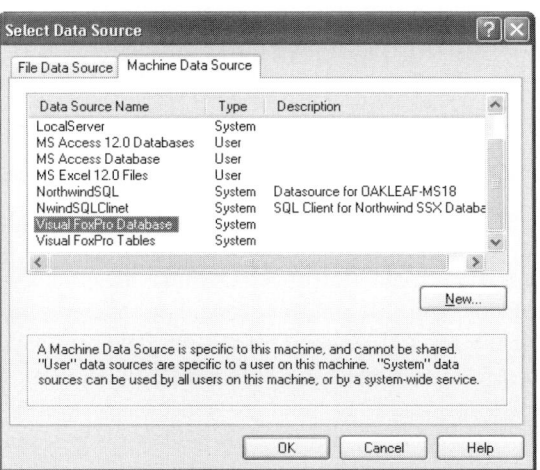

8

4. If you chose the Visual FoxPro Database DSN, select the Visual FoxPro Database (.DBC) option, click Browse to open the Select Database dialog, navigate to the folder containing the .dbc file, and select the file in the list (see Figure 8.34).

Otherwise, accept the Free Table Directory, and click Browse to display the Select Directory Containing Free Tables dialog. If necessary, use the Drives and Directories lists to navigate to the folder in which your FoxPro files are stored in the Folders list. In either case, click Open and OK to display the Link Tables dialog.

Figure 8.34
Select the .dbc file or the folder containing the FoxPro .dbf file(s) to configure the ODBC connection with the Office 2007 FoxPro driver.

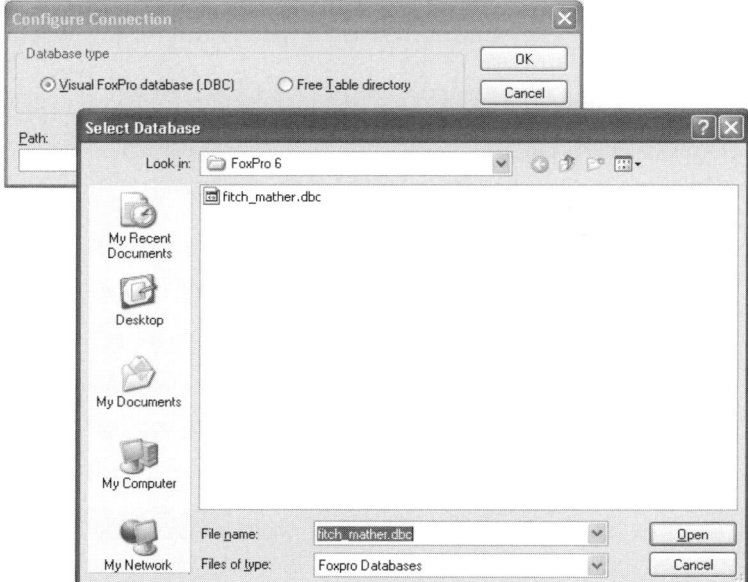

5. The Link Tables dialog lists the FoxPro tables in the folder you selected in step 4. Click each table name to select it, or click Select All. After you select all the tables that you want to link, click OK (see Figure 8.35).

6. If any of the table(s) you selected don't have a primary key index, the Select Unique Record Identifier dialog opens. If you want to update the data in the ODBC-linked table without a primary key index, you must select a field (or combination of fields) that creates a unique record identification for each row in the table—essentially, you create a surrogate primary key for the linked table. To select a field, click it and then click OK. In the example in Figure 8.36, the primary key field of the customers table is customerid.

Figure 8.35
The Link Tables dialog lists all FoxPro tables in the folder or in a .dbc container file. Select the table(s) you want to link to your Access database, and click OK.

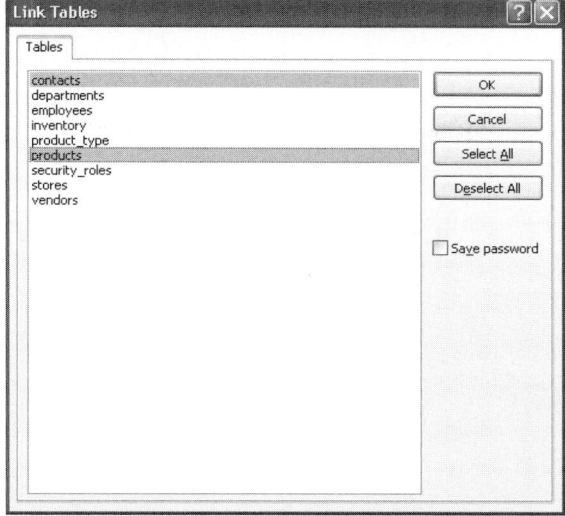

Figure 8.36
If the folder with the tables or the .dbc file doesn't include a primary key index for any of the tables you select to link, you must select a field to act as a surrogate primary key in the Select Unique Identifier dialog.

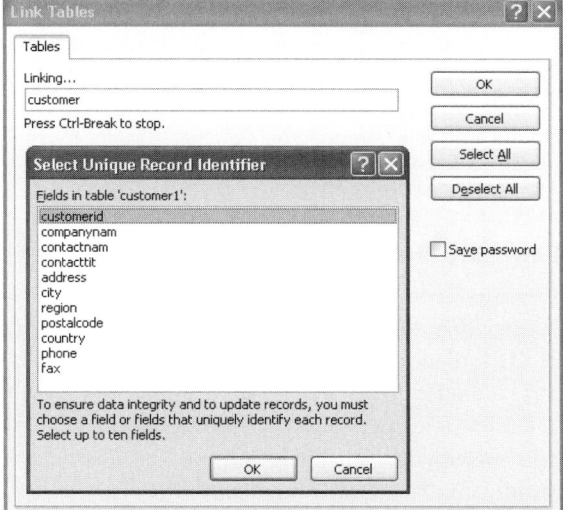

NOTE

All FoxPro 6.0 tables in \Program Files\SEUA12\Chaptr08\FoxPro 6, except the customer.dbf folder, have primary key indexes.

Your linked Visual FoxPro tables appear in the Navigation pane (with the ODBC globe turned to display Africa), as shown in Figure 8.37. Any table linked by ODBC displays the globe icon. Double-click the table icon to display your newly linked Visual FoxPro table. By

8

default, Visual FoxPro table and field names appear in lowercase. The maximum length of a FoxPro or dBASE field name is 10 characters.

Figure 8.37
The FoxPro contacts and products files are linked to the Access database. The linked FoxPro contacts table is updatable, as indicated by the tentative append (*) record at the end of the table records.

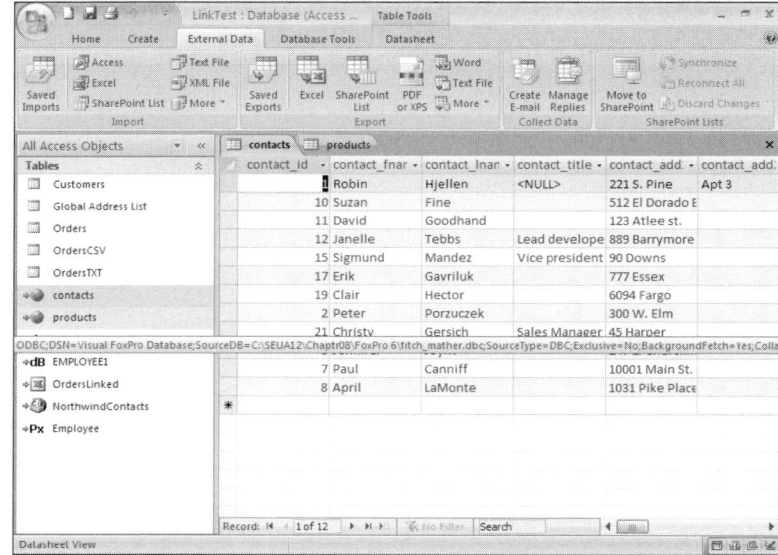

 Access detects problems with linked or imported tables that might cause errors when you try to use the tables with Access. Importing and linking errors are the subject of the "Troubleshooting" section near the end of this chapter.

DEALING WITH IMAGES IN EXTERNAL DATABASE FILES

Most database managers designed for Windows include some form of graphics field data type. Early versions of Paradox, for example, provide a special field data type for graphics; later versions support OLE objects. Although early versions of dBASE lack a field data type for graphics, third-party software firms publish applications that let you store images in dBASE memo fields. Various add-on applications for desktop RDBMSs let programmers display and edit graphic images. The images usually are in individual files, but a few third-party applications continue to place images in memo files.

When you try to import or link desktop database files containing images or other binary data, you might receive an error message that the memo file is corrupted or that you can't import the .db or .dbf file that contains the offending memo or graphics field. In rare cases—usually involving tiny images—you can import the .dbf and .dbt files, but you see random characters in the Access memo field. With Paradox tables, the graphics or binary fields disappear from the table.

The simplest approach to dealing with graphics files missing from imported tables is to convert the individual files to Graphic Interchange Format (.gif) or Joint Photographic Experts Group (.jpg) format, and then use Windows Paint to import the images into an OLE

8

Object field. The following procedure uses the employees table imported from the fitch_mather.dbc FoxPro 6 database of the preceding section, and the nine JPEG files, EMPID1.JPG–EMPID9.JPG, in the \SEUA12\Chaptr08\JPEGImages folder.

NOTE

An alternative is to add a field of the new Attachment data type instead of OLE Object. Attachment fields consume less disk space than corresponding OLE Object fields, but aren't backward compatible with the traditional .mdb format.

To add an OLE Object field and images from files to an imported (or new) table, do this:

1. Open the table in Design view, select the field below the location for the new OLE Object field, and press Insert to add an empty field. This example uses the employees table imported from the FoxProfitch_mather.dbc database.

2. Type the Field Name (**emp_photo** for this example) and select OLE Object as the Data Type setting (see Figure 8.38).

Figure 8.38
Add an OLE Object field to the imported table to hold image data in OLE 2.0 format or to create a link to external image files.

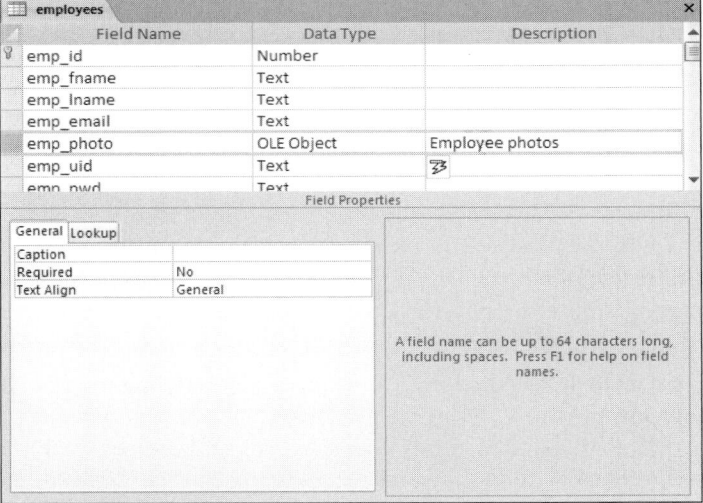

3. Return to Datasheet View, save the design changes, right-click the OLE Object cell in the first row, and choose Insert Object to open the Microsoft Office Access (formerly Insert Object) dialog.

4. Select the Create From File option, click Browse to open the Browse dialog, and navigate to the folder that contains your image files (\SEUA12\Chaptr08\JPEGImages for this example).

5. Double-click the image file you want to embed in the field (EMPID1.JPG for the first image), which adds the well-formed path to the file in the text box (see Figure 8.39).

Figure 8.39
By default, the bitmap data is included in the OLE Object field. Select the Link check box to maintain the image data in the source .png, .gif, .jpg, or .bmp files.

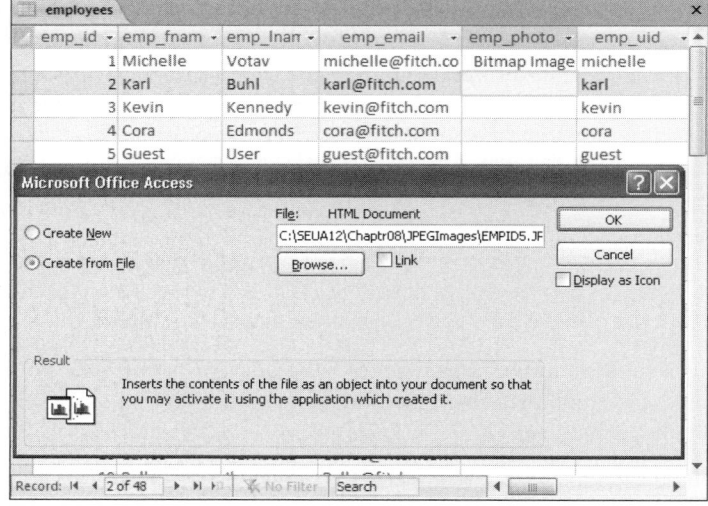

NOTE

Instead of embedding the image in the database, you can create a link to the image's source file by selecting the Link check box. Linking reduces the size of the .accdb file, but requires a permanent path to the source image files. If a network server stores the image files, the path might change. If this happens, you receive an error when attempting to open the linked image file.

6. Click OK to embed or link the image, which adds a Bitmap Image (for .bmp files) or Package (for other image types) value to the cell. Double-click the cell to open the image in Windows Paint (see Figure 8.40). You can edit the image in Paint; Access automatically saves your changes when you close Paint and return to the table.

7. Repeat steps 4, 5, and 6 for each image to add, selecting the row appropriate to the image file.

 The employees table of the LinkTest.accdb database in the \SEUA12\Chaptr08 folder of the accompanying CD-ROM includes several embedded bitmap images. Subfolders contain sets of images in .bmp, .png, and .jpg formats.

CONVERTING FIELD DATA TYPES TO ACCESS DATA TYPES

When you import or link a file, Access reads the header of the file and converts the field data types to Access data types. Access usually is successful in this conversion because it offers a greater variety of data types than most of the other widely used PC RDBMSs. Table 8.2 shows the correspondence of field data types between dBASE, Paradox, and Access files.

Figure 8.40
Double-clicking a Bitmap Image cell opens the image for editing in Windows Paint, if Paint is associated in Windows Explorer with the image's file type. If you've associated a different OLE 2.0–compliant application to the file type, the image opens in that application.

TABLE 8.2   FIELD DATA TYPE CONVERSION BETWEEN ACCESS AND OTHER RDBMSs

dBASE III/IV/5	Paradox 3.x, 4.x, 5.0	Access
Character	Alphanumeric	Text (Specify Size property)
Numeric, Float*	Number, Money, BCD*	Number (Double)
		Number (Single)
		Number (Byte)
	Short Number	Number (Integer)
	Long Number	Number (Long)
	AutoIncrement	AutoNumber
Logical	Logical	Yes/No
Date	Date, Time, Timestamp*	Date/Time
Memo	Memo, Formatted Memo, Binary*	Memo
	OLE	OLE Object

Sometimes two or three types of field data, separated by commas, are shown within a single column in Table 8.2. When Access exports a table that contains a data type that corresponds with one of the two field data types, the first data type is assigned to the field in the exported table. The Float data type is available only in dBASE IV and 5.

TIP

> If you're importing tables, you can change the field data type and the Field Size property to make them more suitable to the type of information contained in the field. When you change a data type or the Field Size property, however, follow the precautions noted in Chapter 5, "Working with Access Databases and Tables."
>
> Remember that you can't change the field data type or Field Size property of linked tables. You can, however, use the Format property with imported or linked tables to display the data in any format compatible with the field data type of imported or linked files. You can change any remaining properties that are applicable to the field data type, such as validation rules and text. By using the Caption property, you can give the field a new and more descriptive name.

→ To review field properties of Access databases, **see** "Choosing Field Data Types, Sizes, and Formats," **p. 213**.

USING THE LINKED TABLE MANAGER ADD-IN TO RELINK TABLES

Moving linked files to another folder or logical drive causes the existing links to break. Access provides an add-in assistant known as the Linked Table Manager to simplify relinking tables.

If you move a file that provides a linked table to an Access database, click the Database Tools tab, and then click the Linked Table Manager. The Linked Table Manager's window lists all tables linked to the database. The list also displays the path to the database containing the linked table(s) at the time the link was created, with the exception of the path to files or databases linked by ODBC. Click the check box of the file(s) whose location(s) might have changed (see Figure 8.41).

Figure 8.41
The Linked Table Manager handles re-creating links to tables or databases that have moved since you created the original links to an Access database.

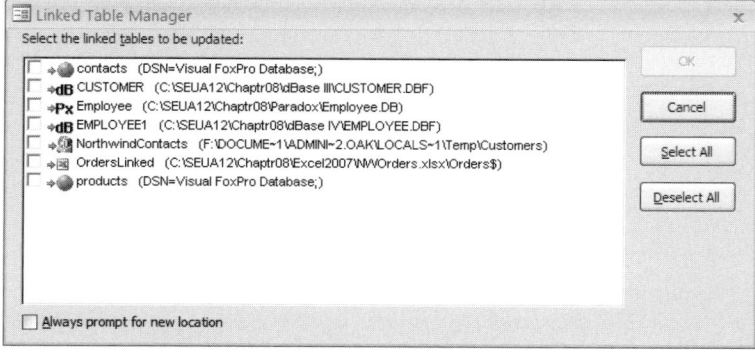

> **TIP**
>
> You also can view the path to the folder containing a linked table by opening the linked table in Design view, opening the Table Properties window, and scrolling through the contents of the Description text box.

Click OK to display the Select New Location of *TableName* dialog shown in Figure 8.42. (If your linked files haven't moved, mark the Always Prompt for New Location check box to open the dialog.) Navigate to the folder where the table or database is located; then double-click the new link file's name and close the dialog. If Access successfully refreshes the table links, it displays a dialog saying so; click OK to close the success message dialog. Click the Close button of the Linked Table Manager to close the add-in.

Figure 8.42
The Select New Location of *TableName* dialog lets you substitute another folder or database file for the broken link.

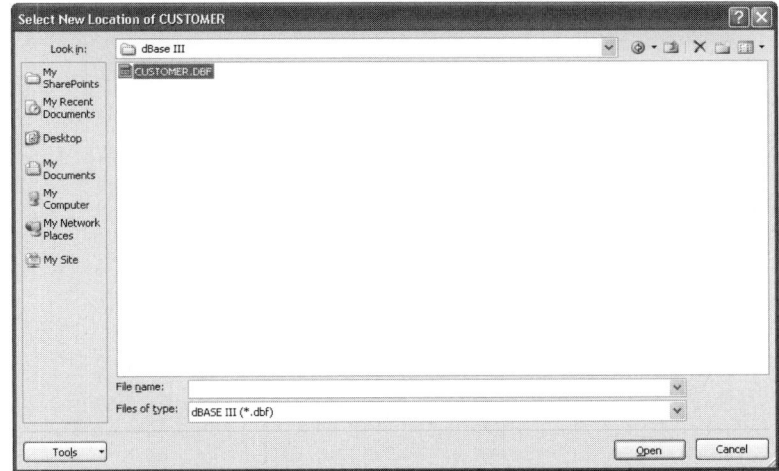

> **NOTE**
>
> If you select a table linked by ODBC, the ODBC Manager's Select Data Source dialog opens so you can re-create the data source for the linked table or database.

> **TIP**
>
> The Linked Table Manager can refresh links only for a table that has been moved to another disk or folder—the table must have the same name. If the linked table's file was renamed, you must delete the table link from your Access database and relink the table under its new name.

USING THE ACCESS MAIL MERGE WIZARD

Access 2007's Mail Merge Wizard can help you create a new mail merge document or employ an existing mail merge document from which to create form letters. The Mail

Merge Wizard uses a table or a query as the data source for the merge data file. The sections that follow describe two methods of creating a form letter:

- Using the Mail Merge Wizard to create a new mail merge document whose merge data source is an Access table

- Using an existing mail merge document with a merge data source from an Access table with a filter or a select query

Access 2000 and earlier used Dynamic Data Exchange (DDE) to send mail merge data to Word. Access 2007 uses an OLE DB data source to generate mail merge documents. OLE DB and Automation is a much more reliable method of interapplication communication than DDE. Using OLE DB also lets you take advantage of Word's filter and sort features, which were unavailable from documents created with earlier versions of the Mail Merge Wizard.

CREATING AND PREVIEWING A NEW FORM LETTER

When you first try a new Wizard, it's customary to create a new object rather than use the Wizard to modify an existing object, such as a mail merge document. The following steps use the Mail Merge Wizard to create a new mail merge document from records in the Customers table of Northwind.accdb:

 1. Open Northwind.accdb, if necessary, click the External Data tab, and select the Customers table in the Navigation pane.

2. Click the Export group's More button to open the gallery and click Merge It with Microsoft Word to launch the Microsoft Word Mail Merge Wizard.

3. Select the Create a New Document and Then Link the Data to It option (see Figure 8.43) to create a new mail merge document using fields from the Customers table.

Figure 8.43
The Mail Merge Wizard's only dialog lets you use an existing merge document (the default) or create a new document.

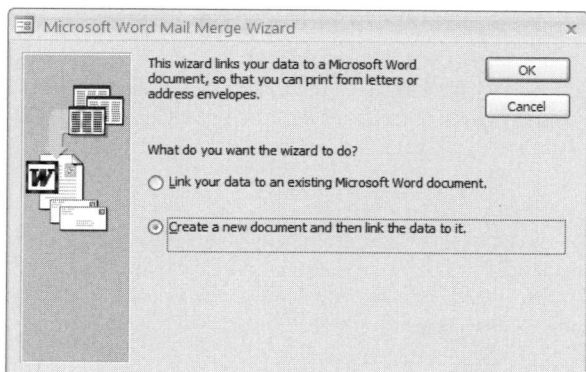

4. Click OK to launch Word 2007, if it isn't running. Word opens a new mail merge main document, Document1, and displays the Mailings ribbon and the Mail Merge page of the task pane.

5. Click the Insert Merge Fields button to verify the available fields from the Customers table in the Insert Merge Field dialog, as shown in Figure 8.44. Click Cancel to close the dialog, and close the task pane.

Figure 8.44
When you start the mail merge process, the Insert Merge Field dialog confirms that you selected the correct table as the merge data source.

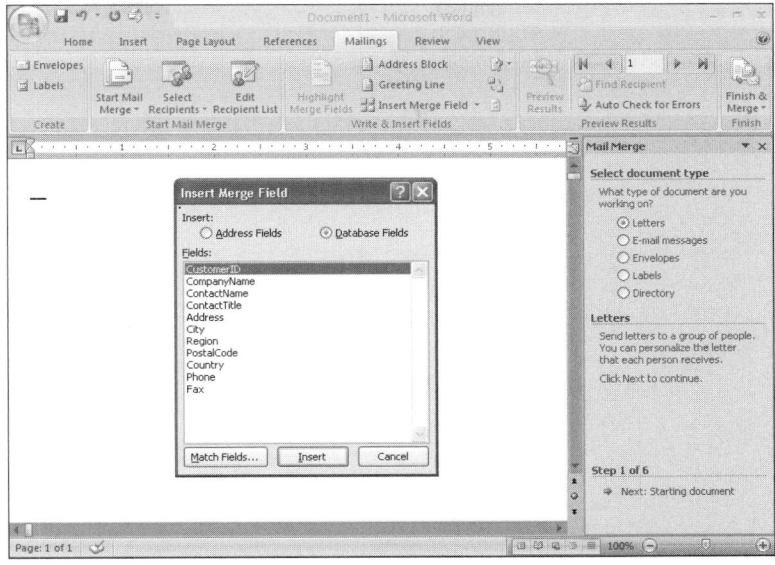

6. With the cursor at the top of the document, click the Insert tab, and then click the Date and Time button to display the Date and Time dialog; choose any date format you want, mark the Update Automatically check box, and click OK to add a date field to the main document.

7. Add two blank lines, click the Mailings tab and the arrow to the right of the Insert Merge Fields button to display the list as a context menu, and click to insert the CompanyName, Address, City, Region, PostalCode, ContactName, and ContactTitle fields from the Customers table to create the address section of the main document. Format the field names, which insert in a single line, as shown in Figure 8.45.

Figure 8.45
Arrange merge fields in letter format after you insert them.

8

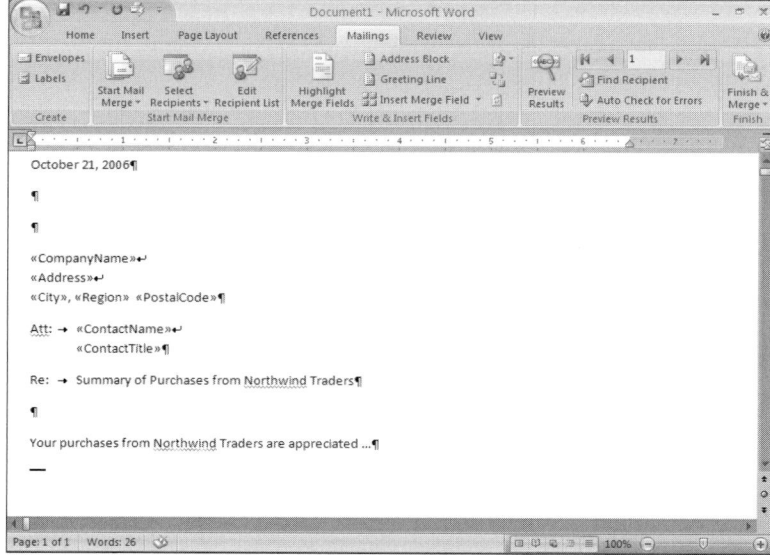

8. Click the Preview Results button of the Mailings ribbon to preview the appearance of the first of your form letters.

9. The form letters go only to customers in the United States, so you should check the address format for United States addresses. Click the Find Recipient button to open the Find in Field dialog, type **USA** in the Find text box, and select Country from the This Field list. Click Find Next to find the first U.S. record. The preview of the form letter for Great Lakes Food Market appears, as shown in Figure 8.46.

Figure 8.46
After clicking the Preview Results button, use the Find in Field dialog to locate the record for the first U.S. customer.

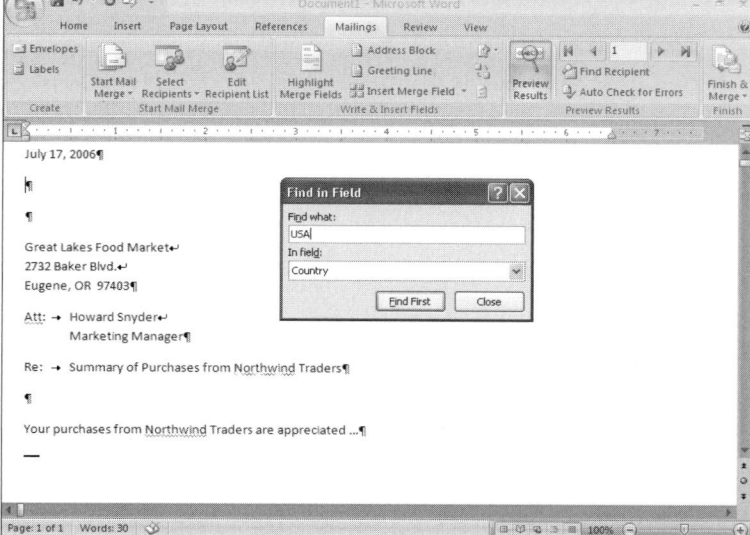

10. To send letters to U.S. customers only, click the Edit Recipients button to open the Mail Merge Recipients dialog with the current record selected. Open the Country field's list and choose (Advanced…), as shown in Figure 8.47, to specify a Word filter on the Country field.

Figure 8.47
Word 2007's Mail Merge Recipients dialog lets you choose how to filter and sort the data source for mail merge documents.

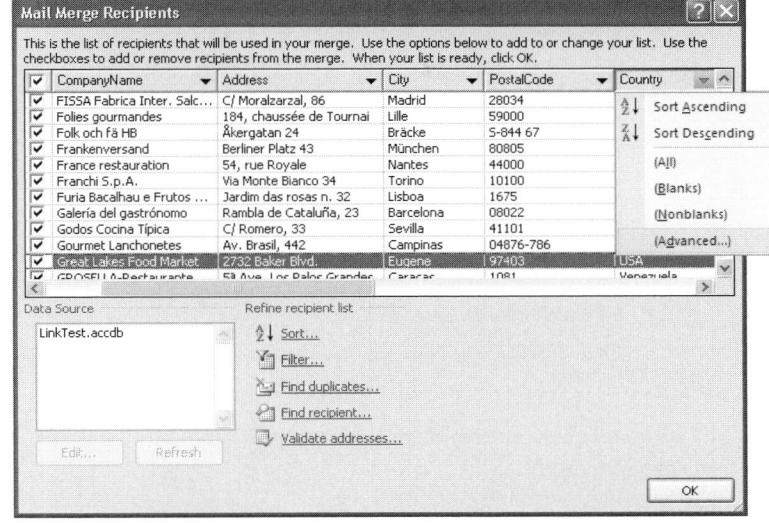

11. In the Filter and Sort dialog, select the Country field, if necessary, accept the default Equal To comparison, and type **USA** in the Compare To text box (see Figure 8.48). You can create complex filters by adding additional criteria and selecting And or Or to determine the filter logic. Click the Sort tab, select PostalCode in the Sort By list, and click OK to close the dialog.

Figure 8.48
The Filter page of the Filter and Sort dialog lets you specify expressions and criteria on which to filter the data source.

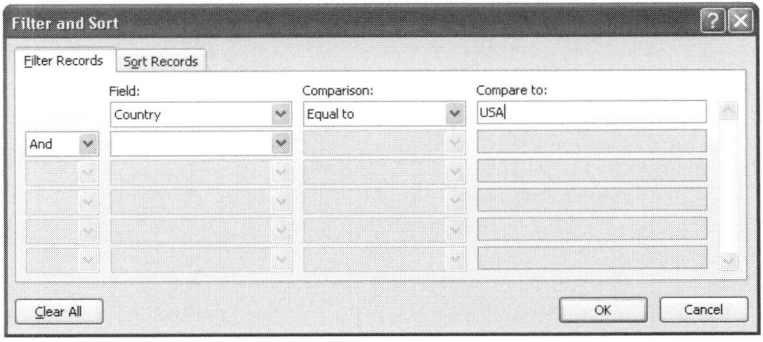

12. Applying a filter marks for inclusion only those records that meet the filter criterion (see Figure 8.49). Click OK to close the dialog.

Figure 8.49
The Wizard marks and sorts the set of filtered records in preparation for generating the mail merge documents.

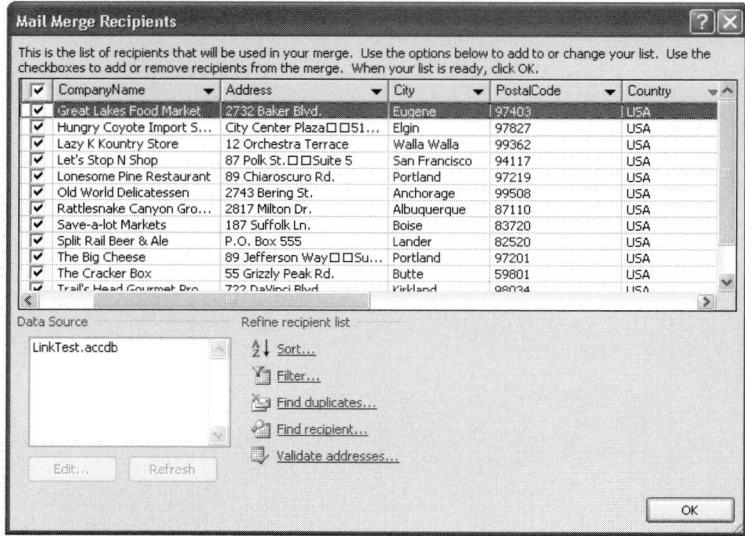

13. The filtered list is applied to the mail merge document. Click the Next Record button to display only the U.S. records in sequence.

14. Click the Finish & Merge and <u>E</u>dit Individual Documents button to open the Merge to New Document dialog. Accept the All (records) option, and click OK to generate the Letters1 document that contains the 13 letters to U.S. customers (see Figure 8.50).

Figure 8.50
The merge document contains a letter for each of the 13 U.S. customers in the filtered list.

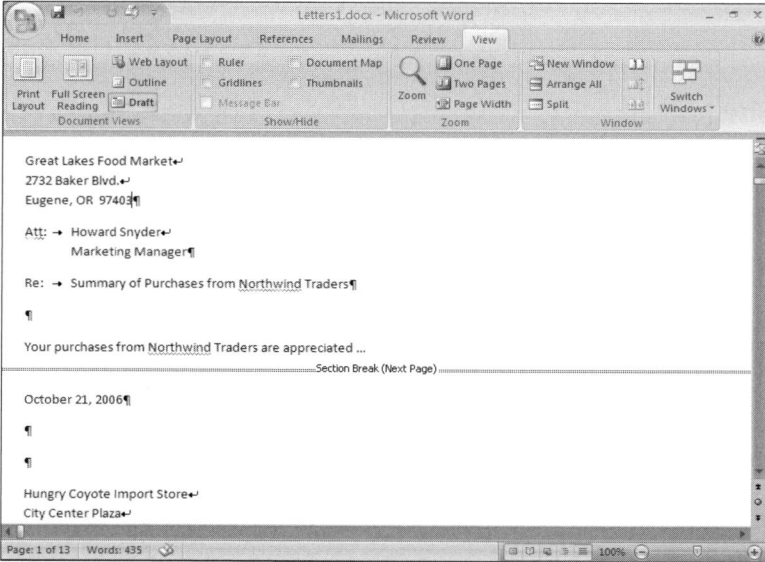

15. Close Letters1 and save it with a descriptive name, such as USCustomersLetters.docx, and do the same for Document1, the mail merge document (USCustomersMerge.docx).

 The two documents created in the preceding steps are located in the \SEUA12\Chaptr08\ MailMerge folder of the accompanying CD-ROM. The merge document doesn't save the filter, so you must reestablish the filter when opening the mail merge document.

USING AN EXISTING MAIL MERGE DOCUMENT WITH A NEW DATA SOURCE

After you create a standard mail merge document, the most common practice is to use different data sources to create form letters by addressee category. Word mail merge documents store database and table connection data as well as retain filter settings. Using Access filters or queries to restrict the recipient list usually is more convenient than performing the same operation in Word.

Take the following steps to use the main mail merge document you created in the preceding section, USCustomersMerge.doc, with a data source based on a filter for the Customers table:

 1. In Access, open the Customers table in Datasheet view, click the Home tab, if necessary, and then click the Advanced Filter Options and <u>F</u>ilter by Form buttons.

2. Scroll to the Country field, open the field list, and select USA.

 3. Click the Apply Filter button to filter the table data and display only U.S. customers.

 4. Click the Advanced Filter Options and <u>A</u>dvanced Filter/Sort buttons to open the Filter Design window, which displays the filter criterion you applied in step 2. Drag the PostalCode field to the second column, and select an Ascending sort (see Figure 8.51).

Figure 8.51
The Filter Design window opened by the Advanced Filter Sort command displays the filter for the Customers table with an ascending sort on the PostalCode field.

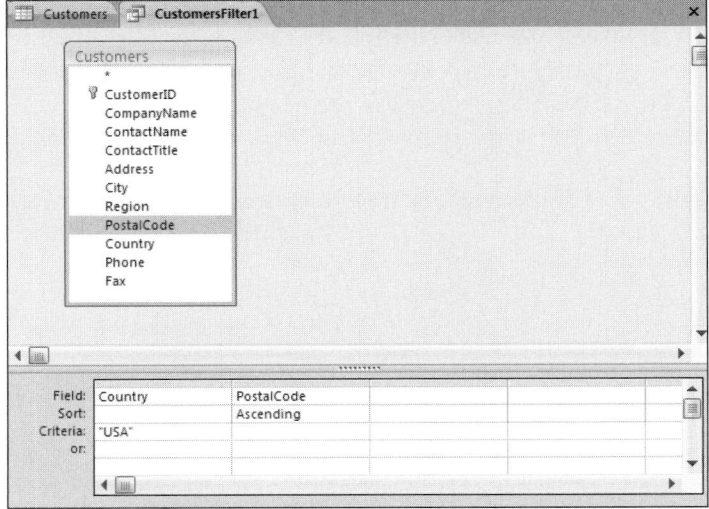

→ To review use of Access's Advanced Filter/Sort feature, **see** "Applying Advanced Filters and Sort Orders," **p. XXX** (Ch 07).

5. Right-click the upper pane of the CustomerFilter1 window, choose Save As Query, give your filter a descriptive name (such as fltUSCustomers), and click OK.

6. Close the Filter window and the Customers table, and don't save your changes.

7. Double-click the filter item (fltUSCustomers for this example) to open the query result set and test the filter. Close the Query Datasheet window.

8. With fltUSCustomers selected in the Navigation pane, click the External Data tab, the Export group's More button, and the Merge It with Microsoft Word button to launch the Mail Merge Wizard. With the Link Your Data to an Existing Microsoft Word Document option marked (the default), click OK to open the Select Microsoft Word Document dialog.

9. Navigate to and double-click the mail merge document you created in the preceding section (USCustomersMerge.doc for this example) in the file list to open the document in Word.

10. If Word can't resolve the data source type, the Confirm Data Source dialog opens to verify the use of an OLE DB data source for the Access query. Accept the default, OLE DB Database Files, and click OK to continue in Word.

TIP

If you attempt to connect to an open document, you might receive a "File in Use" error message. Click Cancel, and then click OK when the "Command Failed" error message appears. Close the merge document and try again.

11. Confirm that the filter is the new merge data source—[fltUSCustomers] in "LinkTest.accdb"—in the task pane's Mail Merge page (see Figure 8.52). Double-check the list by clicking the Mail Merge Recipients button. Only the filtered records appear in the list. Click OK to close the list.

12. You can merge the main document and data source directly to the printer, spam the customers via email, send faxes, or create a series of form letters in a new document, which is identical to the sample document you created in the preceding section.

If you close Word at this point, be sure to save your changes to the main mail merge document.

Figure 8.52
The Mail Merge task pane page confirms the document is using the fltUSCustomers filter.

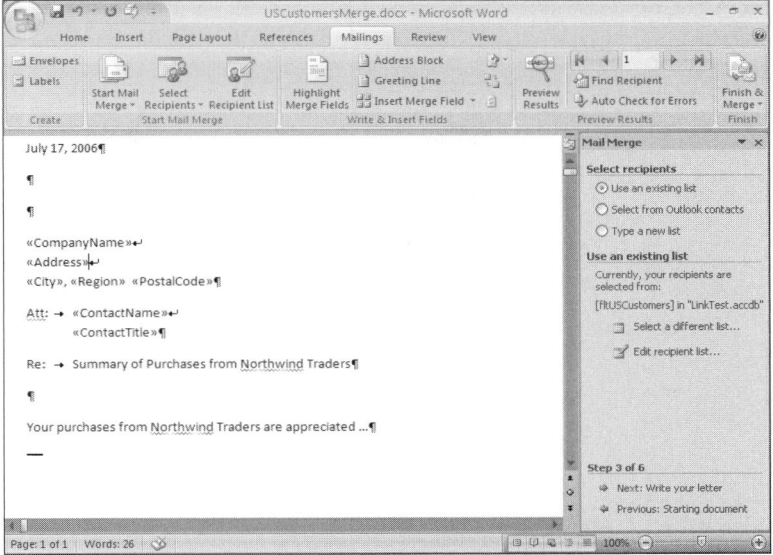

EXPORTING TABLES TO WORD, EXCEL, PDF, AND XPS FILES

You can select the table or query to save in the Navigation pane, click the External Data tab, and then do one or more of the following:

 ■ Click the Word button in the Export group to open the Export RTF File dialog, which lets you generate a Rich Text Format (.rtf) file named for the table or query and, if you marked the Open the Destination File After the Export Operation Is Complete check box, display the table in Word (see Figure 8.53). The .rtf format embeds formatting instructions and data for text, images, and other objects. Most word processing applications, including WordPad, can open .rtf files.

 ■ Click the Excel button in the Export group to generate a workbook (.xls) file named for the table or query and display the worksheet in Excel (see Figure 8.54).

■ Click the PDF or XPS button in the Export group to generate an Adobe Portable Document Format (.pdf) file named for the table or query and display the file in Adobe Reader (see Figure 8.55). PDF is the default file type in the Publish as PDF or XPS dialog's Save As Type list.

Figure 8.53
Clicking the Word button exports an .rtf file of the selected table or query object and opens Word.

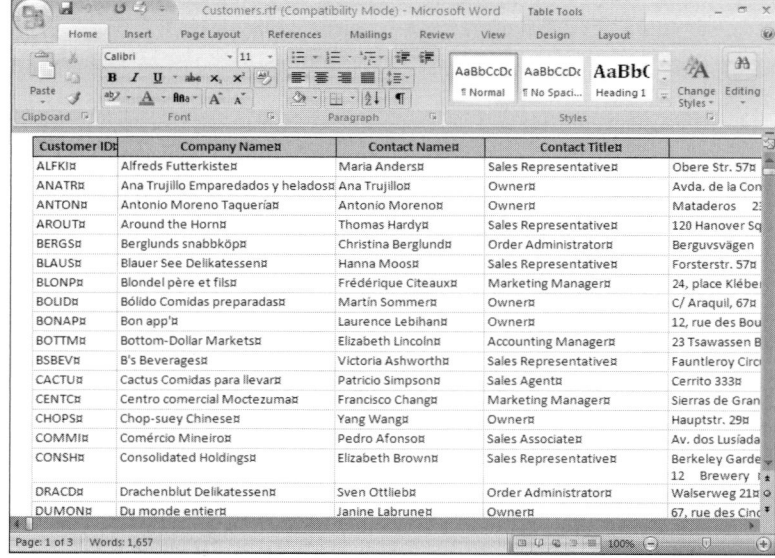

Figure 8.54
Not surprisingly, clicking the Excel button exports an .xls file of the object and opens the worksheet in Excel.

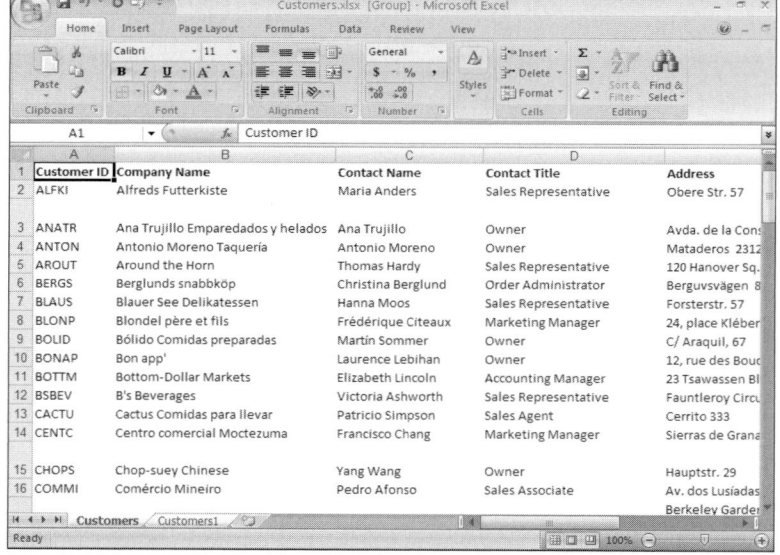

- Alternatively, select XPS in the Files of Type list to export the table in Microsoft XML Paper Specification format (see Figure 8.56). Viewing XPS files requires your computer to have the WinFX API installed. Windows Vista provides WinFX natively; you must install Microsoft .NET Framework 3.0 to obtain the WinFX API if you're not running Windows Vista.

Figure 8.55
As you'd expect by now, clicking the PDF button exports a *TableName*.pdf file of the object and opens the document in Adobe Reader.

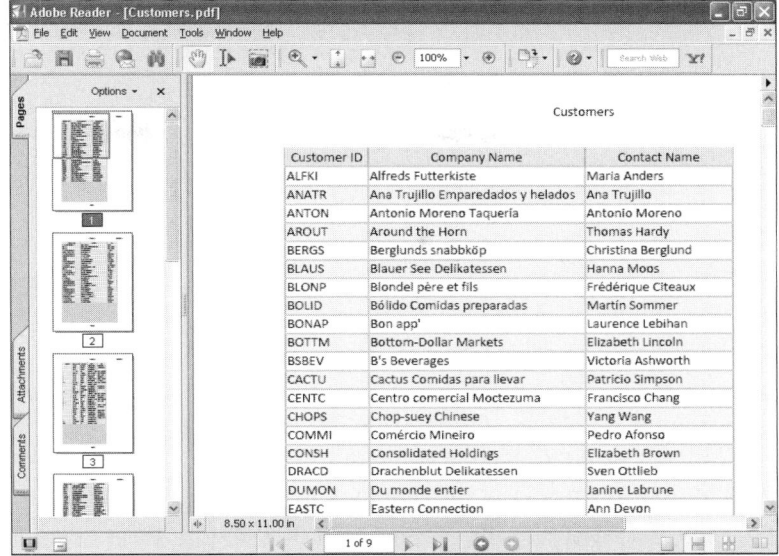

Figure 8.56
Finally, clicking the XPS button exports a *TableName*.xps file of the object and opens the document in the XPS Viewer, if you have WinFX installed by Windows Vista or Microsoft .NET Framework 3.0.

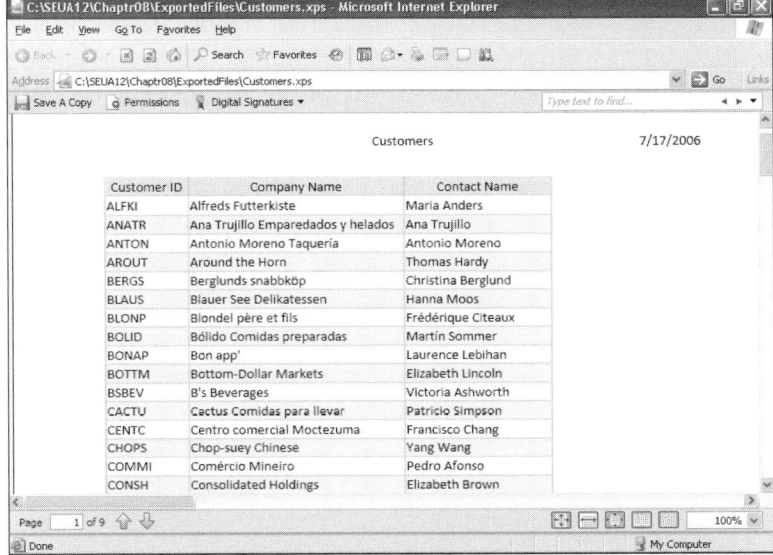

NOTE

The first time you export a table or query to a .pdf or .xps file, Access 2007 automatically downloads the required DLLs from the Microsoft Web site. A mid-2006 threat of legal action by Adobe Software about Microsoft's distribution of the purportedly open-source Adobe Portable Document Format caused this minor inconvenience.

In all cases, Access stores the exported files in your My Documents folder by default. You can change the file's name and path in the Export – *FileType* File dialog's File Name text box.

EXPORTING TABLE DATA AS TEXT FILES

Exporting a table involves a sequence of operations similar to importing a file with the same format. To export a table as a comma- or tab-delimited file that you can use as a merge file with a variety of word processing applications, complete these steps:

1. Select the table you want to export in the Navigation pane (Customers for this example), click the External Data tab, and click the Export group's Text File button to open the Export – Text File dialog.

2. Click Browse to open the File Save dialog, navigate to the location for the text file, and accept the default or edit the *TableName*.txt filename. (This example uses Customers.tab.) Click Save to return to the Export – Text File dialog.

3. Accept the Export Data with Formatting and Layout check box's default (not marked), and click OK to start the Text Export Wizard.

> **NOTE**
>
> Using the Text Export Wizard, including its advanced options, is the same as using the Import Text Wizard described in the "Importing Text Files" section earlier in the chapter, except that the result is an external text file instead of an Access table. You save and reuse export specifications by the method described for import specs.
>
> When exporting a text file, the Text Export Wizard doesn't have a step to edit field names or select field data types; these options aren't relevant when exporting data.

4. Follow the procedures as though you were importing a text file. Figure 8.57 shows the Customers table exported as a tab-separated text file from the Northwind.accdb database and displayed in Windows Notepad.

Figure 8.57
The two highlighted records of the tab-separated text file demonstrate the problem that arises when fields contain newline pairs to, for instance, create a multiline display of address data.

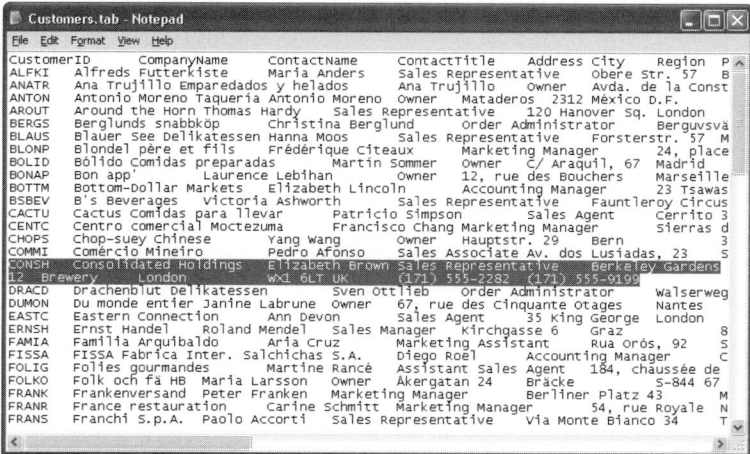

CAUTION

> The two highlighted lines in Figure 8.57 are a single record from the Access table that was split into two text records during the export process. A newline pair is included in the Address field of the record for Consolidated Holdings. The purpose of the newline pair is to separate a single field into two lines: Berkeley Gardens and 12 Brewery. Use of newline pairs within fields causes many problems with exported files. Use of embedded newline pairs in text fields is a bad database design practice. Use two address fields if you need secondary address lines.

The records in files created by Access are exported in the order of the primary key. Any other order you might have created is ignored. If you don't assign primary key fields, the records are exported in the sequence in which you entered them into the table.

EXPORTING DATA IN OTHER FILE FORMATS

In addition to Microsoft Word and text files, you can export data to any other file format that Access can import. Access supports exports to the following file formats:

- Excel .xls files (versions 3.0 through 11).
- Lotus 1-2-3 .wk? files.
- Paradox 3.x, 4.x, 5.0, 7.x, and 8.x files (versions 7.x and 8.x require the BDE).
- dBASE III/III+, IV, 5.0, and 7.0 files (version 7.0 requires the BDE).
- Any format supported by an installed ODBC driver, including client/server databases. Exporting Visual FoxPro files is subject to the limitations described earlier in the chapter.

TROUBLESHOOTING

THE INCORRECT PASSWORD DIALOG

I received a "Can't decrypt file" message, even though the file isn't encrypted.

If you type a wrong password or just press Enter, Access informs you that it can't decrypt the file. You do, however, get another opportunity to type the password or click Cancel to terminate the attempt.

THE NULL VALUE IN INDEX DIALOG

I get a "Can't have Null value in index" message.

Occasionally, older Paradox .px index files don't have an index value for a record; when this situation occurs, you see a warning dialog with the message "Can't have Null value in index." Usually, you can disregard the message and continue linking or importing the file. The offending record, however, might not appear in the table; fixing the file in Paradox and starting over is better than ignoring the message.

THE MISSING MEMO FILE DIALOG

A "Cannot locate the requested Xbase memo file" message appears.

Both dBASE and Paradox use additional memo files to store the data from memo fields in a particular table. dBASE memo files have the .dbt file type, and Paradox memo files have the .mb file type. Access correctly decides that it can't import or link an external table if it can't open the table's associated memo file—either because the memo file doesn't exist, isn't in the same folder as the table with which it is associated, or contains nontext data.

IMPORTING FIXED-WIDTH TEXT FILES

When I import tables created from fixed-width text files, many errors occur.

You probably miscalculated one or more of the starting positions of a field. Locate the first field name with a problem; the names following it usually have problems, too. Close all open tables. From the Navigation Pane, select the table you imported and press Delete. If you have an Import Errors table, delete it, too. You can't delete an open table. Perform the importation process again and reposition the field breaks in the Import Text Wizard. Remember that the Wizard analyzes only the first 20 lines of the text file, so the guesses it makes about where to position the field breaks might be incorrect and might not allow enough room for the actual width of a field.

IN THE REAL WORLD—MICROSOFT GIVETH AND MICROSOFT TAKETH AWAY

Microsoft bundles a raft of no-additional-charge features in Windows Vista, but there's no free lunch at the export/import counter when you upgrade from early Access versions—such as Access 97—to Access 2007. Long-standing dBASE and Paradox import, export, and linking features disappeared in Access 2000, and even Microsoft's Visual FoxPro was slighted by losing its ISAM driver, while gaining limited import/export support with an ODBC driver that has known defects. The loss of updatable linked Excel worksheets is testimony to Microsoft's "not invented here" predilection and reluctance to license others' patents. These defects weren't corrected in Access 2007 and, because VFPODBC.dll is officially in Microsoft "maintenance mode" purgatory, never will be fixed.

Microsoft taketh away updatable linked Excel tables and many desktop database connectivity features, but giveth links to Outlook and Exchange folders, Windows Sharepoint Services, and InfoPath 2007, plus enhanced XML import/export operations and data collection by Outlook email. Fair bargain? Probably, because it's a good bet that more Access users are interested in Outlook/Exchange features than full xBase/Paradox/FoxPro support. These early desktop databases are on their way out because of the success of Access in the desktop database market and the growing popularity of online forms and database applications, such as Dabble DB and QuickBase. If Access, in Microsoft's terms, is "not strategic," support for other desktop RDBMSs must be even lower on Microsoft's database totem pole. Unlike VBA, Visual Basic .NET, and C#, Visual FoxPro's xBase dialect isn't a general-purpose Windows programming language.

8

It remains to be seen if Access 2007's XML import/export features score an immediate hit with Access power users and developers. For most current Access users, XML is more likely to be abbreviated as ineXplicable Munging Language. XML, however, is destined to replace CSV text files and other intermediary formats—such as RTF—for interapplication communication and data exchange between systems. For example, you can export XML data from one or more Access tables and open the XML file in Excel as a formatted worksheet.

N O T E

One of the meanings of the term *munge* is converting data from one format to another, sometimes imperfectly. Early versions of Access used a function named BIFFMunge for Excel import/export. The Free On-Line Dictionary of Computing site offers a brief etymology of *munge* at http://wombat.doc.ic.ac.uk/foldoc/foldoc.cgi?munge, and a more detailed analysis can be found at http://en.wikipedia.org/wiki/Munge.

On the whole, Microsoft gaveth more in Access 2007 than it tooketh away from Access 97. Hopefully, the new features added in Access 2000, 2002, and 2007 will convince more users and developers to migrate from the still all-time favorite version—Access 97.

TRANSFORMING DATA WITH QUERIES AND PIVOTTABLES

DESIGNING QUERIES FOR ACCESS DATABASES

In this chapter

INTRODUCING ACCESS QUERIES

Queries are an essential tool in any database management system. You use queries to select records as well as add, update, and delete records in tables. Most often you use queries to select specific groups of records that meet criteria you specify. You can also use queries to combine information from different tables, providing a unified view of related data items. In this chapter, you learn the basics of creating your own select queries, including specifying selection criteria and using the results of your queries to generate reports and create new tables. You create queries using more than one table in Chapter 11, "Creating Multitable and Crosstab Queries," after you learn the details of how to use operators and create expressions in Chapter 10, "Understanding Access Operators and Expressions."

This chapter covers queries that apply to Access databases and to client/server databases, such as SQL Server, that you link to a conventional Access front-end .accdb file. When you link client/server tables to an Access front end, your application uses the Access query engine to process the back-end data. Access has its own dialect of SQL, called Access SQL, which, for the most part, conforms to the ANSI SQL-92 standard but has several extensions that aren't included in SQL-92. All query techniques you learn in Part III, "Transforming Data with Queries and PivotTables," apply to Access databases and client/server tables linked to an Access front end that stores application objects—queries, forms, reports, and modules—in an .accdb file.

In contrast, Access data projects (ADPs) use SQL Server's query engine. An ADP offers three types of queries—views, functions, and stored procedures—and uses the SQL Server design tools, called the *da Vinci toolset* in this book, for designing queries. (Microsoft used the da Vinci codename for the toolset during its beta cycle, and it stuck). SQL Server uses Transact-SQL (T-SQL), another flavor of SQL-92 that has many proprietary extensions to the language. Most of the Access SQL SELECT query examples in this chapter also work for creating ADP views. Chapter 21, "Moving from Access Queries to Transact-SQL," provides detailed coverage of SQL-92 topics and explains the differences between Access SQL and T-SQL.

> **NOTE**
> The chapters of Part III include examples and brief explanations of the SQL statements the Access query engine generates from your graphical query designs. The objective of these examples is to encourage learning "SQL by osmosis," a process similar to learning a foreign language by immersion rather than from a grammar textbook. By the time you complete Chapter 13, "Creating and Updating Access Tables with Action Queries," you'll have a working knowledge of basic SQL syntax.

TRYING THE SIMPLE QUERY WIZARD

The Simple Query Wizard is aptly named; it's capable of generating only trivial select queries. If you don't have a numeric or date field in the table on which you base the query, the Wizard has only two dialogs—one to select the table(s) and fields to include and the other to name the query. After you create the basic query with the Wizard, you can embellish it in Design view.

Following are the characteristics of the Simple Query Wizard:

- You can't use the Wizard to add selection criteria or specify the sort order of the query.
- You can't use the Wizard to change the order of the fields in the query; fields always appear in the sequence in which you add them in the first Wizard dialog.
- If one or more of your selected fields is numeric, the Wizard lets you produce a summary query that shows the total, average, minimum, or maximum value of the numeric field(s). You also can include a count of the number of records in the query result set.
- If one or more of your selected fields is of the Date/Time data type, you can specify a summary query grouping by date range—day, month, quarter, or year.

> **TIP**
>
> Use crosstab queries for grouping records with numeric values, especially when you're interested in returning a time series, such as multiple monthly, quarterly, or yearly totals or averages. Crosstab queries deliver greatly enhanced grouping capability and show the query result set in a much more readable format compared to that delivered by the Simple Query Wizard. Chapter 11 shows you how to take maximum advantage of Access SQL's powerful crosstab queries.

CREATING A SIMPLE SELECT QUERY

 The queries in this chapter—like the examples in preceding chapters—use the Northwind.accdb sample database tables from the book's accompanying CD-ROM. By default, the CD-ROM's setup program installs Northwind.accdb in your C:\SEUA12\ Nwind folder. The CD-ROM's \SEUA12\Chaptr09\Nwind09.accdb file contains the query and table objects you create in this chapter's examples.

Northwind.accdb's Orders table has a Currency field and several Date/Time fields, so it's the best choice for demonstrating the Simple Query Wizard. To give the Wizard a test drive with the Orders table, do the following:

1. Open Northwind.accdb, if necessary, and click the Create tab and the Query Wizard button to open the New Query dialog.
2. Double-click the Simple Query Wizard item to open the Simple Query Wizard's first dialog.
3. Select Table: Orders in the Tables/Queries list. All fields of the Orders table appear in the Available Fields list.
4. Select the OrderID field in the Available Fields list and click the right-arrow (>) button to add OrderID to the Selected Fields list and remove it from the Available Fields list. Alternatively, you can double-click the field to add it to the query.

5. Repeat step 4 for the CustomerID, OrderDate, and Freight fields. The first Wizard dialog appears as shown in Figure 9.1.

Figure 9.1
You select the source of the query—either a table or a query—in the first dialog of the Simple Query Wizard.

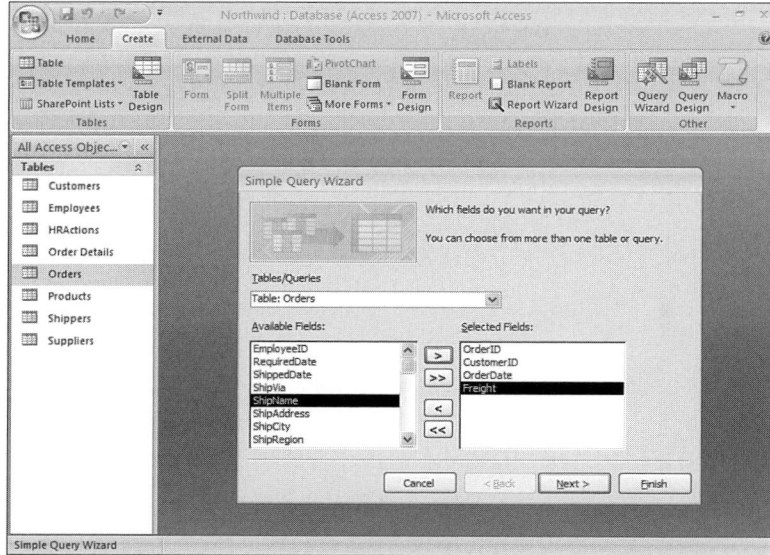

6. Click Next to open the second Wizard dialog, which lets you select between detail and summary queries. Accept the Detail option (see Figure 9.2).

Figure 9.2
The second Wizard dialog, which appears only for data sources with numeric or date fields, gives you the option of displaying all records or generating a summary query.

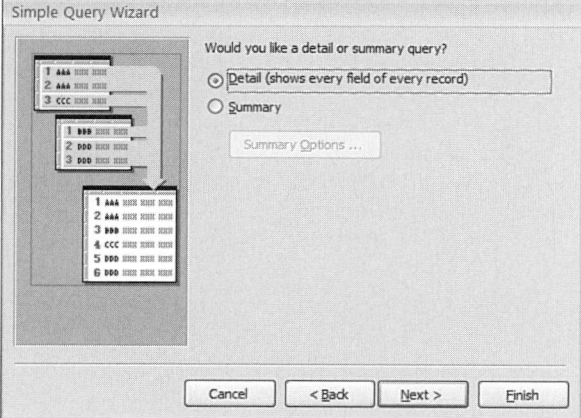

7. Click Next to open the final dialog (see Figure 9.3). Rename the query to **qryOrders1** or the like, and click Finish to display the query result set in Datasheet view (see Figure 9.4).

Figure 9.3
The final Wizard dialog lets you name the query. This book uses a naming convention called Hungarian notation, which adds a two- or three-letter prefix (qry for queries) to Access object names, except names of tables.

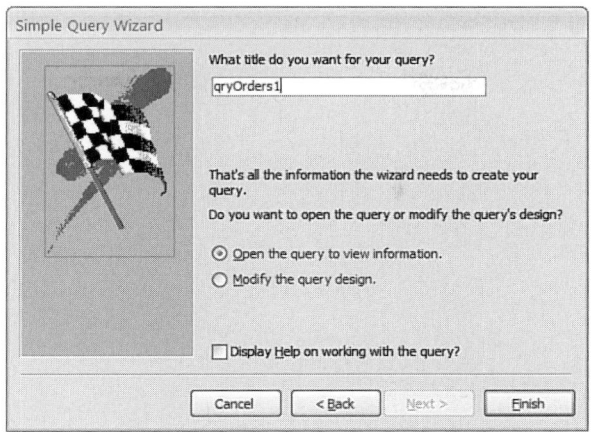

Figure 9.4
The Wizard's query result set substitutes captions for the field names you selected in steps 4 and 5, and the customer name for the CustomerID lookup field. Queries inherit table properties, such as captions and lookup fields, from the data source.

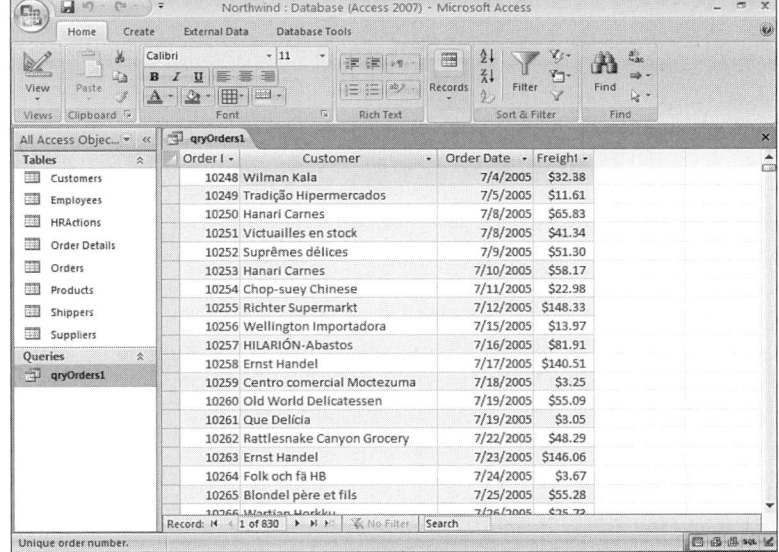

SQL 8. Click the Home tab and the View button caption to open the query View list, and choose SQL View to open the SQL window, which displays the Access SQL version of the query. Click the Query Tools, Design ribbon's Property Sheet button to open the Property Sheet pane for the query (see Figure 9.5).

9. Close the SQL window and save your changes if you altered the query's layout.

Figure 9.5
The SQL window displays the Access SQL statement that the Simple Query Wizard generated from your selections in steps 4–6.

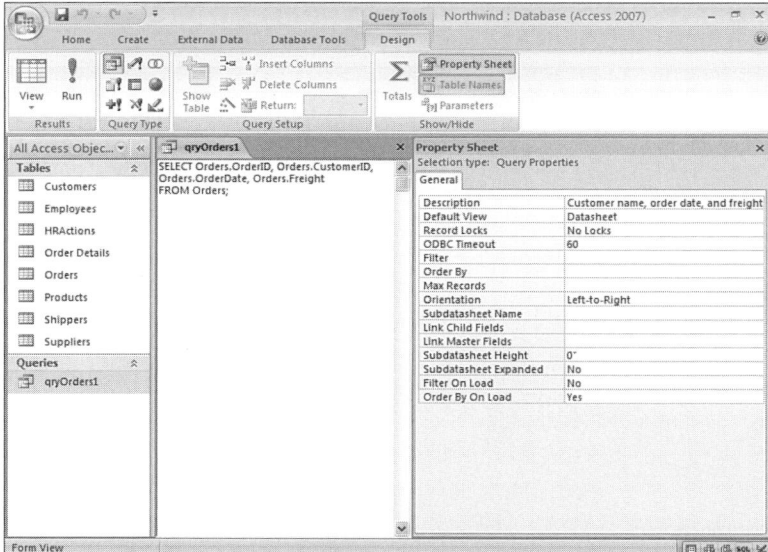

NOTE

The `SELECT Orders.OrderID, Orders.CustomerID, Orders.OrderDate, Orders.Freight FROM Orders;` statement generated by the Wizard is an example of a simple SQL `SELECT` query. The `Orders.` prefixes specify the query's source table name.

The `SELECT` keyword indicates that the query returns records; by tradition, SQL keywords in Access and T-SQL are capitalized. Field lists contain field names, separated by commas. The `FROM` clause, `FROM tablename`, specifies the query's data source. Access SQL uses the semicolon to indicate the end of a query; like the square brackets, the semicolon isn't necessary if the query includes only one complete SQL statement.

If you want to test the Simple Query Wizard's capability to base a query on another query and check the Wizard's summary query capabilities, do the following:

1. Return to the Create ribbon, click the Query Wizard button, and start the Simple Query Wizard. Select Query: qryOrders1 Tables/Queries list.

NOTE

Access calls a query whose source is a query, rather than a table, a *nested query*. You sometimes see the term *subquery* incorrectly applied to a nested query. A subquery is a single SQL statement for a query within a query.

2. Add only the OrderDate and Freight fields to the Selected Fields list.

TIP

> Include only the field(s) by which the data is grouped (OrderDate) and the numeric value(s) to be summarized in a summary query. If you add other fields, such as OrderID, every record appears in the summary query, and you don't obtain the summary you're seeking.

3. Click Next to open the second Wizard dialog (refer to Figure 9.2). Select the Summary option and then click Summary Options to open the identically named dialog. Mark the Avg check box to calculate the average freight cost and mark the Count Records in qryOrders1 check box to add a column with the record count for the group (see Figure 9.6).

Figure 9.6
If you select a summary query, you must specify one of the functions in the Summary Options dialog.

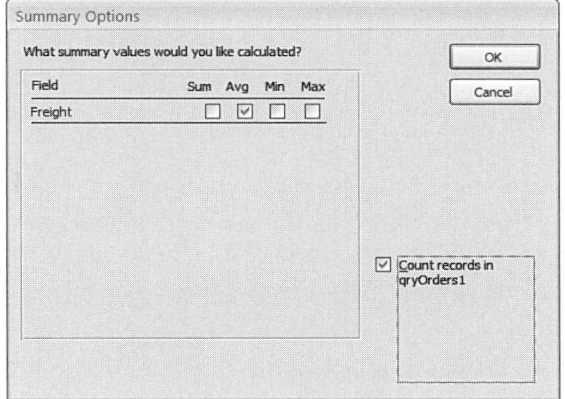

4. Click OK to return to the second Wizard dialog and then click Next to move to the third Wizard dialog. The Wizard has detected the OrderDate Date/Time field and offers you the choice of date grouping; select Quarter (see Figure 9.7).

Figure 9.7
Summary queries with a field of the Date/Time data type open an additional Wizard dialog that lets you group the result set by a date interval.

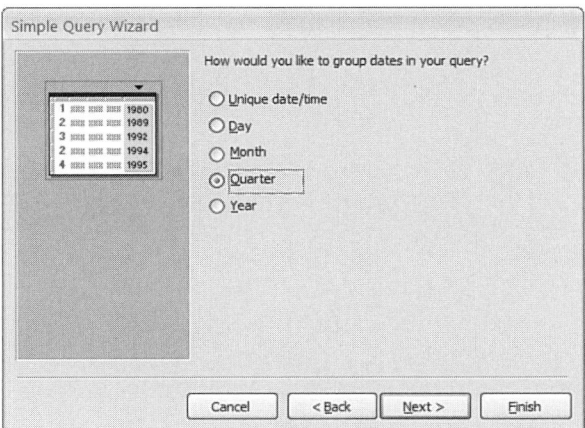

5. Click Next to open the last Wizard dialog and replace the default query name, qryOrders1 Query, with a more descriptive name, such as **qryQuarterlyFreightAverage**.
6. Click Finish to execute the summary query. The query result set appears as shown in Figure 9.8. Open the SQL window to display the SQL statement that generates this considerably more complex query (see Figure 9.9).

OrderDate By Quarter	Avg Of Freight	Count Of qryOrders1
Q3 2005	$54.41	70
Q4 2005	$78.92	82
Q1 2006	$62.27	92
Q2 2006	$88.74	93
Q3 2006	$85.18	103
Q4 2006	$80.94	120
Q1 2007	$83.05	182
Q2 2007	$80.44	88

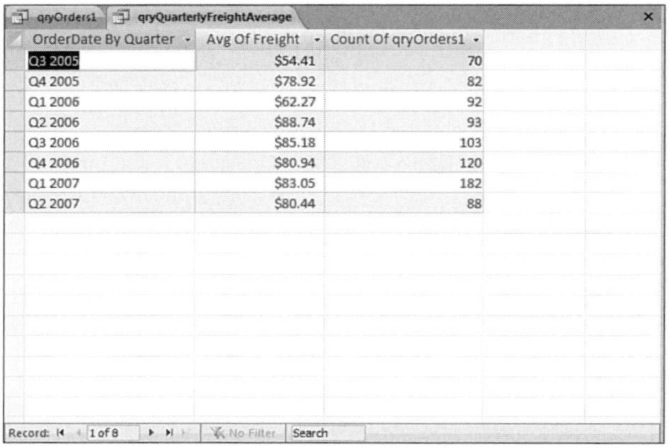

Figure 9.8
The query result set displays the average freight charge and number of orders for each quarter within the range of dates for which data is available.

```
SELECT DISTINCTROW Format$([qryOrders1].[OrderDate],'\Qq yyyy') AS [OrderDate By Quarter],
Avg(qryOrders1.Freight) AS [Avg Of Freight], Count(*) AS [Count Of qryOrders1]
FROM qryOrders1
GROUP BY Format$([qryOrders1].[OrderDate],'\Qq yyyy'),
Year([qryOrders1].[OrderDate])*4+DatePart('q',[qryOrders1].[OrderDate])-1;
```

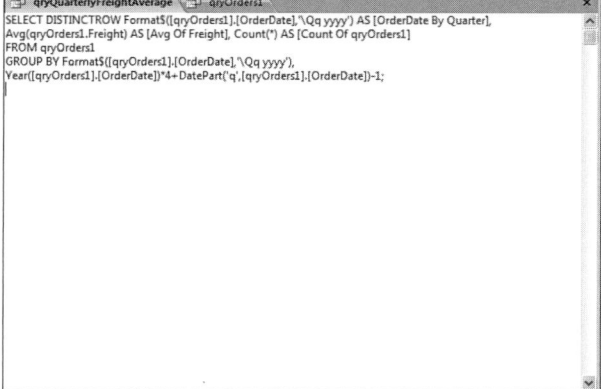

Figure 9.9
The SQL statement for the Wizard's summary query belies the simplicity of the steps required to create the query.

For problems with attempted updates to a summary query, see the "Non-updatable Summary Queries" topic of the "Troubleshooting" section near the end of the chapter.

Access SQL

The SQL statement for the summary query, which is a bit advanced for this point in your SQL learning curve, requires formatting for better readability:

```
SELECT DISTINCTROW
    Format$([qryOrders1].[OrderDate],'\Qq yyyy')
        AS [OrderDate By Quarter],
    Avg(qryOrders1.Freight) AS [Avg Of Freight],
    Count(*) AS [Count Of qryOrders1]
FROM qryOrders1
GROUP BY Format$([qryOrders1].[OrderDate],'\Qq yyyy'),
    Year([qryOrders1].[OrderDate])*4+
    DatePart('q',[qryOrders1].[OrderDate])-1;
```

DISTINCTROW is an Access SQL keyword that isn't required in this query. The Format$ function determines the appearance of the first column (Q# *YYYY*). AS specifies the caption (alias) for the column. Avg is the aggregate function you selected in step 3. Count(*) adds the third column to the result set. Access treats queries as if they were tables, so the FROM clause specifies the source query. GROUP BY is the clause that specifies the date grouping range you chose in step 4 to calculate the values in the second column.

Square brackets ([ ]) surround query column names—such as OrderDate by Quarter—that have spaces or punctuation symbols, which aren't permitted by the SQL-92 specification. In some cases, the Access query processor adds square brackets where they're not needed, as in [qryOrders1].[OrderDate].

Avg, Year, DatePart, and Format$ are VBA functions executed by the Access expression service. The next chapter shows you how to apply these functions to queries. SQL-92 and T-SQL don't include DISTINCTROW and VBA functions, but do support the COUNT function.

Summary queries—more commonly called *aggregate queries*—are a common element of decision-support applications that deliver time-based trend data to management. Aggregate queries also are the foundation for graphical data analysis, which is one of the subjects of Chapter 12, "Working with PivotTable and PivotChart Views." PivotTables and PivotCharts must be based on queries to present meaningful information. PivotTables have built-in aggregation features, so you can use detail queries as PivotTable data sources.

USING THE QUERY DESIGN WINDOW

The Simple Query Wizard has limited usefulness, so the better approach is to design your queries from scratch in Access's graphical Query Design window. The Query Design window is one of Access's most powerful features and has changed very little from the original Access 1.0 version that appeared in late 1992.

To devise a simple query that lets you customize mailing lists for selected customers of Northwind Traders, for example, follow these steps:

9

1. Click the Create ribbon's Query Design button to open the Query Design window. The Show Table dialog is superimposed on the Query Design window, as shown in Figure 9.10. The tabbed lists in the Show Table dialog let you select from all existing tables, all saved queries, or a combination of all tables and queries. You can base a new query on one or more existing tables or queries.

Figure 9.10
When you open a new query in Design view, the Show Table dialog lets you select from lists of tables, queries, or both, to designate the new query's data source.

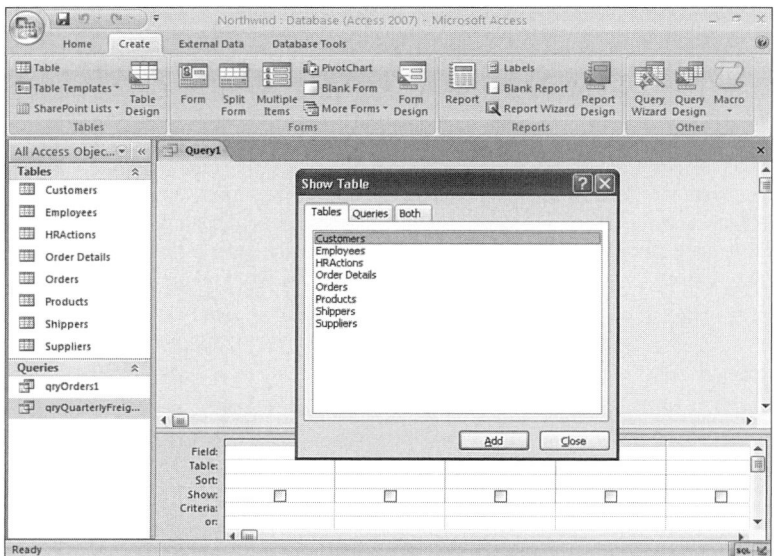

2. This example uses only tables in the query, so accept the default selection of Tables. Click (or use the ↓ key to select) Customers in the Show Table list to select the Customers table and then click the Add button. Alternatively, double-click Customers to add the table to the query. You can use more than one table in a query by choosing another related table from the list and choosing Add again. This example, however, uses only one table. After selecting the tables that you want to use, click Close.

The Fields list for the Customers table appears at the left in the upper pane of the Query Design window, and a blank Query Design grid appears in the lower pane. The Fields list displays all the names of the fields of the Customers table, but you must scroll to display more than five entries with the default Fields list size. The asterisk (*) item at the top of the list is a shortcut symbol for adding all table fields to the query.

SELECTING FIELDS FOR YOUR QUERY

After you add a table from the Show Table dialog, the next step is to decide which of the table's fields to include in your query. Because you plan to use this query to create a customer mailing list, you need the fields that make up a personalized mailing address.

To select the fields to include in the Query Design grid, do this:

1. When you open the Query Design window, the cursor is located in the Field row of the first column. Click the List Box button that appears in the right corner of the first column or press Alt+↓ to open the Field Names list (see Figure 9.11).

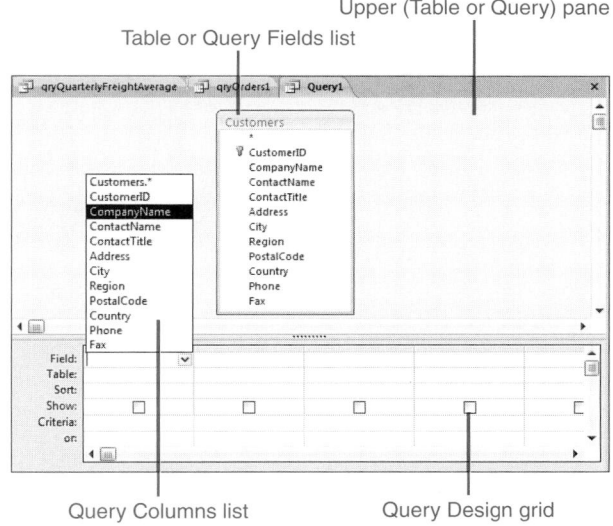

Upper (Table or Query) pane

Table or Query Fields list

Figure 9.11
One way to add a field to your query is to select it in the drop-down query fields list of the Query Design grid.

Query Columns list

Query Design grid

2. Select the ContactName field as the first field header of the query or use the ↓ key to highlight the name and press Enter. The Field list in the lower pane closes.

3. Move the cursor to the second column by using the → or Tab key. Double-click CompanyName in the Customers Field list in the upper pane to add CompanyName as the second field of your query. Double-clicking entries in the upper pane's list is the second method that Access provides to add fields to a query.

4. Access offers a third method of adding fields to your query: the drag-and-drop method. To use the drag-and-drop method to add the Address, City, Region, PostalCode, and Country fields to columns 3 through 7, first select the fields. In the Customers Field list of the upper pane's Query Design window, click Address, and then Shift+click Country. Alternatively, select Address with the ↓ key, hold down the Shift or Ctrl key, and press the ↓ key four more times. You've selected the Address, City, Region, PostalCode, and Country fields, as shown in the Customers field list of Figure 9.12.

5. Position the mouse pointer over the selected fields and click the left mouse button. Your mouse pointer turns into a symbol representing the multiple field names (after you drag the mouse a bit). Drag the symbol for the multiple fields to the third column of your query's Field row, as shown in Figure 9.12, and release the left mouse button.

International Do Not Enter cursor

Figure 9.12
You also can select multiple fields in the table fields list and drag them to the Fields row of the Query Design grid.

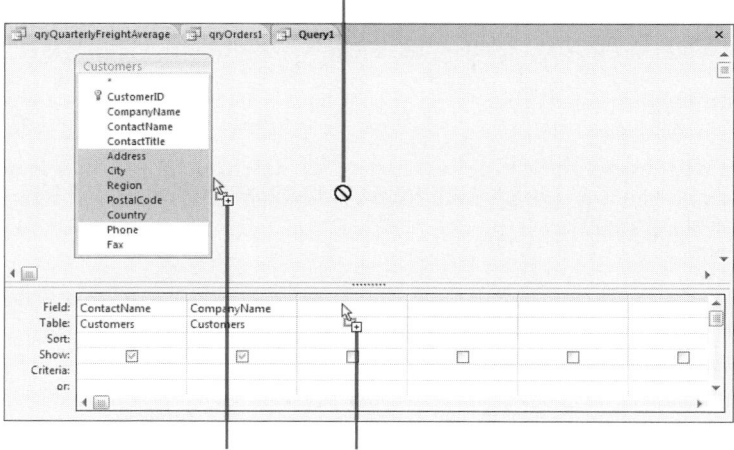

Multiple-field drag-and-drop cursor

NOTE

Access adds the five fields to your query, in sequence, starting with the column in which you drop the symbol. When the mouse pointer is in an area where you can't drop the fields, it becomes the international Do Not Enter symbol shown in the upper pane of the Query Design window of Figure 9.12.

6. To reduce the columns' width, drag the divider of the grid's header bars to the left. Click the scroll-right button (on the horizontal scroll bar at the bottom of the window) or drag the scroll bar slider button to the right to expose the remaining fields. Your Query Design window appears as shown in Figure 9.13.

Figure 9.13
Reduce the width of the columns so Design view displays all columns in your current display resolution (800×600 for most figures in this book).

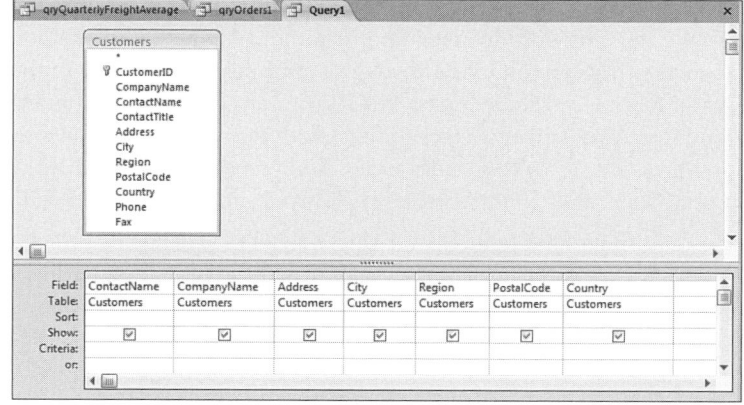

7. Click the Datasheet View or Run button to execute the query.

You haven't yet entered any selection criteria in the Criteria row of the Query Design grid, so your query result set in the Customers table displays all records. These records appear in the order of the primary key index on the CustomerID field because you haven't specified a sorting order in the Sort row of the Query Design grid. (The values in the CustomerID field are alphabetic codes derived from the CompanyName field.) Figure 9.14 shows the result of your first query after the width of the fields have been adjusted.

Figure 9.14
The initial query design in Datasheet view displays the seven selected fields of all records in the Customers table.

Contact Name	Company Name	Address	City	Region	Postal Code	Country
Maria Anders	Alfreds Futterkiste	Obere Str. 57	Berlin		12209	Germany
Ana Trujillo	Ana Trujillo Emparedad	Avda. de la Constituci	México D.F.		05021	Mexico
Antonio Moreno	Antonio Moreno Taquer	Mataderos 2312	México D.F.		05023	Mexico
Thomas Hardy	Around the Horn	120 Hanover Sq.	London		WA1 1DP	UK
Christina Berglund	Berglunds snabbköp	Berguvsvägen 8	Luleå		S-958 22	Sweden
Hanna Moos	Blauer See Delikatessen	Forsterstr. 57	Mannheim		68306	Germany
Frédérique Citeaux	Blondel père et fils	24, place Kléber	Strasbourg		67000	France
Martín Sommer	Bólido Comidas prepara	C/ Araquil, 67	Madrid		28023	Spain
Laurence Lebihan	Bon app'	12, rue des Bouchers	Marseille		13008	France
Elizabeth Lincoln	Bottom-Dollar Markets	23 Tsawassen Blvd.	Tsawassen	BC	T2F 8M4	Canada
Victoria Ashworth	B's Beverages	Fauntleroy Circus	London		EC2 5NT	UK
Patricio Simpson	Cactus Comidas para lle	Cerrito 333	Buenos Aires		1010	Argentina
Francisco Chang	Centro comercial Mocte	Sierras de Granada 99	México D.F.		05022	Mexico
Yang Wang	Chop-suey Chinese	Hauptstr. 29	Bern		3012	Switzerla
Pedro Afonso	Comércio Mineiro	Av. dos Lusíadas, 23	São Paulo	SP	05432-043	Brazil
Elizabeth Brown	Consolidated Holdings	Berkeley Gardens	London		WX1 6LT	UK
Sven Ottlieb	Drachenblut Delikatesse	Walserweg 21	Aachen		52066	Germany
Janine Labrune	Du monde entier	67, rue des Cinquante	Nantes		44000	France

Record: 1 of 91 — No Filter — Search

SELECTING RECORDS BY CRITERIA AND SORTING THE DISPLAY

The mailing for which you're creating a list with your sample query is to be sent to U.S. customers only, so you want to include in your query only those records that have USA in the Country field. Selecting records based on the values of fields—that is, establishing the criteria for the records to be returned (displayed) by the query—is the heart of the query process.

Take the following steps to establish criteria for selecting the records to make up your mailing list:

1. Click the Design View button.
2. To restrict the result of your query to firms in the United States, type **USA** in the Criteria row of the Country column. Entering a criterion's value without preceding the value with an operator, such as = or >, indicates that the value of the field must match the value you type. You don't need to add quotation marks to the expression; Access adds them for you (see the Country column in Figure 9.15).
3. Click the Show check box in the Country column to clear the check mark that appeared when you added the column. After you clear the Show check box, the Country field doesn't appear when you run your query. If you don't clear a Show check box, that field in the query appears in the query's result by default.

4. Move the cursor to the PostalCode column's Sort row and press Alt+↓ to display the sorting options for that field: Ascending, Descending, and (Not Sorted). Select the Ascending option to sort the query by postal code from low codes to high. At this point, the Query Design grid appears as shown in Figure 9.15.

Figure 9.15
Add the USA criterion, hide the Country column, and apply an ascending sort order to the PostalCode column to complete the mailing list query.

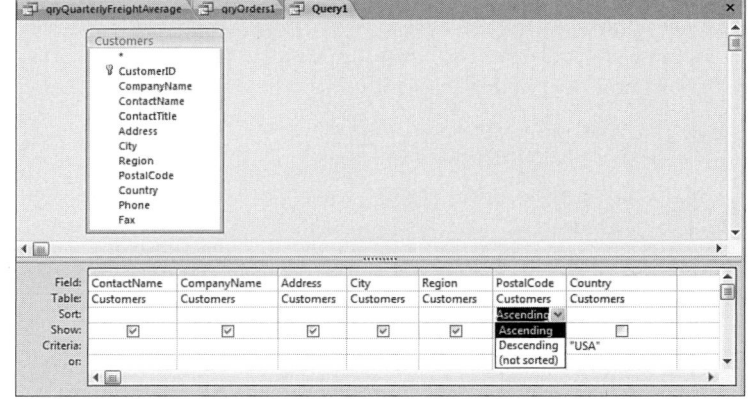

5. Click the Datasheet View or Run button to display the result of the criterion and sorting order.

Figure 9.16 shows the query result set that Access refers to as an *updatable Recordset* (also called a Access *Dynaset*), which is indicated by the tentative append (*) in the last (empty) row of the query result set's leftmost selection column. A `Recordset` object is a temporary table stored in your computer's memory; it's not a permanent component of the database file. You can edit the data in any visible fields of the underlying table(s) in Query Datasheet view if your Recordset is updatable.

Figure 9.16
Datasheet view displays the mailing list query's updatable result set (Recordset).

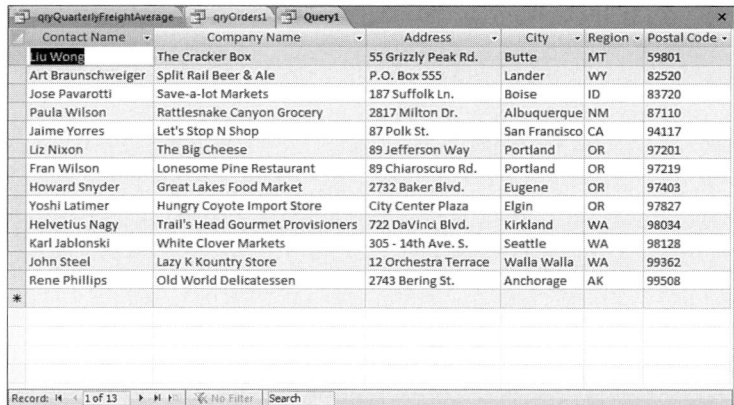

If you encounter problems with updating query result sets, see the "Missing Required Fields" topic of the "Troubleshooting" section near the end of the chapter.

Access SQL

The SQL statement for a sorted `SELECT` query with a criterion is much simpler than the statement of the preceding example:

```
SELECT Customers.ContactName, Customers.CompanyName,
    Customers.Address, Customers.City, Customers.Region,
    Customers.PostalCode
FROM Customers
WHERE (((Customers.Country)="USA"))
ORDER BY Customers.PostalCode;
```

The `WHERE` clause specifies the selection criterion and the `ORDER BY` clause determines the sort order. `ASC[ENDING]` is the default sort order; `DESC[ENDING]` performs a reverse sort. SQL-92 permits abbreviation of the directional keywords. Access adds multiple sets of unneeded parentheses to the `WHERE` clause; if you remove them all, the query executes correctly.

PREVENTING UPDATES TO THE QUERY RESULT SET

You can edit any of the values in the seven columns of the query and, theoretically, add new records because the tentative append record appears in the last row of the query and the new record navigation button is enabled. You can't add a new record, however, because the query doesn't include the primary key field (CustomerID). If you attempt to add a new record by moving to a different record, you receive the message shown in Figure 9.17. You must press Esc to delete all characters you typed in any field of the tentative append record.

Figure 9.17
If you attempt to add a new record to the query, you receive the message shown here because you can't add a value for the primary key field, CustomerID.

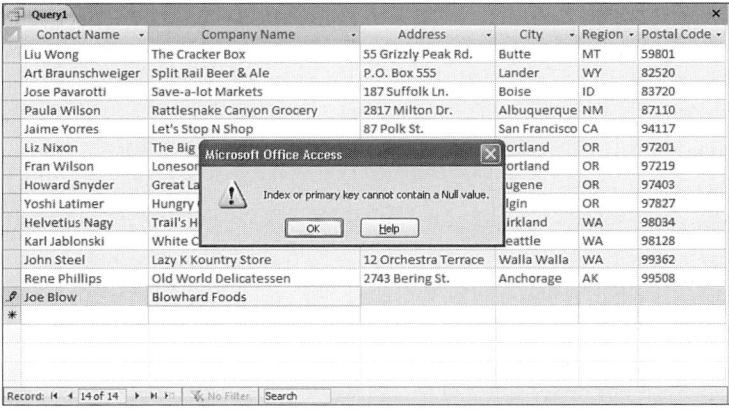

The message that appears to a user of your query who attempts to add a new record is confusing, because most database users don't know what "primary key" and "Null value" mean. It's good database design practice to prevent users from attempting operations they can't complete, so you should designate the query as not updatable by changing the query type to an Access *Snapshot*. The terms *Dynaset* and *Snapshot* refer to the cursor type of the query; a Dynaset has a *read-write (updatable) cursor* and a Snapshot has a *read-only (non-updatable) cursor*. A *cursor* is what RDBMSs use to navigate, read, and—if the cursor is updatable—update the rows returned by the query, add a new row, or delete a row.

To change the type of cursor, which doesn't affect the SQL statement for the query, do this:

1. Click the Design View button to return to Query Design view.

2. Click the Property Sheet toggle button or right-click in an empty area in the upper Query Design pane and then choose <u>P</u>roperties to open the Query Properties dialog.

3. Select the Recordset Type text box, open the drop-down list, and choose Snapshot (see Figure 9.18).

Figure 9.18
Open the Query Properties dialog and select Snapshot as the value of the Recordset Type property to create a read-only query result set.

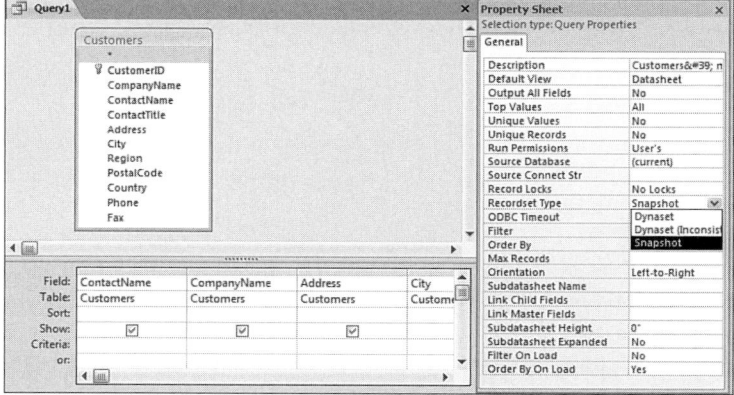

4. Return to Datasheet view to verify that the tentative append record is missing and the new record navigation button is disabled (see Figure 9.19).

Figure 9.19
The read-only Snapshot query doesn't have a tentative append record, and the new record button is disabled.

Contact Name	Company Name	Address	City	Region	Postal Code
Liu Wong	The Cracker Box	55 Grizzly Peak Rd.	Butte	MT	59801
Art Braunschweiger	Split Rail Beer & Ale	P.O. Box 555	Lander	WY	82520
Jose Pavarotti	Save-a-lot Markets	187 Suffolk Ln.	Boise	ID	83720
Paula Wilson	Rattlesnake Canyon Grocery	2817 Milton Dr.	Albuquerque	NM	87110
Jaime Yorres	Let's Stop N Shop	87 Polk St.	San Francisco	CA	94117
Liz Nixon	The Big Cheese	89 Jefferson Way	Portland	OR	97201
Fran Wilson	Lonesome Pine Restaurant	89 Chiaroscuro Rd.	Portland	OR	97219
Howard Snyder	Great Lakes Food Market	2732 Baker Blvd.	Eugene	OR	97403
Yoshi Latimer	Hungry Coyote Import Store	City Center Plaza	Elgin	OR	97827
Helvetius Nagy	Trail's Head Gourmet Provisioners	722 DaVinci Blvd.	Kirkland	WA	98034
Karl Jablonski	White Clover Markets	305 - 14th Ave. S.	Seattle	WA	98128
John Steel	Lazy K Kountry Store	12 Orchestra Terrace	Walla Walla	WA	99362
Rene Phillips	Old World Delicatessen	2743 Bering St.	Anchorage	AK	99508

Record: 14 4 13 of 13 ▶ ▶I ▶ No Filter Search

5. Press Ctrl+S, click the Office button, and choose <u>S</u>ave, or close the query. Then type a name for the query in the text box (**qryCustomersUSA** for this example) and click OK to save the query.

When you save the query, the Northwind.accdb file saves only the design specifications of the query, not the values that the query contains. The query design specification is called a `QueryDef` (query definition) object. When you open the query, Access executes the query and displays the result set in Datasheet view.

CREATING MORE COMPLEX CRITERIA

To limit your mailing to customers in a particular state or group of states, you can add a Criteria expression to the Region or PostalCode field. To restrict the mailing to customers in California, Oregon, and Washington, for example, you can specify that the value of the PostalCode field must be equal to or greater than 90000. Alternatively, you can specify that Region values must be CA, OR, and WA.

Follow these steps to restrict your mailing to customers in California, Oregon, and Washington:

1. Open the query and click the Design View button.

2. Move to the Region column and type **CA** in the first criterion row of the Region column. Access adds the quotation marks around CA (as it did when you restricted your mailing to U.S. locations with the USA criterion).

3. Press the ↓ key to move to the next criterion row in the Region column. Type **OR** and then move to the third criterion row and type **WA**. Your query design now appears as shown in Figure 9.20. Access also adds the required quotation marks to these criteria.

Figure 9.20
You can further restrict records returned by the query with additional criteria in the Region field.

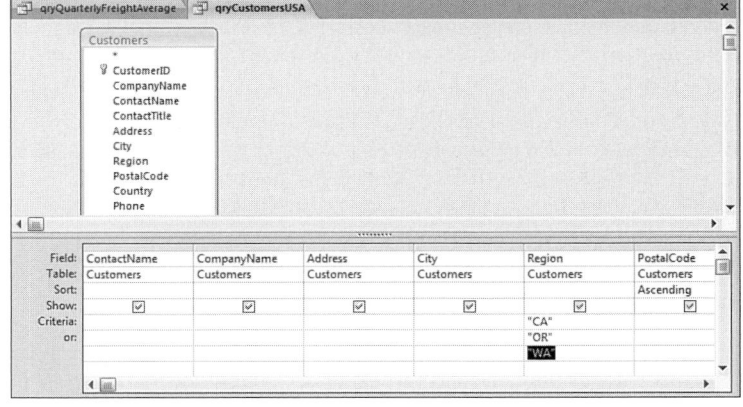

4. Click the Datasheet View or Run button. The query result set appears as shown in Figure 9.21.

Figure 9.21
The query result set with the additional criteria includes only records for the three West Coast states.

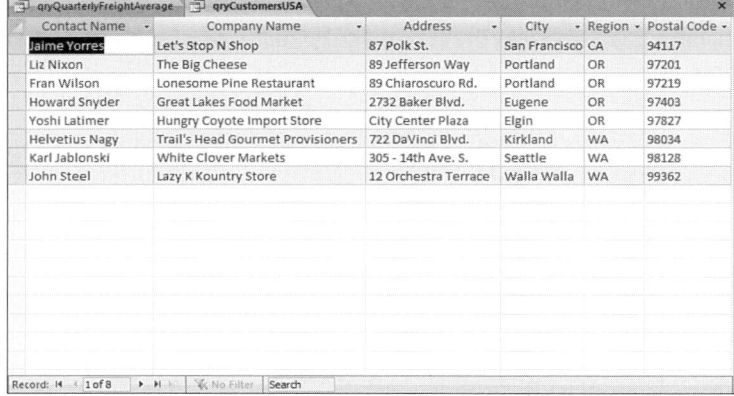

Contact Name	Company Name	Address	City	Region	Postal Code
Jaime Yorres	Let's Stop N Shop	87 Polk St.	San Francisco	CA	94117
Liz Nixon	The Big Cheese	89 Jefferson Way	Portland	OR	97201
Fran Wilson	Lonesome Pine Restaurant	89 Chiaroscuro Rd.	Portland	OR	97219
Howard Snyder	Great Lakes Food Market	2732 Baker Blvd.	Eugene	OR	97403
Yoshi Latimer	Hungry Coyote Import Store	City Center Plaza	Elgin	OR	97827
Helvetius Nagy	Trail's Head Gourmet Provisioners	722 DaVinci Blvd.	Kirkland	WA	98034
Karl Jablonski	White Clover Markets	305 - 14th Ave. S.	Seattle	WA	98128
John Steel	Lazy K Kountry Store	12 Orchestra Terrace	Walla Walla	WA	99362

After you type a criterion on the same line as a previously entered criterion in another field, only those records that meet both criteria are selected for display. In the preceding example, therefore, records with Region values equal to CA and Country values equal to USA, and records with Region values of OR and WA are displayed.

Access SQL

The SQL statement that includes the additional criteria is

```
SELECT Customers.ContactName, Customers.CompanyName,
    Customers.Address, Customers.City, Customers.Region,
    Customers.PostalCode
FROM Customers
WHERE (((Customers.Region)="CA") AND ((Customers.Country)="USA"))
    OR (((Customers.Region)="OR")) OR (((Customers.Region)="WA"))
ORDER BY Customers.PostalCode;
```

Again, Access adds many superfluous parentheses, but the first element of the WHERE clause requires a single pair in the `(Customers.Region ="CA" AND Customers.Country)="USA")` expression.

To be displayed, records for Region values OR and WA need not have Country values equal to USA, because the USA criterion is missing from the OR and WA rows. This omission doesn't affect the selection of records in this case, because all OR and WA records also are USA records. Therefore, the WHERE clause can be simplified to `WHERE Customers.Region="CA" OR Customers.Region="OR" OR Customers.Region="WA"`. If you edit the SQL statement accordingly, the query result set is the same.

CHANGING THE NAMES OF QUERY COLUMN HEADERS

You can substitute a query's field header names with column header names of your choice—a process called *aliasing*—but only if the header name hasn't been changed by an entry in the Caption property of the table's field. If yours is a U.S. firm, for example, you might want to change Region to State and PostalCode to ZIP. (Canadian firms might want to change only Region to Province.)

As demonstrated in the following example, you can't change the PostalCode field for queries based on the Customers table because the PostalCode field previously has been changed (aliased) to Postal Code by the Caption property for the field. You can, however, make the change to the Region field because this field isn't aliased at the table level.

> **TIP**
>
> If you already have a main document for mail merge operations, substitute the main merge document's merge field names for the table's field header names in your query.

→ For more information on merging data with documents, **see** "Using the Access Mail Merge Wizard," **p. 359.**

> **NOTE**
>
> Field names in queries that have been altered by use of the Caption property in the source table can't be aliased, so don't use the Caption property of table fields. If you want to display different field headers, use a query for this purpose. In a client/server RDBMS, such a query is called an SQL VIEW. Aliasing field names in tables rather than in queries isn't considered a generally accepted database design practice.

To change the query column header names, perform the following steps:

1. Click the Design View button. Then place the cursor in the Field column containing the field header name that you want to change—in this case, the Region column.

2. Press F2 to deselect the field; then press Home to move the cursor to the first character position.

3. Type the new name for the column and follow the name with a colon (with no spaces), as in **State:**. The colon separates the new column name that you type from the existing table field name, which shifts to the right to make room for your addition. The result, in this example, is State: Region.

4. Use the arrow key to move to the PostalCode field and repeat steps 2 and 3, typing **ZIP:** as that header's new name. The result is ZIP: PostalCode.

5. Change the column header for the ContactName field to **Contact**; change the column header for the CompanyName field to **Company**.

6. Delete the three criteria (the "CA" Or "OR" Or "WA" criterion you added to the SQL statement described in the preceding section) from the State: Region column so that all records for the United States appear (see Figure 9.22). If you altered the SQL statement, add the Country field to the grid, clear the Show check box, and add **USA** as the criterion.

Figure 9.22
This query design attempts to assign aliases to field names that have Caption property values assigned at the table level.

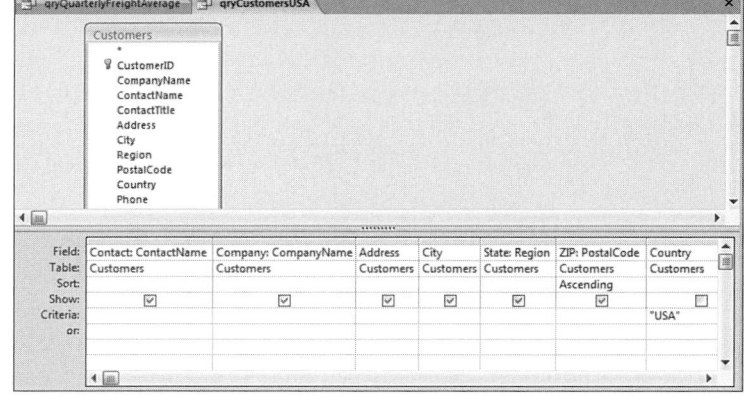

7. Click the Run or Datasheet View button to execute the query. Observe that only the Region column header is changed to State; the other columns are unaffected by the alias entry (see Figure 9.23).

Figure 9.23
The table's Caption property value overrides alias names assigned by the query. Only the Region field, which doesn't have a caption, is aliased to State in this example.

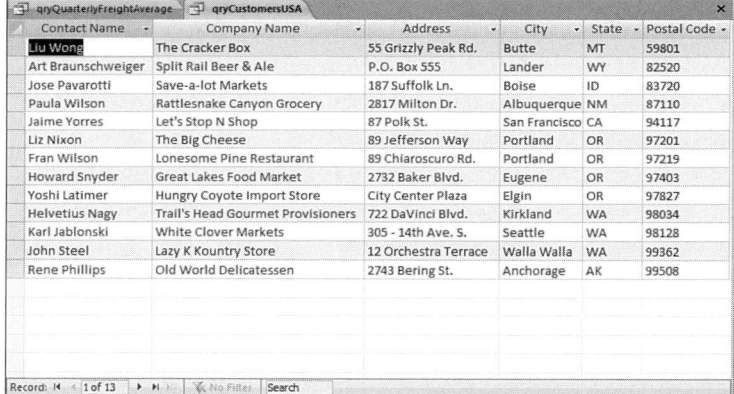

8. Choose File, Save As, and save your query with the name **qryUSMailList**.

Access SQL
The SQL statement that attempts to rename all query columns is

```
SELECT Customers.ContactName AS Contact,
    Customers.CompanyName AS Company,
    Customers.Address, Customers.City,
    Customers.Region AS State,
    Customers.PostalCode AS ZIP
FROM Customers
WHERE (((Customers.Country)="USA"))
ORDER BY Customers.PostalCode;
```

Although the SQL statement renames four fields, only the `Customer.Region` field receives a renamed column.

> To make field aliasing in queries operable, in Table Design view delete the entry in the Caption field for each aliased field of the table. Deleting these entries makes the aliases you entered in the preceding example work as expected.

PRINTING YOUR QUERY AS A REPORT

You often use queries to print quick, ad hoc reports. Access 2007's Print Preview ribbon lets you print your report to a printer or to an Adobe Portable Document Format (.pdf) or Microsoft XML Paper Specification (.xps) file. You also can export the data to a Microsoft Word .rtf (rich-text format) file, an Excel worksheet .xls file, a DOS .txt (text) file, an XML document, a SharePoint list, one of several database formats, or a Microsoft Word merge data source. You also can publish a query as an HTML file to a web server. The table export procedures described in the preceding chapter also apply to queries.

Previewing your query table's appearance to see how the table will appear when printed is usually a good idea. After you determine from the preview that everything in the table is correct, you can print the finished query result set in various formats.

To preview a query result set before printing it, follow these steps:

1. In Query Datasheet view, click the Office button and choose Print, Print Preview. A miniature version of the query table opens in Report Print Preview mode.
2. Position the Zoom pointer (the magnifying glass cursor) anywhere on the query table and click the left mouse button to view the report at approximately the scale at which it will print.
3. Use the vertical and horizontal scroll bar buttons to position the preview in the window (see Figure 9.24).

> Field width in the query table is based on the column width that you last established in Run mode. You might have to drag the right edge of the field header buttons to the right to increase the columns' width so that the printed report doesn't truncate the data. If the query data's width exceeds the available printing width (the paper width minus the width of the left and right margins), Access prints two or more sheets for each page of the report.

4. Right-click the Print Preview window and choose Page Setup to open the Page Setup dialog shown in Figure 9.25. If necessary, click the Print Options tab to display the Margins settings.

Figure 9.24
You can quickly print a query by opening it in the Print Preview window and clicking the image to zoom it to approximately the print scale.

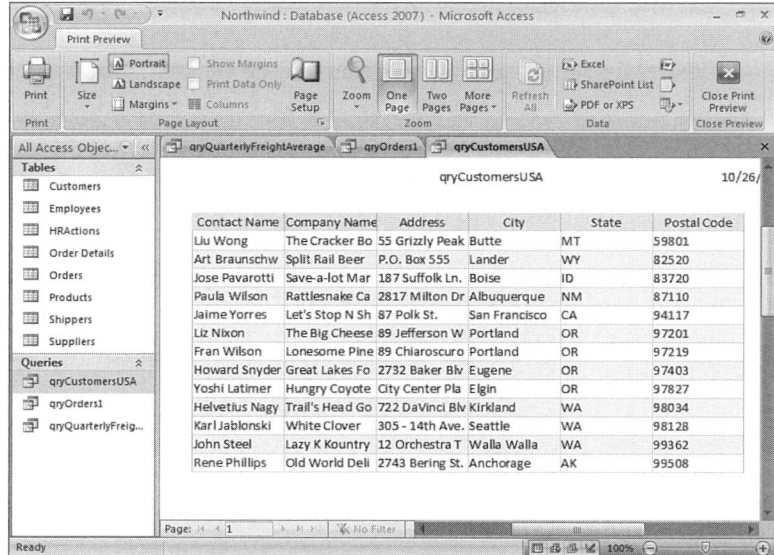

Figure 9.25
The Print Options page of the Print Setup dialog lets you change printing margins from the default 1-inch values. The Page page has orientation, paper size and source, and printer selection options.

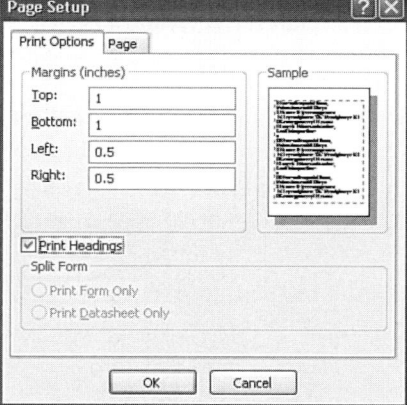

5. Enter any changes that you want to make to the margins; mark the Print Headings check box if you want to print the field header names. Click the Page tab to change the print orientation, paper size or source, or printer. Then click OK to return to Print Preview.

 6. Click the Print button to print your query report, and then click the Close Print Preview button to return to Datasheet view.

TESTING THE OTHER QUERY WIZARDS

In addition to the Simple Query Wizard that you tried early in the chapter, the New Query dialog lets you choose one of the following three specialized Query Wizards:

- **Crosstab Query Wizard** This Wizard helps you create queries that calculate and report the sum, average, or other aggregate value for data grouped by rows and columns. As an example, a crosstab query can calculate total sales for product categories (in rows) and quarters or years (in columns) in a format similar to an Excel PivotTable. Chapter 11, "Creating Multitable and Crosstab Queries," shows you how to use the Crosstab Query Wizard.
- **Find Duplicates Query Wizard** This Wizard finds duplicate values in one or more columns of a single table.
- **Find Unmatched Query Wizard** This Wizard lists values from a column in one table that have no matching values in the corresponding column of a related table.

The following two sections show you how to use the Find Duplicates and Find Unmatched Query Wizards

FINDING DUPLICATE VALUES IN A FIELD

The most common use for the Find Duplicates Query Wizard is to eliminate duplicate values in the field that you want to be the primary key for a table. A primary key that's based on a custom identifying code for or the actual name of an object or person is called a *natural primary key* because it's based on naturally occurring data. The Customers table's CustomerID field, which has values derived from the CompanyName field, is an example of a natural primary key. (A key that's not based on naturally occurring data, such as an Access AutoNumber or SQL Server identity column or uniqueidentifier (rowguid) datatype, is called a *surrogate primary key*.) If you select the candidate field for a natural primary key in table Design view and click the Primary Key button, you receive an error message if the field contains duplicate values.

NOTE

Duplicate values in candidate natural primary key fields most often occur when you import data from spreadsheets or HTML tables and attempt to split the data into multiple related tables.

To test-drive the Find Duplicates Query Wizard with the CustomersWithDups table in the \SEUA12\Chaptr09\Nwind09.accdb sample database, do the following:

1. Open Nwind09.accdb, if necessary, click the Create tab and the Other group's Query Wizard button to open the New Query dialog, and double-click the Find Duplicates Query Wizard item to open the first dialog.

2. With Tables selected in the View group, select the CustomersWithDups table, and click Next.

3. CustomerID is the candidate primary key field, so select it in the Available Fields list, click the > button and click Next.

4. Click the CompanyName in the Available Fields list, click > to add it to the query result set, and Click Next.

5. Replace the default Find Duplicates for CustomersWithDups title with **qryFindDups** and, with the View the Results option selected, click Finish to save the query and display its data sheets with duplicate records for Blondel père et fils (BLONP) and The Big Cheese (THEBI).

Access SQL

The simplified Access SQL statement for the preceding query provides an example of using the GROUP BY and HAVING clauses with the COUNT function in a subquery to find more than one occurrence of a value:

```
SELECT CustomerID, CompanyName FROM CustomersWithDups
    WHERE CustomerID IN
        (SELECT CustomerID FROM CustomersWithDups As Tmp
            GROUP BY CustomerID HAVING Count(*)>1 )
    ORDER BY CustomerID;
```

→ For an example of using the Find Duplicates Query Wizard with an Access table created by importing a large HTML table, **see** "Counting Duplicate Rows with the Find Duplicates Query Wizard," **p. 1013**.

FINDING VALUES IN ONE TABLE WITH NO MATCHING VALUES IN A RELATED TABLE

The Find Unmatched Query Wizard has these two primary applications:

- Finding parent records with no child records in a related table, such as finding records for Customers that have no related Orders records

- Finding child records without parent records in a related table; child records without parent records are called *orphan records*

To demonstrate the Find Unmatched Query Wizard with the Customers and Orders tables of the \SEUA12\Chaptr09\Nwind09.accdb sample database, do the following:

1. Open Nwind09.accdb, if necessary, click the Create tab and the Other group's Query Wizard button to open the New Query dialog, and double-click the Find Unmatched Query Wizard item to open the first dialog.

2. With Tables selected in the View group, select Customers as the parent table, and click Next.

3. With Tables selected in the View group, select Orders as the child table, and click Next.

4. Accept the default CustomerID as the primary key in the Fields in 'Customers' list and foreign key in the Fields in 'Orders' list. The Matching Fields text box displays CustomerID <=> CustomerID. Click Next.

5. Select the CustomerID field, click the > button, select CompanyName, click > to display these two fields for unmatched records, and click Next.

6. Replace the default Customers without Matching Orders name with **qryUnmatched** and click Finish to display in the Datasheet FISSA FISSA Fabrica Inter. Salchichas, S.A. and PARIS Paris spe[ag]cialite[ag]s as the two Northwind customers with no Orders records.

Access SQL

Following is the simplified Access SQL statement for the preceding query:

```
SELECT Customers.CustomerID, Customers.CompanyName
    FROM Customers LEFT JOIN Orders
        ON Customers.CustomerID = Orders.CustomerID
    WHERE Orders.CustomerID Is Null;
```

Chapter 11 covers multitable queries.

→ To learn more about LEFT JOIN SQL syntax, **see** "Creating Outer Joins," **p. 484**.

CREATING OTHER TYPES OF QUERIES

Access lets you create the following five basic types of queries to achieve different objectives:

- *Select* queries extract data from one or more tables and display the data in tabular form. A *union query* is a special type of select query that combines records from two or more tables in a common set of columns.

- *Crosstab* queries summarize data from one or more tables in the form of a spreadsheet. Such queries are useful for analyzing data and creating graphs or charts based on the sum of the numeric field values of many records.

- *Action* queries create new database tables from query tables or make major alterations to a table. Such queries let you add or delete records from a table or make changes to records based on expressions that you enter in a query design. The action query category includes *append*, *update*, *delete*, and *make-table*.

- *Pass-through* queries bypass the Access query processor and send SQL statements directly to the query processor of a back-end database, which returns rows or messages to Access objects. You can't open a pass-through query in Design view; only SQL and Datasheet views are available.

- *Parameter* queries repeatedly use a query and make only simple changes to its criteria. The mailing list query that you created earlier is an excellent candidate for a parameter query because you can change the criterion of the Region field for mailings to different groups of customers. When you run a parameter query, Access displays a dialog to prompt you for the new criterion. Parameter queries aren't actually a separate query type because you can add the parameter function to select, crosstab, and action queries.

Chapter 11 and Chapter 13 explain how to create each of the five query types. Creating a table from the mailing list query to export to a mail merge file is an example of a make-table action query. In fact, this is the simplest example of an action query and also the safest because make-table queries don't modify data in existing tables. A make-table query creates a new table from your query result set.

→ To review the use of tables for Word mail merge operations, **see** "Using the Access Mail Merge Wizard," **p. 359**.

CREATING AND USING A SIMPLE MAKE-TABLE ACTION QUERY

To create a table from your mailing list query, you first must convert the query from a select to an action query. Follow these steps to make this change:

1. Open your mailing list query in Query Design view, click the Design tab, and click the Query Type group's Query Type: Make Table button to open the Make Table dialog.

2. In the Table Name text box, type a descriptive table name for your query table, such as **tblUSMailList** (see Figure 9.26).

Figure 9.26
Specify the table name for your make-table query. When creating a table with a query, it's a good practice to use the tbl prefix to identify the table as one created by a query.

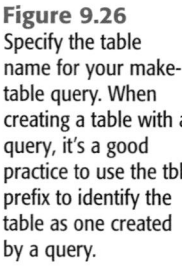 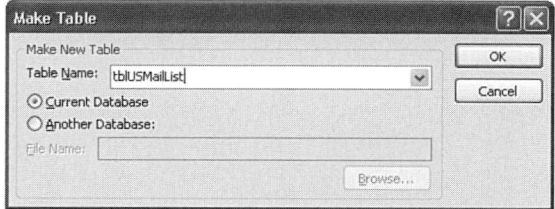

NOTE

> The Make Table dialog lets you define your query table's properties further in two ways. You can add the table to the Northwind database by choosing the Current Database option (the default). You also can pick the Another Database option to add the table to a different database that you specify in the File Name text box.
>
> Your database must be trusted to execute any type of action query.

3. Click OK. Access converts your select query to the make-table type of action query.

4. Save your make-table query with a new name and close it. An exclamation point prefixes the query's icon in the Navigation Pane, which indicates that the query is an action query.

Access SQL

The SQL statement for the make-table query is

```
SELECT Customers.ContactName AS Contact,
    Customers.CompanyName AS Company,
    Customers.Address, Customers.City,
    Customers.Region AS State, Customers.PostalCode AS ZIP
INTO tblUSMailList
FROM Customers
WHERE (((Customers.Country)="USA"))
ORDER BY Customers.PostalCode;
```

The clause that differentiates the make-table query from the select query from which it's derived is `INTO tblUSMailList`. The `INTO` clause lets you specify the table name.

Now that you've converted your query from a select query to an action query, you can create a new U.S. mailing list table. To create the table, follow these steps:

1. Run the newly converted action query table to create your mailing list by double-clicking its name in the Navigation Pane's Queries group. Acknowledge the messages that ask if you want to run the make-table query, confirm that the table, if it exists, will be overwritten, and acknowledge the number of rows to be "pasted" to the new table (see Figure 9.27). Access adds the new tblUSMailList table to the list of tables in the Northwind database.

Figure 9.27
Access displays two or three warning messages before your make-table query creates the table if you haven't cleared the Action Queries and Record Changes text boxes in the Confirm section on the Advanced page of the Access Options dialog.

2. Double-click the tblUSMailList item in the Navigation Pane's Tables group to open the table. Its contents are identical to the contents of the Datasheet view of the make-table query.

After you create the new table, you can export its data to any of the other file formats supported by Access. To do so, use any of the methods described in Chapter 8, "Linking, Importing, and Exporting Data."

ADDING A PARAMETER TO YOUR MAKE-TABLE QUERY

A simple modification to your mailing list query lets you enter a selection criterion, called a parameter, from a prompt generated by Access. Parameterized queries are very useful for generating custom tables for Word mail-merge operations. You can use the same merge specifications with different tables to generate multiple lists for selected regions or types of recipients.

→ For more information on parameterized queries, **see** "Designing Parameter Queries," **p. 500**.

To create a parameterized SELECT query, follow these steps:

1. Close the tblUSMailList table, and then expand the Navigation Pane, if necessary.

2. Right-click the item for the make-table query that you created earlier in the chapter, and choose Design View.

3. Type **[Enter the state code:]** in the first criterion row of the State: Region column, as shown in Figure 9.28. The enclosing square brackets indicate that the entry is a prompt for a parameter when you run the action query.

Figure 9.28
Adding a criterion enclosed in square brackets creates a prompt for a value to filter the query result set.

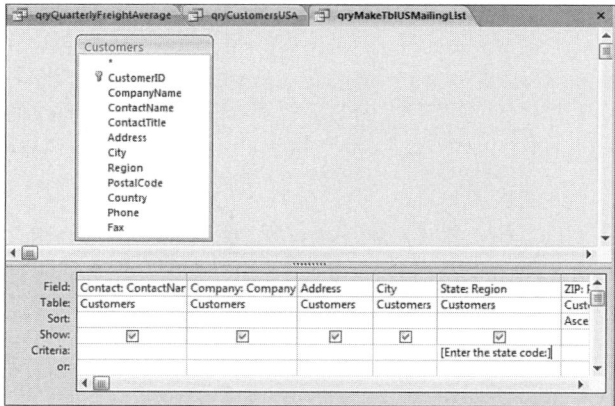

4. Press Ctrl+S to save the query. (You must save the query to re-create the table.)
5. Change to Datasheet view. Access opens the first two warning messages, and then the Enter Parameter Value dialog, which contains the prompt for you to enter the state criterion. Type **WA** for this example (see Figure 9.29), and click OK to open the third warning message and replace the tblUSMailList table (see Figure 9.30).

Figure 9.29
The Enter Parameter Value dialog includes the prompt you added as the criterion of the field for which a value is required.

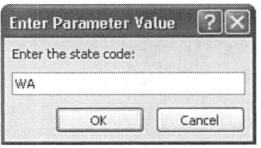

Figure 9.30
This replacement table illustrates the effect of applying a parameter to the WHERE clause of a make-table query.

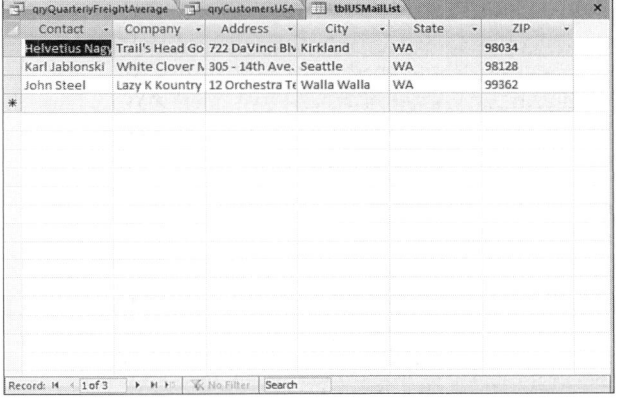

9

Access SQL

The Access SQL statement for the parameterized make-table query is

```sql
SELECT Customers.ContactName AS Contact,
    Customers.CompanyName AS Company,
    Customers.Address, Customers.City,
    Customers.Region AS State, Customers.PostalCode AS ZIP
INTO tblUSMailList
FROM Customers
WHERE (((Customers.Region)=[Enter the state code:])
    AND ((Customers.Country)="USA"))
ORDER BY Customers.PostalCode;
```

The first `Customers.Region)=[Enter the state code:]` criterion of the WHERE clause specifies the prompt and opens the Enter Parameter Value dialog. This syntax is Access-specific and isn't supported by SQL-92 or T-SQL. ADP uses SQL Server functions to return parameterized query result sets.

Access doesn't limit you to using a single parameter. For example, you can replace the "USA" criterion for the Country field with [Enter the country name:], and drag the Country column to the left of the Region column so the country prompt occurs first. In the case of the Orders table, however, you encounter a problem with countries such as Germany and the UK that don't have entries in Region columns. See the "Problems with Null Values in Parameter Fields" of the next section for more information on this issue.

TROUBLESHOOTING

MISSING REQUIRED FIELDS

I created a query that shows the tentative append record, but when I try to add a new record, I receive a "The field 'FieldName' can't contain a Null value because the Required property is set to True" error message. I don't want FieldName in the query.

You must include in your query result set all columns whose Required property value is set to Yes. This means, of course, that each of these fields must have a value typed in it. A unique primary key value is required to add a new record to any table with a primary key. For example, attempting to add a new record to a query on the Customers table that doesn't include CustomerID and CustomerName columns fails, because CustomerID is the primary key and CustomerName is a required field of the table.

NON-UPDATABLE SUMMARY QUERIES

I can't update data in my summary query.

Summary queries aggregate data, so there's no direct relationship between the content of a query row and records in the underlying table(s). This means that there's no way for changes to aggregate values (dates, totals, averages, and the like) to propagate back to the table records. If you want to fudge the figures, change your select summary query to a make-table summary query, and then alter the data in the new table.

PROBLEMS WITH NULL VALUES IN PARAMETER FIELDS

When I enter an empty parameter value to return records without an entry in the specified field, the query returns no records.

You must edit the Access SQL statement for the query to include an OR *FieldName* IS NULL expression to the WHERE clause to return records for fields with missing values. For example, in a query against the Orders table with Region and Country parameters, you must add OR Customers.Region IS NULL to return records for Germany and other countries whose Region values are missing. Following is the SQL statement that corrects the missing records for Germany problem:

```
SELECT Customers.ContactName AS Contact,
    Customers.CompanyName AS Company,
    Customers.Address, Customers.City,
    Customers.Region AS State,
    Customers.PostalCode AS ZIP
INTO tblUSMailList
FROM Customers
WHERE Customers.Country=[Enter the country name:]
    AND (Customers.Region=[Enter the state code:]
    OR Customers.Region IS NULL)
ORDER BY Customers.PostalCode;
```

In the preceding SQL statement, nonessential parentheses added by the Access query designer have been removed. The parenthesis surrounding the `(Customers.Region=[Enter the state code:] OR Customers.Region IS NULL)` expression are required to group the two condition expressions into a single criterion. This issue exemplifies the importance of learning SQL while you're gaining experience with query design.

IN THE REAL WORLD—OPTIMIZING QUERY DESIGN

The objective of select query design is to convert raw data to useful information. The design of decision-support queries in production database applications is a combination of art and science.

THE ART OF QUERY DESIGN

An artful query design returns the result set in the format that's most meaningful to the recipient. For example, a query that displays orders sorted by customer and uses the customer code for identification might be understandable by a salesperson, but not management. Salespeople are likely to know the codes for their particular customers. Few sales or marketing managers, however, are capable of memorizing hundreds or thousands of codes. This is especially true if the codes are numeric, rather than based on the first few letters of customers' names, as is the case for the Northwind Customers table.

Access's table lookup feature propagates to queries; when you specify CustomerID as a query column for the Orders table, a table lookup against Customers automatically substitutes CompanyName for CustomerID in the query result set. On the other hand, database purists object to displaying tables with embedded lookup queries that disguise the actual design of the table.

> **NOTE**
>
> The Access Web site's "The Evils of Lookup Fields in Tables" page (at `http://www.mvps.org/access/lookupfields.htm`) offers eight good reasons why you shouldn't use lookup fields in production databases.

Another aspect of the art of query design is appropriate left-to-right and top-to-bottom ordering of query columns. If your summary query is a time series—such as qryOrdersSummary, which you created in the "Trying the Simple Query Wizard" section at the beginning of the chapter—the Order Date column is the most important, so it appears in the leftmost column. If you're writing Access applications for others, make sure to interview prospective users to determine their column presentation priorities. Use drag and drop to optimize the relative position of columns in Datasheet view.

Most recent data probably is what users want, so applying a descending sort on the Order Date column aids information usability. You can quickly apply a descending sort on a date column in Datasheet view by right-clicking the field-name header and choosing Sort Descending from the context menu.

Apply intuition and inductive reasoning when designing decision-support queries. Access makes it easy to alter the presentation of your queries in Datasheet view. As in music, painting, dance, and the other performing and pictorial arts, practice and experimentation are the keys to query artistry. This is especially true when you design queries that act as the data source for PivotTables and PivotCharts.

THE SCIENTIFIC SIDE OF QUERY DESIGN

The scientific part of query design is optimizing query performance. All production database applications deliver query result sets over some type of network, usually a wired or wireless local area network (LAN) but often a wide area network (WAN), such as the Internet. The performance of queries executed over LANs—and, especially WANs—is dependent on a multitude of factors, the most important of which is the network connection, followed by the amount of network traffic. Broadband Internet access is becoming more widespread, but some Internet users still connect with dial-up modems. Even if you're writing queries for execution on a single PC, plan ahead for networking your application.

The tables of the Northwind.accdb sample database contain far fewer records than you find in typical production databases, and therefore aren't representative of the databases behind real-world applications. The nine-person Northwind Traders sales force produced only 830 orders over a span of almost two years, indicating a serious lack of sales productivity.

To design and run queries for a moderate-size database with a different structure, install the Oakmont.accdb database from the \SEUA12\Oakmont folder of the accompanying CD-ROM and run test queries against its tables. To better emulate network performance, install Oakmont.accdb on a file-sharing server and link the tables to a new .accdb file on your client PC. The Students table has about 30,000 rows, which is more typical of a production customers table. The Enrollments table has 50,000 records.

NOTE

> The CD-ROM's \SEUA12\Nwind folder has several updated versions of the Northwind sample database with and without Access application objects. The number of Orders tables varies from about 1,000 to 50,000 rows, each having four to eight related Order Details rows. The tables include Attachment and multivalued fields and are intended for testing query, data export, and upsizing capabilities and performance.

With networked data, smaller definitely is better. Limit the data returned by your query to only that required by your application's immediate need. It's especially necessary to restrict the amount of data you send to modem-connected mobile users, whether they dial into your LAN or get their data over the Internet. You minimize the amount of data sent "on the wire" to database users' PCs in two ways—setting precise criteria and limiting the number of columns.

Setting precise criteria minimizes the number of rows sent to the client PC. For example, restrict initial queries against large tables—such as those containing orders or invoices—to provide only the current month's or week's orders. Create separate "last month," "this quarter," and "last quarter" queries for users who need historical data. Access's query-expression service lets you write queries that automatically roll over when the month or quarter changes.

There's seldom a reason to include all fields (by using the field list's * choice) in a query. Include in the initial query only those fields necessary to provide the basics. For example, you might want to include the ShipName column in a query on the Orders table to identify the customer, but don't include the ShipAddress, ShipCity, ShipRegion, ShipPostalCode, and ShipCountry columns in management reports. Only salespeople and shipping departments need detailed destination data. Salespeople only need shipping information for their particular accounts, so you can use EmployeeID as a criterion to limit the number of records that have large text fields.

Don't include Attachment, OLE Object (usually images) or Memo fields in initial queries unless they're absolutely essential. Access doesn't automatically retrieve these data types unless the user double-clicks an OLE Object cell or moves the cursor to a Memo field, but data in OLE Object and Memo fields often is very large. A modem-connected user who accidentally double-clicks a 1MB high-resolution image won't be happy when his computer is tied up for several minutes downloading unwanted data. If some users require any of these field data types, create a special query for them.

The science of query design requires detailed analysis and deductive reasoning. Keep these basic query design rules in mind as you progress through the remaining chapters of the "Transforming Data with Queries and PivotTables" part of this book.

CHAPTER 10

UNDERSTANDING ACCESS OPERATORS AND EXPRESSIONS

In this chapter

WRITING EXPRESSIONS FOR QUERY CRITERIA AND DATA VALIDATION

Chapter 6, "Entering, Editing, and Validating Access Table Data," briefly introduced you to operators and the expressions that use them when you added validation rules to table fields. Chapter 9, "Designing Queries for Access Databases," touched on expressions again when you devised selection criteria for the query that you created. Expressions play an important role in all the chapters that follow.

Much of this chapter is devoted to describing the VBA functions available to you for dealing with data of the Numeric, Date/Time, and Text field data types. Functions play important roles in every element of Access—from query criteria, to validation rules for tables and fields of tables, to the control of program flow with VBA. You use functions when creating queries, forms, reports, and even more extensively when writing VBA and VBScript code. To use Access 2007 effectively, you must know what functions are available to you and how to use functions and operators effectively.

> **NOTE**
>
> As mentioned in earlier chapters, the Access expression service enables Access to take advantage of most VBA 6.0 functions in validation rules for Access tables. You use VBA 6.0 functions to set criteria and format fields of queries against Access databases and client/server databases attached to Access front-end .accdbs.
>
> Access data projects (ADPs), which use the SQL Server query processor, don't support VBA functions and use different characters for some operators. You must use corresponding Transact-SQL (T-SQL) built-in functions, where available, for CHECK constraints, VIEW column formatting, WHERE clause criteria, and elsewhere. T-SQL built-in functions aren't the same as SQL Server functions, which are more properly called *user-defined functions*.

An Access 2007 macro security feature—called sandbox mode—proscribes the use of unsafe VBA expressions. Here's how Microsoft describes unsafe expressions: "Unsafe expressions contain methods or functions that could be exploited by malicious users to access drives, files, or other resources for which they do not have authorization." None of the functions of this chapter are blocked unless they are used to supply the default value of a text box control on a form, report, or data access page. However, this and other chapters that make use of the VBA Editor require that the \SEUA12 folder and its subfolders be designated as Trusted Locations. To do this, click the Office button, open the Access Options dialog, click the Trusted Locations link to open the Trusted Locations page, click the Add New Location button to open the Microsoft Office Trusted Location dialog, type the full path to the \SEUA12 folder (usually C:\SEUA12\), mark the Subfolders of This Location Are Also Trusted check box, and click OK.

T-SQL

This chapter provides brief descriptions of the SQL Server Transact-SQL (T-SQL) substitutes for VBA operators and functions, where equivalent or similar operators and functions exist. Chapter 21, "Moving from Access Queries to Transact-SQL," provides more detailed information on differences between T-SQL and Access query syntax.

UNDERSTANDING THE ELEMENTS OF EXPRESSIONS

An *expression* is a statement of intent. If you want an action to occur after meeting a specific condition, your expression must specify that condition. To select records in a query that contains ZIP field values of 90000 or higher, for example, you use the expression

```
ZIP >= 90000
```

if the ZIP field has a numeric data type.

Arithmetic calculations are expressions also. If you need an ExtendedAmount field in a query, for example, use

```
ExtendedAmount: Quantity * UnitPrice
```

as the expression to create calculated values in the data cells of the ExtendedAmount column.

To qualify as an expression, a statement must have at least one operator and at least one literal, identifier, or function. In some cases, such as simple query criteria and field-validation rules, the equals operator (=) is inferred. The following list describes these elements:

- *Operators* include the familiar arithmetic symbols +, -, * (multiply), and / (divide), as well as many other symbols and abbreviations. Some operators are specific to Access or SQL, such as the Between, In, Is, and Like operators.

- *Literals* consist of values that you type, such as **12345** or **ABCDE**. Literals are used most often to create default values and, in combination with field identifiers, to compare values in table fields and query columns.

- *Identifiers* are the names of objects in Access (such as forms and reports) or fields in tables that return distinct numeric or text values. The term *return*, when used with expressions, means that the present value of the identifier is substituted for its name in the expression. For example, the field name identifier CompanyName in an expression returns the value (a firm name) of the CompanyName field for the currently selected record. Access has five predefined named constants that also serve as identifiers: **True**, **False**, **Yes**, **No**, and **Null**. Named constants and variables that you create in Access VBA also are identifiers.

- *Functions* return a value in place of the function name in the expression, such as the Date… and Format… functions, which are used in the examples in Chapter 9. Unlike identifiers, most functions require you to supply an identifier or value as an argument enclosed by parentheses. Later in this chapter, the "Functions" section explains functions and their arguments.

10

When literals, identifiers, or functions are used with operators, these combinations are called *operands*. The following sections explain these four elements of expressions more thoroughly.

> **NOTE**
>
> Expressions in this book appear in `monospace` type to distinguish expressions from the explanatory text. Operators, including symbolic operators, built-in functions, and other reserved words and symbols of VBA, are set in **`monospace bold`** type. (VBA reserved words appear in blue color in the Code-Editing window of modules.) SQL operators and names of Access objects are set in `monospace` type; by convention, SQL-92 reserved words are capitalized.

OPERATORS

Access and VBA provide six categories of operators that you can use to create expressions:

- *Arithmetic* operators perform addition, subtraction, multiplication, and division.
- *Assignment* and *comparison* operators set values and compare values.
- *Logical* operators deal with values that can only be true or false.
- *Concatenation* operators combine strings of characters.
- *Identifier* operators create unambiguous names for database objects so that you can assign the same field name, for example, in several tables and queries.
- Other operators, such as the `Like`, `Is`, `In`, and `Between` operators, simplify the creation of expressions for selecting records with queries.

Operators in the first four categories are available in almost all programming languages. Identifier operators are specific to Access; the other operators of the last category are provided only in RDBMSs that create queries based on SQL. The following sections explain how to use each of the operators in these categories.

ARITHMETIC OPERATORS

Arithmetic operators operate only on numeric values and must have two numeric operands, with the following exceptions:

- When the minus sign (-) changes the sign (negates the value) of an operand. In this case, the minus sign is called the *unary minus*.
- When the equal sign (=) assigns a value to an Access object, property value, or a VBA variable identifier.

Table 10.1 lists the arithmetic operators that you can use in Access expressions.

TABLE 10.1   ARITHMETIC OPERATORS

Operator	Description	Example
+	Adds two operands	Subtotal + Tax
-	Subtracts two operands	Date - 30
- (unary)	Changes the sign of an operand	-12345
*	Multiplies two operands	Units * UnitPrice
/	Divides one operand by another	Quantity / 12.55
\	Divides one integer operand by another	Units \ 2
Mod	Returns the remainder of division by an integer	Units Mod 12
^	Raises an operand to a power (exponent)	Value ^ Exponent

VBA operators are identical to operators used by all current versions of BASIC. If you aren't familiar with BASIC programming, the following operators need further explanation:

Operator	Description
\	The integer division symbol is the equivalent of "goes into," as used in the litany of elementary school arithmetic: 3 goes into 13 four times, with 1 left over. When you use integer division, operators with decimal fractions are rounded to integers, but any decimal fraction in the result is truncated.
Mod	An abbreviation for modulus, this operator returns the leftover value of integer division. Therefore, 13 Mod 4, for example, returns 1.
^	The exponentiation operator raises the first operand to the power of the second. For example, 2 ^ 4, or two to the fourth power, returns 16 (2*2*2*2).

These three operators seldom are used in queries for business applications but often occur in VBA program code.

NOTE

SQL Server supports all Access/VBA operators, except ^ (exponentiation). T-SQL substitutes % for Mod.

ASSIGNMENT AND COMPARISON OPERATORS

Table 10.1 omits the equal sign associated with arithmetic expressions because in Access you use it in two ways—neither of which falls under the arithmetic category. The most common use of the equal sign is as an assignment operator; = assigns the value of a single operand to an Access object, property value, or to a variable or constant. When you use the expression = "Q" to assign a default value to a field, the equal sign acts as an assignment operator.

10

Otherwise, = is a comparison operator that determines whether one of two operands is equal to the other.

Comparison operators compare the values of two operands and return a logical value (**True** or **False**) depending on the relationship between the two operands and the operator. An exception is when one of the operands has the **Null** value. In this case, any comparison returns a value of **Null**. Because **Null** represents an unknown value, you cannot compare an unknown value with a known value and come to a valid **True** or **False** conclusion.

Table 10.2 lists the comparison operators available in Access.

TABLE 10.2   COMPARISON OPERATORS

Operator	Description	Example	Result
<	Less than	123 < 1000	True
<=	Less than or equal to	15 <= 15	True
=	Equal to	2 = 4	False
>=	Greater than or equal to	1234 >= 456	True
>	Greater than	123 > 123	False
<>	Not equal	123 <> 456	True

The principal uses of comparison operators are to create data entry validation rules, to establish criteria for selecting records in queries, to determine actions taken by macros, to create joins using the SQL-89 WHERE and SQL-92 JOIN clauses, and to control program flow in VBA.

LOGICAL OPERATORS

Logical operators (also called *Boolean* operators) are used most often to combine the results of two or more comparison expressions into a single result. Logical operators can combine only expressions that return the logical values **True**, **False**, and **Null**. With the exception of **Not**, which is the logical equivalent of the unary minus, logical operators always require two operands.

Table 10.3 lists the Access logical operators.

TABLE 10.3   LOGICAL OPERATORS

Operator	Description	Example 1 Example 2	Result 1 Result 2
And	Logical and	True And True True And False	True False
Or	Inclusive or	True Or False False Or False	True False

Operator	Description	Example 1 Example 2	Result 1 Result 2
`Not`	Logical not	`Not True` `Not False`	`False` `True`
`Xor`	Exclusive or	`True Xor False` `True Xor True`	`True` `False`

The logical operators **And, Or,** and **Not** are used extensively in Access expressions and SQL statements; in SQL statements these operators are uppercase, as in AND, OR, and NOT. **Xor** is seldom used in queries or VBA. **Eqv** (equivalent) and **Imp** (implication) are rarely seen, even in programming code, so Table 10.3 omits these two operators.

T-SQL

T-SQL has conventional AND, OR, and NOT logical operators. **Xor** is supported by the ^ bitwise comparison operator. Other T-SQL bitwise operators are & (bitwise and) and ¦ (bitwise or).

10

CONCATENATION OPERATORS

Concatenation operators combine two text values into a single string of characters. If you concatenate ABC with DEF, for example, the result is ABCDEF. The ampersand (**&**) is the preferred concatenation operator in VBA and Access. Concatenation is one of the subjects of "The **Variant** Data Type in VBA" section later in the chapter.

> **TIP**
>
> Don't use the + symbol to concatenate strings in queries or Access SQL. In Access SQL and VBA, + is reserved for the addition of numbers; **&** concatenates literals and variables of any field data type. The **&** operator performs implicit type conversion from numbers to text; the **&** operator treats all variables as character strings. Thus, 1234 **&** 5678 returns 12345678, not 6912.

T-SQL

T-SQL uses the + symbol for string concatenation. The SQL-92 specification, however, designates two vertical bars (pipe symbols) as the official concatenation operator, as in 'String1' ¦¦ 'String2'. The string concatenation symbol is one of the least consistent elements of common flavors of SQL.

IDENTIFIER OPERATORS

Earlier versions of Access used identifier operators, **!** (the exclamation point, often called the *bang* operator) and **.** (the period, called the *dot* operator in VBA). As of Access 2000, the period replaces the bang operator, which Access 2007 continues to support for backward compatibility. The period operator performs the following operations:

■ Combines the names of object classes and object names to select a specific object or property of an object. For example, the following expression identifies the Personnel Actions form:

```
Forms.HRActions
```

This identification is necessary because you might also have a table called HRActions.

■ Separates object names from property names. Consider the following expression:

```
TextBox1.FontSize = 8
```

`TextBox1` is a control object, and `FontSize` is a property.

■ Identifies specific fields in tables, as in the following expression, which specifies the CompanyName field of the Customers table:

```
Customers.CompanyName
```

T-SQL

T-SQL uses the bang operator (!) as an alternative to NOT, as in !< (not less than) and !> (not greater than). This usage isn't compliant with SQL-92.

OTHER OPERATORS

The remaining operators are related to the comparison operators. These operators return **True** or **False**, depending on whether the value in a field meets the chosen operator's specification when used in a WHERE clause criterion. A **True** value causes a record to be included in a query; a **False** value rejects the record. When you use these operators in validation rules, entries are accepted or rejected based on the logical value returned by the expression.

Table 10.4 lists the four other operators used in Access queries and validation rules.

TABLE 10.4   OTHER OPERATORS

Operator	Description	Example
Is	Used with **Null** to determine whether a value is **Null** or **Not Null**.	Is **Null** Is **Not Null**
Like	Determines whether a string value begins with one or more characters. (For Like to work properly, you must add a wildcard character , * or one or more ? characters.)	Like "Jon*" Like "FILE????"
In	Determines whether a string value is a member of a list of values.	In("CA", "OR", "WA")
Between	Determines whether a numeric or date value lies within a specified range of values.	Between 1 **And** 5

You use the wildcard characters * and ? with the Like operator the same way that you use them in the Search tool or Command Window. The * (often called *star* or *splat*) takes the place of any number of characters. The ? takes the place of a single character. For example, Like "Jon*" returns **True** for values such as Jones or Jonathan. Like "*on*" returns **True** for any value that contains "on". Like "FILE????" returns **True** for FILENAME, but not for FILE000 or FILENUMBER. Wildcard characters can precede the characters that you want to match, as in Like "*son" or Like "????NAME".

T-SQL
T-SQL supports the IS, LIKE, IN, and BETWEEN logical operators, as described in Table 10.4. However, T-SQL uses the single quote (') as the string identifier, rather than Access's default double quote (").

Except for Is, the operators in this other category are equivalent to the SQL reserved words LIKE, IN, and BETWEEN. Access includes these operators to promote compatibility with SQL. You can create each of these operators by combining other VBA operators or functions. Like "Jon*" is the equivalent of VBA's **InStr**(**Left**(*FieldName*, 3), "Jon"); In("CA", "OR", "WA") is similar to **InStr**("CAORWA", *FieldName*), except that matches would occur for the ambiguous AO and RW combinations. Between 1 **And** 5 is the equivalent of >= 1 **And** <= 5.

> **TIP**
>
> Always use Between...**And**, not the >= and <= comparison operators, to specify a range of dates. You must repeat the field name when using the comparison operators, as in *DateValue* >= #1/1/2006# **And** *DateValue* <= #12/31/2006#. The Between syntax is shorter and easier to understand, as demonstrated by *DateValue* Between #1/1/2006# **And** #12/31/2006#.

LITERALS

VBA provides three types of literals that you can combine with operators to create expressions. The following list describes these types of literals:

- *Numeric* literals are typed as a series of digits, including the arithmetic sign and decimal point if applicable. You don't have to prefix positive numbers with the plus sign; Access assumes positive values unless the minus sign is present. Numeric literals can include E or e and the sign of the exponent to indicate an exponent in scientific notation—for example, -1.23E-02.

- *Text* (or *string*) literals can include any printable character, plus unprintable characters returned by the **Chr** function. The **Chr** function returns the characters specified by a numeric value from the ANSI character table (similar to the ASCII character table) that Windows uses. For example, **Chr**(9) returns the Tab character. Printable characters include the letters A through Z, numbers 0 through 9, punctuation symbols, and other special keyboard symbols such as the tilde (~). VBA expressions require that you enclose string literals within double quotation marks (""). Combinations of printable and unprintable characters are concatenated with **&**. For example, the following expression separates two strings with a newline pair:
  "First line" & Chr(13) & Chr(10) & "Second line"

Chr(13) is the carriage return (CR), and Chr(10) is the line-feed (LF) character; together they form the newline pair. VBA has a string constant, vbCrLf, which you can substitute for Chr(13) & Chr(10).

When you enter string literals in the cells of tables and Query Design grids, Access adds the quotation marks to literal strings for you. In other places, you must enter the quotation marks yourself.

■ *Date/Time* VBA/Access literals are enclosed within number or pound signs (#), as in the expressions #1-Jan-1980# and #10:20:30#. If Access detects that you're typing a date or time in one of the standard Access Date/Time formats into a Design grid, it adds the enclosing pound signs for you. Otherwise, you must type the # signs.

T-SQL

T-SQL numeric literals are identical to Access's, but, as mentioned earlier, string (character) literals are enclosed between single quotes ('string'). T-SQL doesn't have a Date/Time identifier; you must supply date values as quoted strings in one of the standard formats that T-SQL recognizes, such as '3/15/2007'.

IDENTIFIERS

An identifier usually is the name of an object; databases, tables, fields, queries, forms, and reports are objects in Access. Each object has a name that uniquely identifies that object. Sometimes, to identify a subobject, an identifier name consists of a family name (object class) separated from a given name (object name) by a bang symbol or a period (an identifier operator). The family name of the identifier comes first, followed by the separator and then the given name. SQL uses the period as an object separator. An example of an identifier in an SQL statement is as follows:

Customers.Address

In this example, the identifier for the Address field object is contained in the Customers table object. Customers is the family name of the object (the table), and Address is the given name of the subobject (the field). In VBA, however, you use the . symbol to separate table names and field names. (The period separates objects and their properties.) If an identifier contains a space or other punctuation, enclose the identifier within square brackets, as in this example:

[Order Details].Quantity

You can't include periods or exclamation points within the names of identifiers; [Unit.Price], for example, isn't allowed.

In simple queries that use only one table, you can omit the *TableName.* prefix. You use identifiers to return the values of fields in form and report objects. Chapters 14 through 18 cover the specific method of identifying objects within forms and reports.

> **T-SQL**
> T-SQL uses the period to separate table and field names, but adds an *ownername* prefix (dbo for database owner, by default) to the table name, as in dbo.Customers.
> Address. SQL Server queries also enclose table names having spaces or other SQL-Ilegal punctuation with square brackets [ ], as in SELECT * FROM [Order Details].

FUNCTIONS

Functions return values to their names; functions can take the place of identifiers in expressions. One of the most common functions used in VBA/Access expressions is **Now**, which returns to its name the date and time from your computer's system clock. If you type **Now** as the Default Value property of a table's Date/Time field, for example, 12/15/2006 9:00 appears in the field when you change to Datasheet view (at 9:00 a.m. on December 15, 2006).

VBA defines about 150 individual functions. The following list groups functions by purpose:

- *Date and time* functions manipulate date/time values in fields or Date/Time values that you enter as literals. You can extract parts of dates (such as the year or day of the month) and parts of times (such as hours and minutes) with date and time functions.

- *Text-manipulation* functions are used for working with strings of characters.

- *Data-type conversion* functions enable you to specify the data type of values in numeric fields instead of depending on Access to pick the most appropriate data type.

- *Mathematic and trigonometric* functions perform on numeric values operations that are beyond the capability of the standard Access arithmetic operators. You can use simple trigonometric functions, for example, to calculate the length of the sides of a right triangle (if you know the length of one side and the included angle).

- *Financial* functions are similar to functions provided by Lotus 1-2-3 and Microsoft Excel. They calculate depreciation, values of annuities, and rates of return on investments. To determine the present value of a lottery prize paid out in 25 equal yearly installments, for example, you can use the PV function.

- *General-purpose* functions don't fit any of the preceding classifications; you use these functions to create Access queries, forms, and reports.

- *Other* functions include Access domain aggregate functions, SQL aggregate functions, and functions used primarily in VBA programming.

Only the first three groups of functions and SQL aggregate functions commonly are used in Access queries; Chapters 27 through 31 offer examples of the use of some of the members of the last four function groups.

10

USING THE IMMEDIATE WINDOW

When you write VBA programming code in a module, the Immediate window is available to assist you in debugging your code. You also can use the module's Immediate window to demonstrate the use and syntax of functions.

To experiment with some of the functions described in the following sections, open the Northwind.accdb database and perform these steps:

1. Press Ctrl+G to open the VBA Editor and its Immediate window. (You don't need an open database to launch the VBA Editor.)
2. Type **? Now** in the Immediate window (see Figure 10.1) and press Enter. The date and time from your computer's clock appear on the next line. The **?** is shorthand for the VBA **Print** statement (which displays the value of a function or variable) and must be added to the **Now** function call to display the function's value.

Figure 10.1
The VBA editor's Immediate window lets you quickly test the return values of VBA functions.

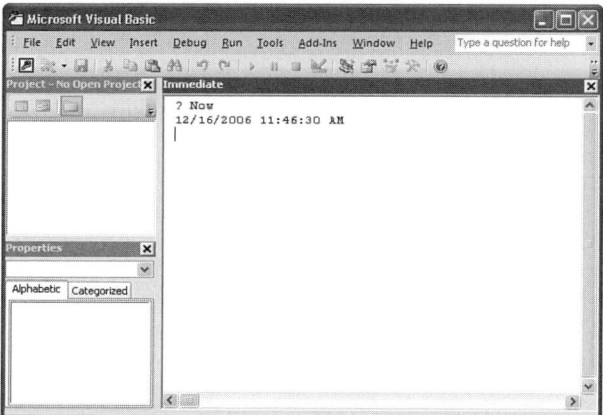

TIP

> If you neglected to precede the function entry with **?** or **Print**, an error message appears, indicating that the VBA editor expected you to type a statement or an equal sign. Click OK and type **?** before the function name in the Immediate window. Press End to return the cursor to the end of the line and then press Enter to retry the test.

3. To reposition the Immediate window more easily, click its title bar and drag the window to a central area of your display where it remains undocked.

GETTING HELP AS YOU WRITE QUERIES

As you type in your functions in the Immediate window, Access displays an Autocompletion ScreenTip, showing the function's name and its complete argument list. You must type a space or opening parenthesis after the function name to make the Autocompletion

ScreenTip appear. An argument list is the list of information that you specify for the function to work on—for example, if you use the **Sqr** function to compute the square root of a number, you must supply a number inside the function's parentheses. Figure 10.2 shows the ScreenTip for the **Sqr** function. You can turn this feature on and off by choosing <u>T</u>ools, <u>O</u>ptions and marking or clearing the Auto Quick Info option on the Editor page.

Figure 10.2
Typing a function in the Immediate window displays the VBA Autocompletion ScreenTip before you add required arguments for the function.

TIP

Obtain online help for a function by placing the cursor within the function name and pressing F1 to display the Visual Basic Reference topic for the function (see Figure 10.3).

10

Figure 10.3
Positioning the cursor within the name of a function and pressing F1 opens the Microsoft Visual Basic Help window and displays the online help topic for the function.

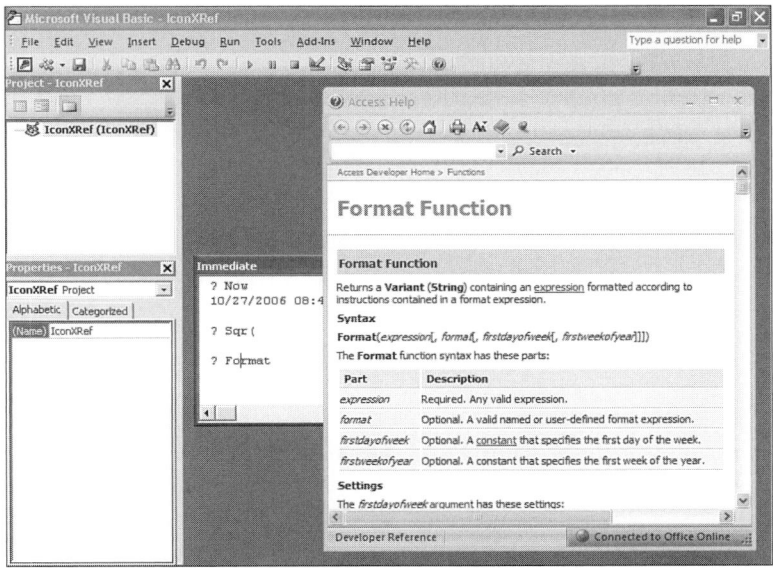

If you click an enabled Example link in any function Help window, the window displays an example of the function used in Access VBA code. Alternatively, scroll to find examples below the function definition. These examples show the syntax of the functions and appropriate arguments. The examples, however, usually aren't applicable to the function's use in an Access query or validation rule. Figure 10.4 illustrates VBA code examples for the VBA **Format** function, which commonly is used in queries.

Figure 10.4
Most examples of VBA function syntax apply to writing VBA code, not formatting the columns of Access query result sets.

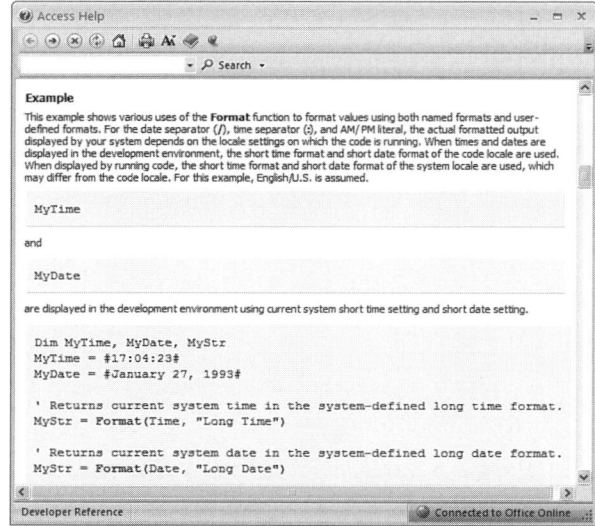

THE Variant DATA TYPE IN VBA

Variant is a special data type unique to Visual Basic dialects. The **Variant** data type enables you to concatenate values that ordinarily have different data types, such as an integer and a character string, which otherwise would result in an error. The capability to concatenate different data types is called *turning off data-type checking* or *evil type coercion (ETC)*. The **Variant** data type also lets you use operands with data of different types, such as adding **Integer** and **Double** values. Internally, Access handles all data in tables and queries as **Variant** data.

The **Variant** data type enables you to concatenate field values of tables and queries that have dissimilar data types without using VBA's data-type conversion functions, such as **Str**. (**Str** converts numeric values to the **String** data type.) The **Variant** data type simplifies expressions that combine field values to create concatenated indexes. The **Variant** data type also enables you to use the **&** symbol to concatenate values of different data types.

Table 10.5 lists the 16 common subtypes of the **Variant** data type of VBA 6.0, along with the names of the intrinsic Visual Basic constants, *vbConstant*, corresponding to the **Variant** subtype value. In addition to the Access intrinsic constants, VBA provides its own set of intrinsic constants, which are prefixed with vb. Access intrinsic constants are prefixed with ac. Intrinsic constants, which you use primarily when writing VBA code, are one of the subjects of Chapter 30, "Understanding Data Access Objects, OLE DB, and ADO."

TABLE 10.5 SUBTYPES OF THE Variant DATA TYPE

Subtype	Constant	Corresponds To	Stored As
0	(None)	Empty	Not applicable (uninitialized)
1	vbNull	**Null**	Not applicable (no valid data)

Subtype	Constant	Corresponds To	Stored As
2	vbInteger	Integer	2-byte integer
3	vbLong	Long	4-byte long integer
4	vbSingle	Single	4-byte single-precision floating point
5	vbDouble	Double	8-byte double-precision floating point
6	vbCurrency	Currency	4-byte fixed point
7	vbDate	Date/Time	8-byte double-precision floating point
8	vbString	String	Conventional string variable
9	vbObject	Object	Automation object
10	vbError	Error	Error data type (error number)
11	vbBoolean	Boolean	**True** or **False** values only
12	vbVariant	Variant	Used with **Variant** arrays
13	vbDataObject	Special	Non-Automation object
17	vbByte	Byte	Numeric value from 0–255
8192	vbArray	Array	Used with **Variant** arrays

You can concatenate **Variant** values with **Variant** subtypes 1 through 8 listed in Table 10.5. You can concatenate a subtype 8 **Variant** (**String**) with a subtype 5 **Variant** (**Double**), for example, without receiving the Type Mismatch error message displayed when you attempt this concatenation with conventional **String** (text) and **Double** data types. Access returns a value with the **Variant** subtype corresponding to the highest subtype number of the concatenated values. This example, therefore, returns a subtype 8 (**String**) **Variant** because 8 is greater than 5, the subtype number for the **Double** value. If you concatenate a subtype 2 (**Integer**) value with a subtype 3 (**Long**) value, Access returns subtype 3 **Variant** data.

T-SQL

SQL Server 2005 supports the sql_variant data type, which can store any SQL Server data type except text (Memo), ntext (Unicode or national text), image (long binary), timestamp, and sql_variant data. Concatenation rules for sql_variant values differ from Access/VBA **Variant**s. The sql_variant data type seldom is used.

Distinguishing between the empty and **Null** subtypes of **Variant** is important. Empty indicates that a variable you created with VBA code has a name but doesn't have an initial value. Empty applies only to VBA variables (see Chapter 27, "Learning Visual Basic for Applications"). **Null** indicates that a data cell doesn't contain an entry. You can assign the **Null** value to a variable, in which case the variable is initialized to the **Null** value, **Variant** subtype 1.

10

THE TempVars COLLECTION

 Access 2007 adds a new `TempVars` collection that lets you define temporary **Variant** text or numeric variables and set and retrieve the variable values with VBA code or macro actions. You set a TempVars member's value with a VBA expression such as `TempVars("tvOne").Value = 3` or `TempVars!tvTwo.Value = "CA"`. Alternatively, you can create and set the value of a `TempVar` member with the SetTempVar macro action.

You can use the value in a query expression, such as `SELECT * FROM Customers WHERE Region = TempVars!tvTwo.Value`. Chapter 26, "Automating Access Applications with Macros 2007," and Chapter 27, "Learning Visual Basic for Applications," provide more information on the use of the `TempVars` collection.

FUNCTIONS FOR DATE AND TIME

Access offers a variety of functions for dealing with dates and times. If you've used Visual Basic, you probably recognize most of the functions applicable to the Date/Time field data types shown in Table 10.6. VBA has several Date/Time functions, such as **DateAdd** and **DateDiff**, to simplify the calculation of date values. **MonthName** and **WeekdayName** functions are new to VBA 6.0.

TABLE 10.6   ACCESS FUNCTIONS FOR DATE AND TIME

Function	Description	Example	Returns
Date	Returns the current system date and time as a subtype 7 date **Variant** or a standard date **String** subtype 8.	Date	3/15/2007 03-15-2007
DateAdd	Returns a subtype 7 date with a specified number of days ("d"), weeks ("ww"), months ("m"), or years ("y") added to the date.	DateAdd("d",31, #3/15/2007#)	4/15/2007
DateDiff	Returns an **Integer** representing the difference between two dates using the d/w/m/y specification.	DateDiff("d", Date, #3/15/2007#)	116 (assuming Date = 11/19/2006)
DatePart	Returns the specified part of a date such as day, month, year, day of week ("w"), and so on, as an **Integer**.	DatePart("w", #3/19/2007#)	2 (Monday)
DateSerial	Returns a subtype 7 **Variant** from year, month, and day arguments.	DateSerial(2007, 3, 15)	3/15/2007
DateValue	Returns a subtype 7 **Variant** that corresponds to a date argument in a character format.	DateValue ("15-Mar-2007")	3/15/2007

Function	Description	Example	Returns
Day	Returns an **Integer** between 1 and 31 (inclusive) that represents a day of the month from a Date/Time value.	Day(Date)	15 (assuming that the date is the 15th of the month)
Hour	Returns an **Integer** between 0 and 23 (inclusive) that represents the hour of the Date/Time value.	Hour(#2:30 PM#)	14
Minute	Returns an **Integer** between 0 and 59 (inclusive) that represents the minute of a Date/Time value.	Minute(#2:30 PM#)	30
Month	Returns an **Integer** between 1 and 12 (inclusive) that represents the month of a Date/Time value.	Month(#15-Jul-06#)	7
MonthName	Returns the full or abbreviated name of a month from the month number (1 to 12). If you omit the second argument, the function returns the full name.	MonthName(10, False) MonthName(10, True)	October Oct
Now	Returns the date and time of a computer's system clock as a **Variant** of subtype 7.	Now	3/15/2007 11:57:28 AM
Second	Returns an **Integer** between 0 and 59 (inclusive) that represents the second of a Date/Time value.	Second(Now)	28
Time	Returns the time portion of a Date/Time value from the system clock.	Time	11:57:20 AM
TimeSerial	Returns the time serial value of the time expressed in hours, minutes, and seconds.	TimeSerial (11, 57, 20)	11:57:20 AM
TimeValue	Returns the time serial value of the time (entered as the **String** value) as a subtype 7 **Variant**.	TimeValue("11:57")	11:57
Weekday	Returns the day of the week (Sunday = 1) corresponding to the date as an **Integer**.	Weekday(#3/15/2007#)	5

10

continues

TABLE 10.6 CONTINUED

Function	Description	Example	Returns
WeekdayName	Returns the full or abbreviated name of the day from the day number (0 to 7). Setting the second argument to **True** abbreviates the name. A third optional argument lets you specify the first day of the week.	WeekdayName(4, False) WeekdayName(4, True)	Wednesday Wed
Year	Returns the year of a Date/Time value as an **Integer**.	Year(#3/15/2007#)	2007

T-SQL

When you use the Upsizing Wizard to convert a conventional Access application with an Access .accdb database to an Access data project with an SQL Server database, the Wizard converts the following Access/VBA Date/Time functions to their T-SQL equivalents:

Access/VBA Function	SQL Server Function
Date	CONVERT(datetime, CONVERT(varchar, GETDATE( ))
DateAdd( )	DATEADD( )
DateDiff( )	DATEDIFF( )
DatePart( )	DATEPART( )
Day( )	DATEPART(dd, *date*)
Hour( )	DATEPART(hh, *time*)
Minute( )	DATEPART(mi, *time*)
Now	GETDATE( )
Second( )	DATEPART(ss, *time*)
Weekday( )	DATEPART(dw, *date*)
Year( )	DATEPART(yy, date)

The Wizard doesn't convert Access/VBA functions that aren't included in the preceding list. You must manually correct conversion failures.

TEXT MANIPULATION FUNCTIONS

Table 10.7 lists the functions that deal with the Text field data type, corresponding to the **String** VBA data type. Most of these functions are modeled on BASIC string functions.

TABLE 10.7 FUNCTIONS FOR THE String DATA TYPE

Function	Description	Example	Returns
Asc	Returns the ANSI numeric value of a character as an Integer	Asc("C")	67
Chr	Returns a character corresponding to the numeric ANSI value as a String	Chr(67) Chr(10)	C (line feed)
Format	Formats an expression in accordance with appropriate format strings	Format(Date, "dd-mmm-yyyy")	15-Mar-2007
InStr	Returns the position of one string within another as a **Long**	InStr("ABCD", "C")	3
InStrRev	Returns the position of one string within another as a **Long**, starting at the end of the string but counting from the start of the string	InStrRev("ABCD", "C")	3
Join	Generates a String from a one-dimension array consisting of strings (spaces separate the array strings)	Join(astrArray)	Depends on the array's contents
LCase	Returns the lowercase version of a string	LCase("ABCD")	abcd
Left	Returns the leftmost characters of a string	Left("ABCDEF", 3)	ABC
Len	Returns the number of characters in a string as a **Long**	Len("ABCDE")	5
LTrim	Removes leading spaces from a string	LTrim(" ABC")	ABC
Mid	Returns a part of a string, beginning at the character position specified by the second argument	Mid("ABCDE", 2, 3)	BCD
PlainText **NEW**	Strips HTML formatting tags from Memo fields with Rich Text as the Text Format property value	PlainText("Hello")	Hello
Replace	Replaces occurrences of a specified substring in a string	Replace("ABCDE", "BC", "YZ")	AYZDE
Right	Returns the rightmost characters of a string	Right("ABCDEF", 3)	DEF
RTrim	Removes trailing spaces from a string	RTrim("ABC ")	ABC
Space	Returns a string consisting of a specified number of spaces	Space(5)	
Split	Returns an array of substrings based on a separator character (the default is a space)	Split("ABC DEF")	(0)ABC (1)DEF
Str	Converts the numeric value of any data type to a string	Str(123.45)	123.45

continues

10

TABLE 10.7 CONTINUED

Function	Description	Example	Returns
StrComp	Compares two strings for equivalence and returns the integer result of the comparison	StrComp("ABC", "abc")	0
String	Returns a string consisting of specified repeated characters	String(5, "A")	AAAAA
StrReverse	Returns a string whose characters are reversed	StrReverse("ABCDE")	EDCBA
Trim	Removes leading and trailing spaces from a string	Trim(" ABC ")	ABC
UCase	Returns the uppercase version of a string	UCase("abc")	ABC
Val	Returns the numeric value of a string in a data type appropriate to the argument's format	Val("123.45")	123.45

NOTE

VBA includes two versions of many functions that return String variables—one with and one without the BASIC-language $ String type identification character. This book doesn't use type identification characters in queries, so the second form of the function is omitted from the tables in this chapter. In VBA code, adding the $ suffix to functions that return strings gives slightly better performance.

T-SQL
The Upsizing Wizard converts the following Access/VBA text manipulation functions to their T-SQL equivalents:

Access/VBA Function	SQL Server Function
Asc( )	ASCII( )
Chr( )	CHAR( )
LCase( )	LOWER( )
Len( )	DATALENGTH( )
LTrim( )	LTRIM( )
Mid( )	SUBSTRING( )
Right( )	RIGHT( )
RTrim( )	RTRIM( )
Space( )	SPACE( )
Str( )	STR( )
UCase( )	UCASE( )

Functions included in Table 10.7 but not in this list cause conversion errors. T-SQL doesn't support the Access/VBA **Format** and **Format...** functions.

Figure 10.5 shows Immediate window examples of common string manipulation functions. The Immediate window is particularly valuable for learning exactly how these functions behave with different types of literal values.

Figure 10.5
Use the Immediate window to verify the syntax of the VBA functions you plan to include in Access queries or validation rules.

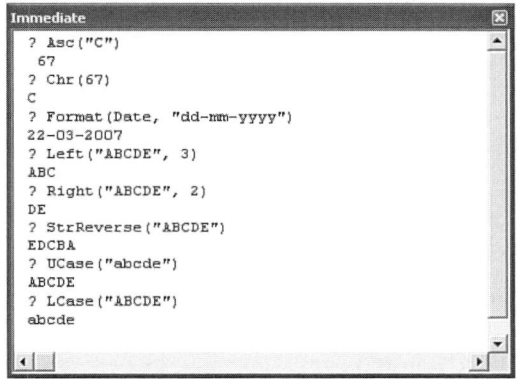

```
Immediate
? Asc("C")
 67
? Chr(67)
C
? Format(Date, "dd-mm-yyyy")
22-03-2007
? Left("ABCDE", 3)
ABC
? Right("ABCDE", 2)
DE
? StrReverse("ABCDE")
EDCBA
? UCase("abcde")
ABCDE
? LCase("ABCDE")
abcde
```

You can use the localized **Format...** functions of VBA 6.0 in Access queries, if you provide numeric values for the functions' arguments (see Figure 10.6). For example, you must substitute the numeric values shown for the vb... constants of the **FormatDateTime** function. Following is the syntax for the **Format...** functions:

- **FormatCurrency**(*NumericValue*[, *DigitsAfterDecimal* [, *IncludeLeadingDigit* [, *ParensForNegativeNumbers* [, *GroupDigits*]]]]) returns a value formatted with the localized currency symbol, including the Euro. With the exception of *NumericValue*, the arguments are optional. If *IncludeLeadingDigit* is **True**, fractional values are prefixed with $0 in North America. Setting *GroupDigits* to **True** applies the group delimiter, which is a comma (as in $1,000) for North America.

- **FormatDateTime**(*DateValue*[, *NamedFormat*]) returns a date string whose format depends on the value of *NamedFormat*. Valid values of *NamedFormat* are vbGeneralDate (0), vbLongDate (1), vbShortDate (2), vbLongTime (3), and vbShortTime (4). Figure 10.6 illustrates the use of the **FormatDateTime** and other **Format...** functions.

- **FormatNumber**(*NumericValue*[, *DigitsAfterDecimal* [, *IncludeLeadingDigit* [, *ParensForNegativeNumbers* [, *GroupDigits*]]]]) returns the same values as **FormatCurrency**, but without the currency symbol.

- **FormatPercent**(*NumericValue*[, *DigitsAfterDecimal* [, *IncludeLeadingDigit* [, *ParensForNegativeNumbers* [, *GroupDigits*]]]]) returns the same values as **FormatNumber**, but multiplies *NumericValue* by 100 and adds a trailing % symbol.

10

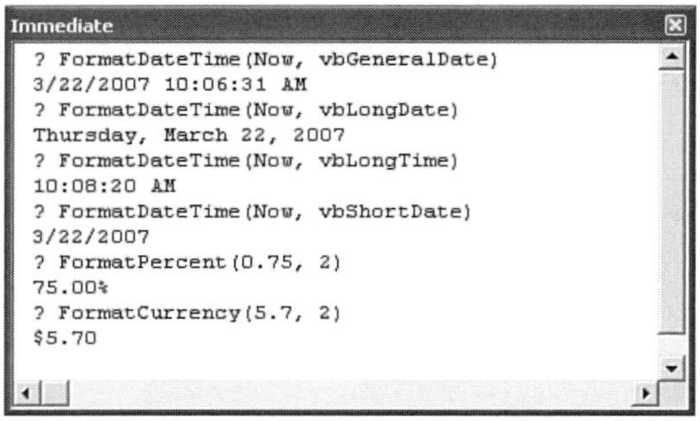

Figure 10.6
The Immediate window displays examples of the use of the VBA 6.0 `Format…` functions.

```
Immediate                                              ☒
    ? FormatDateTime(Now, vbGeneralDate)
    3/22/2007 10:06:31 AM
    ? FormatDateTime(Now, vbLongDate)
    Thursday, March 22, 2007
    ? FormatDateTime(Now, vbLongTime)
    10:08:20 AM
    ? FormatDateTime(Now, vbShortDate)
    3/22/2007
    ? FormatPercent(0.75, 2)
    75.00%
    ? FormatCurrency(5.7, 2)
    $5.70
```

NUMERIC, LOGICAL, DATE/TIME, AND STRING DATA-TYPE CONVERSION FUNCTIONS

You can assign a particular data type to a numeric value with any of the data-type conversion functions. After you freeze (or coerce) a data type with one of the numeric data-type conversion functions, you cannot concatenate that data type with the **String** data type.

Table 10.8 lists VBA's 11 numeric data-type conversion functions. The `NumValue` argument in the Syntax column can be any numeric or **String** value. However, if you use a **String** value as the argument of a numeric-type conversion function, the first character of the argument's value must be a digit, a dollar sign, a plus symbol, or a minus symbol. The most commonly used conversion function in queries is **CCur**.

TABLE 10.8   DATA-TYPE CONVERSION FUNCTIONS FOR NUMERIC, TIME/DATE, AND STRING VALUES

Function	Syntax	Description
CBool	**CBool**(*NumValue*)	Converts a numeric value to the **Boolean** (**True** or **False**) data type
CByte	**CByte**(*NumValue*)	Converts a numeric value to the **Byte** (0–255) data type
CCur	**CCur**(*NumValue*)	Converts a numeric value to the **Currency** data type
CDate	**CDate**(*NumValue*)	Converts a numeric value to a **Date** value (**CDate** replaces **CVDate**, which is obsolete)
CDbl	**CDbl**(*NumValue*)	Converts a numeric value to the **Double** data type
CInt	**CInt**(*NumValue*)	Converts a numeric value to the **Integer** data type
CLng	**CLng**(*NumValue*)	Converts a numeric value to the **Long** integer data type
CSng	**CSng**(*NumValue*)	Converts a numeric value to the **Single** data type
CStr	**CStr**(*varValue*)	Converts a **Variant** value to the **String** data type
CVar	**CVar**(*NumValue*)	Converts a numeric value to a **Variant** data type
CVErr	**CVErr**(*NumValue*)	Converts a valid error number to create user-defined errors
Nz	Nz(*varFieldValue*[, *ReturnValue*]	Converts a **Null** value to 0 or a zero-length string, depending on the context of use

T-SQL

The Upsizing Wizard converts the following Access/VBA data-type conversion functions to their T-SQL equivalents:

Access/VBA Function	SQL Server Function
CCur(*NumValue*)	CONVERT(money, *NumValue*)
CDbl(*NumValue*)	CONVERT(float, *NumValue*)
CInt(*NumValue*)	CONVERT(smallint, *NumValue*)
CLng(*NumValue*)	CONVERT(int, *NumValue*)
CSng(*NumValue*)	CONVERT(real, *NumValue*)
CStr(*NumValue*)	CONVERT(varchar, *NumValue*)
CDate(*NumValue*)	CONVERT(datetime, *NumValue*)
CVDate(*NumValue*)	CONVERT(datetime, *NumValue*)

Functions included in Table 10.8 but not in this list cause conversion errors.

The Nz (Null-to-zero) function accepts only a **Variant** *varFieldValue* argument. Nz returns non-**Null Variant** argument values unchanged. When used in an Access query, Nz returns an empty string ("") for **Null** argument values, unless you specify 0 or another literal, such as "Null" as the value of the optional *ReturnValue* argument. The Access expression service supplies the Nz function; it's not a VBA reserved word, so it doesn't appear in bold type.

> **TIP**
>
> Use Nz to format the result sets of your crosstab queries, replacing **Null** values with 0. (Crosstab queries are one of the subjects of Chapter 11, "Creating Multitable and Crosstab Queries.") When you execute a crosstab query—such as quarterly product sales by region—cells for products with no sales in a region for the quarter are empty. Empty cells might mislead management into believing information is missing. Applying the Nz function puts a 0 in empty cells, which eliminates the ambiguity.

INTRINSIC AND NAMED CONSTANTS

As noted earlier in this chapter, VBA and Access have many predefined intrinsic constants. The names of these constants are considered keywords because you cannot use these names for any purpose other than returning the value represented by the names, such as -1 for **True** and Yes, and 0 for **False** and No. (**True** and Yes are Access synonyms, as are **False** and No, so you can use these pairs of values interchangeably in Access, but not in VBA.) As noted throughout the chapter, **Null** indicates a field without a valid entry. **True**, **False**, and **Null** are the most commonly used VBA intrinsic constants.

T-SQL

T-SQL uses 1 for TRUE and 0 for FALSE. Conversion between -1 for **True** and 1 for TRUE succeeds because **True** accepts any nonzero number as **Not False**. The Upsizing Wizard converts Access **Boolean** fields to the SQL Server bit data type.

Symbolic constants, which you define, return a single, predetermined value for the entire Access session. You can create named constants for use with forms and reports by defining them in the declarations section of an Access VBA module. Chapter 27 describes how to create and use symbolic (named) constants.

→ To find the constants that are built into Access, **see** "Symbolic Constants," **p. 1189**.

CREATING ACCESS EXPRESSIONS

Chapter 6 uses several functions to validate data entry for most fields in the HRActions table. Chapter 9 uses an expression to select the country and states to be included in a mailing-list query. These examples provide the foundation on which to build more complex expressions that define more precisely the validation rules and query criteria for real-world database applications.

→ To review examples using functions to restrict data entry values, **see** "Validating Data Entry," **p. 275**.

→ For information on how to enter expressions in a query, **see** "Selecting Records by Criteria and Sorting the Display," **p. 389**.

The sections that follow provide a few examples of typical expressions for creating default values for fields, validating data entry, creating query criteria, and calculating field values. The examples demonstrate the similarity of syntax for expressions with different purposes. Part IV of this book, "Designing Forms and Reports," provides additional examples of expressions designed for use in forms and reports; Part VII, "Programming and Converting Access Applications," explains the use of expressions with Access VBA code.

EXPRESSIONS FOR CREATING DEFAULT VALUES

Expressions that create default field values can speed the entry of new records. Assigning values ordinarily requires you to use the assignment operator (=). When entering a default value in the properties pane for a table in design mode, however, you can enter a simple literal. An example is the Q default value assigned to the ActionType field of the HRActions table in Chapter 5, "Working with Access Databases and Tables." In this case, Access infers the = assignment operator and the quotation marks surrounding the Q. You often can use shorthand techniques when typing expressions because Access infers the missing characters. If you type = **"Q"**, you achieve the same result.

You can use complex expressions for default values if the result of the expression conforms to or can be converted by Access to the proper field data type. You can type = 1 as the default value for the ActionType field, for example, although 1 is a numeric value and ActionType has the Text data type. The **Variant** data type used for all Access data operations permits this action.

T-SQL

The Upsizing Wizard converts Access default values to SQL Server default values, if the expression for the default value contains functions that have T-SQL equivalents.

→ To review using the assignment operator to assign a default value, **see** "Setting Default Values of Fields," **p. 235**.

EXPRESSIONS FOR VALIDATING DATA

The HRActions table uses several expressions to validate data entry. The validation rule for the EmployeeID field is > 0; the rule for the ApprovedBy field is > 0 Or Is **Null**. The validation rule for the EmployeeID field is equivalent to the following imaginary inline VBA **IIf** function:

```
IIf(DataEntry > 0, EmployeeID = DataEntry,
    MsgBox("Please enter a valid employee ID number."))
```

Access tests *DataEntry* in the validation rule expression. If the validation expression returns **True**, the value of *DataEntry* replaces the value in the current record's field. If the expression returns **False**, a message box displays the validation text that you added. **MsgBox** is a function used in VBA programming to display a message box onscreen. You can't type the imaginary validation rule just described as a property value; Access infers the equivalent of the imaginary **IIf** expression after you add the Validation Rule and Validation Text property values with entries in the two text boxes for the EmployeeID field.

You might want to change the validation expression "H" **Or** "Q" **Or** "Y" **Or** "S" **Or** "R" **Or** "B" **Or** "C" **Or** "T", which you use to test the ActionType field, to a function. The Access **In** function provides a simpler expression that accomplishes the same objective:

```
In("H", "Q", "Y", "S", "R", "B", "C", "T")
```

Alternatively, you can use the following table-level VBA validation expression:

```
InStr("HQYSRBCT",[ActionType]) > 0
```

Instr returns the position of the second argument's character(s) within the first argument's characters. If ActionType is Q, the preceding example returns 2. Both **In** and **Instr** expressions give the same result, but you can use **InStr** only for table-level validation because one of its arguments refers to a field name. Therefore, the **In** function provides the better solution.

T-SQL

The Upsizing Wizard converts Access default values to SQL Server default values, if the expression for the default value contains functions that have T-SQL equivalents.

EXPRESSIONS FOR QUERY CRITERIA

When creating Chapter 9's qryStateMailList query to select records from the states of California, Oregon, and Washington, you type **CA**, **OR**, and **WA** on separate lines; Access adds the equal sign and double quotes around the literals for you. A better expression is **In**(`"CA"`, `"OR"`, `"WA"`), entered on the same line as the =“USA” criterion for the Country field. This expression corrects the query's failure to test the Country field for a value equal to USA for the OR and WA entries.

→ If you're not sure how multiple criteria should look in the grid, **see** "Creating More Complex Criteria," **p. 393**.

You can use a wide range of other functions to select specific records to be returned to a query table. Table 10.9 shows some typical functions used as query criteria applicable to the Northwind Traders tables. (Table 10.9 uses 2006 as the year value, because 2006 has a full calendar year of data in the Northwind.accdb tables.)

TABLE 10.9 TYPICAL EXPRESSIONS USED AS QUERY CRITERIA

Field	Expression	Records Returned
Customers Table		
Country	**Not** `"USA"` **And Not** `"Canada"`	Firms other than those in the United States and Canada.
Country	**Not** (`"USA"` **Or** `"Canada"`)	Firms other than those in the United States and Canada; the parentheses apply the condition to both literals.
CompanyName	`Like "[N-S]*"`	Firms with names beginning with N through S.
CompanyName	`Like S*` **Or** `Like V*`	Firms with names beginning with S or V (Access adds quotation marks for you).
CompanyName	`Like "*shop*"`	Firms with shop, Shop, Shoppe, or SHOPPING in the firm name.
PostalCode	`>=90000`	Firms with postal codes greater than or equal to 90000, including codes that begin with alphabetic characters.
Orders Table		
OrderDate	**Year**(`[OrderDate]`) = `2006`	Orders received in 2006.
OrderDate	`Like "*/*/2006"`	Orders received in 2006; using wildcards simplifies expressions.
OrderDate	`Like "1/*/2006"`	Orders received in the month of January 2006.
OrderDate	`Like "1/?/2006"`	Orders received from the 1st to the 9th of January 2006.
OrderDate	**Year**([OrderDate]) = 2006 **And DatePart**("q", [OrderDate]) = 1	Orders received in the first quarter of 2006.
OrderDate	`Between #1/1/2006# And #3/31/2006#`	Orders received in the first quarter of 2006.

Field	Expression	Records Returned
OrderDate	**Year**([OrderDate]) = 2006 **And DatePart**("ww", [OrderDate])= 10	Orders received in the 10th week of 2006.
OrderDate	>= **DateValue**("1/15/2006")	Orders received on or after 1/15/2006.
ShippedDate	Is **Null**	Orders not yet shipped.
Order Subtotals Query		
Subtotal	>= 5000	Orders with values greater than or equal to $5,000.
Subtotal	Between 5000 **And** 10000	Orders with values greater than or equal to $5,000 and less than or equal to $10,000.
Subtotal	< 1000	Orders less than $1,000.

The wildcard characters used in Like expressions simplify the creation of criteria for selecting names and dates. As in the Windows Search dialog, the asterisk (*) substitutes for any legal number of characters, and the question mark (?) substitutes for a single character. When a wildcard character prefixes or appends a string, the matching process loses case sensitivity, if case sensitivity is specified.

T-SQL
As mentioned earlier in the chapter, T-SQL substitutes % for * and _ (underscore) for ?. Both % and _ comply with ANSI SQL-92.

If you want to match a string without regard to case, use the following expression:

```
UCase(FieldName) = "FIELDNAME"
```

ENTERING A QUERY CRITERION AND ADDING A CALCULATED FIELD

To experiment with query criteria expressions with tables from the Northwind.accdb sample database and add a calculated field value, follow these steps:

1. Click the Create tab, and click the Query Design button to open the Query Design window and the Add Tables dialog.

2. Double-click the Customers, Orders, and Order Details tables in the Tables list of the Show Table dialog, and then click Close, which activates the Query Tools, Design ribbon. The CustomerID fields of the Customers and Orders tables and the OrderID fields of the Orders and Order Details tables are joined; joins are indicated by a line between the fields of the two tables. (Chapter 11, "Creating Multitable and Crosstab Queries," covers joining multiple tables.)

NOTE

> The Order Details table, which has Quantity, UnitPrice, and Discount fields, is required to calculate the total amount of each order.

3. Add the CompanyName, PostalCode, and Country fields of the Customers table to the query. You can add fields by selecting them from the Field drop-down list in the Query Design grid, by clicking a field in the Customers field list above the grid and dragging the field to the desired Field cell in the grid, or by double-clicking a field in the Customers field list above the grid.

4. Add to the query the OrderID, ShippedDate, and Freight fields of the Orders table. Use the horizontal scroll bar slider under the Query Design grid to expose additional field columns as necessary. Place the cursor in the Sort row of the OrderID field, open the Sort list box, and select Ascending Sort. Type an **Is Not Null** criterion for the ShippedDate column to return only orders that have shipped.

Σ 5. Click the ribbon's Totals button to add the Total row to the Query Design grid. The default value, Group By, is added to the Total cell for each field of your query. The Query Design view appears as shown in Figure 10.7.

Figure 10.7
This multitable summary query has one-to-many joins between the Customer and Orders tables, and the Orders and Order Details tables.

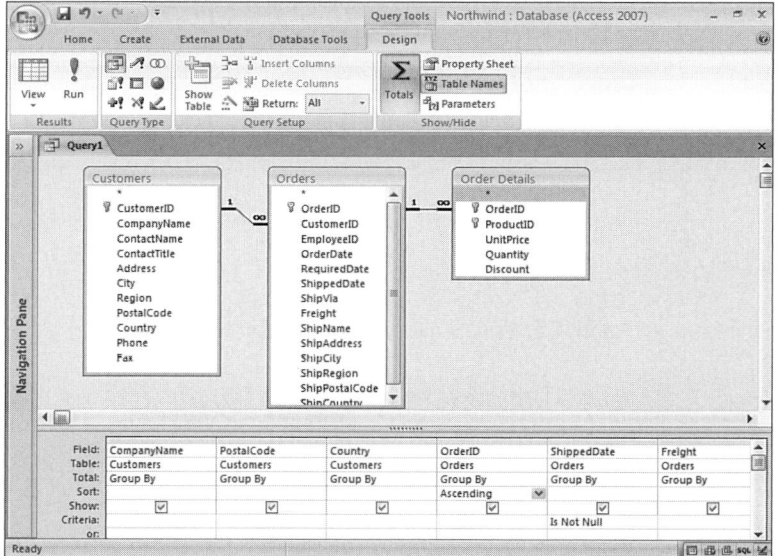

NOTE

> The query requires Group By because the Order Details table has multiple rows for most orders. If you don't specify Totals, the query returns a row for each Order Details record.

6. Click the Query Tools, Design ribbon's Run button to test the result of the interim query design, which returns 809 rows (see Figure 10.8).

Figure 10.8
Datasheet view of the interim query design of Figure 10.7 verifies that only one record appears for each order because of the addition of the Group By expression in the Total row.

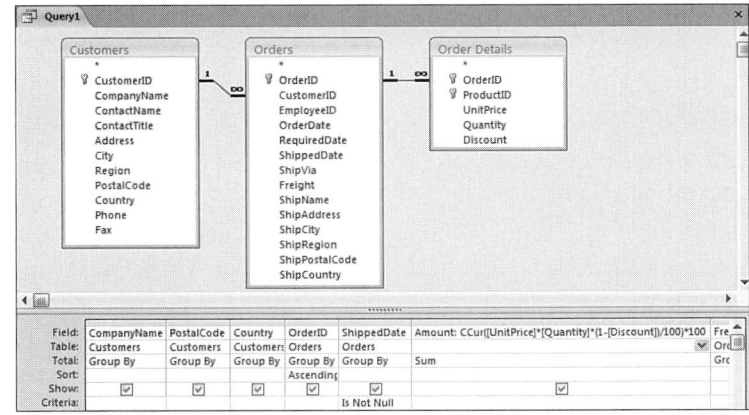

7. Return to Design view by clicking the View button, and scroll the grid so that the Freight column appears. Click the selection bar above the Field row to select the Freight column, and press the Insert key to add a new column.

8. Type **Amount: CCur([UnitPrice]*[Quantity]*(1–[Discount])/100)*100** in the new column's Field cell. This expression calculates the net amount of each line item in the Order Details table, formats the column as if the field data type were **Currency**, and rounds the amount to the nearest cent. The next section discusses how to use expressions to create calculated fields.

9. Move the cursor to the Total row of the new column and open the drop-down list. Select Sum from the list (see Figure 10.9). The Sum option totals the net amount for all line items of each order in the Orders table. In the next chapter, you learn the details of how to create queries that group data.

Figure 10.9
The calculated Amount column supplies the total net amount of the line items of the Order Details records for each order.

→ For other ways you can manipulate results from queries, **see** "Making Calculations on Multiple Records," **p. 495**.

TIP

> The Total row for all other columns of the query shows Group By. Make sure that you mark the Show check box so that your new query column appears when you run the query.
>
> Don't make an entry in the Table row of your new calculated query column; if you do, you receive an error message when you run the query.

10. Click the Query Tools, Design ribbon's Run button to run your new query. Your query appears as shown in Figure 10.10. The Amount column contains the total amount of each order, which is net of any discounts.

Figure 10.10
Datasheet view confirms that the Amount column totals the net amount of each line item for an order.

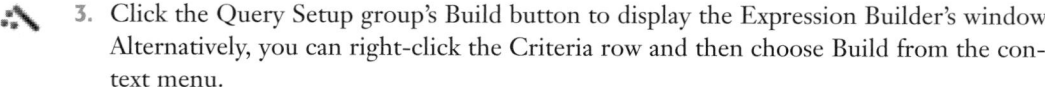

Company Name	Postal Code	Country	Order ID	Shipped Date	Amount	Freight
Wilman Kala	21240	Finland	10248	7/16/2005	$440.00	$32.38
Tradição Hipermercados	05634-030	Brazil	10249	7/10/2005	$1,863.40	$11.61
Hanari Carnes	05454-876	Brazil	10250	7/12/2005	$1,552.60	$65.83
Victuailles en stock	69004	France	10251	7/15/2005	$654.06	$41.34
Suprêmes délices	B-6000	Belgium	10252	7/11/2005	$3,597.90	$51.30
Hanari Carnes	05454-876	Brazil	10253	7/16/2005	$1,444.80	$58.17
Chop-suey Chinese	3012	Switzerland	10254	7/23/2005	$556.62	$22.98
Richter Supermarkt	1203	Switzerland	10255	7/15/2005	$2,490.50	$148.33
Wellington Importadora	08737-363	Brazil	10256	7/17/2005	$517.80	$13.97
HILARIÓN-Abastos	5022	Venezuela	10257	7/22/2005	$1,119.90	$81.91
Ernst Handel	8010	Austria	10258	7/23/2005	$1,614.88	$140.51
Centro comercial Moctezuma	05022	Mexico	10259	7/25/2005	$100.80	$3.25
Old World Delicatessen	99508	USA	10260	7/29/2005	$1,504.65	$55.09
Que Delícia	02389-673	Brazil	10261	7/30/2005	$448.00	$3.05
Rattlesnake Canyon Grocery	87110	USA	10262	7/25/2005	$584.00	$48.29
Ernst Handel	8010	Austria	10263	7/31/2005	$1,873.80	$146.06
Folk och fä HB	S-844 67	Sweden	10264	8/23/2005	$695.62	$3.67
Blondel père et fils	67000	France	10265	8/12/2005	$1,176.00	$55.28

USING THE EXPRESSION BUILDER TO ADD QUERY CRITERIA

After creating and testing your query, you can apply criteria to limit the number of records that the query returns. You can use Access's Expression Builder to simplify the process of adding record-selection criteria to your query. To test some of the expressions listed in Table 10.9, follow these steps:

1. Click the Design View button to change to Query Design mode.

2. Place the cursor in the Criteria row of the field for which you want to establish a record-selection criterion.

3. Click the Query Setup group's Build button to display the Expression Builder's window. Alternatively, you can right-click the Criteria row and then choose Build from the context menu.

4. In the Expression text box at the top of Expression Builder's window, type one of the expressions from Table 10.9. Figure 10.11 shows the sample expression `Like "*shop*"` that applies to the Criteria row of the Company Name column. You can use the Like button under the expression text box as a shortcut for entering `Like`.

Figure 10.11
You can use the Expression Builder to add simple or complex expressions as WHERE clause criteria.

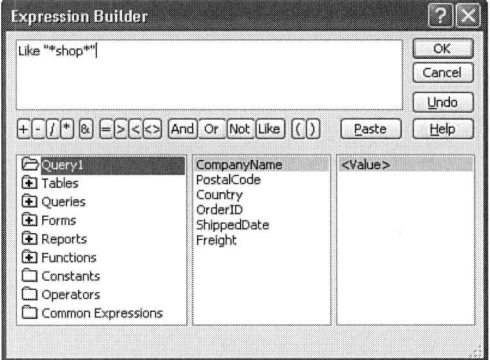

5. Click OK to return to the Query Design grid. The Expression Builder places the expression that you built in the field where the cursor is located (see Figure 10.12).

10

Figure 10.12
The expression you create in the Expression Builder applies to the field you selected when opening the Builder.

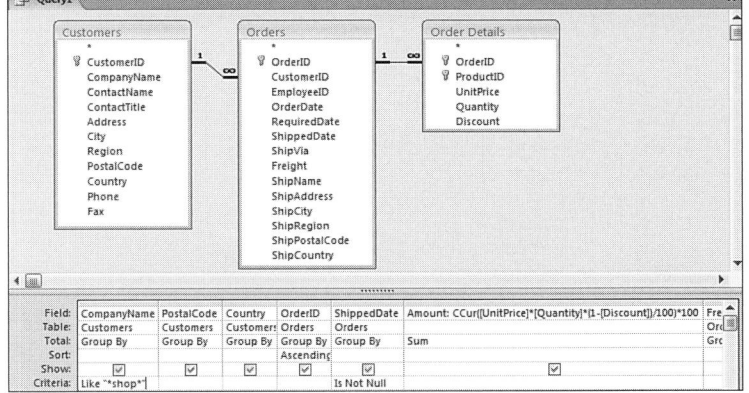

6. Click the Run button on the ribbon to test the expression. The query result for the example in Figure 10.12 appears as shown in Figure 10.13.

7. Return to Query Design mode; then select and delete the added expression by pressing the Delete key.

8. Repeat steps 2 through 7 for each expression that you want to test. When you test expressions using Date/Time functions, sort the OrderDate field in ascending order. Similarly, sort on the Amount field when queries are based on amount criteria. You can alter the expressions and try combinations with the implied **And** condition by entering criteria for other fields in the same row. Access warns you with an error message if you make a mistake in an expression's syntax.

9. After you finish experimenting, save your query with a descriptive name, such as **qryInvoiceAmount**.

Figure 10.13
The `Like "*shop*"` expression displays records only for customers whose names contain "shop", "Shop", or "SHOP".

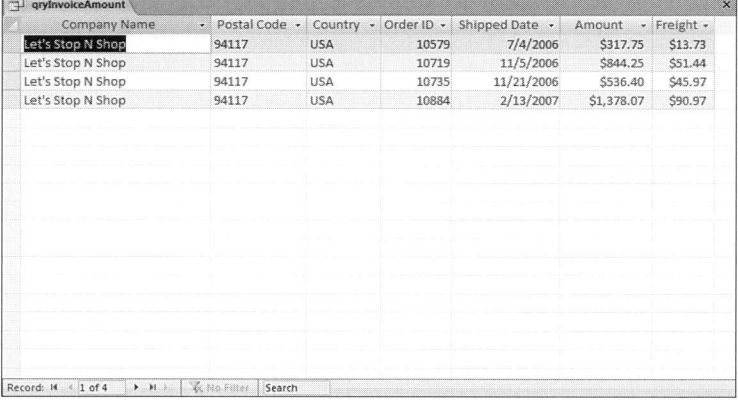

The preceding query and its underlying tables are included in the Chaptr10.accdb sample file, located in the \SEUA12\Chaptr10 folder of the accompanying CD-ROM.

Access SQL

The Access SQL statement for the qryInvoiceAmount query is

```
SELECT Customers.CompanyName, Customers.PostalCode,
    Customers.Country, Orders.OrderID, Orders.ShippedDate,
    Sum(CCur([UnitPrice]*[Quantity]*(1-[Discount])/100)*100) AS Amount,
    Orders.Freight
FROM (Customers
    INNER JOIN Orders
        ON Customers.CustomerID = Orders.CustomerID)
    INNER JOIN [Order Details]
        ON Orders.OrderID = [Order Details].OrderID
GROUP BY Customers.CompanyName, Customers.PostalCode, Customers.Country,
    Orders.OrderID, Orders. ShippedDate, Orders.Freight
    HAVING (((Customers.CompanyName) Like "*shop*") AND
        ((Orders.ShippedDate) Is Not Null))
ORDER BY Orders.OrderID;
```

The `Sum(CCur([UnitPrice]*[Quantity]*(1-[Discount])/100)*100) AS Amount` expression combines the Sum aggregate operation you specified (refer to Figure 10.9) with the expression you typed to define the calculated Amount column.

Each `INNER JOIN...ON` clause defines the joins between two tables; `JOIN` clauses are discussed in the next chapter.

You might think that the `GROUP BY` clause includes more fields than required and only the `Orders.OrderID` field is required for grouping. One of the Total aggregate functions *must* appear in each column of a grouped query.

The `HAVING` clause for grouped rows is the equivalent of the `WHERE` clause for individual rows.

If the Access or SQL Server Query Designer throws an error when you attempt to run a query with aggregate functions, check the "Troubleshooting" section near the end of this chapter.

THE SQL SERVER VERSION OF A QUERY

If you've installed SQL Server Express to support ADPs, you can run the Upsizing Wizard on the Chaptr10.accdb database to create the SQL Server version of the tables and qryOrderAmount query. Chapter 22, "Upsizing Access Applications to Access Data Projects," provides detailed examples of the upsizing process.

→ For instructions on how to install SQL Server Express from the Office 2007 distribution CD-ROM, **see** "SQL Server 2005 Express Edition SP2 Setup," **p. 59**.

The Chaptr10.accdb database that the accompanying CD-ROM installs in your \Program Files\SEUA12\Chaptr10 folder contains the Customers, Orders, and Order Details tables and the qryInvoiceAmount query that you created in the preceding section. To upsize the Chaptr10.accdb database to an SQL Server Chaptr10SQL database and a Chaptr10CS.adp project, do this:

1. Open the Chaptr10.accdb file.
2. Click the Database Tools tab, and click the Move Data group's SQL Server button to start the upsizing process.
3. Accept the default Create New Database option in the first Wizard dialog. Click Next.
4. In the second dialog, accept your *COMPUTERNAME*\SQLEXPRESS as the server name, and accept the default Use Trusted Connection to use your Administrator logon account with Windows authentication for SQL Express. Click Next.
5. In the third dialog, click the >> button to add all three tables to the SQL Server database. Click Next.
6. In the fourth dialog, accept the defaults. Click Next.
7. In the fifth dialog, select the Create a New Access Client/Server Project and accept the default project name (usually C:\SEUA12\Chaptr10\Chaptr10CS.adp). Click Next.
8. In the sixth and last dialog, accept the default Open the New ADP File option, and click Finish to upsize the database. After a minute or so, depending on the speed of your computer, the Chaptr10CS.adp project opens and displays a seven-page Upsizing Wizard report. Page seven shows the T-SQL statement that the Wizard generated from the Access SQL statement.
9. Close the report and, in the Navigation Pane, double-click the qryInvoiceAmount query, which the Wizard upsizes to an SQL Express (user defined) function. The Datasheet view of the query is identical to that of the Access version of the query (refer to Figure 10.10).
10. Click the Design button to open the da Vinci Filter Design window. The three tables and the joins between them appear in the upper pane. Field definitions, including the calculated Amount field definition, appear in the lower pane.
11. Click the small SQL button to display the filter's T-SQL statement. Adjust the position of the table windows and the depths of the three panes as shown in Figure 10.14.

Figure 10.14
The da Vinci Design view of a filter, one of SQL Server's three choices for generating query result sets, has a three-pane window.

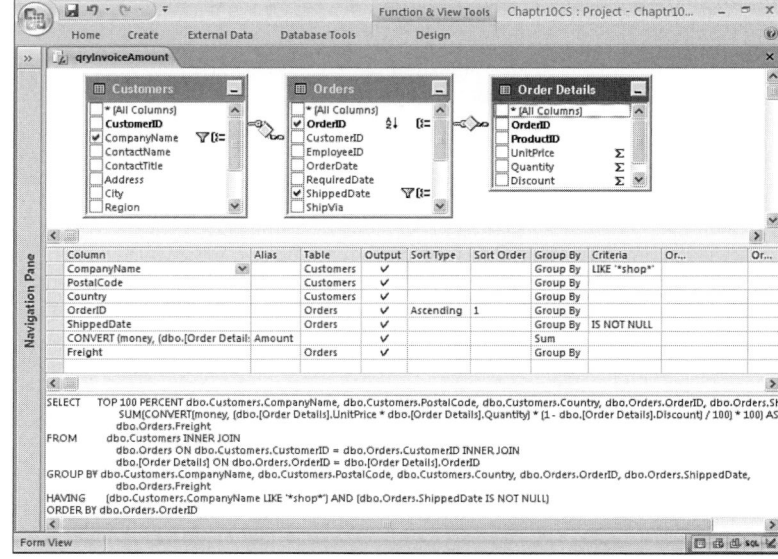

T-SQL

The T-SQL statement for the qryInvoiceAmount function (without a WHERE criterion on the Customers column) is

```
SELECT TOP 100 PERCENT dbo.Customers.CompanyName, dbo.Customers.PostalCode,
    dbo.Customers.Country, dbo.Orders.OrderID, dbo.Orders. ShippedDate,
    SUM(CONVERT(money, (dbo.[Order Details].UnitPrice * dbo.[Order
Details].Quantity) *
        (1 - dbo.[Order Details].Discount)/100)*100) AS Amount,
dbo.Orders.Freight
FROM  dbo.Customers
    INNER JOIN dbo.Orders
        ON dbo.Customers.CustomerID = dbo.Orders.CustomerID
    INNER JOIN dbo.[Order Details]
        ON dbo.Orders.OrderID = dbo.[Order Details].OrderID
GROUP BY dbo.Customers.CompanyName, dbo.Customers.PostalCode,
    dbo.Customers.Country, dbo.Orders.OrderID, dbo.Orders.OrderDate,
    dbo.Orders.Freight
HAVING (dbo.Orders.ShippedDate IS NOT NULL)
ORDER BY dbo.Orders.OrderID
```

The SQL statement is similar to that of the Access query, but substitutes CONVERT(money —) for Access's **CCur** function. The TOP 100 PERCENT prefix is required to permit an ORDER BY clause in a view or function. The dbo. prefix identifies the default database owner.

EXPRESSIONS FOR CALCULATING QUERY FIELD VALUES

The three preceding sections demonstrate that you can use expressions to create new, calculated fields in query tables. Calculated fields display data computed based on the values of other fields in the same row of the query table. Table 10.10 shows some representative expressions that you can use to create calculated query fields. Notice that Access field names must be enclosed with square brackets when typed in the Query Design window.

TABLE 10.10   TYPICAL EXPRESSIONS TO CREATE CALCULATED QUERY FIELDS

Column Name	Expression	Values Calculated
TotalAmount	`[Amount] + [Freight]`	Sum of the OrderAmount and Freight fields
FreightPercent	`100 * [Freight]/[Amount]`	Freight charges as a percentage of the order amount
FreightPct	`Format([Freight]/[Amount], "Percent")`	Freight charges as a percentage of the order amount, but with formatting applied
SalesTax	`Format([Amount] * 0.08, "$#,###.00")`	Sales tax of 8 percent of the amount of the order added with a display that's similar to the **Currency** data type

> **NOTE**
>
> T-SQL doesn't support the VBA **Format** or **Format…** functions, and the Upsizing Wizard won't generate views or functions from Access queries that use these functions.

To create a query containing calculated fields in Chaptr10.accdb, follow these steps:

1. In Query Design view, move to the first blank column of the qryInvoiceAmount query. Type the column name shown in Table 10.10, followed by a colon and then the expression:

   `TotalInvoice: [Amount]+[Freight]`

> **NOTE**
>
> If you don't type the field name and colon, Access provides the default Expr1 as the calculated field name.

2. Place the cursor in the Total cell of the calculated field and select Expression from the drop-down list. If you don't select Expression, your query opens a Parameters dialog or returns an error message when you attempt to execute it.

3. Move to the next empty column, type the following expression, and add the Expression aggregate (see Figure 10.15):

   `FreightPct: Format([Freight]/[Amount],"Percent")`

Figure 10.15
Type one of the expressions of Table 10.10 to add an additional calculated column. The example shown here calculates Total Invoice and Freight Pct column values from another calculated column, Amount, and a table field, Freight.

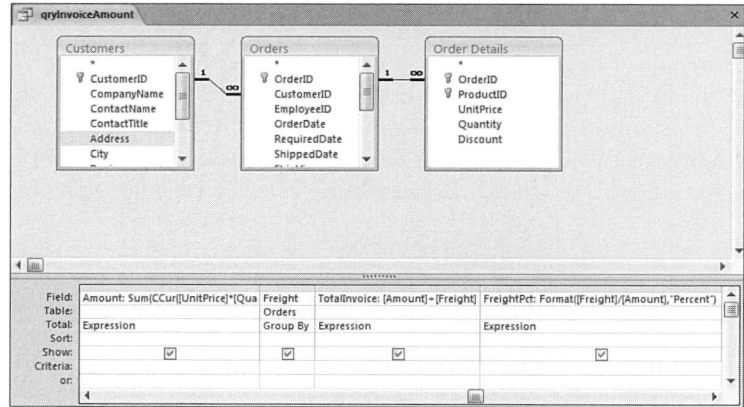

To avoid this error, see "Query Expressions Fail to Execute" in the "Troubleshooting" section near the end of the chapter.

4. Remove the `Like "*shop*"` criterion from the CompanyName column.
5. Run the query. The result set for the query with the added calculated fields appears as shown in Figure 10.16.

qryInvoiceAmount

Company Name	Postal	Country	Order	Shipped Date	Amount	Freight	TotalInvoice	FreightPct
Wilman Kala	21240	Finland	10248	7/16/2005	$440.00	$32.38	$472.38	7.36%
Tradição Hipermerc	05634-03	Brazil	10249	7/10/2005	$1,863.40	$11.61	$1,875.01	0.62%
Hanari Carnes	05454-87	Brazil	10250	7/12/2005	$1,552.60	$65.83	$1,618.43	4.24%
Victuailles en stock	69004	France	10251	7/15/2005	$654.06	$41.34	$695.40	6.32%
Suprêmes délices	B-6000	Belgium	10252	7/11/2005	$3,597.90	$51.30	$3,649.20	1.43%
Hanari Carnes	05454-87	Brazil	10253	7/16/2005	$1,444.80	$58.17	$1,502.97	4.03%
Chop-suey Chinese	3012	Switzerlan	10254	7/23/2005	$556.62	$22.98	$579.60	4.13%
Richter Supermarkt	1203	Switzerlan	10255	7/15/2005	$2,490.50	$148.33	$2,638.83	5.96%
Wellington Importa	08737-36	Brazil	10256	7/17/2005	$517.80	$13.97	$531.77	2.70%
HILARIÓN-Abastos	5022	Venezuela	10257	7/22/2005	$1,119.90	$81.91	$1,201.81	7.31%
Ernst Handel	8010	Austria	10258	7/23/2005	$1,614.88	$140.51	$1,755.39	8.70%
Centro comercial M	05022	Mexico	10259	7/25/2005	$100.80	$3.25	$104.05	3.22%
Old World Delicate:	99508	USA	10260	7/29/2005	$1,504.65	$55.09	$1,559.74	3.66%
Que Delícia	02389-67	Brazil	10261	7/30/2005	$448.00	$3.05	$451.05	0.68%
Rattlesnake Canyor	87110	USA	10262	7/25/2005	$584.00	$48.29	$632.29	8.27%
Ernst Handel	8010	Austria	10263	7/31/2005	$1,873.80	$146.06	$2,019.86	7.79%
Folk och fä HB	S-844 67	Sweden	10264	8/23/2005	$695.62	$3.67	$699.29	0.53%
Blondel père et fils	67000	France	10265	8/12/2005	$1,176.00	$55.28	$1,231.28	4.70%

Record: 1 of 809 No Filter Search

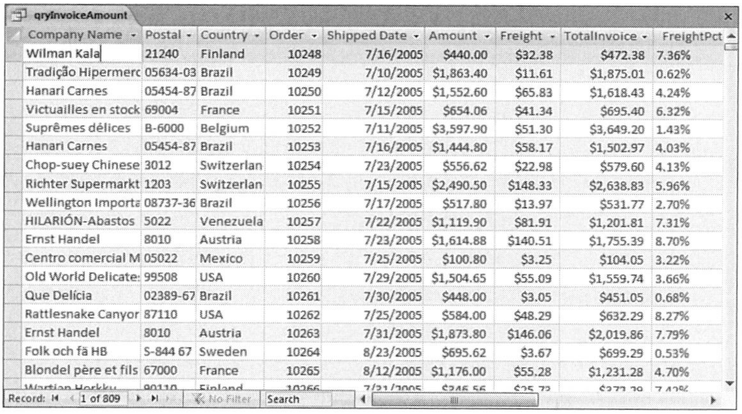

Figure 10.16
Datasheet view displays the query result set of the design shown in Figure 10.15.

6. Repeat steps 3 through 5 for the remaining examples in Table 10.10.

You use the **`Format`** function with your expression as its first argument to display the calculated values in a more readable form. When you add the percent symbol (%) to a format expression or specify "Percent" as the format, the value of the expression argument multiplies by 100 and the percent symbol preceded by a space appends to the displayed value.

If you run into a "Can't evaluate expression" or "Wrong data type" error, check the "Troubleshooting" section near the end of this chapter.

> **TIP**
>
> Use the **Format** function with custom percent formatting if you want fewer or more decimal places. For example, if you only want one digit to the right of the decimal separator, substitute `FreightPct:` **Format**(`[Freight]/[Amount]`,`"#0.0%"`) for the standard formatting in the preceding example. Adding the `%` symbol to the format string automatically multiplies the value argument by 100.
>
> Avoid the use of the **Format** and **Format…** functions in tables you plan to upsize to SQL Server. As mentioned earlier, T-SQL doesn't support these two functions.

TROUBLESHOOTING

QUERY EXPRESSIONS FAIL TO EXECUTE

When attempting to execute a query that contains an expression, a "Can't evaluate expression" or "Wrong data type" message box appears.

The "Can't evaluate expression" message usually indicates a typographic error in naming a function or an object. Depending on the use of the function, an Enter Parameter Value dialog might appear if the named object does not exist. The "Wrong data type" message is most likely to occur as a result of attempting to use mathematic or trigonometric operators with values of the Text or Date/Time field data types. If your expression refers to a control contained in a form or report, the form or report must be open when you execute the function.

AGGREGATE QUERIES THROW ERRORS

I receive a "You tried to execute a query that does not include the specified expression 'ExpressionName' as part of an aggregate function" message when I attempt to run my aggregate query.

An aggregate function is missing from the Totals row of one of the columns. You must select Group By, Expression, or an aggregate function—such as Sum, Avg, Min, Max, or Where—for each column of your query. For T-SQL queries, the da Vinci toolset's "ADO Error: Column 'dbo.*TableName.ColumnName*' is invalid in the select list because it is not contained in either an aggregate function or the GROUP BY clause" error message is more explicit.

TWO-DIGIT YEARS TURN INTO FOUR DIGITS IN QUERY CRITERIA

When I type `Between #1/1/07#` and `#12/31/07#` *in the Criteria cell of Query Design view, Access changes my entry to Between #1/1/2007# and #12/31/2007#.*

Windows Vista, XP, and 2000—and the Office applications that run under these operating systems—are year 2000 (Y2K) compliant. By default, earlier versions of Access running under Windows 9x and Me drop the century digits when creating Access SQL statements to execute queries, regardless of the formatting applied to the underlying table—mm-ddd-yyyy for all date fields in Northwind.accdb. Windows Vista, XP, and 2000 define the short date format as having four-digit years. It's a good data entry practice to require typing four-digit years by adding the appropriate input mask (99/99/0000) with the Input Mask Wizard.

IN THE REAL WORLD—THE ALGEBRA OF ACCESS EXPRESSIONS

A junior high school algebra class provides most students their first introduction to abstract mathematics. Expressions (algebraic formulas) are crucial to the majority of decision-support queries you design, as well as the presentation of calculated data in form and report text boxes and other text-based controls. The colon following the column name of a calculated expression is the equivalent of an equal sign; in mathematical terms, Amount: **CCur**([UnitPrice]*[Quantity]*(1-[Discount])) is the equivalent of curAmount = **CCur**(sngUnitPrice*intQuantity*(1-sngDiscount)) in VBA.

Similarly, functions that convert data types and format query columns also are important to forms and reports. The classic definition of a function is this: If, when X is given, Y is determined, then Y is a function of X. For example, in Price: **Format**([UnitPrice], "#,##0.00"), the value of the UnitPrice field (X) uniquely determines the value of the calculated Price (Y) column. The fact that queries can have calculated and specially formatted columns is one of the reasons this book uses the term *column* with queries and *field* for tables.

In most cases, it's a good design practice to base forms and reports on queries with precalculated and preformatted columns, rather than calculating and formatting values for individual text boxes. It's quicker and easier to check your expressions in the query result set, and you don't need to add expressions or formatting (or both) to every text box, subform, and other control that displays the data.

The only drawback of this approach is that calculating and formatting columns of queries with a large number of rows slows performance, but usually only slightly. For instance, formatting the nine-digit StudentID column of the 45,000-record StudentTransactions table of the Oakmont.accdb database with the ID: **Left**([StudentID], 3) & "-" & **Mid**([StudentID], 4, 3) & "-" & **Right**([StudentID], 3) expression causes an imperceptible effect on query execution speed. Bear in mind, however, that adding calculated columns to queries against networked databases increases the amount of data sent "over the wire." Calculated columns slow networked query execution by the proportion of characters added per row, as does applying formatting that increases the number of characters per column. The alternative is to perform calculations and add formatting by customized controls on Access forms.

Expressions and, to a lesser extent, functions play a major role in query criteria. When you type a criterion—such as CA—in the query design grid, Access converts the criterion to a valid Access SQL expression, in this case WHERE *FieldName* = "CA". In this example, the equal sign is the identity operator. Another use for the identity operator is in creating joins using SQL WHERE clauses, as in WHERE *Table2.PrimaryKey* = *Table1.ForeignKey*. SQL Server required the use of WHERE syntax to define joins prior to adopting the SQL-92 JOIN syntax in SQL Server 6.0 and later.

You can perform logical operations on query result sets with the **IIf** (inline **If**) function, whose arguments can contain other functions. For instance, the equivalent of the Province: Nz([Region], "None") expression is Province: **IIf**(IsNull([Region]),"None",[Region]).

CHAPTER 11

CREATING MULTITABLE AND CROSSTAB QUERIES

In this chapter

INTRODUCING JOINS ON TABLES

You'll only gain a return on your investment in this book and the time you devote to learning about Access if you take full advantage of Access's relational database management capabilities. To do so, you must be able to link related tables based on key fields that have values in common—a process called *joining tables*. Chapter 9, "Designing Queries for Access Databases," and Chapter 10, "Understanding Access Operators and Expressions," showed you how to create simple queries based on a single table. If you tried the examples in Chapter 10, you generated a multiple-table query when you joined the Order Details table to the Orders table and the Customers table to create the query for testing expressions. The first part of this chapter deals exclusively with queries created from multiple tables that you relate through joins.

This chapter provides examples of queries that use each of the four basic types of joins that you can create in Access's Query Design view: inner joins, outer joins, self-joins, and theta joins. It also shows you how to take advantage of UNION queries that you can't create in Access's Query Designer. The chapter also briefly covers subqueries, which you can substitute for nested Access queries. Chapter 13, "Creating and Updating Access Tables with Action Queries," presents typical applications for and examples of four types of action queries: update, append, delete, and make-table.

Some of the sample queries in this chapter use the HRActions table that you created in Chapter 5, "Working with Access Databases and Tables." If you didn't create the HRActions table and have installed the sample databases from the accompanying CD-ROM, click the External Data tab and the Import group's Access button, and import the HRActions table from \SEUA12\Chaptr06\Nwind06.accdb to your working database. Alternatively, open \SEUA12\Chaptr11\Joins11.accdb, which includes all the examples of this chapter.

→ For a detailed description of the HRActions table, **see** "Designing the HRActions Table," **p. 226**.

> TIP
>
> Read this chapter and create the sample queries sequentially, as the queries appear in the text. The sample queries of this chapter build on queries that you create in earlier sections.

JOINING TABLES TO CREATE MULTITABLE QUERIES

Before you can create joins between tables, you must know which fields are related by common values. As mentioned in Chapter 5, assigning identical names to primary key and foreign key fields in different tables that contain related data is a common practice. This approach, used by Microsoft when creating the original Northwind sample database, makes determining relationships and creating joins among tables easier. The CustomerID primary-key field in the Customers table and the CustomerID foreign-key field in the Orders table, for example, are used to join sets of orders with specific customers. A join between tables requires that one field in each table have a common set of values—CustomerID codes for this example.

Figure 11.1 shows the structure of the Northwind.accdb database with a graphical display of the relationships between the tables. Access indicates relationships with lines between field names of different tables. Bold type indicates primary key fields. Each relationship usually involves at least one primary key field. Relationships define *potential* joins between tables, but it's not necessary to have a predefined relationship to create a join.

Figure 11.1
The Relationships window displays the relationships between primary keys and foreign keys in the Northwind database with the HRActions table added. The 1 above the line that shows the join between two tables indicates the "one" side of a one-to-many relationship; the infinity symbol (∞) indicates the "many" side.

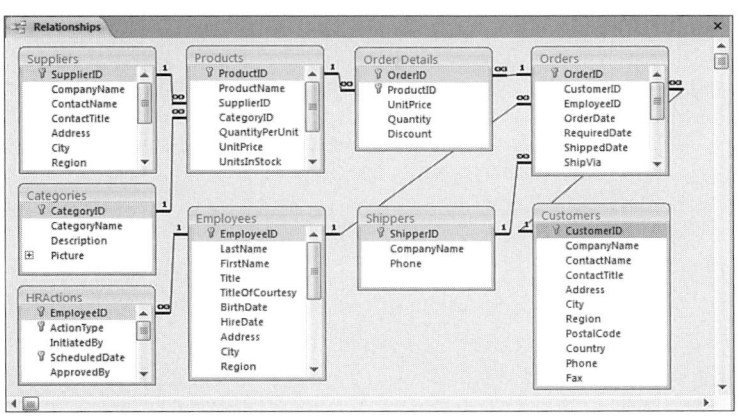

You can display the structure of the joins between the tables in the Northwind by clicking the Database Tools tab and then the Relationship button. Click the Relationship Tools, Design tab to create or edit relationships.

You can choose between displaying only the direct relationships for a single table (the Direct Relationships button on the Relationship Tools, Design toolbar) or all relationships for all tables in a database (the All Relationships button). All tables appear by default when you open the Relationships window of the Northwind sample database. In this case, clicking the Show Direct Relationships button has no effect.

> **TIP**
>
> To show relationships for only one table, click the Clear Layout button, click the Show Table button to display the Show Table dialog, select the table to display in the Tables list, and then click Add and Close. Click the Show Direct Relationships button to display the relationships for the selected table. Clearing the layout of the Relationships window doesn't affect the underlying relationships between the tables. The Show Direct Relationships feature is useful primarily with databases that contain many related tables. Close the Relationships window and don't save the changes.

Access supports four types of joins in the Query Design window:

- *Inner joins* are the most common join for creating select queries. The most common type of an inner join is a *natural join* (also called an *equi-join*), which displays all the records in one table that have corresponding records in another table. The correspondence between records is determined by identical values (WHERE *field1* = *field2* in SQL dialects earlier than SQL-89) in the fields that join the tables. In most cases, joins are based on a unique primary key field in one table and a foreign key field in the other table in a one-to-many relationship. If any records in the table that act as the many side of the relationship have field values that don't correspond to a record in the table of the one side, the noncorresponding records on the one side don't appear in the query result.

> NOTE
>
> Access automatically creates natural joins between tables in Query Design view if there's a relationship defined between the tables or the tables share a common field name that's a primary key of one of the tables.

- *Outer joins* display records in one member of the join, regardless of whether corresponding records exist on the other side of the join.

- *Self-joins* relate data within a single table. You create a self-join in Access by adding to the query a duplicate of the table (Access provides an alias for the duplicate), and then you create a join to the field(s) of the duplicate table.

- *Theta joins* relate data by using comparison operators other than =. Theta joins include not-equal joins (<>) used in queries designed to return records that don't have corresponding values. It's easier to implement theta joins by WHERE criteria rather than by the SQL JOIN reserved word. The Query Design window doesn't indicate theta joins by drawing lines between field names.

The 15.5MB Oakmont.accdb database, in the \SEUA12\Oakmont folder of the accompanying CD-ROM, has a circular set of relationships. Open Oakmont.accdb, either from the CD-ROM or from a copy on your fixed disk, and then click the Database Tools tab and the Relationships button to open the Relationships window (see Figure 11.2). Courses are one-to-many related to Courses, Departments are one-to-many related to Courses, and Employees are one-to-many related to Sections. You also can see a circular relationship between Courses, Enrollments, Students, Grades, and Courses. Oakmont.accdb is useful when you want to test the performance of queries with a large number of records. The fictitious Oakmont University in Navasota, Texas, has about 30,000 students, 2,320 employees, and offers 1,770 sections of 590 courses in 14 academic departments.

CREATING CONVENTIONAL SINGLE-COLUMN INNER JOINS

Joins based on one column in each table are known as *single-column inner equi-joins* and are the most common by far of all join types. The following list details the basic rules for designing a database that lets you use simple single-column inner equi-join for all queries:

- Each table on the one side of the relationship must have a primary key with a No Duplicates index to maintain referential integrity. Access automatically creates a No Duplicates index on the primary key field(s) of a table.

Figure 11.2
The Oakmont.accdb database has a circular set of relationships between the Courses, Enrollments, Students, Grades, and Course tables.

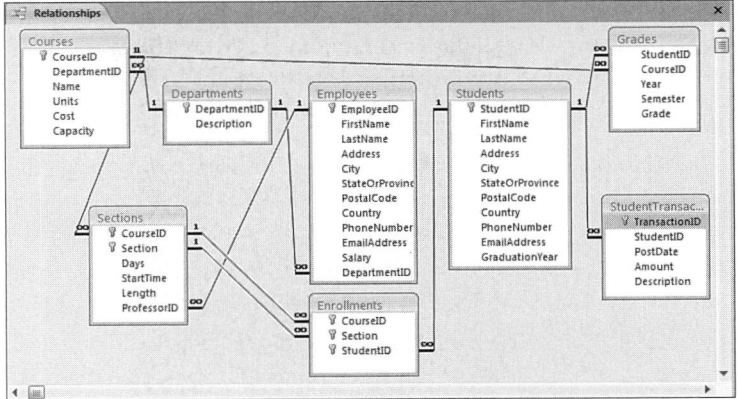

- Many-to-many relationships, such as the relationship of Orders to Products, are implemented by an intermediary table (in this case, Order Details) having a one-to-many relationship (Orders to Order Details) with one table and a many-to-one relationship (Order Details to Products) with another.

> **NOTE**
> Access 2007's new multivalue lookup fields, which have a many-to-many relationship with a lookup table, have a hidden intermediary table that Access creates for you.

- Duplicated data in tables, where applicable, is extracted to a new table that has a primary key, no-duplicates, one-to-many relationship with the table from which the duplicate data is extracted. Using a multicolumn primary key to identify extracted data uniquely often is necessary because individual key fields might contain duplicate data. The combination (also known as *concatenation*) of the values of the key fields, however, must be unique. Access 2007's Table Analyzer Wizard locates and extracts most duplicate data automatically.

→ For more information on make-table queries, **see** "Creating New Tables with Make-Table Queries," **p. 551**.

→ If you're not sure how to create relationships, **see** "Establishing Relationships Between Tables," **p. 237**.

All joins in the Northwind database, shown earlier by the lines that connect field names of related tables in Figure 11.1, are single-column inner joins between tables with one-to-many relationships. Figure 11.2 illustrates the two-column relationship between the CourseID and SectionID fields of the Sections and Enrollments tables. Access uses the ANSI SQL-92 reserved words INNER JOIN to identify conventional inner joins, and LEFT JOIN or RIGHT JOIN to specify outer joins.

Among the most common uses for queries based on inner joins is matching customer names and addresses with orders received. You might want to create a simple report, for example,

11

that lists the customer name, order number, order date, and amount. To create a conventional one-to-many, single-column inner join query that relates Northwind's customers to their orders, sorted by company and order date, follow these steps:

1. With Northwind.accdb open, close all open database objects.

2. Click the Create tab and Query Design button. Access displays the Show Table dialog superimposed on an empty Query Design window.

3. Select the Customers table from the Show Table list and click the Add button. Alternatively, you can double-click the Customers table name to add the table to the query. Access adds the Field Names list for Customers to the Query Design window.

4. Double-click the Orders table in the Show Table list and then click the Close button. Access adds to the window the Field Names list for Orders, plus a line that indicates a join between the CustomerID fields of the two tables. Access creates the join automatically because Access found the relationship with the CustomerID field (a foreign key) in the Orders table.

5. To identify each order with the customer's name, select the CompanyName field of the Customers table and drag the field symbol to the Field row of the Query Design grid's first column.

6. Select the OrderID field of the Orders table and drag the field symbol to the second column's Field row. Drag the OrderDate field to the third column. Your query design appears as shown in Figure 11.3.

Figure 11.3
Access automatically creates the inner join on the CustomerID field between the Customers and Orders table.

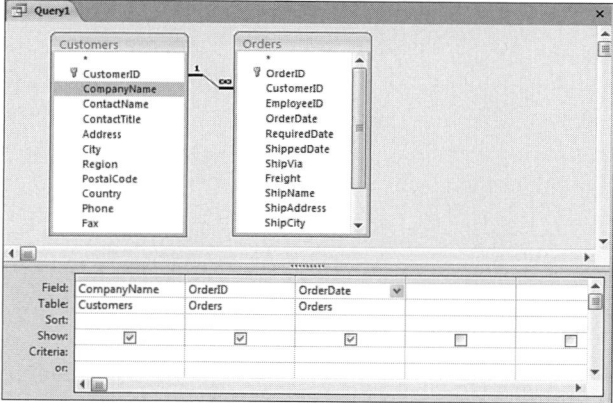

7. Click the Run or Datasheet View button to display the result of the query, the Recordset shown in Figure 11.4. Notice that the field headers of the query result set show the captions for the table fields, which include spaces, rather than the actual field names, which don't have spaces.

Figure 11.4
The Datasheet view of the query design of Figure 11.3 displays the three fields added to the grid.

SPECIFYING A SORT ORDER AND TOP VALUES LIMIT

Access displays query result sets in the order of the index on the primary key field of the table that represents the one side of the topmost one-to-many relationship of query tables, unless you specify sorting on another field, a different sort direction, or both. If the primary key consists of more than one column, Access sorts query result sets in left-to-right key-field column precedence. Because Customers is the topmost one member of the preceding query's Customers-Orders relationship, the query result set displays all orders in CompanyID, OrderID sequence. A query with Orders, Order Details, and Products tables displays rows in ProductID sequence, because Products has a one-to-many relationship with OrderDetails and, indirectly, with Orders. You can override the topmost table's primary key display order by adding a sort order to the query. For example, if you want to see the most recent orders first, you can specify a descending sort by the order date.

→ For more information on primary key indexes, **see** "Adding Indexes to Tables," **p. 242**.

You can use the Top Values option to limit the number of rows returned by the query to those that are likely to be of most interest. For this example with a descending sort, only the most recent orders are relevant. Minimizing the number of rows returned by a query is especially important with client/server queries against large tables or when creating networked applications for remote users having slow dial-up connections.

To add this sort sequence and row limit to your query, follow these steps:

1. Click the Design View button and click the Query Tools, Design tab.
2. Place the cursor in the Sort row of the Order Date column of the Query Design grid and click the arrow or press Alt+↓ to open the drop-down list.
3. Select Descending from the drop-down list to specify a descending sort on date—latest orders first (see Figure 11.5).

Figure 11.5
Add a descending sort on the OrderDate field to display the latest orders first.

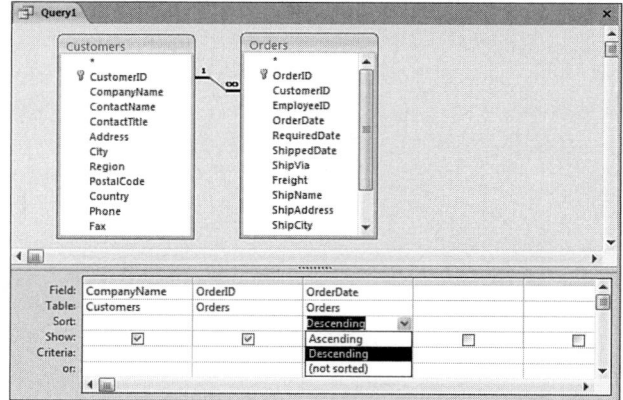

4. Open the Return list of the Query Tools Design ribbon's Query Setup group and select 5%. Adding a Top Values constraint doesn't affect the Query Design grid.

5. Click the Run or Datasheet View button to display the query result set with the new sort order and row limit (see Figure 11.6).

Figure 11.6
Orders appear in descending date sequence in this Datasheet view. With 5% set in the Top Values list, the query returns only 42 rows.

Company Name	Order ID	Order Date
Rattlesnake Canyon Grocery	11077	5/6/2007
Bon app'	11076	5/6/2007
Richter Supermarkt	11075	5/6/2007
Simons bistro	11074	5/6/2007
Pericles Comidas clásicas	11073	5/5/2007
Ernst Handel	11072	5/5/2007
LILA-Supermercado	11071	5/5/2007
Lehmanns Marktstand	11070	5/5/2007
Tortuga Restaurante	11069	5/4/2007
Queen Cozinha	11068	5/4/2007
Drachenblut Delikatessen	11067	5/4/2007
White Clover Markets	11066	5/1/2007
LILA-Supermercado	11065	5/1/2007
Save-a-lot Markets	11064	5/1/2007
Hungry Owl All-Night Grocers	11063	4/30/2007
Reggiani Caseifici	11062	4/30/2007
Great Lakes Food Market	11061	4/30/2007
Franchi S.p.A.	11060	4/30/2007
Ricardo Adocicados	11059	4/29/2007

Record: 1 of 42

6. Open the View list button on the toolbar, and choose SQL View to open the SQL window, which displays the Access SQL statement for the query.

Access SQL
The Access SQL statement for the sorted query with the Top Values limit is

```
SELECT TOP 5 PERCENT Customers.CompanyName,
    Orders.OrderID, Orders.OrderDate
FROM Customers
    INNER JOIN Orders
    ON Customers.CustomerID=Orders.CustomerID
ORDER BY Orders.OrderDate DESC;
```

The INNER JOIN Orders clause specifies a join with the Customers table, and the ON Customers. CustomerID=Orders.CustomerID qualifier names the joined fields.

A pre-SQL-89 alternative method for creating joins is to use the WHERE clause to specify a join. If you edit the SQL statement as follows, you achieve the same result:

```
SELECT TOP 5 PERCENT Customers.CompanyName,
    Orders.OrderID, Orders.OrderDate
FROM Customers, Orders
WHERE Customers.CustomerID=Orders.CustomerID
ORDER BY Orders.OrderDate DESC;
```

Using WHERE clauses to specify INNER, LEFT, and RIGHT JOINs no longer is common practice, because result sets created by WHERE clauses aren't updatable.

DESIGNING NESTED QUERIES

Access lets you use a saved query (QueryDef object) in lieu of that query's tables (TableDef objects) in other queries. The only significant difference between these two objects from a query design standpoint is that queries don't have primary keys. Prior to executing the top-level query, Access executes the QueryDef objects of lower-level (nested) queries, and then creates the join with other tables.

To add a saved query (Northwind.accdb's sample Order Subtotals query for this example) as a nested query in the customer/orders query you created in the preceding section, do this:

1. Return to Query Design view and click the Show Table button to open the dialog.

2. Click the Queries tab of the Show Tables dialog, double-click the Order Subtotals entry in the list, and click Close.

3. Double-click the Subtotal column of the Order Subtotals query to add it to the grid. Double-click the Freight field of the Orders table to add a Freight column to the query (see Figure 11.7). The join line represents a one-to-one relationship between the OrderID fields of the Orders table and the Order Subtotals query, which the Query Designer detects by field name.

4. Add a calculated Totals field by typing **Total: [Subtotal] + [Freight]** in the grid's Field cell to the right of the Freight field.

5. Click the Run button to display the result set (see Figure 11.8).

6. Click the Database Tools tab and the Relationships button to open the Relationships window, click the Show Tables button, click the Queries tab, double-click the Orders Subtotals item in the list, and click Close. Unlike the Query Design process, Access doesn't automatically display the relationship between queries and tables.

7. Drag the OrderID field from the Orders table and drop it on the OrderID column of the Orders Subtotals column to display the Edit Relationships dialog (see Figure 11.9). You can't enforce referential integrity between tables and queries. Click OK to close the dialog.

11

Figure 11.7
Adding a query instead of a table as a query data source adds a relationship between columns and fields of the same name. In this case, the relationship is one-to-one.

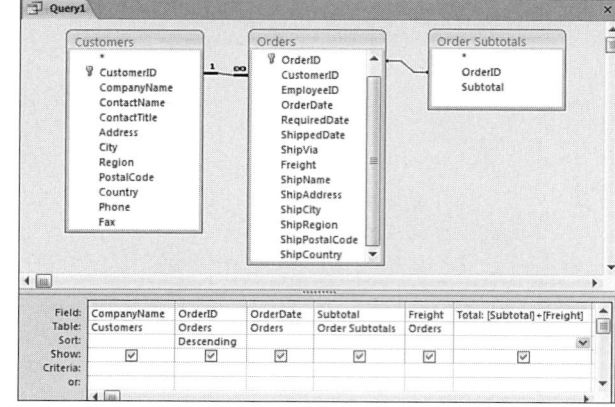

Figure 11.8
The query design of Figure 11.7 adds the Order Subtotals' Subtotal column, the Freight field of the Orders table, and a calculated Totals column.

Figure 11.9
Creating a join between a query and a table disables the referential integrity options of the Edit Relationships dialog.

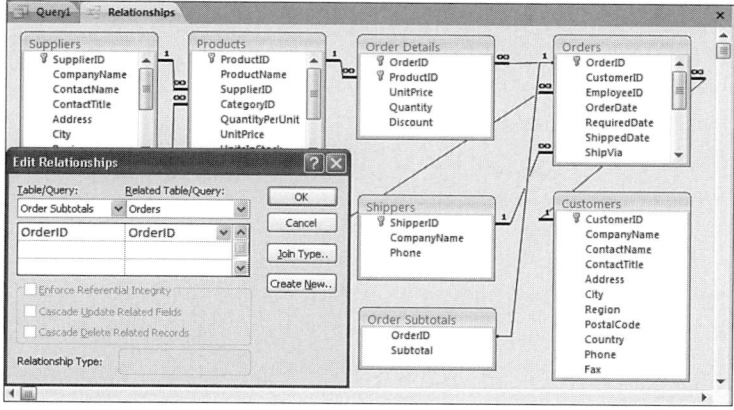

8. Close the Relationships window, and save the layout changes. Then close your query and save it with a descriptive name, such as **qryOrderAmountsRecentTop5%**.

Access SQL

The Access SQL statement for the nested query is

```
SELECT TOP 5 PERCENT Customers.CompanyName, Orders.OrderID,
    Orders.OrderDate, [Order Subtotals].Subtotal, Orders.Freight,
    [Subtotal]+[Freight] AS Total
FROM Customers
    INNER JOIN (Orders
        INNER JOIN [Order Subtotals]
        ON Orders.OrderID = [Order Subtotals].OrderID)
    ON Customers.CustomerID = Orders.CustomerID
ORDER BY Orders.OrderDate DESC;
```

Square bracket pairs ([ ]) surround table or query names having spaces or SQL-illegal punctuation. It's also a common practice to surround field names in expressions for computed columns with square brackets. Indenting the INNER JOIN statements at the same level as the ON prepositions makes the syntax easier to understand.

CREATING QUERIES FROM TABLES WITH INDIRECT RELATIONSHIPS

You can create queries that return indirectly related records, such as the categories of products purchased by each customer. You must include in the queries each table that serves as a link in the chain of joins. If you're designing queries to display the categories of products purchased by each customer, for example, include each of the tables that link the chain of joins between the Customers and Categories tables. This chain includes the Customers, Orders, Order Details, Products, and Categories tables. You often need indirect relationships for data analysis queries.

> **TIP**
>
> Queries with indirect relationships are especially useful to create PivotTable and PivotChart views of data. Several of the next chapter's PivotTable and PivotChart examples use this and related queries as data sources.

To create a query that you can use to analyze customers purchases by category, which requires specifying fields of indirectly related records, follow these steps:

1. Click the Create tab and Query Design button to open the Show Table dialog.

2. Add the Customers, Orders, Order Details, Products, and Categories tables to the query, in sequence; then click the Close button of the Add Table dialog. Access automatically creates a chain of joins between Customers and Categories based on relationships between the primary key field of each intervening table and the identically named foreign key field in the adjacent table.

TIP

> As you add tables to the Query Design window, the table field lists might not appear in the upper pane. Use the upper pane's vertical scroll bar to display the "hidden" tables. You can drag the table field lists to the top of the upper pane and then rearrange the field lists to match the appearance of the upper pane of Figure 11.10.

3. Double-click the CompanyName and CategoryName fields from the Customers and Categories tables to add them to the first two columns of the grid.

4. In the Field row of the third column, type **Amount: CCur([Order Details].[UnitPrice]*[Quantity]*(1-[Discount]))** to calculate the net amount of the purchase of each line item in the Orders Details table (see Figure 11.10).

→ For an explanation of the expression that calculates the Amount column values, **see** "Entering a Query Criterion and Adding a Calculated Field," **p. 437**.

Figure 11.10
The query design shown here calculates the net purchases of each product by every customer.

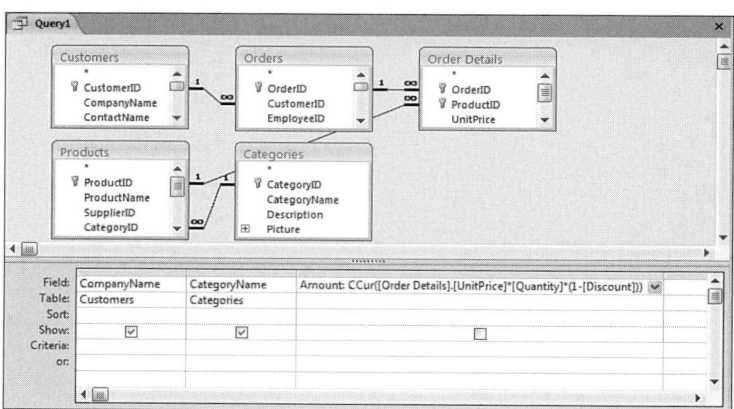

5. Click the Run button to test the query at this intermediate point of the design (see Figure 11.11). The query returns 2,155 rows, which is the number of records in the Order Details table.

6. Return to Design view, click the Query Tools Design tab, and click the Totals button to group the data by CategoryName and CustomerName and to generate total sales by category for each customer. Apply an ascending sort to the CategoryName column, and select Sum from the drop-down list in the Group By row of the Amount column (see Figure 11.12).

7. Run the query to display the summary (aggregated) result set, which now contains 598 records.

8. In the Home ribbon, click the Records group's Totals button to add a totals row to the Datasheet. Open the Amount column's Totals list and select Sum (see Figure 11.13).

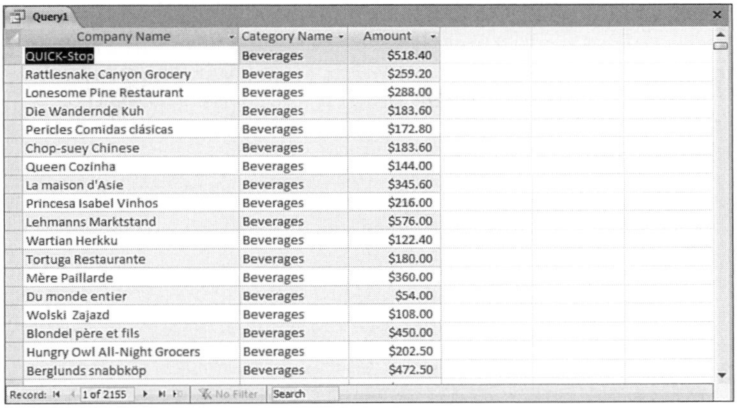

Figure 11.11
The Datasheet view of the query design of Figure 11.10 has too much detail to be usable for sales analysis of product categories.

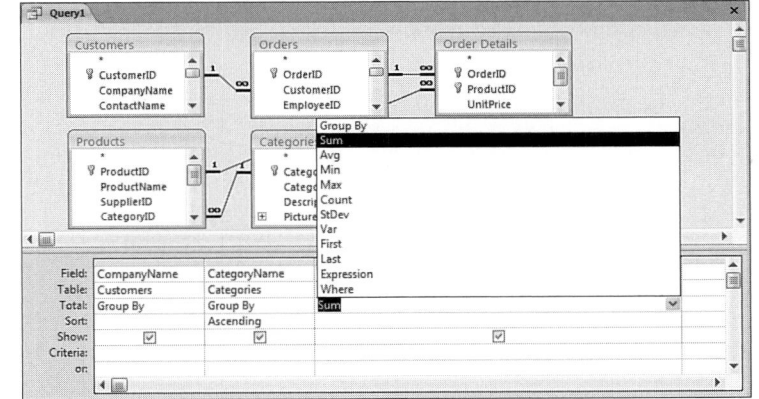

Figure 11.12
To reduce the amount of detail, group the records by the CustomerName and CategoryName fields and calculate the sum of the Amount column.

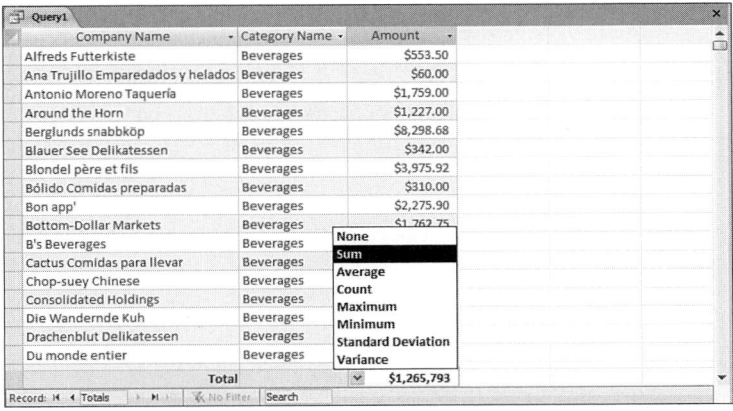

Figure 11.13
This summary query result set totals product sales by category and customer to reduce the number of rows from 2,155 to 598.

11

9. The number of records (598) is still too many for most people to analyze by inspection, so return to Query Design view, open the Field list of the first column, substitute **Country** for CustomerName to reduce the number of records to 165, and re-run the query (see Figure 11.14).

Figure 11.14
Aggregating sales by country and category displays 165 records. If customers in all 21 countries had made purchases in all eight categories, the result set would have 168 records.

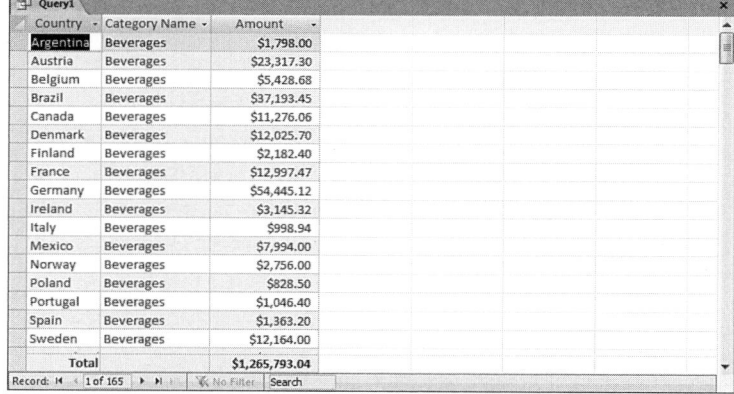

Country	Category Name	Amount
Argentina	Beverages	$1,798.00
Austria	Beverages	$23,317.30
Belgium	Beverages	$5,428.68
Brazil	Beverages	$37,193.45
Canada	Beverages	$11,276.06
Denmark	Beverages	$12,025.70
Finland	Beverages	$2,182.40
France	Beverages	$12,997.47
Germany	Beverages	$54,445.12
Ireland	Beverages	$3,145.32
Italy	Beverages	$998.94
Mexico	Beverages	$7,994.00
Norway	Beverages	$2,756.00
Poland	Beverages	$828.50
Portugal	Beverages	$1,046.40
Spain	Beverages	$1,363.20
Sweden	Beverages	$12,164.00
Total		**$1,265,793.04**

Record: 1 of 165 — No Filter — Search

10. Close the query and save it as **qryOrderAmountsByCountryAndCategory**.

Access SQL

The Access SQL statement for the aggregate query is

```
SELECT Customers.Country, Categories.CategoryName,
   Sum(CCur([Order Details].[UnitPrice]*
   [Quantity]*(1-[Discount]))) AS Amount
FROM (Categories
   INNER JOIN Products
      ON Categories.CategoryID = Products.CategoryID)
   INNER JOIN ((Customers INNER JOIN Orders
      ON Customers.CustomerID = Orders.CustomerID)
   INNER JOIN [Order Details]
      ON Orders.OrderID = [Order Details].OrderID)
      ON Products.ProductID = [Order Details].ProductID
GROUP BY Customers.Country, Categories.CategoryName
ORDER BY Categories.CategoryName;
```

If you write SQL statements for queries with several joins instead of using Access's graphical query design window, it's easier to use a pre-SQL-92 WHERE clause to define the joins, as in:

```
SELECT Customers.Country, Categories.CategoryName,
   Sum(CCur([Order Details].UnitPrice*
   [Quantity]*(1-[Discount]))) AS Amount
FROM Customers, Orders, [Order Details], Products, Categories
WHERE Categories.CategoryID=Products.CategoryID
   AND Customers.CustomerID=Orders.CustomerID
   AND Orders.OrderID=[Order Details].OrderID
   AND Products.ProductID=[Order Details].ProductID
GROUP BY Customers.Country, Categories.CategoryName
ORDER BY Categories.CategoryName;
```

The two preceding SQL statements produce the same result set, but using the WHERE clause causes the join lines to disappear from the Query Design pane. Notice that the WHERE clause elements are identical to the ON elements. Updatability isn't a factor in this case, because aggregate queries aren't updatable.

Queries that use SQL aggregate functions are the foundation of Access crosstab queries. Prior to the release of SQL Server 2005, Access data projects (ADPs) didn't support crosstab queries, because T-SQL lacked the Access SQL reserved words needed to create crosstabs directly. T-SQL now has the PIVOT (and UNPIVOT) keywords, but not TRANSFORM. It remains more common for ADPs to use PivotTables to display aggregate query result sets in crosstab format.

→ For more information on summary queries, **see** "Using the SQL Aggregate Functions," **p. XXX** *(this chapter)*.

→ To learn more about crosstab queries, **see** "Creating Crosstab Queries," **p. XXX** *(this chapter)*.

TIP

> Access's graphical Query Design features are much more comprehensive than those included with Windows programming platforms, such as Visual Studio or Visual Basic Express. If you're a Visual Basic programmer (or plan to learn Visual Basic to create database front ends for Jet/Access databases), use Access to write your programs' Jet/Access SQL statements. SQL Server is the production back end preferred by most Visual Basic programmers, but Jet/Access remains an effective database engine for storing and manipulating local data on Windows clients.

11

CREATING MULTICOLUMN INNER JOINS AND SELECTING UNIQUE VALUES

You can't have more than one join that enforces referential integrity between a pair of tables, but you can have joins on multiple fields. You might, for example, want to create a query that returns the names of customers who have the same billing and shipping addresses. The billing address is the Address field of the Customers table, and the shipping address is the ShipAddress field of the Orders table. Therefore, you need to match the CustomerID fields in the two tables and Customers.Address with Orders.ShipAddress. This task requires a multicolumn inner join.

To create this example of an address-matching, multicolumn inner join, follow these steps:

1. Open a new query in Design view.
2. Add the Customers and Orders tables to the query and close the Add Tables dialog. Access creates the join on the CustomerID fields.
3. Click and drag the Address field of the Customers table's Field List box to the ShipAddress field of the Orders table's Field List box. This creates another join criterion, indicated by the new line between Address and ShipAddress (see the top pane of

Figure 11.15). The new join line between Address and ShipAddress has dots at both ends, indicating that the join is between a pair of fields that doesn't have a specified relationship, the same field name, or a primary key index.

Figure 11.15
This query has an inner join on two fields. You must manually add join criteria between fields with dissimilar names.

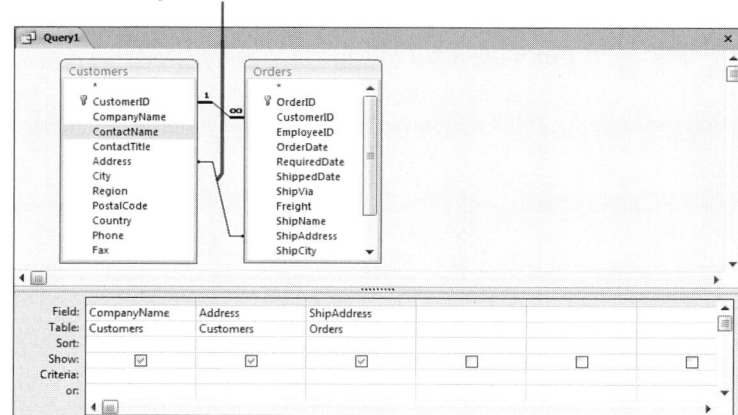

Manually Added Join criterion

4. Drag the Customers table's CompanyName and Address fields to the Field row of the first and second query columns and then drop the fields. Drag the Orders table's ShipAddress field to the query's third column and drop the field in the Field row (refer to the lower pane of Figure 11.15).

5. Click the Run button. Figure 11.16 shows the query's result set.

Figure 11.16
The result set displays records for all orders in which billing and shipping addresses are the same.

6. To eliminate the duplicate rows, you must use the Unique Values option of the Query Property Sheet. To display the Query Property Sheet, click the Design View button, right-click an empty region of the upper pane, and select Properties from the context menu.

7. By default, both the Unique Records query property and the Unique Values property are set to No. Open the Unique Values list and select Yes (see Figure 11.17). Setting the Unique Values property to Yes adds the ANSI SQL reserved word DISTINCT to the query. Close the Query Property Sheet.

Figure 11.17
Setting the Unique Values property to Yes adds the DISTINCT qualifier to the query to display only rows that have different contents.

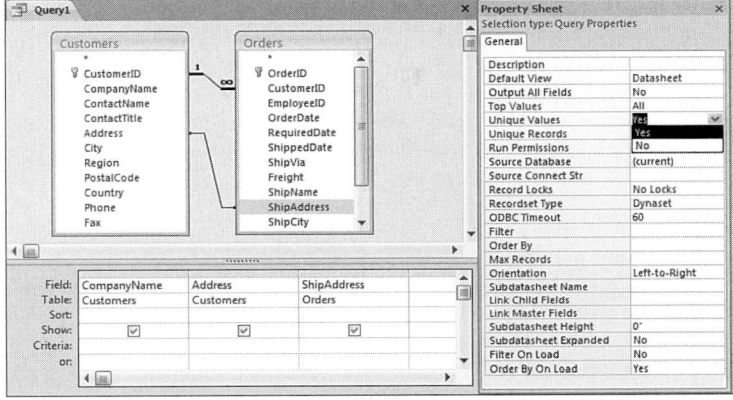

TIP

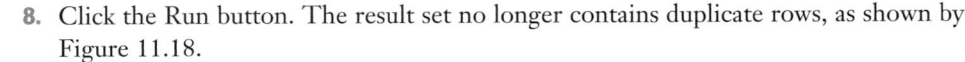

Alternatively, you can change the property settings for the Unique Records and Unique Values properties by double-clicking their text boxes in the Property Sheet. All properties with Yes/No values let you toggle their value by double-clicking.

8. Click the Run button. The result set no longer contains duplicate rows, as shown by Figure 11.18.

Figure 11.18
This result set demonstrates the effect of adding the DISTINCT qualifier to a query.

9. Click the Close Window button to close the query and then save it as **qryShipBillAddresses** for use later in the chapter.

Because most of the orders have the same billing and shipping addresses, a more useful query is to find the orders for which the customer's billing and shipping addresses differ. You can create a not-equal join for this purpose by changing the (`Customers.Address = Orders.ShipAddress`) criterion to (`Customers.Address <> Orders.ShipAddress`). If you make this change, Access displays an error message in Query Design view.

 If you encounter the Enter Parameter dialog when attempting to execute the preceding query, see the "Missing Objects in Queries" member of the "Troubleshooting" section near the end of this chapter.

USING LOOKUP FIELDS IN TABLES

Access's lookup feature for table fields lets you substitute drop-down list boxes or list boxes for conventional field text boxes. The lookup feature is a one-to-many query that the Access Lookup Wizard automatically creates for you. The lookup feature lets you provide a list of acceptable values for a particular field. When you select the value from the list, the lookup feature automatically enters the value in the field of the current record. You can specify either of the following two types of lookup field:

■ *In a field that contains foreign key values, a list of values from one or more fields of a related base table*—The purpose of this type of lookup field is to add or alter foreign key values, preserving relational integrity by assuring that foreign key values match a primary key value. A relationship must exist in the Relationships window between the tables to define a field as containing a foreign key.

As an example, the Products table of Northwind.accdb has two foreign key fields: SupplierID and CategoryID. The lookup feature of the SupplierID field displays the SupplierID and CompanyName field values from the Suppliers table in a drop-down list (see Figure 11.19).

Figure 11.19
A query against the Suppliers table generates the lookup list of the Products table's SupplierID field.

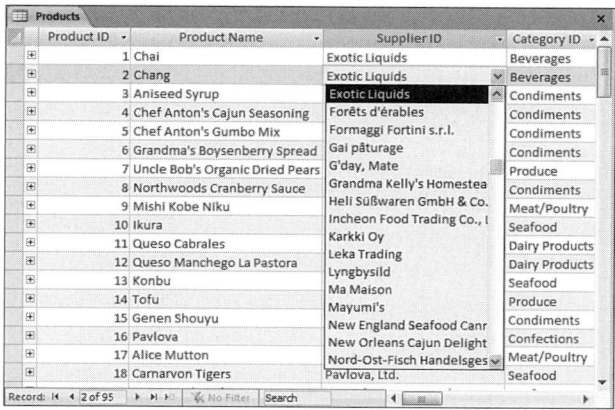

- *In any field except a single primary key field, a list of fixed values from which to select*—Field lists are equivalent to validation rules that specify allowable field values, so a fixed lookup list isn't appropriate in this case.

Access 2007 adds a new Lookup property value, Allow Multiple Values, which lets you add lists with check boxes to enable selecting multiple values. As an example, some Northwind products might have multiple suppliers. Setting the Allow Multiple Values property to Yes, which causes a permanent modification to the table that can't be undone, enables specifying more than one supplier for a product. You also can specify multiple-value lookups for fixed values.

You can add a new lookup field in either Table Design or Table Datasheet view; however, in Design view you can add the lookup feature only to an existing field. In Datasheet view, only the combo box control is displayed, even if you specify a list box control. You can display a combo box or a list box on a form that is bound to a table with lookup fields. In practice, the drop-down list (a combo box with the Limit to List property set to Yes) is the most common type of lookup field control. The following sections describe how to add foreign key and fixed-list lookup features to table fields.

ADDING A FOREIGN KEY DROP-DOWN LIST WITH THE LOOKUP WIZARD

The HRActions table you created in earlier chapters of this book is a candidate for a lookup field that uses a foreign key drop-down list of LastName and FirstName values from the Employees table. If you didn't create and populate the HRActions table, you'll find it in the \SEUA12\Chaptr06\Nwind06.accdb database on the accompanying CD-ROM. Import the HRActions table into your working copy of Northwind.accdb.

TIP

> Before using the imported HRActions table, open it in Design view, select the InitiatedBy field, and set the Text Align property value on the General property page to Left. Alternatively, you can make this change after completing the following example. Otherwise, lookup fields with text values are right-justified, which is inconsistent with the justification of other text fields.

Follow these steps to use the Lookup Wizard to change two fields of the HRActions table to lookup fields:

1. In the Database window, select the HRActions table and press Ctrl+C to copy the table to the Clipboard.

2. Press Ctrl+V to display the Paste Table As dialog. Type a name for the copy, such as **tblHRLookup**, and click the OK button to create the copy with the structure and data.

3. Open the table copy in Design view and select the InitiatedBy field. Click the Lookup tab to display the current lookup properties; a text box control has no lookup properties. Open the Data Type drop-down list and select Lookup Wizard (see Figure 11.20) to open the first dialog of the Lookup Wizard.

11

Figure 11.20
You start the Lookup Wizard from the Data Type field of the Table Design grid, despite the fact that Lookup Wizard isn't an Access data type.

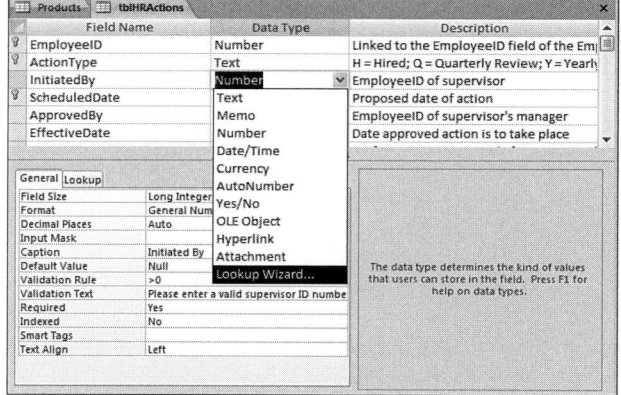

4. You want the field to look up values in another table (Employees), so accept the first (default) option (see Figure 11.21). Click Next to open the Lookup Wizard's second dialog.

Figure 11.21
The first Lookup Wizard dialog has options for the two types of lookup fields.

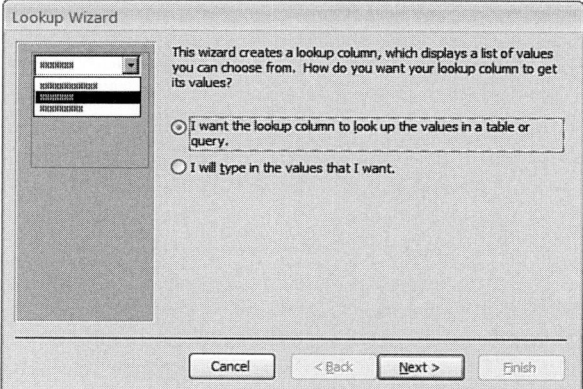

5. With the View Tables option enabled, select the Employees table to which the InitiatedBy field is related (see Figure 11.22). Click Next to display the third dialog.

6. Click the > button three times to add the EmployeeID, LastName, and FirstName fields to your lookup list (see Figure 11.23). You must include the base table's primary key field that's related to your foreign key field. Click Next for the fourth dialog.

7. The fourth dialog lets you sort the list by up to four fields. In this case, you don't need to apply a sort order, so click Next to open the fifth dialog.

8. Adjust the widths of the columns to display the first and last names without excessive trailing whitespace. The Wizard determines that EmployeeID is the key column and recommends hiding the key column by marking the check box (see Figure 11.24). Accept the recommendation, and click Next to display the fifth and final dialog.

Figure 11.22
The second Wizard dialog asks you to select the table to provide data for the lookup columns.

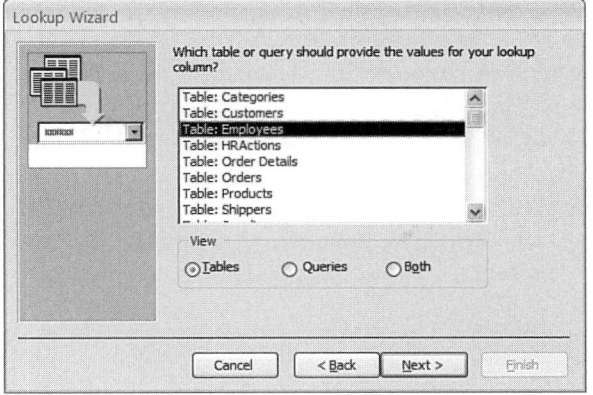

Figure 11.23
The third dialog requests you to specify the fields to include in the lookup list. You must include the table's primary key field.

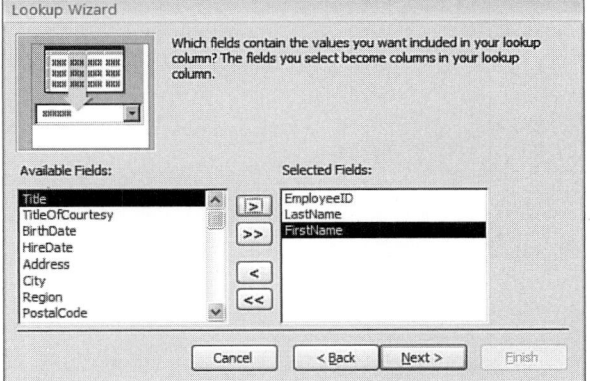

Figure 11.24
Verify the fields to appear in the lookup list, and adjust the column widths to suit the data.

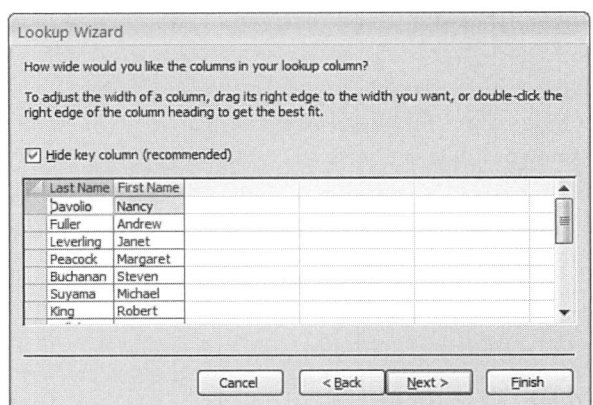

9. Accept the default InitiatedBy as the label for the lookup field in the text box of the final Wizard dialog. The label you specify doesn't overwrite an existing Caption property value. More than one person can't initiate an action, so don't mark the Allow Multiple Values check box. Click Finish to complete the wizard's work.

10. Click Yes when the message asks whether you want to save the table design and create the relationships. Your new lookup field properties appear as shown in Figure 11.25. The simple Access SQL query statement created by the wizard as the Row Source property is `SELECT [Employees].[EmployeeID], [Employees].[LastName], [Employees].[FirstName] FROM [Employees];`.

Figure 11.25
The Lookup page of the InitiatedBy field displays the lookup list property values added by the wizard.

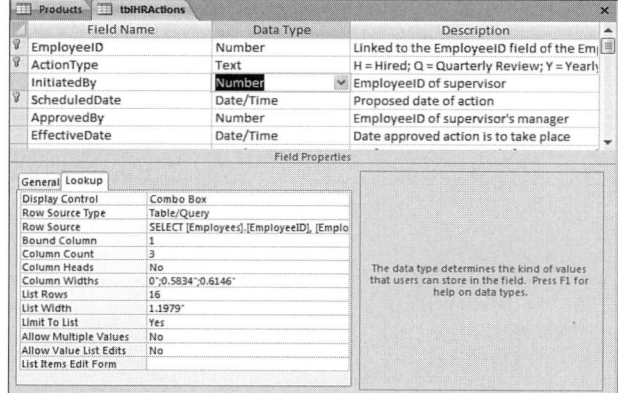

> **TIP**
>
> Preceding step 6 adds fields in their table order, but you can add fields with the Lookup Wizard in any order you prefer. Alternatively, you can rearrange columns by editing the Row Source property's SQL statement after you create the lookup list.

11. Click the Datasheet View button. Only the first visible column of the list appears in the Initiated By column. With the cursor in the Initiated By column, open the drop-down list to display the wizard's work (see Figure 11.26).

12. To change the SQL statement to open a single-column, alphabetized LastName, FirstName list, return to Design view, select the Row Source property of the InitiatedBy field in the Lookup page, and press Shift+F2 to open the Zoom dialog. Edit the SQL statement as follows:

```
SELECT Employees.EmployeeID,
    Employees.LastName & ", " & Employees.FirstName
FROM Employees
ORDER BY LastName, FirstName;
```

Click OK to close the Zoom dialog.

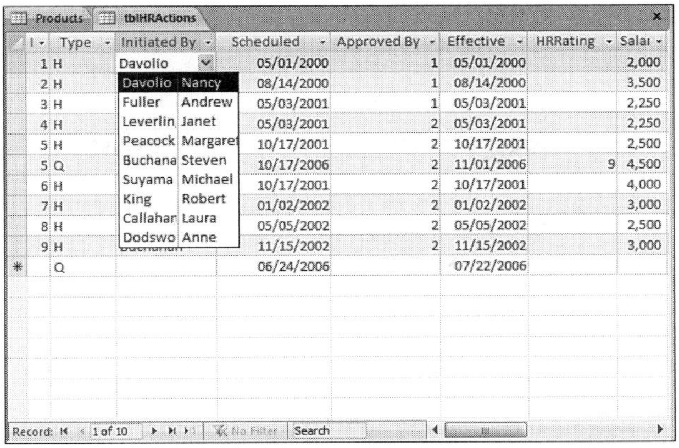

Products | tblHRActions

I	Type	Initiated By	Scheduled	Approved By	Effective	HRRating	Salary
1	H	Davolio	05/01/2000	1	05/01/2000		2,000
2	H		08/14/2000	1	08/14/2000		3,500
3	H		05/03/2001	1	05/03/2001		2,250
4	H		05/03/2001	2	05/03/2001		2,250
5	H		10/17/2001	2	10/17/2001		2,500
5	Q		10/17/2006	2	11/01/2006	9	4,500
6	H		10/17/2001	2	10/17/2001		4,000
7	H		01/02/2002	2	01/02/2002		3,000
8	H		05/05/2002	2	05/05/2002		2,500
9	H		11/15/2002	2	11/15/2002		3,000
*	Q		06/24/2006		07/22/2006		

Davolio	Nancy
Fuller	Andrew
Leverlin	Janet
Peacock	Margaret
Buchana	Steven
Suyama	Michael
King	Robert
Callahar	Laura
Dodswo	Anne

Record: 1 of 10 | No Filter | Search

Figure 11.26 The lookup list of the InitiatedBy field has LastName and FirstName columns. Some FirstName values are truncated, because the column width setting didn't compensate for the width of the vertical scroll bar. The last names in the InitiatedBy field are right-justified if you don't remove the Format property value from the field.

13. Change the value of the Column Count property to **2** and the Column Widths property to **0";1.3"**. Optionally, change the List Rows value to **9** to accommodate Northwind's nine employees without a vertical scroll bar. Click View and then click Yes to save your changes. Then open the lookup list to verify your changes (see Figure 11.27).

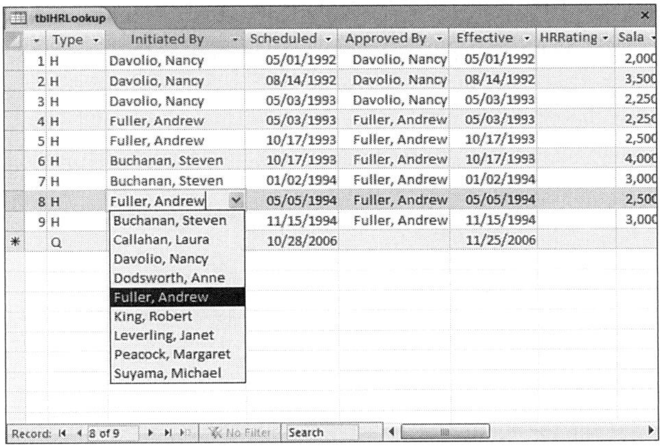

tblHRLookup

	Type	Initiated By	Scheduled	Approved By	Effective	HRRating	Sala
1	H	Davolio, Nancy	05/01/1992	Davolio, Nancy	05/01/1992		2,000
2	H	Davolio, Nancy	08/14/1992	Davolio, Nancy	08/14/1992		3,500
3	H	Davolio, Nancy	05/03/1993	Davolio, Nancy	05/03/1993		2,250
4	H	Fuller, Andrew	05/03/1993	Fuller, Andrew	05/03/1993		2,250
5	H	Fuller, Andrew	10/17/1993	Fuller, Andrew	10/17/1993		2,500
6	H	Buchanan, Steven	10/17/1993	Fuller, Andrew	10/17/1993		4,000
7	H	Buchanan, Steven	01/02/1994	Fuller, Andrew	01/02/1994		3,000
8	H	Fuller, Andrew	05/05/1994	Fuller, Andrew	05/05/1994		2,500
9	H		11/15/1994	Fuller, Andrew	11/15/1994		3,000
*	Q		10/28/2006		11/25/2006		

Buchanan, Steven
Callahan, Laura
Davolio, Nancy
Dodsworth, Anne
Fuller, Andrew
King, Robert
Leverling, Janet
Peacock, Margaret
Suyama, Michael

Record: 8 of 9 | No Filter | Search

Figure 11.27 A single-column lookup list, like that used for the EmployeeID of the Orders table, is better suited to selecting peoples' names.

TIP

> Make sure to correct the lookup field's name to the original value if the Lookup Wizard changes it. The Wizard might change the field name if it isn't the same as the base table's field name. Although Name AutoCorrect can handle field name changes, it's a much better database design practice to freeze the names of tables and fields. Change table and field names during the development process only if absolutely necessary.

→ If you need a list of the properties of the combo box control created by the Wizard, **see** "Adding Combo and List Boxes" **p. 660**.

ADDING A FIXED-VALUE LOOKUP LIST TO A TABLE

You add the alternative lookup feature—a fixed list of values—using the Lookup Wizard in much the same way as you created the foreign key lookup list in the preceding section. To add a fixed-list lookup feature to the ActionType field of your copy of the HRActions table, follow these steps:

1. In Design view, select the ActionType field, open the Data Type list, and select Lookup Wizard to launch the Wizard.

2. In the first Lookup Wizard dialog, select the I Will Type in the Values That I Want option and click the Next button.

3. In the second Lookup Wizard dialog, type **2** in the Number of Columns text box and press the Tab key to create the second list column.

4. Type **H, Hired; Q, Quarterly Review; Y, Yearly Review; S, Salary Adj.; R, Hourly Rate Adj.; B, Bonus Adj.; C, Commission Adj.; T, Terminated** in the Col1 and Col2 columns of eight rows. (Don't include the commas and semicolons.) Adjust the width of the columns to suit the entries (see Figure 11.28). Click the Next button to display the Wizard's third dialog.

Figure 11.28
Specify the number of columns and type values in the second Wizard dialog for a lookup value list.

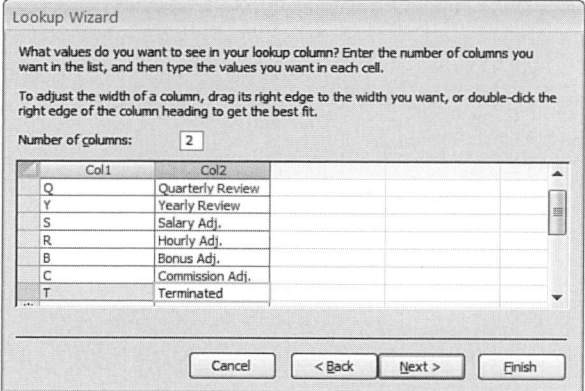

5. The ActionType field uses single-character abbreviations for the type of HRActions, so select Col1 as the "field that uniquely identifies the row." (The ActionType field doesn't uniquely identify the row; Col1 contains the single-character value that you want to insert into the field.) Click the Next button to display the fourth and final Wizard dialog.

6. Accept ActionType as the label for your column and click the Finish button. The lookup properties for the ActionType field appear as shown in Figure 11.29. The Row Source Type is Value List. The Row Source contains the following values:

```
"H";"Hired";"Q";"Quarterly Review";"Y";"Yearly Review";
"S";"Salary Adj.";"R";"Hourly Rate Adj.";"B";
"Bonus Adj.";"C";"Commission Adj.";"T";"Terminated"
```

Figure 11.29
Compare the Lookup properties page for a lookup value list with that for a lookup list based on a related table (refer to Figure 11.25).

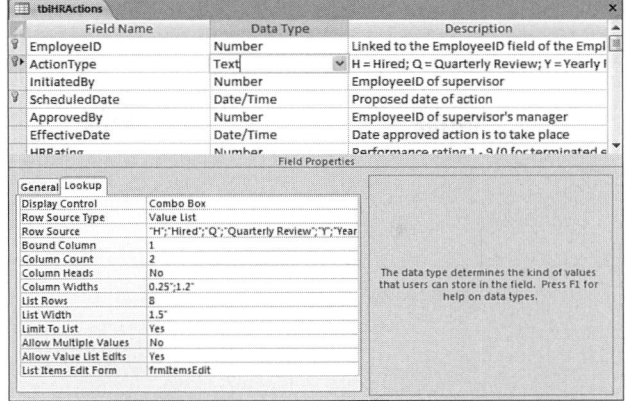

7. Click the Datasheet View button and save the changes to your table. Place the cursor in the Type column, and open the fixed value list to check the wizard's work (see Figure 11.30).

Figure 11.30
Datasheet view displays the fixed-value lookup list for the ActionType field.

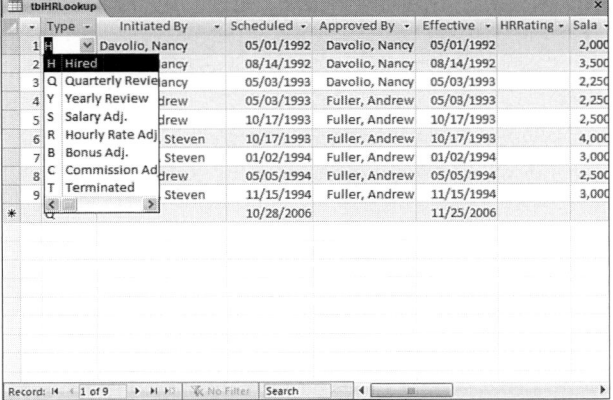

8. If you don't want the abbreviation to appear in the drop-down list, change the first entry of the Column Widths property value to 0.

TIP

> To remove the lookup feature from a field, select the field, click the Lookup tab, and choose Text Box from the Display Control drop-down list.

> **N O T E**
>
> Access 2007 has an Edit List Items dialog that you can use to edit the value list of single-column lookup lists. If you use a single-column combo list, a builder button appears in the Row Source property value text box and the context menu for the field in Datasheet View has an Edit List Items choice.

CREATING MULTIVALUED LOOKUP FIELDS

Multivalued lookup fields are a new Access 2007 feature that lets you emulate a many-to-many relationship between foreign and primary keys of related tables. As an example, each stock-keeping unit in the original Northwind Products table has a single supplier. This book's version of the Products table has 18 generic (not trademarked) Korean and Chinese food products added, and the Suppliers table has two Korean and two Chinese suppliers added. The new Korean suppliers provide nonbranded kimchi and bean pastes, and the Chinese suppliers do the same for traditional sauces. Therefore, the Products table's SupplierID column is a good candidate for conversion to a multivalued lookup field.

> **N O T E**
>
> Another reason for using the SupplierID column is to illustrate issues with displaying multiple items that have lengthy text. Supplier names include commas, which also are the item separator character, so the display can become ambiguous *and* difficult to read.

You first create a foreign-key or value-list lookup field by the procedures illustrated in the two preceding sections, and then set the Allow Multiple Values property value to Yes. This is an irreversible process, so it's a good practice to make a backup copy of the table to be modified—Products for this example—before making the change.

To change the SupplierID column's single-value lookup list to a multivalued lookup list and generate the intermediary table for the underlying many-to-many relationship between the Products and Suppliers table, do the following:

1. Open the Relationships window and temporarily delete the relationship between the Suppliers and Products tables. You can't change the data type of the SupplierID field when it has a relationship defined.

2. Open the Products table in Design view and select the SupplierID column, which has a single-value lookup combo box.

3. In the Lookup properties sheet, change the value of the Allow Multiple Values property to Yes (see Figure 11.31).

4. Click the Datasheet View button, click Yes to save the table, and click Yes again to acknowledge that making this change is irreversible.

5. Open the SupplierID lookup list for one of the kimchi products, such as Hot Cabbage Kimchi (Jar), whose current supplier is Incheon Food Trading Co., Ltd., as indicated by the marked check box.

Figure 11.31
Changing the Allow Multiple Values property value to Yes adds check boxes to the conventional lookup combo box list.

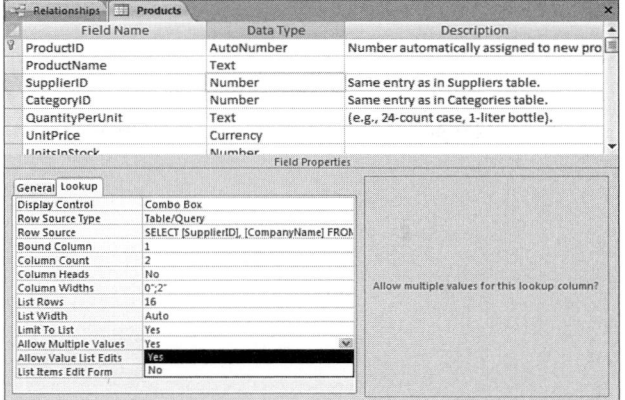

6. Scroll the list to the other kimchi supplier, Seoul Kimchi Co., Ltd., and mark the adjacent check box (see Figure 11.32). Click OK to close the list and save the selection.

Figure 11.32
Add suppliers of the selected product by marking the check boxes in the multiple-values combo box list.

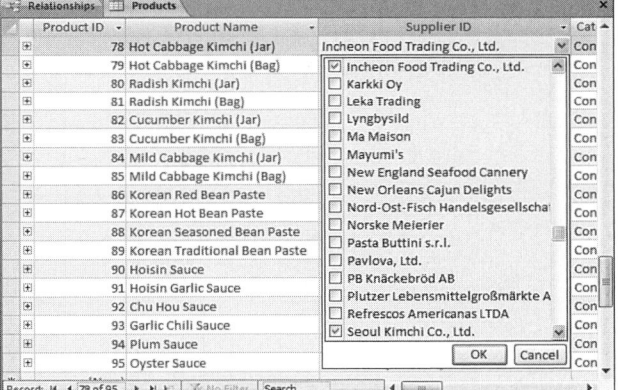

7. Increase the width of the SupplierID datasheet column to display the two suppliers' CompanyName values (see Figure 11.33). Add second suppliers for a few other Asian food products.

8. Click the Relationships tab and notice that the Products field list's SupplierID field has changed to a node with a SupplierID.Value property.

9. Attempt to create a relationship by dragging the SupplierID.Value property to the Suppliers tables' SupplierID field, marking the Edit Relationship dialog's Enforce Referential Integrity check box, and clicking OK. If the Products table is open, you receive the error message shown in Figure 11.34 when you click Create.

Figure 11.33
Displaying two or more suppliers in a multivalued lookup field requires increasing the field's display width greatly.

Figure 11.34
This message box displays the name of the hidden intermediary table to support the many-to-many relationship: 'f_<GUID>_TempField*0'.

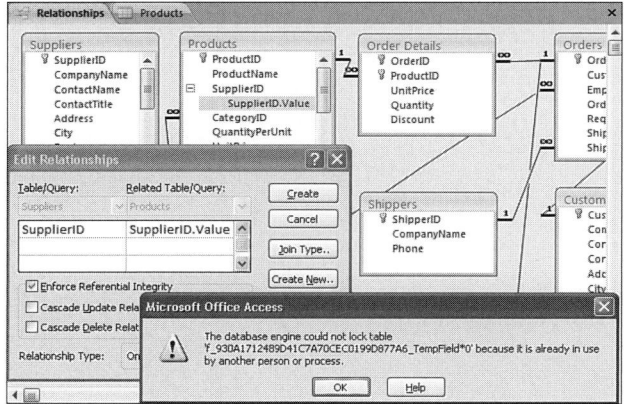

10. Click OK and Cancel to return to the Relationships window, close the Products window, save the layout, and re-create the relationship between the Products and Suppliers tables with referential integrity supported (see Figure 11.35).

11. Close the Relationships window and save the layout changes.

Specifying multivalued fields in queries requires a two- or three-part name, such as [Products].SupplierID.Value. To create a query that displays multiple rows for products with multiple suppliers, do the following:

1. Create a new query in Design view. Add the Products and Suppliers tables.

2. Add the ProductID, ProductName, and SupplierID.Value fields from the Products table as well as the CompanyName field from the Suppliers table to the query (see Figure 11.36).

Figure 11.35
Creating a relationship that maintains referential integrity requires that neither table be opened in Design or Datasheet view.

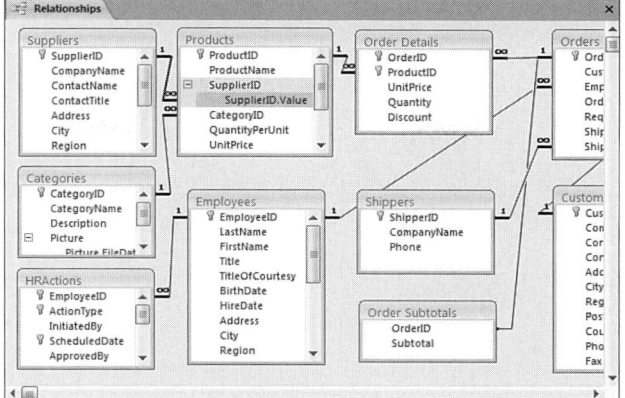

Figure 11.36
Use the Value property of multivalued fields in queries.

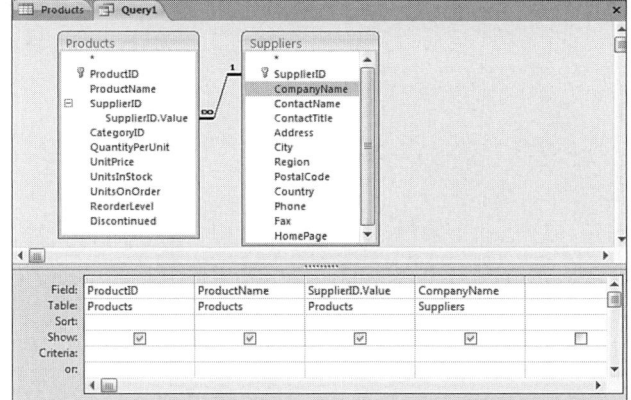

3. Click the Run button and verify that the query returns a row for each product-supplier combination, as shown in Figure 11.37, for Korean food products.

4. Save the query with an appropriate name, such as **qryProductsSuppliersMV**.

> **NOTE**
>
> The lookup feature has generated controversy among seasoned database developers. Relational database purists object to embedding queries as table properties. Another objection to the use of foreign key drop-down lists is that it is easy for uninitiated users to inadvertently change data in a table after opening the list. If you're developing Access applications for others to use, user access to tables should be limited to forms, and lookup operations should use combo or list boxes on forms. Access 2007's lookup feature, however, is a useful tool, especially for new database users creating applications for their own use.
>
> Multivalued fields are even more controversial than lookup fields. Displaying multiple entity values in a single field, even if an intermediary table generates the values, gives

continues

continued

users the impression that storing multiple entity values, such as foreign key values, in a single field is an acceptable practice for relational databases. Microsoft added this feature as an accommodation for SharePoint lists, which aren't relational tables. Use multivalue fields sparingly—if at all—because they won't upsize to SQL Server tables correctly.

Figure 11.37
The Products.
SupplierID.Value
property returns a
row for each product-
supplier combination.

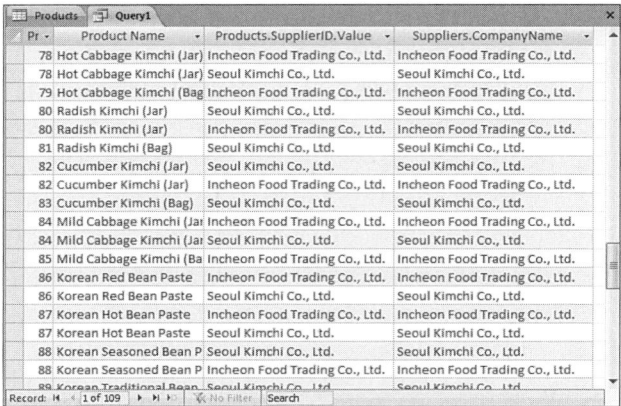

ADDING SUBDATASHEETS TO A TABLE OR QUERY

Subdatasheets are closely related to lookup fields, but serve a different purpose. *Subdatasheets* display related table values in an embedded datasheet, whereas lookup fields display base table values in a combo box or list box. Both of these Access features depend on the equivalent of one-to-many queries; the difference between the queries is that the many side of a subdatasheet is a related table, whereas a lookup field uses a query against a related table to supply the many side values.

You also can cascade subdatasheets to display related data of multiple joined tables, a feature not applicable to lookup fields, but a table or query can't have more than one subdatasheet. Figure 11.38 illustrates the Customers table displaying the Orders subdatasheet for Alfreds Futterkiste with embedded sub-subdatasheets that display Order Details records.

CAUTION

Editing data in subdatasheets can lead to serious data entry errors. For example, if you use the Order Details subdatasheet to change an entry in the Product field, the UnitPrice value doesn't change to correspond to the price for the new product. Subdatasheets are dangerous; if you decide to use them, they should only be used to view, not edit, vital business data.

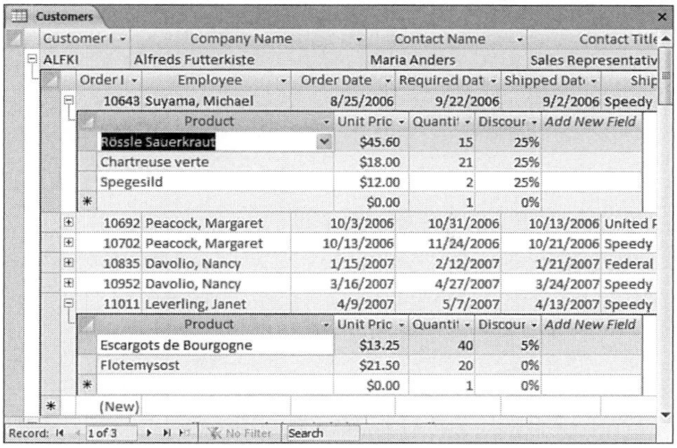

Figure 11.38
The Customers table has a two-level sub-datasheet hierarchy. Note the + and - column at the left of both the Customers and Orders sub-datasheets.

→ For more information on subdatasheets, **see** "Table Properties for Subdatasheets," **p. 208**.

TABLE SUBDATASHEETS

Some of the tables of Northwind.accdb already have subdatasheets; Employees doesn't. To add an HRActions subdatasheet to the Employees table, follow these steps:

1. Verify in the Relationships window that a relationship exists between the EmployeeID fields of the HRActions and Employees tables.

2. Open the Employees table in Datasheet view.

3. Click one of the + symbols in the first column of the Employees datasheet to open the Insert Subdatasheet dialog.

4. Select the HRActions table in the list. The EmployeeID foreign key field of the HRActions table appears in the Link Child Fields drop-down list, and the EmployeeID field of the Employees table appears in the Link Master Fields list (see Figure 11.39). The HRAction table is included in the Relationships window; the relationship supplies the default values for the two drop-down lists.

> **NOTE**
> The Link Master Fields and Link Child Fields values create a one-to-many join on the specified fields.

5. Click OK to add the subdatasheet and close the dialog. The subdatasheet for the selected record opens automatically.

6. Click one or two of the + symbols in the Employees datasheet to display the newly added subdatasheets (see Figure 11.40).

Figure 11.39
Clicking the + symbol in a row of a table that doesn't have a subdatasheet opens the Insert Subdatasheet dialog.

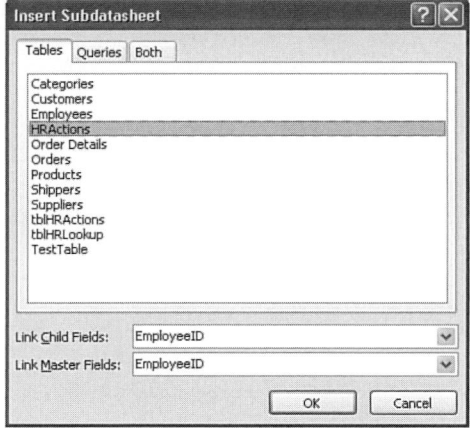

Figure 11.40
Only one HRActions record exists for each employee at this point.

 7. Change to Table Design view, right-click the design grid (upper pane), and choose Properties to display the Table Property sheet. The selections you make in the Insert Subdatasheet dialog appear in the subdatasheet-related properties of the table (see Figure 11.41).

NOTE

The child (foreign key) field, EmployeeID, doesn't appear as a column of the subdatasheet. When you add a new record in the subdatasheet, Access automatically inserts the primary key value of the selected base-table record into the related record. In this case, Access adds the EmployeeID value from the Employees field to the EmployeeID value of the HRActions table.

Figure 11.41
You also can add a subdatasheet by opening the Table Property Sheet and selecting a table or query from the Subdatasheet name list.

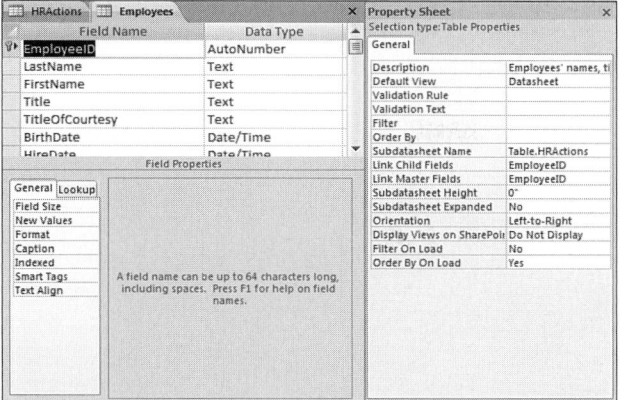

TIP

> The default value of the Subdatasheet Name property for new tables you create is [Auto], which adds the column of boxed + symbols to a new table datasheet. To open the Add Subdatasheet dialog for a new table, choose Insert, Subdatasheet. Alternatively, you can set the subdatasheet properties directly in the Table Properties sheet. To remove a subdatasheet, set the Subdatasheet Name property value to [None]. If you remove a subdatasheet from a table, setting Subdatasheet Name to [Auto] displays the boxed + symbols and lets you open a new subdatasheet in Datasheet view.

QUERY SUBDATASHEETS

If you don't want your subdatasheet to display all the related table's columns, you must design a simple select query with only the desired fields and then use the query to populate the subdatasheet. As an example, you can minimize the width of the Orders subdatasheet of the Customers table by doing the following:

1. In query Design view, create a simple SELECT query that includes only the OrderID, CustomerID (required for the master-child join), OrderDate, ShippedDate, and ShippedVia fields of the Orders table.

2. Click the empty area of the top pane to open the Query Properties sheet, and set the Recordset Type property to Snapshot. Selecting Snapshot creates a read-only subdatasheet to prevent editing. Close the query and save it as **qryShortOrders**.

3. Open the Customers table in Design view, open the Table Property Sheet, and select Query.qryShortOrders from the Subdatasheet Name list. CustomerID remains the value of the linked fields.

4. Return to Datasheet view, saving your changes. The expanded subdatasheet appears as shown in Figure 11.42, without the + sign column. The query is read-only, so the subdatasheet has no tentative append record and you can't edit the data.

Figure 11.42
Use a Snapshot query to create a read-only subdatasheet.

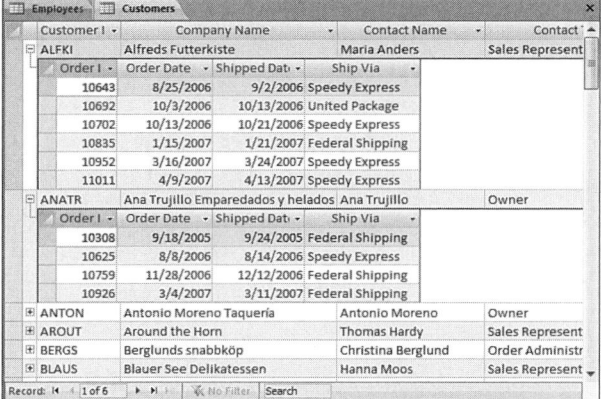

5. In Design view, create another select query that includes all fields (*) of the Order Details table. Open the Query Property Sheet, set the Recordset Type property value to Snapshot, close the windows, and save the query as **qryShortOrderDetails**.

6. Close the Customers table, open qryShortOrders in Design view, click an empty area of the upper pane, and choose Properties to open the Query Property Sheet.

7. Select Query.qryShortOrderDetails in the Subdatasheet Name field and then type **OrderID** in the two Link...Fields text boxes (see Figure 11.43). You must type the field names because you haven't established a relationship between the query and table in the Relationships window.

Figure 11.43
After adding Query.qryOrderDetails as the value of the Subdatasheet Name property, you manually set the Link Child Fields and Link Master Fields property values.

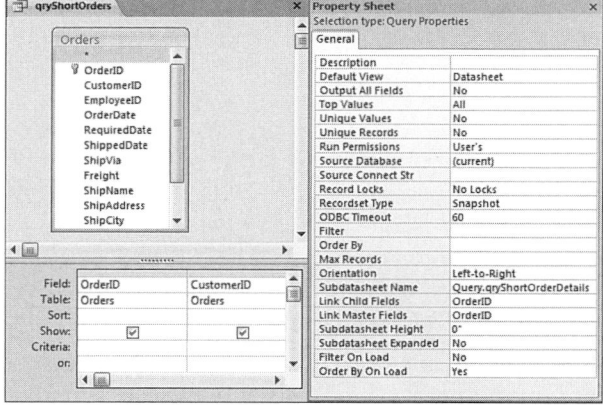

8. Run the query and then expand one or more of the subdatasheets to test your work (see Figure 11.44).

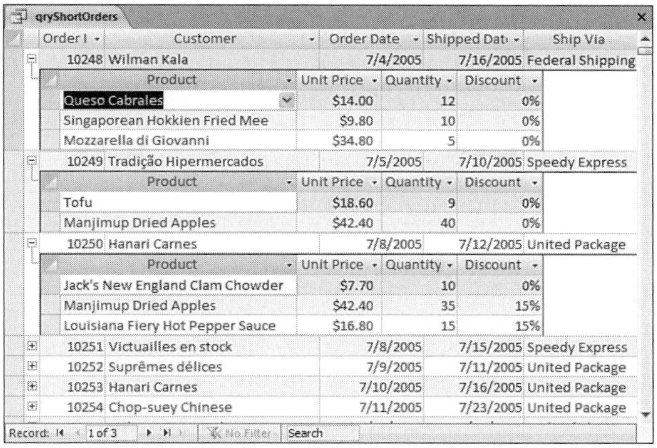

Figure 11.44
The read-only
qryShortOrders query
has a read-only query
subdatasheet
based on
qryShortOrderDetails.

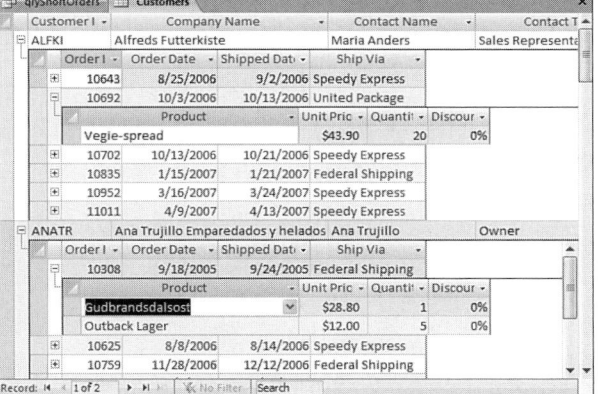

9. Close qryShortOrders, save your changes, open the Customers table, and display the
   subdatasheets. The new version of the Customers table appears as shown in Figure
   11.45. You can open the Products list, but you can't change the value of the Product
   column.

Figure 11.45
The subdatasheet and
sub-subdatasheet are
read-only, but the
Customers table con-
tinues to have read-
write attributes, as
indicated by its tenta-
tive append record.

OUTER, SELF, AND THETA JOINS

The preceding sections of this chapter described the inner join, which is the most common
type of join in database applications. Access also lets you create three other joins: outer, self,
and theta. The following sections describe these three less-common types of joins, which
also apply to SQL Server views, table-returning functions, and stored procedures.

CREATING OUTER JOINS

Outer joins let you display the fields of all records in a table participating in a query, regardless of whether corresponding records exist in the joined table. Access lets you choose between left and right outer joins.

A left outer join query displays all records in the first table you specify, regardless of whether matching records exist in the second table. For example, *Table1* LEFT JOIN *Table2* displays all records in *Table2*. Conversely, a right outer join query displays all records in the second table, regardless of a record's existence in the first table. Records in the second table without corresponding records in the first table usually, but not necessarily, are orphan records; these kinds of records can have a many-to-one relationship to another table.

To practice creating a left outer join to detect whether records are missing for an employee in the HRActions table, follow these steps:

1. Open the Employees table and add a record for a new (bogus) employee. You need only add values for the LastName and FirstName fields.

2. Open a new query and add the Employees and HRActions tables.

3. Drag the EmployeeID field symbol to the EmployeeID field of HRActions to create an inner join between these fields if Access doesn't create the join automatically.

4. Select and drag the LastName and FirstName fields of the Employees table to columns 1 and 2 of the Query Design grid. Select and drag the ActionType and ScheduledDate fields of the HRActions table to columns 3 and 4.

5. Click the line joining EmployeeID with EmployeeID to select it, as shown in Figure 11.46. The thickness of the center part of the line increases to indicate the selection. (In Figure 11.46, the two Field List boxes are separated so that the thin section of the join line is apparent.)

Figure 11.46
Double-clicking the thin region of the join line opens the Join Properties dialog.

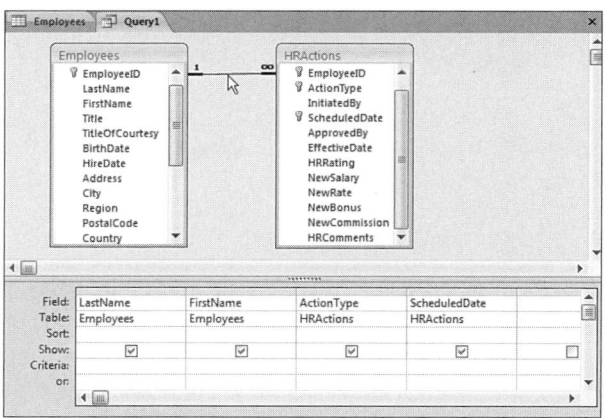

6. Double-click the thin section of the join line to open the Join Properties dialog. (Double-clicking either of the line's thick sections displays the Query Property Sheet.) Type 1 is a conventional inner join, type 2 is a left join, and type 3 is a right join.

7. Select a type 2 join—a left join—by selecting option 2 (see Figure 11.47). Click OK to close the dialog.

Figure 11.47
Select the option for a type 2 join, which includes all records in the left table and only those records of the right table where the two column values match.

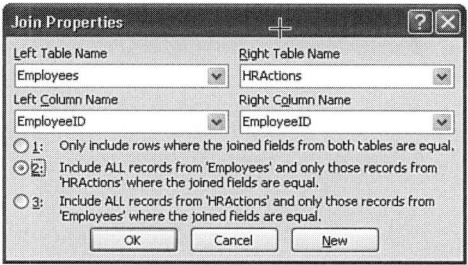

NOTE

Access adds an arrowhead to the line that joins EmployeeID and EmployeeID. The direction of the arrow, left to right, indicates that you've created a left join between the tables, assuming that you haven't moved the field lists from their original position in the table.

8. Click the Run button to display the result of the left join query. In Figure 11.48, the employee you added without a record in the HRActions table appears in the result table's last active row. (Your query result set might differ, depending on the number of entries that you made when creating the HRActions table.)

Figure 11.48
A record for EmployeeID 10 with no HRActions record(s) appears in this left outer join.

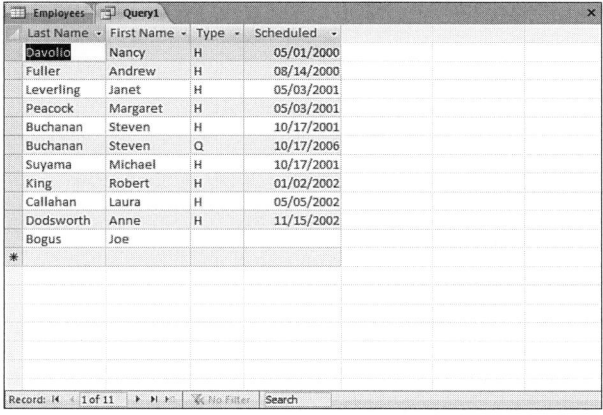

9. Close, but don't save, the query, and then delete the bogus record in the Employees table.

If you could add an HR department action for a nonexistent EmployeeID (referential integrity rules for HRActions table prevent you from doing so), a right join would show the invalid entry with blank employee name fields.

CREATING SELF-JOINS

Self-joins relate values in a single table. Creating a self-join requires that you add a copy of the table to the query and then add a join between the related fields. An example of self-join use is to determine whether supervisors have approved HRActions that they initiated, which is prohibited by the fictitious personnel manual for Northwind Traders.

To create this kind of self-join for the HRActions table, follow these steps:

1. Open a new query and add the HRActions table.
2. Add another copy of the HRActions table to the query by clicking the Add button again. Access names the copy HRActions_1. Close the Show Tables dialog.
3. Drag the original table's InitiatedBy field to the copied table's ApprovedBy field (look ahead to the top pane of Figure 11.49).
4. Drag the EmployeeID and InitiatedBy fields of the original table, and the ApprovedBy and ActionType fields of the copy of the HRActions table, to the Field row of columns 1–4, respectively, of the Query Design grid (see Figure 11.49).

Figure 11.49
A self-join returns rows for which values of two fields in the same table are equal.

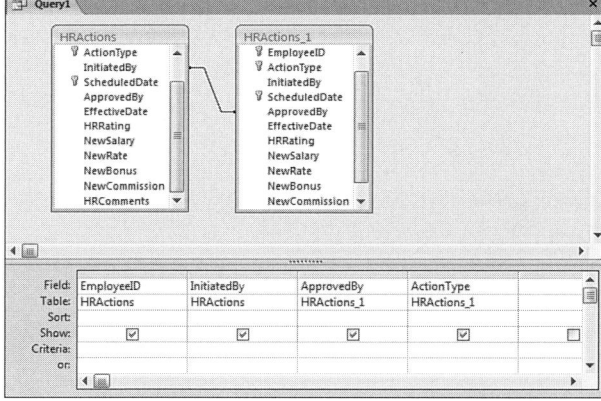

5. With self-joins, you must specify that only unique values are included. (If you don't specify unique values, the query returns every row.) Right-click an empty area in the Query Design window's upper pane, choose <u>P</u>roperties, set the value of the Query Property Sheet's Unique Values property to Yes, and close the Query Property Sheet.

6. Click the Run button to display the records in which the same employee initiated and approved an HR department action, as shown in Figure 11.50. In this case, EmployeeID 1 (Nancy Davolio) was the first employee; EmployeeID 2 (Andrew Fuller)

is a vice-president and can override personnel policy. (Your results might differ, depending on the entries you made in the HRActions table.)

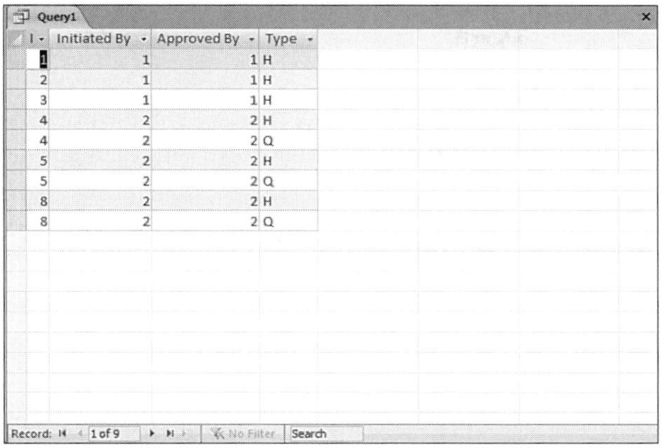

Figure 11.50
This datasheet displays the result set of the design of Figure 11.49. If you don't set the Unique Values property to Yes, the result set has 27 rows.

I	Initiated By	Approved By	Type
1	1	1	H
2	1	1	H
3	1	1	H
4	2	2	H
4	2	2	Q
5	2	2	H
5	2	2	Q
8	2	2	H
8	2	2	Q

Record: ◄ ◄ 1 of 9 ► ►┤ No Filter Search

CREATING NOT-EQUAL (THETA) JOINS WITH CRITERIA

Most joins are based on fields with equal values, but sometimes you need to create a join on unequal fields. Joins that you create graphically in Access are restricted to conventional equi-joins and outer joins. You can create the equivalent of a not-equal theta join by applying a criterion to one of the two fields you want to test for not-equal values.

Finding customers that have different billing and shipping addresses, as mentioned previously, is an example in which a not-equal theta join is useful. To create such a join, follow these steps:

1. Create a new query and add the Customers and Orders tables.

2. Select the Customers table's CompanyName and Address fields and the Orders table's ShipAddress field. Drag them to the Query Design grid's first three columns.

3. Type **<>Customers.Address** in the Criteria row of the ShipAddress column. The Query Design window appears as shown in Figure 11.51.

> **NOTE**
>
> Typing **<>Orders.ShipAddress** in the Address column gives the same result as **<>Customers.Address** in the ShipAddress column.

4. Right-click an empty area in the Query Design window's upper pane and choose Properties to open the Query Property Sheet and set the value of the Unique Values property to Yes. Otherwise, the query returns a record for every order with a different ship address.

Figure 11.51
Not-equal joins require a not-equal (<>) *WHERE* clause criterion to establish the join.

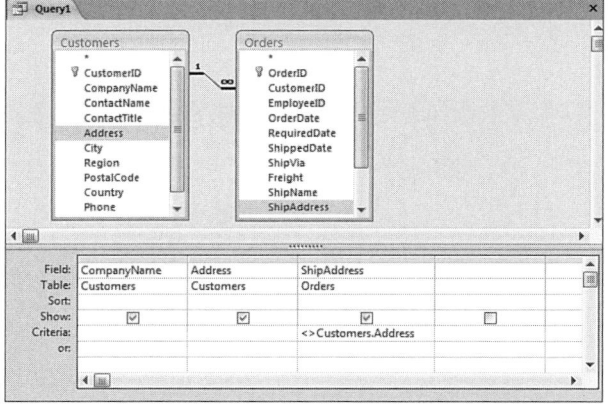

5. Run the query. Only the records for customers that placed orders with different billing and shipping addresses appear, as shown in Figure 11.52.

Figure 11.52
The result set of the not-equal join displays customers with different shipping and billing addresses. If you don't set the Unique Values property to Yes, the query returns 51 rows.

6. Click the Close Window button and save your query if you want.

NOTE

As mentioned in the earlier "Creating Multicolumn Inner Joins and Selecting Unique Values" section, you can create a theta join by changing the operator of an equi-join criterion from = to <>. If you do this, you receive an error message every time you open the query in Design view.

UPDATING TABLE DATA WITH QUERIES

Queries you create with the Unique Values property set to Yes to add the ANSI SQL DISTINCT modifier to the SQL statement aren't updatable. If you set the Unique Records property, instead of the Unique Values property, to Yes, some queries are updatable because Unique Records substitutes Access SQL's DISTINCTROW modifier for DISTINCT.

> **NOTE**
>
> T-SQL doesn't support Access SQL's DISTINCTROW modifier, and the rules that determine the updatability of SQL Server views and table-returning, user-defined functions differ from those of Access. Chapter 21, "Moving from Access Queries to Transact-SQL," covers updatability issues with SQL Server views and functions. Recordsets returned by SQL Server stored procedures aren't updatable.

Unique Records queries create Recordset objects of the updatable Dynaset type. You can't update table data with a query unless you see the tentative (blank) append record (with the asterisk in the select button) at the end of the query result table. The next few sections describe the conditions under which you can update a record of a table included in a query. The following sections also discuss how to use the Output Field Property Sheet to format query-data display and editing.

> **NOTE**
>
> You can't set both the Unique Values and Unique Records properties to Yes—these choices are mutually exclusive. In Access 2007, the default setting of both the Unique Values and Unique Records properties is No.

CHARACTERISTICS THAT DETERMINE WHETHER YOU CAN UPDATE A QUERY

Adding new records to tables or updating existing data in tables included in a query is a definite advantage in some circumstances. Correcting data errors that appear when you run the query is especially tempting. Unfortunately, you can't append or update records in many queries that you create. The following properties of a query prevent you from appending and updating records:

- The Unique Values property is set to Yes in the Query Property Sheet.
- The Recordset Type property is set to Snapshot in the Query Property Sheet.
- Self-joins are used in the query.
- Access SQL aggregate functions, such as Sum(), are employed in the query. Crosstab queries, for example, use SQL aggregate functions.
- The query has three or more tables with many-to-one-to-many relationships. Most queries with indirect relationships fall in this category.

11

- No primary key field(s) with a unique (No Duplicates) index exist for the one table in a one-to-many relationship.

When designing a query to use as the basis of a form for data entry or editing, make sure that none of the preceding properties apply to the query.

TIP

> You can't edit data returned by a query with three or more tables in Query Datasheet view, unless the query is one-to-many-to-many, but you can update values in other types of three-table queries in forms that are bound to the query. To make the query updatable with forms, set the Recordset Type property value to Dynaset (Inconsistent Updates).

If none of the preceding properties apply to the query or any table within the query, you can append records to and update fields of queries in the following:

- A single-table query
- Both tables in a one-to-one relationship
- The many table in a one-to-many relationship or the most-many table in a one-to-many-to-many relationship
- The one table in a one-to-many relationship if none of the fields of the many table appear in the query

Updating the one table in a one-to-many query is a special case in Access. To enable updates to this table, follow these steps:

1. Add to the query the primary key field or fields of the one table and additional fields to update. You don't need to add the primary key field if its Access data type is AutoNumber.
2. Add the foreign key field or fields of the many table that correspond to the key field or fields of the one table; this step is required to select the appropriate records for updating.
3. Add the criteria to select the records for updating to the fields chosen in step 2.
4. Click the Show box so that the many table fields don't appear in the query.

After following these steps, you can edit the nonkey fields of the one table. You can't, however, alter the values of key fields that have relationships with records in the many table, unless you specify Cascade Update Related Fields in the Relationships window's Edit Relationships dialog for the join. Otherwise, such a modification violates referential integrity.

By adding lookup fields to tables, you often can avoid writing one-to-many queries and precisely following the preceding rules to make such queries updatable. For example, the Orders table, which includes three lookup fields (CustomerID, EmployeeID, and ShipVia) is updatable. If you want to allow updates in Datasheet view (called *browse updating*), using lookup fields is a simpler approach than creating an updatable query. Most database developers, however, consider simple browse updating to be a poor practice because of the potential for inadvertent data entry errors. As mentioned earlier, browse updating with lookup fields is especially prone to data entry errors.

→ For more discussion of the browse-mode method and other alternatives, **see** "In the Real World— Alternatives to Action Queries," **p. 575**.

TAKING ADVANTAGE OF ACCESS'S ROW FIX-UP FEATURE

Access queries and SQL Server views have a row fix-up feature (called AutoLookup by Access) that fills in query data when you add a new record or change the value of the foreign key of a many-side record. To take advantage of row fix-up, your query must include the foreign key value, not the primary key value of the join.

Northwind Traders' Orders Qry is an example of a query that uses row fix-up. Orders Qry includes every field of the Customers and Orders tables, *except* the CustomerID field of the Customers table. To demonstrate row fix-up, do the following:

1. Open the Orders Qry in Datasheet view, and scroll to the tentative append record. Alternatively, press Ctrl+End, Home, and ↓ to avoid the scrolling exercise.

2. Tab to the Customer column, open the lookup list, which is bound to the CustomerID field of the Customers table, and select a customer for a new order. The edited record symbol replaces the asterisk, and the datasheet adds a new tentative append row.

3. Scroll the columns to the right until you reach the Address column, which displays the Address field of the Customers table. Row fix-up automatically enters data from the Customer table's record for the selected customer (see Figure 11.53).

Columns from Customers Table

Columns from Orders Table

Figure 11.53
Row fix-up automatically adds data from the table on the one side of a one-to-many relationship when you add a new row. The first three columns of the datasheet are frozen to demonstrate row fix-up when adding a new record to the Orders table.

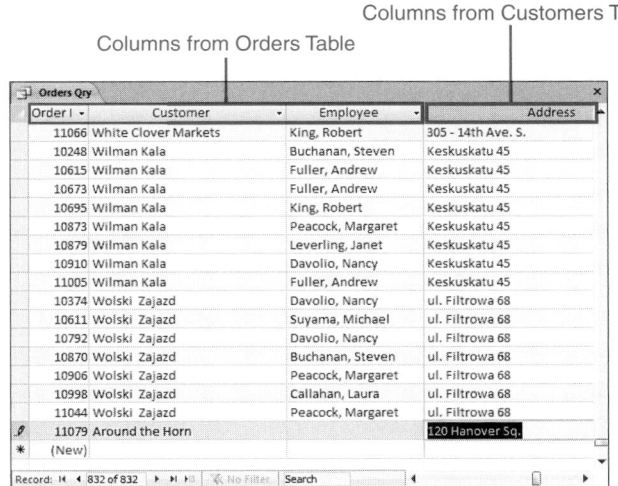

4. Press Esc to cancel the new record addition.

Row fix-up is more useful for forms that are bound to a query than for queries that update data in Datasheet view. Orders Qry is the data source for the sample Orders form. When you add a new order with this form, row fix-up automatically updates its customer data.

FORMATTING DATA WITH THE QUERY FIELD PROPERTY SHEET

The display format of data in queries is inherited from the format of the data in the tables that underlie the query. You can override the table format by using the `Format(ColumnName, FormatString)` function to create a calculated field. In this case, however, the column isn't updatable.

 Access provides an easier query column formatting method—the Field Property Sheet, which you can use to format the display of query data. You also can create an input mask to aid in updating the query data. To open the Field Property Sheet, place the cursor in the Field cell of the query column that you want to format and then click the Properties button of the toolbar. Figure 11.54 shows the Field Property Sheet for the OrderDate column of the Orders Qry. Specifying formats in queries lets you alter the column's display format without affecting the display of table fields.

Figure 11.54
Access's Medium Date format (dd-mmm-yy) doesn't comply with Y2K requirements. To specify a four-year Medium Date format for all Windows operating systems, assign the dd-mmm-yyyy format.

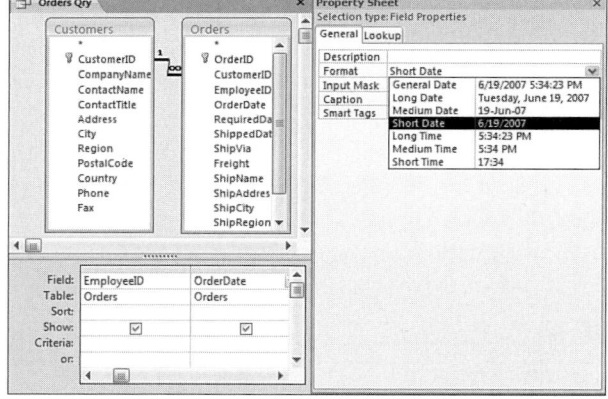

By default, Access 2007's General Date, Long Date, and Short Date formats display four-digit years, which is required for Year 2000 (Y2K) conformance. (Four-digit years is the default for Windows Vista, XP, and 2000.) You can alter the default Short Date or Long Date format in text boxes of the Date page of Control Panel's Customize Regional Options dialog. (Windows 2000's tool is called Regional Options.) Systemwide settings specify the General Date, Long Date, and Short Date formats, but don't affect the Medium Date style. To obtain a four-digit year display with Medium Date format, you must type the Format descriptor string—**dd-mmm-yyyy**—in the Format text box. Most sample tables in Northwind.accdb have the custom dd-mmm-yyyy format applied.

NOTE

The format symbol for month in the [Customize] Regional Options dialog is "M", not "m", which is the systemwide symbol for minutes. Access and VBA use "n" for minutes.

TIP

Always use the default Short Date and Long Date systemwide formats. Don't depend on users to change their default formats. If you want to specify two-digit day and month values, for example, use a custom date format, such as mm/dd/yyyy.

The Field Property Sheet displays the following subset of the properties that apply to a query's fields:

- *Description* lets you enter the text to appear in the status bar when the user selects the field in Datasheet view.

- *Format* lets you control the appearance of the data in Datasheet view, such as Short Date.

- *Input Mask* lets you specify the format for entering data, such as 99/99/0000. (To create an input mask that is appropriate for the field data type, click the ellipsis button to open the Input Mask Wizard.)

➔ For more information on the Input Mask Wizard and a listing of placeholders, **see** "Using Input Masks," **p. 223**.

- *Caption* lets you change the query column heading, such as Received, for the Order Date column.

- *Smart Tags* are a new feature of Access 2007 that enable links to web-based resources and perform other operations, such as propagating changes to field or column properties to dependent forms and reports.

➔ To learn more about smart tags, **see** "Working with Object Dependencies and Access Smart Tags," **p. 248**.

Each of the preceding query properties follows the rules described in Chapter 5 for setting table field properties. Adding a value (Received) for the Caption property of a query against the Orders table is the equivalent of adding a column alias by typing **Received:** as a prefix in the OrderDate column's Field cell. Adding a Caption property value, however, doesn't change the SQL statement for the query. The value of the Input Mask property need not correspond exactly to the value of the Format property, but input mask characters don't appear if you try to use a Short Date mask with a Medium Date format you apply in the query.

TIP

Add captions to queries, not tables. Table Datasheet view should display field names rather than captions to conform to good database design principles. Unfortunately, the tables in Northwind.accdb don't conform to this recommendation.

For example, the Received (OrderDate) column in Figure 11.55, which shows the effect of setting the property values shown in the preceding list, has a single-digit (no leading zero) month and day for the Short Date display format, which overrides the mm/dd/yyyy format of the table field. The input mask (99/99/0000;0;_) permits updating with one-digit or two-digit months and days. Adding or editing a single-digit or two-digit entry gives the same result. Most typists prefer to enter a consistent number of digits in a date field.

Figure 11.55
This query uses m/d/yyyy display format and a 99/99/0000 input mask to allow month and date entries as single- or two-digit values.

Order I ▾	Customer	Employee ▾	Order Date ▾	Required Da ▴
10643	Alfreds Futterkiste	Suyama, Michael	1/25/2006	9/22/2
10692	Alfreds Futterkiste	Peacock, Margaret	10/3/2006	10/31/2
10702	Alfreds Futterkiste	Peacock, Margaret	10/13/2006	11/24/2
10835	Alfreds Futterkiste	Davolio, Nancy	1/15/2007	2/12/2
10952	Alfreds Futterkiste	Davolio, Nancy	3/16/2007	4/27/2
11011	Alfreds Futterkiste	Leverling, Janet	4/9/2007	5/7/2
10308	Ana Trujillo Emparedados y helac	King, Robert	9/18/2005	10/16/2
10625	Ana Trujillo Emparedados y helac	Leverling, Janet	8/8/2006	9/5/2
10759	Ana Trujillo Emparedados y helac	Leverling, Janet	11/28/2006	12/26/2
10926	Ana Trujillo Emparedados y helac	Peacock, Margaret	3/4/2007	4/1/2
10365	Antonio Moreno Taquería	Leverling, Janet	11/27/2005	12/25/2
10507	Antonio Moreno Taquería	King, Robert	4/15/2006	5/13/2
10535	Antonio Moreno Taquería	Peacock, Margaret	5/13/2006	6/10/2
10573	Antonio Moreno Taquería	King, Robert	6/19/2006	7/17/2
10677	Antonio Moreno Taquería	Davolio, Nancy	9/22/2006	10/20/2
10682	Antonio Moreno Taquería	Leverling, Janet	9/25/2006	10/23/2
10856	Antonio Moreno Taquería	Leverling, Janet	1/28/2007	2/25/2
10355	Around the Horn	Suyama, Michael	11/15/2005	12/13/2
10383	Around the Horn	Callahan, Laura	12/16/2005	1/13/2

Record: ◄ ‹ 1 of 832 › ›I ►* No Filter Search

If your query has tables linked to dBASE, FoxPro, or other non-Access tables and you can't update records in or add records to the query result set, see "Queries with Linked Tables Aren't Updatable" in the "Troubleshooting" section near the end of this chapter.

MAKING ALL FIELDS OF TABLES ACCESSIBLE

Most queries you create include only the fields you specifically choose. To choose these fields, you either select them from or type them into the drop-down combo list in the Query Design grid's Field row, or you drag the field names from the field lists to the appropriate cells in the Field row. You can, however, quickly include all fields of a table in a query. Access provides the following three methods for including all fields of a table in a query:

- Double-click the field list title bar of the table to select all fields in the field list, and then drag the field list to the Query Design grid. Each field appears in a column of the grid.

- Drag the asterisk (*) to a single Query Design grid column. To sort on or apply selection criteria to a field, drag the field to the Query Design grid and clear the Show check box for the field.

- Set the Output All Fields property value in the Query Properties sheet to Yes to add with asterisks all fields of all tables to the grid.

MAKING CALCULATIONS ON MULTIPLE RECORDS

One of SQL's most powerful capabilities is obtaining summary information almost instantly from specified sets of records in tables. Summarized information from databases is the basis for virtually all management information systems (MIS) and business intelligence (BI) projects. These systems or projects usually answer questions: What are our sales to date for this month? How did last month's sales compare with the same month last year? To answer these questions, you must create queries that make calculations on field values from all or selected sets of records in a table. To make calculations on table values, you must create a query that uses the table and employ Access's SQL aggregate functions to perform the calculations.

USING THE SQL AGGREGATE FUNCTIONS

Summary calculations on fields of tables included in query result tables use the SQL aggregate functions listed in Table 11.1. These are called aggregate functions because they apply to groups (aggregations) of data cells. The SQL aggregate functions satisfy the requirements of most queries needed for business applications.

TABLE 11.1   SQL AGGREGATE FUNCTIONS

Function	Description	Field Types
Avg()	Average of values in a field	All types except Text, Memo, and OLE Object
Count()	Number of Not Null values in a field	All field types
First()	Value of a field of the first record	All field types
Last()	Value of a field of the last record	All field types
Max()	Greatest value in a field	All numeric data types and Text
Min()	Least value in a field	All numeric data types and Text
StDev(), StDevP()	Statistical standard deviation of values in a field	All numeric data types
Sum()	Total of values in a field	All numeric data types
Var(), VarP()	Statistical variation of values in a field	All numeric data types

Σ StDev() and Var() evaluate population samples. You can choose these functions from the drop-down list in the Query Design grid's Total row. (The Total row appears when you click the Totals button on the toolbar or choose View, Totals.) StDevP() and VarP() evaluate populations and must be entered as expressions. If you're familiar with statistical principles, you recognize the difference in the calculation methods of standard deviation and variance for populations and samples of populations. The following section explains the method of choosing the SQL aggregate function for the column of a query.

NOTE

> ANSI SQL and most SQL (client/server) databases support the equivalent of Access SQL's `Avg()`, `Count()`, `First()`, `Last()`, `Max()`, `Min()`, and `Sum()` aggregate functions as `AVG()`, `COUNT()`, `FIRST()`, `LAST()`, `MAX()`, `MIN()`, and `SUM()`, respectively. T-SQL also provides equivalents of Access's `StdDev()`, `StdDevP()`, `Var()`, and `VarP()` functions with the same names.

MAKING CALCULATIONS BASED ON ALL RECORDS OF A TABLE

Managers, especially sales and marketing managers, are most often concerned with information about orders received and shipments made during specific periods of time. Financial managers are interested in calculated values, such as the total amount of unpaid invoices and the average number of days between the invoice and payment dates. Occasionally, you might want to make calculations on all records of a table, such as finding the historical average value of all invoices issued by a firm. Usually, however, you apply criteria to the query to select specific records that you want to total.

Σ   Access considers all SQL aggregate functions to be members of the Totals class of functions. You create queries that return any or all SQL aggregate functions by clicking the Totals button (with the Greek sigma, Σ, which represents summation) in the Show/Hide group of the Query Tools Design ribbon.

Follow these steps to apply the five most commonly used SQL aggregate functions to the sample Order Subtotals query:

1. Open a new query and add the Order Subtotals query. Click the Query Tools, Design tab.

2. Drag the OrderID column to the first new query column and then drag the Subtotal column four times to the adjacent column to create four Subtotal columns.

Σ   3. Click the Totals button to add the Totals row.

4. Move to the Total row of the OrderID column and press Alt+↓ to display the dropdown list of SQL aggregate functions. Choose Count as the function for the OrderID column, as shown in Figure 11.56.

5. Move to the first Subtotal column, open the list, and choose Sum from the Total dropdown list. Repeat the process, choosing Avg for the second Subtotal column, Min for the third, and Max for the fourth.

6. Place the cursor in the OrderID field and click the Properties button on the toolbar (or right-click in the Count field and then click <u>P</u>roperties in the popup menu) to display the Field Property Sheet. Type **Count** as the value of the Caption property.

7. Repeat step 6 for the four Subtotal columns, typing **Sum**, **Average**, **Minimum**, and **Maximum** as the values of the Caption property for the four columns, respectively. (You don't need to set the Format property, because the Subtotal column is formatted as Currency.)

Figure 11.56
You apply the
Count() function to
one of the rows of
the query that has a
value in every row to
obtain the total num-
ber of rows returned
by the query. The
OrderID column is
the logical choice for
counting.

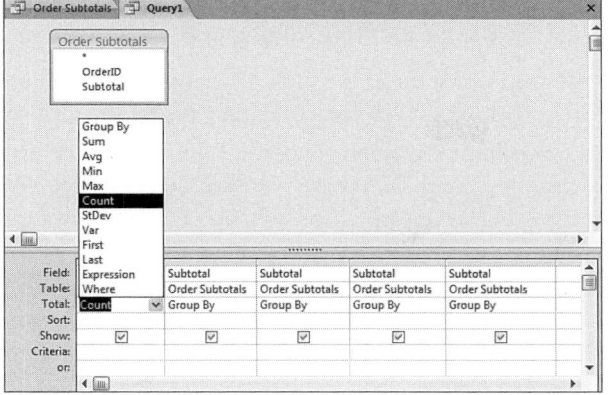

8. Click Run to display the query's result. The query design doesn't have fields suitable for row-restriction criteria, so the result shown in Figure 11.57 is for the whole table.

Figure 11.57
The datasheet dis-
plays five SQL aggre-
gate values for all
records of the Orders
table.

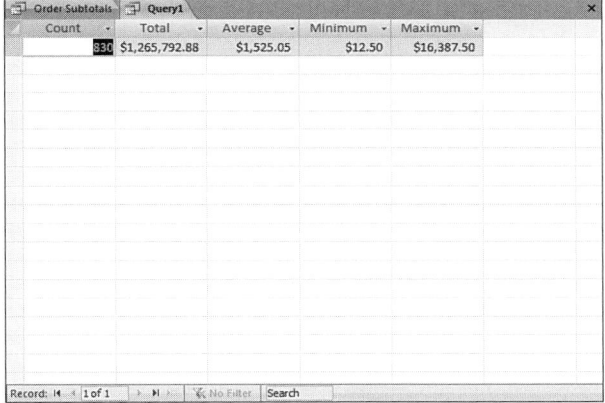

9. Save your query with a descriptive name, such as **qryOrdersAggregates**, because you'll use this query in the two sections that follow.

MAKING CALCULATIONS BASED ON SELECTED SETS OF ROWS OR RECORDS

The preceding sample query performed calculations on all orders received by Northwind Traders that were entered in the Orders table. Usually, you are interested in a specific set of records—a range of dates, for example—from which to calculate aggregate values. To restrict the calculation to orders that Northwind received in March 2006, follow these steps:

1. Return to Query Design view and add the Orders table to the qryOrdersAggregates query. Access automatically creates the join on the OrderID fields. If you didn't create this query, you can import it from the Join11.accdb sample database.

2. Drag the OrderDate field onto the OrderID column to add OrderDate as the first column of the query. You need the OrderDate field to restrict the data to a range of dates.

3. Open the Total drop-down list in the OrderDate column and choose Where to replace the default Group By. Access deselects the Show box of the OrderDate column.

4. In the OrderDate column's Criteria row, type **Like "3/*/2006"** to restrict the totals to orders received in the month of March 2006 (see Figure 11.58). When you use the Like operator as a criterion, Access adds the quotation marks if you forget to type them.

Figure 11.58
The OrderDate field of the Orders table is needed to restrict the aggregate data to orders received within a specified period, March 2006 in this case.

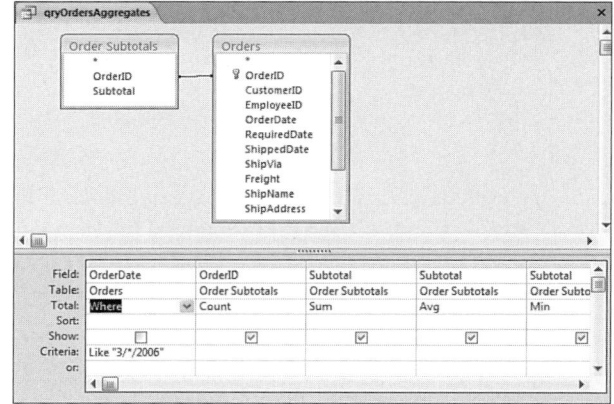

TIP

> Some examples in this chapter use Access `Like "{m¦*}/{d¦*}/yyyy"` expressions as shorthand for `Between #mm/dd/yyyy# And #mm/dd/yyyy#` WHERE clause date constraints. Current versions of the Microsoft Data Access Components and the Access OLE DB driver don't recognize `Like "*/*/yyyy"` and similar `Like` expressions. If you plan to copy Access SQL statements to Visual Basic .NET programs, use the `Between…And` operator, not `Like` for dates.

5. Click the Run button to display the result for orders received during the month of March 2006 (see Figure 11.59).

You can create a more useful grouping of records by replacing the field name with an expression. For example, you can group aggregates by the year and month (or year and quarter) by grouping on the value of an expression created with the Format function. The following steps produce a sales summary record for each month of 2006, the most recent year for which 12 months of data are available in the Orders table:

1. Return to Query Design view, and then click the header bar of the query's OrderDate column to select the first column. Press the Insert key to add a new, empty column to the query.

Figure 11.59
This datasheet shows the effect of adding a date criterion (in this case, orders received in March 2006).

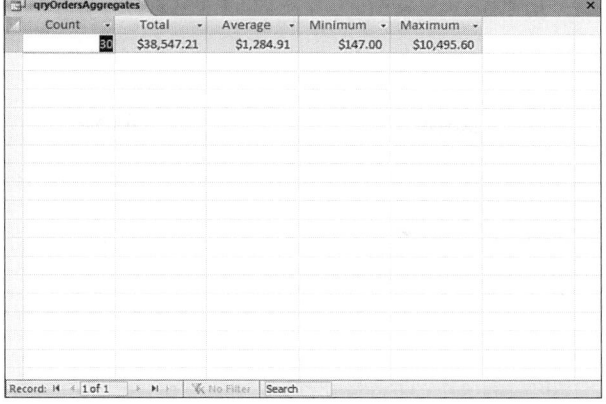

2. Type **Month: Format([OrderDate],"yyyy-mm")** in the first (empty) column's Field row. (You use the "yyyy-mm" format so that the records group in date order. For a single year, you also can use "m" or "mm", but not "mmm", because "mmm" sorts in alphabetic sequence starting with Apr.)

3. Change the Where criterion of the OrderDate column to **Year([OrderDate])=2006** to return a full year of data. Your query design appears as shown in Figure 11.60.

Figure 11.60
This query design returns a row containing aggregate values of orders received in each month of 2006. The Access query parser changes the Year([OrderDate])= 2006 Criteria expression into a Year([OrderDate]) Field expression with 2006 as the criterion value.

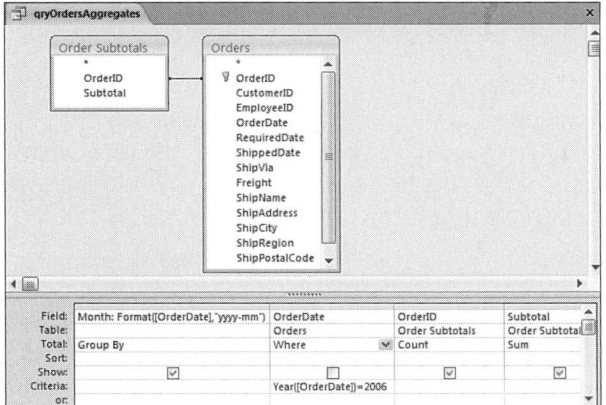

4. Click Run to display the result of your query (see Figure 11.61). The query creates sales summary data for each month of 2006.

Figure 11.61
The datasheet displays aggregate rows for each month of 2006.

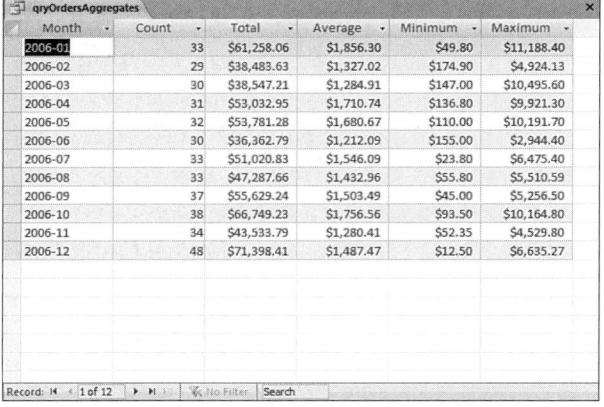

Month	Count	Total	Average	Minimum	Maximum
2006-01	33	$61,258.06	$1,856.30	$49.80	$11,188.40
2006-02	29	$38,483.63	$1,327.02	$174.90	$4,924.13
2006-03	30	$38,547.21	$1,284.91	$147.00	$10,495.60
2006-04	31	$53,032.95	$1,710.74	$136.80	$9,921.30
2006-05	32	$53,781.28	$1,680.67	$110.00	$10,191.70
2006-06	30	$36,362.79	$1,212.09	$155.00	$2,944.40
2006-07	33	$51,020.83	$1,546.09	$23.80	$6,475.40
2006-08	33	$47,287.66	$1,432.96	$55.80	$5,510.59
2006-09	37	$55,629.24	$1,503.49	$45.00	$5,256.50
2006-10	38	$66,749.23	$1,756.56	$93.50	$10,164.80
2006-11	34	$43,533.79	$1,280.41	$52.35	$4,529.80
2006-12	48	$71,398.41	$1,487.47	$12.50	$6,635.27

Record: 14 ◄ 1 of 12 ► ►I No Filter | Search

5. Choose <u>F</u>ile, Save <u>A</u>s and save the query under a different name, such as **qryMonthlyOrders2006**, because you modify the query in the next section.

DESIGNING PARAMETER QUERIES

If you expect to run a summary or another type of query repeatedly with changes to the criteria, you can convert the query to a parameter query. Parameter queries—which Chapter 9 explained briefly—enable you to enter criteria with the Enter Parameter Value dialog. Access prompts you for each parameter. For the qryMonthlyOrders2006 query that you created in the preceding section, the only parameter likely to change is the range of dates for which you want to generate the product sales data. The two sections that follow show you how to add a parameter to a query and specify the data type of the parameter.

ADDING A PARAMETER TO THE MONTHLY SALES QUERY

To convert the qryMonthlyOrders2006 summary query to a parameter query, you first create prompts for the Enter Parameter Value dialog that appears when the query runs. You create parameter queries by substituting the text with which to prompt the user, enclosed within square brackets, for actual values. Follow these steps:

1. Open in Design view the qryMonthlyOrders2006 query that you created in the preceding section.

2. With the cursor in the Month column's Field row, press F2 to select the expression in the Field cell. Then press Ctrl+C to copy the expression to the Clipboard.

3. Move the cursor to the OrderDate column's Field row and press F2 to select OrderDate. Then press Ctrl+V to replace OrderDate with the expression used for the first column.

4. Move to the OrderDate column's Criteria cell and replace Year([OrderDate])=2006 with **[Enter the year and month in YYYY-MM format:]** (see Figure 11.62).

Figure 11.62
Specify the same format for the parameter column as that of the grouping column, and add the prompt for the Enter Parameter dialog.

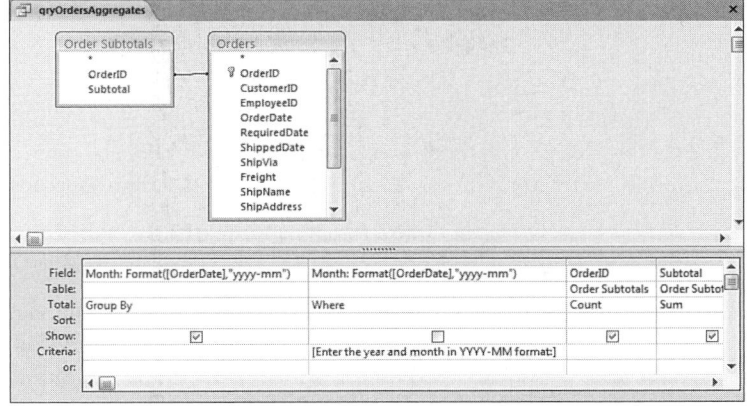

5. Click the Office button, choose Save As, and save the query as **qryMonthlyOrdersParam**.

6. Click the Run button. The Enter Parameter Value dialog opens with the label that you assigned as the value of the criterion in step 4.

7. Type **2006-03** in the text box to display the data for March 2006, as shown in Figure 11.63.

Figure 11.63
You must type the parameter exactly as shown in the Enter Parameter Value dialog's prompt to return rows.

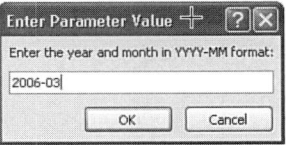

8. Click OK to run the query. The result appears as shown in Figure 11.64.

Figure 11.64
This datasheet shows the result of the parameter value entered in step 7.

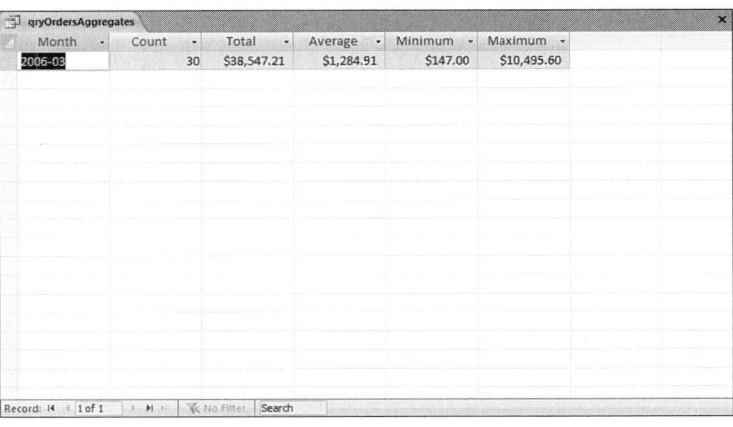

SPECIFYING THE PARAMETER'S DATA TYPE

The default field data type for parameters of Access queries is Text. If the parameter creates a criterion for a query column of the Date/Time or Number field data type, you must assign a data type to each entry that is made through an Enter Parameter Value dialog. Data types for values entered as parameters are established in the Query Parameters dialog. If you have more than one parameter, you can establish the same or a different data type for each parameter.

NOTE

> The data type for the prompt of the qryMonthlyOrdersParam query's parameter is Text (the default), not Date/Time. Therefore, you don't need to apply a data type specification for the query.

Follow these steps to demonstrate adding an optional data type specification to a parameter:

1. Return to Design view, click the Query Tools, Design tab, use the mouse to select the prompt text only in the Month column's Criteria cell (omit the square brackets and colon character), and copy the text of the prompt to the Clipboard by pressing Ctrl+C.

2. Click the Parameters button to display the Query Parameters dialog.

3. To insert the prompt in the Parameter column of the dialog, place the cursor in the column and press Ctrl+V. The prompt entry in the Parameter column must match the prompt entry in the Criteria field exactly; copying and pasting the prompt text ensures an exact match. Don't include the square brackets in the Parameter column.

4. Press Tab to move to the Data Type column, press Alt+↓ to open the Data Type drop-down list, and select Date/Time (see Figure 11.65). Click Cancel to close the dialog without adding the Date/Time data type, because it isn't applicable to this query.

Figure 11.65
Select the data type for the parameter's prompt from the Data Type list in the Query Parameters dialog.

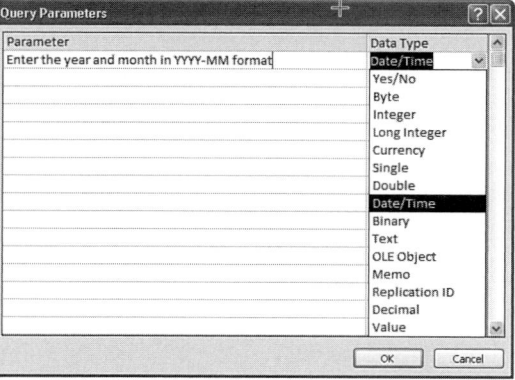

5. If you applied the Date/Time data type to the qryMonthlyOrdersParam query, reopen the Query Parameters dialog and delete the prompt text, which also deletes the data type entry.

Complete your query design and testing before you convert any type of query to a para-meter query. Using fixed criteria with the query maintains consistency during the testing process. Furthermore, you can make repeated changes between Design and Run view more quickly if you don't have to enter one or more parameters in the process. After you finish testing the query, edit the criteria to add the prompt for the Enter Parameter Value dialog.

The parameter-conversion process described in this section applies to all types of queries that you create if one or more of the query columns includes a criterion expression. The advantage of the parameter query is that you or a user of the database can run a query for any range of values—in this case, dates—such as the current month to date, a particular fis-cal quarter, or an entire fiscal year.

CREATING CROSSTAB QUERIES

Crosstab queries are summary queries that let you determine exactly how the summary data appears onscreen. Crosstab queries rotate the axis of the datasheet and display the equivalent of repeating fields (often called *buckets*) in columns. Thus, the datasheet displayed by a crosstab query doesn't conform to first normal form. Crosstab queries are closely related to Access and Excel PivotTables. PivotTable and PivotChart views of queries are the subject of the next chapter.

→ For more information on PivotTables, **see** "Slicing and Dicing Data with PivotTables," **p. 523**.

With crosstab queries, you can perform the following operations:

- Specify the field that creates labels (headings) for rows by using the Group By instruc-tion
- Determine the fields that create column headers and the criteria that determine the val-ues appearing under the headers
- Assign calculated data values to the cells of the resulting row-column grid

The following list details the advantages of using crosstab queries:

- You can display a substantial amount of summary data in a compact datasheet that's familiar to anyone who uses a spreadsheet application or columnar accounting form.
- The summary data is presented in a datasheet that's ideally suited for creating graphs and charts automatically with the Access Chart Wizard.
- Designing queries to create multiple levels of detail is quick and easy. Queries with identical columns but fewer rows can represent increasingly summarized data. Highly summarized queries are ideal to begin a drill-down procedure by instructing the user, for example, to click a Details button to display sales by product.

Using crosstab queries imposes only one restriction: You can't sort your result table on cal-culated values in columns. You can't, therefore, create a crosstab query that ranks products

11

by sales volume. Columns are likely to have values that cause conflicts in the sorting order of the row. You can choose an ascending sort, a descending sort, or no sort on the row label values in the GROUP BY field, which usually is the first column.

USING THE WIZARD TO GENERATE A QUARTERLY PRODUCT SALES CROSSTAB QUERY

Access's Crosstab Query Wizard can generate a crosstab query from a single table, but an individual table seldom contains data suitable as the data source for a crosstab query. If you need more than one table to get the result you want from the wizard, which is almost always the case, you must design a query specifically for crosstab presentation.

Follow these steps to create a query and then use the Crosstab Query Wizard to generate a result set that shows quarterly sales by product for the year 2006:

 1. Create a new query in Design view and add the Orders table and Order Details Extended query. Drag the OrderDate field of the Orders table and the ProductID, ProductName, and ExtendedPrice fields of the Order Details Extended query to the grid. Add **Year([OrderDate])=2006** as the criterion of the OrderDate field to restrict the data to a single year (see Figure 11.66).

Figure 11.66
The source query for the first crosstab query is based on the sample Orders table and Order Details Extended query.

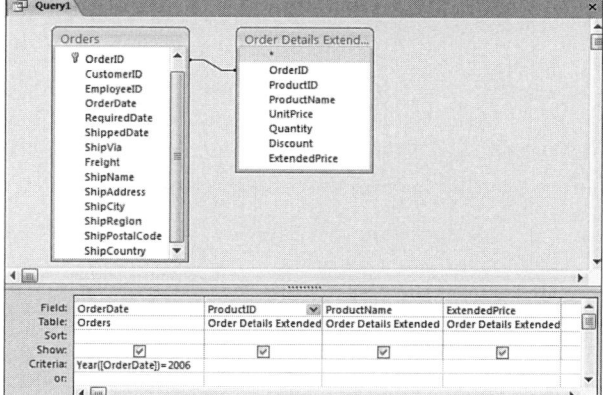

 2. Right-click the ProductID field in the grid, and choose Properties to open the Properties sheet. Click the Lookup tab, and select Text Box in the Display Control to revert from the ProductName lookup to the numeric ProductID value. Click Run to verify your design (see Figure 11.67).

3. Close and save the query as **qryCTWizSource**.

 4. Click the Create ribbon's Query Wizard button to open the New Query dialog and double-click the Crosstab Query Wizard to open the Wizard's first dialog.

5. Select the Queries option and then select qryCTWizSource from the list (see Figure 11.68). Click Next.

Figure 11.67
This datasheet displays the first few rows of the result set from the design of Figure 11.66, which has a row for each Order Details item for orders received in 2006.

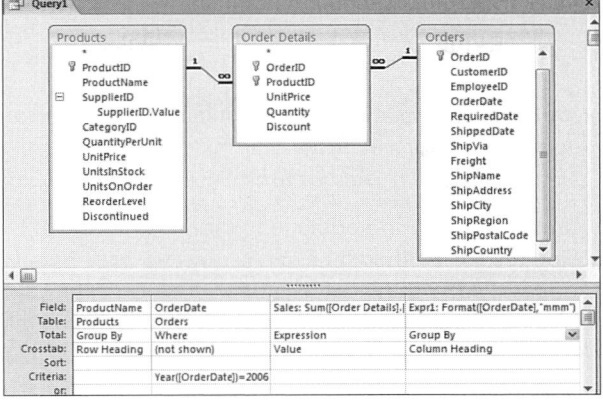

Figure 11.68
Select the data source, usually a query, in the first Crosstab Query Wizard dialog.

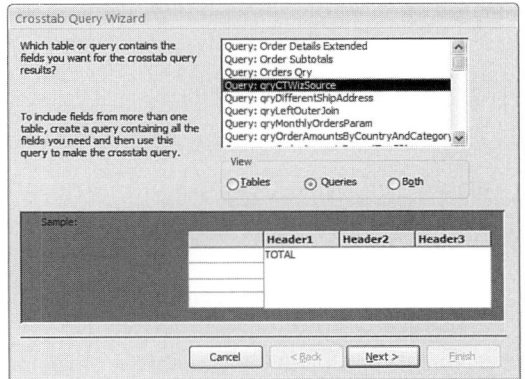

6. Double-click the ProductID column to move ProductID from the Available Fields to the Selected Fields list. Do the same for the ProductName column. The second Wizard dialog appears as shown in Figure 11.69. Click Next.

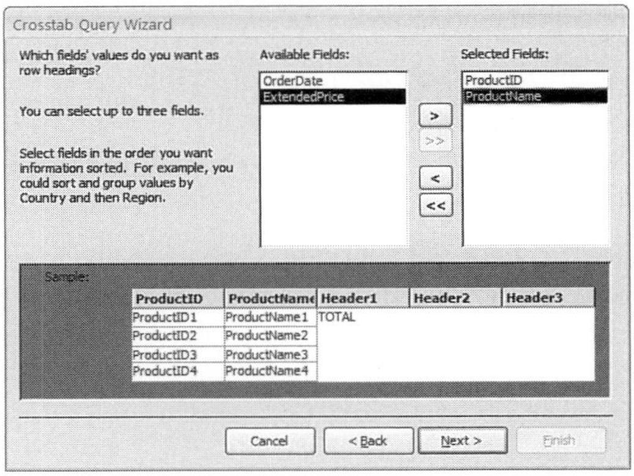

Figure 11.69
Select the query columns to appear as row headers in the second Wizard dialog.

7. Accept the default OrderDate field for the column headings (see Figure 11.70). Click Next.

Figure 11.70
Specify the query column that provides the column headers in the third wizard dialog.

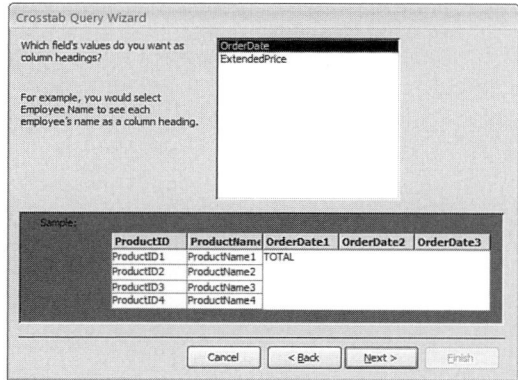

8. Select Quarter as the date interval for the columns (see Figure 11.71). Click Next.

Figure 11.71
Specify the date interval in the fourth dialog's list. This dialog appears only if you specify a date field for row or column headings.

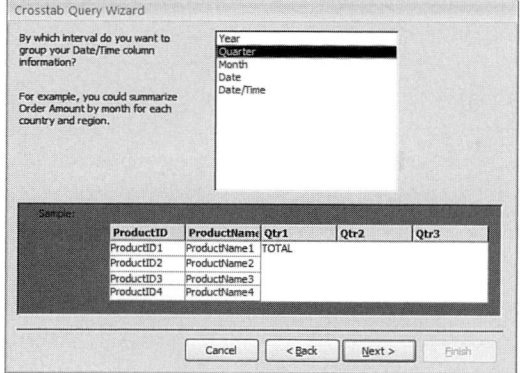

9. Select Sum as the aggregate function to total the ExtendedPrice value (sales) for each quarter. Leave the Yes, Include Row Sums check box marked to include a column that shows the total sales for the four quarters (see Figure 11.72). Click Next.

10. In the final Wizard dialog, type **qry2006QuarterlyProductOrdersCT** as the name of the query and click Finish to display the crosstab query result set (see Figure 11.73).

 11. Change to Design view to check the query the Query Wizard based on the original qryCTWizSource query. Open the list in one of the cells of the added Crosstab row to view the choices for each field of the query (see Figure 11.74).

Figure 11.72
You can specify any aggregate function to summarize the numeric data for the crosstab query, but Sum is the most common.

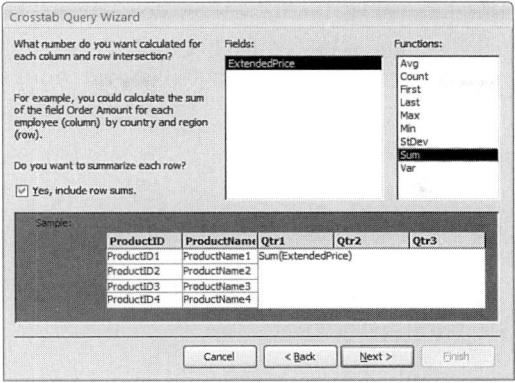

Figure 11.73
The crosstab query has rows for each of the 77 products sold by Northwind Traders in 2006. The new Korean and Chinese products were introduced in 2007.

Product	Product Name	Total Of E	Qtr 1	Qtr 2	Qtr 3	Qtr 4
1	Chai	$4,887.00	$705.60	$878.40	$1,174.50	$2,128.50
2	Chang	$7,038.55	$2,435.80	$228.00	$2,061.50	$2,313.25
3	Aniseed Syrup	$1,724.00	$544.00	$600.00	$140.00	$440.00
4	Chef Anton's Cajun Sea	$5,214.88	$225.28	$2,970.00	$1,337.60	$682.00
5	Chef Anton's Gumbo M	$373.62			$288.22	$85.40
6	Grandma's Boysenberr	$2,500.00			$1,750.00	$750.00
7	Uncle Bob's Organic Dri	$9,186.30	$1,084.80	$1,575.00	$2,700.00	$3,826.50
8	Northwoods Cranberry	$4,260.00		$1,300.00		$2,960.00
9	Mishi Kobe Niku	$6,935.50	$1,396.80	$1,319.20	$3,637.50	$582.00
10	Ikura	$9,935.50	$1,215.20	$688.20	$4,212.90	$3,819.20
11	Queso Cabrales	$6,911.94	$1,630.44	$2,756.25	$504.00	$2,021.25
12	Queso Manchego La Pa	$8,335.30	$456.00	$1,396.50	$4,962.80	$1,520.00
13	Konbu	$812.94	$13.44	$168.00	$469.50	$162.00
14	Tofu	$6,234.48	$1,432.20	$2,734.20	$1,318.27	$749.81
15	Genen Shouyu	$1,474.82		$331.70	$1,143.12	
16	Pavlova	$8,663.40	$1,935.56	$2,395.88	$1,849.70	$2,482.26
17	Alice Mutton	$17,604.60	$2,667.60	$4,013.10	$4,836.00	$6,087.90
18	Carnarvon Tigers	$15,950.00	$1,500.00	$2,362.50	$7,100.00	$4,987.50
19	Teatime Chocolate Bisc	$2,986.75	$943.89	$349.60	$841.80	$851.46

Record: 1 of 77 | No Filter | Search

Figure 11.74
Crosstab queries have an additional row, Crosstab, in the grid.

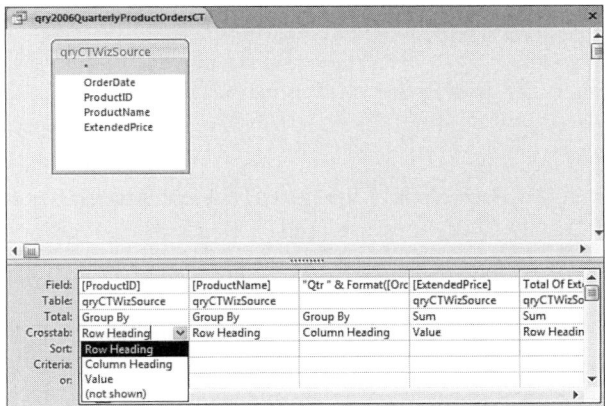

11

The Crosstab row choices—Row Heading, Column Heading, Value, and (Not Shown)—determine the location of field values in the crosstab datasheet.

Access SQL
The Access SQL statement for the crosstab query is

```
TRANSFORM Sum(qryCTWizSource.ExtendedPrice) AS SumOfExtendedPrice
SELECT qryCTWizSource.ProductID, qryCTWizSource.ProductName,
    Sum(qryCTWizSource.ExtendedPrice) AS [Total Of ExtendedPrice]
FROM qryCTWizSource
GROUP BY qryCTWizSource.ProductID, qryCTWizSource.ProductName
PIVOT "Qtr " & Format([OrderDate],"q");
```

The Access SQL PIVOT and TRANSFORM reserved words generate the crosstab query result set. The expression following TRANSFORM defines the numeric values for the matrix. The SELECT field list supplies the row headings and values. The PIVOT expression defines the column headings and acts as an extension to the GROUP BY expression. The "q" format string specifies a quarterly date interval.

DESIGNING A MONTHLY PRODUCT SALES CROSSTAB QUERY

You can bypass the Query Wizard by manually designing a crosstab query from scratch with related tables, rather than a query, as the data source. To create a typical crosstab query in Query Design view that displays products in rows and the monthly sales volume for each product in the corresponding columns, follow these steps:

1. Open a new query in Design view and add the Products, Order Details, and Orders tables to the query.

2. Drag the ProductID and ProductName fields from the Products table to the query's first two columns and then drag the OrderDate field of the Orders table to the third column.

3. Click the Query Design Tools ribbon's Crosstab button to add the Crosstab row to the Query Design grid.

4. Open the drop-down list of the ProductID column's Crosstab row and select Row Heading. Repeat this process for the ProductName column. These two columns provide the required row headings for your crosstab. A crosstab query must have at least one row heading.

5. Open the Total drop-down list of the OrderDate column and select Where. Type **Year([OrderDate])=2006** in this column's Criteria row to restrict the query to orders received in 2006. Leave the Crosstab cell empty or choose (not shown) from the list.

6. Move to the next (empty) column's Field row and type the following:
```
Sales: Sum([Order Details].[Quantity]*[Order Details].[UnitPrice]*
(1-[Order Details].[Discount]))
```

Move to the Total row, choose Expression from the drop-down list, and then choose Value from the Crosstab row. The expression calculates the net amount of the orders received for each product that populates your crosstab query's data cells. (You must specify the Orders Detail table name; if you don't, you receive an "Ambiguous field reference" error message. Alternatively, you can set Order Details as the Table cell value.)

7. Right-click the Sales column, choose Properties to open the Field Properties sheet for the Sales column, and select Currency as the Format property of the column.

8. In the next (empty) column's Field row, type **Format([OrderDate], "mmm")**. Access adds a default field name, Expr1:. Accept the default because the Format function that you added creates the column names, the three-letter abbreviation for the months of the year ("mmm" format), when you run the query. Accept the default Group By value in the Totals cell. The months of the year (Jan through Dec) are your column headings, so move to the Crosstab row and choose Column Heading from the drop-down list. The design of your crosstab query appears as shown in Figure 11.75.

Figure 11.75
This crosstab query design displays order amounts for products by month.

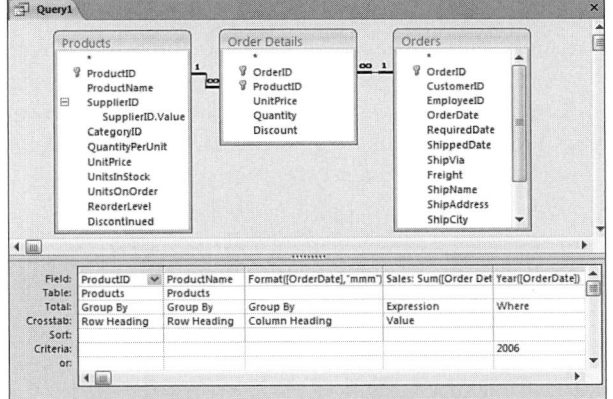

9. Click Run to execute the query (see Figure 11.76).

Figure 11.76
The "mmm" format string for months sorts the columns by month name, not month number.

Product ID	Product Name	Apr	Aug	Dec	Feb
1	Chai	$576.00	$652.50		
2	Chang	$228.00	$1,871.50	$1,505.75	$733.40
3	Aniseed Syrup			$180.00	
4	Chef Anton's Cajun Seasoning	$935.00	$748.00		
5	Chef Anton's Gumbo Mix		$288.22		
6	Grandma's Boysenberry Spread		$1,750.00		
7	Uncle Bob's Organic Dried Pears	$1,275.00	$1,050.00	$1,126.50	$364.80
8	Northwoods Cranberry Sauce	$1,300.00		$960.00	
9	Mishi Kobe Niku	$1,319.20			
10	Ikura	$471.20	$418.50	$1,612.00	$744.00
11	Queso Cabrales		$210.00	$1,601.25	$685.44
12	Queso Manchego La Pastora		$1,162.80		$456.00
13	Konbu	$60.00	$66.30	$102.00	
14	Tofu	$1,627.50	$558.00	$279.00	
15	Genen Shouyu	$176.70			
16	Pavlova	$872.50		$1,483.25	$1,023.73
17	Alice Mutton			$3,480.75	$312.00
18	Carnarvon Tigers	$1,406.25	$5,100.00	$1,875.00	
19	Teatime Chocolate Biscuits		$446.20	$616.76	$458.44

Record: 1 of 77 — No Filter — Search

Notice that the crosstab query result contains a major defect: The columns are arranged alphabetically by month name rather than in calendar order. You can solve this problem by using fixed column headings, which you learn about in the following section.

USING FIXED COLUMN HEADINGS WITH CROSSTAB QUERIES

Access uses an alphabetical or numerical sort on row and column headings to establish the sequence of appearance in the crosstab query result table. For this reason, if you use short or full names for months, the sequence is in alphabetic rather than calendar order. You can correct this problem by assigning fixed column headings to the crosstab query. Follow these steps to modify and rerun the query:

→ To review the ways Access lets you manipulate dates and time, **see** "Functions for Date and Time," **p. 426**.

1. Return to Query Design view, right-click the upper pane, and choose Properties. The Query Properties sheet contains an option that appears only for crosstab queries: Column Headings.

2. In the Column Headings text box, type the three-letter abbreviations of all 12 months of the year. You must spell the abbreviations of the months correctly; data for months with spelling mistakes doesn't appear. You can separate entries with commas or semi-colons, and you don't need to type quotation marks, because Access adds them (see Figure 11.77). Spaces are unnecessary between the Column Headings values. After you complete all 12 entries, close the Query Property sheet.

Figure 11.77
Add month names separated by semi-colons or commas to the Column Headings property of crosstab queries.

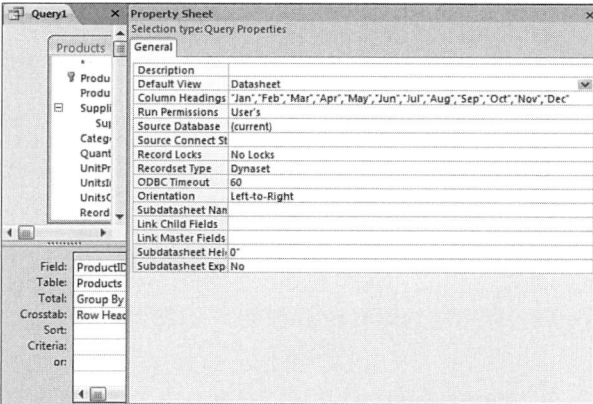

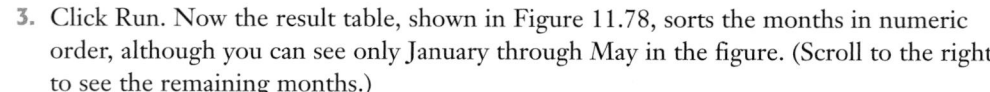

3. Click Run. Now the result table, shown in Figure 11.78, sorts the months in numeric order, although you can see only January through May in the figure. (Scroll to the right to see the remaining months.)

Figure 11.78
Adding the fixed column headers eliminates the sorting problem with the month columns.

Product	Product Name	Jan	Feb	Mar	Apr	May
1	Chai	$489.60		$216.00	$576.00	$122.40
2	Chang	$912.00	$733.40	$790.40	$228.00	
3	Aniseed Syrup	$400.00		$144.00		$600.00
4	Chef Anton's Cajun Seaso			$225.28	$935.00	$2,035.00
5	Chef Anton's Gumbo Mix					
6	Grandma's Boysenberry S					
7	Uncle Bob's Organic Dried		$364.80	$720.00	$1,275.00	$300.00
8	Northwoods Cranberry Sa				$1,300.00	
9	Mishi Kobe Niku	$1,396.80			$1,319.20	
10	Ikura		$744.00	$471.20	$471.20	$62.00
11	Queso Cabrales	$504.00	$685.44	$441.00		$1,832.25
12	Queso Manchego La Pasto		$456.00			$1,396.50
13	Konbu	$8.64		$4.80	$60.00	$108.00
14	Tofu	$1,209.00		$223.20	$1,627.50	
15	Genen Shouyu				$176.70	
16	Pavlova	$248.11	$1,023.73	$663.72	$872.50	$1,334.92
17	Alice Mutton	$2,355.60	$312.00			$2,718.30
18	Carnarvon Tigers			$1,500.00	$1,406.25	
19	Teatime Chocolate Biscui	$295.65	$458.44	$189.80		$92.00

Record: 1 of 77   No Filter   Search

TIP

If your crosstab datasheet differs from that of Figure 11.78, check whether you properly entered the fixed column headings in the Query Property Sheet. A misspelled month causes Access to omit the month from the query result set; if you specified "mmmm" instead of "mmm", only May appears.

4. Save the query with an appropriate name, such as **qry2006MonthlyProductOrdersCT**.

You can produce a printed report quickly from the query by clicking Quick Access Toolbar's Print button. Alternatively, click the Office button, select Print, Print Preview, set orientation and margins, and then click the Print button.

TIP

You might want to use fixed column headings if you use the Group By instruction with country names. Users in the United States will probably place USA first, and Canadian firms will undoubtedly choose Canada as the first entry. If you add a record with a new country, you must remember to update the list of fixed column headings with the new country value. Fixed column headings have another hidden benefit: They often make crosstab queries execute more quickly.

Access SQL
The Access SQL statement for the crosstab query with fixed column headings is

```
TRANSFORM Sum([Order Details].[Quantity]*[Order Details].[UnitPrice]*
    (1-[Order Details].[Discount])) AS Sales
SELECT Products.ProductID, Products.ProductName
FROM Orders
    INNER JOIN (Products
        INNER JOIN [Order Details]
```

```
        ON Products.ProductID = [Order Details].ProductID)
    ON Orders.OrderID = [Order Details].OrderID
WHERE Year([OrderDate])=2006
GROUP BY Products.ProductID, Products.ProductName
PIVOT Format([OrderDate],"mmm")
    In("Jan","Feb","Mar","Apr","May","Jun",
    "Jul","Aug","Sep","Oct","Nov","Dec");
```

The only significant differences between the preceding SQL statement and that for the quarterly crosstab query is the lack of a grand total column for each product, the change of the date interval ("mmm" instead of "q"), and the addition of the In( ) function with the fixed column names list as its argument.

If you want to add a grand totals column, add to the field list of the SELECT statement , Sum(Sales) AS [Total Orders], return to Design view, select the Total Orders column, and set its Format property to Currency. The added column appears in Figure 11.79.

Figure 11.79
You can add a Total Orders column by adding Sum(Sales) AS [Total Orders] to the column list of the SELECT statement. You must specify the Currency format of the column in the Field Property Sheet.

Product	Product Name	Total Orders	Jan	Feb	Mar	Apr
1	Chai	$4,887.00	$489.60		$216.00	$576.0
2	Chang	$7,038.55	$912.00	$733.40	$790.40	$228.0
3	Aniseed Syrup	$1,724.00	$400.00		$144.00	
4	Chef Anton's Cajun Seaso	$5,214.88			$225.28	$935.0
5	Chef Anton's Gumbo Mix	$373.62				
6	Grandma's Boysenberry S	$2,500.00				
7	Uncle Bob's Organic Dried	$9,186.30		$364.80	$720.00	$1,275.0
8	Northwoods Cranberry Sa	$4,260.00				$1,300.0
9	Mishi Kobe Niku	$6,935.50	$1,396.80			$1,319.2
10	Ikura	$9,935.50		$744.00	$471.20	$471.2
11	Queso Cabrales	$6,911.94	$504.00	$685.44	$441.00	
12	Queso Manchego La Pasto	$8,335.30		$456.00		
13	Konbu	$812.94	$8.64		$4.80	$60.0
14	Tofu	$6,234.49	$1,209.00		$223.20	$1,627.5
15	Genen Shouyu	$1,474.82				$176.7
16	Pavlova	$8,663.42	$248.11	$1,023.73	$663.72	$872.5
17	Alice Mutton	$17,604.60	$2,355.60	$312.00		
18	Carnarvon Tigers	$15,950.00			$1,500.00	$1,406.2
19	Teatime Chocolate Biscui	$2,986.75	$295.65	$458.44	$189.80	

Record: 1 of 77   No Filter   Search

WRITING UNION QUERIES AND SUBQUERIES

UNION queries and queries that include subqueries require you to write Access SQL statements. Union is one of the three buttons in the group on the right in the Query Design Tools ribbon's Query Type group: Union, Passthrough, and Data Definition. There is no button for subquery. The following sections provide general syntax examples for writing UNION and subqueries, and they provide simple Access SQL examples. The general syntax examples use the same format as those of Chapter 21, "Moving from Access Queries to Transact-SQL," for T-SQL statements.

USING UNION QUERIES TO COMBINE MULTIPLE RESULT SETS

UNION queries let you combine the result set of two or more SELECT queries into a single result set. Northwind.accdb includes an example of a UNION query, which has the special symbol of two overlapping circles, in the Database window. You can create UNION queries only with SQL statements; if you add the UNION keyword to a query, the Query Design Mode button on the toolbar and the query design choices of the View menu are disabled.

The general syntax of UNION queries is as follows:

```
SELECT select_statement
   UNION SELECT select_statement
     [GROUP BY group_criteria]
     [HAVING aggregate criteria]
  [UNION SELECT select_statement
     [GROUP BY group_criteria]
     [HAVING aggregate criteria]
  [UNION. . .]
  [ORDER BY column_criteria]
```

The restrictions on statements that create UNION queries are the following:

■ The number of fields in the *field_list* of each SELECT and UNION SELECT query must be the same. You receive an error message if the number of fields is not the same.

■ The sequence of the field names in each *field_list* must correspond to similar entities. You don't receive an error message for dissimilar entities, but the result set is likely to be unfathomable. The field data types in a single column need not correspond; however, if the column of the result set contains both numeric and Access Text data types, the data type of the column is set to Text.

■ Only one ORDER BY clause is allowed, and it must follow the last UNION SELECT statement. You can add GROUP BY and HAVING clauses to each SELECT and UNION SELECT statement if needed.

The sample Customers and Suppliers by City query is a UNION query that combines rows from the Customers and Suppliers tables. When you open a UNION query, Query Design view is disabled.

To create a new UNION query, create a new query in Design view, close the Show Table dialog, click the Query Design Tools tab, click the Union query button to open the SQL window, and type the SQL statement.

11

Access SQL

The Access SQL statement for a slightly modified version of the Customers and Suppliers by City query is

```
SELECT City, CompanyName, ContactName,
   CustomerID AS Code, "Customer" AS Relationship
FROM Customers
UNION SELECT City, CompanyName, ContactName,
   SupplierID, "Supplier"
FROM Suppliers
ORDER BY City, CompanyName;
```

The syntax of the preceding SQL statement illustrates the capability of UNION queries to include values from two different field data types, Text (CustomerID) and Long Integer (SupplierID), in the single, aliased Code column (see Figure 11.80).

Figure 11.80
The Code column of this UNION query demonstrates Access's capability to combine values of two different data types. T-SQL UNION queries require compatible data types in a column.

You also can use UNION queries to add (All) or other explicit options to a query result set when populating combo and list boxes. As an example, the following SQL statement adds (All) to the query result set for a combo box used to select orders from a particular country or all countries:

```
SELECT Country FROM Customers
   UNION SELECT "(All)" FROM Customers
ORDER BY Country;
```

The parentheses around (All) causes it to sort at the beginning of the list; the ASCII value of "(" is 40 and "A" is 65. Automatic sorting of combo and list box items uses the ASCII value returned by the VBA **Asc** function.

→ To create a query that returns all rows from joined tables, **see** "Using the tblShipAddress Table in a Query," **p. 567**.

→ To update a table by substituting a string for a specified value, **see** "Using the tblShipAddress Table with UNION Queries," **p. 569**.

→ For examples of using a UNION query to add an (All) item to a combo box, **see** "Adding an Option to Select All Countries or Products," **p. 1266**.

IMPLEMENTING SUBQUERIES

Access traditionally has used nested queries to emulate the subquery capability of ANSI SQL, because early Access versions didn't support subqueries. Access 2007 lets you write a SELECT query that uses another SELECT query to supply the criteria for the WHERE clause. Depending on the complexity of your query, using a subquery instead of nested queries often improves performance. The general syntax of subqueries is as follows:

```
SELECT field_list
   FROM table_list
```

```
WHERE [table_name.]field_name
    IN (SELECT select_statement
[GROUP BY group_criteria]
    [HAVING aggregate_criteria]
[ORDER BY sort_criteria]);
```

Access SQL

Following is the Access SQL statement for a subquery that returns names and addresses of Northwind Traders customers who placed orders between January 1, 2006, and June 30, 2006:

```
SELECT CompanyName, ContactName, ContactTitle, Phone
FROM Customers
WHERE CustomerID IN
    (SELECT CustomerID FROM Orders
      WHERE OrderDate BETWEEN #1/1/2006# AND #6/30/2006#);
```

The SELECT subquery that begins after the IN predicate returns the CustomerID values from the Orders table against which the CustomerID values of the Customers table are compared. Be sure to surround the subquery with parentheses.

Unlike UNION queries, you can create a subquery in Query Design view. You type **IN**, followed by the SELECT statement, as the criterion of the appropriate column, enclosing the SELECT statement within the parentheses required by the IN predicate. Figure 11.81 shows the query design with part of the IN (SELECT…) statement in the Criteria row of the Customer ID column. Figure 11.82 shows the result set returned by the SQL statement and the query design.

Figure 11.81
You can create the base query in Access's Query Design view, but you must type the IN predicate and the subquery's SELECT statement in the Criteria row of the grid.

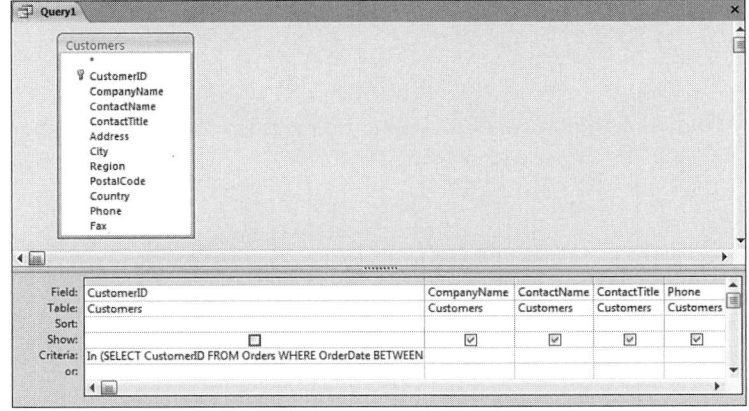

Figure 11.82
This datasheet displays the result set of the subquery design of Figure 11.81.

Company Name	Contact Name	Contact Title	Phone
Antonio Moreno Taqueria	Antonio Moreno	Owner	(5) 555-3932
Around the Horn	Thomas Hardy	Sales Representative	(171) 555-7788
Berglunds snabbköp	Christina Berglund	Order Administrator	0921-12 34 65
Blauer See Delikatessen	Hanna Moos	Sales Representative	0621-08460
Blondel père et fils	Frédérique Citeaux	Marketing Manager	88.60.15.31
Bon app'	Laurence Lebihan	Owner	91.24.45.40
Bottom-Dollar Markets	Elizabeth Lincoln	Accounting Manager	(604) 555-4729
B's Beverages	Victoria Ashworth	Sales Representative	(171) 555-1212
Cactus Comidas para llevar	Patricio Simpson	Sales Agent	(1) 135-5555
Chop-suey Chinese	Yang Wang	Owner	0452-076545
Comércio Mineiro	Pedro Afonso	Sales Associate	(11) 555-7647
Consolidated Holdings	Elizabeth Brown	Sales Representative	(171) 555-2282
Eastern Connection	Ann Devon	Sales Agent	(171) 555-0297
Ernst Handel	Roland Mendel	Sales Manager	7675-3425
Familia Arquibaldo	Aria Cruz	Marketing Assistant	(11) 555-9857
Folies gourmandes	Martine Rancé	Assistant Sales Agent	20.16.10.16
Folk och fä HB	Maria Larsson	Owner	0695-34 67 21
Frankenversand	Peter Franken	Marketing Manager	089-0877310
Franchi S.p.A.	Paolo Accorti	Sales Representative	011-4988260

Record: 1 — No Filter — Search

CREATING QUERIES FROM TABLES IN OTHER DATABASES

Access's Query Properties Sheet includes two properties that let you create a query based on tables contained in a database other than the current database. The database that you open after you launch Access is called the *current database*. Databases other than the current database commonly are called *external databases*. The use of these two properties is as follows:

- The value of the Source Database property for desktop databases is the path to the external database and, for Access databases, the name of the database file. To run a query against tables contained in the Oakmont.accdb sample database from the accompanying CD-ROM, replace (current) in the Source Database text box with the following, as shown in Figure 11.83:

  C:\SEUA12\Oakmont\Oakmont.accdb

  You must have installed the sample files from the CD-ROM in the default C:\SEUA12 folder for this connection string to work.

- The value of the Source Connect Str property depends on the type of external database being used. If your external Access database isn't secure, leave the Source Connect Str text box empty; otherwise, type **UID=*UserID*;PWD=*Password*** to specify the user ID and password needed to open the external database. For other desktop databases, you type the product name, such as Paradox 3.5 or dBASE IV. ODBC data sources require the complete ODBC connect string.

Running a query against an external database is related to running a query against linked tables. When you link tables, the data in the tables is available at any time that your application is running. When you run a query against an external database, the connection to the external database is open only while your query is open in Design or Datasheet view. A slight performance penalty exists for running queries against an external database—each time that you run the query, Access must make a connection to open the database. The connection is closed when you close the query.

Figure 11.83
Specify the full path to the external database as the value of the Source Database property.

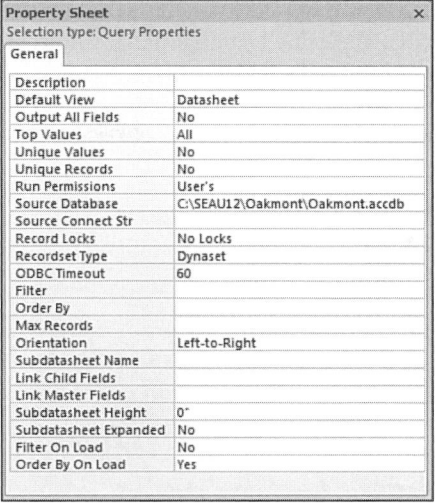

After you specify the external database, its tables appear in the Show Table dialog's list. Figure 11.84 illustrates a query design based on tables in the external Oakmont.accdb sample database. Figure 11.85 shows the result of executing the query design of Figure 11.84.

Figure 11.84
Design view of a query in an external Access database is the same as for a query against tables in the current database. You can create joins between external and current database tables, but you can't enforce referential integrity.

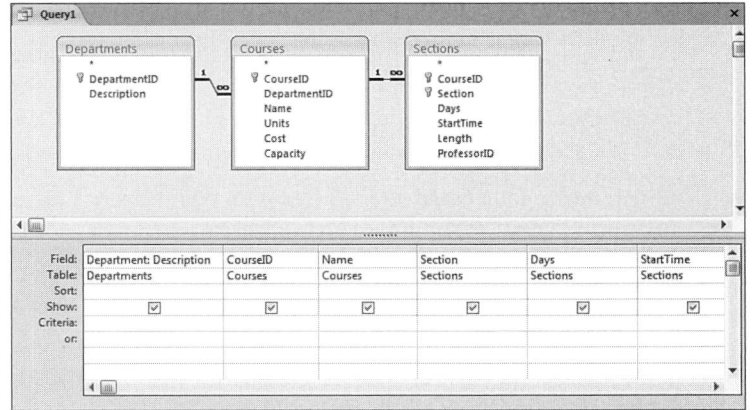

Figure 11.85
This datasheet displays the result set of the query of Figure 11.84 against the external Oakmont. accdb database.

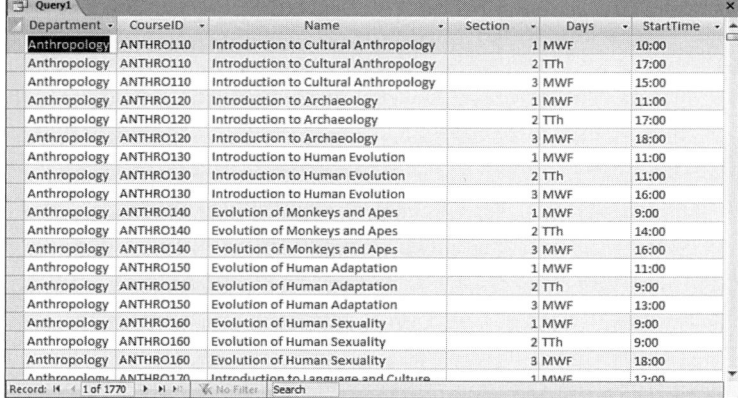

Department	CourseID	Name	Section	Days	StartTime
Anthropology	ANTHRO110	Introduction to Cultural Anthropology	1	MWF	10:00
Anthropology	ANTHRO110	Introduction to Cultural Anthropology	2	TTh	17:00
Anthropology	ANTHRO110	Introduction to Cultural Anthropology	3	MWF	15:00
Anthropology	ANTHRO120	Introduction to Archaeology	1	MWF	11:00
Anthropology	ANTHRO120	Introduction to Archaeology	2	TTh	17:00
Anthropology	ANTHRO120	Introduction to Archaeology	3	MWF	18:00
Anthropology	ANTHRO130	Introduction to Human Evolution	1	MWF	11:00
Anthropology	ANTHRO130	Introduction to Human Evolution	2	TTh	11:00
Anthropology	ANTHRO130	Introduction to Human Evolution	3	MWF	16:00
Anthropology	ANTHRO140	Evolution of Monkeys and Apes	1	MWF	9:00
Anthropology	ANTHRO140	Evolution of Monkeys and Apes	2	TTh	14:00
Anthropology	ANTHRO140	Evolution of Monkeys and Apes	3	MWF	16:00
Anthropology	ANTHRO150	Evolution of Human Adaptation	1	MWF	11:00
Anthropology	ANTHRO150	Evolution of Human Adaptation	2	TTh	9:00
Anthropology	ANTHRO150	Evolution of Human Adaptation	3	MWF	13:00
Anthropology	ANTHRO160	Evolution of Human Sexuality	1	MWF	9:00
Anthropology	ANTHRO160	Evolution of Human Sexuality	2	TTh	9:00
Anthropology	ANTHRO160	Evolution of Human Sexuality	3	MWF	18:00
Anthropology	ANTHRO170	Introduction to Language and Culture	1	MWF	12:00

Record: 1 of 1770 · No Filter · Search

TROUBLESHOOTING

MISSING OBJECTS IN QUERIES

When I run my query, an Enter Parameter Value dialog appears that asks me to enter a value. I didn't specify a parameter for the query.

The Enter Parameter Value dialog appears when the Access engine's query parser can't identify an object specified in the query or evaluate an expression. Usually, the Enter Parameter Value dialog appears because of a typographic error. Intentionally creating parameter queries is the subject of this chapter's "Designing Parameter Queries" section.

QUERIES WITH LINKED TABLES AREN'T UPDATABLE

I can't create an updatable one-to-many query with my linked dBASE or FoxPro tables despite the fact that my query displays only fields from the many side of the relationship.

You must specify (or create) primary key indexes for each dBASE or FoxPro table that participates in the query. The field or fields that you choose must uniquely identify a record; the index doesn't allow duplicate values. Delete the attachment to the dBASE or FoxPro tables and then reattach the table with the primary key indexes. Make sure that you specify which index is the primary key index in the Select Unique Record Identifier dialog that appears after you attach each table.

Also, make sure that you don't include the field of the many-side table on which the join is created in the query. If you add the joined field to the field list, your query isn't updatable.

IN THE REAL WORLD—OPTIMIZING MULTITABLE QUERIES

Chapter 9's "In the Real World—Optimizing Query Design" section discusses the art and science of query design to optimize the presentation of information and query performance. The single-table query design recommendations apply equally to multitable queries.

This chapter is one of the longest in the book because of the importance of multitable SELECT and SQL aggregate queries in production database applications. Joins are fundamental to relational databases. You're likely to find that more than 75% of the queries you create require at least one join, and a substantial percentage need two or more joins.

SUBDATASHEETS

Access 2007's subdatasheet feature is useful for browse-mode editing of related tables, but not much else. *Browse mode* is a term for editing table data in a datasheet. As mentioned earlier in the chapter, it's easy for inexperienced users and data entry operators to make errors when editing datasheets, so minimize or eliminate updatable datasheets and subdatasheets in production Access applications. Instead, use multitable forms—the subject of Chapter 15, "Designing Custom Multitable Forms"—that display a single record of the base table in the main form and show related records in a subform.

NOTE

> Browse-mode editing operations in multiuser and client/server environments are the bane of database administrators (DBAs) because they require multiple database connections and create a substantial amount of network traffic.

→ For more discussion of the browse-mode method and other alternatives, **see** "In the Real World—Alternatives to Action Queries," **p. 575**.

AGGREGATE QUERIES

Aggregate queries generate summary data that's critical for decision-support analysis. Aggregate queries offer quick and easy totaling of orders, sales, and other financial data for one or more time periods. Aggregation methods create large-scale data warehouses and smaller data marts, which are used in online analytical processing (OLAP) applications. Experience with SQL aggregation techniques is a necessity for understanding OLAP methodology.

TIP

> Apply "reasonableness" tests against every summary query you design. Testing becomes increasingly important as the significance of data to others grows. It's very embarrassing to find that you provided data for 2005 when your manager needed 2006 information. Become familiar with trends in the summary data generated by your queries, and compare new query result sets with previous values. If the comparison shows unexpected changes (good or bad), run a simple summary query for one or two periods to verify your data. If the summary data still fails the reasonableness test, you must review the underlying detail data (called *drilling down*). Familiarity with the detail data you summarize is job insurance when your manager says the "numbers don't look right to me."

11

CROSSTAB QUERIES

Most executives prefer the crosstab formats for time series and other comparative financial analyses. Access's Crosstab Query Wizard does a respectable job of generating simple crosstab queries for you. Designing crosstab queries that are more complex than the wizard can handle requires that you first gain experience writing conventional summary queries.

One of the primary issues with Access crosstab queries is that the Access SQL reserved words PIVOT and TRANSFORM, both of which you need to generate crosstab queries, aren't available in SQL Server's T-SQL or any other client/server SQL dialect. Therefore, you can't automatically upsize Access 2007 applications that include crosstab queries to ADP with the Upsize Wizard. (You can't automatically upsize UNION queries, either.) ADPs substitute SQL Server views for select queries; you create views by writing T-SQL SELECT queries for views, functions, or stored procedures. ADPs are the subject of Chapter 20, "Exploring Access Data Projects and SQL Server 2005."

If your data source is a client/server RDBMS, you can use linked server tables with the Crosstab Query Wizard. Alternatively, you can generate the summary query on the server with an Access passthrough query, and then use the Access query result set as the data source for the crosstab query. Passthrough queries, which are more network-efficient than linked tables, are one of the subjects of Chapter 19, "Linking Access Front Ends to Access and Client/Server Tables."

11

CHAPTER 12

WORKING WITH PIVOTTABLE AND PIVOTCHART VIEWS

In this chapter

UNDERSTANDING THE ROLE OF PIVOTTABLES AND PIVOTCHARTS

PivotTables and PivotCharts are powerful tools for summarizing detailed data stored in Access or SQL Server databases. Like crosstab queries, PivotTables present data generated by aggregate queries in a spreadsheet-like format that's familiar to all accounting and management personnel. PivotTable views deliver to Access users the benefits of Excel worksheets without having to launch Excel to manipulate the data. PivotChart views automatically render PivotTable views as line, bar, or area charts. PivotTables and PivotCharts accomplish the primary objective of decision-support front ends—converting online transaction processing (OLTP) data to usable information.

PivotTables replace embedded Excel PivotTables, and PivotCharts supplement or replace Access charts embedded by the Chart Wizard. Excel PivotTables require a local copy of Excel.exe, and the Chart Wizard needs Office 2002's Graph.exe to act as Object Linking and Embedding (OLE) 2+ servers. Many Access developers believe that original Excel PivotTables and OLE-based charts are obsolete. Office PivotTables outperform their earlier Excel counterparts, but conventional Access charts you create with the Chart Wizard have several features that PivotCharts don't offer.

→ To add charts or graphs to forms with the Chart Wizard, **see** "Using the Chart Wizard to Create an Unlinked Graph," **p. 773**.

Access 2002 added two new views to tables, queries, and forms: PivotTable and PivotChart. These views are available in conventional Access applications and Access data projects (ADP). PivotTables and PivotCharts are interdependent; when you design a PivotChart view, you create a corresponding PivotTable view, and vice versa. You can't restrict tables and queries to specific views—such as PivotTable, PivotChart, or both—but you can set the default view. You can set the default view and limit views of forms to include or exclude Pivot... views.

The behavior of the PivotTable and PivotChart views of forms is identical to those of tables or queries. You can use the AutoForm: PivotTable and AutoForm: PivotChart Wizards to create these views of forms from a table or query you specify. Northwind.mdb's sample Sales Analysis form, for example, alternately displays PivotChart and PivotTable form views of a query in a subform.

Forms and reports can contain PivotTable and PivotCharts as conventional ActiveX control objects. You can set the properties of these controls in forms and reports with Visual Basic for Applications (VBA). You can't, however, program these two controls in PivotTable or PivotChart views of tables or queries.

NOTE

> The limitations of PivotTable and PivotChart views might cause you to wonder why this chapter is in Part III, "Transforming Data with Queries and PivotTables," rather than in Part IV, "Designing Forms and Reports." The reason is that well-designed queries— usually based on multiple tables—are fundamental to generating meaningful data for

presentation in PivotTables and PivotCharts. The query and view design techniques you learn in this chapter apply equally to PivotTables and PivotCharts contained in conventional Access and ADP forms.

SLICING AND DICING DATA WITH PIVOTTABLES

PivotTables closely resemble Access crosstab query datasheets, which are one of the main topics of Chapter 11, "Creating Multitable and Crosstab Queries." Both PivotTables and crosstab queries employ aggregate functions—sum, average, count, standard deviation, variance, and the like—to summarize data, but PivotTables can handle the entire aggregation process. This enables PivotTables to selectively display the detail data behind subtotals and grand totals.

Crosstab queries are limited to creating row-by-row subtotals, with optional row (but not column) totals. PivotTables not only provide subtotals but also supply grand totals for rows and columns, plus crossfoot totals. *Crossfooting* is an accounting term for testing the accuracy of a set of numerical values by verifying that the grand totals calculated by row and by column are the same. One of the primary advantages of PivotTables over crosstab datasheets is that the Access application's user, not the database developer who designed the query, can control data presentation.

PivotTables let you swap axes and apply filters to the underlying data. Like filters for tables and queries, you can use PivotTable filters to remove extraneous or unneeded data from the current view.

TIP

Substitute PivotTables for crosstab queries when your data presentation needs crossfooting or you want to apply sophisticated report formatting to the presentation. It's usually much faster to use PivotTable features to generate row totals, subtotals, and grand totals than it is to use crosstab queries. Another advantage of PivotTables is that users can set the amount of detail information that appears in the report and then generate their own graphs or charts from the data.

12

CREATING THE QUERY FOR A SAMPLE PIVOTTABLE VIEW

Queries designed for users who are accustomed to using Excel PivotTable should offer a high degree of flexibility for slicing and dicing the data. For example, sales and marketing managers are likely to want to explore the total value of orders received each quarter by salesperson, customer, product, country, or any combination of these selection criteria. Therefore, your query must supply more than the ordinary amount of data to the PivotTable.

TIP

> Don't assign Caption property values to fields of tables you intend to use with queries for PivotTables and PivotCharts. You can't override the Caption property with query aliases in Access 2007.
>
> To override the Caption property value in aggregate queries, apply a function to the field that doesn't change its values, such as `Trim` for text fields and `Round` for numeric fields. This workaround causes conventional `SELECT` queries to not be updatable, but most PivotTables are based on aggregate queries, which aren't updatable under any condition.

→ For more information on the Caption property issue, **see** "Changing the Names of Query Column Headers," **p. 394**.

One of the most common forms of PivotTables displays time-series data, such as orders or sales by quarter for one or more years. To design a time-series query that supplies the underlying data for a PivotTable to display the quarterly value of orders by salesperson and country, do the following:

1. Open a new query in Design view in \SEUA12\Chaptr12\PivotNW.accdb, \SEUA12\ Northwind\Northwind.accdb, or your working copy of the sample database.

2. Add the Employees and Orders tables as well as the Order Subtotals query, to the new query.

3. Drag the LastName field of the Employees table to the query grid, followed in order by the ShipCountry and OrderDate fields of the Orders table, and the Subtotal field of the Order Subtotals query.

4. Add a **Between #1/1/2006# And #12/31/2006#** criterion to the OrderDate column to restrict the data to the last full year for which order data exists in Northwind.accdb. Clear the Show check box for this column.

5. Drag the OrderDate field from the Orders table to create a new column to the left of the existing OrderDate field. Replace the content of the Field cell of this column with **2006 Quarter: Format([OrderDate],"q")** to create a calculated column to display the number of the calendar quarter in which the order was received.

6. Place the cursor at the beginning of the LastName field, and replace LastName with **Name: Trim(LastName)** to add an alias to the field. Replace ShipCountry with **Country: Trim(ShipCountry)** and add an **Orders:** alias to the Subtotals field. Your query design appears as shown in Figure 12.1.

7. Run the query to check your work, and save the query as **qry2006OrdersByCountryPT** (see Figure 12.2).

Figure 12.1
This query design provides detail data suitable for analyzing employee sales by country.

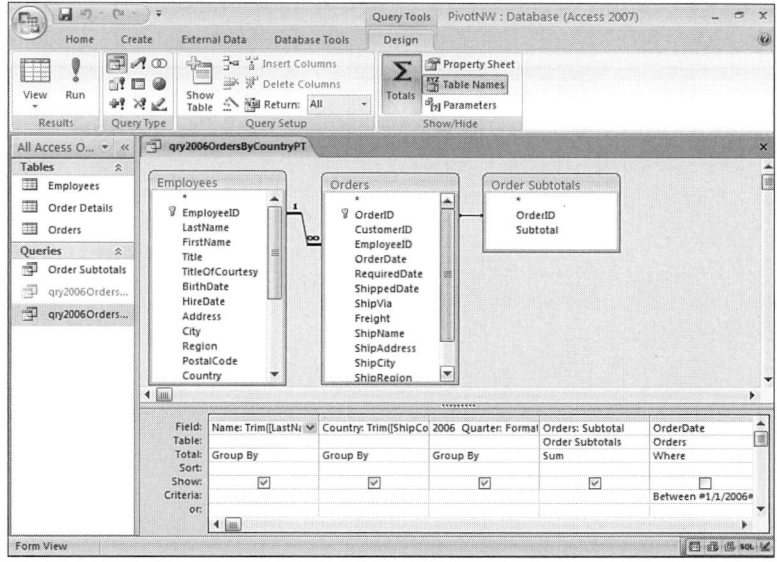

Figure 12.2
The Datasheet view of the query design of Figure 12.1 shows the altered field captions and lists the 408 orders received by Northwind Traders in 2006.

DESIGNING THE PIVOTTABLE VIEW OF THE SAMPLE QUERY

Select the PivotTable View button in the ribbon's Views group; the PivotTable Design ribbon activates. An empty PivotTable view opens with the PivotTable Field List window active and empty Filter Fields, Column Fields, Row Fields, and Totals or Detail Fields drop zones (see Figure 12.3).

12

Figure 12.3
When you open a new PivotTable view of a table or query, the field list of the source table or query has the focus.

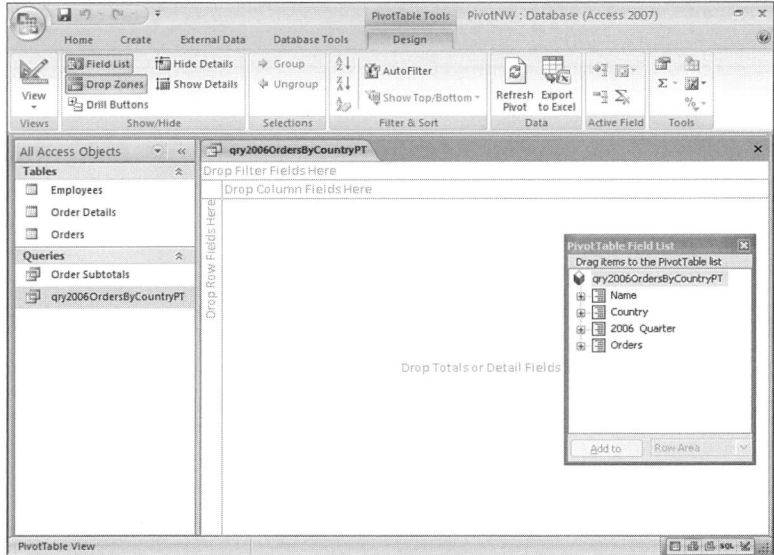

 TIP

If the PivotTable Field List isn't visible, click the Field List button in the ribbon's Show/Hide group.

You drag fields from the PivotTable Field List to the appropriate drop zone, as follows:

- *Column Fields*—Usually hold date-based fields to create a left-to-right time series. If you're not creating a time-series PivotTable, you can select any appropriate field of the table or query. As a rule, the field having the fewest number of rows belongs in columns.

- *Row Fields*—Hold one or more fields that display data by attribute(s). Adding row fields lets you increase the degree of detail displayed by the PivotTable. Increasing the amount of detail data shown is called *drilling down* or *drill-down*.

- *Totals or Detail Fields*—As the central area of the empty PivotTable, these fields display the crosstabulated data. This drop area accepts only fields having numeric values or fields for which you only want to display a count of records.

- *Filter Fields*—One or more optional fields that let you restrict the number of fields that appear in columns, rows, or both. In most cases, you filter data by column or row fields, not fields dropped in the Filter Fields zone. (A field can appear only in one drop zone of a PivotTable.)

GENERATING THE INITIAL PIVOTTABLE

To create the initial PivotTable view of the qry2006OrdersByCountryPT query, do the following:

1. Drag the 2006 Quarter field to the Column Fields drop zone. As the field symbol enters the drop zone, a blue border appears (see Figure 12.4). When you drop the field by releasing the mouse button, a 2006 Quarter filter button appears on the first row, and four columns display quarter numbers 1 through 4. PivotTables automatically add a Grand Total column to the right of the last column you add from the field list.

Figure 12.4
When you drag a field from the PivotTable Field List to a drop zone, the drop zone gains a thicker blue border.

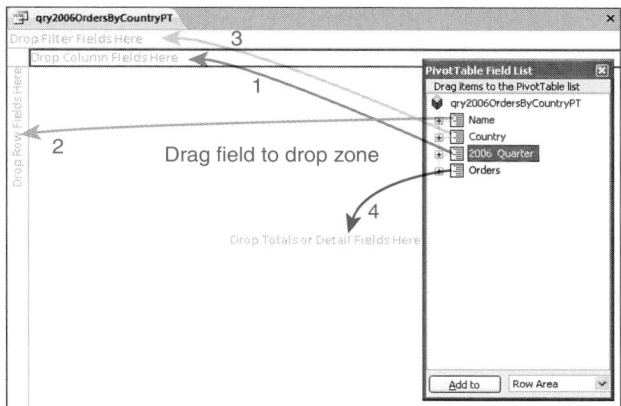

2. Drag the Name field to the Row Fields drop zone, the Orders field to the Totals or Detail Fields drop zone, and the Country field to the Filter Fields drop zone. The PivotTable appears with the rows displaying detail values, as shown in Figure 12.5.

Figure 12.5
After you've dragged the four fields to the locations shown here, the default PivotTable view includes detail values for rows. In this case, the amount of each order obtained by the salesperson appears in the expanded quarter columns.

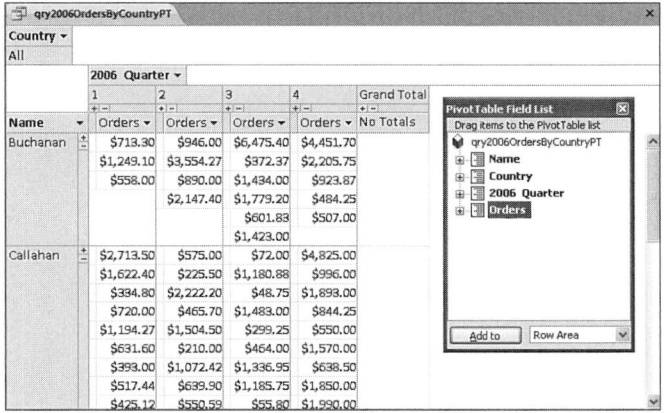

3. You can't identify the countries for the orders in the columns, so drag the Country field from the Filter Fields drop zone to the Name button to group the orders by country. Close the PivotTable Field list.

4. Click the Name button to select it, and click the Bold button on the Home tab to increase the contrast of the selected column (see Figure 12.6).

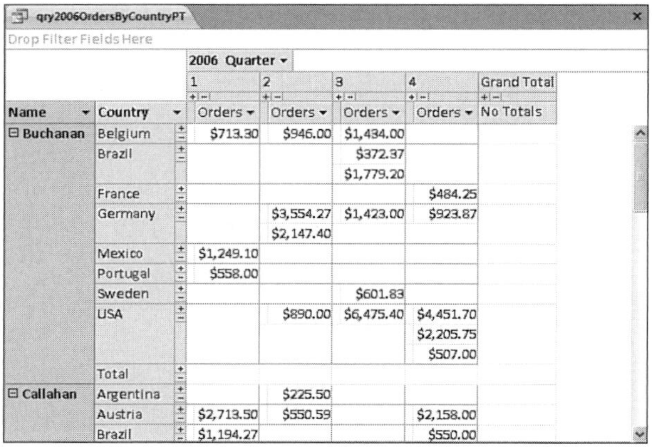

Figure 12.6
Moving the Country field from the Filter Fields to the right of the Name field displays the orders for each country.

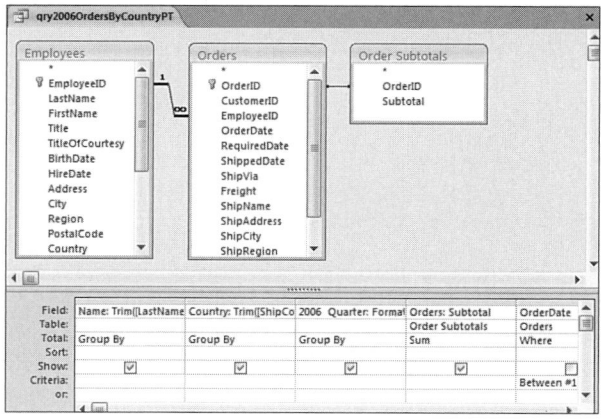

REDUCING THE LEVEL OF DETAIL AND ADDING GRAND TOTALS

Including amounts for each order in the PivotTable shows excessive detail. One approach for this example is to alter the query design to an aggregate (summary) query and group the individual orders by salesperson, country, and quarter.

To modify the query, regenerate the PivotTable data, and add grand totals, do this:

1. Change to Design view.

2. Click the Totals button to group the query data by LastName, ShipCountry, and 2006 Quarter.

3. Open the Total cell for the Orders: Subtotal column and choose Sum as the SQL aggregate function. Open the OrderDate field and select Where. Your modified aggregate query design appears as shown in Figure 12.7.

Figure 12.7
Change the query design to an aggregate query to sum individual orders by LastName, ShipCountry, and 2006 Quarter columns.

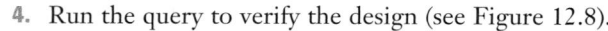

4. Run the query to verify the design (see Figure 12.8).

Figure 12.8
The result set of the query design has 251 records; the original query had 408 records (refer to Figure 12.2).

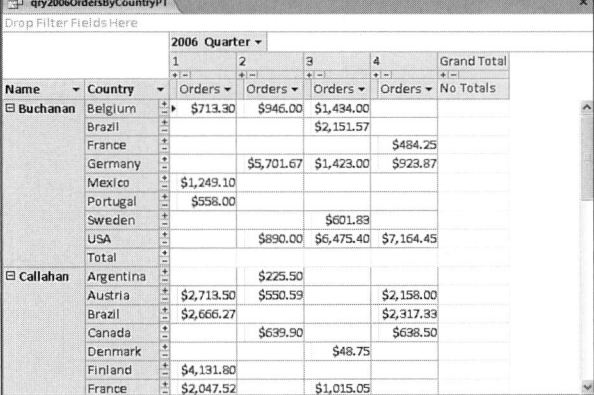

5. Return to PivotTable view, which now displays the summary data (see Figure 12.9).

Figure 12.9
Converting the PivotTable source query to an aggregate query results in a PivotTable with a single value for the total amount of orders from each country.

6. To add Grand Total values, click one of the Orders buttons to select all the Quarter columns, click the PivotTable Tools, Design tab's AutoCalc button, and select Sum from the AutoCalc aggregate functions list. Adding Grand Totals also adds Totals and Sum of Orders items to the PivotTable Field List and totals rows to each Country entry (see Figure 12.10). Close the PivotTable Field List, if it's open.

7. Click the Country button and click Hide Details to display only a single Sum of Orders value for each employee and country. The PivotTable now displays only a single row per country for each employee. Countries from which the employee obtained no orders during the year don't appear.

8. With the Country field selected, click the Subtotals button to add a Totals row for each employee (see Figure 12.11).

12

Figure 12.10
Adding Grand Totals
to the PivotTable also
adds Sum of Orders
totals to the Country
entries.

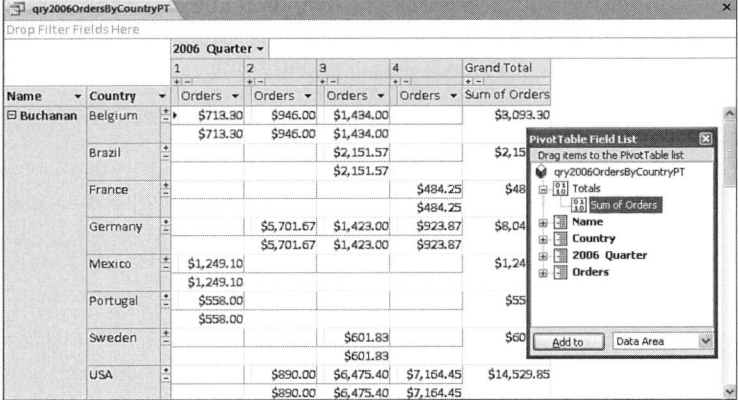

Figure 12.11
Hiding detail rows
and adding subtotals
for each employee
results in a more
meaningful PivotTable
presentation of your
data. Bold formatting
is applied to the Total
label for emphasis.

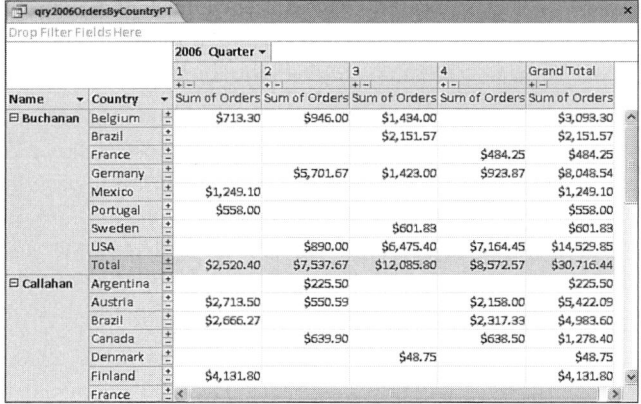

9. Click the Name button to select the column, and click the Active Field group's Collapse button to remove Country values for the employees and display the summary entries for all employees without scrolling (see Figure 12.12). Clicking the adjacent Expand and Collapse buttons toggles display of detail columns.

> **TIP**
>
> You can expand the display for a single employee by clicking the small Show/Hide Details (+) button to the left of the employee's name. The Show/Hide Details button toggles the + and - states.

FILTERING PIVOTTABLE CATEGORY VALUES

Worldwide sales data probably satisfies top management, but regional managers might want to display only orders received from a particular area, such as North America, Europe, or Scandinavia. By default, all field values appear in PivotTable rows or columns and are included in all calculated values, such as totals.

Figure 12.12
Collapsing the Name column eliminates the Country field detail and displays summary data only. Bold formatting is applied to the two Grand Totals labels.

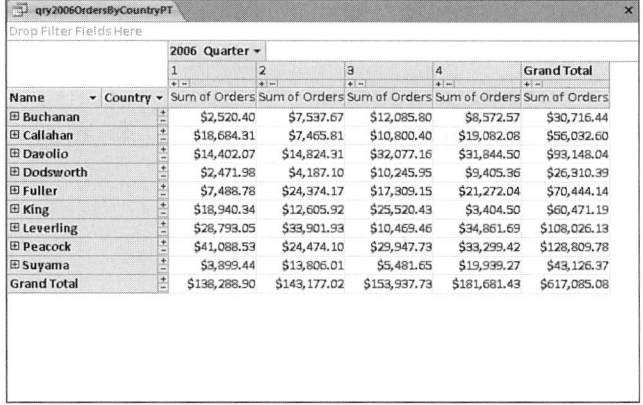

You can filter the PivotTable to display only selected values of a category field, such as Country, by following these steps:

1. Expand the PivotTable display to include the field on which you want to filter. For this example, select the Name field and click the Expand button to display the Countries column.

2. Click the arrow of the field button to filter (Country for this example) in order to open the field value list. The list contains an item for each field value.

3. Click the (All) check box to deselect all fields.

4. Mark the check boxes of the field values you want to include—Canada, Mexico, and USA for this example.

5. Click OK to close the list and apply the filter.

Figure 12.13 illustrates the sample PivotTable with only the Canada, Mexico, and USA fields selected. To return to displaying all fields, open the list and click the (All) check box.

Figure 12.13
This filtered PivotTable view restricts the visible values to orders received from Canada, Mexico, and the USA.

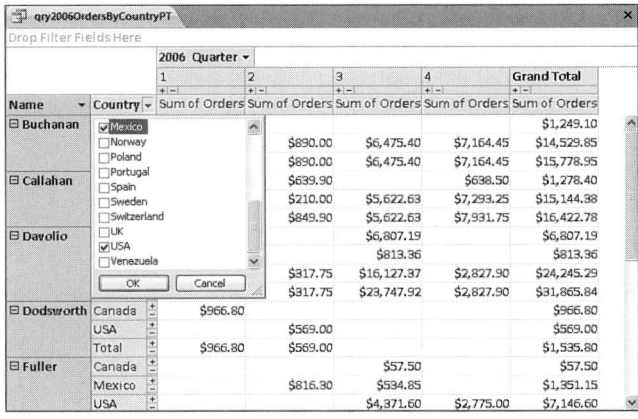

12

You also can filter data by rank, such as the top- or bottom-performing salesperson, or the countries with the highest or lowest sales. To test the PivotTable's Top/Bottom Items feature with the sample query, do the following:

 1. Select the Name column, click the Filter and Sort group's Show Top/Bottom Items button, choose Show Only the Top, and choose 1 from the submenu. The PivotTable displays data only for Margaret Peacock, the top salesperson for North American orders.

2. Click the Show Top/Bottom Items button, choose Show Only the Bottom, and choose 1 from the submenu. The PivotTable shows Anne Dodsworth occupies the lowest rung on the North America sales ladder.

3. Remove the filter on the Names column by clicking the Show Top/Bottom Items button and choosing Show All.

> **TIP**
>
> Use the Filter and Sort group's AutoFilter button to toggle between filtered and unfiltered display quickly.

4. Select the Country column, click the Show Top/Bottom Items button, choose Show Only the Top, and choose 2 from the submenu. The PivotTable displays data for Germany and the USA for all employees (see Figure 12.14).

Figure 12.14
The PivotTable's Top/Bottom Items feature lets you filter items by the value rank. Germany and the USA rank by order amount as the top two countries.

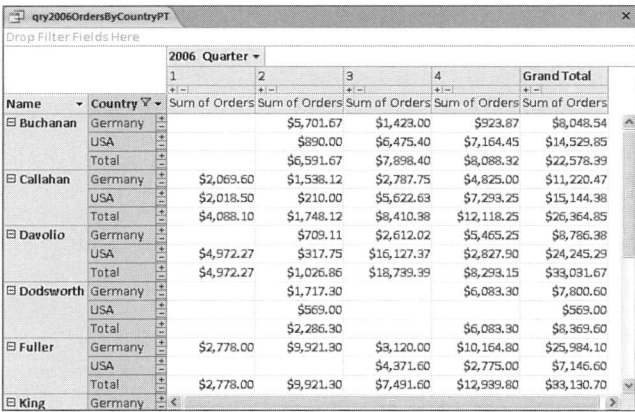

5. Remove the filter on the Country column by clicking the Show Top/Bottom Items button and choosing Show All.

If you select Other in the list of values, the Properties dialog opens to the Filter and Group page, where you can set custom filtering options by numeric or percentage rank.

INCREASING THE LEVEL OF DETAIL FOR DRILL-DOWN

The preceding section demonstrates the capability to reduce to a manageable level the amount of detail information displayed by the PivotTable. Total amounts of the orders obtained by employees for each country might satisfy the vice-president of sales, but sales managers and salespersons might want to review values of individual orders. Commissioned salespersons want order number and date information to ensure that all orders they book are assigned to them.

Providing additional drill-down information requires you to modify the underlying sample query and regenerate the value data, as follows:

1. Return to Query Design view.

2. Click the Totals button to remove the Totals row and eliminate data grouping.

3. Drag the OrderID and OrderDate fields of the Orders table field list to the right of the LastName field. (The column sequence isn't important.)

4. Return to PivotTable view, click the Show Details button, and click the Field List button to display the PivotTable Field List, which now has Order ID, Order Date, Order Date by Week, and Order Date by Month items added.

5. Right-click the Sum of Orders item in the Field List, and choose Delete to replace the Sum of Orders labels with Orders.

6. Drag the Order ID field to the immediate left of the Orders button. Drag the Order Date field to the immediate right of the Order ID button. Select the Orders button, click the AutoCalc button, and select Sum to add a Sum of Orders row rather than a column (see Figure 12.15), and then close the PivotTable Field List. If the Order… fields aren't in the correct sequence, drag their buttons to the proper relative position.

Figure 12.15
The PivotTable now displays Order ID and Order Date values for each order.

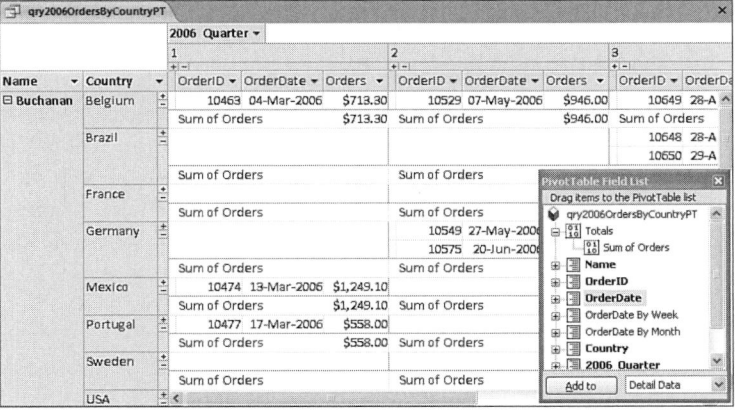

7. Click the Hide Details button to reduce the PivotTable's level of detail.

> Be judicious when increasing the detail level of PivotTables by eliminating grouping in your query. The later "Optimizing Performance of PivotTables" section describes performance problems that result from large query result sets.

CHANGING FILL/BACKGROUND AND TEXT COLORS

 You can increase the contrast of the PivotTable's display or emphasize elements by changing their color with the Fill Color tool of the Home tab's Font group. For example, you can remove the gray tint from the Name, Country, Quarter, and Grand Total labels by selecting each field in sequence, clicking the Fill/Back Color tool, and choosing white in the color picker (see Figure 12.16). Alternatively, you can apply a new color scheme to the display by choosing appropriate Access Theme colors.

Figure 12.16
Substituting a white background for the default gray color of the Name, Country, Quarter, and Grand Total field labels increases the contrast of the PivotTable.

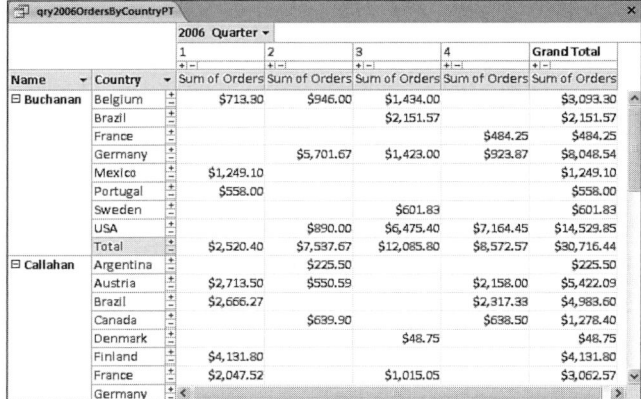

EXCHANGING PIVOTTABLE AXES AND CATEGORY HIERARCHIES

The term PivotTable derives from the capability to exchange (pivot) the x (horizontal) and y (vertical) axes of the table. PivotTables also let you exchange the hierarchy of category columns, which often is more useful than pivoting the table. If you're more interested in sales by country than by employee, drag the sample PivotTable's Country button to the left of the Name button. The All Orders values now represent quarterly sales by country (see Figure 12.17).

> If you accidentally drag the field out of the PivotTable window, which removes the field from the PivotTable, open the Field List and drag the missing field to the proper location.

qry2006OrdersByCountryPT

Country	Name	2006 Quarter 1	2	3	4	Grand Total
		Sum of Orders	Sum of Orders	Sum of Orders	Sum of Orders	Sum of Orders
Argentina	Callahan		$225.50			$225.50
	Dodsworth				$12.50	$12.50
	King		$110.00			$110.00
	Leverling	$319.20				$319.20
	Peacock	$443.40			$706.00	$1,149.40
	Total	$762.60	$335.50		$718.50	$1,816.60
Austria	Callahan	$2,713.50	$550.59		$2,158.00	$5,422.09
	Davolio				$8,665.67	$8,665.67
	Dodsworth				$344.00	$344.00
	Fuller			$6,129.45		$6,129.45
	King			$7,765.47		$7,765.47
	Leverling	$1,792.00	$12,803.45			$14,595.45
	Peacock	$6,405.21			$3,436.45	$9,841.66
	Suyama	$439.20			$4,198.85	$4,638.05
	Total	$11,349.91	$13,354.04	$13,894.92	$18,802.97	$57,401.84
Belgium	Buchanan	$713.30	$946.00	$1,434.00		$3,093.30
	Dodsworth					

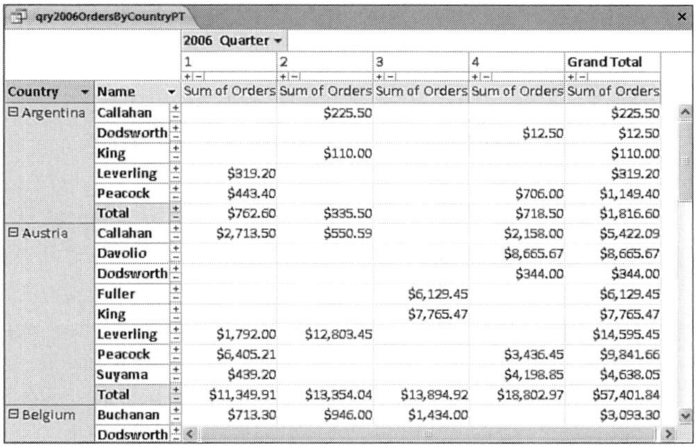

Figure 12.17 Interchanging the Country and Names fields recalculates the PivotTable to display values for quarterly sales by country. Details are hidden with the Hide Details button in this example.

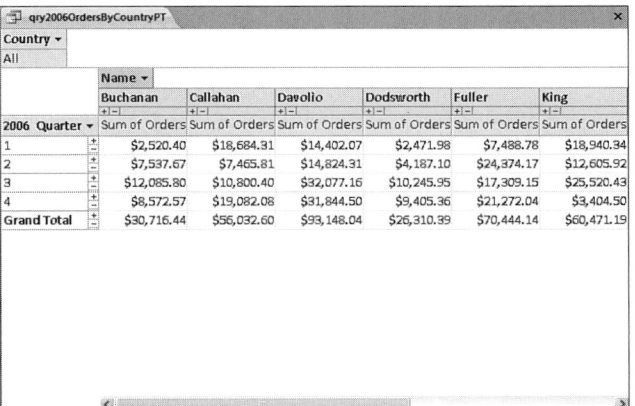

Interchanging the axes lets you view the data from a different perspective. In many cases, users want data presented in a familiar format. For example, the sales manager might be accustomed to comparing the quarter-by-quarter performance of his or her salespeople with quarterly data in rows, not columns. To exchange the Name and 2006 Quarter axes, drag the Name button to its original position (left of the Country button), drag the 2006 Quarter button to the left of the Name button, and then drag the Name button to the empty Column Fields drop zone. Optionally, drag the Country field to the Filter Fields drop zone (see Figure 12.18).

qry2006OrdersByCountryPT

Country: All

2006 Quarter	Name: Buchanan	Callahan	Davolio	Dodsworth	Fuller	King
	Sum of Orders	Sum of Orders	Sum of Orders	Sum of Orders	Sum of Orders	Sum of Orders
1	$2,520.40	$18,684.31	$14,402.07	$2,471.98	$7,488.78	$18,940.34
2	$7,537.67	$7,465.81	$14,824.31	$4,187.10	$24,374.17	$12,605.92
3	$12,085.80	$10,800.40	$32,077.16	$10,245.95	$17,309.15	$25,520.43
4	$8,572.57	$19,082.08	$31,844.50	$9,405.36	$21,272.04	$3,404.50
Grand Total	$30,716.44	$56,032.60	$93,148.04	$26,310.39	$70,444.14	$60,471.19

Figure 12.18 Rotating the axes of a PivotTable lets you conform data presentation to the users' preference. In this example, the Employees field includes only the first six employees in the filter list.

SETTING PIVOTTABLE PROPERTY VALUES

The Properties dialog has four pages of PivotTable property settings for active elements. Right-click a field and choose Properties to open the dialog. Following are brief descriptions of the purpose of each page:

- *Format*—Lets you select a field name and select the font name, size, color, attributes (bold, italic, underlined), and justification (left, right, and centered). You also can set the background color, column width, and sort the column or row in ascending (default) or descending order. The value in the Select list determines the field to which properties you set in the Filter and Group and Captions pages apply (see Figure 12.19, left).

- *Filter and Group*—Enables customer top/bottom value filtering of the field you select on the Format page. If you have ungrouped items in a field, you can use the Grouping controls to aggregate them (see Figure 12.19, right).

Figure 12.19
The Format (left) page's Select value determines the field to which the settings of the Filter and Group (right) and Captions pages apply.

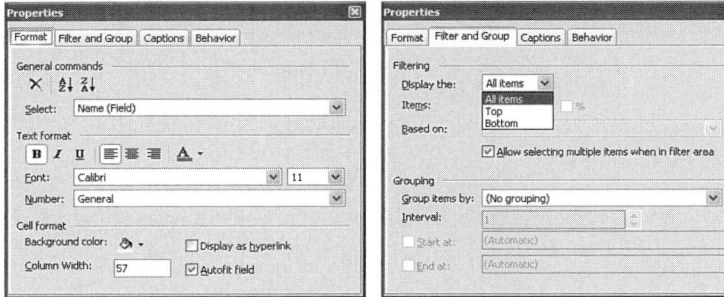

- *Captions*—Lets you change the caption for the field you selected in the Format page. For example, you can change Sum of Orders caption to All Orders, Order ID to Number, or Order Date to Date. The captions page also has a list of uninteresting property values (see Figure 12.20, left).

- *Behavior*—Options apply to the entire PivotTable. You can hide the Show/Hide Details buttons of fields and the drop zones. In the case of the PivotTable of the sample query, you can hide the Filter Fields drop zone, because there is no suitable field available to drop in the zone. PivotTable views of tables and queries don't have a title bar or built-in toolbar, so two of the check boxes are disabled (see Figure 12.20, right). PivotTable view of forms have a title bar.

Figure 12.20
The most important feature of the Captions page (left) is the ability to change the caption of any PivotTable field. The options you set in the Behavior page (right) apply to all fields.

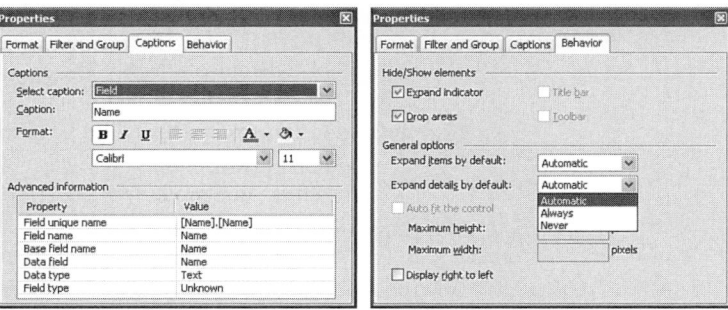

- *Report*—These options also apply to the entire PivotTable. The Report page only appears when you right-click an empty region of the PivotTable. The most important options are Always Display Empty Rows and Empty Columns. Marking either of these check boxes generates a row or column, regardless of whether a value is present. Accept the default options, unless you have a good reason to do otherwise.

If you right-click an empty area of the PivotTable and choose Properties, only the Captions, Report, and Behavior pages appear. In this case, the Captions page lets you change captions for the four drop zones and the title bar.

TIP

> To make PivotTable view the default for your query, change to Design mode, open the Query Properties dialog, and change the Default View property value to PivotTable.
>
> To print a PivotTable, choose File, Print in PivotTable view. You might need to widen the columns slightly to print Grand Total columns correctly.

EXPORTING THE PIVOTTABLE TO EXCEL

You can export the PivotTable as a *FileName*.htm file, together with supporting .xml, .htm, and .css files, or as a single-file web page (*FileName*.mht) to a pseudo-PivotTable in an Excel workbook. This isn't a very exciting feature, because the process exports the data as a static XML rowset (Cachedata.xml in the …*FileName*_files folder). The temporary workbook is read-only and doesn't update as the underlying data from the query changes.

Click the Export to Microsoft Excel button to generate the PivotTable workbook. Figure 12.21 shows the default view of the PivotTable exported to Sheet1 of a workbook with the Excel PivotTable Tools, Design tab and PivotTable Field List pane active. You might need to drag a field to the worksheet and enable data transfer to complete the PivotTable import. Sheet 2 contains data exported by the source query of the PivotTable, which Excel translates from the Cachedata.xml file.

Clicking Excel's Chart Wizard button automatically generates a PivotChart from the PivotTable. To create a readable chart, clear the Country check box in the PivotTable Field List pane to eliminate the Country detail data before you click the Chart Wizard button. Otherwise, the chart is impossible to decipher. Figure 12.22 shows the PivotChart created from the collapsed PivotTable.

NOTE

> The files required to create the Excel workbook described in this section are included in the \SEUA12\Chaptr12 folder of the accompanying CD-ROM. Double-click the 2006OrdersByEmployee&CountryPT.mht file to open a static PivotTable in IE 5+. Opening the *PivotTableName*.mht or .htm file of a PivotTable saved as a web page adds an Edit with Microsoft Office Excel choice to IE 7's Page menu.

Figure 12.21
This Excel workbook was created by exporting the sample PivotTable from the earlier "Increasing the Level of Detail for Drill-Down" section.

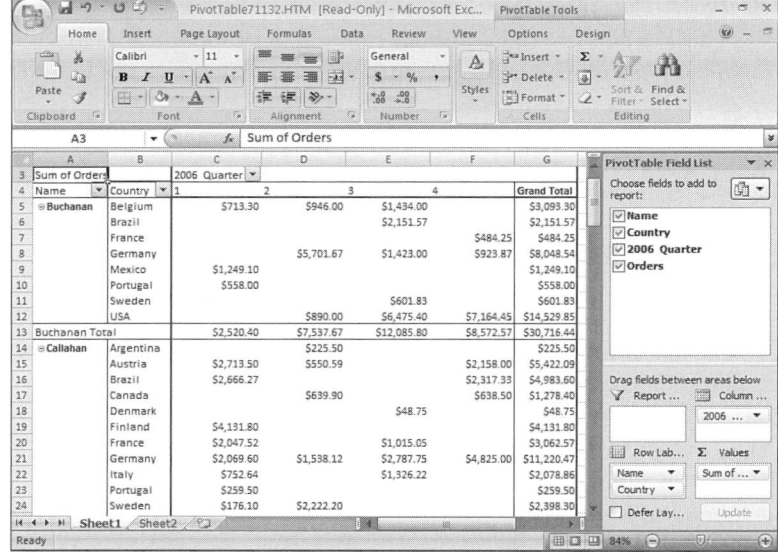

Figure 12.22
The Excel Chart Wizard displays in another worksheet a PivotChart based on each row and column displayed in the PivotTable.

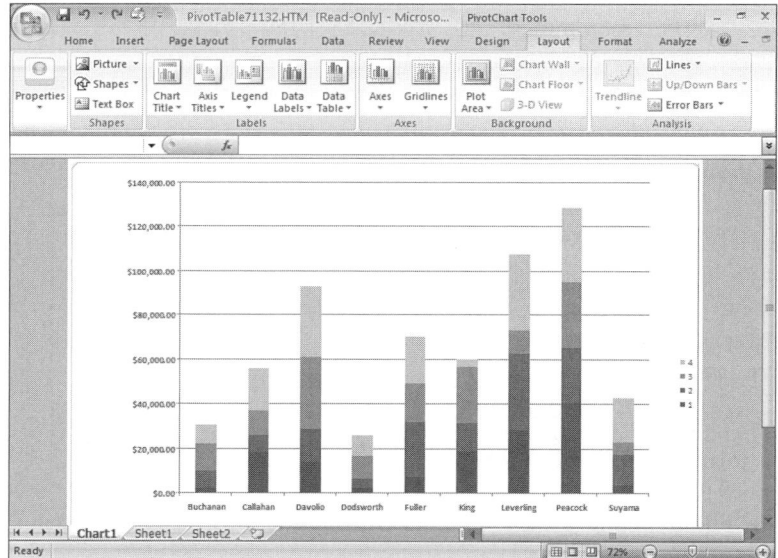

OPTIMIZING PERFORMANCE OF PIVOTTABLES

The first and most important rule of PivotTables is, *Minimize the number of rows returned by queries that you intend to use as the data source for PivotTable views.* Access returns only the first 100 rows of the query result set to the initial Datasheet view, so response is almost instantaneous for a default Dynaset-type query without GROUP BY or other operations that require operations on the entire result set. The Access database engine retrieves additional rows as you scroll the datasheet. Unfortunately, PivotTables don't take advantage of Access's incremental row retrieval feature.

The Oakmont.mdb sample database has a sufficient number of records to bring a PivotTable view to its knees with a simple query. For example, you might want to analyze tuition revenue by student graduation year and course. The average Oakmont student is enrolled in only two courses, so the query returns 59,996 rows. The objective of the query is to return total revenue and an enrollment count for all sections of each of the 590 courses offered by the college, and to summarize the data by academic department. In theory, the PivotTable's AutoCalc feature should be able to total the revenue and count the number of enrollment records. Figure 12.23 shows the initial design of a query that's capable of providing the required data.

Figure 12.23
This sample query against four tables of the Oakmont.mdb database returns 59,996 rows.

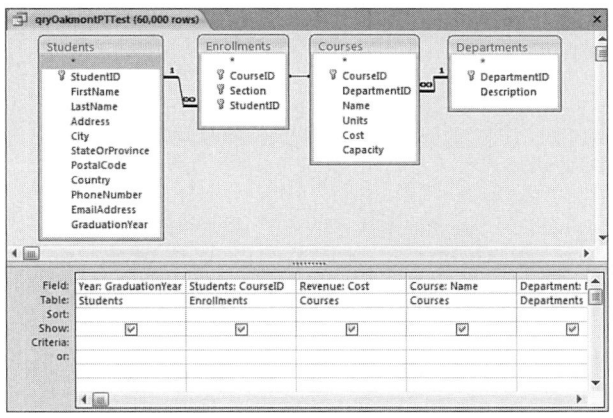

NOTE

The three qryOakmontPTTest sample queries (60,000, 2,350, and 52 rows) discussed in this section are included in the PivotOM.accdb database in the \SEUA12\Chaptr12 folder of the accompanying CD-ROM. You must install the Oakmont.accdb database from the CD-ROM to its default location, C:\SEUA12\Oakmont, for these queries to execute from the default linked tables. If you've installed Oakmont.accdb to another location, click the Database Tools tab's Linked Table Manager button and then change the links to the correct path before attempting to open a table or query.

→ To review how to use the Linked Table Manager, **see** "Using the Linked Table Manager Add-in to Relink Tables," **p. 358**.

Opening the 60,000-row query design of Figure 12.23 in PivotTable view takes six seconds or more on a fast computer (a 2.1GHz Pentium 4 system with 1GB RAM and a fast Serial-ATA (SATA) drive running Windows XP Professional). This delay occurs every time you move from Query Datasheet or Design view to PivotTable view, because all rows of the

12

query must be loaded into the PivotTable to compute totals. An equal delay occurs between PivotTable and PivotChart views. If the Oakmont.mdb file is on a network server, opening the PivotTable view can take up to 30 seconds and consume a large part (or all) of the network's available bandwidth. Clicking Show Details requires about five seconds to regenerate the local PivotTable view.

 If you're using large Access tables shared from a network server and experience performance problems with PivotTables, see the "PivotTable Performance Problems with Networked Tables" topic of the "Troubleshooting" section near the end of this chapter.

If the opening delay doesn't sufficiently deter you, dropping fields of this query to rows or columns can consume 100% of your CPU cycles and take even longer. If you don't select Hide Details beforehand, dropping the Year field on the Column Fields zone takes a minute or two for the four year (2003 through 2006) columns to appear. Clicking Hide Details and dropping the Year field takes only a few seconds to display the columns. With details hidden, dropping Department on the Row Fields zone, and Revenue and Students on the Totals and Detail Fields zones, takes only about a second to regenerate totals (see Figure 12.24).

Figure 12.24
This PivotTable performs grouping and aggregation operations on a 60,000-row query result set. Performing these operations in the PivotTable can take a long time.

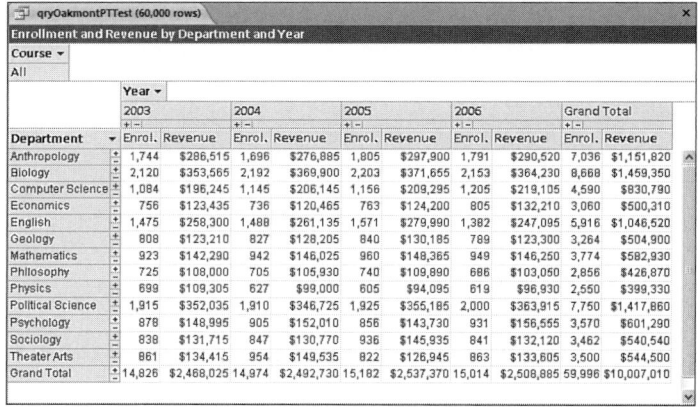

The solution to the preceding performance hit is to use Access's Totals (Group By) feature to reduce the number of query rows. Grouping by year, course, and department; counting Enrollments records; and summing the Cost field of the Courses table lets the Access query engine—instead of the PivotTable—handle the initial aggregation (see Figure 12.25).

The PivotTable—identical to that shown earlier in Figure 12.24—better digests the result set of the aggregate query, which now contains 2,348 rows. Access takes only about two seconds to execute this query from a local database, and the same PivotTable view opens in a bit more than three seconds. The detail data is consolidated by the query, so the Show Detail/Hide Detail toggle operation is almost instantaneous. Reducing the number of rows of the local query result set, however, doesn't reduce network traffic if you're connected to a remote database.

12

Figure 12.25
Adding a GROUP BY expression to the query and summing the enrollment count and tuition revenue in the Access query reduces the number of query rows from 59,996 to 2,348.

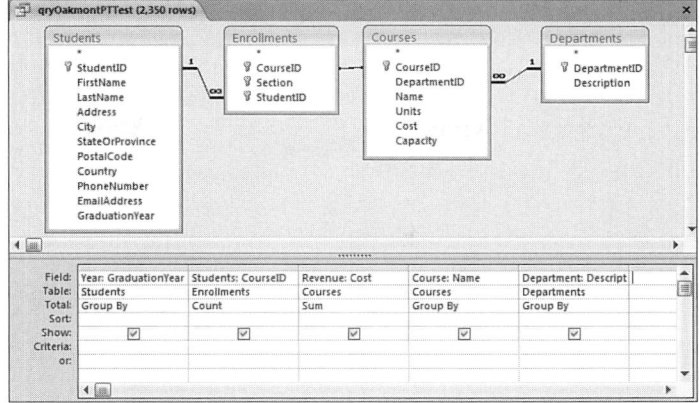

If you don't need detail enrollment and revenue data for each course, you can speed PivotTable operations by removing the Course: Name field from the query design of Figure 12.25 to return only 52 rows. Execution of the Access query with 52 rows takes about the same time as for 2,348 rows, but PivotTable operations are almost instantaneous.

FORMATTING AND MANIPULATING PIVOTCHARTS

When you define a PivotTable view, you also automatically generate a corresponding PivotChart view of tables, queries, and forms. Access links PivotTable and PivotChart views, so there's no need for a Chart Wizard to specify the initial design. For example, open the PivotTable view of the qry2006OrdersByCountryPT sample query you created in the "Creating the Query for a Sample PivotTable View" section near the beginning of the chapter and collapse the Name category, if Country fields are visible. Choose PivotChart view to open the chart, as shown in Figure 12.26.

ADDING LEGENDS, AXIS TITLES, AND FILTERS

Following are some of the PivotChart property values you can alter to change the format of PivotCharts and filter the data presented:

- *Legends*—The default PivotChart style is Clustered Column; each column of each category—quarterly sales columns for the Name category for this example—is color coded. Clicking the Show/Hide group's Legend button on the PivotChart Tools, Design ribbon toggles the legend below the 2006 Quarters field button.

- *Axis titles*—Titles for the x- and y-axes of the sample chart are missing. To add axis titles, right click the axis title, choose <u>P</u>roperties to open the Properties dialog, and click the Format page. You can change the font, size, and attributes, and type the title in the Caption text box.

12

Figure 12.26
The PivotTable automatically creates a PivotChart view of the qry2006OrdersByCountryPT sample query. Be sure to minimize the amount of category detail in the PivotTable before opening a PivotChart.

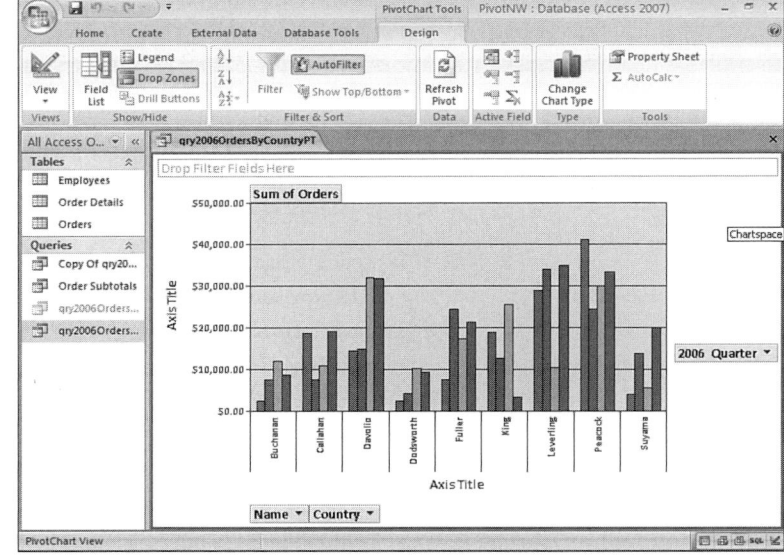

- *Category filters*—Filters on category fields limit the chart's display to selected values. As you change filter values, the chart automatically reformats the display and changes the scale of the y-axis to optimize the display. Adding filters to category fields also affects the PivotTable view.

Figure 12.27 shows the legend and axis titles added, and filters applied to the Name and Country categories. Axis totals and a legend have been added. X-axis category values rotate 90 degrees counterclockwise if their width fits the divisions.

Figure 12.27
The sample PivotChart displays totals of North American orders for the first five employees.

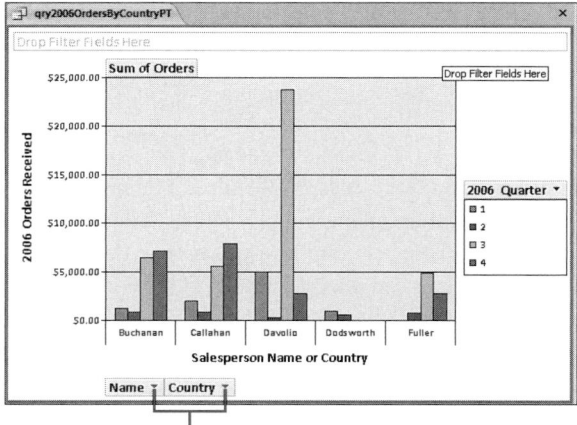

Arrows change from black to blue to indicate that a filter is applied

TIP

Remove filters applied to category fields as soon as you no longer need them. The only visible feedback that a filter is applied is a change to the color of the small arrows from black to blue, which isn't readily apparent. Accidentally leaving a filter in place when changing the chart's layout can lead to interpretation errors.

ALTERING CATEGORY PRESENTATION

PivotCharts have Filter Fields and Category Fields drop zones similar to those of PivotTables, and field buttons corresponding to those of the source PivotTable. An additional field button (All Orders for this example) represents the PivotTable's values displayed by the chart, called a *series*. You can change category presentation by dragging category fields to the Filter Fields drop zone and changing the chart's display as follows:

- *Coalesce clusters to totals*—To display total sales for each employee for the year 2006, drag the 2006 Quarter button to the Filter Fields drop zone (see Figure 12.28). The y-axis scale changes to reflect the larger totals.

Figure 12.28
Dragging a category field button to the Filter Fields drop zone changes the clustered columns to a single total column for each category.

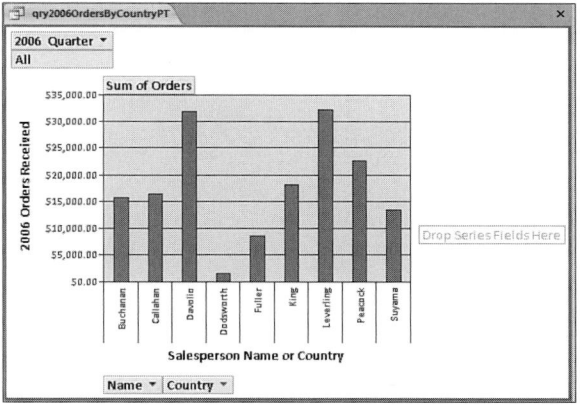

NOTE

Filter Field buttons indicate that a filter is applied by changing the All label to the filter selection. If you select more than one filter criterion, the label displays "(multiple items)."

- *Replace categories*—Drag the Name button to the Filter Fields drop zone to display total 2006 sales for each country (see Figure 12.29). Passing the mouse pointer over the chart's bars opens a ScreenTip, which displays detail data.

Figure 12.29
Dragging the leftmost (primary) category field button to the Filter Fields drop zone displays data for the remaining category button.

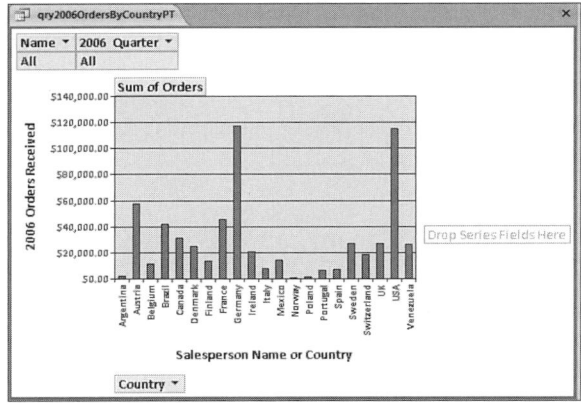

> **TIP**
>
>
>
> If you accidentally drag a field button outside the PivotChart's window and remove it from the PivotChart (and the PivotTable), open the Field List and drag the field to the appropriate drop zone.

- **Remove excessive detail**—When you return the Name and 2006 Quarter fields to their original locations—the Category and Series Fields drop zones, respectively—the category axis of the chart becomes an unreadable jumble. To remove the Country bars from the chart, select the Name button and click the Active Field group's Collapse button on the PivotChart Tools, Design ribbon, or right-click the chart and choose Collapse from the context menu.

- **Drill down into a category**—The Active Field group's Drill Into toolbar button or context menu choice lets you display the second (or lower) level of detail for a category. To display sales by country for a single salesperson, right-click the name in the category axis and choose Drill Into to display sales by country and quarter for the person (see Figure 12.30). To return to the original chart format, right-click the name and choose Drill Out. The Drill Into and Drill Out buttons and context menu choices are enabled only when you select a category item.

CHANGING THE CHART TYPE

 PivotCharts come in a remarkable variety of types and styles, ranging from the default Clustered Column to Radar, which displays values relative to a centerpoint (as in the radar display of an airport approach control facility). To change the chart's style, click outside the chart area and then click the PivotChart Tools, Design ribbon's Chart Type button to open the Properties dialog to the Type page. Click one of the styles to preview the chart's appearance. Figure 12.31 shows the sample chart type changed from Clustered to Stacked Column. Choosing a 100% Stacked Column style changes the y-axis units to percent.

Figure 12.30
Selecting a primary category item in the x-axis, such as Peacock, and clicking the ribbon's Drill Into button displays secondary category values—in this case, sales for Margaret Peacock by country and quarter.

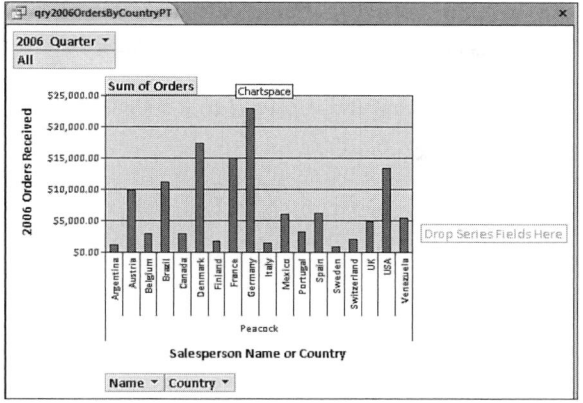

Figure 12.31
Column charts are one of 12 types you can select from the Types page of the Properties dialog. Each type has between 2 and 10 styles, and most types offer 3D versions.

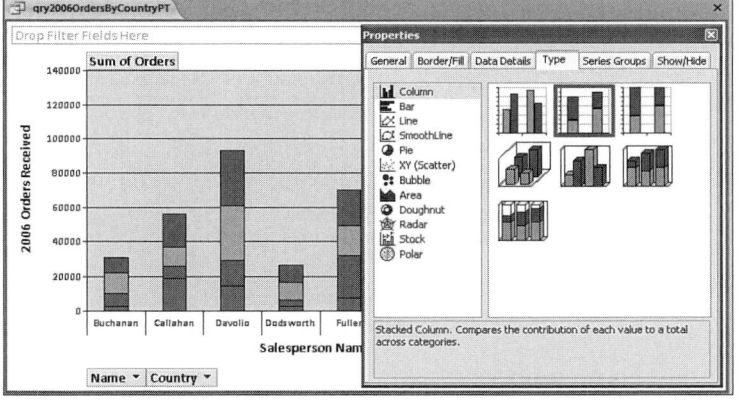

12

> **TIP**
>
> Don't change to a 100% Stacked Column—or any other 100%… style—unless you specifically need this style. When you return to another style, the format of the y-axis values change to General Number. You then must select the values, click the Format tab, and reset the numeric format.

The most useful formats for conventional PivotCharts are as follows:

- *Stacked Column charts*—Display contribution of series elements, such as quarters, to a total value. ScreenTips display the numeric value of each element of the column but, unfortunately, not the total value.

- *Bar charts*—Rotate the axes 90 degrees counterclockwise; offer the same styles as Column charts.

- *Stacked Area charts*—Better suited to time-series data, such as monthly, quarterly, or yearly categories. Figure 12.32 shows a Stacked Area chart from a slightly modified (monthly) version of the sample query. Unlike Stacked Bar or Column charts, ScreenTips of stacked area charts don't display numeric values.

Figure 12.32
This Stacked Area chart displays the month-to-month trend of each employee's contribution to total sales order value.

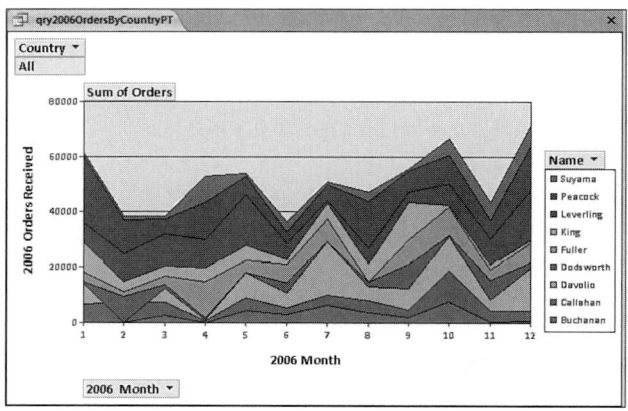

 The qry2006OrdersByCountryPT sample query and the completed PivotChart and PivotTable are included in the PivotNW.accdb sample database located in the \SEUA12\ Chaptr12 folder of the accompanying CD-ROM. The Oakmont queries are in the PivotOM.accdb database.

TROUBLESHOOTING

PIVOTTABLE PERFORMANCE PROBLEMS WITH NETWORKED TABLES

When I link large back-end tables on a network server as the data source for PivotTables, I experience serious deterioration in performance.

Opening PivotTables based on aggregate queries against remote Access tables requires moving all affected rows of the underlying tables across the network, because the query that performs the aggregation runs on your local computer. In a lightly loaded 100BaseT network, the added opening time for a PivotTable isn't a serious issue. If your network uses 10BaseT media or you're connected to a hub (not a switch), and the network has a substantial amount of traffic, aggregate queries against large tables can slow dramatically. For historical (static) data, consider converting the aggregate query to a make-table query and changing the data source to the table. Using a table with fewer rows also helps solve performance problems that result from overtaxed server disk drives.

If you upsize your application to SQL Server, queries run as views, functions, or stored procedures on the server, not the client PC. One of the primary advantages of client/server RDBMSs, such as SQL Server, is that only query result sets move across the network.

IN THE REAL WORLD—VISUALIZING DATA

Database developers, who deal with tables and query result sets on a daily basis, tend to forget that consumers of their products aren't necessarily fond of tabular data. Having to scan—let alone digest—reams of tabular data, whether on paper or PC monitor, is one of the curses of the cubicle.

Management executives primarily are interested in trends and exceptions. Only when trends go the wrong way or exceptions hit the bottom line are suits (middle management) or pinstripes (top execs, bankers, eastern venture capitalists) likely to be interested in detail data. Well-designed PivotTables let users control the amount of detail displayed, subject to the performance issues that result from using very large data sets to provide multiple drill-down levels. PivotChart's Drill Into and Out feature makes drill-down simple enough for management types to use.

THE PERILS OF PIVOT MANIPULATION

Before the advent of PivotTables and PivotCharts, application programmers had to design individual forms or write complex VBA code to let users slice and dice data according to their preferences. PivotTables and PivotCharts in Access forms let users choose the fields to display, change category hierarchies, and swap axes. The problem with this approach, of course, is that users who aren't familiar with PivotTables and PivotCharts get into trouble and call for help. After a few calls from users who've lost field buttons, it's tempting to lock down the view by clearing all the check boxes except ScreenTips in the Show/Hide page of the PivotChart's Properties dialog.

A better alternative to lockdown is user education. PivotTables are the cornerstone of Microsoft's approach to delivering crosstabs from SQL Server and other client/server tables linked to SQL Server databases. As Web Parts for delivering information to browser-based applications, such as Windows SharePoint Services version 3 and Microsoft Office SharePoint Server 2007, become more popular, you can expect PivotCharts to play an important role in all data-intensive presentation formats.

MEANING, SIGNIFICANCE, AND VISUALIZATION

Data becomes information when one grasps the meaning and significance of the data. Well-designed charts and graphs based on summary queries make the data contained in millions of rows of transactional tables meaningful. The significance of information is in the eye of the beholder. If your bonus is based on sales, trends in sales determine much of your income; if you're a profit-sharing participant, the bottom line counts the most. As noted at the beginning of the chapter, time-series graphs and charts are most common, because spotting trends and taking action based on trends is one of management's primary responsibilities. Trends inherently are historical in nature; regression analysis and other statistical methods enable projecting historical performance to the future with varying degrees of risk. In many cases, the experienced eye of a seasoned executive can better project future trends than the most sophisticated statistical algorithms.

12

Data visualization, the foundation of graphs based on queries, is more of an art than a science. Edward R. Tufte's self-published 1983 classic, *The Visual Display of Quantitative Information*, is still a bestseller—at least by computer book standards. Tufte's sequel, *Envisioning Information* (1990), deals primarily with cartography. The final volume of the trilogy, *Visual Explanations: Images and Quantities, Evidence and Narrative* (1997), covers presentation of dynamic data. Tufte describes his three books as "pictures of numbers, pictures of nouns, and pictures of verbs." Anyone designing Access graphs and charts for any purpose other than entertainment should own a copy of *The Visual Display of Quantitative Information*. After you become acquainted with Tufte's seminal work, you're very likely to acquire his other two books.

Management by Trend Exception

Most managers and executives suffer from information overload. One of the approaches to making information delivered to management more effective is to flag situations in which performance falls outside of the expected or budgeted range. Multiline graphs, which present actual versus projected performance, are especially useful for flagging poor or exceptional results at the region, department, division, or corporate level. Regression methods often are more useful in actual-versus-budgeted graphs, because extrapolated trend lines that cross budget lines in the wrong direction are immediately visible to the most harried executive. Adding budgetary data usually requires nested queries, views, or functions to combine summary results from transaction data and presummarized budget data.

12

CHAPTER 13

CREATING AND UPDATING ACCESS TABLES WITH ACTION QUERIES

In this chapter

GETTING ACQUAINTED WITH ACTION QUERIES

Action queries create new tables or modify the data in existing tables. Access offers the following four types of action queries:

- *Make-table* queries create new tables from the data contained in query result sets. One of the most common applications for make-table queries is to create tables that you can export to other applications or that summarize data from other tables. A make-table query provides a convenient way to copy a table to another database. In some cases, you can use make-table queries to speed the generation of multiple forms and reports based on a single, complex query.

- *Append* queries add new records to tables from the query's result set.

- *Delete* queries delete records from tables that correspond to the rows of the query result set.

- *Update* queries change the existing values of fields of table records that correspond to rows of the query result set.

By default, new queries you create are SELECT queries. After opening a new or existing query in Design view, you can change its type to one of the four action queries by clicking the Query Tools, Design tab's corresponding Query Type: Make Table, Query Type: Append, Query Type: Delete, and Query Type: Update buttons. Your Access database must trusted to execute Action queries. If the database isn't in a trusted location or signed by a valid code-signing certificate, execution will fail silently with a "The action or event has been blocked by Disabled Mode" message in the status bar.

> **NOTE**
>
> Access data projects (ADPs) offer similar Query menu choices for action queries when you create a new stored-procedure query. Stored procedures have an additional type of append query, called an *Append Values* procedure, which lets you add a new record with values you type in the da Vinci Query Design grid. SQL Server functions and views don't support make-table queries.

This chapter shows you how to create each of the four types of Access action queries and how to use Access's cascading deletions and cascading updates of related records. Cascading deletions and cascading updates are covered here because these referential-integrity features are related to delete and update action queries, respectively.

> **TIP**
>
> Always make a backup copy of a table that you intend to modify with an action query. This is especially important when using the Northwind.accdb sample database from \SEUA12\Nwind folder in this chapter's examples. Changes made to table data with action queries are permanent; an error can render a table useless. Invalid changes made to a table with an action query containing a design error often are difficult to detect.

CREATING NEW TABLES WITH MAKE-TABLE QUERIES

In the following sections, you learn how to use a make-table query to create a new table, tblShipAddresses, for customers that have different shipping and billing addresses. This process enables the deletion of the tblShipAddresses data that, in most of the records in the Orders table, duplicates the address data in the Customers table. Removing duplicated data to new tables is an important step when you're converting data contained in a flat (nonrelational) database to a relational database structure.

You can use the Table Analyzer Wizard, described in Chapter 5, "Working with Access Databases and Tables," to perform an operation similar to that described in the following sections. Removing duplicated data manually, however, is one of the best methods of demonstrating how to design make-table queries.

→ To use a wizard to remove duplicate data, **see** "Using the Table Analyzer Wizard," **p. 255**.

A modification of the query that you created in the "Creating Not-Equal Theta Joins with Criteria" section of Chapter 11, "Creating Multitable and Crosstab Queries," generates the data for the new tblShipAddresses table. Make-table queries are especially useful in converting flat-file tables that contain duplicated data, including tables created by spreadsheet applications, to relational form.

NOTE

Completed versions of most sample queries in this chapter are included in the Action13.accdb database located in the \SEUA12\Chaptr13 folder of the accompanying CD-ROM.

DESIGNING AND TESTING THE SELECT QUERY

To create the new tblShipAddresses table from the data in the Orders table, you first must build the following SELECT query:

1. Open your working copy of Northwind.accdb, create a new select query, and add the Customers and Orders tables to it.

2. Drag the CustomerID field from the Customers table and drop it in the query's first column. The CustomerID field links the tblShipAddresses table to the Orders table.

3. Drag the ShipName, ShipAddress, ShipCity, ShipRegion, ShipPostalCode, and ShipCountry fields from the Orders table and drop them in columns 2–7, respectively. You use these fields, in addition to CustomerID, to create the new tblShipAddresses table.

To add criteria to select only those records of the Orders table in which the ShipName doesn't match the CompanyName or the ShipAddress doesn't match the Customers table's address, do this:

13

1. In the ShipName column's first Criteria row, type the following:

   <>[Customers].[CompanyName]

2. In the next row of the ShipAddress column, type the following:

   <>[Customers].[Address]

3. To ensure against the slight possibility that the same address might occur in two different cities, in the third row of the ShipCity column, type this:

   <>[Customers].[City]

> **NOTE**
>
> Each not-equal criterion must be on a separate Criteria row to specify the OR operator for the three criteria. Multiple criteria on the same row use the AND operator. If you add the three criteria in the previous steps to the same row, the sample query returns only three Northwind Orders records.

4. Right-click an empty area in the Query Design window's upper pane, and choose Properties to open the Query Properties window. Open the Unique Values drop-down list, select Yes, and close the Query Properties window. The query design appears as shown in Figure 13.1.

Figure 13.1
The design of the qryMakeShip Addresses make-table query requires that the not-equal criteria be added on separate rows of the grid.

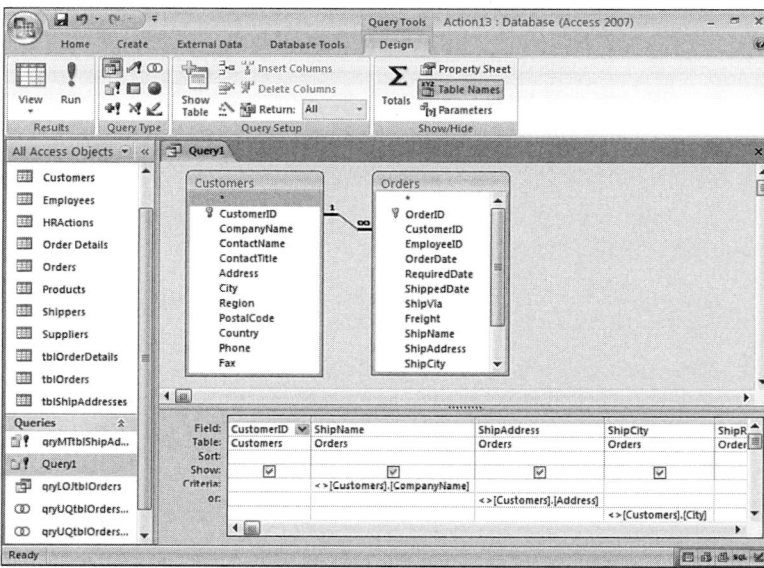

5. Click Run to execute the select query and test the result (see Figure 13.2).

Figure 13.2
The query design of Figure 13.1 returns 10 rows of shipping addresses that differ from the customers' billing addresses.

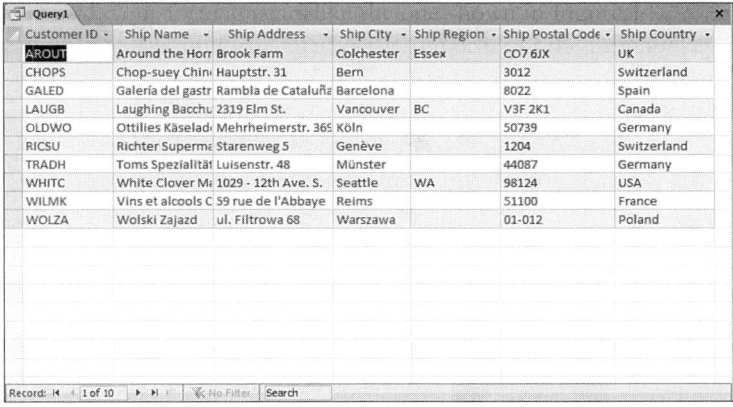

Access SQL

If you don't add the Unique Values property, which adds the DISTINCT qualifier to the query's SELECT statement, the query returns a row for each order with a different shipping address. Following is the Access SQL statement for the preceding query, with unneeded parentheses and square brackets removed for readability:

```
SELECT DISTINCT Customers.CustomerID, Orders.ShipName,
    Orders.ShipAddress, Orders.ShipCity, Orders.ShipRegion,
    Orders.ShipPostalCode, Orders.ShipCountry
FROM Customers
    INNER JOIN Orders
    ON Customers.CustomerID = Orders.CustomerID
WHERE Orders.ShipName<>Customers.CompanyName
    OR Orders.ShipAddress<>Customers.Address
    OR Orders.ShipCity<>Customers.City;
```

CONVERTING THE SELECT QUERY TO A MAKE-TABLE QUERY

Now that you've tested the select query to make sure that it creates the necessary data, create the table from the query by following these steps:

1. Return to Query Design view, click the Design tab, and click Query Type: Make Table to open the Make Table dialog. Type the name of the table, tblShipAddresses, in the Table Name text box (see Figure 13.3) and click OK.

Figure 13.3
The Make Table dialog lets you type a new name for the table or select an existing table to replace with new data.

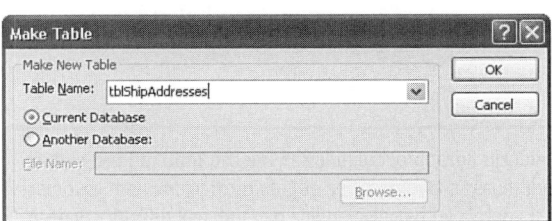

13

2. Click Run. A message confirms the number of records that you are about to add to the new table. Click Yes to create the new table, whose icon and name appear in the Navigation Pane's Tables group.

3. Close and save your query with an appropriate name, such as **qryMTtblShipAddresses**.

4. Double-click the tblShipAddresses table item in the Navigation Pane. The records appear as shown in Figure 13.4.

Figure 13.4
Caption property values of a make-table query don't propagate to the newly created table. Compare the field names of this table with the query result set of Figure 13.2.

Now complete the design of the new tblShipAddresses table by following these steps:

1. Change to Table Design view. The table's basic design is inherited from the Field Name and Data Type properties of the fields of the tables used to create the new table. The tblShipAddresses table doesn't inherit the primary key assignment from the Customers table's CustomerID field.

2. Choose the CustomerID field, open the Indexed property drop-down list, and choose the Yes (Duplicates OK) value. Indexing improves the performance of queries when you have multiple ShipAddresses for customers.

3. The CustomerID, ShipName, ShipAddress, ShipCity, and ShipCountry fields are required, so set the value for each of these fields' Required property to Yes and set the Allow Zero Length property to No.

4. Many countries don't have values for the ShipRegion field, and a few countries don't use postal codes, so verify that the Allow Zero Length property is set to Yes for the ShipRegion and ShipPostalCode fields.

Access SQL

The only difference between the select and make-table queries is the addition of the INTO *tablename* clause that specifies the name of the new table to create. Following is the Access SQL statement for the sample make-table query:

```
SELECT DISTINCT Customers.CustomerID, Orders.ShipName,
    Orders.ShipAddress, Order's.ShipCity, Orders.ShipRegion,
    Orders.ShipPostalCode, Orders.ShipCountry
```

```
    INTO tblShipAddresses
FROM Customers
    INNER JOIN Orders
    ON Customers.CustomerID = Orders.CustomerID
WHERE Orders.ShipName<>Customers.CompanyName
    OR Orders.ShipAddress<>Customers.Address
    OR Orders.ShipCity<>Customers.City;
```

This query and the preceding query are SQL-92 and T-SQL compliant. You can copy and paste either query into the SQL pane of the da Vinci stored procedure design window, save the stored procedure, and execute it. The da Vinci toolset, also called the Project Designer, adds SQL Server's `dbo.` (database owner) prefix to each table name before creating the stored procedure.

→ For more information on using the da Vinci toolset to create T-SQL stored procedures, **see** "Examining Stored Procedures," **p. XXX** *(Ch 20)*.

ESTABLISHING RELATIONSHIPS FOR THE NEW TABLE

Now you must complete the process of adding the new table to your database by establishing default relationships and enforcing referential integrity so that all records in the tblShipAddresses table have a corresponding record in the Customers table. Access's graphical Relationships window makes this process simple and intuitive. To establish the relationship of tblShipAddresses and the Customers table, follow these steps:

1. Close the tblShipAddresses table. Answer Yes when asked whether you want to save changes to the table's design and answer Yes again when asked whether you want to apply the new data integrity rules to the table.

2. Click the Database Tools tab and then the Relationships button to open the Relationships window.

3. Click the Show Table button and double-click the tblShipAddresses table to add the table to the Relationships window; then close the Show Table dialog. Move the tblShipAddresses field list to the lower-right position shown in Figure 13.5.

4. Click the Customers table's CustomerID field, drag the field symbol to the tblShipAddresses table's CustomerID field, and drop the symbol to open the Edit Relationships dialog.

5. Mark the Enforce Referential Integrity check box. Access sets the default relation type, One-To-Many, which is the correct choice for this relation. Access also establishes a conventional INNER JOIN as the default join type, so in this case you don't need to click the Join Type button to display the Join Properties window.

6. Mark the Cascade Update Related Fields and Cascade Delete Related Records check boxes to maintain referential integrity automatically (see Figure 13.6).

13

Figure 13.5
Add the new tblShipAddresses table to the Relationships window.

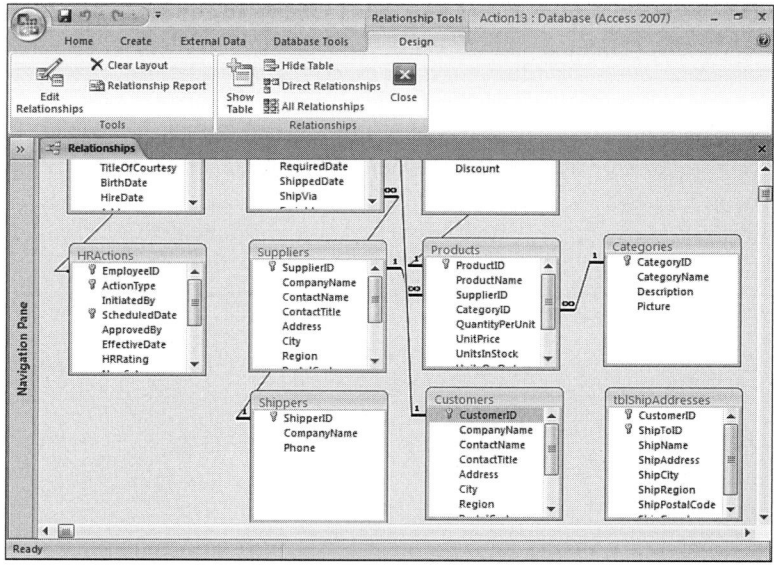

Figure 13.6
Establish a one-to-many relationship between the Orders and tblShipAddresses tables and specify cascade updates and deletions to maintain referential integrity of the tblShipAddresses table.

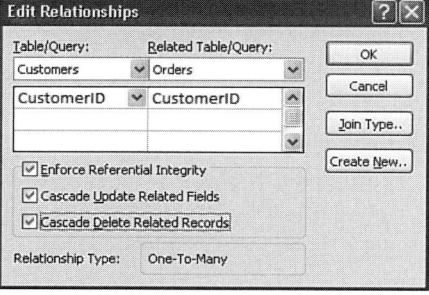

7. Click the Create button in the Edit Relationships dialog to close it. Your Relationships window appears as shown in Figure 13.7.

8. Close the Relationships window and click Yes to save your changes.

USING THE NEW tblShipAddresses TABLE

The purpose of creating the new tblShipAddresses table is to eliminate the data in the Orders table that duplicates information in the Customers table. The additional steps that you must take to use the new table include the following:

Figure 13.7
An infinity (∞) symbol indicates the many-to-one relationship of the tblShipAddress table with the Customers table.

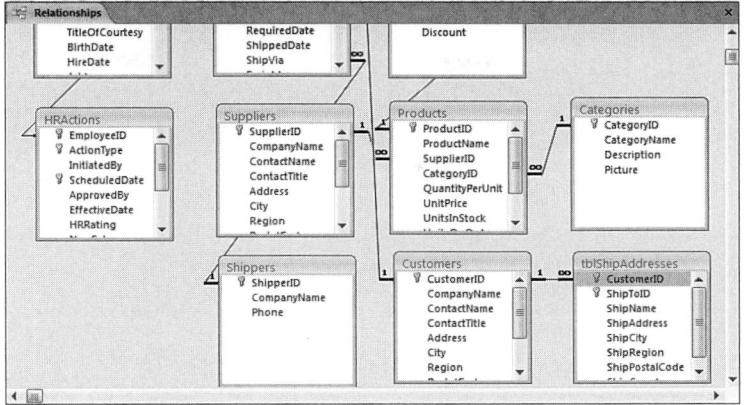

- You need a new Number (Long Integer) field, ShipToID, for the tblShipAddresses and Orders tables. In the Orders table's ShipToID field, you can have a 0 value to indicate that the shipping and billing addresses are the same. You then assign a sequential number to each tblShipAddresses for each customer. (In this case, the value of the ShipToID field is 1 for all records in tblShipAddresses.) By adding the ShipToID field to the tblShipAddresses table, you can create a composite primary key on the CustomerID and ShipToID fields.

- Don't delete fields that contain duplicated data extracted to a new table until you confirm that the extracted data is correct and modify all the queries, forms, and reports that use the table. You use the update query described later in this chapter to assign the correct ShipToID field value for each record in the Orders table. After you verify that you've assigned the correct value of the ShipToID field, you can delete the duplicate fields.

- Add the new table to any queries, forms, reports, or VBA procedures that require the extracted information.

- Change references to fields in the original table in all database objects that refer to fields in the new table.

During this process, you have the opportunity to test the modification before deleting the duplicated fields from the original table. Making a backup copy of the table before you delete the fields also is a low-cost insurance policy.

CREATING ACTION QUERIES TO APPEND RECORDS TO A TABLE

A make-table query creates the new table structure from the structure of the records that underlie the query. Only the fields of the records that appear in the Datasheet view of the query are added to the new table's structure. If you design and save a tblShipAddresses table before extracting the duplicated data from the Orders table, you can use an append query to add the extracted data to the new table.

To remove and then append records to the tblShipAddresses table, for example, follow these steps:

1. Open the tblShipAddresses table in Datasheet view, press Ctrl+A to select all records, and then press the Delete key to delete all records from the table. Click Yes when asked to confirm the deletion and then close the table.

2. Open your make-table query, qryMTtblShipAddresses, from the Navigation Pane in Design view.

> **TIP**
>
> Take extra care when designing action queries not to execute the query prematurely. If you double-click the query in the Navigation Pane or open the query in Datasheet view, you run the make-table query.

3. Click the Query Tools, Design tab's Query Type: Append button. The Append dialog—a renamed version of the Make Table dialog—opens with tblShipAddresses as the default value in the Table Name drop-down list.

4. Click OK to close the Append dialog and add the Append To row to the Query Design grid (see Figure 13.8).

Figure 13.8
Changing a select or make-table query adds an Append To row to the grid. You can specify appending values to a field by opening the Append To list for the query field and selecting the field name.

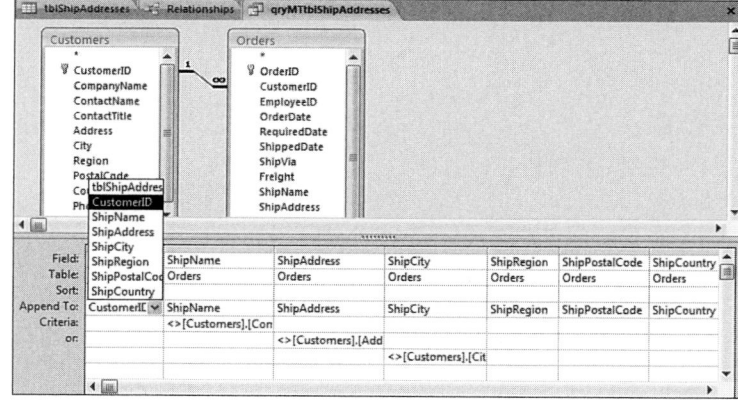

> **TIP**
>
> To append data to a table, the field names of the query and of the table you are appending the records to must be identical, or you must specify the field of the table that the append query column applies to. Access doesn't append data to fields in which the field name differs by even a single space character. The Query Design grid for append queries has an additional row, Append To (shown in Figure 13.8), that Access attempts to match

> by comparing field names of the query and the table. Default values appear in the Append To row of columns for which a match occurs. If a match doesn't occur, open the Append To row's drop-down list and select the destination table's field.

5. Click Run to execute the append query. A message box displays the number of records that the query will append to the table. Click Yes to append the records, and then save the query.

6. Open the tblShipAddresses table to verify that you've added the 10 records. If the table was open when you appended the records, you must close and reopen it to view the added records.

7. Close the query without saving the changes, and then close the table.

 If you can't add a primary key on a table you've appended new records to, see the "Appending Records Causes Primary Key Problems" topic of the "Troubleshooting" section near the end of the chapter.

Access SQL

Append queries—more commonly called `INSERT` queries—add an `INSERT INTO` *tablename(field list)* clause to the `SELECT` statement. The field list argument is what lets you append data to a field with a different name. Following is the SQL statement for the `INSERT` version of the make-table query:

```
INSERT INTO tblShipAddresses ( CustomerID, ShipName,
    ShipAddress, ShipCity, ShipRegion, ShipPostalCode, ShipCountry )
SELECT DISTINCT Customers.CustomerID, Orders.ShipName,
    Orders.ShipAddress, Orders.ShipCity, Orders.ShipRegion,
    Orders.ShipPostalCode, Orders.ShipCountry
FROM Customers
    INNER JOIN Orders
    ON Customers.CustomerID = Orders.CustomerID
WHERE Orders.ShipName<>Customers.CompanyName
    OR Orders.ShipAddress<>Customers.Address
    OR Orders.ShipCity<>Customers.City;
```

Like the select and make-table versions, the Access SQL statement is SQL-92 compliant, so the preceding statement also executes as an SQL Server stored procedure.

13

You can't append records containing values that duplicate those of the primary key fields or other fields with a no-duplicates index in existing records. If you try to do so, a message box indicates the number of records that cause key-field violations. Unlike with the paste append operation, however, Access doesn't create a Paste Errors table that contains the unappended records.

DELETING RECORDS FROM A TABLE WITH AN ACTION QUERY

Often you need to delete a specific set of records from a table. For example, you might want to delete records for canceled orders or for customers who have made no purchases for several years. Deleting records from a table with a DELETE query is the reverse of the append process. You create a SELECT query with all fields (using the * choice from the field list) and then add the individual fields to be used to specify the criteria for deleting specific records. If you don't specify any criteria, Access deletes all the table's records when you convert the SELECT query into a DELETE query and run it against the table.

> **TIP**
>
> It's a good practice to run a SELECT query to display the records that you are about to delete and then convert the SELECT query to a DELETE query.

To give you some practice at deleting records—you stop short of actual deletion in this case—suppose that Northwind Traders' credit manager has advised you that Austrian authorities have declared Ernst Handel (CustomerID ERNSH) insolvent and that you are to cancel and delete any orders from Ernst Handel not yet shipped. To design the query that selects all of Ernst Handel's open orders, follow these steps:

1. Open a new query in Design view and add the Orders table to it.

2. Drag the * (all fields) item from the field list to the Field cell of the query's first column.

3. Drag the CustomerID field to the second column's Field cell. You need this field to select a specific customer's record. The fields that make up the query must be exactly those of the Orders table, so clear the Show box to prevent the CustomerID field from appearing in the query's result twice. This field is already included in the first column's * indicator.

4. In the CustomerID field's Criteria cell, type **ERNSH** to represent Ernst Handel's ID.

5. A Null value in the ShippedDate field indicates orders that have not shipped. Drag the ShippedDate field from the field list to the third column's Field cell. Click the Show box to prevent the ShippedDate field from appearing in the select query's result twice, because the * in the first column also includes that field.

6. In the ShippedDate field's Criteria cell, type **Is Null**. To ensure that you delete only records for Ernst Handel *and* only those that have not been shipped, you must place this criterion on the same line as that of the CustomerID field (see Figure 13.9).

7. Run the select query to display the records to delete when the delete query runs (see Figure 13.10).

Figure 13.9
The test select query design returns all unshipped orders for CustomerID equal to ERNSH.

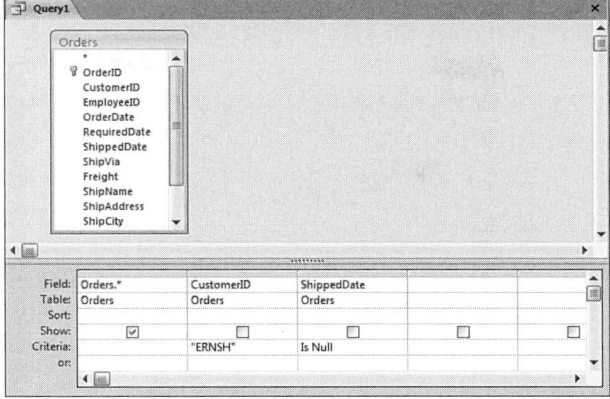

Figure 13.10
The select query displays the two orders for Ernst Handel that haven't been shipped.

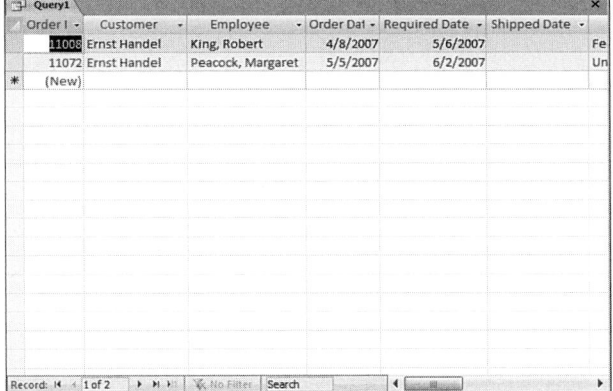

To proceed with the simulated deletion, which would delete the Order Details records for the two orders, follow these steps:

1. Create a copy of the Orders table by selecting the Orders table item in the Navigation Pane and pressing Ctrl+C to copy the table to the Clipboard. Press Ctrl+V to open the Paste Table As dialog. Type **tblOrders** as the name of the new table copy, and press Enter.

2. Repeat step 1 for the Order Details table, naming it **tblOrderDetails**. These two tables are backup tables in case you actually delete the two records for Ernst Handel. The relationship between the Orders table and its related Order Details table specifies Cascade Delete Related Fields but not Cascade Update Related Fields.

 3. Open your select query in Design view. Click the Design tab and the Query Type: Delete button. Access replaces the select query grid's Sort and Show rows with the Delete row, as shown in Figure 13.11. The From value in the Delete row's first column, Orders.*, indicates that Access will delete records that match the Field specification

from the Orders table. The Where values in the remaining two cells indicate fields that specify the deletion criteria.

Figure 13.11
Specifying a delete query adds a Delete row to the grid that identifies From and Where fields.

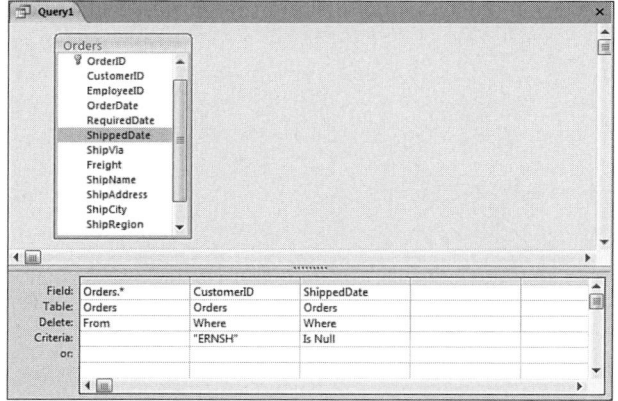

4. Click the Run button. A message box asks you to confirm the deletion of the rows. Click No to prevent the deletion.

5. Close and then save your query if you want.

NOTE

Deleting records in a *one* table when records corresponding to the deleted records exist in a related *many* table violates the rules of referential integrity; the records in the *many* table would be made orphans. In this situation, referential integrity is enforced with cascading deletions for the Order Details and Orders table. If you delete the two ERNSH records, the Access query engine first deletes the corresponding Order Detail records and then deletes the Orders records.

By default, Access uses a transaction when applying action queries to multiple tables. In this example, if the query can't delete the two Orders records and their seven related Order Details records, the transaction is rolled back, and no deletions occur. Otherwise, the transaction commits and permanently deletes all base and related records. If you set the action query's Use Transactions property value to No, the query deletes any records it can without violating referential integrity rules.

If you accidentally delete records for Ernst Handel, reverse the process that you used to make the backup tables: Copy the backup tables—tblOrders and tblOrderDetails—to Orders and Order Details, respectively. You use the tblOrders table in the following section.

Access SQL

Following is the Access SQL statement for the sample delete query:

```
DELETE Orders.*, Orders.CustomerID, Orders.ShippedDate
    FROM Orders
WHERE Orders.CustomerID="ERNSH"
    AND Orders.ShippedDate) Is Null;
```

The field list is optional for delete queries, but you must have at least one field in the field list to satisfy the Access query designer. If you delete the field list in SQL view, the query executes, but won't open in Query Design view.

Like all other Access action queries, the Access SQL and T-SQL statements are identical.

UPDATING VALUES OF MULTIPLE RECORDS IN A TABLE

Update queries change the values of data in a table. Such queries are useful when you must update field values for many records with a common expression. For example, you might need to increase or decrease the unit prices of all products or products within a particular category by a fixed percentage.

To see how an update query works, you perform some of the housekeeping chores discussed earlier in the chapter that are associated with using the tblShipAddresses table. To implement this example, you must have created the tblShipAddresses table, as described in the "Creating New Tables with Make-Table Queries" section earlier in this chapter.

NOTE

> If you didn't create the tblShipAddresses table and you've installed the sample files from the accompanying CD-ROM, you can import this table from the \SEUA12\Chaptr13\Action13.accdb database.

ADDING A SHIPTOID FIELD TO THE TBLORDERS TABLE

You must modify the tblOrders and tblShipAddresses tables to include a field for the ShipToID code that relates the two tables. To add the ShipToID field to the tblOrders table, do this:

1. Open the tblOrders table in Design mode. If you didn't create the tblOrders table as a backup table for the example of the preceding section, do so now.

2. Select the ShipVia field by clicking the selection button and then press Insert to add a new field between ShippedDate and ShipVia. (Access inserts fields in tables above the selected field.)

3. Type **ShipToID** as the field name, select Number as the field data type, and accept the default Long Integer as the field's Field Size. Set the Default Value property to 0 and the Required property value to Yes. Access automatically adds a Duplicates OK index to

13

fields whose names end with "ID". You don't need an index on this field, so set the Indexed property value to No. The table design pane appears as in Figure 13.12, which shows the new ShipToID field selected.

Figure 13.12
Add the ShipToID field as the foreign key for a relationship with the ShipToID field you add to the tblShipAddress table.

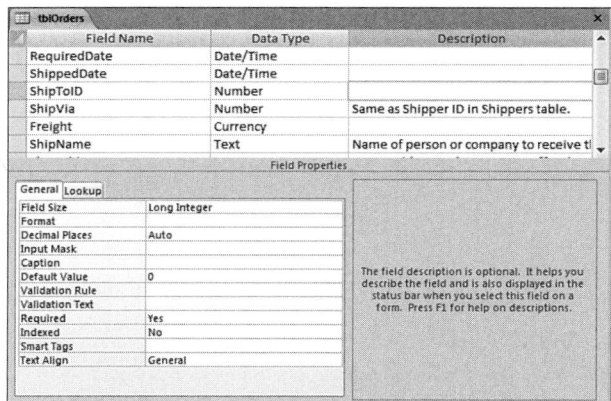

4. Close the tblOrders table and save the changes to your design. You changed the domain integrity rules when you added the Required property, so a message box asks whether you want to test domain integrity. Click No to avoid the test, which would fail because no values have been added to the ShipToID field. (Default values don't replace Null values in newly added fields.)

ADDING A SHIPTOID FIELD AND COMPOSITE PRIMARY KEY TO THE TBLSHIPADDRESSES TABLE

Now add the ShipToID field and establish a composite primary key for the tblShipAddresses table by doing the following:

 1. Open the tblShipAddresses table in Datasheet view.

2. Click the ShipName field header and choose Insert, Column to add a Field1 field between the CustomerID and the ShipName fields.

3. Type **1** in the Field1 cell for each record of the tblShipAddresses table.

 4. Change to design mode and change the name of Field1 to **ShipToID**. Access detects from your data entries that the field should be a Number field and assigns Long Integer as the default Field Size property value. Change the value of the Required property to Yes.

5. Click the CustomerID field and Shift+click the ShipToID field to select both fields.

6. Click the Design Tools' Primary Key button to create a composite primary key on the CustomerID and ShipToID fields. Optionally, click the Indexes button to display the indexes added to the table. Your table design appears as shown in Figure 13.13.

Figure 13.13
The ShipToID and CustomerID fields comprise a composite primary key of the tblShipAddresses table. Access adds the indexes automatically.

7. Close the tblShipAddresses table. This time you test the changes that you made to the table, so click Yes when the Data Integrity Rules message box opens.

WRITING UPDATE QUERIES TO ADD FOREIGN KEY VALUES TO THE TBLORDERS TABLE

To indicate where the orders were shipped, you must update the ShipToID field in tblShipAddresses. The value 1 (or greater) indicates a shipping address other than the customer's address; the value 0 indicates the order is shipped to the customer's billing address. You can accomplish this by running an update query:

1. Close all open tables, create a new query, and add the Customers and tblOrders tables to it. Relationships haven't been specified between the two tables, so the join line between the tables doesn't have one-to-many symbols.

2. Drag the tblOrders table's ShipName and ShipAddress fields to the first two columns of the Query Design grid.

3. Type **<>[Customers].[CompanyName]** in the first Criteria row of the ShipName column and **<>[Customers].[Address]** in the second Criteria row of the ShipAddress column. (Prior tests show that you don't need to test the City, PostalCode, and Country fields.) Your query design appears as shown in Figure 13.14.

4. Run the query to verify that you have correctly selected the set of records to be updated. In this case, you *don't* specify Unique Values, because you must change every tblOrders record that meets the query criteria.

After ensuring that you've selected the appropriate records of the tblOrders table for updating, 63 rows for the sample query, you're ready to convert the select query to an update query by following these steps:

1. Return to Query design mode and drag the tblOrders table's ShipToID field to the query's first column.

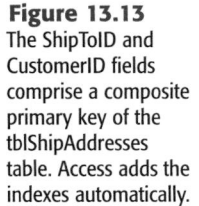

Figure 13.14
This query design, which is similar to qryMTShipAddresses, returns all orders for which the ship-to name or ship-to address differs from the billing data.

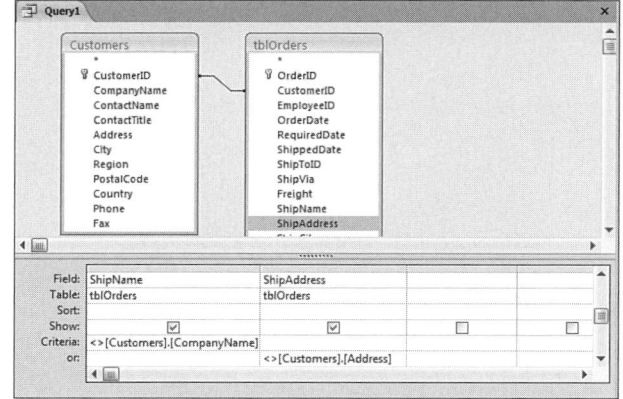

 2. Click the Query Type: Update button. A new Update To row replaces the Sort and Show rows of the select Query Design grid.

3. In the ShipToID column's Update To cell, type **1** to set ShipToID's value to 1 for orders that require the use of a record from the tblShipAddresses table. The Update Query Design grid appears as shown in Figure 13.15. The Update To cells of the remaining fields are blank, indicating that Access is not to update values in these fields.

Figure 13.15
Type the value (1) for the update to the ShipToID field of records that require a join to a record in the tblShipAddresses table.

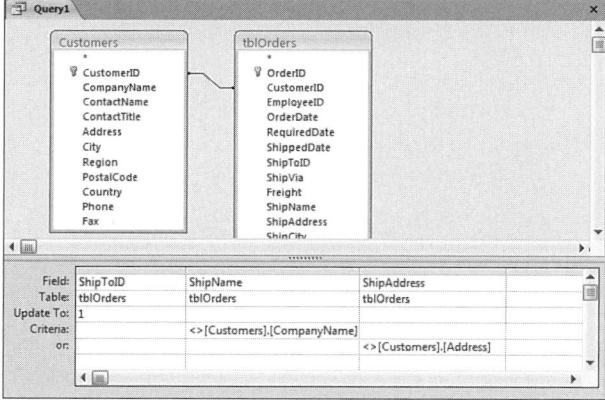

 4. Save and run the update query. A message box indicates the number of records to be updated (63 for this example). Click Yes to continue.

5. Click the Database Window button and open the tblOrders table. Check a few records to see that you correctly added the ShipToID value of 1.

6. Close the update query.

Access SQL

Update queries substitute UPDATE for SELECT as well as a SET list for the SELECT field list. An update query can set multiple field values by additional, comma-separated `TableName.FieldName = Value` statements. Following is the Access SQL statement for the sample update query:

```
UPDATE Customers
    INNER JOIN tblOrders
        ON Customers.CustomerID = tblOrders.CustomerID
    SET tblOrders.ShipToID = 1
WHERE tblOrders.ShipName<>[Customers].[CompanyName]
    OR tblOrders.ShipAddress<>[Customers].[Address];
```

The Access SQL and T-SQL statements are identical.

Finally, you must add 0 values to the ShipToID cells of records that have the same shipping and billing address by following these steps:

1. Create a new query, and add only the tblOrders table.

2. Drag the ShipToID field to the query's first column and Query Type: Update button.

3. Type **0** in the Update To row and **Is Null** in the Criteria row. Before running the query, check it in Datasheet view; all fields should be empty.

4. When you're sure the query is correct, click Run to replace Null values in the ShipToID column with 0. Close and don't save the query.

After you check the tblOrders table to verify the result of your second update query, you can change to Table Design view and safely delete the ShipName, ShipAddress, ShipCity, ShipRegion, ShipPostalCode, and ShipCountry fields from the table.

USING THE TBLSHIPADDRESS TABLE IN A QUERY

When you join the tblOrders and tblShipAddresses tables in a query to regenerate the appearance of the original Orders table, you must specify a LEFT OUTER JOIN on the CustomerID and ShipToID fields of the tables to return all tblOrders records, not just those with records in the tblShipAddresses table.

To create a query that returns all rows of the tblOrders table with empty Ship... fields for records with 0 ShipToID values, do the following:

1. Open a new query, and add the tblOrders and tblShipAddresses tables.

2. Click the OrderID field and Shift+click the Freight field of the tblOrders field list in the upper pane to select the first nine fields, and then drag the selected fields to the grid. Add an ascending sort to the OrderID column.

3. Click the ShipName field in the tblShipAddresses field list, Shift+click the ShipCountry field, and drag the six selected fields to the right of the Freight field in the grid.

4. In the upper pane, drag the CustomerID field of tblOrders and drop it on the CustomerID field of tblShipAddresses to create an INNER JOIN. Do the same for the

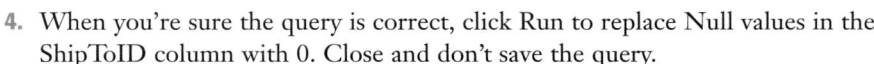

13

ShipToID fields. The direction in which you drag the field symbol (the same direction as the other join, left-to-right) is important. Your query design appears as shown in Figure 13.16. The query grid is scrolled to the right to show the first two fields from the tblShipAddresses table.

Figure 13.16
This query design has INNER JOINS between tblOrders and tblShipAddresses, so the query returns only rows for which records exist in the tblShipAddresses table.

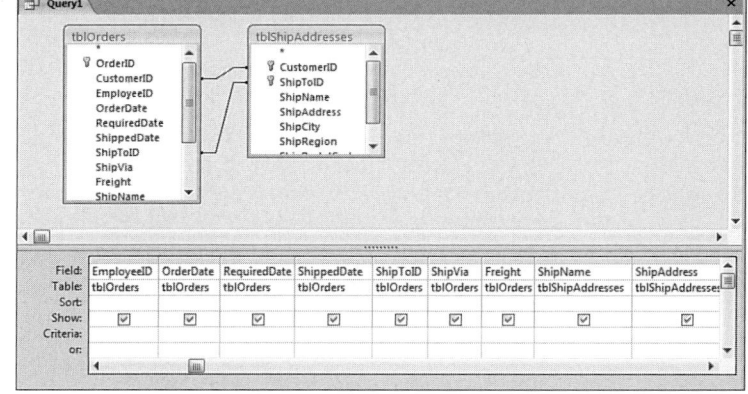

5. Select and then double-click the join line between the CustomerID fields to open the Join Properties dialog. Select option 2, a LEFT OUTER JOIN, and click OK. Specifying this join adds a right-pointing arrow to the join line.

6. Repeat step 5 for the ShipToID field (see Figure 13.17). Both joins must be LEFT OUTER JOINs to return all tblOrders records.

Figure 13.17
Specifying a LEFT (OUTER) JOIN (option 2) in the Join Properties dialog adds an arrow to the join line.

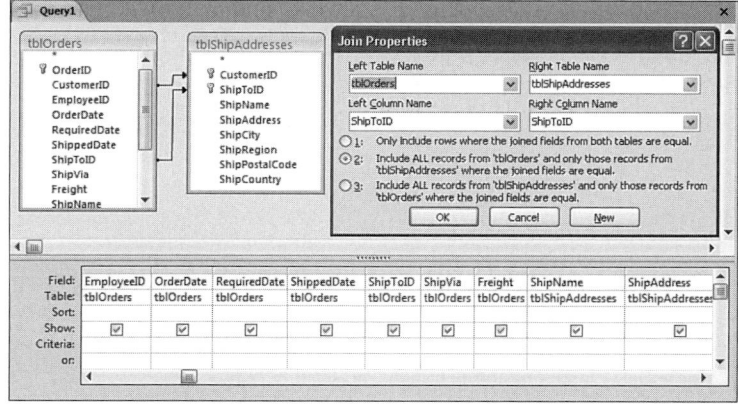

7. Run the query to verify that records for orders with and without ship addresses appear (see Figure 13.18). Save the query as **qryLOJtblOrders** or a similar name, but don't close it.

Figure 13.18
This Datasheet view of the query result set from the design of Figure 13.17 returns all orders. The first two columns are frozen.

Order ID	Customer	ShipToID	Ship Via	Freight	ShipName	ShipAddress	Ship
10248	Wilman Kala	1	Federal Shipping	$32.38	Vins et alcools	59 rue de l'Abb	Reims
10249	Tradição Hipermercados	1	Speedy Express	$11.61	Toms Spezialit	Luisenstr. 48	Müns
10250	Hanari Carnes	0	United Package	$65.83			
10251	Victuailles en stock	0	Speedy Express	$41.34			
10252	Suprêmes délices	0	United Package	$51.30			
10253	Hanari Carnes	0	United Package	$58.17			
10254	Chop-suey Chinese	1	United Package	$22.98	Chop-suey Chi	Hauptstr. 31	Bern
10255	Richter Supermarkt	1	Federal Shipping	$148.33	Richter Superm	Starenweg 5	Genè
10256	Wellington Importadora	0	United Package	$13.97			
10257	HILARIÓN-Abastos	0	Federal Shipping	$81.91			
10258	Ernst Handel	0	Speedy Express	$140.51			
10259	Centro comercial Moctezu	0	Federal Shipping	$3.25			
10260	Old World Delicatessen	1	Speedy Express	$55.09	Ottilies Käsela	Mehrheimerst	Köln
10261	Que Delícia	0	United Package	$3.05			
10262	Rattlesnake Canyon Groce	0	Federal Shipping	$48.29			
10263	Ernst Handel	0	Federal Shipping	$146.06			
10264	Folk och fä HB	0	Federal Shipping	$3.67			
10265	Blondel père et fils	0	Speedy Express	$55.28			

Record: 1 of 830 — No Filter — Search

USING THE tblShipAddress TABLE WITH UNION QUERIES

If you want to substitute "Same as Bill To" or the like as the Ship To address on invoices for those orders in which the value of the ShipToID field is 0, you can either write VBA code or a UNION query to accomplish this task; however, the latter approach is much simpler.

→ To review creating UNION queries, **see** "Using UNION Queries to Combine Multiple Result Sets," **p. XXX** (Ch. 11).

To quickly write the SQL statement for a UNION query that adds a text value—Same as Bill To—to the ShipName field for 0 ShipToID values, do this:

SQL 1. Open the SQL view of qryLOJtblOrders, select the entire SQL statement, and press Ctrl+C to copy it to the Clipboard. Close the query.

2. Open a new query, close the Show Table dialog, and click the Union Query button to open the SQL window.

3. Press Ctrl+V to paste the SQL statement to the window.

4. Replace LEFT in LEFT JOIN with **INNER** to return only the rows with values in the tblShipAddresses table.

5. Delete the trailing semicolon of the pasted text, press Enter twice, and type the following UNION SELECT statement as shown here:

```
UNION SELECT tblOrders.OrderID, tblOrders.CustomerID,
    tblOrders.EmployeeID, tblOrders.OrderDate, tblOrders.RequiredDate,
    tblOrders.ShippedDate, tblOrders.ShipToID, tblOrders.ShipVia,
    tblOrders.Freight,
    "Same as Bill To", " ", " ", " ", " ", " "
FROM tblOrders
WHERE tblOrders.ShipToID = 0;
```

Your SQL window appears as shown in Figure 13.19. The five space values (" ",) in the added statement are required because both components of the UNION query result set must have the same number of columns.

13

Figure 13.19
This SQL statement consists of a copy of the SELECT query of the preceding example with an INNER JOIN instead of a LEFT JOIN and a UNION SELECT statement to add the rows with the 0 ShipToID values.

> **TIP**
>
> You can save some typing by copying the tblOrders... elements of the field list after the UNION SELECT statement.

6. Run the query to verify that the result set contains the Same as Bill To values in the ShipName column (see Figure 13.20). Save the query as **qryUQtblOrdersShipTo**.

Figure 13.20
The UNION query Access SQL statement of Figure 13.18 returns the expected result set. (The first two columns are frozen.)

CustomerID	OrderID	ShipToID	ShipVia	Freight	ShipName	ShipAddress	ShipC
WILMK	10248	1	3	$32.38	Vins et alcools Chevalier	59 rue de l'Abbaye	Reims
TRADH	10249	1	1	$11.61	Toms Spezialitäten	Luisenstr. 48	Münste
HANAR	10250	0	2	$65.83	Same as Bill To		
VICTE	10251	0	1	$41.34	Same as Bill To		
SUPRD	10252	0	2	$51.30	Same as Bill To		
HANAR	10253	0	2	$58.17	Same as Bill To		
CHOPS	10254	1	2	$22.98	Chop-suey Chinese	Hauptstr. 31	Bern
RICSU	10255	1	3	$148.33	Richter Supermarkt	Starenweg 5	Genève
WELLI	10256	0	2	$13.97	Same as Bill To		
HILAA	10257	0	3	$81.91	Same as Bill To		
ERNSH	10258	0	1	$140.51	Same as Bill To		
CENTC	10259	0	3	$3.25	Same as Bill To		
OLDWO	10260	1	1	$55.09	Ottilies Käseladen	Mehrheimerstr. 369	Köln
QUEDE	10261	0	2	$3.05	Same as Bill To		
RATTC	10262	0	3	$48.29	Same as Bill To		
ERNSH	10263	0	3	$146.06	Same as Bill To		
FOLKO	10264	0	3	$3.67	Same as Bill To		
BLONP	10265	0	1	$55.28	Same as Bill To		

Record: 3 of 830 — No Filter — Search

The Query Datasheet view of an Access query you generate from an SQL statement differs from queries you create in the Access query designer. Queries based on SQL statements that Access can't display in Query Design view don't inherit table properties, such as captions and lookup fields.

Access SQL

You can regenerate an exact duplicate of the original Orders table that has ship-to addresses for each order with the following lengthy SQL statement:

```
SELECT tblOrders.OrderID, tblOrders.CustomerID, tblOrders.EmployeeID,
    tblOrders.OrderDate, tblOrders.RequiredDate, tblOrders.ShippedDate,
    tblOrders.ShipToID, tblOrders.ShipVia, tblOrders.Freight,
tblShipAddresses.ShipName,
    tblShipAddresses.ShipAddress, tblShipAddresses.ShipCity,
    tblShipAddresses.ShipRegion, tblShipAddresses.ShipPostalCode,
    tblShipAddresses.ShipCountry
FROM tblOrders
    INNER JOIN tblShipAddresses
        ON (tblOrders.ShipToID = tblShipAddresses.ShipToID)
            AND (tblOrders.CustomerID = tblShipAddresses.CustomerID)

UNION SELECT tblOrders.OrderID, tblOrders.CustomerID, tblOrders.EmployeeID,
    tblOrders.OrderDate, tblOrders.RequiredDate, tblOrders.ShippedDate,
    tblOrders.ShipToID, tblOrders.ShipVia, tblOrders.Freight,
Customers.CompanyName, Customers.Address, Customers.City, Customers.Region,
    Customers.PostalCode, Customers.Country
FROM tblOrders
    INNER JOIN Customers
        ON (Customers.CustomerID = tblOrders.CustomerID)
WHERE tblOrders.ShipToID = 0;
```

You can save time by copying the basic structure of the first SELECT statement to the UNION SELECT statement, changing tblShipAddresses… field names to corresponding Customers… field names, and altering the INNER JOIN statement to join the Customers and tblOrders tables on the CustomerID field. (The name of this query is qryUQtblOrdersShipTo; Figure 13.21 shows its query result set.)

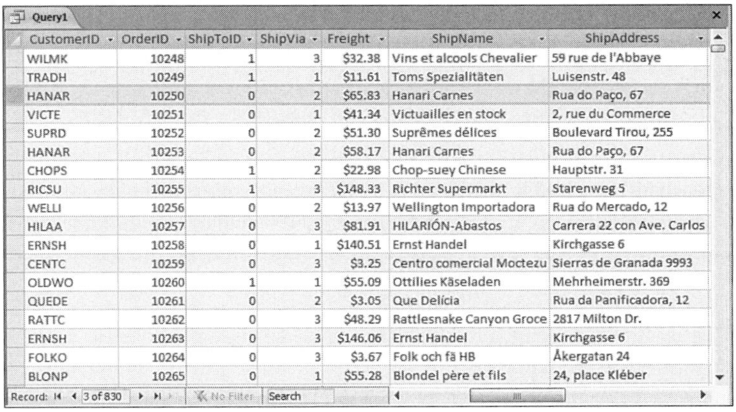

Figure 13.21
You can produce a query result set that's an exact duplicate of the original Orders table with a UNION query that returns Bill To addresses from the Customers table.

CustomerID	OrderID	ShipToID	ShipVia	Freight	ShipName	ShipAddress
WILMK	10248	1	3	$32.38	Vins et alcools Chevalier	59 rue de l'Abbaye
TRADH	10249	1	1	$11.61	Toms Spezialitäten	Luisenstr. 48
HANAR	10250	0	2	$65.83	Hanari Carnes	Rua do Paço, 67
VICTE	10251	0	1	$41.34	Victuailles en stock	2, rue du Commerce
SUPRD	10252	0	2	$51.30	Suprêmes délices	Boulevard Tirou, 255
HANAR	10253	0	2	$58.17	Hanari Carnes	Rua do Paço, 67
CHOPS	10254	1	2	$22.98	Chop-suey Chinese	Hauptstr. 31
RICSU	10255	1	3	$148.33	Richter Supermarkt	Starenweg 5
WELLI	10256	0	2	$13.97	Wellington Importadora	Rua do Mercado, 12
HILAA	10257	0	3	$81.91	HILARIÓN-Abastos	Carrera 22 con Ave. Carlos
ERNSH	10258	0	1	$140.51	Ernst Handel	Kirchgasse 6
CENTC	10259	0	3	$3.25	Centro comercial Moctezu	Sierras de Granada 9993
OLDWO	10260	1	1	$55.09	Ottilies Käseladen	Mehrheimerstr. 369
QUEDE	10261	0	2	$3.05	Que Delícia	Rua da Panificadora, 12
RATTC	10262	0	3	$48.29	Rattlesnake Canyon Groce	2817 Milton Dr.
ERNSH	10263	0	3	$146.06	Ernst Handel	Kirchgasse 6
FOLKO	10264	0	3	$3.67	Folk och fä HB	Åkergatan 24
BLONP	10265	0	1	$55.28	Blondel père et fils	24, place Kléber

Record: 3 of 830 | No Filter | Search

13

After you've verified that you can reproduce the data in the original Orders table with a union query, it's safe to delete the ShipName through ShipCountry fields of the tblOrders table.

TESTING CASCADING DELETION AND CASCADING UPDATES

When you delete a record in a primary or base table on which records in a related table depend, cascading deletions automatically delete the dependent records. Similarly, if you modify the value of a table's primary key field and a related table has records related by the primary key field's value, cascading updates change the value of the related foreign key field for the related records to the new primary key field value.

Cascading deletions and cascading updates are special types of action queries that the Access engine executes for you. The following three sections show you how to use Access's cascading deletions and cascading updates features with a set of test tables copied from the Orders and Order Details tables of Northwind.accdb.

CREATING THE TEST TABLES AND ESTABLISHING RELATIONSHIPS

When experimenting with database features, you should work with test tables rather than live data. As mentioned in the note at the beginning of this chapter, using copied test tables is particularly advisable when the tables are participants in action queries. The remaining sections of this chapter use the two test tables, tblOrders and tblOrderDetails, that you created in preceding sections:

1. Open the tblOrders table in Table Design view.
2. Change the field data type of the OrderID field from AutoNumber to Number and make sure that the Field Size property is set to Long Integer. (This change is necessary to test cascading updates in the next section.)
3. Close tblOrders and save your changes.

Cascading deletions and updates require that you establish a default relationship between the primary and related tables as well as enforce referential integrity. To add both cascading deletions and updates to the tblOrderDetails table, follow these steps:

1. If you haven't created tblOrderDetails, use the Clipboard to copy the Order Details table to tblOrderDetails.
2. Click the Database Tools tab and the Relationships button to display the Relationships window.
3. Scroll right to an empty area of the Relationships window.
4. Click the Show Table button to display the Add Table dialog.
5. Double-click the tblOrders and tblOrderDetails items in the list, and then close the Show Table dialog.

6. Click and drag the OrderID field of tblOrders to the tblOrderDetails table's OrderID field to establish a one-to-many join on the OrderID field and open the Relationships dialog.

7. Mark the Enforce Referential Integrity check box, which enables the two cascade check boxes.

8. Mark the Cascade Update Related Fields and Cascade Delete Related Records check boxes, as shown in Figure 13.22.

Figure 13.22
Add Access's Cascade Update Related Fields and Cascade Delete Related Records features to automatically maintain the tblOrderDetails table's referential integrity.

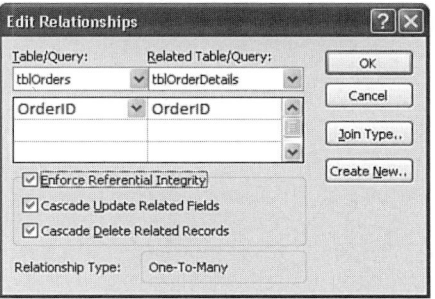

9. Click OK to make your changes to the join effective and close the Relationships window. Click Yes when Access asks if you want to save your changes to the window's layout.

 If you receive an error message when you click the OK button, see the "Access Won't Create a Relationship to a New Table" topic of the "Troubleshooting" section near the end of the chapter.

TESTING CASCADING DELETIONS

To try cascading deletions with the test tables, follow these steps:

1. Open the tblOrders and tblOrderDetails tables in Datasheet view.

2. Click tblOrders datasheet's tab to make it the active window and then click a record-selection button to pick an order in tblOrders to delete.

3. Press the Delete key to tentatively delete the selected records and the related order's line-item records in tblOrderDetails.

4. A message asks you to confirm the deletion. Click Yes to delete the records.

To verify that you've deleted the related records, click the tblOrderDetails tab and scroll to the related record or records for the order that you deleted in the tblOrderDetails table. The data cell values for the deleted related records are replaced with #Deleted. (These values aren't saved with the table.) Press F5 to refresh the Datasheet and remove the #Deleted rows.

13

TESTING CASCADING UPDATES

Cascading updates to the foreign key field of records that depend on a primary key value that you want to change in a primary table are a valuable Access feature. Performing updates of primary key values while enforcing referential integrity is not a simple process; Chapter 5 briefly discusses the problems associated with performing such updates manually. To see how Access takes the complexity out of cascading updates, follow these steps:

1. Click the tblOrders tab, and change the value of the OrderID cell of the first record to the order number that you deleted in the preceding section. Alternatively, change the value of the OrderID cell to a value such as **20000**, which is outside the range of the values of the test table.

2. Move the cursor to another record to cause the cascading update to occur. You immediately see the changes in the OrderID foreign key field of the related dependent records (see Figure 13.23).

Figure 13.23
Changing the OrderID value in the base table automatically changes the OrderID values of related records, if you specify cascading updates.

No confirmation message appears when you execute a cascading update, because the effect is reversible. If you make an erroneous entry that causes an undesired cascading update, you can change the entry to its original value by reentering the original or the correct value manually.

TROUBLESHOOTING

APPENDING RECORDS CAUSES PRIMARY KEY PROBLEMS

After appending records to an existing table, I can't create a primary key on the table.

The Unique Values Only test that you specify in the Query Properties window applies only to the query, not to the table to which you append the records. If possible, create a primary key for the destination table before appending records. For example, if you want to preclude the possibility of appending duplicate records to the tblShipAddresses table, you must first create the composite primary key, discussed in the "Using the New tblShipAddresses Table" section, which creates a No Duplicates index on the primary key, and then append the records.

ACCESS WON'T CREATE A RELATIONSHIP TO A NEW TABLE

When I try to enforce referential integrity, I get a "Can't create relationship to enforce referential integrity" message.

You dragged the field symbols in the wrong direction when you created the relationship. The related (to-many) table is in the Table/Query list and the primary (one-to) table is in the Related Table/Query list. Close the Edit Relationships dialog, click the thin area of the join line to select the join, and then press the Delete key to delete the join. Make sure that you drag the field name that you want from the primary table to the related table. Alternatively, you can make these changes in the Edit Relationships dialog.

IN THE REAL WORLD—ALTERNATIVES TO ACTION QUERIES

Microsoft calls any Access query that alters table data an *action* query; the more common name is *update* query, as in updating the database. With Access, however, there's a good reason to distinguish graphical action queries from the update queries used in online transaction processing (OLTP). Access's graphical action queries are intended primarily for bulk operations—adding, altering, or deleting large numbers of records in a single operation. OLTP usually deals with a single record or a few related records per operation. Creating a new Access action query each time you must update a single record clearly is an inefficient process, even if you add a parameter to designate the record you want to update or delete.

NOTE

> The sections that follow deal with advanced Access topics, which are covered in detail by chapters later in this book. In the real world, production databases reside on a file or application server and multiple users connect their client PC's front-end applications to networked client/server (SQL Server Express, or SQL Server 2005) databases. Chapter 19, "Linking Access Front Ends to Access and Client/Server Tables," and Chapter 20, "Exploring Access Data Projects and SQL Server 2005," deal with client/server databases. The purpose of this "In the Real World" episode is to demonstrate the many options that Access and SQL Server offer for executing action queries and their equivalents.

BROWSE-MODE UPDATING

Browse-mode table editing in Datasheet view is the obvious alternative to action queries when you need to add, alter, or delete only one or a few records. In the real world of networked multiuser databases, however, database administrators (DBAs) discourage or prohibit browse-mode editing because browsing usually requires multiple database connections for a single client PC and generates a substantial amount of network traffic.

Furthermore, multiuser browse-mode editing often results in concurrency (contention) problems when two users attempt to edit the same record. Access's optimistic record-locking approach minimizes concurrency conflicts, but resolving which user's edit of a record is correct often requires manual intervention by the DBA or a supervisor. DBAs, especially, don't like to get involved with table-level contention issues. DBAs suffer perpetual contention with information technology managers and chief financial officers.

FORM-BASED UPDATING

Form-based updates are the most common approach for production Access applications using Access databases. Designing Access forms for OLTP applications is the subject of the next two chapters. Typically, the main form displays field values of a single record (for example, an invoice) in text boxes. Data from related tables, such as invoice line items, appear in a multirow subform. Conventional Access form-based updating, however, is a variation on the browse-mode datasheet updating process. The client PC maintains at least one connection to the database tables while the editing application is open and generates a significant amount of network traffic during the editing process.

The primary advantage of form-based over datasheet updating is that you can add to the form VBA code that resolves contention issues with error-handling procedures. An even better approach to contention problems is to write VBA code that takes advantage of the data-related events of ActiveX Data Objects (ADO). You must be a fluent VBA programmer, however, to write effective event-handling subprocedures for Access's form Recordsets.

UPDATING WITH SQL STATEMENTS

Sending SQL INSERT (append), UPDATE, or DELETE queries over the network to the database server is a much more efficient process than browse-mode editing with datasheets or forms. You send an SQL SELECT query to the database to retrieve only the record(s) you need, disconnect from the database, edit the records, open a connection, send one of the three types of SQL update queries, and then close the connection. Following is a typical T-SQL statement to add a new order with three line items to the Orders and Order Details tables of the NorthwindCS SQL Server database:

```
INSERT INTO Orders
   VALUES(11093, 'KOENE', 1,
      '5/15/2007', '6/1/2007', NULL, 3, NULL,
      'Königlich Essen',
      'Maubelstr. 90',
      'Brandenburg', '', '14776',
      'Germany')
INSERT INTO [Order Details]
   VALUES(11093, 24, 4.5, 24, 0)
INSERT INTO [Order Details]
   VALUES(11093, 36, 19, 36, 0)
INSERT INTO [Order Details]
   VALUES(11093, 42, 9.8, 12, 0)
```

The preceding SQL INSERT statement contains a substantial amount of text overhead, but executes very quickly over a network connection. You can quickly convert the statement into an SQL Server transaction by adding a BEGIN TRANS[ACTION] prefix and a COMMIT [TRANS[ACTION]] suffix. Wrapping the statement in a transaction ensures that either all INSERT operations succeed or the entire operation fails and no change occurs to either of the tables. Adding TRANS[ACTION] statements qualifies the operation for OLTP. Chapter 21, "Moving from Access Queries to Transact-SQL," describes T-SQL TRANSACTION syntax.

Another update alternative is to use an ADO 2.7 disconnected Recordset object to retrieve and update Access or SQL Server 2005 records. The advantage of disconnected Recordset objects is that ADO handles most of the disconnecting and reconnecting chores for you. Disconnected Recordsets also let you edit multiple groups of records, and then send only the changes to the database with the UpdateBatch method. Sending only the changes is especially efficient for UPDATE operations.

Updating with SQL Server Stored Procedures

The most efficient and secure method of updating tables is by using a parameterized stored procedure with a client/server database, such as SQL Server 2005. A stored procedure is a precompiled query that's similar to a stored Access query (called a QueryDef object). Chapter 21 shows you how to write T-SQL parameterized stored procedures. SQL Server 2005— and thus SQL Server Express—execute stored procedures faster than previous SQL Server versions.

You send the new values to add or change as stored procedure parameters. It's a common practice to write separate stored procedures for INSERT, UPDATE, and DELETE operations. DBAs greatly appreciate developers who take full advantage of stored procedures. Well-written stored procedures let DBAs spend more of their time contending with management, instead of putting out fires started by contentious OLTP users.

13

DESIGNING FORMS AND REPORTS

CREATING AND USING ACCESS FORMS

UNDERSTANDING THE ROLE OF ACCESS FORMS AND CONTROLS

Access forms create the user interface to your tables. Although you can use Table view and Query view to perform many of the same functions as forms, forms offer the advantage of presenting data in an organized and attractive manner. You can arrange the location of fields on a form so that data entry or editing operations for a single record follow a natural left-to-right, top-to-bottom sequence. You can limit the number of fields that appear on the form, and allow or prevent editing of specific field values. A properly designed form speeds data entry and minimizes operator keying errors.

Forms are constructed from a collection of individual design elements called *controls* or *control objects*. An Access form consists of a window in which you place the following classes of Access controls:

- *Bound controls* display the data from the table or query that serves as the data source of the form. Access's native bound controls include text boxes, combo and list boxes, subforms, and object frames for graphics. You can bind many Microsoft and third-party ActiveX controls to a form's data source. For example, you can bind the PivotTable, PivotChart, and Spreadsheet controls of the Office Web Components (OWC) to the data source of your form.

- *Unbound dynamic controls*, also called *calculated controls*, can display data from sources other than the table or query that serves as the data source for the form. For example, you can use an unbound text box to display the current date and time.

- *Unbound static controls* display, for example, fixed-text labels and logo graphics.

In most cases, you base an Access form on a table or query, which you specify during the initial form design step, to serve as the master data source for your form. This chapter concentrates on creating bound forms with dynamic text-based controls and subforms. A *subform* is another form contained within a form. The primary use of subforms is to display detail data from a table or query that has a many-to-one relationship with the form's master data source.

NOTE

The form design techniques you learn in this chapter also apply to designing forms of Access data projects (ADP), one of the subjects of Chapter 20, "Exploring Access Data Projects and SQL Server 2005." Forms for ADP are identical in almost all respects to forms that use Access tables or queries as data sources. The primary differences are ADP's connection to the SQL Server data source (instead of a native Access connection) and Access's method of storing the forms in an .adp file (rather than in an .accdb file).

Chapter 29, "Programming Combo and List Boxes," provides examples of unbound forms that don't have a data source.

→ For an example of an unbound Switchboard form with embedded macros, **see** "Exploring Access 2007's Macro-based Switchboard Manager," **p. 1164**.

AUTO-GENERATING A BASIC TRANSACTION-PROCESSING FORM

The content and appearance of your form depend on its use in your database application. Database applications fall into two basic categories:

- *Transaction-processing* applications add new records to tables, or edit or delete existing records. Transaction-processing applications require write access to (permissions for) the tables that are linked to the form.

- *Decision-support* applications supply information as graphs, tables, or individual data elements but don't allow the user to add or edit data. Decision-support applications require only read access to the tables that are linked to the form.

The form that you create in this example is typical of transaction-processing forms used to add new records to the many side of a one-to-many relationship. Adding line items to an invoice is an example of when a form of this kind—called a *one-to-many* or *master/child* form—is necessary. The objective of the HRActions form is to add new records to the HRActions table or let you edit the existing records.

Maintaining a record of employee performance reviews and actions resulting from the reviews is one of the primary responsibilities of personnel departments. For organizations with more than a few employees, a database is an effective tool for recording dates on which employees were hired, promoted, demoted, or terminated, and the justification for actions taken. This information often is critical in the defense of wrongful termination or other litigation brought by disgruntled former (or even current) employees. Human resources (HR) databases—the more politically correct term for personnel databases—also can handle scheduling of periodic reviews and aid in ensuring that managers or supervisors handle their HR responsibilities in a timely manner.

CREATING A MASTER/CHILD FORM FROM RELATED TABLES

The "Default Form and Report Layouts" section of Chapter 1, "Access 2007 for Access 200x Users: What's New," mentions that clicking the Create ribbon's form button with a table or query selected creates a form with Access 2007's default format, which has one or two columns of stacked controls, depending on the number of table fields or query columns. If the selected table has a single one-to-many relationship with another table, the form-generation process adds a Datasheet-style subform. The subform is bound to the related table, which in turn links to the main or master form.

NOTE

> This book uses the term *master/child* to describe the form/subform relationship because the property names for the linkage are Link Master Fields and Link Child Fields.

14

You can't use the Northwind.accdb sample database to auto-generate the master/child form because the Employees table has relationships with the Orders table as well as the HRActions table. Ordinarily, you would start with a new database, import the Employees and HRActions tables into it, and then establish a many-to-one relationship between them on the EmployeeID field. To save time, you'll find a pre-built HRActions14.accdb database with the two related tables in your \SEUA12\Chaptr14 folder.

To auto-generate the master/child form with the HRActions.accdb database, do the following:

1. Open the \SEUA12\Chaptr14\HRActions.accdb database.

2. Select the Employees table in the Navigation pane, click the Create tab, and click the Forms group's Form button to create and open the Employees master/child form in form Layout view (see Figure 14.1).

Figure 14.1
The basic Employees form auto-generated from the Employees and HRActions tables is the starting point of the final form layout process.

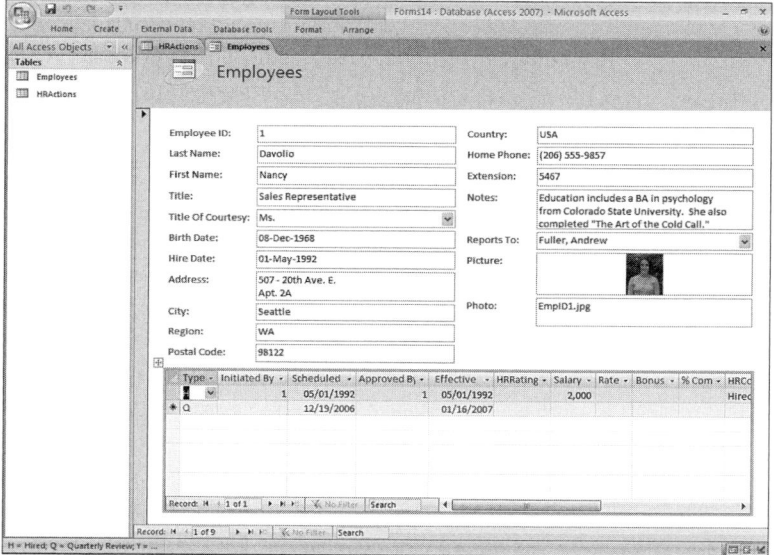

3. Press Ctrl+S to open the Save As dialog, type **frmHRActions** as the form name, and click OK to save the form.

EXPLORING THE frmHRActions FORM IN LAYOUT VIEW

The master (main) form consists of two columns of text boxes—each with an associated label—for entering or editing data values in all but the EmployeeID and Picture fields of the Employees table. The subform contains all fields from the HRActions table (except the EmployeeID field) arranged in a tabular layout. Access uses the fields' Caption property values as default text box labels and also as column headings for the tabular subform.

In Figure 14.1, notice that a horizontal scroll bar appears in the subform area. The subform is larger than the area created for it in the main form, so Access automatically adds one or two scroll bars to let you access all data displayed in the subform. The subform's record navigation buttons let you scroll all records related to the current record of the main form.

The basic form needs many cosmetic adjustments to the layout of the main form and the subform. The remaining discussions and exercises in this chapter show you how to modify auto-generated forms and those created with the Form Wizard; you can apply these form-editing skills when you create your own forms from scratch, as described in the next chapter.

TIP

> No matter how adept you become at designing Access forms, auto-generating them or using the Form Wizard to create the basic form design saves you time.

FORM LAYOUT VIEW'S CONTEXTUAL RIBBONS

NEW Access 2007's new Layout view for forms and reports speeds the design process by enabling grouped controls in stacked or tabular styles and letting you manipulate controls or groups of controls with live data visible. Selecting Layout View in the Home ribbon's View gallery adds two contextual ribbons to the UI: Form Layout Tools – Formatting (see Figure 14.2, top) and Form Layout Tools – Arrange (see Figure 14.2, bottom). The following two sections describe these two ribbons in detail.

Figure 14.2
Form Layout view adds Form Layout Tools – Formatting (top, split horizontally) and Form Layout Tools – Arrange contextual ribbons (bottom).

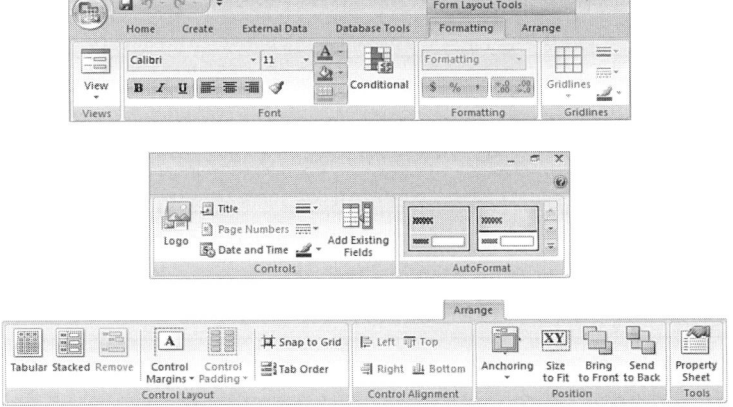

THE FORM LAYOUT TOOLS – FORMAT RIBBON

The Formatting contextual ribbon has control button groups for specifying the view, formatting text and numbers, modifying Datasheet gridlines, setting control properties, and applying AutoFormats to forms. Table 14.1 lists the icon, name, KeyTips, and a brief description of each command button of the Form Layout Tools – Format ribbon. The keyboard shortcut to display KeyTips is Alt+G.

14

TABLE 14.1 ICONS, COMMAND BUTTONS, KEYTIP SHORTCUTS, AND COMMAND BUTTON ACTIONS FOR THE FORM LAYOUT TOOLS – FORMAT RIBBON

Icon	Command Button	Shortcut Alt+G,	Command Action
Views Group			
	Form View	WF	Displays selected form in Form view
	Layout View	WY	Displays selected form in Layout view
	Design View	WD	Displays selected form in Design view
Font Group			
Calibri	Font	FF	Sets font family from list
11	Font Size	FS	Sets font size from list
B	Bold	1	Sets selected text bold
I	Italic	2	Sets selected text italic
U	Underline	3	Underlines selected text
	Align Left	AL	Aligns selected text left
	Center	AC	Centers selected text
	Align Right	AR	Aligns selected text right
	Format Painter	FP	Applies selected format to other controls
A	Font Color	FC	Opens color picker to apply color to selected text
	Fill/Back Color	FB	Opens color picker to apply color to control background
	Alternate Fill/ Back Color	FA	Opens color picker to select a color to shade controls in alternate rows
	Conditional Formatting	O	Opens the Conditional Formatting dialog to enable formatting a control based on the result of an expression or the control receiving the focus (see Figure 14.3)
Formatting Group			
Currency	Formatting	R	Sets number format from list
$	Currency	AN	Applies currency format
%	Percent	P	Multiplies display value by 100 and adds % symbol

14

Icon	Command Button	Shortcut Alt+G,	Command Action
	Comma Format	K	Applies commas as thousands separators
	Increase Decimals	0	Adds decimal digits
	Decrease Decimals	9	Reduces decimal digits

Gridlines Group

Icon	Command Button	Shortcut Alt+G,	Command Action
	Gridlines	B	Opens a gallery of eight gridline patterns for Datasheets
	Gridline Thickness	G	Opens a gallery of six line thicknesses ranging from Hairline to 6 points
	Gridline Type	J	Opens a gallery of eight gridline styles
	Gridline Color	FL	Opens a color picker to set gridline color

Controls Group

Icon	Command Button	Shortcut Alt+G,	Command Action
	Logo	L	Opens an Insert Picture dialog to select a graphic for an Attachment control in the form's Header section
	Title	T	Inserts a Title label in the form's Header section
	Page Number	N	Opens the Page Number dialog to insert a formatted page number into the form's header or footer (enabled in Design view only)
	Date and Time	D	Opens a Date and Time dialog to insert a date value, time value, or both, in the form's Header section
	Border Thickness	CH	Opens a gallery of six line thicknesses ranging from Hairline to 6 points
	Border Type	CY	Opens a gallery of eight gridline styles
	Border Color	CL	Opens a color picker to set gridline color
	Add Existing Fields	X	Opens the Field List from which to drag additional master and child fields to the form

AutoFormat Group (see the later "Using AutoFormat" section)

Icon	Command Button	Shortcut Alt+G,	Command Action
	AutoFormat	SQ	Opens a gallery of 25 prebuilt Access AutoFormats
	AutoFormat Wizard	F	Starts the AutoFormat Wizard, which enables modifying or creating new AutoFormats

14

APPLYING CONDITIONAL FORMATTING

The Conditional Formatting dialog lets you specifiy one or more conditions that format the text and background color of a control in response to changes in the value of the control, the value of a Boolean expression (**True**), or the control receiving the focus (see Figure 14.3). You select the condition type—Field Value Is, Expression Is, or Field Has Focus—in the leftmost drop-down list.

Figure 14.3
These two conditional formatting expressions set the Country text box's value bold for UK and USA addresses, and color the text red for USA or green for UK addresses.

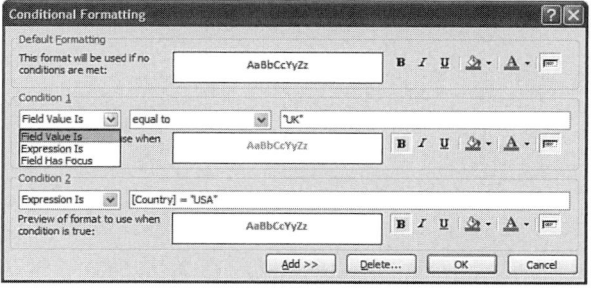

Condition 1 creates an expression based on the control's numeric or alphabetic value. You can select from equal to (=), not equal to (<>), greater than (>), less than (<), greater than or equal to (>=), and less than or equal to (<=_) conditions.

Condition 2 requires typing in the text box a VBA expression that evaluates to **True** or **False**. Chapter 10, "Understanding Access Operators and Expressions," describes expressions that return **Boolean** values.

THE FORM LAYOUT TOOLS – ARRANGE RIBBON

The Arrange contextual ribbon has groups for managing control groups, setting text margins and padding for controls, toggling the Snap to Grid layout feature, setting tab order, aligning and positioning controls, and displaying the Property Sheet. Table 14.2 lists the icon, name, KeyTips, and a brief description of each command button of the Form Layout Tools – Arrange ribbon. The keyboard shortcut to display KeyTips is Alt+L.

TABLE 14.2   ICONS, COMMAND BUTTONS, KEYTIP SHORTCUTS AND COMMAND BUTTON ACTIONS FOR THE FORM LAYOUT TOOLS – ARRANGE RIBBON

Icon	Command Button	Shortcut Alt+L,	Command Action
Control Layout Group			
	Tabular		Adds the selected controls to a tabular control group
	Stacked		Adds the selected controls to a stacked control group
	Remove		Removes the selected controls from their control group

Icon	Command Button	Shortcut Alt+L,	Command Action
	Control Margins		Opens a gallery from which you can select the space between control borders and text: None, Narrow, Medium, or Wide
	Control Padding		Opens a gallery from which you can select the space between adjacent controls: None, Narrow, Medium, or Wide
	Snap to Grid	SR	Toggles the snap-to-grid layout feature on and off
	Tab Order	AT	Opens the Tab Order dialog to enable modifying or resetting controls' tab order (see Figure 14.4)

Control Alignment Group

Icon	Command Button	Shortcut Alt+L,	Command Action
	Left	L	Aligns the left edge of two or more controls
	Right	R	Aligns the right edge of two or more controls
	Top	T	Aligns the top edge of two or more controls
	Bottom	B	Aligns the bottom edge of two or more controls

Position Group

Icon	Command Button	Shortcut Alt+L,	Command Action
	Anchoring	C	Opens a gallery of nine options for positioning a control when resizing the form's window
	Size to Fit	F	Sizes the selected control to fit its contents
	Bring to Front	I	Sets the Z-order of the selected control in front of other controls
	Send to Back	K	Sets the Z-order of the selected control behind other controls

Tools Group

Icon	Command Button	Shortcut Alt+L,	Command Action
	Property Sheet	Alt+ Enter	Toggles the appearance of the Property Sheet

NOTE

You must select at least one control to enable most control buttons except Snap to Grid and Tab Order. You must select two or more controls to enable the Control Alignment group's buttons.

14

THE TAB ORDER DIALOG

The Tab Order dialog lets you customize the sequence of movement of focus between controls. The default Form layout's tab order is top to bottom for controls in a Stacked group and left to right between groups.

Figure 14.4
The Tab Order dialog simplifies rearranging the order in which controls in the form Header, Detail, or Footer section receive the focus. Most forms place all active controls in the Detail section.

To change the tab order of a form section, select one or more controls and then drag the selection to another location.

REARRANGING THE DEFAULT FORM LAYOUT

You can rearrange a form's layout in traditional Design view or the new Layout view, but Layout view accompanies the layout process with live data in the form's controls. Some form and control property values can only be changed in Design view.

> **TIP**
>
> Select Normal windows mode for Access with a window size of 800×600 pixels to make the instructions example easier to follow and the figures more representative. This book uses primarily 800×600-pixel screen captures for readability.

The sample main form has two stacked control groups; the HRActions Datasheet at the bottom of the form is a single Subform control. The most obvious problems with the default form layout are, from top to bottom:

- The depth of the form's standard Header section is excessive.
- The label (Auto_Title0) in the form's Header section needs changing to reflect the form's purpose.

- The width of the two stacked control groups is excessive for all fields except Notes.
- Including Birth Date data on a data entry form is not politically correct and might violate government regulations.
- The size of the Picture field's Attachment control is too small and its aspect ratio is incorrect.
- The Photo field's TextBox and Label controls (inherited from earlier Northwind versions) isn't needed.
- The HRActions subform (Child36) has more depth than necessary.

To start the form rearrangement process and learn how to work with grouped (stacked) controls, do the following:

1. Navigate through the nine Employees records to verify the approximate width of the content in each text box.

2. Select the Employee ID text box (not the label) and drag its right edge to the left to reduce the width of all text boxes in the group (see Figure 14.5).

Figure 14.5
Changing the width (or position) of a single grouped (stacked) control changes the width of all controls in the group. When you release the mouse button, the outline of the original group disappears.

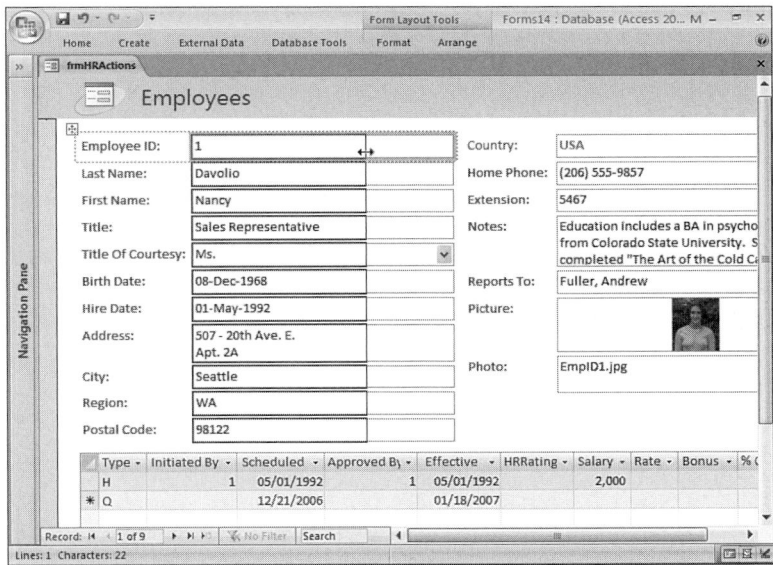

3. Select and then click to activate the Employees label. Replace Employees with **Northwind Human Resources Actions** as the label's caption, and then click the Format Layout Tools – Arrange ribbon's Size to Fit button.

4. Click the group selection button, which adds the move group (four-headed) cursor to the select cursor, and then drag the right-hand group to within about 20 pixels of the left-hand text boxes.

14

5. Repeat step 2 for the right-hand group.

6. Select the Birth Date label and text box, and press Delete to remove them. The Hire Date and lower controls move up to fill the gap.

7. Repeat step 5 for the Photo label and text box.

8. Select the Country label and text box, and drag them together from the top of the right group to the bottom of the left group. Move the right group up to align horizontally with the left group.

9. Drag the bottom of the Picture Attachment control to align with the bottom of the Country text box. When correctly aligned, the photo fills the entire Attachment control (look ahead to Figure 14.6).

10. Drag the two control groups closer to the top of the Details section, and then drag the subform closer to the bottom of the Country text box.

11. Drag the subform's right border to the left and align it with the right group's right border, and, optionally, drag the bottom of the subform up to reduce its depth.

12. Click the Form Layout Tools – Format tab or the Home tab and change to Design view. Drag the form's right border to within about 0.25 inch of the right control group's right border.

13. Change to Form view. Figure 14.6 shows the redesigned form in Form view.

Figure 14.6
A few minutes of redesign reduces the form's obesity greatly. Form size isn't a major issue when viewed as a tabbed document, but minimizing bloat is a good policy for forms you want to display in modal or nonmodal pop-up windows.

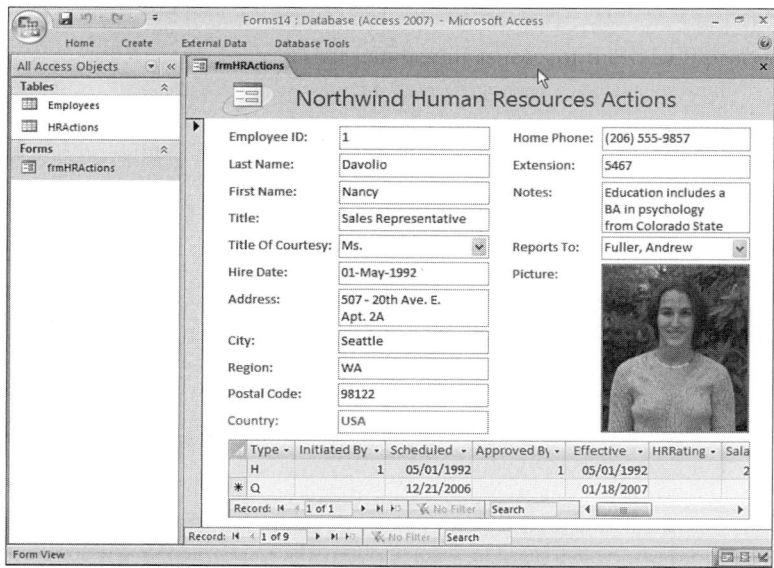

14. Optionally, right-click the Navigation pane's frmHRActions item, choose Rename, and change the friendly name of the form to the friendlier **Human Resources Actions**.

15. Press Ctrl+S to save your changes so far.

CHANGING FORM VIEW FROM A TABBED DOCUMENT TO A MODAL POP-UP WINDOW

The alternative to tabbed documents for displaying forms is a modal pop-up window that's the default display mode for *TableName* Details forms generated from Access 2007 templates.

To change frmHRActions' display mode to a modal pop-up window, do the following:

1. Open frmHRActions, if necessary.

2. In <u>L</u>ayout View, press Alt+Enter to open the Property Sheet, and click the vertical Record Selector button at the left of the form to specify Form as the selected object.

3. Click the Other tab, and change the Pop Up and Modal property values from No to Yes.

4. Close the Property Sheet and frmHRActions, and click Yes when asked if you want to save your changes.

5. Double-click the Navigation Pane item for the form to open it as a modal pop-up window (see Figure 14.7).

Figure 14.7
Users can minimize or maximize a modal pop-up form, but can't shift the focus to Access or another window without closing the form.

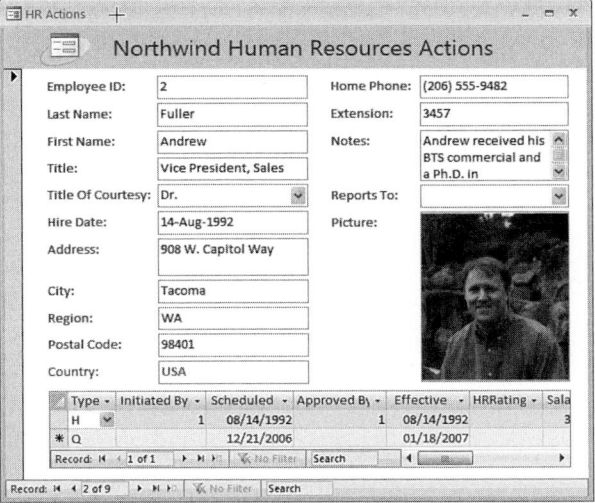

6. To experiment with a nonmodal pop-up form, close the form, open it in Layout view, open the Property Sheet for the form, click the Other tab, and set the Modal property value to No.

7. Close the form, save your changes, then double-click the item to open the form. With a nonmodal form, you can change the focus to the Access UI or any other window while the form is open. However, the **True** Pop Up property causes the window to remain on top of all other windows, even when minimized.

14

8. To return to the default tabbed document mode, open the Property Sheet for the form, click the Other tab, set the Pop Up property value to No, close the form, and save your changes.

It's a common practice to add a Close button, Save & Close button, or both, to the Header or Details section of pop-up forms.

SETTING FORM APPEARANCE PROPERTIES

Access offers several formatting properties that you can use to customize the appearance of your forms and the control objects they contain. You also can apply many of the property settings described in the following sections to subforms that you open in separate windows.

DEFAULT VALUES FOR FORMS

You can change a few default values used in the creation of all forms by clicking the Office and Access Options buttons to open the Access Options dialog, clicking the Object Designers button, and scrolling to the Forms/Reports section (see Figure 14.8). The Selection Behavior options determine how you select control objects with the mouse. You can create a form to use as a template and replace the standard (Normal) template, and mark the Always Use Event Procedures check box to permit only VBA code for automating applications and prevent embedding Access macros in forms.

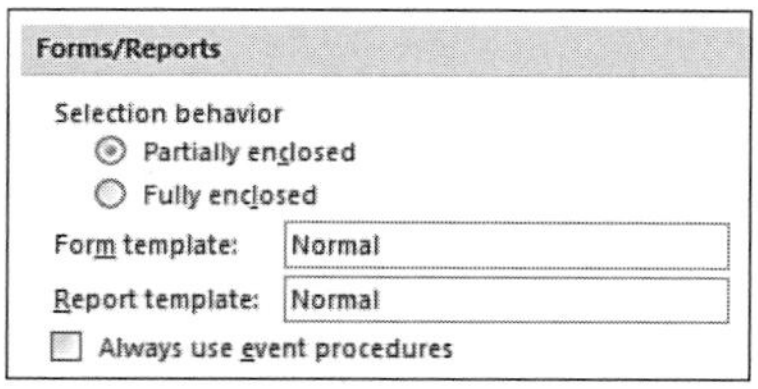

Figure 14.8
You can change a few default form values that apply to all databases you create in the Forms/Reports section of the Access Option dialog's Object Designers page.

The Application Options section of the Access Options dialog's Current Database page (see Figure 14.9) has several items that apply default values to the forms of the current database.

Following are the application options that apply to forms and their controls:

- **Application Icon**—Specify the path and filename of a desktop and toolbar icon to replace Access's icon.

- **Use as Form and Report Icon**—Mark to replace the Access icon with the small version of the icon on a form or report's tabbed document or window.

- **Display Form**—Select the form to open automatically when the user launches the database.

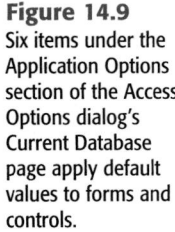

Figure 14.9
Six items under the Application Options section of the Access Options dialog's Current Database page apply default values to forms and controls.

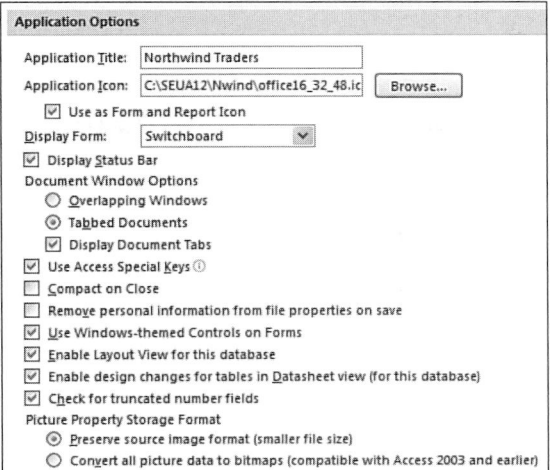

- **Document Window Options**—Select the Overlapping Windows option to replace tabbed documents with modal pop-up forms. Clear Display Document Tabs to hide the tabs of tabbed documents, which requires users to employ the Navigation pane to select the active form.

- **Use Windows-themed Controls on Forms**—Clearing this check box removes Windows XP or Vista themes from form controls.

- **Enable Layout View for This Database**—Clearing this check box prevents users from opening forms in Layout view.

 All form, form section, and control properties have default values. You can change the default values for the current form, section, or controls by choosing the object and then changing the default values displayed in the Properties window for that object. You can also use the AutoFormat feature to quickly apply a predefined format to all controls in the form. The next section describes using AutoFormat to change a form's appearance, and subsequent sections describe ways to change the format of text or controls manually on a form.

TIP

Check the Selection Type and object name of the Property Sheet before you change property values to make sure the selected object is the one whose properties you want to change. It's a common practice to leave the Property Sheet open as you alter the form design, and the selected object might not be the object you intend.

USING AUTOFORMAT

 AutoFormat lets you apply a predefined format to an entire form with only a few mouse clicks. Access 2007 comes with 25 predefined formats and an AutoFormat Wizard, and you also can create or customize your own formats for use with the AutoFormat Wizard.

14

APPLYING AN AUTOFORMAT FROM THE GALLERY

To apply a format to a form with one of Access 2007's 25 standard AutoFormats, follow these steps:

1. Click the Form Layout Tools – Format tab and then the AutoFormat group's button to open the AutoFormat gallery shown in Figure 14.10.

Figure 14.10
An AutoFormat that you select from the gallery applies a pre-defined format to the entire form.

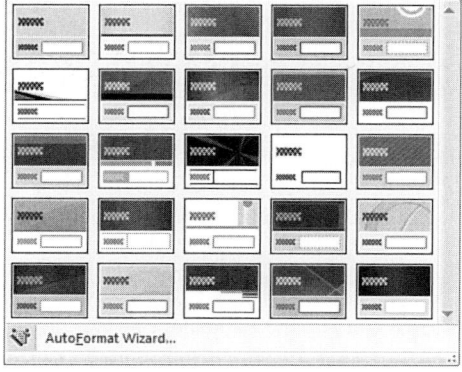

2. Click the preview image to apply the format to the form. Figure 14.11 shows the frmHRActions form after the None format has been applied. Applying other formats requires moving the two control groups down to accommodate the AutoFormat style's standard form Header depth.

Figure 14.11
The frmHRActions form has the None (plain vanilla) format applied to the main form.

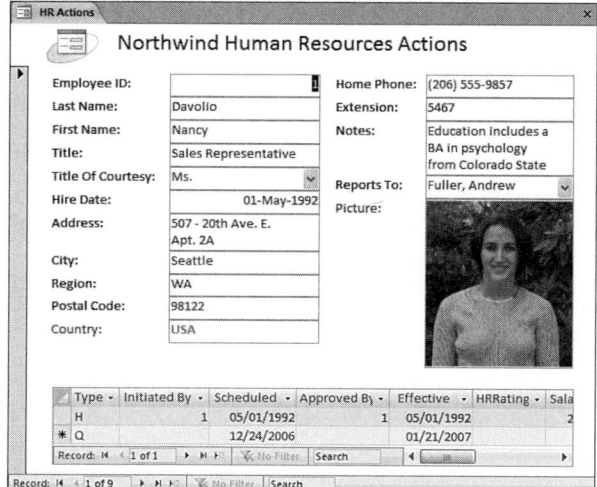

3. Press Ctrl+Z to return to the original format you selected when creating the form, if you want. You can undo initial application of an AutoFormat from the gallery but not by the AutoFormat Wizard.

> **TIP**
>
> Don't depend on the preview image to provide a faithful representation of the appearance of the form after applying the AutoFormat. Some AutoFormats differ from their previews markedly.

USING THE AUTOFORMAT WIZARD

Clicking the AutoFormat Wizard button at the bottom of the gallery (refer to Figure 14.10) opens the AutoFormat Wizard's main dialog, which includes the same 25 AutoFormats as the gallery. Select an AutoFormat name in the list and click OK to apply it to the current form.

The AutoFormat dialog, when expanded by clicking the Options button, lets you omit the application of font, color, or border style information to your form when you apply the AutoFormat (see Figure 14.12). Deselect the check box for the elements of the AutoFormat that you don't want AutoFormat to apply to your form.

Figure 14.12
The AutoFormat Wizard lets you selectively apply a style to the current form's fonts, colors, or border styles.

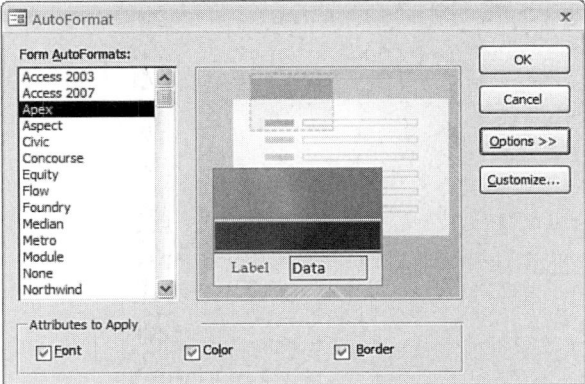

> **TIP**
> If you don't have an AutoFormat selection for the Access 2007 default format and don't like the choices offered by the wizard, close the form and don't save the changes. As mentioned in the preceding section, you can't undo the application of an AutoFormat by the wizard.

14

CREATING AND CUSTOMIZING AUTOFORMATS

The predefined AutoFormat styles might not suit your tastes, or you might want to create AutoFormat styles specific to your organization or application.

Applying formatting to a form through an AutoFormat style is by far the easiest way to create standardized forms for your database application—especially because the Form Wizard uses the same format style list as the AutoFormat feature. In other words, any AutoFormat you create also becomes available in the Form Wizard dialog.

> **NOTE**
>
> Access stores the standard set of AutoFormat styles in a \Program Files\Microsoft Office\Office12\ACCWIZ\ACWZUSR12.accdu folder. The extension for wizard user settings files is .accdu.
>
> When you add, delete, or customize an AutoFormat, Access creates a user-specific file, \Documents and Settings*UserName*\Application\Data\Microsoft\Access\ACWZUSR12.accdu (Windows XP) or \Users*UserName*\AppData\Roaming\Microsoft\Access\ACWZUSR12.accdu (Windows Vista).

To create a new AutoFormat or customize an existing one, follow these steps:

1. Create a form and alter its appearance (using the techniques described in the next five sections of this chapter) so that the form has the font, border, background picture, and other options adjusted exactly the way you want them for your new or customized AutoFormat. This example uses the default Form format, which has a "Web 2.0-ish" style.

2. Click the Form Layout Tools – Format tab and the AutoFormat or More button to display the AutoFormat gallery. If you want to modify an existing AutoFormat, select it in the Form AutoFormats list now. This example creates a new Default style.

3. Click the Customize button to open the Customize AutoFormat dialog and select the Create a New AutoFormat Based on the Form 'HR Actions', as shown in Figure 14.13.

Figure 14.13
The Customize AutoFormat dialog is used to create, modify, or delete an AutoFormat. This selection creates a new format from the currently selected form.

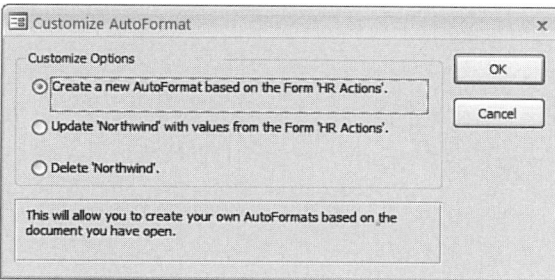

4. Click OK. The New Style Name dialog opens with the default *FormName*1 value. Type an appropriate name for your new AutoFormat (**Default** for this example) and click OK. Access creates the AutoFormat style and returns you to the AutoFormat dialog.

NOTE

> The AutoFormat Wizard doesn't save the form Header style, so you can only depend on the wizard to apply the saved custom style to a form's Details section.

5. Click Close to close the AutoFormat dialog.

DELETING AUTOFORMATS

If you've created your own AutoFormats, you might want to delete an AutoFormat that you no longer use. To delete an AutoFormat, follow these steps:

1. Open any form in Design view.
2. Click the AutoFormat button to display the AutoFormat dialog.
3. Click to select the AutoFormat you want to delete in the Form AutoFormats list and then click the Customize button. Access displays the Customize AutoFormat dialog (refer to Figure 14.13).
4. Select the Delete '*FormatName*' option and click OK. Access deletes that AutoFormat from the list.

TIP

> Be sure to select the correct AutoFormat for deletion before you click OK. Access doesn't ask for confirmation when you delete an AutoFormat.

5. Click Close to close the AutoFormat dialog.

CHANGING AN OBJECT'S COLORS

You select object colors with color pickers, as well as by setting form and control property values in the Property Sheet. The following sections describe how to use the Formatting toolbar controls and the Property Sheet to change background and foreground colors of form sections and control objects, as well as border properties of control objects.

THE ACCESS COLOR PALETTE

The Access color palette consists of 20 Access theme colors, which the current or default AutoFormat specifies, 70 standard (named) colors, 31 Windows system colors, and up to 10 recent colors. The theme colors are divided into 10 colors for specific objects, such as Background Light Header and Access Theme Color 1 through 10.

14

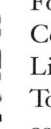

Figure 14.14 shows the color picker that opens when you click the drop-down button of the Form Layout Tools – Format ribbon's Font Color, Fill/Back Color, or Alternate Fill/Back Color button in the Font group; the Gridlines group's Color button; or the Controls group's Line Color button. The color picker is the same for all buttons, and each color button has a ToolTip to display the color name. The color picker doesn't include Windows System colors, which depend on the user's Windows theme; you select Windows System colors in the Property Sheet for the object.

Figure 14.14
Access's standard color picker offers a total of 90 predefined colors, up to 10 recently used colors, and a More Colors button to open a Colors dialog with additional color selection options.

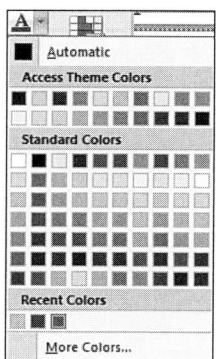

Following are the color names for the first row of the color picker's buttons, from left to right:

Title Text	Light Header Background
Light Label Text	Dark Header Background
Dark Label Text	Alternate Row
Description	Borders/Gridlines
Background	Highlight

BACKGROUND COLORS

The background color (Back Color property) of a form section (Header, Detail, or Footer) applies to all areas of that section except areas occupied by control objects that don't have a transparent background. The default background color of form Detail and Footer sections is white; the form Header section is Background Light Header.

If you're creating a form that you intend to print, a dark or deeply textured background will not only be distracting but will also consume substantial amounts of printer toner. Data entry operators often prefer a white or light gray background rather than a colored or textured background. Colored and textured backgrounds tend to distract users.

There's no command button to format a section's background color. To change the background color of a section of a form in Layout view, follow these steps:

1. Click an empty area within the section of the form (Header, Detail, or Footer) whose background color you want to change. (In Design view, you can click the section's header bar.) This step selects the appropriate section.

2. Press Alt+Enter to open the Property Sheet, verify that the section you want is selected, and click the Format tab.

3. Click the builder button to open the color picker (see Figure 14.15).

Figure 14.15
Use the Property Sheet's color property builder buttons to open the color picker.

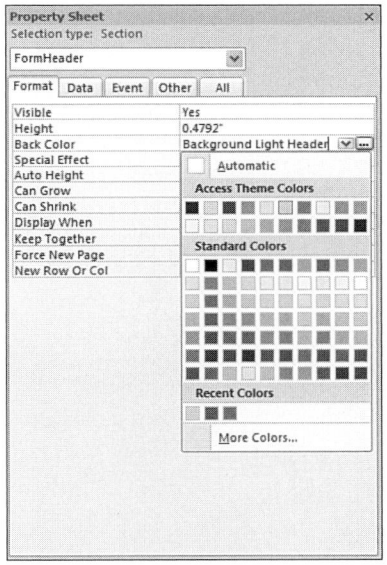

4. Click the button for the color you want to use.

Because the background color of each form section is independent, you must repeat the process if you want to change the color for other sections of your form. Clicking the Automatic button sets the Back Color property to white (#FFFFFF).

You choose the background color for a control object, such as a label, by selecting the control and clicking the Form Layout Tools – Format button and the Fill/Back Color dropdown button to open the color picker. Alternatively, use the Home ribbon's Font buttons. The default value of the Back Color property of text boxes is white so that text boxes (and the data they contain) contrast with the form's background color.

14

TIP

> In most cases, the preferred background color of labels is the same as that of the form. Set labels' Back Style color to transparent so the background color shows.

BACKGROUND IMAGES AND LOGOS

You can use a bitmap or vector image as the background for a form. Unlike background colors that you assign to form sections, you select a single bitmap picture for the entire form. Access 2007 comes with a few .gif bitmaps that you can tile as form backgrounds, plus the Globe.wmf metafile from an AutoFormat of an earlier Access version. Access stores these images in the Program Files\Microsoft Office\Office12\Bitmaps\Styles folder as the background for the form. You can use any .bmp, .dib, .emf, .gif, .ico, .jpg, .pcx, .png, or .wmf graphics file as a background for a form.

TIP

> Forms with background logos can look dramatic and, therefore, are best suited for decision-support forms intended for management personnel. (Management types are known to prefer form over substance.) For accurate, high-speed data entry, keep your transaction-processing forms visually simple so that users can easily distinguish data fields on the form and easily read text labels.

You set or remove a form's background image through the form's Property Sheet; you can also specify several viewing and formatting properties for the background picture. Follow these steps to set the background image properties of a form:

1. Open the form in Layout view if necessary.

2. Click the Form (Record) Select button.

3. If the Property Sheet isn't already open, press Ctrl+Enter.

4. Click the Format tab in the Property Sheet to display the various Picture properties: Picture, Picture Tiling, Picture Alignment, Picture Type, and Picture Size Mode. These properties and their effects are described in the list following these numbered steps.

5. Specify the path and filename for the graphics file in the Picture text box, and set the various Picture properties until you're satisfied with the appearance of the form. As you change each property, results of the change become immediately visible on the form. Figure 14.16 illustrates use of a tiled Acbluprt.gif image to create a simple grid pattern.

6. Optionally, close the Property Sheet.

The following list summarizes form properties related to the background picture, available choices for each property, and the effects of each choice:

Figure 14.16
A tiled bitmap can create a uniform pattern or texture for the form's background.

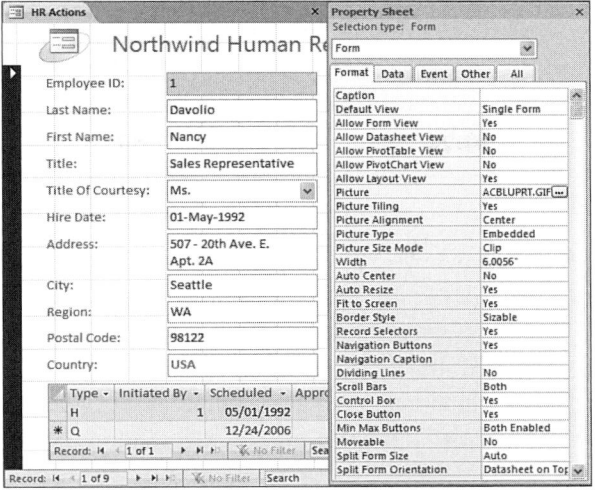

■ The Picture property contains the folder path and filename of the graphics file that Access uses as the form's background. You can either type the folder path and filename directly in the Picture property text box or use the Builder to help you select the background graphics file. To use the Builder, click the Picture property field to select that field and then click the Build button that appears next to the text box. Access opens the Insert Picture dialog; navigate to the location and select the graphics file to use, as shown in Figure 14.17.

Figure 14.17
Use the Insert Picture dialog to select a graphics file for a form's background.

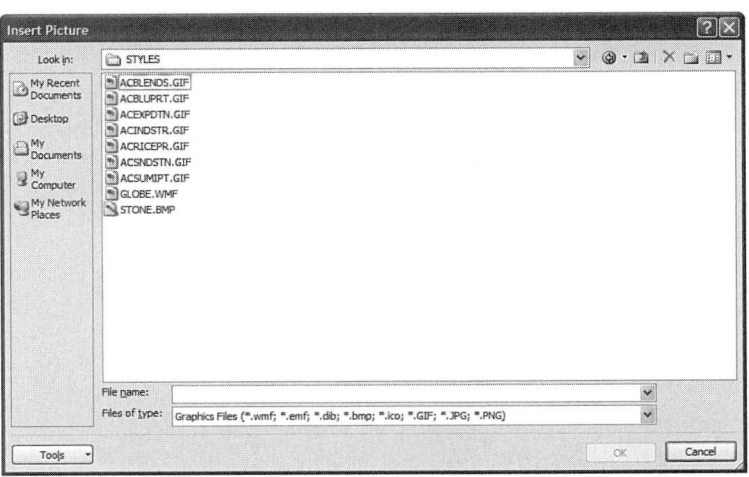

TIP

To remove a background picture, delete the entry in the Picture text box and click Yes when asked if you want to remove the picture from the form.

14

- The Picture Type property specifies the method that Access uses to attach the background picture to the form. You can select either Embedded or Linked as the picture type. Use the Embedded picture type, especially if you intend to distribute your database application; the resulting form is self-contained and doesn't rely on the presence of external files that might be moved or deleted. If you have many forms that use the same background bitmap graphic, linking the background picture can save some disk space.

- The Picture Size Mode property controls how Access sizes the background picture. The available choices are Clip, Stretch, and Zoom. Clip causes Access to display the picture at its full size behind the form; if the picture is larger than the form, the picture is clipped to fit the form. If the picture is smaller than the form, the form's own background color shows in any part of the form background not covered by the picture. Stretch causes Access to stretch the picture vertically and horizontally to match the size of the form; the Stretch option permits distortions in the picture. Zoom causes Access to magnify the picture, without distortion, to fit the size of the form.

- The Picture Alignment property controls where Access positions the background picture. The available choices are Top-left (aligns the upper-left corner of the picture with the upper-left corner of the form window), Top-right (aligns the upper-right corner of the picture with the upper-right corner of the form window), Center (places the picture in the center of the form window), Bottom-left (aligns the lower-left corner of the picture with the lower-left corner of the form), Bottom-right (aligns the lower-right corner of the picture with the lower-right corner of the form), and Form Center (centers the picture on the form).

> **TIP**
>
> To ensure that a background picture is displayed relative to the form, rather than the form's window, select Form Center as the value for the Picture Alignment property.

- The Picture Tiling property has two permissible values: Yes and No. Tiling means that the picture is repeatedly displayed to fill the entire form or form window (if the Picture Alignment property is set to Form Center, the tiling fills just the form).

Now that you know how to adjust the background picture and colors of a form, the next section describes how to adjust the foreground colors and border properties of the form and objects on the form.

FONT COLOR, BORDER COLOR, AND BORDER STYLE

You can set the font color, border color, and border width with buttons on the Form Layout Tools – Format ribbon or directly in the Property Sheet for a selected control.

 Font color (the Fore Color property) is applicable only to control objects. (The Font Color ribbon button is disabled when you select a form section.) Font color specifies the color for the text in labels and text boxes. The default value of the Fore Color property is black. You choose border colors, pattern, and thickness for control objects that have borders by clicking the appropriate Controls group button.

To set a control's foreground color, border width, or border color by using the Font or Controls group's buttons, first click the control whose properties you want to change and then click the command button for the property you want to change: Font Color, Line Thickness.

 To set a control's foreground color, border width, border color, or border style in the Properties window, first select the control whose properties you want to change by clicking it. Click the Format tab in the Property Sheet and then scroll to the text box for the property you want to change. Most of the border properties are selected from drop-down lists; color properties require you to select a named color or open the color picker and click one of the standard color buttons. Alternatively, you can use the Color Builder described in the following section.

CREATING CUSTOM COLORS WITH THE COLOR BUILDER

If you aren't satisfied with one of the predefined colors for your form sections or control objects, you can specify your own custom colors by following these steps:

1. Place the cursor in the Back/Fill Color, Fore Color, or Border Color text box of the Properties window for a form section or control.

 2. Click the Builder button to open the color picker, and then click More Colors to open the Colors dialog (see Figure 14.18, left). If one of the colors of the hexagonal palette suits your taste, select the color button, click OK to assign that color as the value of the property, and then close the dialog. If you want a more customized color, proceed to step 3.

Figure 14.18
Choose a custom color from the Color dialog's Standard (left) or Custom page (right). The Custom page lets you choose the RGB (red, green, blue) or HSL (hue, saturation, luminance) color model.

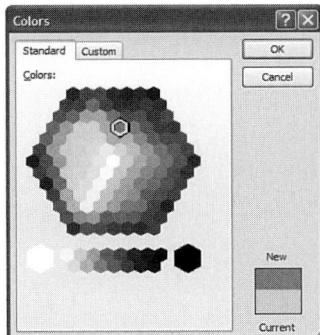 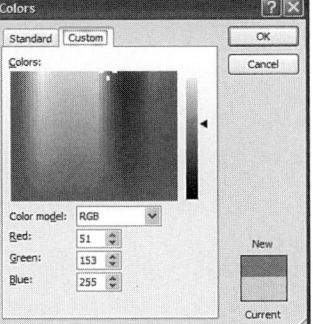

3. Click the Custom tab and accept the default RGB (red, green, blue) color model, as shown in Figure 14.18 (right), or choose HSL (hue, saturation, luminance) if you prefer.

4. Click and drag the cursor within the square Hue/Saturation area to choose the color you want.

5. Click and drag the arrow at the right of the rectangular luminance area while observing the Color block; release the mouse button when the Color block has the luminance (brightness) value you want.

6. Click OK to add this color value to the property, and close the Color dialog.

USING THE WINDOWS CLIPBOARD AND DELETING CONTROLS

 All conventional Windows Clipboard commands apply to control objects. You can cut or copy a selected control or group of controls to the Clipboard. After that, you can paste the control or group to the form with the Windows keyboard shortcut keys: Ctrl+X to cut, Ctrl+C to copy selected controls to the Clipboard, and Ctrl+V to paste the Clipboard contents.

You can delete a control by selecting it and then pressing Delete. If you accidentally delete a label associated with a control and pressing Ctrl+Z or clicking the Quick Access Toolbar's Undo button doesn't solve the problem, do the following: Select another label, copy it to the Clipboard, select the control the label needs to be associated with, and paste the label to the control.

CHANGING THE CONTENT OF TEXT CONTROLS

You can edit the content of text controls by using conventional Windows text-editing techniques. When you place the mouse pointer within the confines of a text control and click the mouse button, the mouse pointer becomes the Windows text-editing cursor that you use to insert or delete text. You can select text by dragging the mouse over it or by holding down Shift and moving the cursor with the arrow keys. All Windows Clipboard operations are applicable to text within controls. Keyboard text selection and editing techniques using the arrow keys in combination with Shift are available as well.

Most Access text boxes are bound to table or query fields. If you change the name of a field in a text box and make an error naming the field, you receive a "#Name?" error message in the offending text box when you select Run mode. Following is a better method of changing a text box with an associated label:

1. Delete the existing field control by clicking to select it and then pressing Delete.

 2. Click the Controls group's Add Existing Fields button in the Form Layout Tools – Format ribbon to display the Field List dialog.

3. Scroll through the entries in the list until you find the table or query field name you want.

4. Click the field name to select it; then drag the field name to the location of the deleted control. Release the mouse button to drop the new name.

5. Close the Field List dialog when you're finished.

You can relocate and resize the new field caption and text box (or edit the caption) as necessary. If you drag the field name inside a Tabular or Stacked control group, the caption and text box resize automatically.

USING THE FORMAT PAINTER

 The Format Painter lets you quickly copy the format of any control on the form to any other control on the form. The Format Painter copies only those formatting properties that are relevant to the control on which you apply the Format Painter. To use the Format Painter, follow these steps:

1. Select the control with the formatting you want to copy.

 2. Click or double-click the Format Painter button on the toolbar; the mouse cursor changes to a pointing arrow with a paintbrush icon attached to it. (Double-clicking "locks" the Format Painter on. Double-click the Format Painter button only if you want to copy the formatting to more than one control.)

3. Click any control that you want to copy the formatting to; the Format Painter copies all relevant formatting properties to this control. If you didn't double-click the Format Painter button, the Format Painter turns itself off after copying the formatting properties to one control.

4. If you locked the Format Painter on by double-clicking its button, you can repeat step 3 as many times as you want. Click the Format Painter button again to turn off the Format Painter.

Typically, you use the Format Painter to quickly set the formatting properties for field text labels, or in any situation where selecting several controls by dragging a selection rectangle seems undesirable. By locking the Format Painter, it's easy to format several controls one after another.

 If you encounter problems when you open the form in Form view, see the "Form Problems" topic of the "Troubleshooting" section near the end of the chapter.

CREATING A MASTER/CHILD FORM WITH THE FORM WIZARD

An alternative to auto-generating a master/child form by clicking the Create ribbon's Form button is to use the Form Wizard to generate the master form and its child subform. The advantage to using the Form Wizard is that you can use the wizard to customize the form design and create a subform that you can further customize in form Design view. You don't need to select a table or query prior to running the Form Wizard. However, forms created by the Form Wizard require much effort to create a layout that optimizes data entry efficiency.

14

To use the Form Wizard to create a frmEmployees form similar to frmHRActions, do the following:

1. Close frmHRActions (HR Actions) if it's open, and click the Create tab and the More Forms button to open the gallery. Click the Form Wizard button to launch the Form Wizard.

2. In the first wizard dialog, select the Employees table for the master form and click the >> button to add all fields. Select the BirthDate field and click < to remove it. Then do the same for the Photo field

3. Select the HRActions table for the child subform, click the >> button to move all fields. Select the HRActions.EmployeeID field and click < to remove it. Do the same for New Rate and New Commission because Northwind doesn't have hourly employees or commissioned salespeople (see Figure 14.19).

Figure 14.19
Select the tables to act as the record sources for the master and child forms and fields to display in the first Form Wizard dialog.

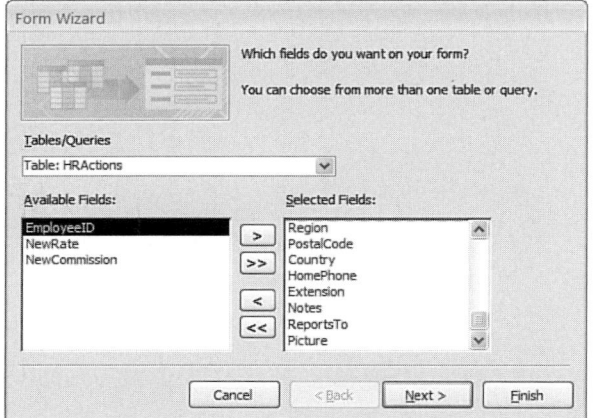

4. Click Next and accept the default setting By Employees (as the way to view data) and the Form with Subform(s) option (see Figure 14.20). (You can add more than one subform in step 3.)

5. Click Next and select Tabular as the default layout for the subform. (You can change the layout Datasheet view later, if you want.)

6. Click Next and select Default as the AutoFormat style for the form (see Figure 14.21). If you didn't create the Default style in the earlier "Creating and Customizing AutoFormats" section, select None.

7. Click Next and change the form name to **frmEmployees** and the subform name to **sbfHRActions**. Also, accept the option Open the Form to View or Enter Information (see Figure 14.22), and click Finish to generate the new master/child form.

14

Figure 14.20
Specify Employees as the record source for the master form and use a subform (rather than a linked form) for the child form.

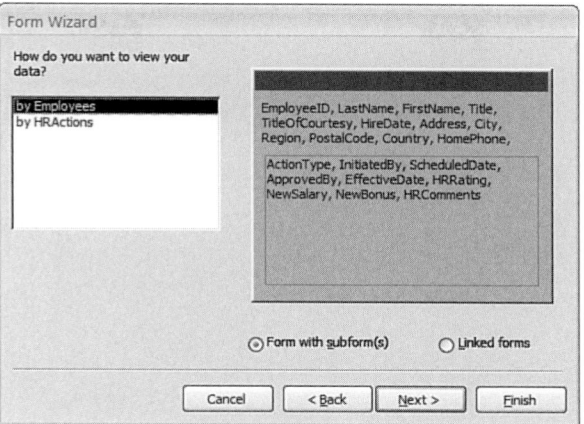

Figure 14.21
Select the AutoFormat style to apply in the third Form Wizard dialog.

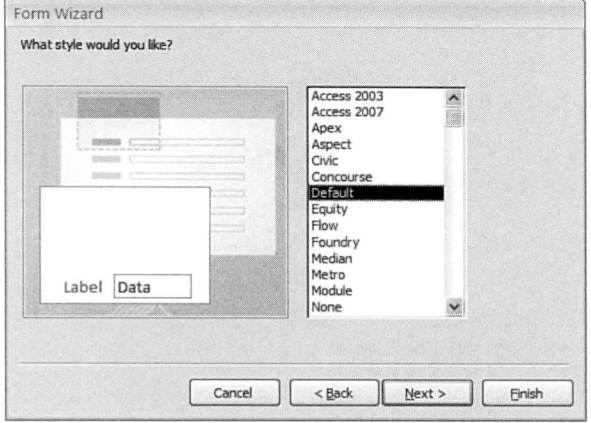

Figure 14.22
The final Form Wizard dialog lets you name the master and child forms.

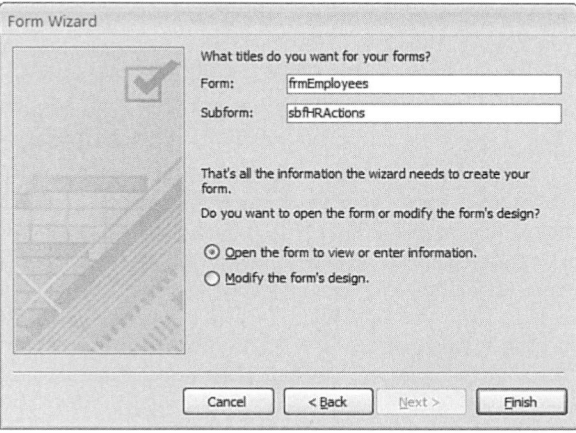

14

Figure 14.23 shows the initial master/child form in Form view. Four stacked control group columns contain the master form's label/text box control pairs. The form's layout obviously needs substantial modification, including regrouping the label and text box controls, and making substantial changes to the tabular subform.

Figure 14.23
The Form Wizard creates the necessary Access objects but the initial layout won't win any design awards.

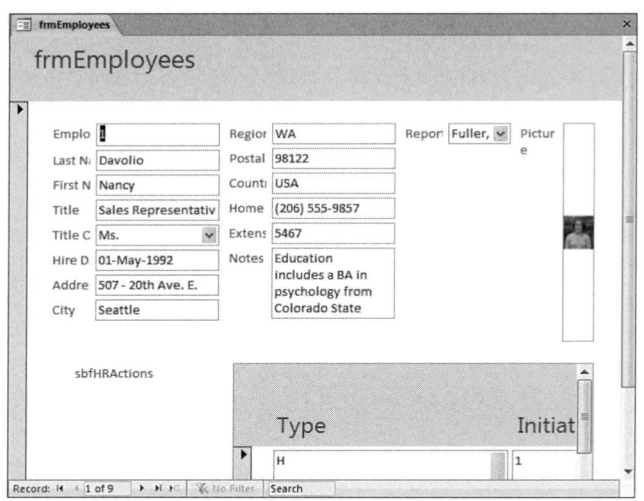

REFINING THE WIZARD-GENERATED FORM'S LAYOUT

The primary objective of this section is to emulate the layout of the master/child form you created early in the chapter, taking advantage of grouped controls where practical. Another goal is to demonstrate how to manipulate grouped control stacks.

To adjust the layout while minimizing use of form Design view, do the following:

1. Change to form Layout view, select the frmEmployees label, and reduce its height to about 0.5 inch.

2. Move the sbfHRActions subform and its label down about 2 inches to make room for three more label/text box pairs in the first column.

3. Click and drag the Region label and text box in the second column to the bottom of the first control stack. Do the same for the Postal Code and Country fields.

NOTE

You can drag controls from one stacked control group to another stacked control group or a tabular control to another tabular control group. However, you can't drag a control from a stacked control group to a tabular control group, and vice versa. You can't drag an ungrouped control into another control group, but you can create a control group by selecting a single control and clicking the Stacked or Tabular button.

4. Click and drag the Reports To field below the Notes field, and the Picture field below the Notes field. Drag the right edge of each group to the right to increase the label and text box width, then align the two stacked control groups to emulate the frmHRActions form. Optionally, drag the bottom up one grid notch to reduce the stacks' height (look ahead to Figure 14.24.)

TIP

Click and drag controls vertically within the stacked control group to relocate them. You also can drag controls horizontally within a tabular control group.

5. Replace the frmEmployees label text with **Northwind Human Resources Data Entry**.

6. Select sbfHRActions, click the Arrange ribbon's Remove button to ungroup the subfrom, select its label, click delete, and reposition the subform (see Figure 14.24).

Figure 14.24
The rearranged main form is now ready for subform redesign.

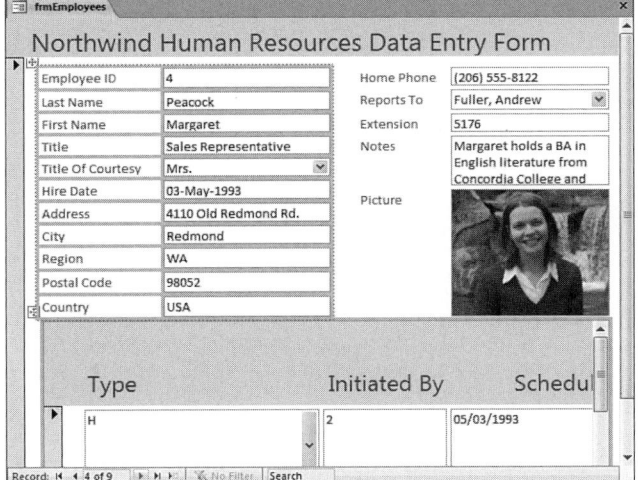

SETTING SUBFORM PROPERTIES

You can learn about modifying the properties of a subform by working with the subform that's used to create the history of prior HRActions for an employee. In this example, editing or deleting entries using the subform isn't allowed, but you can add new entries. The subform needs to be modified so that all its columns are readable without horizontal scrolling. When you complete the following steps, the sbfHRActions subform appears as shown in Figure 14.25.

14

Figure 14.25
The sbfHRActions subform in the frmHRActions form appears as shown here after its field sizes and overall dimensions have been modified.

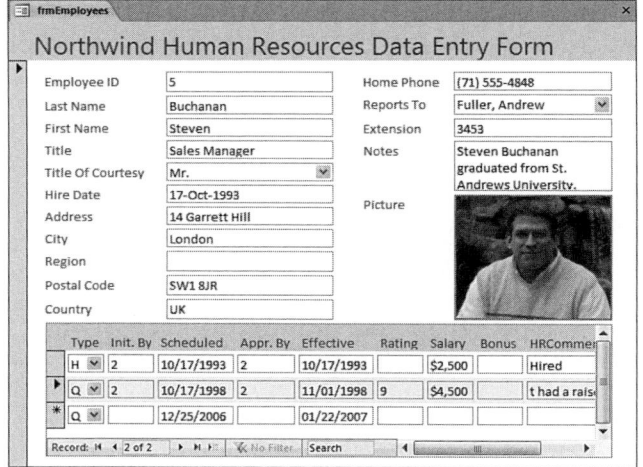

Although you can use the in-situ subform-editing feature to alter the design of a subform, in most cases it's easier to use the traditional method of subform design modification. In-situ editing is better suited for changing subform property values than for altering subform dimensions.

To change the properties of the sbfHRActions subform, follow these steps:

1. Open frmEmployees in Design view, right-click the sbfHRActions subform, and choose Subform in New Window from the context menu. Alternatively, click the Form Design Tools – Design tab, and click the Tools group's Subform in New Window button. The new subform window replaces the in-situ subform.

TIP

When you close a subform that's been opened in its own window, the in-situ subform disappears from Form Design view. To regain the in-situ version, click Form view and then Form Design view.

2. Press Ctrl+A to select all controls on the subform. Click the Form Design Tools – Remove tab to remove all controls from the default tabular control group.

3. Open the Property Sheet, set the Font Name property value to Calibri, Font Size to 11 points, Height to 0.20 inch, and Text Align to Left. Drag the Footer bar up to within one grid division of the Detail section's text boxes.

4. Click the Details bar to select the Details section and set the Alternate Back Color property value to Alternate Row.

5. Close the Property Sheet and drag the mouse pointer over all the labels to select them, drag the group to the top of the form Header section, then drag the Details bar to the bottom of the labels.

6. Press Ctrl+A to select all controls and click the Tabular button to create a Tabular control group. Re-creating the control group lets you change the widths of labels and text boxes simultaneously.

7. Change to Layout view, select each column in sequence, abbreviate the field name, and adjust the widths of the columns (except the Comments column) to accommodate their data. Set the format of the Salary and Bonus fields to Currency with 0 decimal places (see Figure 14.26).

Figure 14.26
Choosing New Window from the context menu opens the subform in a separate window. Change the field names and adjust the widths of the subform's labels and fields as shown here.

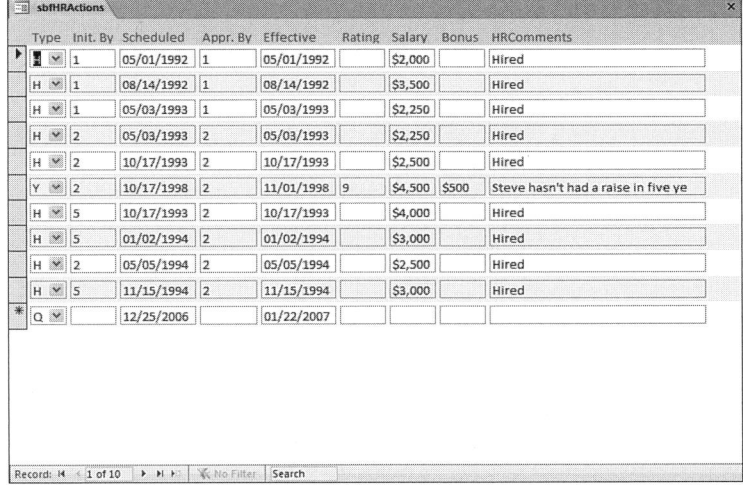

Type	Init. By	Scheduled	Appr. By	Effective	Rating	Salary	Bonus	HRComments
I	1	05/01/1992	1	05/01/1992		$2,000		Hired
H	1	08/14/1992	1	08/14/1992		$3,500		Hired
H	1	05/03/1993	1	05/03/1993		$2,250		Hired
H	2	05/03/1993	2	05/03/1993		$2,250		Hired
H	2	10/17/1993	2	10/17/1993		$2,500		Hired
Y	2	10/17/1998	2	11/01/1998	9	$4,500	$500	Steve hasn't had a raise in five ye
H	5	10/17/1993	2	10/17/1993		$4,000		Hired
H	5	01/02/1994	2	01/02/1994		$3,000		Hired
H	2	05/05/1994	2	05/05/1994		$2,500		Hired
H	5	11/15/1994	2	11/15/1994		$3,000		Hired
Q		12/25/2006		01/22/2007				

Record: 1 of 10   No Filter   Search

TIP

As you make changes to the subform, press Ctrl+S to save them. It's frustrating to spend several minutes adjusting the positions and formatting of fields, and then lose your changes by an inadvertent error.

8. Return to form Design view, and drag the right edge of the form to the left until the form is slightly wider than the fields (about 7 ½ inches). Then drag the form Footer section upward so that the Detail section is about ⅜ inches high.

9. With the subform window active, open the Property Sheet, select Form in the selection type list, and click the Data tab.

10. Set the Allow Edits and Allow Deletions property values to No (to prevent modifying previous actions) and set Allow Additions to Yes.

14

NOTE

> You can set the Data Entry property to Yes to achieve a result that is similar to setting the Allow Edits and Allow Deletions property to No and the Allow Additions property to Yes. When you set the Data Entry property to Yes, however, only the tentative new record appears—no previous entries appear in the subform.

 11. Save your changes, close the sbfHRActions subform, and close and reopen the frmEmployees form in Design view.

TIP

> You must close and reopen the main form to make changes you apply to a subform in the window appear in Form view. The form embeds a copy of the subform; the embedded copy doesn't change until you close and reopen the form.

 12. Save your changes and then close and reopen the frmEmployees form in Form view. Your form appears as shown in earlier Figure 14.25.

 If problems occur when you attempt to add a new subform record for an employee, see the "Subform Problems" topic of the "Troubleshooting" section near the end of the chapter.

GENERATING MULTIPLE ITEMS AND SPLIT FORMS

Selecting a table or query and clicking the Create Ribbon's Multiple Items button in the Forms group generates a Datasheet-style tabular list of all table fields and records or query columns and rows. This form style is very similar to that which the Form Wizard creates for subforms if you choose the Datasheet instead of the Tabular style with the Default AutoFormat. The primary differences are in the Header section: the addition of a logo and minor changes to the column header format. Figure 14.27 shows a multiple-items form generated from the HRActions table.

TIP

> You can use the Multiple Items button to create a Datasheet-style form for a subform with a style similar to the default main form, but using the Form Wizard to do this is faster and offers more flexibility.

 Chapter 2, "Building Simple Tracking Applications," introduced you to the split form design. A split form lets you display multiple records in Datasheet format above the split. You also can type data for the selected record in the text boxes of a panel below the split. The idea behind the split form is the ability to quickly select the record of interest from a large number of records in the Datasheet and edit the record more efficiently in stacked text boxes. A vertically adjustable splitter bar divides the main form with stacked text boxes and an Attachment control from the lower datasheet section (see Figure 14.28).

Figure 14.27
The HRActions multiple-items form appears as shown here after the column widths and row height have been adjusted.

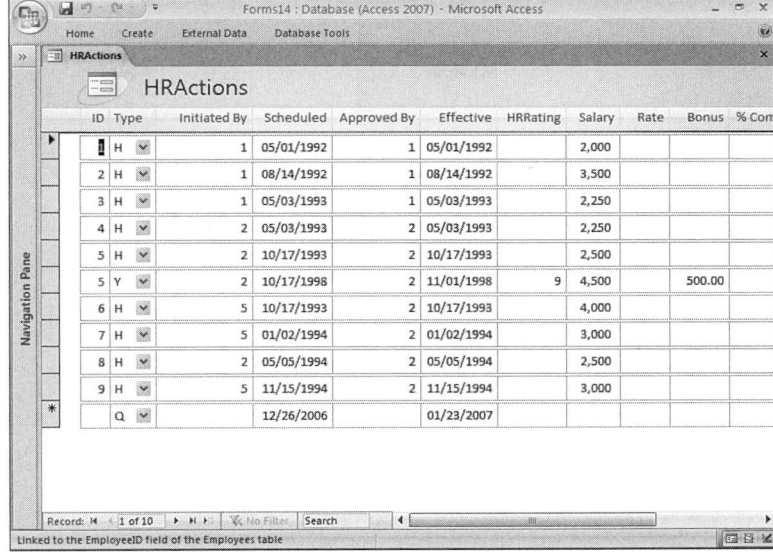

Figure 14.28
This split form shows the main form above and Datasheet below the splitter bar; you can reverse these positions or display the Datasheet to the left or right of the main form.

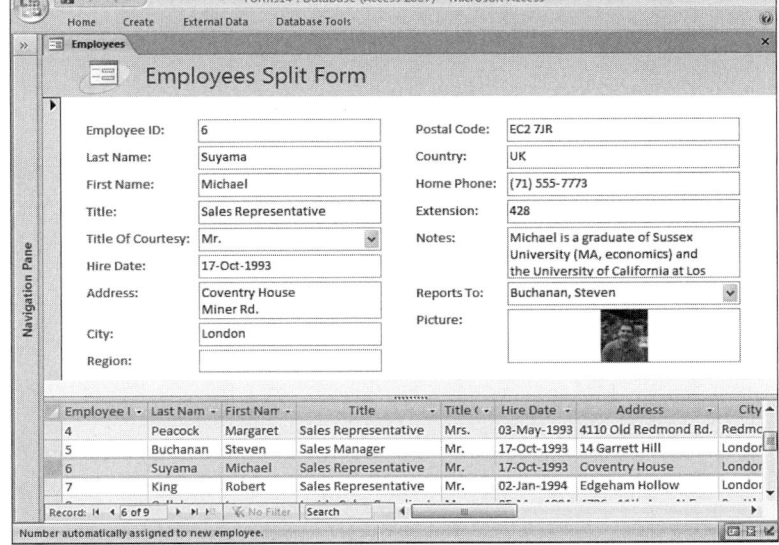

USING TRANSACTION-PROCESSING FORMS

As noted near the beginning of this chapter, the purpose of transaction-processing forms is to add new records to, delete records from, or edit data in one or more tables that underlie the form. The sections that follow describe how to add new records to the HRActions table with the frmHRActions form.

Forms you create with the Create ribbon's Form button and the Form Wizard use the standard record-navigation buttons located at the bottom of the form. The record-navigation buttons perform the same functions with forms as they do with tables and queries. You can select the first or last records in the table or query that is the source of data for your main form, or you can select the next or previous record. Subforms include their own set of record-selection buttons that operate independently of the set for the main form.

NOTE

If you didn't create the frmHRActions form in the preceding sections of this chapter, the forms, subforms, and Employees and HRActions objects are included in the Forms14.accdb database in your \Program Files\Seua12\Chaptr14 folder.

Navigation between the text boxes used for entering or editing data in the form is similar to navigation in queries and tables in Datasheet view except that the up-arrow and down-arrow keys cause the cursor to move between fields rather than between records. Accept the values you've entered by pressing Enter or Tab.

APPENDING NEW RECORDS TO THE HRACTIONS TABLE

In Datasheet view of a table or query, the last record in the datasheet is provided as a tentative append record (indicated by an asterisk on the record-selection button). If you enter data in this record, the data automatically is appended to the table and Access starts a new tentative append record. Forms also provide a tentative append record, unless you set the Allow Additions property value for the form to No.

The following comments apply to adding HRAction records with the frmHRActions form:

- Because data from the Employees table is included in the main form, the ID number, name, and title of the employee appear in the text boxes on the main form. Your form design lets you edit the LastName, FirstName, and Title data, although these fields are incorporated in the table (Employees) on the one side of a one-to-many relationship. The editing capability of a form is the same as that for the underlying table or query that serves as its source unless you change the form's editing capabilities by setting the form's Allow Editing property and other related properties.

- After you add a new record to the HRActions table, you can't delete or edit it, because the Allow Edits and Allow Deletions property values are set to No.

TIP

When experimenting with adding records to the HRActions table, temporarily set the subform's Allow Edits and Allow Deletions property values to Yes.

- If you added an entry for the chosen employee ID when you created the HRActions table in Chapter 5, "Working with Access Databases and Tables," the entry appears in the subform's fields. The subform's data display is linked to the data in the main form through the one-to-many relationship between the Employees table and the HRActions table. The subform only displays records from the HRActions table whose EmployeeID fields match the value of the EmployeeID field of the record currently displayed by the main form.

To append a new record to the HRActions table and enter the required data, follow these steps:

1. Open the frmHRActions form if it isn't already open or click the Form View button if you're in Design view. Data for the first record of the Employees table—with the matching data from the corresponding record(s) in the HRActions table—appears in the text-box controls of your form.

2. Access places the cursor in the first text box of the main form, the ID text box. The first example uses Steven Buchanan, whose employee ID is 5, so type **Steve** in the Search text box. Access displays the Employees table data for Steven Buchanan in the main form and his HRActions records in the subform.

> **NOTE**
>
>
> Alternatively, click the Next Record button of the lower set of navigation buttons four times to open the record for Mr. Buchanan.

> **TIP**
>
> If you change the value of the AutoNumber ID field (for instance to 5), you receive a "Field can't be updated" message when you move the cursor to another field. Press Esc to cancel the change. (Typing the original value generates the same message.)
>
> You can prevent editing of this or any other field of a form or subform by changing the Locked property of the field's text box to Yes.

3. Click in the Type field of the tentative append record in the subform. If the tentative append record in the subform isn't visible, click the New Record button of the subform's navigation control to move to the tentative append record at the end of the existing HRActions table entries for Steven Buchanan.

4. Type a valid HRAction type (**H, Q, Y, S, R, B, C,** or **T** because of the field's validation rule) in the Type text box. (If you added the lookup list to the Action field, you can select the type code from the list.) Default date values appear in the Scheduled and Effective date fields. In this example, you bring Steven Buchanan's HRActions records up to date by adding yearly performance review information. Type **Y** and then press Tab or Enter to accept the default Type value and move the cursor to the next data-entry text box, Initiated By.

5. Mr. Buchanan reports to the vice president of sales, Andrew Fuller, whose employee ID is 2. Type **2** in the Initiated By text box and press Enter.

14

NOTE

> The pencil symbol, which indicates that you're editing a record, replaces the triangle at the top of the Record Selector bar to the left of the record that you are entering. The Description property you entered for the field in the table underlying this query appears in the status bar and changes as you move the cursor to the next field. (To change a previous entry, press Shift+Tab, or use the up- and down-arrow keys to maneuver to whichever text box contains a value you want to change.)

6. Mr. Buchanan was hired on 10/17/1993, but Northwind Traders had no Human Resources (HR) department to maintain HR data until mid-1998, so type **10/17/1998** in the Scheduled field if you didn't add this entry earlier. If there is a 10/17/1998 entry, type **10/17/1999**.

7. Because Mr. Fuller is a vice-president, he has the authority to approve salary increases. Type Mr. Fuller's employee ID, **2**, in the Approved By text box and then press Enter to move the cursor to the next field.

8. The effective date for salary adjustments for Northwind Traders is the 1st or 15th day of the month in which the performance review is scheduled. Type the appropriate date in the Effective text box.

9. You can type any number from **0** (terminated) to **9** (excellent) in the Rating text box, which reflects the employee's performance.

10. You can be as generous as you want with the salary and bonus that you enter in the Salary and Bonus text boxes. The value of the Salary field is a new monthly salary, not an incremental value.

11. In the Comments multiline text box to the right of the New Amount field, add any comments you care to make concerning how generous or stingy you were with this salary increase. The multiline text box includes a scroll bar that appears when the cursor is within the text box, but the text box shows only one line.

12. When you complete your entries, Access stores them in a memory buffer but doesn't add the new record to the HRActions table. You can add the record to the table by choosing <u>R</u>ecords, Save Recor<u>d</u>; clicking the New Record button; or changing the position of the record pointer with the Previous or Next record selector button. If you want to cancel the addition of a record, press Esc twice.

13. Repeat steps 3 through 12 to add a few additional records.

TIP

> If you click the Next Record selector button to select the tentative append record, and then decide that you don't want to add any more data, click the Previous Record button to make sure this new record isn't added to the table. If the table has required fields without default values, however, you must enter a value for each required field, and then delete the added record. Deleting records requires setting the subform's Allow Deletions property value to Yes.

When you add a record, your form appears like the one shown in Figure 14.29. Each record for an employee appears in the subform datasheet in the order of the primary key fields of the HRActions table.

Figure 14.29
The frmEmployees form appears as shown here after a new subform record has been appended for an employee.

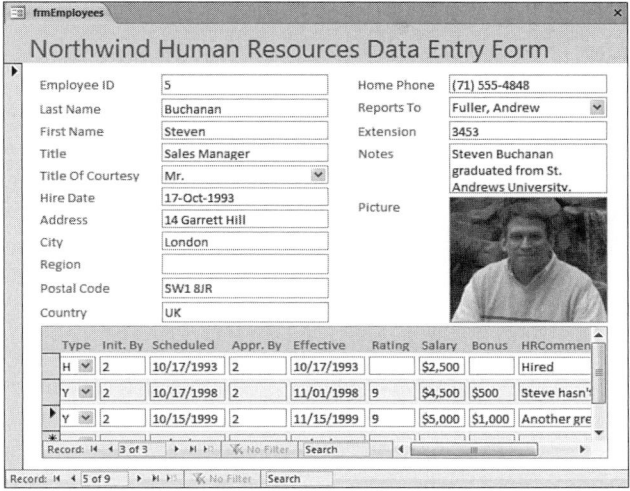

MODIFYING THE PROPERTIES OF A FORM OR CONTROL AFTER TESTING

The entries you added and edited gave you an opportunity to test your form. Testing a form to ensure that it accomplishes the objectives you have in mind usually takes much longer than creating the form and the query that underlies it. During the testing process, you might notice that the order of the fields isn't what you want or that records in the subform aren't displayed in an appropriate sequence. The following two sections deal with modifying the properties of the form and subform control.

REMOVING FIELDS FROM THE TAB ORDER

Access lets you set the value of the Tab Stop property to No to prevent controls from receiving the focus in the tab order. To remove a control from the tab order, select the control, open the Properties window, select Other, and change the value of the Tab Stop property to No. You can't edit the EmployeeID field, so set the Tab Stop property to No for this control.

NOTE

Setting the Tab Stop property's value to No doesn't disable a given control, but it removes the control from the tab sequence. As a result, the control can't be selected by pressing the Tab key, but can still be selected by clicking it with the mouse.

14

DISABLING EDITING OF SPECIFIC CONTROLS

It's a common practice to disable controls that users can't or shouldn't edit. For example, the Employee ID text box is read-only because it's bound to an AutoNumber EmployeeID field. It's tempting to disable this field by setting its Enabled property value to No, but doing this grays the label and text box text, and displays an unattractive text box background color. Therefore, the better choice, along with removing disabled controls from the tab order, is to set the control's Locked property value to Yes. When the user opens the form, focus is on the next control in the tab order.

TROUBLESHOOTING

FORM PROBLEMS

I can't add a new record to a form or subform that's bound to an Access query.

The most likely cause of this problem is that the query you're using as the record source for the form or subform isn't updatable. Run the query and verify that the tentative append record appears after the last record with data. If the tentative append record is present in the datasheet and not in the form or subform, then you might have accidentally set the Allow Additions property value to No.

The text boxes on my form are empty, the Next and Previous record navigation buttons are disabled, and the First and Last record buttons don't work.

You accidentally set the Data Entry property value of the form to Yes. Setting the Data Entry property permits adding new records, but prevents the user from seeing existing records. Why the First and Last buttons are enabled is a mystery. This problem also occurs with subforms and often results from selecting the form instead of the subform when setting the Data Entry property value.

No controls appear on my form in Form view.

You've set the Allow Additions property to No, and accidentally set the Data Entry property value of the form to Yes. In this case, subforms don't appear on the form. There have been many requests by Access users and developers to display an error message when these mutually exclusive property values are specified. (New Access users have been known to panic after having spent several hours designing a form and then seeing their work disappear in Form view.) The problem also applies to subforms but isn't as dramatic.

SUBFORM PROBLEMS

The subform I added to the main form doesn't change its data when I move the main form's record pointer with the navigation buttons.

You didn't create the required link between the main form and the subform in the Data page of the main form's Properties window, or the link is broken as the result of changing a table or query name.

Select the subform container of the main form (not the subform itself) by clicking the edge of the subform in form Design view, open the Properties window, and click the Data tab. Click the Builder button to open the Subform Field Linker dialog, and add or correct the field names of the linked tables or queries.

IN THE REAL WORLD—THE ART OF FORM DESIGN

Creating an effective form design for data entry requires a unique combination of graphic design and programming skills. Whether your goal is to develop front ends for Access or SQL Server databases, or SharePoint lists, the basic methodology of form design is the same. Large database-development projects usually begin with a detailed specification for the database, plus a set of descriptions of each data display and entry form. Small- to medium-sized organizations, however, seldom have the resources to develop an all-encompassing specification before embarking on a project. If your objective is to develop from-scratch Access forms for decision-support or online transaction processing (OLTP) applications, keep in mind the guidelines of this and the following chapter's "Real World" sections.

UNDERSTAND THE AUDIENCE

Your first task is to determine how your Access application fits into the organization's business processes. If the application is for decision support, determine its audience. Most executives want a broad-brush, organization-wide view of the data, which usually entails graphical presentation of the information. Generating graphs is the primary topic of Chapter 18, "Adding Graphs, PivotCharts, and PivotTables," and one of the topics of Chapter 12, "Working with PivotTable and PivotChart Views." Managers commonly request graphs or charts for trend analysis, together with tabular summary information for their area of responsibility. PivotTables, described in Chapter 12, let managers "slice and dice" the data to present multiple views of the data. Supervisors need detailed information to handle day-to-day employee performance and productivity issues. Thus, your decision-support application is likely to require several forms, each tailored to the information needs of users at different levels in the organization's hierarchy.

OLTP front ends require a different design approach than decision-support applications. For heads-down OLTP—typified by telephone order or reservation applications—keyboard-only data entry in a single form is the rule. One of the primary objectives of OLTP form design is minimizing operator fatigue; tired operators tend to enter inaccurate data. OLTP forms need to be simple, fast, and easily readable. Easy reading implies larger-than-standard fonts—at least 10 points—and subdued form colors. Designing forms in which the field sequence is in the order that the data entry operator expects, such as finding or adding customer information before entering an order, is especially important for telephone order entry forms.

DESIGN IN CLIENT MONITOR RESOLUTION

You might have a 19-inch or larger 1,280×960 monitor and a 3D graphics accelerator with 32-bit color depth, but it's not very likely that all the users of your Access application are so fortunate. In the Access 2.0 era, designing for 640×480 resolution was the rule; in those days, most laptop and many desktop PCs had standard 256-color VGA displays. Today, almost all laptop and desktop PCs support at least 1,024×768 (XVGA) resolution and 32-bit color depth. When designing your forms for lower (SVGA) resolution, switch to 800—600 display mode, even if you have a 21-inch monitor. Make sure to test your form designs with the 15-inch monitors that organizations commonly—but mistakenly—assign to data entry operators.

If your application must support mobile users having a variety of laptop and notebook hardware, make sure to check for adequate contrast and text readability on lower-end laptop and notebook PCs with 12-inch displays.

STRIVE FOR CONSISTENCY AND SIMPLICITY

Microsoft's goal for the Office suite is visual and operational consistency among members. Design your Access decision-support forms to emulate the "look and feel" of other Office XP members, especially Microsoft Excel. It's a likely bet that most decision-support users are familiar with Excel.

Simplicity is the watchword when designing OLTP forms. Provide only the elements—forms, subforms, and controls—required for data entry operators to get their work done. Above all, attempt to design a single form that handles all aspects of the OLTP process, if possible. Opening a new form for each step in the data entry process causes visual discontinuities that lead to operator fatigue. Substitute visually simple list boxes for read-only datasheets; show and hide the list boxes with VBA code to minimize screen clutter. Chapter 29, "Programming Combo and List Boxes," shows you how to take full advantage of combo and list boxes in decision-support and OLTP applications.

Figure 14.30 shows the single form of an Access demonstration OLTP application, A12oltp.accdb, in order lookup mode. A12oltp.accdb originated as a Microsoft Tech*Ed presentation for designers of Access 2.0 client/server OLTP front ends for SQL Server 6.0. The application has been upgraded for each succeeding Access and SQL Server version. Typing the first letter or two of a customer name in the Bill To text box and pressing Enter opens a list box of customer matches. This process speeds determination of whether the customer's data is present in the database.

NOTE

A version of A12oltp.accdb that's restricted to use of a linked Access database, A12data.accdb, is included in the \Seua12\Chaptr14 folder of the accompanying CD-ROM. The application expects to find A12data.accdb in your C:\\Seua11\Chaptr14 folder after you install the sample applications from the CD-ROM to the default location. If you installed the book's sample files to another location, acknowledge the two error messages that appear when you open the database. Click the Database Tools tab and click the Linked Table Manager button to change the path to A12data.accdb.

Figure 14.30
This demonstration OLTP application uses a single form for heads-down entry of telephone orders and order status reporting. The time values below the list boxes compare performance between Access and client/server operating modes. Client/server mode for the Microsoft Data Engine isn't enabled in this version.

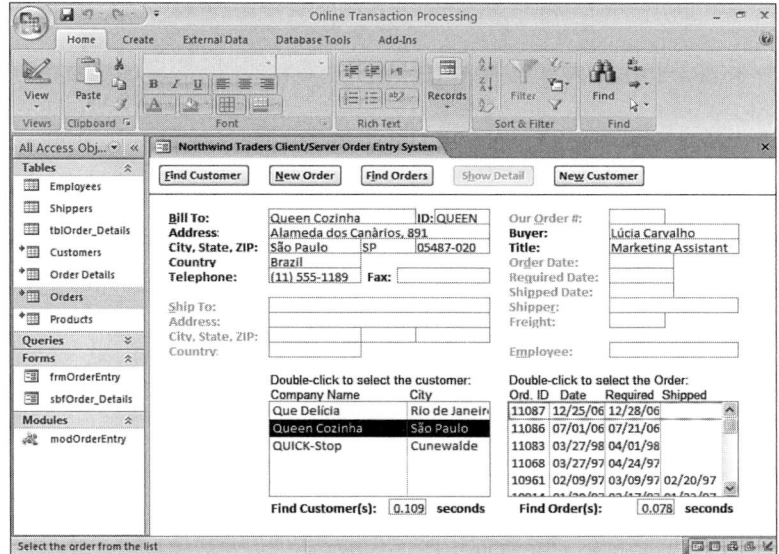

Select the customer in the left list box with the down-arrow key and press Enter to open the right text box. Use the down-arrow key to select an existing order to review from this text box. Pressing Enter again fills the Ship To information text boxes and shows a list box of order line items (see Figure 14.31). Each command button and data field group has a shortcut key to eliminate the need for mouse operations.

Figure 14.31
Selecting a customer and order in the two list boxes shown in Figure 14.30 adds information from the Orders and Order Details tables to the form.

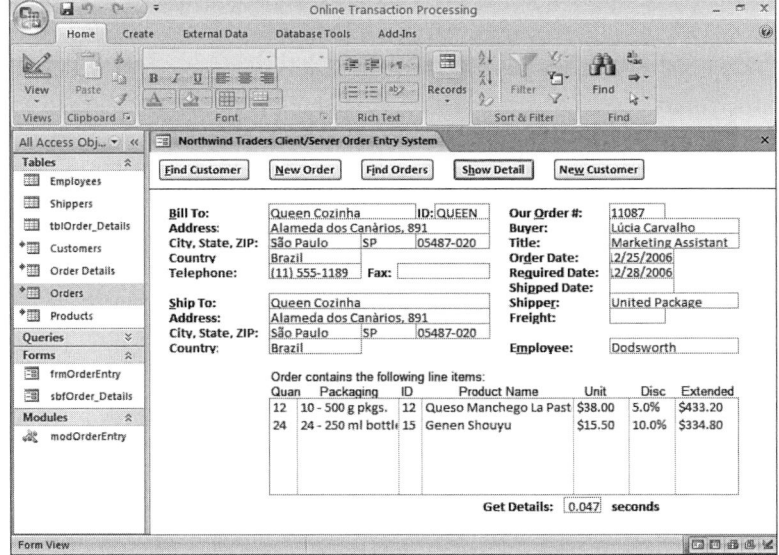

14

To add a new order for a customer, press Alt+N to replace the Order Details list box with a subform for adding line items. Mark the Same as Bill To check box, type a value in the Required Date field, select a Shipper and Employee, and then type a quantity and product ID value in the first two fields of the subform. When you tab past the ID field, a lookup operation completes the Product Name, Packaging, and Unit Price fields, and calculates the Extended (amount) value. If you add a discount, the Extended value updates automatically (see Figure 14.32). Use screen tips to prompt inexperienced operators for appropriate entries, as shown for the Quan[tity] subform field in Figure 14.32. Pressing Alt+A or clicking Add New Order adds the order and its line items to the Orders and Order Details tables, and displays the result in the Order Details list box.

Figure 14.32
It's easy to add line items in the subform, because VBA code automatically completes the entries after you make quantity and product ID entries.

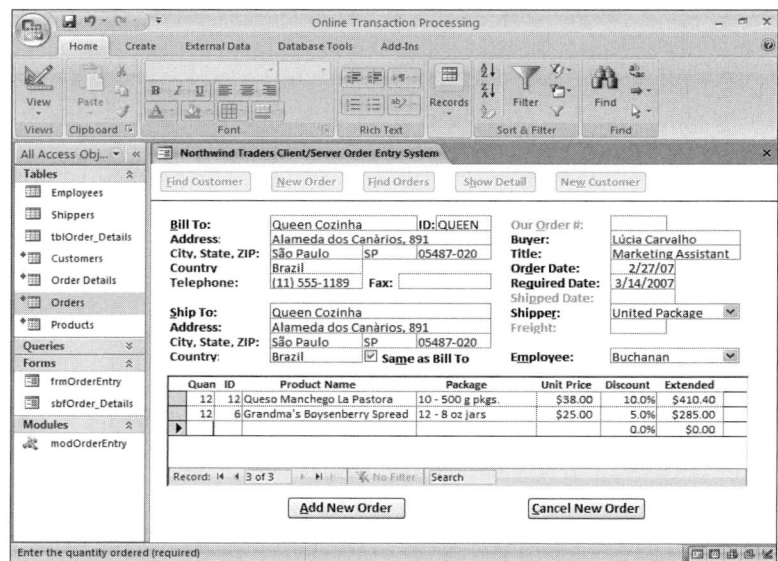

The A12oltp.accdb application is almost a full-fledged order entry system; the only missing element is the ability to edit existing orders that haven't been shipped. Give the application a test drive to sharpen your data entry skills in subforms, and consider layouts similar to A12oltp.accdb when you design forms for production use.

14

CHAPTER 15

DESIGNING CUSTOM MULTITABLE FORMS

In this chapter

EXPANDING YOUR FORM DESIGN REPERTOIRE

This chapter emphasizes use of form Design mode and shows you how to get the most out of those form controls that aren't covered in other chapters. Chapter 18, "Adding Graphs, PivotCharts, and PivotTables" covers the Chart control, as well as PivotChart and PivotTable forms. The "Opening Forms from the Navigation Pane and Adding Records" section of Chapter 2, "Building Simple Tracking Applications," describes how to use the Attachments dialog to add images to Attachment fields.

Working in form Layout view, the primary subject of the preceding chapter, lets you customize the design of forms that you auto-generate with the Create ribbon's Form, Split Form, or Multiple Items button, or with the Form Wizard. Layout view limits the types of controls that you can add to a form to text boxes, combo boxes, attachments, check boxes, and subforms. These controls must be bound to table fields or query columns and have an attached label; deleting a label deletes the associated control also. You can add new controls only by dragging them from the Field List dialog or by clicking the Logo, Title, Page Number, or Date & Time button. The benefit you gain from this abridgement of your form design freedom is the ability to relocate and resize controls with live data visible.

Form Design mode, on the other hand, offers virtually unbridled freedom to add any of Access's 20 native control types or hundreds—perhaps thousands—of Access-compatible ActiveX controls to the form. (The term *native controls* means those that Access 2007 provides in its Form Design Tool – Design contextual ribbon.) Several native controls have associated wizards to guide you in their usage. You aren't restricted to adding controls bound to table fields or query columns; unbound controls can supply values to VBA code or Access macros.

> **NOTE**
>
> The form-design techniques you learn in this chapter also apply to Access data projects (ADP). ADP forms are identical to conventional Access forms, except that the forms and controls bind to objects in SQL Server 2005 databases—not Access databases.

GETTING ACQUAINTED WITH FORM DESIGN VIEW'S CONTEXTUAL RIBBONS

Form Design view replaces Layout view's Form Layout Tools – Format ribbon with the Form Design Tools – Design ribbon, and it replaces Form Layout Tools – Arrange with the almost identical Form Design Tools – Arrange ribbon. The following two sections include tables that describe all the buttons of both ribbons for completeness.

THE FORM DESIGN TOOLS – DESIGN RIBBON

The Design contextual ribbon has control button groups for specifying the view, formatting text, modifying Datasheet gridlines, adding native Access controls, setting control properties, opening Field List and Property Sheet dialogs, opening the VBA code editor, and opening a subform in a new window (see Figure 15.1).

Figure 15.1
The Form Design Tools – Design contextual ribbon includes buttons to add 18 Access native controls to forms.

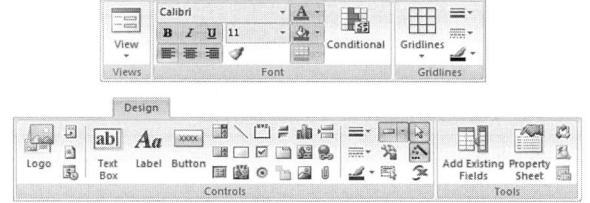

Table 15.1 lists the icon, name, KeyTips, and a brief description of each command button of the Form Design Tools – Design ribbon. The keyboard shortcut to display KeyTips is Alt+G, the same as the Form Layout Tools – Format ribbon.

TABLE 15.1 ICONS, COMMAND BUTTONS, KEYTIP SHORTCUTS, AND COMMAND BUTTON ACTIONS FOR THE FORM DESIGN TOOLS – DESIGN CONTEXTUAL RIBBON

Icon	Command Button	Shortcut Alt+G,	Command Action
Views Group			
	Form View	WF	Displays selected form in Form view
	Layout View	WY	Displays selected form in Layout view
	Design View	WD	Displays selected form in Design view
Font Group			
Calibri	Font	FF	Sets font family from list
11	Font Size	FS	Sets font size from list
B	Bold	1	Sets selected text bold
I	Italic	2	Sets selected text italic
U	Underline	3	Underlines selected text
	Align Left	AL	Aligns selected text left
	Center	AC	Centers selected text

continues

15

TABLE 15.1   CONTINUED

Icon	Command Button	Shortcut Alt+G,	Command Action
☰	Align **R**ight	AR	Aligns selected text right
◁	Format **P**ainter	FP	Applies selected format to other controls
A	Font **C**olor	FC	Opens a color picker to apply color to selected text
◬	Fill/**B**ack Color	FB	Opens a color picker to apply color to control background
▦	**A**lternate Fill/Back Color	FA	Opens a color picker to select a color to shade controls in alternate rows
▦	C**o**nditional Formatting	O	

Gridlines Group

Icon	Command Button	Shortcut Alt+G,	Command Action
▦	Gridlines	B	Opens a gallery of eight gridline patterns for Datasheets
≡	**G**ridline Thickness	G	Opens a gallery of six line thicknesses ranging from Hairline to 6 points
⦂	Gridline Type	J	Opens a gallery of eight gridline styles
◢	Gridline Color	FL	Opens a color picker to set gridline color

Controls Group

Icon	Command Button	Shortcut Alt+G,	Command Action
🖻	**L**ogo	L	Opens an Insert Picture dialog to select a graphic for an Image control in the form's Header section
🖻	**T**itle	T	Inserts a Title label in the form's Header section
🔢	Page **N**umber	N	Opens the Page Number dialog to insert a formatted page number into the form Header or Footer (enabled in Design view only)
🕔	**D**ate and Time	D	Opens a Date and Time dialog to insert a date or time value, or both, in the form's Header section
ab|	Text Bo**x**	CX	Enables drawing a text box with an associated label on the form
A*a*	Lab**e**l	CE	Enables drawing a standalone label on the form
▬	**B**utton	CB	Enables drawing a control button on the form and starts the Command Button Wizard*

Icon	Command Button	Shortcut Alt+G,	Command Action
	Combo Box	CO	Enables drawing a combo box on the form and starts the Combo Box Wizard*
	List Box	CS	Enables drawing a list box on the form and starts the List Box Wizard*
	Subform/Subreport	CF	Enables drawing a subform on the form and starts the Subform Wizard*
	Line	CN	Enables drawing a line on the form
	Rectangle	CR	Enables drawing a rectangular box on the form
	Bound Object Frame	CW	Enables drawing a rectangle to display the contents of an OLE Object field on the form (obsolescent, use an Attachment control)
	Option Group	CG	Enables drawing a container for option buttons, check boxes, command buttons, or toggle buttons on the form and starts the Option Group Wizard*
	Check Box	CK	Enables drawing a check box on the form to represent Boolean (Yes/No) values
	Option Button	CJ	Enables drawing an option button on the form to represent Boolean (Yes/No) values
	Toggle Button	CT	Enables drawing a button that changes from a Yes to No to Yes value when clicked repeatedly
	Tab Control	CC	Enables drawing a tabbed container for other controls on a form
	Insert Page	CC	Not enabled in Form Design view
	Insert Chart	CM	Enables drawing a rectangle to hold a graph or chart and starts the Chart Wizard (see Chapter 18)
	Unbound Object Frame	CU	Enables drawing a rectangle to display a static OLE Object (obsolescent, use an Image control)
	Image	CI	Enables drawing a rectangle to display a static image from a variety of bitmap and vector image files
	Insert or Remove Page Break	CV	Toggles a page break in a form section (for printing)

continues

15

TABLE 15.1   CONTINUED

Icon	Command Button	Shortcut Alt+G,	Command Action
	Insert Hyperlink	I	Opens the Insert Hyperlink dialog to add a button that opens an existing file or web page, a database object, or Outlook to author an email to the recipient
	Attachment	CZ	Opens the Attachments dialog to add, modify, or delete a MIME attachment
	Border Thickness	CH	Opens a gallery of six line thicknesses ranging from Hairline to 6 points
	Border Type	CY	Opens a gallery of eight gridline styles
	Border Color	CL	Opens a color picker to set gridline color
	Special Effect	K	Applies a special effect to the default Flat control
	Set Control Defaults	CD	Removes custom attribute values applied to controls
	Select All	CA, Ctrl+A	Selects all controls on a form
	Select	S	Returns to the Select cursor to deselect a control command button
	Use Control Wizards	P	Specifies using wizards to design command buttons, combo boxes, list boxes, option groups, subforms, and charts
	Insert ActiveX Control	M	Opens the Insert ActiveX Control dialog, which lets you select any ActiveX control registered on the local computer
Tools Group			
	Add Existing Fields	X	Opens the Field List dialog from which to drag additional master and child fields to the form
	Property Sheet	HP	Opens the Property Sheet dialog for the selected form, section, or control
	View Code	V	Opens the VBA Editor
	First 10 Records Preview	E	Not enabled in Form view
	Subform in New Window	R	Opens the selected embedded subform in its own window

* Wizards start only if the Use Control Wizards toggle button is active.

→ To review how to specify conditional formatting, **see** "Applying Conditional Formatting," **p. 588**.

To add a control to the form, click to set the command button for the control you want, place the mouse cursor in the section and at the location where you want the upper-left corner of the control, press the left mouse button, and draw a rectangle to specify the control's size. When you release the mouse button, the control materializes or a wizard starts, depending on the control type and the state of the Use Control Wizards toggle button.

CONTROL CATEGORIES

Three control object categories apply to Access forms and reports:

- *Bound controls* are associated with a field in the data source for the form or subform. *Binding a control* means connecting the control to a data source, such as a field of a table or a column of a query that supplies the current value to or accepts an updated value from a control. Bound controls display and update values of the data cell in the associated field of the currently selected record. Text boxes are the most common bound control. You can display the content of graphic objects or play audio files embedded in a table with a bound OLE object. You can bind toggle buttons and check boxes to Yes/No fields. Option button groups bind to fields with numeric values. All bound controls have associated labels that display the Caption property of the field; you can edit or delete these labels without affecting the bound control.

- *Unbound controls* display data you provide that is independent of the form's or subform's data source. You use the image or unbound OLE object control to add a drawing or bitmapped image to a form. You can use lines and rectangles to divide a form into logical groups or simulate boxes used on the paper form. Unbound text boxes are used to enter data that isn't intended to update a field in the data source but is intended for other purposes, such as establishing a value used in an expression. Some unbound controls, such as unbound text boxes, include labels; others, such as unbound OLE objects, don't have labels. Labels also are unbound controls.

- *Calculated controls* use expressions as their source of data. Usually, the data source expression includes the value of a field, but you also can use values created by unbound text boxes in calculated control expressions.

THE FORM DESIGN TOOLS – ARRANGE RIBBON

The Arrange contextual ribbon has groups for auto-formatting forms, managing control groups, setting text margins and padding for controls, grouping and ungrouping controls, toggling the Snap to Grid layout feature, setting tab order, aligning, sizing and positioning controls, and controlling the visibility of the grid, ruler, and form and page headers and footers (see Figure 15.2).

Table 15.2 lists the icon, name, KeyTips, and a brief description of each command button of the Form Design Tools – Arrange ribbon. The keyboard shortcut to display KeyTips is Alt+L, which is the same as that for the Form Layout Tools – Arrange ribbon.

Figure 15.2
The Form Design Tools – Arrange contextual ribbon has sets of command buttons that are similar to the Form Layout Tools – Arrange ribbon.

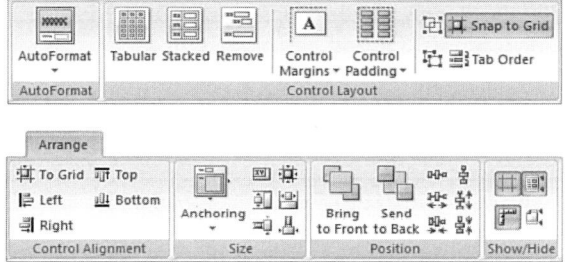

TABLE 15.2 ICONS, COMMAND BUTTONS, KEYTIP SHORTCUTS, AND COMMAND BUTTON ACTIONS FOR THE FORM DESIGN TOOLS – ARRANGE CONTEXTUAL RIBBON

Icon	Command Button	Shortcut Alt+L,	Command Action
AutoFormat Group (see Chapter 14's "Using AutoFormat" section)			
	AutoFormat	SQ	Opens a gallery of 25 prebuilt Access AutoFormats
	AutoFormat Wizard	F	Starts the AutoFormat Wizard, which enables modifying or creating new AutoFormats
Control Layout Group			
	Tabular	SU	Adds the selected controls to a tabular control group
	Stacked	O	Adds the selected controls to a stacked control group
	Remove	N	Removes the selected controls from their control group
	Control Margins	M	Opens a gallery from which you can select the space between control borders and text: None, Narrow, Medium, or Wide
	Control Padding	P	Opens a gallery from which you can select the space between adjacent controls: None, Narrow, Medium, or Wide
	Group	G	Groups one or more selected controls to act as a single unit
	Ungroup	U	Removes selected controls from a group
	Snap to Grid	SR	Toggles the snap-to-grid layout feature on and off
	Tab Order	AT	Opens the Tab Order dialog to enable modifying or resetting controls' tab order

Icon	Command Button	Shortcut Alt+L,	Command Action
Control Alignment Group			
	Align to Grid	F	Aligns the left and top edges to the closest grid dot
	Left	L	Aligns the left edge of two or more controls
	Right	R	Aligns the right edge of two or more controls
	Top	T	Aligns the top edge of two or more controls
	Bottom	B	Aligns the bottom edge of two or more controls
Size Group			
	Anchoring	C	Opens a gallery of nine options for positioning a control when resizing the form's window
	Size to Fit	SF	Sizes the selected control to fit its contents
	Size to Tallest	ST	Sizes the height of all selected controls to the tallest member
	Size to Shortest	SS	Sizes the height of all selected controls to the shortest member
	Size to Grid	SG	Sizes the height and width of the selected controls to the closest grid coordinates
	Size to Widest	SW	Sizes the width of all selected controls to the widest member
	Size to Narrowest	SN	Sizes the width of all selected controls to the narrowest member
Position Group			
	Bring to Front	I	Sets the Z-order of the selected control in front of other controls
	Send to Back	K	Sets the Z-order of the selected control behind other controls
	Make Horizontal Spacing Equal	E	Equalizes the horizontal spacing between selected controls
	Increase Horizontal Spacing	YY	Increases the horizontal spacing between selected controls

continues

15

TABLE 15.2 CONTINUED

Icon	Command Button	Shortcut Alt+L,	Command Action
	Decrease Horizontal Spacing	D	Decreases the horizontal spacing between selected controls
	Make Vertical Spacing Equal	Q	Equalizes the vertical spacing between selected controls
	Increase Vertical Spacing	YZ	Increases the vertical spacing between selected controls
	Decrease Vertical Spacing	X	Decreases the vertical spacing between selected controls
Show/Hide Group			
	Grid	V	Toggles grid dot visibility
	Ruler	W	Toggles ruler visibility
	Form Header/ Footer	J	Toggles Form Header and Footer sections
	Page Header/ Footer	H	Toggles Page Header and Footer sections

→ To learn more about auto-formatting, **see** "Using AutoFormat," **p. 595**.

→ To review how to set the tab order, **see** "The Tab Order Dialog," **p. 590**.

> **NOTE**
>
> You must select at least one control to enable most control buttons except Snap to Grid and Tab Order. You must select two or more controls to enable the Control Alignment group's buttons.

WORKING IN FORM DESIGN VIEW

It's a common practice to start with a blank form in Design mode, but you'll probably find it more efficient to start with one of the Create ribbon's three default forms. Figure 15.3 is an abbreviated version of the HRActions form that you created in Chapter 14, "Creating and Using Basic Access Forms," open in form Design view. Clicking the form context menu's Page Header/Footer choice adds Page Header and Footer sections, which only appear when you print the form.

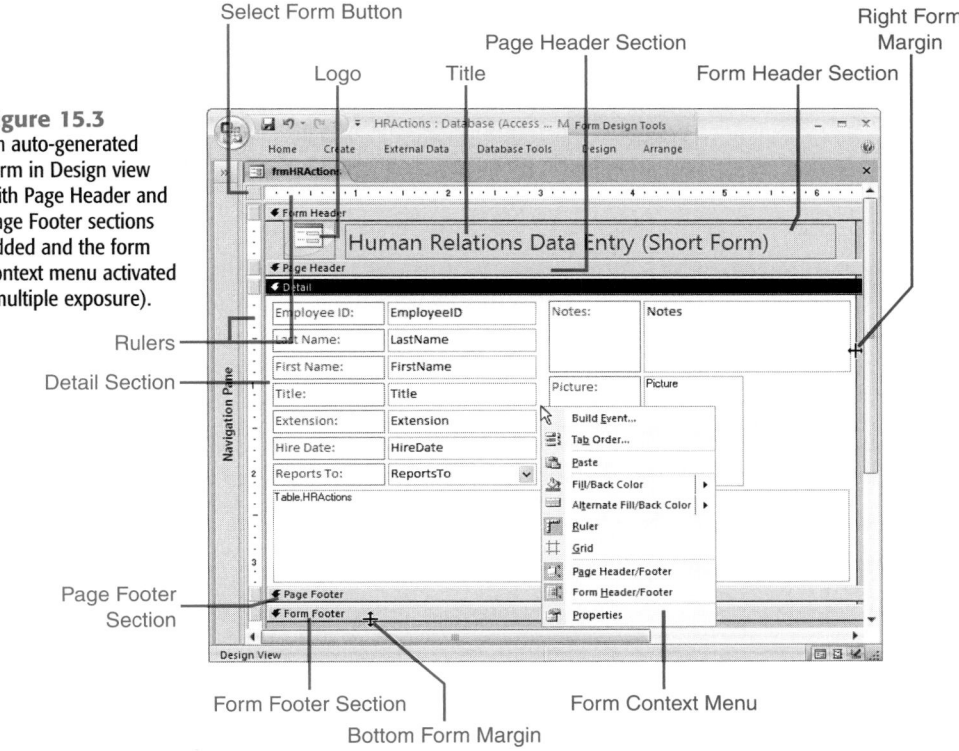

Figure 15.3
An auto-generated form in Design view with Page Header and Page Footer sections added and the form context menu activated (multiple exposure).

SELECTING FORM ELEMENTS AND CONTROLS

The following list describes how to select and display the properties of form sections and control objects:

- **Entire form**—To select the entire form, which includes all the following elements, click the Select Form button. The Property Sheet displays properties that apply to the form as a whole.

- **Header section only**—To select a Header section, click the Form Header or Page Header bar. The Property Sheet has items for the Form Header or Page Header section only.

- **Detail section only**—To select the Detail section, click the Detail bar. The properties are similar to those of the Form Header section, but all apply to the Detail section.

- **Footer section only**—To select a Footer section, click the Form Footer or Page Footer bar. A set of properties identical to the header properties is available for the footer sections. A Form Footer appears only if a Form Header has been added. The same applies to Page Headers and Footers, which appear only when you print the form.

- **Control object (or both elements of a control with an associated label)**—Click the surface of the control to select the control. A thick orange border with a solid square anchor handle at the upper-left corner identifies a selected individual control. If the control has a grouped label, the control/label pair replaces the solid anchor handles with a handle that contains a cross-cursor symbol. Each control type has its own set of properties.

CHANGING THE SIZE OF THE FORM AND ITS SECTIONS

You can change the height of a form section by dragging the Form Header, Page Header, Detail, Page Footer, or Form Footer bar vertically with the mouse. When you position the mouse pointer at the top edge of a section divider bar, it turns into a line with two vertical arrows (refer to Figure 15.1). You drag the pointer with the mouse to adjust the size of the section above the mouse pointer.

The height of the Detail section is determined by the vertical size of the window in which the form is displayed, less the combined heights of all header and footer sections. When you move the vertical scroll bar, only the Detail section scrolls.

SELECTING, MOVING, AND SIZING A SINGLE CONTROL OR LABEL/CONTROL PAIR

When you select a single control object by clicking its surface, the control is enclosed by an orange rectangle with an anchor rectangle at its upper-left corner and seven smaller, rectangular sizing handles (see Figure 15.4). This section's examples use text boxes, but the techniques you learn apply to most other controls except the Line, Insert Page, and Page Break controls. Some controls, such as Button, Toggle Button, Hyperlink, and Tab controls, don't have associated labels.

Figure 15.4
The appearance of selection or sizing handles and the mouse pointer depend on the moving or sizing operation in progress and whether the control is associated or grouped with another control. A missing example in the Grouped Label column indicates that the operation isn't supported.

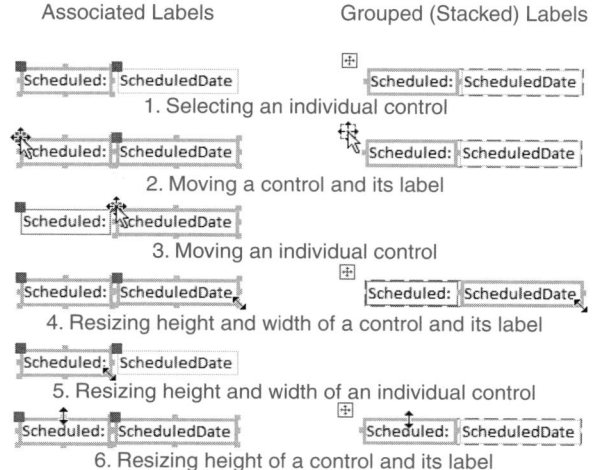

NOTE

Controls you generate by dragging a field from the Field List dialog or add from the Form Design Tools – Design ribbon in form Design view have associated labels. Selecting the control or its associated label activates the single-control selector of the unselected member.

You can group a control and its associated label by right-clicking the control and choosing Layout, Stacked or Layout, Tabular. (Choosing a tabular layout adds a Form Header section and moves the label to the section.) Clicking either the control or label of a grouped label/control pair activates the grouped control and selects the clicked object. Stacked grouping is used in most of this chapter's examples because it's the most flexible grouping method.

Alternatively, you can group controls by selecting them and clicking the Form Design Tools – Arrange ribbon's Group button, as described in the later section "Selecting and Moving Multiple Controls."

Selecting and deselecting controls is a toggling process. *Toggling* means repeating an action with the effect of alternating between On and Off conditions. The Property Sheet, for example, appears and disappears if you repeatedly click the Form Design Tools – Design ribbon's Property Sheet button.

The following choices are available for moving or changing the size of a control object (the numbers correspond to the numbers in Figure 15.2):

1. *To select a control* (and activate or select its associated or grouped label, if any), click anywhere on its surface.

TIP

If you have trouble selecting a small control, such as a thin line (particularly one that is adjacent to a section bar), you can select the control from the drop-down list at the top of the Property Sheet.

2. *To move the control* (and its associated label, if any) to a new position, click to select the control. If the control has an associated label, press Shift and click the label to select it. Press and hold down the left mouse button while dragging either control anchor to the new location for the control(s). If the control has a grouped label, drag the grouped control anchor to the new location. An outline of the control indicates its position as you move the mouse. When the control is where you want it to be, release the mouse button to drop the control in its new position.

TIP

You can use the arrow keys to move the selected control(s) to a new location in default increments of 1/24 inch. When using the arrow keys to move a control with an associated label, you don't need to select the label to move the pair in unison.

3. *To separately move the elements of a control that has an associated label,* position the mouse pointer on the anchor handle in the upper-left corner of the control that you want to move. Click and drag the individual element to its new position and then release the mouse button. (You can't drag individual elements of grouped controls to new locations.)

4. *To simultaneously adjust the height and width of a control* (and its associated or grouped label, if any), click the small sizing handle at any of the three corners of the outline of the selected control(s) or the corners of a grouped control pair. The mouse pointer becomes a diagonal two-headed arrow. Click and drag this arrow to a new position and then release the mouse button.

5. *To simultaneously adjust the height and width of an individual control,* click and drag one of the three corner sizing handles. (You can't resize individual elements of grouped controls.)

6. *To adjust only the height or width of the control,* click the sizing handle on one of the horizontal or vertical surfaces of the outline or the center of the control for a grouped control pair. The mouse pointer becomes a vertical or horizontal two-headed arrow. Click and drag this arrow to a new position and then release the mouse button.

ALIGNING CONTROLS TO THE GRID

The Form Design window includes a grid that consists of one-pixel dots with a default spacing of 24 to the inch horizontally and 24 to the inch vertically. When the grid is visible, you can use the grid dots to assist in maintaining the horizontal and vertical alignment of rows and columns of controls. Even if the grid isn't visible, you can cause controls to "snap to the grid" by clicking the Form Design Tools – Arrange ribbon's Snap to Grid button. This command is a toggle, and when Snap to Grid is active, the button is activated (refer to Figure 15.2). Whenever you move a control while Snap to Grid is activated, the upper-left corner of the object jumps to the closest grid dot.

You can cause the size of control objects to conform to grid spacing by right-clicking the control and choosing Size, To Grid. You also can make the size of the control fit its content by choosing Size, To Fit.

> **TIP**
>
> If Snap to Grid is on and you want to locate or size a control without reference to the grid, press and hold the Ctrl key while you move or resize the control.

Toggling the Form Design Tools – Arrange ribbon's Grid command button controls the visibility of the grid; by default, the grid is hidden for all new forms. If the grid spacing is set to more than 24 per inch or 10 per centimeter, the dots aren't visible. For "non-metrified" users, better values are 16 per inch for Grid X and 12 per inch for Grid Y. This grid dot spacing is optimum for text controls that use the default 8-point MS Sans Serif font. To change the grid spacing for a form, follow these steps:

1. Click the Form Select button or press Ctrl+R to select the entire form.

2. Press F4 to open the Property Sheet.

3. Click the Format tab, and then scroll through the list until the Grid X and Grid Y properties are visible.

4. Change the value of Grid X and Grid Y to 16 dots if you want controls to align with inch ruler ticks. Metrified users are likely to prefer a value of 10 or 20 for Grid X and Grid Y.

SELECTING AND MOVING MULTIPLE CONTROLS

You can select and move several objects at a time by using one of the following methods:

- *Enclose the objects with a selection rectangle.* Begin by clicking the surface of the form outside the outline of a control object. Press and hold down the mouse button while dragging the mouse pointer to create an enclosing rectangle that includes each of the objects you want to select (see Figure 15.5, top left). Release the mouse button to select the objects. You can now move the selected objects (see Figure 15.5, top right) by clicking and dragging the anchor handle of any one of them.

Figure 15.5
Selecting a group of objects by dragging a selection rectangle (top left) or holding the Shift key down and clicking to select the individual controls (top right). You can group the controls so they act in unison (bottom left), or add them to a control stack.

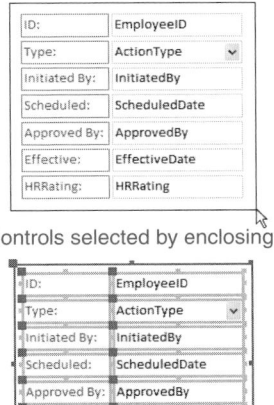

Controls selected by enclosing

Selected controls

Grouped controls

Stacked controls

- *Click to select one object; then hold down the Shift key while you click to select the next object.* You can repeat this step as many times as necessary to select all the objects you want (see Figure 15.5, top right).

- *To remove a selected object from a group*, hold down the Shift key and click the object with the mouse to deselect it. To deselect an entire group, click any inactive area of the form. An inactive area is an area outside the outline of a control.

- *To create a group of the multiselected objects*, click the Form Design Tools – Layout ribbon's Group command button. The selection rectangle permanently encloses the objects. Click the Ungroup button to remove the Group attribute from the enclosed objects.

- *To create a control stack from multiselected objects*, click the Form Design Tools – Layout ribbon's Stack command button. To remove a control from the stack, select it and click the ribbon's Remove button. Alternatively, right-click the group and choose Layout, Stacked or Layout, Remove.

If you select or deselect a control with an associated label, the label is selected or deselected along with the control. You can change some property values—such as the font size or family and the foreground or background color—of all multiple-selected controls.

> **NOTE**
>
> The selection rectangle selects a control if any part of the control is included within the rectangle. This behavior is unlike many drawing applications in which the entire object must be enclosed to be selected. You can change the behavior of Access's selection rectangle to require full enclosure of the object by opening the Access Options dialog, selecting the Object Designers page, and changing the value of the Selection Behavior option from Partially Enclosed to Fully Enclosed.

ALIGNING A GROUP OF CONTROLS

You can align selected individual controls, or groups of controls, to the grid or each other by choosing Format, Align and completing the following actions:

- To fine-adjust the position of a control by the width of a single pixel, select the control and press Ctrl+*arrow key*.
- To align a selected control (or group of controls) to the grid, right-click the group and choose Align, To Grid from the context menu.
- To adjust the positions of controls within a selected columnar group so that their left edges fall into vertical alignment with the leftmost control, choose Align, Left from the context menu.
- To adjust the positions of controls within a selected columnar group so that their right edges fall into vertical alignment with the right edge of the rightmost control, choose Align, Right from the context menu.
- To align rows of controls at their top edges, choose Align, Top from the context menu.
- To align rows of controls at their bottom edges, choose Align, Bottom from the context menu.

Your forms have a more professional appearance if you take the time to align groups of controls vertically and horizontally.

> **TIP**
>
> To quickly select a group of controls in a column or row, click within the horizontal or vertical ruler. This shortcut selects all controls intersected by the vertical or horizontal projection of the arrow that appears when you move the mouse within the ruler.

Almost all control management techniques you learn in this chapter apply to Access reports. Using controls in the design of reports is discussed in Chapter 16, "Working with Simple Reports and Mailing Labels" and Chapter 17, "Preparing Advanced Reports." Using command buttons to execute VBA code is covered in Part VII of this book, "Programming and Converting Access Applications."

ADDING LABEL AND TEXT BOX CONTROLS TO A BLANK FORM

Using one of the Create ribbon's Forms group buttons or the Form Wizard simplifies the generation of standard forms for displaying and updating data in tables. Creating forms from scratch in form Design view by adding controls from the Form Design Tools – Design ribbon provides much greater design flexibility than automated form generation. The examples in this chapter use the HRActions table you created in Chapter 5, "Working with Access Databases and Tables," and used with Layout mode in Chapter 14, as well as a query called qryHRActions, which you create in the next section.

→ For more information on creating the data source for this chapter and establishing the correct relationships, **see** "Creating the HRActions Table in Design View," **p. 229**.

> **TIP**
>
>
>
> If you haven't created the HRActions table, you can import it from the Forms15.accdb database in your \SEUA12\Chaptr15 folder.

CREATING THE QUERY DATA SOURCE FOR THE MAIN FORM

The HRActions table identifies employees uniquely by their sequential ID numbers, located in the EmployeeID field. As before, you need to display the employee's name and title on the form to avoid entering records for the wrong person. The form design example in this chapter uses a one-to-many query to provide a single source of data for the new, custom HRActions form.

To create the HRActions query that serves as the data source for your main form, follow these steps:

1. If Northwind.accdb or your working database is open, close all open objects; otherwise, open the database.

2. Click the Create tab and the Query Design button to open Query1 and the Show Table dialog. Select the HRActions table and click Add. (Don't worry if your query's name contains a different number.)

3. Select the Employees table in the Show Table dialog, and click Add to add the Employees table to your query. Click the Close button to close the Show Table dialog.

4. If you defined relationships for the HRActions table as described in Chapter 5, the line connecting the two tables indicates that a many-to-one relationship exists between the EmployeeID field in the HRActions table and the EmployeeID field of the Employees table.

TIP

> If you didn't define any relationships, the join line doesn't appear. In this case, you need to drag the EmployeeID field from the HRActions Field List to the EmployeeID field of the Employees Field List to create a join between these two fields.

5. Click the * field of the HRActions table, and then drag and drop it in the first column of the Query Design grid. This adds all the fields of the HRActions table to your query.

6. From the Employees table, click and drag the LastName, FirstName, Title, HireDate, Extension, ReportsTo, Notes, and Picture fields to columns 2 through 9 of the Query grid, respectively, as shown in Figure 15.6.

Figure 15.6
The query includes all fields (*) from the HRActions table and eight fields from the Employees table.

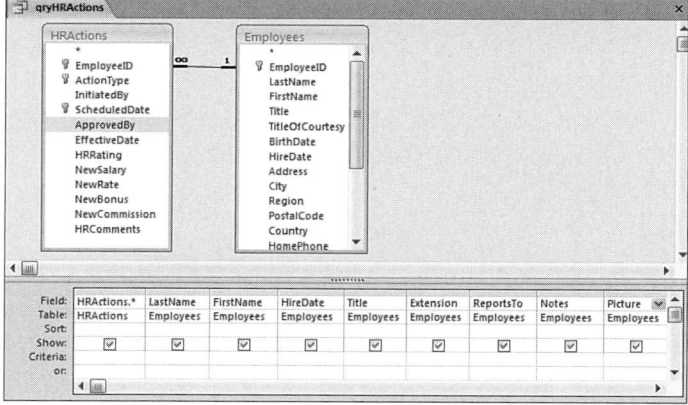

7. To simplify finding an employee, click the Sort row of the LastName column and select an Ascending sort.

8. Click the Run button to check your work, and then close the new query. Click Yes when the message box asks if you want to save the query.

9. In the Save As dialog, name the query **qryHRActions** and click OK.

Now that you've created the query that provides a unified data source for the main form, you're ready to begin creating your custom multitable form.

CREATING A BLANK FORM WITH A HEADER AND FOOTER

Understanding the entire form design process requires starting from a *tabula rasa* (blank slate). To open a blank form, assign qryHRActions as its data source, and add Form Header and Footer sections to emulate a simplified version of the form you auto-generated in Layout view and created with the Form Wizard in Chapter 14, do the following:

1. Click the Create tab and the Blank Form button to open a new, empty form (Form1) with an empty Field List in Layout view. Right-click the form and choose <u>D</u>esign View. Choosing Design View adds the Form Design Tools – Design and Layout contextual ribbon tabs with Design selected.

2. Click the Property Sheet button to open the Property Sheet. Click the Form Select button at the intersection of the two rulers, click the Data tab, and select qryHRActions in the Record Source property's drop-down list (see Figure 15.7). Accept the remaining defaults and click OK.

Figure 15.7
Select qryHRActions as the record source for the new form in the Property Sheet.

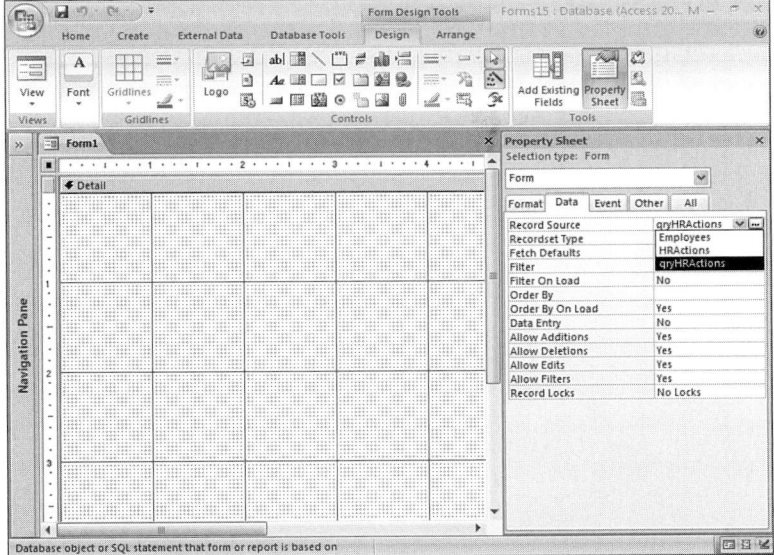

3. Click the Add Existing Fields button to open the Field List dialog, which displays fields of the Employees and HRActions tables. Click the Show Only Fields in the Current Record Source button (link) at the bottom of the dialog to display columns of the qryHRActions query. (The link changes to Show All Tables.).

4. Right-click the form's Detail section and choose Form <u>H</u>eader/Footer to add a header and footer to the form.

The default width of blank forms is about 6.12 inches. The default height of the Form Header and Footer sections is 0.25 inch, and the height of the Detail section is 5.25 inches. To adjust the height of the form's Detail section and the width of the form, do this:

1. Place the mouse pointer on the top line of the Form Footer bar. The mouse pointer becomes a double-headed arrow with a line between the heads. Hold down the left mouse button and drag the bar to create a Detail section height of about 3.5 inches, measured by the left vertical ruler. The active surface of the form, which displays the default 24×24 grid dots, shrinks vertically as you move the Form Footer bar upward.

> **TIP**
>
> If the grid dots aren't visible, click the Form Design Tools – Arrange tab and the Show/Hide group's Grid button.

2. Minimize the Form Footer section by dragging the bottom margin of the form to the bottom of the Form Footer bar.

3. Drag the right margin of the form to 6 inches as measured by the horizontal ruler at the top of the form, as shown in Figure 15.8.

Figure 15.8
Create a starting form that has a Detail section of approximately 6×3.5 inches with Form Header and minimized Form Footer sections.

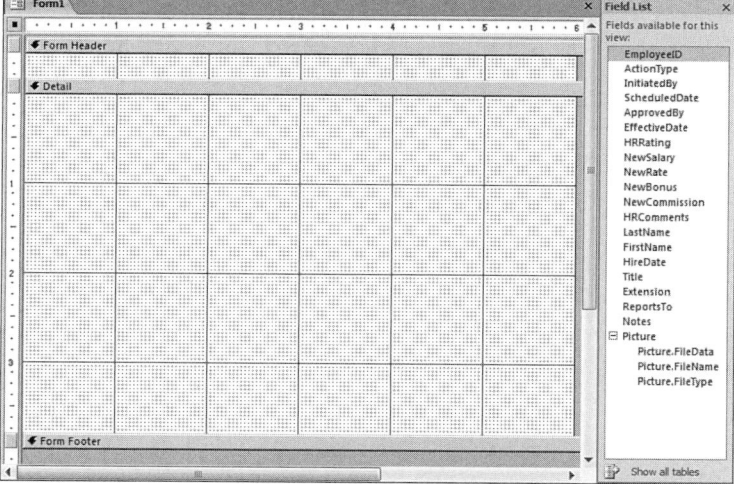

ADDING A LABEL TO THE FORM HEADER

The label is the simplest Access control to use. By default, labels are unbound and static, and they display only the text you enter. Static means that the label retains the value you originally assigned as long as the form is displayed, unless you change the Caption property value with VBA code or an Access macro. To add a label to the Form Header section, complete the following steps:

Aa 1. Click the Form Design Tools – Design ribbon's Label button. When you move the mouse pointer to the form's active area, the pointer becomes the symbol for the Label button, combined with a crosshair. The center point of the crosshair defines the position of the control's upper-left corner.

2. Locate the crosshair at the upper-left of the Form Header section. Press and hold down the left mouse button while you drag the crosshair to the position for the lower-right corner of the label (see Figure 15.9).

Figure 15.9
Drag the symbol for the control (a label in this example) from the upper left to the lower right to define a rectangle that represents the size of the control.

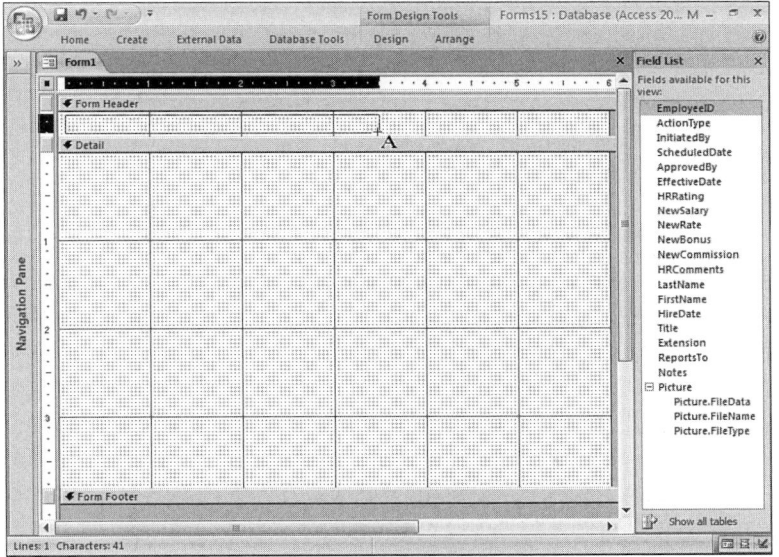

> **NOTE**
>
> As you drag the crosshair, the outline of the container for the label follows your movement. The number of lines and characters that the text box can display in the currently selected font appears in the status bar.

3. If you move the crosshair beyond the bottom of the Form Header section, the Form Header bar moves to accommodate the size of the label after you release the left mouse button. When the label is the size you want, release the mouse button.

4. The mouse pointer becomes the text-editing cursor inside the outline of the label. Type **Human Resources Action Entry** as the text for the label, and click anywhere outside the label to finish its creation. If you don't type at least one text character in a label after creating it, the box disappears the next time you click the mouse.

5. Press Ctrl+S and type the name **frmHRActionEntry** in the Form Name text box of the Save As dialog. Click OK.

→ For tips on manipulating elements of a form, **see** "Selecting, Moving, and Sizing a Single Control or Label/Control Pair," **p. 636**.

You use the basic process described in the preceding steps to add most of the other types of controls to a form. (Some control command buttons, such as the Combo Box, List Box, and Insert Chart buttons, launch a Control Wizard to help you create the control if the Use Control Wizards button is activated.)

After you add the control, you use the anchor and sizing handles described earlier in this chapter to move the control to the desired position and to size the control to accommodate the content. The location of the anchor handle determines the Left (horizontal) and Top (vertical) properties of the control. The sizing handles establish the control's Width and Height property values.

FORMATTING TEXT AND ADJUSTING TEXT CONTROL SIZES

When you select a control that accepts text as the value, the typeface and font size combo boxes appear in the ribbon's Font Group (refer to Figure 15.1). The default is 11-point Calibri, the same font used by Datasheets. To format the text that appears in a label or text box, do the following:

1. Click the Human Resources Action Entry label you created in the preceding section to select it. If the Property Sheet isn't open, click the ribbon's Property Sheet button.

2. Open the Font list in the Fonts group and select the typeface family you want. Calibri is Access 2007's default, and Tahoma was Access 2003's default font.

3. Open the Font Size list and select 18 points.

4. Click the Bold attribute button.

5. The size of the label you created probably isn't large enough to display the larger font. To adjust the size of the label to accommodate the content of the label, right-click the label and choose _S_ize, To _F_it. Access resizes the label's text box to display the entire label; if necessary, Access also increases the size of the Form Header section.

When you change the properties of a control, the new values are reflected in the Property Sheet for the control, as shown in Figure 15.10. If you move or resize the label, you see the label's Left, Top, Width, and Height property values change in the Property Sheet's Format page. You usually use the Property Sheet to change the property values of a control only if a ribbon command button or context-menu choice isn't available.

Figure 15.10
The Property Sheet reflects changes you make to the property values of a control with ribbon controls.

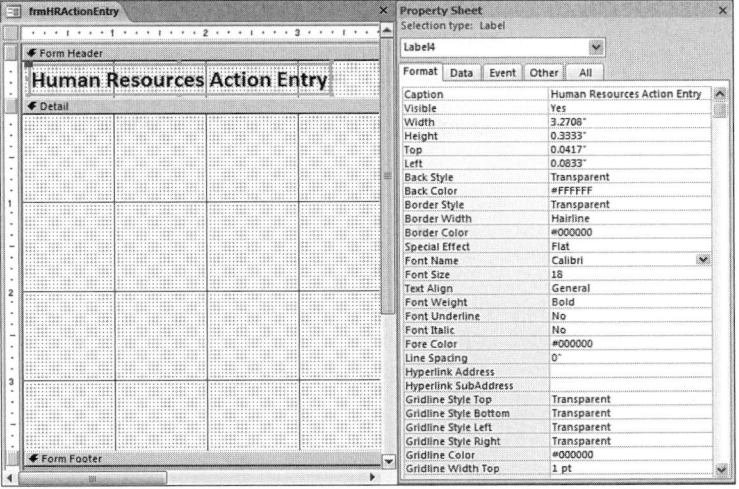

15

NOTE

You can select different fonts and the Bold, Italic, and Underline attributes (or a combination) for any label or caption for a control. Good design practices dictate use of a single font family, such as Calibri, for all controls on a form. If the PC running your Access application doesn't have the font family you specified, Windows selects the closest available match—usually Arial for sans serif fonts. Changes you make to the formatting of data in controls doesn't affect the data's display in Datasheet view.

TIP

Change the default format of a control, such as a label, by doing this: Select the control with the properties you want to set as the default for other instances of the control type, then click the ribbon's Set Control Defaults button.

CREATING BOUND AND CALCULATED TEXT BOXES

Following are the most common attributes of Access text boxes:

- *Single-line text boxes* usually are bound to Text or numeric fields of a table or columns of a query.

- *Multiline text boxes* usually are bound to fields of the Memo type and include a vertical scroll bar to allow access to text that doesn't fit within the box's dimensions.

- *Calculated text boxes* obtain values from expressions that begin with an equal sign (=) and are usually a single line. Most calculated text boxes get their values from expressions that manipulate table field or query column values; but the **=Now** expression to supply the current date and time also is common. Calculated text boxes are unbound and read-only. You can't edit the value displayed by a calculated text box.

■ *Unbound text boxes* can be used to supply values—such as limiting dates—to Access VBA procedures. As a rule, an unbound text box that doesn't contain a calculation expression can be edited. (An unbound text box control can be set to inhibit editing, but doing so negates the control's purpose in most cases.)

The following sections show you how to create the first three types of text boxes.

ADDING BOUND TEXT BOX/LABEL PAIRS

The most common text box used in Access forms is the single-line bound Text Box control, which makes up the majority of the controls for the frmHRActions form of Chapter 14. Access associates a label with the field or column name with bound text boxes. To add a bound text box and an associated label in Design view, do the following:

1. If necessary, click the ribbon's Add Existing Fields button to redisplay the Field List dialog and click the Show Only Fields in the Current Record Source link to display the qryHRActions query's columns.

2. Click and drag the EmployeeID field from the Field List dialog to the upper-left corner of the form's Detail section. When you move the mouse pointer to the active area of the form, the pointer becomes a field symbol, but no crosshair appears. The position of the field symbol indicates the upper-left corner of the text box, not the label, so drop the symbol in the approximate position of the text box anchor handle, as shown in Figure 15.11.

Figure 15.11
Add a bound text box with an associated label by dragging the field name to the position where you want the text box to appear.

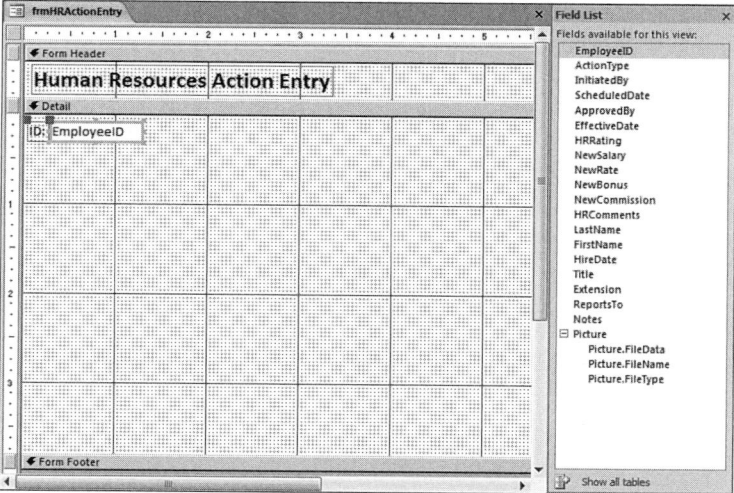

3. Drag the text box by the anchor handle closer to the ID label, and decrease the box's width.

B 4. Small type sizes outside a field text box are more readable when you turn the Bold attribute on. Select the ID: label and click the Bold button.

NOTE

When Access creates a label for a text box that's associated with a form control, the bound object's name is the value for the text label. If the form control is bound to a table or query object, such as a field, that has a Caption property (and the Caption property isn't empty), Access combines the value of the Caption property with a colon suffix (the colon is a default you can inhibit) as the default value for the text label of the bound form control. When you created the HRActions table in Chapter 5, you set the Caption property for each field name. The EmployeeID field has a Caption property set to ID, so the label for the text box bound to the EmployeeID field is also ID plus a colon.

5. Drag the HRComments field from the Field List to the form about 0.75 inch below the ID label, delete the label, and resize the text box to about 1×2.5 inches, as shown later in Figure 15.12. When you add a text box bound to a Memo field, Access automatically sets the Scrollbars property to Vertical, and they appear when the memo is longer than the text box space or when you place the cursor in the text box.

6. Press Ctrl+S to save your work.

When you drag fields from the Field List in this manner, you automatically create a bound control. By default, however, all controls you add from the Ribbon are *unbound* controls. You can bind a control to a field by creating an unbound control with a tool and selecting a field in the Control Source property drop-down list (reach the Control Source list by clicking the Data tab in the Property Sheet for the control).

ADDING A CALCULATED TEXT BOX AND FORMATTING DATE/TIME VALUES

You can display the result of all valid Access expressions in a calculated text box. An expression must begin with = and can use VBA functions to return values. To create a calculated text box that displays the current date and time, do the following:

1. Close the Property Sheet, click the Text Box button on the ribbon, and draw an unbound text box at the right of the Form Header section of the form.

2. Edit the label of the new text box to read **Date/Time:**, and relocate the label so that it is adjacent to the text box. Apply the Bold attribute to the label.

3. Type **=Now** in the text box to display the current date and time from your computer's system clock; Access adds a trailing parentheses pair for you. Adjust the width of the label and the text box to accommodate the approximate length of the text.

4. Change to Form Layout view and inspect the default date format (MM/DD/YYYY HH:MM:SS AM/PM for North America).

5. To delete the seconds value, open the Property Sheet for the text box and click the Format tab. Select the Format property and type **mm/dd/yyyy hh:nn ampm** in the text box.

Your reformatted Date/Time text box appears as shown below the ID label/text box in Figure 15.12. Access lets you alter properties of text boxes and other controls in the form Layout *and* form Design views. When you change the focus to another control, the format string (mm/dd/yyyy hh:nn ampm for this example) properly reformats the text box.

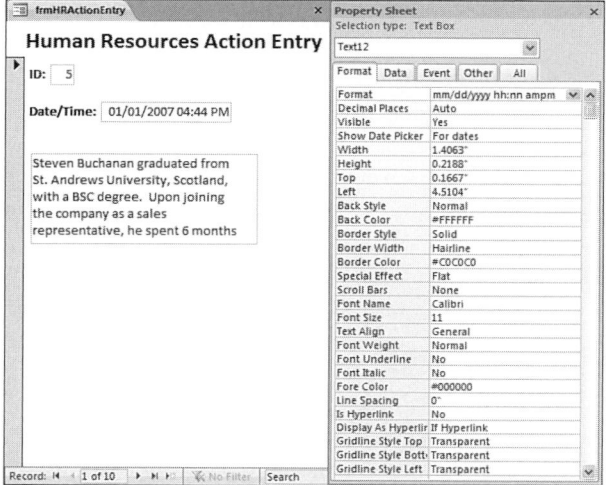

Figure 15.12
A copy of the Form Header section's Date/Time control, which you create in the next section, demonstrates the formatted unbound text box value. (The Property Sheet obscures the original control). Multiline text boxes don't display vertical scroll bars in Layout view.

NOTE

When you return to Design view, the Human Resources Action Entry label you added to the form header might have an error correction flag. An error correction flag is a small green triangle in the top-left corner of the control. The "Accepting or Declining Control Error Correction" section, which follows shortly, describes dealing with error correction on forms.

USING THE CLIPBOARD WITH CONTROLS

You can use the Windows Clipboard to make copies of controls and their properties. As an example, create a copy of the Date/Time control, as shown in Figure 15.12, with the Clipboard by performing the following steps:

1. Return to form Design view and select the unbound Date/Time control and its label by clicking the text box. Both the label and the text box are selected, as indicated by the selection handles on both controls.

2. Copy the selected control to the Clipboard by pressing Ctrl+C.

3. Click the Detail bar to select the Detail section, and paste the copy of the control below the original version by pressing Ctrl+V. (Access pastes the control into the top-left corner of the Detail section, so you'll need to reposition it.)

4. Click the Format property in the Property Sheet for the copied control, and select Long Date from the drop-down list.

 5. To check the appearance of the controls you've created, right-click the form and choose Form View.

 6. Return to Design view and delete the added Date/Time text box and label. To do so, enclose both with a selection boundary created by dragging the mouse pointer across the text boxes from the upper-left to the lower-right corner. Press Delete. (You need the Date/Time text box only in the Form Header section for this form.)

ACCEPTING OR DECLINING CONTROL ERROR CORRECTION

After you add a text box control to the Form Header section, Access 2007's control error-correction feature becomes evident in Form Design view. The Date/Time: label sports a green flag in its upper-left corner. When you select a control with an error flag, the error-checking smart tag icon—a diamond-shaped sign with an exclamation point—appears to the right of the control.

When you pass the mouse pointer over the icon, an error message screen tip describing the problem appears (in this case, "This is a new label and is not associated with a control"). Clicking the icon's arrow opens the following list (see Figure 15.13):

Figure 15.13
When you add an unbound label control that's not associated with a text box, Access 2007 flags the control for error correction and offers these selections to ignore or correct the purported error.

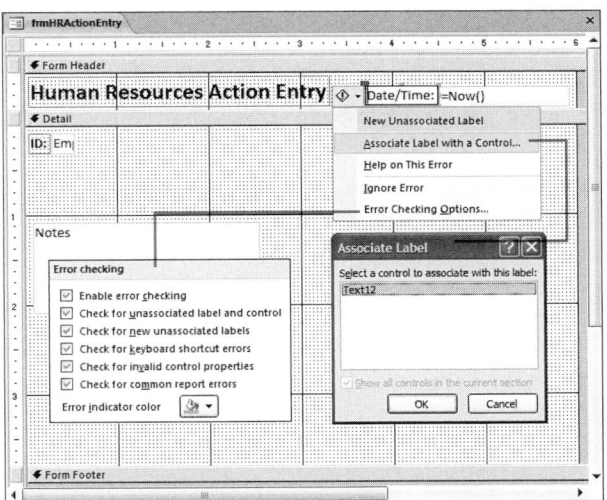

- **New Unassociated Label**—Error description, not a menu choice.
- **Associate Label with Control**— Opens an Associate Label dialog with a list of text box(es) in the section to which the label can be associated.
- **Help on This Item**—Opens a Microsoft Access Help window, which should (but doesn't) display the topic relating to the error.

- **Ignore Error**—Removes the flag from the selected control.
- **Error Checking Options**—Opens the Access Options dialog's Object Designers page, which has an Error Checking group at the bottom to let you specify the errors to be flagged or turn off error checking. Clearing the Check for Unassociated Label and Control check box and clicking OK removes the flag from the selected control. Clicking OK with a check box cleared prevents further error checking for the selection.

Adding new unassociated labels is a common task, so removing this error check is a good form and report design practice. Changes you make in the error checking Options dialog apply to all databases.

CHANGING THE DEFAULT VIEW AND OBTAINING HELP FOR PROPERTIES

A form that fills Access's Design window might not necessarily fill the window in Run mode. Run mode might allow the beginning of a second copy of the form to appear. A second copy appears if the Default View property has a value of Continuous Forms. Forms have the following six Default View property values from which you can choose:

- *Single Form* displays one record at a time in one form.
- *Continuous Forms* displays multiple records, each record having a copy of the form's Detail section. You can use the vertical scroll bar or the record selection buttons to select which record to display. Continuous Forms view is the default value for subforms created by the Form Wizard.
- *Datasheet* displays the form fields arranged in rows and columns.
- *PivotTable* displays an empty PivotTable design form, unless you've previously designed the PivotTable.
- *PivotChart* displays an empty PivotChart design form, unless you've previously designed the PivotChart.
- *Split Form* adds a Datasheet to the top of the form with a column for each field assigned to a control on the form.

> **NOTE**
>
> PivotTable and PivotChart views of the data source for a data entry form seldom are useful. These views require aggregate values, which are uncommon except in decision-support forms. Rather than use a PivotTable or PivotChart view of the data, add these views as controls to a form. Chapter 18 describes how to add PivotTable and PivotChart controls to forms.

To change the form's Default View property, do the following:

  1. Return to form Design view, if necessary.

  2. Right-click the form and choose Properties.

  3. Click the Form Select button to display form-wide properties and then click the Format tab.

4. Click the Default View property and open the list.

5. Select the value you want for this property for the current form. For this exercise, select Single Form (the default) from the list.

6. While Default view is selected, press F1 to open the Help window for the Default View property. This Help window also explains how the Default View and Views Allowed properties relate to each another.

NOTE

> The vertical scroll bar disappears from the form in Form view if a single form fits within its tabbed document or overlapping window.

ADDING GROUP BOXES WITH THE WIZARD

Option buttons, toggle buttons, and check boxes ordinarily return only Yes/No (–1/0 or **True/False**) values when used by themselves on a form. These three controls also can return Null values if you change the TripleState property value to Yes. Individual bound option button controls are limited to providing values to Yes/No fields of a table or query. When you place any of these controls within an option group, however, the buttons or check boxes can return a number you specify for the value of the control's Option Value property.

The capability to assign numbers to the Option Value property lets you use one of the preceding three control types inside an option group frame for assigning values to the HRRating field of the HRActions table. Option buttons are most commonly used in Windows applications to select one value from a limited number of values.

The Option Group Wizard is one of three Control Wizards that take you step-by-step through the creation of complex controls. To create an option group for the HRRating field of the HRActions table with the Option Group Wizard, follow these steps:

1. Click the Use Control Wizards button to turn on the wizards if the toggle button isn't On (the default value).

NOTE

> Access's toggled ribbon command buttons indicate the On (True) state by a border with a colored background under Windows Vista and XP. This differs from toggle buttons on forms, which use a very light gray background and a sunken effect to indicate the On (pressed) state. Background colors differ if you've applied a nondefault Windows Vista or XP desktop theme.

2. Click the Option Group tool, position the pointer where you want the upper-left corner of the option group, and click the mouse button to display the first dialog of the Option Group Wizard.

3. For this example, type five of the nine ratings in the Label Names datasheet (pressing Tab, not Enter to separate them): **Excellent**, **Good**, **Acceptable**, **Fair**, and **Poor** (see Figure 15.14). Click Next.

Figure 15.14
Type the caption for each option button of the option group in the first dialog of the Option Group Wizard.

TIP

You can specify accelerator keys in the captions of your option buttons by placing an ampersand (**&**) before the letter to be used as an accelerator key. Thereafter, pressing Alt in combination with that letter key selects the option when your form is in Run mode. To include an ampersand in your caption, type **&&**.

4. The second dialog lets you set an optional default value for the option group. Select the option named Yes, the Default Choice Is, and open the drop-down list. Select Good, as shown in Figure 15.15, and click Next. If you need to, you can return to any previous step by clicking Back one or more times.

Figure 15.15
Select a default value in the second Option Group Wizard dialog.

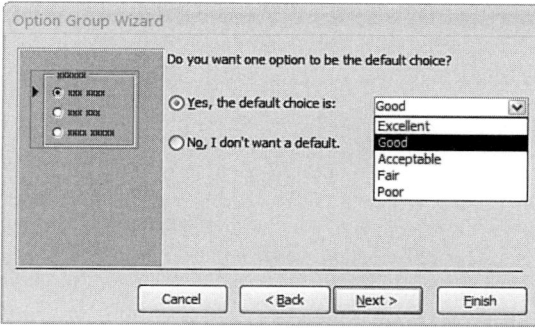

5. The third dialog of the Option Group Wizard lets you assign option values to each option button of the group. The default value is the numbered sequence of the buttons. Type **9**, **7**, **5**, **3**, and **1** in the five text boxes, as illustrated in Figure 15.16, and click Next.

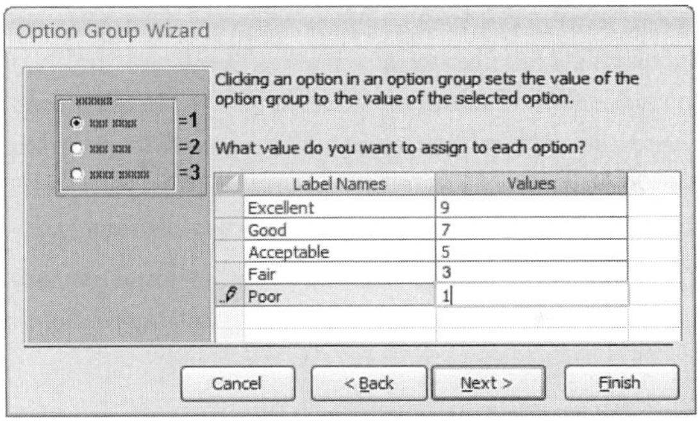

Figure 15.16
Assign a numeric value to each option button in the group. In Form view, clicking an option button assigns its value to the option frame.

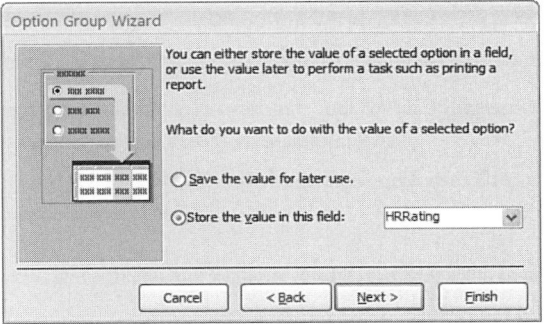

NOTE

> The domain integrity rule for the HRRating field provides for nine different ratings. Nine option buttons, however, occupy too much space on a form, so this example uses only five of the nine ratings. (In the real world, you wouldn't just eliminate options because there are too many; you would substitute a combo box control.)

6. The fourth Wizard dialog lets you bind the option group to a field of a table or a column of a query that you specified as the Record Source property value of the bound form. Select the HRRating column of the qryHRActions query to which your form is bound (see Figure 15.17). Click Next.

Figure 15.17
Bind the option group value to a numeric field (HRRating for this example).

7. The fifth dialog lets you determine the style of the option group, as well as the type of controls (option buttons, check boxes, or toggle buttons) to add to the option group. You can preview the appearance of your option group and button style choices in the Sample pane. For this example, select Option Buttons and Flat (see Figure 15.18). The flat effect matches the default effect applied to all controls by Access 2007.

Figure 15.18
The fifth Wizard dialog lets you choose the option frame's control type and appearance.

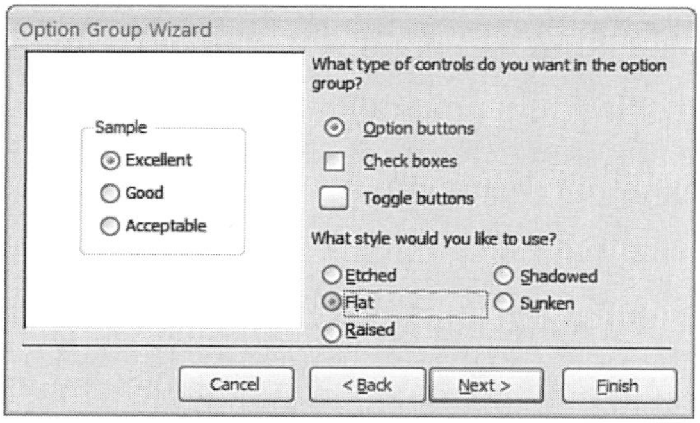

NOTE

Check boxes are an inappropriate choice for controls in an option group. Windows programming standards reserve multiple check boxes for situations in which more than one option choice is permissible.

The sunken and raised styles of option groups, option buttons, and check boxes are applicable only to control objects on forms or option groups with a Back Color property other than white.

8. The last dialog provides a text box for entering the Caption property value of the label for the option group. Type **Rating**, as shown in Figure 15.19, and click Finish to let the Wizard complete its work.

Figure 15.19
Add the caption for the option group in the last wizard dialog.

9. Open the Properties dialog for the option group, and assign the control a name (**grpRating** for this example). Figure 15.20 shows the completed Rating option group and its Property Sheet in Form Design view.

Figure 15.20
The Properties dialog for the grpRating option group (originally called an *option frame*) displays the property values assigned by the wizard.

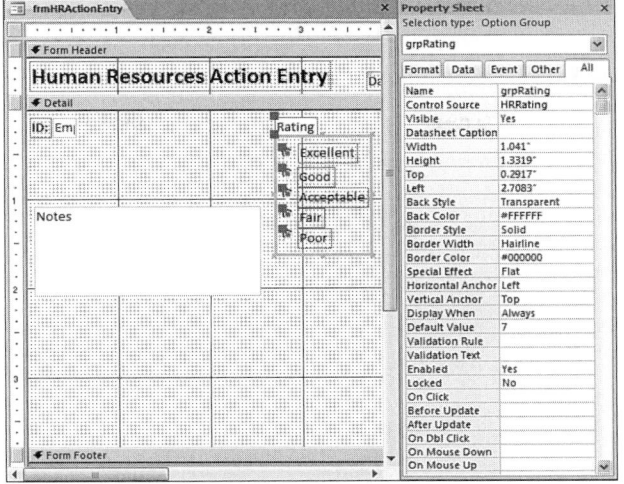

TIP

Name the controls you add to identify their use, rather than accepting the Access default value for the Name property. This book uses object-naming conventions that consist of a three-letter, lowercase abbreviation of the object type—*grp* for option groups, *txt* for text boxes, *frm* for forms, and the like—followed by a descriptive name for the control. Using a consistent object-naming convention makes it much easier to write (and later interpret) VBA code for automating your application.

Access 2000 added the capability to change property values in Form view; Access 2007 no longer supports displaying the Property Sheet in Form view, but compensates by adding Layout view. However, you can change the Name property value of an object only in Form Design view.

→ For more information on Access and VBA naming conventions, **see** "Typographic and Naming Conventions Used for VBA," **p. 1174**.

To test your new bound option group, select the Text Box tool and drag the HRRating field from the field list to the form to add a text box that's bound to the HRRating column. Figure 15.21 shows the option group in Form view with the Bold attribute applied to the option group label and the Rating text box added. Click the option buttons to display the rating value in the text box. Although your entry on the form tentatively updates the value onscreen, the value in the table doesn't change until you move the record pointer or change the view of the form. Press Ctrl+S to save your form.

Figure 15.21
Clicking an option button displays its value in the HRRating text box and makes a tentative change to the HRRating field of the current record of the HRActions table.

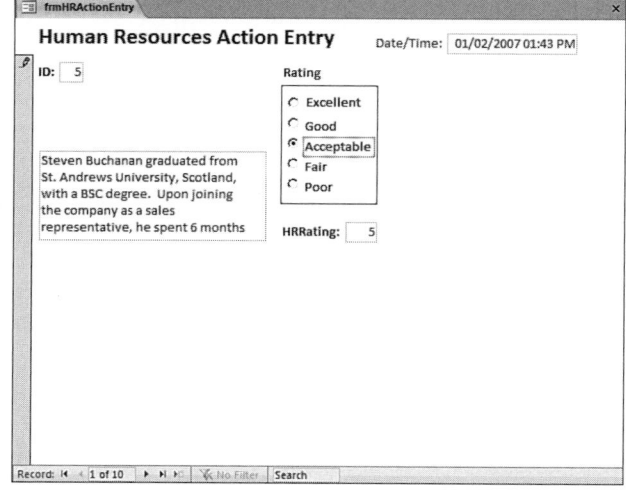

CHANGING ONE CONTROL TYPE TO ANOTHER

Access lets you "morph" a control of one type to become a control of a compatible type. You can change an option button to a check box, for example, or you can change a toggle button to an option button. You can't, however, change a text box to an object frame or other control with a different field data type. To change a control to a different type, follow these steps:

1. In the form's Design view, right-click the control whose type you want to change.

2. Choose Change to see a submenu of form control types. Only the submenu choices for control types that are compatible with the selected control are enabled.

3. Choose the control type you want from the submenu's active choices. Access changes the control type.

USING THE CLIPBOARD TO COPY CONTROLS TO ANOTHER FORM

Access's capability of copying controls and their properties to the Windows Clipboard lets you create controls on one form and copy them to another. You can copy the controls in the header of a previously designed form to a new form and edit the content as necessary. The form that contains the controls to be copied need not be in the same database as the destination form in which the copy is pasted. This feature lets you create a library of standard controls in a dedicated form that is used only for holding standard controls. If your library includes bound controls, you can copy them to the form, and then change the field or column to which they're bound.

The Date/Time calculated text box is a candidate to add to Chapter 14's frmHRActions form. You might want to add a Time/Date text box to the Form Header or Detail section of all your transaction forms. To add the Date/Time control to the frmHRActions form, assuming both forms are in the same database, do the following:

1. With the frmHRActionEntry form open, click the Design View button, and select the Date/Time control and its label by clicking the text box.

2. Press Ctrl+C to copy the selected control(s) to the Clipboard.

3. Open the HR Actions form from the Navigation Pane and change to Design view. Reduce the title's font size to 16 points and move the title label to the left to make room for the date/time text box.

4. Click the Header section selection bar, and press Ctrl+V. A copy of the control appears in the upper-left corner of the form header.

5. Deselect the text box and press Delete to remove the Date/Time label.

6. Hold down the mouse button and drag the text box to a position to the right of the Title label. Optionally change the Back Style and Border Style property values to Transparent to allow the header background color to show through.

7. Click Form view to display the modified HR Actions form (see Figure 15.22).

Figure 15.22
Copying a previously formatted control from one form to another saves design time.

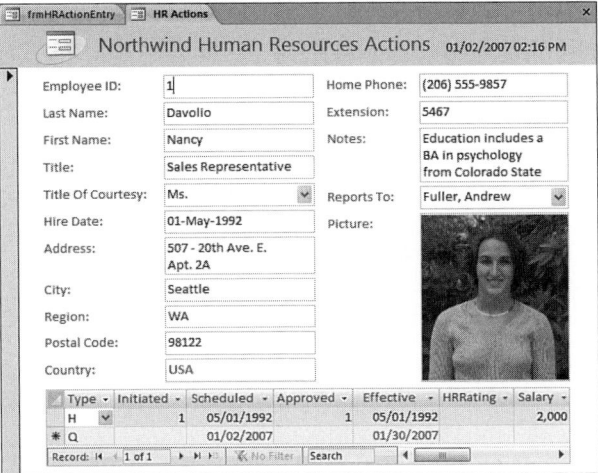

8. Return to Form Design view, press Ctrl+S to save your changes, and close the HR Actions form.

If you receive an error message when the focus moves to controls you've copied to another form, see the "Error Messages on Copied Controls" topic in the "Troubleshooting" section near the end of this chapter.

ADDING COMBO AND LIST BOXES

Combo and list boxes both serve the same basic purpose by letting you pick a value from a list, rather than type the value in a text box. These two kinds of lists are especially useful when you need to enter a code that represents the name of a person, firm, or product. You don't need to refer to a paper list of the codes and names to make the entry. The following list describes the differences between combo and list boxes:

- *Combo boxes* consume less space than list boxes in the form, but you must open these controls to select a value. You can allow the user to enter a value in the text box element of the drop-down combo list or limit the selection to just the members in the drop-down list. If you limit the choice to members of the drop-down list (sometimes called a *pick list*), the user can still use the text box to type the beginning of the list value— Access searches for a matching entry. This feature reduces the time needed to locate a choice in a long list.

- *List boxes* don't need to be opened to display their content; the portion of the list that fits within the size of the list box you assign is visible at all times. Your choices are limited to values included in the list.

In most cases, you bind the combo or list box to a field so that the choice updates the value of this field. Two-column controls often are the most common. The first column contains the code that updates the value of the bound field, and the second column contains the name associated with the code. A multiple-column list is most useful when assigning supervisor and manager employee ID numbers to the InitiatedBy and ApprovedBy fields in the frmHRActionEntry form, for example.

USING THE COMBO BOX WIZARD

Designing combo boxes is a more complex process than creating an option group, so you're likely to use the Combo Box Wizard for every combo box you add to forms. Follow these steps to use the Combo Box Wizard to create the cboInitiatedBy drop-down list, which lets you select from a list of Northwind Traders' employees:

1. Open the frmHRActionEntry form (which you created and saved earlier in this chapter) from the Navigation Pane in Form Design view if it isn't presently open.

2. Click the Use Control Wizards button, if necessary, to turn on the wizards.

3. Click the Combo Box tool in the Form Design Tools – Design ribbon. The mouse pointer turns into a combo box symbol while on the active surface of the form.

4. Click the Add Existing Fields button to display the Field List dialog.

5. Drag the InitiatedBy field to an empty region form's Detail section. The first Combo Box Wizard dialog opens.

6. You want the combo box to look up values in the Employees table, so accept the default option (see Figure 15.23). Your selection specifies Table/Query as the value of the Row Source Type property of the combo box. Click Next.

Figure 15.23
The first Combo Box Wizard dialog lets you select the type of combo box to create. This example uses a lookup-type combo box.

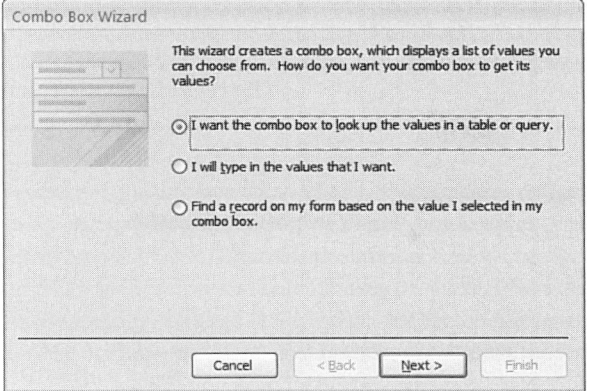

7. In the second wizard dialog, select Employees from the list of tables (see Figure 15.24) and click Next.

Figure 15.24
Select the table or query to provide the list items of the combo box in the Combo Box Wizard's second dialog. Use a base table (Employees for this example) to ensure that the list doesn't contain multiple entries for a single lookup value.

8. For this example, the combo box needs the EmployeeID and LastName fields of the Employees table. EmployeeID is the field that provides the value to the bound column of the query, and your combo box displays the LastName field. EmployeeID is selected in the Available Fields list by default, so click the > button to move EmployeeID to the Selected Fields list. LastName is then selected automatically, so click the > button again to move LastName to the Selected Fields list. Your Combo Box Wizard dialog appears as shown in Figure 15.25. This selection generates the Access SQL SELECT query that serves as the value of the combo box's Row Source property and populates its list. Click Next.

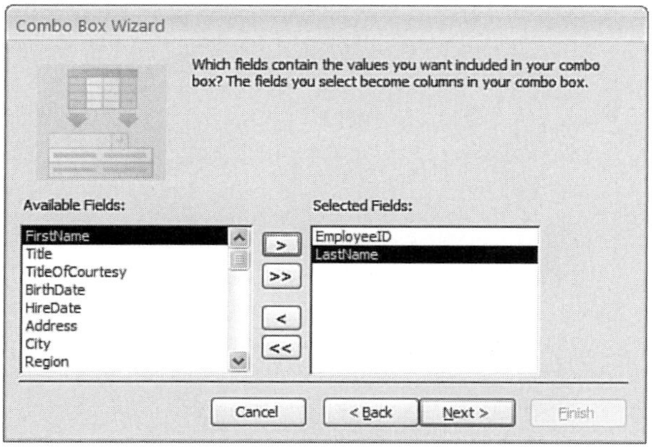

Figure 15.25
In the third Combo Box Wizard dialog, add the bound column and one or more additional columns to display in the combo box list.

TIP

If two or more employees have the same last name, add the FirstName field to the combo list. Unlike conventional combo and list boxes, Access controls can display multiple columns.

9. To sort the list by last name, open the first list and select the LastName field (see Figure 15.26). Selecting a sort on one or more fields adds an ORDER BY clause to the combo box's SELECT query.

Figure 15.26
In the new Combo Box Wizard sorting dialog, select the field(s) on which to apply an ascending or descending sort. Clicking an Ascending button toggles a descending or ascending sort.

10. The fifth dialog displays the list items for the combo box. Access has successfully determined that the EmployeeID field is the key field of the Employees table and has assumed (correctly) that the EmployeeID field binds the combo box.

The Hide Key Column check box is selected by default; this option causes Access to hide the bound column of the combo box. You've selected two columns for the combo box, but only one column (the LastName field) displays in the combo box's list. The EmployeeID column is hidden and used only to supply the data value for the InitiatedBy field.

11. Resize the LastName column by dragging the right edge of the column to the left—you want the column wide enough to display everyone's last name but not any wider than absolutely necessary (see Figure 15.27). Click Next.

Figure 15.27
The Combo Box Wizard queries the combo box's data source (the Employees table) and displays the control's list items. Double-click the right edge of the list to size the list's width to fit the list items.

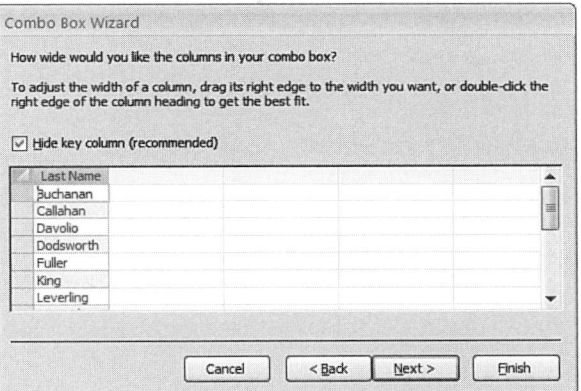

Resizing the list width doesn't accomplish its objective. The Combo Box Wizard adds a combo box of the size you created when dragging the tool on the form, regardless of the width you specify at this point.

12. Your combo box updates the InitiatedBy field with the EmployeeID value corresponding to the name you select. You previously specified that the Control Source property is the InitiatedBy column when you dragged the field symbol to the form in step 5. The Combo Box Wizard uses your previous selection as the default value of the Control Source property (see Figure 15.28), so accept the default by clicking the Next button to display the sixth and final dialog.

13. The last dialog lets you edit the label associated with the combo box (see Figure 15.29). Type **Initiated by:** and click Finish to add the combo box to your form.

Figure 15.28
The fifth Combo Box Wizard dialog specifies the column of the query to be updated by the combo box selection.

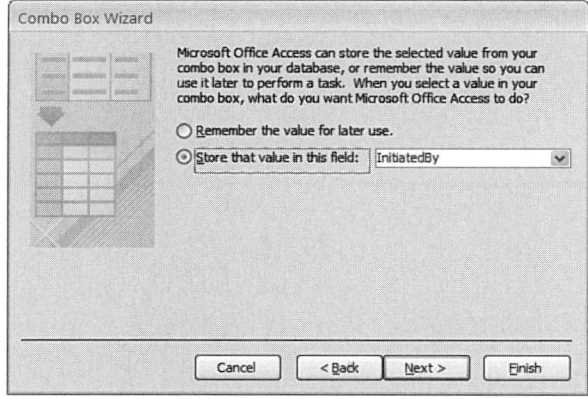

Figure 15.29
Type the label caption for the combo box in the sixth and last Combo Box Wizard dialog.

B

14. Press Ctrl+B to apply the bold attribute to the combo box label, and adjust the width and position of the label. Open the Property Sheet for the combo box, and change its name to **cboInitiatedBy**. Figure 15.30 shows the new combo box in form Design view.

NOTE

> The Row Source property is the SQL SELECT statement that fills the combo box's list. Specifying a Column Width value of 0 hides the first column. The Description property of the EmployeeID field provides the default Status Bar Text property value.

15. Close the Property Sheet and drag the combo box and its label to the top of the right side of the form.

Figure 15.30
The Combo Box Wizard sets the property values for the combo box, but leaves it up to you to specify a meaningful control name.

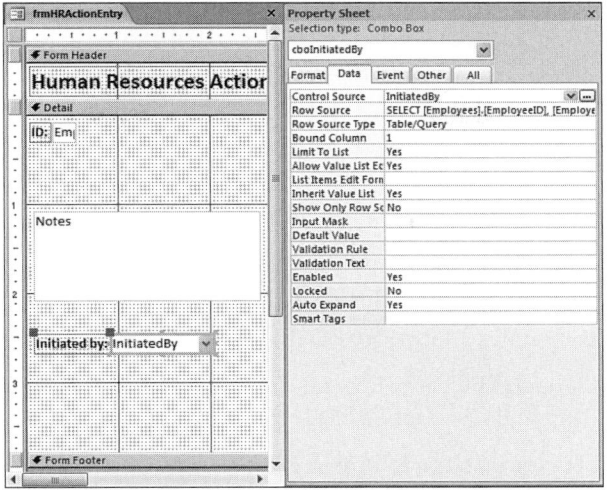

16. Change to Form view to test your combo box. Change the Initiated By value to another person, and then use the navigation buttons to move the record pointer and make the change permanent. Return to the original record, and verify that the combo box is bound to the InitiatedBy field (see Figure 15.31). Optionally, change the Text Align property value to Left.

Figure 15.31
The combo box in Form view displays a list with the default maximum of eight items. The default Text Align property value is General, so the text box is aligned right because the InitiatedBy field is numeric.

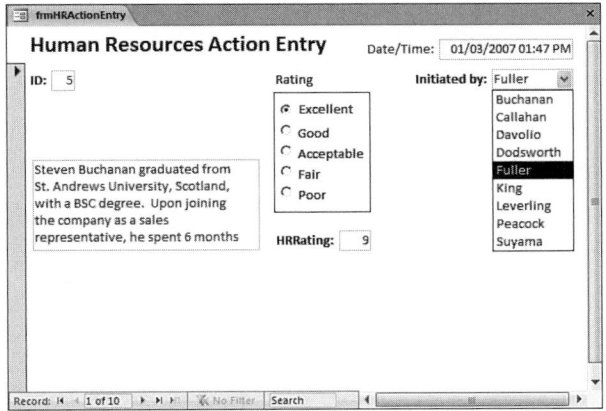

Access SQL

The Access SQL statement generated by the Combo Box Wizard for cboInitiatedBy is

```
SELECT Employees.EmployeeID, Employees.LastName
FROM Employees
ORDER BY [LastName];
```

> **TIP**
>
> If you don't use the Combo Box Wizard to generate the combo box, you can select an existing table or query to serve as the Row Source for the combo box.

USING THE QUERY BUILDER TO POPULATE A COMBO BOX

If the Row Source Type property for a combo box is Table/Query, you can substitute a custom SQL statement for a named table or query as the value of the Row Source property. For either tables or queries, you can choose only the fields or columns you want for the text box, eliminating the need to hide columns. In addition, you can specify a sort order for the list element of your combo box and specify criteria to limit the list.

To invoke Access's Query Builder and create an SQL statement for populating a manually added Approved By combo box, follow these steps:

1. Return to or open frmHRActionEntry in Design view, and click to disable the ribbon's Use Control Wizards button to add the combo box manually. Click the Add Existing Fields button, if necessary, to display the Field List dialog.

2. Click the Combo Box button in the Form Design Tools – Design ribbon, and then drag the ApprovedBy field to add a new combo box in the original position of the Initiated By combo box you added in the preceding section. Select the new control and open the Property Sheet if necessary.

3. Select the Row Source property, and click the Builder button to launch the Query Builder with the Show Table dialog open. The Query Builder window is identical in most respects to the Query Design window, but its title and behavior differ.

4. Add the Employees table to the query, and then close the Show Table dialog. Drag the EmployeeID, LastName, and Title fields to the Query Design grid.

5. You want an ascending sort on the LastName field, so select Ascending in the Sort check box. Only presidents, vice-presidents, managers, and supervisors can approve HR actions, so type **Like *President*** in the first Criteria row of the grid's Title column, **Like *Manager*** in the second, and **Like *Supervisor*** in the third. Access adds the quotation marks surrounding the Like argument for you. Clear the Show check box of the Title column. Your query design appears as shown in Figure 15.32.

> **TIP**
>
> Test the results of your query by clicking the Query Tools – Design ribbon's Run button. Access executes the query and displays a Datasheet view of the query's results. For this example, only Mr. Buchanan and Dr. Fuller meet the criteria.

6. Close the Query Builder. The message box shown in Figure 15.33 appears to confirm your change to the Row Source property value, instead of asking if you want to save your query. Click Yes, and the SQL statement derived from the graphical Query Design grid becomes the value of the Row Source property.

Figure 15.32
This query design limits approval to employees whose titles include President, Manager, or Supervisor.

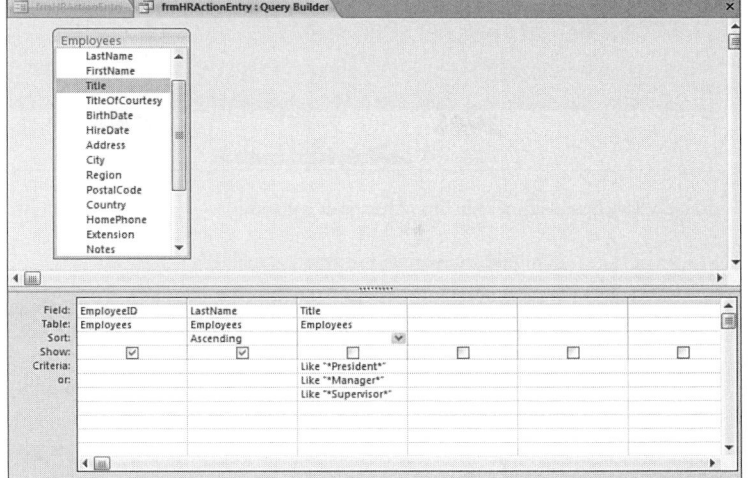

Figure 15.33
This query design supplies the corresponding Access SQL statement as the value of the combo box's Row Source property.

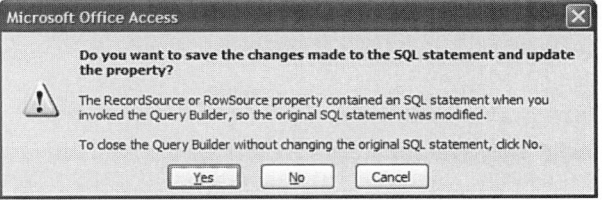

7. In the combo box's Property Sheet, change the name of the combo box to **cboApprovedBy**. Change the Column Count property value to **2** and type **0.2;0.8** in the Column Widths text box. You specify column widths in inches, separated by semicolons, and Access adds the units for inches (") to the widths. (Metrified users specify column widths in cm.) Finally, change the Limit to List value to **Yes**.

TIP

You can display only the LastName field in the combo box, making the combo box similar in appearance to that for the InitiatedBy field, by setting the first Column Width value to **0**.

8. Change the label caption to **Approved by:** and apply the Bold attribute, and move the combo box and its label below the Initiated By control/label pair.

9. Switch to Form view to test the effect of adding the sort (the ORDER BY clause) and criteria (the WHERE clause) to the query (see Figure 15.34). Press Ctrl+S to save your form changes.

Figure 15.34
The combo box list contains items for employees whose titles comply with the Like criteria.

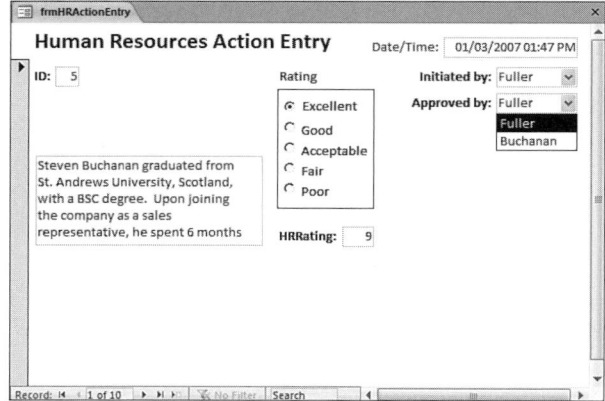

Access SQL

The Access SQL statement generated by the Query Builder is

```
SELECT Employees.EmployeeID, Employees.LastName
FROM Employees
WHERE (((Employees.Title) Like "*President*")) OR
       (Employees.Title) Like "*Manager*") OR
       (Employees.Title) Like "*Supervisor*"))
ORDER BY Employees.LastName;
```

Access SQL uses the DOS and UNIX * and ? wildcards for all characters and a single character, respectively. T-SQL requires the ANSI SQL wildcards % and _, and surrounds character strings with a single-quote rather than double-quotes. The table name prefixes aren't needed, and the parentheses in the WHERE clause are superfluous.

T-SQL

The simplified T-SQL equivalent of the preceding Access SQL statement for an ADP is

```
SELECT EmployeeID, LastName
FROM dbo.Employees
WHERE Title LIKE '%President%' OR
      Title LIKE '%Manager%' OR
      Title LIKE '%Supervisor%'
ORDER BY LastName
```

The dbo. prefix—called the *schema* component of the table name—in the preceding statement is optional, but is a common practice in T-SQL statements.

It's a more common practice for ADP to use SQL Server 2005 views, stored procedures, or table-returning functions to provide the Row Source for forms, combo boxes, and list boxes.

CREATING A COMBO BOX WITH A LIST OF STATIC VALUES

Another application for list boxes and combo boxes is picking values from a static list of options that you create. A drop-down list to choose a Rating value saves space in a form compared with the equivalent control created with option buttons within an option group.

As you design more complex forms, you find that display "real estate" becomes increasingly valuable.

The option group you added to the frmHRActionEntry form provides a choice of only five of the possible 10 ratings. To add a drop-down list with the Combo Box Wizard to allow entry of all possible values, do the following:

1. Change to Form Design view, and click the Use Control Wizards button to enable the Combo Box Wizard.

2. Open the Add Existing Fields dialog, and then click the Combo Box tool in the Form Design Tools – Design ribbon. Drag the HRRating field symbol to the original position of the cboApprovedBy combo box you added previously.

3. In the first wizard dialog, select the I Will Type in the Values That I Want option (refer to Figure 15.23), and then click Next to open the second dialog.

4. The Rating combo box requires two columns: The first column contains the allowable values of HRRating, 0 through 9, and the second column contains the corresponding description of each rating code. Type **2** as the number of columns.

5. Access assigns value-list Row Source property values in column-row sequence; you enter each of the values for the columns in the first row and then do the same for the remaining rows. Type **9 Excellent, 8 Very Good, 7 Good, 6 Average, 5 Acceptable, 4 Marginal, 3 Fair, 2 Sub-par, 1 Poor, 0 Terminated** (use the Tab key to separate the value sets; don't type the commas).

6. Set the widths of the columns you want by dragging the edge of each column header button to the left, as shown in Figure 15.35. If you don't want the rating number to appear, drag the left edge of column 1 fully to the left to reduce its width to 0. When you've adjusted the column widths, click Next to open the third dialog.

Figure 15.35
Type the values for the two columns in the list, and then adjust the column widths to suit the list's contents.

15

7. Select Col1, the HRRating code, as the bound column for your value list—that is, the column containing the value you want to store or use later (see Figure 15.36); this column must contain unique values. Click Next to open the fourth dialog.

Figure 15.36
Select the column that contains the unique value to identify the rows of the list (in most cases, Col1).

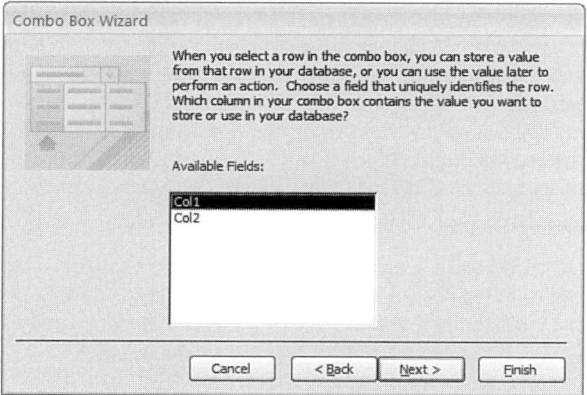

8. Accept the default value (the HRRating column) in the fourth dialog, and click Next to open the final dialog of the Combo Box Wizard.

B 9. Type **Rating:** as the label for the new combo box control, apply the Bold attribute to the label, and then click Finish to complete the combo box specification and return to Form Design view.

10. Open the Property Sheet for the combo box, change the Name to **cboRating**, and then click the Property Sheet's Data tab. Set Limit to List to Yes to convert the drop-down combo to a drop-down list. Quickly review the Row Source property. Notice that the wizard has added semicolons between the row entries, and quotation marks to surround the text values in the Row Source property. You use this format when you enter list values manually.

11. Click the Property Sheet's Format tab, replace the Column Width property value with **0;1,** which forces the rating names to replace the numeric values, type **Auto** as the List Width, and then set Text Align to Left.

12. Change to Form view. The open Rating static-value combo box and its Property Sheet appear as shown in Figure 15.37.

Another opportunity to use a static-value combo box is as a substitute for the Type text box. Several kinds of performance reviews exist: Quarterly, Yearly, Bonus, Salary, Commission, and so on, each represented by an initial letter code.

Figure 15.37
The value-list version of the cboRating combo box closely resembles the cboApprovedBy combo box.

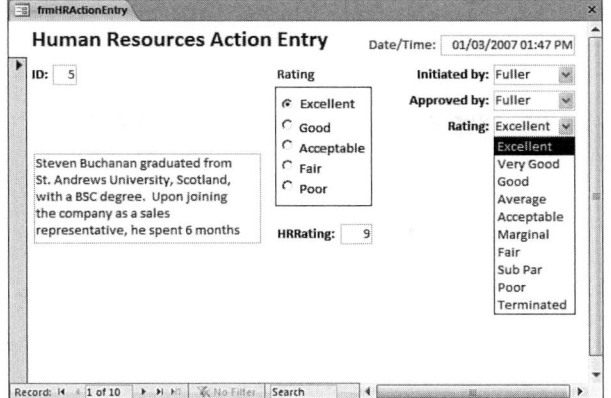

TIP

> You can improve the appearance of columns of labels and associated text, list, and combo boxes by right-aligning the text of the labels and left-aligning the text of the boxes. Select all the labels in a column with the mouse, and click the Align Right button on the Home ribbon. Then select all the boxes and click the Align Left button.

CREATING A COMBO BOX TO FIND SPECIFIC RECORDS

The Combo Box Wizard includes a third type of combo list box that you can create—a combo list that locates a record on the form based on a value you select from the list. You can use this type of combo box, for example, to create a Find box on the frmHRActionEntry form that contains a drop-down list of all last names from the Employees table. Thus, you can quickly find HRActions records for employees.

To create a combo box that finds records on the form based on a value you select from a drop-down list, follow these steps:

1. Change to Design view, and click the Use Control Wizards button in the Form Design Tools – Design ribbon, if necessary, to enable the Combo Box Wizard.

2. Click the Combo Box tool in the Form Design Tools – Design ribbon, and then click and drag on the surface of the form's Detail section to create the new combo box in a position underneath the cboRating combo box you created previously. Release the mouse, and the first Combo Box Wizard dialog appears. When you don't drag a column name to the form, you create an unbound combo box.

3. Select the Find a Record on My Form Based on the Value I Selected in My Combo Box option, and click Next (refer to Figure 15.23).

4. In the second wizard dialog, scroll the Available Fields list until the LastName field is visible. Click to select this field, and then click the > button to move it to the Selected Fields list (see Figure 15.38). Click Next to open the third dialog.

Figure 15.38
Select the name of the field to search in the Available Fields list, and click > to add the entry to the Selected Fields list.

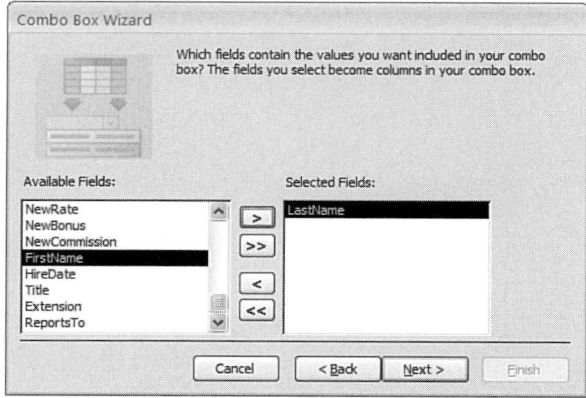

> **TIP**
>
> When creating a combo box to find records, select only one field. The combo box won't work for finding records if you select more than one field for the combo box's lists.
>
> If the record source contains more than one person with the same last name, you need to add a calculated FullName query column to use the find-record combo box version. For this example, the expression to create a FullName query column is `FullName:` `[LastName] & ", " & [FirstName]`.

5. The Combo Box Wizard now displays a list of the field values from the column you just selected. Double-click the right edge of the LastName column to get the best column-width fit for the data values in the column, and then click Next to go to the fourth and final step of the Wizard.

B 6. Type **Find:** as the label for the new combo box, and then click Finish to complete the new combo box control. After applying the bold attribute to the label, aligning its text right, and adjusting its size, your form appears in Design view as shown in Figure 15.39.

Figure 15.39
The record-finding version of the combo box uses an event procedure to move the record pointer to the first record matching the combo box selection.

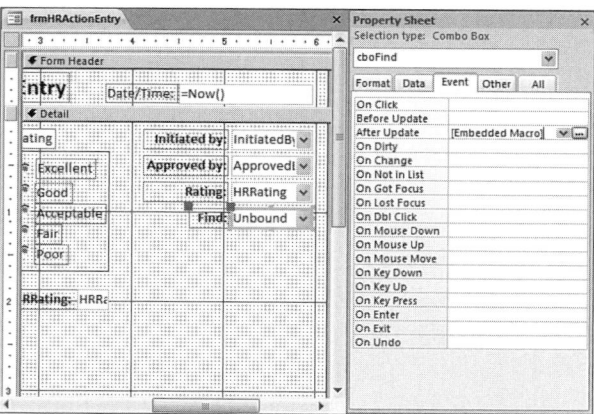

7. Click the Form View button to display the form. The open Find: combo box appears as shown in Figure 15.40.

8. Press Ctrl+S to save your work so far.

Figure 15.40
The combo box finds the records for last name Buchanan. If you have more than one record for an employee, multiple instances of the LastName value appear in the list at this point.

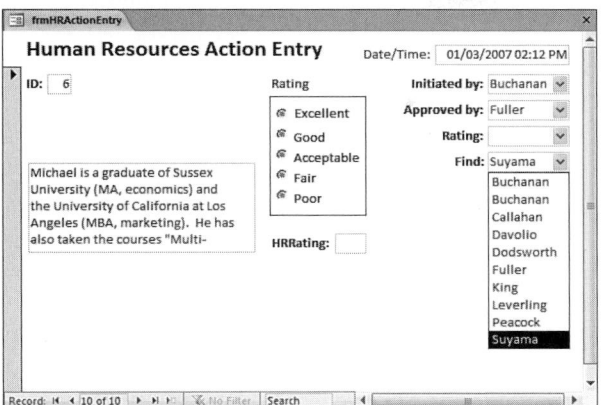

> **TIP**
>
> Always use unbound combo box controls for record selection. If you bind a record-selection combo box to a field, the combo box updates field values with its value.

 When you create this type of combo box, the Combo Box Wizard automatically creates an embedded macro for the After Update property of the combo box (refer to the Property window in Figure 15.39). Access automatically executes the assigned embedded macro whenever a particular event occurs—in this case, updating the combo box. Chapter 26, "Automating Access Applications with Macros 2007," describes embedded and standalone Access macros, and Chapter 28, "Handling Events with VBA and Macros," describes how to write event-handling macros and VBA subprocedures.

 To view the embedded macro sheet that the wizard created for your new combo box, change to Design view, open the Property Sheet for the Find: combo box, click the Events tab in the window, select the After Update property text box, and then click the Builder button. Access opens the macro sheet designer tabbed document for the cboFind:After Update event and its Macro Tools – Design contextual ribbon shown in Figure 15.41. Close the macro sheet designer and return to Design view.

To use a combo box of this type, select a value from the list. As soon as you select the new value, Access updates the combo box's text box, which then invokes the embedded macro for the After Update event. The Search for Record macro action finds the first record in the form's Recordset with a matching value and displays it.

15

Figure 15.41
The Combo Box Wizard generates the cboFind:After Update embedded macro to find the first record containing the selected last name.

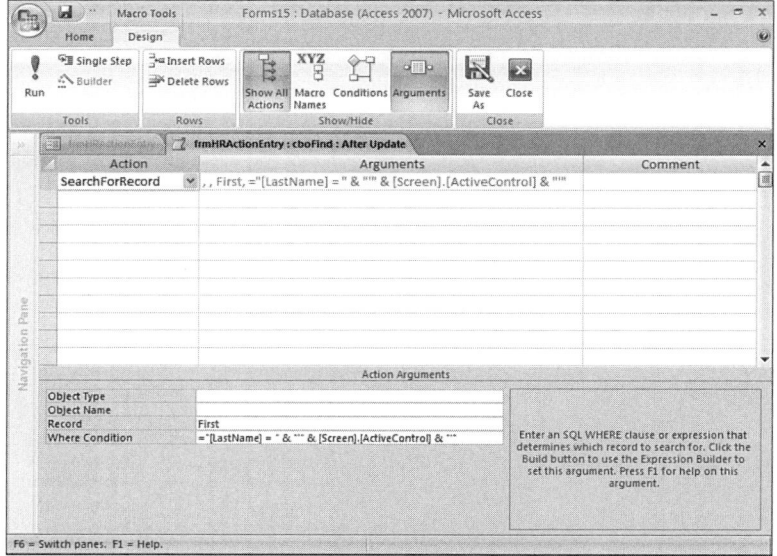

Because the field on the form is based on the LastName column of the form's underlying query, you see an entry in the list for every last name entry in the Recordset produced by the qryHRActions query. If, for instance, more than one HRActions records exist for Steve Buchanan, Buchanan appears in the combo list as many times as there are records for him. If all employees have at least one record, you can change the Record Source's Access SQL Statement to the following:

```
SELECT DISTINCT [qryHRActions].[LastName] FROM [qryHRActions];
```

If an employee doesn't have a record in the qryHRActions query result set, the name doesn't appear in the list. To display a unique list of all employee last names, change the Row Source property to obtain the LastName field values for the combo box list with an SQL statement based on a query from the Employees table.

 To change the Row Source property, follow the procedure you learned in the "Using the Query Builder to Populate a Combo Box" section, earlier in this chapter: Open the Property Sheet of the cboFind combo box, click the Data tab, select the Row Source text box, and then open the Query Builder. Change the query so that it uses the LastName field of the Employees table, add an ascending sort, as shown in Figure 15.42, and change the Limit to List property value to Yes.

Figure 15.42
Changing the Row Source of the combo box to a query against the Employees table eliminates duplicate items in the cboFind combo box.

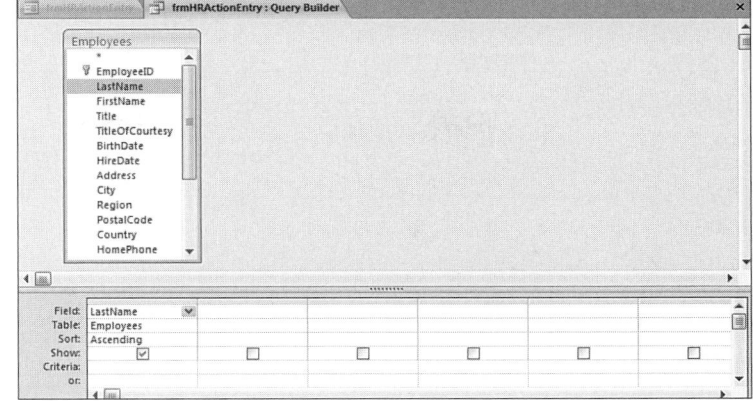

ADDING AN ATTACHMENT CONTROL FOR IMAGES

Previous versions of Access used OLE Object fields to store images, sounds, or other non-textual content and Bound Object Frame controls to display or play back the content. Bound Object Frame controls relied on OLE 2.0 full servers, such as Windows Paintbrush, Paint, or Sound Recorder, as an editing intermediary between the OLE Object fields' content and the form's user. The choice of content data type was limited to those from the set of OLE 2.0 servers installed on users' computers.

 As noted in earlier chapters, Access 2007's new Attachment data type lets users store a wide variety of file-based content in Access tables. A unique feature of the Attachment data type is the ability to store multiple images or the contents of other file types in a single table cell. By default, the control displays the first image (or icons for nongraphics items) from an internal list that's sorted by source filename.

Table 15.3 lists the graphics file extensions and format names that the Attachment control renders natively. The Compressed column indicates if adding the content type to the column compresses the data to save space.

TABLE 15.3   GRAPHICS FORMATS RENDERED BY THE ATTACHMENT CONTROL

Extension	Graphics Format	Compressed
.bmp	Windows Bitmap	Yes
.dib	Device Independent Bitmap	Yes
.emf	Enhanced Metafile	Yes
.exif	Exchangeable File Format	Yes
.gif	Graphics Interchange Format	No
.ico, .icon	Icon	Yes

continues

TABLE 15.3   CONTINUED

Extension	Graphics Format	Compressed
.jpg, .jpeg, .jpe	Joint Photographic Experts Group	No
.rle	Run Length Encoded Bitmap	Yes
.png	Portable Network Graphics	No
.tif, .tiff	Tagged Image File Format	Yes
.wmf	Windows Metafile	Yes

To manage attachments, including opening content added from nongraphics files, do one of the following to open the Attachments dialog:

- Double-click the Attachment control's surface.
- Click the Attachment symbol (a paperclip) on the floating mini-toolbar that appears when you hover the mouse over the control.
- Right-click the Attachment control and choose Manage Attachments.

→ To review an early example of working with the Attachment data type and Attachments control, **see** "Opening Forms from the Navigation Pane and Adding Records," **p. 87**.

The Attachments dialog lets you add files of almost any type except those that have the following extensions:

.ade	.csh	.lnk	.mda	.pif	.vb
.adp	.exe	.mad	.mdb	.prf	.vbe
.app	.fxp	.maf	.mde	.prg	.vbs
.asp	.hlp	.mag	.mdt	.pst	.vsmacros
.bas	.hta	.mam	.mdw	.reg	.vss
.bat	.inf	.maq	.mdz	.scf	.vst
.cer	.ins	.mar	.msc	.scr	.vsw
.chm	.isp	.mas	.msi	.sct	.vsw
.cmd	.its	.mat	.msp	.shb	.ws
.com	.js	.mau	.mst	.shs	.wsc
.cpl	.jse	.mav	.ops	.tmp	.wsf
.crt	.ksh	.maw	.pcd	.url	.wsh

NOTE

The Attachment control embargoes file extensions for earlier Access versions (.ade, .adp, .mda, .mdb, .mde, .mdt, .mdw, .mdz) but not their Access 2007 equivalents (.accdb, .accde, and so on).

The Attachment control embargoes the preceding extensions because files of these types might contain executable content and thus have the potential to be malicious.

The qryHRActions query includes the Picture Attachment field. To experiment with the Attachment data type and control's Attachments dialog, do the following:

1. With the frmHRActionEntry form open in Layout view, delete the Rating option frame, the Rating text box, and the two Rating labels.

2. Click the Form Layout Tools – Design ribbon's Add Existing Fields button to open the Field List, click the Show Only Fields in the Current Record Source link, and drag the Picture field to the form at the right of the Notes text box.

3. Adjust the height of the control to that of the Notes text box and the width of the control to match that of the image. Pass the mouse over the image to activate the mini-toolbar (see Figure 15.43).

Figure 15.43
A mini-toolbar lets you scan multiple images or other content in the selected Attachment cell. Clicking the paperclip icon opens the Attachments dialog.

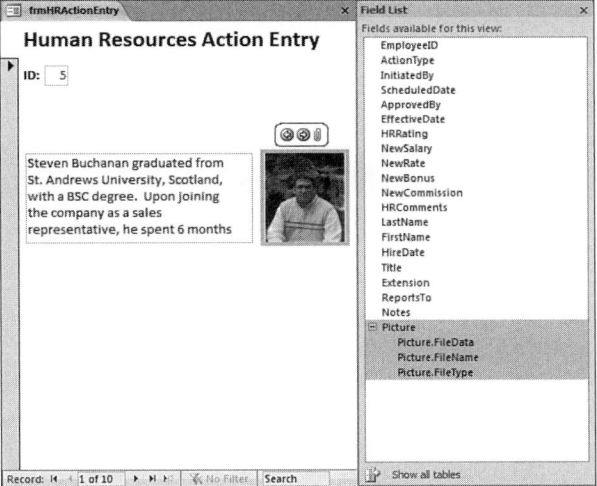

4. You can't add or remove content in Layout view, so change to Form view and double-click the control to open the Attachments dialog and display the content imported from one of the EMPID1.JPG through EMPID9.JPG files in the \SEUA12\Nwind folder.

5. Click the Add button to open the Choose File dialog, navigate to a source of temporary files to add to the selected Attachment table cell, select a file, and then click Open to close the Choose File dialog and add the file to the Attachments dialog's list (see Figure 15.44).

6. Verify that you can open the added content in its default application by double-clicking the list item or selecting the item and clicking Open. You can save an individual item with the Save button or save all items to a specified folder by clicking the Save All button.

15

Figure 15.44
The Attachments dialog displays the contents of a table cell with three Windows Media Audio (.wma) files, a JPEG image of Steven Buchanan, and an Access 2007 database.

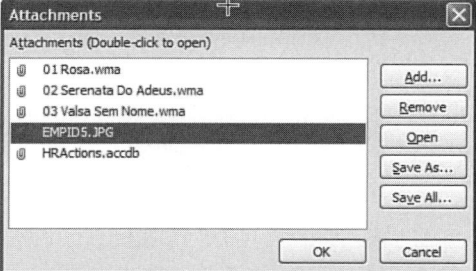

7. Select each item you added in steps 5 and 6 and click Remove to set it for deletion from the list. Click OK to remove the items and close the dialog.

TIP

> Use the Image control—not an Unbound Object Frame control—to display static images, such as logos and background bitmaps. The Image control accepts an even wider range of graphics formats than the Attachment control.

WORKING WITH TAB CONTROLS

The tab control lets you easily create multipage forms in a single tabbed dialog, similar to Access 2007's tabbed documents. The tab control is a very efficient alternative to creating multipage forms with the Page Break control. You can use the tab control to conserve space onscreen and show information from one or more tables. The sections that follow show you how to add images to a new OLE object field of the Employees table, add a tab control to a form, and display images in a bound image control on a tab control page. You also learn to set the important properties of the tab control as a whole, as well as the properties of individual pages of the tab control.

ADDING THE TAB CONTROL TO A FORM

To add a tab control to the frmHRActionEntry form, follow these steps:

1. Click the Design View button if the frmHRActionEntry form isn't already in Design view. No wizard for the tab control exists, so the status of the Use Control Wizards button doesn't matter.

2. Click the Tab Control button on the Form Design Tools – Design ribbon; the mouse cursor changes to the Tab Control icon while it's over the active surface of the form.

3. Click and drag on the surface of the form's Detail section to create the new tab control near the bottom center of the form (see Figure 15.45).

Figure 15.45
Access's default tab control has two pages.

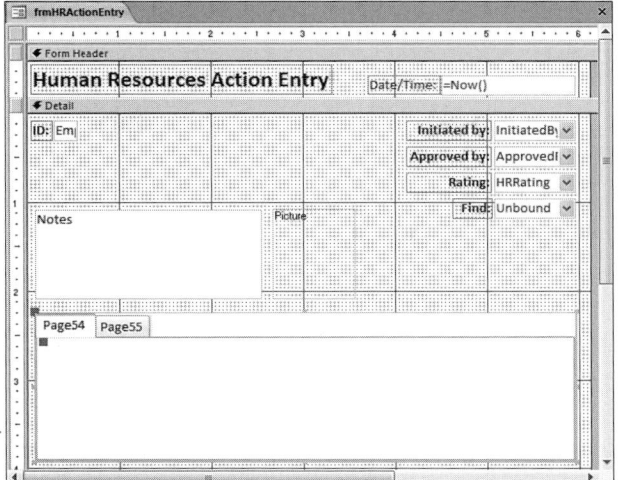

By default, Access creates a tab control with two pages. Each page's tab displays the name of the page combined with a sequential number corresponding to the number of controls you placed on your form in this work session. The next few sections describe how to change the page tab's caption, add or delete pages in the tab control, add controls to the pages, and set the page and tab control properties.

ADDING TAB CONTROL PAGES

Depending on the data you want to display and how you want to organize that data, you might want to include more than two pages in your tab control. To add a page to a tab control, follow these steps:

1. In Design view, right-click the tab control to open the context menu.
2. Choose Insert Page; Access inserts a new page in the tab control to the right of the last page.

CHANGING THE PAGE ORDER

Because Access adds a new page only after the last page, it isn't possible to add a new page at the beginning or middle of the existing tab pages. As a result, if you want the new tab control page to appear in another location in the tab control, you must change the order of pages in the tab control. You might also want to change the order of tab control pages as you work with and test your forms—in general, you should place the most frequently used (or most important) page at the front of the tab control.

To change the order of pages in a tab control, follow these steps:

1. Right-click one of the tabs and choose Page Order to open the Page Order dialog shown in Figure 15.46.

Figure 15.46
Change the left-to-right sequence of the tabs with the Page Order dialog.

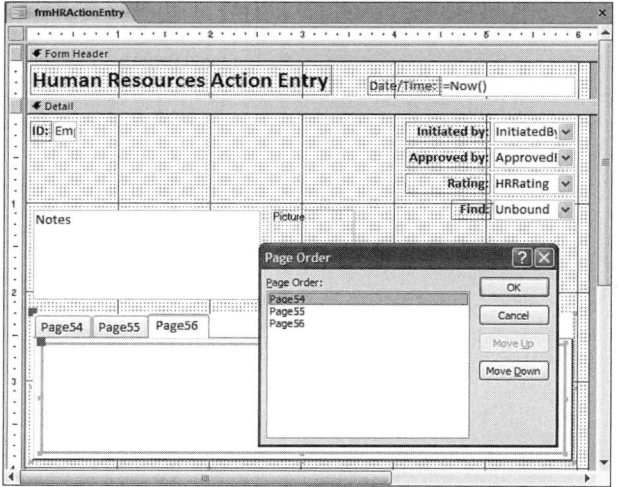

2. In the Page Order list, select the page whose position you want to change.
3. Click the Move Up or Move Down buttons, as appropriate, until the page is in the position you want.
4. Repeat steps 3 and 4 until you have arranged the tab control pages in the order you want, and then click OK to close the Page Order dialog and apply the new page order to the tab control.

DELETING A TAB CONTROL PAGE

At some point, you might decide that you don't want or need a page in a tab control. The frmHRActionEntry form needs only two pages in its tab control. If you added a page to the tab control by following the steps at the beginning of this section, you can delete a page from the tab control by following this procedure:

1. Right-click the page tab of the page you want to delete; Access brings that page to the front of the tab control.
2. Choose <u>D</u>elete Page; Access deletes the currently selected tab control page.

SETTING THE TAB CONTROL'S PROPERTIES

Two sets of properties govern the appearance and behavior of a tab control. A set of properties exists for the entire tab control, and a separate set of properties applies to each page in the tab control. The following list summarizes the important properties of the tab control and its pages; the remaining property settings for the tab control and its pages are similar to those you've seen for other controls (height, width, color, and so on):

- *Caption* is a text property. It controls the text that appears on the page's tab and applies to individual tab control pages only. If this property is empty (the default), then the page's Name property is displayed on the page's tab.

- *MultiRow* is a Yes/No property. It applies to the tab control as a whole and determines whether the tab control can display more than one row of tabs. The default setting is No; in this case, if there are more tabs than fit in the width of the tab control, Access displays a scroll button in the tab control. If you change this property to Yes and there are more page tabs than will fit in the width of the tab control, Access displays multiple rows of tabs.

- *Picture* displays an icon in any or all the page tabs. You can use any of Access's built-in icons or insert any bitmapped (.bmp) graphics file as the page's tab icon.

- *Style* applies to the tab control as a whole and controls the style in which the tab control's page tabs are displayed. The default setting, Tabs, produces the standard page tabs you're accustomed to seeing in the Property Sheet and in various dialogs in Access and Windows. Two other settings are available: Buttons and None. The Buttons setting causes the page tabs to be displayed as command buttons in a row across the top of the tab control. The None setting causes the tab control to omit the page tabs altogether. Use the None setting if you want to control which page of the tab control has the focus with command buttons or option buttons located outside the tab control. However, using command buttons external to the tab control to change pages requires writing a macro or Access VBA code. You should use the default Tabs setting unless you have a specific reason for doing otherwise—using the Tabs setting ensures that the appearance of your tab controls is consistent with other portions of the Access user interface. Using this setting also saves you the effort of writing VBA program code.

- *Tab Fixed Height* and *Tab Fixed Width* apply to the tab control as a whole and govern the height and width of the page tabs in the control, respectively. The default setting for these properties is 0. When these properties are set to 0, the tab control sizes the page tabs to accommodate the size of the Caption for the page. If you want all the page tabs to have the same height or width, enter a value (in inches or centimeters, depending on your specific version of Access) in the corresponding property text box.

To display the Property Sheet for the entire tab control, right-click the edge of the tab control, and choose <u>P</u>roperties from the resulting context menu. Alternatively, click the edge of the tab control to select it (clicking the blank area to the right of the page tabs is easiest), and then press F4 to display the Property Sheet.

To display the Property Sheet for an individual page in the tab control, click the page's tab to select it, and then press F4 to display the page's Property Sheet.

The tab control in the frmHRActionEntry form uses one page to display current information about an employee: the employee's job title, supervisor, company telephone extension, hire date, and photo. The second tab control page displays a history of that employee's HRActions in a subform you add later in the chapter.

Follow these steps to set the Caption property for the frmHRActionEntry form's tab control:

1. Open the frmHRActionEntry form, and change to Form Design view, if necessary.
2. Click the first page of the tab control to select it, and then click the Properties button on the toolbar to display that page's Property Sheet.
3. Click the Format tab, if necessary, to display the Format properties for the tab control page.
4. Type **Employee Info** in the Caption property's text box.
5. Click the Other tab and change the Name property value to **pagEmployeeInfo**.
6. Click the second page of the tab control to select it; the contents of the Property dialog change to show the properties of the second tab control page. Click the Format tab.
7. Type **History** in the Caption property text box for the second page of the tab control, type **pagHistory** in the Name property of the Other page, and close the Property Sheet.
8. Click outside the tabbed region to select the entire tab control, and type **tabHRAction** as the name of the control.

Figure 15.47 shows the tab control with both page captions set and the first page of the tab control selected. Notice that the sizing handles visible in the tab control are inside the control—this position indicates that the page, not the entire control, is currently selected. When the entire tab control is selected, the sizing handles appear on the edges of the tab control.

Placing Other Controls on Tab Pages

You can place any of Access's 17 other types of controls on the pages of a tab control—labels, text boxes, list boxes, even subforms. To add a control of any type to a tab control's page, follow this procedure:

1. In Design view, click the page tab you want to add the control to; Access selects the page and brings it to the front of the tab control.
2. Add the desired control to the tab control's page using the techniques presented earlier in this chapter for creating controls on the main form.

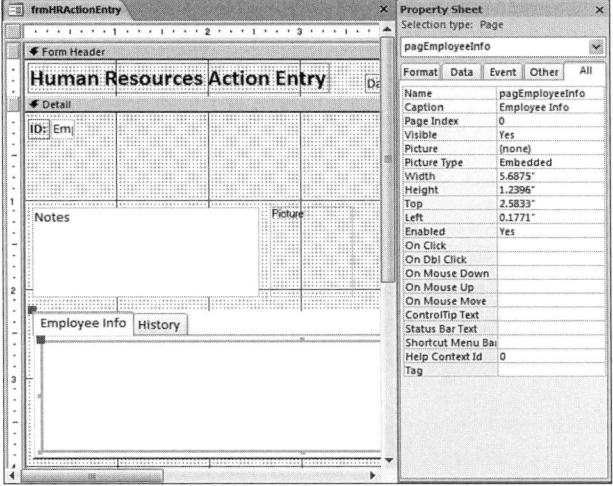

Figure 15.47
Set the Page properties by clicking the tab of one of the pages. Click the empty area to the right of the tabs to set the properties of the entire tab control.

Alternatively, you can copy controls from the same or another form and paste them into the tab control's pages by using the same techniques you learned for copying and pasting controls on a form's Detail and Header/Footer sections. You can't drag controls from the form's Detail or Header/Footer sections onto the tab control's page, and vice versa.

As you proceed with the examples in this chapter and complete the frmHRActionEntry form, you place various bound and unbound controls on the pages of the tab control.

OPTIMIZING THE FORM'S DESIGN

The preceding sections of this chapter have shown you how to use Form Design Tools – Design ribbon controls without regard to positioning the controls to optimize data entry operations. In this section, you add more controls from the qryHRActions query's field list to the main form's Detail section and the Company Info page of the tab control. You place new controls for adding or editing fields of the HRActions table on the main form, and relocate the controls you added earlier into a logical data entry sequence. The Employee Info page of the tab control displays reference data from the Employees table. Multipage tab controls are especially effective for displaying data that's related to the entries you make on the main form.

To add and rearrange the form's controls to optimize data entry, follow these steps (look ahead to Figure 15.48 for control placement and formatting):

  1. Return to Design view, if necessary, and delete the Picture Attachment control and Notes text box. You add these controls to the tab control in later steps.

  2. Click the Add Existing Fields button to open the Field List dialog if it isn't already open.

3. Drag the LastName field from the Field List to a position to the right of the ID field text box; delete the field's label.

4. Drag the FirstName field from the Field List to a position to the right of the LastName field; delete the FirstName field's label.

5. Drag the ActionType field from the Field List to a position at the right of the FirstName field to add a combo box.

6. Repeat step 4 for the ScheduledDate, EffectiveDate, NewSalary, and NewBonus fields (see Figure 15.48 for field positioning and sizing). You must move the InitiatedBy, ApprovedBy, HRRating, and Name text boxes that you placed on the form earlier in this chapter.

7. Resize the HRComments field so that it's underneath the EmployeeID and name fields (see Figure 15.48). Next, resize the tab control so that it fills the width of the form and extends from an area below the HRComments field to the bottom of the form. The tab control needs to be as large as possible to display as much data as possible in the subform that you add later to its second page.

8. Click the first tab of the tab control to bring it to the front, and then drag the Title field from the Field List to a position near the top-left corner of the Company Info page.

9. Repeat step 8 for the ReportsTo, Extension, and HireDate fields (see Figure 15.48 for field placement).

10. Drag the Picture field onto the right side of the tab control's first page, and delete its label (the fact that this field displays a photo of the employee is enough to identify the field). Size and position the Photo field at the right edge of the tab control's page; you might need to resize the tab control and the form after inserting the Photo field.

11. Drag the Notes field to the bottom-left corner of the tab control's first page and delete its label.

12. Use the techniques you learned in Chapter 14 to move, rearrange, and change the label formats to match the appearance of Figure 15.48. (All labels are bold, sized to fit, and right-aligned.)

TIP

Use the Format Painter to format the text labels of the fields.

→ For more information on creating a uniform appearance with the Format Painter, **see** "Using the Format Painter," **p. 607**.

13. Change the Format property value of the ScheduledDate and EffectiveDate text boxes to **mm/dd/yyyy** to ensure Y2K compliance, and change the Format property value of the Salary and Bonus text boxes to Currency to add a dollar sign and change the Decimal Places property value to 0.

Figure 15.48
Here's the final design of the form with new controls and formatting.

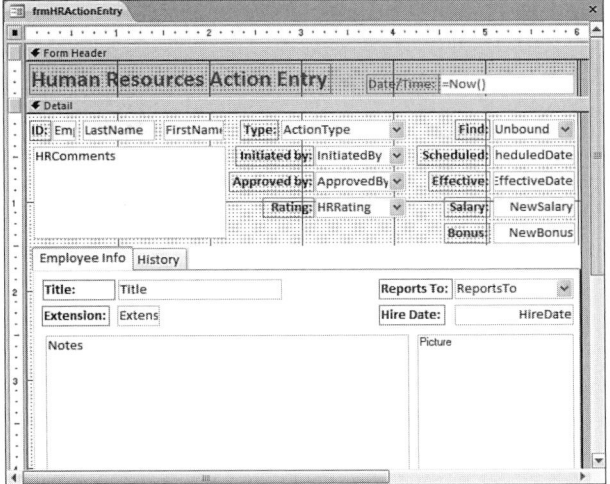

14. To replace the letter code or number with text in the Type, ApprovedBy, and Rating combo boxes, change the Column Widths property value of the Type control to **0";1.2"** and ApprovedBy and Rating to **0";0.65"**.

15. Click the Select Form button, and set the Caption property value of the form to **Human Resources Action Entry**.

16. Press Ctrl+S to save your changes, and test your new and modified controls by changing to Form view (see Figure 15.49).

Figure 15.49
The form is now complete, except for the addition of a subform to the History page of the tab control.

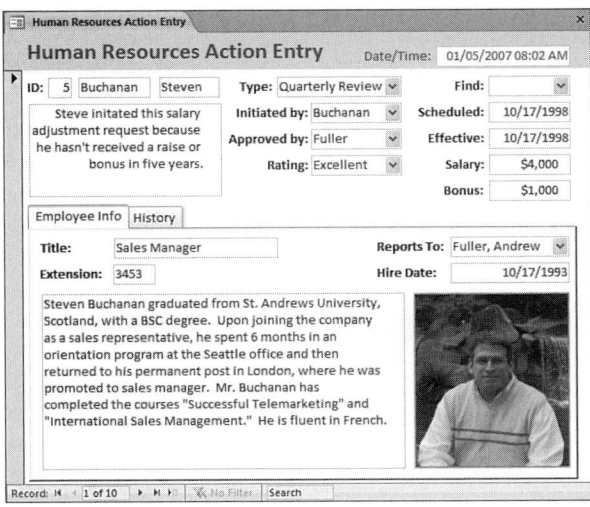

ADDING A HISTORY SUBFORM TO A TAB CONTROL PAGE

The frmHRActionEntry form needs a subform to display the history of HRActions for the employee displayed in the main part of the form. The HRActions table provides the data source for the subform. Access's Subform/Subreport control offers the Subform Wizard, which lets you quickly add an existing form as a new subform, as described in the following sections.

CREATING A MODIFIED HRACTIONS SUBFORM

If you didn't create the sbfHRActions subform in the preceding chapter, import the sbfHRActions subform from your \Program Files\Seua11\Chaptr14\Forms14.accdb database.

Follow this drill to adapt the sbfHRActions subform for use on the History page of the tab control:

1. Select sbfHRActions in the Navigation Pane, and press Ctrl+C and Ctrl+V to create a copy of the subform named **sbfHRActionsTab** and open it in Design view.

2. Delete the HRComments column's header and text box.

3. Right-click the ActionType combo box, and choose Change To, Text Box.

4. Shift-click to select the ActionType, InitiatedBy, ApprovedBy, and HRRating text boxes, and click the Home ribbon's Center button to center the text and labels.

5. Select all labels and drag them to the middle of the Form header section. Click the Bold button to apply the bold attribute to all labels. Drag the Detail section bar up to the bottom of the labels.

6. Select all text boxes and drag them to the bottom of the Detail bar. Drag the Form Footer bar up to the bottom of the text boxes.

7. Reduce the width of the subform to about 5.38 inches, and save your changes (see Figure 15.50).

Figure 15.50
Form Design view shows the changes you make to the layout for the sbfHRActionsTab subform for addition to the History tab page.

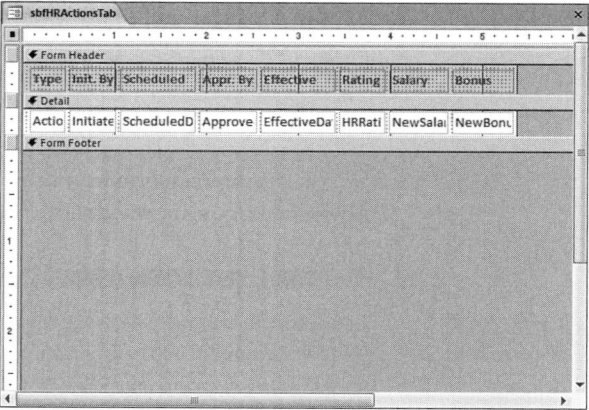

8. Change to form Design view to check your work (see Figure 15.51) and close the sub-form.

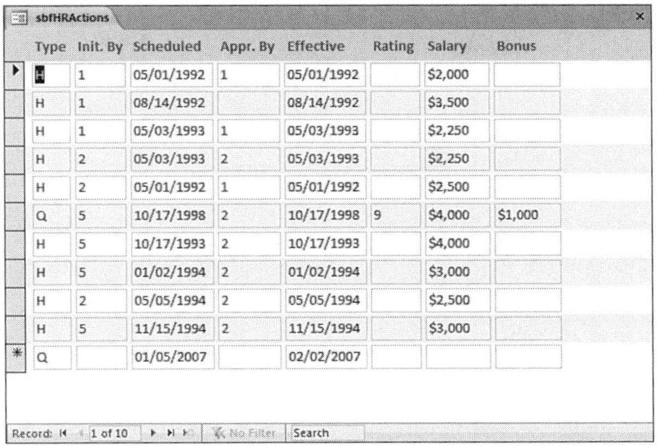

Figure 15.51
The final version of the read-only sub-form to be added to the History tab page.

Type	Init. By	Scheduled	Appr. By	Effective	Rating	Salary	Bonus
H	1	05/01/1992	1	05/01/1992		$2,000	
H	1	08/14/1992		08/14/1992		$3,500	
H	1	05/03/1993	1	05/03/1993		$2,250	
H	2	05/03/1993	2	05/03/1993		$2,250	
H	2	05/01/1992	1	05/01/1992		$2,500	
Q	5	10/17/1998	2	10/17/1998	9	$4,000	$1,000
H	5	10/17/1993	2	10/17/1993		$4,000	
H	5	01/02/1994	2	01/02/1994		$3,000	
H	2	05/05/1994	2	05/05/1994		$2,500	
H	5	11/15/1994	2	11/15/1994		$3,000	
Q		01/05/2007		02/02/2007			

Record: 1 of 10 — No Filter — Search

ADDING THE sbfHRActionsTab SUBFORM WITH THE WIZARD

To add the sbfActionsTab subform to the History page of the tab control with the Subform Wizard, do the following:

1. With the Wizard activated, open frmHRActionEntry in Design view, click the History tab of the tab control, and select the Subform/Subreport tool in the Form Design Tools – Design ribbon.

2. Drag the mouse pointer icon, which assumes the shape of the Subform/Subreport tool, to the History page. The icon changes to a pointer when you reach the active region of the History page, which changes from white to black.

3. Release the mouse to open the Subform Wizard's first dialog.

4. Select the Use an Existing Form option and select sbfHRActionEntryTab in the list (see Figure 15.52). Click Next.

5. In the second Wizard dialog, accept the Choose from a List option and then select Show HRActions for Each Record in qryHRActions Using Employee[ID] (see Figure 15.53). Click Next.

6. Accept sbfHRActionEntryTab as the name of the subform, and click Finish to dismiss the Wizard.

7. Delete the label and adjust the size of the subform to occupy most of the available area of the History page (see Figure 15.54).

Figure 15.52
The Subform Wizard's first dialog lets you select the existing form to use as a subform.

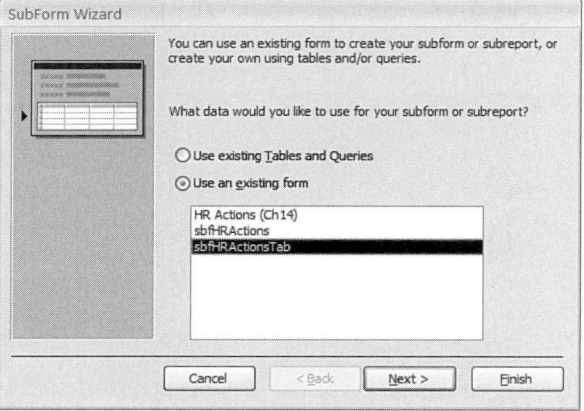

Figure 15.53
The second dialog is where you specify the value of the LinkChildFields and LinkMasterFields properties (EmployeeID for this example).

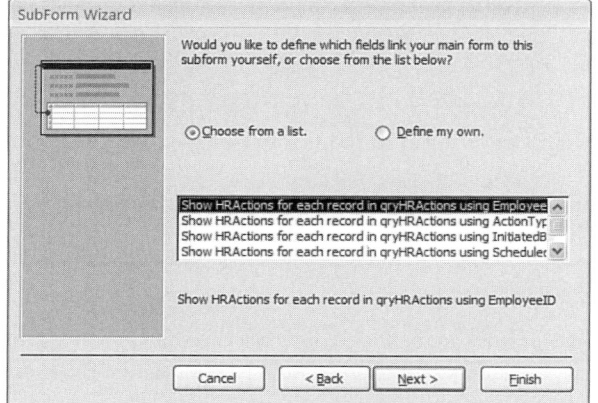

Figure 15.54
After the Wizard adds the subform, adjust its dimensions to suit the active area of the tab control's page.

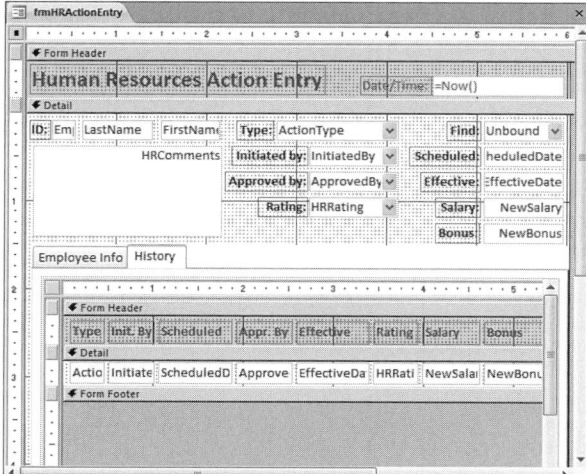

8. Change to Form view, select Buchanan in the Find list, and click the History tab to display the hired entry for Steven Buchanan and a tentative append record (see Figure 15.55).

Figure 15.55
Form view with the History page selected displays HRActions record(s) for the employee selected in the Find combo box.

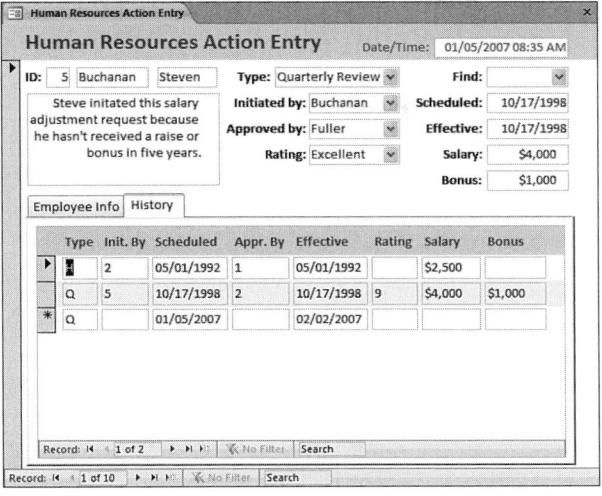

MODIFYING THE DESIGN OF CONTINUOUS FORMS

The default design of the History page's subform as created by the Subform Wizard lets you edit records of the HRActions table. The term *History* implies read-only access to the table in the tab control. Therefore, you should alter the properties of the subform to make the form read-only and remove unnecessary controls. For example, the vertical scroll bar lets you display any HRActions record for the employee, so you don't need record navigation buttons, nor do you need record selectors.

Access's in-situ subform editing feature lets you change many of the properties of subforms with the main form open in Design view. Unfortunately, you can't change property values, such as Record Selectors and Navigation Buttons, that affect the structure of the subform. Therefore, you must change the design of the subform independently of its main form container. Access has a command—Subform in New <u>W</u>indow—that provides a shortcut for changing subform properties.

To further optimize the design of the sbfHRActionEntryTab subform, follow these steps:

1. Return to Design view, click the History tab, select and right-click the subform, and choose Subform in New <u>W</u>indow to open sbfHRActionEntryTab in Design view, and then pres F4 to display the Property Sheet for the subform.

2. In the Format page of the Property Sheet, set Scroll Bars to Vertical Only, Record Selectors to No, and Navigation Buttons to No.

3. In the Data page, set the Recordset Type to Snapshot. Doing so has the same effect as setting Allow Edits, Allow Deletions, and Allow Additions to No. Your subform is now read-only because all snapshot-type Recordsets are read-only.

4. Select all text boxes and set the Tab Stop property to No for the group. Close the subform and save your changes.

5. In the now-empty History page, reduce the width of the subform and the tab control by about ⅛-inch to reflect removal of the Record Selector buttons. You can reduce the width of the subform container only when the subform isn't open for in-situ editing.

6. In the main form, select the tab control, and set it's Tab Stop property to No. Do the same for the EmployeeID, LastName, and FirstName text boxes.

7. Set the tab order by clicking the Form Design Tools – Arrange tab and the Tab Stop button to open the Tab Order dialog. Click Auto Order to set the tab order of the controls for which the Tab Order property is Yes. Select and move the cboFind combo box to the top of the tab order. The default control tab order is top-to-bottom, left-to-right. Click OK to close this dialog.

8. Return to Form view and click the History tab to verify your changes to the subform (see Figure 15.56).

Figure 15.56
Form view reflects subform linking on the EmployeeID field and the changes you made to the design and dimensions of the subform.

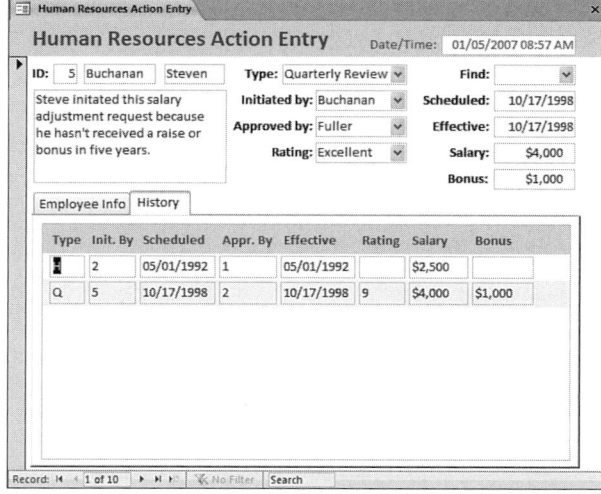

TIP

Removing text boxes and other controls from the tab order that you seldom or can't edit speeds data entry. To further optimize data entry, set the Tab Stop property of all controls on both pages of the tab control to No. Labels don't have a tab stop control; if you multiselect all controls on a page, use Shift+click to deselect the labels to set Tab Stop to No for all other controls.

ADDING NEW RECORDS IN THE HRACTIONENTRY FORM

Unlike Chapter 14's frmHRActions form, the Record Source for the main frmHrActionEntry form is a query. The query design takes advantage of Access' row fix-up feature when you add a new record to the HRActions table in the form. Row fix-up works in this case because the source of the qryHRActions query's EmployeeID column is a field of the HRActions table, not the Employees table.

→ For a review of row fix-up in one-to-many queries, **see** "Taking Advantage of Access's Row Fix-up Feature," **p. 491**.

To add a new record to the HRActions table, do the following:

1. Open frmHRActionEntry in Form view, and click the tentative append (new) record button to add a new record. All data disappears from the form.

2. Type a number in the [Employee]ID text box; for this example type **5** for Steven Buchanan. Press Tab or Enter to add data for the selected employee in the query columns from the Employees table and default values from the HRActions table to the form's controls (see Figure 15.57).

Figure 15.57
Adding a new record and typing an employee ID in the ID text box fills the form with employee data and default values from the qryHRActions query.

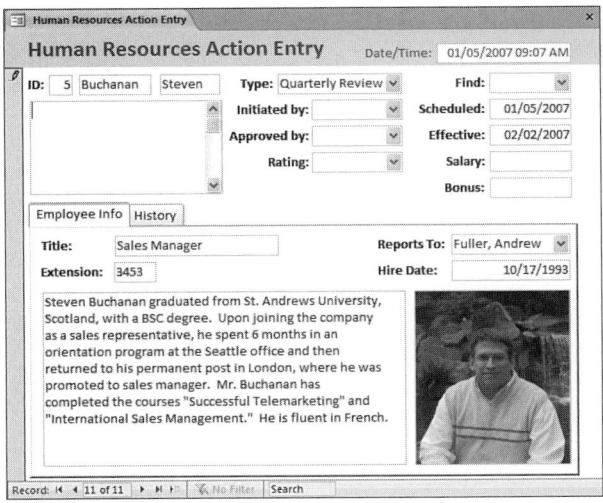

3. Make selections in the combo boxes, change the default dates, if necessary, and add a note regarding the action. If your cursor isn't in the Notes multiline text box, press Shift+Enter to save the record (see Figure 15.58). Shift+Enter in a multiline text box adds a newline character and doesn't save the record.

Figure 15.58
Completing the record addition requires only a few combo box selections, changes to dates, and an optional note.

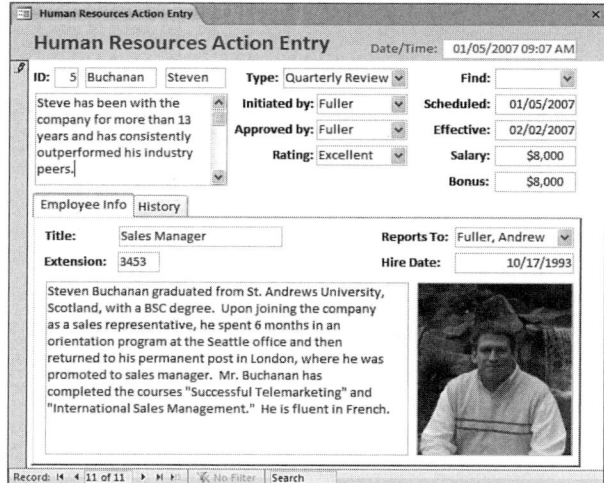

4. Verify that you added the record correctly by selecting the employee for whom you added the action—in this case Steven Buchanan—in the Find combo box. Click the History tab to display the employee's entries (see Figure 15.59). The History subform's snapshot Recordset must be refreshed to display the added record.

Figure 15.59
After you refresh the History subform by selecting the employee in the Find combo box, the newly added record appears.

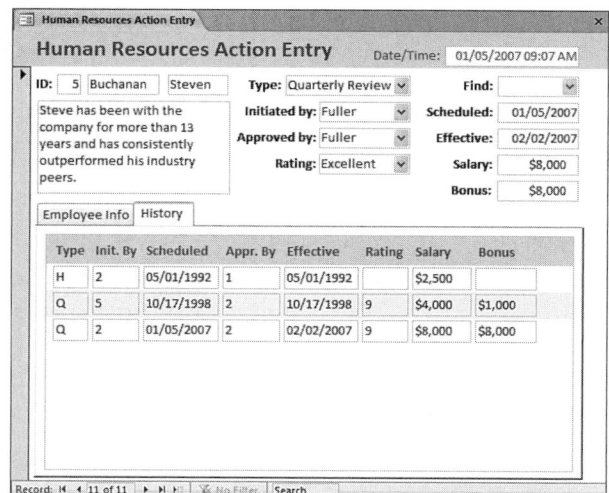

At this point in its development, frmHRActionEntry would be dangerous to release for use by data entry operators. For example, all fields in the main form are updatable. Thus, an operator could change the FirstName, LastName, and other values of the Employees table, as well as the EmployeeID for an existing HRActions record. You can set the Locked property to Yes for all controls linked to the Employees table, but you can't lock the EmployeeID text box that's required to specify the EmployeeID of a new record. You can control the locked status of form controls by adding VBA event-handling code for the form's Before Insert and After Insert events.

TIP

> You can make frmHRActionEntry safe for data entry operators by setting the Data Entry property of the form to Yes. Specifying Data Entry prevents operators from viewing existing records and only allows them to enter new records. In this case, you must change the Recordset Type property value of the subform to Dynaset, and set the AllowEdits, AllowDeletions, and AllowAdditions property values to Yes. Otherwise, the added record won't appear in the History subform.

OVERRIDING THE FIELD PROPERTIES OF TABLES

Access uses the table's property values assigned to the fields as defaults. The form or subform inherits these properties from the table or query on which the form is based. You can override the inherited properties, except for the Validation Rule property, by assigning a different set of values in the Property Sheet for the control. Properties of controls bound to fields of tables or queries that are inherited from the table's field properties are shown in the following list:

- Format
- Decimal Places
- Status Bar Text
- Typeface characteristics (such as Font Name, Font Size, Font Bold, Font Italic, and Font Underline)

- Validation Rule
- Validation Text
- Default Value

Values of field properties that you override with properties in a form apply only when the data is displayed and edited with the form. You can establish validation rules for controls bound to fields that differ from properties of the field established by the table, but you can only narrow the rule. The table-level validation rule for the content of the HRType field, for example, limits entries to the letters H, Q, Y, S, R, B, C, and T. The validation rule you establish in a form can't broaden the allowable entries; if you add F as a valid choice by editing the validation rule for the HRType field to InStr("HQYSRBCTF",[HRType])>0, you receive an error when you type F.

However, you can narrow the range of allowable entries by substituting `InStr("SQYB",[HRType])>0`. Notice that you can use expressions that refer to the field name as validation-rule expressions in forms; such expressions aren't permitted as field-level validation-rule expressions in Access 2007.

ADDING PAGE HEADERS AND FOOTERS FOR PRINTING FORMS

Access lets you add a separate pair of sections, Page Header and Page Footer, that appear only when the form prints. You add both of these sections to the form at once by choosing View, Page Header/Footer. The following list shows the purposes of Page Header and Footer sections:

- Page Header sections enable you to use a different title for the printed version. The depth of the page header can be adjusted to control the location where the Detail section of the form is printed on the page.

- Page Footer sections enable you to add dates and page numbers to the printed form.

Page Header and Page Footer sections appear only in the printed form, not when you display the form onscreen in Form view. Figure 15.60 shows the frmHRActionEntry form in Design view with Page Header and Page Footer sections added.

Figure 15.60
Page Header and Page Footer sections appear when you print the form, but not in Form view.

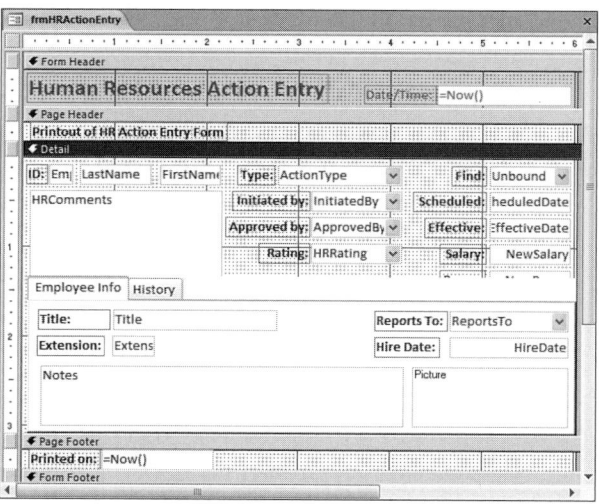

With the Display When (Format) property of the Property Sheet for the Form Header and Form Footer sections, you can control whether these sections appear in the printed form. In Figure 15.60, the Form Header section duplicates the information in the Page Header section (except for the Date/Time label and text box), so you might not want to print both. To control when a section of the form prints or is displayed, perform the following steps:

1. Double-click the title bar of whichever section of the form you want to change; this opens the related Property Sheet. (The Page Header and Page Footer sections don't have a Display When property; these sections appear only during printing.)
2. Click the Format tab if the formatting properties aren't already showing. Click to drop down the Display When list.
3. To display but not print this section in Form view, select Screen Only.
4. To print but not display this section, select Print Only.

TROUBLESHOOTING

ERROR MESSAGES ON COPIED CONTROLS

A control copied to another form throws error messages whenever that control gets the focus.

When you copy a control to a form that uses a data source different from the one used to create the original control, you need to change the Control Source property to correspond with the field the new control is to be bound to. Changing the Control Source property doesn't change the Status Bar Text, Validation Rule, and Validation Text properties for the new control source. You must enter the appropriate values manually.

IN THE REAL WORLD—ACCESS WIZARDRY

Access 1.0 had only a few wizards; Access 2007 has 42, four fewer than Access 2003 because Access 2007 doesn't include the four Data Access Page wizards. Microsoft defines a wizard as "a Microsoft Access tool that asks you questions and creates an object according to your answers." The "Wizards, builders, and add-ins in Access 2003" help topic from the Office Online site lists 51 wizards, but four items in the list—Documentor, Macro-To-Module Converter, Subform/Subreport Field Linker, and Switchboard Manager—don't carry the wizard suffix and are better classified as utilities.

NOTE

> When this book was written, there was no "Wizards, builders, and add-ins in Access 2007" help topic. However, you can search the Internet for "Wizards, builders, and add-ins in Access 2003" to locate the list for the previous edition.

Form-related wizards are the most numerous. The following nine wizards, listed in alphabetical order, assist you in creating custom forms:

- **AutoForm Wizard**—Automatically generates a form. Access 2007 has added the PivotTable and PivotChart types.
- **AutoFormat Wizard**—Applies a specific format to a form.
- **Chart Wizard**—Adds to a form a graph or chart bound to a table or query.

15

- **Combo Box Wizard**—Generates one of three classes of bound and unbound combo box controls on a form.
- **Command Button Wizard**—Adds a command button control.
- **Form Wizard**—Generates a new form. Access 2002 added the capability to generate a PivotTable or PivotChart form.
- **Option Group Wizard**—Adds a group of option buttons.
- **Subform/Subreport Field Linker**—Creates or alters links between a main form and subform.
- **Subform/Subreport Wizard**—Adds a new subform.

One of the reasons that Access 2007 has the largest wizard population of all Office 2007 applications is that Access is the most complex of the Office 2007 members—from both the user and developer standpoint. Access's complexity, compared with Word, Excel, PowerPoint, and Outlook, undoubtedly is the reason that Microsoft doesn't include Access 2007 in the Basic, Standard, and Small Business editions of Office 2007. The omission of Access from the Small Business edition is surprising, because establishing and maintaining databases is crucial for almost every enterprise, regardless of size. It's a good bet that Access loses many potential users to competing products as a result of its omission from the Small Business edition.

Wizards are classified as Access add-ins, which also include builders, menu add-ins, and a new class of Component Object Model (COM) add-ins. The standard set of wizards and builders that come with Access appear in the `HKEY_LOCAL_MACHINE\Software\Microsoft\Office\12.0\Access\Wizards` key of the Registry. Figure 15.61 shows the top-level Registry keys for the Control Wizards used in this and the preceding chapter. Microsoft classifies Access builders as Property Wizards in the Registry.

Figure 15.61
The Registry includes keys for each Access wizard and builder.

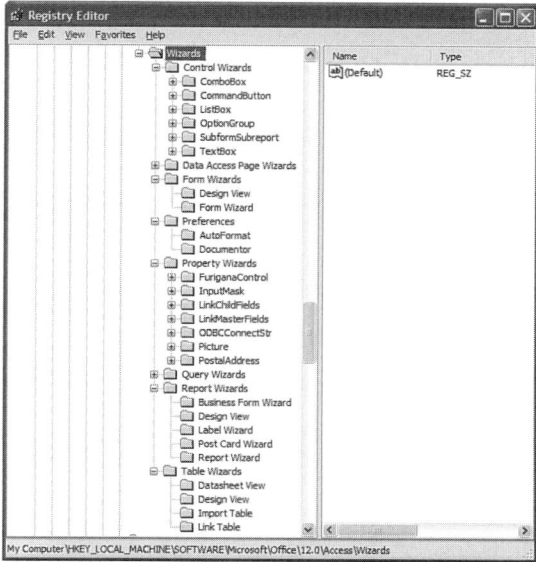

Most of the wizards are contained in the Acwzmain.mde file in your …\Office12\ACCWIZ folder; the ACWZTOOL.ACCDE Advanced Wizards file includes the Add-In Manager and some builders; and ACWZLIB.ACCDE holds the Import/Export Wizards. You can open the ACWZ….ACCDE files and their forms in Access 2007, but you can't open modules or make changes to objects. It's unfortunate that Microsoft uses the .accde format to prevent viewing the wizard VBA code; Access wizards are excellent examples of VBA power programming in action.

15

CHAPTER 16

WORKING WITH SIMPLE REPORTS AND MAILING LABELS

In this chapter

UNDERSTANDING THE RELATIONSHIP BETWEEN FORMS AND REPORTS

The final product of most database applications is a report. Access combines data from tables, queries, and—in some cases—forms to produce a report that you can print for people who need or request it. One of Access's major selling points is its capability to generate fully formatted reports easily and quickly. No other report generator application comes close to rivaling Access's flexible report-generation capabilities.

> **NOTE**
>
> SQL Server 2005 SP2 (Service Pack 2) Reporting Services is an enterprise-grade, server-based report generator for SQL Server and Oracle databases. SQL Server Express (SSX) SP2 includes a Reporting Services version that runs on the same computer as SSX. It's much easier and faster to create Access reports than Report Server reports.

With the expansion of email and the growth of intranets and the Internet, it's becoming more common for people to read and, when necessary, print their own reports. Access offers the following methods of distributing paperless reports:

- Adobe Portable Document Format (.pdf) files, for viewing in or printing from Adobe Reader.

- Microsoft XML Paper Specification (.xps) files, for viewing in or printing with the XPS Viewer add-in for Internet Explorer. *Metro* was the codename for XPS during its development.

> **NOTE**
>
> Saving reports in PDF or XPS format requires the Microsoft Save as PDF or XPS Add-in for 2007 Microsoft Office programs, which you download from the Office Online site when you first use either feature.
>
> XPS is a Microsoft "open" format that's based on the Windows Presentation Foundation's (WPF's) eXtensible Application Markup Language (XAML). XAML is part of Windows Vista and available as an add-in for Windows XP and Windows 2003 Server.

> → For more information on sending reports as email attachments, **see** "Mailing Reports as Attachments," **p. 765**.

- Report Snapshots, which are self-contained .snp files that you can send as an email attachment with Outlook, Outlook Express, or any other Windows email program. Users must have a local copy of the freely distributable Snapshot Viewer application to open and print the reports, which are exact replicas of the conventional Access report. Report Snapshots are present for backward compatibility with previous Access versions.

- Rich Text Format (.rtf) files, for opening in and printing from Microsoft Word, primarily for backward compatibility.

- Text (.txt) files, for backward compatibility only.

- Static web reports, which apply an Extensible Stylesheet Language Transformations (XSLT) document to an Extensible Markup Language (XML) file to generate an HTML 4.0 simulation of the original report. You can export static—also called *snapshot*—web reports to a web server from conventional (Access) applications or Access data projects (ADPs). Recipients print the report from the browser.

- Live web reports, which are similar to static XSL/XML web reports, but deliver current data by executing an Active Server Pages (ASP) or HTML template query against SQL Server when opening the page in a browser.

→ To learn more about static and live Web reports, **see** "Exporting Static Reports as XML and Web Pages," **p. 1071**, "Exporting Reports to HTML Tables," **p. 1026**, and "Displaying Dynamic Tables in Active Server Pages," **p. 1037**.

Some reports consist of a single page, such as an order acknowledgment, invoice, graph, or chart. Multipage Access reports—typified by catalogs, general ledgers, and financial statements—are more common than the single-page variety. A multipage report is analogous to a continuous form that has been optimized for printing.

Most methods of creating Access forms, which you learned about in Chapter 14, "Creating and Using Basic Access Forms," and Chapter 15, "Designing Custom Multitable Forms," also apply to reports. The following list details the principal differences between reports and forms:

- Reports are intended primarily for printing and, unlike forms, usually aren't designed for display in a window. When you view an 8 ½×11-inch report in the default Print Preview, its content might not be legible. In the zoomed (full-page) view, only a part of the report might be visible in the Print Preview or Layout Preview window, depending on your monitor's resolution.

- You can't change the value of the underlying data for a report with a control object from the toolbox as you can with forms. With reports, Access disregards user input from combo boxes, option buttons, check boxes, and the like. The primary controls you use on forms are labels and text boxes. You can use a check box to indicate the value of fields of the Yes/No (**Boolean**) data type.

- Reports don't provide a Datasheet view. Only Print Preview, Report, Layout, Design views are available. Report and Layout views are new in Access 2007.

- In multicolumn reports, the number of columns, the column width, and the column spacing are controlled by settings in the Printer Setup dialog, not by controls that you add or properties that you set in Design view.

Access reports share many characteristics of forms, including the following:

- *Basic reports* are generated by clicking the Create ribbon's Report button. The default basic report is a tabular list of all fields of all records in the table or query you select in the Navigation pane.

- *Report Wizards* create the three basic kinds of reports: single-column, groups/totals, and mailing labels. You can modify as necessary the reports that the Report Wizards create. The function of the Report Wizard is similar to that of the Form Wizard discussed in Chapter 14. The Label Wizard creates mailing labels for popular label brands and sizes.

- *Sections* include report headers and footers, which appear once at the beginning and at the end of the report, and page headers and footers, which print at the top and bottom of each page. The report footer often is used to print grand totals. Report sections correspond to similarly named form sections.

- *Group sections* of reports, as a whole, comprise the equivalent of the Detail section of forms. Groups often are referred to as *bands*, and the process of grouping records is known as *banding*. You can add group headers that include a title for each group, and group footers to print group subtotals. You can place static (unbound) graphics in header and footer sections and bound graphics within group sections.

- *Controls* are added to reports from the Access toolbox and then moved and sized with their handles. Reports support embedded bitmaps, attachments, OLE objects (such as graphs and charts you create with MSGraph.exe), and ActiveX controls (such as the PivotChart and PivotTable).

- *Subreports* can be incorporated into reports the same way you add subform controls within main forms.

CATEGORIZING TYPES OF ACCESS REPORTS

Reports created by Access fall into six basic types, also called *layouts*, as detailed in the following list:

- **Tabular reports**—Provide a column for each field of the table or query and print the value of each field of the records in rows under the column header. If you have more columns than can fit on one page, additional pages print in sequence until all columns are printed; then the next page-length group of records is printed. The Create ribbon's Report button auto-generates a tabular report from the selected table or query. The AutoReport feature also can create a tabular report automatically.

- **Single-column reports**—List in one long column of text boxes the values of each field in each record of a table or query. A label indicates the name of a field, and a text box to the right of the label provides the values. Access's AutoReport feature can create a single-column report with a single click of the toolbar's AutoReport button. You seldom use single-column reports because the format wastes paper.

- **Multicolumn reports**—Display single-column reports in multiple columns by using the "newspaper" or "snaking" column approach of desktop publishing and word processing applications. Information that doesn't fit in the first column flows to the top of the second column, and so on. The format of multicolumn reports wastes less paper than the single-column variety, but the uses of multicolumn reports are limited because the column alignment is unlikely to correspond with what you want.

- **Groups/totals reports**—The most common kind of report. Access groups/totals reports summarize data for groups of records and then add grand totals at the end of the report.

- **Mailing labels**—A special kind of multicolumn report that prints names and addresses (or other multifield data) in groups. The design of the stock adhesive label on which you print determines how many rows and columns are on a page.

- **Unbound reports**—Contain subreports based on unrelated data sources, such as tables or queries.

The first five types of reports use a table or query as the data source, as do forms. These kinds of reports are said to be bound to the data source. The main report of an unbound report isn't linked to a table or query as a data source. The subreports contained by an unbound report, however, must be bound to a data source.

AUTO-GENERATING A SIMPLE TABULAR REPORT

The process for auto-generating a tabular report from a table or query is dead simple. For example, following is the process for creating a Products report from the \SEUA12\Chaptr16\Reports16.accdb database's qryInventory query:

1. Open the Reports16.accdb file from the \SEUA12\Chaptr16 folder and select the qryInventory query in the Navigation pane.

2. Click the Create tab and its Report button to generate the qryInventory report in Layout view (see Figure 16.1).

It's obvious that the default layout for auto-generated reports is much better suited to forms than reports. The 11-point font size is too large for ordinary reports, and row height and column width is excessive. It's easy to adjust font sizes and column widths in Layout view, but Design view is more practical for making other adjustments. Figure 16.2 is a print preview of the report's final version after the adjustments described have been made.

Figure 16.1
The default format of auto-generated reports is very similar to auto-generated forms.

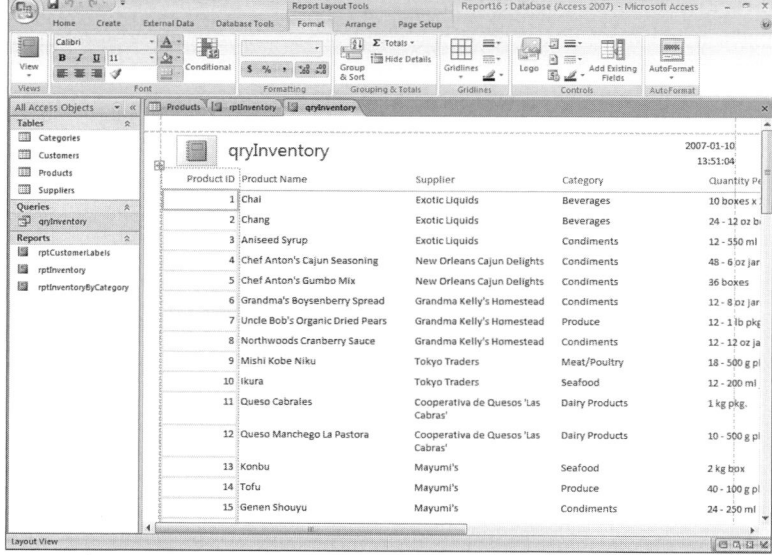

Figure 16.2
Modifying the layout of the auto-generated report shows all columns and their values across a single page and reduces the number of pages from eight to four.

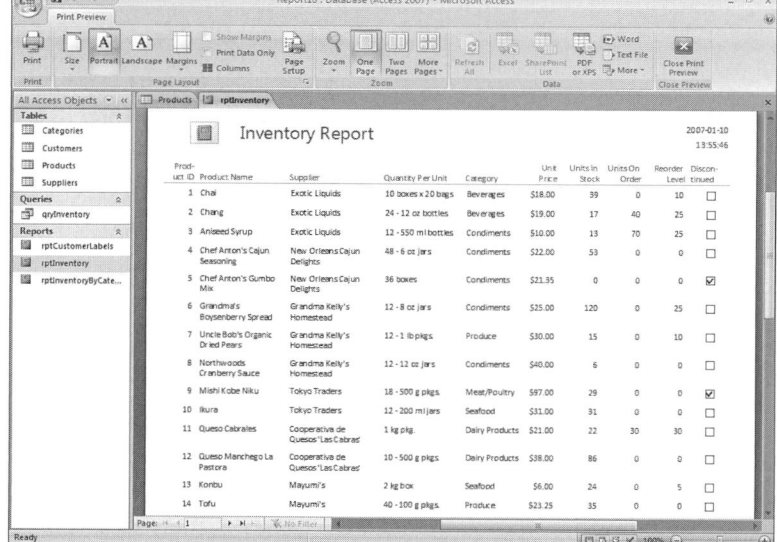

CREATING A GROUPED REPORT WITH THE REPORT WIZARD

This section shows you how to use the Report Wizard to create a grouped report based on data in the Products and Suppliers tables of the Northwind Traders sample database. (Like the Form Wizard, the Report Wizard lets you create reports that contain data from more than one table without first creating a query.) This report displays the quantity of each specialty food product in inventory, grouped by product category.

NOTE

> The process of designing an Access data project (ADP) report is, for the most part, identical to that for conventional reports based onAccess data sources. The difference is that ADP uses an SQL Server table, view, function, or stored procedure as the data source for the report. ADP doesn't support some Access features, such as domain aggregate functions, but the workarounds for ADP limitations are relatively simple. Chapter 22, "Upsizing Access Applications to Access Data Projects," describes the principal workarounds required when migrating from Access applications to ADP.

Creating an inventory report begins with modifying the basic report created by the Report Wizard. The process of creating a basic report with the Report Wizard is similar to the process that you used to create a form with a subform in Chapter 14. An advantage of using the Report Wizard to introduce the topic of designing Access reports is that the steps for this process are parallel to the steps you take when you start with a default blank report. Chapter 17, "Preparing Advanced Reports," explains how to start with a blank report and create more complex reports. Many of the adjustments you make to this report also apply to the sample auto-generated report in the preceding section.

To create an Inventory by Category report in Northwind.accdb, follow these steps:

1. Click the Create tab and then click the Report Wizard button to open the first Report Wizard dialog. Select Table: Products from the Tables/Queries list.

2. The fields that you select to display represent columns of the report. You want the report to print the product name and supplier so that users don't have to refer to another report to associate codes with names. The fields from the Products table that you need for this report are CategoryID, ProductID, ProductName, SupplierID, and UnitsInStock. With the > button, select these fields in sequence from the Available Fields list. As you add fields to the Selected Fields list, Access removes the field names from the Available Fields list. Alternatively, you can double-click the field name in the Available Fields list to move the field name to the Selected Fields list. The fields appear from left to right in the report, based on the top-to-bottom sequence in which the fields appear in the Selected Fields list.

3. To demonstrate how the Wizard deals with reports that bind to more than one table, add the CompanyName field from the Suppliers table. Open the Tables/Queries dropdown list and select Table: Suppliers.

TIP

> You can retrace your steps to correct an error by clicking the Back button whenever it is enabled. The Finish button accepts all defaults and jumps to the end of the Wizard, so you shouldn't use this button until you're familiar with the Report Wizard's default selections.

4. Instead of presenting the supplier name as the report's last field, you want the report's CompanyName column to follow the SupplierID report column. Select the SupplierID field in the Selected Fields list. Now select the CompanyName field from the Available Fields list and click the > button. Access moves the CompanyName field from the Available Fields list and inserts the field into the Selected Fields list (see Figure 16.3). Click Next.

Figure 16.3
After selecting the fields from the primary table, select the SupplierID field, and add the CompanyName field of the Suppliers table in the first Report Wizard dialog.

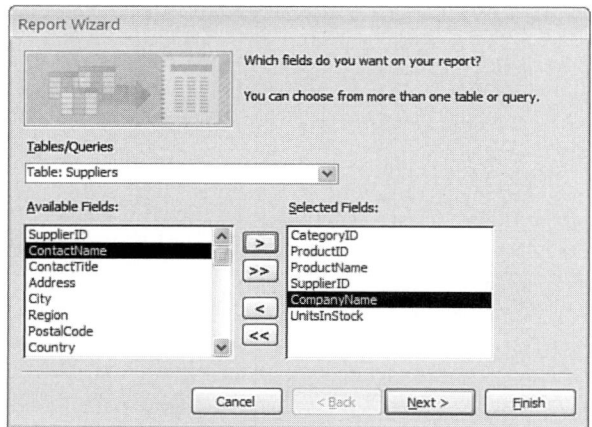

NOTE

The purpose of adding the CompanyName field of the Suppliers table is to demonstrate how the Wizard handles the design of reports based on more than one table. If you don't add the CompanyName field, the Report Wizard dialog of step 5 doesn't appear. The SupplierID field of the Products table is a lookup field, so CompanyName appears in lieu of the numeric SupplierID value. You remove the duplicate field when you modify the report later in the chapter.

5. The Report Wizard asks how you want to view the data in the report, so select By Products, as shown in Figure 16.4.

NOTE

Notice the Show Me More Information button near the left center of the Wizard dialog. Click this button to display the first of a series of hint dialogs for the Report Wizard. If you click the Show Me Examples option, Access displays additional hint screens. These screens use examples from the Sales Reps, Customers, and Orders tables to show you the different groupings that the Report Wizard can automatically add to the report. Click the Close button repeatedly until you return to the Report Wizard dialog shown in Figure 16.3.

Figure 16.4
Select the Products table as the basis for your report in the second Report Wizard dialog.

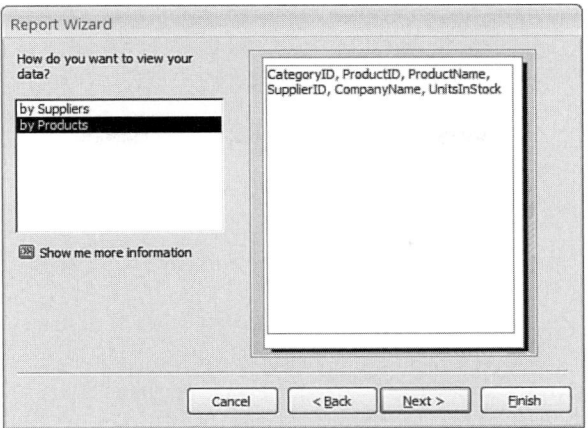

6. Click Next to open the third Report Wizard dialog, which asks whether you want to add any grouping levels to the report. Select the CategoryID field in the list and click the > button to establish the grouping by the products' category, as shown in Figure 16.5.

Figure 16.5
Specify the field on which you want to group your report in the third Report Wizard dialog.

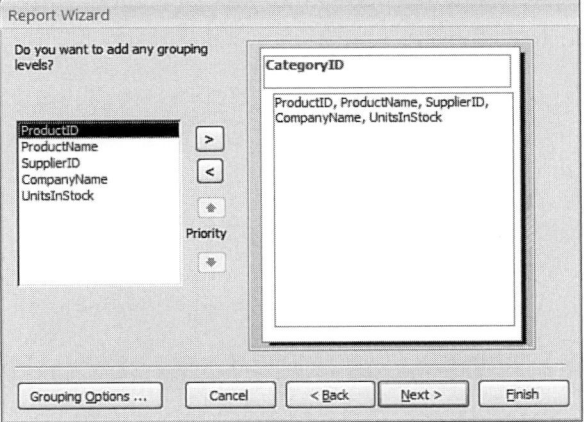

7. Click the Grouping Options button to open the Grouping Intervals dialog shown in Figure 16.6. By changing the grouping interval, you can affect how Access groups data in the report. For numeric fields, you can group items by 10s, 50s, 100s, and so on. For text fields, you can group items based on the first letter, the first three letters, and so on. The Wizard checks the field data type and suggests appropriate grouping intervals.

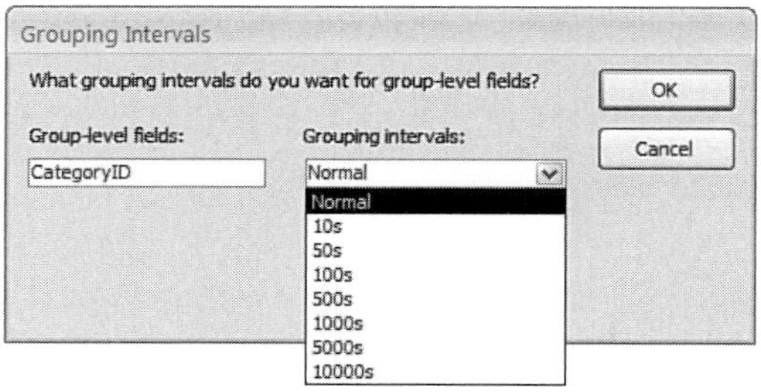

Figure 16.6
The Normal option groups numeric fields by individual values. You also have the option to group numeric fields by seven ranges of values.

Grouping Intervals	
What grouping intervals do you want for group-level fields?	OK
Group-level fields: Grouping intervals:	Cancel
CategoryID Normal ▼	
Normal	
10s	
50s	
100s	
500s	
1000s	
5000s	
10000s	

16

TIP

> If your application uses a text-coding scheme, such as BEVA for alcoholic beverages and BEVN for nonalcoholic beverages, you can combine all beverages in a single group by selecting 1st 3 Characters from the Grouping Intervals list. Access provides this option for fields of the Text data type.

→ For additional methods of grouping data by characters in the field, **see** "Grouping and Sorting Report Data," **p. 746**.

8. This report doesn't require any special grouping interval, so accept Normal in the Grouping Intervals list, click OK to return to the Report Wizard, and click Next.

9. You can sort the records within groups by any field that you select (see Figure 16.7), with up to four different sorted fields. The dialog doesn't offer CategoryID as a choice because the records already are grouped on this field, and the field on which the grouping is based is sorted automatically by the table's primary key. Select ProductName in the first drop-down list.

Figure 16.7
In the fourth Report Wizard dialog, select the field on which to sort records within the group you specified in the third dialog.

NOTE By default, the sort order is ascending; if you want a descending sort order, click the button to the right of the drop-down list. (This button is a toggle control; click it again to return to an ascending sort.)

10. Click the Summary Options button to display the Summary Options dialog. If you want to add summary information to a report column, you set the options for that column in this dialog. The Report Wizard lists all the numeric fields on the report that aren't AutoNumber fields and offers you check boxes to select a Sum, Average, Minimum, and Maximum for that report column. Depending on the check boxes that you select, the Report Wizard adds those summary fields to the end of the report.

11. The Show option group lets you select whether the report shows the summary fields only or the full report with the summary fields added at the end of each group and at the end of the report. For this report, select the Sum and Avg check boxes for the UnitsInStock field, the Detail and Summary option, and the Calculate Percent of Total for Sums check box (see Figure 16.8). The Calculate Percent of Total for Sums check box displays the group's total as a percentage of the grand total for all groups. Click OK to return to the Report Wizard dialog, and click Next.

Figure 16.8
The Summary Options dialog lets you add to your report values based on calculations on numeric fields (other than AutoNumber fields).

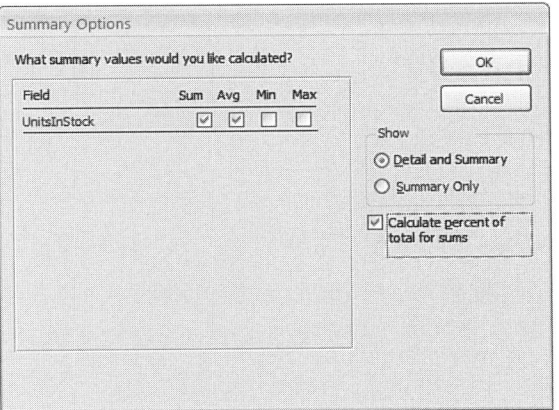

12. The Wizard asks you to select a layout for your report. The window on the left shows a preview of the layout style that you select; click each of the six option buttons to check the layouts. For this report, select Stepped in the Layout option group (see Figure 16.9).

13. By default, the Report Wizard selects the Adjust the Field Width So All Fields Fit on a Page check box. As a rule, you should select this option to save paper and make reports with a few columns more legible. In the Orientation option group, you select the report's printing orientation. For this example, select the default Portrait option. Click Next.

Figure 16.9
The Stepped report layout is the most common choice for reports with a few columns. You can increase the number of columns per page by choosing one of the Align Left layouts.

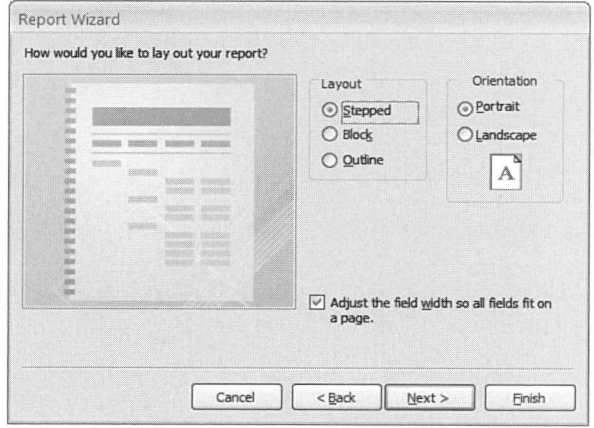

TIP

When you restrict field widths to fit all fields on a page, fields with long lines of text often are truncated in the final report. You can adjust field widths in Report Design view to accommodate long text lines or change to multiline text boxes that expand automatically.

14. Select one of the 25 predefined report styles for your report. The window on the left shows a preview of the selected style (see Figure 16.10). Select the None style to use the Calibri font, include a title and print in monochrome, and then click Next to display the final Report Wizard dialog.

Figure 16.10
Choose one of the 25 predefined printing styles for the report.

15. Type **rptInventoryByCategory** as the title for the new report; the Report Wizard uses this title as the name of the saved report it creates (see Figure 16.11). Accept the Preview the Report option, and click Finish to complete your report specification. The

Report Wizard creates the report and displays it in Print Preview. Click the Close Print Preview button to show Report view.

Figure 16.11
Type the name for your report in the last Report Wizard dialog. You change the report's caption to "Inventory by Category" later in the chapter.

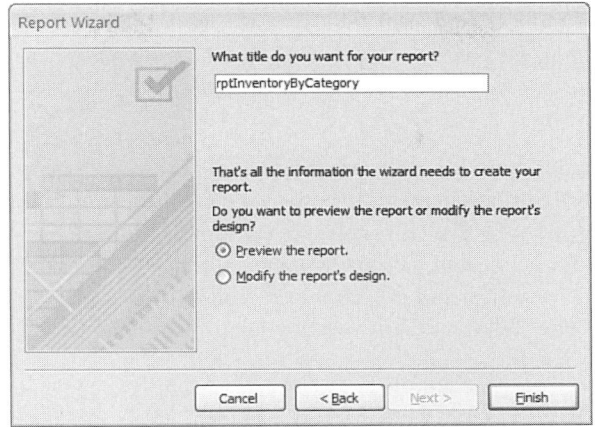

Figure 16.12 shows in Report view the basic report that the Report Wizard creates, which has some major design deficiencies that you correct in the sections that follow. Use the vertical and horizontal scroll bars, if necessary, to position the preview as shown. When you're finished previewing the report, close it.

Figure 16.12
The report generated by the Wizard doesn't provide sufficient space to display the full supplier names or the percent of total Units in Stock as the Standard value.

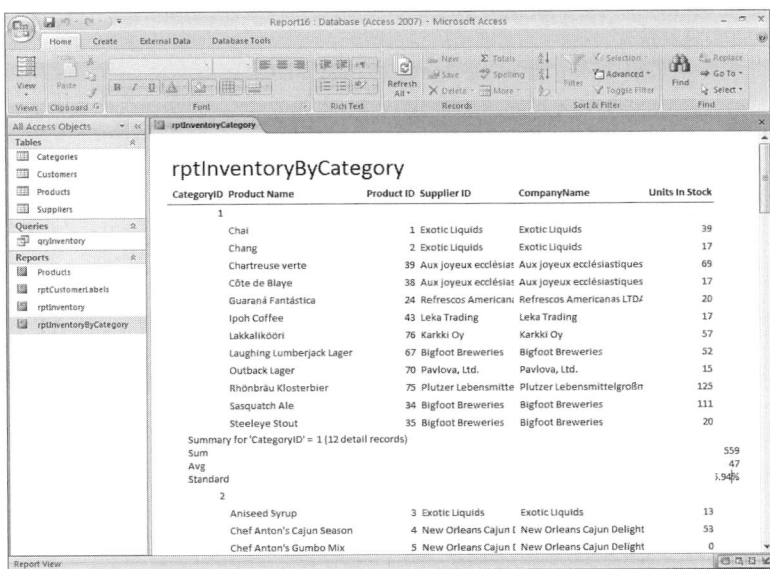

TIP

Unlike Access's record navigation text boxes, Print Preview's Page text box shows only the current report page. To obtain a page count, the Access report engine must paginate the report; pagination can take a considerable period of time for very long reports. To display the total number of report pages in the Pages text box, click the Last Page button (arrow and bar) at the bottom of the Print Preview window.

With a few design modifications, you can obtain a finished report with the information necessary to analyze Northwind's current inventory. The modifications correct obvious defects in the wizard-designed report, such as the excess width of the CategoryID column, cut-off names in the Product Name and CompanyName columns, duplication of the Supplier ID and CompanyName columns, and the truncated Standard value. You make these changes in the "Modifying a Basic Wizard Report" section later in this chapter.

USING ACCESS'S CONTEXTUAL REPORT RIBBONS

NEW Access 2007's new Layout view for reports speeds the report layout process by enabling grouped controls in stacked or tabular styles and letting you manipulate individual controls or groups of controls with live data visible. Selecting Layout View in the Home or a contextual ribbon's View gallery adds three contextual ribbons to the UI: Report Layout Tools – Format, Report Layout Tools – Arrange, and Report Layout Tools – Page Layout. The following three sections describe these contextual ribbons' report-specific groups in detail.

NOTE

The following sections provide cross-references to tables that describe command buttons of groups that are identical for form and report ribbons.

THE REPORT LAYOUT TOOLS – FORMAT RIBBON

The Format contextual ribbon has control button groups for specifying the view, formatting text and numbers, modifying Datasheet gridlines, setting control properties, and applying AutoFormats to forms. With the exception of the Grouping & Totals group, the Report Layout Tools – Format ribbon and the Form Layout Tools – Format ribbon are identical and serve the same purposes (see Figure 16.13).

Figure 16.13
Report Layout view adds the Report Layout Tools – Formatting contextual ribbon shown here and the Report Layout Tools – Arrange contextual ribbon (bottom).

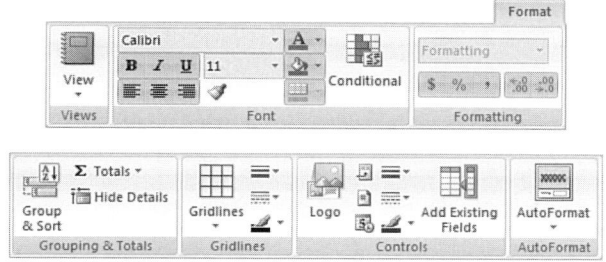

→ For descriptions of command buttons of the Font, Formatting, Gridlines, Controls, and AutoFormat groups, **see** "The Form Layout Tools – Format Ribbon," **p. 585**.

Table 16.1 shows the icon, name, KeyTips, and a brief description of each command button of the Report Layout Tools – Format ribbon's Views and Grouping & Totals groups. The keyboard shortcut to display KeyTips is Alt+M.

TABLE 16.1   ICONS, COMMAND BUTTONS, KEYTIP SHORTCUTS, AND COMMAND BUTTON ACTIONS FOR THE REPORT LAYOUT TOOLS – FORMAT RIBBON

Icon	Command Button	Shortcut Alt+M,	Command Action
Views Group			
	Report View	WF	Displays selected report in Form view
	Print Preview	WV	Displays a print preview of the selected report
	Layout View	WY	Displays selected report in Layout view
	Design View	WD	Displays selected report in Design view
Groupings & Totals Group			
	Group and Sort	HG	Opens the Group, Sort, and Total frame at the bottom of the report Layout view
Σ	Totals	HT	Opens a gallery to add one of the following aggregate values to a column: Sum, Average, Count Records, Count Values, Max, Min, Standard Deviation, or Variance
	Hide Details	HD	Toggles visibility of the Details section and its controls

→ To learn how to take advantage of the Group, Sort, and Total frame, **see** "Grouping and Sorting Report Data," **p. XXX** *(Ch 17)*.

THE FORM DESIGN TOOLS – DESIGN RIBBON

The Design contextual ribbon has control button groups for specifying the view, formatting text, modifying control gridlines, adding native Access report controls, setting control properties, opening Field List and Property Sheet dialogs, and opening the VBA code editor (see Figure 16.14).

Except for the Group & Sort icon and the Controls group, the Report Design Tools – Design and Report Design Tools – Format contextual ribbons are identical.

Figure 16.14
The Report Design Tools – Design contextual ribbon adds the Grouping & Totals group to the Report Design Tools – Design ribbon.

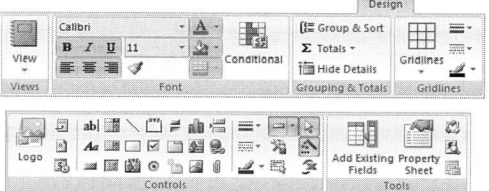

THE REPORT LAYOUT AND DESIGN TOOLS – ARRANGE RIBBON

The Report Layout Tools – Arrange and Report Design Tools – Arrange contextual ribbons have identical groups for managing control groups, setting text margins and padding for controls, toggling the Snap to Grid layout feature, setting tab order, aligning and positioning controls, and displaying the Property Sheet. The Arrange ribbon is the same as the Form Layout Tools – Arrange contextual ribbon (see Figure 16.15).

Figure 16.15
The Arrange contextual ribbon is present for the active Report Design Tools – Layout and Report Design Tools – Design tabs.

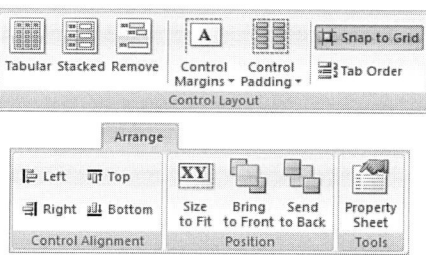

→ For descriptions of all groups and command buttons of the Report Layout Tools and Report Design Tools Arrange ribbon, **see** "The Form Layout Tools – Arrange Ribbon," **p. 585**.

THE REPORT LAYOUT AND DESIGN TOOLS – PAGE SETUP RIBBON

Like the Arrange contextual ribbon, the Page Setup ribbon is present when either the Report Layout Tools or Report Design Tools tab is active (see Figure 16.16). The Page Setup contextual ribbon's controls duplicate many functions of the Page Setup dialog.

Figure 16.16
The Page Setup contextual ribbon's command buttons emulate those of the tabbed Page Setup dialog, which has only one group.

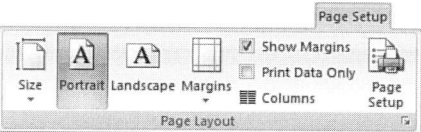

Table 16.2 lists the icon, name, KeyTips, and a brief description of each command button of the Report Layout Tools – Arrange and Report Design Tools – Arrange ribbons' groups. The keyboard shortcut to display KeyTips is Alt+S.

TABLE 16.2   ICONS, COMMAND BUTTONS, KEYTIP SHORTCUTS, AND COMMAND BUTTON ACTIONS FOR THE REPORT LAYOUT TOOLS – ARRANGE AND REPORT LAYOUT TOOLS – ARRANGE RIBBONS

Icon	Command Button	Shortcut Alt+S,	Command Action
	Size	SZ	Opens a gallery of standard English and metric paper sizes.
	Portrait	R	Selects portrait orientation (default).
	Landscape	L	Selects landscape orientation.
	Margins	M	Opens a gallery of Normal (0.75"), Wide (1.00"), and Narrow (0.25", default) margins.
	Show Margins	I	Toggles margins' visibility in Layout view only.
	Print Data Only	D	Prints only data in bound text boxes; labels aren't printed.
	Columns	O	Opens the Page Setup dialog with the Columns page active.
	Page Setup	SP	Opens the Page Setup dialog with the Print Options page active.

→ To learn how to customize print settings with the Page Setup dialog, **see** "Adjusting Margins and Printing Conventional Reports," **p. 731**.

THE PRINT PREVIEW RIBBON

The Print Preview ribbon is common to most Office 2007 applications, but the command button collection and layout differs among Office members. Access 2007's ribbon incorporates the basic set of controls provided by the earlier Print Preview dialog the ribbon replaces. Figure 16.17 shows Access's Print Preview ribbon with a report selected.

Figure 16.17
The Print Preview ribbon's command buttons emulate those of the former Print Preview dialog.

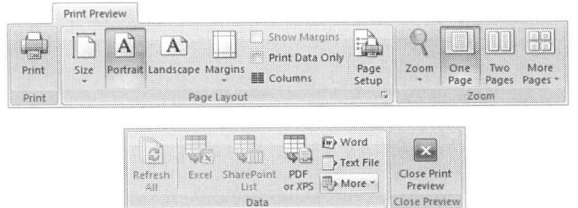

Table 16.3 shows the icon, name, KeyTips, and a brief description of each command button of the Print Preview ribbon's Print, Page Layout, Zoom, Data, and Close Preview groups. The keyboard shortcut to display KeyTips is Alt+P.

16

TABLE 16.3 ICONS, COMMAND BUTTONS, KEYTIP SHORTCUTS, AND COMMAND BUTTON ACTIONS FOR THE PRINT PREVIEW RIBBON

Icon	Command Button	Shortcut Alt+P,	Command Action
Print Group			
	Print	PD	
Group			
	Size	SZ	Opens a gallery of standard English and metric paper sizes.
	Portrait	R	Selects portrait orientation (default).
	Landscape	L	Selects landscape orientation.
	Margins	M	Opens a gallery of Normal (0.75"), Wide (1.00"), and Narrow (0.25", default) margins.
	Show Margins	I	Toggles margins' visibility in Layout view only.
	Print Data Only	D	Prints only data in bound text boxes; labels aren't printed.
	Columns	O	Opens the Page Setup dialog with the Columns page active.
	Page Setup	SP	Opens the Page Setup dialog with the Print Options page active.
Zoom Group			
	Zoom	PZ	Toggles one page and 100% view.
	One Page	1	Show one page in window.
	Two Pages	2	Show two pages in window.
	More Pages	U	Opens a gallery of Four Pages, Eight Pages, and Twelve Pages choices.
Data Group			
	Refresh All	A	Refreshes the contents of all databound controls.
	Excel	X	Exports to Excel (disabled for reports).
	SharePoint List	H	Exports to Excel (disabled for reports).
	PDF or XPS	F	Saves as a Portable Document File or XML Paper Specification file.

Icon	Command Button	Shortcut Alt+P,	Command Action
	Word	W	Saves as an Rich Text File (RTF).
	Text File	T	Saves as an ASCII text file (TXT).
	More	G	Opens a gallery of Save As selections: Access Database, XML File, Snapshot Viewer, HTML Document (Merge It with Microsoft Office Word is disabled for reports).

Close Print Preview Group

N/A	Close Print Preview	C	Closes Print Preview and returns to Report view.

MODIFYING A BASIC WIZARD REPORT

The Report Wizard tries to create the optimum final report in the first pass. Usually, the wizard comes close enough to a finished product that you spend far less time modifying a wizard-created basic report than creating a report from the default blank template.

In the following sections, you use Access's report design features to make the rptInventoryByCategory report more attractive and easier to read. In the process, you learn report design editing techniques in Access's new report Layout and Design views. Report Layout view makes many design changes much easier.

DELETING, RELOCATING, AND EDITING EXISTING CONTROLS

The first step in modifying the Wizard's report is to relocate the existing controls on the report. Access 2007's new report Layout view makes relocating controls *much* easier. You don't need to align the labels and text boxes precisely during the initial modification; the "Aligning Controls Horizontally and Vertically" section later in this chapter covers control alignment.

This report is more useful if you include the unit cost of each product and its current inventory value, which is the product of unit cost and number of units on hand. To accommodate two additional columns, you must compress the horizontal space consumed by the current columns. To rename the report and start creating space for additional controls on the report, follow these steps:

1. Open rptInventoryByCategory in report Layout view, if it's not already open, and click the Format tab.

2. Click outside the report's default margins to select the entire report, and press F4 to open the Properties Sheet.

3. Change the Format page's Caption property value to **Inventory by Category**.

4. Click the title label at the top of the page and make the same change, and then change its Font Size property value from 24 to 18.

5. The SupplierID and CompanyName columns are redundant in this report because the SupplierID column displays a lookup field. Select the Company Name label in the Page Header section, and press Delete to remove the stacked label and text box from the report. The Units in Stock column moves to the left and occupies the vacated space.

NOTE

> SupplierID and CompanyNames are added to demonstrate that the Wizard treats lookup fields inconsistently. ProductID is a lookup field for ProductName, CategoryID is a lookup field for CategoryName, and SupplierID is a lookup field for CompanyName. The ProductID and CategoryID columns show the expected numeric values, but the SupplierID column shows the unexpected CompanyName values.

6. Select the three small text boxes in the CategoryID Footer section and drag them to the left until their right side aligns with the right side of the Units in Stock text box. Drag the Grand Total text box to align with the three text boxes. Increase the width of all four text boxes and reduce the width of the Page 1 of # text box. (Look ahead to Figure 16.18 for approximate control dimensions).

 7. CategoryID occupies a column, but you can display this column's content in the CategoryID footer (or header) without consuming the extra column space. Right-click the CategoryID text box and choose <u>L</u>ayout, <u>R</u>emove to enable it to be moved, and then delete the CategoryID label.

 8. For this report, you'll put the CategoryID text box in the footer section of the group. You can't cut and paste controls between sections in Layout view, so change to Design view. Select the CategoryID text box, press Ctrl+X, select the CategoryID Footer bar, and then press Ctrl+V to paste the text box. Drag the text box to a temporary location in the middle of the CategoryID Footer section.

9. Drag the Detail section bar upward to eliminate the space occupied by the now-empty CategoryID Header, and drag the Page Header up to reduce the space below the report caption. Drag the ProductName label within one grid dot of the left margin.

 10. Applying the sort on ProductName moved the ProductID column after the ProductName column. Most reports require IDs before names. Change to Layout view and drag the ProductID label to the report's left margin. To save space, change the label from Product ID to **ID** and reduce the width of the column. Change the Units in Stock label to **Units** and reduce the column width.

11. Increase the width of the Product Name and Supplier ID columns to accommodate the width of most items (about 2 inches), and change the Supplier ID label to **Supplier**. Finally, drag the text boxes at the right of the CategoryID Footer, Page Footer, and Report Footer to align with the Units column's right edge. Your report now appears in Design view as shown in Figure 16.18.

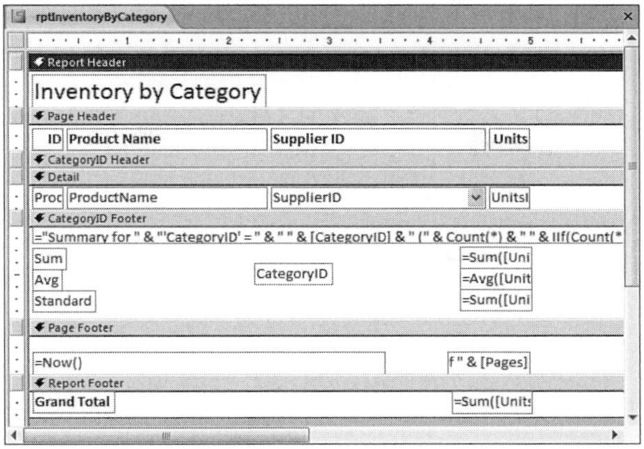

Figure 16.18
Design view shows the first set of changes to the report to accommodate new columns. Grid dots are hidden to improve legibility.

PRINTING THE LOOKUP FIELDS OF A TABLE

By default, the Report Wizard adds to the CategoryID Footer a calculated field that's visible in Figure 16.18. The calculated field displays the group's field name (CategoryID) and value to help identify the group footer's summary fields. For example, for CategoryID 1, the calculated field displays the following in Print Preview mode:

```
Summary for 'CategoryID' = 1 (12 detail records)
```

For this report, you want a more explicit description of the product category—more than just the CategoryID number. You replace the Category ID Footer's calculated field that starts with ="Summary for" in a later section with the category name. As usual, save your changes frequently.

USING THE DLookUp DOMAIN AGGREGATE FUNCTION FOR LOOKUPS

Not every table that you use in your reports will have lookup fields, nor is it necessarily desirable to create lookup fields for all numeric code fields (such as CategoryID and SupplierID). If you want to display a looked-up value for a field that isn't defined as a lookup field, you use Access's domain aggregate function, DLookUp, to find values from another table that correspond to a value in one of the report's fields. For example, to display both the actual CategoryID number and the CategoryName in the CategoryID Footer of the Inventory by Category report, you can use the DLookUp function to display the text of the CategoryName field from the Categories table, and a bound text field to display the CategoryID number from the Products table. The expression you use is

```
=DLookUp("[CategoryName]","Categories","[CategoryID] =
Report!CategoryID") & " Category"
```

[CategoryName] is the value that you want to return to the text box. Categories is the table that contains the CategoryName field. [CategoryID] = Report!CategoryID is the criterion that selects the record in the Categories table with a CategoryID value equal to the value in your report's CategoryID text box. The Report identifier is necessary to distinguish between the CategoryID field of the Categories table and a control object of the same name. (`Report!` is necessary in this example because Access has automatically named the report's CategoryID text box control as CategoryID. Remember that the DLookUp function isn't available in ADP reports.

TAKING ADVANTAGE OF AN EXISTING LOOKUP FIELD

CategoryID is a lookup field, but the Wizard didn't take advantage of this feature when generating the report. To add a new field to display the CategoryName field in the CategoryID footer, and complete the redesign of the report, do the following in Design view:

1. Delete the =`"Summary for "` ... text box and the temporary CategoryID label you moved from the CategoryID Header section. For this report, the Avg field is unnecessary, so delete it and its label.

2. To add a bound text box to act as the label for the subtotal in the CategoryID Footer section, click the Design tab and the Add Existing Fields button, and select CategoryID from the Field List.

3. Drag the CategoryID field to the position of the text box you deleted. Because the CategoryID field is a lookup field, it displays as a drop-down list when you drag it from the Field List (see Figure 16.19). When printed or displayed in Print Preview, this field shows the CategoryName rather than the numeric code. Close the Field list.

Figure 16.19
Replace the calculated field in the CategoryID Footer with the CategoryID lookup field.

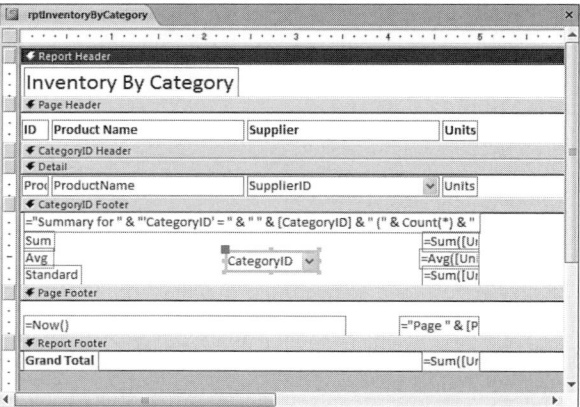

COMPLETING THE INITIAL REPORT MODIFICATIONS

Do the following to complete and review the report design prior to adding your own calculated controls to the report:

1. Drag the two calculated fields (=Now and =`"Page…"`) in the Page Footer section until they are one grid mark away from the top of the Page Footer section. Drag the Report Footer bar upward to reduce the Page Footer's height.

2. Click and drag the =Sum([UnitsInStock])/[UnitsInStock] text box from its present location below the =Sum([UnitsInStock]) text box to a position at the top of the CategoryID Footer, near the center of the page. Then drag the Standard label to the left of the text box you moved, and change its caption to **Percent:** (look ahead to Figure 16.20).

3. Select the text box and Shift+click the Percent label. Then open the smart tag's list and select Associate Label## with Standard of UnitsInStock to associate the label with the text box.

4. Drag the =Sum([UnitsInStock]) field up to the bottom of the CategoryID footer and the Sum label to the left of the text box you moved, and change Sum to **Total:**. Move the right edge of the text box to align with right edge of the UnitsInStock text box, if necessary. Move up the Page Footer divider bar to reduce the footer's depth (again, look ahead to Figure 16.20).

5. Repeat step 3 for the Total label and text box.

TIP

> To differentiate between calculated field text boxes that show only the first few characters of the expression, temporarily increase their width. Shift+F2 doesn't open the Zoom window for report text boxes, and there's no Zoom choice in the text boxes' context menu.

B   6. To distinguish the category section breaks, select all controls in the CategoryID Footer section and press Ctrl+B to set them bold.

  7. Underline the column headers by selecting the ID label, clicking the Format tab, clicking the Gridlines control, and selecting Bottom from the gallery.

B   8. Select the Grand Total label and text box in the Report Footer section and move the text box to align its right edge with the right edge of the text boxes above it. Your final report design appears as shown in Figure 16.20. Press Ctrl+S to save your report design.

Figure 16.20
At this point, the initial redesign of the Inventory by Category report is ready for a test run.

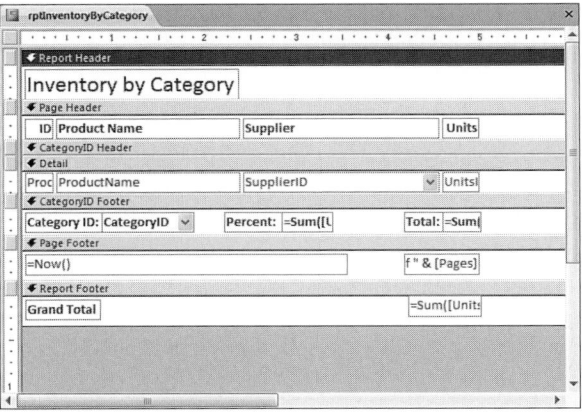

If you get a blank page after each page when you print or preview a report, see the suggestion in "Eliminating Empty Pages" in the "Troubleshooting" section near the end of this chapter.

 To check the progress of your work, periodically click the Print Preview button to display the report prior to printing. Figure 16.21 shows your Inventory by Category report in Print Preview mode.

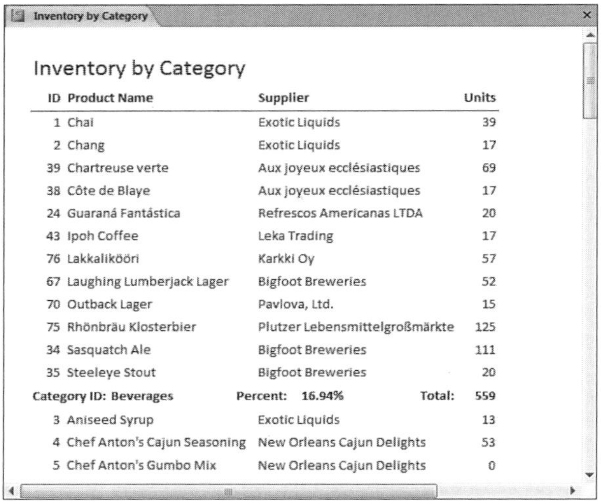

Figure 16.21
Report view displays the report design of Figure 16.20 at the equivalent of Print Preview's actual size (100% zoom).

	Inventory by Category			✕

Inventory by Category

ID	Product Name	Supplier	Units
1	Chai	Exotic Liquids	39
2	Chang	Exotic Liquids	17
39	Chartreuse verte	Aux joyeux ecclésiastiques	69
38	Côte de Blaye	Aux joyeux ecclésiastiques	17
24	Guaraná Fantástica	Refrescos Americanas LTDA	20
43	Ipoh Coffee	Leka Trading	17
76	Lakkalikööri	Karkki Oy	57
67	Laughing Lumberjack Lager	Bigfoot Breweries	52
70	Outback Lager	Pavlova, Ltd.	15
75	Rhönbräu Klosterbier	Plutzer Lebensmittelgroßmärkte	125
34	Sasquatch Ale	Bigfoot Breweries	111
35	Steeleye Stout	Bigfoot Breweries	20
Category ID: Beverages		**Percent: 16.94%** **Total:**	**559**
3	Aniseed Syrup	Exotic Liquids	13
4	Chef Anton's Cajun Seasoning	New Orleans Cajun Delights	53
5	Chef Anton's Gumbo Mix	New Orleans Cajun Delights	0

CHANGING THE REPORT'S RECORD SOURCE AND ADDING CALCULATED CONTROLS

Calculated controls are very useful in reports. You use calculated controls to determine extended values, such as quantity times unit price or quantity times cost. Now you have enough space at the right of the report to add two columns: one for the Cost field, which is calculated as a percentage of UnitPrice, and one for the extended inventory value, which is UnitPrice multiplied by UnitsInStock. The following subsections explain how to provide the data for and add these controls.

CHANGING THE REPORT'S RECORD SOURCE

You created the Inventory by Category report by selecting fields directly from the Products and Suppliers tables in the Report Wizard. Therefore, the Record Source property for the report as a whole is an SQL statement that selects only the fields that you chose initially in the Report Wizard. Although you can add fields to the report by creating unbound text box controls and using the Expression Builder to create an expression to retrieve the desired value, it's a more straightforward process to create a query to select the desired fields and then substitute the new query as the report's data source. You also can specify record-selection criteria in a query.

Access SQL

Following is the Access SQL statement generated by the Report Wizard:

```
SELECT Products.CategoryID, Products.ProductID,
    Products.ProductName, Products.SupplierID,
    Suppliers.CompanyName, Products.UnitsInStock
FROM Suppliers INNER JOIN Products
    ON Suppliers.SupplierID=Products.SupplierID;
```

Northwind.accdb's Products table includes some products that have been discontinued. Inventory reports shouldn't include counts and valuations of products that no longer are available for sale.

> **TIP**
>
> Alternatively, you can use the Filter and Filter On property values on the Data page of the report's Property Sheet to prevent discontinued products from inclusion in the report. Another approach would be to add a `WHERE NOT Discontinued` clause to the Record Source SQL statement. As a rule, however, it's easier to troubleshoot report problems if you use a query as the Record Source property of the report. The query lets you quickly preview the result set on which your report is based.

To create a query that eliminates discontinued products from the result set, follow these steps:

1. Open a new query in Design view by clicking the Queries shortcut in the Database window and then double-clicking the Create Query in Design View shortcut.
2. Double-click the Products table in the Show Table dialog and then close the dialog.
3. Drag * from the field list to the first column of the query.
4. Drag the Discontinued field to the query grid's second column.
5. Clear the Show check box for the Discontinued field and then type **False** in the Discontinued field's first Criteria row.
6. If you want to list products alphabetically by product name, add the ProductName field and select an ascending sort (see Figure 16.22). Alternatively, you can specify ProductName in the Order By list and set the Order By On property value to Yes.
7. Run the query to test your work, close the Query window, and save your changes using the name **qryInventory**.

> **TIP**
>
> You don't need to add the Suppliers table to the query because the SupplierID field of the Products table supplies the CompanyName lookup value to the table.

Figure 16.22
This query prevents the Inventory by Category report from including discontinued products.

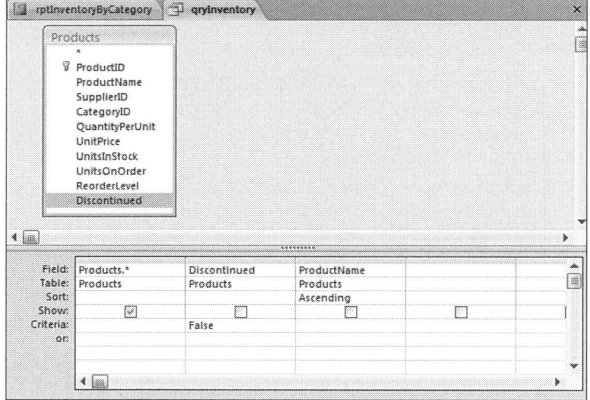

To change the report's Record Source property value to the new query, follow these steps:

1. Open the Inventory by Category report in Report Design view, and click the Select Report button to select the report.

2. Press F4 to open the report's Property Sheet. Then click the Data tab to display the report's data properties.

3. Click the Record Source text box and then use the drop-down list to select the qryInventory query as the report's new Record Source property (see Figure 16.23).

Figure 16.23
Replace the Wizard-generated SQL statement with the new query to serve as the Record Source property value for the report.

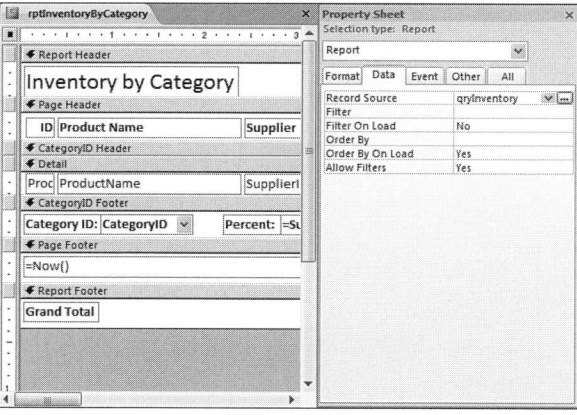

4. Check the report in Print Preview mode, and then save the changes to the report.

ADDING THE CALCULATED CONTROLS

Now that you've changed the report's record source, you have easy access to the UnitPrice field, which you need for adding the calculated Cost and Value fields to the report.

UnitPrice is the selling price of the product, not its cost to Northwind Traders. For this example, assume that Northwind Traders sells its goods at a uniform markup of 50%. In retailing terminology, this means that a product costing $1.00 sells for $1.50, and the inventory value is 66.7% of the UnitPrice value. Thus, the text box expression for the cost of the product is `=[UnitPrice]*0.667` and the value is `=[UnitsInStock]*[UnitPrice]*0.667`.

To add the Cost and Value calculated fields to the report, follow these steps:

1. Return to Design view, and click the Report Design Tools – Design tab.

Aa

2. Click the Label tool in the Controls group and draw a label to the right of the Units label in the Page Header section. Type **Cost** as the caption and click Ctrl+B to set it bold.

B

3. Add another label to the right of Cost and type **Value** as the caption. Then click Ctrl+B to set it bold.

≣

4. If necessary, change the font and size to match the other labels in the Page Header. For this example, click the Right Align button in the Font group. (Access automatically sets the font name, but not the size, bold, alignment, or other font attributes.)

abl
≣|

5. Click the Text Box tool, and add two unbound text boxes in the Detail section under the new labels. Delete the attached labels, and align the right edge of the text boxes under the right edge of the Page Header labels.

6. Click the Arrange tab, select the Cost text box and label, and click the Control Layout group's Tabular button to associate the two controls. Do the same for the Value text box and label.

> **TIP**
>
> A faster method of adding text boxes and labels is to select both the label and the text box and then press Ctrl+C and Ctrl+V to superimpose a copy that has an associated label over the existing controls. Drag the copy to its new location.

7. Select the new Cost text box, open the Property Sheet, click the All tab, type **Cost** in the Name text box, select Currency as the format, and type **=[UnitPrice]*0.667** in the Control Source text box (see Figure 16.24).

8. Select the Value text box, click the All tab, type Value in the Name text box, select Currency as the format, and type **=[UnitsInStock]*[UnitPrice]*0.667** as the expression. Change to Report view to check your work.

> **TIP**
>
>
>
> A good way to enter long, complex expressions is to click the Builder button to open the Expression Builder, which provides a larger text box in which to type the expression.

16

Figure 16.24
Type as the Data Source property value the expression for the value to print in the calculated field text box.

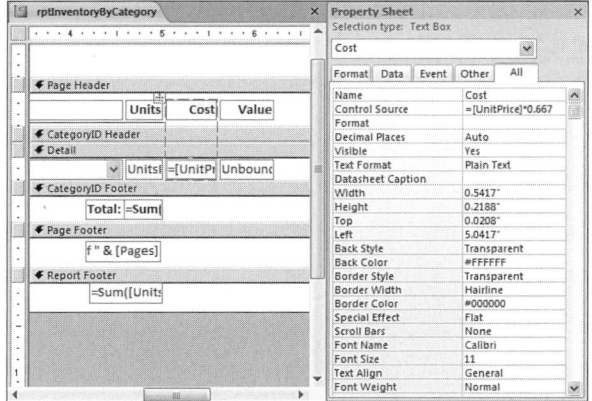

9. Return to Design view, drag the Percent label and text box to the left, and change the label caption to **% Units:**.

10. Add a text box in the CategoryID Footer section under the Value label, but type **=Sum([UnitsInStock]*[UnitPrice]*0.667)** as the Control Source, CatValue as the name, and Currency as the format. Click Ctrl+B to set the Font Weight property to Bold.

11. Repeat step 10 to create the grand total value text box with the **=Sum([UnitsInStock]*[UnitPrice]*0.667)** expression as the control source in the Report Footer section, and set this text box's Name property to **TotalValue**. Set the Font Weight to Bold, and delete the associated label. Also apply the Bold attribute to the Grand Total label.

12. Add another unbound text box to the right of the % Units text box in the CategoryID Footer section. Type **=[CatValue]/[TotalValue]** as the value of the Control Source property, and set the Format property's value to Percent and the Font Weight to Bold. Change the label caption to **% Value** and conform the font.

13. Drag the form's right margin to within about one grid dot of the right edge of the text boxes. The report design at this point appears as shown in Figure 16.25. Press Ctrl+S to save your report.

> *If a Parameters dialog appears when you test your report in Preview mode, see the "Unexpected Parameters Dialogs" topic of the "Troubleshooting" section near the end of the chapter.*

14. Click Print Preview to check the result of your additions. Use the vertical scroll bar, if necessary, to display the category subtotal. The next section describes how you can correct any values that are not aligned properly and the spacing of the Detail section's rows.

15. Click the Bottom of Report page selector button to display the grand totals for the report (see Figure 16.26). The record selector buttons become page selector buttons when you display reports in Print Preview mode.

Figure 16.25
The enhanced report design with added Cost, Value, Cat(egory) Value, and Grand Total Value calculated fields.

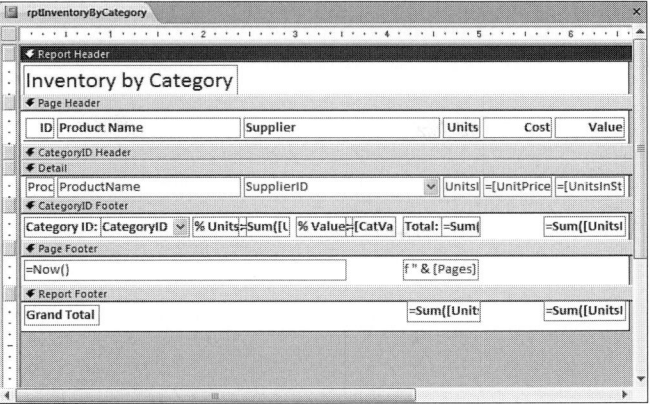

Figure 16.26
The last page of the report displays grand totals for units and inventory values.

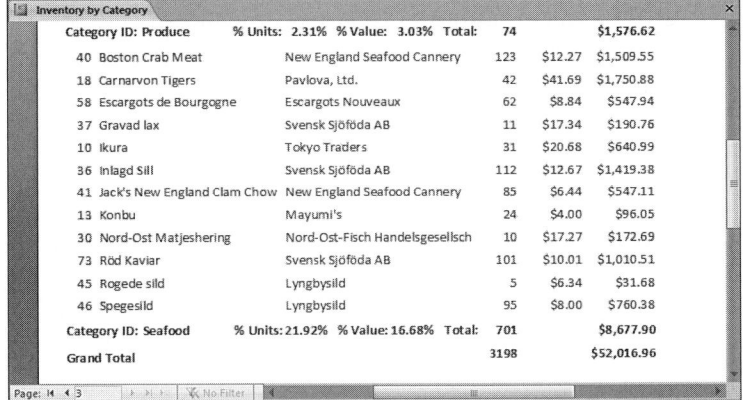

ALIGNING AND FORMATTING CONTROLS AND ADJUSTING LINE SPACING

The exact alignment of label and text box controls is more important on reports than it is on forms because in the printed report any misalignment is obvious. Formatting the controls further improves the report's appearance and readability.

The spacing of the report's rows in the Detail section is controlled by the section's depth. Likewise, you can control the white space above and below the headers and footers by adjusting the depth of their sections and the vertical position of the controls within the sections. To create a professional-looking report, you must adjust the controls' alignment and formatting as well as the sections' line spacing.

ALIGNING CONTROLS HORIZONTALLY AND VERTICALLY

You align controls by first selecting the rows to align and then aligning the columns. Access provides several control-sizing and alignment options to make the process easier.

NOTE

The combination of the Report Wizard's accurate control placement and alignment assistance by the new Layout features minimizes the need to align controls for the preceding scenario. You probably won't see much change when you complete the following steps.

To size and align the controls that you created, follow these steps:

1. If you still have the Inventory by Category report open in Print Preview, click the Close button to return to Design view.

2. Select all labels in the Page Header sections and click the Control Alignment's group's Align Top button. This process aligns the tops of each selected label with the uppermost selected label. Click a blank area of the report to deselect the labels.

3. Select all text boxes in the Detail section and repeat step 2 for the text boxes.

4. Select the labels and text boxes in the CategoryID Footer and Report Footer sections and repeat step 2.

5. Select all controls in the Units column and click the Align Right button so that Access aligns the column to the right edge of the text farthest to the right of the column. Then click the Font group's Align Right button to right-align the contents of the labels and text boxes. (The first part of this step aligns the controls themselves to the rightmost control, and the second part right-aligns the text or data displayed by the selected controls.)

6. Select all controls in the Cost column and repeat step 5.

7. Select all controls in the Values column (except the Page Footer text box) and repeat step 5.

8. Click Report View to display the report with the improved alignment of rows and columns.

FORMATTING CONTROLS

You formatted the currency columns and percent fields as you added them in the preceding sections. However, following are typical changes you need to make to apply accounting-style numeric formats, underlines, and align the header labels with currency columns:

1. In Design view, select the three text boxes related to the Units[inStock] column, press F4 to open the Property Sheet, and type **#,##0** as the Format template to add a thousands separator and display a 0 for null values.

2. The Value column's text box in the Details section is formatted for currency. Accountants prefer individual items to apply currency formatting only to the first item of a group. Access doesn't offer this formatting, but you can remove the currency symbol for all members of a group by specifying Standard format, which corresponds to a **#,##0.00** Format template. Select the Cost and Value text boxes in the Detail section and change the format from Currency to Standard.

3. Standard format doesn't reserve space for accounting-standard parentheses to indicate negative numbers. Therefore, you must move the CatValue and TotalValue text boxes to the right to realign their content with that of the Value items. (It's easier to do this in Layout view).

4. To apply subtotal and grand total lines above and below the appropriate text boxes, select the Line tool and draw lines above the Units and Value subtotal and grand total text boxes and add a pair of lines under the grand total text boxes. (Setting the Font Underline property to Yes only adds a single underline.)

5. Open the report in Report view and scroll to the last page to inspect your handiwork (see Figure 16.27).

Figure 16.27
The last page of the report in Report view displays the changes to item values and the formatting of subtotals/grand totals.

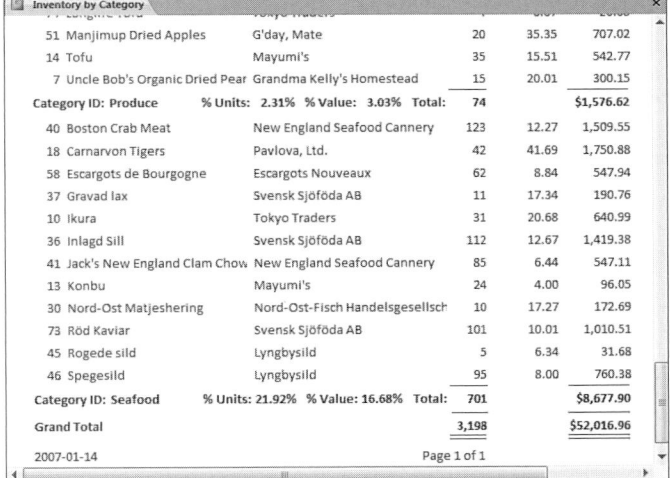

ADJUSTING LINE SPACING

The line spacing of the Inventory by Category report's sections is satisfactory, but you can also change this spacing. Minimizing line spacing allows you to print a report on fewer sheets of paper. You also can use the Can Grow property of text boxes to prevent truncation of long text items.

To change the spacing of the report's Page Header and Detail sections, follow these steps:

1. Change to report Design view.

2. Select all labels in the Page Header and move the group to the top of the section. The gridline moves with the labels.

3. Drag the CategoryID Footer section up to the bottom of the Detail section's text boxes.

4. A few ProductName and supplier CompanyName items exceed the width of their text boxes and are truncated. You can eliminate the truncation by setting the Can Grow property value for the text boxes to Yes. However, you have a substantial amount of free horizontal space, which allows widening the text boxes if you keep the printing margins within bounds.

5. Change to Report view to check the Page Header depth and line spacing of the Detail section. You can't reduce a section's line spacing to less than that required by the tallest text box or label by reducing the section's Height property in the Properties box. If you try this approach, Access rejects the entry and substitutes the prior value.

6. Select all controls in the Detail section and press F4 to open the Property Sheet. Change the Height property value to 0.18", which changes to 0.1799". Figure 16.28 illustrates the resulting truncation of text descenders.

7. Attempting to change the Top property value from the default 0.0208" to 0" fails because the Top Padding property value is set to 0.0208". Change the Top Padding property value to 0" and try again. Drag the CategoryID footer up to the bottom of the text boxes.

Figure 16.28
The report shows the effect of adjusting the depth of the Report Header, Page Header, and Detail sections, and reducing the Height of the Detail section's text boxes below about 0.185" (see the truncated letter g's in Laughing and Big).

Inventory by Category

ID	Product Name	Supplier	Units	Cost	Value
1	Chai	Exotic Liquids	39	12.01	468.23
2	Chang	Exotic Liquids	17	12.67	215.44
39	Chartreuse verte	Aux joyeux ecclésiastiques	69	12.01	828.41
38	Côte de Blaye	Aux joyeux ecclésiastiques	17	175.75	2,987.83
43	Ipoh Coffee	Leka Trading	17	30.68	521.59
76	Lakkalikööri	Karkki Oy	57	12.01	684.34
67	Laughing Lumberjack Lager	Bigfoot Breweries	52	9.34	485.58
70	Outback Lager	Pavlova, Ltd.	15	10.01	150.08
75	Rhönbräu Klosterbier	Plutzer Lebensmittelgroßmärkte	125	5.17	646.16
34	Sasquatch Ale	Bigfoot Breweries	111	9.34	1,036.52
35	Steeleye Stout	Bigfoot Breweries	20	12.01	240.12
Category ID: Beverages	**% Units: 16.85% % Value: 15.89% Total:**		**539**		**$8,264.30**
3	Aniseed Syrup	Exotic Liquids	13	6.67	86.71
4	Chef Anton's Cajun Seasoning	New Orleans Cajun Delights	53	14.67	777.72
92	Chu Hou Sauce	Zhongshan Sauces Co., Ltd.	5	8.17	40.85
83	Cucumber Kimchi (Bag)	Seoul Kimchi Co., Ltd.	4	150.08	600.30
82	Cucumber Kimchi (Jar)	Seoul Kimchi Co., Ltd.	8	28.35	226.78
93	Garlic Chili Sauce	Zhongshan Sauces Co., Ltd.	10	7.84	78.37
15	Genen Shouyu	Mayumi's	39	10.34	403.20
6	Grandma's Boysenberry Spread	Grandma Kelly's Homestead	120	16.68	2,001.00
44	Gula Malacca	Leka Trading	27	12.97	350.28
91	Hoisin Garlic Sauce	Zhongshan Sauces Co., Ltd.	15	7.00	105.05

8. Change the Height property to 0.185", which Access changes to 0.1847", to eliminate the text truncation and then press Ctrl+S to save your changes.

The Inventory by Category report, completed to this point, is included on the accompanying CD-ROM as Report16.accdb in the \SEUA12\Chaptr16 folder.

ADJUSTING MARGINS AND PRINTING CONVENTIONAL REPORTS

 Clicking the One Page button in Print Preview shows the report as it would print using Access 2007's new default printing margins of 0.25" on the top, bottom, and sides of the report (see Figure 16.29). In the Print Preview's Print Setup dialog, you can adjust the printed version of the report. The procedure for printing a report applies to printing the data contained in tables and queries as well as single-record or continuous forms.

16

Figure 16.29
One Page view shows the report with the default 0.25" printing margins.

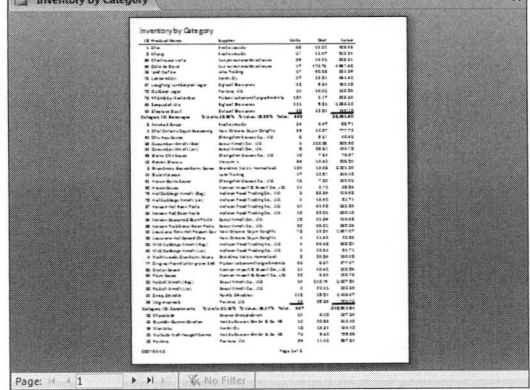

NOTE

You also can change the printing margins by clicking the Print Preview ribbon's Margins button and selecting <u>N</u>ormal or <u>W</u>ide. However, these margins might not meet your requirements.

To change the printing margins for a report, follow these steps:

1. Open the report, choose Print Preview mode, and click the ribbon's Page Setup button to open the Page Setup dialog.

2. The Page Setup dialog is similar to the Print and Page Setup dialogs of other Windows applications, with a section for printing margins included. To increase the amount of information on a page, decrease the top and bottom margins. By selecting the Print Data Only check box, you can print only the data in the report; the Report and Page Headers and Footers don't print.

16

NOTE

The Page Setup dialog's default settings are 0.75" top and bottom, and 0.35" left and right, which correspond to the Margins gallery's Normal choice.

3. In the Left text box, type **1** to specify a 1.0" left margin for a three-hole punch. Type **0.5** in the Right text box. In the Top and Bottom text boxes, type **0.5** (see Figure 16.30). Click OK to see a One Page view of the report with the revised margins (see Figure 16.31).

Figure 16.30
The Page Setup dialog lets you set margins and other property values for printing reports, forms, datasheets, and other Access objects.

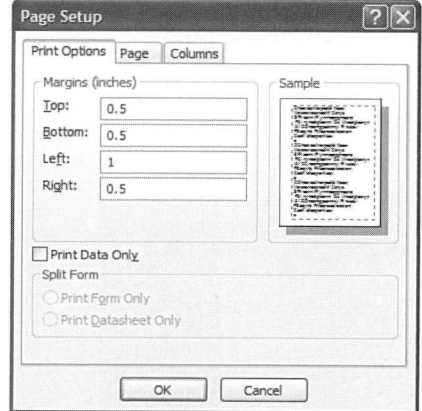

Figure 16.31
The One Page preview shows the effect of applying the margin settings shown in Figure 16.30.

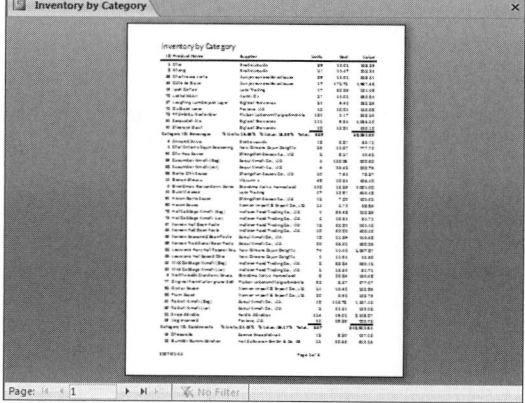

TIP

The printing margins that you establish for a report in the Page Setup dialog apply to the active report only; each report has a unique set of margins. When you save the report, Access saves its margin settings.

4. To print the report, click the Print button. The standard Print dialog appears for the printer specified in Windows as the default printer. Figure 16.32 shows, as an example, the Print dialog for a networked Brother laser printer. The Setup button opens the Page Setup dialog (refer to Figure 16.30).

Figure 16.32
The Print dialog lets you select the printer, pages to print, number of copies, and collation sequence.

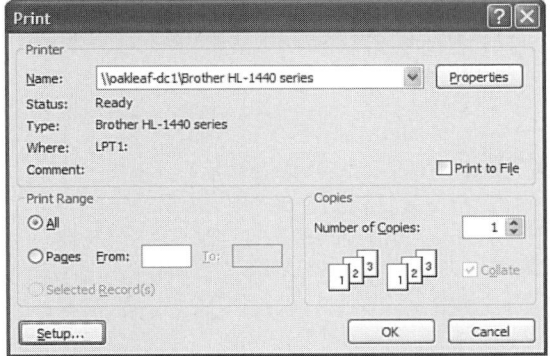

> **TIP**
>
> You can print the report without displaying the Print dialog by clicking the Office button and clicking Print, Quick Print.

5. You can print all or part of a report or print the report to a file for later printing; you can also select the number of copies to print. By clicking the Properties button, you can change the parameters that apply to the selected printer. Click OK to print the report.

The Page Setup dialog includes a Columns page that allows you to establish specifications for printing mailing labels and other multiple-column reports. The "Printing Multicolumn Reports as Mailing Labels" section describes these specifications and how you set them.

PREVENTING WIDOWED RECORDS WITH THE GROUP KEEP TOGETHER PROPERTY

Access includes a property for groups, called Keep Together, that prevents widowed records from appearing at the bottom of the page. Depending on your report section depths, you might find that only a few records of the next group (called widowed records) appear at the bottom of the page. The report designs shown in Figures 16.29 and 16.31 have five and two widowed records at the bottom of the first report page, respectively.

You can force a page break when an entire group doesn't fit on a page by following these steps:

 1. With the report in Design view, click the Group & Sort button to open the Group, Sort, and Total pane below the report Design window.

2. Select the group that you want to keep together. For this example, select CategoryID.

3. Click the More link to expand the grouping options, open the Do Not Keep Group Together on One Page option's list, and choose Keep Whole Group Together on One Page, as shown in Figure 16.33.

Figure 16.33
Select the group to keep together (CategoryID), and select Keep Whole Group Together on One Page.

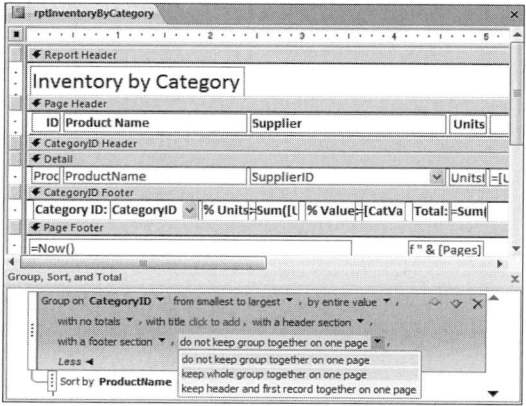

 4. Click the Sort & Group button again to close the Group, Sort, and Total pane and then select Report View to see the result of applying the group Keep Together property.

The Report Wizard makes the entries in the Sorting and Grouping dialog for you. The next chapter describes how to use the Group, Sort, and Total pane to design reports without the aid of the Wizard.

PRINTING MULTICOLUMN REPORTS AS MAILING LABELS

Access lets you print multicolumn reports. You can create a single-column report with the Report Wizard, for example, and then arrange the report to print values from the Detail section in a specified number of columns across the page. The most common application of multicolumn reports is the creation of mailing labels.

CREATING A MAILING LABEL WITH THE LABEL WIZARD

You can create mailing lists with the Label Wizard, or you can start with a blank form. The Label Wizard's advantage is that it includes the dimensions of virtually every kind of adhesive label for ink-jet and laser printers made by the Avery Commercial Products division and several other North American and overseas manufacturers. You select the product number of the label that you plan to use, and Access determines the number of columns, rows per page, and margins for the report's Detail section. You also can customize the Label Wizard for labels with unusual sizes or those produced by manufacturers who aren't included in the Wizard's repertoire. Several label manufacturers include a note with their products that indicates the corresponding Avery label number.

To create mailing labels with the Label Wizard, using the Customers table for this example, do the following:

1. Select the Customers table in the Navigation Pane.

2. In the Create ribbon's Reports group, click the Labels button to start the Label Wizard.

3. If you're using Avery labels, select the product code (5160 for this example). Otherwise, select the manufacturer in the list, and select the product code for a three-across label. Accept the Sheet Feed option if you're using laser-printer labels (see Figure 16.34). Click Next.

Figure 16.34
The first dialog of the Label Wizard lets you select a manufacturer and then a label size available from the manufacturer.

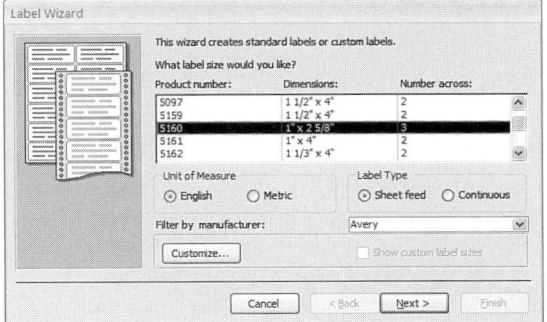

4. In the second Wizard dialog, select the font family, size, and weight for the label. The defaults—8-point Arial light—make the labels hard to read. This example uses 9-point Courier New medium (see Figure 16.35). Click Next.

Figure 16.35
Specify the printer font and its attributes in the second Label Wizard dialog.

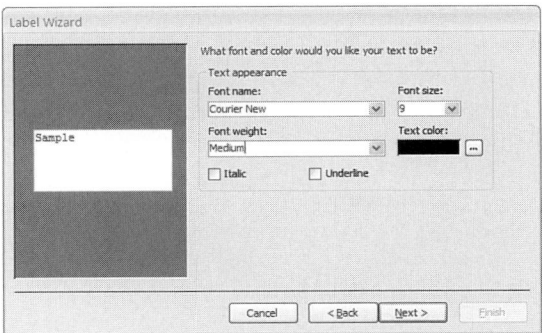

5. In the third Wizard dialog, select the field of the record source for the label's first row—ContactName for this example—and click the > button to add it to the Prototype Label text box. Press Enter to add a new line.

6. Repeat step 4 for the CompanyName and Address fields.

7. Select City, click >, and add a comma and a space.

8. Select Region, click >, add two spaces, select PostalCode, and click >. Your Prototype label appears as shown in Figure 16.36.

Figure 16.36
The Prototype Label text box displays the label design as you add fields from the Available Fields list.

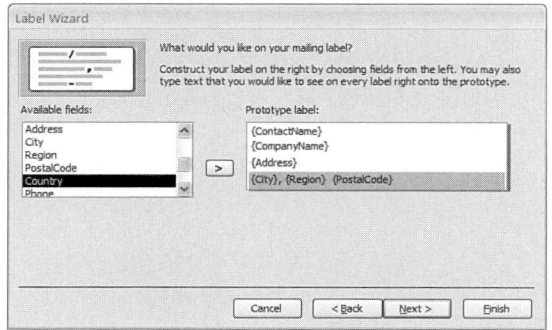

9. If the mailing is international, add an additional line for the Country field.

NOTE

Although the Avery 5160 label has sufficient depth to add the Country field with 9-point type, the Wizard doesn't let you add more than four lines.

10. Click Next and specify the fields on which to sort the labels. Even if you couldn't add the Country field, double-click Country in the Available fields list and then double-click PostalCode (see Figure 16.37). Click Next.

Figure 16.37
Specify the sort order for the labels in the fourth Label Wizard dialog.

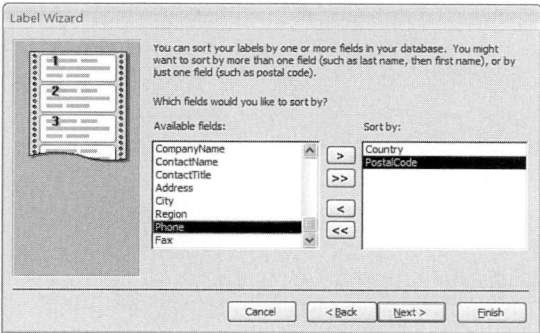

11. In the fifth Wizard dialog, type a name for the report, such as **rptCustomerLabels**, and click Finish to display the labels in Report view.

In many cases, you receive the error message shown in Figure 16.38 prior to opening the report in Report view or Print Preview. The error message for the preceding example is due to the Wizard's miscalculation of column widths, which you correct in the next section. Click OK to dismiss the message and display the labels in Report view or Print Preview (see Figure 16.39).

Figure 16.38
This error message occurs when using Avery 5160 labels, because the Label Wizard's page layout settings require a page width of 8.625 inches.

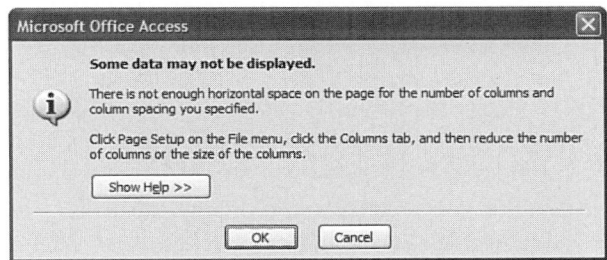

NOTE

If the right margin is set to 0.25, you don't receive the error message shown in Figure 16.38. If you receive the message, choose File, Page Setup to open the Page Setup dialog, and set the right margin value to 0.25.

Figure 16.39
Print Preview with the Navigation Pane hidden shows the first few labels in 1,024×768 resolution. Choose 75% in the Zoom button's gallery to check the top and side margins if your monitor is set to 800×600 resolution.

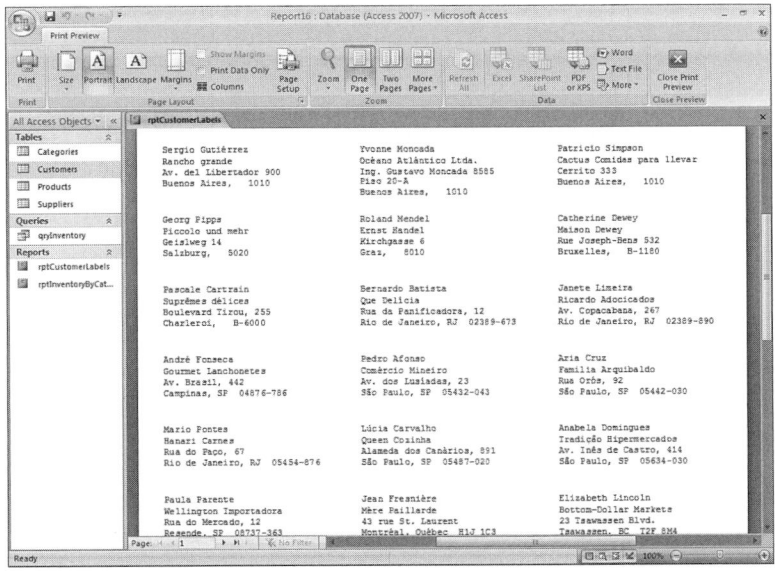

MODIFYING AN EXISTING MAILING LABEL REPORT

The Wizard doesn't let you add a line for Country, so you must alter the design of the report manually. To add the Country field to the label you created in the preceding section, do the following:

1. Change to report Design view, press Ctrl+A to select all the text boxes, and move them up within one grid dot of the bottom of the Detail section header.

2. Click outside the text boxes to deselect them, select the ContactName text box, press Ctrl+C and Ctrl+V to add a copy of the text box to the Detail section.

3. Move the added text box directly under the Trim([City]... text box.

4. Right-click the added text box, choose Properties to open the Property Sheet, click the Data tab, and select Country in the Control Source list.

5. If you didn't add Country as the first sorting field in the fourth Wizard dialog, click the Sorting and Grouping button to open the dialog of the same name, select PostalCode, click Insert, and add Country above Postal Code in the Field/Expression list. Then close the dialog.

6. To prepare for fixing the Wizard's column width miscalculation, press Ctrl+A to select the text boxes and move them one grid dot to the left.

7. Click the Select Report button, click the Format tab of the Property Sheet, and replace the 2.625 Width property value with **2.583**. When you move the cursor to another text box, 2.583 becomes 2.5826. Your modified design appears as shown in Figure 16.40.

Figure 16.40
The modified label report design has the Country field added, text boxes relocated, and the width reduced.

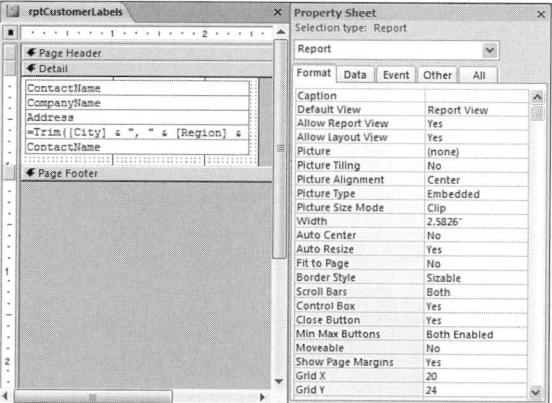

> **NOTE**
>
> Following is the explanation of the 2.583-inch width for the label report: The Control Wizard calculates the required page width in inches as follows: 0.25 (left margin) + 3 * 2.625 (label width) + 2 * 0.125 (column spacing) + 0.25 (right margin) = 8.625. (In some cases, the right margin is 0.30, but you can change that to 0.25.) You need to reduce the width of the labels so the page width is 8.5 or less. Dividing 0.125 by 3, rounding up to 0.042, and subtracting from 2.625 results in a required width of 2.583.
>
> The result of the preceding calculation isn't perfect, because you need to take into account the reduced column width in setting the column spacing.

8. Click Print Preview and zoom the report to 100% scale. Verify that label spacing is consistent. In this example, the label for Yvonne Moncada has an extra address line. The added line pushes down labels below the row with the extra line, which results in a print registration error (see Figure 16.41). Registration errors of this type are cumulative, so if more than one row of a label page has an extra line, the registration problem becomes serious.

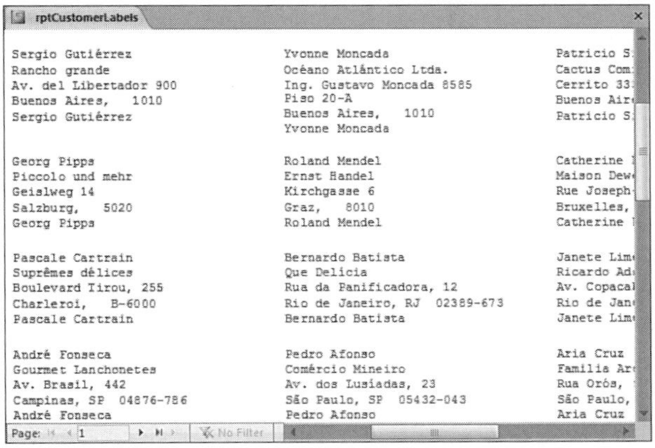

Figure 16.41
The increased space between the first and second lines of the labels is due to an extra line in the Address field of the label for Yvonne Moncada.

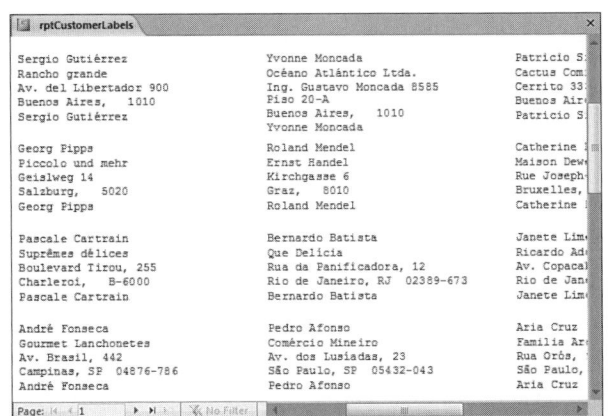

9. To correct the spacing problem, return to Design view, select the Details section's header bar, open the Property Sheet, click the Format tab, and set the Can Grow property value to No. Preventing the Detail section from expanding results in all rows having the same spacing (compare Figure 16.42 with Figure 16.41).

Figure 16.42
Setting the Can Grow property value of the Detail section of the label report prevents print registration problems. The space for four-line addresses between the first and second rows is now the same as that between other rows.

16

10. Press Ctrl+S to save your design changes, change to Print Preview, and print a sample of all pages on plain paper. If your labels appear to print correctly, print the first page on label stock for a test. If registration is correct, print the remaining pages.

> **NOTE**
>
> Tests with Avery 5160 labels and a Brother HL-1440 laser printer demonstrate that the left, top, and bottom margins set by the Wizard are satisfactory. You can fit six lines of 9-point type on a one-inch-deep label.

The Page Setup dialog lets you tweak the Wizard's settings and your adjustments to improve label printing registration. You specify the number of columns in a row and the number of rows on a page by selecting settings in the Columns page of the Page Setup dialog, as shown in Figure 16.43. This dialog opens when you choose File, Page Setup in either Print Preview or Report Design view. The Label Wizard sets these values for you automatically, and they change when you set new printing-related property values, but you might need to tweak them for the label stock or printer you use.

Figure 16.43
The Columns page of the Page Setup dialog lets you set the printing properties for reports using newspaper (snaking) columns. You also can change the column spacing and width, and the height (depth) of the labels.

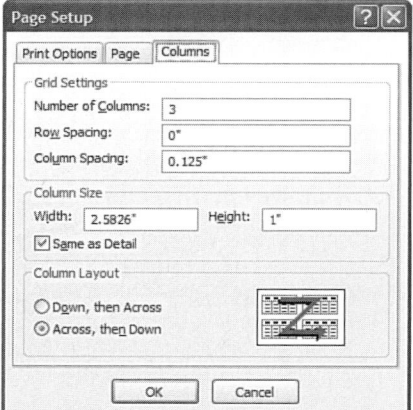

The dialog's text boxes, check boxes, and option buttons let you set the following printing properties:

- The Number of Columns property sets the number of labels across the page. In this example, this property is set to 3, so the labels print three across.

> **NOTE**
>
> The Left and Top margin settings (which you set on the Margins tab of the Page Setup dialog) specify the position at which Access prints the upper-left corner of the first label on the page. For most laser and inkjet printers, these values can't be less than about 0.25 inches. Labels designed for laser and inkjet printers are die cut so that the marginal areas remain on the backing sheet when you remove the individual labels.

- Row Spacing and the Height property determine the number of labels that fit vertically on a page and the vertical distance between successive labels. If you set Row Spacing to 0, the depth of your Detail section determines the vertical spacing of the labels.

- Column Spacing specifies the position of the left edge of columns to the right of the first column.

- The Width property in the Column Size group overrides the left margin, and the Height property overrides the bottom margin that you establish in Report Design view only if you clear the Same as Detail check box.

- The Down, Then Across option causes the labels to print in snaking column style. The first column is filled from top to bottom, then the second column is filled from top to bottom, and so on.

- The Across, Then Down option, the default for Wizard-created labels, causes the labels to print in columns from left to right and then in rows from the top to the bottom of the page. This setting is preferred for mailing labels because it wastes less label stock when using continuous-feed printers to print on stock with more than one label across.

NOTE

> You might have to make minor alignment adjustments because the upper-left corner of the printer's image and the upper-left corner of the paper might not correspond exactly.

The rptCustomerLabels report is included in Report16.accdb on the accompanying CD-ROM in the \SEUA12\Chaptr16 folder.

TROUBLESHOOTING

ELIMINATING EMPTY PAGES

When previewing or printing a report, Access displays or prints a blank page after each page with data.

If a report's width becomes greater than the net printable width (the paper width minus the sum of the left and right margins), the number of report pages doubles. Columns of fields that don't fit a page's width print on a second page, similar to the printing method used by spreadsheet applications. If you set your right margin beyond the right printing margin or if the right edge of any control on the report extends past the right printing margin, the added pages often are blank. Change the printing margins or reduce the width of your report so that it conforms to the printable page width. (See the section "Adjusting Margins and Printing Conventional Reports" earlier in this chapter.)

UNEXPECTED PARAMETERS DIALOGS

A Parameters dialog appears when I change to report Preview mode, but the query to which the report is bound doesn't have parameters.

You misspelled one or more objects—usually text box or query field names—in expressions for text boxes or other controls that use calculated values. Click Cancel and verify that the expression in the Record Source property for each text box or other control on the report contains valid object names.

IN THE REAL WORLD—THE EPHEMERAL PAPERLESS OFFICE

Business magazines of the 1980s and early 1990s touted the forthcoming "paperless office." Articles envisioned scanning incoming documents, storing the images in disk files, and handling all document processing on PC workstations. Document imaging and storage system vendors introduced a wide range of expensive hardware to support the paperless office concept. A new breed of consultants arrived on the scene to develop the workflow systems required to integrate document-processing hardware with existing business processes. Document imaging, workflow, and portal-based collaboration systems have become a multi-billion dollar industry. Windows SharePoint Services 3.0 supports Windows Workflow Foundation to define workflows for collaborative document management.

Automotive and other large firms developed electronic document interchange (EDI) to process orders, invoices, and payments electronically. Email became a top contender to eliminate ever-growing piles of interoffice memos. Now large and small organizations alike are replacing complex EDI systems and their high-cost private (called *value-added*) networks with XML documents, XML Schema Definition (XSD) language, XSLT transformations, and the Internet.

XML-based business-to-business (B2B) communication was one of the hot topics of the 2000 dot-net boom. Despite the subsequent decline of stock market valuation of firms at the bleeding edge of the erstwhile business-to-consumer (B2C) revolution, B2B transactions with standards-based XML web services continue to replace B2C e-commerce as a major source of revenue for an army of software vendors and consultants. Much of Microsoft's .NET Framework and Visual Studio .NET marketing effort is directed to early adopters of XML web services and other accouterments of Service-Oriented Architecture (SOA), such as Windows Communications Framework (WCF). Office 2007 isn't immune to web services propaganda because Microsoft offers an Office Web Services Toolkit, as well as Visual Studio Tools for Office, to simplify consumption of XML web services.

Paperless office is an oxymoron—the most popular PC peripheral component continues to be the printer. Sales of printer paper continue to grow at better than 10% per year, and the market for copiers and fax machines shows no signs of a significant slowdown, despite the dramatic year-over-year decreases in disk drives' cost per gigabyte. According to Hewlett-Packard, 90% of information in 1997 was stored on paper and 10% was in digital format; by

2004, HP estimated that paper-based storage had dropped to 30%, with digital files holding 70%. The total amount of stored information doubles every four years or so. Thus, HP projects a continuing increase in the demand for printers and paper, and printers continue to deliver HP's highest margins.

Beginning with version 1.0, one of Access's strongest selling points has been its versatile, integrated report-printing capabilities. The report event model lets you write VBA code to customize report generation. Most other database front-end development platforms have add-on report generators, such as Crystal Decisions' Crystal Reports. Visual Basic 6.0's Report Designer, which replaces prior versions' Crystal Reports add-on, doesn't even come close to offering the rich feature set of Access 2007 reports. Visual Studio .NET 1.0 lacks an integrated report designer and relies on a "Lite" add-on version of Crystal Reports. SQL Server 2000 and 2005's Reporting Services rivals the flexibility of Access reports and offers enterprise-scale deployment options. However, designing complex reports isn't as easy with Reporting Services as it is with Access.

As this chapter demonstrates, designing and implementing informative, attractive reports can be a tedious process. Exact alignment and proper formatting of labels, text boxes, lines, and other report controls is far more important to reports than forms. Spending the time needed to make reports concise and graphically appealing is worthwhile, especially when you consider that paper reports most likely are destined for management. Cubicle operatives now fulfill most of their information needs electronically.

There have been surprisingly few changes to Access's report printing engine over the years, and Access 2007 incorporates no new report design features. (Access 2007 has inherited the Avery 5160 bug, discussed in this chapter's "Modifying an Existing Mailing Label Report" section, from Access 97). Access 2002 delivered the capability to export live and static reports in XML format, as well as in HTML for web distribution. Chapter 23, "Importing and Exporting Web Pages," covers web-based reports in detail.

16

CHAPTER 17

PREPARING ADVANCED REPORTS

In this chapter

CREATING REPORTS FROM SCRATCH

Access 2007's Report Wizard can create reports that you can use "as is" or modify to suit most of your database reporting requirements. In many cases, however, you must create reports that are more complex than or different from those offered by the Report Wizard. For example, you might have to apply special grouping and sorting methods to your reports. Including subreports within your reports requires that you start from a blank report form instead of using the Report Wizard. Like subforms, subreports use master-child relationships to provide detail information, such as the orders placed by each customer by year, quarter, or month.

Reports make extensive use of unbound fields having calculated values. To understand fully the process of designing advanced Access reports independently of the Report Wizard, you must be familiar with VBA and Access functions, which are two of the subjects of Chapter 10, "Understanding Access Operators and Expressions." You also must understand the methods that you use to create and design forms, which are covered in Chapter 14, "Creating and Using Basic Access Forms," and Chapter 15, "Designing Custom Multitable Forms." Reports make extensive use of Access functions such as `Sum()` and VBA expressions such as `="Subtotal of" & [FieldName] & ":"`. If you skipped Chapters 10, 14, or 15, you might want to refer to the appropriate sections of those chapters whenever you encounter unfamiliar subjects or terminology in this chapter.

NOTE

> The report design techniques you learn in this chapter apply, for the most part, to Access data projects (ADPs). The queries on which you base reports in an ADP must conform to Transact-SQL syntax. For example, you can't use Access SQL's `TRANSFORM…PIVOT` statements to create ADP reports based on crosstab queries. You also can't include Access-specific functions, such as `DLookup()`, that are provided by the Access expression service. Chapter 22, "Upsizing Access Applications to Access Data Projects," describes the workarounds you need to adapt Access-based reports to ADPs.

GROUPING AND SORTING REPORT DATA

Most reports you create require that you organize the data into groups and subgroups in a style similar to the outline of a book. The Report Wizard lets you establish the initial grouping and sorting properties for your data, but you might want to rearrange your report's data after reviewing the Report Wizard's first draft.

The Group, Sort, and Total pane (see Figure 17.1) lets you modify these report properties in design mode. The sections that follow modify the Inventory by Category report that you created in the preceding chapter. The sorting and grouping methods described here, however, apply to any report that you create. To display the pane, open the report in Layout or Design view and click the Format or Design ribbon's Group & Sort button.

Figure 17.1
Use the Group, Sort, and Total pane to classify and sort your reports by numeric or alphabetic values.

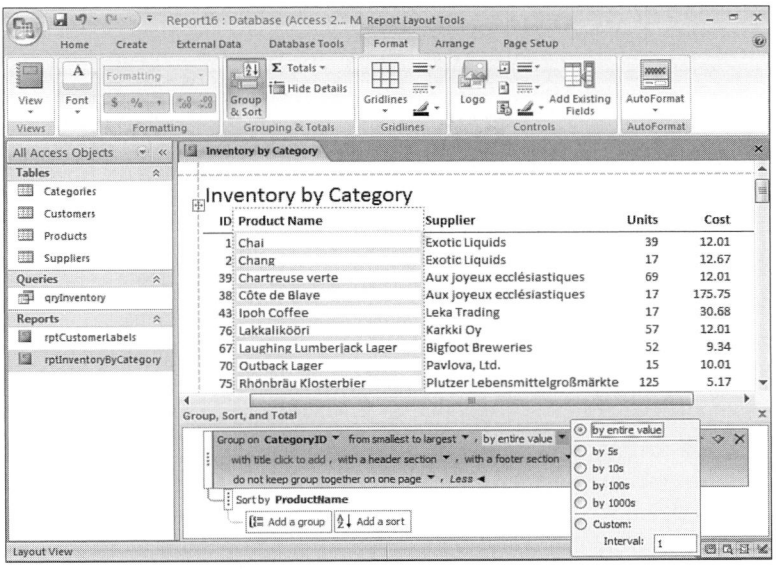

Property values you set in the Group, Sort, and Total pane determine the fields or expressions on which Access is to group the products, up to a maximum of 10 fields or expressions. You can sort the groups and grouped data in ascending (from smallest to largest, or *A* on top) or descending (from largest to smallest, or *Z* on top) order, but you must select one or the other; "unsorted" isn't an option.

NOTE

Apparently, the Access 2007 team wasn't confident Access users would understand the terms *ascending* and *descending order* for numeric and alphabetic values.

GROUPING DATA

The method that you use to group data depends on the type of data in the field you plan to group. You can group by categories, in which case a unique value must represent each category. You can group data by a range of values, which usually is numeric but also can be alphabetic. You can use the data in a field to group the report rows, or you can substitute an expression as the basis for the grouping.

NOTE

Reports demonstrating the grouping examples in the following sections are included in the Report17.accdb database in the \SEUA12\Chaptr17 folder of the accompanying CD-ROM.

GROUPING BY NUMERIC VALUES

When you told the Report Wizard in the preceding chapter to use CategoryID as the field by which to group, you elected to group by a numeric value. You can alter the grouping sequence easily by using the Group, Sort, and Total pane. For example, you can group the inventory report by SupplierID to aid in comparing the inventory turnover rate of products from multiple suppliers. The report you create in the later "Working from a Blank Report" section provides some insight into inventory turnover by product category, not by supplier.

→ To review the Report Wizard process, **see** "Creating a Grouped Report with the Report Wizard," **p. 704.**

To group the Inventory by Category report by SupplierID, do the following:

1. If you don't already have it open, open the rptInventoryByCategory report in Design view, and save the report as **rptInventoryBySupplier**. Change the title text box and report Caption property value to **Inventory by Supplier**.

2. Click the Design tab and the Group & Sort button, open CategoryID's drop-down list in the Group, Sort, and Total pane, and select SupplierID as the first group field. When you change the group field, Access automatically renames the Group Header and Footer sections from CategoryID to SupplierID. Close the Group, Sort, and Total pane.

3. Delete the CategoryID label and lookup list in the SupplierID Footer section; CategoryID isn't appropriate to the new grouping.

4. Click the Add Existing Fields button to open the Field List and drag the SupplierID field to the SupplierID Footer section. Then drop it in the position formerly occupied by CategoryID. SupplierID is a lookup field, so the new control for the field is a drop-down list.

5. Delete the SupplierID label and position the SupplierID list at the top left of the Footer section. Remove the % Units label and text box to make room for the long CompanyName values displayed by the SupplierID list. Widen the SupplierID control to about 3 inches, and apply the Bold attribute (see Figure 17.2).

Figure 17.2
You can quickly repurpose an existing report by changing its Group By property value and making minor design changes to the new report.

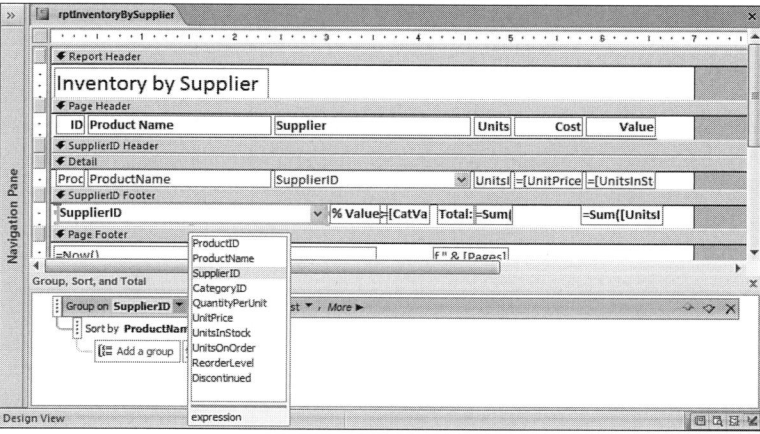

6. Save your design changes, and open the report in Print Preview (see Figure 17.3).

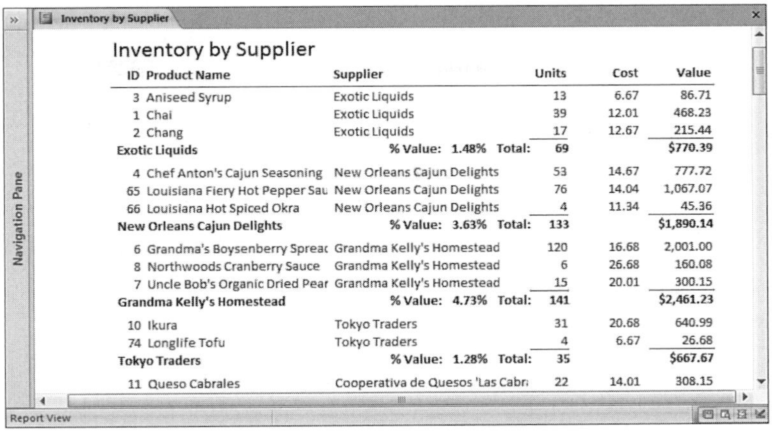

Figure 17.3
The Supplier column in the repurposed inventory report is redundant, but doesn't detract from the overall value of the report.

	Inventory by Supplier					✕
	Inventory by Supplier					
ID	**Product Name**	**Supplier**	**Units**	**Cost**	**Value**	
3	Aniseed Syrup	Exotic Liquids	13	6.67	86.71	
1	Chai	Exotic Liquids	39	12.01	468.23	
2	Chang	Exotic Liquids	17	12.67	215.44	
Exotic Liquids		% Value: 1.48% Total:	69		$770.39	
4	Chef Anton's Cajun Seasoning	New Orleans Cajun Delights	53	14.67	777.72	
65	Louisiana Fiery Hot Pepper Sau	New Orleans Cajun Delights	76	14.04	1,067.07	
66	Louisiana Hot Spiced Okra	New Orleans Cajun Delights	4	11.34	45.36	
New Orleans Cajun Delights		% Value: 3.63% Total:	133		$1,890.14	
6	Grandma's Boysenberry Sprea	Grandma Kelly's Homestead	120	16.68	2,001.00	
8	Northwoods Cranberry Sauce	Grandma Kelly's Homestead	6	26.68	160.08	
7	Uncle Bob's Organic Dried Pear	Grandma Kelly's Homestead	15	20.01	300.15	
Grandma Kelly's Homestead		% Value: 4.73% Total:	141		$2,461.23	
10	Ikura	Tokyo Traders	31	20.68	640.99	
74	Longlife Tofu	Tokyo Traders	4	6.67	26.68	
Tokyo Traders		% Value: 1.28% Total:	35		$667.67	
11	Queso Cabrales	Cooperativa de Quesos 'Las Cabri	22	14.01	308.15	

Report View

NOTE

It only requires a bit more work to change the SupplierID field in the detail section to CategoryID, reduce the width of the list text box, move the field to the right, and increase the width of the Product Name column to display the entire names.

GROUPING BY ALPHABETIC CODE CHARACTERS

If you use a systematic code for grouping, you can group by the first five or fewer characters of the code field. With an expression, you can group by any set of characters within a field. To group by the second and third digits of a code, for example, use the following expression:

```
=Mid([FieldName], 2, 2)
```

Mid's first numeric argument is the position of the starting character on which to group, and the second is the number of characters to use for grouping.

GROUPING WITH SUBGROUPS

If your table or query contains appropriate data, you can group reports by more than one level by creating subgroups. The Employee Sales by Country report (one of the Northwind Traders sample reports), for example, uses groups (Country) and subgroups (the employee's name—the actual group is a VBA expression that combines the FirstName and LastName fields) to organize orders received within a range of dates. Open the Employee Sales by Country report in Design view to view the additional section created by a subgroup. Change to Print Preview, and type **1/1/2006** and **12/31/2006** as the values of the Beginning Date and Ending Date Enter Parameter Value dialogs to view all orders.

USING A FUNCTION TO GROUP BY RANGE

You often must sort reports by ranges of values. (If you opened the Employee Sales by Country report, close it and reopen the rptInventoryByCategory report in Design mode.) If you want to divide the Inventory by Category report into a maximum of nine sections—each beginning with a three-letter group of the alphabet (*A* through *C*, *D* through *F*, and so on) based on the ProductName field—the entries in the Group, Sort, and Total pane should look like the entries in Figure 17.4.

Figure 17.4
Set the Group By properties to those shown here to group product names by a three-initial-letter interval.

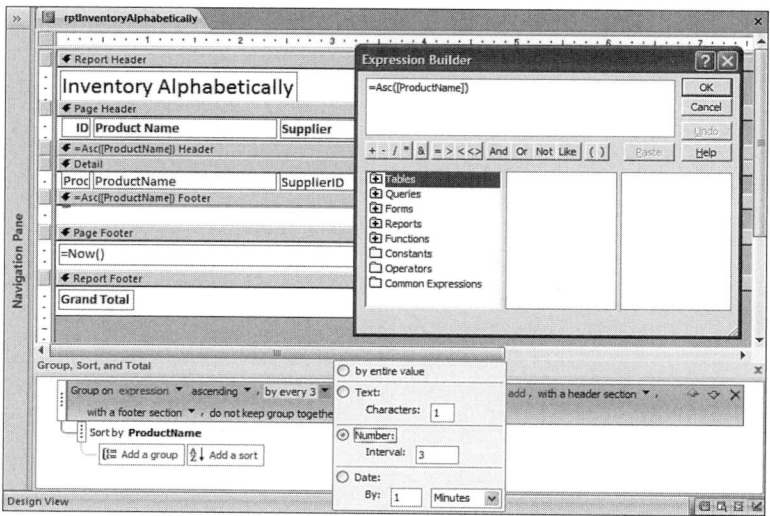

NOTE

Requiring users to type an expression in a separate, unrelated dialog is an example of poor interface design. The single Sorting and Grouping dialog of earlier Access versions is much more straightforward than this approach.

Alphabetic grouping demonstrates a grouping bug that has been present since Access 2.0. VBA's `=Asc([ProductName])` function returns the ASCII (numeric) value of the first character of its string argument, the ProductName field. You set the Group On specification to Expression to open the Expression Builder, type **=Asc([ProductName])**, and then set the interval (by every) to 3. This setup *theoretically* groups the data into names beginning with *A* through *C*, *D* through *F*, and so on. You must add an ascending sort on ProductName to ensure alphabetic sorting within the group (see Figure 17.5). You can replace all text boxes in the Group Footer with a separation line because subtotals by alphabetic groups aren't significant. Although of limited value in this report, an alphabetic grouping often is useful for formatting long, alphabetized lists to assist readers in finding a particular record.

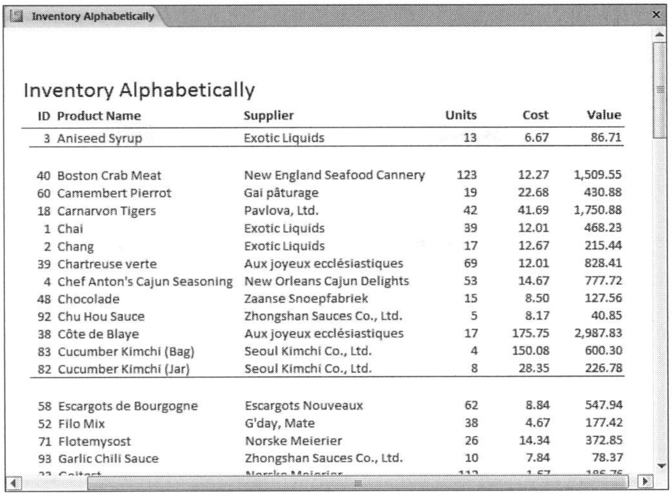

Figure 17.5
A bug in Access's interval grouping process when using a VBA expression causes grouping by *A*, *B* to *D*, *E* to *G*, and so on. This bug has been present since Access 2.0.

GROUPING ON DATE AND TIME

If you group data on a field with a Date/Time data type, Access lets you set the Group, Sort, and Total pane's Group On property to Year, Qtr (quarter), Month, Week, Day, Hour, or Minute. To group records so that values of the same quarter for several years print in sequence, type the following in the Field/Expression column of the Sorting and Grouping dialog:

```
=DatePart("q",[FieldName])
```

→ For a full listing of ways you can sort by date or time, **see** "Functions for Date and Time," **426**.

SORTING DATA GROUPS

Although most data sorting within groups is based on the values contained in a field, you also can sort by expressions. When an inventory evaluation list is compiled based on the original Inventory by Category report, the products with the highest extended inventory value are the most important. The report's users might want these products listed first in a group. This decision requires sorting the records within groups on the expression `=[UnitsInStock]*[UnitPrice]`, which is similar to the expression that calculates the report's Value column. (You don't need to account for the constant markup multiplier when sorting.) A descending sort is necessary to place the highest values at the top of the report. Figure 17.6 shows the required entries in the Expression Builder and the Group, Sort, and Total pane.

The descending sort on the inventory value expression results in the report shown in Figure 17.7. As expected, the products with the highest inventory value appear first in each category.

rptInventoryByCategory
Report Header
Inventory by Category
Page Header
ID Product Name
CategoryID Header
Detail
Proc ProductName
CategoryID Footer
Category ID: CategoryID % Units
Page Footer
=Now()
Report Footer
Grand Total
Expression Builder
=[UnitPrice]*[UnitsInStock]
OK
Cancel
Undo
Help
Paste
+ - / * & = > < <> And Or Not Like ( )
Tables
Queries
Forms
Reports
Functions
Constants
Operators
Common Expressions
Group, Sort, and Total
Group on CategoryID
Sort by expression descending , More ▶
Add a group
ascending
descending

Figure 17.6
The expression in the second row of the Group, Sort, and Total pane places items with the largest inventory value at the top of each CategoryID group.

Inventory by Category and Value
Inventory by Category and Value
ID Product Name Supplier Units Cost Value
38 Côte de Blaye Aux joyeux ecclésiastiques 17 175.75 2,987.83
34 Sasquatch Ale Bigfoot Breweries 111 9.34 1,036.52
39 Chartreuse verte Aux joyeux ecclésiastiques 69 12.01 828.41
76 Lakkalikööri Karkki Oy 57 12.01 684.34
75 Rhönbräu Klosterbier Plutzer Lebensmittelgroßmärkte 125 5.17 646.16
43 Ipoh Coffee Leka Trading 17 30.68 521.59
67 Laughing Lumberjack Lager Bigfoot Breweries 52 9.34 485.58
1 Chai Exotic Liquids 39 12.01 468.23
35 Steeleye Stout Bigfoot Breweries 20 12.01 240.12
2 Chang Exotic Liquids 17 12.67 215.44
70 Outback Lager Pavlova, Ltd. 15 10.01 150.08
Category ID: Beverages % Units: 16.85% % Value: 15.89% Total: 539 $8,264.30
61 Sirop d'érable Forêts d'érables 113 19.01 2,148.07
6 Grandma's Boysenberry Spreac Grandma Kelly's Homestead 120 16.68 2,001.00
81 Radish Kimchi (Bag) Seoul Kimchi Co., Ltd. 10 116.73 1,167.25
65 Louisiana Fiery Hot Pepper Sau New Orleans Cajun Delights 76 14.04 1,067.07
4 Chef Anton's Cajun Seasoning New Orleans Cajun Delights 53 14.67 777.72
63 Vegie-spread Pavlova, Ltd. 24 29.28 702.75
83 Cucumber Kimchi (Bag) Seoul Kimchi Co., Ltd. 4 150.08 600.30
89 Korean Traditional Bean Paste Seoul Kimchi Co., Ltd. 20 28.01 560.28
87 Korean Hot Bean Paste Incheon Food Trading Co., Ltd. 15 35.02 525.26
85 Mild Cabbage Kimchi (Bag) Incheon Food Trading Co., Ltd. 6 83.38 500.25

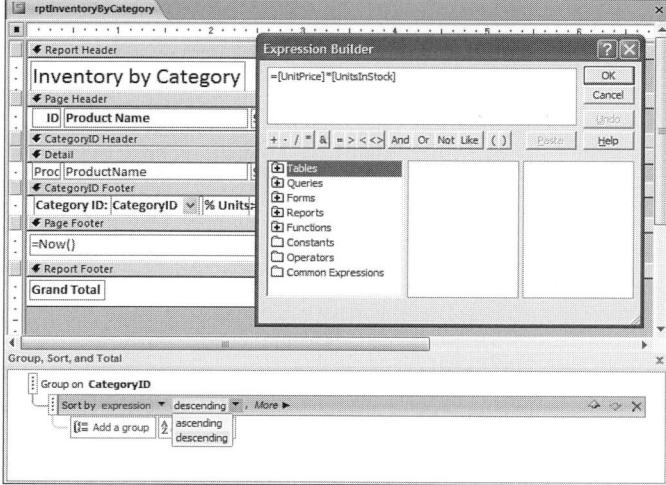

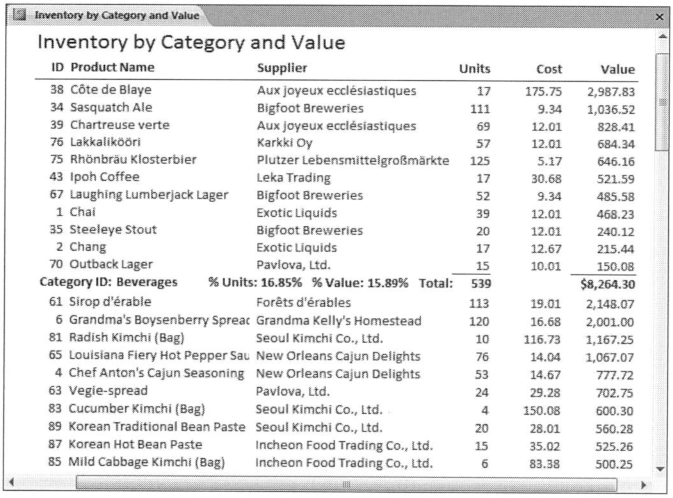

Figure 17.7
The grouping and sorting properties shown in Figure 17.6 result in a report that places emphasizes on the most important elements within a group.

Working from a Blank Report

Usually, the fastest way to set up a report is to use the Report Wizard to create a basic report and then modify the basic report as described in Chapter 16, and previous sections of this chapter. If you're creating a report style that the wizard can't handle or a report containing a subreport, however, modifying a standard report style created by the Report Wizard could take longer than creating a report by using the default blank report that Access provides.

USING A REPORT AS A SUBREPORT

The report you design in the following sections includes information about total monthly orders for products by category. Comparing the monthly orders to the inventory level of a category allows the report's user to estimate inventory turnover rates. This report serves two purposes—a primary report, and a subreport within another report. You add the Monthly Orders by Category report as a subreport of the Inventory by Category report in the "Incorporating Subreports" section, later in this chapter.

To create a report to use as the Monthly Orders by Category subreport (rpt2006MonthlyCategoryOrders) in the following section of this chapter, "Adding and Deleting Sections of Your Report," you need to base the subreport on a query (qry2006MonthlyProductOrdersCT) adapted for this purpose.

 A copy of the qry2006MonthlyProductOrdersCT query is included in the Report17.accdb database in the \SEAU12\Chaptr17 folder of the accompanying CD-ROM.

→ To review how to create this crosstab query, **see** "Designing a Monthly Product Sales Crosstab Query," **p. 508**.

To modify the query for this subreport, follow these steps:

1. From the Navigation Pane, open the qry2006MonthlyProductOrdersCT query in Design view.

2. In the grid, change the first column's field name from ProductID to CategoryID by opening the Field drop-down list and clicking the CategoryID field name. You need the CategoryID field to link with the CategoryID field in the qryInventory query that the rptInventoryByCategory report uses as its data source.

3. Delete the ProductName column. The modified query appears as shown in Figure 17.8.

Figure 17.8
The query for inventory analysis uses RequiredDate rather than OrderDate to more accurately reflect the date on which an order became a sale.

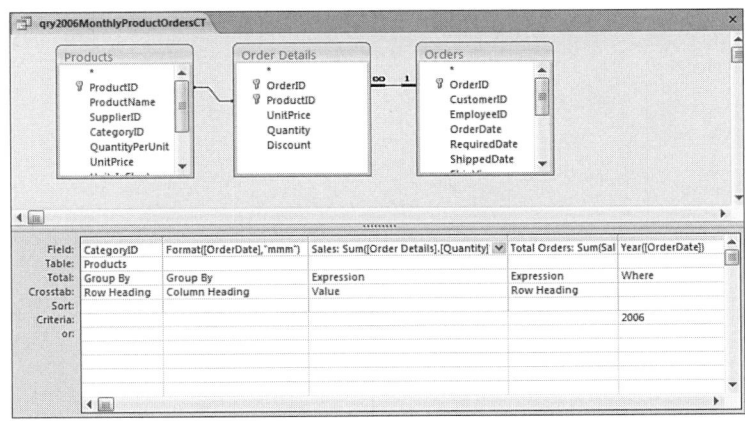

4. Click the Office button, choose Save <u>A</u>s, Save Object <u>A</u>s, and name the modified query **qry2006MonthlyCategoryOrdersCT**. Click Run to check the query. Your query result set appears as shown in Figure 17.9.

Figure 17.9
The query includes a Total Orders column that's useful for calculating inventory turns (total yearly sales divided by inventory value).

5. Click the Create tab and the Report Design button to open a new report in Design view.

6. Press F4 to open the Property Sheet. Click the Data tab and select qry2006MonthlyCategoryOrdersCT as the Record Source property value (see Figure 17.10).

Figure 17.10
This blank report with qry2006Monthly CategoryOrdersCT as the Record Source is the starting point for the subreport you add to the Inventory by Category report later in the chapter.

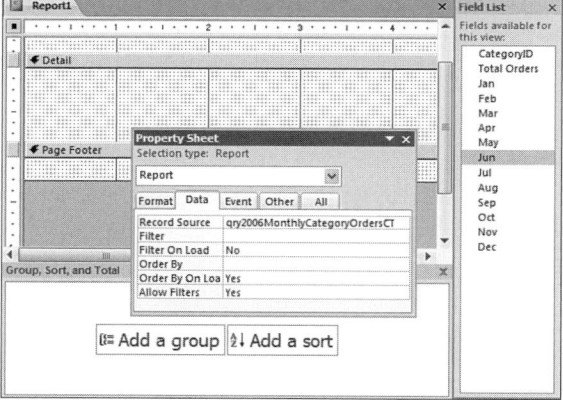

CREATING THE MONTHLY SALES BY CATEGORY REPORT

The crosstab query that acts as the Monthly Sales by Category report's data source is closely related to a report, but the crosstab query doesn't include detail records. Each row of the query consists of subtotals of sales for a category for each month of the year. One row appears below the inventory value subtotal when you link the subreport (child) to the main (master) report, so this report needs only a Detail section. Each detail row, however, requires a header label to print the month. The CategoryID field is included so that you can verify that the data is linked correctly.

To complete the Monthly Sales by Category report (and later a subreport), follow these steps:

1. In the blank report you opened in the preceding section, remove the default Page Header and Page Footer sections by right-clicking the report and choosing Page Header/Footer to clear the toggle. This subreport only requires a Detail section.

2. Drag the right margin of the Detail section to the right so that the report is about 6 ½ inches wide.

3. Click the Design ribbon's Add Existing Fields button, select CategoryID, and drag its field symbol to the Detail section.

4. Click the CategoryID label and relocate the label to the upper left of the Detail section directly over the CategoryID combo box. (CategoryID appears as a combo box, not a text box, in Report Design view because CategoryID is a lookup field.) Adjust the width of the label and text box to 1 ⅛ inch. Edit the label's text to **Category**.

5. Click and drag the field list's Jan field to the right of the CategoryID field. Move the label to the top of the section, adjacent to the right border of the field to its left. Move the text box under the label. Adjust the label and text box width to 21 dots (⅞ inch). Edit the label's text to delete the colon.

6. Repeat step 5 for the month fields of Feb through Jun. The report design now appears as shown in Figure 17.11.

Figure 17.11
Start the report design by adding the CategoryID field and the Jan through Jun fields of the query to the first row of labels and text boxes.

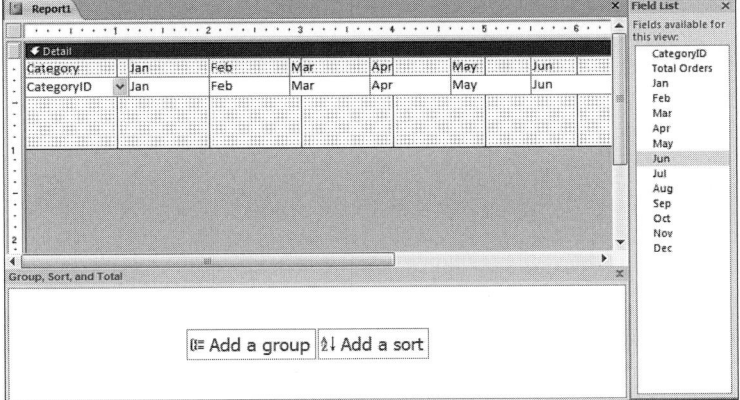

7. Click each month label while holding down the Shift key so that you select all six month labels (but only the labels).

8. Press Ctrl+B to apply the bold attribute to all month labels. Then click the Font group's Center button to center the labels above the text boxes.

9. Select the CategoryID text box and the label, and press Ctrl+B.

10. Select the six month text boxes, and click the Right button to right-align the dollar amounts.
11. Click the Design ribbon's Line control and add a line at the top edge of the labels. Drag the line's right-end handle to the right edge of the Jun text box.
12. Repeat step 11 for another identical line but add the new line under the text boxes.
13. Drag the Detail section's margins to within three dots of the bottom and right edges of the controls. The report's design appears as shown in Figure 17.12.

Report1
Detail
Category
Jan
Feb
Mar
Apr
May
Jun
CategoryID
Jan
Feb
Mar
Apr
May
Jun
Group, Sort, and Total
Add a group
Add a sort

Figure 17.12 Format and align the labels, align the text boxes, and add two one-point lines to dress up the report.

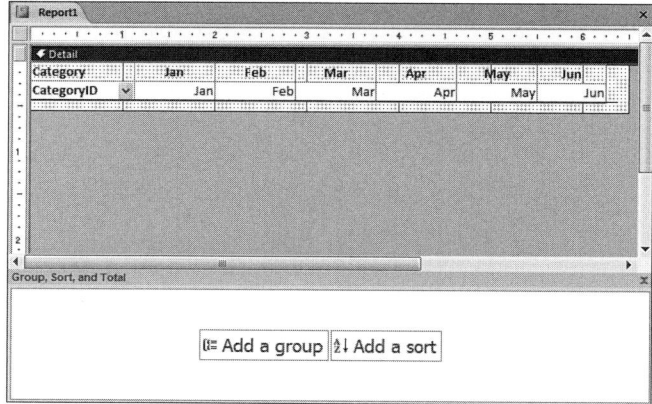

14. Click Report View to verify the design (see Figure 17.13).

Report1
Category Jan Feb Mar Apr May Jun
Beverages $21,904.16 $2,845.84 $10,636.88 $7,074.35 $15,422.25 $3,485.42
Category Jan Feb Mar Apr May Jun
Condiments $5,252.07 $6,128.86 $1,645.13 $5,544.40 $5,453.02 $1,855.27
Category Jan Feb Mar Apr May Jun
Confections $9,128.11 $6,978.87 $3,209.92 $11,538.61 $7,689.82 $2,174.88
Category Jan Feb Mar Apr May Jun
Dairy Products $9,066.40 $5,584.84 $9,728.90 $5,775.60 $10,435.57 $8,455.80
Category Jan Feb Mar Apr May Jun
Grains/Cereals $4,547.80 $4,693.70 $3,167.60 $6,544.40 $2,267.25 $6,345.85
Category Jan Feb Mar Apr May Jun
Meat/Poultry $6,842.85 $7,561.02 $2,998.48 $6,613.44 $3,395.51 $4,923.50
Category Jan Feb Mar Apr May Jun
Produce $2,704.92 $2,679.60 $3,676.80 $5,893.86 $3,099.60 $5,823.70
Category Jan Feb Mar Apr May Jun
Seafood $1,811.75 $2,010.90 $3,483.50 $4,048.29 $6,018.26 $3,298.37

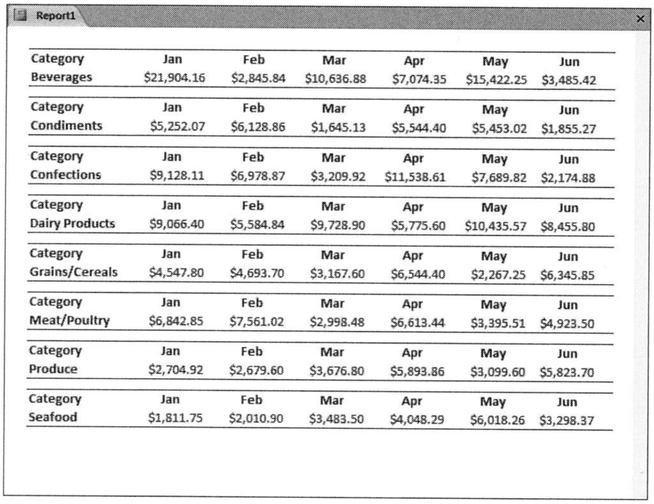

Figure 17.13 Confirm the first phase of the report's design in Print Preview.

15. Press Ctrl+S and type **rpt2006MonthlyCategoryOrders** as the report's name.

To add the remaining months of the year and the Grand Total field to your report, follow these steps:

1. To accommodate another row of labels and text boxes, return to Design view and increase the depth of the Detail section by dragging the bottom margin down about 1 inch.

2. Press Ctrl+A to select all the controls in the Detail section.

3. Press Ctrl+C to copy the labels, text boxes, and lines to the Clipboard.

4. Press Ctrl+V to paste a copy of the labels and text boxes to the Detail section.

5. Move this copy directly under the original labels and text boxes.

6. Click a blank area of the report to deselect the controls; then select and delete the new CategoryID text box. When you delete this text box, you also delete the associated label.

7. Edit both the labels and text boxes to display Jul through Dec. (Access automatically sets the text boxes' Control Source property to match the field name you type into the text box.)

8. Open the field list, if necessary, and add the Total Orders field and label in place of the second CategoryID field and label you deleted in step 6. Change the label caption to **Year Total**, select the label and text box, and apply the Bold attribute. Adjust the width of the label and text box to match the controls above.

9. Press Ctrl+A to select all the controls, and click the Arrange tab's Align to Grid button to correct any minor alignment discrepancies.

10. Drag the right side of the Jun and Dec text boxes to the right two dots, drag the right report margin to the edge of these two text boxes, and drag the bottom margin up to within two dots of the bottom of the text boxes in the second row. Figure 17.14 shows the final report design.

17

Figure 17.14
Copying the first row of controls to create a second row. Editing the labels and text boxes is faster than adding and adjusting another set of six controls.

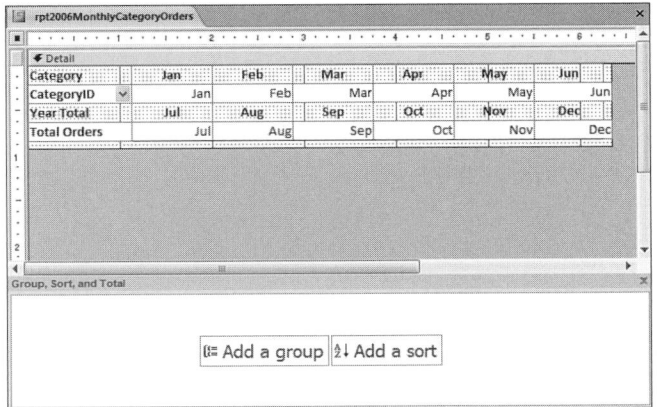

11. Click Report View to display the double-row report (see Figure 17.15).

Figure 17.15
Report view displays
the report design of
Figure 17.14.

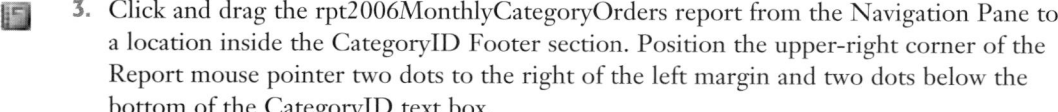

Category	Jan	Feb	Mar	Apr	May	Jun
Beverages	$21,904.16	$2,845.84	$10,636.88	$7,074.35	$15,422.25	$3,485.42
Year Total	Jul	Aug	Sep	Oct	Nov	Dec
$103,924.30	$7,889.22	$5,836.92	$5,726.70	$8,374.90	$3,851.00	$10,876.65
Category	Jan	Feb	Mar	Apr	May	Jun
Condiments	$5,252.07	$6,128.86	$1,645.13	$5,544.40	$5,453.02	$1,855.27
Year Total	Jul	Aug	Sep	Oct	Nov	Dec
$55,368.59	$5,519.83	$4,220.02	$3,575.18	$6,565.91	$3,784.67	$5,824.20
Category	Jan	Feb	Mar	Apr	May	Jun
Confections	$9,128.11	$6,978.87	$3,209.92	$11,538.61	$7,689.82	$2,174.88
Year Total	Jul	Aug	Sep	Oct	Nov	Dec
$82,657.75	$6,462.60	$7,105.63	$6,708.59	$7,800.70	$5,081.85	$8,778.15
Category	Jan	Feb	Mar	Apr	May	Jun
Dairy Products	$9,066.40	$5,584.84	$9,728.90	$5,775.60	$10,435.57	$8,455.80
Year Total	Jul	Aug	Sep	Oct	Nov	Dec
$115,387.64	$12,387.35	$6,826.55	$11,420.30	$12,869.00	$12,992.47	$9,844.85
Category	Jan	Feb	Mar	Apr	May	Jun
Grains/Cereals	$4,547.80	$4,693.70	$3,167.60	$6,544.40	$2,267.25	$6,345.85

12. Close the rpt2006MonthlyCategoryOrders report and save the changes.

The technique of copying controls to the Clipboard, pasting copies to reports, and then editing the copies is often faster than creating duplicate controls that differ from one another only in the text of labels and the field names of bound text boxes.

INCORPORATING SUBREPORTS

Reports, like forms, can include subreports. Unlike the Form Wizard, however, the Report Wizard offers no option for automatically creating reports that include subreports. You can add subreports to reports that you create with the Report Wizard, or you can create subreports from blank reports, like you did in the earlier section "Working from a Blank Report."

ADDING A LINKED SUBREPORT TO A BOUND REPORT

If a main report is bound to a table or query as a data source and the subreport's data source can be related to the main report's data source, you can link the subreport's data to the main report's data.

To add and link the rpt2006MonthlyCategoryOrders report as a subreport to the Inventory by Category report, for example, follow these steps:

1. Open the original version of the rptInventoryByCategory report from Chapter 16 in Design view.

2. Drag down the top of the Page Footer border to make room for the subreport in the CategoryID Footer section (about ⅞ inch).

3. Click and drag the rpt2006MonthlyCategoryOrders report from the Navigation Pane to a location inside the CategoryID Footer section. Position the upper-right corner of the Report mouse pointer two dots to the right of the left margin and two dots below the bottom of the CategoryID text box.

4. When you release the right mouse button, Access adds a subreport control, which displays the subreport in Design view within a frame for in-site editing. Delete the subreport's label (see Figure 17.16).

Figure 17.16
Drag a report's icon to a section of another report and drop it to automatically add the subreport.

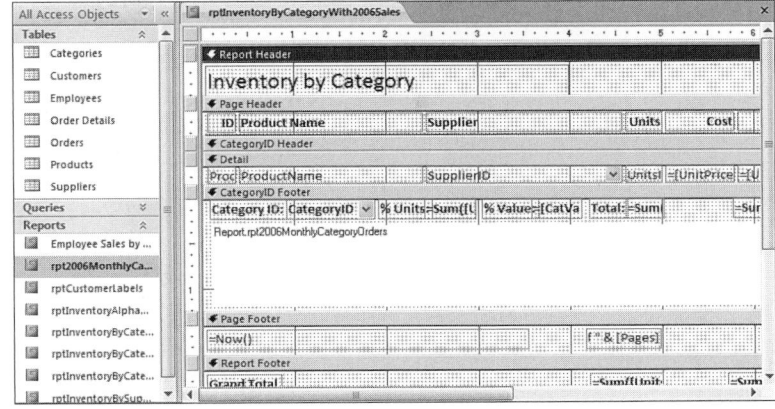

5. Adjust the CategoryID Footer's depth to provide about 0.1-inch margins above and below the section's controls.

6. You need to link the data in the subreport to the data of the main report so that only the sales data corresponding to a specific group's CategoryID value appears in the CategoryID Footer section. Select the subreport and click the Property Sheet button to display the subreport's Property Sheet. Click the Data tab, and type **CategoryID** in the LinkChildFields and LinkMaster Fields text boxes (see Figure 17.17).

N O T E

If you click the Builder button to open the Subreport Field linker dialog, you receive the error message "The expression you entered refers to an object that is closed or doesn't exist." This message occurs because the subreport isn't embedded in the parent report. You can close and reopen the parent report to correct the error, but it's easier just to type the linking field name twice.

7. Click the Report View button to display the report. The subreport appears as shown at the bottom of Figure 17.18. Scroll the report to confirm that the linkage is correct for all categories.

8. Save the modified report as **rptInventoryByCategoryWith2006Sales**.

You can add and link several subreports to the main report if each subreport has a field in common with the main report's data source.

rptInventoryByCategoryWith2006Sal...
Report Header
Inventory by Category
Page Header
ID Product Name
CategoryID Header
Detail
ProductName
CategoryID Footer
Category ID: CategoryID
% Units:=Su
Report.rpt2006MonthlyCategoryOrders
Page Footer
=Now()
Report Footer
Grand Total
Property Sheet
Selection type: Subform/Subreport
rpt2006MonthlyCategoryOrders
Format
Data
Event
Other
All
Source Object
Report.rpt2006MonthlyCategoryOrders
Link Master Fields
CategoryID
Link Child Fields
CategoryID
Filter On Empty Ma
Yes
Enabled
Yes

Figure 17.17
If you don't see the subreport's Design view in the subreport frame, type the Link Master Field and Link Child Field names in the Property Sheet.

Inventory by Category
Inventory by Category
ID Product Name Supplier Units Cost Value
1 Chai Exotic Liquids 39 12.01 468.23
2 Chang Exotic Liquids 17 12.67 215.44
39 Chartreuse verte Aux joyeux ecclésiastiques 69 12.01 828.41
38 Côte de Blaye Aux joyeux ecclésiastiques 17 175.75 2,987.83
43 Ipoh Coffee Leka Trading 17 30.68 521.59
76 Lakkalikööri Karkki Oy 57 12.01 684.34
67 Laughing Lumberjack Lager Bigfoot Breweries 52 9.34 485.58
70 Outback Lager Pavlova, Ltd. 15 10.01 150.08
75 Rhönbräu Klosterbier Plutzer Lebensmittelgroßmärkte 125 5.17 646.16
34 Sasquatch Ale Bigfoot Breweries 111 9.34 1,036.52
35 Steeleye Stout Bigfoot Breweries 20 12.01 240.12
Category ID: Beverages % Units: 16.85% % Value: 15.89% Total: 539 $8,264.30
Category Jan Feb Mar Apr May Jun
Beverages $21,904.16 $2,845.84 $10,636.88 $7,074.35 $15,422.25 $3,485.42
Year Total Jul Aug Sep Oct Nov Dec
$103,924.30 $7,889.22 $5,836.92 $5,726.70 $8,374.90 $3,851.00 $10,876.65
3 Aniseed Syrup Exotic Liquids 13 6.67 86.71
4 Chef Anton's Cajun Seasoning New Orleans Cajun Delights 53 14.67 777.72
92 Chu Hou Sauce Zhongshan Sauces Co., Ltd. 5 8.17 40.85
83 Cucumber Kimchi (Bag) Seoul Kimchi Co., Ltd. 4 150.08 600.30
82 Cucumber Kimchi (Jar) Seoul Kimchi Co., Ltd. 8 28.35 226.78

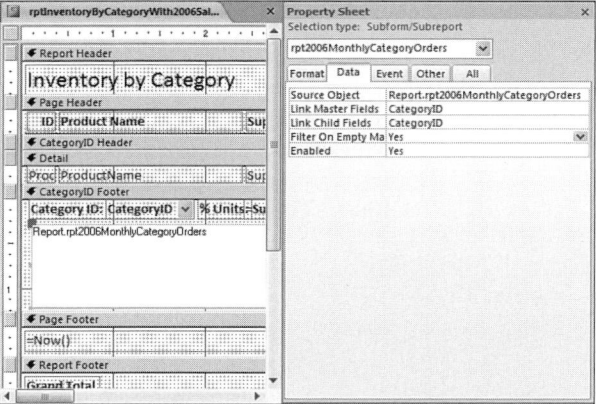

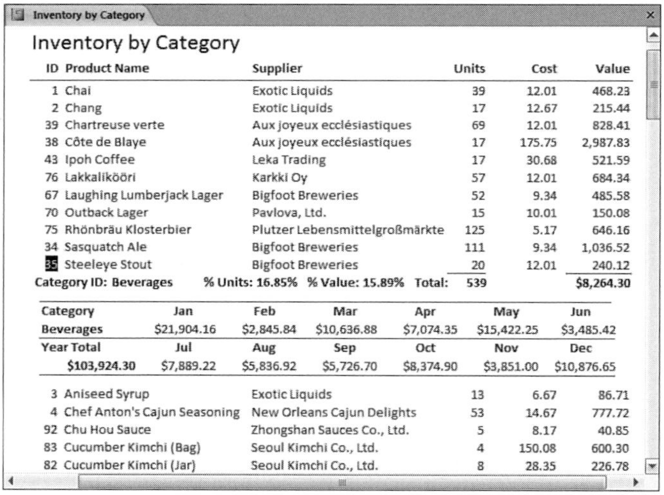

Figure 17.18
The appropriate rows of the linked subreport print below the text boxes in the CategoryID Footer section.

TIP

You can use calculated values to link main reports and subreports. Calculated values often are based on time–months, quarters, or years. To link main reports and subreports by calculated values, you must create queries for both the main report and subreport that include the calculated value in a field, such as Month or Year. You create the calculated field in each query by using the corresponding Access date function, `Month` or `Year`. To group by quarters, select Interval for the Group On property and set the value of the Group Interval property to 3. You can't use Qtr as the Group On property because the calculated value lacks the Date/Time field data type.

If you receive an error message when you try to create a link between the main report and subreport when the subreport is visible in Design view, turn to "Link Expression Errors" in the "Troubleshooting" section at the end of this chapter.

USING UNLINKED SUBREPORTS AND UNBOUND REPORTS

Most reports that you create use subreports that are linked to the main report's data source. You can, however, insert independent subreports within main reports. In this case, you don't enter values for the Link Child Fields and Link Master Fields properties. The subreport's data source can be related to or completely independent of the main report's data source.

Figure 17.19 illustrates the effect of including an unlinked subreport in a main report. The figure shows a part of page 1 of the rpt2006MonthlyCategoryOrders subreport within the rptInventoryByCategoryWith2006Sales report after deleting the CategoryID values of the Link Child Fields and Link Master Fields properties, prior to saving the report with a new name. Notice that without the link, the subreport displays all records instead of just those records related to the particular category in which the subreport appears. You might need to set the CategoryID Footer section's Keep Together property to No to display the subform on the first page. The Keep Together property is one of the subjects of the "Controlling Page Breaks and Printing Page Headers and Footers" section later in the chapter.

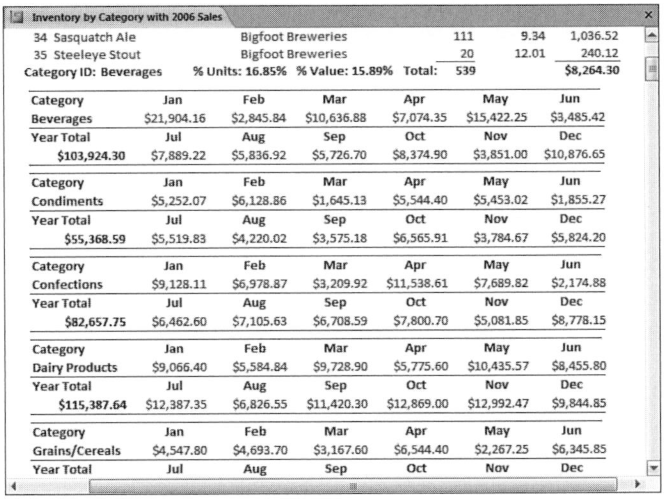

Figure 17.19
Removing the link between the master and child fields causes each instance of the CategoryID Footer section to display all rows of the subreport.

Inventory by Category with 2006 Sales						
34 Sasquatch Ale	Bigfoot Breweries			111	9.34	1,036.52
35 Steeleye Stout	Bigfoot Breweries			20	12.01	240.12
Category ID: Beverages	% Units: 16.85%	% Value: 15.89%	Total:	539		$8,264.30
Category	Jan	Feb	Mar	Apr	May	Jun
Beverages	$21,904.16	$2,845.84	$10,636.88	$7,074.35	$15,422.25	$3,485.42
Year Total	Jul	Aug	Sep	Oct	Nov	Dec
$103,924.30	$7,889.22	$5,836.92	$5,726.70	$8,374.90	$3,851.00	$10,876.65
Category	Jan	Feb	Mar	Apr	May	Jun
Condiments	$5,252.07	$6,128.86	$1,645.13	$5,544.40	$5,453.02	$1,855.27
Year Total	Jul	Aug	Sep	Oct	Nov	Dec
$55,368.59	$5,519.83	$4,220.02	$3,575.18	$6,565.91	$3,784.67	$5,824.20
Category	Jan	Feb	Mar	Apr	May	Jun
Confections	$9,128.11	$6,978.87	$3,209.92	$11,538.61	$7,689.82	$2,174.88
Year Total	Jul	Aug	Sep	Oct	Nov	Dec
$82,657.75	$6,462.60	$7,105.63	$6,708.59	$7,800.70	$5,081.85	$8,778.15
Category	Jan	Feb	Mar	Apr	May	Jun
Dairy Products	$9,066.40	$5,584.84	$9,728.90	$5,775.60	$10,435.57	$8,455.80
Year Total	Jul	Aug	Sep	Oct	Nov	Dec
$115,387.64	$12,387.35	$6,826.55	$11,420.30	$12,869.00	$12,992.47	$9,844.85
Category	Jan	Feb	Mar	Apr	May	Jun
Grains/Cereals	$4,547.80	$4,693.70	$3,167.60	$6,544.40	$2,267.25	$6,345.85
Year Total	Jul	Aug	Sep	Oct	Nov	Dec

You can add multiple subreports to an unbound report if all the subreports fit on one page of the report or across the page. In the latter case, you can use the landscape printing orientation to increase the available page width.

CUSTOMIZING DE NOVO REPORTS

Most of the preceding examples in this chapter are based on a standard report structure and template you chose when creating the Inventory by Category report in Chapter 16. When you start a report from scratch, you must add sections required by your reports, set up printing parameters, and, if the number of records in the data source is large, consider limiting the number of detail rows to supply only the most significant information.

ADDING AND DELETING SECTIONS OF YOUR REPORT

When you create a report from a blank template or modify a report created by the Report Wizard, add new sections to the report by using the following guidelines:

- To add report headers and footers as a pair, right-click the report and choose Report Header/Footer.

- To add page headers and footers as a pair, right-click the report and choose Page Header/Footer.

- To add a group header or footer to a report with a Group By value specified, click the Group & Sort button on the Report Design Tools – Design ribbon and set the Group Header or Group Footer property value, or both, to Yes.

Figure 17.20 shows a blank report in Design view, with the headers and footers for each section that you can include in a report. (Although Figure 17.20 shows only one group, you can add up to 10 group levels to your report.)

Figure 17.20
A report with a single Group By property value has a total of seven sections.

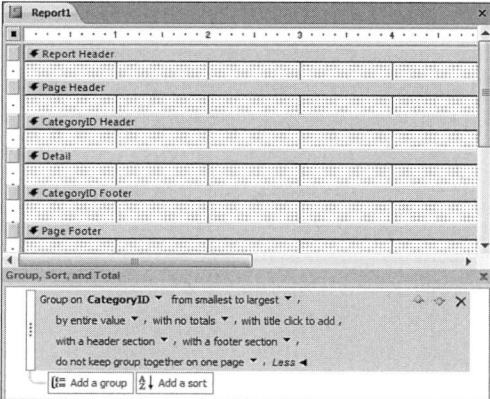

If you group the data in more than one level (group, subgroup, sub-subgroup), you can add a group header and footer for each level of grouping. This action adds to your report another pair of sections for each subgroup level.

You delete sections from reports by using methods similar to those that you use to create the sections. To delete unwanted sections, use the following guidelines:

- To delete the Detail section or an individual Report Header, Report Footer, Page Header, or Page Footer section, delete all controls from the section, and then drag the divider bar up so that the section has no depth. To delete a Report Footer section, drag the report's bottom margin to the Report Footer border. These actions do not actually delete the sections, but sections with no depth do not print or affect the report's layout.

- To delete Report Header and Footer sections as a pair, right-click the report and choose Report <u>H</u>eader/Footer. If the Report Header or Footer section includes a control, a message box warns you that you will lose the controls in the deleted sections.

- To delete Page Header and Footer sections as a pair, right-click the report and choose P<u>a</u>ge Header/Footer. A warning message box appears if either section contains controls.

 - To delete a Group Header or Footer section, click the Group & Sort button, click More, and change the properties to Without Header, Without Footer, or both.

TIP

Page and report headers and footers that incorporate thin lines at the upper border of the header or footer can be difficult to delete individually. To make these lines visible, click Ctrl+A to add sizing anchors to the lines. Hold down the Shift key and click the controls you want to save to deselect these controls. Then press the Delete key to delete the remaining selected lines.

CONTROLLING PAGE BREAKS AND PRINTING PAGE HEADERS AND FOOTERS

The Force New Page and Keep Together properties of the report's Group Header, Detail, and Group Footer sections control manual page breaks. To set these properties, double-click the group's section header to display the section's Property Sheet. Force New Page causes an unconditional page break immediately before printing the section. If you set the Keep Together property to Yes and insufficient room is available on the current page to print the entire section, a page break occurs and the section prints on the next page.

To control whether Page Headers or Footers print on the first, last, or all pages of a report, press Ctrl+R or click the Select Report button, and then press F4. You then select the Page Headers and Page Footers option in the Format page of the Property Sheet (see Figure 17.21).

Figure 17.21
Specify when page headers or page foot-ers appear in the report in the Format page of the Report Property Sheet.

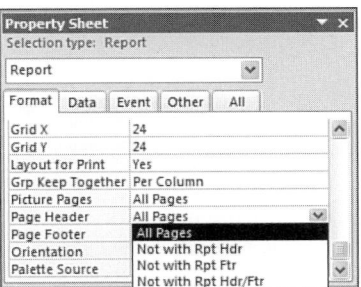

ADDING OTHER CONTROLS TO REPORTS

Access places no limit on the native controls you can add to reports. So far, the controls that you've modified or added have been limited to labels, text boxes, lines, and the combo boxes that Access places automatically for fields configured as lookup fields. These four kinds of controls are likely to comprise more than 90% of the controls used in the reports you create. Controls that require user interaction, such as lists and combo boxes, can be used in a non-printing section of the report, but practical use of these controls in reports is limited. The following list describes other controls that you might want to add to reports:

- **Attachment**—Print the first image or other attchment type.
- **Bound object frames**—Print the contents of the OLE Object field data type, including bound charts you design in the next chapter. An OLE object can be a still or animated graphic, a video clip, CD audio track, or even MIDI music. Reports are designed only for printing, so animated graphics, video, and sound are inappropriate for reports.
- **Unbound object frames**—Display OLE objects created by OLE server applications, such as the Graph Wizard, Windows Paint, Microsoft Word, or Excel. Usually, you place unbound objects in the report's Form Header or Form Footer section, but you can add a logo to the top of each page by placing the image object in the Page Header section. A graph or chart created by the Chart Wizard is a special kind of unbound OLE object; you can't create a bound chart with the Wizard.
- **ActiveX controls**—Similar to objects within unbound object frames. You can add PivotTables and PivotCharts to reports, but you must establish the design parameters for the PivotTable or PivotChart before printing.
- **Lines and rectangles (also called shapes)**—Add graphic design elements to reports. Lines of varying widths can separate the sections of the report or emphasize a particular section.
- **Check boxes and option buttons**—Can be used to indicate the values of Yes/No fields or used within group frames to indicate multiple-choice selections. Group frames, option buttons, and check boxes used in reports indicate only the value of data cells and do not change the values. Reports seldom use option or toggle buttons.

Adding graphs in bound and unbound object frames and placing PivotTables and PivotCharts in reports are subjects covered in Chapter 18, "Adding Graphs, PivotCharts, and PivotTables."

REDUCING THE LENGTH OF REPORTS

A report's properties or controls don't limit the number of rows of detail data that a report presents. One way of minimizing detail data is to write a TOP *N* or TOP *N* PERCENT query using Access or Transact-SQL. Chapter 21, "Moving from Access Queries to Transact-SQL," has examples of the use of SELECT TOP *N* [PERCENT] statements. All rows of a table or query appear somewhere in the report's Detail section, if the report includes a Detail section with at least one control. To include only a selected range of dates in a report, for example, you must base the report on a query with the criteria necessary to select the Detail records or apply a filter to the report. If the user is to select the range of records to include in the report, use a parameter query as the report's data source.

MAILING REPORTS AS ATTACHMENTS

NEW Outlook or Outlook Express lets you send a report as an email attachment in several common formats: .html, Adobe Portable Document (.pdf), Rich Text (.rtf), Snapshot (.snp), Text (.txt), and XML Paper Specification (.xps).

NOTE

> Microsoft released Report Snapshots (.snp) as an add-in for Access 97; the Report Snapshot feature is built into later Access versions. The advantage of a Report Snapshot is that recipients don't need Access to view the reports. If recipients don't have the Snapshot viewer (Snapview.exe and Snapview.hlp) installed, they must obtain it from the Microsoft website:
>
> http://support.microsoft.com/support/kb/articles/q175/2/74.asp
>
> For widest usability, choose PDF format.

SENDING A REPORT WITH AN OUTLOOK MESSAGE

In Outlook to send a report as a PDF attachment to an email message, follow these steps:

1. Make sure that your email client (Outlook or Outlook Express) and current profile is operational. You must have a functioning email system to export a report Snapshot.

2. In the Navigation Pane, select a report. You don't need to open the report to send it.

3. Click the Office button and choose <u>E</u>-mail to open the Send Object As dialog.

4. Select PDF from the Select Output Format list (see Figure 17.22). Click OK to close the Send dialog. (You might be prompted to identify your email system at this point). Access creates the attachment file and opens your email application. The attachment icon appears in the body of the message.

NOTE

> Access 2007 has added support for PDF and XPS files and removed Excel 5–7 and 97–2002 formats.

5. Complete the message and send it to the recipient. To test the attachment, send the message to yourself.

 If you receive an error message when you try to open the Snapshot on another computer, check the "Report Snapshots Won't Open" topic in the following "Troubleshooting" section.

Figure 17.22
Select the format you want in the Send Object As dialog, and click OK to generate the file and open your email application with the file as an attachment.

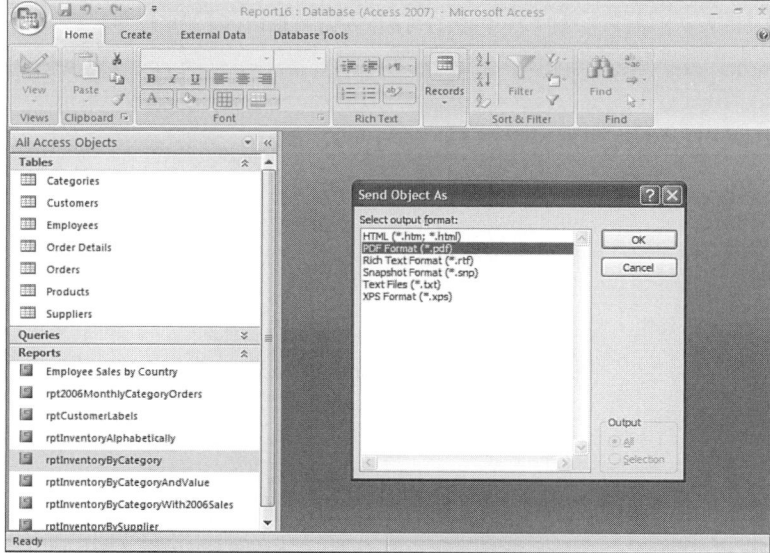

TROUBLESHOOTING

LINK EXPRESSION ERRORS

Attempting to create a link between the main report and subreport causes a "Can't evaluate expression" error message.

The most likely cause is that you are trying to create a master-child (or, more properly, parent-child) link with an incompatible data type. Parent-child linkages are similar to joins of queries that use the WHERE *SubreportName.FieldName* = *ReportName.FieldName* criterion. As with joins, the data types of the linked fields of tables or columns of queries must be identical. You can't, for example, link a field of the Text data type with a field of the Integer data type, even if your text field contains only numbers. If you use an expression to create the link, the data type that the expression returns must match the field value. You can use the data type conversion functions described in Chapter 10 to change the data type that the expression returns to that of the linked field. For example, you can link a text field that contains numbers to a field of the Long Integer data type by entering =**CLng**(TextField) as the linking value.

REPORT SNAPSHOTS WON'T OPEN

Selecting the Open It option in the Opening Mail Attachment dialog results in the error message "The Managed Software Installer failed to install the program associated with this file" or a similar error message.

The most likely cause of this error is that SnapView.exe is missing from your or the recipient's PC. In this case, open Control Panel, and double-click the Add/Remove Programs icon to open the Add/Remove Programs dialog. Select Microsoft Office XP, and click Add/Remove to open the Microsoft Office Maintenance Mode dialog. Click Change to open the installer's Microsoft Office XP Setup dialog, and select the Add or Remove Features option. Click Next and expand the Microsoft Access for Windows node, set Snapshot Viewer to Run from My Computer, and click Update.

NOTE

> The Snapshot Viewer hasn't changed since the version supplied as an Access 97 add-in. Prior versions of the Snapshot viewer are compatible with Access 2007 reports.

If Snapview.exe is present, you have a Registry problem—the association between the .snp file extension and SnapView.exe is missing. In this case, repeat the preceding Add/Remove Programs process to enter Office 2007 Maintenance Mode, but click the Repair Office button instead of the Add or Remove Features button.

IN THE REAL WORLD—THE ART OF REPORT DESIGN

Designing reports that deliver useful information in a graphically appealing format is a challenge. The challenge becomes acute when you're faced with the prospect of designing a complex report, such as a physician's patient history, that derives its information from multiple related tables. In the case of a patient history, some of the tables contain memo fields with large blocks of formatted text that describe diagnosis and treatment. Specialists often want reports that print from OLE Object fields or linked graphics files, embedded images generated from digital cameras, scanned photographs, or single-frame captures from a video camera. Most physicians also need billing reports that conform to state and federal government agency standards, as well as health insurers' requirements.

Fortunately, Access 2007's report engine and graphical Report Design mode can handle just about any report format imaginable. Report generation flexibility is one of the primary reasons that database developers haven't abandoned Access for Visual Basic .NET, which offers a more traditional approach to programming structure than Access, and SQL Server Reporting services, which is included with SQL Server 2005 Express with Advanced Services Service Pack 2.

It's impossible for two chapters of reasonable length to cover every feature of the Access report engine in detail. This chapter and its predecessor provide only an introduction to report design and demonstrate the basic elements of reports and subreports. Complete coverage of Access's reporting capabilities, including the use of VBA to respond to report events and set printer properties, would fill a book of 500 pages or more.

CHAPTER 18

ADDING GRAPHS, PIVOTCHARTS, AND PIVOTTABLES

In this chapter

GENERATING GRAPHS AND CHARTS WITH MICROSOFT GRAPH

Microsoft Graph 12—called *MSGraph* in this book—is a 32-bit, OLE 2.0 mini-server application (Graph.exe) that's identical to Access 200x's Graph.exe and Access 97's Graph8.exe. An OLE mini-server is an application that you can only run from within an OLE container application, such as Access 2007. Word 2007 and Excel 2007 also use MSGraph, which originated as the charting component of Microsoft Excel 5.0. Microsoft encourages use of the PivotChart control for new Access applications, but there's no "PivotChart Wizard" to lead you through the steps to design a PivotChart. The AutoForm: PivotChart option generates a data-bound form with a PivotChart that you must configure manually, as described in Chapter 12, "Working with PivotTable and PivotChart Views," and in more detail in the "Working with PivotChart Forms," section near the end of this chapter.

The sections that follow describe how to use Access's Chart Wizard to add graphs and charts to conventional Access 2007 forms and reports. Access Data Projects (ADP) don't support the Chart Wizard, which generates an Access crosstab query to use as its final data source. As mentioned in Chapter 11, "Creating Multitable and Crosstab Queries," SQL Server doesn't support the Access SQL TRANSFORM and PIVOT keywords for crosstab queries. (SQL Server 2005's new PIVOT operator uses a different syntax to generate crosstabs.) Sections later in the chapter describe how to add bound PivotChart and PivotTable controls to Access- and SQL Server–based forms and reports.

CREATING THE QUERY DATA SOURCE FOR THE GRAPH

Most graphs required by management are the time-series type. Time-series graphs track the history of financial performance data, such as orders received, product sales, gross margin, and the like. Time-series graphs usually display date intervals (months, quarters, or years) on the horizontal x-axis—sometimes called the *abscissa*—and numeric values on the vertical y-axis—also called the *ordinate*.

CHOOSING DATA SOURCES FOR SUMMARY QUERIES

In smaller firms, the numerical data for the y-axis comes from tables that store entries from the original documents (such as sales orders and invoices), which underlie the summary information. Queries sum the numerical data for each interval specified for the x-axis.

Detail data for individual orders or invoices, such as that found in the sample Order Details table, often is called a *line-item source*. Because a multibillion-dollar firm can accumulate millions of line-item records in a single year, larger firms usually store summaries of the line-item source data in tables; this technique improves the performance of queries. Summary data often is referred to as *rolled-up data* (or simply as *rollups*). Rollups of data on mainframe computers often are stored in client/server databases running under Windows Server 2003+ or various UNIX flavors to create data warehouses or data marts.

Although rolling up data from relational tables violates two of the guiding principles of relational theory—don't duplicate data in tables and don't store derived data in tables—databases consisting solely of rolled-up data are very common. As you move into the client/server realm with ADP and SQL Server, you're likely to encounter many rollup tables derived from production online transaction processing (OLTP) databases.

NOTE

The Developer, Standard, Enterprise, and Datacenter editions of Microsoft SQL Server 2005 include Microsoft Analysis Services, formerly called *OLAP services*. OLAP is an acronym for online analytical processing, which manipulates multidimensional data from production databases. OLAP can operate directly on OLTP databases, but it's more common to roll up online data into OLAP data structures, often called *cubes*, and then perform analysis on the cubes.

These editions incorporate Business Intelligence Management Studio (BIDS). BIDS, an acronym for an earlier product name (Business Intelligence Development Studio), is a Visual Studio 2005 add-in (shell) for creating OLAP roll-ups (cubes) from OLTP and historical databases. BIDS hosts the Report Designer for SQL Server 2005 Reporting Services, which SSX with Advanced Services SP2 supports.

DESIGNING A QUERY BASED ON OLTP TABLES

Northwind Traders is a relatively small firm that receives very few orders, so it isn't necessary to roll up line-item data to obtain acceptable query performance on a reasonably fast (Pentium IV or better) computer. The Chart Wizard handles time-series grouping for you, so you don't need to base your chart on a crosstab query.

To create a summary query designed specifically for use with the Chart Wizard, follow these steps:

1. Click the Create tab and Query Design button to open a new query in Design view, and add the Categories, Products, Order Details, and Orders tables to the query.

2. Drag the CategoryName field of the Categories table to the first column.

3. Type the expression

```
Amount: CCur([Order Details].[UnitPrice]*[Order Details].[Quantity]*
(1 -[Order Details].[Discount]))
```

in the second column's Field row.

NOTE

The CCur VBA function is required to change the field data type to Currency when applying a discount calculation.

TIP

With the cursor in the Field row of the second column, press Shift+F2 to open the Zoom window to make entering the preceding expression easier.

4. Drag the ShippedDate field of the Orders table to the third column. Add an ascending sort on this column.

5. Add the criterion **Between #1/1/2006# And #12/31/2006#** to the ShippedDate column to include only orders shipped in 2006. This example uses the year 2006 instead of 2007 because data is available for all 12 months of 2006.

6. Save your query with the name **qry2006SalesChart** (see Figure 18.1).

Figure 18.1
This query calculates the net value of all Northwind orders shipped in 2006 classified by product category and shipped date.

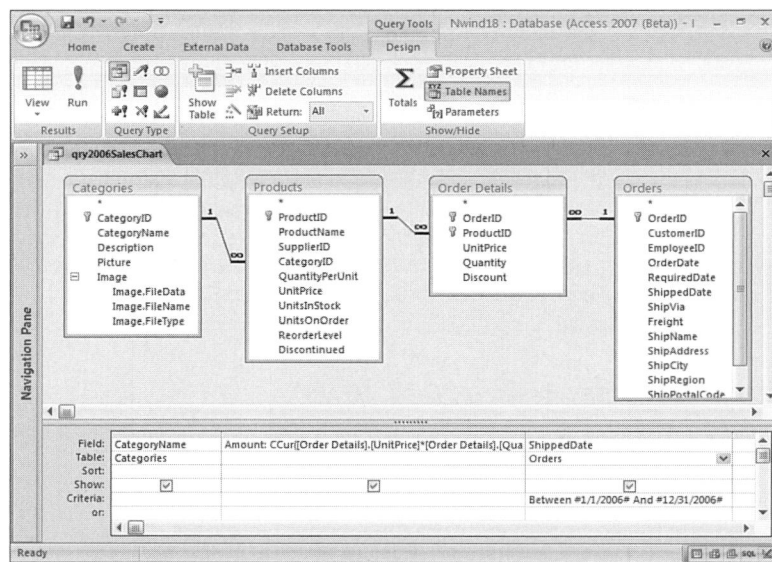

7. Click the Run button to test your query (see Figure 18.2), and then close it.

Figure 18.2
The query returns a row for each date on which an order was shipped and provides the total amount of the sale for the product categories.

Category Name	Amount	Shipped Date
Seafood	$335.34	1/16/2006
Meat/Poultry	$471.60	1/16/2006
Dairy Products	$146.88	1/16/2006
Beverages	$360.00	1/16/2006
Dairy Products	$1,440.00	1/1/2006
Beverages	$285.00	1/3/2006
Produce	$585.90	1/3/2006
Confections	$58.80	1/3/2006
Confections	$1,307.25	1/3/2006
Dairy Products	$320.00	1/3/2006
Seafood	$48.00	1/3/2006
Confections	$394.00	1/3/2006
Seafood	$241.92	1/3/2006
Meat/Poultry	$1,650.60	1/3/2006
Dairy Products	$230.40	1/3/2006
Grains/Cereals	$288.00	1/6/2006
Dairy Products	$1,032.00	1/6/2006
Dairy Products	$583.80	1/6/2006
Confections	$68.00	1/3/2006

The design of the qry2006SalesChart query is a typical sample data source for time-series graphs and charts you generate with MSGraph as well as PivotCharts.

USING THE CHART WIZARD TO CREATE AN UNLINKED GRAPH

It's possible to create a graph or chart by choosing Insert, Object and selecting Microsoft Graph Chart in the Object Type list, but the Chart Wizard makes this process much simpler. You can use the Chart Wizard to create two different classes of graphs and charts:

- *Unlinked* (also called nonlinked) line graphs display a line for each row of the query. You can also create unlinked stacked column charts and multiple-area charts.

- *Linked* graphs or charts are bound to the current record of the form in which they are contained and display only a single set of values from one row of the table or query at a time.

This section shows you how to create an unlinked line graph based on a query. The "Changing the Graph to a Chart" section describes how to use MSGraph to display alternative presentations of your data in the form of bar and area charts. In the later section "Creating a Linked Graph from an Access Crosstab Query," you generate a graph that's linked to a specific record of a query result set.

To create an unlinked graph that displays the data from the qry2006SalesChart query, follow these steps:

 1. Click the Create tab and the Blank form button, and change to Design view to display the Form Design Tools, Design ribbon.

2. Click the Controls group's Chart button, draw a reasonably large frame on the form, and release the mouse to open the Chart Wizard's first dialog. Select the Queries option and then select qry2006SalesChart in the list box (see Figure 18.3). Click Next.

Figure 18.3
Select the Queries option and then select the query for the graph or chart in the list box.

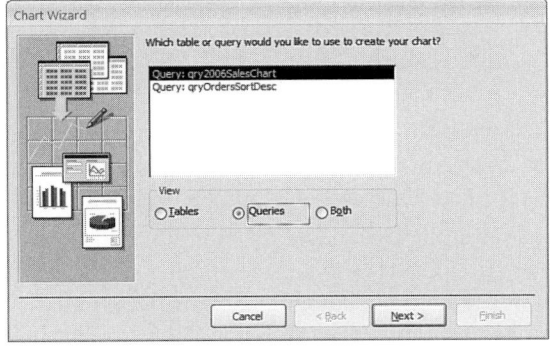

3. In the second Wizard dialog, click the >> button to add all three fields to your graph (see Figure 18.4). Click Next to move to the third dialog.

Figure 18.4
Time-series charts require at least date and value columns (ShippedDate and Amount, respectively). Creating a multiple-line chart requires a classification field (CategoryID) to provide the data for each line.

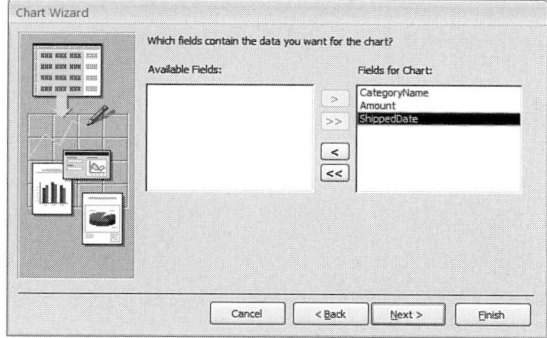

4. Click the Line Chart button, shown selected in Figure 18.5. Click Next.

Figure 18.5
A line graph is the best initial choice for data presentation, because lines make it easy to determine whether the data meets reasonableness tests.

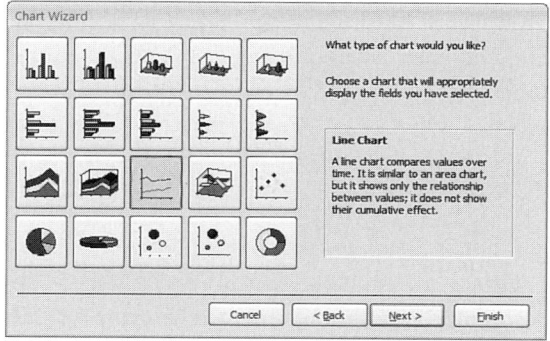

NOTE

This book uses the term *graph* when the presentation consists of lines, and *chart* for formats that use solid regions—such as bars, columns, or areas—to display the data.

5. The Wizard designs a crosstab query based on the data types of the query result set. In this case, the Chart Wizard makes a mistake by assuming you want months in the legend box and product categories along the graph's horizontal x-axis (see Figure 18.6).

6. You want the categories in the legend and the months of 2006 across the x-axis. Drag the CategoryName button from the right side of the dialog to the drop box under the legend to the right of the chart, and drag the ShippedDate button to the drop box under the x-axis. The button title, partly obscured, is ShippedDate by Month (see Figure 18.7).

Figure 18.6
Time-series graphs and charts almost always plot time on the horizontal axis, but the Chart Wizard's initial design puts classifications (CategoryName) on the x-axis.

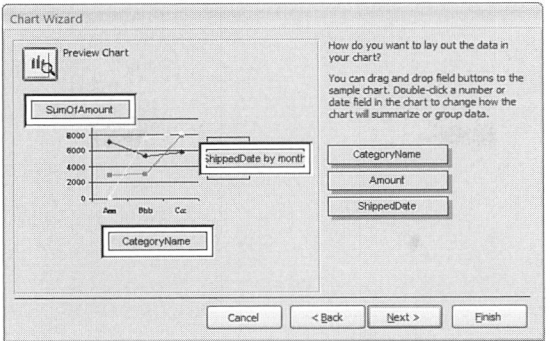

Figure 18.7
Drag the date column button from the right to the x-axis and the classification column button to the legend. The Wizard's default time-series interval is month.

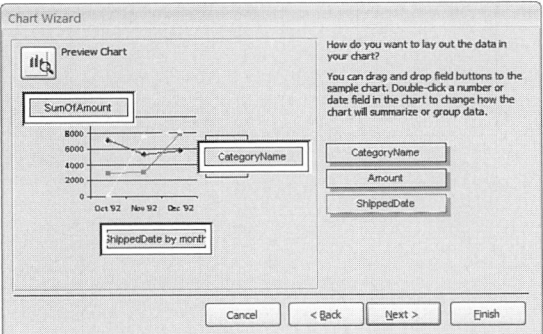

TIP

> You can double-click the ShippedDate by Month button and select from a variety of GROUP BY date criteria, ranging from Year to Minute, and specify an optional range of dates (refer to Figure 18.7). Marking the Use Date Between check box lets you add a WHERE *DateValue* BETWEEN *#StartDate#* AND *#EndDate#* clause to the crosstab query's SQL statement.

7. Click the Preview Chart button to display an expanded—but not full-size—view of your graph. The size relationship between objects in Chart Preview isn't representative of your final graph or chart. Click Close.

8. Click the Next button to go to the fourth and final Chart Wizard dialog. Type **2006 Monthly Sales by Category** in the text box to add a title to your graph. Accept the default Yes, Display a Legend option to display the Category legend (see Figure 18.8).

Figure 18.8
The last Wizard dialog's default options are satisfactory for most graphs and charts. If your source query doesn't have a classification column, you don't need a legend.

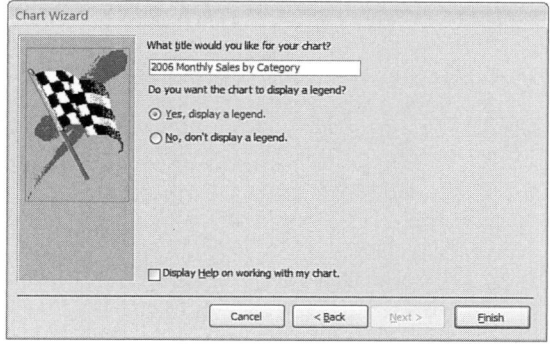

9. Accept the remaining default, and click Finish. Click the Form View button to display the initial graph layout (see Figure 18.9).

Figure 18.9
The Wizard makes a poor guess at the form, font, and the unbound object frame size needed to display the elements the Wizard generates.

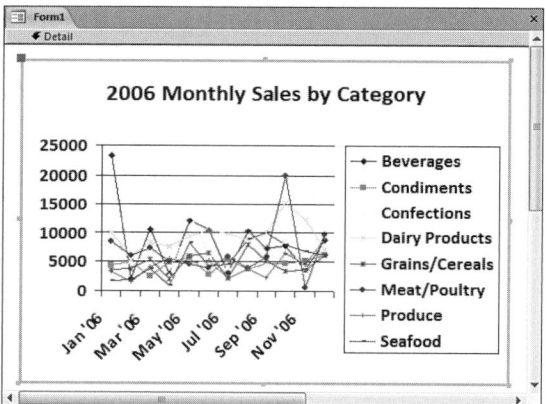

NOTE

In the small version of the graph illustrated by Figure 18.9, some month labels are missing and the legend crowds the graph and label. You fix these problems in the next section of this chapter, "Modifying the Design Features of Your Graph."

10. Click the Design View button and increase the size of your graph to at least 7.5 inches wide by 4.5 inches high. Click the Properties button to display the Properties Sheet for the graph (see Figure 18.10).

Figure 18.10
The All page of the unbound object frame that contains the chart lets you check the crosstab query's SQL statement and set the Enable and Locked properties. Graph.exe's version number is 12, but the Class version (8) hasn't changed since Office 97.

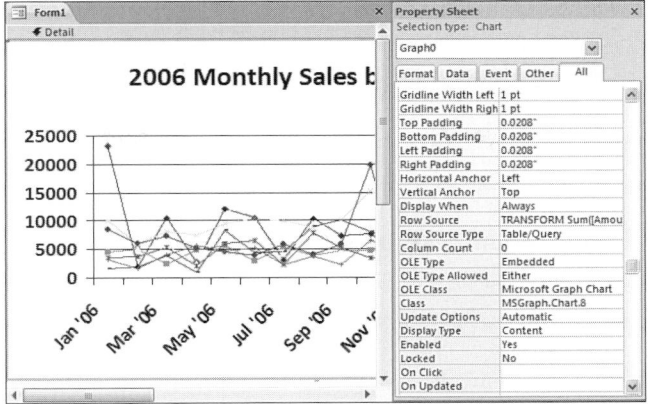

11. Click the Data tab of the Properties dialog, and make sure the Enabled property value of the unbound object frame (OLEUnbound0) is set to Yes and the Locked Property is set to No (the defaults).

12. The chart is in an unbound object frame, so you don't need form adornments for record manipulation. Select Form in the Selection Type list, click the Format tab of the Properties window, and set the Scroll Bars property of the form to Neither, the Record Selectors property to No, and the Navigation Buttons property to No.

13. Use the sizing handles of the unbound object frame to create a 1/8-inch form border around the frame. Leaving a small form area around the object makes the activation process more evident.

14. Save your form with a descriptive name, such as **frm2006SalesByCategoryChart**. Return to Form view in preparation for changing the size and type of your graph.

Access SQL

The Wizard writes the following Access crosstab query to generate the data for the chart:

```
TRANSFORM Sum([Amount]) AS [SumOfAmount]
    SELECT (Format([ShippedDate],"MMM 'YY"))
    FROM [qry2006SalesChart]
    GROUP BY (Year([ShippedDate])*12 + Month([ShippedDate])-1),
        (Format([ShippedDate],"MMM 'YY"))
PIVOT [CategoryName];
```

The GROUP BY clause permits display of monthly data for multiple years, which isn't applicable to the sample query. The Format expression generates x-axis labels, such as Jan '06.

SQL Server's T-SQL doesn't support Access SQL's TRANSFORM...PIVOT statements, so you can't use the Chart Wizard with ADP. You can, however, write T-SQL statements to emulate a crosstab query, so it's possible to use the Insert Object approach to adding an MSGraph chart or graph to forms of ADP.

→ For an example of the SQL Server equivalents of Access crosstab queries, **see** "Emulating Access Crosstab Queries with T-SQL " **p. 980**.

> **TIP**
>
> When you complete your design, set the value of the Enabled property for the form to No so that users of your application can't activate the graph and alter its design. It's also a good practice to set the values of the Allow Datasheet, PivotTable, and PivotChart View properties to No.

MODIFYING THE DESIGN FEATURES OF YOUR GRAPH

MSGraph (Graph.exe) is an OLE 2.0 mini-server, so you can activate MSGraph in place and modify the design of your graph. MSGraph also supports *Automation*, which lets you use VBA code to automate design changes. This section shows you how to use MSGraph to edit the design of the graph manually, as well as how to change the line graph to an area or column chart.

To activate your graph and change its design with MSGraph, follow these steps:

1. Display the form in Form view and then double-click the graph to activate MSGraph in place, which opens a Datasheet window that displays the values returned by the crosstab query (see Figure 18.11). A diagonally hashed border surrounds the graph; MSGraph's menus replace or supplement those of Access 2007. (The activation border is missing from the left and top of the object frame if you didn't create some additional space on the form around the object frame in step 12 of the preceding section.)

Figure 18.11
Activating the unbound object frame grafts MSGraph's menu commands to Access's and opens the Datasheet window.

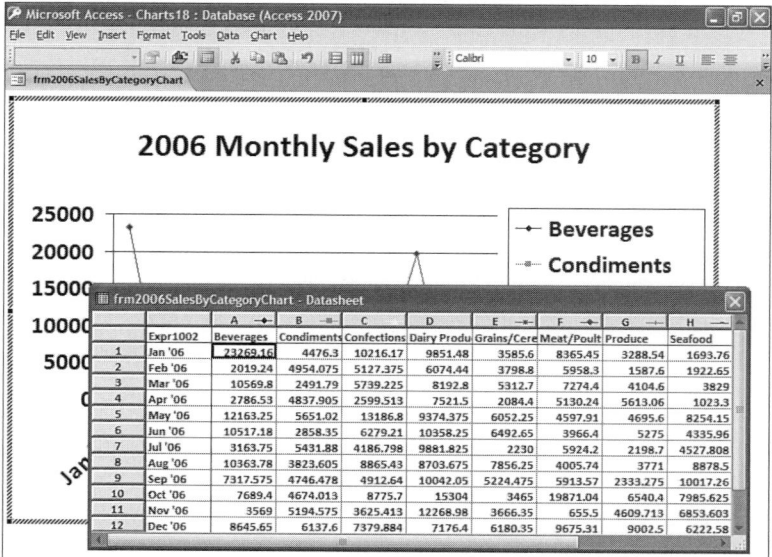

NOTE

> Menu commands of an OLE server or mini-server added to those of the container application are called *grafted menus* or *object menus*. The process that adds the menu commands is called *menu negotiation*.

2. Change the type family and font size of your chart's labels and legend to better suit the size of the object. Double-click the graph title to open the Format Chart Title dialog. Click the Font tab, set the chart title's font size to 18 points, regular (see Figure 18.12), clear the Auto Scale check box, and then click OK to close the dialog.

Figure 18.12
MSGraph has properties dialogs for most of its objects, including chart titles, legends, and axes. Reduce the font size of the Chart Title object to 18 points, and clear the Auto Scale check box to retain the font size regardless of the object frame's dimensions.

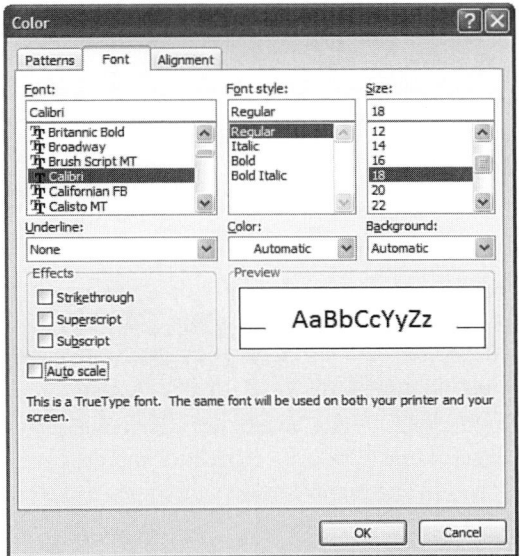

3. Double-click the legend to open the Format Legend dialog. Set the size of the legend font to 10-points, regular, and clear the Auto Scale check box.

4. The y-axis labels should be smaller and formatted as currency, so double-click one of the labels on the y-axis to display the Format Axis dialog. Set the font to 11-points, regular, and clear the Auto Scale check box.

5. Click the Number tab, select Currency in the Category list, and enter **0** in the Decimal Places text box (see Figure 18.13). Click OK to close the Format Axis dialog.

Figure 18.13
Reduce the font size of the y-axis labels to 11 points and apply currency formatting in the Format Axis dialog.

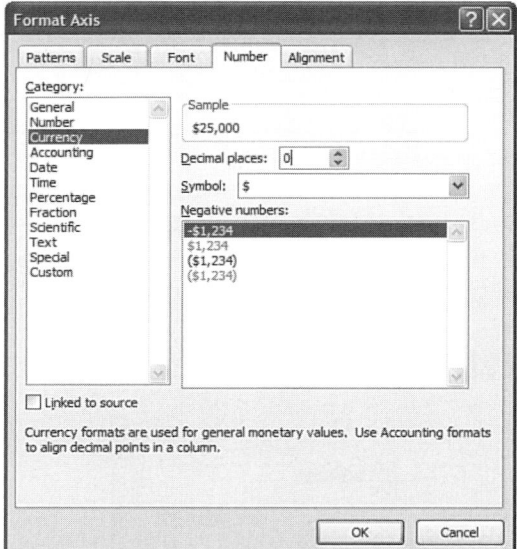

6. The default font size for axis labels at a graph size of 7.5×4.5 inches is 15.25 points, which causes MSGraph to label the x-axis diagonally. Double-click the x-axis and change its font size to 11 points, and also clear the Auto Scale check box. Click OK to close the dialog and apply the new format.

7. Resize the elements of the graph to take maximum advantage of the available area within the unbound object frame. Click the chart title and drag it to the top of the frame. Click an empty area in the graph to select the plot area, which adds a shaded rectangle around the region, and increase its size.

8. Click the form region outside the graph to deactivate MSGraph, and then save your changes. Your line graph now appears as shown in Figure 18.14.

Depending on the use of the graph or chart, consider increasing its size to increase the accuracy of data interpretation for users. If you plan to print the chart, you can increase the width to about 8 inches without changing the default (Narrow) printing margins. You can save vertical space by deleting the chart title and changing the form's Caption property to that of the deleted title. The figures in the following sections reflect these design changes.

CHANGING THE GRAPH TO A CHART

You might want to change the line graph to some other type of chart (such as area or stacked column) for a specific purpose. Area charts, for example, are especially effective as a way to display the contribution of individual product categories to total sales. To change the line graph to another type of chart, follow these steps:

Figure 18.14
The modified graph design corrects the poor choices the Wizard made for the title, axis, and legend font sizes.

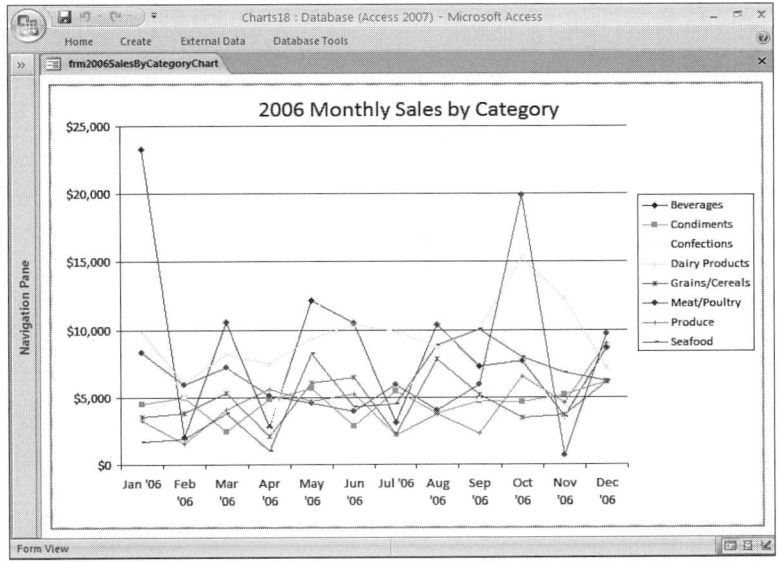

1. Double-click the graph to activate it and then choose Chart, Chart Type to open the Chart Type dialog with the Standard Types page active.
2. Select Area in the Chart Type list (see Figure 18.15).

Figure 18.15
MSGraph's Chart Type dialog offers many more choices of chart and graph styles than the Chart Wizard.

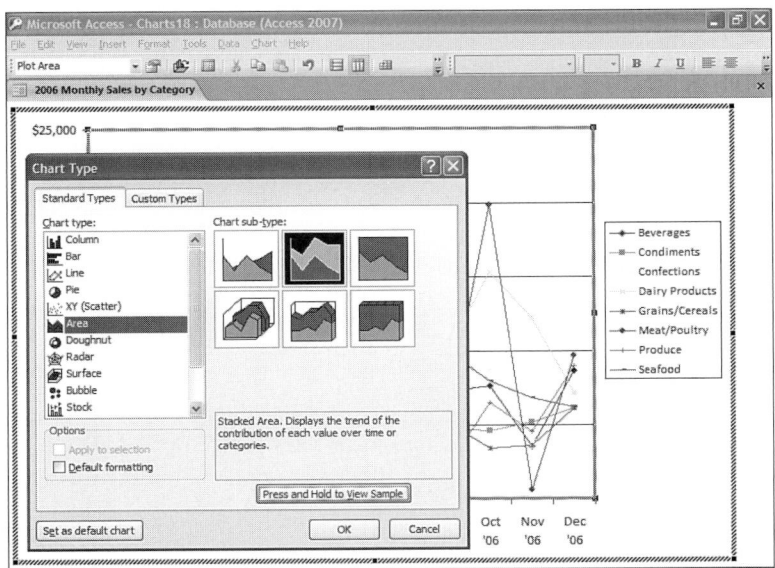

18

TIP

You can preview your chart by clicking and holding down the left mouse button on the Press and Hold to View Sample button.

3. Select the stacked area chart as the Chart Sub-type setting (the middle chart in the first row—refer to Figure 18.15). Click OK to change your line graph into an area chart, as shown in Figure 18.16. The contribution of each category appears as an individually colored area, and the top line segment represents total sales.

Figure 18.16
The stacked area chart shows the contribution of each category to total sales.

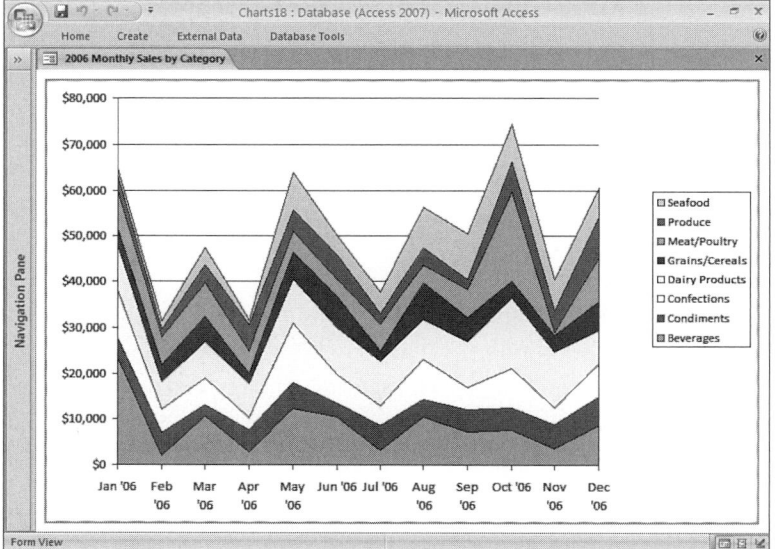

4. To convert the area chart into a stacked column chart, choose Chart, Chart Type to display the Standard Types page of the Chart Type dialog. Select Column in the Chart Type list, and then select as the chart subtype the stacked column chart (selected in Figure 18.17).

5. Click OK to close the Chart Type dialog. Your stacked column chart appears as shown in Figure 18.18.

6. Another subtype of the area chart and stacked column chart is the percentage distribution chart. To create a distribution-of-sales graph, repeat steps 4 and 5 but select the 100% Stacked Column picture (the third thumbnail in the top row) with equal column heights as the Chart Sub-type setting. Click OK to close the Chart Type dialog.

Figure 18.17
You can select a 3D stacked column chart, but conventional 2D column charts are easier to interpret.

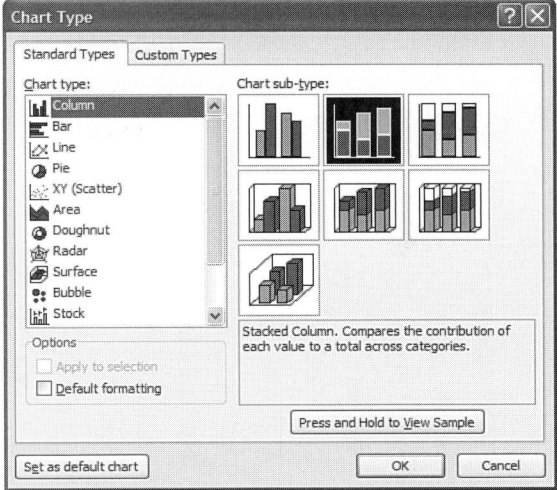

Figure 18.18
A stacked column chart is a less-dramatic alternative to a stacked area chart.

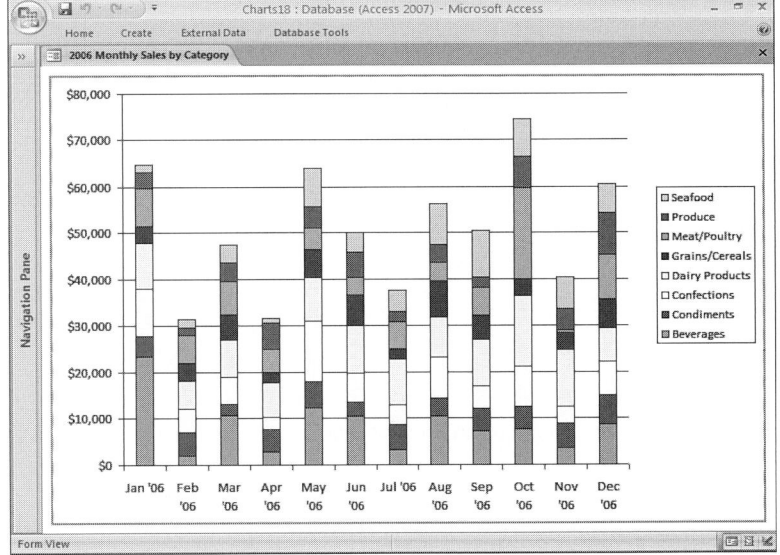

7. Because you previously set the format of the y-axis to eliminate the decimals, you need to change the format of the y-axis manually to Percentage. Double-click the y-axis to open the Format Axis dialog and click the Number page (refer to Figure 18.13). Select Percentage in the Category list, make sure that Decimal Places is set to 0, and then click OK to apply the format. Your chart appears as shown in Figure 18.19.

Figure 18.19
A 100% stacked column shows the distribution of sales by category.

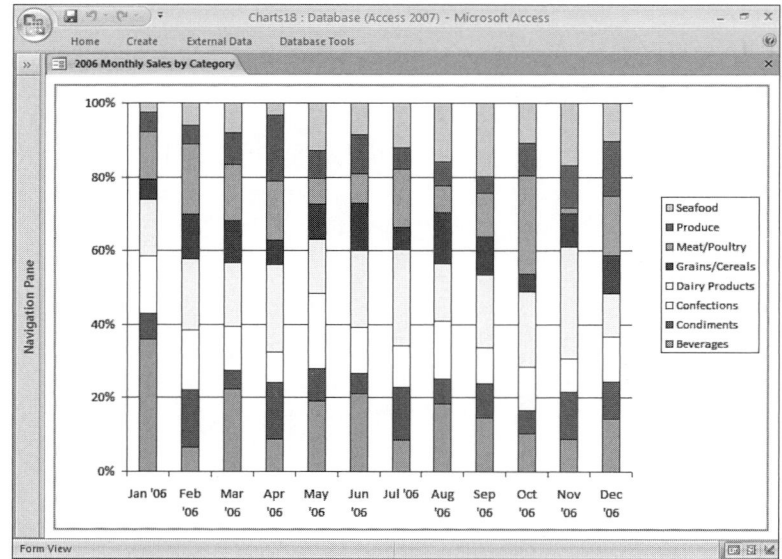

8. Change the chart type back to a line graph in preparation for the linked graph example later in "Creating a Linked Graph from an Access Crosstab Query." Change the y-axis format to Currency, click inside the form region outside the object frame to deactivate the graph, and then save your form.

Of the four types of charts demonstrated, most users find the area chart best for displaying time-series data for multiple values that have meaningful total values.

PRINTING GRAPHS OR CHARTS IN REPORTS

The process of adding an unbound MSGraph object to an Access report is identical to that for forms. Unless all your users have access to a color printer, you should select a line graph subtype that identifies data points with a different symbol for each category. For area and stacked column charts, a series of hatched patterns differentiate the product categories. The Custom Types page of the Chart Types dialog offers a selection of B&W... chart types specifically designed for monochrome printers.

You can save a form created by the Chart Wizard to a report by choosing File, Save As, and selecting Report in the Save As dialog. It's almost as easy to create a new report and copy the form's unbound object frame to it, which also demonstrates how to add a graph to an existing report. Follow these steps:

 1. Open the form with the graph or chart in Design view, select the unbound OLE object frame, and press Ctrl+C to copy the control to the Clipboard. For this example, copy frm2006SalesByCategoryChart's OLEUnbound0 object.

2. Click the Create tab and Blank Report button to open a new report in Layout view. Change to Report Design view.

3. Click the Report Design Tools, Arrange tab and click the Show/Hide group's Report Header/Footer button to add Report Header and Footer sections to the report. If you plan to add fields to the Detail section, you usually add the chart or graph to the report Footer section. Click the Page Header/Footer button to eliminate these default sections, close up the Detail and Report Footer sections of the report, and select the Report Header section.

4. Press Ctrl+V to paste the graph or chart to the selected Report Header section.

5. Adjust the height and width of the unbound object frame within the printing limits of the page. Optionally, move the object frame down, and add a label with a report title. Alternatively, you can add a chart title.

6. Double-click the object frame to activate the object, close the Datasheet window, and choose Chart, Chart Type to open the Chart Type dialog.

7. Click the Custom Types tab, and choose B&W Area to change the style to an area chart with hatching (see Figure 18.20).

Figure 18.20
The B&W Area style is a better selection for printing (in most cases) than B&W Column, which includes a data table.

8. Click OK to apply the style. Click outside the graph to deselect it and display the monochrome chart, which has a gray background and unformatted y-axis labels, and change to Report view (see Figure 18.21).

Figure 18.21
Selecting a different chart style removes much of the formatting you applied to the copied chart.

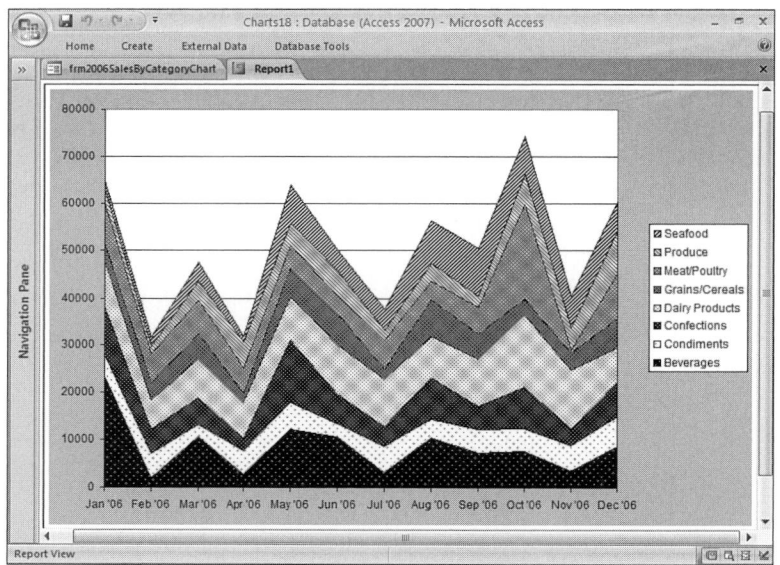

9. To remove the gray background, which consumes toner or ink but doesn't contribute to readability, change to Design view and double-click the object frame to activate it. Right-click the gray region, and choose Format Chart Area to open the dialog of the same name. On the Patterns page, select the None option in the Area frame to make the background transparent and then click OK.

10. Double-click the y-axis labels to open the Format Axis dialog, click the Number tab, select Currency, set Decimal Places to 0, and click OK.

11. Click the Report Header bar to deactivate the object, change to Design view, and open the Properties window for the object frame (OLEUnbound0 for this example).

12. Click the Format tab, and set the Border Style property value to Transparent.

> **NOTE**
>
> Selecting the None option in the Border frame of the Format Chart Area dialog's Patterns page doesn't remove the default border of the object frame.

13. Select the Report in the Selection Type list, and set the Caption property value to **2006 Monthly Sales by Category**.

14. Change to Report View to display your modified report design (see Figure 18.22).

You can't activate the chart object for editing in Report mode.

Figure 18.22
Monochrome reports use hatching and shading to differentiate areas by classification. Unfortunately, many laser printers don't distinguish dark regions, such as Confections and Beverages, in this example.

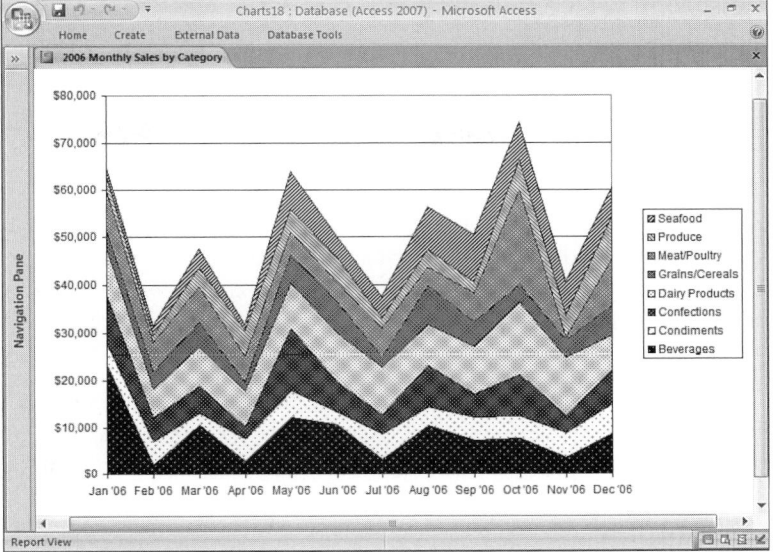

15. Save your report with a descriptive name, such as **rpt2006SalesByCategoryChart** for this example.

You can increase the printed width of the graph by returning to Design view and double-clicking the legend to open the Format Legend dialog. Click the Placement tab and select the Bottom option. Optionally, click the Format tab and select the None option in the Border frame. Figure 18.23 shows the report with the relocated legend.

Figure 18.23
Relocating the legend to the bottom of a report (or form) lets you increase the printed (or displayed) width of the chart.

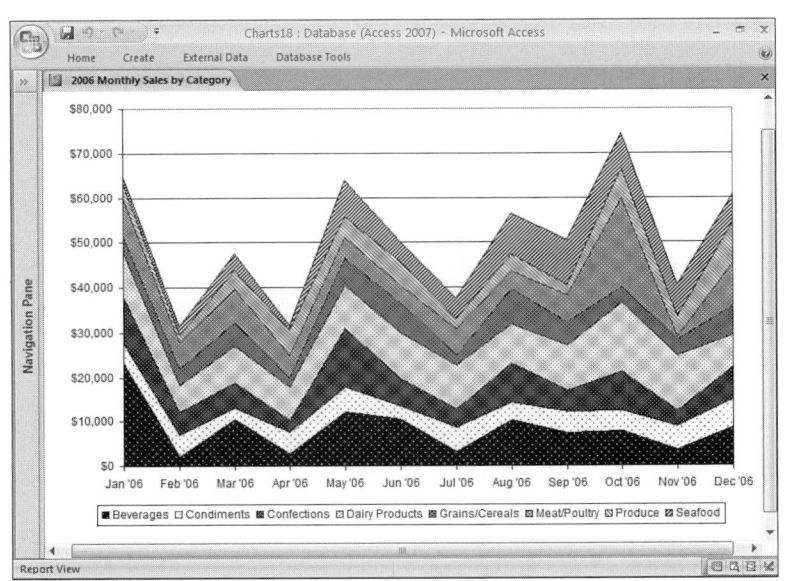

CREATING A LINKED GRAPH FROM AN ACCESS CROSSTAB QUERY

Access's Chart Wizard is quite parochial: It insists on creating a crosstab query for you. After you've created a chart with the Chart Wizard, however, you can change the graph's Row Source property value to specify a previously created crosstab query of your own design.

Linked graphs or charts display a succession of graphical representations of related data. Linked graphs are useful for delivering more detailed information than bar or area charts can impart. For example, it's difficult to interpret trends for sales of product categories in a stacked area chart. Linked graphs let you drill down into the data behind summary charts and add features to aid data interpretation—such as trendlines. Linked graphs are one of Access 2007's most powerful features.

For this linked graph example, you create the qry2006SalesChartCT crosstab query and use the query as the Row Source setting of the unbound object frame to complete the linked graph example in the following section. The linked graph example doesn't work with the crosstab query created by the Chart Wizard in the preceding steps. The Chart Wizard's crosstab query result set has months in rows and categories in columns.

DESIGNING THE CROSSTAB QUERY FOR THE GRAPH

To create the qry2006SalesChartCT query from qry2006SalesChart, follow these steps:

1. Create a new query in Design view, add the qry2006SalesChart query, and click the Query Types group's Crosstab button.

2. Drag the CategoryName field to the first column of the query and select Row Heading in the Crosstab row. Accept the default Group By value in the Total cell.

3. Alias the CategoryName field by typing **Categories:** at the beginning of the Field text box.

4. Type the expression **Month:Format([ShippedDate], "mmm")** into the second Fields cell to use three-letter month abbreviations. Then, select Column Heading in the Crosstab cell. Accept the default Group By value in the Total cell.

5. Drag the Amount field to the third column, set the Total cell to Sum, and set the Crosstab cell to Value (see Figure 18.24).

6. Click the Property Sheet button to open the query's property sheet. In the Column Headings text box, type the 12 month abbreviations (**Jan,...Dec**), separated by commas to arrange the columns in date, not alphabetic, sequence. Access adds the quotes around the month abbreviations for you (see Figure 18.25).

Figure 18.24
An Access crosstab query for a linked graph requires specifying Row Heading, Column Heading, and Value in the Crosstab row of the query design grid.

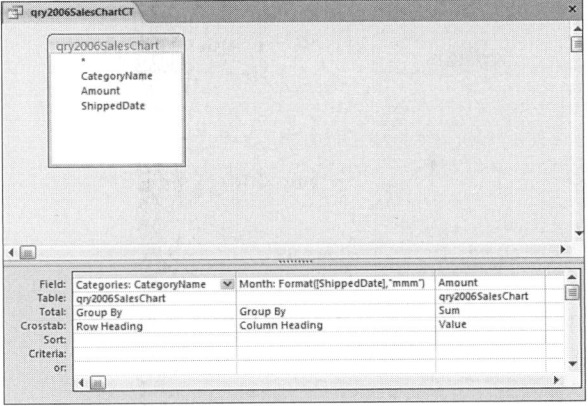

Figure 18.25
In the query's property sheet, add a comma-separated list of column headings that correspond to your crosstab query's Format expression for the Column Heading values.

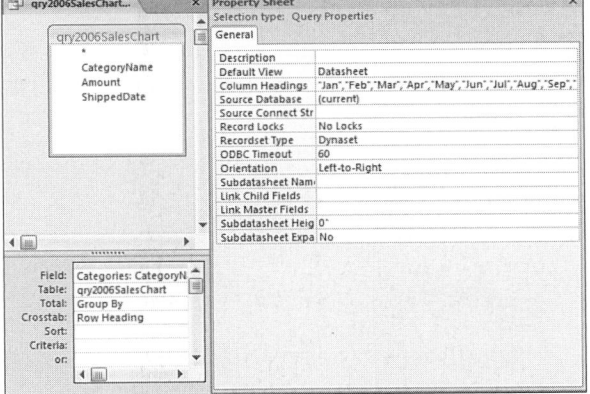

7. Save your query as **qry2006SalesChartCT**.

8. Click the Run button to check your query result set (see Figure 18.26).

Access SQL

The crosstab query for the linked chart differs from that created by the Chart Wizard for an unlinked chart or graph. Following is the Access SQL statement for the linked chart's data source:

```
TRANSFORM Sum(qry2006SalesChart.Amount) AS SumOfAmount
SELECT qry2006SalesChart.CategoryName AS Categories
FROM qry2006SalesChart
GROUP BY qry2006SalesChart.CategoryName
PIVOT Format([ShippedDate],"mmm")
    In ("Jan","Feb","Mar","Apr","May","Jun",
        "Jul","Aug","Sep","Oct","Nov","Dec");
```

The primary difference between the two queries is the GROUP BY clause, which groups the data by the CategoryName column, rather than by a date expression. In this case, the In predicate is required to return the monthly data in date (instead of alphabetic) order.

18

Figure 18.26
This Access crosstab query provides the value of the Row Source property for the linked graph.

Category Name	Jan	Feb	Mar	Apr	May	Jun
Beverages	$23,269.16	$2,019.24	$10,569.80	$2,786.53	$12,163.25	$10,517.18
Condiments	$4,476.30	$4,954.08	$2,491.79	$4,837.91	$5,651.02	$2,858.35
Confections	$10,216.17	$5,127.38	$5,739.23	$2,599.51	$13,186.80	$6,279.21
Dairy Products	$9,851.48	$6,074.44	$8,192.80	$7,521.50	$9,374.38	$10,358.25
Grains/Cereals	$3,585.60	$3,798.80	$5,312.70	$2,084.40	$6,052.25	$6,492.65
Meat/Poultry	$8,365.45	$5,958.30	$7,274.40	$5,130.24	$4,597.91	$3,966.40
Produce	$3,288.54	$1,587.60	$4,104.60	$5,613.06	$4,695.60	$5,275.00
Seafood	$1,693.76	$1,922.65	$3,829.00	$1,023.30	$8,254.15	$4,335.96

Record: 1 of 8 — No Filter — Search

ASSIGNING THE CROSSTAB QUERY AS THE GRAPH'S ROW SOURCE

The next stage in the process is to take advantage of your existing MSGraph design by changing its data source from the Chart Wizard's Access SQL statement to the new crosstab query. Do the following:

1. Open frm2006SalesByCategoryChart in Design view, select the chart's object frame (OLEUnbound0), and open its Property Sheet.

2. Open the Row Source list box, and select qry2006SalesChartCT as the value of the Row Source property. The graph displays category labels on the x-axis and month labels in the legend.

3. Return to Form view, double-click to activate the graph, and click the toolbar's By Row button or choose Data, Series in Rows from the Chart menu. Verify that your line graph appears the same as the graph that the Chart Wizard created in the earlier section "Modifying the Design Features of Your Graph" (refer to Figure 18.14).

 If you're having trouble getting labels into the correct location, see "Reversing the X-Axis and Legend Labels" in the "Troubleshooting" section at the end of this chapter.

LINKING THE GRAPH TO A SINGLE RECORD OF A TABLE OR QUERY

You create a linked graph or chart by setting the values of the MSGraph object's Link Child Fields and Link Master Fields properties. The link is similar to that between a form and subform. A linked graph displays the data series from the current row of the table or query that serves as the Record Source of the form. As you move the record pointer with the record navigation buttons, the graph is redrawn to reflect the data values in the selected row.

→ To review the linking process between master and child forms or reports, **see** "Adding the SBF HRActions Tab Subform with the Wizard" **p. 687**.

To change the 2006frmSalesByCategoryChart form to accommodate a linked graph, follow these steps:

1. Change to Form Design view, select Form in the Selection Type list, and then click the Property Sheet button to open the Property Sheet for the form.

2. Click the Data tab, open the Record Source list box, and select qry2006SalesChartCT as the value of the Record Source property of the form, which binds the form to the crosstab query.

3. Your form needs record-navigation buttons for a linked graph or chart, so click the Format tab and set the value of the Navigation Buttons property to Yes.

4. Select the unbound object frame (OLEUnbound0) and then click the Data tab. Verify that qry2006SalesChartCT is the Row Source for the chart. Type **Categories** as the value of the Link Child Fields and Link Master Fields properties (see Figure 18.27). Disregard the "Can't build a link between unbound forms" error messages that might appear after typing the Link Child Fields value.

Figure 18.27
Type the column name of the field on which to link the graph and the form in the Link Master Fields and Link Child Fields text boxes. You can't use the Builder button to create the link; you receive an error message if you try.

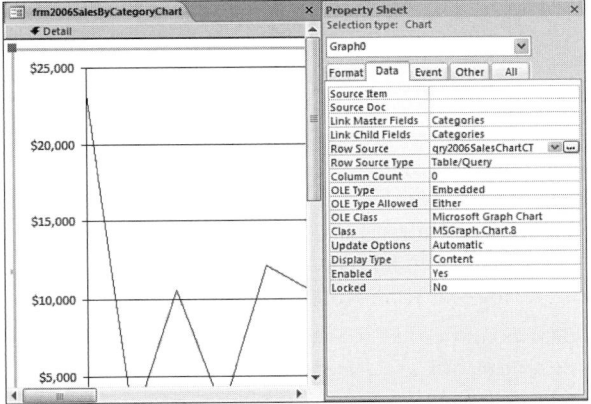

NOTE

Using this technique, you create the link between the current record of the form and the row of the query that serves as the Row Source property of the graph (through the aliased Categories column of the query).

5. To test your linked graph, click the Form View button. If (in the earlier "Changing the Graph to a Chart" section) you saved the line graph version of the form, your graph initially appears as shown in Figure 18.28.

Figure 18.28
The linked graph displays a single line and legend entry for each of the eight product categories.

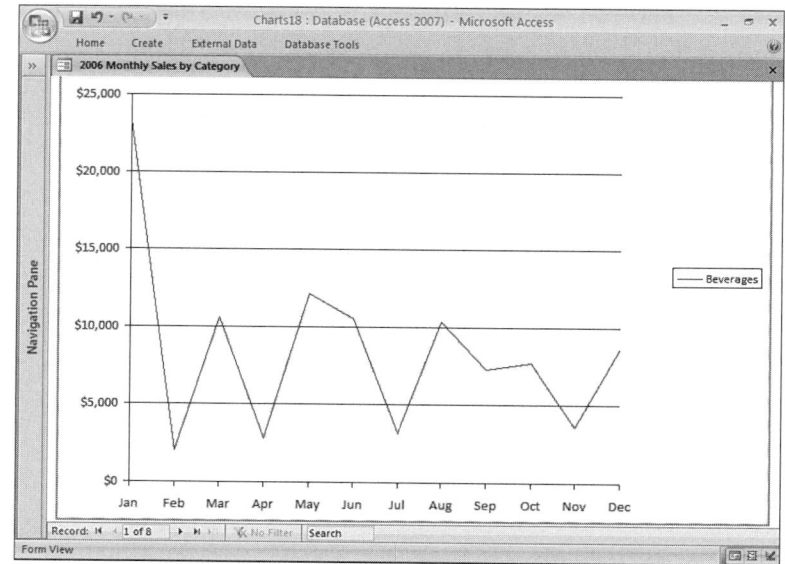

6. The single line appears a bit anemic for a graph of this size, so double-click the graph to activate it in place. Right-click the line with all data points selected, and choose Format Data Series to display the Format Data Series dialog. Click the Patterns tab, select the Custom option, open the Weight drop-down list, and choose the thickest line it offers. Optionally, change the color from Automatic to a color from the pick list.

7. To change the data-point marker, select the Custom option, open the Style drop-down list, and select the square shape. Use the drop-down lists to set the Foreground and Background colors of the marker to Automatic to add solid markers of the line color. Optionally, increase the size of the markers by a couple of points (see Figure 18.29). Click OK to close the dialog and implement your design changes.

8. Double-click the legend box to open the Format Legend dialog. On the Patterns page, click the None option in the Border frame to remove the border from the legend. Click the Font tab, turn the Bold attribute on, and change the font size to 18 points. Click OK to close the dialog and apply your modification to the legend.

9. To use your enhanced legend as a title for the chart, delete the existing title, if present, and click and drag the legend to a location above the graph. Click the plot area to display the chart's sizing handles; drag the middle sizing handle to the right to increase the width of the plot area (see Figure 18.30).

10. Click the record navigation buttons to display a graph of the sales for each of the eight categories. As you change categories, notice that the y-axis scale changes. The maximum range for the Beverages category is $25,000, while that for Condiments is $7,000.

Figure 18.29
The Format Data Series dialog lets you change the thickness and color of the graph's line, add and format data markers, and change the line segment to a continuous curve between data points (called *smoothing*, which is shown later in Figure 8.31).

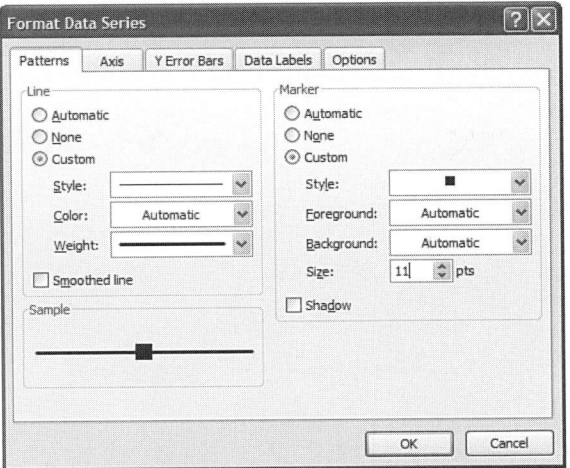

Figure 18.30
This graph is reformatted with increased line thickness, added data points, and a modified legend to act as the chart title.

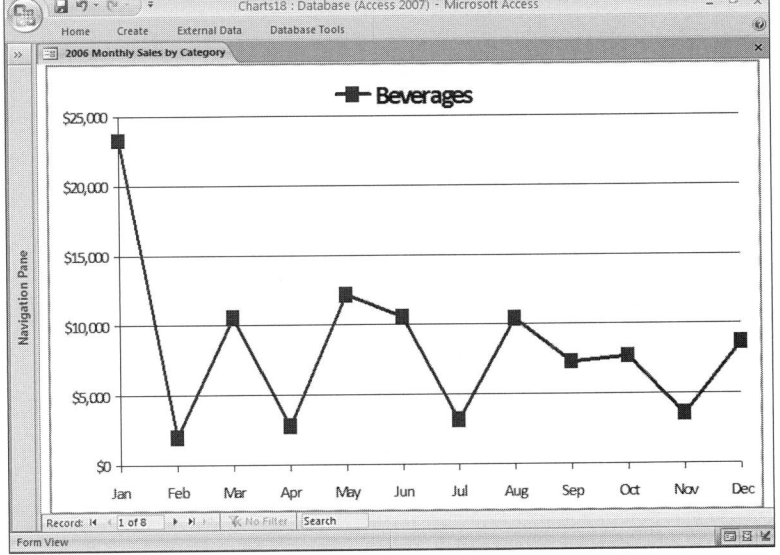

11. To add a trendline to your graph, activate the graph and choose Chart, Add Trendline to open the Add Trendline dialog. Accept the default Linear trendline on the Type page, and click the Options tab. Select the Custom option, type a legend for the trendline, such as **2006 Sales Trend**, and click OK.

12. To remove the sizing handles from the Form view of the deactivated object, change to Design view, select the object frame, and open the Property Sheet. Click the Data tab, and change the Enabled property value to No and Locked to Yes. (You can't change Locked to Yes in Form view.) Changing these two property values prevents users from activating the graph. With the Smoothed Line check box of the Data Series dialog marked, your modified graph appears in Form view as shown in Figure 18.31. Refer to Figure 18.29 for setting the Smoothed Line option.

Figure 18.31
Adding a trendline to the graph aids in interpreting the data. Smoothing the data series line implies the existence of additional data points between those in the datasheet, such as the slower decline from May to June.

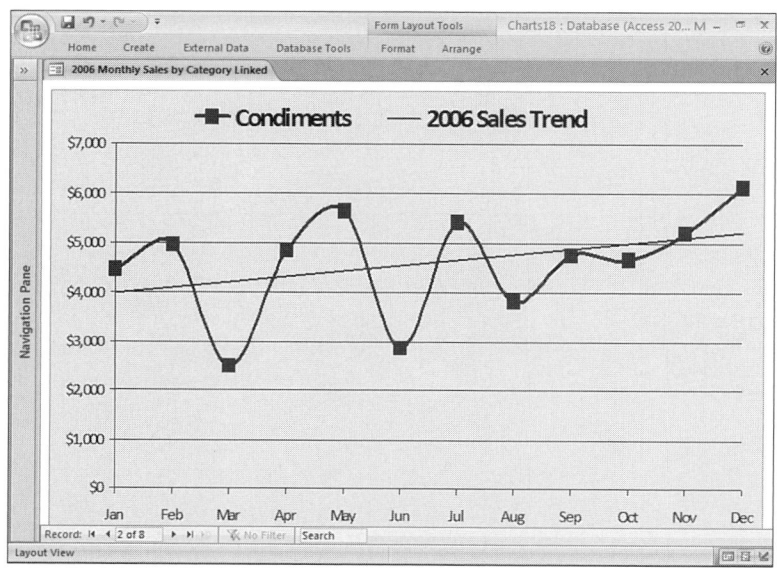

13. Click the Office button, choose Save As, and then save your bound graph form with a new name, such as **frm2006SalesByCategoryChartLinked**.

WORKING WITH PIVOTCHART FORMS

Microsoft promotes Office 2007 PivotCharts as a substitute for MSGraph OLE Objects for a good (marketing) reason: MSGraph requires a crosstab query (or equivalent) and, as mentioned earlier, SQL Server's T-SQL doesn't support crosstab queries directly. If you want to add graphs or charts to ADP, PivotCharts are the least-effort answer. The same is true if you anticipate upsizing your Access databases to SQL Server and upgrading conventional Access objects to ADP forms and reports.

The sections that follow describe how to use PivotCharts to emulate the unlinked and linked MSGraph objects you created in the preceding sections of this chapter. The sample PivotCharts use the qry2006SalesChart query, because the Access SQL and T-SQL versions of the query are identical. The PivotTable created from the query acts as the data source for the PivotChart by handling the data restructuring ordinarily accomplished by Access SQL `PIVOT...TRANSFORM` statements.

→ To review PivotChart design basics, **see** "Formatting and Manipulating PivotCharts," **p. 541**.

CREATING A PIVOTCHART FORM FROM A QUERY

PivotCharts don't have the formatting flexibility of MSGraph objects, but they let you duplicate most MSGraph chart types satisfactorily. To generate a stacked area PivotChart based on the qry2006SalesChart query, do the following:

1. Select the qry2006SalesChart query in the Navigation Pane.

2. Click the Create tab, and then click the Forms group's PivotChart button to open a PivotChart named qry2006SalesChart with the Field List superimposed. (If the Field list isn't visible, click an empty area of the form.) Expand the Field List's ShippedDate by Month node to display period options (see Figure 18.32).

Figure 18.32
The quickest way to create a PivotChart form is to select a table or query and click the Create ribbon's PivotChart button.

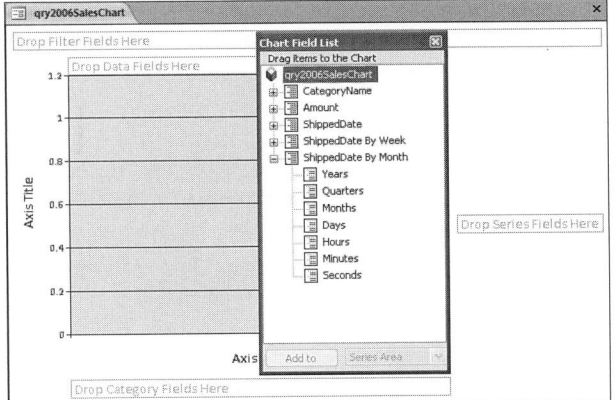

3. Drag the Amount field from the Chart Field List to the Drop Data Fields Here zone and the CategoryName field to the Drop Series Fields Here zone. Each product category is a member of Series 1 of the PivotChart.

> **N O T E**
>
> The PivotChart detects the currency format of the Amount query column and applies standard currency formatting to the y-axis. Unlike with MSGraph, you can't remove the two digits after the decimal point without writing a considerable amount of VBA code.

4. From the Field List's ShippedDate By Month node, drag the Months field to the Drop CategoryFields Here node. The default chart type is the conventional (not stacked) column version, so Months has one column for each of the eight product categories (see Figure 18.33).

Figure 18.33
Adding value, category (classification), and series fields (columns) from the qry2006SalesChart query generates this default multiple column chart.

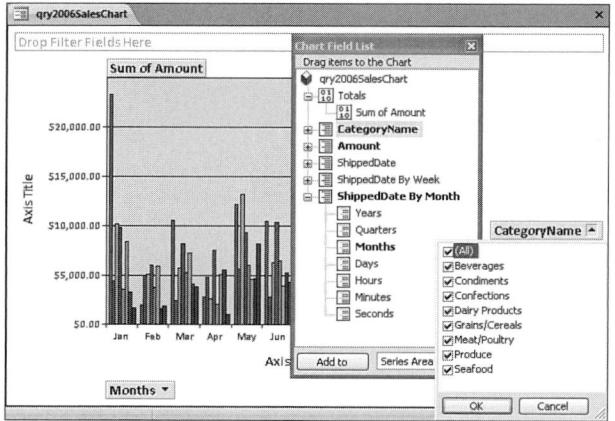

5. Click the PivotChart Tools, Design tab's Change Chart Type button to open the Type page of the Properties dialog. Select the Area chart type and click the Stacked Area subtype to emulate the MSGraph chart you created in the "Changing the Graph to a Chart" section early in the chapter (see Figure 18.34). (If the button is disabled, select the chart to enable it.)

Figure 18.34
The PivotChart's Stacked Area chart type is almost identical to that of MSGraph's. Notice that the month abbreviations are centered under—instead of between—the x-axis value markers.

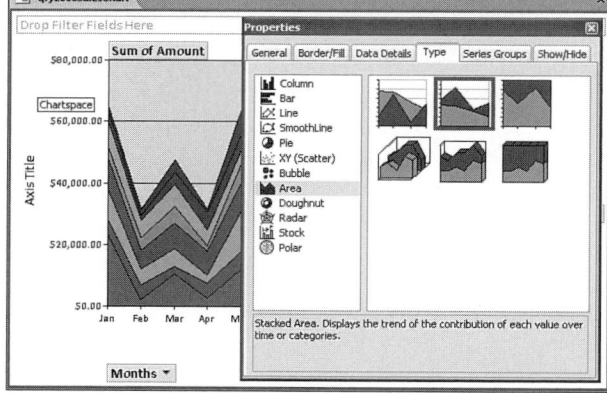

6. Click the Show/Hide tab and clear all check boxes except Screen Tips and Commands and Options Dialog Box. Removing the field buttons prevents users from rearranging the chart.

NOTE

"Commands and Options" was the original name of the Properties dialog. Microsoft's developers overlooked changing the caption of the check box.

7. With the Properties dialog open, click the y-axis line and then click the Format tab. Change the font size to 9 points, and apply the Bold attribute to the labels.

8. Repeat step 6 for the x-axis labels.

9. Select in the General page's list the Value Axis 1 Title, click the Format tab, and delete its Caption property value. Do the same for the Category Axis 1 Title. The form caption defines the axis titles adequately.

10. Optionally, select the legend and change the Position setting to Bottom. (If the legend isn't visible, choose PivotChart, Show Legend).

11. Change to Form Design view, click the Form Selector button, open the Form properties window, click the Format tab, and type **2006 Monthly Sales By Category** as the value of the Caption property. Your PivotChart in Form view now appears as shown in Figure 18.35.

Figure 18.35
With the exception of the two decimal digits of the y-axis labels, this PivotChart successfully emulates the MSGraph stacked area chart shown earlier in Figure 18.16.

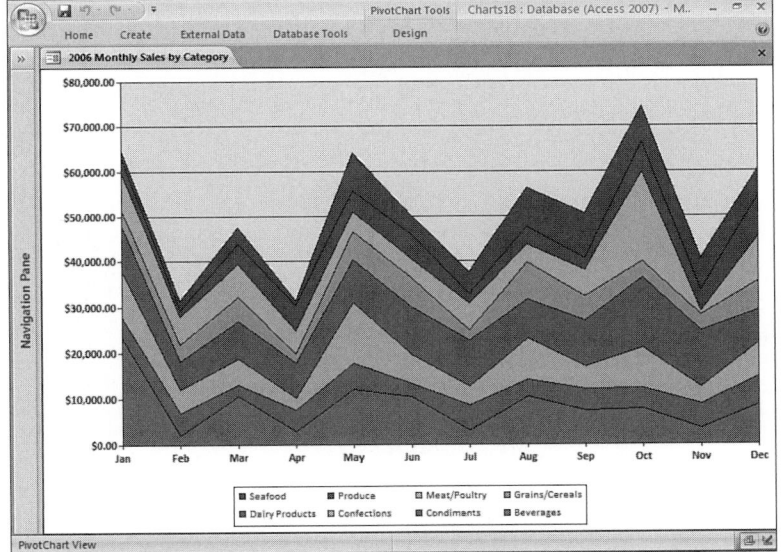

12. In Form Design view, open the form's Properties window again and set the Allow Form View, Allow Datasheet View, and Allow PivotTable View property values to No. Restricting the view of the form is important because it keeps users from being confused by extraneous views of nonmeaningful data.

13. Save your form with a descriptive name, such as **sbf2006SalesPivotChart**, and close it. You apply the **sbf** prefix because you use the PivotChart form as a subform in the next section.

> **NOTE**
>
> PivotCharts on forms don't have a fixed size in Form view. As you change the dimensions of the form, the PivotChart expands or contracts accordingly.

USING THE PIVOTCHART FORM AS A SUBFORM

The PivotChart view of a form prevents you from altering the overall design of the form. For instance, you can't add a visible page header/footer or add extra space to the detail section in which to place a label for a chart title. To achieve form layout flexibility, use the PivotChart form as a subform by following these steps:

 1. Click the Create tab and the Blank Form button to open a new empty form. The Field list displays a node for each table.

2. Expand the Detail section of the form to accommodate a chart or graph of reasonable size, approximately 7.5 inches wide by 4.5 inches deep for this example.

 3. In the Form Design Tools, Design ribbon's Control group, make sure the Control Wizards button is selected.

 4. Select the Subform/Subreport tool, and draw a subform container of moderate size. When you release the mouse, the SubForm Wizard opens.

5. In the first SubForm Wizard dialog, select the Use an Existing Form option, and select the PivotChart form to use as the subform. For this example, select the sbf2006SalesPivotChart you created in the preceding section (see Figure 18.36). Click Next.

Figure 18.36
In the first SubForm Wizard dialog, select the PivotChart form you saved to serve as a subform of the new form you opened.

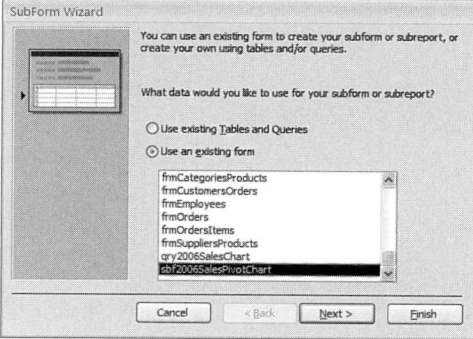

6. Accept the default name for the subform container and its label in the last Wizard dialog, and click Finish to add the subform, which has a default size of about 8.5×1.5 inches. Reduce the width of the form to the original 7.5 inches. Disregard the appearance of the Form Header/Footer sections in Form Design view; PivotChart forms don't display these sections in Design or Form view.

7. Use the sizing handles to expand the subform to within about 3/8 inch from the top, and 1/8 inch or so from the left, right, and bottom edges of the form.

8. Change to Layout view to verify that the subform displays the PivotChart, and adjust the depth of the form to fit the available space (see Figure 18.37).

Figure 18.37
Perform a quick check of the initial appearance of your PivotChart subform to verify that it opens in PivotChart view.

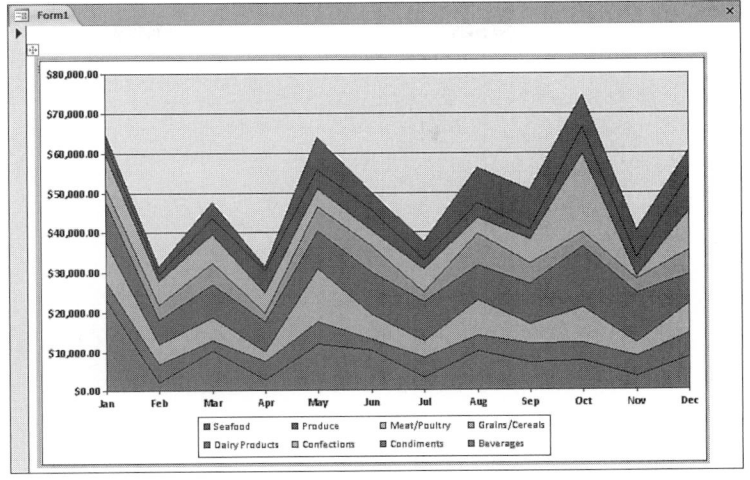

> **TIP**
>
> If the subform opens in Form or Datasheet view, you forgot to disable all but PivotChart view in step 11 of the preceding section.

9. Return to Design view and open the form's property sheet. On the Format page, set the Caption property value to **2006 Monthly Sales By Category**, Allow Datasheet View to No, Allow PivotTable View to No, Allow PivotChart View to No, Scroll Bars to Neither, Record Selectors to No, and Navigation Buttons to No.

10. Add a **2006 Monthly Sales By Category PivotChart** Form label above the subform to serve as a chart title (see Figure 18.38).

11. Select the subform, and set the Border Style property value to Transparent. Return to Form view, select an empty area of the form and click the Property Sheet button of the PivotChart Tools, Design ribbon's Tools group. Verify that Chart Workspace is selected on the General page, click the Border/Fill tab, open the Border group's Color picker and click None. The form/subform combination appears as shown in Figure 18.39.

12. Save your form with the usual descriptive name (**frm2006SalesPivotChart** for this example) and close it.

Figure 18.38
Here's the final design of the form/subform combination to display the unlinked PivotChart.

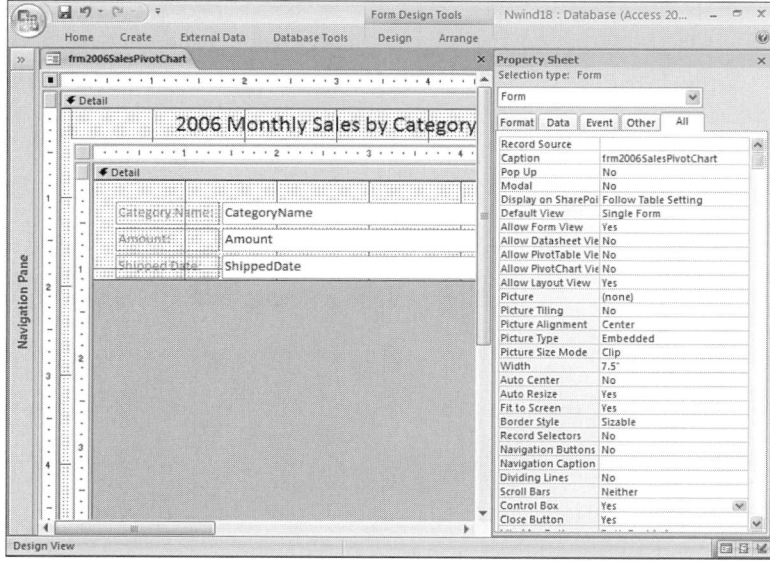

Figure 18.39
Adding the PivotChart form as a subform adds flexibility to the form layout and also enables conversion of the combination to a linked graph. Placing the mouse pointer on a data point shows a ScreenTip with the series name and value.

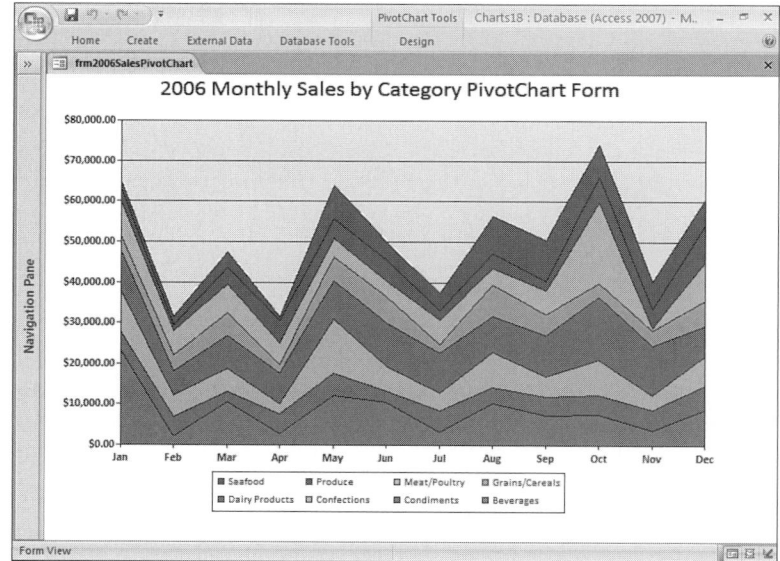

> **TIP**
>
> Use the design process described in this and the preceding section to create a report/subreport combination for printing. You can select a set of textures for the individual data series members of the PivotChart if your users need to print black-and-white reports.
>
> You can print the form to color printers, but you might not be pleased with the initial aspect ratio of the chart. By default, the chart expands vertically to fill the entire printable area of the page. To retain the aspect ratio, set the Format page's Can Grow property value to No.

LINKING THE PIVOTCHART TO THE MAIN FORM'S CURRENT RECORD

Creating a linked PivotChart isn't as simple as the method described in the earlier "Creating a Linked Graph from an Access Crosstab Query" section. The basic steps required to link a PivotChart form/subform combination are as follows:

1. Bind the form to a table or query that you can link to the query that provides the data source for the subform and its graph or chart.

2. Set the values of the Link Master Fields and Link Child Fields properties to the common fields of the main form and subform data sources.

3. Add Record Navigation buttons to the main form.

4. Modify the form and PivotChart design to take advantage of chart linking.

The following two sections describe how to modify copies of the form and PivotChart subform you created in the preceding two sections to link a graph to the Categories table.

CLONING A LINKED PIVOTCHART FORM/SUBFORM PAIR

Take the following steps to create renamed copies of the form and subform, and link them:

1. Make a copy of the sbf2006SalesPivotChart subform, and name it **sbf2006SalesPCLinked**. (Select original subform in the Navigation pane and press Ctrl+C, Ctrl+V to quickly create the copy.)

2. Open the subform copy in Form view, click the Pivot Chart Tools, Design Change ribbon's Chart Type button, and select Line or Smoothline in the Chart Type Dialog's list. Click the first subtype, a standard line graph, and then close and save changes to the subform. Changing the chart to a graph verifies that you're using the correct subform when you make changes to the main form.

3. Make a copy of the frm2006SalesPivotChart as **frm2006SalesPCLinked**, and open the copy in Design view.

4. Open the Property Sheet for the form, click the Data tab, and set the Record Source property to the Categories table. The CategoryName field of the Categories table links to the CategoryName column of the subform's qry2006SalesChart data source.

5. Set the Allow Filters, Allow Edits, Allow Deletions, and Allow Additions property values to No to create a read-only (decision-support) form.

6. Click the Format tab and set the value of the Navigation Buttons property of the form to Yes.

7. Right-click the label at the top of the form and choose Change To, Text Box to replace it with a text box of the same size. Click the Data tab and set the Control Source property to =**"2006 Sales for " & [CategoryName]**, and the Locked property value to Yes.

8. To emulate a label with a text box, click the Format tab and set the text box's Back Style property value to Transparent.

9. Click the edge of the subform to select the subform container, click the Data tab, and select sbf2006SalesPCLinked as the Source Object property value.

10. Click the Builder button of the Link Master Fields property text box to open the Subform Field Linker dialog. If CategoryName isn't selected in both the Master Fields and Child Fields lists, select that field (see Figure 18.40). Click OK.

Figure 18.40
Use the Subform Field Linker to set the Link Master Fields and Link Child Fields property values.

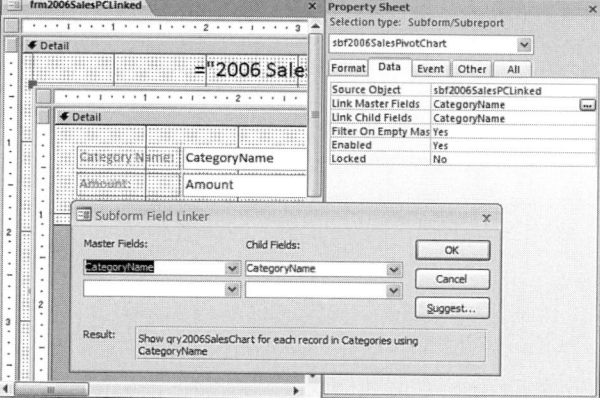

11. Click Form view to display the linked line graph. Navigate the Recordset to verify that the category name in the caption and the legend track one another (see Figure 18.41). Close the form/subform combination, and save your changes.

Figure 18.41
The linked PivotChart subform resembles the linked MSGraph object shown earlier in Figure 18.28.

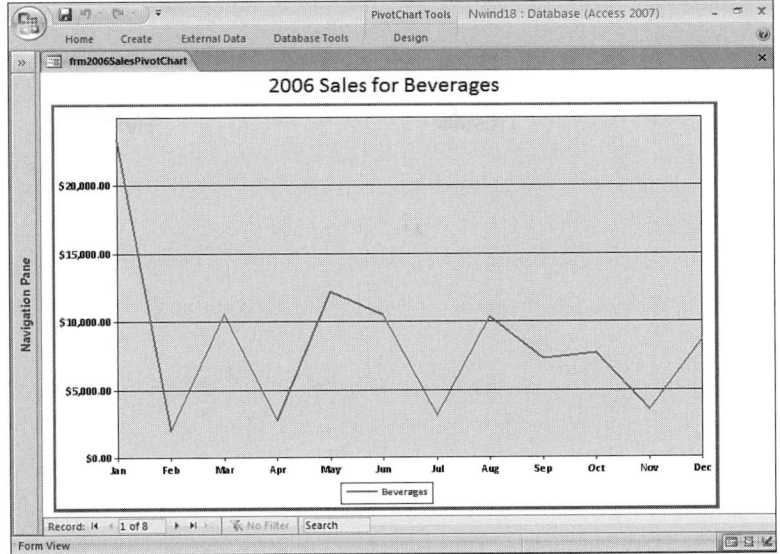

TWEAKING THE DESIGN OF THE PIVOTCHART SUBFORM

After you've verified that linking is working, you can delete the legend to devote more space on the form to the graph. Like with MSGraph objects, you can change the line (series member) formatting properties and add trendlines to PivotCharts. However, the process is much more tedious than that for linked MSGraph objects, because you must alter each member of the series.

To delete the legend, increase the line thickness, and add a trendline to a series member, do the following:

1. Open the sbf2006SalesPCLinked form in PivtoChart view. Then activate the PivotChart Tools, Design ribbon, right-click an empty area of the graph, and click Property Sheet to open the Properties dialog for the Chart Workspace. Be sure to open the subform, not the main form.

2. In the Select list, choose Legend and then click the Delete button to remove the Legend, which isn't necessary for a linked graph.

3. Open the Select list and choose Beverages to select the first series member. Click the Line/Marker tab, and set the Weight property to thick. On the General Page, click the Add Trendline button (the middle button below the Add line) to add a linear trendline to the graph.

4. Return to the General page, and select the added Beverages Trendline 1. Click the Line/Marker tab, and set the Weight property to thick.

18

5. Click the Trendline tab, and clear the Display Equation and Display R-squared Value check boxes.

6. Repeat steps 3–5 for the Condiments category.

7. Press Ctrl+S to save your final changes, and close the subform.

 8. Open the frm2006SalesPCLinked form in Form view to check your design changes (see Figure 18.42).

Figure 18.42
Thickening the PivotChart's series line and adding a trendline duplicates the final MSGraph linked chart of Figure 18.31, except for the data points and line smoothing.

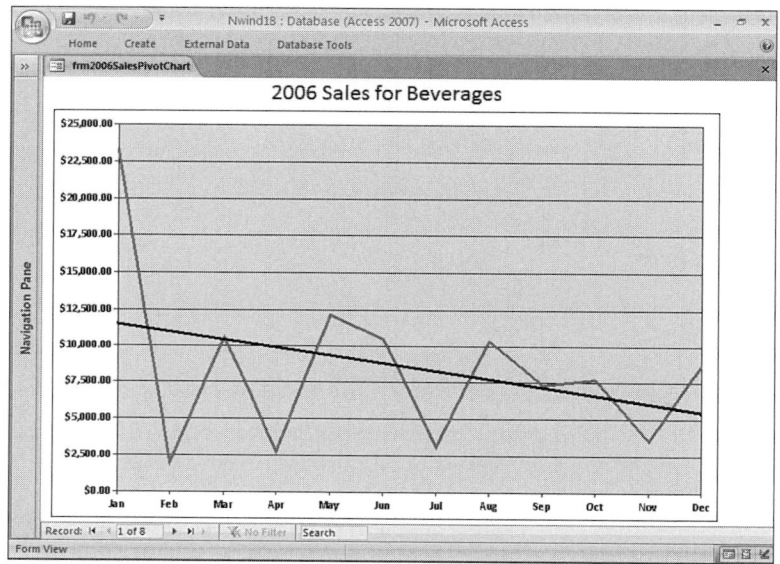

NOTE

The final versions of the forms and subforms you create in this chapter are included in the Charts18.mdb sample database, which is located in the \SEUA12\Chaptr18 folder of the accompanying CD-ROM.

PERSISTING LINKED PIVOTCHART PROPERTIES WITH VBA CODE

A defect in the PivotChart Web Component causes the PivotChart to lose the design changes you made in the preceding section when you move the record pointer with the Navigation buttons. This bug appeared in Access 2002 and persists in Access 2007. You must add VBA code to reapply the properties for each category's graph. The code behind the frm1997SalesPCLinked form of the Charts18.mdb sample database performs the following functions:

■ Changes the number format of the y-axis labels from Currency to the custom $#,##0 format, which removes the unnecessary decimal digits.

- Sets the scale of all graphs to $25,000 so users aren't misled by scale changes when comparing results of categories with different maximum sales values for the year.
- Establishes a thick line weight.
- Adds a trendline and hides the equation and R-squared text.
- Changes the color of the trendline from black to red and the weight to thick.

> **NOTE**
>
> Access 2007 has a bug in the setup program that omits the required reference to Microsoft Office XP Web Components. This reference must be present to persist the linked PivotChart properties.
>
> If this reference is missing from the Visual Basic editor's References list, click Browse, navigate to the \Program Files\Microsoft Office\Office 12 folder, and double-click OFFOWC.dll to add the Office XP Web Components reference to your Access project.

Figure 18.43 shows the frm2006SalesPCLinked form of Charts18.mdb with formatting applied by the Form_Current event handler. To view the VBA code, with the form open in Design view, click the toolbar's Code button to open the VBA editor.

Figure 18.43
Code in the Form_ Current event handler of Charts18.mdb's frm2006SalesPCLinked form applies the linked PivotChart formatting changes shown here.

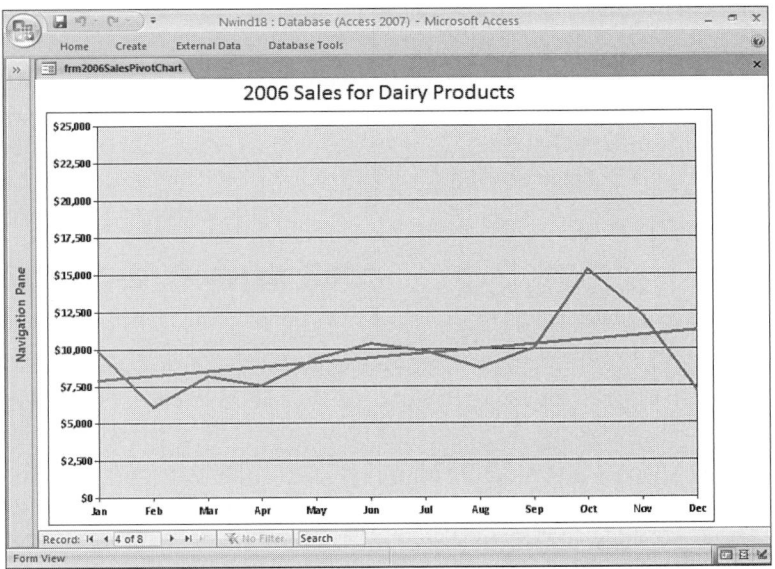

→ For the details on adding VBA formatting code for PivotCharts, **see** "Using the On Current Event to Set Linked PivotChart Properties" **p. XXX** *(Ch 28)*.

SUBSTITUTING OR ADDING A PIVOTTABLE IN A FORM

PivotCharts rely on an underlying PivotTable to supply data to the chart or graph. Thus, it's easy to alter a form or subform to display a PivotTable instead of a PivotChart. For example, you can open the sbf2006SalesPivotChart subform in Design view and change its AllowPivotChartView property value to No, AllowPivotTableView to Yes, and DefaultView to PivotTable.

When you open the modified frm2006SalesPivotChart, the PivotTable appears as shown in Figure 18.44. Months are row headings and product categories are column headings, so you might want to pivot the table to correspond to the graph layout. In this case, you must mark the Field Buttons/Drop Zones check box on the PivotChart Property dialog's Show/Hide page to enable pivoting when you change to PivotTable view.

Figure 18.44
To substitute this PivotTable for a PivotChart, change the Allow…View and Default View property values on the Format page of the PivotChart subform.

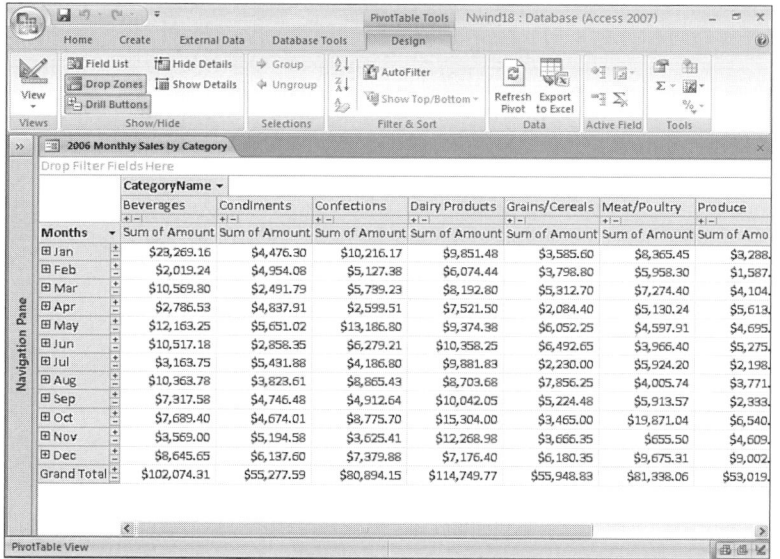

Another approach is to create individual PivotTable and PivotChart subforms. You can locate an additional PivotTable subform below the PivotChart. Alternatively, you can add a command button and VBA event-handling code to alternate between the two subforms as the Source Object property value of the subform container. The Access 2007 version of Northwind.mdb's sample Sales Analysis form uses this method to alternately display Sales Analysis Subform1 and Sales Analysis Subform2.

To examine the Sales Analysis approach, open Northwind.mdb from the \Seua12\Nwind folder, open the Sales Analysis form in Design view, and click the Code button to display the `btnEdit_Click` event handler's code.

TROUBLESHOOTING

REVERSING THE X-AXIS AND LEGEND LABELS

After the Row Source property of a chart is changed to the qry2006SalesChartCT crosstab query, the product categories appear in the chart as the x-axis labels, and the month abbreviations appear in the legend.

In the example in the "Assigning the Crosstab Query as the Graph's Row Source" section, you didn't change to Series in Rows in step 3. Crosstab queries you design can have the legend values (representing a series of lines) as column headers or row headers. If your x-axis and legend labels are wrong, activate the chart, choose Data, and then choose either Series in Columns or Series in Rows to make the change.

CONNECTING A PIVOTCHART (MICROSOFT OFFICE CHART 10.0) OR PIVOTTABLE (MICROSOFT OFFICE PIVOTTABLE 10.0) ACTIVEX CONTROL

Using Insert Object to add a PivotChart or PivotTable ActiveX control to a form or report, and setting up the Microsoft.Access.OLEDB.4.0 provider to connect to the current database results in a Data Link Error message.

When you have an Access object open in Design view, the Access database is locked in the read-only state to prevent others from modifying objects simultaneously. The lock prevents opening the second connection to the database, which is required to support the ActiveX control version of these objects. This problem doesn't occur with ADP, because you can establish multiple simultaneous connections to SQL Server in Design view. The advantage to the ActiveX control version of the PivotChart or PivotTable control, however, is that you don't need to add a subform to add design elements to the form. The downside is that your ADP requires additional connections to SQL Server to support each PivotChart or PivotTable.

IN THE REAL WORLD—A HOBSON'S CHOICE: MSGRAPH OBJECTS VERSUS PIVOTCHARTS

 Webster's New Collegiate Dictionary defines a Hobson's choice as an "apparently free choice with no real alternative." You are free to continue to use MSGraph with Access databases and Access SQL crosstab queries. MSGraph is a mature and stable product with no significant bugs. Its precursors date back to Excel 5.0, and MSGraph is backward-compatible with the Access 97, 2000, and 2002 versions. If you intend to use VBA to customize MSGraph objects, however, be prepared for a long learning curve. MSGraph's object model is the epitome of obfuscation. Check http://msdn.microsoft.com//library/en-us/odeomg/html/deovrmicrosoftgraph2000.asp for an object model diagram of MSGraph 9.0. Compare the MSGraph object model with the ChartSpace object model at http://msdn.microsoft.com/library/en-us/owcvba10/html/octocChartWorkspaceObjectModel.asp.

General-purpose OLE 2.0 objects created by mini-servers, such as MSGraph, are endangered species because web browsers, including IE, don't support them directly. You can open a Word document or Excel spreadsheet in IE and display an embedded MSGraph chart because Word and Excel are OLE 2.0 full servers and act as the graph's container. The catch is that you must have Microsoft Office installed to open the Word or Excel document, plus MSGraph (which Office installs automatically) to view the embedded graph or chart. The Access 2007 runtime version includes a redistributable runtime version of Graph.exe; the runtime version's design features are disabled.

PivotCharts and their underlying PivotTables are ActiveX controls, so they're Web-enabled and programmable with VBScript or JavaScript, as well as with VBA, when they're used in conventional Access forms and reports. The hierarchy of the PivotChart object model is much simpler and more straightforward than that of MSGraph. PivotTables accept XML-encoded data, so they fit into Microsoft's .NET framework. PivotTables—and thus PivotCharts—also can manipulate DataCubes generated by SQL Server's Analysis (OLAP) Services. You can expect Microsoft to enhance these versatile controls in subsequent Office upgrades.

MSGraph has been in maintenance mode since Office 2000, and Microsoft provides it only for backward compatibility; there won't be any additions to its current feature set or changes to its object model. As of Office 2007, Office Web Components (OWC) have suffered a similar fate. Microsoft has removed the capability to author OWC-based web pages from Access and Excel. Mainstream support for OWC XP (2002) will end on December 31, 2008, and for OWC 11 (2003) support will end three years later.

NEW Office 2000's OWC license restrictions prevented Access developers from using PivotCharts and PivotTables in runtime Access applications. (Access 2007 Runtime Edition includes the runtime versions of both MSAccess.exe and MSGraph.exe). OWC version 9.0 required users to have Office 2000 installed to open a form or report containing a PivotTable or PivotChart. Office XP changed the licensing terms. The Office 2002 and later OWC license lets you distribute OFFOWC.dll with your runtime applications for users who don't have Office 11 installed. This policy is similar to that for Graph.exe. Alternatively, users of Web-enabled Access applications can download the Office XP Web Components from Microsoft's website (http://office.microsoft.com/downloads/2002/owc10.aspx).

→ For more information about the freely downloadable Access 2007 Runtime Edition, see "Access Runtime and Developer Extensions," **p. 68**.

The only difference between the licensed and distributable behavior of OFFOWC.dll is lack of design-mode features in the latter. For instance, users can't alter the field complement of PivotTables or perform pivoting operations, but expansion/contraction and setting filters are permitted. This is more of an issue with PivotTables than with PivotCharts; most applications set the properties of PivotCharts either in the Properties dialog for the object or with VBA code. Spelunking the MSGraph object model is an overwhelming task.

There's no "real alternative" to PivotCharts in the new Access 2007 applications you create or, as mentioned early in the chapter, for existing applications you upgrade to ADP and SQL Server. The workaround for the lack of SQL Server crosstab queries described in Chapter 22's "Emulating Access Crosstab Queries with T-SQL" section is a short-term approach. Dedicate your graph and chart learning investment to PivotCharts; PivotCharts will be around for a while, but MSGraph is a dead end.

MOVING TO NETWORKED MULTIUSER APPLICATIONS

LINKING ACCESS FRONT ENDS TO ACCESS AND CLIENT/SERVER TABLES

In this chapter

CREATING MULTIUSER ACCESS APPLICATIONS BY LINKING TABLES

A single .accdb file that contains Access *application objects* (forms, reports, macros, and VBA code modules) and Access *data objects* (tables and queries) is one of Access's strongest selling points. Other desktop database management applications—such as Visual FoxPro and Visual Basic—require multiple files for a single database application. The obvious advantage of a single .accdb file for a complete Access application is simplicity. You can deploy your application by copying its .accdb file to another computer that has Access 2007 installed.

Sharing your Access application with other users in a Windows XP or Vista workgroup, or Windows Server 2003 or later domain, requires separating the application objects from database objects. It's *theoretically* possible for multiple users to simultaneously share a single .accdb application on a network or use the Terminal Services feature of Windows Server 2003 or later to run multiple instances of the application. In practice, however, application response time and network traffic issues make the single .accdb approach impractical for all but the simplest database projects. Another disadvantage of the single .accdb approach is that making changes to any Access object by opening it in Design mode prevents all other users from interacting with the object.

Making your Access application accessible to more than one user at a time requires dividing the application into *front-end* and *back-end* components. For Access databases, the front end contains all application elements plus queries; the back end contains only Access tables. If you use the Upsizing Wizard and choose to link your Access application to the Microsoft SQL Server 2005 Standard or Express Edition (SSX), SQL Server tables replace Access tables. The linking process for Access tables is similar to that for linking dBASE or Paradox files; linking SSX tables parallels linking Visual FoxPro files with an Open Database Connectivity (ODBC) driver.

→ To review the table linking process, **see** "Linking Visual FoxPro Tables with ODBC," **p. 350**.

NOTE

Sections later in the chapter cover linking to SQL Server 2005 Express, Developer, Workgroup, Standard, and Enterprise editions, Microsoft Desktop Engine (MSDE) 2000, and the four SQL Server 2000 editions—Personal, Developer, Standard, and Enterprise. This chapter uses *SQL Server* to refer to any SQL Server 2005 or 2000 edition, except when discussing features that are specific to SSX.

Chapter 20, "Exploring Access Data Projects and SQL Server 2005," and Chapter 22, "Upsizing Access Applications to Access Data Projects" describe Access data projects (ADP). ADP connect directly to SQL Server tables, and Access queries become back-end SQL Server views, functions, or stored procedures.

Multiuser Access applications usually require that each user have a copy of the front-end .accdb file and network access to the back-end .accdb file or an SQL Server *instance*. Alternatively, users can run multiple front-end Terminal Server sessions. You can share Access back ends in a peer-to-peer Windows XP or 2000 Professional workgroup environment or within a Windows Server 2003 or later Active Directory domain. A single front end can link to multiple back ends. Providing network access to SSX in a Windows XP or Vista workgroup environment requires modifying SSX's security settings. For workgroups, linked tables in Access back ends are simpler to implement.

NOTE

An SQL Server instance is simply an installation of the server software. A single computer can host multiple SQL Server instances, each of which has its own name. For example, the default instance name of an SSX instance is *ComputerName*\SQLEXPRESS.

NOTE

The following sections describe creating and securing back-end databases shared by a Windows Server 2003 domain controller or member server. Windows Server 2003 is used for the examples because that operating system supports Windows SharePoint Services (WSS) 3.0 and Microsoft Office SharePoint Server (MOSS) 2007, which are commonly used by Access 2007 clients. The process for sharing files with a Windows Vista or XP Professional workgroup member is similar, but the share and file security settings differ. The examples assume that you're familiar with creating file shares, have an administrative account for the server, and know how to manage Windows Vista or XP users and security groups.

CREATING LINKED ACCESS TABLES WITH THE DATABASE SPLITTER

19

You use the Database Splitter utility to create a conventional multiuser Access/Access application from a copy of the application's single .accdb file. The Database Splitter automatically creates a new .accdb file for the tables, moves the tables from the front-end to the back-end .accdb file, and creates individual table links between the two files.

Take the following steps to create and link the back-end database to the front-end application objects:

1. If the computer on which you're running Access 2007 has a network connection to a server or another workstation, create a share on the server or another workstation in your workgroup to store the back-end .accdb file. The server or other workstation doesn't need to have Office 2007 installed to share the back-end file. Otherwise, add a new folder to store the shared back-end .accdb file on your client machine.

 2. If you're splitting a production database, create and use a copy of the database. This example uses a copy of the Northwind.accdb sample database named NWClient.accdb, which you'll find in the \SEUA12\Chaptr19 folder.

3. Open the Access database to split, click the Database Tools tab, and click the Move Data group's Access Database button to open the utility's first and only dialog (see Figure 19.1).

Figure 19.1
The Database Splitter utility has only a single dialog.

4. Click the Split Database button to open the Create Back-End Database dialog. The default name of the back-end .accdb is the front-end name with a _be suffix. Change the name to whatever you want; this example uses NWData.accdb as the name.

5. Navigate to the server share (or local folder, if you're not using a network server). This example uses the Northwind share on the OAKLEAF-DC1 domain controller for the OAKLEAF domain (\\OAKLEAF-MS10\Northwind), which also runs an SSX instance (see Figure 19.2).

Figure 19.2
Specify a share on a workstation or server in your Windows Server 2003 or later domain or another workstation in your Windows Vista or XP workgroup.

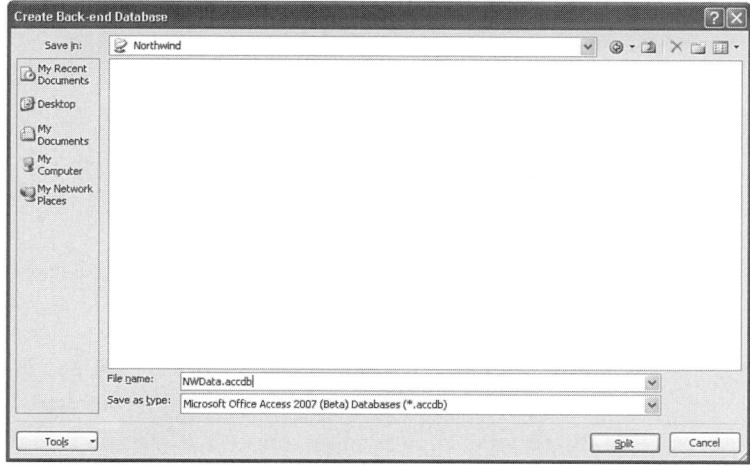

Assigning the Uniform Naming Convention (UNC) name–//*SERVERNAME*/*ShareName*– to connect to the server share is a better practice than allocating a local logical drive letter to the share. Users can delete or change the drive letter assignment. Converting the front end to the .accde format prevents users from changing the UNC link to the back-end file with the Linked Table Manager.

6. Click the Split Button to create the new back-end database and move the tables to it. Click OK to acknowledge the completion message. The links to the back-end tables appear in the front-end application, as shown in Figure 19.3.

Figure 19.3
The table icons of the Database window gain an arrow to indicate that they're linked to the back-end .accdb file.

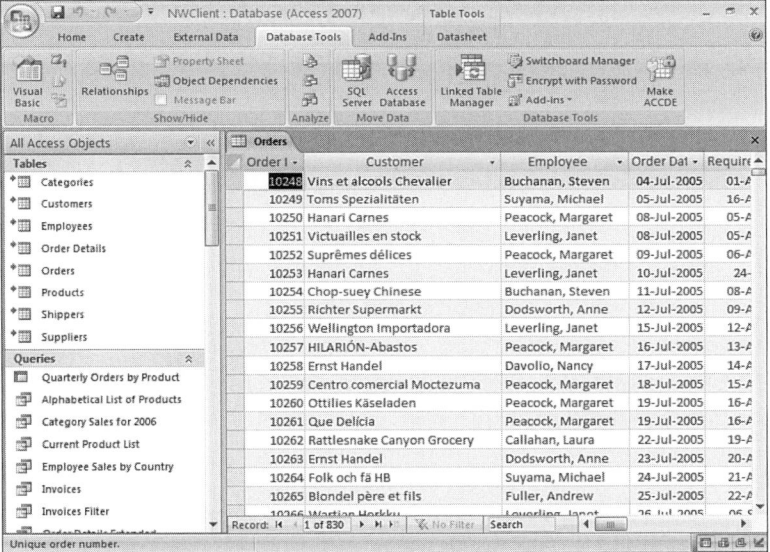

7. Verify that the linked tables are operational by opening each table in sequence and navigating to the last record to ensure that the tables are updatable.

8. Open one of the tables in Design view. You receive a message that some properties of linked tables can't be modified in Design view. Click Yes and then click the Properties button to open the Table Properties window. The Description property value defines the link to the back-end .accdb file (see Figure 19.4).

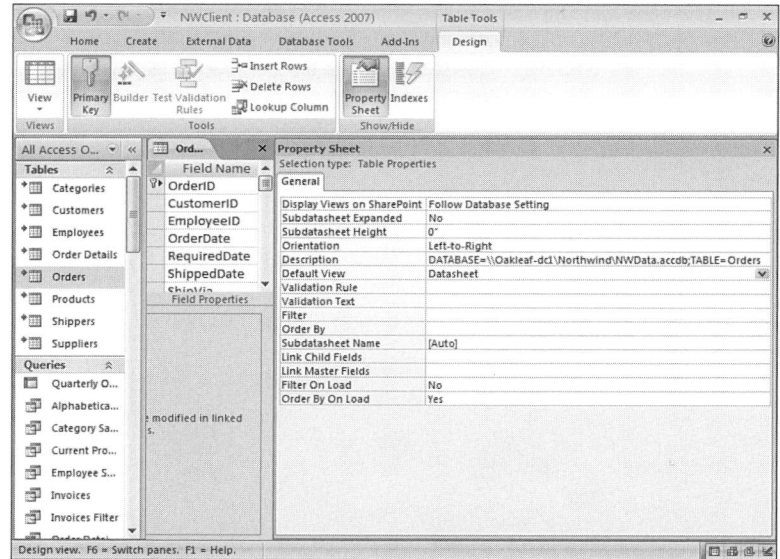

Figure 19.4
The Description property value of the linked table contains the linking information.

9. Run a few queries, and open the forms and reports to verify that the application objects behave as expected with the linked tables.

ESTABLISHING NETWORK SHARE, FOLDER, AND FILE SECURITY FOR THE BACK END

The first step after you share a back-end database is to set share, folder, and file permissions on the .accdb file. If ordinary network users have Full Control permissions of the share and file, your back-end database is vulnerable to deletion, copying, or moving by any network user who has access to the server. Removal from Access 2007 of Access 2003 and earlier's user- and group-level security features means that network share, folder, and file-level security is your only defense against unauthorized users gaining access to your back-end database file, the data in the file, or both.

By default, the share, folder, and files you create as a network administrator inherit permissions assigned to the parent drive or folder. Windows 2000's default share permissions give the Everyone group Full Control; Windows Server 2003 assigns Read share permissions to the Everyone group. This section's examples assume that the Everyone group has no default or inherited permissions for the share or the back-end .accdb file.

All users of your front-end application need Read permissions for the share, and Read, Write, Create, and Delete permissions for the folder. These permissions enable the first user to create the .laccdb locking file (NWData.laccdb for this example) when opening the .accdb file during login and the last user to delete the file when logging off the application.

NOTE

The locking file contains the computer name and Access security name—typically Admin—of each person who has an active link to the back-end .accdb file. This file can contain up to 255 records, which is Access's limit for concurrent database users.

You can assign permissions to security groups or users; this example assigns permissions to two security groups in the `oakleaf.org` Windows 2003 domain: NWReaders and NWWriters. You then assign an NWReader1 user to NWReaders and an NWWriter1 account to the NWReaders and NWWriters groups. Table 19.1 shows the permissions required by the NWReaders and NWWriters groups. You must remove the default Users security group to prevent ordinary users from accessing the folder or its files.

TABLE 19.1 THESE PERMISSIONS ARE REQUIRED TO AUTHORIZE SECURITY GROUPS TO ENABLE READ OR READ/WRITE ACCESS TO BACK-END DATA FILES ON A WINDOWS SERVER 2003 SHARE

Group	Share	Folder	Back-end .accdb File
Users	(Removed)	(Removed)	(Removed)
NWReaders	Read	Read & Execute	Read
NWReaders	Change	Create Files / Write Data, Delete Subfolders and Files	
NWWriters			Write

NOTE

The following procedure assumes that you have or a domain administrator has used Active Directory Users and Computers to add the NWReaders security group and added the NWReader1 and NWReader1 account to it, as well as the NWWriters security group with the NWWriter1 account.

19

Following are the steps required to secure the Northwind network share, Northwind folder, and the NWData.accdb file:

1. Log on to the server with an account that has Administrator privileges.

2. In Explorer, right-click the shared folder (Northwind) and choose properties to open the *FolderName* Properties dialog. Click the Sharing tab, and then click the Permissions button to open the Permissions for *ShareName* dialog.

3. If it's present, select the Everyone security group in the Name list and click Remove.

4. Click Add to open the Select Users, Computers or Groups dialog, and type the name(s) of the users or groups to add in the text box, separated by semicolon, and click the Check Names button to verify your spelling (see Figure 19.5).

Figure 19.5
Type the groups or users to add in the Select Users, Computers, or Groups dialog. If the names (NWReaders and NWWriters groups for this example) are present in Active Directory, clicking the Check Names button underlines them.

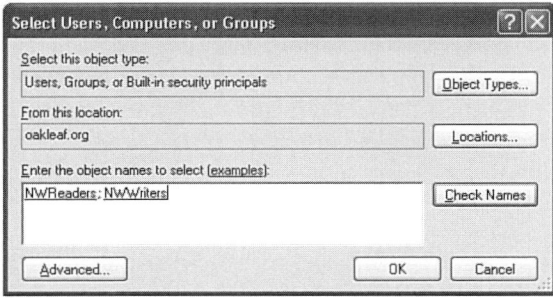

5. Click OK to add the groups or users to the Name list, and then grant them Read and Change permissions (see Figure 19.6). You need Change permissions for the share to enable all users in the designated groups to create and delete the .ldb file. Click OK to close the Permissions dialog.

Figure 19.6
You must grant specific Access groups or users Read and Change permissions for the share.

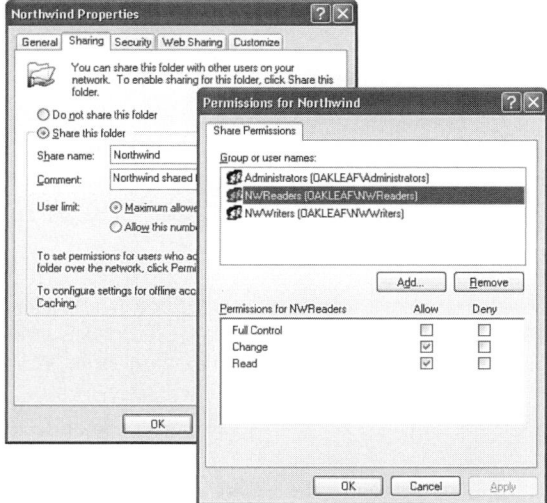

6. Click the Security tab. If the Users group has been added to the Group or User Names list, click Advanced to open the Advanced Security Settings for *ShareName* dialog, clear the Allow Inherited Permissions from the Parent to This Object and All Child Objects check box, and click OK to open the Security message box (see Figure 19.7). Click Copy to copy all inherited Users permissions; then click OK again to close the dialog. On the Security page, select Users and click Remove.

Figure 19.7
To prevent ordinary domain users from gaining access to the back-end database file, you must remove inherited permissions, if any, and then remove the Users group from the folder's Group or User Names list.

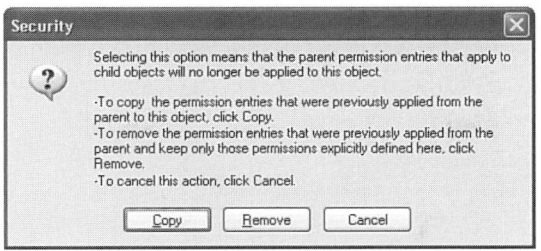

7. Add the groups or users to the folder Permissions list and grant them Read & Execute permission, which enables List Folder Contents and Read permissions. Grant the read/write group or users Write permission (look ahead to Figure 19.9).

8. Click Advanced to open the Advanced Security Settings dialog, select the read-only group or user name in the list, and click Edit to open the Permission Entry for *GroupName* dialog and mark the Create Files/Write Data and Delete Subfolders and Files check boxes to enable the users or groups to open and close .laccdb files (see Figure 19.8). (Previous permission settings marked the other check boxes.)

Figure 19.8
Access users or groups must have Create Files/Write Data and Delete Subfolders and Files permissions to add and delete the .laccdb locking file in the shared folder, even if they don't have Write permissions.

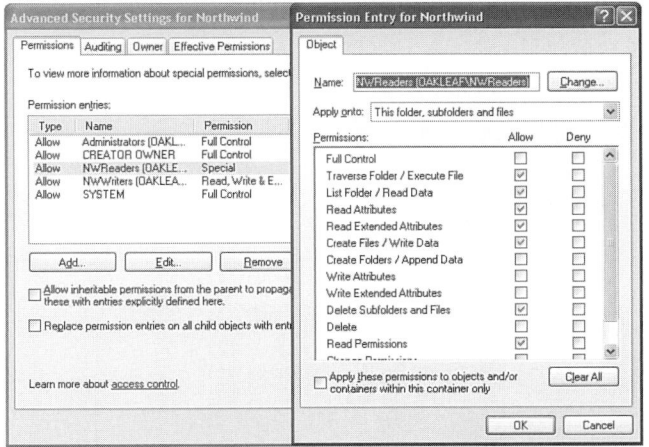

19

9. Click OK twice to save your permission changes, close the Permission Entry for *ShareName* and Advanced Security Settings for *ShareName* dialogs, and return to the *ShareName* Properties dialog (see Figure 19.9).

Figure 19.9
Read-write users or groups must have folder Write, as well as Read & Execute, List Folder Content, and Read permissions. For this example, in which read-write users are members of the NWReaders and NWWriters groups, it isn't necessary to add Read & Execute permissions for the NWWriters group.

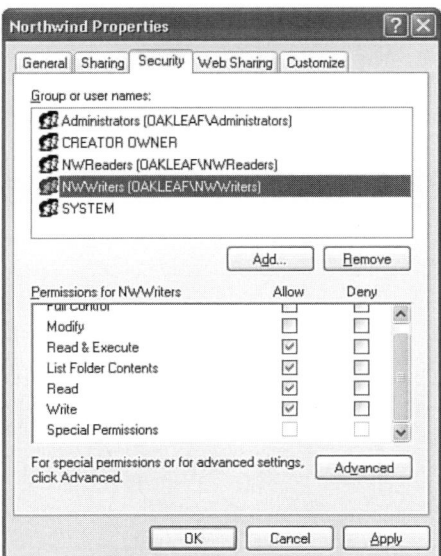

10. Click OK to close the *ShareName* properties dialog, right-click the back-end data .accdb file, choose Properties to open the *FileName* Properties dialog, and click the Security tab. Verify that read-only users or groups have inherited the permissions Read & Execute, Read, and Special Permissions, and that read-write users or groups have these and Write permissions (see Figure 19.10).

Figure 19.10
Users or groups inherit file permissions from the folder permissions you set.

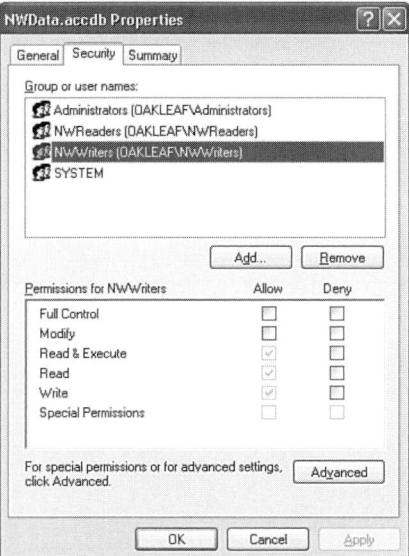

19

11. Click OK to accept the file permissions and close the Security dialog.

Your back-end database files are now secured against access or updates by unauthorized users and inadvertent or intentional deletion or modification by non-administrators.

VERIFYING BACK-END DATABASE NETWORK SECURITY

It's a good practice to verify that your security settings work by following these steps:

1. Log off the server and log on to the client with the read/write account (NWWriter1), launch Access, and open the front-end .accdb file (NWClient.accdb). By default, the Access front-end opens in read-only mode and displays Security Warning and Read-Only messages. (Users are prompted to create a read/write copy of the front-end database, and can dispense with the Security Warning by trusting the client file's location.)

2. Open a table and verify that the tentative append record is present, which verifies that the back-end database is read/write for this user (see Figure 19.11).

Figure 19.11
NWWriters members open the front-end .accdb file and see the Security Warning and Read-Only messages, as well as a tentative append record for tables they open.

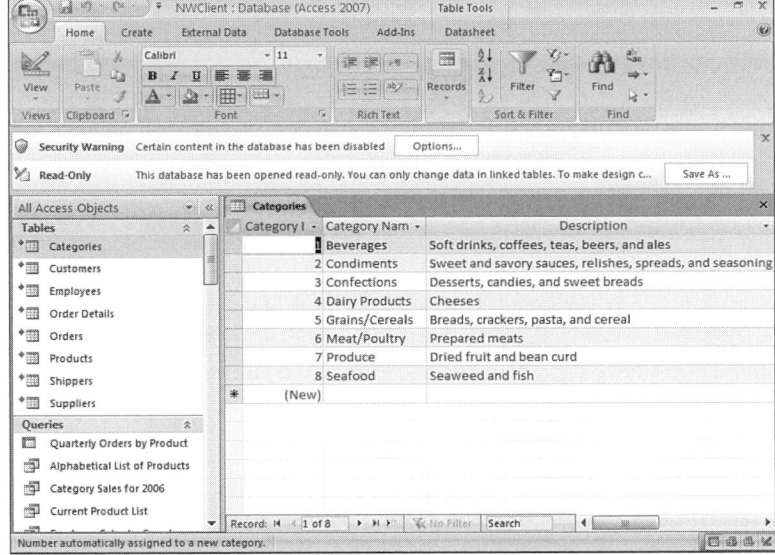

3. Log off and log on with the read-only account (NWReader1) and launch Access, which displays the same messages.

4. Open a table in the front-end client and verify that the tentative append record is missing, which confirms that back-end data isn't updatable. Attempts to edit table data also fail.

5. Finally, log off and log on with an account that's a member of the Users or Power Users group but doesn't have permissions for the back-end share or file.

6. Attempt to open a table in the front-end client. You receive a message that the table is locked by another user or you need permission to view the data (see Figure 19.12).

Figure 19.12
Users who don't have read or write permissions for the back-end data field (NWData.accdb) receive this error message when they attempt to open a table.

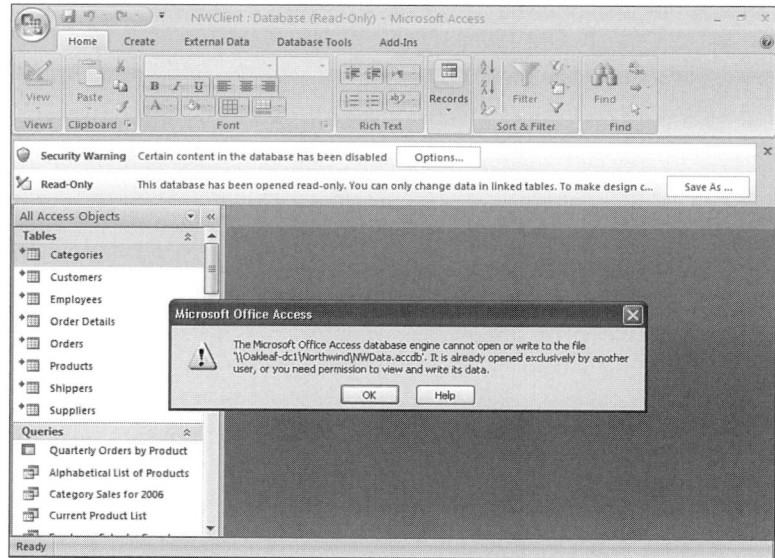

Shared Access back-end databases are satisfactory for Access multiuser applications that support up to about 25 concurrent users, with five or fewer making simultaneous data changes. In this case, you can skip the following sections about SQL Server and implement user-level security for your front end. If your application involves heavy-duty online transaction processing (OLTP) or the data is vital to the economic survival of your organization, you should consider linking to an SQL Server back end or migrating to Access data projects (ADP), which connect directly to SQL Server tables.

CAUTION

After you split a database, Access 2007's Manage, Back Up Database button on the Office menu backs up the front end only. Unless you have automated nightly backup for the server or workstation that shares the back-end data, you must back up the data .accdb file manually. Backing up the .accdb file requires administrative access to the server or workstation.

TIP

As an administrator, you can open the back-end data .accdb file in Access and take advantage of Access 2007's database backup and compact/repair utilities. For the preceding example, you would open \\OAKLEAF-DC1\Northwind\NWData.accdb.

EVALUATING THE BENEFITS OF MIGRATING TO CLIENT/SERVER DATABASES

Modern client/server databases, typified by Microsoft SQL Server 2005, provide a much more *reliable* and *scalable* data storage environment than shared-file databases, such as Access. The vast majority of production databases used by all but very small organizations follow the client/server model. Oracle currently claims the lion's share of the client/server relational database management system (RDBMS) business, but IBM, Microsoft, and Sybase each own significant market share. There also are several popular open-source RDBMSs that run under Windows—My SQL, PostgreSQL, and Firebird.

Client/server technology ordinarily offloads much of the data-processing workload to the server. When an RDBMS client instructs the server to execute an SQL SELECT * statement having WHERE clause criteria, only those rows that meet the criteria pass over the network to the client. If you replace * with an explicit field list, the RDBMS only populates query columns that correspond to the specified fields. Minimizing the amount of data transmitted to the client saves costly network bandwidth and improves performance, especially for remote users who access the database over virtual private network (VPN) connections.

Another advantage of migrating from conventional multiuser Access applications to client/server back-end databases is elimination of routine compact/repair operations to remove deleted records from Access tables. When you delete records from a table, Access marks the records as deleted but doesn't remove them from the table. You must compact the database periodically to remove deleted records and regain the disk space they occupy. Using a client/server back end also eliminates the Access database locking problems that often occur after a power outage or unscheduled shutdown when users are in the process of making changes to Access tables.

CLIENT/SERVER RELIABILITY AND SCALABILITY BENEFITS

Reliability—also called *availability* in this context—is the most important property of a production database. The goal of most database administrators is to ensure that the database is available to users at least 99.99% of the time. 99.99% (called "four nines") availability means that the database has a maximum downtime of 45 minutes per month. Five nines, which is expected of banking, other financial, and national security databases reduces downtime to about five minutes per year. Achieving 99.999% or better database availability requires very costly server clusters, but it's reasonable to expect at least four nines from SQL Server 2005 running under Windows Server 2003 or later.

Database scalability primarily is hardware-related. You can increase the number of concurrent users without suffering a performance slowdown by increasing the amount of RAM, CPU speed, and number of CPUs in the server(s). Unlimited-use licenses for most RDBMSs are based on the number of CPUs. You can compare licensing costs of Oracle, SQL Server, and IBM DB2 for different software editions, and server CPU and CPU speed configurations at http://www.microsoft.com/sql/prodinfo/compare/.

19

SQL SERVER 2005 EXPRESS EDITION FEATURES AND LIMITATIONS

SQL Server 2005 Express Edition (called *SQL Express or SSX* when referring specifically to this version of SQL Server) running under Windows Server 2003 has the same level of reliability as SQL Server 2005 Standard or Enterprise Edition running on a single server. You can achieve similar reliability when running SSX under Windows Vista or XP Professional, if you dedicate the machine to running SSX and don't use the machine to run desktop applications. The source code of SSX is identical to that of other SQL Server 2005 editions; the scalability limitations applied to the freely distributable edition don't affect its reliability.

TIP

> One of the advantages of running SSX or other SQL Server 2005 editions under Windows Server 2003 or later is the capability to manage the server from a Windows Vista or XP Professional workstation by running Terminal Services in administrative mode.
>
> You don't need to install Active Directory on the Windows server to run SQL Server 2005 versions. If your network uses Active Directory, installing SSX on a member server, not a domain controller, devotes more of the server's available resources to database operation and management, and thus improves performance.

Microsoft limits the scalability of SSX by restricting it to using a single CPU, regardless of how many processors you plug into your multiprocessing server or workstation or how many cores each processor contains. Similarly, SSX will use a maximum of 1GB RAM, regardless of the amount of RAM on the machine, and the maximum database size is 4GB. However, you can run up to 16 named instances (installations) of SSX on a single computer. SSX can't act as a replication publisher, which is unfortunate because Access 2007 no longer supports replication. However, this limitation isn't likely to affect most Access users and developers. SSX can act as a snapshot, merge, or transactional replication subscriber with SQL Server 2005 or 2000.

NOTE

> As mentioned earlier, shared Access databases have a fixed limit of 255 concurrent users. There's no limit on the number of Access clients simultaneously connected to SSX on a Windows server. However, Windows Vista and XP Professional have a fixed maximum of 10 inbound (client) connections, so the maximum number of simultaneous networked users connected to SSX running under either of these operating systems is 10.

Access 2003's lack of graphical RDBMS management tools for MSDE 2000 discouraged many Access power users and developers from migrating to linked or directly connected SQL Server databases. Several third-party tools became available for managing MSDE 2000 user logins and database security, but these GUI tools didn't measure up to the quality of SQL Server Enterprise Manager (EntMan) for SQL Server 2000 Developer Edition and higher.

SSX offers SQL Server Management Studio Express (SSMSX) Service Pack (SP) 2, a slightly restricted version of the full SQL Server 2005 Management Studio that comes with SQL Server 2005 Developer Edition and higher. SSMSX is a full-featured graphical RDBMS management tool and query designer (see Figure 19.13).

Figure 19.13
SQL Server Management Studio Express (SSMSX) SP2 has almost all the bells and whistles of the version that comes with SQL Server 2005 Workgroup, Standard, and Enterprise editions.

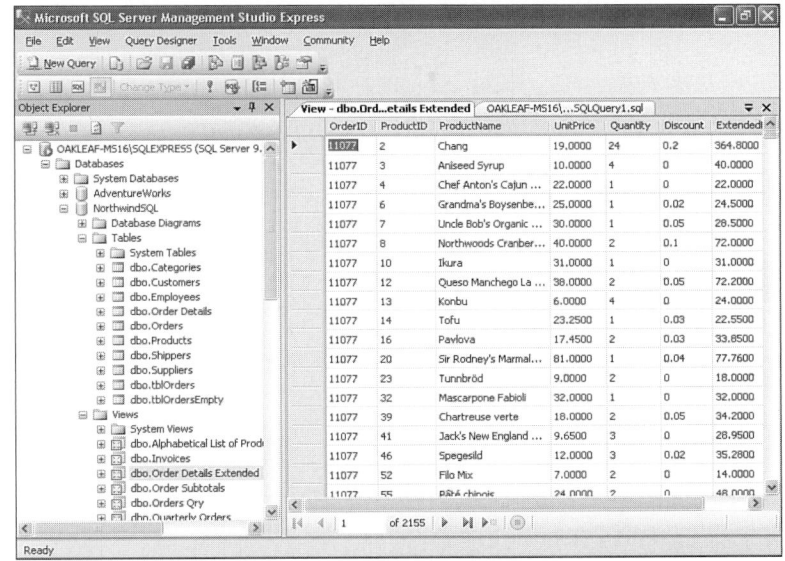

> **NOTE**
>
> SSMSX SP2 is required to run under Windows Vista. Windows Vista supports SSX SP1 or SP2. SSX SP2 is required to support a new option into the setup process that you automatically add the user who runs SSX setup into the SysAdmin Fixed Server Role, which overcomes a problem with Windows Vista's User Access Control restriction on logging in as a member of the local Administrators group.

CHOOSING A CLIENT/SERVER MIGRATION STRATEGY

Prior to the introduction of Access 2000, linking was the only method of migrating Access applications from Access tables to client/server databases. The primary advantage of linking client/server tables is that the Access 2007 database engine running on the client processes your Access SQL queries. Thus, crosstab queries continue to execute as expected, and you can use MSGraph objects in your forms and reports without reconstructing their Record Source property as an SQL Server 2005 PIVOT view.

Linked client/server tables let you take advantage of Access pass-through queries to send Transact-SQL (T-SQL) statements directly to SQL Server, PL/SQL to Oracle, or any other SQL dialect to your RDBMS. The downside of linking is that you lose the efficiency of server-side query processing, which is one of the most important features of client/server

RDBMSs. The sections that follow describe Access 2007 options for moving to SQL Server databases.

→ To learn more about pass-through queries, **see** " Writing and Executing Pass-through Queries," **p. XXX** *(this chapter).*

MIGRATING ACCESS APPLICATIONS TO SQL SERVER WITH THE UPSIZING WIZARD

Access 2007 supports the following three automated migration—called *upsizing*—scenarios from conventional Access applications to SQL Server:

- **Splitting, upsizing, and linking a single-user Access database**—If your .accdb file contains application objects (queries, forms, pages, reports, modules, macros, or any combination) and data objects (tables), you can split and upsize the tables, and link the application objects to the server tables in a single process. An example of this scenario is upsizing Northwind.accdb.

- **Upsizing and linking a multiuser Access application**—If you've used the Database Splitter utility to segregate application and data objects into front-end and back-end .accdb files, respectively, you upsize only the front-end .accdb file. Upsizing the back-end .accdb doesn't work directly; you receive a "Can't find *TableName*" error message when you attempt to open the upsized linked table in the front-end application's Datasheet view or in a form or report.

- **Upsizing an Access application to an Access data project**—This scenario moves your Access tables to SQL Server and attempts to update your queries to T-SQL stored procedures. Chapter 22, "Upsizing Access Applications to Access Data Projects," describes this upsizing method and how to overcome problems with Access queries that T-SQL can't handle.

19

TIP

> SQL Server doesn't have data types that correspond to Access 2007's new Attachments and multivalued lookup field (MVLF) data types. The Upsizing Wizard skips Attachments fields and upsizes MVLF fields to SQL Server's `ntext` (Unicode text) data type, which disables lookups.
>
> If these data types are important to your application, but you want to take advantage of the benefits of client/server tables, you can elect to not update some tables during the upsizing process or rename and use the local table that the wizard leaves in the front-end .accdb file after completing its task.

You use the Access 2007 Upsizing Wizard—which works only with SQL Server 6.5 (having SP5 installed), 7.0, 2000 (including MSDE 2000), or 2005 (including SSX)—for the preceding three scenarios, but this chapter focuses only on the first two. The client/server examples in this book use SSX as the server, but most examples also accommodate all SQL Server 2000 editions, including MSDE 2000. None of the examples have been tested with SQL Server 6.5 or 7.0, for which mainstream support ended on 1/1/2002 and 12/31/2005, respectively.

SQL Server enforces referential integrity by triggers or declarative referential integrity (DRI), if specified in the Relationships window for the Access tables. Access uses DRI, which conforms to ANSI-92 SQL syntax, and DRI is the preferred approach for SQL Server 2005 databases. SQL Server 2005 also supports Access's cascading updates and deletions; SQL Server 7.0 and earlier don't. No version of SQL Server has a field data type that corresponds to Access's Hyperlink data type, so the wizard converts Hyperlink fields to plain text.

→ For a brief description of SQL Server 2005's feature set, **see** " SQL Server 2005 Express Edition SP2 Setup," **p. 59**.

N O T E

> Access 2007 doesn't include SQL Server 2005's Books Online documentation. Microsoft has published an online version of updated SQL Server 2005 documentation at http://go.microsoft.com/fwlink/?LinkId=65208.

EXPORTING TABLES TO OTHER RDBMSS

Access uses the Open Database Connectivity application programming interface (ODBC API) to link conventional Access (.accdb) front ends to client/server RDBMSs. Office 2007 installs ODBC drivers for SQL Server and Oracle 8i or earlier databases. If you're using Oracle, IBM DB2, Sybase, Informix, or another RDBMS as your application's data source, you can't use the Upsizing Wizard to automate the table export and linking process; the Wizard supports SQL Server only. You must manually export (copy) your Access tables to the RDBMS and then link the RDBMS tables to your Access front end. You also must set up primary keys, relationships, and indexes for the tables manually.

→ For an introduction to the ODBC table-linking process, **see** "Linking Visual FoxPro Tables with ODBC," **p. 350**.

N O T E

> Linking to databases of an RDBMS other than SQL Server or Oracle 8i requires a vendor-supplied or third-party ODBC driver. You can't use an OLE DB data provider to link client/server tables to Access front ends.
>
> An alternative to linking tables in "foreign" databases to Access front ends is to use the *linked server* feature of SQL Server 2000. Linking a server—other than another SQL Server instance—requires an OLE DB data provider for the linked server. Linking servers to SQL Server 2005 is required to use ADP with other RDBMSs. Linking SQL Server to other RDBMSs is beyond the scope of this book.

Migrating tables and linking to databases other than SQL Server involve the following basic steps:

1. You or your organization's database administrator (DBA) must create the database, and you must have permissions to create, read, and write to objects in the database.

19

2. Back up the Access database, and verify the integrity of the backup.

3. Use the External Data ribbon's More, ODB<u>C</u> Database button in the Export group to export the Access tables to the new database.

4. Use the RDBMS's management tools to designate primary keys, add indexes, default values, and validation rules, and to enforce referential integrity between the tables. Add cascading updates and deletions, if the RDBMS supports them (most do).

5. Rename the existing Access tables, and use the Import group's More, ODB<u>C</u> Database to establish links to the database tables.

6. Delete the existing Access tables after you confirm that the linked tables operate properly and have been backed up on the server.

> **TIP**
>
>
>
> Microsoft has reported many issues with exporting and linking Oracle tables to Access 2002 applications, many of which also apply to Access 2007. To review the known problems, click the Knowledge Base link in the Microsoft.com front page's Resources group, search the Microsoft Knowledge Base (KB) with Access 2003 selected in the Search Product list, and type **Oracle** in the For box; then repeat the process with Access 2007 as the product.

UPSIZING A SINGLE-FILE APPLICATION TO SQL SERVER 2005

If you've created a single-file Access application and want to make it available to your colleagues who have Access 2007 installed, the Upsizing Wizard makes the process easy and fast. You must, of course, have downloaded and installed SSX from or have access to another version of SQL Server 200x before you can upsize your application. If your application is encrypted, you must decrypt it before upsizing. All examples of this chapter assume you are logged in to Windows Vista, XP, or Server 2003+ as a member of the Administrators group.

→ For instructions on how to download and install SSX and SSMSX SP2, **see** "SQL Server 2005 Express Edition SP2 Setup," **p. 59**.

> **TIP**
>
> For a production application, install SSX on the production server, if you don't intend to create the new database on an existing installation of SQL Server 2005 Workgroup, 200x Standard, or 200x Enterprise Edition. The network name of the server—called the SQL Server *instance name*—is embedded in the Description property value of each table. SSX instances have a default \SQLEXPRESS suffix.

If you specify the local instance of SSX installed on your client computer, you must change the property value–called the *ODBC connection string*–to reflect the NetBIOS name change when you move the database to a production server. Making this change isn't a simple process; you must update each link manually or use a VBA subprocedure to regenerate the links to the new server.

→ For details on the required subprocedure, **see** "Changing the Link Connection String with a VBA Subprocedure," **p. 840**.

MODIFYING TABLE PROPERTIES TO ENSURE SUCCESSFUL UPSIZING

The Upsizing Wizard has several limitations, most of which are imposed by SQL Server 2005 or earlier. In some cases, the upsizing process fails silently, and the final upsizing report doesn't indicate the reason for the failure.

Following is a check list of modifications you must make to your tables—and a few other recommendations—to ensure upsizing success:

- **Validation rule and default value expressions**—T-SQL can't handle many Access-specific or VBA expressions that establish default field values, or table- or field-level validation rules. In such cases, the Upsizing Wizard might not create the SQL Server table. You must remove the offending expressions and run the Upsizing Wizard again to link only the missing tables. Then you must rewrite the expressions to comply with T-SQL syntax rules using SSMSX.

NOTE

Chapter 21, "Moving from Access Queries to Transact-SQL," includes examples of T-SQL expressions you can use for default values and validation rules, and shows you how to use SSMSX to change the property values of SQL Server tables and fields.

19

- **Hidden tables**—If you've applied the Hidden attribute to any of the tables you want to upsize, the wizard ignores the hidden tables during the upsizing process.
- **Fields added by Access replication**—If you've implemented Access replication, you must remove all replication system fields from the tables before upsizing. Tables with replication fields don't upsize.

TIP

Michael Kaplan's Trigeminal Software website, http://www.trigeminal.com/, has a TSI Access 2000 Un-Replicator for Access 2000 and a TSI Replication System Fields Utility for Jet 3.5x and 4.0. Both utilities work with Access 2007, but only if your database uses the default Access 2000 format.

- **Tables without unique indexes**—You can update an Access table that doesn't have a Unique Values Only index, but SQL Server tables require a unique index for updatability. Make sure all tables have a unique index. Add an AutoNumber field to the table if you can't create a unique index from the data in the table. (AutoNumber fields become `integer` fields with the `identity` property in SQL Server tables.) The unique index usually is on the table's primary key field.

- **Related fields with unequal Field Size property values**—Access lets you create relations on Text fields having different sizes, but SQL Server doesn't. The tables upsize, but the Wizard doesn't establish the relationship between them. Make sure that the size of the primary- and foreign-key field pair is the same in both related tables. Specify the longer of the two size values to prevent inadvertently truncating data.

- **Very large tables**—During addition of data to an upsized table, SQL Server adds entries to the transaction log file. If you have a very large table and are short on disk space, the combination of the table and log file might exceed the free space on the destination disk. Make sure that the destination drive has free space greater than three times your .accdb file size.

TIP

Microsoft has published a whitepaper titled "Using the Access 2002 Upsizing Tools" that you can download from Knowledge Base article Q294407. The whitepaper hadn't been updated for Access 2007 when this book was written. Search the Knowledge base at http://search.support.microsoft.com/search/ with Access 2007 as the product and **upsizing tools** as the text to find the updated version and other troubleshooting data. Search with Access 2003, if you don't find the information you want for Access 2007.

RUNNING THE UPSIZING WIZARD

Following are the steps to upsize a simple, single-file Access application with the Upsizing Wizard:

1. Make a backup copy of the Access database to upsize, and verify that the backup copy works.

2. Open the original database file, but don't open any database objects. This example uses NwindSQL.accdb, a modified upgrade of the Access 2000 version of the Northwind.accdb database with images embedded in the Photo field of the Employees table and the Employees form imported from Access 2000's Northwind.accdb file.

→ For an explanation of how to embed the EmpID#.bmp bitmap files in an OLE Object field, **see** "Dealing with Images in External Database Files," **p. 354**.

NOTE

The NwindSQL.accdb database used for this example is included in the \SEUA12\ Chaptr19 folder of the accompanying CD-ROM. NwindSQL.accdb includes the VBA sub-procedure required to change the server name when you move the SQL Server database from one machine to another.

3. Click the Database Tools tab and click the Move Data group's SQL Server button to start the upsizing process.

4. Accept the default Create a New Database option in the first Wizard dialog (see Figure 19.14) and then click Next.

Figure 19.14
The first Upsizing Wizard dialog lets you add your tables to an existing database or create a new database. You create a new SQL Server database unless you're running the Wizard to upsize a table that wasn't upsized because of an error.

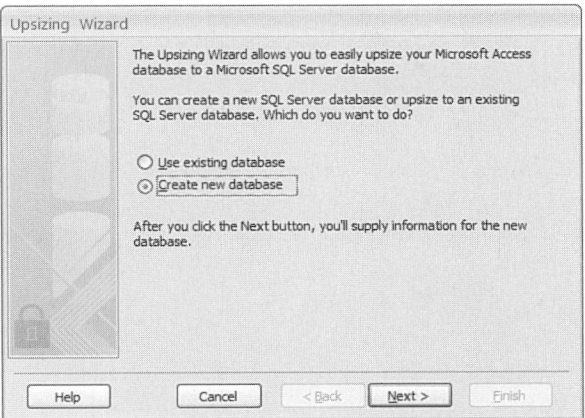

5. In the second Wizard dialog, open the What SQL Server Would You Like... list and select the name of a production server or peer workstation server that has SQL Server 2005 or SSX installed. This example uses SQL Server 2005 Standard Edition installed on a Windows Server 2003 domain controller (OAKLEAF-CD1). The client computer (OAKLEAF-XP15) runs Office 2007 under Windows XP Professional SP2.

> **NOTE**
> If you're upsizing a sample database to become familiar with the process, you can select (local) or your computer's name and, if SSX is installed, an \SQLEXPRESS suffix.

6. SQL Server 2005 and SSX install by default with Windows authentication only enabled, which prevents use of the sa (system administrator) login and SQL Server–based security. Mark the Use Trusted Connection check box.

> **NOTE**
> A trusted connection to SQL Server uses Windows integrated authentication for database connections, and is the *much* preferred method of managing client/server database security.
>
> Using Windows authentication requires your logon account to have at least CREATE DATABASE privileges for SQL Server. A member of the local Administrators group of the machine running SQL Server (BUILTIN\Administrators) has system administrator (sa) rights for the server and all databases by default.

19

7. Accept the default database name, the name of your .accdb file with an "SQL" suffix, or change it to a name you like better (see Figure 19.15). Don't use spaces or punctuation symbols in the name; doing so violates generally accepted database naming practices. Click Next.

Figure 19.15
The second Upsizing Wizard dialog requires you to select the machine running SQL Server, specify the authentication method for your connection, and provide a name for the new database.

8. After a brief delay, the third Wizard dialog opens with a list of the tables in the Access database in the Available Tables list. Click the >> button to export all the tables to SQL Server (see Figure 19.16). If you want to retain temporary or local tables on the client, select the table(s) and click the < button to move them from the Export to SQL Server list back to the Available Tables list. Click Next.

Figure 19.16
The only Access tables you should retain in the front-end application are temporary tables or local tables that you use to set user preferences.

9. In the fourth Wizard dialog, accept the default options unless you have a specific reason for doing otherwise (see Figure 19.17). Click Next.

Figure 19.17
The fourth Upsizing Wizard dialog proposes the most common set of options for the upsizing process.

NOTE

> As mentioned earlier in the chapter, SQL Server's DRI features are preferred over triggers to enforce referential integrity. Prior to SQL Server 7.0, triggers were the only method of enforcing referential integrity.
>
> SQL Server can use optional timestamp fields to determine quickly whether large Memo fields (SQL Server `ntext` fields) and OLE Object fields (SQL Server `image` fields) have been updated. If your Access table includes lengthy Memo fields or if OLE Object fields contain large images or other data, accept the Yes, Let The Wizard Decide or Yes, Always choice in the Add Timestamp Fields to Tables list.

10. In the fifth Wizard dialog, select the Link SQL Server Tables to Existing Application option (see Figure 19.18). If you accept the default No Application Changes option, you must manually link the tables to your database front-end application. Click Next to open the final Wizard dialog and then click Finish to start the upsizing process.

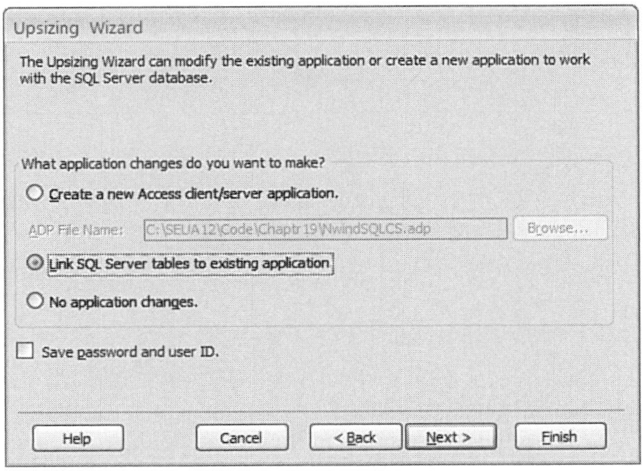

Figure 19.18
Be sure to select the Link SQL Server Tables to Existing Application option to have the Upsizing Wizard handle the table-linking process for you.

19

NOTE

The Save Password and User ID check box only applies to SQL Server security, which isn't enabled by default. Even if you could save your administrative logon name and password, doing so would breach security rules—users would be able to impersonate your administrative account to gain full control over the SQL Server instance.

→ To learn how to pre-create SQL Server user accounts and add users to roles, before or after running the Upsizing Wizard, **see** "Adding SQL Server User Logins with SQL Server Management Studio," **p. 852**.

11. A progress indicator dialog appears for a period that depends on the size of the tables, the speed of your computer and, if the database is remote, network and server performance. After the Wizard completes its task, an Upsizing Wizard Report appears in Print Preview. Click the report to zoom to 100% scale and review its contents (see Figure 19.19).

Figure 19.19
After the Upsizing Wizard updates and links the table, it generates a report summarizing the upsizing process. Look for errors and "not upsized" entries. (The report for upsizing the sample NwindSQL.accdb tables is 15 pages long.)

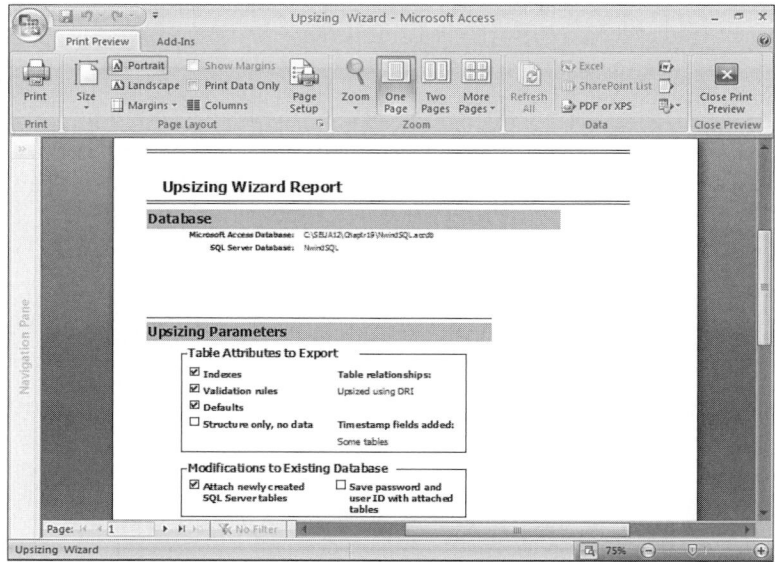

12. Click the Data group's PDF or XPS button to save the report as an Adobe PDF or Microsoft XML Paper Specification (XPS) file. Print the report, if you want, and then close the Upsizing Wizard window. The Wizard does not automatically save the report.

VERIFYING THE UPSIZING AND LINKING PROCESS

The wizard renames your Access tables by adding a "_local" suffix to the table names and adds links—identified by the ODBC symbol—to the SQL Server tables. The Wizard creates a new Custom Group 1 in the Navigation Pane with tables as unassigned objects. Select

Object Type and All Access Objects to display the local and linked tables (see Figure 19.20). When you pass the mouse pointer over a linked table item, a ScreenTip displays in a single line part of the ODBC connection string for the database.

Figure 19.20
The Navigation Pane displays linked tables with the original Access table names and the Access tables renamed with a "_local" suffix.

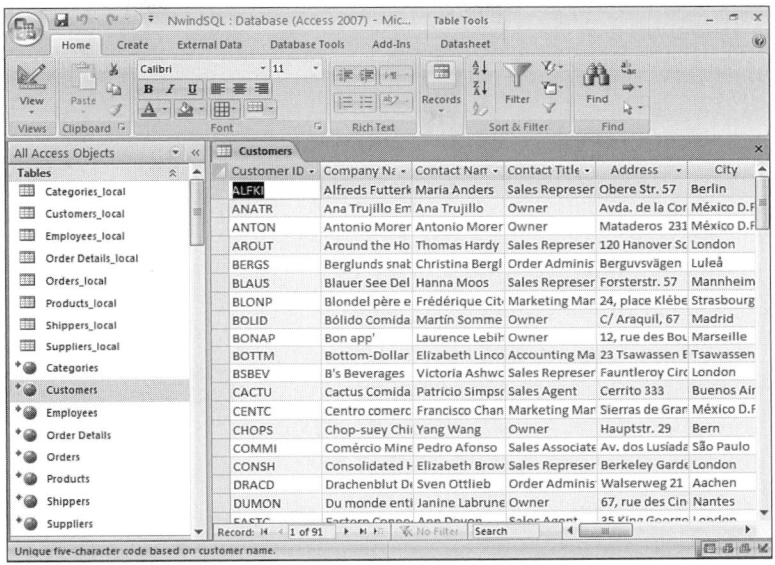

 If some tables don't upsize to SQL Server, indicated by a missing link entry for the tables, see the "Access Tables Fail to Upsize" topic of the "Troubleshooting" section at the end of the chapter.

After you've verified that all required server tables have links, do the following to confirm that the tables are operable with your front end:

1. Open the front-end forms and reports to verify that the upsizing process completed satisfactorily.

2. Verify in Form or Table Datasheet view that default values, formats, input masks, field and table validation rules, and other special property values you've specified for tables have upsized successfully. SQL Server 7.0 doesn't support extended properties, so display formats, input masks, and other Access-specific properties aren't updated. Also, verify by the presence of the tentative append record that the tables are updatable.

3. If your tables have lookup fields, verify that these extended property features work as they did in the Access tables. Linked tables don't support subdatasheets because they cause a performance hit with tables that have a large number of rows.

4. Open the upsized tables in Design view, and acknowledge the message that warns you that you can't change some table properties. Check the data type of an Access Hyperlink field, which changes to an Access Memo field (see Figure 19.21). Access

19

Memo fields upsize to SQL Server's `ntext` (Unicode text) data type. No version of SQL Server supports the Allow Zero Length property, so this value is No for all fields, regardless of your original setting. The upsize_ts field is the `timestamp` field added by the Upsizing Wizard.

Figure 19.21
Upsizing Access Hyperlink fields results in a change to the SQL Server data type (`ntext`) that corresponds to a Access Memo field. Design view of a linked SQL Server database displays Access, not SQL Server, field data type names.

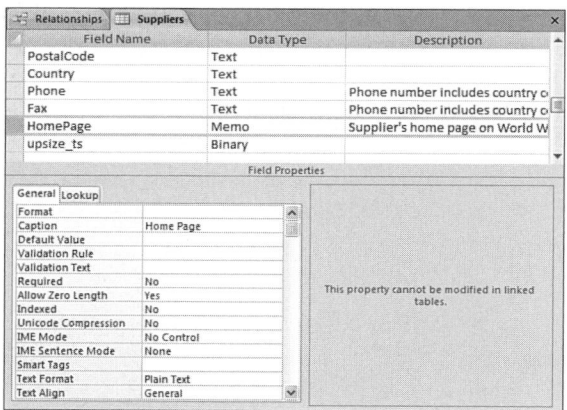

5. Right-click the Table Design view window, and choose Properties to open the Table Properties dialog with the Description text box selected. Press Shift+F2 to open the Zoom dialog to view the full connection string for the table. Figure 19.22 shows the connection string for the Suppliers table with the Zoom dialog's font size changed to 10 points and newline characters added to format the string for readability.

Figure 19.22
The Zoom dialog displays a formatted version of the ODBC connection string for the Suppliers table.

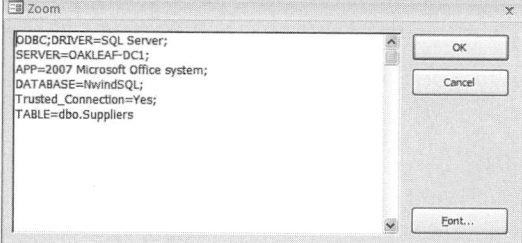

6. Execute every `SELECT` query to make sure the Wizard hasn't modified the query and rendered it inoperable. Don't execute action queries that update table values. Some queries—such as Northwind.accdb's Sales by Year query—require entering parameter values.

7. Open the Relationships window. Upsized tables lose their relationships, and you must depend on SQL Server's DRI to maintain referential integrity. To make creating new queries easier, reestablish the relationships between the tables. (Referential integrity options are disabled in the Edit Relationships window for client/server tables.)

After you've verified the success of the upsizing process, you can safely delete the ..._local tables, if you made a backup of your application. If not, export the ..._local tables to a new Access database and then delete them.

> **TIP**
>
>
>
> To return a test application to its original condition, delete the links to the table and rename the Access tables by removing the _local suffix.

UPSIZING AN APPLICATION WITH LINKED TABLES

As mentioned earlier in the chapter, the process for upsizing Access front ends with linked Access tables is identical to that for upsizing single-file applications. You run the Upsizing Wizard from the front-end .accdb. The Wizard connects to the shared .accdb back end and generates the SQL Server tables from the linked Access database. This example uses the NWClient.accdb front end and NWData.accdb back end you created at the beginning of the chapter.

To create an SQL Server database on your local machine that you move to a production server later in the chapter, using the NWClient.accdb and NWData.accdb pair as an example, do the following:

1. Make backup copies of NWClient.accdb and NWData.accdb, if you haven't done this.

2. Open the NWClient.accdb front end, click the Database Tools tab, click the SQL Server button to start the Upsizing Wizard, accept the default Create New Database option in the first dialog, and click Next.

3. In the second Wizard dialog, specify *ComputerName*/SQLEXPRESS as the SSX instance, change the name of the database to NWDataSQL, and click Next.

4. In the third dialog, select all tables, and in the fourth dialog, accept the defaults.

5. In the fifth dialog, make sure to select the Link SQL Server Tables to Existing Application option and clear the Save Password and User ID check box, if it's marked. Click Next and Finish to upsize the linked tables.

6. Verify the upsizing process with the methods described in the preceding section.

EXAMINING THE ODBC TABLE CONNECTION STRING

When you choose the Create a New Database option in the first Upsizing Wizard dialog, the ODBC connection string for each table contains all the information Access needs to connect to the server and link each table (refer to Figure 19.22). This type of ODBC connection doesn't require you to create a named ODBC user or system data source (user or system DSN) or a file data source to establish the connection. Using a DSN-less connection simplifies the process of making your linked-table application available to users, because they don't need a user or system DSN on their computer or a link to a file data source on the server.

19

A DSN-less ODBC connection string consists of the following elements, separated by semi-colons:

- `ODBC` designates the connection as using the ODBC API.
- `DRIVER=SQL Server` specifies the version of the SQL Server ODBC driver to use. (SQL Native Client is the current version for SQL Server 2005, but the Upsizing Wizard uses the preceding version for compatibility with SQL Server 2000 and earlier.)
- `SERVER=SERVERNAME` designates the computer name of the machine running the instance of SQL Server with the upsized database, followed by \SQLEXPRESS for SSX or a custom instance name for SQL 2000 or 2005. In a Windows 2003 domain, the computer name often is called the *down-level* name of a computer. (The "up-level" name is the full *hostname.domainname.ext* of the computer—oakleaf-dc1.oakleaf.org for example.)
- `UID=UserName` specifies the SQL Server logon name if you aren't using Windows integrated security.
- `PWD=Password` is the SQL Server logon name if you aren't using Windows integrated security. Notice that the password is in clear text, which is a serious security violation. Using Windows authentication is recommended strongly, because it's integrated with Windows networking, and is much more secure and easier to administer than SQL Server's username/password security approach.
- `APP=2007 Microsoft Office system` is for information only.
- `WSID=COMPUTERNAME` is your computer name (workstation ID) and is for information only.
- `DATABASE=DatabaseName` designates the name of the upsized database.
- `Trusted_Connection=Yes` specifies use of Windows integrated authentication; `No` or a missing entry specifies SQL Server security and requires `USR` and `PWD` entries.
- `TABLE=dbo.TableName` specifies the SQL Server table and its owner prefix. (SQL Server 2005 calls the owner prefix the *schema* name.) The default prefix is `dbo`, which is the abbreviation for the system administrator (sa) as the object's owner (database owner). When you log on to SQL Server with an administrative account, you are sa.

NOTE

> The linked table's Description property value doesn't contain `UID`, `PWD`, or `WSID` values. The `dbo.TableName` element isn't present in the `Connect` property value of the link's `TableDef` object. (Access local or linked tables are members of the database's `TableDefs` collection). Access appends `TABLE=` and the `SourceTableName` property value of the `TableDef` to the Description property value.

If you select the Use an Existing Database option in the first Upsizing Wizard dialog, you must use an existing—or create a new—machine or file data source. If one of your tables won't upsize, you must run the Wizard again to create the table and add the link to an existing database. If you delete a link and must restore it, you must click More in the External Data ribbon's Import Data group, choose ODB<u>C</u> Database to open the Get External Data dialog, select the Link to the Data Source option, click OK to open the Select Data Source dialog, and select or create the DSN to use.

→ To learn how to create a temporary or permanent ODBC DSN, **see** "Linking Client/Server Tables Manually," **p. XXX** (this chapter).

NOTE

When you use the Select Data Source dialog to link a table with ODBC, the link name gains a dbo_ prefix. Delete the prefix to enable existing Access objects to connect to the table.

In either case, your tables end up with a combination of conventional and DSN-less convention strings. If you don't change the `Connect` property of the `TableDef` object to specify a DSN-less connection, all users of your application must add the ODBC DSN to their computer or have access to a server share holding a file data source.

The standard DSN for an SQL Server table replaces the `Driver=SQL Server` element with `DSN=DataSourceName`, and replaces the `SERVER=SERVERNAME` element with `Description=OptionalText` in the Description and `Connect` property values. Otherwise, the elements of the connection string are the same as in the preceding DSN-less connection list. The `ChangeServer` VBA subprocedure, which is described later in the "Changing the Link Connection String with a VBA Subprocedure" section, also changes DSN to DSN-less connections.

MOVING THE UPSIZED DATABASE TO ANOTHER SERVER

If you upsize the database to a local SSX instance and then decide to move the database to another server, be prepared to add a substantial amount of VBA code to your project to regenerate the links. There's no Access wizard or utility to automatically change the `SERVER=SERVERNAME` element of a DSN-less connection string for each linked table.

19

CAUTION

Don't try to use the Linked Table Manager database utility to change the server name in a DSN-less connection string. The Linked Table Manager requires an ODBC user or system DSN, or a file data source, instead of modifying the current DSN-less connection string. If you use the Linked Table Manager to change the link, you must set up a machine DSN on each user's computer or create a file data source on the server and specify the Uniform Naming Convention (UNC) path to the file in the connection string. The `ChangeServer` procedure requires at least one DSN-less connection to change DSN connections.

MOVING OR COPYING THE SQL SERVER DATABASE FILES

You can move or copy an SQL Server database from one machine to another by any of the following methods:

- Create a temporary ADP with existing data, connect to the SQL Server database, open the Office menu, and choose Server, Transfer Database to install the database on the new SSX instance. The original database is retained. This is the simplest and most foolproof method.

→ For an example of using the Transfer Database command to move an SQL Server database, **see** "Transferring the Project's Database to a Server," **p. 906**.

- Select Server, Copy Database File instead of Transfer Database in the preceding method. This process leaves the original database intact..

- Close all connections to the database, stop SQL Server on the source computer, and use Explorer to copy *DatabaseName*.mdf (database) and *DatabaseName*.ldf (log file) from the \Program Files\Microsoft SQL Server\MSSQL\Data folder to the same folder on the new server. After copying the files, create a temporary ADP with existing data. In the DataLink Properties dialog, select the Attach a Database File as a Database Name option and specify the database name and the *DatabaseName*.mdf file, which must be on the same machine as the SQL Server instance you specify.

CHANGING THE LINK CONNECTION STRING WITH A VBA SUBPROCEDURE

After you've moved the linked tables to the new server, you face the challenge of changing the SERVER=*SERVERNAME* element of the DSN-less connection string to the new server name. Properties of linked table definitions, which Access calls TableDefs, are read-only. You can't persist changes to the Description property value of a linked table. If you alter the server name in the connection string of the Description property, and close and save your changes to the table design, the connection string doesn't change.

NwindSQL.accdb in the \SEUA12\Chaptr19 folder of the accompanying CD-ROM contains a modChangeServer module with a single VBA subprocedure: ChangeServers. You can use this procedure to change the connection string to point to the new server or change a DSN connection string to the DSN-less type. To add modChangeServer and its subprocedure to your front-end .accdb file, import the module from NwindSQL.accdb. The following example uses NWClientSQL.accdb, upsized to your local computer in the earlier "Upsizing an Application with Linked Tables" section. Running the example requires you to have a networked computer running SQL Server 2005 or SSX.

→ To review the process for working with VBA modules, **see** "Using the Immediate Window," **p. 422**.

To run the ChangeServer subprocedure in an application that has tables linked to SQL Server and the modChangeServer module installed, do this:

1. Click the Modules shortcut in NWClient.accdb's Database window, and double-click modChangeServer to open the VBA editor with the ChangeServer subprocedure active.

2. Press Ctrl+G to open the Immediate window. Type **ChangeServer** *"CurrentServerName"*, *"NewServerName"*. For this example, the procedure call is **ChangeServer "OAKLEAF-MS16\SQLEXPRESS", "OAKLEAF-DC1"** (see Figure 19.23). If you haven't copied or moved the tables to another server, use the current workstation or server name as the value of both arguments.

Figure 19.23
Call the ChangeServer subprocedure with two literal string arguments: the current server name followed by the destination server.

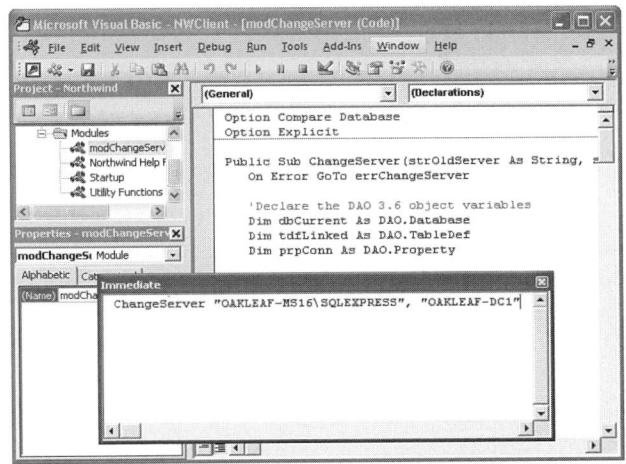

3. Press Enter to execute the procedure. The first stage of the procedure creates an array of the new connection data for each linked table, and displays a message asking you to confirm the change (see Figure 19.24, top).

Figure 19.24
You see one of these two messages, depending on the validity of your source instance argument values.

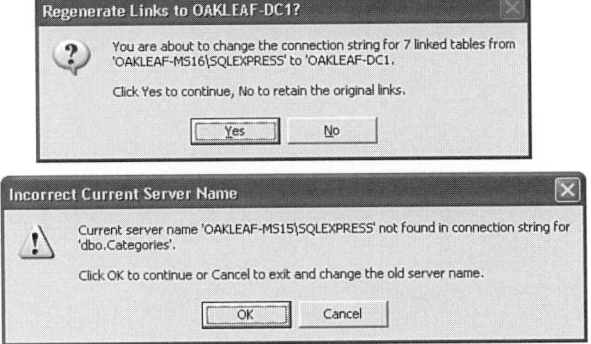

4. After a second or more, depending on the speed of your machine and the network, a **Debug**.Print statement confirms all new connection strings in the Immediate window (see Figure 19.25).

19

Figure 19.25
The Immediate window displays the new connection strings for the links.

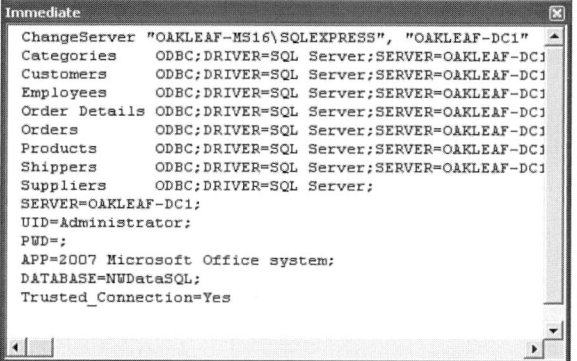

If you type a nonexistent server name as the second argument value, or the database isn't present on the destination server you specify, you receive the two error messages shown in Figure 19.26. The upper message from SQL Server appears after about 30 seconds of inactivity. Clicking OK opens an SQL Server Login dialog (see Figure 19.26, middle). Click Cancel to dismiss the dialog and display the procedure's error message (see Figure 19.26, bottom). Click OK to cancel execution and leave the connection strings unaffected.

Figure 19.26
These three error messages appear in sequence if you type an invalid destination server name and don't correct it in the SQL Server Login dialog.

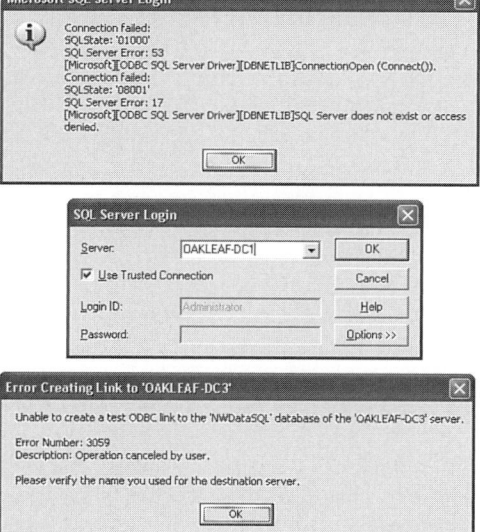

NOTE

ChangeServer creates a test connection to the destination server to prevent deleting the first existing link. The properties of linked `TableDef` objects are read-only, so the existing link must be deleted before adding the new `TableDef`.

LINKING CLIENT/SERVER TABLES MANUALLY

As mentioned in the earlier section "Examining the ODBC Table Connection String," you must create an ODBC data source when you use the Upsizing Wizard with an existing SQL Server database. You also must create a DSN when you manually export Access tables to an RDBMS other than SQL Server, and then link the tables to your Access front end. The number and appearance of the dialogs varies according to the ODBC driver you use to make the connection to the existing database on the RDBMS.

After you create the DSN, you can use the Upsizing Wizard to add new tables to an SQL Server database. For other RDBMSs, you must manually export your Access tables to the database. You use the same DSN to export the data from and attach the tables to your Access front end.

CREATING THE ODBC DATA SOURCE

To create a DSN for any RDBMS for which you've installed an ODBC 2.x or 3.x driver, do the following:

1. Launch Control Panel's ODBC Data Source Administrator tool. Under Windows XP and Server 2003, the Data Sources (ODBC) icon is in Control Panel's Administrative Tools subfolder. The Administrator opens with the User DSN page active.

   > **NOTE**
   >
   > If you select the Use Existing Database option in the first Upsizing Wizard dialog, the Wizard opens the Select Data Source dialog.

2. If you're preparing a temporary data source for the addition of tables to an SQL Server database you created with the Upsizing Wizard, you can create a User or System DSN on your workstation. Otherwise, click the File DSN tab and navigate to a server share for which users of your application have at least read access.

3. Click the Add button to open the Create New Data Source dialog, and select the driver for the RDBMS with the database for your application (see Figure 19.27). This example uses the new SQL Native Client driver for SQL Server 2005 installed by SQL Server 2005 or SSX.

4. Click Next to open the second Create New Data Source dialog, and type the UNC path and name of the data source file (**\\OAKLEAF-DC1\Northwind\ NWDataSQL.dsn** for this example). The standard extension for DSN files is, not surprisingly, *dsn*.

19

Figure 19.27
Select the ODBC driver for your RDBMS in the Create New Data Source dialog. Don't set Advanced properties, unless the driver vendor instructs otherwise.

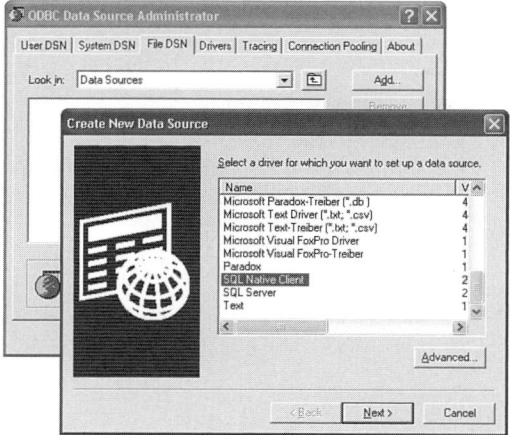

> **TIP**
>
> The default location for a file DSN is the \Program Files\Common Files\ODBC\Data Sources on your computer. The best location for the file DSN for an upsized multiuser application is the share in which you placed the Access back-end database. Use UNC's *ServerName**ShareName* network path format, not a mapped drive, to specify the file location.

5. Click Next to confirm your initial settings and then click Finish to open the first driver-specific dialog: Create a New Data Source for SQL Server in this case.

6. Type a description of the DSN, and open the Server list to select the RDBMS server (OAKLEAF-DC1 for this example; see Figure 19.28).

Figure 19.28
The first driver-specific dialog for the SQL Server driver lets you add a description of the DSN and specify the server name.

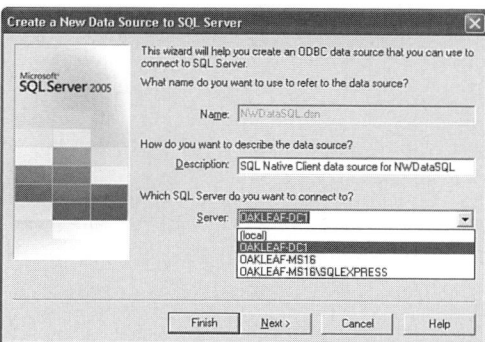

7. Click Next to open the second driver-specific dialog. For SQL Server, accept the default Windows NT Authentication option (see Figure 19.29). Alternatively, select With SQL Server Authentication..., which requires a user account and password having at least CREATE DATABASE privileges.

Figure 19.29
The SQL Server driver's second dialog lets you select the authentication method.

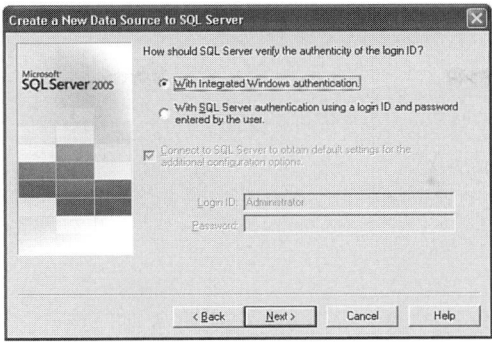

8. Click Next to make a temporary connection to the server. Mark the Change the Default Database To check box, open the drop-down list, and select the database name (NwindSQL for this example). Accept the default Use ANSI… settings (see Figure 19.30).

Figure 19.30
Select the default database for the DSN in the third SQL Server–specific dialog. SSX doesn't support SQL Server mirroring, so leave the Mirror Server text box empty.

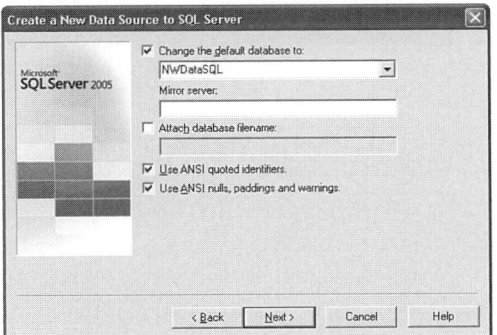

9. Click Next to open the fourth SQL Server dialog. The single default option, Perform Translation for Character Data, is satisfactory for most DSNs. Specify logging options only if you need to debug performance problems when using the DSN.

10. Click Finish to display a summary of your settings, and click Test Data Source to confirm connectivity to the database on the server (see Figure 19.31).

11. Click OK twice to save the file DSN, and then click OK to close the ODBC Administrator tool.

19

Figure 19.31
The final step when configuring an SQL Server ODBC data source is to test connectivity to the specified database.

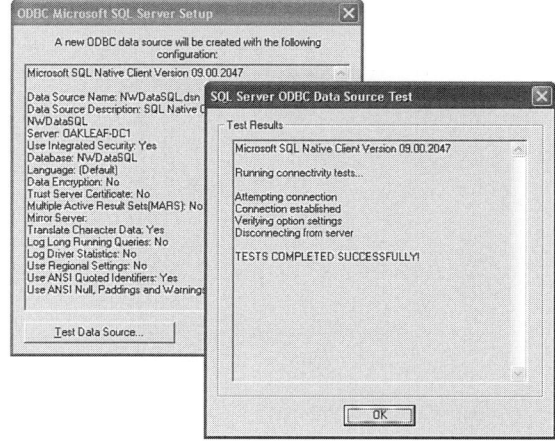

> **NOTE**
>
> If you use a temporary user or system DSN to add table(s) to a new SQL Server database you created with the Upsizing Wizard, run the `ChangeServer` subprocedure, described in the earlier section "Changing the Link Connection String with a VBA Subprocedure," to change to DSN-less connections for added tables.

EXPORTING ACCESS TABLE DATA TO THE RDBMS

Manually exporting Access tables to an ODBC-connected client/server database is a straightforward process, but the manual export procedure creates only the basic table structure with a simple `CREATE TABLE` statement and then populates the table with an `INSERT` statement for each row. Unlike the Upsizing Wizard, exporting a table doesn't establish primary keys, add indexes, or enforce referential integrity with DRI. You or the DBA must handle these tasks after exporting all tables.

Following are the steps to export Access tables to RDBMSs other than SQL Server:

1. Open the .accdb file containing the Access table(s) to export (HRActions from Northwind.accdb for this example) and click the External Data tab.

2. Click the More button and choose ODB<u>C</u> Database to open the Export dialog with *TableName* in the Export *TableName* To text box (see Figure 19.32, top).

3. Click OK to open the Select Data Source dialog with the File DSN page active. If you specified a default folder for file DNSs in step 3 of the preceding section, the file you created appears in the list. If not, navigate to the server share in which you stored the DSN. Select the file (see Figure 19.32, bottom), and click OK to close the dialog and start the export process.

Figure 19.32
When you select ODBC Databases in the Export group's More list, the Export dialog (top) opens with the selected table. Clicking OK opens the ODBC Administrator's Select Data Source dialog.

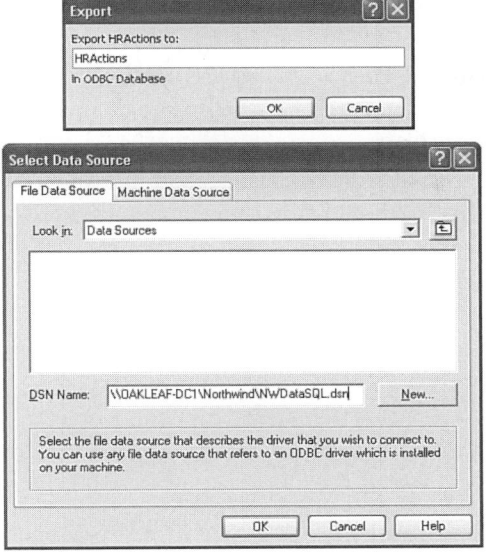

4. Repeat steps 2 and 3 for each table to export. You don't need to wait for the export process to complete before selecting another table to export.

5. Use the RDBMS's toolset to specify primary key fields, add indexes, and establish referential integrity to emulate—as closely as possible—your original Access database.

Use SQL Server Management Studio to perform step 5's operations for SQL Server 2005 databases or SSMSX for SSX instances. Alternatively, you can add SQL Server indexes and create relationships (called constraints) by opening an Access data project for the database. The process for adding indexes and other table accouterments is tedious when upsizing many tables, so use the Upsizing Wizard for all Access export operations to SQL Server if possible.

ATTACHING THE EXPORTED TABLES

Attaching the tables to your front-end application with the file DSN follows the same process as that described for FoxPro databases in Chapter 8, "Linking, Importing, and Exporting Tables." Unfortunately, you can't use the Linked Table Manager to change front-end links from an .accdb file to a .dsn file.

To attach the client/server tables you exported, do this:

1. Open the front-end .accdb, click the External Data tab, click the Imports Data group's More button, and choose ODBC Database to open the Get External Data – ODBC Database dialog.

19

2. Select the Link to the Data Source option to open the File DSN page of the Select Data Source dialog.

3. Type the path and name of the DSN file (**\\OAKLEAF-DC1\Northwind\ NWDataSQL.dsn** for this example) or navigate to and double-click the *FileName*.dsn file to open the Link Tables dialog.

4. Multiselect the tables to attach to the front-end .accdb file. Figure 19.33 shows the seven upsized SQL Server Northwind tables and an imported HRActions table selected.

Figure 19.33
Select in the Link Tables dialog each exported table to attach to the front end.

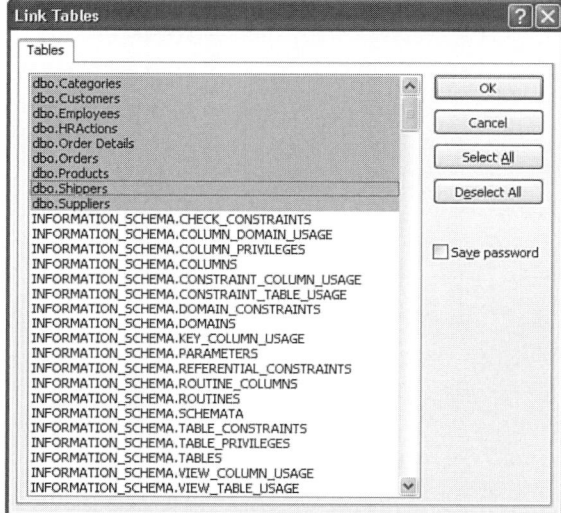

5. If you specified Windows authentication when you created the DSN, the Save Password check box should be cleared. Most Windows NT versions of client/server RDBMSs accommodate Windows authentication. For RDBMS-based security, you can mark the Save Password check box if you didn't use sa (or its equivalent) as the account when you created the DSN. Click OK to begin the linking process.

6. If Access can't determine the primary key field(s) of linked tables, the Select Unique Record Identifier dialog opens for each table (see Figure 19.34). Select the key field(s) for the table; if you click Cancel, the table won't be updatable.

7. The prefix of the attached table names depends on the RDBMS's table naming conventions. As mentioned earlier in the chapter, SQL Server tables gain a dbo_ prefix. Temporarily rename the original tables or links, if any, and then rename the new ODBC links by removing the prefix.

Figure 19.34
Specify the name(s) of the primary key field(s) if Access can't detect a table's primary key.

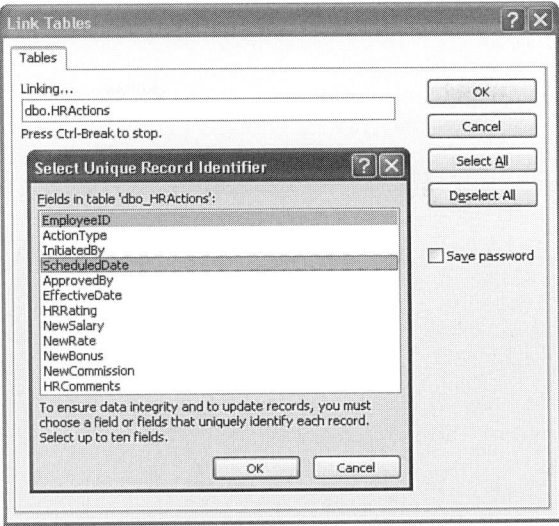

8. Open the Relationships windows to verify all tables are present in the Show Table list. Add all tables to the Relationships window, and verify that every table has key field(s) identified by a key symbol. Reestablish the relationships between the primary- and foreign-key fields of the tables.

9. Check all queries for proper execution, and make sure your forms and reports operate as before.

After you've verified that all's well with the attached tables, you can delete the renamed Access tables or their links, if present.

WRITING AND EXECUTING PASS-THROUGH QUERIES

The conventional approach to executing SQL commands against back-end, client/server databases is by opening persistent (stored) views, table-valued functions, and stored procedures. An alternative method is to send SQL statements as batch commands directly to the database server's query processor with *pass-through queries*. The term *pass-through* is apropos because the SQL statements pass through Access to the back-end server without touching the Access query engine.

For applications that have linked client/server tables, pass-through queries let you use the server's SQL dialect, rather than Access SQL. The server's dialect might offer capabilities that Access SQL can't match, such as SQL Server 2005's new T-SQL ranking functions— ROW_NUMBER, RANK, DENSE_RANK, and NTILE— or the UNPIVOT operator. Like row-returning stored procedures, all pass-through SELECT queries return read-only Recordsets.

19

> **NOTE**
>
> An explanation of T-SQL ranking functions is beyond the scope of this chapter, but ROW_NUMBER is obvious. This section's example includes a ROW_NUMBER (RowNumber) column ranked by average ShippedDate value for a quarter. For more information on these T-SQL keywords, type **ranking functions** in the SQL Server Books Online's Look In list.

To execute a pass-through query against linked SQL Server 2005 tables using NWClientSQL.accdb as the example, do the following:

1. Open the front-end database (NWClientSQL.accdb) that has tables linked from a back-end server (OAKLEAF-DC1).

2. Click the Create tab, and click the Other group's Query Design button to open the Query1 window with the Show Table dialog active. Click Close to close the dialog without adding a table.

3. In the Query Tools, Design ribbon, click the Query Type group's Pass-Through button to clear objects from the Query1 window, which becomes a large text box for writing SQL batches.

4. Click the Property Sheet button, and select the ODBC Connect Str text box, which contains an ODBC; stub, to activate its builder button.

5. Click the Builder button to open the Select Data Source dialog with the File Data Source page active. Open the Look In list and navigate through My Network Places to the server share (//OAKLEAF-DC1/Northwind) that stores the file DSN (NWDataSQL.dsn), as shown in Figure 19.35.

Figure 19.35
Navigate to and select the file DSN stored on a server share with the Look In list, unless the DSN is mapped to a local drive letter.

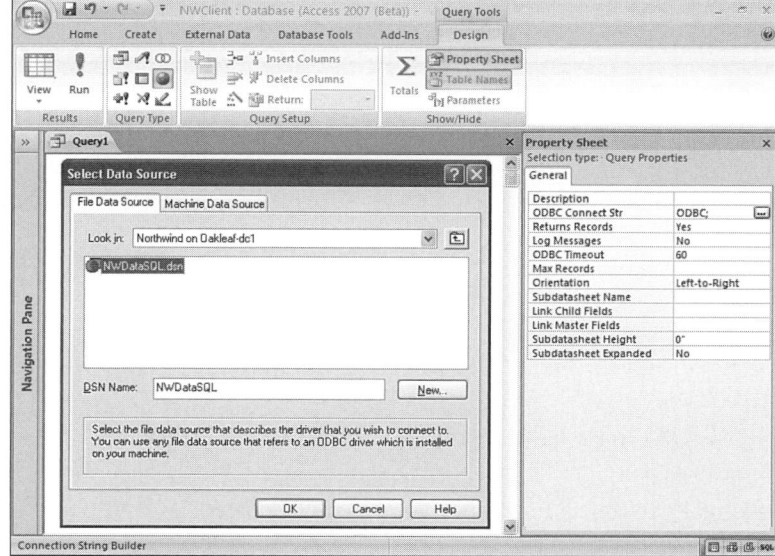

N O T E

> You must navigate to My Network Places and then to server shares with the Look In list, because the Navigate Up button to the right of the Look In list stops at My Computer.

6. Select the file DSN and click OK to paste a DSN-less connection string as the ODBC Connect Str property value and close the Select Data Source dialog. Click No when asked if you want to store the password in the connection string.

7. Type the SQL batch statement to be executed by the server in the text box. If the batch statement is a select query, set the Returns Records property value to Yes; otherwise, set the value to No.

8. Click the Run button to execute the pass-through query and, if the query returns rows, fill the Datasheet (see Figure 19.36).

Figure 19.36
A complex query produces this result set, which includes a RowNumber column whose values represent the rank of average ShippedDate values for products ordered in the quarter. A green globe identifies pass-through queries in the Navigation Pane.

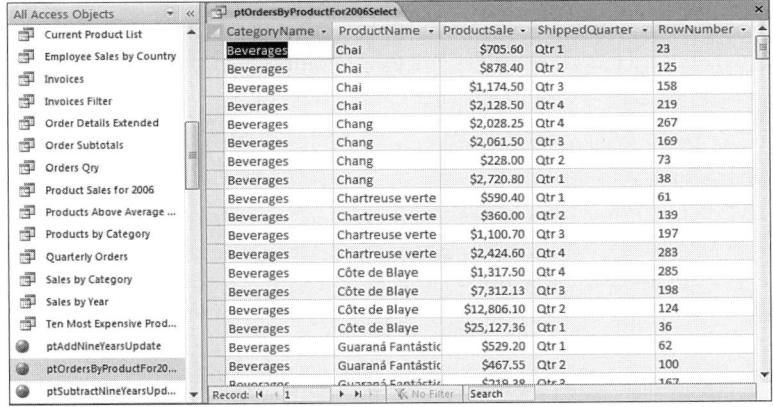

T-SQL
Here's the T-SQL Select statement for the ptOrdersByProductFor2006Select pass-through query that creates the result set shown in Figure 19.36:

```
SELECT Categories. CategoryName, ProductName,
    SUM(CONVERT(money, ([Order Details].UnitPrice * Quantity)
    * (1 - Discount) / 100) * 100) AS ProductSales,
    'Qtr ' + CONVERT(char(1), DATEPART(q, ShippedDate)) AS ShippedQuarter,
    ROW_NUMBER() OVER(ORDER BY AVG(CONVERT(integer, ShippedDate)))
    AS RowNumber
FROM Categories INNER JOIN
    Products ON Categories.CategoryID = Products.CategoryID INNER JOIN
        Orders INNER JOIN [Order Details]
        ON Orders.OrderID = [Order Details].OrderID
            ON Products.ProductID = [Order Details].ProductID
WHERE (ShippedDate BETWEEN '1/1/2006' AND '12/31/2006')
GROUP BY Categories.CategoryName, ProductName,
    'Qtr ' + CONVERT(char(1), DATEPART(q, Orders.ShippedDate))
ORDER BY Categories.CategoryName, ProductName
```

19

UPDATE, INSERT, and DELETE pass-through queries execute without warning. If you don't set the Returns Records property value to No, you receive a "Pass-through query with ReturnsRecords property set to True did not return any rows" message.

CAUTION

> The ChangeServer VBA subprocedure, which is described in the earlier section "Changing the Link Connection String with a VBA Subprocedure," doesn't change the server for pass-through queries. You must change the SERVER= item manually.

ADDING SQL SERVER USER LOGINS WITH SQL SERVER MANAGEMENT STUDIO

It isn't practical to protect data in linked client/server tables with folder and file access to the back-end database. To restrict read and write access to a database or specific tables within a database, you must establish user logins for the database, grant permissions to these logins, and then add user accounts to the logins. Security features differ greatly between RDBMSs, so this section deals only with SQL Server 2005 [Express] and its management toolset, SQL Server Management Studio [Express]. There are no significant security differences between the Enterprise, Standard, Workgroup, and Express versions.

NOTE

> There are many aspects of SQL Server security, such as administrative security, file and folder encryption, and data protection, that this section doesn't cover because they're beyond the scope of this book. The purpose of this section is to show you how to set up SQL Server security for ordinary database users.

Two of SQL Server's security principals are *logins* to a server instance and *users* of individual databases. With Windows integrated security, logins correspond to Windows security groups and users as Windows users who are members of one or more of the login groups.

Installing SQL Server 2005 or SSX SP1 or later on a computer in an Active Directory domain creates the following logins for Windows groups and services (look ahead to Figure 19.37):

- **BUILTIN\Administrators**—The local group containing the Administrator account, and the Domain Admins and Enterprise Admins security groups. Members have the System Administrator (sysadmin) role for all databases. Each member of this group has permissions to do *anything* to the SQL Server instance. Microsoft recommends that you create a new user login in the sysadmin role and then delete this login.

- **BUILTIN\Users**—The local group with default (`public`) database role for all Domain Users. The `public` role has no default access permissions to any objects.

- *COMPUTERNAME***SQLServer2005MSSQLUser$***COMPUTERNAME**$-**SQLEXPRESS**—A Domain Local user group with Log on as a Service, Log on as a Batch Job, and other permissions for SQL Server. This security group has explicit Read & Execute, List Folder Contents, and Read permissions on the SQL Server …\MSSQL.1\MSSQL folder that contains the data and related files.

- *COMPUTERNAME***SQLServer2005MSFTEUser$***COMPUTERNAME**$-**SQLEXPRESS**—A Domain Local user group with the Log on as a Service right for the SQL Server Full Text [Search] Engine. Installing the Full Text Search service is an option when you set up SSX and SSMSX SP2 with the SQL Server 2005 Express with Advanced Features installer.

- **NT AUTHORITY\NETWORK SERVICE**—The default local service account under which SQL Server runs. Microsoft recommends that you create a domain user account with minimal privileges and run SQL Server 2005 under that account.

- **NT AUTHORITY\SYSTEM**—The local service account that has access to all machine resources.

All security groups in the preceding list contain the Active Directory Administrator account if you used that account to install SSX. Otherwise, the SQLServer2005…User group contains the account you used when installing SSX.

You take advantage of the NWReaders and NWWriters security groups and NWReader1 and NWWriter1 domain user accounts that you created in the earlier section "Establishing Network Share, Folder, and File Security for the Back End" to create SSX logins and NWDataSQL users in the next section.

UNDERSTANDING SERVER AND DATABASE ROLES

Roles simplify assigning privileges to logins or users. SQL Server provides the following two types of roles:

- Server roles—Roles for server-wide administrative permissions that you assign to logins, such as sysadmin, dbcreator, and securityadmin. Table 19.2 lists server roles and their permissions in approximate descending order of authority.

- Database roles—Roles for database-scoped data access, data entry, and administrative permissions that you assign to logins or users. Table 19.3 lists database roles and their permissions in approximate descending order of authority.

TABLE 19.2 SQL SERVER 2005 SERVER ROLES AND THEIR PERMISSIONS

Server Role	Server-wide Permissions
sysadmin	Perform any server action.
dbcreator	CREATE, ALTER, DROP, and RESTORE any database.
securityadmin	GRANT, DENY, and REVOKE server-level and database-level permissions, and reset login passwords.
diskadmin	Manage SQL Server disk files.
serveradmin	Change server-wide configuration options and shut down the server.
processadmin	Terminate running processes of an SQL Server instance.
setupadmin	Add and remove linked servers, and also execute some system stored procedures.
bulkadmin	Execute the BULK INSERT statement.
public	Read server metadata (VIEW ANY DATABASE).

TABLE 19.3 SQL SERVER 2005 DATABASE ROLES AND THEIR PERMISSIONS

Database Role	Permissions
db_owner	Perform all configuration and maintenance actions, including dropping the database.
db_ddladmin	Execute CREATE, ALTER, DROP, and any other Data Definition Language (DDL) command in the database.
db_accessadmin	GRANT or REVOKE database access by Windows logins or groups, or SQL Server logins.
db_backupoperator	Back up—but not restore—the database.
db_datareader	SELECT data from user tables.
db_datawriter	INSERT, UPDATE, and DELETE data in user tables.
db_denydatawriter	Deny INSERT, UPDATE, and DELETE operations on user tables.
db_denydatareader	Deny SELECT on user tables.

You must be in the securityadmin server role or db_owner database role to add logins and db_datareader and db_datawriter permissions. For this example, the NWReaders login requires db_datareader, and the NWWriters login requires db_datareader and db_datawriter roles for the NWDataSQL database.

CREATING THE NWREADER AND NWWRITER LOGINS WITH SSMSX

Most Access users who upsize single-file or front-end/back-end Access applications to linked SQL Server tables or Access data projects are members of an Active Directory (AD) domain. Thus, this procedure for creating SQL Server logins and granting permissions uses AD security principals—security groups and user accounts in the Domain Users group. You can emulate this process for workgroups or even a single computer by creating local groups for NWReaders and NWWriters, and local NWReader1 and NWWriter 1 user accounts that correspond to the AD accounts.

To create logins for the NWReaders and NWWriters security groups and assign the groups database roles, do the following:

1. If you didn't create the NWReaders and NWWriters groups with NWReader1 and NWWriter1 user accounts in the earlier section "Establishing Network Share, Folder, and File Security for the Back End," do it now.

2. Log on with an administrative account to your local computer that has the NWClientSQL front end with tables linked to an SQL Server 2005 instance.

3. Open SSMSX and connect to the SQL Server 2005 instance on your local machine or a remote server. This example uses the local OAKLEAF-MS16\SQLEXPRESS instance.

4. Expand the server-wide Security\Logins node that's below the last database node (see Figure 19.37).

Figure 19.37
SQL Server Management Studio Express displays the default Security\ Logins node for an SQL Server Express SP1 installation. Default logins correspond to Windows security groups.

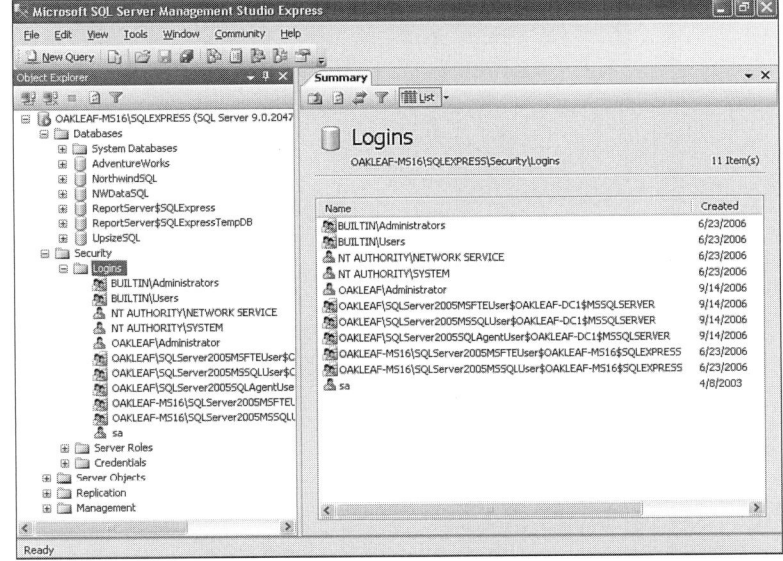

5. Right-click the Logins node and select New Logins to open the Login – New dialog with the General page active.

6. Click the Search button to the right of the Login Name text box to open the Add User or Group dialog, and click its Object Types dialog to open the Object Types dialog, which has Built-in Security Principals and Users selected by default.

7. Mark the Groups check box, click OK to return to the Select User or Group dialog, and click the Locations button to open the Locations dialog.

8. Expand the Entire Directory node, and select your domain (oakleaf.org for this example). If you're not a member of an AD domain, select your local computer name. Click OK to return to the Select User or Group dialog.

9. Type **NWReaders** in the text box, and click Test Names to verify that the group exists, indicated by an underline (see Figure 19.38). Click OK to close the dialog and return to the Login – New dialog.

Figure 19.38
The Select User or Group Dialog lets you select a Windows group for a login from the entire directory, a specific domain, or a computer in a workgroup.

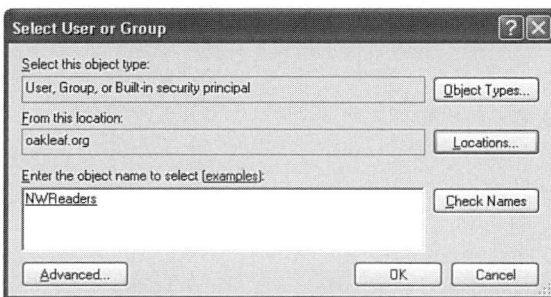

10. Open the Default Database list and select the database for the login—NWDataSQL for this example (see Figure 19.39).

Figure 19.39
Specify the Windows security group and default database for the new login on the General page.

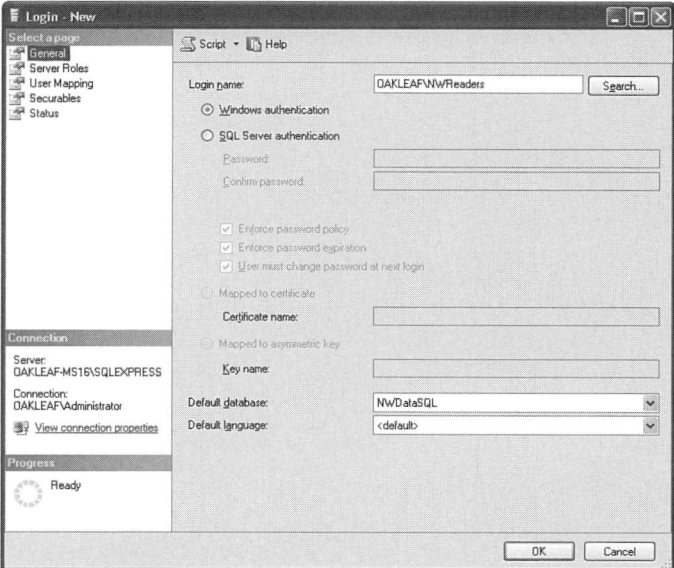

11. Select the User Mapping page, mark the Map check box adjacent to the default database (NWDataSQL) to enable the Database Role Membership list, and mark the db_datareader role (see Figure 19.40). Click OK to close the dialog.

Figure 19.40
Map the login to the default database and assign database roles on the Mapping User page.

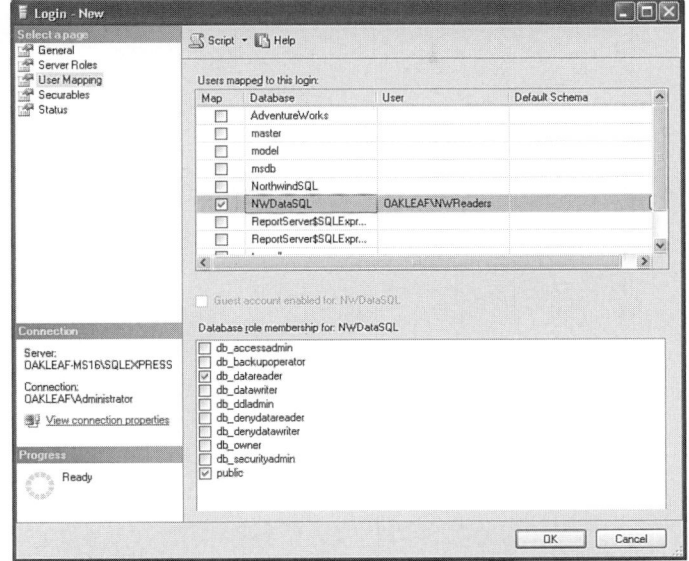

NOTE

Specifying a Default Schema for a group login opens an error message. Only individual user logins can specify a Default Schema. (The default Default Schema is dbo).

19

12. Repeat steps 5 through 11, but type **NWWriters** in step 8 and mark db_datareader and db_datawriter role check boxes in step 11.

13. The new logins appear in the Security\Logins list and under the Databases\ NWDataSQL\Security\Users node (see Figure 19.41).

The NWReaders group's SELECT permissions enable members to open views, invoke inline table-valued functions, and execute SELECT pass-through queries. NWWriters members can execute pass-through queries that perform INSERT, UPDATE, or DELETE operations on tables.

GRANTING EXECUTE RIGHTS TO STORED PROCEDURES

Unfortunately, SQL Server 2005 doesn't have a db_executor database role that would enable a user or group to execute all user-defined stored procedures in the database. It's uncommon to execute stored procedures from front ends to linked client/server tables, but the requirement sometimes occurs. You use a pass-through query with EXEC[UTE] StoredProcedureName as its query expression.

Figure 19.41
Adding logins to the server and mapping the logins to a database adds the group as a user to the mapped database.

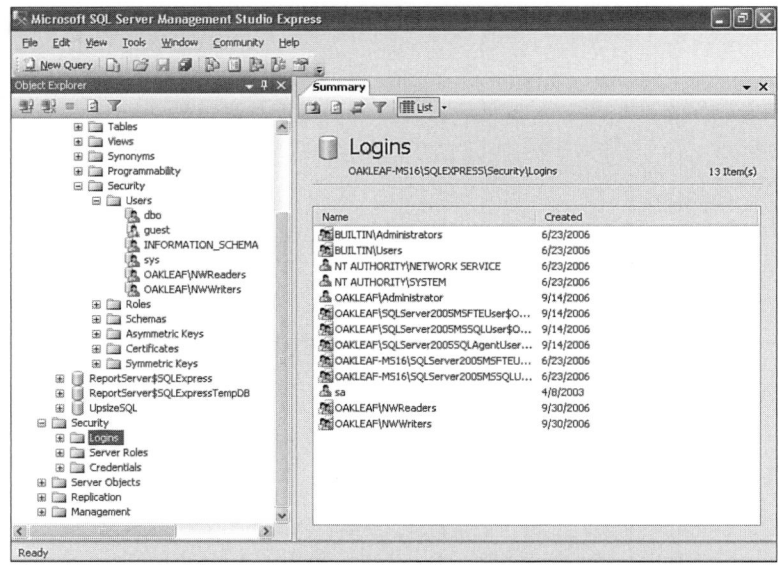

When you upsize Access databases to ADPs, the Upsizing Wizard creates stored procedures for several classes of SELECT queries and all action queries. ADP queries are the equivalent of pass-through queries, because their SQL statements execute directly against the back-end tables, rather than passing through the Access query processor.

To enable members of login groups—NWReaders and NWWriters for this example—to execute a set of stored procedures with explicit permissions, do the following:

1. In SSMSX, double-click the \NWDataSQL\Security\Users\NWReaders node to open the Database User – OAKLEAF\NWReaders dialog, and select the Securables page.

2. Click the Add button to open the Add Objects dialog, select the All Objects of the Types button, and click OK to open the Select Objects dialog. Click the Object Types button to open the Select Object Types dialog, mark stored procedures, and click OK to return the Database User dialog.

3. Scroll to the user stored procedures in the Securables list—dbo.spProductSalesFor2006Select, dbo.spAddNineYearsUpdate, and dbo.spSubtractNineYearsUpdate for this example.

4. Only NWWriters should have execute permissions for the two …Update procedures, so mark the check box for dbo.spProductSalesFor2006Select and click OK twice to return to the Database User – OAKLEAF\NWReaders' Securables page.

5. Mark the Execute and View Definition check boxes for the select stored procedure in the Grant column (see Figure 19.42). (With Grant check boxes enable the user to grant the permission to other users.) Click OK to close the dialog.

Figure 19.42
Select the stored pro-
cedure(s) to enable in
the Securables list of
the Database User –
Domain\UserName
dialog.

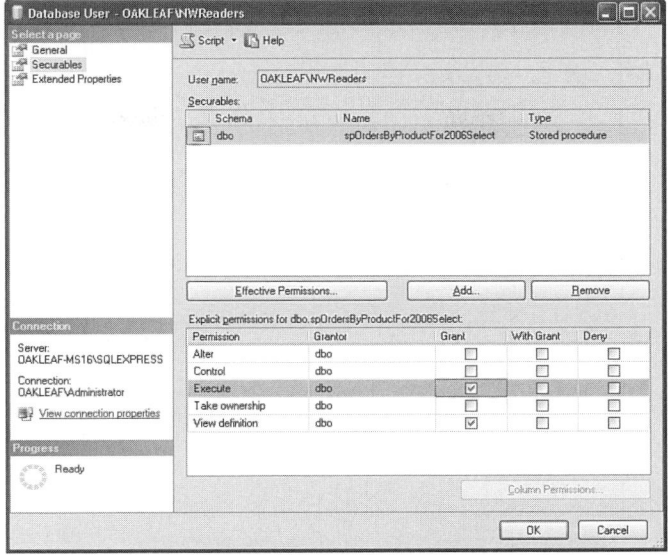

6. Repeat steps 1 through 5 for the NWWriters user, but add all three stored procedures in step 3, and mark the Grant check boxes for each procedure in step 5.

VERIFYING DATABASE SECURABLES PROTECTION

The process of verifying the SQL Server linked table permissions for members of the NWReaders and NWWriters Windows security groups is similar to—but more complex than—that for the linked Access tables scenario in the earlier section "Verifying Back-end Database Network Security." Here's the drill:

- Log on to the front-end computer as NWWriter1, and verify that you can read and update tables in Datasheet View, run Access queries, execute pass-through SELECT and UPDATE queries, and execute stored procedures.

- Log on as NWReader1 and verify that you read—but not update—tables, run Access SELECT but not UPDATE queries, and execute only SELECT pass-through queries and stored procedures. Figure 19.43 shows typical error messages resulting from attempts to update tables and executing stored procedures without appropriate permissions.

- Log on as User1 and verify that you cannot open any linked table, run any Access or pass-through query, or execute any stored procedure (see Figure 19.44).

Figure 19.43
These error messages occur when the NWReader1 user attempts to update a table (top) or execute a stored procedure without execute permissions (bottom).

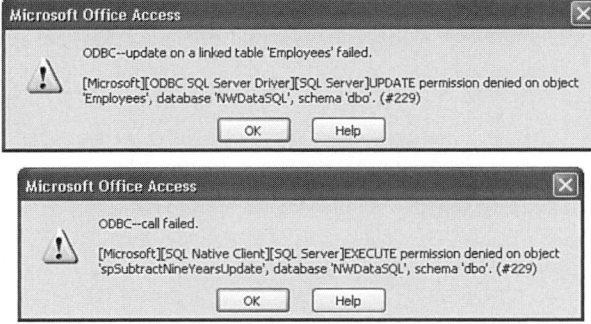

Figure 19.44
You receive the top error message when a user with no permissions for database objects attempts to open or execute an object. The second error message occurs after acknowledging the top message for a linked table.

PASSWORD-PROTECTING AND ENCRYPTING ACCESS FRONT ENDS

All production database applications should have at least some level of security applied. The minimum level of security is password-protecting the front-end .accdb file. The problem with password protection is that users can copy the front-end .accdb file and then open any Access object—except password-protected VBA code—in Design view and make design changes.

The only method of preventing unauthorized design changes to a password-protected .accdb file is to distribute the front end as an .mde file or supply a runtime version of your application. A runtime version requires the Access 2007 Developer Extensions' runtime version of MSAccess.exe, which was included with the Microsoft Office Developer Edition (MOD) for earlier Office versions. Creating an .mde version from a copy of your front-end .accdb file or use of runtime Access prevents users from opening any object in Design view.

As a general rule, don't password-protect or create .mde versions of back-end .accdb files. Instead, use share- and file-level security, as described in the earlier section "Establishing Network Share, Folder, and File Security for the Back End."

Providing your application's users with a password-protected .mde version of your front-end database is the simplest method to achieve nominal security. You set only the initial password for the .accdb precursor of the .mde file; users can change the password of an .mde file. This means that everyone running your front end can unset the password, which can compromise security. You or your network administrator can minimize security breaches by requiring network users to change their logon passwords periodically. Changing logon passwords doesn't require changes to file-based or SQL Server security parameters for the back end.

ADDING A DATABASE PASSWORD

To password-protect and encrypt a front-end .accdb file, do this:

1. Close the database if it's open, and store an unprotected backup copy of the front end on a secure medium, such as a recordable or rewritable CD or a floppy disk. Most front-end .accdb files will fit on a 1.44MB floppy disk. Use the backup copy if you forget the password. This copy also serves as the backup for an .mde version.

2. Click the Office button, and choose Open to display the Open dialog.

3. Select the file to protect, and click the arrow to the right of the Open button to display a list of Open... options (see Figure 19.45). Choose Open Exclusive to open the file for exclusive use.

Figure 19.45
Use the Open button's list to open the .accdb file in exclusive mode. You need exclusive access to set the database password and encrypt the front end.

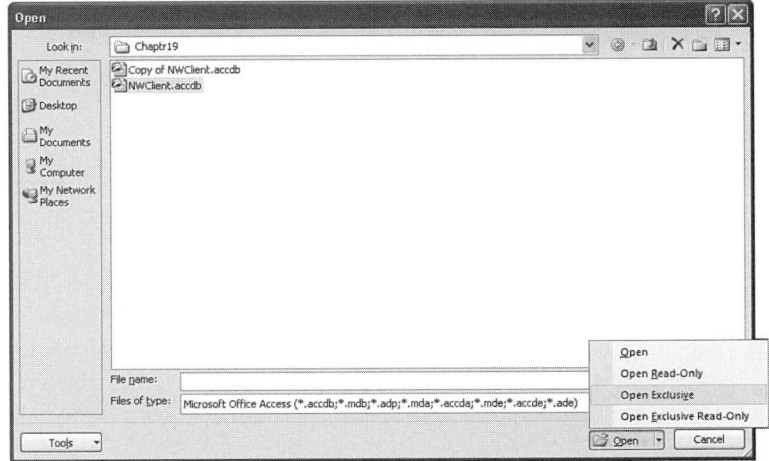

4. Click the Database Tools tab and click Encrypt with Password to open the dialog of the same name. If you didn't open the file for exclusive use in step 3, you receive an error message.

5. Type and confirm the password in the two text boxes (see Figure 19.46), click OK, and close the database.

Figure 19.46
Type and confirm the front-end password in the Set Database Password text boxes.

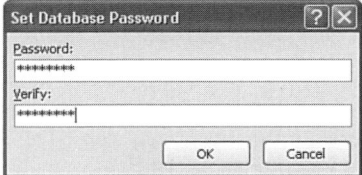

NOTE

For maximum password security, use a combination of at least eight upper- and lower-case letters, numbers, and allowed punctuation characters. You can't use the following characters in a password: " \ [ ] : | < > + = ; , . ? *..

6. Reopen the .accdb file, type the password in the Password Required dialog's Enter Database Password text (see Figure 19.47), and click OK.

Figure 19.47
Users must type the database-specific password to open the front end. Password-protecting a database doesn't prevent users from making design changes or other modifications to database objects.

To remove the password, repeat steps 2–4, but click Decrypt Database in step 4. Type the password again in the text box and click OK.

PASSWORD-PROTECTING VBA CODE

Access 2000 introduced password protection for VBA 6.0 code in conventional modules and Class Modules. You don't need to password-protect VBA code if you convert your front end to an .mde file, which compiles your source code and removes it from the .mde file. *Class Modules* (also called *Microsoft Access Class Objects*) hold the VBA code behind forms and reports. You might want to protect your VBA code against modification by users who have design privileges for the front end.

You can prevent users from viewing or modifying the VBA code in your entire front end by taking the following steps:

 1. Open any module, or open a form or report in Design view, and click the Code button to open the VBA editor. Exclusive access isn't necessary to password-protect VBA code.

2. Choose <u>T</u>ools, *ProjectName* Prope<u>r</u>ties to open the *ProjectName* Properties dialog, and click the Protection tab.

3. Mark the Lock Project for Viewing check box, and type and confirm a password in the two text boxes (see Figure 19.48). Click OK.

Figure 19.48
Prevent front-end users from viewing and modifying your VBA code behind forms and reports and in modules by password-protecting the code for the entire project.

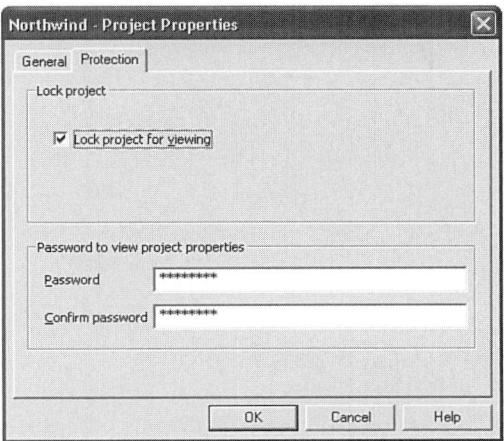

TIP

Don't use the same or a similar password for the VBA code and the database. The database password will be the first choice of curious users. More determined users will try variations on the database password, such as adding a numeric suffix.

4. Close and reopen the database, and then repeat step 1. Type the password in the *ProjectName* Password dialog, and click OK.

To remove the VBA code password, repeat steps 1 and 2, clear the Lock Project for Viewing check box, and click OK.

CREATING AND TESTING AN .ACCDE FRONT END

As mentioned earlier, .accde files provide a quick way to protect your front ends from modification by users. Users can't add, delete, or view in design mode forms, reports, and modules. Users have unrestricted access to tables and queries, which means they can wreak havoc on their own copy of the program by deleting links to tables, rewriting queries, and performing other mischief. Applying user-level security is the only means of securing local and linked tables, and preserving the integrity of queries and macros (if you use macros).

Open your Access front-end .accdb file, click the Database Tools tab, and click the <u>M</u>ake ACCDE button to open the Save As dialog. Accept the default *AccdbFileName*.accde or rename the file. Click Save to create the new .accde file. Open the .accde file and verify user

19

restrictions for tables, forms (see Figure 19.49), reports, and modules. Users might be able to open the Visual Basic Editor but can't view source code, because creating the .mde file removes the source code.

Figure 19.49
The context menu for a form illustrates user restrictions by disabled choices. Unfortunately, there are no user restrictions for Design view of tables, queries, and macros.

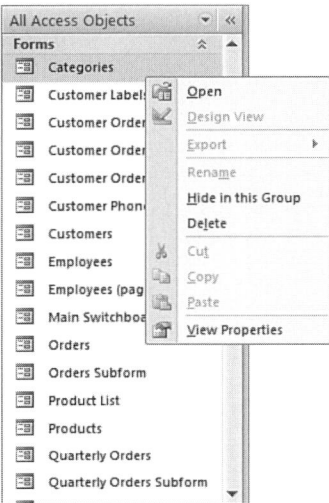

TROUBLESHOOTING

ACCESS TABLES FAIL TO UPSIZE

I receive error messages during the upsizing process, and some tables don't upsize.

The most common cause of failure is the presence of complex Access or VBA expressions in table or field validation rules. SQL Server has counterparts for many Access query expressions, but only a few for VBA functions. SQL Server 2000's extended properties accommodate Access input masks, data display formatting, subdatasheets, and lookup fields. The Upsizing Wizard, however, handles a surprisingly broad range of validation rules. For example, you can upsize with no difficulty the Forms14.accdb application whose HRActions table has several table and field validation rules.

If you adhere to the recommendations in the "Modifying Table Properties to Ensure Successful Upsizing" section near the middle of this chapter, there's little probability of encountering table upsizing failures.

SQL SERVER EXPRESS PERFORMANCE PROBLEMS

Performance of my multiuser Access applications is significantly slower after upsizing the tables to SSX or other SQL Server 2005 editions.

If your SSX back end appears to be running out of steam as you add more users, the first step is to optimize your queries to minimize the amount of data returned to the client.

Revisit all queries with SELECT * statements to determine whether you need all columns returned. For example, don't include the shipping address fields of Northwind.accdb's Orders table in your query if you're only interested in order dates or customer billing information. Avoid Access-specific or VBA expressions in WHERE clause criteria, because the server must return all records for processing by the Access expression service. Both Access and SQL Server support SELECT TOP *n* [PERCENT] queries, but ODBC doesn't. Thus, the server must return all records to the client for TOP *n* processing by Access.

Try to design your form queries with WHERE clause criteria that return fewer than 100 rows. Such queries require only a single connection to the server.

After you've streamlined your queries, the next step is to add RAM. Minimum RAM for reasonable performance with five or fewer users is 512MB for Windows XP or 1GB for Windows Vista.

If some—but not all—users experience performance problems, check their client PCs for adequate RAM to run Office 2007 or the Access 2007 runtime version. The "System Requirements for Access 2007" section of the Introduction lists the RAM requirements for Office 2007. Network connectivity between the client and server also can be a problem; solving networking issues is beyond the scope of this book.

IN THE REAL WORLD—THE (ALMOST) FREE LUNCH

Controversy over the future of conventional shared-file multiuser Access applications continues unabated among Access developers and Microsoft marketers. The shared-file, "Access is alive and well" axis insists that Access is a viable back end for workgroup-size online transaction processing (OLTP) applications. The "Access is dead" cabal, whose membership is dominated by SQL Server marketing folks, consider SSX to be Microsoft's "strategic database" for Office applications and SQL Server 2005 to be the natural back-end choice for everyone else, including users of hand-held devices running SQL Server Compact Edition (SSCE). Regardless of the rhetoric, you can't beat the price of SSX; it's free.

Shared-file proponents tend to favor traditional Data Access Objects (DAO), a mature technology that's been renamed the Microsoft Office Access 2007 Database engine Object Library. Members of the MSDE/SQL Server clan justifiably promoted OLE DB and ActiveX Data Objects (ADO) as being where the action was for database connectivity. Microsoft's .NET Framework is centered on SQL Server and an enhanced version of ADO called ADO.NET, which was in version 2.0 when this book was written. The SQL Server and Visual Studio teams are devoting all current development efforts to ADO.NET.

The reality is that multiuser Access back ends do run out of steam in heavy-duty OLTP applications having many simultaneous users. The point at which concurrency and file corruption problems begin to appear in Access back-end databases depends on a variety of factors. Each upgrade to Access has improved multiuser reliability, but many developers still consider 20 to 30 simultaneous updating users to be the practical limit for Access 2007. The absolute maximum number of concurrent user connections to any Access database is 255.

Therefore, Access isn't a serious contender for an e-commerce orders database on a highly trafficked website. The 1GB maximum table size and 32-index limit (including indexes created by relationships) makes Access impractical for use in data marts and warehouses of medium or larger scope.

Access offers the advantage of easy conversion from single-user, single-file mode to shared-file multiuser mode. The Database Splitter utility makes the transition automatic. Descriptions of the Access user-level security system range from Byzantine to Machiavellian, but Access's file-system security is almost as easy to manage as SQL Server security.

If you seek multiuser simplicity in a small Windows Vista or XP workgroup environment, shared-file Access probably is your best bet. For more sizable projects, linking Access front ends to SSX under Windows Server 2003—followed ultimately by a transition to a full version of SQL Server—is the natural choice, especially if you also want full compatibility with Windows SharePoint Services (WSS) 3.0. File-system security and password protection apply to front-ends with links to SQL Server tables, but don't secure the back-end database itself against marauding members of the local Administrators group who have a copy of SSMSX.

SSX is substantially more robust than Access, especially for OLTP. You don't need to periodically compact SQL Server files as users edit and delete records. SSX offers automated backup and restore operations and provides a transaction log that you can use to return restored tables to their exact state at the time of a crash.

If you're starting an Access project from scratch, and you expect more than about 20 users to update database tables simultaneously, seriously consider starting directly with an ADP. Although you can use the Access Upsizing Wizard to convert a conventional Access application to ADP, the upsizing process isn't bulletproof. You must rewrite Access queries that contain Access-specific reserved words and functions missing from the Wizard's bag of tricks. You save time in the short and long run by conforming to SQL Server's T-SQL dialect when you design your queries. Chapter 22, "Upsizing Access Applications to Access Data Projects," describes typical workarounds for Access queries that won't upsize to T-SQL.

Your free lunch ticket expires when you must upgrade your server from SSX to the $5,995 SQL Server 2005 Standard Edition for a single processor with unlimited cores. To mitigate the pain of SQL Server license costs, Microsoft gives you a free copy of SQL Server Analysis (formerly OLAP) Services and Business Intelligence Management Studio. Of course, the SQL Server folks hope you'll build data marts so large that they require their own dedicated server cluster (and thus pairs of even more costly SQL Server 2005 Enterprise Edition licenses).

EXPLORING ACCESS DATA PROJECTS AND SQL SERVER 2005

In this chapter

MOVING ACCESS TO THE CLIENT/SERVER MODEL

Access 2007's Access data projects (ADPs), also called *Microsoft Access projects* or *Access client/server applications*, let you connect to Microsoft SQL Server 2005 SP2 or SQL Server Express (SSX) SP2 on your PC; on a peer server running Windows Vista, XP Professional, or 2000 Professional; or on a network server running Windows 2003 Server or later. You also can connect to networked SQL Server 2000 SP4 or Microsoft Desktop Engine (MSDE) 2000 SP4 databases. As in the previous chapters of this book, the term *SQL Server* refers to any of these four SQL Server versions. *SQL Server 2005* is used when discussing new features that aren't also supported by SQL Server 2000 or MSDE 2000.

> **NOTE**
>
> It's possible to connect ADP front ends to SQL Server 6.5 and 7.0 databases, but doing this is beyond the scope of this book.
>
> You cannot install MSDE 2000 on machines running Windows Vista, so there are no examples that demonstrate how to use MSDE 2000 in this book. Using SSX or MSDE 2000 as the ADP back-end server is essentially an identical process.

Following are the most important characteristics of ADPs:

- Like upsized Access applications, ADPs rely on SQL Server tables, but they don't use .accdb files to store database front-end forms, reports, and other application objects. ADPs store application objects in a single .adp or .ade (encrypted) compound document file (DocFile).

- Unlike upsized Access front-end .accdb files, the .adp file doesn't contain queries; SQL Server stores SELECT queries as views. A view is a precompiled SQL SELECT query, which replaces conventional Access SELECT queries saved as Access QueryDef (query definition) objects.

- SQL Server stored procedures replace Access action queries. Like views, stored procedures are precompiled queries, but stored procedures aren't limited to SELECT queries. Stored procedures are especially efficient at processing INSERT, UPDATE, and DELETE operations and managing transactions.

- Project designer windows substitute for Access's Table and Query Design windows. The da Vinci windows perform functions similar to—but differ in layout from—their Access counterparts. Table and Query Datasheet views are almost identical to those for Access back ends.

- SQL Server offers *user-defined functions (UDFs)*, which you can use to return the equivalent of a table to an ad-hoc query, view, or stored procedure. User-defined functions support SQL Server's *linked servers* feature to connect to other client/server RDBMSs, Active Directory, and Index Service. For example, you can connect an ADP to an Oracle database linked to MSDE. You also can use UDFs to return scalar (character or numeric) values.

- SQL Server uses *extended properties* to support Access's lookup field and subdatasheet features, so you don't lose these capabilities when migrating to the client/server model. Extended properties also support input masks, captions, and data display formatting. SQL Server includes system stored procedures to add, read, and remove custom extended properties from the database.

- SQL Server has its own panoply of new Extended Markup Language (XML) features, which are independent of those offered by Access 2007. For example, you can write an XML file that contains a query and add an XML Stylesheet Language transform (XSL/T) to return data directly from SQL Server to a fully formatted table in a web page. SQL Server 2005 has a new xml data type, but Access doesn't support it.

- ADPs dispense with Open Database Connectivity (ODBC) and Data Access Objects (DAO), substituting OLE DB data providers and ActiveX Data Objects (ADO) for database connectivity and data manipulation, respectively. OLE DB and ADO are the subjects of Chapter 30, "Understanding Data Access Objects, OLE DB, and ADO."

- You design ADPs in Access's standard Form and Report views and use the standard Toolbox to add native Access and ActiveX controls to forms and reports. You can import Access objects—other than tables and queries—from existing Access databases.

You can use the Upsizing Wizard to convert a conventional Access .accdb application to an Access project, instead of retaining the Access .accdb front end.

ADPs are best suited to the following types of Access 2007 applications:

- Front ends to new or existing SQL Server databases. Access 2007 is a very effective rapid application development (RAD) tool for client/server front ends.

- New projects that require more robust data storage than an Access database or need the capability to selectively encrypt individual tables, columns, or even cells with public key cryptography. Any project that is likely to have more than 25 simultaneously connected users is a candidate for an SQL Server back end.

- Applications that you expect to upsize to SQL Server 2005 Express, Standard, or Enterprise Edition in the near future or even long term. Microsoft has made it easy to migrate ADPs from SSX or MSDE on your PC to SQL Server running under Windows 2003 Server or later. Using ADPs, rather than Access tables, ensures a quick and seamless transition from a local SSX or MSDE database to SQL Server 2000 or 2005.

- Applications that need to restrict data editing or access to specific tables or queries to specific users or groups. Access 2007 doesn't support user-level or group-level security for any objects, including Access data tables. SQL Server provides very granular permissions.

- Projects that use two-way SQL Server 2005 replication to synchronize multiple copies of the database. SQL Server replication is more robust and flexible than the version offered by Access 2003 and earlier. (Access 2007 doesn't support replication).

20

Users of your Access project must have Access 2000 or later installed, unless you use the Access 2007 runtime version to create a distributable version of your ADP. Access 2007 saves ADPs in Access 2002/2003 format by default or, optionally, Access 2000 format; ADPs don't support the Access 2007 format. The runtime version of MSAccess.exe is a member of the Access 2007 Developer Extensions. If your Access project requires a local database, users also must install SSX. If the application connects to an SQL Server database (not the Express or Desktop Edition), users must have the requisite client licenses for Windows 2003+ Server and SQL Server.

TIP

> Consider linking SQL Server tables to an Access .accdb front end if your application requires local tables. The Upsizing Wizard gives you the choice of linking or moving your tables to SQL Server.
>
> You can use a local Access database with ADP client applications, but you must write VBA code to connect to the local database and manipulate its contents. You can use either DAO or ADO to make the connection to the local .accdb, but using ADO is much more efficient. If you use DAO to connect to the local .accdb file, clients must load both DAO and ADO, which consumes additional resources.

UNDERSTANDING THE ROLE OF SQL SERVER AND ADP

Microsoft's announcement in mid-1995 that Access 2000 would include an "alternate database" led to a flurry of "Jet is dead" pronouncements in the computer press. These stories gained credence when members of the SQL Server 2005 team described their forthcoming product as "Microsoft's strategic database direction." The reality is that Access obituaries are very premature. Jet plays a major role in more than 25 Microsoft products, and variants of the Jet database engine serve as the message store for Microsoft Exchange. Access, with its customized Jet database engine, is likely to be alive and well, at least through the first few decades of the twenty-first century.

Regardless of the Access version of Jet's prospects for long-term survival, there's a definite trend toward the use of client/server back ends when database reliability and security is the primary objective. Production web-based applications require client/server back ends for security and scalability. Thus, SQL Server 2005 will play an increasingly important role as even small firms migrate database applications to intranets and the Internet.

SQL SERVER EDITIONS, LICENSING, AND FEATURES

SQL Server 2005 comes in Compact, Express, Evaluation, Developer, Workgroup, Standard, and Enterprise editions. The Standard and Enterprise editions usually run under Windows 2003+ Server, and the Developer Edition is restricted from use as a production server. SQL Server Compact Edition (SSCE) is a lightweight relational database that someday might substitute for local Access tables in ADP.

Unlike MSDE 2000, which is licensed as a "stand-alone desktop device," SSX has no significant license restrictions on its use. SSX is "redistributable software," which means you can provide an installable copy of SSX with a commercial Access application. If you want to redistribute SSX, you must obtain a no-charge distribution license from Microsoft.

NOTE

> Links from Microsoft's SQL Server web pages at http://www.microsoft.com/sql/ offer product and licensing information for all SQL Server 2005 editions. The http://www.microsoft.com/sql/express page has links to pages for downloading SSX SP2 and optional accessories, as well as feature comparisons and specifications.

All SQL Server editions, except Compact, share a common code base, and data files are fully interchangeable between the versions. All editions use Transact-SQL (T-SQL), which includes many extensions to ANSI-92 SQL. The primary difference between SSX and the other SQL Server 2005 editions (except SSCE) is that SSX doesn't include SQL Server OLAP (Online Analytical Processing) Services, Service Broker, Native Web Services, or a few other advanced features. Installing SSX SP2 with Advanced Services adds SQL Server 2005 Management Studio Express, a graphic tool for creating and managing databases and executing T-SQL queries; Reporting Services that run from a local SSX database; and Full-Text Search capability.

→ For instructions for downloading and installing SSX, **see** "SQL Server 2005 Express Editions SP2 Setup" **p. 59**.

BENEFITS AND DRAWBACKS OF ACCESS DATA PROJECTS

Chapter 19, "Linking Access Front Ends to Access and Client/Server Tables," describes the benefits of moving multiuser applications from shared-file to client/server back ends. There's little controversy among application developers that client/server or multi-tier architecture ultimately will replace all shared-file databases for production applications.

The benefits of moving from Access front ends with linked client/server databases to ADPs aren't so clear-cut. The newer OLE DB and ADO technology is more flexible and efficient than ODBC and Access's Data Access Objects (DAO). ADO is compatible with scripting languages—such as VBScript and JavaScript—for web applications, but DAO isn't. All application objects in the project share a single OLE DB connection to SQL Server, and consume inconsequential server resources when they're idle. Access applications usually require multiple, active connections to the back-end .accdb file that links to the client/server tables.

You should be aware, however, that SQL Server doesn't support new Access 2007 data types, such as Attachments and append-only Memo fields, multivalued lookup fields (MVLF), or the traditional OLE Object data type.

→ For more detailed information on Access features not supported by ADP, see "Upsizing with the Trial-and-Error Approach" **p. 949**.

20

OLE DB and ADO don't offer dramatic performance improvements over ODBC and DAO for databases having tables with 100,000 rows or fewer. However, connecting projects directly to SQL Server lets you take advantage of predefined views and stored procedures that do offer improved server response, especially with databases having tables with a very large number of records. If you expect your databases ultimately to grow to hundreds of thousands or even millions of rows, your best bet is to connect directly to SQL Server with ADP. ADPs are best viewed as an advanced form and report engine for SQL Server. Unlike Access .accdb applications, which can connect to any client/server RDBMS having an ODBC 2+ driver, ADPs connect only to SQL Server. If you need to connect to an IBM DB2, Informix, Oracle, or Sybase RDBMS, you must set up SQL Server views on linked server tables. Using ADPs requires a long-term commitment to SQL Server for your production databases.

Access is unsurpassed as an RDBMS instructional tool, and ADPs with SSX combine to form an ideal method of learning up-to-date client/server database design and programming techniques. If your goal is to become proficient in managing client/server RDBMSs in general—and SQL Server in particular—ADP is a far better choice than working with linked Access tables.

EXPLORING THE NORTHWINDSQL SAMPLE PROJECT

The \Seua12\Chaptr20 folder contains a sample NorthwindSQL.adp project. NorthwindSQL.adp requires a connection to the NorthwindSQL database on SSX, which—in turn—requires installing SSX and attaching the \Seua12\Nwind\NorthwindSQL.mdf database file and its NorthwindSQL.ldf log file.

→ To get instructions for downloading and installing SSX, and attaching the Seua12\Nwind\ NorthwindSQL.mdf as the NorthwindSQL database, **see** "SQL Server 2005 Express Edition SP2 Setup" **p. 59**.

To start the NorthwindSQL project, click the Office button, choose Open, navigate to the \Seua12\Chaptr20 folder, and double-click NorthwindSQL.adp. Double-click the Orders item in the Navigation Pane's Tables group (see Figure 20.1).

> **TIP**
>
> The project uses the default SQL Server instance name for SSX on the local machine: . \SQLEXPRESS. If your SSX or SQL Server 2005 instance is on a different server, click the Office button, choose Server, Connection to open the Data Link Properties dialog, change Server Name to a valid instance name, and click OK.

The Navigation Pane for Access data projects differs considerably from the conventional Access Navigation pane with linked table connections. The most important alterations are as follows:

Figure 20.1
The Navigation Pane of an Access data project file displays table items without linked indicators, and view, stored procedure, and function items in the Queries group.

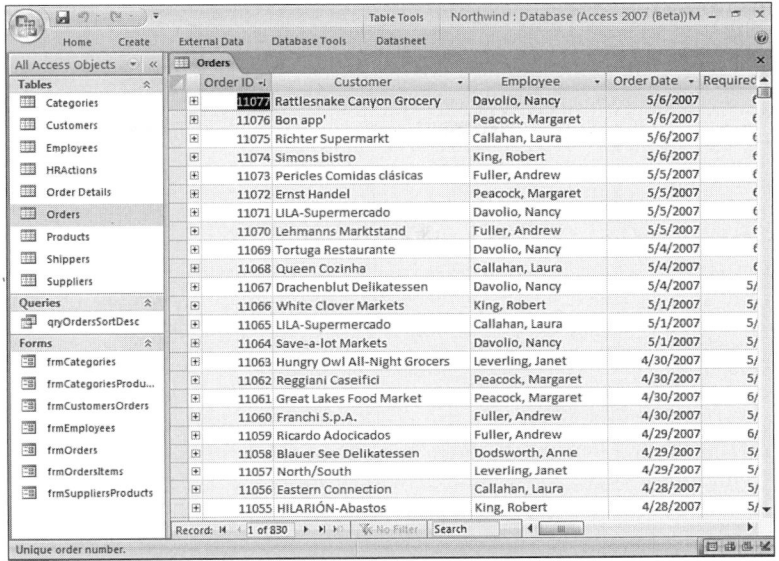

- *Tables* stored in SQL Server databases appear in the Tables group as though they are local tables. The right-pointing arrow symbol, which indicates a linked table of any type, including client/server tables, is missing. Opening an SQL Server table, such as Orders, in Datasheet view displays the same lookup fields and subdatasheet views as its Access counterpart.

- *Queries* groups saved views (Ten Most Expensive Products, for example), stored procedures (Customers and Suppliers), and functions (Invoices Filter).

- *Views* (in the Queries group) use the Access select query symbol, because views most closely correspond to simple Access QueryDefs.

- *Functions* (in the Queries group) that return tables are similar to views, but support parameters.

T-SQL
Views and functions require an explicit field list to support SQL Server's extended properties. If your query contains SELECT * FROM *TableName*, subdatasheets and lookup fields don't appear in the view or function. Recordsets returned by stored procedures don't support extended properties.

- *Stored procedures* (in the Queries group) execute parameterized and action queries as precompiled Transact-SQL statements. Stored procedures provide a substantial performance improvement over direct execution of complex SQL statements.

- *Database diagrams* serve the same purpose as Access relationships (and have the same icon) but differ considerably in their visual presentation.

20

The remaining Access application objects—forms, reports, pages, macros, and modules—are identical, with a few exceptions, to the corresponding objects of conventional Access applications that employ .accdb files for storage. The exceptions primarily are minor changes to form and report properties; as an example, you can set the Record Source property of a form or report to a view, function, or stored procedure.

WORKING WITH SQL SERVER TABLES IN THE PROJECT DESIGNER

ADPs use a set of client/server graphical design tools called the *da Vinci toolset* during their development. Microsoft also calls the da Vinci toolset *MS Design Tools*, but the most common name for Access's implementation of the toolset is the *project designer*. Access's project design mode lets you alter the structure of tables, relationships, views, functions, and stored procedures directly from the user interface. SQL Server and other client/server RDBMSs rely on SQL CREATE, ALTER, and DROP statements for design changes. The project designer executes the SQL statements for your design changes each time you confirm saving changes when exiting design mode. The ability to alter the design of SQL Server tables, which you can't do with linked tables, is an important feature of projects.

> **NOTE**
>
> The SQL panes of Access 2007's product designer don't include the CREATE VIEW¦FUNCTION¦PROC[EDURE] AS *Name* component of the T-SQL statement to create a new object. The project designer adds a CREATE... statement for a new object or an ALTER... statement for an existing object when sending the command to SQL Server.

Server Management Studio (SSMS), SQL Server Management Studio Express (SSMSX), and Visual Studio 2005+ also use the da Vinci toolset for client/server database design. Thus, the project designer brings Access 2007 into conformance with other Microsoft application design platforms and database management tools, at least for client/server databases.

> **TIP**
>
> ADPs are an excellent learning aid and prototyping tool for large-scale client/server database projects. You can quickly and easily create new SSX databases, add tables, establish relationships, design views, and write stored procedures in the project designer. Creating data-enabled forms and reports with Access 2007 is a much faster process than that of other design platforms. After you've tested your prototype SSX database design, you can deploy the database's .mdf and .ldf files directly to SQL Server 2005 versions running under Windows 2003+ Server.

 Tables appear in conventional Access Datasheet view (see Figure 20.2). Date values appear in short date format, and money (Currency) fields default to the currency format you specify in the Currency page of Control Panel's Regional Settings tool.

Figure 20.2
The Datasheet view of NorthwindSQL's Orders table demonstrates the use of SQL Server extended properties.

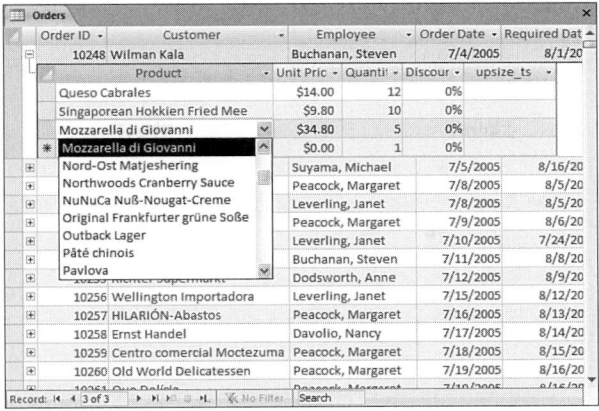

PROJECT DESIGNER'S TABLE DESIGN VIEW

 Table Design view differs dramatically from that of tables linked with Access. Figure 20.3 shows the Orders table in the Access 2007 project designer. Four basic column properties (Column Name, Data Type, Length, and Nulls) plus an extended property (Description) appear in the columns grid, and the Columns and Lookup properties pages display additional property values for the selected column. Property labels and text boxes are enabled only for those properties that are applicable to the column's data type. After you become familiar with the table-creation features of the project designer, you'll find that adding new SQL Server tables is almost as easy as creating new Access tables.

Figure 20.3
Access 2007's project designer Table Design view has some features in common with Access's Table Design view for local and attached client/server tables.

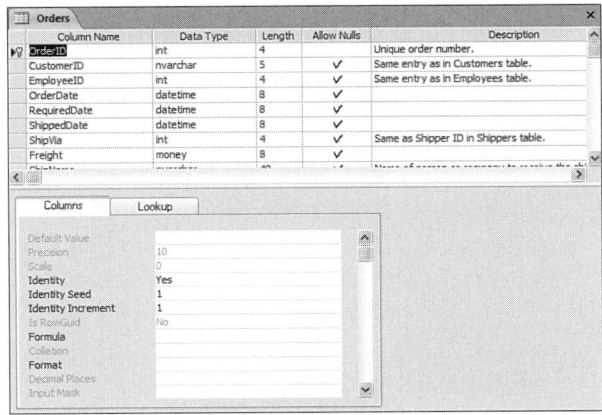

20

SQL Server data type names are in lowercase, a holdover from Microsoft SQL Server's origin as the PC version of Sybase SQL Server for Unix. Table 20.1 lists the names and the correspondence of each project designer grid and the Columns properties page values you set in Access's Table Design grid and General properties page for Access.

> **NOTE**
>
> Client/server databases commonly substitute the term *column* for *field*; this book uses *field* for tables and *column* for query result sets, views, functions, and data-returning stored procedures.

TABLE 20.1 A COMPARISON OF PROJECT DESIGNER AND ACCESS TABLE PROPERTIES

Property	Correspondence to Access Table Properties
Column Name	Same as Access's Field Name. Spaces are permitted in SQL Server column names, but aren't recommended.
Data Type	Same as the combination of Access's Data Type and Field Size, except data types use SQL Server terminology.
Length	Same as Access's Field Size for text fields, except that `char` columns are fixed length.
Allow Nulls	The inverse of Access's Required property; a check mark (the default) allows null values in fields.
Description	Same as Access's Description property (an extended property).
Default Value	Same as Access's Default Value.
Precision	Applicable primarily to numeric or decimal fields; specifies the total number of digits of the column (the precision property of int[eger] and money fields is fixed).
Scale	Applicable to numeric or decimal fields; specifies the number of digits to the right of the decimal point (the scale of money fields is fixed at 4).
Identity	Equivalent to Access's AutoNumber field data type with Increment as the New Values property; Yes specifies that an int (same as Access's Long Integer) field automatically creates a new value when appending a record. (SQL Server doesn't support Access's Random option for AutoNumber fields.)
Identity Seed	Specifies the starting value of a field with the identity property set (usually 1).
Identity Increment	Specifies the increment between successive identity values (usually 1).
Is RowGuid	Yes specifies that the row contains a globally unique identifier (GUID, pronounced "goo id") used primarily in conjunction with timestamp fields for replication. Access has no direct counterpart.
Formula	For tables, this is the expression (formula) for creating a computed column value; Access has no equivalent table property.
Collation	Sets the collating (sorting) sequence for the character column; the default value is `<database default>`. Access has no equivalent property.
Format	Lets you select a predefined display format from a drop-down list (extended property); same as Access's Format property.
Decimal Places	Lets you select Auto or from zero to six characters after the decimal point (extended property); same as Access's Decimal Places property.

Property	Correspondence to Access Table Properties
Input Mask	Lets you type a format string, such as **>LLLLL** for uppercase letters, or open the Input Mask Wizard to generate the string (extended property); same as Access's Input Mask property.

The Lookup properties page (see Figure 20.4) lets you specify extended property values that are identical to those of Access's Lookup page. The Row Source property value for a lookup field can be a T-SQL statement, an SQL Server table, view, or function, or a value or field list.

Figure 20.4
SQL Server extended properties in the Lookup properties page correspond exactly to Access's Lookup properties.

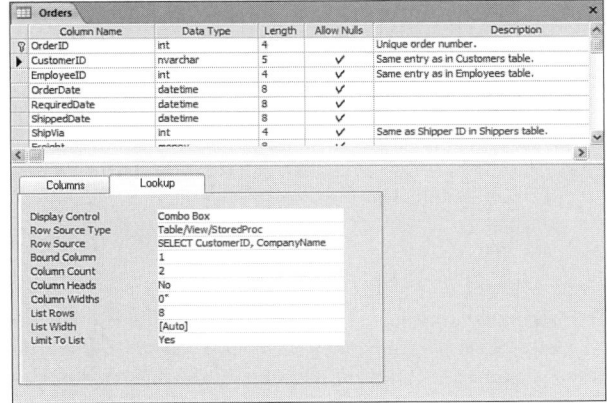

THE TABLE PROPERTIES DIALOG

 The Properties dialog for SQL Server tables also differs greatly from Access's table properties dialog. In Table Design view, click the Table Tools Design tab and then click the Show/Hide group's Properties button to open the Properties dialog, which has five pages—Tables, Relationships, Indexes/Keys, Check Constraints, and Data. (Alternatively, right-click the columns grid and choose <u>P</u>roperties.) You set extended property values for Access table and field properties that aren't included in Table 20.1 and the Lookup Properties page in pages of the Properties dialog.

THE TABLES PROPERTIES PAGE

Figure 20.5 shows the Tables page of the Properties dialog for the Order Details table. The Order Details table is used for this and the following sections because this table has several unique properties.

20

Figure 20.5
The Tables page only displays a few of the properties of the selected table.

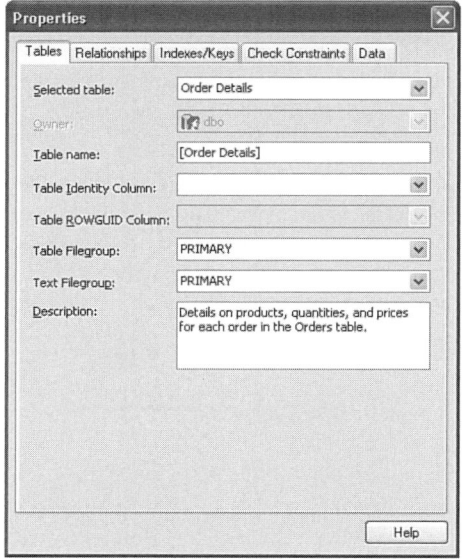

> **NOTE**
>
> The Properties dialog doesn't have OK, Apply, and Cancel buttons. As you make changes on the four pages, the SQL statements to alter the properties accumulate in a cache. When you close the Table Design window or click the Datasheet View button, message boxes offer you the option of saving the table design or abandoning the changes.

Following are brief descriptions of the elements on the Tables page:

- **Selected Table**—Although Selected Table is a drop-down list, you can only select the currently open table from the list.

- **Owner**—The default database owner (dbo) appears here as a read-only value. SQL Server 2005 enables substituting a *schema name* for the database owner value. A schema is a container within a database for a group of tables, views, stored procedures, functions, constraints, aggregates, and other table-level objects.

- **Table Name**—ANSI SQL doesn't allow table names with spaces or punctuation (except underscores), so field names containing illegal characters must be enclosed between square brackets.

> **NOTE**
>
> Microsoft opened a Pandora's box by allowing Access databases to include spaces and other nonalphanumeric symbols in database, table, and field names. The Northwind.mdb sample database developers finally removed spaces from field names in Access 9x, but the space remains in the Order Details table name. Access developers have complained long and loudly, but to no avail, about Microsoft's continuing use of spaces in Access object names.

- **Table Identity Column**—You can assign the `identity` property to a field from a drop-down list of fields with numeric data types.

- **Table ROWGUID Column**—If this property is enabled, you can specify a field to contain automatically generated GUIDs. (Refer to the Is RowGuid property in Table 20.1.)

- **Table Filegroup and Text Filegroup**—SQL Server lets DBAs create multiple operating system files for a single (usually very large) table. DBAs also can assign SQL Server `text` fields, the equivalent to Access's Memo data type, to their own filegroup. Users of MSDE aren't likely to need to create filegroups.

- **Description**—You can add a text description of the table as the value for this extended property, which corresponds to Access's table Description property.

THE RELATIONSHIPS PAGE

Figure 20.6 shows the Relationships page of the Order Details table. Table relationships established by T-SQL declarative referential integrity (DRI) statements also appear in the Database Diagram for the database, which is the subject of the later "Diagramming Table Relationships" section. Many of the properties on this page have counterparts in Access's Edit Relationships dialog.

→ To review Access's Edit Relationships dialog, **see** "Establishing Relationships Between Tables," **p. 237**.

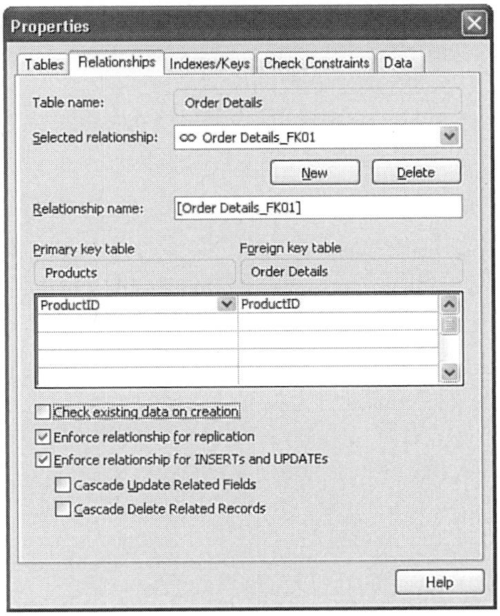

Figure 20.6
The two fields of the primary composite key of the Order Details table have foreign key (FK) relationships with the primary keys of the Orders and Products table. Only one of the relationships (Order_Details_FK01 to the ProductID field of the Products table) appears here.

20

Following are descriptions of the Relationship page's elements:

- **Selected Relationship**—The Order details table has a composite primary key (OrderID and ProductID). These two fields have a foreign key (FK) relationship with the Orders table's OrderID field and the Product table's ProductID field, respectively. The list box opens to select the `FK_Order_Details_Products` relationship.

- **Relationship Name**—SQL Server automatically names the keys as `FK_TableName_FieldName`.

- **Primary Key Table and Foreign Key Table, and fields lists**—Table names are read-only, except when you click Add to create a new relationship. The field lists are similar to those of Access's Edit Relationships dialog.

- **Check Existing Data on Creation**—If you mark this check box, data in the table is tested for relational integrity when you add a new relation. Access always tests existing data when establishing a new relationship.

- **Enforce Relationship for Replication**—Marking this check box requires replicated copies of the table to enforce the relationship. Access doesn't have this property.

- **Enforce Relationship for INSERTs and UPDATEs**—This check box has the same effect as marking Access's Enforce Referential Integrity check box.

- **Cascade Update Related Fields and Cascade Delete Related Records**—These two check boxes correspond to Access's check boxes of the same names.

The Indexes/Keys Page

Figure 20.7 shows the Indexes/Keys page for the Order Details table, which displays the table's primary key by default. This page bears only a faint resemblance to Access's Indexes dialog.

Following are descriptions of the controls on the Indexes/Keys page:

- **Selected Index**—Open this list to select an index on the table. Order Details has a primary key (composite) and a foreign key index (on ProductID). The Type label changes, depending on the type of index you select: Primary Key, Index, or Unique Constraint.

- **Index Name**—SQL Server names indexes as `PK_TableName` for the primary key and `IX_TableName` for other indexes. You can rename the index, if you want. (The `ProductID` index doesn't have the `IX_` prefix.)

- **Column Name and Order**—These two list fields correspond to the Field Name and Sort Order columns of Access's Indexes dialog.

- **Index Filegroup**—This list is enabled only when adding a new index. Like text filegroups, it's uncommon to create a special filegroup for SSX indexes.

Figure 20.7
The Indexes/Keys page for the Order Details table displays the properties of the composite, clustered primary key.

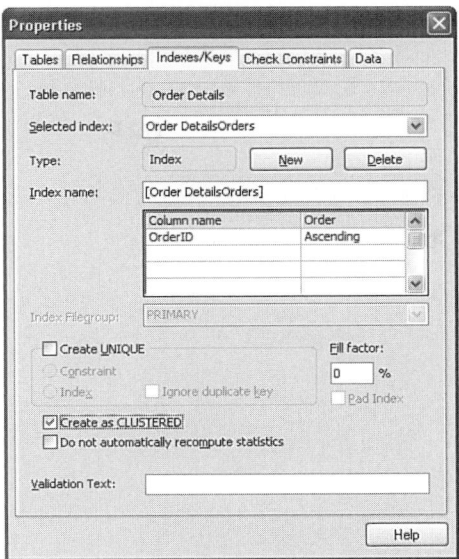

- **Create UNIQUE: Constraint, Index, and Ignore Duplicate Key**—These check boxes and options determine index properties when creating a new index. Create UNIQUE is equivalent to Access's No Duplicates modifier. SQL Server lets you choose to enforce unique values with a CHECK constraint or an index; Access relies on an index. The Ignore Duplicate Key property applies only to bulk insert operations, which aren't common for SSX databases.

- **Create as CLUSTERED**—This check box causes SQL Server to physically order the table records by the primary key value. Clustered indexes improve performance of INSERT and DELETE operations. It's a common practice to specify a clustered index on each table's primary key to improve database performance.

- **Fill Factor and Pad Index**—If records aren't added to the table in the order of the primary key, adding some empty space (usually 10% to 20%) to the index page can improve INSERT performance. Pad Index reserves empty space (two rows) in clustered tables.

- **Do Not Automatically Recompute Statistics**—Marking this check box speeds creation of indexes on large tables at the possible expense of query performance.

- **Validation Text**—This extended property sets the text of the error message you receive when attempting to INSERT or UPDATE a value that conflicts with the UNIQUE constraint. Access has built-in message text for attempted violation of the No Duplicates rule.

20

THE CHECK CONSTRAINTS PAGE

Figure 20.8 shows the Check Constraints page for the Order Details table. Access 2002 moved the constraint property settings to their own page and added a Validation Text property.

Figure 20.8
The Check Constraints page lets you establish the equivalent of Access Validation Rule and Validation Text properties.

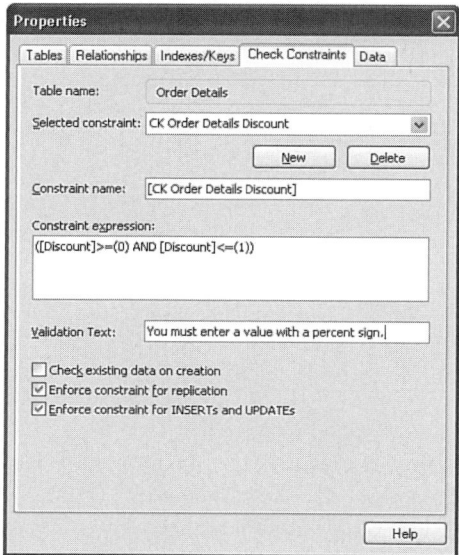

Following are descriptions of the elements of the Check Constraints page:

- **Selected Constraint**—CHECK constraints are the SQL Server equivalent of Access table- and field-level validation rules. You can specify multiple CHECK constraints; the Order Details table has three CHECK constraints—CK_Discount, CK_Quantity, and CK_UnitPrice—which you select from the drop-down list.

- **Constraint Name**—This text box lets you rename the default name assigned by SQL Server, CK_FieldName.

- **Constraint Expression**—The CHECK expression must evaluate to TRUE or FALSE. You add new constraints by clicking the New button and typing the expression and name in the text boxes.

- **Validation Text**—This extended property sets the text of the error message you receive when attempting to INSERT or UPDATE a value that conflicts with the selected constraint. The property corresponds to Access's Validation Text property.

- **Constraint properties**—You can test existing data for conformance to constraints, enable constraints for data addition and updates, and apply constraints to replicated data with the three check boxes at the bottom of the page.

THE DATA PAGE

Figure 20.9 shows the Data page for the Order Details table. All elements on this page are SQL Server extended properties that provide ADP counterparts of Access table features, such as subdatasheets.

Figure 20.9
The Data page has a collection of extended properties to support upsizing existing Access tables.

TIP

> Avoid setting Access-specific table features and properties, such as subdatasheets, lookup fields, links for subforms and subreports, Filter, and Order By in new Access data projects. These features and properties are intended to support upsizing Access tables to SQL Server and have no counterparts in ANSI SQL. Browse-mode editing in Datasheet view with subdatasheets and lookup fields isn't recommended for production client/server applications because this type of editing increases the probability of data entry errors. To prevent subdatasheet open buttons from appearing in Datasheet view, set the Subdatasheet Name property to [None].
>
> Use views with WHERE criteria to avoid use of the Filter property. Filter property values, as well as filters applied by ribbon buttons, are applied by Access to the locally cached copy of the table's Recordset. However, applying custom sort orders to views and inline table-valued functions locally is a better database design practice than using the TOP operator and ORDER BY clauses to return all rows in the desired order.

20

→ To review how Access handles lookup fields and subdatasheets, **see** "Using Lookup Fields in Tables," **p. 466** and "Table Properties for Subdatasheets," **p. 208**.

EXPLORING SQL SERVER VIEWS

Like tables, views open in conventional Access datasheets. Figure 20.10 shows the Order Details Extended view, which is almost identical to the Access version. Like tables, the Sort Ascending, Sort Descending, Filter by Form, Filter by Selection, and Find buttons of the Home ribbon's Sort & Filter group operate on the locally cached copy (snapshot) of the view's Recordset, not the view itself.

Figure 20.10
NorthwindSQL's Order Details Extended view is similar to the corresponding Access `QueryDef` object. The Order Details Extended (TVF) is the table-valued function version of the view.

Order I	Product	Product Name	Unit Pric	Quanti	Discour	ExtendedPri
10248	11	Queso Cabrales	$14.00	12	0%	$168.00
10248	42	Singaporean Hokkien Fri	$9.80	10	0%	$98.00
10248	72	Mozzarella di Giovanni	$34.80	5	0%	$174.00
10249	14	Tofu	$18.60	9	0%	$167.40
10249	51	Manjimup Dried Apples	$42.40	40	0%	$1,696.00
10250	41	Jack's New England Clam	$7.70	10	0%	$77.00
10250	51	Manjimup Dried Apples	$42.40	35	15%	$1,261.40
10250	65	Louisiana Fiery Hot Pepp	$16.80	15	15%	$214.20
10251	22	Gustaf's Knäckebröd	$16.80	6	5%	$95.76
10251	57	Ravioli Angelo	$15.60	15	5%	$222.30
10251	65	Louisiana Fiery Hot Pepp	$16.80	20	0%	$336.00
10252	20	Sir Rodney's Marmalade	$64.80	40	5%	$2,462.40
10252	33	Geitost	$2.00	25	5%	$47.50
10252	60	Camembert Pierrot	$27.20	40	0%	$1,088.00
10253	31	Gorgonzola Telino	$10.00	20	0%	$200.00
10253	39	Chartreuse verte	$14.40	42	0%	$604.80
10253	49	Maxilaku	$16.00	40	0%	$640.00
10254	24	Guaraná Fantástica	$3.60	15	15%	$45.90
10254	55	Pâté chinois	$19.20	21	15%	$342.72

Record: 1 of 2155   No Filter   Search

> **NOTE**
>
> The Data properties page of ADP forms and reports has two properties—Server Filter and Server Filter by Form—added by Access 2002. These properties let you apply a server-side filter to a table, view, or function instead of the cached Recordset for the form or report. Using server-side filters minimizes the amount of data sent to the client, which reduces network traffic and improves performance.

 Changing to Design view opens the graphical view designer, the structure of which resembles the Access query designer. The primary difference between the two designers is a 90-degree rotation (transposition) of the axes of the design grid. Click the SQL button of the Function & View Tools Design ribbon's Tools group to display the SQL statement that creates the view (see Figure 20.11). The upper diagram pane displays field lists for each table with a symbolic join. The key symbol indicates the primary key field(s) and the infinity symbol (∞) specifies the foreign key field. Primary key field(s) of the tables appear in bold type.

Figure 20.11
The project designer's equivalent of Access's Query Design view adds a convenient SQL pane.

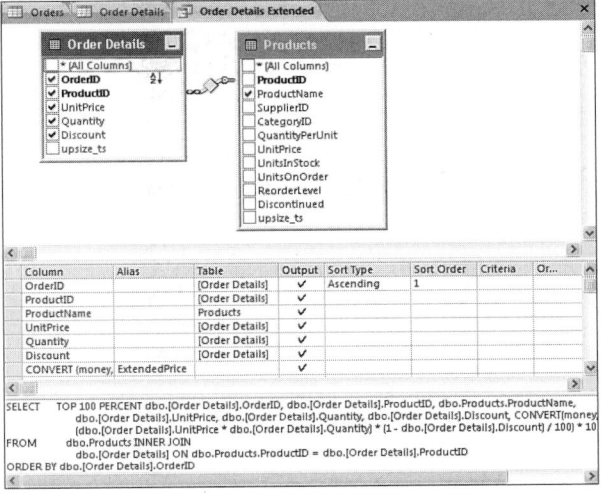

The Access Upsize Wizard adds an upsize_ts field of the `timestamp` data type to some or all tables, depending on a wizard setting. Timestamp fields consist of auto-generated numeric values, which are guaranteed to be unique within a table and increment whenever a cell value changes. You use timestamp fields to resolve *concurrency conflicts*. Concurrency conflicts occur when two concurrent users edit the value of the same cell.

The view designer adds the following five design-related buttons that aren't present in the Query Tools Design ribbon to the Function & View Tools' Design ribbon:

- **Diagram**—Toggles the display of the diagram in the upper pane. You specify the type of join in a properties sheet.

- **Grid**—Toggles the display of the column information, which is where you alias columns, select the source table for the column, specify whether column data appears in the view, and add an ORDER BY clause or WHERE criteria.

- **SQL**—Toggles the lower text box that displays the Transact-SQL statement that generates the view.

- **Verify SQL Syntax**—Runs a grammar check on the SQL statement but doesn't execute the query to create the view.

- **Group By**—Adds a GROUP BY expression that includes every member of the SELECT statement's field list. Group By properties let you add a ROLLUP, CUBE, or ALL modifier for complex aggregation.

The SQL statement for the Order Details Extended view illustrates substitution of the SQL CONVERT function for VBA's **CCur** function to change the data type of the calculated ExtendedPrice column to money. The dbo schema prefix provides three of the four elements of SQL Server's four-part naming convention. Linked databases require use of three-part names to resolve duplicate table and field names in local and linked servers.

The complete SQL SELECT statement for the view is as follows:

```
SELECT TOP 2147483647 dbo.[Order Details].OrderID, dbo.[Order Details].ProductID,
    dbo.Products.ProductName, dbo.[Order Details].UnitPrice,
    dbo.[Order Details].Quantity, dbo.[Order Details].Discount, CONVERT(money,
    (dbo.[Order Details].UnitPrice * dbo.[Order Details].Quantity) *
    (1 - dbo.[Order Details].Discount) / 100) * 100 AS ExtendedPrice
FROM dbo.Products INNER JOIN dbo.[Order Details]
    ON dbo.Products.ProductID = dbo.[Order Details].ProductID
ORDER BY dbo.[Order Details].OrderID DESC, dbo.[Order Details].ProductID
```

> **TIP**
>
> An ORDER BY clause in a view or an inline table-valued function requires a TOP operator in the SELECT clause. It was a common practice to use SELECT TOP 100 PERCENT ... for SQL Server 2000 views and inline functions. However, SQL Server 2005's query optimizer "optimizes out" the TOP 100 PERCENT operator *and* the ORDER BY clause too. Thus, a specified sort order doesn't appear when you open the view or function in Access 2007's Datasheet view, or right-click a view in SSMSX's Object Explorer and choose Open View.
>
> The better workaround for this problem is to set the Order By property of the view or function to the column name(s), separating the names with a comma if there's more than one. The other alternative is to substitute TOP (2147483647) for TOP 100 PERCENT. 2147483647, which is the maximum value accepted by the query parser.

To explore adding new tables and setting JOIN properties, do the following:

1. Move the Products and Order Details tables to the right to make room for the addition of the field list of the Suppliers table.

2. Click the Add Table button to open the Add Table dialog, which has Tables, Views, and Functions pages. On the Tables page, select Suppliers and click Add to add an INNER JOIN between the SupplierID fields (see Figure 20.12).

3. Close the Add Table dialog, and click the SupplierID and CompanyName check boxes of the Suppliers table to add the columns to the view.

4. Right-click the join line between the Suppliers and Products tables, and choose Properties to open the Join Properties dialog. You select the type of join from a drop-down list of the available operators. Mark the All Rows from Suppliers check box to create a RIGHT OUTER JOIN, which squares the left side of the diamond join symbol (see Figure 20.13). (Marking both check boxes creates a FULL OUTER JOIN; the join symbol becomes a square. Scroll the SQL pane to read the JOIN changes to the view's SQL statement.)

Figure 20.12
The process of adding a new table and its columns to a view is similar to that for Access `QueryDefs`.

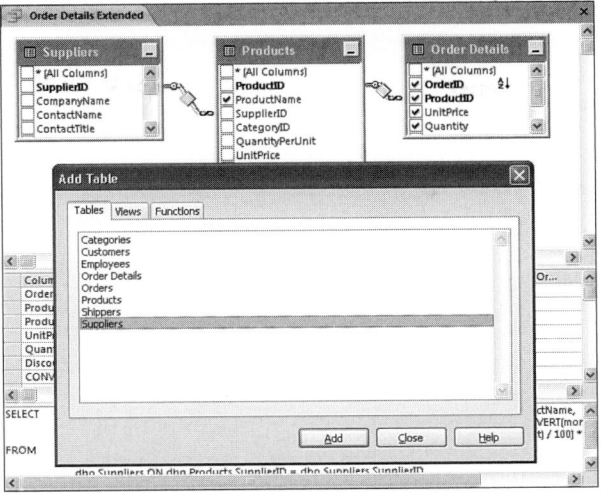

Figure 20.13
The Properties dialog for JOINS in a view offers the same functions as Access's Join Properties dialog in a different format. SQL Server adds the capability to specify the JOIN operator.

Symbol for RIGHT OUTER JOIN

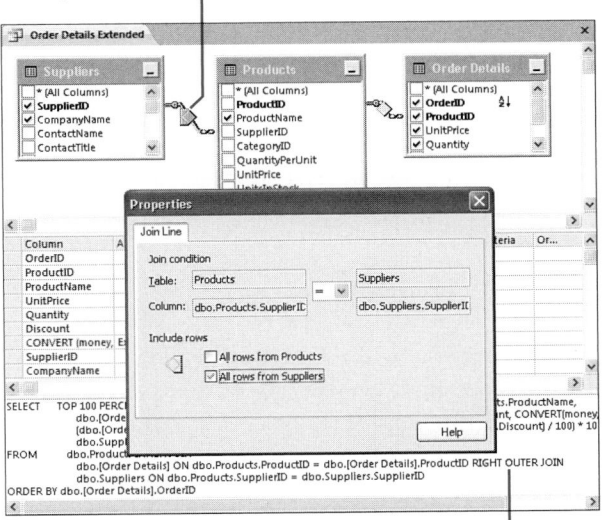

RIGHT OUTER JOIN replaces INNER

20

5. Clear the All Rows from Suppliers and All Rows from Products check boxes if you marked them, and close the Join Properties dialog. Click the Group By button to add a GROUP BY clause containing all columns, which adds Group By symbols to fields selected in the field lists. Like Access Totals queries, tabbing or selecting the Group By cell for each column lets you choose Group By, Sum, Avg, Min, Max, Count, Expression, Where, and many additional SQL Server–specific options from a drop-down list (see Figure 20.14).

Figure 20.14
Clicking the ribbon's Group By button adds a Group By column to the design grid and a `GROUP BY` clause to the `SELECT` statement. The effect is similar to specifying an Access Totals query.

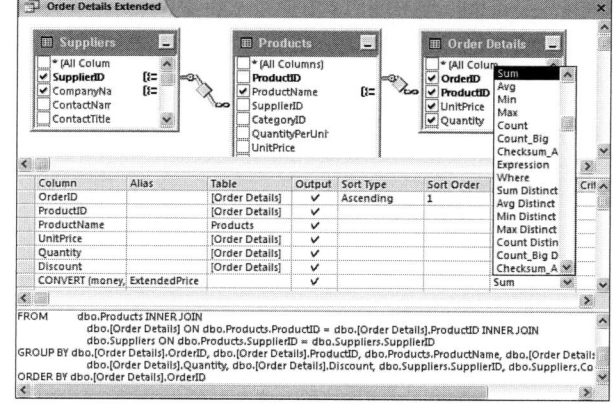

6. Click the ribbon's Properties button or right-click the window and choose <u>P</u>roperties to open the Properties dialog for views (see Figure 20.15). On the View page, you can add the `DISTINCT` qualifier to eliminate duplicate rows; specify `CUBE`, `ROLLUP`, or `ALL` extensions to the `GROUP BY` clause; and specify a `TOP` *n* [`PERCENT`] view by marking the TOP check box, typing the *n* value in the text box, and marking the PERCENT, WITH TIES, or both check boxes. You also can add text to the extended Description and SQL Comment properties.

Figure 20.15
Access 2007's View Properties dialog sets many special properties of SQL Server views.

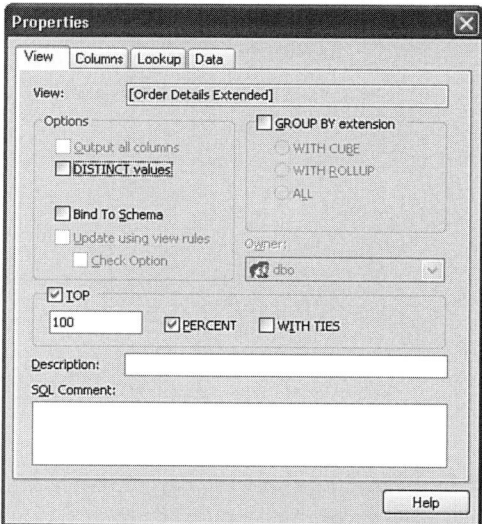

N O T E

Many of the properties on the View page have counterparts in Access's Query Properties dialog. The other property values of the View page—such as Bind to Schema and Update Using View Rules—require familiarity with T-SQL, the subject of the next chapter.

7. Click the Columns tab, and select the Discount column in the Column Name text box. The enabled labels indicate extended properties whose values you can set for the specific field data type, such as Description, Format, Decimal Places, and Caption for most numeric data types (see Figure 20.16). Close the Properties dialog.

Figure 20.16
The Columns page lets you set additional extended property values.

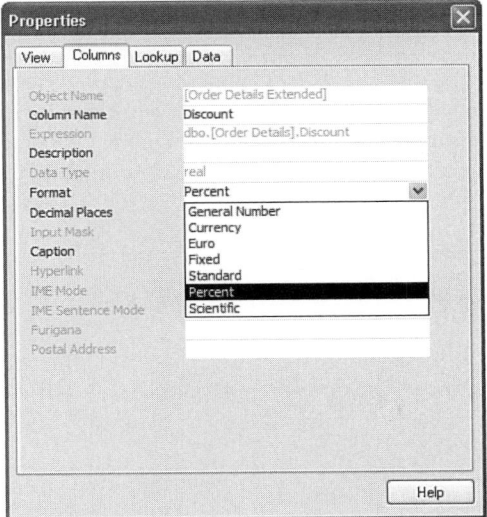

N O T E

The Lookup and Data pages of a view have the same set of properties as those for tables.

20

8. Click the Verify SQL Syntax button on the toolbar to check the changes you made in the preceding steps. You receive a message box confirming the statement's validity. Deliberately introducing an error results in a message providing the approximate location of the mistake. Figure 20.17 illustrates the message that occurs if you delete the left bracket from the second instance of [Order Details] in the query's SQL pane and click Verify SQL Syntax.

Figure 20.17
You receive an error message if the SQL Server query parser detects incorrect syntax. In this case, the parser interprets 'Order' as the SQL keyword ORDER because of a missing left bracket.

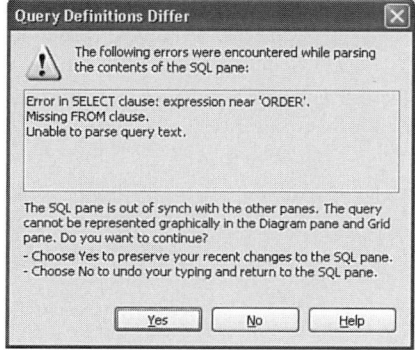

9. Close the view designer and don't save the changes you made. Modifications to the database are temporary until you close the designer or run the query and elect to save changes.

TAKING ADVANTAGE OF INLINE FUNCTIONS

SQL Server 2005's inline functions let you emulate Access's parameterized queries. Views don't accept parameters, but you can choose between table-returning functions and stored procedures to emulate read-only parameterized views. Functions and stored procedures accept one or more input parameters, which correspond to Access parameters. One of the advantages of a parameterized in-line function is that it can substitute for a table name in the FROM clause of a SELECT query.

→ To review Access parameterized queries, **see** "Designing Parameter Queries," **p. 500**.

CREATING A PARAMETERIZED TABLE-VALUED FUNCTION

In-line table-valued functions are an alternative to stored procedures for creating the equivalent of parameterized views. (SQL Server views don't support parameters). The process of creating a function is identical to that for creating a view, except for the added parameter.

Do the following to create a new parameterized inline table-valued function based on the Orders table:

1. In the Create ribbon's Other group, click Query Wizard to open the New Query dialog (see Figure 20.18). The choices in the list differ greatly from those of the conventional Access database version.

2. Double-click the Design In-Line Function item to open Function1 in Design view with the Add Table dialog active.

3. Select the Orders table, click Add, and close the Add Table dialog.

4. Mark the OrderID, CustomerID, OrderDate, RequiredDate, and ShippedDate check boxes of the field list to add these columns to the grid. Add a descending sort on the OrderDate column.

Figure 20.18
The New Query dialog for ADPs gives you the choice between using the project designer (Design…) or typing T-SQL statements in a text editor window (Create Text…).

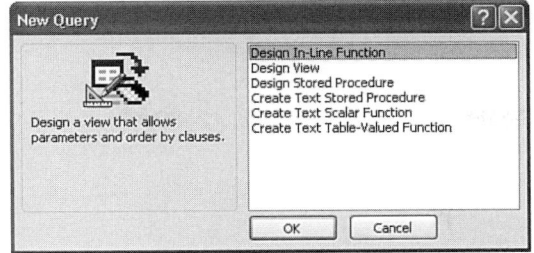

5. To add date-based input parameters to the OrderDate field, type the Access version of a pair of date parameters—**BETWEEN [Start Date] AND [End Date]**—in its Criteria cell (see Figure 20.19). In this case, the square brackets specify an input parameter, *not* that the parameter names include a space. When you tab past the cell, the statement changes to T-SQL parameter syntax—`BETWEEN @Start_Date AND @End_Date`. T-SQL doesn't permit spaces in parameter names.

Figure 20.19
Specifying function parameters is similar to adding Access query parameters. The query parser converts the Access to T-SQL parameter format.

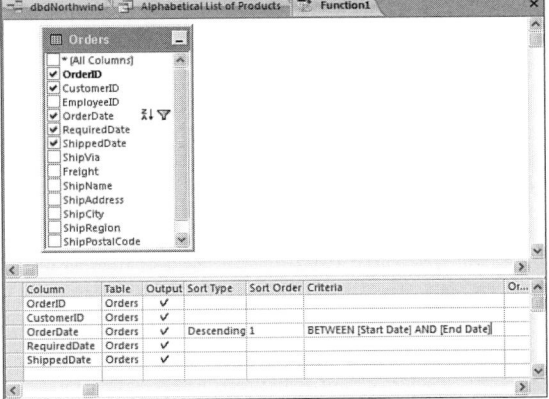

SQL 6. Click the SQL button to open the SQL pane and change `TOP 100 PERCENT` to `TOP 2147483647`.

7. Click the Run button, click Yes when asked whether you want to save your query, type a name for the function—such as **fnOrdersByDate**—in the Save As dialog, and click OK.

8. A slightly modified version of the Access Enter Parameter Value dialog opens for the `Start_Date` parameter. Type **6/12/2006** and click OK to open the `End_Date` dialog. Type **12/31/2006** and click OK to view the result set of the function in Datasheet view (see Figure 20.20).

Figure 20.20
Datasheet view of the function confirms the End_Date parameter works. Scroll to the bottom of the datasheet to check for the Start_Date parameter.

ADDING DEFAULT VALUES FOR THE INPUT PARAMETERS

Access's Enter Parameter Value dialog doesn't support default values but ADP's do.

To add default values for the Start_Date and End_Date parameters, do this:

1. Return to Design view, click the Property Sheet button, or right-click the window and choose Properties to open the function's Properties dialog.

2. Click the Function Parameters tab to display a list with the two parameter names and their data type (datetime).

3. Type the default values for the two parameters in the default column. As you move to the second parameter, the first default value is enclosed by single quotes (see Figure 20.21).

Figure 20.21
The Function Parameters page is blank, unless you add input parameters by the procedure in the preceding section. Add default values for the parameters in the Default column.

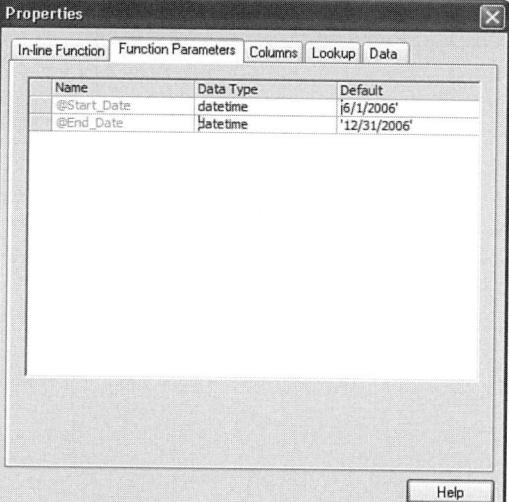

NOTE

SQL Server accepts only character values for dates. The default delimiter for T-SQL character values is the single quote or apostrophe ('). Access's # delimiter doesn't apply to T-SQL date values.

4. Click the Run button, save your changes, and open the drop-down list of the Start_Date Enter Parameter Value dialog and select <DEFAULT> (see Figure 20.22). The other option is <NULL>, which passes a NULL value to the parameter. Stored procedures and functions often include T-SQL code to act on NULL parameter values. Click OK to display the End_Date Enter Parameter Value dialog.

Figure 20.22
Enter Parameter Value dialogs for functions and stored procedures have a drop-down list from which you can select a previously specified default or a NULL value.

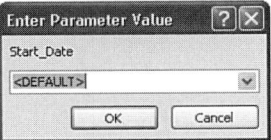

5. Select <DEFAULT>, and then click OK in the End_Date Enter Parameter Value dialog to open the function's datasheet.

EXAMINING STORED PROCEDURES

Access 2007's project designer lets you create many common types of stored procedures without writing any T-SQL code. This feature provides parity between Access and SQL Server action queries, because you can create make-table, update, append values, and delete queries in the designer, instead of writing T-SQL in the text editor. Like Access UNION queries, you must write SQL Server UNION queries for views, functions, and stored procedures in the text editor. The project designer doesn't have a Query, SQL Specific, Union menu choice.

NorthwindSQL includes only parameterized SELECT stored procedures, which you create using the same process as that for parameterized inline functions. Open one or more of the sample stored procedures in Design view to see the similarity between the grid and T-SQL statements for stored procedures. Simple parameterized inline functions are updatable in Datasheet view; stored procedures—parameterized or not—aren't updatable.

20

CREATING AND EXECUTING MAKE-TABLE AND UPDATE STORED PROCEDURES

To give the project designer a test run with make-table and update queries, do this:

1. Click Query Wizard to open the New Query dialog, and double-click the Design Stored Procedure item.

2. Double-click the Orders item in the Add Table dialog, close the dialog, and click the SQL button. By default, a SELECT query skeleton statement opens in the SQL pane. Mark the * (All Columns) check box.

3. Click the Make-Table Query button to open the Make Table dialog. Type a table name, such as **tblOrders**, in the text box, and click OK to create a SELECT dbo.Orders.* INTO dbo.tblOrders FROM dbo.Orders statement (see Figure 20.23).

Figure 20.23
The process of creating a make-table stored procedure is identical to that for creating an Access make-table query.

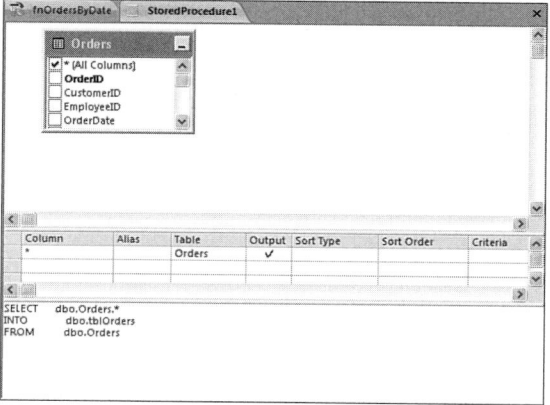

NOTE

It's an SQL Server convention to use two-letter object type prefixes for views (vw), stored procedures (sp or xp), and functions (fn). Microsoft and many developers add an underscore, especially when naming objects with the even more traditional all lowercase convention. However, adding an underscore to the sp or xp prefixes conflicts with SQL Server's use of sp_ for system stored procedures and xp_ for extended procedures. It's not common to prefix table names with tb or tb_, but tmp or tmp_ often precedes temporary table names. The examples of this chapter use the tbl prefix for consistency with the Access tables you created in earlier chapters.

4. Click the Run button, and save your stored procedure as **spMakeOrdersTable**. After SQL Server stores and executes the stored procedure, a message confirms that the stored procedure executed, but didn't return any records. Click OK, and then close the project designer.

> The new tblOrders table you created has a structure that's identical to the Orders source table, including the Identity property of the OrderID field. Make-table queries don't set a primary key field, so the tblOrder table isn't updatable in Datasheet view. (SQL Server tables require a primary key for the cursor-based updates used by datasheets, but not for updates by stored procedures.)
>
> To add a primary key field, open tblOrders in Design view, select the OrderID field, click the Primary Key button on the toolbar, close the table, and save the changes.

5. Repeat steps 1 and 2, but use the tblOrders table you just created to avoid making changes to the sample Orders table.

6. Click the Update Query button to change the grid and skeleton UPDATE dbo.tblOrders SET statement to the make-table syntax.

7. Mark the OrderDate, RequiredDate, and ShippedDate check boxes of the field list to add the fields to the SET statement, which defines the fields to be updated and their new values. Pencil icons in the check boxes indicate a pending UPDATE operation.

8. Type **DATEADD(yyyy, 1, OrderDate)**, **DATEADD(yyyy, 1, RequiredDate)**, and **DATEADD(yyyy, 1, ShippedDate)** in each column's corresponding New Value cell to add a year to date values. Type **not null** in the Criteria cell of the ShippedDate row to prevent an attempt to add a year to a NULL value. The designer changes the entry to NOT IS NULL and adds the WHERE NOT ShippedDate IS NULL criterion (see Figure 20.24).

Figure 20.24
Stored procedures that update table values also follow Access's methodology.

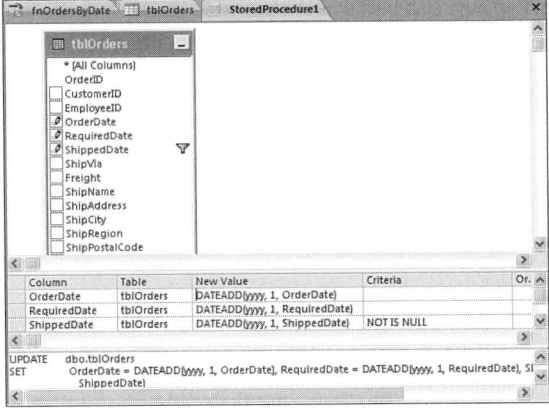

> Like the Access query designer, the project designer adds multiple parenthesis pairs to the WHERE clause. Parentheses aren't required for simple criterion, but are needed to specify the application sequence of operators—such as AND, OR, and NOT—in complex WHERE clauses.

9. Click the Verify SQL Syntax button, click OK to dismiss the syntax confirmation message, and click the Run button. Save the stored procedure as **spUpdateOrders**. Click OK to dismiss the execution confirmation message, and close the project designer.

10. Open tblOrders from the Navigation pane, not by changing to Datasheet view of the designer, to verify the updates. Changing to Datasheet view executes the stored procedure again, which adds another year to the dates.

> **CAUTION**
>
> Access UPDATE queries post a warning message that indicates the number of rows to be changed, if you haven't cleared the Confirm Record Changes check box of the Option dialog's Edit/Find page. You receive no warning when you execute a stored procedure that updates tables.

> **NOTE**
>
> The IS NOT NULL criterion appears on the same line as ShippedDate, which implies that the criterion only applies to that column and that the query would update the OrderDate and RequiredDate columns for orders with missing ShippedDate values. This is not the case. The criterion applies to all columns included in the SET statement. To update all dates, you need to run two queries—one for OrderDate and RequiredDate and one for ShippedDate.

ADDING RECORDS WITH APPEND STORED PROCEDURES

To execute an append (INSERT INTO) stored procedure, you need a table with the same structure as the source table. For example, if you use tblOrders as the source table, you need a new empty table with the same structure as tblOrders. Create a new copy of the Orders (not the tblOrders) table by selecting Order, pressing Ctrl+C, Ctrl+V, typing **tblOrdersEmpty**, and selecting Structure Only in the Paste Table dialog.

DEALING WITH IDENTITY FIELDS

The tblOrders and tblOrdersEmpty tables have an OrderID field of the int data type with the Identity property set to Yes, which is equivalent to an Access AutoNumber field. You have the following choices when appending new records to a table that has an Identity field:

- Change the Identity property value in the target table to No. This approach lets you append records with the source table's value in the former identity column. (You can use SELECT * FROM SourceTable in the SELECT INTO statement.) After you append the records, you can set the Identity property to Yes. You don't need to change the Identity Seed property value from the default (1).

- Change the Identity Seed value to the same starting number as the records you're appending (10248 for tblOrders) or to another value to renumber the records consecutively. In this case, you specify all except the identity field in the SELECT field list.

N O T E

It's much easier to change the identity starting value for an SQL Server table than the initial value of an Access AutoNumber field.

Follow these steps to prepare for testing the second of the preceding choices:

 1. Open the tblOrdersEmpty table in Design view, select the OrderID column, and change the Identity Seed value to any number you want. This example uses **1010248**, which represents a change to increase the number of digits for order numbering without renumbering the significant five digits of older orders. (Unfortunately, you can't use 010248, because the leading zero is stripped when you save the table design.)

2. Click Table Datasheet view, save your design changes, and verify that tblOrdersEmpty displays the (New) default in the OrderID field of the only (empty) record.

3. Close the table. If you leave the table open, the appended records don't appear until you close and reopen it.

CREATING THE APPEND QUERY

To append and renumber records from the tblOrders table, do the following:

 1. Click the Create ribbon's Stored Procedure button, add tblOrders in the Add Table dialog, and click the SQL button.

2. Mark each field name check box for the CustomerID through the ShipName fields but omit ShippedDate and Freight, and then click the Stored Procedure Tools, Design ribbon's Append Query button to open the Choose Target Table for Insert Results dialog (see Figure 20.25).

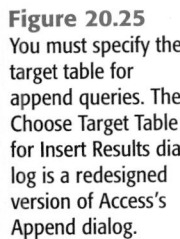

Figure 20.25
You must specify the target table for append queries. The Choose Target Table for Insert Results dialog is a redesigned version of Access's Append dialog.

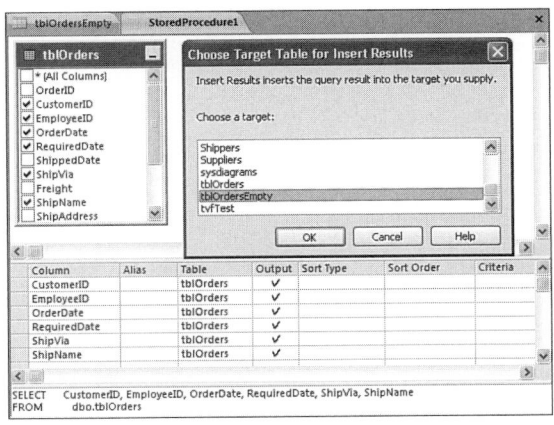

3. Select the tblOrdersEmpty table in the list and then click OK to change the grid layout to the append query format, add an Append field list column to the grid, and add the `INSERT INTO TableName (FieldList)` statement to the query (see Figure 20.26). The field list's check box icons change to plus (+) signs.

Figure 20.26
The grid for an append query has columns that correspond to the Access append query design grid's rows.

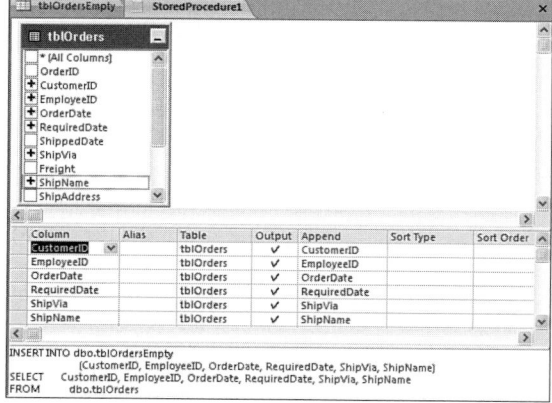

4. Click Run, save your stored procedure as **spAppendOrders**, and acknowledge the execution confirmation message.

5. Open the table with the appended records to confirm the renumbering process (see Figure 20.27).

Figure 20.27
The appended records have one million added to the original order number.

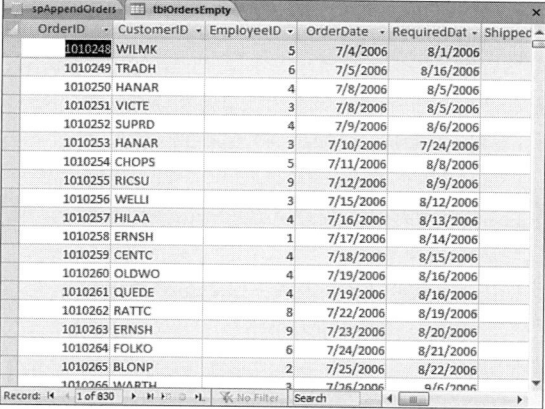

Stored procedures have an append values query option that Access doesn't offer. An append values query lets you add one record at a time (perform an `INSERT`) with a stored procedure. Practically speaking, append values queries are only useful as parameterized stored procedures; in most cases, you supply the parameter values with VBA code.

To test-drive an append values query with the tblOrdersEmpty table, do this:

1. Close the table, create a new stored procedure, and add the tblOrdersEmpty table to it.

2. Mark the check boxes for the fields, except the OrderID field, that are valid when entering an order. ShippedDate and Freight, for example, don't receive values until the order goes out the door, assuming that your organization complies with generally accepted accounting practices (GAAPs). You can skip the ShipAddress through ShipCountry fields for this example.

3. Choose Query, Append Values Query to change the grid to a Column and Value list.

4. Type appropriate values in each of the Value cells. You must type a value into each cell; use NULL to specify a value that's unknown or not applicable. Character identifiers (') are added automatically to ...char and datetime fields, and ...char fields receive a N prefix indicating Unicode encoding. Typing the values adds them to the query's VALUES list, with a CONVERT function added for datetime fields (see Figure 20.28).

Figure 20.28
Append value stored procedures let you add a single record with values you type in the grid. Without parameters, stored procedures of this type aren't very useful.

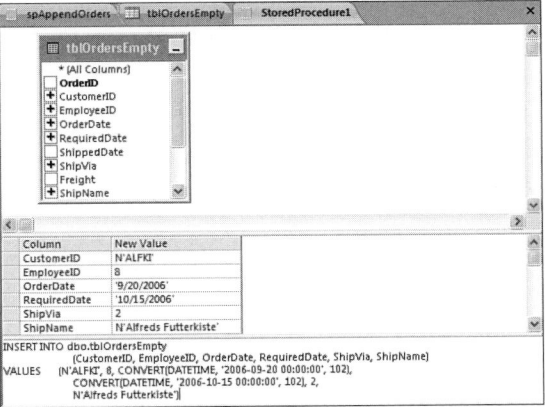

5. Click Run, save your stored procedure as **spAppendBogusOrder** or the like, acknowledge the confirmation message, close the procedure, and open the table to verify the appended order.

UPDATING RECORDS

Updating one or more record(s) is a process that's almost identical to appending a single record. Click the Update Query button instead of the Append Values Query, mark the fields to update, type the updated values, and add a criterion row, as shown in Figure 20.29.

Like append values procedures, update procedures aren't very useful without parameters or an SQL statement that supplies the update values from another table or query.

Figure 20.29
The process of creating update stored procedures is similar to that for the append values type. Update stored procedures include a Criteria column for specifying the set of row(s) to update.

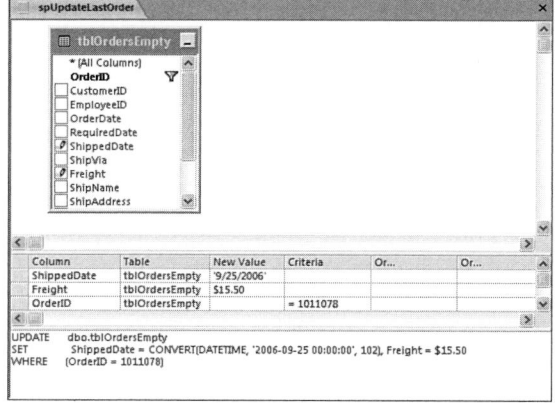

DELETING RECORDS

Delete queries saved as stored procedures without parameters aren't much more useful than parameterless append value or update queries. To create a simple parameter query to delete older records from the tblOrdersEmpty or tblOrders table, run the following drill:

1. Create a new stored procedure, and add tblOrdersEmpty to it.

2. Click the Delete Query button to set up the grid, add a skeleton DELETE FROM *TableName* statement, and change the * (All Columns) item's icon to the delete symbol.

3. Drag the column(s) on which to establish deletion criterion—ShippedDate for this example—to the grid.

4. Type the parameter criterion, **<=@Delete_Date**, in the Criteria column.

5. ShippedDate is NULL for some orders, so drag a second copy of ShippedDate to the grid and type **NOT IS NULL** in the Criteria column. The stored procedure design appears as shown in Figure 20.30.

Figure 20.30
The query for this stored procedure that deletes older records requires compound criteria for the ShippedDate field that consists of a Delete_Date parameter and NOT IS NULL criterion.

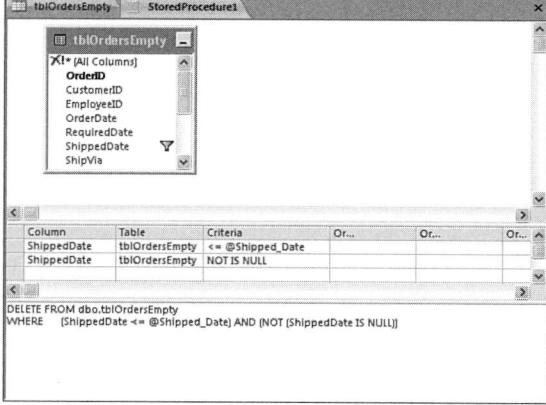

6. Click Run, save the stored procedure as **spOrdersDeleteParam** (or similar), and type a date that's valid for the table to delete records for shipments on or before the date.

DIAGRAMMING TABLE RELATIONSHIPS

Double-clicking the dbdNorthwind item in the Navigation pane's Database Diagrams group opens the dbdNorthwind diagram. da Vinci Database diagrams derive from Access's Relationships window. Right-click the diagram, select Zoom, and then select the percentage that displays all tables without scrolling (75% for Figure 20.31).

Figure 20.31
The Relationships database diagram displays the same information as Access's Relationships window in a different format.

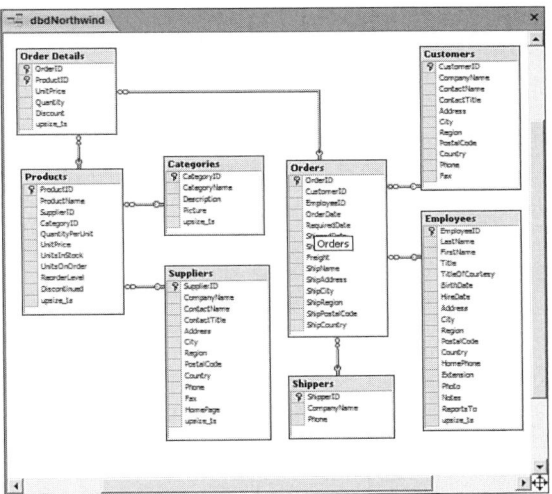

You can do the following in the Relationships diagram:

- Modify the properties of any table in the database, including adding and deleting fields or changing the properties of fields. Right-clicking the table header opens a versatile context menu with 18 choices. Choosing Column Properties expands the selected table window to display a reduced-size version of Table Design view (see Figure 20.32). Choose Column Name to return to the default view.

- Add or drop tables of the database. You can also start with a new SQL Server database, and then add all the required tables, fields, and relationships in the window.

- View and alter relationships between tables by right-clicking the join line and choosing Properties.

- Hide tables. Hiding a table also causes relationship symbols connecting the table to disappear.

- Print the diagram. If the size of the diagram exceeds the maximum paper size of your printer, you must cut and paste several sheets to obtain a complete diagram.

20

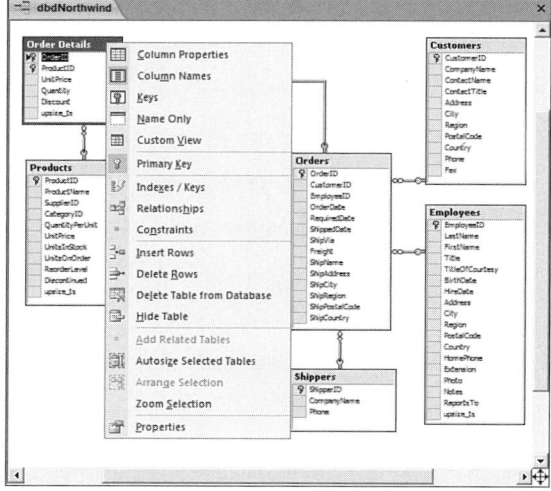

Figure 20.32
You can display column properties (shown here for the Categories table) or make one of 17 other choices from the database diagram's context menu.

> To create a new database diagram, click to expand the Create ribbon's Macro list and select Diagram. The process of adding tables and relationships to the da Vinci diagram is almost identical to that for Access Relationships window diagrams.

BACKING UP AND RESTORING DATABASES

Unlike Access databases, which you can back up by a manual copying process, ADPs have a built-in snapshot copy process. The best feature of the ADP backup process is that you don't need exclusive access to the database; you can generate a backup while you and other users are connected to the database.

TIP

> Use SQL Server Management Studio Express to back up large databases to tape manually or automatically. Access's backup and restore features are limited to creating conventional disk files on fixed or removable media. If you intend to back up to a CD-R or CD-RW drive, make a fixed-disk copy and then burn the CD-ROM from the disk copy.

To create a snapshot backup of your project's current database (NorthwindSQL for this example), do the following:

1. Click the Office button, choose Server to open the Manage Server Information window (see Figure 20.33), and then select Back Up SQL Database to open the Backup dialog.

Figure 20.33
The Manage Server
Information window
offers nine action
choices. The ninth
choice, Set Login
Password, isn't visible
here. Later sections
show you how to per-
form the most impor-
tant tasks.

2. Accept or change the proposed name of the backup file. By default, SQL Server backup
   files use the name of the database with a .dat extension—NorthwindSQL.dat for this
   example (see Figure 20.34).

Figure 20.34
Use the backup fea-
ture to quickly create
live snapshot backups
of your project's data-
base.

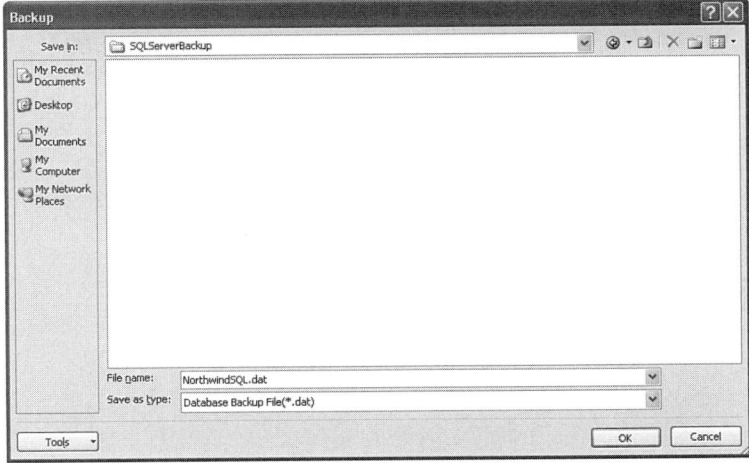

3. Navigate to a backup folder, preferably on a network server or a second local physical
   drive. When you click OK, you receive the message shown in Figure 20.35.

Figure 20.35
This message confirms creation of the snapshot backup and suggests backing up your .adp file by making a conventional copy.

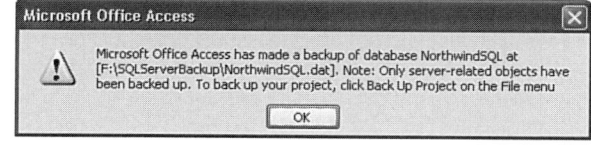

You restore a backup .dat file when, for instance, you accidentally delete a table or other database object. You can't restore a database while you or users are connected to it.

To perform a restore, do the following:

1. Click the Office button and choose Server, Restore SQL Database. You receive the message shown in Figure 20.36.

Figure 20.36
This message indicates that you can't perform a live restore of a database. All connections to the database must be closed before proceeding.

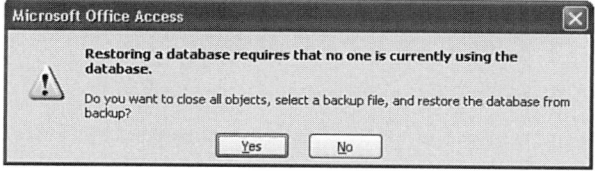

2. Click Yes to dismiss the message. Then navigate to the backup file, select it, and click OK. Your project disconnects from the database, and the message box shown in Figure 20.37 appears after a delay that depends on the size of the database and network performance.

Figure 20.37
Restoring a database from a .dat backup copy requires temporarily disconnecting the project from the database.

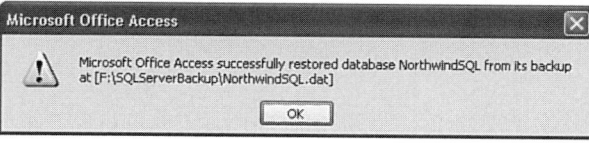

3. Click OK to acknowledge the message and automatically reconnect to the restored database.

TIP

> If you receive the message shown in Figure 20.38, other users have open connections to the database or there's a spurious lock on the database. If no other users are connected, you might be able to remove the lock by stopping and starting SQL Server with SQL Server Management Studio or Computer Management\Services and Applications\SQL Server Configuration Manager. In some cases, however, you must reboot the machine for the restore operation to succeed.

Figure 20.38
This message indi-
cates that there are
open connections or
a residual lock on the
database.

> **Microsoft Office Access**   ☒
>
> [Microsoft][ODBC SQL Server Driver][SQL Server]Exclusive access could not be obtained because
> the database is in use.
> [Microsoft][ODBC SQL Server Driver][SQL Server]RESTORE DATABASE is terminating abnormally.
>
> OK

If you need to restore the .adp and .dat files as the result of a catastrophic failure, such as a
crashed fixed disk, do this:

1. Copy the .adp file from the backup and open it in the disconnected state.

2. Restore the database, as described in the preceding set of steps. Your project remains
   disconnected from the database.

3. Click the Office button and choose Server, Connection to open the Data Link
   Properties dialog.

4. Type **.\SQLEXPRESS** or **.** as the server name, and select the restored database in the
   Select the Database on the Server list (see Figure 20.39).

Figure 20.39
If you restore the .adp
and .dat files, you
must reconnect man-
ually to the project's
database.

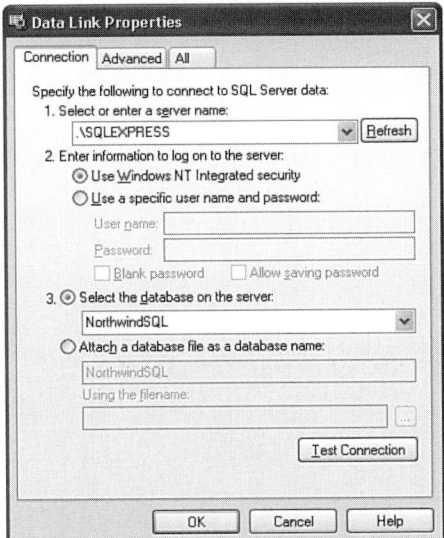

20

5. Click Test Connection to verify your settings, and click OK to reconnect your project
   to the restored database.

TRANSFERRING THE PROJECT'S DATABASE TO A SERVER

The Server page's Transfer Database and Copy Database File choices manage the SQL Server instance on which your database resides. The Transfer Database choice uses SQL Server 2005's Integration Services (formerly Data Transformation Service) to create a copy of the current database on another machine running SQL Server. The most common use for this utility is to place a database you've developed into production on a workgroup server. Transfer Database is a live copying process; you don't need to disconnect from the current database.

To transfer your project's database to a server, do the following:

1. Click the Office button and choose Server, Transfer Database to open the Transfer Database Dialog.

2. Select the destination server—OAKLEAF-DC1 for this example—in the drop-down list or type the server name if it isn't present in the list (see Figure 20.40).

Figure 20.40
Specify the target server for the current database in Transfer Database dialog.

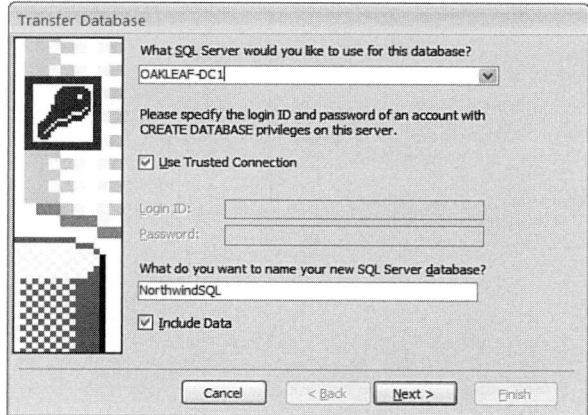

3. Click Next and then Finish to start the transfer process, which displays a progress dialog (see Figure 20.41).

Figure 20.41
This progress dialog displays each step in the Transfer Database operation.

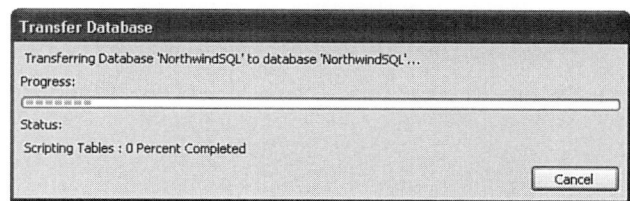

4. When the transfer process completes, your project remains connected to the local (original) database.

The Copy Database File choice copies the database files to the location you specify. When you make this choice, the message shown in Figure 20.42 opens, advising that you must close all connections to the source database. If you click Disconnect, the Open dialog appears to let you make a copy of the SQL Server database (.mdf) file in another location that you can attach to SQL Server.

Figure 20.42
Before you can copy the project's database file to another location, you must close all connections to the database.

Connecting to a Remote SQL Server Database

CONNECTING TO A REMOTE SQL SERVER DATABASE

To connect to an SQL Server database on a production server, such as the database you transferred in the preceding section, do this:

1. Choose File, Connection, to open the Data Link Properties dialog.

2. Open the Select Server or Enter a Server Name drop-down list and select the NetBIOS name of the server and, if the remote instance is SSX or MSDE 2000, add **\SQLEXPRESS** or **\INSTANCENAME** (see Figure 20.43). If the server doesn't appear in the list, type its name in the list's text box.

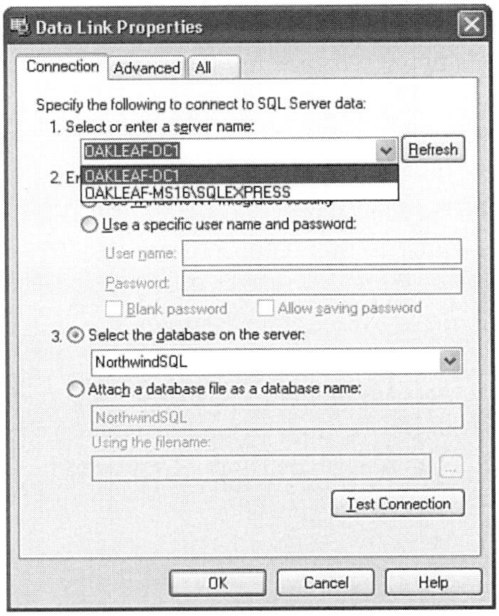

Figure 20.43
All instances of SQL Server on machines running Windows 2000 Server or Windows Server 2003+ appear in the server name list.

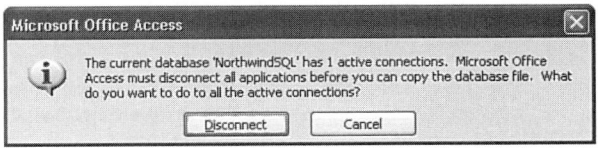

20

3. Accept the default Use Windows NT Integrated Security option, select the database name, and click Test Connection.

4. Click OK to connect to the remote SQL Server database.

NOTE

If you used the Copy Database File feature to copy an .mdf file, you can attach the copied file to a remote or local instance of SQL Server as a database name, as shown in Figure 20.44.

Figure 20.44
If you need to attach an SQL Server .mdf file to a database, you can do so by selecting the Attach a Database File as a Database Name option, typing the database name to use, and navigating to the location of the file.

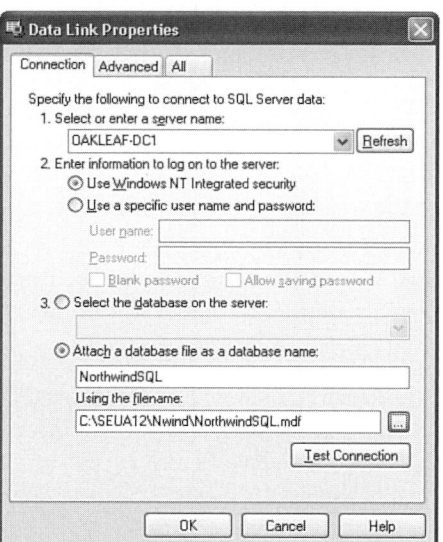

DESIGNING FORMS AND REPORTS WITH SQL SERVER DATA SOURCES

The appearance and behavior of forms and reports bound to SQL Server tables, views, and inline table-valued functions are similar to their counterparts in .accdb files. If the .accdb file's queries are updatable, forms based on corresponding SQL Server views or inline functions usually are updatable.

You can set a Server Filter or Server Filter by Form property value, which serves as a WHERE clause constraint to restrict the number of rows returned from the back-end table or query. This contrasts with a conventional Filter or Filter by Form operation that applies the filter on the client. Using a server-side filter minimizes network traffic and improves project performance.

Unfortunately, ADPs don't support Layout view for forms or reports. If you find Layout View indispensable, consider linking SQL Server tables to an .accdb front end.

SECURING YOUR PROJECT AS AN .ade FILE

When you distribute Access projects to users, the only security you can apply on the client side is compiling the project to an encoded .ade file. Like .accde files, projects stored in .ade format prevent users from making design changes to the front end and gaining access to your VBA source code. When you use the default integrated Windows authentication for the back-end SQL Server database, which is the recommended configuration for SQL Server, you can't apply password protection to the project. Windows authentication prevents users who haven't been assigned server logins and database permissions from opening the project's connection to the server.

→ To learn how to use SSMS[X] to add logins and database permissions to SSX, **see** "Adding SQL Server User Logins with SQL Server Management Studio Express," **p. 852**.

To create an .ade version of your .adp file, follow the same procedure as described in Chapter 19 for creating an .acce from an .accdb file:

1. Create an archive of the .adp file on removable media and then make a backup copy with a different name. Most .adp files fit on a high-density diskette and all will fit on a CD-ROM.

2. If your .adp file uses Access 2000 format, you must convert the backup copy to Access 2002-2003 format before creating the .ade file. Only users with Access 2002 or later installed can open the file.

> **TIP**
>
> Use Access 2000 to create .ade files for Access 2000 users. You can't create an Access 2000–compatible .ade file in Access 2007.

3. Open the backup copy, and then choose Tools, Database Utilities, Make ADE File to open the Save ADE As dialog.

4. Type the name of the .ade file to save in the File Name text box, and click Save to create the .ade file.

TROUBLESHOOTING

REMOTE DATABASE CONNECTION PROBLEMS

Access hangs or throws an error message when I attempt to connect my project to an instance of SQL Server running on a server.

There are many causes for connection failures to remote databases, the most obvious being network problems. Verify that you can connect to the server PC and open server shares with Explorer. If you can connect to a server share but not the database, you probably have a TCP/IP problem. Use Control Panel's Network tool and verify the TCP/IP settings for your network interface card (NIC).

IN THE REAL WORLD—STRATEGIC DATABASE SCHIZOPHRENIA

Several computer press columnists have derided Access as difficult for non-experts to use. The simpler alternatives that these pundits propose usually are flat-file managers with lookup fields that are similar to SharePoint lists. These simple programs, which often are online applications that run in a browser, don't require the data management capabilities offered by full-featured RDBMSs.

Microsoft's primary objective for Access 2007 is to make it easier for database novices to create tables, queries, forms, and reports for basic tracking applications. The jury's still out on whether replacing traditional menus and toolbars with the new ribbon UI achieves this objective. However, there's no question that the new Office Online templates ease creation of common tracking applications. But simplifying Access caused Microsoft to abandon important developer features, such as user-level security with workgroup files.

Microsoft declared SQL Server to be the company's "strategic database" in mid-1999 when releasing Access 2000, the first Access version to offer ADP and MSDE 1.0. Articles with "Jet Is Dead" headlines appeared in the computer press because Microsoft promoted MSDE heavily and implied that Jet was on its way to oblivion. Microsoft invested a substantial amount of development time and energy to make the transition from Access back ends to SQL Server databases more palatable to Access users and developers. An improved user interface for designing SQL Server database objects in recent Access versions, and easy addition of parameters to functions and stored procedures, bring ADP close to parity with Access's Table and Query Design views.

MSDE's lack of even rudimentary menu-based or graphical database management tools made ordinary database administration chores difficult for developers and next to impossible for ordinary Access users. Using command-line OSQL for server and database management required familiarity with T-SQL data definition and data security language commands, plus experience executing SQL Server 2000 system stored procedures. Thus, it's fair to conclude that ADP and MSDE were tactical, not strategic features of Access 2000 through 2003.

Microsoft now offers the SQL Server Management Studio Express Edition tools for SQL Server Express. SSMSX's full-featured tools for managing databases overcome the final obstacle to adoption of ADP and SQL Server back-end databases. However, Microsoft's Access team now recommends linked SharePoint lists as an enterprise back end for Access applications, despite the fact that SharePoint doesn't offer relational features, such as joins or referential integrity maintenance, or data validation rules. Access 2007 front ends for Windows Share Point Services (WSS 3.0) or Microsoft Office SharePoint Server (MOSS) 2007 have glacial performance compared to SQL Server 2007 or .accdb databases. Access might enhance SharePoint but SharePoint doesn't enhance Access, as you'll see in Chapter 25, "Collaborating with Windows SharePoint Services."

Most users of SSX in medium-sized and larger concerns probably will migrate to SQL Server 2005 Standard Edition when putting ADPs into full-scale production, fulfilling

Microsoft's strategic objective in providing a free distribution license for SSX. The US$5,999 price tag for a single-processor, unlimited-user license for SQL Server 2005 Standard Edition or US$3,889 for the Workgroup Edition undoubtedly will deter small firms from upgrading. The performance of SSX, which no longer has the five-simultaneous-query throttle, is likely to meet the needs of most small- to medium-sized businesses.

TIP

> Small firms with 75 users or fewer should consider licensing Microsoft Small Business Server (SBS) 2003 R2 Premium editions, which include SQL Server 2005 Workgroup edition. A server and five client licenses costs U.S.$1,299 and additional client licenses cost slightly less than U.S.$100 each. Multicore processors count only as a single CPU for licensing purposes. (SBS 2003 R2 is limited to a total of 75 connected users or devices.) All Access 2007 clients that connect to or replicate with the SQL Server instance must have a client license. For more information on SBS 2003 R2, go to http://www.microsoft.com/sbserver/.

Where SQL Server 2005 shines is in ease of installation, maintenance, and administration. You can run medium-sized SQL Server 2005 installations without a trained DBA, and you'll probably find that SQL Server 2005 databases require less maintenance attention than shared-file Access back ends. Unlike Access, SQL Server 2005 databases are largely self-tuning and self-managing. Choosing the optimum set of indexes for server tables traditionally has been a hit-or-miss operation based on DBA intuition. If you have the Workgroup or Standard edition, SQL Server's Profiler and Index Tuning Wizard analyze table usage, and the wizard recommends the fields to index. This is an especially important feature for databases having usage patterns that change significantly over time.

If you decide to stick with Access front ends linked to SSX, instead of moving to ADP, you gain most of the advantages of SQL Server 2005 without the pain and suffering of rewriting complex Access applications for ADP compliance. Query performance won't match that of views and stored procedures, but your crosstab queries execute without modification, and all Access and VBA query functions remain intact.

20

CHAPTER **21**

MOVING FROM ACCESS QUERIES TO TRANSACT-SQL

In this chapter

UNDERSTANDING THE ROLE OF SQL IN ACCESS 2007

This chapter describes Structured Query Language (SQL), the grammar of the language, and SQL Server's dialect of ANSI-92 SQL called *Transact-SQL (T-SQL)*. Earlier chapters have demonstrated how Access translates queries you build in its Query Design view into Access SQL statements. Access SQL is another SQL dialect that closely resembles T-SQL, but Access SQL lacks T-SQL's support for views and its extensions for functions, stored procedures, and linked servers. Access SQL is unique in its support for VBA functions—such as `CCur()` and `DatePart()`—in queries. T-SQL has equivalents to many VBA functions, but the usage syntax differs.

SQL (usually pronounced "sequel" or "seekel," but more properly "ess-cue-ell") is the common language of client/server database management. The principal advantage of SQL is that it's standardized—you can use a common set of SQL statements with all SQL-compliant database management systems. The first U.S. SQL standard was established in 1986 as ANSI X3.135-1986. The commonly implemented version is ANSI X3.135-1992, usually known as SQL-92. ANSI is an acronym for the American National Standards Institute. X3.135 is the code name for the ANSI subcommittee that's responsible for editing and publishing SQL standards documentation. The corresponding International Standards Organization (ISO) standard is ISO/IEC 9075:1992.

SQL is an application language for relational databases, not a system or programming language. SQL is a set-oriented language, not a procedural language like VBA. ANSI SQL includes neither a provision for program flow control (branching and looping) nor keywords to create data-entry forms and print reports. Publishers of ANSI SQL–compliant RDBMSs are free to extend the language if the basic ANSI commands are supported in accordance with the standards. Unlike standards (called *recommendations*) for HTML, XML, and other Web-related languages coordinated by the World Wide Web Consortium (W3C), updates to ANSI SQL are few and far between. A later standard is SQL:1999 (called *SQL3* during the seven-year standards process), which supports hierarchical, network, and other database models, not just relational databases. SQL:2003 is the current ANSI standard, which formalizes XML data type features and columns with auto-generated values, such as Access AutoNumber and SQL Server IDENTITY columns.

> **NOTE**
> Access SQL is based on SQL-92 and supports some SQL:1999 core features. SQL Server 2005 supports most SQL:1999 core features and the XML requirements of SQL:2003's Section 14. Access 2007 doesn't support SQL Server 2005's XML data type, so it's not covered in this book.

An SQL background helps you understand the query process, and design more efficient Access SQL and T-SQL queries. You need a basic knowledge of SQL to write subqueries and UNION queries and for any application that uses VBA to generate Recordsets for populating list and combo boxes. Simple examples of Access SQL and T-SQL are presented in other chapters in this book. These examples demonstrate what occurs behind the scenes when you create a query using either of Access's visual Query by Example (QBE) tools. QBE is the original name for pre-Windows query tools that emulate query-design grids in text-only displays. Almost all graphical query-design tools are based on early QBE techniques.

You probably can use Access's Query Design window to generate the SQL statements for 90% or more of the queries you need to support conventional Access applications. (You must write UNION and pass-through queries in the SQL window.) The graphical project designer (also called the *da Vinci toolset*) is likely to cover 75% or so of your query needs for Access Data Projects (ADP); you must write the remaining 25% in T-SQL. T-SQL offers many additional features, such as IF...ELSE and WHILE statements for flow control within queries. Taking advantage of most of the features of SQL Server 2005 requires at least the ability to modify T-SQL statements you create with the project designer.

TIP

> Learn SQL by osmosis. Each time you design a query in Access's Query Design view or the project designer for ADPs, open the SQL window or pane and read the underlying SQL statement. The relationship between the SQL statement and graphic query design is evident for simple queries. As you advance to more complex queries with joins and aggregate functions, carefully compare the SQL statement with the contents of the QBE grid. Over time, you'll find that SQL lives up to its original name, SEQUEL–Structured *English* Query Language.

UNDERSTANDING SQL GRAMMAR

When you learn the grammar of a new language, it's helpful to categorize the vocabulary of the language by usage and then into the familiar parts of speech. SQL commands, there-fore, first are divided into six usage categories:

- *Data Query Language (DQL)* consists of commands that obtain data from tables and determines how the results of the retrieval are presented. The SELECT command is the principal instruction in this category.

- *Data Manipulation Language (DML)* provides INSERT and DELETE commands, which add or delete entire rows, and the UPDATE command, which changes the values of data in specified columns within rows.

- *Transaction Processing Language (TPL)* includes BEGIN TRAN[SACTION], COMMIT [TRAN[SACTION]¦WORK], and ROLLBACK [TRAN[SACTION]¦WORK], which group multiple DML operations. If one DML operation of a transaction fails, the preceding DML operations are canceled (rolled back). Access 4.0 SQL and T-SQL implement BEGIN TRANSACTION, COMMIT TRANSACTION¦WORK, and ROLLBACK TRANSACTION¦WORK; only T-SQL supports the TRAN abbreviation.

- *Data Definition Language (DDL)* includes CREATE¦ALTER TABLE, ADD¦ALTER COLUMN, and CREATE VIEW instructions that define the structure of tables and views. DDL commands also are used to modify tables and to create and delete indexes. The keywords that implement declarative referential integrity (DRI) are used with DDL statements.

21

Access SQL and T-SQL support the `[CREATE¦ALTER]` `TABLE` and `[CREATE¦ALTER}` `INDEX` instructions; T-SQL offers non-ANSI `ALTER` `VIEW`, `[CREATE¦ALTER]` `FUNCTION`, and `[CREATE¦ALTER]` `PROCEDURE` statements.

- *Cursor Control Language (CCL)* can select a single row of a query result set for processing. Cursor control constructs, such as `UPDATE` `WHERE` `CURRENT`, are handled by ADO's cursor engine or the Access database engine, so these commands aren't discussed in this chapter.

- *Data Control Language (DCL)* performs administrative functions that grant and revoke privileges to use the database, such as `GRANT` and `REVOKE`, a set of tables within the database, or specific SQL commands. DCL sometimes is called *Data Security Language*.

Keywords that make up the vocabulary of SQL are identified further in the following categories:

- *Commands*, such as `SELECT`, `EXECUTE`, `CREATE`, and `ALTER`, are verbs that cause an action to be performed.

- *Qualifiers*, such as `WHERE`, limit the range of values of the entities that constitute the query.

- *Clauses*, such as `ORDER` `BY`, modify the action of an instruction.

- *Predicates*, such as `IN`, `ALL`, `ANY`, `SOME`, `LIKE`, and `UNIQUE`, are expressions that test facts about data values. Predicates can return a `TRUE`, `FALSE`, or, in some cases, `NULL` (unknown) result. These three values are SQL keywords.

- *Operators*, such as =, <, or >, compare values and specify joins with a `WHERE` clause or `JOIN` syntax. Access SQL and T-SQL use `JOIN` syntax by default. Operators also are called *comparison predicates*.

- *Group aggregate functions*, such as `AVG()`, `COUNT()`, `MAX()`, `MIN()`, and `SUM`, return a single result for a set of values.

- *Data type conversions functions* change values from one data type to another. `CAST()` and `CONVERT()` are the most commonly used conversion functions.

- *Utility functions* return values determined by expressions. You can use `NULLIF()`, for example, to return a `NULL` value if the function's expression evaluates to `TRUE`. Date/time and string manipulation functions also fit into the utility category.

→ For more information on the relationship between VBA and T-SQL utility functions, **see** "VBA Functions That Upsize to SQL Server Functions," **p. 979**, and "VBA Functions That You Must Manually Convert to Related SQL Server Functions," **p. 980**.

- *Other keywords* (or reserved words) modify the action of a clause or manipulate cursors that are used to select specific rows of queries. The T-SQL `FOR` `XML` `[AUTO¦RAW¦EXPLICIT]` modifier, for example, returns an XML document or subdocument instead of a conventional Recordset from a `SELECT` query. `FOR` `XML` isn't included in ANSI SQL.

> **NOTE**
>
> SQL keywords usually are capitalized, but the keywords aren't case sensitive. The upper-case convention is used in this book, and SQL keywords are set in monospace type. You use parameters, such as `column_list`, to define or modify the action specified by keywords. Names of replaceable parameters are printed in lowercase italicized monospace type.
>
> ANSI SQL defines *reserved words*, such as `SELECT`, and *nonreserved words*, such as `DATA` and `FORTRAN`. *Keywords* include both reserved and nonreserved words. All the keywords used in this chapter are reserved words; you can't use a reserved word as the name of a database object, such as a table.

WRITING SELECT QUERIES IN SQL

The heart of SQL is the `SELECT` statement, used to return a specified set of records from one or more tables. The following lines of syntax are used for an SQL `SELECT` statement that returns a virtual query table (called a *result set*, usually a `Recordset` object) of all or selected columns (fields) from all or qualifying rows (records) of a source table:

```
SELECT [ALL¦DISTINCT¦DISTINCTROW] [TOP (n) [PERCENT]] [WITH TIES] select_list
  FROM table_names
  [WHERE search_criteria]
  [ORDER BY column_criteria [ASC¦DESC]]
```

The following list shows the purpose of the elements in this basic select query statement:

- `SELECT` is the basic command that specifies a query. The `select_list` parameter determines the fields (columns) that are included in the result table of the query. When you design a graphical query, the `select_list` parameter is determined by the fields you add to the Fields row in the Query grid. Only those fields with the Show check box marked are included in the `select_list`. Multiple field names are separated by commas.

  The optional `ALL`, `DISTINCT`, and `DISTINCTROW` qualifiers determine how rows are handled. `ALL` specifies that all rows are to be included, subject to subsequent limitation. `DISTINCT` eliminates rows with duplicate data in both Access SQL and T-SQL. `DISTINCTROW` is an Access SQL keyword, similar to T-SQL's `DISTINCT`, that eliminates duplicate rows but also enables you to change values in the query result set. T-SQL doesn't support `DISTINCTROW`, so the preceding is the only example in this chapter that includes this qualifier.

  The optional `TOP (n) [PERCENT]` modifier limits the query result set to returning the first *n* rows or *n* percent of the result set prior to the limitation. `TOP` and `PERCENT` are Access SQL and T-SQL, not ANSI SQL, keywords. Omit the parentheses for Access queries. You use the `TOP` modifier to speed display when you want to display only the most significant rows of a query result set. `TOP (100) PERCENT`, which returns all rows, is required to create SQL Server views that you can sort with the `ORDER BY` clause. The optional T-SQL-only `WITH TIES` modifier requires an `ORDER BY` clause and returns additional rows that result from equal values in the `ORDER BY` field. SQL Server 2005 permits a variable or expression to replace the *n* argument.

21

- FROM `table_name` specifies the name or names of the table or tables that form the basis for the query. The `table_name` parameter is created in QBE by the selections you make in the Add Table dialog. If fields from more than one table are included in the `select_list`, each table should be specified in the `table_name` parameter. You must prepend table names to field names that are present in both tables (see the following Caution). Commas separate the names of multiple tables.

- WHERE `search_criteria` determines which records from the select list are displayed. The `search_criteria` is an expression with a predicate, such as LIKE or = for text fields, or a numeric operator, such as <, > or >=, for fields with numeric values. The WHERE clause is optional; if you don't add a WHERE clause, the query returns all the rows from the table specified by FROM `table_name`.

- ORDER BY `column_criteria` specifies the sorting order of the result set. Like the WHERE clause, ORDER BY is optional. You can specify an ascending or descending sort by the optional ASC or DESC keyword, respectively. If you don't specify a sort direction, ascending is the default.

CAUTION

> If you add fields from two or more tables and don't join the tables by a WHERE `Table1.Field1 = Table2.Field2` clause or a JOIN statement, the statement returns a combination of all rows of all tables, called a *Cartesian product*. Executing such a statement against tables on a remote machine can generate enough traffic to bring a network to its knees. ADP datasheets have a default maximum of 10,000 rows to prevent an accidental Cartesian product from consuming all SQL Server resources for a substantial period.

USING SQL PUNCTUATION AND SYMBOLS

In addition to the comparison operators used for expressions, SQL uses commas, periods, semicolons, and colons as punctuation. The following list of symbols and punctuation is used in T-SQL, which follows ANSI standards, and Access SQL; differences between the two SQL dialects are noted where appropriate:

- *Commas*—Used to separate members of lists of parameters, such as multiple field names, as in Name, Address, City, ZIP.

- *Square brackets*—Square brackets surrounding field names are required only when the field name includes spaces, keywords, or other symbols—including punctuation—not allowed by ANSI SQL, as in [Order Details]. Square brackets also must surround names you assign in the grid to input parameters for Access queries.

- *Periods*—Used to separate named objects of a subordinate class. For example, if fields of more than one table are involved in the query, a period is used to separate the table name from the field name, as in [Order Details].OrderID. Four-part names of linked tables in FROM statements use the `Server.Database.Schema.Table` format.

→ For an example of linked tables and four-part names, **see** "Connecting to a Remote SQL Server Database," **p. 907**.

- *String identifiers (also called delimiters)*—Designate literal character values. ANSI SQL requires the single quote symbol (') to enclose literal string values. You can use the double quote (") or the single quote symbol to enclose literal values in Access SQL statements. Using the single quote makes writing SQL statements in VBA easier. For backward compatibility with SQL Server 7.0 and earlier, as well as databases that specify the QUOTED_IDENTIFIER option, T-SQL interprets the double quote as a square bracket.

- *Wildcards*—Differ in Access and ANSI SQL. ANSI SQL uses % and _ (underscore) symbols as the wildcards for the LIKE statement, rather than the * (asterisk) to specify zero or more characters and ? to specify a single character in Access SQL.

- *Date/time identifier*—Access requires the # symbol to enclose date/time values in expressions. ANSI SQL accepts date values in a variety of character formats enclosed by single quotes. Access also uses the # wildcard for the LIKE statement to represent any single digit. ANSI SQL doesn't support the use of the # symbol in queries.

- *: and @ identifiers for variables*—ANSI SQL uses : as a prefix to identify variables that receive parameter values (sometimes called *host variables*). T-SQL uses @ for conventional variables (including variables to receive parameter values) and @@ for variables whose values SQL Server supplies, such as @@IDENTITY, which returns the current value of the identity column of a table. Access SQL handles input parameters by an entirely different method, and doesn't support declaring variables in SQL statements.

- *! (the exclamation mark or bang symbol)*—Synonym for NOT in ANSI SQL. ANSI SQL uses != for not equal; T-SQL and Access SQL use <>, but T-SQL also supports !=.

As the preceding list demonstrates, relatively minor differences exist in the availability and use of punctuation and symbols between ANSI and Access SQL. These minor differences, however, can cause a major difference in the behavior of Access and SQL Server

TRANSLATING SQL STATEMENTS INTO QBE DESIGNS

When you create a SELECT query in Query Design mode, Access translates the graphical query design into an Access SQL SELECT statement. Similarly, the project designer for ADPs generates T-SQL from your selections in the fields list and entries in the designer grid. The SQL translation operation is bidirectional; when you type an SQL statement into Access's SQL window or the SQL pane of the project designer, the graphical QBE view changes. Access's query designer requires that you change from Query Design to SQL view, and vice versa, to view the query changes. Clicking the Check SQL Syntax button updates the project designer's top and middle panes.

> **TIP**
>
> If you want to compare Access and SQL Server QBE translation directly, open two instances of Access 2007—one with Northwind.accdb as the current database and the other with NorthwindCS.adp as the current project. The NorthwindCS.adp client front end and NorthwindSQL.mdf SQL Server 2005 back-end database file are provided in the \Seua12\Nwind folder.

→ If you haven't downloaded and installed SSX or attached Seua12\Nwind\NorthwindSQL.mdf as the NorthwindSQL database, **see** "SQL Server 2005 Express Edition SP2 Setup" **p. 59**.

21

CREATING ACCESS QUERY DEFINITIONS

To generate Access query definitions (QueryDef objects) from SQL statements in Northwind.accdb, do this:

1. Open Northwind.accdb, click the Create tab, and click the Query Design button to open a new query in Design view.

2. Close the Show Table dialog, and click the SQL View button to open the Query1: Select Query SQL window. The window opens with a default SELECT; query fragment.

3. Type the SQL statement in the window (see Figure 21.1 and the following Access SQL box), and select Design View to display the graphical version of the query.

Figure 21.1
Type the SQL statement in Access's SQL window. Unfortunately, the standard font size is 8 points, which makes reading what you type difficult in high-resolution modes. You can't change the font size.

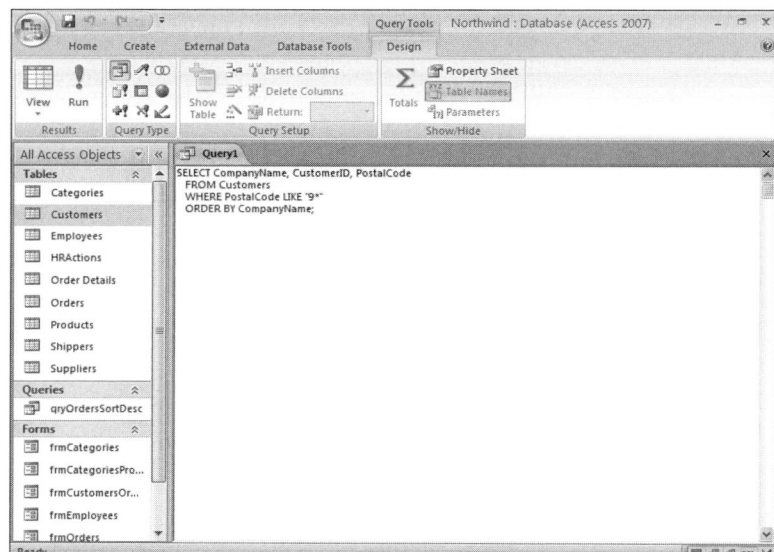

4. Click Run to display the result of your query in Datasheet view.

Saving the queries is optional. To generate a new query, delete the SQL text and start over.

Access SQL
The following lines are an example of a simple Access SQL query statement using default character identifiers and the * wildcard:

```
SELECT CompanyName, CustomerID, PostalCode
    FROM Customers
    WHERE PostalCode LIKE "9*"
    ORDER BY CompanyName;
```

Access SQL terminates statements by adding a semicolon immediately after the last character on the last line. If you don't type the semicolon, Access's query parser adds it for you.

NOTE

Examples of SQL statements in this book are formatted to make them more readable. Access doesn't format its SQL statements. When you enter or edit SQL statements in the SQL window, formatting these statements so that commands appear on individual lines makes the SQL statements more intelligible. Indented lines indicate continuation of a preceding line or a clause that is dependent on a keyword in a preceding line. Use Ctrl+Enter to insert newline pairs (the carriage return and newline characters, CrLf) before SQL keywords. Access SQL and T-SQL ignore spaces and newline pairs (called *whitespace*) when processing the SQL statement.

The preceding Access SQL statement creates the query design shown in Figure 21.2.

Figure 21.2
The Access SQL statement of Figure 21.1 creates this simple query design. The Access query parser causes changes you make in the SQL window to appear immediately in the Query Design window.

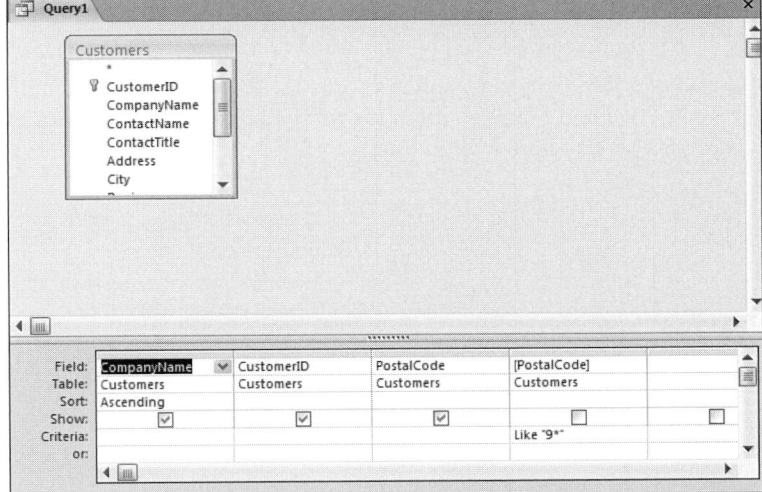

WORKING WITH SQL SERVER VIEWS

Views are SQL Server's most common incarnation of SELECT queries, but you also can return query result sets from inline functions and stored procedures. A view is a stored SELECT query definition that serves the same purpose as an Access QueryDef object. To create a view from an SQL statement in the project designer for ADPs, do this:

1. Open NorthwindCS.adp, click the Create tab and Query Wizard button to open the New Query dialog (see Figure 21.3).

2. Select Design View, which means "design a view" in this case, and click OK to open the Add Table dialog.

3. Close the Add Table dialog, click the Function & View Tools tab, and click the SQL button to add the SQL text pane. The pane contains a default SELECT…FROM fragment.

21

Figure 21.3
The New Query dialog lets you select one of six predefined T-SQL query types.

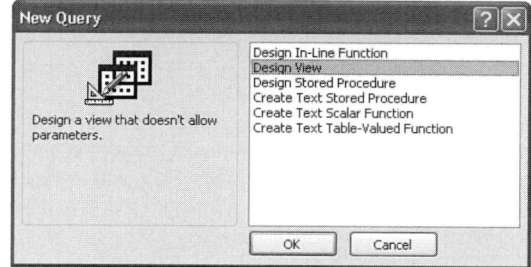

4. Type the SQL statement in the pane. If you use the preceding Access SQL query, the designer automatically adds the TOP 100 PERCENT to accommodate the ORDER BY clause, but it's a good practice to add the modifier yourself. You must change LIKE "9*" to LIKE '9%' to comply with T-SQL syntax (see Figure 21.4).

5. Click Check SQL Syntax, and acknowledge the syntax verification message, to display the QBE version of the query in the top two panes (see Figure 21.5). Clicking either of the QBE panes also refreshes them.

Figure 21.4
This T-SQL query parser adds the TOP 100 PERCENT modifier, which is intended to support the ORDER BY clause. Project queries also require T-SQL–compliant string identifiers and wildcards.

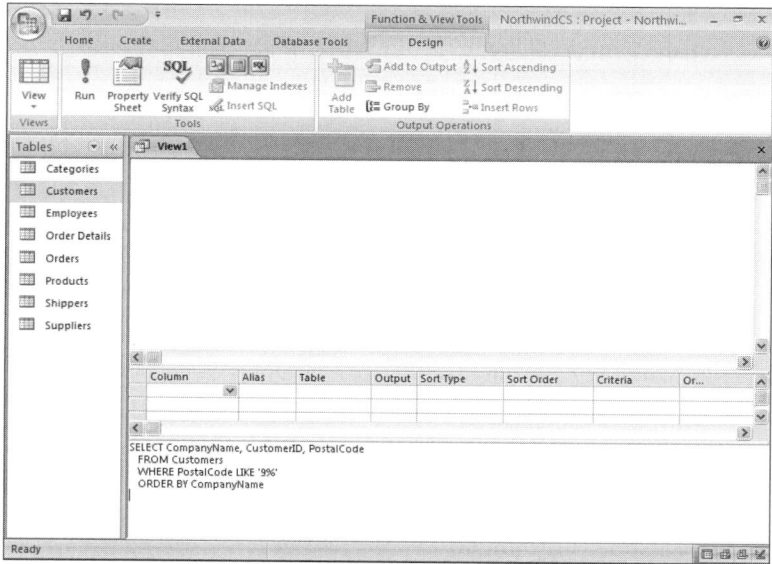

6. Click Run to display the result of your query in Datasheet view (see Figure 21.6). Unlike with Access, you must save the view to the SQL Server database before you can execute it.

Figure 21.5
When you check the SQL syntax, the project designer reformats the SQL statement, adds the dbo. (schema) prefix to table name(s), and adds parentheses to the WHERE clause.

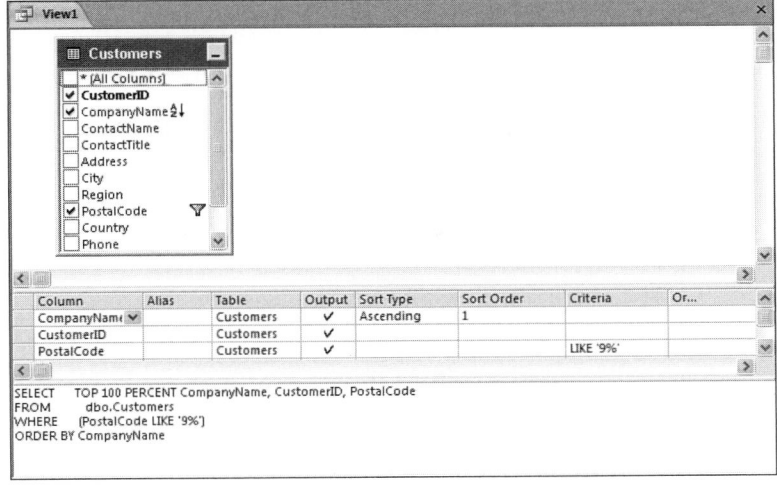

```
SELECT    TOP 100 PERCENT CompanyName, CustomerID, PostalCode
FROM      dbo.Customers
WHERE     (PostalCode LIKE '9%')
ORDER BY CompanyName
```

Figure 21.6
The query result set of the view design of Figure 21.5 is updatable, as indicated by the empty tentative append record, but the TOP 100 PERCENT modifier doesn't sort PostalCode in ascending order.

Company Name	Customer ID	Postal Code
Great Lakes Food Market	GREAL	97403
Hungry Coyote Import Store	HUNGC	97827
Lazy K Kountry Store	LAZYK	99362
Let's Stop N Shop	LETSS	94117
Lonesome Pine Restaurant	LONEP	97219
Old World Delicatessen	OLDWO	99508
The Big Cheese	THEBI	97201
Trail's Head Gourmet Provisioners	TRAIH	98034
Wartian Herkku	WARTH	90110
White Clover Markets	WHITC	98128

Record: 1 of 10   No Filter   Search

TIP

The TOP 100 PERCENT modifier enables sorting SQL Server 2000/MSDE 2000 tables with an ORDER BY clause, but the SQL Server 2005/SQL Express query engine ignores this modifier. To sort the view, change to Design View, open the view's Property Sheet, click the Data Tab, add the ORDER BY clause (without ORDER BY) as the Order By property value (PostalCode [ASC]) for this example, and close the Property Sheet. Then remove the modifier and ORDER BY clause from the SQL statement.

→ For more information on the TOP 100 PERCENT modifier and ORDER BY clauses in views, **see** "Exploring SQL Server Views," **p. 884**.

21

SQL If you copy or type the preceding Access SQL statement into the project designer's SQL pane without making the changes described in step 3, and then click the Check SQL Syntax button, you receive an "ADO error: Invalid column name '9*'" error message, because SQL Server's query parser interprets the double-quotes as a column identifier. Changing the double-quotes to single-quotes eliminates the error message, adds TOP 100 PERCENT, changes the statement's format, and removes the trailing semicolon. When you execute the SQL statement, the view has no rows because T-SQL doesn't recognize the * wildcard and interprets the LIKE predicate as the two-character string '9*'. Change * to %, and the view returns the expected Recordset.

T-SQL

Following is the T-SQL statement corresponding to the earlier Access SQL version, with the required changes in bold type:

```
CREATE VIEW vwTest1 AS
[SELECT TOP 100 PERCENT] CompanyName, CustomerID, PostalCode
   FROM Customers
   WHERE PostalCode LIKE '9%'
   [ORDER BY CompanyName]
```

The project designer's SQL pane hides the required [CREATE¦ALTER] VIEW *view_name* AS statement.

USING THE SQL AGGREGATE FUNCTIONS AND WRITING INLINE FUNCTIONS

If you want to use the aggregate functions to determine totals, averages, or statistical data for groups of records with a common attribute value, you must add a GROUP BY clause to your SQL statement. The GROUP BY clause specifies the set of rows on which the aggregate function(s) operate.

> **TIP**
>
> T-SQL queries that use the SUM() aggregate function and GROUP BY clauses are the first step in the process of emulating Access crosstab queries with T-SQL's new PIVOT operator.

→ For instructions on how to emulate crosstab queries with T-SQL, **see** "Emulating Access Crosstab Queries with T-SQL," **p. 980**.

You can further limit the result of the GROUP BY clause with the optional HAVING qualifier:

```
SELECT [ALL¦DISTINCT] [TOP n [PERCENT]]
      aggregate_function(field_name) AS alias_name
   [, select_list]
 FROM table_names
[WHERE search_criteria]
 GROUP BY group_criteria
   [HAVING aggregate_criteria]
 [ORDER BY column_criteria]
```

21

The *select_list* includes the *aggregate_function* with a *field_name* as its argument. The field used as the argument of an aggregate function must have a numeric data type. The following list describes the additional required and optional SQL keywords and parameters to create a GROUP BY query:

- AS *alias_name* assigns a caption to the column. The caption is created in an Access query by the *alias:aggregate_function(field name)* entry in the Field row of the Query grid.

- GROUP BY *group_criteria* establishes the column(s) on which the grouping is based. In this column, GROUP BY appears in the Totals row of the Query grid. The GROUP BY clause is required for aggregate queries.

- HAVING *aggregate_criteria* applies one or more criteria to the column that contains the *aggregate_function*. The *aggregate_criteria* of HAVING is applied after the grouping is completed. The HAVING clause is optional.

- WHERE *search_criteria* operates before the grouping occurs; at this point, no aggregate values exist to test against *aggregate_criteria*. Access substitutes HAVING for WHERE when you add criteria to a column with the *aggregate_function*. The WHERE clause is optional, but it is seldom missing from an aggregate query.

Access queries and SQL Server views that include aggregate functions aren't updatable.

TIP

> Current releases of most client/server RDBMSs support the ANSI SQL AS *alias_name* construct. Early versions of SQL Server, Sybase System 10+, and IBM DB2, as examples, substitute a space for the AS keyword, as in SELECT *field_name alias_name*, ... (SQL Server 7+ accepts either AS or a space.) Some ODBC drivers for these databases use special codes (called *escape syntax*) to change from the Access/ANSI use of AS to the space separator. If you use Access SQL pass-through queries with some client/server RDBMSs, you might need to use the space separator, not the AS keyword.

Access SQL
The following Access GROUP BY query is written in ANSI SQL, except for the # symbols that enclose date and time values:

```
SELECT ShipRegion,
       SUM(Freight) AS [Total Freight]
   FROM Orders
   WHERE ShipCountry='USA'
       AND OrderDate BETWEEN #1/1/2006# AND #12/31/2006#
   GROUP BY ShipRegion
   HAVING SUM(Freight)>=100
   ORDER BY SUM(Freight) DESC
```

The query returns a result set that consists of two columns: ShipRegion (states) and the totals of Freight for any shipping region where the total freight charges for that region is greater than or equal to 100 in 2006.

21

Figure 21.7 illustrates the Access Query Design View for the preceding SQL statement.

Figure 21.7
The only clue to the presence of a HAVING criterion in Access Query Design View is the >=100 criterion in the Freight aggregate (Sum) column.

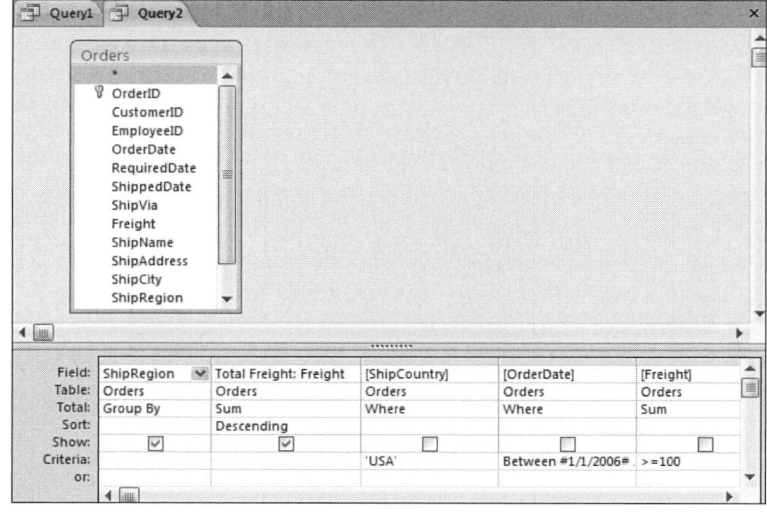

The Access query design of Figure 21.7 returns seven rows with ShipRegion and Total Freight columns. If you remove the HAVING expression, the result set has eight rows.

 If you encounter an Enter Parameter dialog when you attempt to run an Access SQL query, see "Unexpected Enter Parameter Dialogs" of the "Troubleshooting" section near the end of the chapter.

Table-valued functions (TVFs) can substitute for or augment views and, unlike views, support parameters. To create an SQL Server inline table-valued function from an SQL statement, do this:

 1. On NorthwindCS's Create ribbon, click Query Wizard to open the New Query dialog.

2. Double-click Design In-line Function to open the Function1: Function window and the Add Table dialog.

 3. Close the Add Table dialog to activate the Function & View Tools, Design ribbon, and click the SQL button to add the SQL pane.

4. Type the following T-SQL statement in the SQL pane.

T-SQL
You also must substitute single-quotes for the # date/time delimiters of the Access SQL query to create the following T-SQL version:

```
SELECT TOP (2147483647) ShipRegion,
      SUM(Freight) AS [Total Freight]
   FROM Orders
   WHERE ShipCountry='USA'
      AND OrderDate BETWEEN '1/1/2006' AND '12/31/2006'
   GROUP BY ShipRegion
   HAVING SUM(Freight)>=100
   ORDER BY SUM(Freight) DESC
```

---

5. Click the Check SQL Syntax button to verify the syntax and populate the upper two panes of the project designer (see Figure 21.8).

Figure 21.8
Other than the name in the designer's title bar, inline table-valued functions appear identical in the project designer to a view with the same SQL statement.

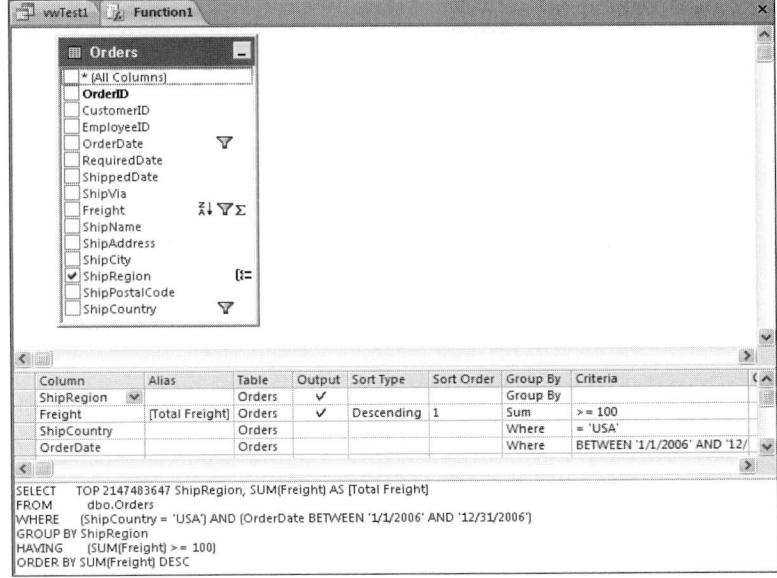

6. Click the Run button and save your function with a descriptive name, such as fn2006Freight.

Datasheet view of the result set returned by the function is identical to that of the Access query, with the exception of the name. In this case, substituting TOP (2147483647) for TOP 100 PERCENT causes the ORDER BY clause to sort the table-valued function's result set.

> **TIP**
>
> Use inline table-valued functions instead of stored procedures to generate the equivalent of a parameterized view. Result sets returned by simple table-valued SELECT functions are updatable in Datasheet view. SQL Server views don't support parameters, and the Recordsets returned by stored procedures aren't updatable.

→ To review adding parameters to inline functions, **see** "Creating a Parameterized Table-Valued Function," **p. 890**.

21

CREATING JOINS WITH SQL

Joining two or more tables with the Access query designer or the project designer uses the ANSI-92 JOIN...ON structure that specifies the table to be joined and the relationship between the fields on which the JOIN is based:

```
SELECT [ALL¦DISTINCT]select_list
   FROM
   table_name [INNER¦LEFT [OUTER]¦RIGHT [OUTER]]¦FULL [OUTER]]
      JOIN join_table ON join_criteria
   [table_name [INNER¦LEFT [OUTER]¦RIGHT [OUTER]]¦FULL [OUTER]]
      JOIN join_table ON join_criteria]
   [WHERE search_criteria]
   [ORDER BY column_criteria]
```

The following list describes the elements of the JOIN statement:

- *table_name* [INNER¦LEFT [OUTER]¦RIGHT [OUTER]]¦ JOIN *join_table* specifies the name of the table that's joined with other tables listed in *table_name*. When you specify a self-join by including two copies of the field list for a single table, the second table is distinguished from the first by adding an underscore and a digit to alias the table name.

  NOTE

  > One of the four types of joins, INNER, FULL, LEFT, or RIGHT, must precede the JOIN statement in Access queries, but INNER is optional in T-SQL. INNER specifies an inner join; LEFT specifies a left outer join; RIGHT specifies a right outer join. The OUTER qualifier for LEFT and RIGHT joins is optional. OUTER is optional for FULL joins.

- ON *join_criteria* specifies the two fields to be joined and the relationship between the joined fields. One field is in *join_table* and the other is in a table that's included in *table_names*. The *join_criteria* expression usually contains an equal sign (=) comparison operator and returns a true or false value. You can substitute other comparison operators, such as If *expression*, for =; in this case, if the value of the expression is true, the record in the joined table is included in the query.

The number of JOIN statements you can add to a query usually is the total number of tables participating in the query minus one. You can create more than one JOIN between a pair of tables, but the result often is difficult to predict.

Access SQL

The following Access SQL statement, which was created in Query Design view, defines INNER JOINs (also called natural joins) between the Orders, Order Details, Products, and Categories tables:

```
SELECT Orders.OrderID, Products.ProductName,
   Categories.CategoryName
FROM Categories INNER JOIN
      (Products INNER JOIN
         (Orders INNER JOIN
         [Order Details] ON Orders.OrderID =
         [Order Details].OrderID) ON Products.ProductID =
```

```
[Order Details].ProductID) ON Categories.CategoryID =
        Products.CategoryID
```

The result set returns a list of products and their category for every order. You can copy this SQL statement from the Access SQL window into the project designer for a view, table-valued function, or stored procedure to generate the same result set.

If you copy the preceding SQL statement to the SQL pane of an SQL Server view or function and click Check SQL Syntax, the designer adds the dbo. prefix to all table and field references, reformats the SQL statement, and reverses the left-to-right order of the tables in the top pane. Figure 21.9 shows the T-SQL version with additional manual formatting of the JOIN statements to clarify the nesting of the JOIN and ON elements of the query.

Figure 21.9
Multiple, nested JOIN statements aren't easy to write from scratch or read after you've defined them. If you omit the optional INNER prefixes, the SQL Server query parser inserts them when you test the syntax.

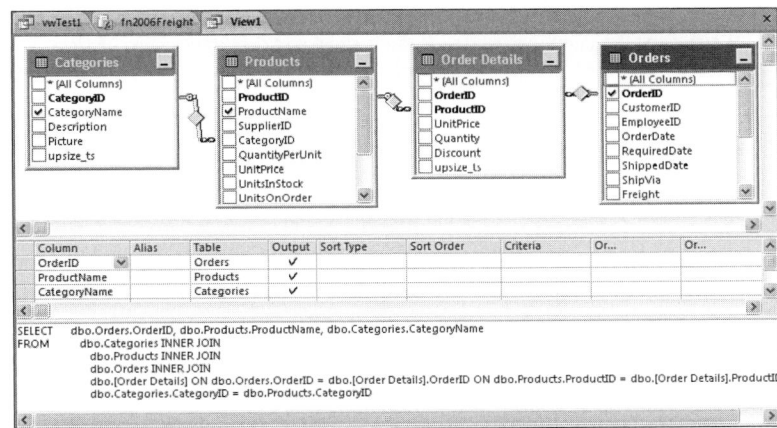

You can create joins in ANSI SQL with the WHERE clause, using the same expression to join the fields as that of the ON clause in the JOIN command. It's much simpler to write SQL statements using WHERE clauses to create relationships than to employ the JOIN syntax. Queries using WHERE clauses to create joins, however, aren't updatable.

Access SQL
The following ANSI SQL-89 statement returns the same result set as the preceding Access SQL statement in Figure 21.8, except that the result set isn't updatable:

```
SELECT Orders.OrderID, Products.ProductName,
    Categories.CategoryName
  FROM Orders, [Order Details], Products, Categories
  WHERE Orders.OrderID = [Order Details].OrderID
    AND Products.ProductID = [Order Details].ProductID
    AND Categories.CategoryID = Products.CategoryID;
```

In versions of SQL Server prior to 7.0, you could specify joins only with WHERE clauses.

21

T-SQL

If you type or copy the preceding Access SQL statement into the project designer and then click Check SQL Syntax, the query parser insists on converting the WHERE clause to INNER JOIN structures:

```
SELECT dbo.Orders.OrderID, dbo.Products.ProductName,
    dbo.Categories.CategoryName
FROM INNER JOIN dbo.[Order Details]
        ON dbo.Orders.OrderID =
            dbo.[Order Details].OrderID
    INNER JOIN dbo.Products
        ON dbo.[Order Details].ProductID =
            dbo.Products.ProductID
    INNER JOIN dbo.Categories
        ON dbo.Products.CategoryID =
            dbo.Categories.CategoryID
```

In this case, however, the JOINs aren't nested, which makes them easier to read. If you remove the "optional" INNER qualifiers, the query parser inserts them when you check the syntax or save the view.

If you want to preserve WHERE clause join syntax in a T-SQL query, you must write the query in a query execution tool, such as SQL Server Management Studio's Query pane.

WRITING UNION QUERIES

UNION queries let you combine the result set of two or more SELECT queries into a single result set. Northwind.accdb includes an example of a UNION query—Customers and Orders by City—that's identified by an icon with two overlapping circles, the symbol for a union set. The NorthwindCS database doesn't include a corresponding union view. You can create Access and SQL Server UNION queries only with SQL statements. The general syntax of UNION queries is as follows:

```
SELECT select_statement
    UNION SELECT select_statement
        [GROUP BY group_criteria]
        [HAVING aggregate criteria]
    [UNION SELECT select_statement
        [GROUP BY group_criteria]
        [HAVING aggregate criteria]]
    [UNION...]
    [ORDER BY column_criteria]
```

The following are the restrictions on statements that create UNION queries:

- The number of fields in the *field_list* of each SELECT and UNION SELECT query must be the same. You receive an error message if the number of fields isn't identical.

- The sequence of the field names in each *field_list* must correspond to similar entities. You don't receive an error message for dissimilar entities, but the result set is likely to be unfathomable. In Access UNION queries, the field data types in a single column need not correspond; if the column of the result set contains Access numeric and text data types, the data type of the column is set (coerced) to Text. T-SQL doesn't support automatically coercing dissimilar data types in a single column.

21

■ Only one ORDER BY clause is allowed, and it must follow the last UNION SELECT statement. You can add GROUP BY and HAVING clauses to each SELECT and UNION SELECT statement if needed.

The following SQL statement creates a UNION query combining rows from the Customers and Suppliers tables:

```
SELECT  City, CompanyName,
     ContactName, 'Customer' AS Relationship
  FROM Customers
UNION  City, CompanyName,
     ContactName, 'Supplier'
  FROM Suppliers
ORDER BY City, CompanyName
```

The preceding statement, which illustrates adding a field (Relationship) with a constant value (Customer) in each row, is valid in Access SQL and T-SQL. Enclosing an element of a field list in single quotes defines it as a constant value. TOP 2147483647 in a SELECT statement is required for use of the ORDER BY clause in T-SQL, but the ORDER BY clause doesn't sort SQL Server 2005/SQL Express union queries. (SQL Server 2000/MSDE 2000 union queries sort with TOP 100 PERCENT and ORDER BY.)

Access SQL

You can alter the preceding statement to include the CustomerID and SupplierID fields in an Access SQL query, as follows:

```
SELECT City, CustomerID AS Code, CompanyName,
     ContactName, 'Customer' AS Relationship
  FROM Customers
UNION SELECT City, SupplierID AS Code, CompanyName,
     ContactName, 'Supplier'
  FROM Suppliers
ORDER BY City, CompanyName;
```

The syntax of the SQL statement illustrates the capability of Access UNION queries to include values from two different field data types, Text (CustomerID) and Long Integer (SupplierID), in the single, aliased Code column. SQL Server won't execute this query.

T-SQL

You must use the T-SQL CAST() or CONVERT() function to conform dissimilar data types to a single data type for a column returned by a UNION query. Use the CAST() function as shown in the following example:

```
SELECT City, CustomerID AS Code,
     CompanyName, ContactName,
     'Customer' AS Relationship
  FROM Customers
UNION SELECT  City,
     CAST(SupplierID AS varchar(5)) AS Code,
     CompanyName, ContactName, 'Supplier'
  FROM Suppliers
```

21

You can't convert five-character CustomerID values to integers, but you can convert integer SupplierID values to a string. You must know the target SQL Server data type (`varchar(5)`, a five-character variable-length character field in this example) to use `CAST()`. `CAST()` is the most common replacement for the VBA type conversion functions, such as `CCur()`. Open the table (Customers) in Design view to obtain the SQL Server data type for the `CAST()` function.

To sort a SQL Server 2005/SQL Express `UNION` query, set the Property Sheet Data page's Order By property value to the `ORDER BY` expression, **City, CompanyName** for this example.

CAUTION

> Copy the SQL statement to the Clipboard before setting the Order By property value. Closing the Property Sheet replaces your union query with the `SELECT ... FROM` stub. Paste the SQL statement, and then click Run and save the modified view definition.

→ For examples of the use of SQL Server's `CAST()` and `CONVERT()` functions, **see** "Conforming Computed Columns to the ANSI SQL Standard," **p. 959**, "Modifying the Upsized qry2006SalesChart View," **p. 987**.

After you click Check SQL Syntax with a `UNION` query statement in the project designer's SQL pane and acknowledge the syntax check, a "Query Definitions Differ" error message appears. In some cases, the error message occurs before the syntax verification message. These error messages appear because the project designer can't represent `UNION` queries graphically; you can ignore them by clicking Yes in the Query Definitions Differ dialog.

Figure 21.10 shows the Datasheet view of the preceding T-SQL query. The Datasheet view of the equivalent Access query is identical. `UNION` queries, like queries returning SQL aggregate functions, aren't updatable.

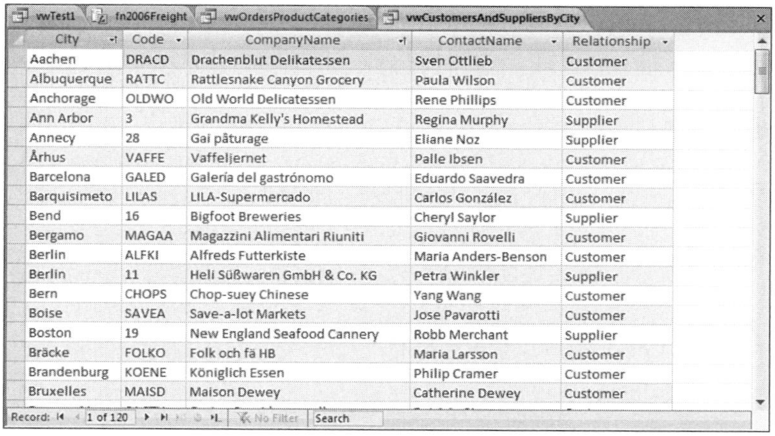

Figure 21.10
The result set for the Access SQL and T-SQL versions of the UNION query against the Customers and Suppliers tables is the same.

City	Code	CompanyName	ContactName	Relationship
Aachen	DRACD	Drachenblut Delikatessen	Sven Ottlieb	Customer
Albuquerque	RATTC	Rattlesnake Canyon Grocery	Paula Wilson	Customer
Anchorage	OLDWO	Old World Delicatessen	Rene Phillips	Customer
Ann Arbor	3	Grandma Kelly's Homestead	Regina Murphy	Supplier
Annecy	28	Gai pâturage	Eliane Noz	Supplier
Århus	VAFFE	Vaffeljernet	Palle Ibsen	Customer
Barcelona	GALED	Galería del gastrónomo	Eduardo Saavedra	Customer
Barquisimeto	LILAS	LILA-Supermercado	Carlos González	Customer
Bend	16	Bigfoot Breweries	Cheryl Saylor	Supplier
Bergamo	MAGAA	Magazzini Alimentari Riuniti	Giovanni Rovelli	Customer
Berlin	ALFKI	Alfreds Futterkiste	Maria Anders-Benson	Customer
Berlin	11	Heli Süßwaren GmbH & Co. KG	Petra Winkler	Supplier
Bern	CHOPS	Chop-suey Chinese	Yang Wang	Customer
Boise	SAVEA	Save-a-lot Markets	Jose Pavarotti	Customer
Boston	19	New England Seafood Cannery	Robb Merchant	Supplier
Bräcke	FOLKO	Folk och fä HB	Maria Larsson	Customer
Brandenburg	KOENE	Königlich Essen	Philip Cramer	Customer
Bruxelles	MAISD	Maison Dewey	Catherine Dewey	Customer

Record: 1 of 120

TIP

Use UNION queries to add an (All) option or other options when populating combo and list boxes with SELECT queries. As an example, the following SQL statement adds (All) to the query result set for a combo box used to select orders from a particular country or all countries:

```
SELECT TOP (2147483647) Country FROM Customers
    UNION SELECT '(All)'
    FROM Customers
ORDER BY Country;
```

The parenthesis around (All) causes it to sort at the beginning of the list; the ASCII value of "(" is 40 and "A" is 65. Automatic sorting of combo and list box items uses the ASCII value returned by the VBA **Asc** function.

→ For examples of using a UNION query to add an (All) item to a combo box, **see** "Adding an Option to Select All Countries or Products," **p. 1266**.

Implementing Subqueries

Early versions of Access used nested queries to emulate the subquery capability of ANSI SQL. (A *nested query* is a query executed against the result set of another query; thus, a nested query requires two QueryDefs. Similarly, a *nested view* executes against another view.) Access SQL and T-SQL let you write a SELECT query that uses another SELECT query to supply the criteria for the WHERE clause. Depending on the complexity of your query, using a subquery instead of nested queries often improves performance, especially with SQL Server. The general syntax of subqueries is as follows:

```
SELECT [TOP (2147483647)] field_list
    FROM table_list
    WHERE [table_name.]field_name
        IN (SELECT [TOP (2147483647)] select_statement
            [GROUP BY group_criteria]
            [HAVING aggregate_criteria]
            [ORDER BY sort_criteria])
    [ORDER BY sort_criteria]
```

T-SQL

Following is the T-SQL statement for a sample subquery that returns names and addresses of Northwind Traders customers who placed orders between January 1, 2006, and June 30, 2006:

```
SELECT TOP (2147483647) Customers.ContactName,
        Customers.CompanyName, Customers.ContactTitle,
        Customers.Phone
    FROM Customers
    WHERE Customers.CustomerID
        IN (SELECT Orders.CustomerID
                FROM Orders
                WHERE Orders.OrderDate
                    BETWEEN '1/1/2006' AND '6/30/2006')
    ORDER BY Customers.CompanyName
```

21

The SELECT subquery that begins after the IN predicate returns the CustomerID values from the Orders table against which the CustomerID values of the Customers table are compared. The only difference between Access SQL and T-SQL syntax for subqueries is delimiter characters.

Unlike UNION queries, Access Query Design view and the project designer support the graphical design of subqueries. You type IN, followed by the SELECT statement as the criterion of the appropriate column, enclosing the SELECT statement within the parentheses required by the IN predicate. Figure 21.11 shows the view design generated by the preceding T-SQL statement; Figure 21.12 shows the result set.

Figure 21.11
The subquery specified for the IN predicate appears in the Criteria cell of the field name designated in the WHERE clause of the project designer (shown here) and Access's Query Design view.

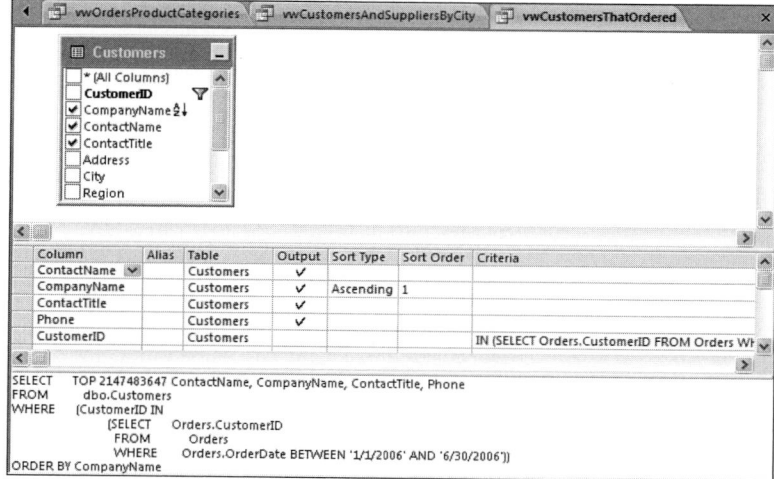

NOTE

The simple subquery design of Figure 21.11 offers no benefit over a conventional query that has an INNER JOIN between the Customers and Orders table and the WHERE clause applied to the query result set. Subqueries are most commonly used when the subquery's SQL statement is much more complex than that of this example.

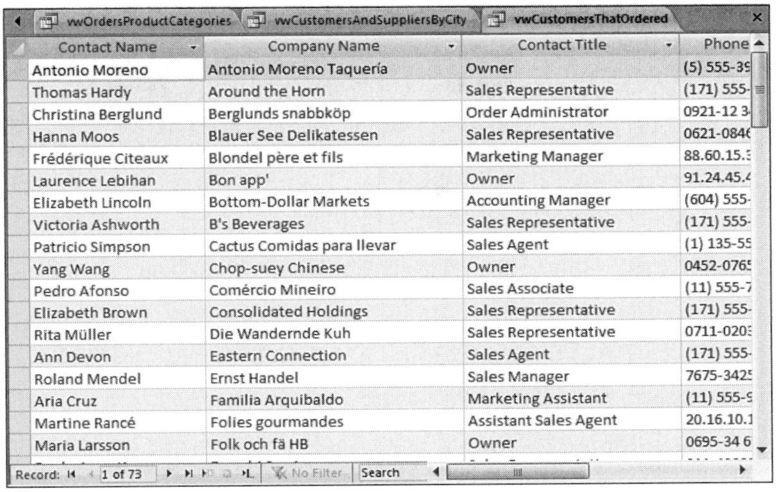

vwOrdersProductCategories | vwCustomersAndSuppliersByCity | vwCustomersThatOrdered

Contact Name	Company Name	Contact Title	Phone
Antonio Moreno	Antonio Moreno Taquería	Owner	(5) 555-39
Thomas Hardy	Around the Horn	Sales Representative	(171) 555-
Christina Berglund	Berglunds snabbköp	Order Administrator	0921-12 3
Hanna Moos	Blauer See Delikatessen	Sales Representative	0621-0846
Frédérique Citeaux	Blondel père et fils	Marketing Manager	88.60.15.3
Laurence Lebihan	Bon app'	Owner	91.24.45.4
Elizabeth Lincoln	Bottom-Dollar Markets	Accounting Manager	(604) 555-
Victoria Ashworth	B's Beverages	Sales Representative	(171) 555-
Patricio Simpson	Cactus Comidas para llevar	Sales Agent	(1) 135-55
Yang Wang	Chop-suey Chinese	Owner	0452-0765
Pedro Afonso	Comércio Mineiro	Sales Associate	(11) 555-7
Elizabeth Brown	Consolidated Holdings	Sales Representative	(171) 555-
Rita Müller	Die Wandernde Kuh	Sales Representative	0711-0203
Ann Devon	Eastern Connection	Sales Agent	(171) 555-
Roland Mendel	Ernst Handel	Sales Manager	7675-3425
Aria Cruz	Familia Arquibaldo	Marketing Assistant	(11) 555-9
Martine Rancé	Folies gourmandes	Assistant Sales Agent	20.16.10.1
Maria Larsson	Folk och fä HB	Owner	0695-34 6

Record: 1 of 73 No Filter Search

Figure 21.12
This datasheet displays the result set of the view with the subquery design of Figure 21.11. Data such as CompanyName and ContactName is updatable, but you can't add new records to the Customers table because the primary key field (CustomerID) isn't present.

Writing Action Queries and Stored Procedures

Data Manipulation Language (DML) commands are implemented by action queries: append, update, delete, and make-table. Access uses QueryDefs for action queries; ADP requires stored procedures or functions to support `INSERT`, `UPDATE`, `DELETE`, and `SELECT…INTO` statements. This section shows the standard syntax for each type of action query, which is identical in Access SQL and T-SQL.

Append queries use the following syntax:

```
INSERT INTO dest_table
   SELECT [ALL¦DISTINCT] select_list
   FROM source_table
  [WHERE append_criteria]
```

If you omit the `WHERE` clause, specified field values of all records of *`source_table`* are appended to *`dest_table`*. The *`source_table`* must exist and have columns that correspond to those you specify in *`select_list`*.

➔ For an example of a stored procedure that appends records, **see** "Adding Records with Append Stored Procedures," **p. XXX** *(Ch 20)*.

`UPDATE` queries use the `SET` command to assign values to individual columns:

```
UPDATE table_name
   SET column_name = value [, column_name = value[,…]]
  [WHERE update_criteria]
```

Separate multiple *`column_name = value`* entries by commas if you want to update the data in more than one field. If you omit the `WHERE` clause, the `SET` expression acts on every record of the table, which probably isn't your intention.

Access SQL and T-SQL support the ANSI SQL VALUES keyword for adding records to or updating tables the hard way (specifying the value of each column of each record). The later "Taking Advantage of Transactions in Stored Procedures" section has a T-SQL statement that uses the VALUES approach.

DELETE queries take the following form:

```
DELETE FROM table_name
  [WHERE delete_criteria]
```

If you omit the optional WHERE clause in a DELETE query, you delete all records from table_name.

→ To review creating DELETE stored procedures in the project designer, **see** "Deleting Records," **p. 900**.

Make-table queries use the following syntax:

```
SELECT [ALL¦DISTINCT] select_list
   INTO new_table
   FROM source_table
  [WHERE append_criteria]
```

To copy the original table, substitute an asterisk (*) for select_list and omit the optional WHERE clause. Data types and sizes in the new_table are the same as those of the source_table. If your SQL Server source_table has a computed column, the corresponding column in the new_table contains the computed values, not the expression used to compute the column.

→ For an example of a simple make-table stored procedure, **see** "Creating and Executing Make-Table and Update Stored Procedures" **p. 894**.

You can execute any of the preceding SQL statements directly against Access or SQL Server tables from VBA code and an ActiveX Data Objects (ADO) Connection object. Using VBA code to execute SQL statements directly, rather than designing stored procedures for action queries—or views and functions to return Recordsets—is an option for ADPs. Chapter 30, "Understanding Data Access Objects, OLE DB, and ADO," provides examples of generating and executing SQL statements with VBA code.

SPECIFYING PARAMETERS FOR CRITERIA AND UPDATE VALUES

When you design Access queries or stored procedures to update table data, you specify parameters to supply values to WHERE clause criteria and, for INSERT and UPDATE queries, field values. If you specify the data type for input parameters, Access adds a PARAMETERS declaration that precedes the SQL statement. The sequence of the parameter values in the declaration determines the order in which the Enter Parameter Value dialogs appear.

→ For more information on the AddOrders.accdb application that adds records to SQL server tables by executing SQL statements directly or with stored procedures, **see** "Exploring the AddOrders.adp Sample Project," **p. 1328**.

21

Access SQL

The Access SQL statement for a typical Access parameterized UPDATE query for the quantity field of the Order Details table is

```
PARAMETERS [Type Order Number] Long,
           [Type Product Code] Long,
           [Type New Quantity] Short;
UPDATE [Order Details]
   SET [Order Details].Quantity =
       [Enter New Quantity]
   WHERE [Order Details].OrderID =
         [Type Order Number] AND
         [Order Details].ProductID =
             [Type Product Code];
```

The semicolon at the end of the PARAMETERS declaration indicates the start of an independent SQL statement.

T-SQL uses variables to store parameter values; SQL Server identifies user variables by an @ prefix. T-SQL supports input and output parameters, and return values; this section deals only with input parameters, which are by far the most common type and the only type that Access queries support.

T-SQL

Following is an example of standard T-SQL syntax to create a parameterized UPDATE stored procedure:

```
CREATE PROCEDURE tsql_edititems
   (@OrderID int,
    @ProductID int,
    @Quantity smallint)
AS UPDATE [Order Details]
SET Quantity = @Quantity
WHERE OrderID = @OrderID AND
      ProductID = @ProductID
```

Parentheses surrounding the three parameter declarations are optional.

If you type the entire statement into the project designer's SQL pane, you receive an error when you click Verify SQL Syntax. The designer wants only the UPDATE statement with the variables. To avoid the error message, open the New Query dialog, choose Create Text Stored Procedure, and replace the SQL window's skeleton CREATE PROCEDURE statement with the preceding code.

The right side of the SET expression, = @Quantity, appears in the New Value cell of the Quantity row of the project designer's grid. The WHERE clause variables appear as = @OrderID and = @ProductID in the Criteria column. Unlike with Access parameters, you can't change the sequence or appearance of the Enter Parameter Value dialogs by rearranging the rows of the grid; the dialog to enter the UPDATE variable always opens first.

21

N O T E

When you execute the preceding UPDATE query, you receive a "The stored procedure executed successfully, but did not return records" message no matter what values you type in the three parameter dialogs (including nothing). Stored procedures that update tables should include T-SQL code to test for parameter value entry errors, especially when you execute them interactively. The "Programming Stored Procedures" topic of SQL Server Books Online has an example of a test for a missing (NULL) parameter value.

If you don't clear the Confirm Action Queries check box on the Option dialog's Edit/Find page, Access action queries display the number of rows that will be affected by execution. The Confirm Record Changes check box values don't apply to execution of T-SQL stored procedures or functions.

TAKING ADVANTAGE OF TRANSACTIONS IN STORED PROCEDURES

Unless you specify otherwise, Access automatically uses transaction processing when updating data in multiple tables with a single SQL statement. SQL Server requires explicit declaration of the beginning of the transaction and its end. When you write a T-SQL statement that makes changes to more than one table, wrap the statement with BEGIN TRAN[SACTION] and COMMIT TRAN[SACTION] statements, as illustrated by the following simple example.

T-SQL

This simple DELETE stored procedure uses a transaction to ensure that the Order Details table doesn't end up with orphan records after the parent Orders record is deleted:

```
CREATE PROCEDURE tsql_delorder
    @OrderID int
AS
BEGIN TRAN
    DELETE FROM [Order Details]
        WHERE OrderID = @OrderID
    DELETE FROM Orders
        WHERE OrderID = @OrderID
COMMIT TRAN
```

If you want to create the preceding stored procedure, choose Create Text Stored Procedure (not Design Stored Procedure) in the New Query dialog.

The following stored procedure is one of several that were used to create the NwindXL19. accdb files for Chapter 19, "Linking Access Front Ends to Access Client/Server Tables." The AddOrders.adp application adds four stored procedures to a modified copy of the NorthwindCS database, including the preceding example. The only modification to the copy of the database is the removal of the IDENTITY attribute from the OrderID field of the Orders table to permit the adding and deleting of records while adding records that have consecutive order numbers. Instead of an identity column, the procedure checks for the last OrderID value and adds 1 for the new order number.

T-SQL

This sample stored procedure adds a new order to an Orders table (which doesn't have an `identity` field) and then adds the first line item for the order to the Order Details table:

```
CREATE PROCEDURE tsql_addorder
    @CustID varchar(5),
    @EmpID int,
    @OrdDate datetime,
    @ReqDate datetime,
    @ShipVia int,
    @ShipName varchar(40),
    @ShipAddr varchar(60),
    @ShipCity varchar(15),
    @ShipReg varchar(15) = NULL,
    @ShipZIP varchar(10) = NULL,
    @ShipCtry varchar(15),

    @ProdID int,
    @Price money,
    @Quan int,
    @Disc real

AS DECLARE @OrderID int

SET NOCOUNT ON
BEGIN TRAN
    SELECT @OrderID = MAX(OrderID) FROM Orders
    SELECT @OrderID = @OrderID + 1
    INSERT Orders
        VALUES(@OrderID, @CustID, @EmpID,
          @OrdDate, @ReqDate, NULL, @ShipVia,
          NULL, @ShipName, @ShipAddr, @ShipCity,
          @ShipReg, @ShipZIP, @ShipCtry)
    INSERT [Order Details]
        (OrderID, ProductID, UnitPrice, Quantity, Discount)
        VALUES(@OrderID, @ProdID, @Price, @Quan, @Disc)
COMMIT TRAN
SET NOCOUNT OFF
IF @@error = 0
    RETURN @OrderID
ELSE
    RETURN 0
```

Don't even *think* about typing this or a similar stored procedure into the SQL pane of the project designer. The designer can't handle even moderately complex stored procedures. Instead, type the stored procedure in the window opened by the Create Text Stored Procedure selection in the project designer's New Query dialog.

Following are brief descriptions of the new T-SQL elements in the preceding example:

- The `@ShipReg varchar(15) = NULL` and `@ShipZIP varchar(10) = NULL` parameter declarations have default `NULL` values to accommodate addresses that don't have a `ShipRegion` or `PostalCode` value. Unlike Access parameters, you can assign default values to T-SQL parameters.

- The DECLARE @OrderID int statement creates an internal @OrderID variable to return the order number to the VBA subprocedure that calls the stored procedure and supplies the parameter values.

- The two SELECT statements obtain the last OrderID value and add 1 to specify the new value.

- SET NOCOUNT ON eliminates a roundtrip to the server to report the number of records affected.

- The two INSERT statements illustrate different methods of using the VALUES function. The first example doesn't include a field list, so the comma-separate list of values must correspond to the sequence of fields in the table. The second example includes a field list that defines the sequence for the following VALUES list.

- SET NOCOUNT OFF is optional, but is included here as a good stored procedure programming practice (GSPPP).

- The IF @@error conditional statement assigns the new @OrderID value to the RETURN value if the transaction commits (@@error = 0). @@error is an SQL Server system variable that returns a nonzero value when an execution error is encountered. The RETURN value is 0 if the transaction fails. Error handling is one of the primary uses for T-SQL's flow-control structures.

 This section's example appears complex, but it pales in comparison with stored procedures and SQL scripts that are used in production databases. Instnwnd.sql is a truly complex script for creating the Northwind member of the Microsoft SQL Server 2000 Sample Databases. You can download the SQL2000SampleDb.msi installer from go.microsoft.com/fwlink/?LinkId=31995, and run the installer to create a copy of Instnwnd.sql in your C:\SQL Server 2000 Sample Databases folder. Make a copy as Northwind.txt, and then open it in Notepad. Go to the end of the file, and then Page Up to view the INSERT statements that Microsoft generated to populate the Suppliers and Products tables.

> **NOTE**
>
> Use the Northwind.txt copy to prevent making inadvertent changes to Instnwnd.sql. Most of Northwind.txt's 2MB is devoted to binary data for the bitmaps stored in the OLE Object fields of the Categories and Employees tables.

WORKING WITH TABLES IN ANOTHER DATABASE

Access lets you open only one database at a time unless you write code to open another table with a VBA function or subprocedure, or specify a linked server. However, you can use Access SQL's IN predicate with a make-table, append, update, or delete query to create or modify tables in another database. ANSI SQL doesn't support the IN reserved word as a modifier for SELECT...INTO statements.

Access SQL

Following is a sample SQL statement to create a copy of Northwind.accdb's Customers table in another Access database:

```
SELECT *
    INTO Customers
    IN 'c:\Databases\Illwind.accdb'
FROM Customers
```

You receive an error message if the Customers table exists in the target database or if the path or filename is invalid.

The project designer uses SQL Server three-part names to specify tables in another database of the SQL Server instance to which you're connected. Three part names use the `Database.Schema.Table` format; for most RDBMSs, the `Schema` element is the database owner name—dbo by default for SQL Server. For example, the three-part name for the Customers table of the NorthwindCS database is `NorthwindCS.dbo.Customers`.

> **NOTE**
>
> Three-part names are a shortened version of the four-part names you use to refer to tables in a linked database. The missing fourth element is the `ServerName` prefix that you would need to add to specify a table in a linked database.

SQL Server's default database is master, which the setup program creates during the installation process. You can use the master database as a temporary destination for tables you copy by SELECT…INTO statements. However, adding user tables to the master database isn't a recommended practice.

T-SQL

Following is a simple T-SQL statement for a stored procedure that creates a copy of NorthwindCS's Customers table in the master database:

```
SELECT dbo.Customers.*
    INTO master.dbo.Customers
FROM dbo.Customers
```

You receive an error message if the Customers table exists in the target database or if you don't have CREATE TABLE permission for the target database. You also receive an error if you don't add the dbo. prefix to both instances of Customers.

After you create the table in the other database, you can create a view, function, or stored procedure with tables in both databases. To create a view between the Customers table in the master database and the Orders table in the NorthwindCS database, do the following:

21

 1. Create a new view or function in the project designer and add the Customers and Orders tables from NorthwindSQL.

2. Mark the check boxes for a couple of fields from each table—CustomerID, CompanyName, OrderID, and OrderDate for this example.

[SQL] 3. Open the SQL pane and add the prefix **master.** to each instance of dbo.Customers.

[SQL] 4. Click Check SQL Syntax to verify your T-SQL modifications. The Customers field list adds an arrow and (master) to its title bar, and the join line loses its key and ∞ symbols (see Figure 21.13).

Figure 21.13
Joins between tables in different databases don't display symbols representing relationships.

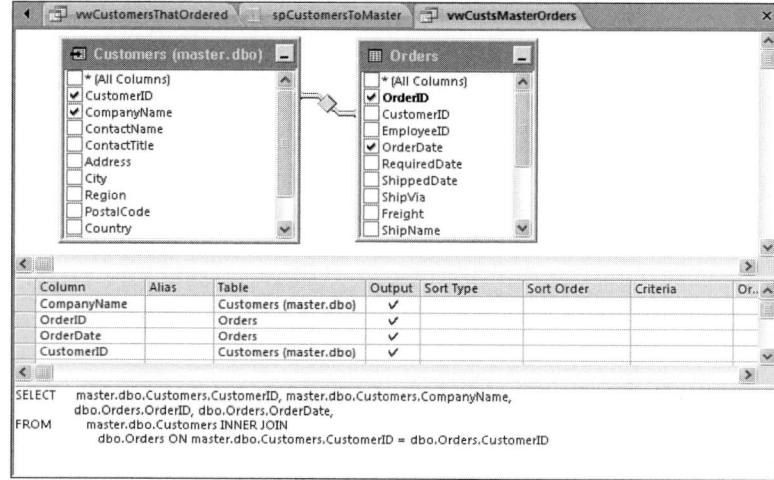

You lose the benefit of referential integrity enforcement between tables in different databases, because the relationships between tables are defined only within a single database. Views across multiple databases aren't updatable in Datasheet view, but you can write functions or stored procedures to perform INSERT, UPDATE, and DELETE operations. Production stored procedures that update tables in multiple databases require a substantial amount of additional code to protect tables against violation of referential integrity rules.

NOTE

> Transactions across linked SQL Server databases are managed by the Distributed Transaction Coordinator (DTC), which all versions of SQL Server install during the setup process. Operations on multiple databases running on a single SQL Server instance each use a single ODBC or OLE DB connection and don't employ DTC.

21

CREATING TABLES WITH ANSI-92 DDL

You can create new tables in your current database with DDL reserved words, which are identical for Access and SQL Server 2000 and later. Using SQL to create new tables is of primary interest to developers, not users, of Access applications because it's much easier to create new tables with the Access or SQL Server graphical table design tools than writing the equivalent DDL statements. In some cases, however, you might need to create tables with SQL statements. You can write Access DDL statements in the text box that opens by clicking Insert, Query Wizard, Query Design, then closing the Show Table dialog, and finally clicking SQL Specific and choosing Data Definition.

Following is a brief description of the basic ANSI SQL-92 DDL syntax for creating, altering, and dropping (deleting) tables and related objects:

- `CREATE TABLE` *table_name* `(`*field_name data_type* `[(`*field_size*`)][,` *field_name data_type*...`])` creates a new table with the fields specified by a comma-separated list. Properties of fields are space delimited, so you need to enclose entries for field names with spaces in square brackets (`[ ]`). For Access SQL, the *data_type* can be any valid Access SQL field data type, such as `TEXT(`*field_size*`)` or `INTEGER`. T-SQL accepts any valid SQL Server data, such as `int`, `datetime`, `nvarchar(`*field_size*`)`, and `text`. (The default field *data_type* for Access is `Text` and for SQL Server is `char`. The default `field_size` argument value is 50 characters for Access and SQL Server.)

> **TIP**
>
> If you don't specify a *data_type* for a field, the default values for *data_type* and *field_size* apply. You can change the default field data type and size in the Tables/ Queries page of the Options dialog for Access and ADPs.

> **NOTE**
>
> If you use the Access `TEXT` modifier without a *field_size* argument (in parentheses), Access interprets `TEXT` as the Memo field data type for conformance to SQL Server's `text` data type. Access SQL includes many new data type modifiers, such as `CHARACTER`, `VARCHAR`, `NATIONAL CHAR`, `NATIONAL CHAR VARYING`, and others for localization and Unicode preferences. The corresponding SQL Server data types are `char`, `varchar`, `nchar`, and `nvarchar`.

- `CONSTRAINT` *constraint_name* `{PRIMARY KEY¦UNIQUE¦REFERENCES` *foreign_table* `[(`*foreign_field*`)]}` establishes DRI for the table. Access and SQL Server create an index on the field name that precedes the expression. You can specify the index as the `PRIMARY KEY` or as a `UNIQUE` index. SQL Server lets you specify `[CLUSTERED¦ NONCLUSTERED]` for a `PRIMARY KEY` or `UNIQUE` index. You also can establish a relationship between the field and the field of a foreign table with the `REFERENCES` *foreign_table* `[`*foreign_field*`]` entry. (The `[`*foreign_field*`]` item is required if the *foreign_field* is not a primary key field.)

- `CHECK (`*expression*`)` creates an additional constraint that's similar to but more flexible than Access's table-level validation. The expression argument can compare values obtained from other tables by means of a `SELECT` statement.

21

- CREATE [UNIQUE] INDEX *index_name* ON *table_name* (*field_name* [ASC¦DESC][, *field_name* [ASC¦DESC], ...]) [WITH {PRIMARY¦DISALLOW NULL¦IGNORE NULL}] creates an index on one or more fields of a table. If you specify the WITH PRIMARY modifier, UNIQUE is assumed (and not required). You can only create one primary key index/constraint on a table. DISALLOW NULL prevents the addition of records with NULL values in the indexed field; IGNORE NULL doesn't index records with NULL *field_name* values.

- ALTER TABLE lets you add new fields (ADD COLUMN *field_name*...) or delete existing fields (DROP COLUMN *field_name*...).

- ALTER COLUMN *table_name* (*field_name* *data_type* [*field_size*]) lets you change the properties of a single column.

- DROP COLUMN *column_name* ON *table_name* deletes the column from a table specified by *table_name*.

- DROP INDEX *index_name* ON *table_name* deletes the index from a table specified by *table_name*.

- DROP TABLE *table_name* deletes a table from the database.

The syntax examples of the preceding list, other than DROP COLUMN, DROP INDEX, and DROP TABLE, cover only the basic syntax common to Access and SQL Server objects. The "Data Definition Language" topic under the "Microsoft Access SQL Reference" node of online help's Contents pane provides more complete syntax examples. For a full description of T-SQL's CREATE TABLE statement, search for **CREATE TABLE** in the Index pane of SQL Server Books Online.

USING SQL STATEMENTS WITH FORMS, REPORTS, AND CONTROLS

If you create many forms and reports based on queries, views, or stored procedures, the query list in your Database window can become cluttered. The clutter becomes worse as you add queries, views, or functions to populate list and combo boxes. You can use SQL queries you write or copy from the SQL dialog in place of the names of query or view objects as the data source for forms, reports, and lists. After you verify proper operation of the object whose data source you changed, delete the corresponding object from your database. You can use Access SQL or T-SQL statements for the following purposes:

- **Record Source property of forms and reports.** Substitute the SQL query text for the name of the query in the Record Source text box.

- **Row Source property in lists and drop-down combo lists on a form.** Using an SQL statement rather than a query or view object can give you greater control over the sequence of the columns in your list.

- **Value of the SQL property of a QueryDef object or the strSource argument of the OpenRecordset method in VBA code for Access databases.** You use SQL statements extensively as property and argument values when programming applications with VBA, especially for SQL pass-through queries.

- **Source property of a `DAO.Recordset` object specified as the `Recordset` property of an Access form, report, or control.** The capability to bind Access objects to `DAO.Recordset` objects was new in Access 2002.

- **Source property of an `ADODB.Recordset` object specified as the `Recordset` property of a form, report, or control.** Access 2000 introduced the capability to bind Access form and report objects to ADO Recordsets. Access 2007 ADPs can use disconnected Recordsets to minimize active connections to the database.

You can create and test your Access SQL statement in Query Design view or the project designer's SQL pane for views. You can copy unformatted Access SQL statements directly to the Clipboard. Paste text of T-SQL statements formatted by the project designer into Notepad, remove the formatting (with WordWrap on), and copy the unformatted text to the Clipboard. Paste the text into the text box for the property or into your VBA module. Then close the test query or view design without saving it.

TROUBLESHOOTING

UNEXPECTED ENTER PARAMETER DIALOGS

When I try to execute a query from my SQL statement, an Enter Parameter Value dialog appears.

You misspelled one of the table names in your `table_list`, one of the field names in your `field_list`, or both. If the Access engine's query parser can't match a table name or a field name with those specified in the FROM clause, Access assumes that the entry is a parameter and requests its value. Check the spelling of the database objects in your SQL statement. (If you misspell an SQL keyword, you usually receive a syntax error message box.)

IN THE REAL WORLD—SQL AS A SECOND LANGUAGE

It's tempting to use Access's Query Design view or the project designer to generate all SQL statements behind the scenes. Graphical QBE bypasses the need to learn *two* languages—SQL and VBA—to become a proficient Access database developer. The reality is that you ultimately must master both SQL and VBA, because the two languages are inextricably intertwined in all nontrivial Access database front ends to Access and SQL Server databases. SQL is the *lingua franca* of all relational databases, just as VBA is the common programming language of Microsoft Office, Visual Basic 6.0, Visio, and many third-party applications.

> **NOTE**
>
> SQL is the foundation for several Microsoft query-language extensions, including SHAPE syntax for generating hierarchical Recordsets and Multidimensional Expressions (MDX) for DataCubes and the PivotTable Service for online analytical processing (OLAP) with Microsoft Analysis Services (formerly OLAP Services and Decision Support Services). As more organizations adopt the Standard or Enterprise editions of SQL Server 2005, which include Analysis Services, data warehouses will become commonplace in medium-sized enterprises, and smaller firms will set up data marts.

If English is your native language, make SQL your second tongue and VBA your third. Access is an exceptionally valuable tool for mastering Access SQL and T-SQL. If your plans include becoming proficient in client/server database technology, concentrate on ADPs and T-SQL.

21

UPSIZING ACCESS APPLICATIONS TO ACCESS DATA PROJECTS

In this chapter

TAKING A HARD LOOK AT THE UPSIZING PROCESS

Upsizing an Access application to an SQL Server 2005 or SQL Server Express (SSX) back-end database and an Access data project (ADP) is a drastic operation. The Upsizing Wizard banishes all vestiges of Access data objects—Tables and QueryDefs—from your application. As a general rule, the probability of initial upsizing success is inversely proportional to the size and complexity of your .accdb-based Access application. If you've designed your initial Access applications with upsizing in mind, the likelihood of upsizing success greatly increases. It's a safe bet, however, that only a small percentage of existing Access applications were developed with ease of upsizing as a design parameter.

Following are the basic steps that the Upsizing Wizard takes when you select the New Database option in the first Wizard dialog and the Create a New Access Client/Server Application option in the fifth dialog:

- Log on to your test machine with an account that's a member of the local Administrators security group if the SQL Server instance is on the same machine. Otherwise, use a Domain Admins account.

- Create a new SQL Server database. By default, the new database is the name of the existing database with an "SQL" suffix.

- Copy the structure of Access tables to new tables in the database, and add the data to the tables.

- Add indexes to the tables.

- Add extended properties to the tables and set the values of the properties.

- Create in the Navigation pane's Queries group a view for each Access SELECT QueryDef object that doesn't have a GROUP BY clause.

- Create an inline table-valued function (TVF) for each Access SELECT QueryDef object that has a GROUP BY clause in the Queries page.

- Create an inline TVF for parameterized SELECT queries.

- Create a stored procedure for each insert, update, delete, or make-table QueryDef object in the Queries group.

- Create a new project (.adp) file with a connection to the new SQL database.

- Copy all Access forms, subforms, reports, subreports, macros, and modules in the .accdb file to the new .adp file. The Wizard makes no changes to VBA code behind forms or reports, or in modules.

Upsizing tables, queries, and Access SQL statements is subject to the limitations described in the sections later in this chapter. This chapter covers upsizing conventional single-file and front-end/back-end Access applications.

PREPARING TO UPSIZE YOUR ACCESS APPLICATIONS

There are two basic approaches to increasing the probability of a fully successful upsizing operation:

- **Trial and error**—Run the Wizard early and often to determine the scope of the additional effort necessary to upsize your Access application successfully. If you have very large tables, you can use the structure-only option to minimize upsizing time. Read the Upsizing Wizard's report, make the changes necessary to upgrade missing objects, and try again.
- **Planned migration**—Make changes to the Access tables, queries, and application objects to minimize the likelihood of upsizing problems. For example, convert your VBA code that uses Data Access Objects (DAO) to ActiveX Data Objects (ADO) that use the OLE DB data provider for Access. Thoroughly test your changes.

If your Access application is relatively simple or in the early development stage and doesn't include VBA code that has a reference to any version of DAO, the trial-and-error method might be your best choice. The most efficient upsizing method usually is a combination of the two approaches.

> **TIP**
>
> Replace all instances of `Like` expressions for date constraints in Access query WHERE clauses with `Between…And…` expressions. For example, change `Like "*/*/2007"` to `Between #1/1/2007# And #12/31/2007#`. The Wizard upsizes `Like "*/*/2007"` to `LIKE '%/%/2007'`, but the upsized query returns no rows in the project designer.

→ For more information on the LIKE problem, **see** "Access Functions and Operators Used in Place of ANSI SQL Keywords," **p. 975**.

UPSIZING WITH THE TRIAL-AND-ERROR APPROACH

An initial test of the Upsizing Wizard lets you see how much work is in store to upsize your application. For a complex Access application, the test drive might convince you to abandon a full-fledged upsizing operation and use SQL Server tables linked to your Access front end. In this case, Chapter 19, "Linking Access Front Ends to Access and Client/Server Tables," describes the quick-and-easy way to gain most of the advantages of an SQL Server back end.

If you don't have a production Access application to test and you've created the queries, forms, and reports used as examples in the preceding chapters in a copy of the Northwind.accdb sample database, you have a good starting point for determining what types of Access objects the Upsizing Wizard can handle without modification.

NOTE

If you didn't perform all the exercises, Upsize22.accdb in the \SEUA12\Chaptr22 folder of the accompanying CD-ROM contains most of the sample objects created in Chapters 5 through 19. Between…And… replaces instances of Like expressions in the Upsize22.accdb queries.

TIP

Be sure that your .accdb file is in a trusted location before starting the Upsizing Wizard. If you don't, the Security Warning dialog opens when the Wizard starts upsizing tables and a blank Access window obscures the Wizard's progress message box.

PERFORMING AN INITIAL TEST OF THE UPSIZING PROCESS

To give the Upsizing Wizard a test drive with a new SQL Server database, do the following:

1. Create a backup copy of the database you plan to upsize, unless you're using the Upsize22.accdb sample database. You can upsize either a single-file or split (front-end/back-end) application. The upsizing process doesn't affect the source .accdb file under ordinary circumstances, but there's always the chance of an extraordinary occurrence.

2. If you've encrypted the database with a password, click the Database Tools tab and the Decrypt Database button to return it to the unencrypted state before upsizing. You must open the database in single-user mode and supply the encryption password to do this.

3. If any Access database table or query objects are hidden, right-click the item in the Navigation pane and choose Properties to open the *TableName* or *ObjectName* Properties dialog's General page. Clear the Attributes, Hidden check box and then click OK.

4. Click the Database Tools ribbon's SQL Server button to start the Upsizing Wizard. In the Wizard's first dialog, accept the default Create New Database option and then click Next.

5. In the second Wizard dialog, open the list box and select or type the computer name of the machine running SQL Server 2005 Developer Edition or higher, or the *ComputerName/InstanceName* for SSX. The default SSX *InstanceName* is SQLEXPRESS.

6. If you're logged on as a Windows user having administrative privileges for the destination SQL Server or SSX instance, mark the Use Trusted Connection check box. Alternatively, use sa or your assigned SQL Server administrator login ID and type your password, if the server uses SQL Server security. By default, SQL Server 2005 and SSX require a trusted connection, which uses Windows integrated security for authentication.

7. Accept or change the name of the new SQL Server database. This example uses **UpsizeSQL** as the database name (see Figure 22.1). Click Next.

Figure 22.1
Select the computer name of the computer running SQL Server (with SQLEXPRESS as the instance name for SSX), the type of authentication (integrated Windows or SQL Server), and the name of the new SQL Server database in the second Wizard dialog.

Figure 22.2
Select all Access tables for upsizing, unless you have a good reason to do otherwise.

8. In the third Wizard dialog, click the >> button to move all tables from the Available Tables list to the Export to SQL Server list (see Figure 22.2). The HRActions table and all tables with a tbl prefix are sample tables created in earlier chapters. Click Next.

9. In the fourth dialog, accept the defaults for table attributes (all check boxes marked), accept the default Use DRI (declarative referential integrity) option, and select "Yes, let the Wizard decide" in the Add Timestamp Fields to Tables list. Unless you have tables with 250,000 or more records, don't mark the Only Create the Table Structure; Don't Upsize Any Data check box (see Figure 22.3). Click Next.

22

Figure 22.3
Marking all attribute check boxes is satisfactory for most upsizing operations. It's a good practice to let the Wizard add `timestamp` fields where necessary to upsized tables.

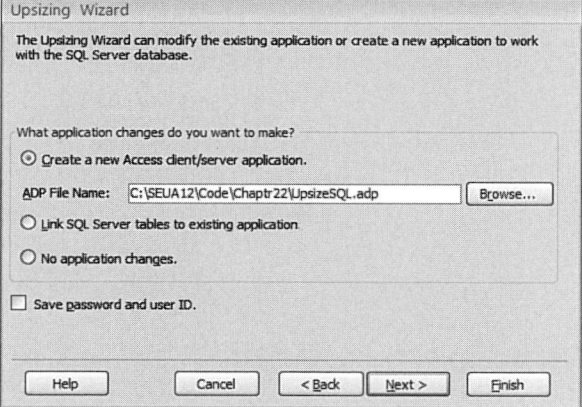

10. The fifth dialog offers the choices of creating a new project or linking SQL Server tables to the Access application. Select the Create a New Access Client/Server Application option. The Wizard proposes to name the front-end file *AccdbName*CS.adp. For this initial example, the name is **UpsizeSQL.adp** (see Figure 22.4). Click Next.

Figure 22.4
Specify a new Access project and give the .adp file a name in the fifth Wizard dialog.

TIP

Clear the Save Password and User ID box if you want to maintain the security of your back-end database. Default integrated Windows security lets you control database access by the user's group membership in a Windows Server 2003+. If you specified SQL Server security in step 5, users must type their preassigned login ID and password to connect to the database.

→ To learn more about granting users access to your upsized database, **see** "Securing Upsized Projects and Their Data," **p. 997**.

11. Accept the Open the New ADP File option and click Finish to start the upsizing operation.

The Wizard begins the upsizing process and displays a progress dialog (see Figure 22.5).

Figure 22.5
The progress dialog briefly describes each Upsizing Wizard operation. The width of the progress bar is based on the number of objects upsized, not the time required for upsizing.

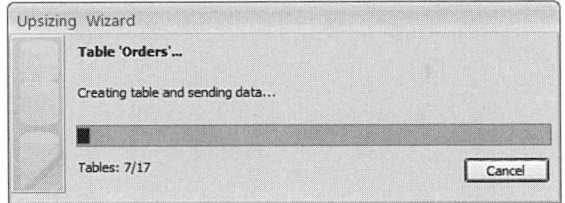

NOTE

The Wizard reports that it's adding triggers to the tables, regardless of whether you specify the default Use DRI (declarative referential integrity) or Use Triggers option in the fourth Wizard dialog.

After the Wizard copies the table structures, data, and extended properties, you receive a series of error messages when the Wizard starts upsizing queries. Figure 22.6 illustrates a typical query error message, which occurs because the Wizard can't handle VBA expressions in SQL statements. Click OK after reading each message to complete the upsizing process.

Figure 22.6
Several queries include the VBA Format function to format number data type values as currency, which opens an Errors from Server message similar to that shown here. SQL Server doesn't have a Format function, nor does it support most VBA expressions in query strings.

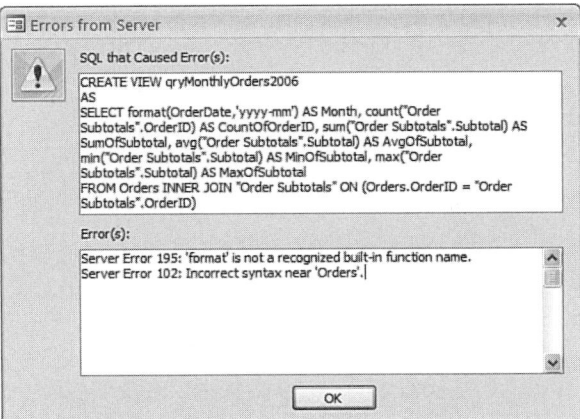

When the Wizard completes copying forms and other application objects, which is a much slower process than copying other objects (except large tables), the Upsizing Wizard Report opens in the Print Preview window. Upsizing Upsize22.accdb takes about five minutes on a moderately fast (2.6GHz Pentium 4) computer. The auto-generated report for the initial upsizing of Upsize22.accdb is 43 pages, of which pages 32–43 contain results for queries. (Your page numbers might differ.) Figure 22.7 illustrates results for two successfully upsized queries. The Wizard uses SQL Server quoted ("...") identifiers for object names with spaces instead of the more conventional square bracket ([...]) pairs.

> **TIP**
>
> You lose the Upsizing Wizard Report if you click the Close Print Preview button without saving the report explicitly. To save it, click the Data group's PDF or XPS button to open the Publish as PDF or XPS dialog, select the type of document to save (*.pdf or *.xps) in the Files of Type list, and then click Publish. By default, these reports publish to Access's default database folder, which you specify on the Popular page of the Access Options dialog, not in the working folder that contains the source .accdb or destination .adp file.

Figure 22.7
Report elements for a simple SELECT query upsized to an inline, table-valued function and a UNION query upsized to a stored procedure.

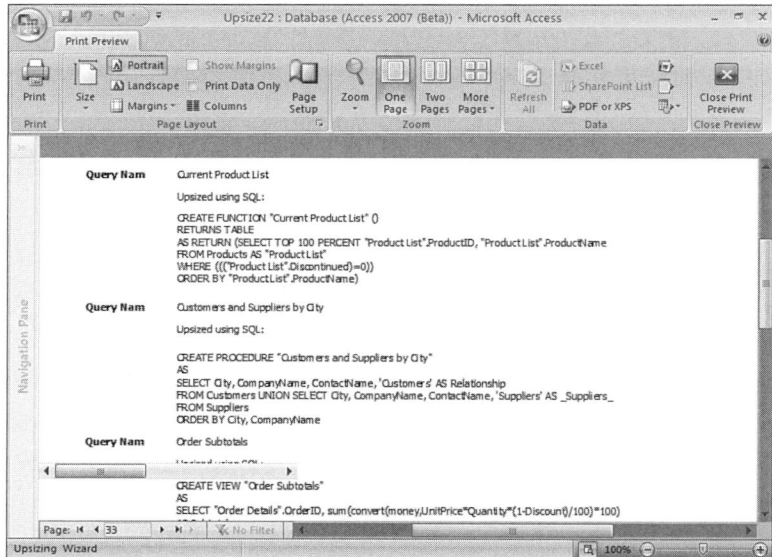

Following are the Upsizing Wizard's limitations and initial workarounds, where available, based on the report for the initial test run with Upsize22.accdb:

- The Wizard doesn't remove Access SQL's DISTINCTROW reserved word or convert it to T-SQL's DISTINCT modifier. Access 95 and earlier automatically added DISTINCTROW to all SELECT queries, so this problem is likely to occur only with seasoned Access applications. The "Access's DISTINCTROW and ANSI SQL's DISTINCT Keywords" section later in the chapter compares the difference in effect of these two modifiers on query result sets. Changing DISTINCTROW to DISTINCT solves this problem, but might have side effects, such as making the query result set not updatable. You seldom need the DISTINCT modifier; if you do, add it to the upsized query when you test it.

- The Wizard won't upsize Access crosstab queries, because SQL Server 2005 doesn't support Access's SQL's TRANSFORM keyword and doesn't use the same syntax for the common PIVOT keyword. The workaround for this problem isn't simple, as demonstrated in the later "Emulating Access Crosstab Queries with T-SQL" section.

- The Wizard bails out when it encounters VBA reserved words, such as **Format**, for which T-SQL has no direct equivalent. The qry2006OrdersByCountryPT, qryMonthlyOrders2006, qryMonthlyOrdersParam, qryMonthlySales2006, qryOrderAmount, and Sales by Year queries use the **Format** function. The initial workaround for these queries is to remove the function and its format definition string to verify that the unformatted query is upsizable. If WHERE, GROUP BY, or ORDER BY clauses use the **Format** function, the query result set won't be valid.

→ For some examples of the use of T-SQL functions to replace the **Format** function, **see** "Modifying the Upsized qry2006SalesChart View," **p. 987**.

- Nested queries fail to upsize when the source query (also called the *outer query*) won't upsize. Fixing the outer query solves the problem, if the nested (inner) query that's specified in the FROM clause can be upsized.

- Access SELECT and action queries that use the IN predicate to specify another .accdb file won't upsize. The four qryOakmont… queries can't be upsized, because the IN predicate specifies the Oakmont.accdb file. The only workaround is to upsize the Oakmont.accdb database and then write queries that use three-part SQL Server names to specify tables in the OakmontSQL database.

→ For more information on three-part names, **see** "Working with Tables in Another Database," **p. 940**.

- Action queries with parameters don't upsize. SELECT queries with parameters upsize to inline, table-valued functions with parameters. Parameterized SELECT queries with spaces in the parameter names, such as qryStateMailList, don't upsize.

→ To review inline functions that use parameters, **see** "Creating a Parameterized Table-Returning Function," **p. 890**.

- The Wizard fails to upsize queries with column alias names that are SQL Server reserved words. For example, OrderDate AS Date or CostPerUnit AS Cost as a member of a field list prevents upsizing the query. In most cases, surrounding reserved words with […] delimiters—as in OrderDate AS [Date]—solves the problem.

- The Wizard won't upsize queries that aren't executable because of a table- or field-naming error. The tblOrders table doesn't have Ship… fields, so upsizing qryUQtblOrders1 fails. The SalesOrders query fails because Table1 is missing. Delete test queries or action queries you ran once to modify tables.

Modifying complex queries to work around upsizing problems is a tedious process, especially if you have a large number of queries that fail. Be sure to test each query whose Access SQL statement you modify to verify the changes you make. Deleting crosstab and other queries that the Wizard can't upsize is optional.

RUNNING A SECOND UPSIZING PASS

 After performing the first set of query fixes and temporary workarounds, you must run the Upsizing Wizard again. The sample Upsize22A.accdb file has most of the fixes described in the preceding section.

To make a second upsizing pass from scratch, do the following:

1. Close all open objects in the new .adp file except the Database window.

2. Click the Office button, choose Ser<u>v</u>er, and click <u>D</u>rop SQL Database. A message box asks you to confirm dropping the current database (UpsizeSQL for this example).

3. Click Yes to drop SQL Server's reference to the database files and delete the corresponding .mdf and .ldf files. Your database disconnects, and the Tables and Queries pages of the Database window empty.

4. Close the project, and use Windows Explorer to delete the .adp file you created (UpsizeSQL.adp for this initial example).

5. Open Upsize22A.accdb (or whatever file you're upsizing) and repeat steps 4–11 of the earlier "Performing an Initial Test of the Upsizing Process" section.

Table 22.1 is a scorecard for the Upsizing Wizard's successive passes on the Upsize22.accdb and Upsize22A.accdb queries. The numbers in the Pass 2 column reflect modification or deletion after the first pass of queries that the Wizard won't attempt to upsize. (Upsize22a.accdb generates the Pass 2 data).

TABLE 22.1   SUCCESS AND FAILURE OF UPSIZE22.ACCDB QUERIES IN TWO TRIALS WITH THE UPSIZING WIZARD

Query Upsize Status	Pass 1	Pass 2
Successfully upsized	29	46
Failed (DISTINCTROW)	13	0
Failed (PIVOT...TRANSFORM)	5	0
Failed (VBA **Format** function)	5	0
Failed (missing source query)	4	0
Failed (tables in another database)	4	0
Failed (missing field or table)	2	0
Failed (mishandled parameter)	1	0
Failed (other reasons)	1	2

At this point, only two of Upsize22.accdb's queries fail to upsize, so it's not an efficient use of your time to attempt to modify the Access SQL statements and rerun the Upsizing Wizard. The better approach is to correct the remaining problems in the new project, UpsizeSQL.adp, which is used in the following examples.

CORRECTING WIZARD ERRORS

The first of the two queries that fail to upsize for "other reasons" is qry2006OrderDataPT. This nested query, which requires the Order Details Extended query as a data source, is intended as the data source for a PivotTable to display quarterly or monthly orders by employee and category. Figure 22.8 shows the upsizing report entry for the query. This error relates to the decision by the Upsizing Wizard's developers to upsize Access queries with ORDER BY clauses to inline, table-valued functions instead of views with the TOP 100 PERCENT or TOP 2147483647 modifier. The Access Order Details Extended query upsizes to a view, but the Wizard doesn't handle references to functions correctly.

Figure 22.8
Failure to upsize the qry2006OrderDatePT query results from the `[Order Details Extended]()` `"Order Details Extended"` frag-ments.

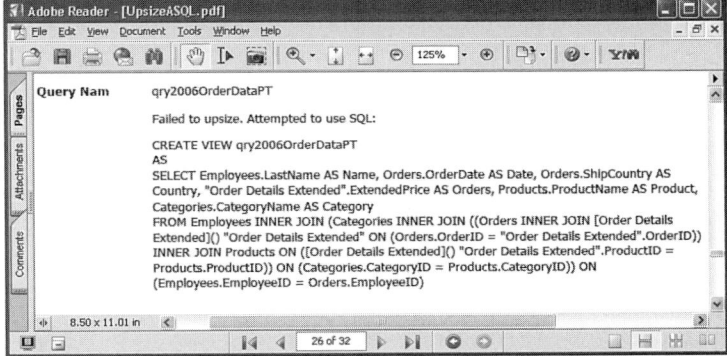

Access SQL
The Access SQL version of the qry2006OrderDataPT query is

```
SELECT Employees.LastName AS Name,
       Orders.OrderDate AS [Date],
       Orders.ShipCountry AS Country,
       [Order Details Extended].ExtendedPrice AS Orders,
       Products.ProductName AS Product,
       Categories.CategoryName AS Category
FROM Employees
   INNER JOIN (Categories
      INNER JOIN ((Orders
         INNER JOIN [Order Details Extended]
         ON Orders.OrderID =
             [Order Details Extended].OrderID)
            INNER JOIN Products
            ON [Order Details Extended].ProductID =
                Products.ProductID)
      ON Categories.CategoryID = Products.CategoryID)
         ON Employees.EmployeeID = Orders.EmployeeID;
```

The Wizard erroneously translates the FROM clause of the Access SQL statement to

```
FROM Employees
    INNER JOIN (Categories
        INNER JOIN ((Orders
            INNER JOIN [Order Details Extended]()
                "Order Details Extended"
            ON Orders.OrderID =
                "Order Details Extended".OrderID)
            INNER JOIN Products ON [Order Details Extended]()
            "Order Details Extended".ProductID =
                Products.ProductID)
    ON Categories.CategoryID = Products.CategoryID)
        ON Employees.EmployeeID = Orders.EmployeeID
```

The error is mixing delimiter types in the statement that calls the Order Details Extended function. Deleting both added [Order Details Extended]() function calls solves the problem if Order Details Extended is a view. The nested query failed to upsize, so you can't just edit the T-SQL for the query. Following is what you must do to fix the problem:

- Replace the Order Details Extended function with a view. Copy the T-SQL statement of the function to the Clipboard, delete the function, create a new view in the project designer, and paste the T-SQL statement in the view's SQL pane. The nested query didn't upsize, so you must copy the original Access SQL statement to the Clipboard, create a new view, and paste the text to the SQL pane of the view.

T-SQL

The T-SQL for the view of the Order Details Extended query is

```
SELECT TOP 2147483647 dbo.[Order Details].OrderID,
    dbo.[Order Details].ProductID,
    dbo.Products.ProductName,
    dbo.[Order Details].UnitPrice,
    dbo.[Order Details].Quantity,
    dbo.[Order Details].Discount,
    CONVERT(money, (dbo.[Order Details].UnitPrice *
        dbo.[Order Details].Quantity) *
        (1 - dbo.[Order Details].Discount) / 100) *
        100 AS ExtendedPrice
FROM dbo.Products
    INNER JOIN dbo.[Order Details]
        ON dbo.Products.ProductID =
            dbo.[Order Details].ProductID
ORDER BY dbo.[Order Details].OrderID
```

You can remove / 100 and * 100 without affecting the values in the ExtendedPrice column.

- Copy the original Access SQL statement to the Clipboard, create a new view, and paste the text to the SQL pane of the view.

→ For more information on the use of the TOP 2147483647 operator, **see** "Exploring SQL Server Views," **p. 884**.

Alternatively, you can use the existing function as the inner query and modify the outer query. Add the function name with empty parentheses to the INNER JOIN element as follows: INNER JOIN **[Order Details Extended]()** [Order Details Extended]. (Square bracket delimiters work if you don't combine them with double-quote delimiters.) If you use AS to explicitly declare the alias, clicking Check SQL Syntax removes it.

The better of the two preceding options is to change the function to a view, because multiple nested queries or the Record Source property value of forms and reports might depend on the source query.

TIP

> If you change a function to a view, test all nested queries that rely on the changed view or function. If the outer query expects a function but opens a view (or vice versa), you receive an error message and must delete (or add) empty parentheses.

The qryCTWizSource view illustrates the importance of testing each successfully upsized object in the project designer to verify the correctness of column names and data values. The qryCTWizSource view upsizes, but contains an upsizing error—in this case a spurious alias for the ProductID column. Following is the offending SELECT statement's column list with the bad alias in bold:

```
SELECT dbo.Orders.OrderDate,
    [Order Details Extended].ProductID
      AS [_Order Details Extended.ProductID_],
    [Order Details Extended].ProductName,
    [Order Details Extended].ExtendedPrice
```

Remove the alias, and the view executes correctly.

CONFORMING COMPUTED COLUMNS TO THE ANSI SQL STANDARD

Access SQL lets you use the value of one computed column as a source for another computed column. It's common to use such compound-computed columns to store values that include sales or value-added taxes.

Access SQL
The following sample field list with multiple aliased computed columns works when you use Access SQL but fails with T-SQL:

```
SELECT OrderTotal * 0.06 AS StateTax,
    OrderTotal * 0.01 AS CountyTax,
    OrderTotal * 0.005 AS CityTax,
    StateTax + CountyTax +
      CityTax AS Taxes,
    OrderTotal + Taxes AS InvoiceTotal
FROM Orders
```

The ANSI-92 SQL standard requires that each member of the SELECT column list must have an unambiguous reference to a field of a table specified in the FROM clause. The computed Taxes column of the preceding example fails this test, because it's defined only in the query and not in the table, so SQL Server's query parser won't compile the statement.

Figure 22.9 shows the error message the query parser returns when the Upsizing Wizard encounters the Access qryOrderAmount query, which computes freight cost as a percentage of the order amount for each order. (The **Format**() function to display percent was removed from the query prior to upsizing.) The Access query used the VBA **CCur** function to convert the Access data type of the Amount from Double to Currency; the Wizard substituted the T-SQL CAST(*float expression*) AS money function.

Figure 22.9
The qryOrderAmount query fails to upsize to a function, because the FreightPct column is dependent on the computed Amount column.

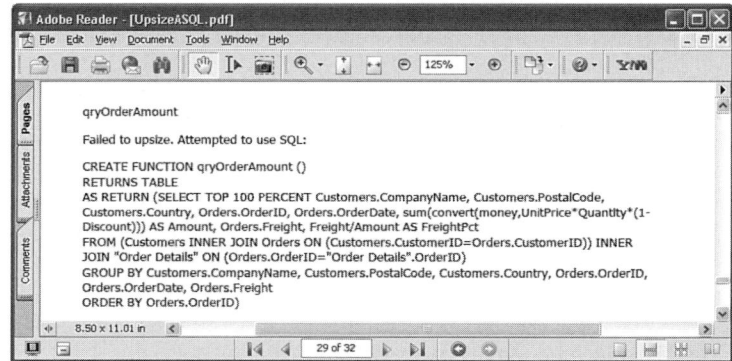

Access SQL

The Access SQL statement for the qryOrderAmount query is

```
SELECT Customers.CompanyName,
       Customers.PostalCode, Customers.Country,
       Orders.OrderID, Orders.OrderDate,
       Sum(CCur([UnitPrice]*[Quantity]*
          (1-[Discount]))) AS Amount,
       Orders.Freight, [Freight]/[Amount] AS FreightPct
FROM (Customers
       INNER JOIN Orders
          ON Customers.CustomerID = Orders.CustomerID)
       INNER JOIN [Order Details]
          ON Orders.OrderID = [Order Details].OrderID
GROUP BY Customers.CompanyName, Customers.PostalCode,
    Customers.Country, Orders.OrderID,
    Orders.OrderDate, Orders.Freight
ORDER BY Orders.OrderID;
```

The column definition that conflicts with ANSI SQL is in bold type.

You can correct the problem in the source query by substituting the Sum…AS Amount aggregate statement for the [Amount] value in the second computed column. If you correct the source query, you must rerun the Upsizing Wizard. It's faster to create a new view in the project designer by doing the following:

1. Copy the Access SQL statement of the source query to the Clipboard.

2. Create a new view in the upsized project, click the SQL button, and paste the statement to the SQL pane.

3. Substitute the T-SQL CONVERT or CAST function for VBA type conversion statements, if they are used in value expressions. For this example, the CAST(*Expression* AS money) function substitutes for the VBA **cCur**(*Expression*) function.

4. Temporarily remove the element of the column definition that prevents compiling the view (/[Amount] for this example). Click Check SQL Syntax to verify your changes. The project designer automatically adds TOP 100 PERCENT to accommodate the ORDER BY clause, which you must change to TOP 2147483647 (see Figure 22.10).

Figure 22.10
The first step in conforming an Access SQL query with computed column values based on aliased columns is to substitute T-SQL functions for unsupported VBA functions and test the result without the offending aliased value.

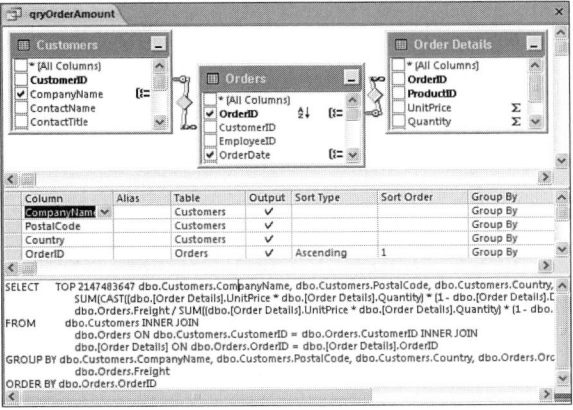

5. Substitute the expression of the calculated column for the alias name you deleted. For this example, / SUM((dbo.[Order Details].UnitPrice * dbo.[Order Details].Quantity) * (1 - dbo.[Order Details].Discount)) substitutes for /[Amount]. The CAST function isn't required here because the column value is a decimal fraction, not a monetary amount.

T-SQL

The final T-SQL statement for the qryOrderAmount view is

```
SELECT TOP 2147483647 dbo.Customers.CompanyName,
    dbo.Customers.PostalCode, dbo.Customers.Country,
    dbo.Orders.OrderID, dbo.Orders.OrderDate,
    SUM(CAST((dbo.[Order Details].UnitPrice *
      dbo.[Order Details].Quantity) *
     (1 - dbo.[Order Details].Discount) AS money)) AS Amount,
    dbo.Orders.Freight,
    dbo.Orders.Freight /
      SUM((dbo.[Order Details].UnitPrice *
      dbo.[Order Details].Quantity) *
     (1 - dbo.[Order Details].Discount)) AS FreightPct
FROM dbo.Customers
    INNER JOIN dbo.Orders
      ON dbo.Customers.CustomerID =
          dbo.Orders.CustomerID
    INNER JOIN dbo.[Order Details]
      ON dbo.Orders.OrderID =
          dbo.[Order Details].OrderID
GROUP BY dbo.Customers.CompanyName,
    dbo.Customers.PostalCode, dbo.Customers.Country,
    dbo.Orders.OrderID, dbo.Orders.OrderDate,
    dbo.Orders.Freight
ORDER BY dbo.Orders.OrderID
```

6. Verify your changes, and save the view with the original query name (**qryOrderAmount** for this example).

7. Run the view and verify that the result set is identical to that of the original Access query. In this case, the FreightPct column values are unformatted decimal fractions, not the desired percentage values.

8. To change the format of the FreightPct column, right-click anywhere in the project designer window and choose Properties to open the Properties dialog for the view. Click the Columns tab, select FreightPct from the Column Name list, and select Percent from the Format list (see Figure 22.11). Extended property values apply only to Access objects, such as datasheets.

9. Close the Properties dialog, save the change to the view, and rerun the view. Figure 22.12 shows the resulting datasheet with the column sequence rearranged to match that of the column list.

> **NOTE**
>
> Access saves column widths and other datasheet properties you change in Datasheet view, but doesn't save changes you make to the sequence of columns. When you close and reopen the view, the column sequence reverts to the original sequence.

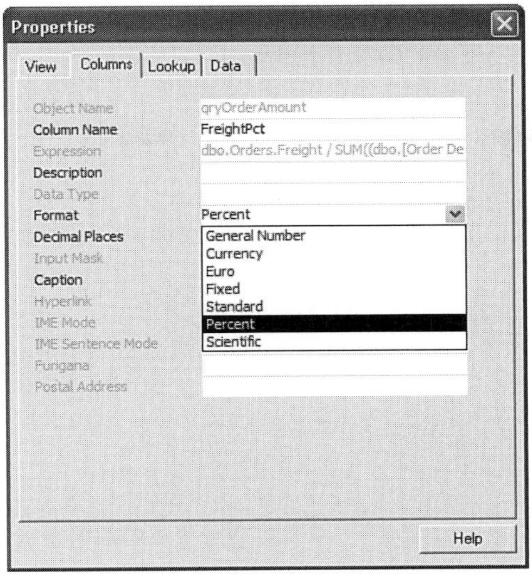

Figure 22.11 Set the extended Format property value of columns you want to display as percentages in Datasheet view. Format property values override the default display of SQL Server formatted data types, such as `money`, `smallmoney`, and `datetime`.

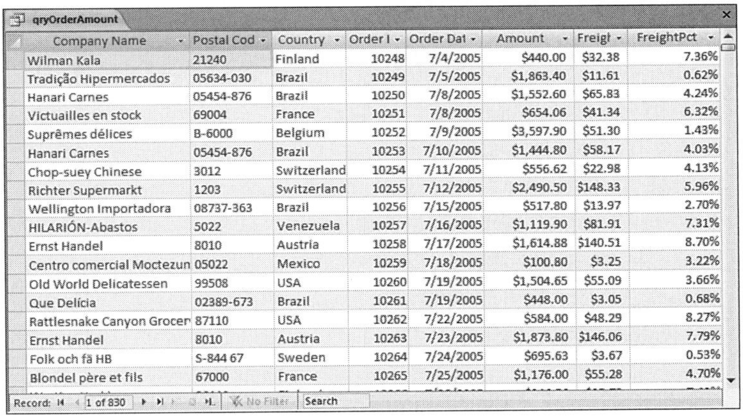

qryOrderAmount

Company Name	Postal Cod	Country	Order I	Order Dat	Amount	Freigl	FreightPct
Wilman Kala	21240	Finland	10248	7/4/2005	$440.00	$32.38	7.36%
Tradição Hipermercados	05634-030	Brazil	10249	7/5/2005	$1,863.40	$11.61	0.62%
Hanari Carnes	05454-876	Brazil	10250	7/8/2005	$1,552.60	$65.83	4.24%
Victuailles en stock	69004	France	10251	7/8/2005	$654.06	$41.34	6.32%
Suprêmes délices	B-6000	Belgium	10252	7/9/2005	$3,597.90	$51.30	1.43%
Hanari Carnes	05454-876	Brazil	10253	7/10/2005	$1,444.80	$58.17	4.03%
Chop-suey Chinese	3012	Switzerland	10254	7/11/2005	$556.62	$22.98	4.13%
Richter Supermarkt	1203	Switzerland	10255	7/12/2005	$2,490.50	$148.33	5.96%
Wellington Importadora	08737-363	Brazil	10256	7/15/2005	$517.80	$13.97	2.70%
HILARIÓN-Abastos	5022	Venezuela	10257	7/16/2005	$1,119.90	$81.91	7.31%
Ernst Handel	8010	Austria	10258	7/17/2005	$1,614.88	$140.51	8.70%
Centro comercial Moctezun	05022	Mexico	10259	7/18/2005	$100.80	$3.25	3.22%
Old World Delicatessen	99508	USA	10260	7/19/2005	$1,504.65	$55.09	3.66%
Que Delícia	02389-673	Brazil	10261	7/19/2005	$448.00	$3.05	0.68%
Rattlesnake Canyon Grocer	87110	USA	10262	7/22/2005	$584.00	$48.29	8.27%
Ernst Handel	8010	Austria	10263	7/23/2005	$1,873.80	$146.06	7.79%
Folk och fä HB	S-844 67	Sweden	10264	7/24/2005	$695.63	$3.67	0.53%
Blondel père et fils	67000	France	10265	7/25/2005	$1,176.00	$55.28	4.70%

Record: 1 of 830 No Filter Search

Figure 22.12 Datasheet view of the upsized qryOrderAmount query confirms that it's identical to the result set of the original Access version.

TIP

To force the datasheet column sequence to conform to that of the column list, create a stored procedure instead of a view. You can quickly create the stored procedure version of a view by copying the view's T-SQL statement and pasting it into the SQL pane of a new stored procedure.

22

DEALING WITH FUNCTIONS THAT REFER TO VALUES OF ACCESS CONTROL OBJECTS AND OTHER OBSCURE ISSUES

Access queries accept values returned by Access objects, such as bound text, combo, and list boxes. For example, the Invoices Filter query uses the value of the OrdersID text box of the Orders form as the WHERE clause criterion to filter the Invoices query.

Dealing with the Invoices Filter demonstrates three important rules for testing upsized projects:

- **Don't trust the Wizard**—Despite the known inability of the Wizard to upsize Access queries that refer to Access object values, the Wizard attempts to do so and creates inoperable functions or stored procedures in the SQL Server database. Compare the execution behavior of every upsized query with its Access counterpart in the source .accdb.

- **Find and test each Access object that relies on an upsized query**—If you have a large number of application objects, this process is challenging. Take advantage of the Object Dependencies task pane to find references to the query.

> **TIP**
>
> Alternatively, export a Database Documenter report to an .rtf or .txt file, and use the Find feature of Word or your text editor to locate references to specific query names.

- **Verify whether query upsizing issues are the source of apparent form or report malfunction**—This example demonstrates that the upsized Invoices Filter and Invoices queries require you to modify the Orders form and the associated Invoice report.

→ To review use of the Database Documenter, **see** "Generating a Data Dictionary with the Database Documenter," **p. 259**.

This section addresses upsizing a specific set of objects, but the process described typifies the hurdles you face when upsizing even a relatively simple set of interdependent database and application objects.

Access SQL

The Access SQL statement for the Invoices Filter query (after changing DISTINCTROW to DISTINCT) is

```
SELECT DISTINCT Invoices.*
FROM Invoices
WHERE (((Invoices.OrderID)=
    Forms!Orders![OrderID]));
```

T-SQL

The Upsizing Wizard treats the `Forms!Orders![OrderID]` element of the `WHERE` clause as a conventional input parameter:

```
SELECT DISTINCT dbo.Invoices.*
FROM dbo.Invoices
WHERE (OrderID = @Forms_Orders__OrderID_)
```

The Wizard replaces Access's bang (!) object separator and square bracket ([ ]) delimiters with underscores (_), so there are two underscores between Orders and OrderID, and another underscore following OrderID. The parameter naming problem is moot for this example, because a parameterized function won't work in the context by which it's called in the Orders form.

SPELUNKING APPLICATION OBJECTS FOR QUERY REFERENCES

It's not easy to determine how the Orders form employs the Invoices Filter query, because it doesn't—and shouldn't—appear as a value of the Filter property in the Data page of the Properties dialog for the Orders form or Orders subform. The Print Invoice button of the Orders form executes a VBA event handler, `PrintInvoice_Click`, to print an invoice for the currently selected order; event-handling code calls the Invoices Filter. Clicking the Print Invoice button opens a message that states the following:

The multi-part identifier "Customers.CompanyName" could not be bound

The reference to the Invoices Filter is in the VBA code behind the Orders form. Following is the code for the `PrintInvoice_Click` event handler:

```
Sub PrintInvoice_Click()
' This code created by Command Button Wizard.
On Error GoTo Err_PrintInvoice_Click

    Dim strDocName As String

    strDocName = "Invoice"
    ' Print Invoice report, using Invoices Filter query to print
    ' invoice for current order.
    DoCmd.OpenReport strDocName, acViewNormal, "Invoices Filter"

Exit_PrintInvoice_Click:
  Exit Sub

Err_PrintInvoice_Click:
    ' If action was cancelled by the user,
    ' don't display an error message.
    Const conErrDoCmdCancelled = 2501
    If (Err = conErrDoCmdCancelled) Then
      Resume Exit_PrintInvoice_Click
    Else
      MsgBox Err.Description
      Resume Exit_PrintInvoice_Click
    End If
End Sub
```

22

NOTE

> Working with VBA code is the subject of Part VII of this book, "Programming and Converting Access Applications," so including code examples at this point might appear to be premature. If you're considering upgrading existing Access applications to SQL Server, however, it's a reasonable assumption that you have at least some familiarity with VBA.

The `DoCmd.OpenReport strDocName, acViewNormal, "Invoices Filter"` instruction opens the Invoice report and applies the Invoices Filter to the report before printing. The data source for the Invoice report is the Access Invoices query, which the Wizard has upsized to an inoperative view. Before attempting to change the event-handler code to print a single invoice, however, test the report to determine whether it works with the T-SQL view. Not surprisingly, it doesn't work, but the incorrectly upsized Invoices Filter isn't the culprit.

CORRECTING DUPLICATE COLUMN NAMES IN VIEWS

To detect the source of the "column prefix" problem and correct it, do the following:

1. In the Navigation Pane's Reports group, double-click the Invoice report. You receive the "multipart identifier" error message, which indicates the problem is related to the upsized Invoices query.

   TIP

   > Unlike Access queries, SQL Server views and functions don't support table prefixes to resolve ambiguous references to columns having the same name. T-SQL doesn't permit duplication of column names in views or functions, so it aliases a duplicate name with a numeric suffix.

2. Change to Report Design view, and find the controls bound to duplicate column names. The `CompanyName` field is common to the Customers and Shippers tables. Views don't support table names, so delete the `Customers.` and `Shippers.` prefixes from the text boxes adjacent to the Bill To and Ship Via labels.

3. Open the Invoices view in Design view to find the aliased `CompanyName` field, which is associated with the Shippers table. Change the `CompanyName1` alias to the more descriptive **ShipperName** (see Figure 22.13). Save your change.

   TIP

   > Don't confuse captions with aliases. Captions are extended properties; aliases appear in the SQL SELECT statement's field list. The Wizard has upsized Access Caption property values to extended properties of the view, so Company Name appears as the caption for both the CompanyName and ShipperName columns. To avoid Datasheet view confusion, open the Properties dialog for the query, change the Caption property value of the column to **Shipper Name**, and save the change.

Figure 22.13
T-SQL views require unique column names, so the Wizard generates an alias for duplicate column names in the SELECT list. Changing the CompanyName1 alias to ShipperName clarifies the view's output.

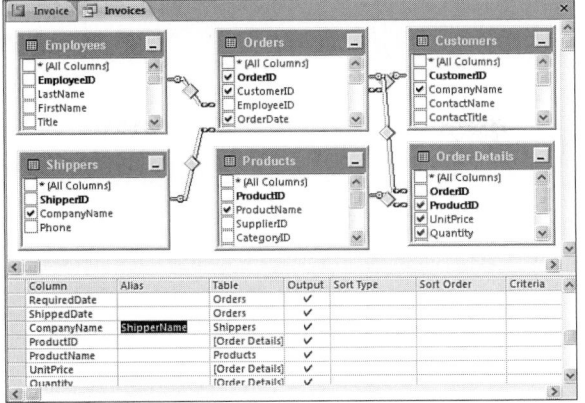

4. Return to the Invoice report and change the name of the CompanyName text box under the ShipVia label from CompanyName to **ShipperName** (see Figure 22.14).

Figure 22.14
Changing the alias of a column of a view requires a corre-sponding change to the name of all appli-cation objects that are bound to the column.

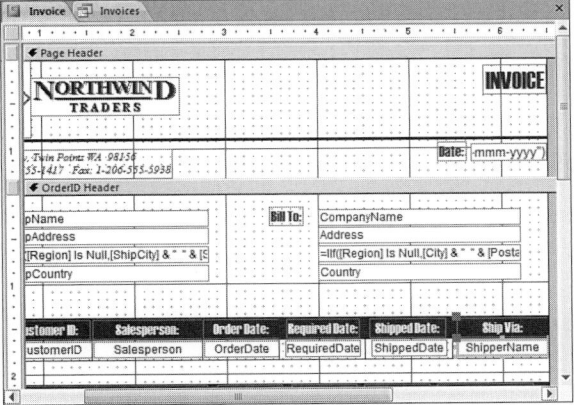

5. Change to Print Preview to verify that your changes work properly (see Figure 22.15). Close the Invoices report and save the changes.

6. Reopen the Orders form, if you closed it, and click the Print Invoices button. Be pre-pared to quickly click the Cancel button, because this operation now prints an invoice for every order.

Figure 22.15
Opening the Invoice report in Print Preview demonstrates that your changes to the report and its view data source correct the initial problem.

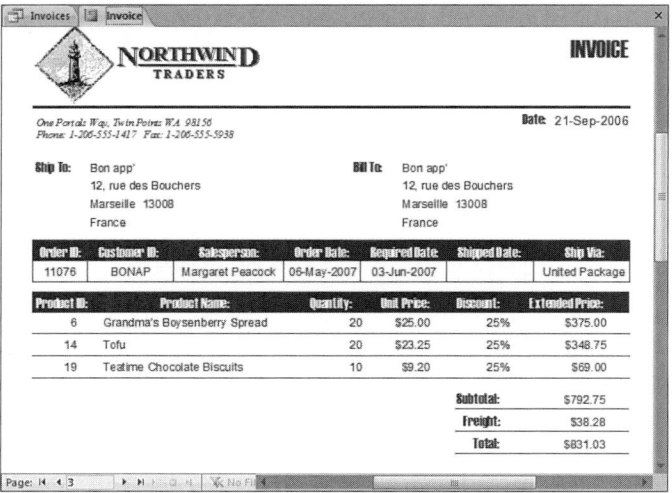

> **NOTE**
>
> Printing every invoice instead of printing no invoice or displaying an error message is unexpected behavior. No argument value is passed as a parameter to the Invoices Filter function, so you would expect the Enter Parameter Value dialog to appear. All invoices are printed because the `DoCmd.OpenReport` method disregards the filter if it can't open it, instead of displaying an error message.

REMOVING REFERENCES TO THE INVOICES FILTER FROM THE ORDERS FORM

Applying filters saved as query objects is a holdover from the early days of Access when macros were popular for automating applications. There's no simple method of modifying the Invoices Filter to enable its use in this scenario, and it's much more efficient to specify a server filter in the VBA code that opens the Invoice report. Unlike the conventional Access Filter property of a form or report, which applies the WHERE clause expression (without the WHERE) against all rows of the RecordSource on the client, the ServerFilter applies the WHERE expression at the server. Sending only the selected record(s) over the network speeds execution time and reduces network traffic.

The syntax of the `OpenReport` method of the Access-specific `DoCmd` object is

```
DoCmd.OpenReport strReportName, [intMode,
    [strFilterName, [strWHERECondition,
    [intWindowMode, [varOpenArguments]]]]]
```

All the arguments except `strReportName` are optional. In this case, you delete the reference to the Invoices Filter as the `strFilterName` argument because conventional client-side filters don't work with ADPs. For this example, you set the report's ServerFilter property value to a `strFilter` argument value that provides the OrderID value of the Orders form's current order to the Invoices report. The `strFilter` value is a valid WHERE clause without the WHERE keyword (OrderID = *intOrderID* for this example).

To fix the `DoCmd.OpenReport` statement of the `PrintInvoice_Click` event handler and add the other VBA code required to print the specified invoice, do the following:

1. Open the Orders form in Design view, and click the Code button to open the VBA editor.

2. Scroll to the `DoCmd.OpenReport…` line of the `PrintInvoice_Click` subprocedure.

3. Delete the `"Invoices Filter"` argument value and its preceding comma.

4. Add **strFilter = "OrderID = " & CStr(Me.OrderID.Value)** to a new line above the `DoCmd.OpenReport…` line, and add `strFilter = ""` to a new line after the `DoCmd.OpenReport…` line (see Figure 22.16). The **CStr** function converts the **Variant** OrderID value of the **Long** (Integer) type to a **String** variable. **Me** is a self-reference to the report. Use of **Me** and Value is optional, but is good VBA programming practice. The three related `DoCmd.OpenReport` statements are

```
strFilter = "OrderID = " & CStr(Me.OrderID.Value)
DoCmd.OpenReport strDocName, acViewNormal
strFilter = ""
```

Figure 22.16
Add the highlighted code to the `DoCmd.OpenReport` instruction after deleting the reference to the Invoices Filter view.

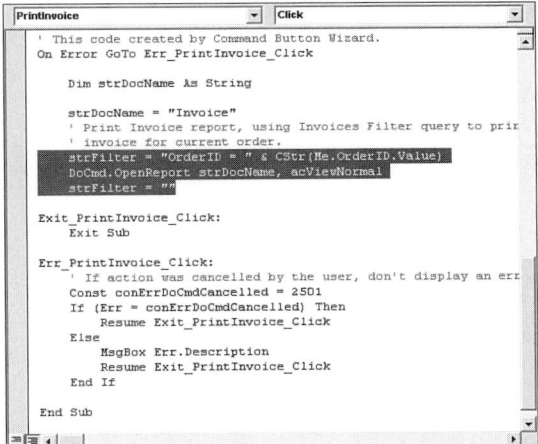

```
PrintInvoice                    ▼   Click                        ▼
    ' This code created by Command Button Wizard.
    On Error GoTo Err_PrintInvoice_Click

        Dim strDocName As String

        strDocName = "Invoice"
        ' Print Invoice report, using Invoices Filter query to print
        ' invoice for current order.
        strFilter = "OrderID = " & CStr(Me.OrderID.Value)
        DoCmd.OpenReport strDocName, acViewNormal
        strFilter = ""

    Exit_PrintInvoice_Click:
        Exit Sub

    Err_PrintInvoice_Click:
        ' If action was cancelled by the user, don't display an err
        Const conErrDoCmdCancelled = 2501
        If (Err = conErrDoCmdCancelled) Then
            Resume Exit_PrintInvoice_Click
        Else
            MsgBox Err.Description
            Resume Exit_PrintInvoice_Click
        End If

    End Sub
```

> **T I P**
>
> If you want to display the report in Print Preview mode before printing, change the `acViewNormal` Access constant to `acViewPreview`.

5. Open the Utility Functions module and type **Public strFilter As String** below the Option Explicit line to create a public string variable that's visible to code behind the Invoices report and Orders form.

22

6. With the Invoices report open in Design view, open the Properties Sheet, click the Events tab, select the Form by clicking the square button in the upper-left corner, and select Event Procedure in the On Open event's list to open a window with a Report_Open event handler stub.

7. Type **Me.ServerFilter** = **strFilter** between the Sub Report_Open and End Sub lines.

8. Close the Invoices report and save your changes. The ServerFilter property value won't be refreshed if the Invoices report is open in your project.

9. Return to the Orders form, click Form view, and click the Print Invoice button. If you change the mode, the invoice for the selected order appears in the Print Preview window; otherwise, the default printer prints the invoice.

10. Close the Orders form and save your changes.

If you judge the amount of work required to upsize a relatively simple set of interrelated queries and application objects to be daunting, consider abandoning the upsizing process and linking SQL Server tables to your Access application. However, your application isn't likely to perform as well with very large tables and many simultaneous users.

→ For more information on upsizing linked Access tables, **see** " Upsizing a Single-File Application to SQL Server 2005," **p. 828**.

UPSIZING ACCESS SQL STATEMENTS EXECUTED BY FORMS, REPORTS, AND CONTROLS

Many Access developers use SQL SELECT statements, instead of saved (persistent) queries, to supply the record source for bound forms, reports, and controls on forms and reports. Tracking down problems with application objects that execute SQL statements directly is even more of a challenge than fixing objects that refer to SQL Server views, functions, and stored procedures. Access 2007's Upsizing Wizard doesn't attempt to convert Access SQL statements used as the values of Record Source and Row Source properties to SQL Server views or stored procedures.

Northwind.accdb—and thus Upsize22.accdb—includes an example of a form (Sales Analysis) that fails to open as a result of an Access SQL keyword (DISTINCTROW) that T-SQL doesn't support. When you double-click the Sales Analysis form, an "Incorrect syntax near '.'" error message opens.

The culprits in this case are the Sales Analysis form's two alternating subforms—Sales Analysis Subform1 and Sales Analysis Subform2. Both subforms have SQL statements as the value of the Record Source property. Unfortunately, the Microsoft developers added DISTINCTROW to the SELECT statement, which renders the SQL statement unusable in a project.

To correct problems with SQL statements that serve as the record source for bound objects, do this:

1. Open the form or report in Design view, click Properties to open the Properties window for the object, and click the Data tab. For this example, open Sales Analysis Subform1 (see Figure 22.17).

Figure 22.17
Sales Analysis
Subform1 has a
superfluous
DISTINCTROW modifier in the SELECT
statement for the
form's Record Source
property. Why
Microsoft's developers added this modifier is a mystery.

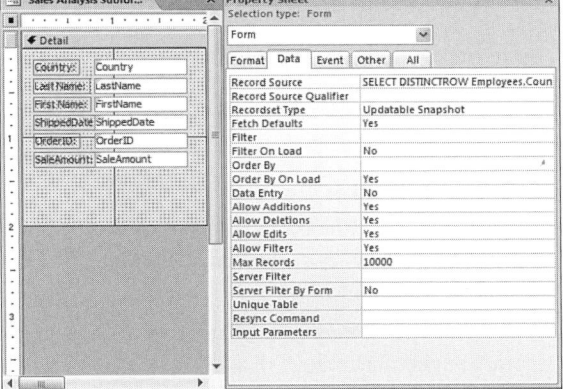

2. If the Record Source property has an SQL statement as its value, remove the DISTINCTROW modifier, if present, and click the Builder button to open the project designer's SQL Statement: Query window.

3. If the problem with the SQL statement isn't immediately evident, click the Check SQL Syntax button, which opens an error message that *might* assist in locating the errant element.

SQL 4. Use of DISTINCTROW is the obvious problem in this example, so delete it and click the Check SQL Syntax button. After you delete DISTINCTROW, the project designer's window appears as shown in Figure 22.18.

Figure 22.18
Clicking the Builder button of the Record Source property's text box opens the project designer's SQL Statement: Query window. The Diagram and Grid panes don't open until you click Check SQL Syntax.

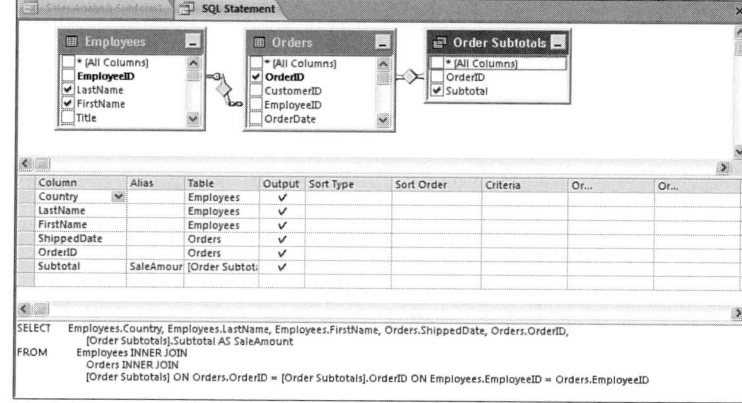

5. Close the project designer, click Yes to save your changes, close the Properties window, and close the form or report, again saving your changes.

6. For this example, repeat step 1 for the Sales Analysis Subform2 form, delete DISTINCTROW from the SQL statement in the Record Source text box, close the Properties window and the form, and save your changes.

 7. Test the form to verify that the changes you made to the SQL statements don't lead to incorrect values. Compare the data values displayed by the upsized form with that of the original Access version. Figure 22.19 shows that deleting DISTINCTROW doesn't affect the data of the subform's PivotTable.

Figure 22.19
The upsized PivotTable form displays data that's identical to its Access counterpart in Upsize22.accdb or Northwind.accdb.

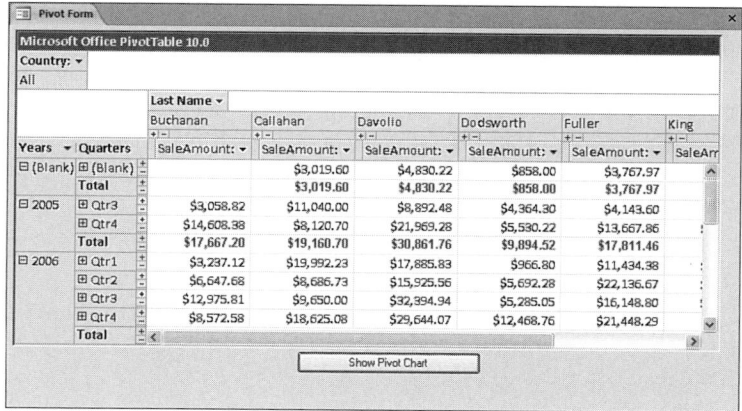

The preceding process also applies to Row Source property value of list boxes, combo boxes, and most other objects bound to SQL statements. An exception is the Row Source property of Chart objects you create with the Chart Wizard. The later "Emulating Access Crosstab Queries with T-SQL" section shows you how to handle T-SQL's lack of crosstab query capability.

Comparing ANSI-92 SQL, T-SQL, and Access SQL

Access SQL and T-SQL don't include many of the approximately 200 keywords incorporated in the ANSI standard for SQL-92. Most of the common SQL keywords missing from Access's implementation are provided by the expressions you create with operators, built-in functions, or user-defined functions you write in Access's VBA flavor. Understanding the similarities and differences between Access and ANSI-92 SQL is important when you upsize Access applications to ADP. This knowledge is even more important if you take the "planned migration" route, described near the beginning of the chapter, to upsizing your database front ends.

> **NOTE**
>
> The information in the following sections applies to all SQL Server 2005 editions: Developer, Workgroup, Standard, Enterprise, and Express.

ANSI-92 SQL Reserved Words in Access SQL

Access doesn't support all the ANSI SQL keywords with identical reserved words in the Access SQL language, but each update to Access converges on the SQL-92 standard, as does each successive version of SQL Server. In this chapter, keywords are defined as the commands and functions that make up the vocabulary of the ANSI SQL language. Access SQL commands and functions are referred to here as *reserved words* to distinguish them from ANSI SQL.

The tables in the following two sections also are intended to acquaint readers who are familiar with ANSI or similar implementations of SQL in other RDBMSs or database front-end applications with the Access implementation of Access SQL and SQL Server 2000's version of T-SQL. If you haven't used any version of SQL, the tables demonstrate that SQL is a relatively sparse language, having far fewer keywords compared to programming languages such as VBA, and that Access SQL is even more sparse. Access SQL has few reserved words to learn. T-SQL implements most ANSI-92 keywords and has many useful additions to ANSI-92 SQL.

Access SQL Reserved Words Corresponding to ANSI SQL and T-SQL Keywords

Access supports the ANSI SQL and T-SQL keywords listed in Table 22.2 as identical reserved words in Access SQL. Don't use these reserved words as the names of tables, fields,

22

or variables. The reserved words in Table 22.2 appear in all capital letters in the SQL statements Access creates for you when you design a query or when you add a graph to a form or report. Reserved words marked with an asterisk were introduced by Access 2000, are accessible only from VBA code, and, if you're using ActiveX Data Objects (ADO), require a reference to the Microsoft ADO Ext. 2.x for DDL and Security library (Msadox.dll).

TABLE 22.2   RESERVED WORDS COMMON TO ANSI-92 SQL, ACCESS SQL, AND T-SQL

ADD	ALIAS	ALL
ALTER	ANY	AS
ASC	AVG	BEGIN*
BETWEEN	BY	CHECK*
COLUMN*	COMMIT*	CONSTRAINT
COUNT	CREATE	DELETE
DESC	DISALLOW*	DISTINCT
DROP	EXISTS	FOREIGN
FROM	HAVING	IN
INDEX	INNER	INSERT
INTO	IS	JOIN
KEY	LEFT	LIKE
MAX	MIN	NOT
NULL	ON	OR
ORDER	OUTER	PARAMETERS
PRIMARY*	PROCEDURE	REFERENCES
RIGHT	ROLLBACK*	SELECT
SET	SOME*	TRANSACTION*
UNION	UNIQUE	UPDATE
VALUE	VALUES	VIEW
WHERE		

The keywords that relate to data types—CHAR[ACTER], FLOAT, INT[EGER], and REAL—aren't included in Table 22.2 because Access SQL uses a different reserved word to specify these SQL data types (refer to Table 22.4 later in this chapter). The comparison operators (=, <, <=, >, and =>) are common to both ANSI SQL and Access SQL. Access and T-SQL substitute the <> operator for ANSI SQL's not-equal (!=) operator.

As in ANSI SQL, the IN reserved word in Access SQL can be used as an operator to specify a list of values to match in a WHERE clause or the result set of a subquery.

ACCESS FUNCTIONS AND OPERATORS USED IN PLACE OF ANSI SQL KEYWORDS

Table 22.3 shows reserved words in Access SQL that correspond to ANSI SQL keywords but are operators or functions used in Access SQL expressions. Access doesn't use ANSI SQL syntax for aggregate functions; for example, you can't use the SUM(DISTINCT *field_name*) or AVG(DISTINCT *field_name*) syntax of ANSI SQL. Access distinguishes between its use of the Sum() aggregate function and the SQL implementation, SUM(), by initial-letter-only capitalization. Expressions that use operators such as **And** and **Or** are enclosed in parentheses in Access SQL statements; Access SQL uses uppercase AND and OR when criteria are added to more than one column.

TABLE 22.3   ACCESS SQL RESERVED WORDS THAT SUBSTITUTE FOR ANSI SQL KEYWORDS

Access SQL	ANSI SQL	Access SQL	ANSI SQL
And	AND	Max()	MAX()
Avg()	AVG()	Min()	MIN()
Between	BETWEEN	Not	NOT
Count()	COUNT()	Null	NULL
Is	IS	Or	OR
In	IN	Sum()	SUM()
Like	LIKE		

The Wizard upsizes Access SQL Like expressions for DateTime values to the ANSI SQL LIKE operator, as mentioned near the beginning of this chapter. For example, WHERE *DateColumn* Like "*/*/2006" upsizes to WHERE *DateColumn* LIKE '%/%/2006'. (The next section discusses differences between Access and ANSI SQL wildcard characters.) T-SQL statements containing LIKE constraints for columns of the datetime data type fail to return rows. If you attempt to edit the LIKE expression, you receive a "Your entry cannot be converted to a valid date time value" message. This use of LIKE is valid in T-SQL; T-SQL statements containing LIKE datetime constraints work fine in the SQL Query Analyzer or from OSQL. The problem with LIKE datetime expressions in the project designer appears to stem from the SQL Server OLE DB provider (SQLOLEDB).

The Access IsNull() function that returns **True** (–1) or **False** (0), depending on whether IsNull()'s argument has a Null value, has no equivalent in ANSI SQL, and isn't a substitute for IS NULL or IS NOT NULL qualifiers in WHERE clauses.

Access SQL doesn't support DISTINCT aggregate function references, such as AVG(DISTINCT *field_name*); the default DISTINCTROW qualifier added to the SELECT statement by Access serves this purpose in Access SQL.

ACCESS SQL RESERVED WORDS, OPERATORS, AND FUNCTIONS NOT IN ANSI SQL

Access SQL contains a number of reserved words that aren't ANSI SQL keywords (see Table 22.4). Most of these reserved words define Access data types; some reserved words have equivalents in ANSI SQL and T-SQL, and others don't. You use Access DDL reserved words to establish or modify the properties of tables and columns. Access SQL's DISTINCTROW modifier is described in the following section. Access uses PIVOT and TRANSFORM to create the crosstab queries that are unique to Access databases.

> **NOTE**
>
> SQL Server 2005's T-SQL finally has PIVOT (and UNPIVOT) operators. PIVOT exchanges columns (on the x-axis) and rows (y-axis) by pivoting the result set 90 degrees counter-clockwise. UNPIVOT undoes a PIVOT operation. The later "Emulating Access Crosstab Queries with T-SQL" section explains how T-SQL and Access SQL PIVOT operators differ.

TABLE 22.4   ACCESS SQL RESERVED WORDS NOT IN ANSI SQL

Access SQL	ANSI SQL	Category	Purpose
BINARY	No equivalent	DDL	Not an official Access field data type
BOOLEAN	No equivalent	DDL	Access Yes/No field data type
BYTE	No equivalent	DDL	Byte field data type, 1 byte integer
CURRENCY	No equivalent	DDL	Access Currency field data type
DATETIME	No equivalent	DDL	Access Date/Time field data type
DISTINCTROW	No equivalent	DQL	Updatable Access Recordset objects
DOUBLE	REAL	DDL	High-precision decimal numbers
LONG	INT[EGER]	DDL	Long Integer field data type
LONGBINARY	No equivalent	DDL	OLE Object field data type
LONGTEXT	VARCHAR	DDL	Memo field data type
OWNERACCESS	No equivalent	DQL	Run with owner's privileges parameters
PIVOT	No equivalent	DQL	Used in crosstab queries
SHORT	SMALLINT	DDL	Integer field data type, 2 bytes
SINGLE	No equivalent	DDL	Single-precision real number
TEXT(*n*)	CHAR[ACTER]	DDL	Text field data type
TRANSFORM	No equivalent	DQL	Creates crosstab query
&	|| (two pipe symbols)	DQL	String concatenation
? (LIKE wildcard)	_ (wildcard)	DQL	Single character
* (LIKE wildcard)	% (wildcard)	DQL	Zero or more characters

Access SQL	ANSI SQL	Category	Purpose
# (LIKE wildcard)	No equivalent	DQL	Single digit, 0–9
# (date specifier)	No equivalent	DQL	Encloses date/time values
<> (not equal)	!=	DQL	Access uses ! as a object name separator

Access provides four statistical aggregate functions that aren't incorporated in ANSI SQL. These functions are listed in Table 22.5.

TABLE 22.5   AGGREGATE SQL FUNCTIONS IN ACCESS SQL BUT NOT ANSI SQL

Access Function	Category	Purpose
StdDev()	DQL	Standard deviation of a population sample
StdDevP()	DQL	Standard deviation of a population
Var()	DQL	Statistical variation of a population sample
VarP()	DQL	Statistical variation of a population

ACCESS'S DISTINCTROW AND ANSI SQL's DISTINCT KEYWORDS

Access SQL's DISTINCTROW reserved word that follows the SQL SELECT keyword causes Access to eliminate duplicated rows from the query's result. The effect of DISTINCTROW is especially dramatic in queries used to display records in tables that have indirect relationships. As mentioned earlier in the chapter, you're likely to encounter DISTINCTROW in Access queries created prior to Access 97.

DISTINCTROW is related to, but not the same as, the DISTINCT keyword in ANSI SQL. Both words eliminate duplicate rows of data in query result tables, but they differ in execution. DISTINCT in ANSI SQL eliminates duplicate rows based only on the values of the data contained in the rows of the query, from left to right. You cannot update values from multiple-table queries that include the keyword DISTINCT.

DISTINCTROW eliminates duplicate rows based on the content of the underlying table, regardless of whether additional field(s) that distinguish records in the table are included. DISTINCTROW allows values in special kinds of multiple-table Recordset objects to be updated.

NOTE

> You can use the Unique Table property value of a form's record source to make most one-to-many queries updatable. Specify the name of the table on the many side of the relationship as the value of the Unique Table property.

To distinguish between these two keywords, assume that you have a table with a LastName field and a FirstName field and only 10 records, each with the LastName value, Smith. Each record has a different FirstName value. You create a query that includes the LastName field, but not the FirstName field. DISTINCTROW returns all 10 Smith records because the FirstName values differ in the table. DISTINCT returns one record because the FirstName field that distinguishes the records in the table is absent in the query result table.

Versions before Access 97 included the default reserved word DISTINCTROW unless you purposely replaced it with the DISTINCT keyword by using the Query Properties dialog's Unique Values Only option. The Access Query Properties dialog sets the default value of the Unique Values (DISTINCT) and Unique Rows (DISTINCTROW) properties to No. Don't specify Unique Rows in Access queries you intend to upsize to ADP.

ACCESS AND CORRESPONDING SQL SERVER DATA TYPES

SQL Server 2005 has more data types than those specified by the ANSI-92 standard (refer to Table 22.2). For example, ANSI-92 doesn't require conforming RDBMSs to support Unicode characters. Access and SQL Server both support Unicode data types; SQL Server identifies Unicode data type by an n (for National Character) prefix.

The Upsizing Wizard automatically converts Access data types to corresponding SQL Server 2000 data types. Table 22.6 lists Access data types, the SQL Server data type to which the Wizard converts the Access data type, if supported, and SQL Server data types that are related to the upsized data type, if any. Parentheses enclose SQL Server property or extended property values that must be set to emulate Access data types.

TABLE 22.6   ACCESS DATA TYPES AND THE DIRECTLY CORRESPONDING AND RELATED SQL SERVER 2000 DATA TYPES

Access Datatype	Upsizes To SQL Server Datatype	Related SQL Server Datatypes
SQL Server 2000		
Yes/No	bit	
Number (Byte)	tinyint	
Number (Integer)	smallint	
Number (Long Integer)	int	
Number (Single)	float	
Number (Double)	float	
Number (Decimal)	decimal	numeric
Number (Replication ID) (GUID)	uniqueidentifier	
AutoNumber	int (Identity)	
Currency	money	smallmoney

Access Datatype	Upsizes To SQL Server Datatype	Related SQL Server Datatypes
Date/Time	`datetime`	`smalldatetime`
Text(*n*)	`nvarchar(n)`	`varchar(n)`
Hyperlink	`ntext (Hyperlink)`	
Memo	`ntext`	`text`
OLE Object	(Does not upsize)	
Attachments	(Does not upsize)	
Multivalued (Lookup)	(Does not upsize)	

Access doesn't have data types that correspond to SQL Server 2005's `bigint`, `xml`, `char`, `nchar`, `sql_variant`, `user-defined`, `varchar`, `[n]varchar(max)`, `varbinary`, and `varbinary(max)` data types.

VBA FUNCTIONS THAT UPSIZE TO SQL SERVER FUNCTIONS

T-SQL has many functions that correspond to VBA functions that you commonly use in Access queries. Table 22.7 lists the VBA functions that the Upsizing Wizard converts to their T-SQL counterparts. The table doesn't include the SQL functions listed earlier in Tables 22.2 and 22.3. You can safely use these VBA functions in Access queries that you plan to upsize to SQL Server.

TABLE 22.7   VBA FUNCTIONS THAT THE WIZARD AUTOMATICALLY CONVERTS TO T-SQL FUNCTIONS

`Ccur`	`Hour`	`Right$`
`Cdbl`	`Lcase$`	`Right`
`Chr$`	`Lcase`	`Rtrim$`
`Chr`	`Left`	`Second`
`Cint`	`Len`	`Space$`
`Clng`	`Ltrim$`	`Str$`
`Csng`	`Mid$`	`Ucase$`
`Cstr`	`Mid`	`Ucase`
`Cvdate`	`Minute`	`Weekday`
`Day`	`Month`	`Year`

VBA FUNCTIONS THAT YOU MUST MANUALLY CONVERT TO RELATED SQL SERVER FUNCTIONS

The Upsizing Wizard doesn't automatically convert the VBA functions listed in Table 22.8 into the corresponding T-SQL functions that perform similar or identical operations. In most cases, the reason the Wizard doesn't perform the translation is minor syntax differences. Eliminate, if possible, or minimize use of these functions in Access queries you plan to upsize.

TABLE 22.8 VBA FUNCTIONS THAT THE WIZARD AUTOMATICALLY DOES NOT CONVERT TO T-SQL FUNCTIONS

VBA Function	T-SQL Function	VBA Function	T-SQL Function
Asc	ASCII	Lower	LOWER
Date	GETDATE	Now	GETDATE
DateAdd	DATEADD	Space	SPACE
DateDiff	DATEDIFF	Str	STR
DatePart	DATEPART	String	REPLICATE
Format	DATENAME	StrReverse	REVERSE
Instr	CHARINDEX		

The **Format** function is one of the most commonly used VBA functions in Access queries, and DATENAME only handles one of many possible **Format** expressions.

→ For examples of the use of T-SQL DATEPART, DATENAME, DATEDIFF, and GETDATE functions, **see** "The Better Approach for Dynamic *and* Static Data—PIVOT Views or Stored Procedures," **p. 986**.

TIP

> SQL Server 2005 Books Online has the standard syntax for T-SQL functions and examples of their use. Click the Index tab and type the function name in the text box to open the Transact-SQL Reference topic for the function. The "Date and Time Functions" topic has links to all functions that accept or return date or time values. If you haven't downloaded the current SQL Server 2005 Books Online release, you can find it at http://www.microsoft.com/sql/downloads/2005/.

EMULATING ACCESS CROSSTAB QUERIES WITH T-SQL

Regardless of your upsizing strategy, you must roll your own T-SQL equivalents of Access crosstab queries to provide the data source for upsized charts you created with Microsoft Graph and the Chart Wizard. Your only alternative is to convert all graphs and charts to PivotCharts and re-create their source queries.

Access SQL

This is the generalized Access SQL syntax for crosstab queries:

```
TRANSFORM aggregate_function(field_name) [AS alias]
SELECT [ALL|DISTINCT] select_list
   FROM table_name
   PIVOT Format(field_name),"format_type")
[IN (column_list)]
```

TRANSFORM defines a crosstab query, and PIVOT specifies the GROUP BY characteristics plus the fixed column names specified by the optional IN predicate.

➔ To review Access crosstab query design, **see** "Creating Crosstab Queries," **p. 503**.

SQL Server 2005 Books Online calls crosstab queries "cross-tab reports" and equates cross-tab reports with PivotTables. The example creates a trivial result table with explicit numeric values for four quarters of two years. Unfortunately, the topic doesn't show you how to write a stored procedure that emulates the capabilities of Access's crosstab queries.

The frm2006SalesByCategoryChart form you created in Chapter 18, "Adding Graphs, PivotCharts, and PivotTables," has a generic crosstab SQL statement that the Chart Wizard generates from the query you specify as the data source for the chart. The Chart Wizard stores the crosstab SQL statement as the value of the Row Source property of the chart. The Upsizing Wizard upsizes this form, but when you try to open it, you receive an error message that the SQL statement exceeds a maximum length of 128 characters. When you click OK, another error message appears with possible causes of the problem. The fundamental problem—repeated several times earlier in this and preceding chapters—is that T-SQL finally supports a PIVOT keyword, but it's *not* the equivalent of Access SQL's TRANSFORM and PIVOT keywords.

You must find a way to deliver the data to the chart in the appropriate format. The following sections describe two methods of emulating the result set of crosstab queries in ADP.

THE PRAGMATIC APPROACH FOR STATIC DATA—CHEAT

If your chart or graph displays historical data that isn't subject to revision, you can save considerable time and effort by creating an SQL Server table from the output of the crosstab query the Chart Wizard generates.

TIP

> Check with your organization's chief financial or executive officer before committing to a static version of historical financial data. Retroactive revision of prior financial data—sometimes involving several years of data—became increasingly common in the first decade of the 21st century.

CREATING A WORKSHEET FROM THE CROSSTAB QUERY RESULT SET

Cheating by creating a static table isn't as straightforward as you might expect. You use an Excel worksheet as an intermediary in the process. To create the initial worksheet, do the following:

 1. Open the original Access .accdb version of the form with a graph or chart created by the Chart Wizard. This example uses the frm2006SalesByCategoryChart form you created in Chapter 18. A copy of this form is included in Upsize22.accdb; this example uses the copy.

 2. Change to Design view, right-click the unbound object frame (usually OLEUnbound0), and choose Properties to open the object's Properties window.

 3. Click the Data tab, select the entire SQL statement in the text box of the Row Source property, and copy the statement to the Clipboard.

 4. Open a new query in Design view, close the Show Table dialog, and click the SQL view button.

Access SQL

Following is the Access SQL statement for the Record Source of frm2006SalesByCategoryChart's OLEUnbound0 unbound object frame:

```
TRANSFORM Sum([Amount]) AS [SumOfAmount]
    SELECT (Format([ShippedDate],"MMM 'YY"))
    FROM [qry2006SalesChart]
    GROUP BY (Year([ShippedDate])*12 +
        Month([ShippedDate])-1),
        (Format([ShippedDate],"MMM 'YY"))
PIVOT [CategoryName];
```

The crosstab query uses the qry2006SalesChart query, which upsizes successfully.

→ To review the process for creating the graph, **see** "Generating Graphs and Charts with Microsoft Graph," **p. 770**.

 5. Paste the SQL statement into the SQL window, and click Run to verify the data returned. Figure 22.20 shows the query result set from the sample chart.

> **TIP**
>
> Changing the crosstab query type to a make-table query doesn't create a table with the crosstab structure. However, you can use the crosstab query as the data source for a make-table query. Another approach is to save the crosstab query and export its result set to a worksheet, but copying the cells to a worksheet is faster, especially if you have many upsized charts to fix.

6. Press Ctrl+A to select all records in the datasheet, and press Ctrl+C to copy the cell values to the Clipboard.

7. Launch Excel with a new workbook. With the cursor in cell A1, press Ctrl+V to paste the cells to Sheet1.

Figure 22.20
Datasheet view of the chart's crosstab query shows the tabular data structure required to populate the chart's datasheet.

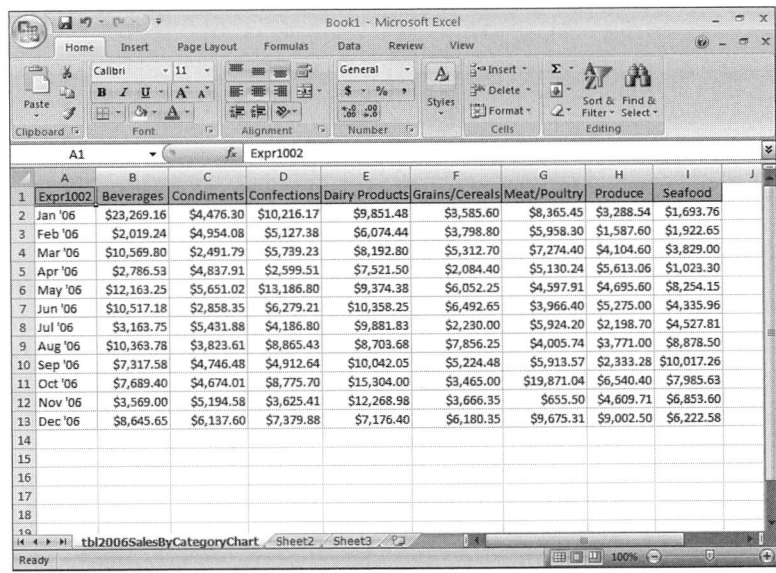

Expr1002	Beverages	Condiments	Confections	Dairy Produc	Grains/Cere	Meat/Poultr	Produce
Jan '06	$23,269.16	$4,476.30	$10,216.17	$9,851.48	$3,585.60	$8,365.45	$3,288.
Feb '06	$2,019.24	$4,954.08	$5,127.38	$6,074.44	$3,798.80	$5,958.30	$1,587.
Mar '06	$10,569.80	$2,491.79	$5,739.23	$8,192.80	$5,312.70	$7,274.40	$4,104.
Apr '06	$2,786.53	$4,837.91	$2,599.51	$7,521.50	$2,084.40	$5,130.24	$5,613.
May '06	$12,163.25	$5,651.02	$13,186.80	$9,374.38	$6,052.25	$4,597.91	$4,695.
Jun '06	$10,517.18	$2,858.35	$6,279.21	$10,358.25	$6,492.65	$3,966.40	$5,275.
Jul '06	$3,163.75	$5,431.88	$4,186.80	$9,881.83	$2,230.00	$5,924.20	$2,198.
Aug '06	$10,363.78	$3,823.61	$8,865.43	$8,703.68	$7,856.25	$4,005.74	$3,771.
Sep '06	$7,317.58	$4,746.48	$4,912.64	$10,042.05	$5,224.48	$5,913.57	$2,333.
Oct '06	$7,689.40	$4,674.01	$8,775.70	$15,304.00	$3,465.00	$19,871.04	$6,540.
Nov '06	$3,569.00	$5,194.58	$3,625.41	$12,268.98	$3,666.35	$655.50	$4,609.
Dec '06	$8,645.65	$6,137.60	$7,379.88	$7,176.40	$6,180.35	$9,675.31	$9,002.

Record: 1 of 12   No Filter   Search

TIP

If you want to use the crosstab table as a record source for other queries in the project, select the columns with numerical data, and format the cells as Number or Currency.

8. Rename Sheet1 to identify the table (**tbl2006SalesByCategoryChart** for this example) and save the workbook in Excel 97-2003 format (.xls), not Excel 2007 format (.xlsx), with a descriptive name such as **AccessCrosstabs.xls** (see Figure 22.21).

Figure 22.21
This Excel 97 - 2003 format worksheet serves as the data source for a new SQL Server table you can use as the row source for the upsized frm2006SalesBy-CategoryChart form.

	A	B	C	D	E	F	G	H	I
1	Expr1002	Beverages	Condiments	Confections	Dairy Products	Grains/Cereals	Meat/Poultry	Produce	Seafood
2	Jan '06	$23,269.16	$4,476.30	$10,216.17	$9,851.48	$3,585.60	$8,365.45	$3,288.54	$1,693.76
3	Feb '06	$2,019.24	$4,954.08	$5,127.38	$6,074.44	$3,798.80	$5,958.30	$1,587.60	$1,922.65
4	Mar '06	$10,569.80	$2,491.79	$5,739.23	$8,192.80	$5,312.70	$7,274.40	$4,104.60	$3,829.00
5	Apr '06	$2,786.53	$4,837.91	$2,599.51	$7,521.50	$2,084.40	$5,130.24	$5,613.06	$1,023.30
6	May '06	$12,163.25	$5,651.02	$13,186.80	$9,374.38	$6,052.25	$4,597.91	$4,695.60	$8,254.15
7	Jun '06	$10,517.18	$2,858.35	$6,279.21	$10,358.25	$6,492.65	$3,966.40	$5,275.00	$4,335.96
8	Jul '06	$3,163.75	$5,431.88	$4,186.80	$9,881.83	$2,230.00	$5,924.20	$2,198.70	$4,527.81
9	Aug '06	$10,363.78	$3,823.61	$8,865.43	$8,703.68	$7,856.25	$4,005.74	$3,771.00	$8,878.50
10	Sep '06	$7,317.58	$4,746.48	$4,912.64	$10,042.05	$5,224.48	$5,913.57	$2,333.28	$10,017.26
11	Oct '06	$7,689.40	$4,674.01	$8,775.70	$15,304.00	$3,465.00	$19,871.04	$6,540.40	$7,985.63
12	Nov '06	$3,569.00	$5,194.58	$3,625.41	$12,268.98	$3,666.35	$655.50	$4,609.71	$6,853.60
13	Dec '06	$8,645.65	$6,137.60	$7,379.88	$7,176.40	$6,180.35	$9,675.31	$9,002.50	$6,222.58

tbl2006SalesByCategoryChart / Sheet2 / Sheet3

9. Repeat steps 1–8 for each form or report that contains a Wizard-created chart. In step 7, use the saved workbook and add a new worksheet to store the additional query result set copies.

10. Close the workbook. You can't import the worksheet data if the workbook is open.

 The AccessCrosstabs.xls workbook is included in the \SEUA12\Chaptr22 folder of the accompanying CD-ROM. The three worksheets have cells formatted as Text, Number, and Currency.

IMPORTING THE WORKSHEET TO AN SQL SERVER TABLE

Do the following to import the workbook data to SQL Server for your project and enable forms and reports that include charts:

1. Open the project that contains the upsized form with the inoperable chart (UpsizeASQL.adp for this example).

2. Click the External Data tab and the Import group's Excel button to open the Get External Data – Excel Spreadsheet dialog.

3. Click Browse to open the Open File dialog, navigate to the location of the workbook you saved, and double-click the file to return to the Get External Data – Excel Spreadsheet dialog. With the Import the Source Data… option selected, click OK to start the Import Spreadsheet Wizard.

4. In the first Wizard dialog, select the worksheet for the SQL Server table to create (see Figure 22.22) and then click Next.

Figure 22.22
Importing the crosstab worksheet with the Import Spreadsheet Process is quick, because you accept all but one default value.

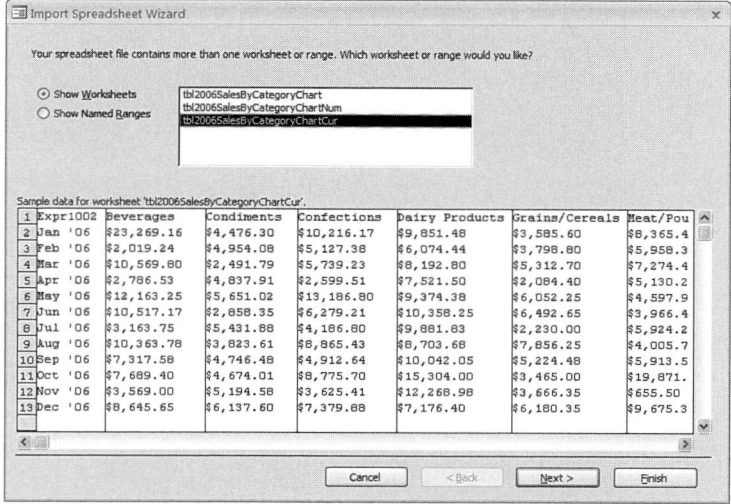

5. In the second dialog, mark the First Row Contains Column Headings check box and click Next.

6. If you renamed the worksheet to correspond to the SQL Server table name in step 8 of the preceding section, accept the worksheet name as the table name, and click Finish to create the table in the current SQL Server database (UpsizeSQL for this example).

7. Click Close to close the Save Import Steps dialog. Then open the new SQL Server table to verify the import process, and verify the data types in Design view; for this example, all categories columns should be money. Change the column name of the first column to MonthYear, if you want.

8. Right-click the chart and choose Properties to open the Properties window for the unbound object frame. (The presentation of the graph in Design view is static.)

9. Click the Data tab, open the Row Source list, and select the imported table corresponding to the crosstab query to replace (see Figure 22.23).

Figure 22.23
Specify the new SQL Server table you created as the value of the Row Source property of the chart.

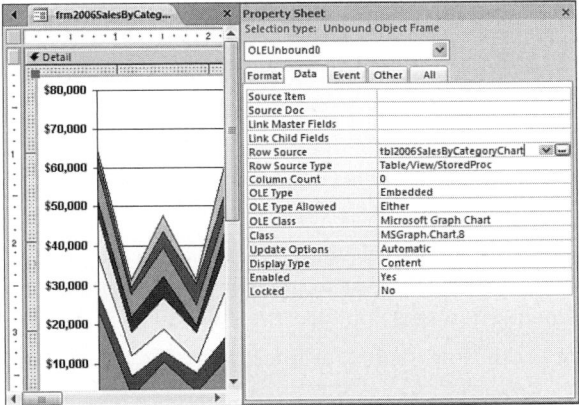

10. Close the Properties window, and change to Form or Report view to test the data source. Figure 22.24 shows the upsized frm2006SalesByCategoryChart form.

11. Repeat steps 2–10 for each worksheet in your crosstab workbook.

MODIFYING THE TABLE TO ACCOMMODATE A LINKED CHART

Linked charts require that the crosstab table column names for the Link Master Fields and Link Child Fields correspond. Forms having linked charts usually specify the name of a table or query as the record source for the form and a crosstab query as the row source for the chart.

→ To review linking graphs, **see** "Creating a Linked Graph from an Access Crosstab Query," **p. 788**.

Figure 22.24
The upsized 2006
Monthly Sales by
Category form
(frm2006SalesBy-
CategoryChart) is
almost identical to its
Access counterpart.

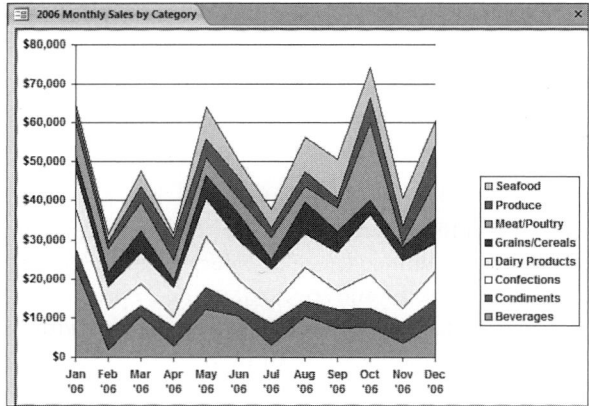

Using the upsized frm2006SalesByCategoryChartLinked form you created in Chapter 18 as an example, follow these steps to fix linked MSGraph 10 objects:

1. Open the form in Design view, right-click the graph, open the Properties window, and click the Data tab.

2. Verify that the table(s) that provide the Record Source property of the form and the Row Source property of the chart have the fields specified by the Link Master Fields and Link Child Fields properties.

3. The linking field of the tbl2006SalesByCategoryChart table is Expr1002 (refer to Figure 22.21), so open the table in Design view and change the name of the first field to **Categories**. (Nonlinked graphs don't use the field name of the first column.)

4. Specify the table as the Row Source for the chart.

5. If the form uses a crosstab query as its record source, change the Record Source property value to the name of the crosstab table, tbl2006SalesByCategoryChart in this case.

6. Verify that the linked form behaves and appears identically to the original Access version, and save your changes.

THE BETTER APPROACH FOR DYNAMIC *AND* STATIC DATA—PIVOT VIEWS OR STORED PROCEDURES

Creating crosstab tables from the contents of datasheets isn't a generally accepted programming practice, so this section describes how to emulate the Access SQL crosstab statement for the record source of frm2006SalesByCategoryChart's OLEUnbound0 unbound object frame. You can use a view to replace crosstabs that are dedicated to a specific time period and format. A single parameterized stored procedure can handle multiple time periods, such as years, that you specify by the parameter value.

There are two basic steps to the stored procedure approach:

- **Design a view that returns the values you need for the table**—For this example, the values are eight category names, total sales amounts for each category by month, and the month number. The upsized qry2006SalesChart view is the starting point for the final view design.

- **Write a view or stored procedure that uses the PIVOT operator, the FOR clause, and the IN predicate to create the crosstab table from the view's output**—A PIVOT query requires columns for unique GROUP BY values to be added to the SELECT column list—where they can be aliased—and specified in the IN predicate. The IN predicate of the FOR clause is identical to that for Access crosstab queries with fixed column headers. The PIVOT operator's arguments are an aggregate function to supply values, and the FOR clause to specify the source of the IN predicate's values. Writing PIVOT queries isn't difficult once you've designed and tested a few.

> **TIP**
>
> As a general rule, you should substitute ActiveX PivotCharts for MSGraph OLE charts in your new Access applications. Relatively simple views, functions, or stored procedures serve as the data source for PivotCharts and their underlying PivotTables in ADP. The Chart Wizard isn't available within ADP because it depends on Access crosstab queries.

MODIFYING THE UPSIZED QRY2006SALESCHART VIEW

The upsized qry2006SalesChart view returns one record with the total sale amount of products in a category for each date on which a product shipped in 2006. The total number of records returned by the query is about 1,042 if you haven't added or deleted Orders records with OrderDates in 2006. You must group the records to return totals for each category by month.

Following are the steps to modify UpsizeASQL.adp's qry2006SalesChart view:

1. Open the view in Design view, and click the SQL button to open the SQL pane. Adjust the position of the field lists and the depth of the panes.

2. Click the Group By button, change the Group By criterion of the aliased Amount column to Sum, and change the ShippedDate column to Where. Making this change adds another ShippedDate entry to the columns list (see Figure 22.25).

3. A numeric month value is required to sort the output of the view by Category and calendar (not alphabetic) month. Replace the column name of the ShippedDate column that has Group By in the Group By column with the following new column definition:
   ```
   DATEPART(month, dbo.Orders.ShippedDate)
   ```

Figure 22.25
The upsized qry2006SalesChart adds the dbo. prefix to all table and column names, and translates the VBA CCur function to CONVERT(money, ColumnValue). Initial grouping is based on the values or the CategoryName and ShippedDate columns.

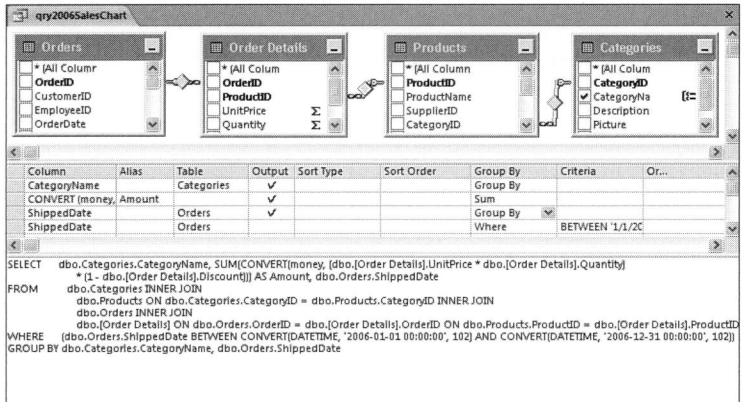

T-SQL

DATEPART([month¦quarter¦year], *DateTimeField*) returns the numeric value of the time period.

---

4. Replace the added Expr1 alias with **MonthNum** in the Alias column.

5. Specify an Ascending sort on the CategoryName column and another Ascending sort on the MonthNum column. Adding the ORDER BY clauses automatically adds TOP 100 PERCENT to the SELECT statement; change the operator to TOP 2147483647. Your view design appears as shown in Figure 22.26.

Figure 22.26
The final design of the qry2006SalesChart view illustrates the complexity of T-SQL statements with fully qualified table and field identifiers.

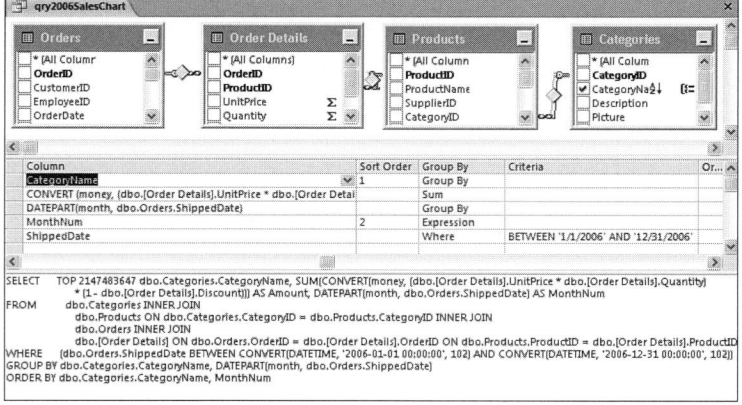

6. Click Check SQL Syntax to verify your changes, and run the view—saving your changes—to display its output (see Figure 22.27).

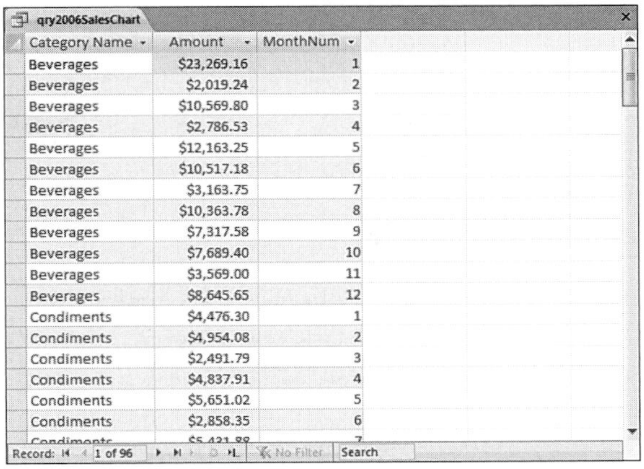

qry2006SalesChart

Category Name	Amount	MonthNum
Beverages	$23,269.16	1
Beverages	$2,019.24	2
Beverages	$10,569.80	3
Beverages	$2,786.53	4
Beverages	$12,163.25	5
Beverages	$10,517.18	6
Beverages	$3,163.75	7
Beverages	$10,363.78	8
Beverages	$7,317.58	9
Beverages	$7,689.40	10
Beverages	$3,569.00	11
Beverages	$8,645.65	12
Condiments	$4,476.30	1
Condiments	$4,954.08	2
Condiments	$2,491.79	3
Condiments	$4,837.91	4
Condiments	$5,651.02	5
Condiments	$2,858.35	6
Condiments	$5,431.88	7

Record: 1 of 96 No Filter Search

Figure 22.27 The output of the modified qry2006SalesChart view provides the required 96 rows of source data for the stored procedure.

T-SQL

Following is the full T-SQL statement for the modified view:

```
SELECT TOP 2147483647 dbo.Categories.CategoryName,
   SUM(CONVERT(money, (dbo.[Order Details].UnitPrice *
   dbo.[Order Details].Quantity) *
  (1 - dbo.[Order Details].Discount))) AS Amount,
   LEFT(DATENAME(month, dbo.Orders.ShippedDate), 3) +
   ' ''' + SUBSTRING(DATENAME(year,
   dbo.Orders.ShippedDate), 3, 2) AS Month,
   DATEPART(month, dbo.Orders.ShippedDate) AS MonthNum
FROM dbo.Orders
   INNER JOIN dbo.Categories
      INNER JOIN dbo.Products
         ON dbo.Categories.CategoryID =
            dbo.Products.CategoryID
      INNER JOIN dbo.[Order Details]
         ON dbo.Products.ProductID =
            dbo.[Order Details].ProductID
         ON dbo.Orders.OrderID =
            dbo.[Order Details].OrderID
WHERE (dbo.Orders.ShippedDate BETWEEN
   CONVERT(DATETIME, '2006-01-01 00:00:00', 102) AND
   CONVERT(DATETIME, '2006-12-31 00:00:00', 102))
GROUP BY dbo.Categories.CategoryName,
      LEFT(DATENAME(month, dbo.Orders.ShippedDate), 3) +
      ' ''' + SUBSTRING(DATENAME(year,
      dbo.Orders.ShippedDate), 3, 2),
   DATEPART(month, dbo.Orders.ShippedDate)
ORDER BY dbo.Categories.CategoryName,
   DATEPART(month, dbo.Orders.ShippedDate)
```

The `CONVERT(DATETIME, '2006-01-01 00:00:00', 102)` expression changes the standard SQL Server date format to the ANSI yyyy.mm.dd standard without the time data. Specifying 101 as the second argument value accepts the U.S. m/d/yyyy format.

UNDERSTANDING PIVOT SYNTAX

SQL Server 2005's PIVOT query syntax shares PIVOT, SELECT, and IN keywords with Access's TRANSFORM … PIVOT crosstab syntax with fixed column headers. However, the PIVOT operator's arguments and SELECT lists differ between Access and SQL Server.

Access crosstab queries are simpler to write than SQL Server 2005 PIVOT queries because Access has a Crosstab Query Wizard to assist in their design and you don't need to add explicit pivoted column names to the outer SELECT statement. You only need an IN predicate with explicit column names if your pivoted column names don't sort in the left-to-right sequence you want.

Access SQL

Access's Crosstab Query Wizard only takes a single table or query as its data source. If you want to use the Crosstab Query Wizard, you must first join the tables in a SELECT query (qry2006OrdersByCountry) as follows:

```
SELECT Orders.ShipCountry, Sum(CCur(UnitPrice * Quantity
    *(1-Discount))) AS Subtotal,
    "2006Q" & CStr(DatePart("q",OrderDate)) AS Quarter
FROM Orders INNER JOIN [Order Details] ON Orders.OrderID =
    [Order Details].OrderID
WHERE ((Year(OrderDate)=2006))
GROUP BY Orders.ShipCountry, "2006Q" & CStr(DatePart("q",[OrderDate]));
```

Then use the Crosstab Query Wizard to pivot the preceding query's result set (qry2006OrdersByCountryCTWiz) as shown here:

```
TRANSFORM Sum(qry2006OrdersByCountry.[Subtotal]) AS Amount
SELECT qry2006OrdersByCountry.[ShipCountry]
FROM qry2006OrdersByCountry
GROUP BY qry2006OrdersByCountry.[ShipCountry]
PIVOT qry2006OrdersByCountry.[Quarter]
```

The Wizard-added **qry2006OrdersByCountry** qualifier isn't required in the preceding example.

You can combine the crosstab and inner SELECT queries (qry2006OrdersByCountryCT) as shown here:

```
TRANSFORM Sum(Subtotal) AS Amount
SELECT ShipCountry FROM
    (SELECT ShipCountry, Sum(CCur(UnitPrice*Quantity*(1-Discount)))
    AS Subtotal,
    "2006Q" & CStr(DatePart("q", OrderDate)) AS Quarter
    FROM Orders INNER JOIN [Order Details] ON Orders.OrderID =
    [Order Details].OrderID
    WHERE ((Year(OrderDate)=1997))
    GROUP BY Orders.ShipCountry, "2006Q" & CStr(DatePart("q", OrderDate)))
GROUP BY ShipCountry
PIVOT Quarter [IN ("2006Q1", "2006Q2", "2006Q3", "2006Q4")]
```

The IN predicate's fixed column headers are optional because the Quarter format shown sorts in the correct order for multiple years. Access's Query Designer can't display the preceding nested query.

Figure 22.28 shows the resultset for the preceding Access SQL query.

Figure 22.28
The
qry2006OrdersByCou
ntryCT query delivers
the crosstab report
shown here.

Ship Countr	2006Q1	2006Q2	2006Q3	2006Q4
Argentina	$762.60	$335.50		$718.50
Austria	$11,349.92	$13,354.04	$13,894.92	$18,802.97
Belgium	$6,109.48	$946.00	$1,434.00	$2,945.00
Brazil	$9,469.82	$4,848.82	$13,443.55	$14,179.00
Canada	$13,933.61	$4,382.25	$9,225.70	$3,756.50
Denmark	$13,706.40	$835.20	$2,127.25	$8,523.69
Finland	$4,131.80	$4,935.20	$1,161.85	$3,208.44
France	$13,401.84	$10,187.22	$9,788.05	$11,886.27
Germany	$11,929.90	$42,017.22	$23,575.24	$39,797.80
Ireland	$1,441.38	$6,948.55	$6,969.50	$5,094.98
Italy	$2,585.69	$488.70	$1,504.43	$3,367.60
Mexico	$1,249.10	$10,576.71	$2,203.47	$320.00
Norway		$200.00	$500.00	
Poland			$808.00	$399.85
Portugal	$3,277.99	$1,677.30	$1,519.24	
Spain	$338.20	$838.30	$2,775.05	$3,026.85
Sweden	$1,703.82	$9,760.44	$5,920.68	$9,778.75
Switzerland	$2,097.60	$4,138.00	$4,666.94	$7,478.28

Record: I◄ ◄ 1 of 21 ► ►I ►※ No Filter | Search

T-SQL's PIVOT syntax appears more complex than Access's crosstab query syntax because pivoted column names *must be added explicitly* to the outer SELECT query and the IN predicate. Also, the three-part *Schema.Table.Column* names complicate the query.

T-SQL

SQL Server 2005 Books Online's "Using PIVOT and UNPIVOT" topic provides the following annotated syntax for the PIVOT operator:

```
SELECT <first non-pivoted column>,
    ...
    [last non-pivoted column] AS <column name>,
    [first pivoted column] AS <column name>,
    [second pivoted column] AS <column name>,
    ...
    [last pivoted column] AS <column name>
FROM
    ( <SELECT query that produces the data> )
    AS <alias for the source query>
PIVOT
    (<aggregation function>( <column being aggregated> )
FOR
    [<column that contains the values that will become column headers>]
    IN ( [first pivoted column], [second pivoted column],
    ...
    [last pivoted column] )
) AS <alias for the pivot table>
```

The emphasized line is added to indicate that the SELECT column list can have two or more nonpivoted related columns, such as CategoryName and ProductName.

The <SELECT query that produces the data> can be a SELECT query or the name of a table or view that contains the nonpivoted columns, <column being aggregated>, and <column that contains the values that will become column headers>. If the table or view has additional columns, you must supply a SELECT query to return only those specific columns. If you don't, the IN predicate list will return one row for each row in the source table or query.

The <aggregation function> is required even if the source table or query has pre-aggregated the <column being aggregated> values with a GROUP BY clause.

T-SQL

The following relatively simple example (vw2006OrdersByCountryCT) creates a crosstab view that displays the net value of Northwind orders for 2006 by quarter and country:

```
SELECT ShipCountry, [1] AS [2006Q1], [2] AS [2006Q2],
   [3] AS [2006Q3], [4] AS [2006Q4]
FROM
   (SELECT dbo.Orders.ShipCountry,
      CONVERT(money, SUM((dbo.[Order Details].UnitPrice *
         dbo.[Order Details].Quantity) *
         (1 - dbo.[Order Details].Discount))) AS Amount,
      DATEPART(quarter, dbo.Orders.OrderDate) AS Quarter
   FROM dbo.[Order Details] INNER JOIN dbo.Orders
      ON dbo.[Order Details].OrderID = dbo.Orders.OrderID
   WHERE DATEPART(year, dbo.Orders.OrderDate) = 2006
   GROUP BY DATEPART(quarter, dbo.Orders.OrderDate),
      dbo.Orders.ShipCountry) AS Source
PIVOT (SUM(Amount)
   FOR Quarter
      IN ([1], [2], [3], [4])) AS Dest
```

Here's a more readable version (vw2006OrdersByCountryAbbr) with two-part names used only where required:

```
SELECT ShipCountry, [1] AS [2006Q1], [2] AS [2006Q2],
   [3] AS [2006Q3], [4] AS [2006Q4]
FROM
   (SELECT ShipCountry,
      CONVERT(money, SUM((UnitPrice * Quantity) *
         (1 - Discount))) AS Amount,
      DATEPART(quarter, OrderDate) AS Quarter
   FROM [Order Details] INNER JOIN Orders
      ON [Order Details].OrderID = Orders.OrderID
   WHERE DATEPART(year, OrderDate) = 2006
   GROUP BY DATEPART(quarter, OrderDate), ShipCountry) AS Source
PIVOT(SUM(Amount)
   FOR Quarter
      IN ([1], [2], [3], [4])) AS Dest
```

ShipCountry is the sole nonpivoted column header, and [1] AS [2006Q1] ... [4] AS [2006Q4] are the four aliased pivoted column headers. The FROM clause's SELECT statement provides the country name, net amount of each order, and quarter number (1 to 4) that defines the pivoted columns.

PIVOT (SUM(Amount) ...) generates the aggregated values around which the result set pivots. FOR Quarter specifies the column name that supplies the pivoted column names, and IN (...) is the predicate that determines which pivoted columns receive data. Notice that CONVERT(money, SUM(...)) is required to cast the Amount value to the money data type.

Figure 22.29 shows the vw2006OrdersByCountryCTAbbr view's result set.

Figure 22.29
The vw2006OrdersBy-
CountryCT query
delivers the crosstab
report shown here,
which is identical to
the Access
qry2006OrdersBy-
CountryCT crosstab
query.

ShipCountry	2006Q1	2006Q2	2006Q3	2006Q4
Argentina		$762.60	$335.50	$718.50
Austria	$11,349.92	$13,354.04	$13,894.92	$18,802.97
Belgium	$6,109.48	$946.00	$1,434.00	$2,945.00
Brazil	$9,469.82	$4,848.82	$13,443.55	$14,179.00
Canada	$13,933.61	$4,382.25	$9,225.70	$3,756.50
Denmark	$13,706.40	$835.20	$2,127.25	$8,523.69
Finland	$4,131.80	$4,935.20	$1,161.85	$3,208.44
France	$13,401.84	$10,187.22	$9,788.05	$11,886.27
Germany	$11,929.90	$42,017.22	$23,575.24	$39,797.80
Ireland	$1,441.38	$6,948.55	$6,969.50	$5,094.98
Italy	$2,585.69	$488.70	$1,504.43	$3,367.60
Mexico	$1,249.10	$10,576.71	$2,203.47	$320.00
Norway		$200.00	$500.00	
Poland			$808.00	$399.85
Portugal	$3,277.99	$1,677.30	$1,519.24	
Spain	$338.20	$838.30	$2,775.05	$3,026.85
Sweden	$1,703.82	$9,760.44	$5,920.68	$9,778.75
Switzerland	$2,097.60	$4,138.00	$4,666.94	$7,478.28
UK	$7,229.70	$9,500.66	$1,295.50	$10,027.24

Record: 1 of 21   No Filter   Search

N O T E

Text files containing the Access SQL code—qry2006OrdersByCountry.sql,
qry2006OrdersByCountryCTWiz.sql, and qry2006OrdersByCountryCT.sql—and the T-SQL
examples—vw2006OrdersByCountryCT.sql and vw2006OrdersByCountryCTAbbr.sql—are
included in the \SEUA12\Chaptr22 folder of the accompanying CD-ROM. Open the file in
Notepad, copy the text to the Clipboard, and paste the statement to the SQL pane of a
new query or view. You can import the T-SQL scripts directly into SQL Server
Management Studio [Express] (SSMSX).

WRITING THE qryCATEGORIESCT PIVOT VIEW

Creating a PIVOT view to provide the data source for the qryCategoriesCT data source of the
frm2006SalesByCategoryChart and frm2006SalesByCategoryChartLinked forms and
sbf2006SalesPivotChart and sbf2006SalesPCLinked subforms isn't a complex process. The
data source that you created in the earlier "Modifying the Upsized qry2006SalesChart View"
section minimizes the amount of code you need to write. The most tedious part of the modification is typing the 12 explicit column names twice and aliases once.

T-SQL
Here's the T-SQL code for the qryCategoriesCT PIVOT view:

```
SELECT TOP 2147483647 CategoryName AS Category, [1] AS [Jan '06],
    [2] AS [Feb '06], [3] AS [Mar '06], [4] AS [Apr '06], [5] AS [May '06],
    [6] AS [Jun '06], [7] AS [Jul '06], [8] AS [Aug '06], [9] AS [Sep '06],
    [10] AS [Oct '06], [11] AS [Nov '06], [12] AS [Dec '06]
FROM (SELECT CategoryName, Amount, MonthNum
    FROM dbo.qry2006SalesChart) AS Source
PIVOT(SUM(Amount)
    FOR MonthNum
        IN ([1], [2], [3], [4], [5], [6], [7], [8], [9], [10], [11], [12]))
        AS MonthlyOrders
ORDER BY CategoryName
```

Notice that the FROM clause includes a subselect for the three required data items—CategoryName, Amount, and MonthNum. The qry2006SalesChart also returns the Month column values, which are formatted as MMM 'YY. Using Month instead of MonthNum eliminates the need to type aliases in the first SELECT statement, but requires the use of the formatted column names for the IN predicate's argument.

Figure 22.30 shows most of the Datasheet view of the query. The resulting stacked area chart is the same as for the 2006 Monthly Sales by Category form version with the copied crosstab values (refer to Figure 22.24).

Figure 22.30
The qryCategoriesCT query delivers the crosstab report shown here, which is identical in appearance to the original Access crosstab produced by the Query Wizard.

Category	Jan '06	Feb '06	Mar '06	Apr '06	May '06	Jun '06	Jul '06	Aug '06	Sep '0
Beverages	$23,269.16	$2,019.24	$10,569.80	$2,786.53	$12,163.25	$10,517.18	$3,163.75	$10,363.78	$7,31
Condiments	$4,476.30	$4,954.08	$2,491.79	$4,837.91	$5,651.02	$2,858.35	$5,431.88	$3,823.61	$4,74
Confections	$10,216.17	$5,127.38	$5,739.23	$2,599.51	$13,186.80	$6,279.21	$4,186.80	$8,865.43	$4,91
Dairy Products	$9,851.48	$6,074.44	$8,192.80	$7,521.50	$9,374.38	$10,358.25	$9,881.83	$8,703.68	$10,04
Grains/Cereals	$3,585.60	$3,798.80	$5,312.70	$2,084.40	$6,052.25	$6,492.65	$2,230.00	$7,856.25	$5,22
Meat/Poultry	$8,365.45	$5,958.30	$7,274.40	$5,130.24	$4,597.91	$3,966.40	$5,924.20	$4,005.74	$5,91
Produce	$3,288.54	$1,587.60	$4,104.60	$5,613.06	$4,695.60	$5,275.00	$2,198.70	$3,771.00	$2,33
Seafood	$1,693.76	$1,922.65	$3,829.00	$1,023.30	$8,254.15	$4,335.96	$4,527.81	$8,878.50	$10,01

Record: 1 of 8 · No Filter · Search

NOTE

Text files containing the T-SQL code for the modified qry2006SalesChart view (vw2006SalesChart.sql) and the qryCategoriesCT view (vwCategoriesCT.sql) are in the \Seua12\Chaptr22 folder of the accompanying CD-ROM. If you didn't perform the preceding exercises, open the file in Notepad, copy the text to the Clipboard, and paste the statement to the SQL pane of a new view or stored procedure.

CROSSFOOTING CROSSTAB QUERIES

Access's Query Wizard lets you add an optional row totals column but not a column totals row. T-SQL's PIVOT syntax doesn't support optional row totals. Management usually wants crosstab reports with row and column totals, which accountants commonly call *crossfooting* or *crossfoot totals*. You can define reports that print calculated crossfoot total values, but management might have access to Datasheet views that ordinarily don't have these features.

You can open the Home ribbon's Records menu and click Totals to toggle a row of column totals, but you can't display a column of row totals without some additional work. The column totals are a Datasheet artifact, so they would not be present when users export the table data to another application. Crosstabs primarily are management tools; it's a good application development practice to give management types what they want.

Adding crossfoot totals to a crosstab view requires T-SQL code in a stored procedure that performs the following steps:

1. Create a temporary table (#tblCategoryCT) with structure and data identical to the PIVOT table query result set by executing a SELECT … INTO #tblCategoryCT FROM qryCategoriesCT statement.

2. Add a Totals column of the money data type to the table with an ALTER TABLE #tblCategoryCT ADD Totals money statement.

3. Populate the Totals column with the sum of all non-NULL row values with an UPDATE #tblCategoryCT SET Totals = IsNull([Jan '06],0) + … IsNull([Dec '06],0) statement. (The IsNull(value, 0) function returns 0 for NULL column values).

4. SQL Server 2005 won't execute the following instructions:

```
INSERT tblCategoryCT (Category, [Jan '06], [Feb '06], [Mar '06], ...)
    VALUES(N'Totals', SUM(IsNull([Jan '06],0)), SUM(IsNull([Feb '06],0)),
        SUM(IsNull([Mar '06],0)) ...)
```

Therefore, you must store the sum of non-NULL column values into variables with a set of 12 of these statements:

```
DECLARE @Jan money
SET @Jan = (SELECT SUM(IsNull([Jan '06],0)) FROM #tblCategoryCT)
...
DECLARE @Totals money
SET @Totals = (SELECT SUM(IsNull([Totals],0)) FROM #tblCategoryCT);
```

Then, add the row of column totals with INSERT #tblCategoryCT VALUES('Totals', @Jan, @Feb, @Mar, @Apr, @May, @Jun, @Jul, @Aug, @Sep, @Oct, @Nov, @Dec, @Totals).

5. Finally, return the rows and drop the temporary table:

```
SELECT * FROM #tblCategoryCT ORDER BY Category;
DROP TABLE #tblCategoryCT;
```

T-SQL

Here's the full T-SQL batch to create the spCategoriesCrossfoot stored procedure:

```
CREATE PROCEDURE spCategoriesCrossfoot
AS
SET NOCOUNT ON
—Create the temporary tblCategoryCT table from the PIVOT query
SELECT Category, [Jan '06], [Feb '06], [Mar '06], [Apr '06],
[May '06], [Jun '06], [Jul '06], [Aug '06],
[Sep '06], [Oct '06], [Nov '06], [Dec '06]
INTO #tblCategoryCT FROM qryCategoriesCT;

—Add a Row Totals Field
ALTER TABLE #tblCategoryCT ADD Totals money;

—Update the Total Field
UPDATE #tblCategoryCT SET Totals =
IsNull([Jan '06],0) + IsNull([Feb '06],0) + IsNull([Mar '06],0) +
IsNull([Apr '06],0) + IsNull([May '06],0) + IsNull([Jun '06],0) +
```

```
IsNull([Jul '06],0) + IsNull([Aug '06],0) + IsNull([Sep '06],0) +
IsNull([Oct '06],0) + IsNull([Nov '06],0) + IsNull([Dec '06],0);

—Get the column totals
DECLARE @Jan money
SET @Jan = (SELECT SUM(IsNull([Jan '06],0)) FROM #tblCategoryCT)
DECLARE @Feb money
SET @Feb = (SELECT SUM(IsNull([Feb '06],0)) FROM #tblCategoryCT)
DECLARE @Mar money
SET @Mar = (SELECT SUM(IsNull([Mar '06],0)) FROM #tblCategoryCT)
DECLARE @Apr money
SET @Apr = (SELECT SUM(IsNull([Apr '06],0)) FROM #tblCategoryCT)
DECLARE @May money
SET @May = (SELECT SUM(IsNull([May '06],0)) FROM #tblCategoryCT)
DECLARE @Jun money
SET @Jun = (SELECT SUM(IsNull([Jun '06],0)) FROM #tblCategoryCT)
DECLARE @Jul money
SET @Jul = (SELECT SUM(IsNull([Jul '06],0)) FROM #tblCategoryCT)
DECLARE @Aug money
SET @Aug = (SELECT SUM(IsNull([Aug '06],0)) FROM #tblCategoryCT)
DECLARE @Sep money
SET @Sep = (SELECT SUM(IsNull([Sep '06],0)) FROM #tblCategoryCT)
DECLARE @Oct money
SET @Oct = (SELECT SUM(IsNull([Oct '06],0)) FROM #tblCategoryCT)
DECLARE @Nov money
SET @Nov = (SELECT SUM(IsNull([Nov '06],0)) FROM #tblCategoryCT)
DECLARE @Dec money
SET @Dec = (SELECT SUM(IsNull([Dec '06],0)) FROM #tblCategoryCT)
DECLARE @Totals money
SET @Totals = (SELECT SUM(IsNull([Totals],0)) FROM #tblCategoryCT);

—Add and populate a Column Totals row
INSERT #tblCategoryCT VALUES('Totals', @Jan, @Feb, @Mar, @Apr, @May,
@Jun, @Jul, @Aug, @Sep, @Oct, @Nov, @Dec, @Totals);

—Return the rows and drop the temporary table
SELECT * FROM #tblCategoryCT ORDER BY Category;
DROP TABLE #tblCategoryCT;
```

Figure 22.31 shows, in a double exposure, the result of executing the spCategoriesCrossfoot stored procedure. The T-SQL code to create the stored procedure is in the \SEUA12\Chaptr 22\spCategoriesCrossfoot.sql file.

Figure 22.31
The spCategoriesCrossfoot stored procedure adds column and row crossfoot totals to the qryCategoriesCT PIVOT view's result set.

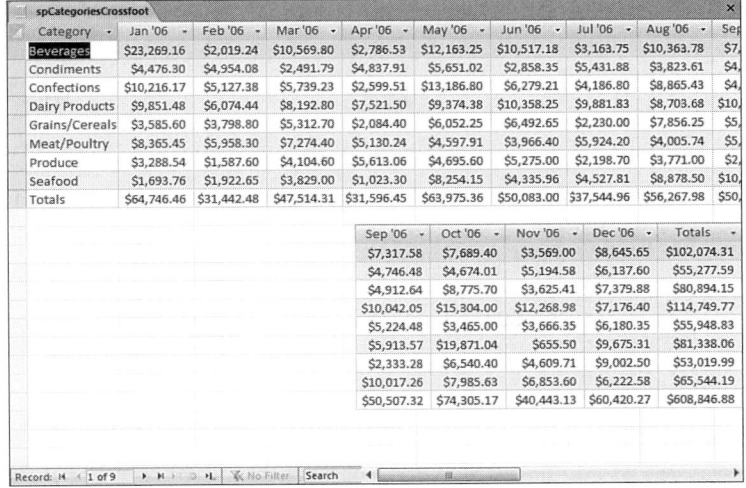

SECURING UPSIZED PROJECTS AND THEIR DATA

Converting your upsized project to an encoded (.ade) file doesn't provide security for your back-end SQL Server database. You must provide groups or individual users with logins to the server and permissions to read and update specific tables, as well as to open views and execute stored procedures.

→ For more information on creating .ade files and using SSMSX, **see** "Securing Your Project as an .ade File," **p. 909** and **see** "Adding SQL Server User Logins with SQL Server Management Studio," **p. 852**.

Chapter 19 covers granting read permissions for tables, views, and functions to Windows groups or users by adding them as members of the db_datareader database role and granting write permissions for tables with the db_datawriter role. However, there's no predefined db_executors role that has automatic permissions for stored procedures.

In Chapter 19, you created the NWReaders security group and assigned it the db_datareader database role, and you created the NWWriters group and assigned it db_datareader and db_datawriter roles. Members of NWReaders automatically gain read permission on views or functions that serve as data sources for SELECT (row-returning) stored procedures.

You must manually add execute permission for each stored procedure that returns result sets to the NWReaders group. Add execute permission for each stored procedure that performs UPDATE, INSERT, or DELETE operations to the NWWriters group. Adding view definition permission for stored procedures to the NWReaders, NWWriters, or both groups is optional.

To add execute permission for the NWReaders group to all row-returning stored procedures in the UpsizeSQL database, as an example, do the following:

1. Open SSMSX and connect to your ADP's SSX instance (OAKLEAF-MS16 for this example).

2. Expand the Databases, UpsizeSQL, Security, and Users nodes.

3. Add the [DomainName\]NWReaders login as an UpsizeSQL database user with the db_datareader role, as described in Chapter 19's "Adding SQL Server User Logins with SQL Server Management Studio" section.

4. If the Database User [DomainName\]NWReaders dialog isn't open, right-click the [DomainName\]NWReaders item under the \UpsizeSQL\Security\Users node and select Properties. Select the Securables page.

5. Click Add to open the Add Objects dialog, select the All Objects of the Types option, and click OK to open the Select Object Types dialog.

6. Mark the Stored Procedures check box (see Figure 22.32), and click OK to close the dialog and display the Securables list of the database's stored procedures, including system stored procedures with dbo.dt_ and sys.sp_ prefixes.

Figure 22.32
The Select Object Types dialog lets you grant execute permissions for a database user on any stored procedure (or other object type) in the database.

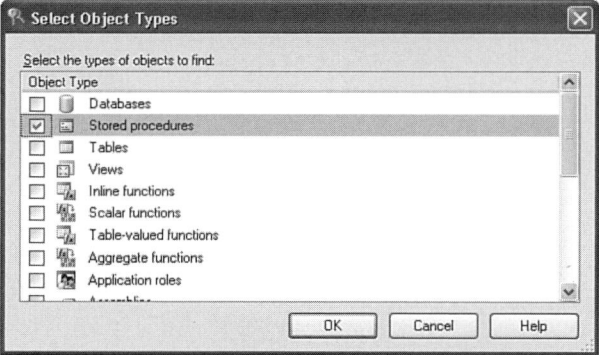

7. With the Customers and Suppliers by City stored procedure item selected, mark the Grant check box and, optionally, the View Definition check box (see Figure 22.33).

8. Repeat step 7 for other row-returning stored procedures in the database, such as qryUnionQuery, qryUSMailList, and spCategoriesCrossfoot, if present.

9. Log off Windows with your administrative account and log in with an account that's a member of the NWReaders security group and verify that you can execute the row-returning stored procedures.

10. Optionally, repeat steps 4–8 for the NWWriters login and then add permissions for the qryAQtblShipAddresses (INSERT), qryDQOrders (DELETE), and qryMTtblShipAddresses (make-table) action queries.

Figure 22.33
The Securables page of the database user's properties dialog lets you assign explicit permission for all stored procedures in the database, including system stored procedures.

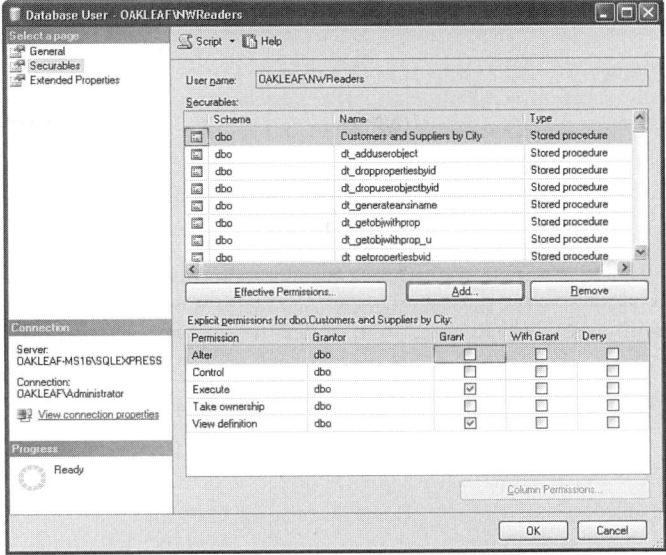

Managing SQL Server security is an even more complex task than using the Access user- and group-level security features of Access 2003 and earlier.

TROUBLESHOOTING

STORED PROCEDURES DON'T RETURN THE EXPECTED RECORDSET

My `SELECT * FROM TableName` *statement at the end of a stored procedure that includes* `INSERT [INTO]`, `UPDATE`, *or* `DELETE` *statements doesn't return any rows.*

`SET NOCOUNT ON` wasn't added automatically by the stored procedure designer as the first statement of your procedure or was deleted as a result of modifying the stored procedure code in SSMSX. T-SQL and VBA can handle combinations of multiple return values and Recordsets from a stored procedure, but ADP can't. If you don't add `SET NOCOUNT ON`, the server returns the number of records affected for each operation, which generates an unneeded data transfer from the server to the client. In the case of the spCategoriesCT procedure, the server returns 10 values before sending the Recordset. Unless you're using VBA code to execute the query and need the `RecordsAffected` values returned after execution, verify in SSMX that `SET NOCOUNT ON` is the first statement of your stored procedures.

22

IN THE REAL WORLD—STRATEGIC OR NOT?

Access data projects (ADP) and SQL Server once represented Microsoft's strategic migration path to client/server applications. Only those technologies that Microsoft deems *strategic* receive significant development funding. As an example, when Microsoft decided in 1998 that SQL Server was its *strategic* database, Jet development ground to an immediate halt with the release of Access 2000. Jet 4.0 was the end of the line for this venerable database engine.

The Access team has decided that ADP and SQL Server are no longer a strategic combination for the Office product group. The official recommendation is to link Access front ends to Windows Server 2003's free Windows SharePoint Services (WSS 3.0) or the costly Microsoft Office SharePoint Server (MOSS) 2007. If loss of almost all benefits of a relational database management system doesn't meet your requirements, the Access team recommends linking SQL Server 2005 tables to an Access 2007 front end.

 Similarly, Data Access Objects (DAO) and Open Database Connectivity (ODBC) aren't strategic; DAO was terminal at version 3.6 and, when this book was written, there were no references to ODBC on Microsoft's website (http://www.microsoft.com/data/odbc/default.htm). Microsoft Data Access Components (MDAC), which include ActiveX Data Objects (ADO) and OLE DB, *were* strategic, but are no longer as strategic as ADO.NET. Windows XP, Server 2003, and Vista install MDAC 2.8 as part of the operating system, but MDAC 2.8 doesn't include Jet or the Jet OLE DB or ODBC driver. (Windows Vista's Windows Data Access Components (DAC) 6.0 is a slightly modified version of MDAC 2.8 SP1.) Mainstream support for MDAC 2.8 retires on July 8, 2008, a few months more than a year after the release of Access 2007. Almost all of Microsoft's data connectivity efforts are directed to the .NET Framework's ADO.NET, ASP.NET, and Visual Studio 2005 and later.

The Access team decided that ADO wasn't strategic and created its own version of Jet called the *Access database engine* and replaced DAO 3.6 with the Microsoft Office 2007 Access database engine Objects (ACEDAO.dll). Access 2007 and ACEDAO support new features, such as multivalued lookup tables, the Attachments data type, and layout view for forms and reports. Support for the new Access database format and object library is subject to Office 2007 support policy.

Circumstances might dictate that you upgrade your Access application from Access to SQL Server. A common reason for upsizing is that your application has become critical to the continued success of your organization, so management wants to put it under the aegis of the information technology (IT) department. In this case, you and the IT department must decide whether to link the Access application to the server or upsize the front-end .accdb to an .adp. Most linked Access applications consume several simultaneous ODBC connections per user to SQL Server, but ADP consumes only one or two OLE DB connections. Poorly designed Access queries can require the server to send thousands of rows to clients when only one or a few rows suffice for the application. If your application has many users, it's likely that the SQL Server database administrator(s) will insist on the more efficient ADP approach.

If you're using Access as an RDBMS learning tool, and want to expand your *weltanschauung* from the desktop to the client/server world, Access 2007 is your best bet. The project designer makes it easy to design views, functions, and stored procedures based on SELECT statements, as well as stored procedures for INSERT, UPDATE, DELETE, and make-table queries. After you've mastered the transition from Access SQL to T-SQL, you can experiment with writing increasingly complex stored procedures from scratch. Like a working knowledge of VBA, expertise in stored-procedure programming boosts your career potential.

What's more, unlike the transition from Visual Basic 6.0 to Visual Basic .NET, T-SQL in SQL Server 2005 is fully backward-compatible with SQL Server 2000's T-SQL. It's also certain that the next version (code-named *Katmai*) of SQL Server's implementation of T-SQL will be fully backward-compatible with that of SQL Server 2005. Another bonus is that T-SQL is the query language for the freely redistributable SQL Server Compact Edition (SQLce, formerly SQL Server Anywhere Edition), the lightweight, embeddable SQL Server version that replaces SQL Server Consumer Edition (SQLS CE).

COLLABORATING WITH ACCESS DATA

CHAPTER 23

IMPORTING AND EXPORTING WEB PAGES

In this chapter

Hypertext Markup Language (HTML) is the *lingua franca* of the World Wide Web. *Hypertext* refers to a computer document that has cross-references (*hyperlinks*) to other related documents, which are accessible from the local machine or other, networked computers. When you select (click) a hyperlink, a web browser on your computer displays the linked document. HTML defines markup tags, enclosed by angle brackets, to specify the type, purpose, or formatting of a blog of text or graphic image. For example, <p> … </p> tags specify the beginning and end of a paragraph, <img … /> defines a graphic image, and <a …>…</a> tags specify a hyperlink (anchor). Most tags occur in pairs, but empty tags, such as <img … /> and
 (line break), are single markup elements.

 The World Wide Web Consortium (W3C, http://www.w3c.org) maintains HTML standards as recommendations; the latest W3C recommendation when this book was written was the HTML 4.01 Specification of December 24, 1999 (http://www.w3.org/TR/html4/).

The growth of the Internet, spurred by the Web's popularity, caused HTML to become the most widely used of all document formats. Fortunately, HTML contains tags to define tables and their column/row structure; tables are the most popular method of laying out web pages. Therefore, the capability to import or link HTML tables to Access tables has gained importance as more reference and other useful information moves from private text files in various—often proprietary—formats to public HTML pages. Similarly, the popularity of HTML requires many Access users to export table data to HTML files for posting to Websites on intranets or the Internet.

> **NOTE**
>
> Joel Spolsky, a highly respected software developer and former Microsoft employee, says at the end of a June 2004 article titled "How Microsoft Lost the API War" (where API is an abbreviation of Application Programming Interface): "The new API is HTML, and the new winners in the application development marketplace will be the people who can make HTML sing" (http://www.joelonsoftware.com/articles/APIWar.html).

IMPORTING OR LINKING DATA FROM HTML TABLES

One of the most common—and most risky—processes is importing others' data from Web-based HTML content to Access tables. First, the originator of the information usually has a copyright to the content by default. One exception to this general rule is content published by federal agencies, such as the Federal Register or Code of Federal Regulations (CFR). Other exceptions are content in the public domain and documents published with an appropriate Creative Commons license.

> **NOTE**
>
> Brief explanations and links to full text copies of the six types of Creative Commons licenses can be found at http://creativecommons.org/about/licenses/meet-the-licenses/.

Unless the content falls within the preceding exceptions, you must have permission to import or link to original content. Linking HTML content to a database table is not the same process as creating a hyperlink to the same material on the author's or designee's site.

CAUTION

> Nothing in this or other chapters of this book should be construed as legal advice. Engage an attorney if you have questions concerning the propriety or legality of incorporating others' works in your Access tables.

 Second, you'll often need to modify the HTML code to import the content correctly—or at all. This chapter's sections on importing HTML use as the source simple HTML tables from the United States International Trade Commission's (USITC) searchable Harmonized Tariff Schedule (HTS) Database (http://www.usitc.gov/tata/hts/other/dataweb/). This site typifies public reference data sources on the Web.

ANALYZING AN HTML TABLE'S STRUCTURE

The <table> and </table> tag pair identify the beginning and end of an HTML table structure. The <tr> and </tr> (table row) tag pair create rows; the <td> ... </td> (table data) tags create cells that hold data. Optional <th colspan="#"> and </th> pairs define a table heading that spans # columns. Following is the HTML code for a page with a simple four-column, four-row table with a table heading that spans all four columns, table column headings in the first row, and a border around all cells:

```
<html>
  <head>
    <title>Web Page with a Simple Table</title>
  </head>
  <body>
    <table border="1">
      <tr>
        <th colspan="4">Simple Four-Column Table</th>
      </tr>
      <tr>
        <th>Col1</th><th>Col2</th><th>Col3</th><th>Col4</th>
      </tr>
      <tr>
        <td>R1C1</td><td>R1C2</td><td>R1C3</td><td>R1C4</td>
      </tr>
      <tr>
        <td>R2C1</td><td>R2C2</td><td>R2C3</td><td>R2C4</td>
      </tr>
      <tr>
        <td>R3C1</td><td>R3C2</td><td>R3C3</td><td>R3C4</td>
      </tr>
    </table>
  </body>
</html>
```

Access 2007's Import HTML Wizard detects the `<table>` tag to create a list of the table(s) in an HTML document, and it parses the `<tr>` elements to add records and the `<td>` elements to add fields.

NOTE

The \SEUA12\Chaptr23\SimpleTable.htm file contains the preceding code. Open the file in any web browser to view the table.

IMPORTING HTML TABLES FROM WEB PAGES

Internet Explorer's <u>V</u>iew, Sour<u>c</u>e menu choice opens Notepad with the HTML code for most web pages. As an example, Figure 23.1 shows part of the USITC web page of eight-digit HTS8 codes, product descriptions, and tariffs for Chapter 95, "Toys, Games and Sports Requisites; Parts and Accessories Thereof" (HTS8 code >= 95000000).

Figure 23.1
The U.S. International Trade Commission publishes a Harmonized Tariff Schedule database with eight-digit HTS8 product codes and tariff rates for various countries of origin. This is the start of the display page for Chapter 95, "Toys, Games and Sports Equipment; Parts and Accessories Thereof."

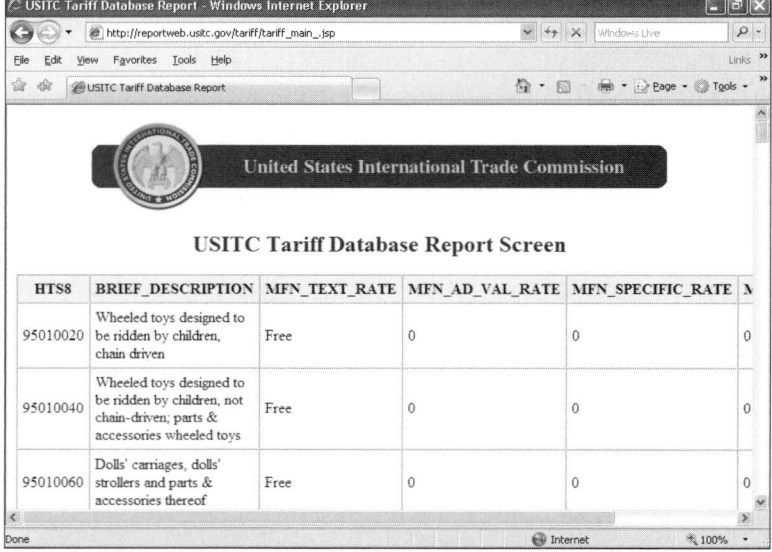

To create an HTML file for a simple table that's part of a basic web page for reference data, such as the table shown in Figure 23.1, do the following:

1. Launch Internet Explorer (IE) 6.0 or later, and navigate to the site that contains the data you want to import or link (http://reportweb.usitc.gov/tariff/tariff_form_.jsp for this example).

2. If the database is searchable and enables displayed field selection, specify the fields to include in the web page: HTS8, BRIEF_DESCRIPTION, MFN_TEXT_RATE (most-favored nation tariff rate), MFN_AD_VAL_Rate (ad valorem rate), MFN_

SPECIFIC_RATE, and MFN_OTHER_RATE for this example (see Figure 23.2). Click Proceed To Next Step to open the Query Screen.

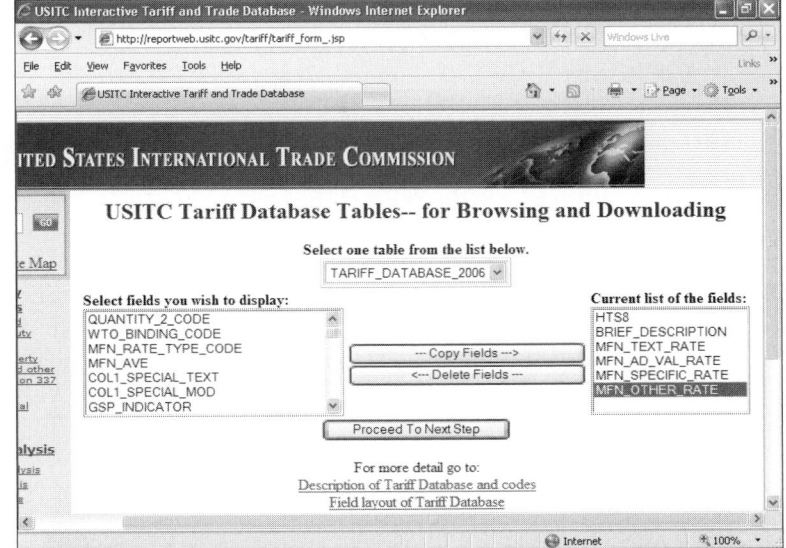

Figure 23.2
Select the fields to include in the tariff display page in this USITC Database Tables page.

3. For this example, select HTS8 in the first list, >= in the second, and type **95000000** in the third field. Also, accept 100 in the Number of Records to Display text box (see Figure 23.3). Click Run Report to open the page shown earlier in Figure 23.1.

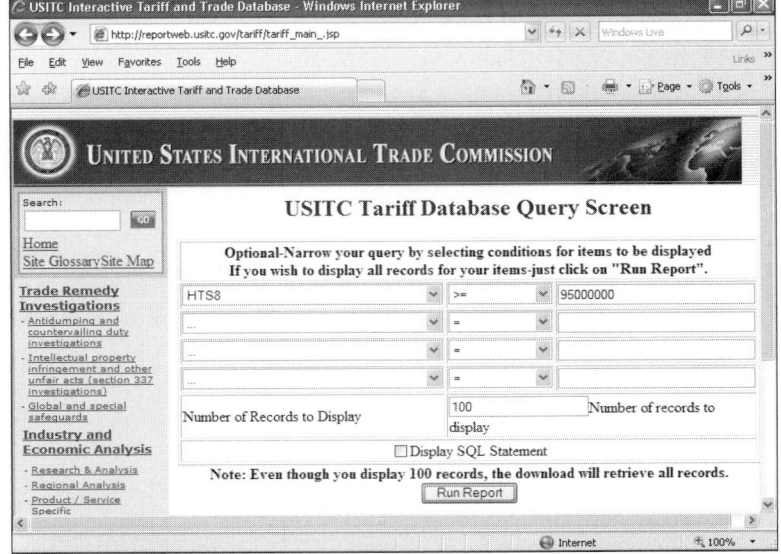

Figure 23.3
Specify the starting eight-digit HTS8 code and the number of rows to display in the USITC Tariff Database Query Screen.

4. In IE, choose <u>V</u>iew, Sour<u>c</u>e to open Notepad with the HTML content of the page. Scroll until you reach the HTML code that starts the data table (`<TABLE BORDER cellpadding=5 cellspacing=0>` for this example).

5. In Notepad, choose <u>F</u>ile, Save <u>A</u>s to open the Save As dialog, select All Files in the Save As Type list, name the file **HTSTest1.htm** or the like, and save it in your working folder (\Seau12\Chaptr23).

To import the HTML file you created with Access's Import HTML Wizard, follow these steps:

1. Launch Access if necessary, open a new database named **HTMLOperations.accdb** in your working folder, close Table1, click the External Data tab, and click the Import group's More button to open the gallery. Click the <u>H</u>TML Document button to open the Get External Data – HTML Document dialog.

2. Accept the Import the Source Data into a New Table in the Current Database option, click the Browse button to open the File Open dialog, navigate to the location of your saved .htm file, double-click the file item to return to the Get External Data – HTML Document dialog, and click OK to start the Import HTML Wizard.

If you receive an error message at this point and can't continue to the next step, see the "Errors Importing HTML Files Obtained from the Web" topic in the "Troubleshooting" section near the end of this chapter.

3. If the .htm file contains more than one table, you must select the table to export in the list box, which displays the page title with a sequential suffix number. For this example, select the second table (USITC Tariff Database Report1), which contains the data to export (see Figure 23.4). Click Next.

Figure 23.4
The first Import HTML Wizard dialog lets you select the table with the data to import, if the file contains more than one HTML table.

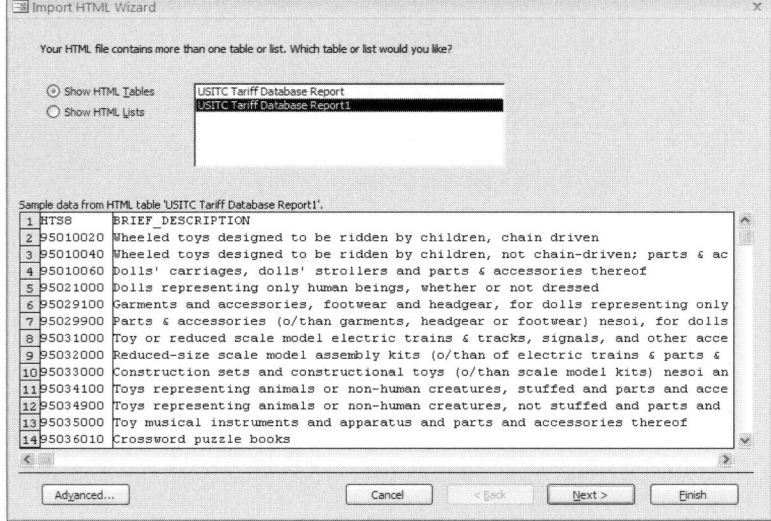

4. In the second Wizard dialog, mark the First Row Contains Column Headings and then click Next.

5. In the third Wizard dialog, accept the HTS8 field's default Long Integer data type and specify a Duplicates OK index (see Figure 23.5). Select the BRIEF_DESCRIPTION field and specify the Memo data type to accommodate text more than 255 characters long. Accept the default Text data type for the MFN_TEXT_RATE field, and replace the remaining three fields' Long Integer with the Double data type. Click Next.

NOTE

The Wizard doesn't detect the presence of numbers with decimal fractions in the last three columns, because it tests only the first 24 rows of the table and finds 0 in each cell. The first item with a nonzero tariff is row 38. (Look ahead to Figure 23.8.)

Figure 23.5
The HTS8 (product code) field ordinarily would be used as the primary key, but it has several duplicate values.

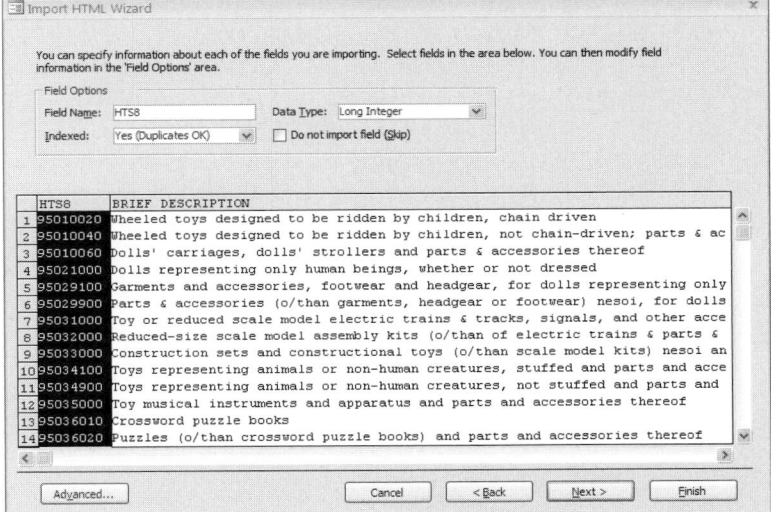

6. In the fourth Wizard dialog, select the No Primary Key option so you can run the … Duplicates query, remove the duplicate rows, and then assign the HTS8 field as the table's primary key. Click Next.

7. In the fifth and final Wizard dialog, rename the table to **HTS8Chapter95** or the like, and click Finish to display the Get External Data – HTML Document dialog's Save Import Steps page.

8. If you want to save the import specification, mark the Save Import Steps check box and add the required information, as illustrated by Figure 23.6, and click the Save Import button.

Figure 23.6
You can save the import specification for the table and schedule recurring imports in Outlook with the Microsoft Office Access Outlook Add-in for Publishing and Data Collection.

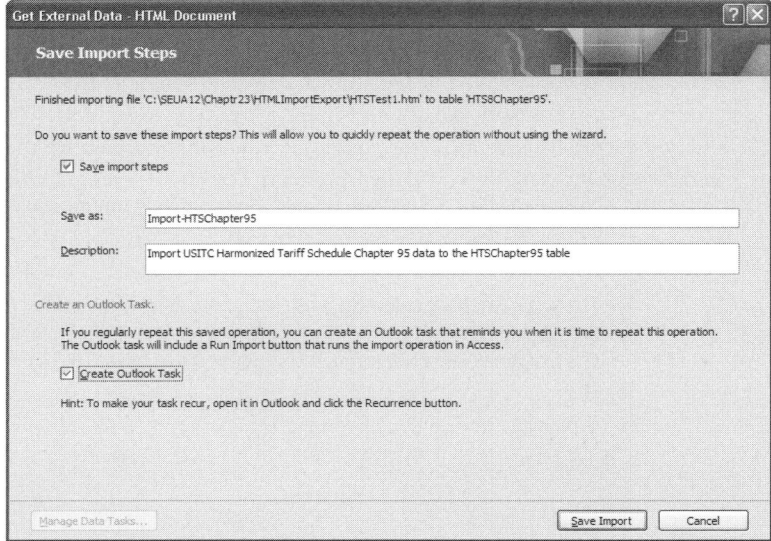

23

9. If you marked the Create Outlook Task check box in the Get External Data – HTML Document dialog, after a few seconds an Outlook Task message opens. Click the Recurrence button to specify the interval between repeated imports in the Task Recurrence dialog (see Figure 23.7).

TIP

Mark the Outlook Task message's Reminder check box to remind you of the impending task so that you can repeat preceding steps 1–5 prior to the import process.

Figure 23.7
If you want to repeat the importation periodically, set the recurrence interval in the Outlook Task message's Task Recurrence dialog.

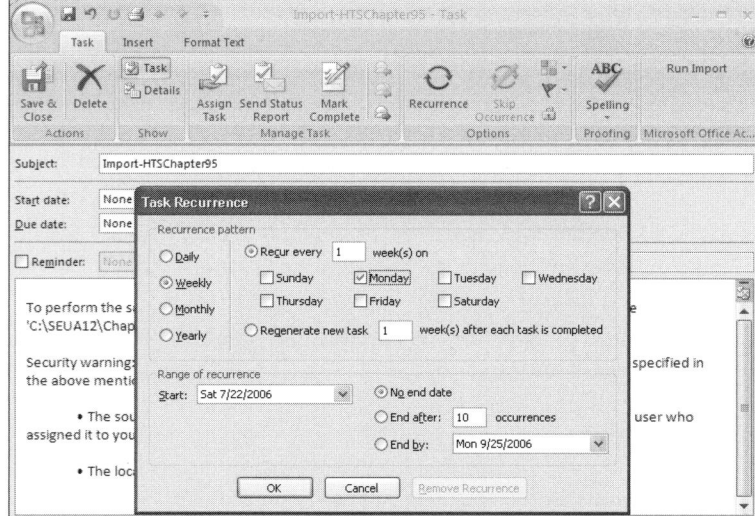

10. Close the Task Recurrence dialog, click Save & Close to return to Access, and open the HTS8Chapter95 table (see Figure 23.8).

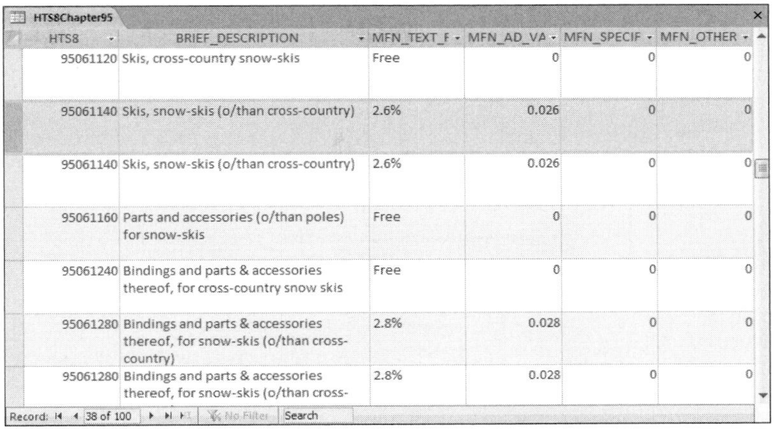

Figure 23.8
The imported HTS8Chapter95 table contains duplicate rows for product code 95061140 (heading 9506.11.40) and 95061280 (9506.12.80).

HTS8	BRIEF_DESCRIPTION	MFN_TEXT_F	MFN_AD_VA	MFN_SPECIF	MFN_OTHER
95061120	Skis, cross-country snow-skis	Free	0	0	0
95061140	Skis, snow-skis (o/than cross-country)	2.6%	0.026	0	0
95061140	Skis, snow-skis (o/than cross-country)	2.6%	0.026	0	0
95061160	Parts and accessories (o/than poles) for snow-skis	Free	0	0	0
95061240	Bindings and parts & accessories thereof, for cross-country snow skis	Free	0	0	0
95061280	Bindings and parts & accessories thereof, for snow-skis (o/than cross-country)	2.8%	0.028	0	0
95061280	Bindings and parts & accessories thereof, for snow-skis (o/than cross-	2.8%	0.028	0	0

Record: 38 of 100 · No Filter · Search

COUNTING DUPLICATE ROWS WITH THE FIND DUPLICATES QUERY WIZARD

Duplicate rows in tables imported from an HTML document don't occur frequently, but you ordinarily should remove those that prevent you from creating a primary key for the table from one or more of its fields. Unlike most other import errors, duplicate rows in the source table don't generate rows in an Import Errors table when you specify the primary key field. Instead, the Import Wizard ignores the duplication errors by abandoning the attempt to add the primary key.

You remove duplicates by running an append query to add nonduplicate rows to a new table of the same structure as the source table. You need to know the number of duplicates so that you can verify that the number of records in the new table is correct. The Find Duplicates Query Wizard makes it easy to create a result set that contains a row for each duplicate row in the source table, regardless of the number of duplicates of a particular row.

You use the Find Duplicates Query Wizard to create a Find Duplicates for HTS8Chapter95 query, which contains a row for each of the 22 duplicate entries in the HTS8Chapter95 table that you created in the preceding section. If you have any source values with more than two duplicates, you sum the query's NumberOfDups field to compare the value with the message you receive when appending the rows to the new table.

NOTE

If the USITC has removed the duplicates since this book was published, you can create the HTS8Chapter95 file from the HTSTest1.htm file in the \SEUA12\Chaptr23 folder.

To create the Find Duplicates for HTS8Chapter95 query in your HTMLOperations database, do this:

1. Click the Create tab and the Query Wizards button to open the New Query Wizard. Double-click the Find Duplicates Query Wizard item to start the process.

2. In the first Wizard dialog, select the item Table: HTS8Chapter95 in the list and click Next.

3. In the second Wizard dialog, select HTS8 in the Available Fields list and click the > button to move it to the Selected Fields list (see Figure 23.9).

Figure 23.9
The HTS8 and BRIEF_DESCRIPTION fields contain the duplicate data, but the wizard doesn't add Memo fields to the Available Fields list.

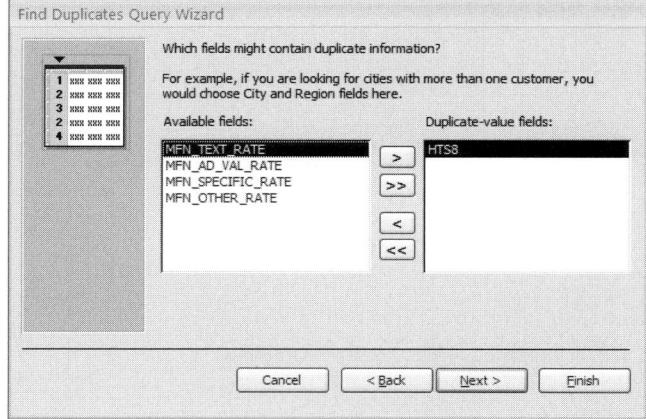

4. The Wizard doesn't enable testing fields of the Memo data type for duplication or displaying them for reference, so click Finish to create the query and open it in Datasheet view (see Figure 23.10).

Figure 23.10
The Find Duplicates Query Wizard generates a result set containing at least the field containing the duplicated values and the NumberOfDups column.

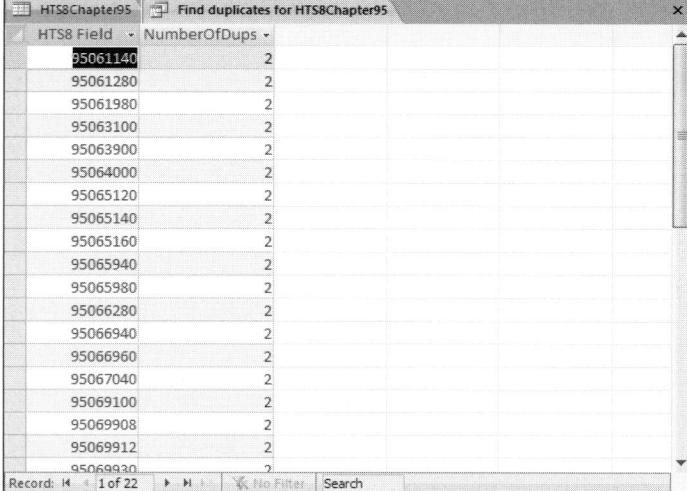

5. If you have a large number of rows, open a new query in SQL view, type SELECT MAX([NumberOfDups]) AS MaxDups FROM [Find Duplicates for HTS8Chapter95] in the text box, and click the Run button. For this example, MaxDups is 2.

6. If MaxDups is greater than 2, replace the preceding SQL statement with SELECT SUM([NumberOfDups]) AS TotalDups FROM [Find Duplicates for HTS8Chapter95].

7. Close the query and save your changes.

For a small duplicate result set, inspection can take the place of steps 5 and 6, but it's a good audit practice to always run MaxDups and, if MaxDups is greater than 2, TotalDups queries.

REMOVING DUPLICATE ROWS WITH AN APPEND QUERY

To create a copy of the HTS8Chapter95 table without the duplicates and add nonduplicate records to it, do the following:

1. Close the HTS8Chapter95 table and rename it **HTS8Chapter95Dups** or the like for this example.

2. Select the renamed table and press Ctrl+V, Ctrl+C to open the Paste Table As dialog. Change the table name to **HTS8Chapter95** for this example, and select the Structure Only option (see Figure 23.11). Click OK.

Figure 23.11
Clone the structure of the source table to start the process of creating a table without duplicate rows.

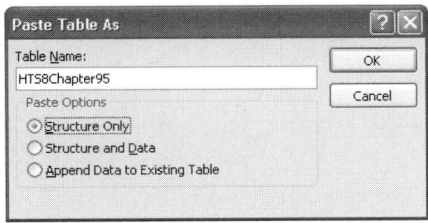

3. Open the new empty table in Design view and, with the candidate key field (HTS8 for this example) selected, click the Primary Key button, close the table, and save your changes.

4. Click the Create tab, and click the Query Design button to create a new query. Add the source table to the query, drag the all fields (*) item to the query grid, and click the Query Tools, Design ribbon's Append Query button to open the Append dialog.

5. Select the destination table in the Table Name list or edit the table name in the text box. Accept the default Current Database option (see Figure 23.12), and click OK.

6. Click the Run button to prepare to append nonduplicate records. Click Yes to acknowledge the number of rows in the source table (100) and display the message box shown in Figure 23.13.

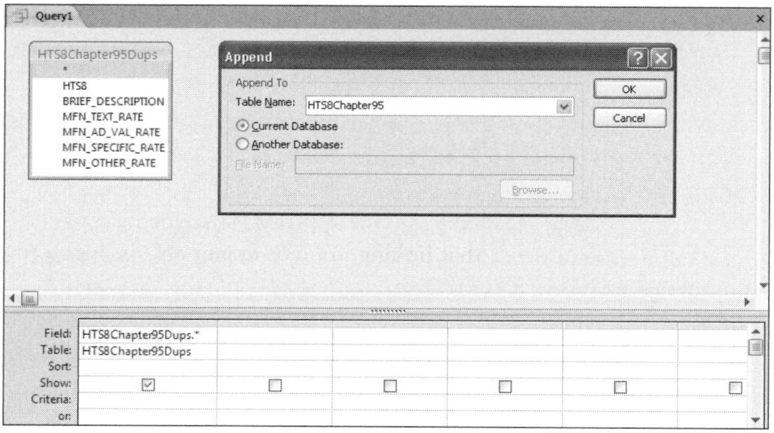

Figure 23.12
Specify the destination table for the appended records in the Append dialog.

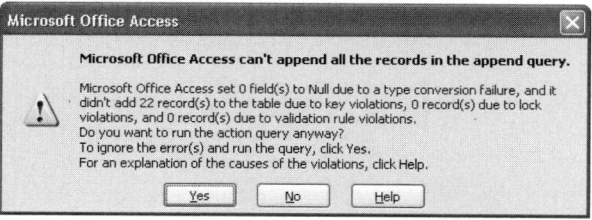

Figure 23.13
This message box opens when you attempt to append duplicate records to a destination table with a primary key field. The transaction reports the number of type conversion errors, primary key uniqueness violations, and validation rule violations. Clicking No rolls back the transaction.

7. Compare the number of records that the query didn't add to the table due to key violations to the TotalDups value you obtained in the preceding section. If the two values are the same, click Yes to commit the transaction; otherwise, click No to roll back the transaction.

8. Inspect the new table for consistency (other than missing duplicate rows) with the source table. When you're convinced it's safe, you can delete or archive the source table.

It's clear that periodically importing up-to-date HTML data from a typical website that provides reference data and then correcting problems with the resulting tables involves a very complex workflow.

NOTE

The USITC simplifies the process of importing data by providing downloadable files in comma-separated, tab-separated, and other text formats for the query. However, you must enter the HTS8 query criteria each time you want to update the table.

LINKING HTML DOCUMENTS TO ACCESS TABLES

You can substitute a link to the HTML file for the import process described in the preceding sections but, as is the case with linked Excel worksheets, the linked table is read-only. Linking also prevents making corrections for duplicate fields and the other problems with the source content that the following sections describe. Unless you write VBA code to obtain the HTML content directly from the website or have network access to the source .htm file, you must use the View Source approach described early in this chapter. On the whole, you'll probably find that linking HTML documents is impractical for all but a few, very simple scenarios.

IMPORTING HTML LISTS TO ACCESS TABLES

The Import HTML Wizard enables importing data from HTML ordered (numbered, `<ol>`) and unordered (bulleted, `<ul>`) lists. The `<li>` … `</li>` list item tag pairs surround the text for each list item. The following HTML code generates a three-node ordered list and a hierarchical nested list that has three parent nodes with three child nodes each:

```
<html>
  <head>
    <title>Web Page with Ordered and Unordered Lists</title>
  </head>
  <body>
    <ol>
      <li>Ordered List Item 1</li>
      <li>Ordered List Item 2</li>
      <li>Ordered List Item 3</li>
    </ol>
    <ul>
      <li>Unordered List Item 1
        <ol>
          <li>Nested Ordered List Item 1</li>
          <li>Nested Ordered List Item 2</li>
          <li>Nested Ordered List Item 3</li>
        </ol>
      </li>
      <li>Unordered List Item 2
        <ol>
          <li>Nested Ordered List Item 1</li>
          <li>Nested Ordered List Item 2</li>
          <li>Nested Ordered List Item 3</li>
        </ol>
      </li>
      <li>Unordered List Item 3
        <ol>
          <li>Nested Ordered List Item 1</li>
          <li>Nested Ordered List Item 2</li>
          <li>Nested Ordered List Item 3</li>
        </ol>
      </li>
    </ul>
  </body>
</html>
```

Figure 23.14 shows how Firefox 1.5 and all other browsers render the preceding code.

Figure 23.14
Access imports the simple ordered list correctly, but doesn't preserve the hierarchical structure of the unordered list.

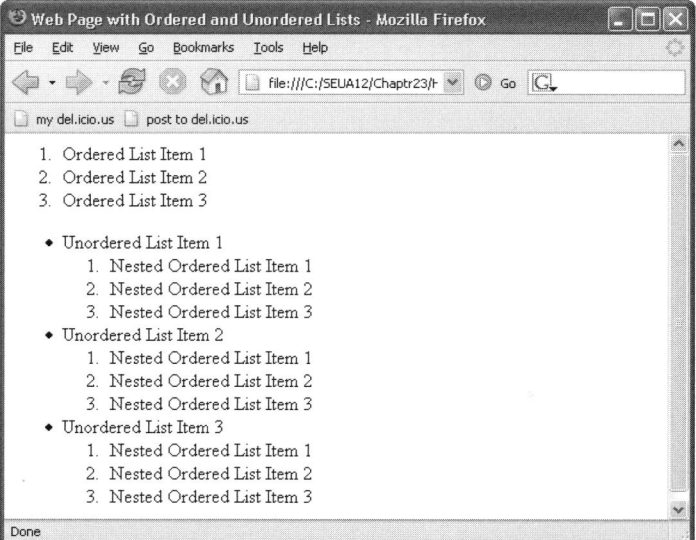

You can import both lists to a single table column with the Import HTML Wizard, but the nested unordered list is hierarchical. This Wizard can't translate hierarchical structures to relational tables, so it adds all list items to the memo field shown in Figure 23.15.

Figure 23.15
The Import HTML Wizard imports each list item in a nested list as a separate line of text. Fortunately, nested lists are seldom found on websites.

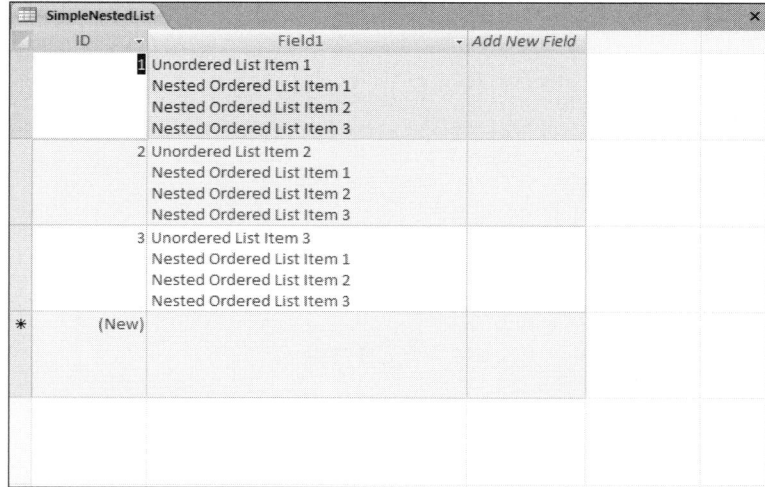

NOTE

The \SEUA12\Chaptr23\SimpleLists.htm file contains the code for the preceding example.

List items often consist of or contain hyperlinks. As an example, Figure 23.16 shows the last three of five lists of hyperlinks in the ArticlesFromOakLeafOL.htm file that was generated from the sidebar code of the OakLeaf Weblog (http://oakleafblog.blogspot.com).

Figure 23.16
The first of these three lists has all list item text contained in the hyperlink's anchor tag. All but one list item (Atom 0.3 site feed) of the other two lists has text outside the anchor tag.

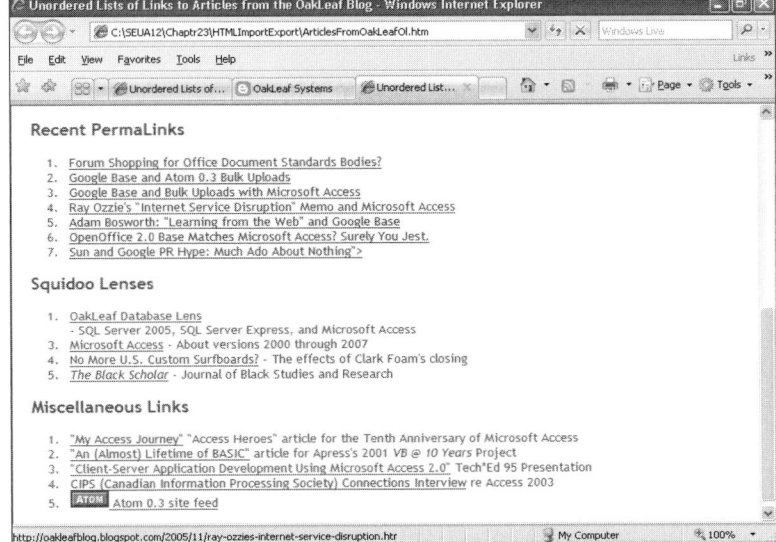

When you use the Import HTML Wizard to create a table with a Hyperlink field, all items in the Recent PermaLinks and preceding lists create live hyperlinks to articles, blog entries, or other Web pages. These three tables have list items with anchor tags that surround *all the item's text*, as in:

```
<li>
  <a href="http://oakleafblog.blogspot.com/2005/11/ray-ozzies-internet-
    service-disruption.html">
  Ray Ozzie's "Internet Service Disruption" Memo and Microsoft Access</a>
</li>
```

However, the Wizard has a problem with importing list items whose anchor tags *do not include all the item's text*, such as:

```
<li>
  <a href="http://www.microsoft.com/Office/previous/access/10years/jennings.asp">
 "My Access Journey"</a> "Access Heroes" article for the Tenth Anniversary of
    Microsoft Access
</li>
```

Only `"My Access Journey"` appears as text in the hyperlink field; `"Access Heroes"` article for the Tenth Anniversary of Microsoft Access is missing. The hyperlink field's Address value is empty, as you can see by right-clicking the cell and choosing Hyperlink, Edit Hyperlink to open the Insert Hyperlink dialog. The Wizard's parser isn't consistent; as an example, all the following list item's text appears in the Hyperlink field, as you can see in Figure 23.17:

```
<li>
  <a href="http://www.stephenibaraki.com/cips/v119/rjen.html">CIPS
    (Canadian Information Processing Society) Connections Interview</a>
    re Access 2003
</li>
```

Figure 23.17
All but the Atom 0.3 Site Feed hyperlink are inactive. The items in the first three rows have text missing from the original list item content.

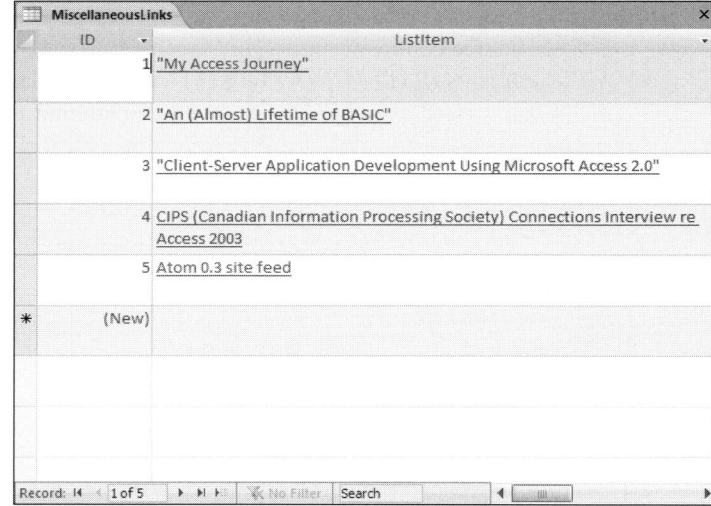

The problem with `<li>` element content that contains an anchor element for part of the text content also occurs with similar `<td>` elements.

NOTE

> Access doesn't have the capability to export tables or reports to HTML lists.

FIXING SOURCE CONTENT BEFORE IMPORTING WITH HTML TIDY

When you attempt to import complex HTML tables to Access tables, you often encounter the message shown in Figure 23.18.

Figure 23.18
Either or both of these messages might appear when you open an HTML file with content that the Import HTML Wizard can't parse correctly.

Many web page designers and authors use simple text editors—such as Windows Notepad—to create "free-hand" HTML documents, which are subject to tagging errors and omissions. Web browsers are very forgiving of HTML markup errors, such as missing closing tags (`</p>` or `</a>`) or improperly nested elements (such as `<p>…<a …>…</p></a>` instead of `<p>…<a …>…</a></p>`). Therefore, many HTML syntax errors aren't detected by the Web page rendered in the browser. Missing closing tags or incorrectly nested table elements make it very difficult or impossible for the wizard to import HTML tables into relational tables automatically.

HTML Tidy is an open source command-line utility for fixing HTML syntax errors and conforming HTML documents to HTML 4.01 or XHTML 1.0 standards where possible. If the Import HTML Wizard rejects the HTML document you attempt to convert to an Access table, chances are that running HTML Tidy on the file will solve the problem.

NOTE

> XHTML 1.0 is HTML 4+ expressed as an XML document. The later "Converting HTML 4.01 Files to XHTML 1.0 with Tidy" topic describes XHTML 1.0 and how you use HTML Tidy to generate valid XHTML from the process's nonconforming HTML output.

 W3C offers a description of HTML Tidy at `http://www.w3.org/People/Raggett/tidy/` and an online HTML Tidy Web service at `http://cgi.w3.org/cgi-bin/tidy`. The Web service accepts the URL of any Web page, runs Tidy on the source HTML, and displays the processed page. You can view the effect of Tidy on the code by opening the source of the original and processed page in Notepad.

DOWNLOADING AND RUNNING HTML TIDY

 To use HTML Tidy to fix errant HTML files, download the current version of tidy.exe for 32-bit Windows from the Source Forge site as tidy-060405-exe.zip at `http://prdownloads.sourceforge.net/int64/tidy-060405-exe.zip?download`. Download from `http://prdownloads.sourceforge.net/int64/tidy-060405-setup.exe?download` if you prefer a Windows installer package that includes Dave Raggett's overview and a quick-reference guide to Tidy options. In either case, expand tidy.exe to your \Windows folder so it's on your computer's path.

You can run tidy.exe from VBA's Shell command to automate applying HTML Tidy to files you import programmatically. However, a better approach is to use a COM component (DLL) to add Tidy functionality to an Access application. André Blavier has wrapped the August 4, 2000, Tidy version to create TidyCOM.dll, which you can download from `http://perso.orange.fr/ablavier/TidyCOM/TidyCOM.zip`.

Alternatively, you can download André Blavier's TidyUI, a GUI version of Tidy, as tidyui.exe and related files in tidiui.zip from `http://users.rcn.com/creitzel/tidy.html#tidyui`. Unfortunately, this application also uses the August 4, 2000, Tidy version; February 14, 2006, was the latest Tidy release when this book was written. Expand these files into a \Program Files\TidyUI folder.

The primary advantage of the GUI version is that you can view and edit the original (see Figure 23.19) and processed (Tidied, see Figure 23.20) versions of the document (see \SEUA12\Chaptr23\Tidy\HTSTest.htm for the examples in this and the following sections). The tabbed panel lets you view and set Markup, Layout, Encoding, Warnings, and Misc(ellaneous) options that ordinarily require authoring a Tidy configuration file.

Figure 23.19
The TidyUI GUI version (tidy.exe) displays the start of the HTS8 table in the original version of HTSTest.htm from the USITC. The left panel displays HTML Tidy's Markup configuration options.

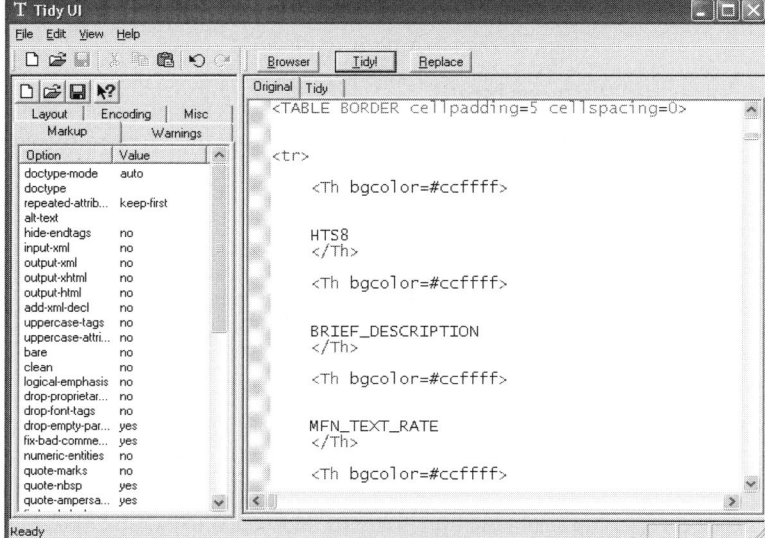

Figure 23.20
TidyUI has corrected tag case issues, quoted attribute values, indented the code with two spaces, and removed empty lines from the original version shown in Figure 23.21. The left panel shows HTML Tidy's Layout configuration options.

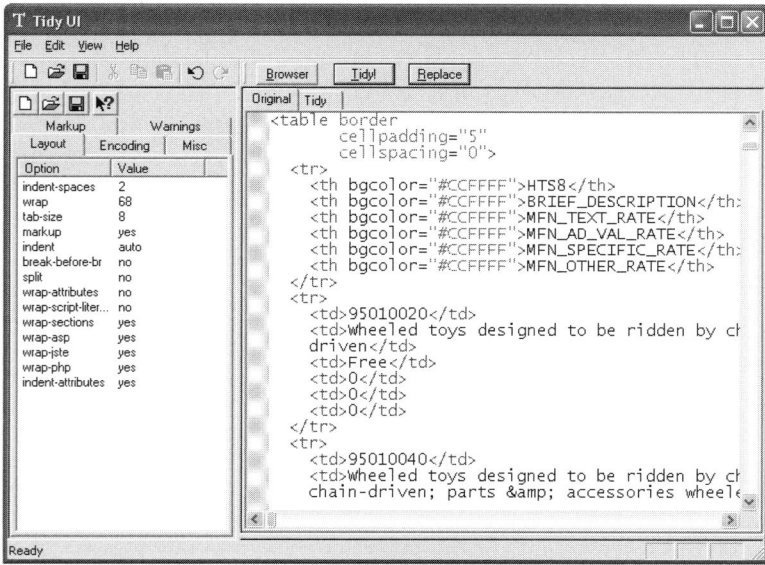

To obtain a list of HTML Tidy's command-line options, type **tidy.exe -h > TidyHelp.txt** at the command prompt. The \SEUA12\Chaptr23\Tidy folder contains a copy of TidyHelp.txt. Documentation for HTML Tidy's configuration options can be found at `http://tidy.sourceforge.net/docs/quickref.html`.

RUNNING TIDY.EXE FROM THE COMMAND PROMPT

Following is the simplest HTML Tidy command-line syntax, which tidies a file with default configurations settings by overwriting it in place:

tidy -m [*path*\]*filename*.htm[l]

The preceding command outputs error and warning messages to the command window. To send these messages to a TidyErrors.txt file, use add **-f** switch and filename as in the following command:

tidy -f TidyErrors.txt -m [*path*\]*filename*.htm[l]

If you want to preserve the original *filename*.htm[l] file, replace the **-m**[odify] switch with the **-o**[utput] switch and the output filename, as in:

tidy -f TidyErrors.txt -o *tidyfile*.htm[l]
[path\]*filename*.htm[l]

USING HTML TIDY CONFIGURATION FILES

HTML Tidy configuration files enable fine-grained specification of Tidy's transformation process. Following is the content of a simple documented configuration file (HTMLConfig.txt) for fixing HTML documents:

```
doctype: auto            # Add the DOCTYPE declaration (Tidy guesses)
bare: yes                # Remove proprietary Microsoft Word tags
add-xml-decl: no         # Add XML declaration to provide encoding info
output-html: yes         # Produce HTML output
drop-empty-paras: yes    # Drop empty <p> tags automatically
fix-backslash: no        # Replace \ with / in URLs
literal-attributes: yes  # Keep whitespace in attribute values
lower-literals: no       # Change attribute values to lower case
replace-color: yes       # Replace hex color codes with name (#ffffff = white)
quote-ampersand: no      # Replace & with &amp;
quote-marks: no          # Replace " with &quot;
quote-nbsp: no           # Replace Unicode 160 with  
indent: yes              # Indent code automatically
indent-spaces: 2         # Indent two spaces
char-encoding: ascii     # Character encoding for input and output
ascii-chars: no          # Replace entities with closest ASCII character
tidy-mark: no            # Omit Tidy-generated information in output file
newline: CRLF            # Use CRLF for newlines
```

Add the **-config** switch and configuration filename to use a configuration file:

tidy -f TidyErrors.txt -config *configfile.ext*
-o *tidyfile*.htm[l] [*path*\]*filename*.htm[l]

As an example, the following command from the TidyCommands.txt file processes HTSTest.htm with HTMLConfig.txt, saving errors to HTMLErrors.txt and the output as HTSTest1.htm:

tidy -f HTMLErrs.txt -config HTMLConfig.txt
-o HTSTest1.htm HTSTest.htm

> **NOTE**
>
> The TidyCommands.txt file contains commands to produce XHTML 1.0 documents. You use the XHTML commands to convert the Output HTML Wizard's old-timey HTML 3.0 format documents to XHTML 1.0 and Cascading Style Sheets (CSS).

EXPORTING ACCESS TABLES TO HTML FILES

Exporting an Access table or query to an HTML file is a quick-and-easy process. Your only options are to specify an HTML template file and change the file encoding from the ASCII (ANSI) default to Unicode (UTF-16) or UTF-8.

> **NOTE**
>
> If your working file doesn't have the Northwind Customers and Categories tables, import them from the \SEUA12\Nwind\Northwind.accdb database.

To create a typical HTML page from an Access table, do the following:

1. Select the Customers table in the Navigation Pane, click the External Data tab, click the Export group's More button to open the gallery, and click the <u>H</u>TML Document button to open the Export – HTML Document dialog.

2. Click Browse to open the File Save dialog, navigate to the designation folder for the exported Customers.html file, and click Save to return to the Export – HTML Document dialog.

3. Mark the Export Data with Formatting and Layout check box and the Open the Destination File After the Export Operation Is Complete check box (see Figure 23.21), and click OK to start the HTML Output Options dialog.

4. UTF-8 encoding is becoming the accepted standard for Web pages with non-English characters, so select the Unicode (UTF-8) option (see Figure 23.22), and click OK to generate the Customers.html file (see Figure 23.23).

Figure 23.21
If you don't mark the Export Data with Formatting and Layout check box, the resulting HTML table uses the default font (Times New Roman) and borders.

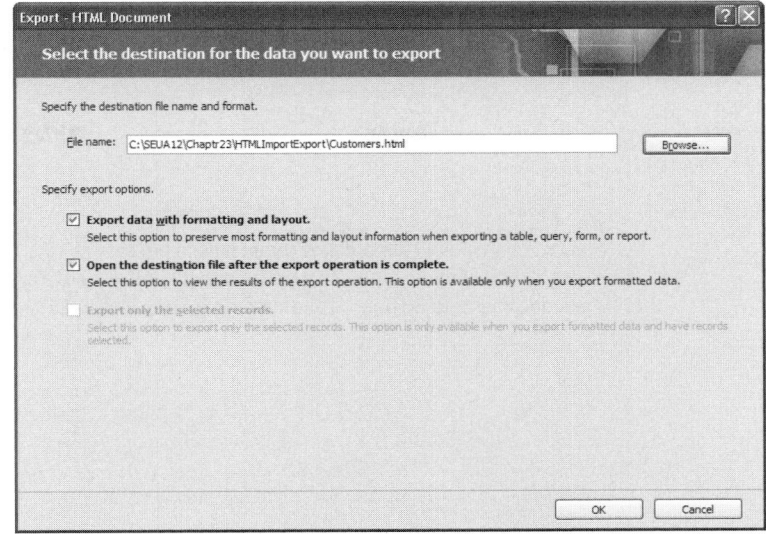

Figure 23.22
HTML file encoding options are Default Encoding (which is ASCII/ANSI), Unicode, and Unicode (UTF-8).

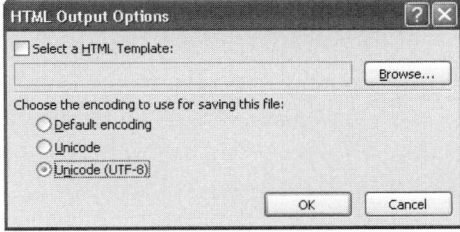

Figure 23.23
Displaying all columns of the Customers table in Customers.html without scrolling requires 1024×768 (minimum) screen resolution.

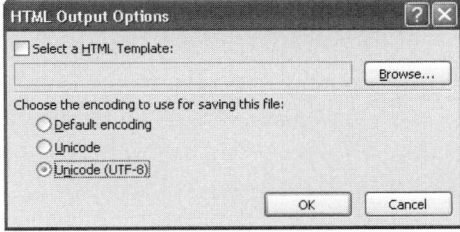

5. Click View, Source to scan the HTML code in Windows Notepad (see Figure 23.24).

Figure 23.24
The HTML export process generates HTML 3.0 code for tables with uppercase tags and attributes, as well as repetitive STYLE attributes for each table cell.

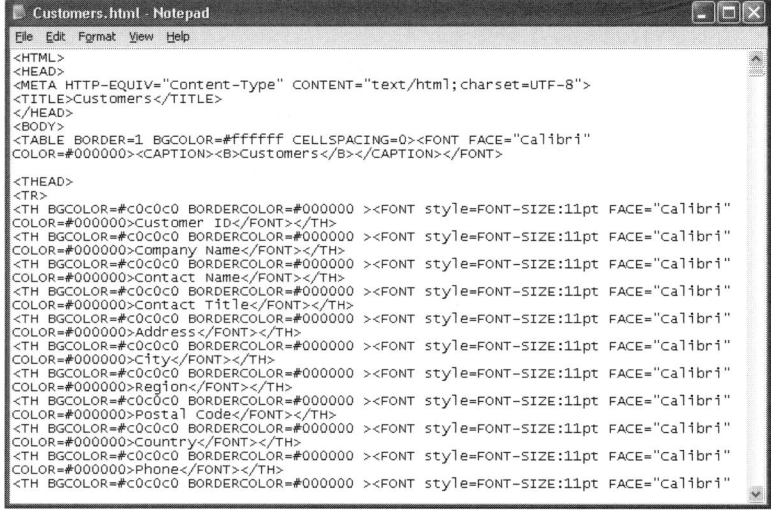

6. Close Notepad and IE.

Access's HTML export process hasn't been updated significantly since Access 97, so the markup follows HTML 3.2 standards. The later "Upgrading Access HTML Documents to HTML 4.01 and CSS" section shows you how to use HTML Tidy to "clean" the HTML files to current standards.

EXPORTING REPORTS TO HTML TABLES

Access 2007 includes RPT2HTML4.XSL, an XML style sheet/transform (XSLT) file that generates HTML 4.01 tables from reports. The resulting tables faithfully duplicate the original report design, but don't support graphics.

The process of creating HTML tables from reports is similar to that for creating HTML tables from Access tables. To create a report from the Northwind Categories table, modify it to optimize the resulting table, and create a Categories.html file, do the following:

1. Select the Categories table in the Navigation Pane, click the Create tab, and then click the Report button to create a default Report object from the table in Layout view.

2. Reduce the width of the Category ID and Category Name columns, select the Picture column, click Delete, select the Picture column, and click Delete. The report export process doesn't handle images in OLE Object or Attachment fields. Widen the Description field so that the descriptions occupy a single line.

3. The report export process doesn't handle static bitmaps either, so delete the icon to the left of the Categories field and move the Categories label to the report's left margin.

4. Click the Page Setup tab, click the Page Layout group's Margins button, and click the Wide button in the gallery. Adjust the report controls to fit the reduced width, delete the time text box, and move the date text box down to the time text box's position.

5. Click the Page Layout group's Columns button to open the Page Layout dialog. Click the Print Options tab, set the top and bottom margins to 0.25 inches, and click OK.

6. Delete the count text box at the bottom of the Category ID column. Layout view of the report should appear as shown in Figure 23.25.

Figure 23.25
The Categories report, shown here in Layout view, is ready to export to an HTML file.

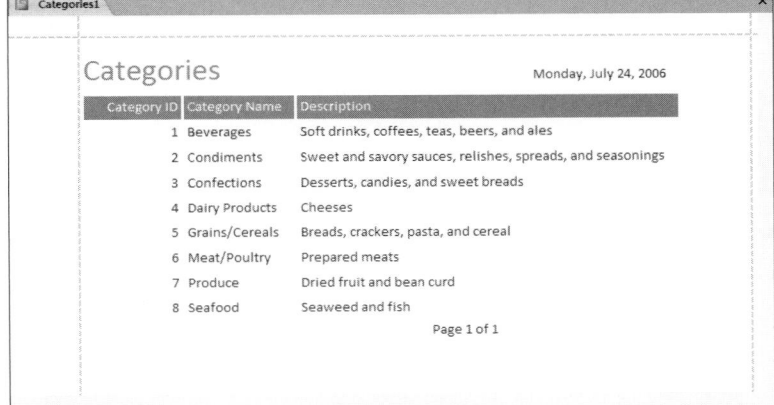

7. Change to Report view, close the report, and save it as **rptCatsHTML** or the like.

8. Right-click rptCatsHTML in the Navigation Pane, and choose Export, HTML Document to open the Export – HTML Document dialog. If you want to change the location or name of the rptCatsHTML.html file, click Browse.

9. Mark the Open the Destination File After the Export Operation Is Complete check box, and click OK to open the HTML Output Options dialog.

10. Accept the Default Encoding option in this case, and click OK to create and open the rptCatsHTML.html file in IE (see Figure 23.26).

11. Choose View, Source to open the HTML document in Windows Notepad. Notice that the report export process creates a separate table for each report row (see Figure 23.27).

12. Close Notepad, IE, and the Export – HTML Document dialog.

Figure 23.26
The export report feature creates a very close HTML replica of the source Access report.

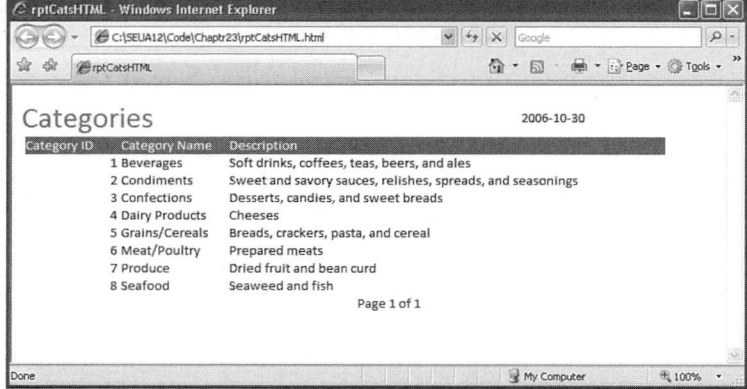

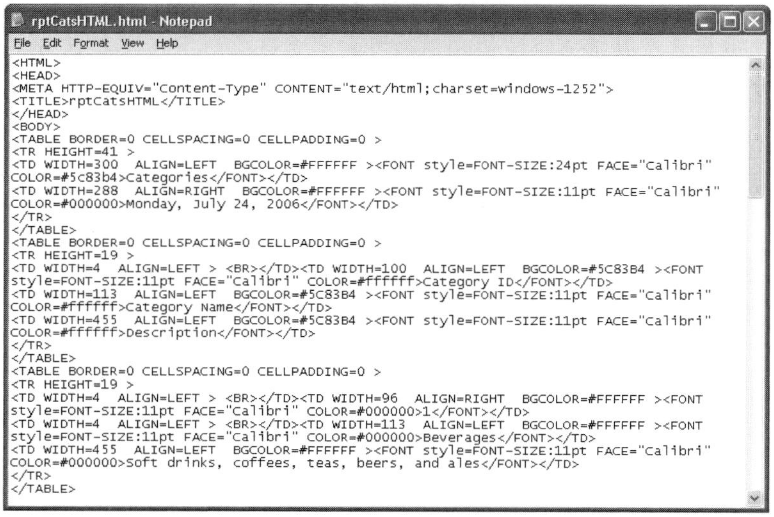

Figure 23.27
RPT2HTML4.XSL generates a separate table for the header and each data row of the report.

If the Access report has more than one page, RPT2HTML4.XSL generates consecutively numbered *Filename*Page#.htm[l] files for page 2 and greater. The transform adds navigation links to additional pages at the bottom of the page, as shown for a three-page Suppliers report in Figure 23.28.

NOTE

The first Suppliers report page shown in Figure 23.28 is Suppliers.html in the \SEUA12\Chaptr23 folder. The SuppliersPage2.html and SuppliersPage3.html files contain code for the remaining two pages.

Figure 23.28
Multipage reports exported to HTML files add First, Previous, Next, and Last links for page navigation.

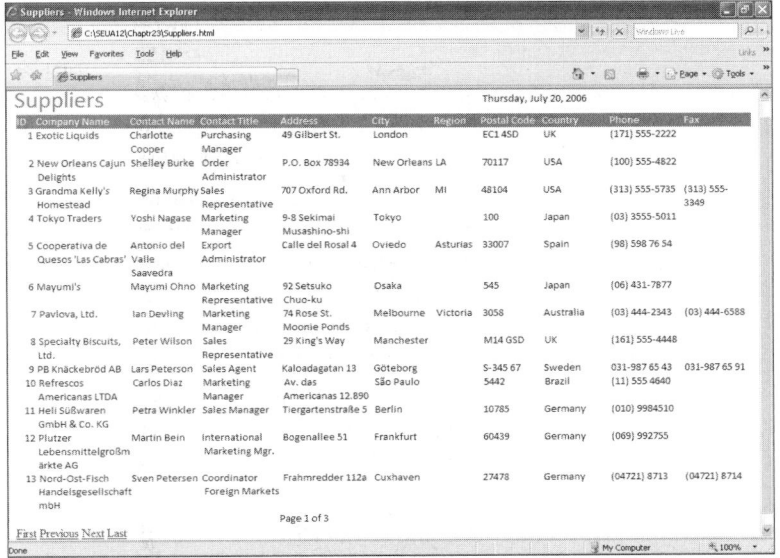

23

> Be sure to design your source report with a page width that accommodates all fields. Navigating report pages left to right, then down isn't generally accepted by browser users.

MODIFYING PAGE LAYOUT WITH HTML TEMPLATES

An HTML template file lets you merge the title and body elements of an HTML file created from an Access table, query, or report. If the source of the HTML file is a report, you can also merge the navigation anchors with your document. Following are valid tokens for HTML template files:

Template Token	Replacement
`<!—AccessTemplate_Title—>`	The name of the table, query, or report placed in the title bar of the web browser
`<!—AcessTemplate_Body—>`	The output of the table, query, or report
`<!—AccessTemplate_FirstPage—>`	An HTML anchor tag that links to the first page of a report
`<!—AccessTemplate_PreviousPage—>`	An HTML anchor tag that links to the page previous to the current report page
`<!—AccessTemplate_NextPage—>`	An HTML anchor tag that links to the next page after the current report page
`<!—AccessTemplate_LastPage—>`	An HTML anchor tag that links to the last page of a report
`<!—AccessTemplate_PageNumber—>`	The current page number

Following is the HTML code for a simple template (ASCIITableTemplate.html) that you can use with exported tables:

```html
<html>
  <head>
    <title>
      <!—AccessTemplate_Title—> Table with HTML Template
    </title>
  </head>
  <body>
    <div style="font-family: Calibri, Verdana, Arial, sans-serif; font-weight:
      bold;text-align: center;" >
      <p style="font-size: 18pt;color: #add1ff">
        Access Table with HTML Template</p>
      <span><!—AccessTemplate_Body—></span>
    </div>
  </body>
</html>
```

Marking the HTML Output Option dialog's Select a HTML Template check box disables the Encoding options because the template's encoding determines the final file's encoding (see Figure 23.29). Figure 23.30 shows the CustomersTempl.html page with the ANSITableTemplate.html template file applied.

Figure 23.29
Mark the Select a HTML Template check box and browse for (or type the path and filename of) the template to use when exporting a table or report as HTML.

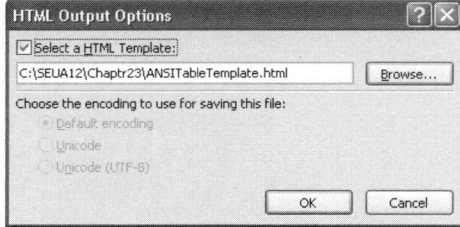

Figure 23.30
The code for the CustomersTempl.html page consists of the ANSITableTemplate.html files' code merged with that generated by the HTML export process for the Customers table.

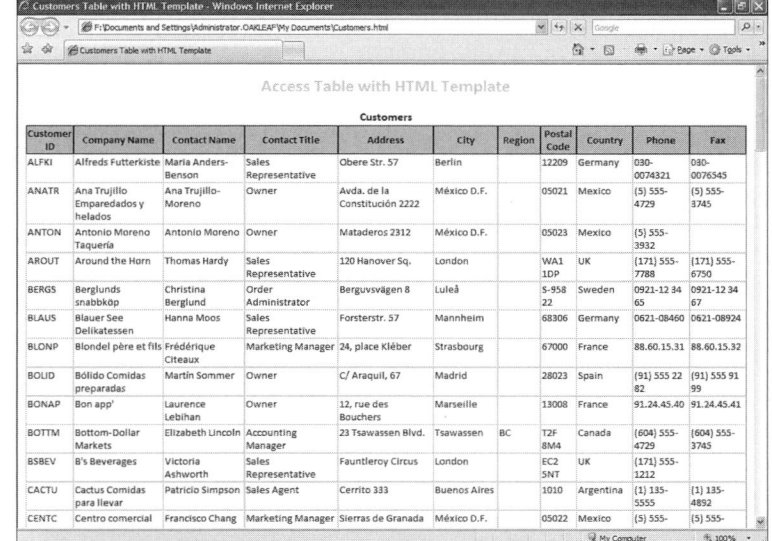

The following template (ASCIIReportTemplate.html) conforms the font for the navigation anchors (links) of exported reports:

```
<html>
  <head>
    <title>
      <!—AccessTemplate_Title—> Report with HTML Template
    </title>
  </head>
  <body>
    <div style="font-family: Calibri, Verdana, Arial, sans-serif;
      font-weight: bold;text-align: center;" >
      <p style="font-size: 18pt;color: #add1ff">
        Access Report with HTML Template</p>
      <span><!—AccessTemplate_Body—></span>
      <br />
      <span style="font-size: 12pt;">
        <!—AccessTemplate_Body—>
        <a href="<!—AccessTemplate_FirstPage—>">First</a>
        <a href="<!—AccessTemplate_PreviousPage—>">Previous</a>
        <a href="<!—AccessTemplate_NextPage—>">Next</a>
        <a href="<!—AccessTemplate_LastPage—>">Last</a>
      <span>
    </div>
  </body>
</html>
```

If you don't add the template, IE renders the navigation anchors with the default font (New Times Roman, refer to Figure 23.28).

TIP

> Double-click the ANSITableTemplate.html and ANSIReportTemplate.html files in the \SEUA12\Chaptr23 folder to display the template layout in IE.

UPGRADING ACCESS HTML DOCUMENTS TO HTML 4.01 AND CSS

HTML 3.2 added formatting capabilities to HTML with <FONT> tags, which turned out to be a major error. Code for web pages became littered with difficult-to-maintain code, such as this HTML 3.2 example for a single table cell:

```
<TD BORDERCOLOR=#add1ff >
  <FONT style=FONT-SIZE:11pt FACE="Calibri" COLOR=#000000>
    Alfreds Futterkiste
  </FONT>
</TD>
```

NOTE

> The preceding element is one of 1,092 similar code blocks in the \SEUA12\Customers. html file exported from the Northwind Customers table. The formatting code comprises 90 percent or more of the file's content.
>
> Specifying the Calibri face, which is a new, proprietary Windows font installed by Office 2007, and not specifying fallback to Tahoma, Arial, or (generic) sans-serif, causes the page to render in the default Times [New] Roman font if Office 2007 isn't installed.

HTML 4.0 and 4.01 enable separating formatting from layout code by transferring all formatting tags and attributes from an HTML 3.2 document to a cascading style sheet, which can be incorporated into the `<head>` element of the HTML document or linked from a separate .css file. If you routinely export tables, queries, or reports to HTML documents for publication on an organization's public Internet or private intranet website, the webmaster is likely to require your pages to conform to HTML 4.01 or XHTML 1.0 standards.

NOTE

> Access 2007's XML export feature enables generating HTML (presentation) files from static XML data documents that the feature creates from tables, queries, and the data behind forms or reports. The HTML files have an empty `<style type="text/css">` `</style>` element but don't use CSS rules for formatting. Tags are lowercase, but unsupported HTML 3.2 attributes—such as `link`, `vlink`, `bgcolor`, and `align`—prevent validation to the HTML 4.01 Strict standard.

→ To learn more about exporting Access tables in XML format, **see** "Exporting Tables and Queries to XML and HTML," **p. XXX** *(Ch 24)*.

USING HTML TIDY'S CLEAN OPTION

HTML Tidy offers a **-c[lean]** command-line switch to replace `<CENTER>` and `<FONT>` tags, which are deprecated in HTML 4+, and the nonstandard `<NOBR>` (no break) tag with CSS style properties and rules. HTML files exported by Access also contain a nonstandard `<BORDERCOLOR>` tag, which Tidy identifies as *proprietary*. You can instruct Tidy to remove these tags by adding the `drop-proprietary-attributes: yes` instruction to Tidy's configuration file.

TIP

> W3 Schools has a set of HTML 4.01 / XHTML 1.0 reference pages that start at http://www.w3schools.com/tags/. The reference pages list valid tags, core attributes, color names, and ASCII and common symbol entities.

Here's the command-line instruction for running Tidy with the clean option:

```
tidy -c -f HTMLErr.txt -config UTF8Config.txt -o Customers1.html Customers.html
```

Following is an abbreviated version of the output that results from running the preceding instruction once on Customers.html and again on Customers1.html to add the DOCTYPE declaration on the first line:

```html
<!DOCTYPE html PUBLIC "-//W3C//DTD HTML 4.01 Transitional//EN">
<html>
  <head>
    <meta http-equiv="Content-Type" content="text/html; charset=utf-8">
    <title>
      Customers
    </title>
    <style type="text/css">
      span.c3 {color: black; font-family: Calibri}
      span.c2 {FONT-SIZE: 11pt; color: black; font-family: Calibri}
      caption.c1 {font-weight: bold}
    </style>
  </head>
  <body>
    <table border="1" bgcolor="white" cellspacing="0">
      <caption class="c1">
        Customers
      </caption>
      <thead>
        <tr>
          <th bgcolor="silver">
            <span class="c3"><span class="c2">Customer ID</span></span>
          </th>
          ...
          <th bgcolor="silver">
            <span class="c2">Fax</span>
          </th>
        </tr>
      </thead>
      <tbody>
        <tr valign="top">
          <td>
            <span class="c2">ALFKI</span>
          </td>
          ...
          <td>
            <span class="c2">030-0076545</span>
          </td>
        </tr>
        ...
      </tbody>
    </table>
  </body>
</html>
```

Tidy does the following to the HTML 3.2 source document to create the preceding HTML 4.01 destination document:

- Lowercases tags and attribute name-value pairs because lowercase is preferred by the HTML 4.01 specification

- Moves most formatting tags to a style sheet enclosed by <style> tags in the document's <head> element

- Adds a class attribute to the table's `<caption>` element
- Surrounds heading and value cell content with `<span>` tags having a class attribute

The complete version of the preceding document (\SEUA12\Chaptr23\Tidy\Customers1.html) passes the W3C's validation test for HTML 4.01 – Transitional, which isn't surprising because the author of the original HTML Tidy program, Dave Raggett, was the lead editor of the HTML 4.01 specification (see Figure 23.31).

Figure 23.31
The W3C's Markup Validation Service gives Customers1.html thumbs-up for HTML 4.01 Transitional conformance but not for HTML 4.01 Strict.

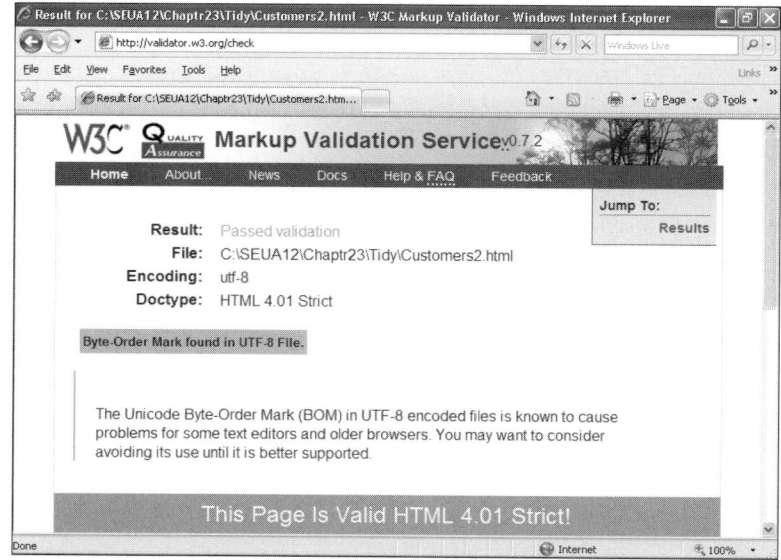

NOTE

The W3C Markup Validation Service page is found at http://validator.w3.org. To check an HTM[L] file for conformance to the HTML 4.01 Specification, scroll to the Validate by File Upload section, click Browse, navigate to and double-click the file to test, and then click Check. The DOCTYPE declaration is required to specify whether Transitional or Strict validation is required.

You also can test the CSS code that Tidy generates with the W3C's CSS Validation Service at http://jigsaw.w3.org/css-validator/. Copy the CSS code only (without the surrounding `<style>` tag pairs) to the Validate by Direct Input text area and click the Check button.

FIXING TIDY-GENERATED CSS CODE

The CSS code that Tidy's clean option generates is valid but returns the warnings shown in Figure 23.32. The three warnings about the lack of an alternative generic font for the font family attribute reflect the warning about the Calibri font in the note near the beginning of this section.

Figure 23.32
The W3C CSS Validation Service displays four warnings about missing generic font attribute values and two warnings about missing background color values.

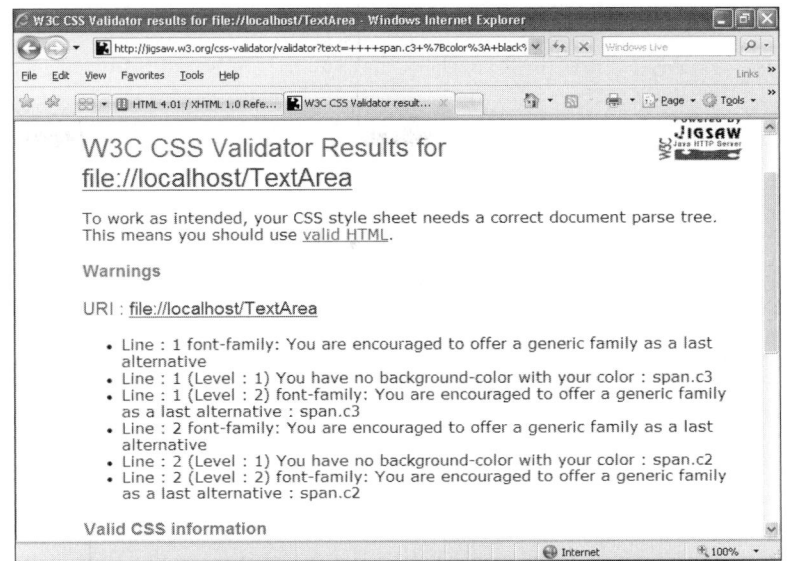

The `span.c3` style is superfluous because it duplicates the color and font family, so it and the `<span class="c3">` element can be deleted; the CSS code should be edited to the following:

```
table.t0 {border: solid skyblue 2px; border-collapse: collapse}
th.t1 {background-color:skyblue; border: solid skyblue 2px}
td.t2 {background-color:white; border: solid skyblue 2px}
tr.r1 {vertical-align: top}
span.c2 {font-size: 11pt; color: black;
  font-family: Calibri,Tahoma,Arial,sans-serif}
caption.c1 {font-size: 14pt; font-weight: bold; color: darkorange;
font-family: Calibri,Tahoma,Arial,sans-serif}
```

Remove the `<table>` element's `border="1"` and `bgcolor="white"` attributes because these values are set by the `table.t0`, `th.t1`, and `td.t2` styles. The `bgcolor` attribute prevents validation as HTML 4.01 Strict because `bgcolor` is deprecated in HTML 4+. Replace the `cellspacing="0"` attribute with `class="t0"` to use a style that makes all borders 2px wide.

Optionally, use the `tr.r1 {vertical-align: top}` style, which removes the last HTML 3.2 format attribute, by replacing all `valign="TOP"` instances with `class="r1"`.

After making the preceding changes, saving the edited file as Customers2.html, and validating the HTML and CSS code, delete `Transitional` from the `DOCTYPE` specification to specify validation as HTML 4.01 Strict.

NOTE

The \SEUA12\Chaptr23\Tidy\Customers2.html file passes HTML 4.01 Strict validation.

LINKING DOCUMENTS TO A CSS FILE

You probably can use the style sheet that you design for an exported HTML table with many similar exported tables to conform to your organization's standards for table appearance. You can avoid adding style sheet code to all your exported HTML documents by adding the CSS code to a *StyleName*.css file and replacing the `<style type="text/css">` … `</style>` block with the following line:

```
<link rel="stylesheet" type="text/css" href="StyleName.css" />
```

As an example, the Customers3.html file links to the Web20Style.css file.

CONVERTING HTML 4.01 FILES TO XHTML 1.0 WITH TIDY

To further standardize HTML, the W3C promulgated the Extensible HTML Markup Language (XHTML) 1.0 recommendation, which was last revised on August 1, 2002 (`http://www.w3.org/TR/xhtml1/`). XHTML 1.0 is HTML 4.01 content expressed as an Extensible Markup Language (XML) 1.0 document or, as the W3C puts it, "a reformulation of HTML 4 in XML 1.0." Applications or components, such as Microsoft XML, v6.0 (Msxml6.dll), that can manipulate well-formed XML documents work equally well with XHTML 1.0 documents. Chapter 24, "Integrating with XML and InfoPath 2007," provides detailed information about the XML 1.0 standard.

XHTML 1.0 and CSS 2.0 is on its way to becoming the standard for new web pages authored by most organizations. IE 6 "fully supports" CSS 1.0 (level 1) and "some pieces of" CSS 2.0 (level 2), according to an "IE and Standards" post on Microsoft's IE blog (`http://blogs.msdn.com/ie/archive/2005/03/09/391362.aspx`). The extent to which IE 7 will meet the CSS 2.0 or 2.1 (level 2, revision 1) specification wasn't public information when this book was written.

Once you've used Tidy to process the exported HTML 3.2 file to HTML 4.01, the only basic change that's required is to add the XML 1.0 declaration and conform the DOCTYPE definition to the XHTML 1.0 standard, as shown here:

```
<?xml version="1.0"?>
<!DOCTYPE html PUBLIC "-//W3C//DTD XHTML 1.0 Strict//EN"
    "http://www.w3.org/TR/xhtml1/DTD/xhtml1-strict.dtd">
```

Making the preceding changes requires ensuring that the Tidy configuration file includes the following instructions:

```
add-xml-decl: yes        # Add XML declaration to provide encoding info
output-xhtml: yes        # Produce valid XHTML output
lower-literals: yes      # Change attribute values to lower case
quote-ampersand: yes     # Replace & with &amp;
quote-marks: yes         # Replace " with &quot;
quote-nbsp: yes          # Replace Unicode 160 with  
char-encoding: utf8      # Character encoding for input and output
```

The XHTMLConfig.txt configuration file includes the preceding changes. Following is the command to generate the XHTML 1.0 version of Customers2.html as Customers4.html:

```
tidy -c -f XHTMLErrs.txt -config XHTMLConfig.txt -o Customers4.html
  Customers2.html
```

UTF-8 is the default encoding for XML files, but it's a good practice to specify the encoding in the XML declaration:

```
<?xml version="1.0" encoding="UTF-8"?>
```

Customers4.html validates as XHMTL 1.0 Strict, as illustrated by Figure 23.33.

Figure 23.33
Making a few minor changes to a Tidied HTML 4.01 document generates an XHTML 1.0 Strict document that the W3C test validates.

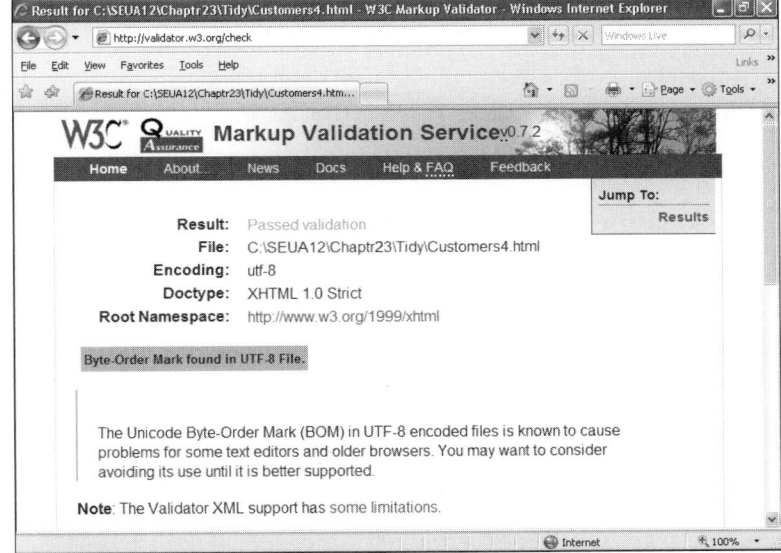

DISPLAYING DYNAMIC TABLES IN ACTIVE SERVER PAGES

Active Server Pages (ASP) overcome the need for periodic refreshing of static .htm[l] pages by generating pages with *dynamic tables*. Dynamic tables read the table data or execute a query to return the required data and render the table each time a user opens a page. Delivering web pages with tables generated by ASP guarantees up-to-date data. Access 97 through 2003 offered the option to export tables or queries to ASP files directly. Microsoft removed this feature from Access 2007.

NOTE

Microsoft relegated ASP to downlevel technology status after releasing ASP.NET 1.0.

CREATING AN ASP TEMPLATE FILE

You can work around Access 2007's lack of the Export to ASP Page feature by preparing a generic ASP template from an ASP file created in Access 2003 or earlier. A rudimentary knowledge of Visual Basic Script (VBS) and ASP coding techniques is all that's required to create the template. Customizing the template requires only a search-and-replace operation if your page displays all table fields, and use of field names instead of column captions is acceptable. Otherwise, you must write an SQL statement to specify the fields to display and add caption aliases.

You create the template in these steps:

1. In Access 2003 or earlier, export a Northwind table, such as Suppliers, to a Step1.asp file.

2. Rewrite the VBS code to iterate the Recordset's fields and return the Field.Name to populate the table header's `<tr>` elements.

3. Rewrite the nested rows loop to iterate the Recordset's fields to populate the `<td>` cells with the Field.Value values. Save the file as Step2.asp.

4. Copy the file to the \IntetPub\wwwroot folder, and test the page with Internet Information Services (IIS) 7.0 running under Windows Vista, IIS 6/0 for Windows Server 2003 SP-1 or R2, or IIS 5.1 for Windows XP Professional Edition (see Figure 23.34).

Figure 23.34
The first edit of the ASP template file replaces the field captions with field names in the table header. Otherwise, the first two field versions display identical tables.

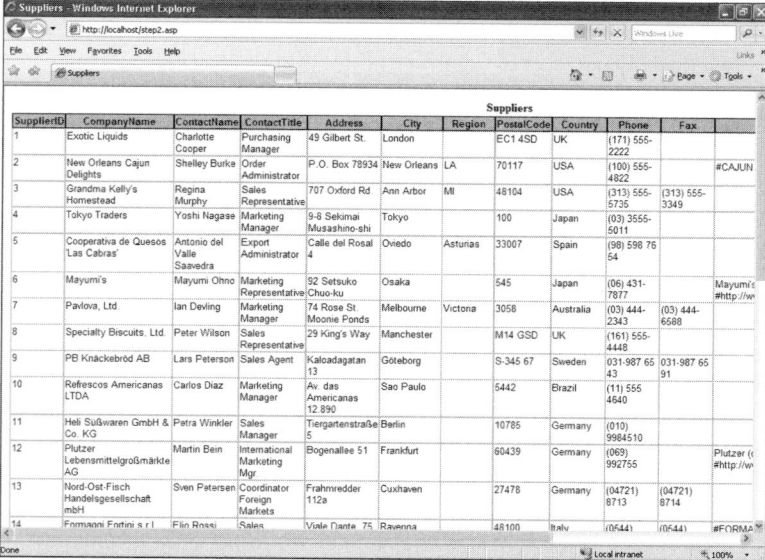

5. Replace the HTML 3.2 formatting code with the HTML 4.01 and CSS code as described in the earlier section "Upgrading Access HTML Documents to HTML 4.01 and CSS."

6. Search and replace the table with a different table in the same database, if you want, and save the file as *TableName*CSS.asp.

7. Repeat step 4's test with *TableName*CSS.asp. Figure 23.35 shows the CustomersCSS.asp page that results from replacing Products with Customers in step 6.

Figure 23.35
Rendering of the CustomersCSS.asp page is almost identical to the Customers2.html page created earlier in the chapter.

Following is the VBS and ASP code in the CustomersCSS.asp page:

```
<!DOCTYPE html PUBLIC "-//W3C//DTD HTML 4.01//EN">
<html>
  <head>
    <meta HTTP-EQUIV="Content-Type" CONTENT="text/html;charset=windows-1252">
    <title>Customers</title>
    <style type="text/css">
      table.t0 {border: solid skyblue 2px; border-collapse: collapse}
      th.t1 {background-color:skyblue; border: solid skyblue 2px}
      td.t2 {background-color:white; border: solid skyblue 2px}
      tr.r1 {vertical-align: top}
      span.c2 {font-size: 11pt; color: black;
        font-family: Calibri,Tahoma,Arial,sans-serif}
      caption.c1 {font-size: 14pt; font-weight: bold; color: darkorange;
        font-family: Calibri,Tahoma,Arial,sans-serif}
    </style>
  </head>
  <body>

<% 'Set up session and open ODBC machine-level connection
Session.timeout = 5
If IsObject(Session("NwindAccess_conn")) Then
  Set conn = Session("NwindAccess_conn")
Else
  Set conn = Server.CreateObject("ADODB.Connection")
```

```
conn.Open "NwindAccess","Administrator",""
  Set Session("NwindAccess_conn") = conn
End If %>

<% 'Create a Recordset
If IsObject(Session("Customers_rs")) Then
  Set rs = Session("Customers_rs")
Else
  sql = "SELECT * FROM [Customers]"
  Set rs = Server.CreateObject("ADODB.Recordset")
  rs.Open sql, conn, 3, 3
  If rs.Eof Then
    rs.AddNew
  End If
  Set Session("Customers_rs") = rs
End If %>

<!-- Start HTML -->
  <table class="t0">
    <caption class="c1">Customers</caption>
    <thead>
      <tr>
      <!-- Add tables headers (field names) -->
      <% For col = 0 To rs.Fields.Count -1 %>
        <th class="t1">
          <span class="c2">
            <!-- Add field names -->
            <%=Server.HTMLEncode(rs.Fields(col).Name)%>
          </span>
        </th>
      <% Next %>
      </tr>
    </thead>
    <tbody>
      <% On Error Resume Next
        'Add rows and cells
        rs.MoveFirst
        Do While Not rs.Eof %>
        <tr class="r1">
        <% For col = 0 to rs.Fields.Count -1 %>
          <td class="t2">
            <span class="c2">
              <%=Server.HTMLEncode(rs.Fields(col).Value)%>
            </span>
          </td>
        <% Next %>
        </tr>
      <% rs.MoveNext
        Loop %>
    </tbody>
  </table>
  </body>
</html>
```

RUNNING THE TEMPLATE FROM YOUR WEB SERVER

Running CustomersCSS.asp requires an ODBC data source for the Northwind sample database. If you don't have a System DSN for Northwind.accdb, you must create one. This section assumes that you're running IIS 5.1+ on the computer you use to create the ASP file(s). Alternatively, you can use a networked instance of IIS that has Access 2007 installed.

SETTING UP THE ODBC DATA SOURCE

To create a NwindAccess ODBC data source for the ASP page, do the following:

1. From Control Panel, open the Administrative Tools folder and launch the ODBC Administrator tool by double-clicking the Data Sources (ODBC) icon.

2. Click the System DSN tab to create a data source that's available regardless of who's logged on to the web server, and click the Add button (the New button in Windows 2000) to open the Create New Data Source dialog.

3. Select the Microsoft Access 12.0 Driver (*.mdb, *.accdb) in the Name list, and click Finish to open the ODBC Microsoft Access Setup dialog.

4. Type a short name (**NwindAccess** for this example) in the Data Source Name text box and an optional description of the data source in the Description text box. The name must match the `Connection` name in the ASP page.

5. Click Select to open the Select Database dialog, select All Files (*.*) in the List Files of Type list, navigate to Northwind.accdb in the \SEUA12\Nwind folder, and double-click the file in the Database Name list to close the dialog. The ODBC Microsoft Access Setup dialog appears as shown in Figure 23.36. Access 2007 doesn't support user-level security, so don't specify a system database (workgroup file).

Figure 23.36
Create a new NwindAccess ODBC System DSN for the database that contains the source tables for your ASP pages.

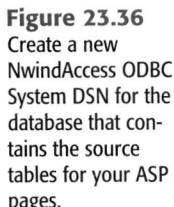
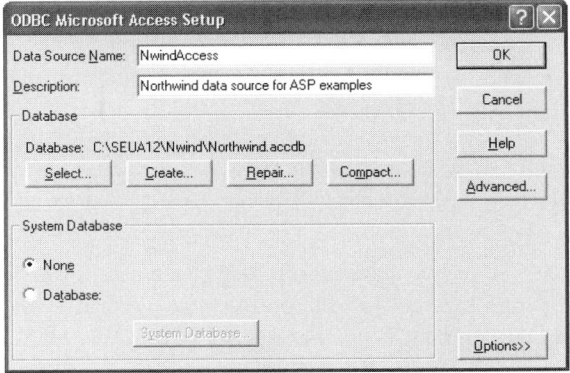

6. Click OK twice to close the two dialogs.

SETTING UP INTERNET INFORMATION SERVICES TO RUN THE ASP FILE

IIS isn't installed by default by Windows XP Professional Edition, Windows Server 2003, or Windows Vista Home Premium, Professional, or Ultimate editions. You must specify IIS installation during the OS setup operation, or use Add/Remove Windows Components or the Configure Your Server dialog to install it from your original media.

> **NOTE**
>
> The RazorX website has detailed, illustrated instructions for setting up IIS 5.1 on Windows XP Professional at `http://www.razorx.com/tutorials/IISonXPPro/`. Microsoft's instructions for setting up IIS 7.0 on Windows Vista Home Premium, Professional, or Ultimate editions are at `http://www.iis.net/default.aspx?tabid=2&subtabid=25&i=957`.

IIS 6.0 and 7.0 require enabling the web server to run ASP 3.0 applications in the Internet Information Services (IIS) Manager. For IIS 6.0, you enable ASP 3.0 by selecting the Web Service Extensions node, selecting Active Server Pages in the right pane, and clicking the Allow button (see Figure 23.37).

Figure 23.37
Enable IIS 6.0 to run ASP by enabling Active Server Pages on the Windows Server 2003 IIS Manager's Web Service Extensions page.

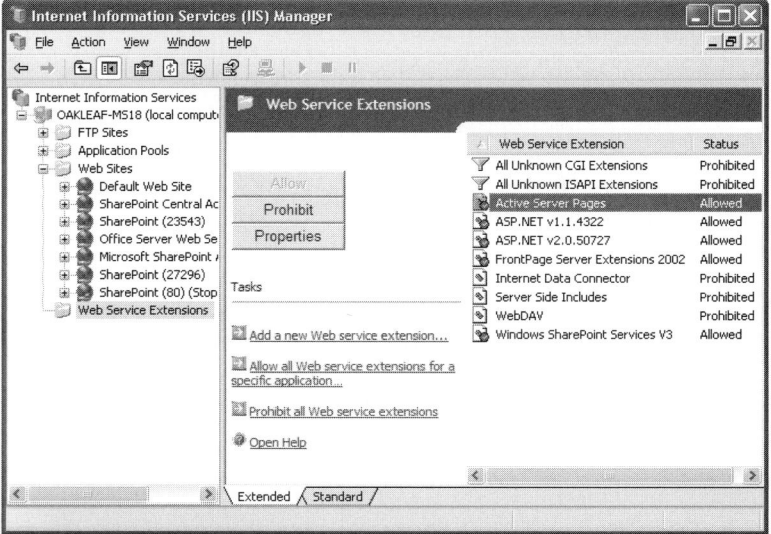

For IIS 7.0 you enable ASP 3.0 by marking the ASP check box in the Turn Windows Features On or Off dialog's Internet Information Services\World Wide Web Services\Application Development Features category (see Figure 23.38).

Figure 23.38
Enable IIS 7.0 to run ASP by enabling Active Server Pages on the Windows Vista IIS Manager's ISAPI and CGI Restrictions page.

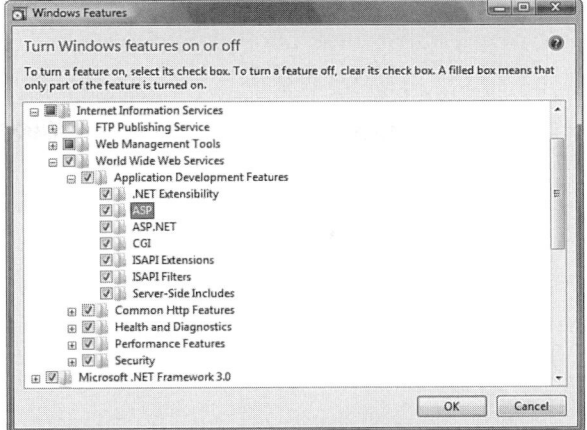

After you copy CustomersCSS.asp to \Inetpub\wwwroot, type **http://localhost/customerscss.asp** as the address to display the sample page.

 If you encounter a "not found" (404) error at this point, see the "Errors Testing the CustomersCSS.asp Page" topic of the "Troubleshooting" section near the end of this chapter.

GATHERING DATA BY EMAIL WITH HTML FORMS

Collecting data by email is a new Access 2007 feature that enables users who can't connect to the database to insert or update table rows by invitation. Unlike with popular web-based forms programs, such as DabbleDB (http://www.dabbledb.com) or Wufoo (http://www.wufoo.com), you can't use Access's system to collect data from Internet users at large. However, it's much more common to restrict data insert and update operations to trusted members of a team, department, or division.

NOTE

For an example of a Wufoo form that anyone can complete from a blog post, visit http://oakleafblog.blogspot.com/2006/07/wufoo-challenges-infopath-for-form.html. The post includes links to several other web-based forms applications.

Following is the basic process for creating and processing an HTML update form, which involves a combination of Microsoft Office Access and Outlook 2007:

1. If the source table to be updated doesn't contain an email field with the address of the person who's responsible for keeping the data up to date, add the field and the data for the rows to be updated. Alternatively, create a new table that contains the email addresses and a one-to-one or one-to-many relationship to the table to be updated.

2. Select the source table and run the Collect Data Through E-Mail Messages wizard. Specify an HTML form (rather than an InfoPath form), select Update Existing Information, specify the fields to be included in the form, and specify whether completed and returned forms are to be processed automatically on receipt.

→ To learn how to update *and* add new rows with an InfoPath form, **see** "Gathering Data by Email with InfoPath 2007 Forms," **p. 1081**.

3. Complete the wizard's steps and send the form to the recipient. The recipient must have a forms-enabled email client such as Outlook.

4. The recipient replies by editing the form as necessary and sending the form to the originator.

5. The originator processes the form automatically or manually. Processing the form updates the original table's data.

6. The person in charge of the process can resend the form to addresses from which no response has been received within the desired time span.

NOTE

> You can use Outlook contacts or other sources of email addresses for forms that insert new rows in the table. Forms that update tables must use email addresses from a table in the database.

Form design is entirely automatic, and most elements of the workflow are automated. Once you've processed a few test forms, you probably can create and send a bulk update form for several thousand recipients in less than an hour. However, monitoring, reviewing, and analyzing the responses is likely to take much more time.

CREATING AN HTML FORM FOR THE CUSTOMERSUPDATE TABLE

You need at least two valid email addresses to run an effective test of the email data gathering process. You send forms to be filled out and receive completed forms from your default email address. The secondary email address lets you emulate actions of the form's recipient. The email addresses for the following example are oakleaf@sbcglobal.net (primary) and rogerj@sbcglobal.net (secondary, recipient). It's assumed that you have Outlook accounts for both email addresses.

Follow these steps to test the email data gathering process with the CustomersUpdate table of the sample \Seau12\Chaptr23\HTMLImportExport.accdb database:

1. Add your secondary email address to one or more of the CustomersUpdate table's ContactEmail cells. The wizard processes only those records that have an email address.

2. Click the External Data tab, and click the Collect Data group's Create E-Mail button to start the Collect Data Through E-Mail Messages wizard and display the introductory dialog. Click Next.

3. In the Choose the Type of Data Entry Form That You Want to Send to Users dialog, accept the default HTML Form option and click Next.

4. In the Are You Collecting New Data or Updating Existing Data? dialog, select the Update Existing Information option and click Next.

5. In the Specify the Data That You Want to Collect dialog, click the >> button to add all fields to the email message. You don't want others to edit the CustomerID field, so select CustomerID in the Fields to Include in E-Mail Message list and mark the Read-Only check box (see Figure 23.39). Click Next.

Figure 23.39
Specify the fields that recipients can edit and those that are visible but read-only in the third wizard dialog.

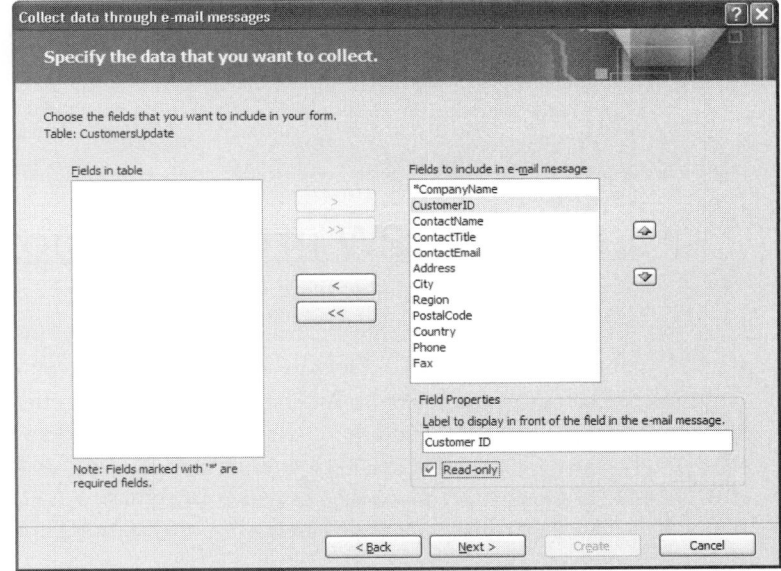

The wizard automatically inserts a space before capitalized letters within a PascalCase word to create more readable captions. You can edit the field text box's label that's seen by the recipient if you want.

6. In the Specify How You Want to Process the Replies dialog, mark the Automatically Process Replies and Add Data to CustomersUpdate check box and the Only Allow Updates to Existing Data check box (see Figure 23.40). (Recipients can't insert new data because the CustomerID field is read-only.)

Figure 23.40
Specify whether you want to process updates automatically. The Set Properties to Control the Automatic Processing of Replies link opens the Collecting Data Using E-Mail Options dialog.

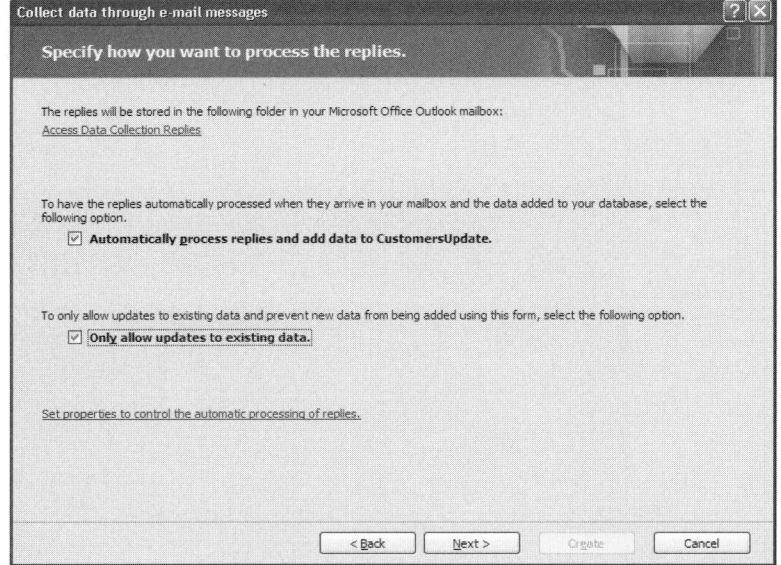

7. Click the Set Properties to Control the Automatic Processing of Replies link to open the Collecting Data Using E-Mail Options dialog. Mark the Discard Replies from Those to Whom You Did Not Send the Message check box and the Accept Multiple Replies from Each Recipient check box. The latter selection allows recipients to change their minds about edits. Set the Number of Replies to Be Processed option to a reasonable number (150 replies for 91 customers should be sufficient) and, if necessary, click the calendar button to select a cut-off date for responses (see Figure 23.41). Click OK to close the dialog and click Next.

Figure 23.41
For this example, only the recipient can respond to the request. Also, the recipient can reply multiple times, but can't submit multiple rows.

8. The wizard proposes to use any field in the source table that contains the word *mail*, so accept the default Current Table or Query option and ContactEmail as the field. Click Next.

9. The suggested text for the title of the email is imperious, so reword the Subject and Introduction text for politeness (see Figure 23.42). Click Next.

Figure 23.42
Regardless of how you reword the request to update a customer record, it still rings the "phishing request" bell.

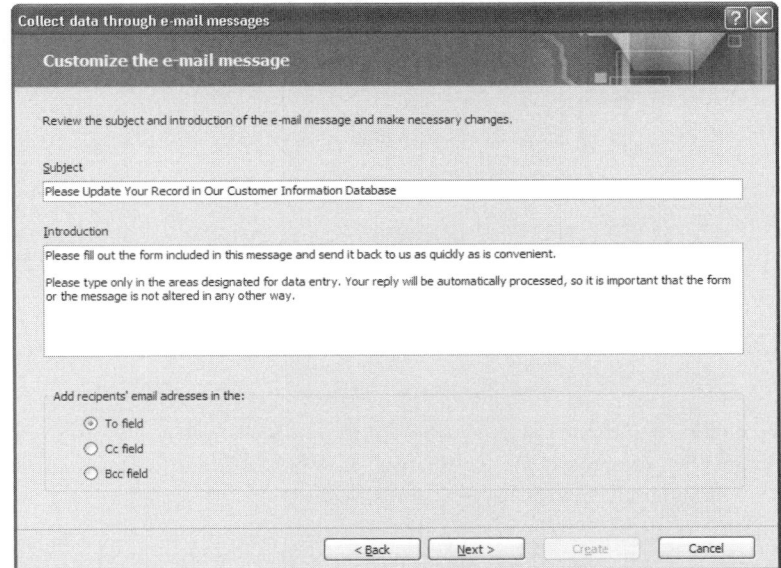

10. Review the Create the E-Mail Message dialog, which has an omnipresent warning about confidential or sensitive information and a second warning that not all rows of the table have email addresses. Click Next to display a list of recipients with selection check boxes.

11. Click Send to send the message(s) from your default email account, close the dialog, and dismiss the wizard.

EMULATING THE RECIPIENT BY EDITING THE FORM(S)

The next step is to test the editing and update processing system by emulating a recipient. Do the following:

1. If it's not open, launch Outlook, click Send/Receive All, and identify the incoming message. Figure 23.43 shows a single message received from OakLeaf Systems, which contains three forms (for ALFKI, ANATR, and AROUT).

Figure 23.43
Outlook displays a data gathering message received by RogerJ from OakLeaf Systems. The message contains three forms.

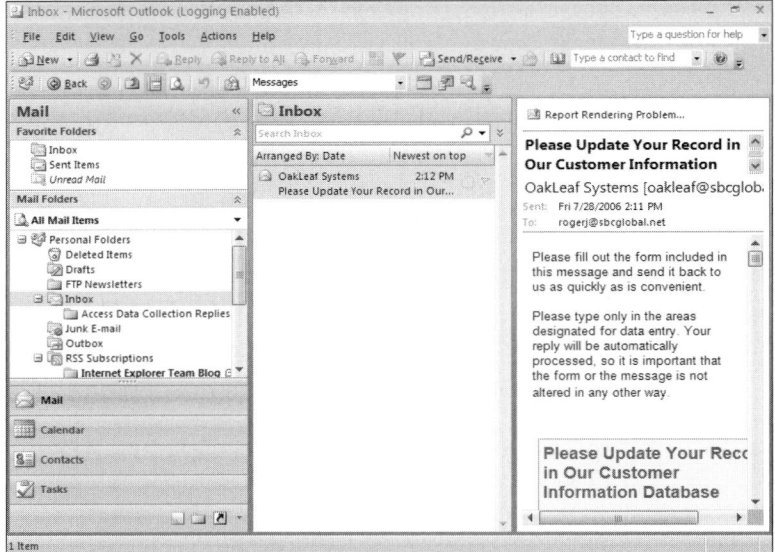

2. Right-click the message, choose <u>R</u>eply, and make a few edits to the data (see Figure 23.44). Notice that the Company Name field is identified as Required and the Customer ID field is flagged as read-only.

Figure 23.44
Edits have been made to the Company Name, Contact Name, Contact Title, and ContactEmail fields of the ALFKI form. Only Company Name and Contact Name changes are visible here.

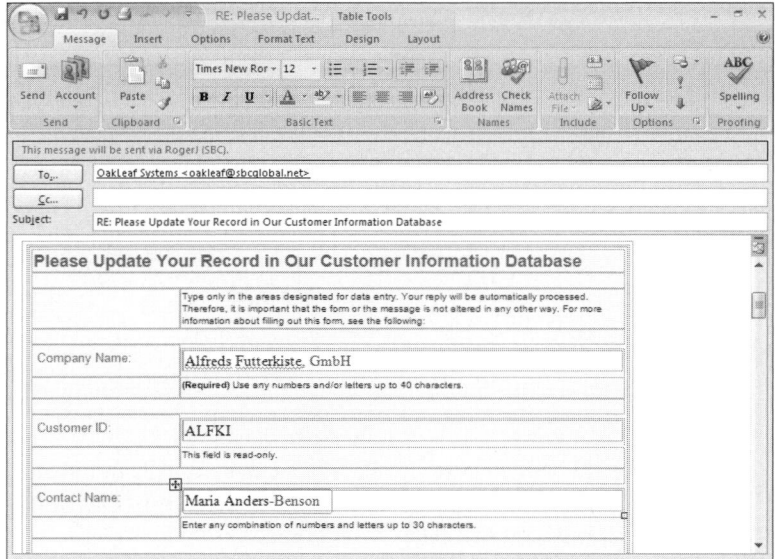

3. After completing cursory edits, click the Send button to return the message with the completed forms to the originator.

4. Click Send/Receive All to receive the message with the completed forms into the Access Data Collection Replies folder.

5. Click the Access Data Collection Replies folder item to display the forms' processing status: Collecting data using email was successful (see Figure 23.45).

Figure 23.45
Automatic processing applies the form edits to the table data as messages arrive. After a message is processed, the status changes to "Collecting data using e-mail was successful."

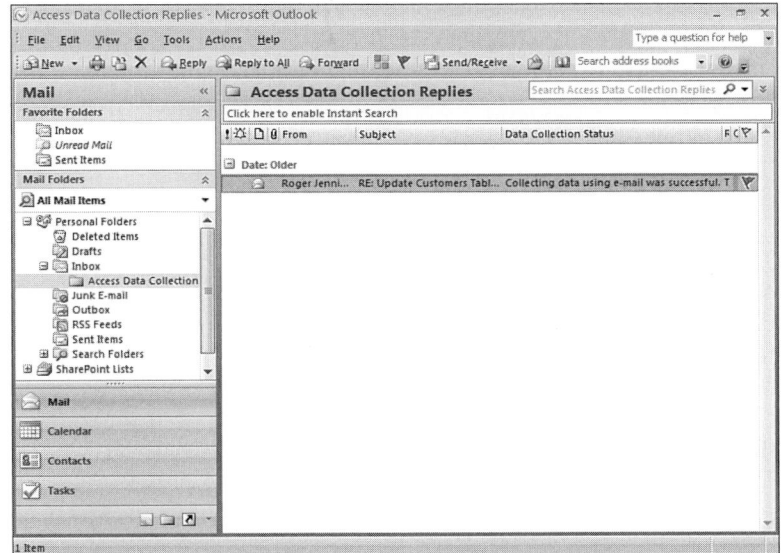

6. Open the destination table (CustomerUpdates for this example) and verify that the table data reflects the edits you made to the forms (see Figure 23.46.)

Figure 23.46
Datasheet view confirms that the edits have been applied to the table.

CREATING A MESSAGE TO ADD A RECORD TO A TABLE

Adding records to a table follows a similar course. Here's a brief description of the process for creating a form to add a new record to the Suppliers table:

1. Select the Suppliers table in the Navigation Pane, start the wizard, skip the first dialog, select HTML Form in the second dialog, and accept the default Collect New Information Only in the third dialog.

2. In the fourth dialog, click >> to add all but the SupplierID field to the form. AutoNumbered primary key fields don't appear in the Field in Table list.

3. In the fifth dialog, the only option is Automatically Process Replies and Add Data to Suppliers.

4. The sixth dialog lets you select between Enter the E-Mail Addresses in Microsoft Office Outlook or Use the E-Mail Addresses Stored in a Field in the Database.

5. When you complete the wizard steps, the Add *TableName* Form opens with empty form text boxes. Click the To button to open the Select Names: Outlook Address book to designated recipients, if you selected the Enter the E-Mail Addresses in Microsoft Office Outlook option in step 4.

Editing, returning, and processing the form's data is similar to that for update forms.

TROUBLESHOOTING

ERRORS IMPORTING HTML FILES OBTAINED FROM THE WEB

When I attempt to import to Access tables some .htm or .html files that I obtain from others' websites, I receive error messages, such as "Reserved error (-5016); There is no message for this error" or "The Microsoft Office Access database engine could not find the object 'd:\path\filename.htm[l]'. Make sure the object exists and you spell its name and the path name correctly."

Browsers are much more tolerant than Access's HTML import process of syntax and other errors in HTML documents. In almost all cases, running the HTML Tidy program on the document solves the initial import problem. This chapter's "Upgrading Access HTML Documents to HTML 4.01 and CSS" section describes the HTML Tidy program and how to use it.

EXPORTED HTML FILES CONTAIN BORDERCOLOR ATTRIBUTES AFTER RUNNING HTML TIDY

The exported .html files I create include a BORDERCOLOR=#000000 (or similar) attribute for each <th> and <td> element, although I've run HTML Tidy on the document.

You forgot to add the drop-proprietary-attributes: yes instruction to Tidy's configuration file. Tidy considers BORDERCOLOR to be a proprietary attribute. Delete all instances of this attribute and specify the border color for table headings and cells with CSS code.

Exported HTML Files Contain HTML 3.2 `bgcolor` And `valign` Attributes After Running HTML Tidy

Unlike `<FONT>` *elements and their attributes, HTML Tidy doesn't upgrade HTML 3.2* `bgcolor="white"`, `bgcolor="silver"`, `border="1"`, `cellspacing="0"`, *and* `valign="TOP"` *attributes to CSS.*

If you need or want to express all formatting instructions as CSS, you must complete the process manually. The Customers2.html file or Customers3.html/Web20Style.css files show the required changes.

Errors Testing the CustomersCSS.asp Page

I receive a "page not found (404)" error when testing the CustomersCSS.asp page.

If you're running Windows SharePoint Services (WSS) or Microsoft Office SharePoint Services (MOSS) on TCP port 80, you'll incur an error because the default website also runs on port 80. Temporarily stop the WSS or MOSS site with IIS to enable viewing your pages from the \Inetpub\wwwroot folder.

Otherwise, type **http://localhost/** to test the default home page of the default website. If you receive a 404 error, verify in IIS Manager that the site isn't stopped. If the site's running, check for the presence of the CustomersCSS.asp page in the \Inetpub\wwwroot folder.

In the Real World—HTML Versus XML as Computing's *Lingua Franca*

Bill Gates delivered his celebrated "embrace and extend the Internet" proclamation to Wall Street analysts on December 7, 1995. From that time forward, the capability to generate HTML documents from Office members and Microsoft development platforms became *de rigeur*. On the Office front, Microsoft released Access for Windows 95 on August 30, 1995, and, almost immediately thereafter, offered the Internet Assistant for the Microsoft Access add-in on April 8, 1996. Microsoft's November 1996 whitepaper, "Choosing the Appropriate Database Development Tool," described the Access add-in:

> "The Internet Assistant for Microsoft Access for Windows 95 has been integrated into Microsoft Access. The Publish to the Web Wizard is a flexible tool that allows users to publish any object in their database either statically or dynamically. It allows for custom HTML formatting using templates and remembers all of the settings used to output the objects in the form of a configuration. The Publish to the Web Wizard integrates with the Microsoft WebPost Wizard to automatically move the published objects to the Web server of choice, whether it is on the Internet or corporate intranet."

Access 97 provided a built-in Publish to the Web Wizard for creating HTML, ASP, or Internet Data Connector (IDC/HTC) files. Access 2000 introduced the HTML import feature and Data Access Pages (DAP), HTML files that emulated many features of Access forms and reports. Unfortunately, DAP didn't become ready for prime time on intranets until the release of the Access 2003 version.

In the web development platform market, Microsoft acquired Vermeer Technologies, Inc. for its FrontPage HTML page design tool about a month after the December 1995 meeting. ASP 1.0 was released with IIS 3.0 in December 1996. Microsoft described the new Visual InterDev 1.0 development environment, which arrived on March 10, 1997, as "a complete solution for building *database-driven* Web applications" with ASP.

> **NOTE**
>
>
> *BusinessWeek* magazine offers the first of a two-part cover story, "Inside Microsoft: The untold story of how the Internet forced Bill Gates to reverse course," from the July 15, 1996, issue at http://www.businessweek.com/1996/29/b34841.htm. The second part is b34842.htm.

ACCESS'S HTML FEATURE SET GETS SHORT SHRIFT AFTER ACCESS 97

Microsoft's unrelenting emphasis on Web-based technologies during the 11+ years following the 1995 Gates proclamation has generated interesting new HTML technologies, such as ASP.NET and SharePoint, plus the Windows Live and Office Live Web platforms. Access's HTML feature set, on the other hand, has been the victim of not-so-benign neglect.

Microsoft hasn't enhanced Access's HTML export features since Access 97 or import capabilities after Access 2000. Exported HTML documents remain rooted in HTML version 3.2, which became obsolete on December 18, 1997, when the W3C released HTML 4.0. The HTML 4.01 recommendation became effective December 24, 1999. Access 2007's export features don't implement CSS level 1, whose W3C recommendation is dated December 17, 1996.

Surprisingly, you can't create or edit Data Access Pages in Access 2007, or produce dynamic HTML reports from auto-generated ASP files. (It's *not* surprising that Access 2007 doesn't support IDC/HTC files because Microsoft has deprecated the Internet Data Connector, HTTPOdbc.dll, as of IIS 7.0). However, ASP 3.0 remains a viable and very popular dynamic web development platform. Fortunately, this chapter's "Displaying Dynamic Tables in Active Server Pages" section demonstrates that rolling your own ASP code from a template generated by an earlier Access version isn't very difficult.

ACCESS XML IN THE SHADOW OF THE "OPEN" XML FORMAT WAR

The Microsoft Office Open XML formats for Word, Excel, and PowerPoint 2007 files generated substantial controversy as they sped through the ECMA (previously European Computer Manufacturers Association) standards process in 2006. ECMA approved Open XML on December 7, 2006, as an ECMA standard (ECMA 376) and started in January 2007 the fast-track process for approval of ECMA 376 as an ISO international standard.

The Open XML formats are intended to compete with the OpenDocument Format for Office Applications (ODF) 1.0 standard approved on May 1, 2005, by the Organization for the Advancement of Structured Information Standards (OASIS). The International Standards Organization (ISO) approved the draft ODF specification on May 3, 2006, and probably will have issued the final ISO 26300 standard by the time you read this book.

OpenOffice.org's free OpenOffice 2.0+ and Sun Microsystems' $80 StarOffice 8.0 support ODF. Government agencies have shown the most interest in "Open" XML formats because of a recent reluctance to depend on archiving public documents in proprietary Microsoft Office .doc, .xls, and .ppt binary file formats. Non-governmental Office customers, who represent the vast majority of its users, aren't likely to be concerned with the vagaries of proprietary file formats; they simply want compatibility with earlier versions' files. If Microsoft had submitted its binary file formats to a recognized standards organization before OpenOffice.org submitted their XML formats, .docx, .xlsx, and .pptx formats probably would be moot.

Obviously, Microsoft doesn't relish being cornered into supporting someone else's file format, especially when the format was developed by—and is being shepherded through the standards process by—today's most viable competitors to Microsoft Office. Access isn't a participant in the XML format wars because OpenOffice Base, OpenOffice.org's erstwhile competitor to Access, doesn't store data in XML documents. However, Microsoft has diverted to Open XML resources that might have been devoted to, for instance, bringing Access's HTML import and export feature set up to date.

NOTE

> For a detailed comparison of OpenOffice.org Base and Access 2003, see the "OpenOffice 2.0 Base Matches Microsoft Access? Surely You Jest" article at http://oakleafblog.blogspot.com/2005/10/openoffice-20-base-matches-microsoft.html.

XML import and export features got a lift in Access 2003 with the added capability of supporting hierarchical document structures created from child and lookup tables. However, it's problematic for Access to import hierarchical XML files that any application other than Access exports. Thus, the primary use for Access's XML import and export features is as a replacement for comma-separated value (CSV) files in data interchange between instances of identically structured Access databases.

When you compare the number of HTML and XML files that deliver useful data, Access's HTML import/export operations should receive substantially more development effort than XML. Here's hoping for a significant improvement of HTML import and export features in Access v.*Next*.

CHAPTER 24

INTEGRATING WITH XML AND INFOPATH 2007

In this chapter

ADOPTING XML AS A DATA INTERCHANGE FORMAT

One of Microsoft's primary selling points for Office 2007 is the capability of Word, Excel, PowerPoint, and Access to export and import documents and data in Extensible Markup Language (XML) 1.0. Structured documents and relational data stored as XML files can be exchanged between multiple business applications running under different operating systems. Interchangeability is the driving force behind the widespread adoption of XML as the century standard for sharing information.

Microsoft's stated goal for Office 2007 is to make the Microsoft Office Open XML format an "open standards" alternative to proprietary Microsoft file formats and the competitive OpenDocument Format (ODF) 1.0 specification. On December 7, 2006, ECMA International approved Office Open XML formats as an ECMA standard and voted to submit the new standards to the International Organization for Standardization (ISO) for consideration as an ISO standard through the fast-track process. Theoretically, Access could import structured XML documents—such as resumes, employee performance reviews, and expense reports—prepared in Word 2007 or Excel 2007 to relational data stored in an Access table. The key to the document import process is a consistent document structure that's defined by a *schema*. (The next section defines XML schemas.) Access expects an XML document structure with upper-level elements to define rows, and child elements to define columns and insert data in table cells. Word .docx and Excel .xlsx files don't adhere to this structure.

NOTE

The XML documents and schemas that Access generates as part of the XML export process are not an "open standard" or part of the Open XML standardization process.

→ For more information about the Open XML format, **see** "Access XML in the Shadow of the 'Open' XML Format War," **p. 1052**.

Access 2002 introduced importing and exporting XML-encoded data to and from Access and SQL Server tables. Access 2002 was limited to the import/export of flat (nonrelational) data. Access 2003 and 2007 handle hierarchical XML representations of relational data. This feature lets you export documents from related tables to create multiple tables from a single XML document and schema. In some cases, you can append records to multiple tables from an XML document; doing this usually requires that the exporting and importing databases are exact duplicates of one another.

This chapter begins with definitions of important XML terms and then covers the use of XML documents exported by Access to generate HTML documents for deployment on intranets and the Internet. Sections at the end of the chapter describe exporting and importing XML data documents, generating and using XML schemas, and transforming XML data with custom XSLT files.

The chapter concludes with a section about substituting Microsoft Office InfoPath 2007 XML-based forms for the HTML forms described in the "Gathering Data by Email with HTML Forms" section of Chapter 23, "Importing and Exporting Web Pages."

> **TIP**
>
> If you're only interested in the end result and want to defer learning the underpinnings of Access 2007's XML features, skip to the "Exporting Static Reports as XML and Web Pages" section.

GAINING AN XML VOCABULARY

SQL has formal grammar rules that depend on the structure of relational databases. XML has a hierarchical structure based on Standard Generalized Markup Language (SGML) for formatting text documents. XML-related "programming" languages, which manipulate XML documents, have a very complex grammar. Before you can begin to interpret—not to mention write and manipulate—XML documents, you need to know a few basic XML terms.

> **NOTE**
>
> The quotes around "programming" in the preceding paragraph are to contrast procedural code that you write in VBA or other familiar programming languages with XML code that manipulates XML documents. XML document-manipulation code, written in Extensible Stylesheet Language Transformations (XSLT), deals with the entire document as a single "chunk." An example near the end of this chapter illustrates the use of VBScript code to process XML data documents with XSLT.

Following are brief definitions of XML-related terms used in this and the following two chapters; some definitions include simple XML examples:

- **XML document**—Any document that follows all XML syntax rules is a *well-formed* document. An XML document must have at least one pair of tags that define the document root (`<root>`…`</root>`) and usually has an *XML header*. The tags can have any name, but the case must match; unlike HTML, XML is case-sensitive. In this and the following chapters, an XML document is assumed to be a document containing Access 4.0 or SQL Server 2000 data, with or without an embedded *XML schema*. XML data documents usually carry an .xml extension; by default, Access names exported data files *TableName*.xml or *QueryName*.xml.

- **Element**—An element is a unit of an XML document that's enclosed between a pair of tags, as in `<tag>element</tag>`. Elements can be—and almost always are—nested within other elements to form a hierarchical document structure.

- **Attribute**—An attribute is a `name="value"` pair that follows the first tag name of an element, as in `<tag attribName="attribValue">`…`</tag>`. Attributes usually represent properties of an element.

- **XML header**—The `<?xml version="1.0" ?>` header technically is optional, but all XML documents should include the header, which usually specifies the encoding method, as in `<?xml version="1.0" encoding="UTF-8" ?>`. UTF-8 is an abbreviation for Universal Character Set Transformation Format 8-bit, a transformation of 16-bit Unicode that's supported by most web browsers.

- **Well-formed**—A well-formed document is one that an XML parsing tool, such as the MSXML parser included with IE 5+, can display without reporting syntax errors (for instance, `<ROOT>...</root>`). Well-formed isn't the same as *validated*.

XML

Following is an example of the simplest well-formed XML data document that conveys some information:

```
<?xml version="1.0" encoding="UTF-8" ?>
<dataroot>
    This is data.
</dataroot>
```

If you type the preceding text in Notepad and save the file as **Simple.xml**, you can open it in IE 5+. IE's XML parser color codes XML elements: The first line is blue, tags are brown, and values (in this example, "This is data.") are black and bold face.

- **Validated**—The original definition of a validated XML document is one that conforms to a predefined Document Type Definition (DTD), which is a holdover from SGML, on which XML (and HTML) is based. DTDs use an arcane syntax and are very difficult to write. An *XML schema* is more appropriate than a DTD for data documents, but is at least equally difficult to compose. Fortunately, Access generates the schemas for the XML documents you export. All XML document examples in this and the following chapters are well-formed and many are validated against XML schemas during import processing.

- **XML schema**—XML schemas define the structure of XML documents and the types of data they contain. For data documents exported by Access, schemas include field data type definitions and, if a query returns data from more than one table, a description of the relationship between the tables. Access names exported schema files *TableName*.xsd or *QueryName*.xsd.

NOTE

> Schemas exported by Access 2007 conform to the W3C's final recommendation of May 2, 2001, for XML Schema 1.0 (http://www.w3.org/TR/xmlschema-0/ for Part 0: Primer). The accepted file extension for schemas conforming to this recommendation is .xsd.

- **XML namespace**—XML namespaces are intended to define standard elements and attributes for specific software products, such as Microsoft Office. The namespace attribute (`xmlns`) usually—but not necessarily—has a unique Uniform Resource Identifier (URI) as its value. There's a recent recommendation for XML namespace attribute names and values at (http://www.w3.org/TR/1999/REC-xml-names-19990114/). Note that `urn:` as a prefix to a namespace URI is an acronym for Universal Resource Name.

XML

The following header and namespace declaration appears at the beginning of each XML data document/schema pair you export from an Access 2007 table or query:

```
<?xml version="1.0" encoding="UTF-8" ?>
<dataroot xmlns:od="urn:schemas-microsoft-com:officedata"
xmlns:xsi="http://www.w3.org/2001/XMLSchema-instance"
xsi:noNamespaceSchemaLocation="TableOrQueryName.xsd">
```

Namespaces for the entire document are declared as attributes of the document root. Access doesn't use the `od` (`officedata`) element type when exporting XML data documents; `od` appears in schemas. The `xmlns:xsi=...` line specifies a URI to indicate that the document has an associated schema. The `xsi:noNamespaceSchemaLocation=` line asserts that the document's data elements are defined by the specified XML schema file: *TableOrQueryName.xsd*. If the location doesn't have a path or an http://... URL, the .xsd file must be in the same folder as the .xml file.

- **Element-centric**—XML documents that contain a single value, such as a number or a block of text, within an element are called *element-centric*. XML data documents exported by Access are element-centric. Element-centric XML stores table data in a `<row>` element with `<column>value</column>` subelements.

XML

The shortest XML document that you can generate by exporting an Access object is the Shippers.xml file:

```
<?xml version="1.0" encoding="UTF-8" ?>
<dataroot xmlns:od="urn:schemas-microsoft-com:officedata"
    xmlns:xsi="http://www.w3.org/2001XMLSchema-instance"
    xsi:noNamespaceSchemaLocation="Shippers.xsd">
  <Shippers>
     <ShipperID>1</ShipperID>
     <CompanyName>Speedy Express</CompanyName>
     <Phone>(503) 555-9831</Phone>
  </Shippers>
  <Shippers>
     <ShipperID>2</ShipperID>
     <CompanyName>United Package</CompanyName>
     <Phone>(503) 555-3199</Phone>
  </Shippers>
  <Shippers>
     <ShipperID>3</ShipperID>
     <CompanyName>Federal Shipping</CompanyName>
     <Phone>(503) 555-9931</Phone>
  </Shippers>
</dataroot>
```

Each subelement (child) of the Shippers (parent) element consists of a single-valued piece of data that represents field values from the Shippers table.

- **Attribute-centric**—XML documents with multivalued elements are called *attribute-centric*. For data documents, the attribute name usually is the field or column name, and the value is a text representation of the field value.

24

XML

Following is an edited version of the attribute-centric XML document for the Shippers table, which is created by saving an ActiveX Data Object (ADO) Recordset:

```
<xml xmlns:rs='urn:schemas-microsoft-com:rowset'
    xmlns:z='#RowsetSchema'>
    <rs:data>
        <z:row ShipperID='1' CompanyName='Speedy Express'
          Phone='(503) 555-9831'/>
        <z:row ShipperID='2' CompanyName='United Package'
          Phone='(503) 555-3199'/>
        <z:row ShipperID='3' CompanyName='Federal Shipping'
          Phone='(503) 555-9931'/>
    </rs:data>
</xml>
```

Attribute-centric XML can hold the data for an entire row of a table or query result set in a single element. In this example, a set of `z:row` elements nest within a single `rs:data` element for the entire Recordset. The attribute-value pairs are `FieldName='value'`. Single- or double-quotes must enclose text values. (XML documents created by saving ADO Recordsets in XML format include the schema as a separate set of elements. The schema elements have been removed from the preceding document.)

- **XML style sheets**—Extensible Stylesheet Language (XSL) can serve two purposes: transforming one XML document into another XML document with a different structure or into an HTML (presentation) document. XSLT is the language in which you— or more likely others at this point—write XML style sheets. Style sheets are stored in files that carry an .xsl extension (.xslt also is used).

NOTE

The October 2001 W3C recommendation for Extensible Stylesheet Language (http://www.w3.org/TR/xsl/) was current when this book was written. XSLT 1.0's finale recommendation of November 1999 is at http://www.w3.org/TR/xslt.html.

EXPORTING TABLES AND QUERIES TO XML AND HTML

Access 2007's XML table and query export feature generates a static XML document and, optionally, an XSLT transform and plain-vanilla HTML table. Fortunately, you can dress up the table by editing the XSLT code that transforms the XML data to HTML. (Why the Access XML developers didn't emulate with XSL the more attractive conventional HTML export format is a mystery.) The later "Reformatting HTML Tables and Adding Page Elements" section shows you how to alter the XSLT style sheet to format the table to your liking.

→ To generate a dynamic (live) HTML table from an Access database, **see** "Displaying Dynamic Tables in Active Server Pages," **p. 1037**.

Do the following to create an HTML page by exporting a table or query as XML:

1. Right-click the table or query to export in the Navigation pane, and choose <u>E</u>xport, <u>X</u>ML File to open the Export – XML File dialog. This example uses vwUnion, which is a modified version of Northwind.accdb's Customers and Suppliers view.

NOTE

The XMLXSL24.accdb sample database in the \SEUA12\Chaptr24 folder of the accompanying CD-ROM includes vwUnion and the other tables and queries for the examples of this chapter. To use SQL Server, which is recommended as the data source for most production XML and web applications, upsize XMLXSL24.accdb to an SQL Server database (XMLXSL24SQL) and an Access project (XMLXSL24CS.adp).

→ To review the upsizing process, **see** "Upsizing with the Trial-and-Error Approach," **p. 949**.

2. Click browse to navigate to the folder in which to store the XML, XSLT, and HTML files, change the filename if you want, and click Save and OK to open the Export XML dialog.

3. Mark the Presentation of Your Data (XSL) option to add an XSLT style sheet (*ObjectName*.xsl) to the XML data (*ObjectName*.xml) and schema (*ObjectName*.xsd) files in the current folder (see Figure 24.1). The default settings generate separate data and schema files.

Figure 24.1
The basic version of the Export XML dialog generates the selected XML file types in the folder you specify in the Export – XML File dialog. Mark the Presentation of Your Data (XSL) check box to create .xsl and .htm files in addition to the default .xml file.

4. Click OK to start the export process, which takes only a second or so for the small query result set generated by vwUnion. In addition to the three files mentioned in step 3, specifying a style sheet generates an *ObjectName*.htm file. Click Close to close the Export – XML File dialog.

5. Open Explorer, navigate to the folder you specified in step 2, and double-click the *ObjectName*.htm file (vwUnion.htm for this example) and enable ActiveX objects to open the page in IE 7 (see Figure 24.2).

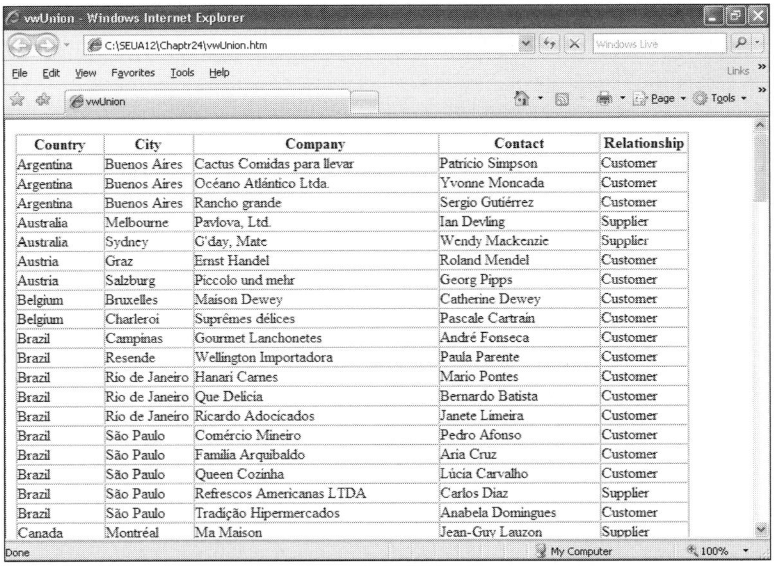

Figure 24.2
The unformatted HTML table created from the .xml, .xsl, and .htm files generated by the XML export process won't win any design awards.

TIP

If your goal is simply to deliver the output of a table or query to a single static web page, use conventional HTML or ASP export as described in Chapter 23, "Importing and Exporting Web Pages." Exporting static data as XML is overkill in this case. The example in the preceding section is the starting point for gaining an understanding of how .xml and .xsl files interact to create an .htm file.

ANALYZING THE EXPORTED XML SCHEMA AND DATA

As mentioned earlier in the chapter, a primary purpose of XML is to enable interchange of information between multiple, networked applications that can run on different operating systems. The capability of XML data to pass through corporate or personal firewalls lets you exchange selected data from your Access or SQL Server databases with other organizations over the Internet. A major benefit of extracting the data as an XML file is that allowing outsiders to connect to your database isn't required to obtain needed information.

By default, XML data is Unicode (UTF-8) text; the data document isn't aware of the data type of the table fields or query columns that generate the text. If you create an XML data document from a table or query that includes fields of the Access DateTime or SQL Server `datetime` data type, such as the Northwind Orders table, the date elements appear in XSD `dateTime` data type format as

```
<OrderDate>2006-07-04T00:00:00</OrderDate>
<RequiredDate>2006-08-01T00:00:00</RequiredDate>
<ShippedDate>2006-07-16T00:00:00</ShippedDate>
```

XSD's `dateTime` text format is well suited to sorting, but isn't easily readable in a table. Thus, the recipient's XSL code must have access to the schema of the table or query to determine how to interpret and, if necessary, transform the data. The XML schema, which you can embed in the XML data file or save as an independent .xsd file, supplies the field data type and other field or column properties. Any application—such as Access 2007—that supports XSD can either import the data directly to a table or use XSLT to transform the schema attributes, such as `sqlSType="varchar"`, to name-value pairs for the target RDBMS, such as Oracle or IBM DB2.

> **TIP**
>
> Don't embed the schema in the .xml data document you send to others. The XML applications used by your recipients might not be able to handle embedded schemas. Send the .xsd schema file with the first transmission of the .xml document, and then send updates to the data as individual .xml files.

24

THE VWUNION.XSD SCHEMA FILE

Listing 24.1 shows the content of the vwUnion.xsd file you exported in the preceding section with indenting applied for easier reading. The schema defines the XML data as a `complexType` that contains a `sequence` of six `simpleType` column elements. Column elements that may be empty have a `minOccurs="0"` attribute. The combination of the `od:sqlSType=` `"varchar"` attribute and `<xsd:maxLength value="15"/>` element, for example, define a `varchar(15)` data type. Each named element of the associated XML data file has a corresponding `<xsd:element name="name">… </xsd:element>` entry in the XSD schema file.

LISTING 24.1   THE XML SCHEMA FOR THE VWUNION VIEW CONTAINED IN VWUNION.XSD.

```
<?xml version="1.0" encoding="UTF-8"?>
<xsd:schema xmlns:xsd="http://www.w3.org/2001/XMLSchema"
            xmlns:od="urn:schemas-microsoft-com:officedata">
   <xsd:element name="dataroot">
      <xsd:complexType>
         <xsd:choice maxOccurs="unbounded">
            <xsd:element ref="vwUnion"/>
         </xsd:choice>
      </xsd:complexType>
   </xsd:element>
   <xsd:element name="vwUnion">
      <xsd:annotation>
         <xsd:appinfo/>
      </xsd:annotation>
      <xsd:complexType>
         <xsd:sequence>
            <xsd:element name="Country" minOccurs="0"
                  od:AccessType="text" od:sqlSType="varchar">
               <xsd:simpleType>
                  <xsd:restriction base="xsd:string">
                     <xsd:maxLength value="15"/>
                  </xsd:restriction>
```

```
            </xsd:simpleType>
          </xsd:element>
          <xsd:element name="City" minOccurs="0"
              od:AccessType="text" od:sqlSType="varchar">
            <xsd:simpleType>
              <xsd:restriction base="xsd:string">
                <xsd:maxLength value="15"/>
              </xsd:restriction>
            </xsd:simpleType>
          </xsd:element>
          <xsd:element name="Company" od:AccessType="text"
              od:sqlSType="varchar">
            <xsd:simpleType>
              <xsd:restriction base="xsd:string">
                <xsd:maxLength value="40"/>
              </xsd:restriction>
            </xsd:simpleType>
          </xsd:element>
          <xsd:element name="Contact" minOccurs="0"
              od:AccessType="text" od:sqlSType="varchar">
            <xsd:simpleType>
              <xsd:restriction base="xsd:string">
                <xsd:maxLength value="30"/>
              </xsd:restriction>
            </xsd:simpleType>
          </xsd:element>
          <xsd:element name="Relationship" od:AccessType="text"
              od:sqlSType="varchar"
            <xsd:simpleType>
              <xsd:restriction base="xsd:string">
                <xsd:maxLength value="8"/>
              </xsd:restriction>
            </xsd:simpleType>
          </xsd:element>
        </xsd:sequence>
      </xsd:complexType>
    </xsd:element>
</xsd:schema>
```

The schema for a table with a variety of data types is more interesting than that for a view having only text/varchar data types. Figure 24.3 shows IE 7 displaying the xsd:appinfo node of the schema for the Orders table. This node specifies the properties of the indexes on the Orders table; the node is empty in the code of Listing 24.1 because the view isn't indexed. Export the Orders table to XML and specify a schema file, open the Orders.xsd file in IE 7, and scroll to the xsd:element nodes for fields to see how SQL Server and Jet data types map to the predefined xsd data types.

The vwUnion.xml Document File and Entities

Figure 24.4 shows IE 7 displaying the vwUnion.xml file's XML dataroot root element, its namespace attributes, and the elements of the first two rows. The XML code for all rows of the view has a consistent structure.

Figure 24.3
The XSD schema for Northwind's Orders table includes the properties of the table's indexes.

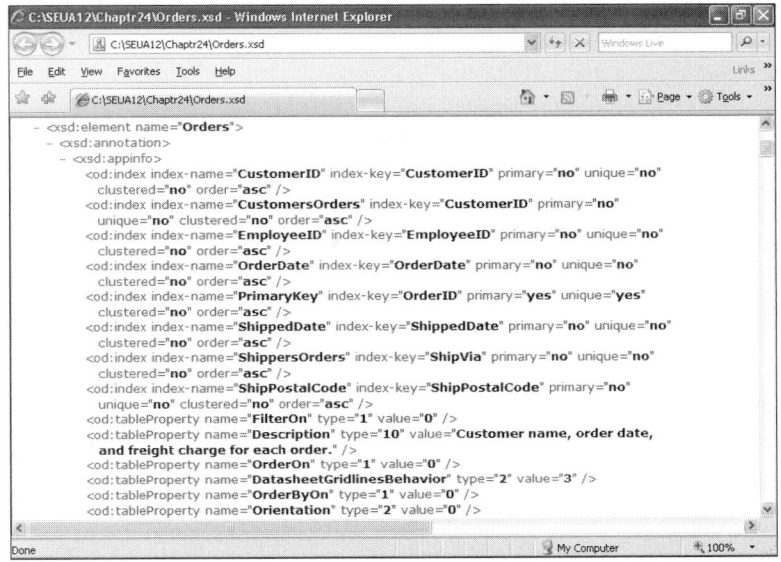

Figure 24.4
IE 7's built-in style sheet improves readability of XML data documents by indenting the subnodes (subtrees). If the XML document is malformed, an "XML page cannot be displayed" message occurs at the location of the error.

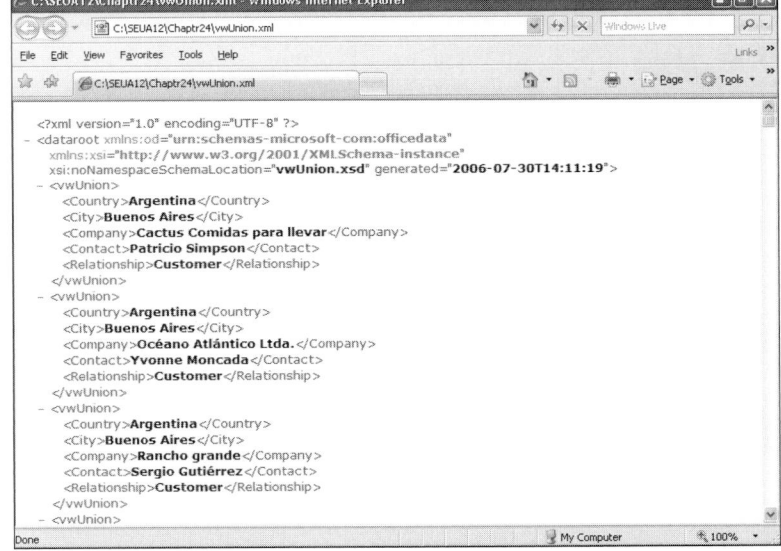

If you choose <u>V</u>iew, Sour<u>c</u>e to open the file in Notepad, scroll to the second row for Australia. You see the following line:

```
<Company><G&apos;day, Mate></Company>
```

' is called an *entity*; in this instance, it represents an apostrophe (') , which XML doesn't permit in content. Table 24.1 lists the ASCII characters that are forbidden in XML text and must be replaced by entities, a process called *entititzing*.

TABLE 24.1. ENTITIES TO REPLACE CHARACTERS THAT ARE ILLEGAL IN XML

Char	Name	Entity
&	Ampersand	&amp;
'	Apostrophe	&apos;
"	(Double) quote	&quot;
<	Less than	&lt;
>	Greater than	&gt;

CDATA ELEMENTS

A CDATA (character data) section permits inclusion of characters that XML interprets as delimiters or large blocks of text that contain special characters or formatting that doesn't conform to XML syntax rules. The ![CDATA[*free text*]] format is required to ensure that the XML parser doesn't inadvertently interpret ordinary data as CDATA. A common use for CDATA sections is to contain binary data for bitmaps in XML and scripting code in XSLT documents.

SPELUNKING THE VWUNION.XSL FILE

The vwUnion.xsl file performs the translation from XML to HTML in accordance with rules specified with a template. Figure 24.5 shows the first few lines of vwUnion.xsl.

Figure 24.5
The vwUnion.xsl style sheet starts with the declaration of a template for generating HTML. A collection of VBScript functions that return values to XPath expressions is located in a CDATA section at the end of the file.

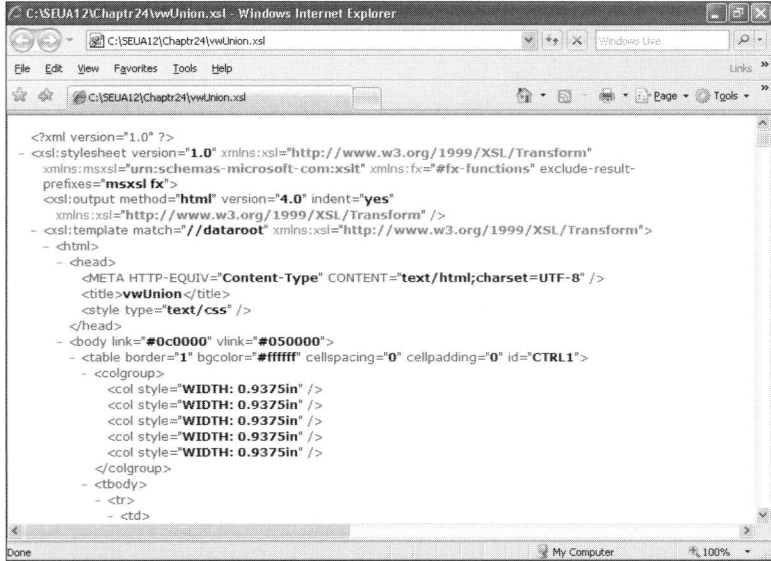

The `<xsl:template match="/">` line defines the beginning of the body of the template. Literal values—such as `<html>` and `<head>`—export directly to the .htm file. XSL elements—such as `<xsl:for-each select="dataroot/vwUnion">`—are template processing rules expressed in an XSLT sublanguage called XML Path Language (XPath). The W3C issued its November 1999 recommendation for XPath 1.0 (`http://www.w3.org/TR/xpath`) in conjunction with the XSLT 1.0 recommendation. Coverage of XSLT and XPath coding techniques is beyond the scope of this book.

> **TIP**
>
>
>
> If you're interested in learning more about XSLT, Microsoft offers a comprehensive XSLT Developer's Guide. Search for **"XSLT Developer's Guide"** (include the quotes) at http://msdn.microsoft.com/ to find the latest version.

REFORMATTING HTML TABLES AND ADDING PAGE ELEMENTS

Fortunately, you don't need to master XSL/XSLT and XPath to improve the formatting of the default table style. Basic knowledge of HTML and Cascading Style Sheets (CSS) is all you need to change the table design and add other elements to the page.

> **NOTE**
>
> You might find it simpler to create Access reports with a design that emulates an HTML table, and save the report design as XML with a presentation transform. Working with XSLT-generated HTML tables, however, lets you apply your HTML authoring skills to create custom pages that comply with specific website design standards. You also can apply the techniques you learn in the following two sections to the much more complex .xsl files of exported Access reports.

APPLYING CSS RULES TO TABLE AND TEXT ELEMENTS

If you have an organization-wide style for displaying tabular information—such as phone directories and other data that's suited to a simple table—you can conform the design of exported tables and queries by altering the HTML code of the *ObjectName*.xsl style sheet. It's a common practice to remove formatting from structural markup by specifying standard styles as a set of CSS rules.

→ To learn more about CSS for formatting web pages, **see** "Upgrading Access HTML Documents to HTML 4.01 and CSS," **p. 1031**.

To use CSS to change the font, border, and background color of the table header and rows in the style sheet, using vwUnion.xsl as an example, do this:

1. Make a backup copy of *ObjectName*.xsl in case you run into problems you can't fix easily.

2. Open *ObjectName*.xsl in Notepad, and change the text between the `<title>`...`</title>` tags to a more descriptive name—**Customers and Suppliers by Country and City** for this example.

3. Add the following lines between the `<style type="text/css"></style>` lines to specify an 11-point Calibri font, set `skyblue` as the background color for the table header, and specify `skyblue` as the table border color:

```
body {font-size: 11pt; color: black;
   font-family: Calibri,Tahoma,Arial,sans-serif}
table {border: solid skyblue 2px; border-collapse: collapse}
td {background-color: white; border: solid skyblue 2px; padding: 2px}
       div {background-color: skyblue; border: 0px; padding: 5px}
```

NOTE

> Access 2007 XSLT for tables generates separate `<tbody>` elements for header and data cells, and adds `<div align="center"><strong>` elements to format the header cells. Thus, the `div` rule applies header formatting. This HTML syntax is unconventional.

4. Remove the `<colgroup>` ... `</colgroup>` block, which sets each column's width to 1 inch, and delete the `border="1"` `bgcolor="#ffffff"` `cellspacing="0"` `cellpadding="0"` attributes from the `<table>` tag, which becomes `<table id="CTRL1">`.

5. Save the .xsl file, open *ObjectName*.htm in IE 6+ to test your changes, and then close the .htm file.

 If Internet Explorer goes into an infinite loop at this point and consumes all or most of your computer's resources, see the "IE 7 Problems Rendering XML Export with Presentation" topic of the "Troubleshooting" section near the end of the chapter.

Figure 24.6 illustrates the effect of the preceding changes.

Figure 24.6
Adding a few CSS style rules, which include changing HTML border attributes, modernizes the table's appearance.

6. To prevent accidentally overwriting your changes when updating the XML data document, save the .xsl file with a new name—**CityUnion.xsl** for this example.

> **TIP**
>
> Select All Files in Notepad's Save As Type list and UTF-8 in the Encoding list when saving XSL, HTML, and XML files. When saving changes with Ctrl+S, you don't need to alter the Save As Type and Encoding selections.

7. Open the .htm file in Notepad, and change the filename argument value in the `LoadDOM` `objStyle`, `"vwUnion.xsl"` line to **CityUnion.xsl**.

8. Save the edited .htm file with a different name—**CityUnion.htm** for this example—so you don't accidentally overwrite it.

9. Open the new .htm file in IE 6+ to verify the changes you made to the .htm script.

> **NOTE**
>
> Sample files for the preceding example—CityUnion2.xsl, CityUnion2.htm, CityUnion2.asp, and CityUnion2.html—are in the \SEUA12\Chaptr24 folder. CityUnion2.html is the HTML source document generated from CityUnion2.htm.

ADDING A TABLE HEADER AND CAPTION

Adding elements to the style sheet is even easier than modifying existing elements. For example, to add a full-width table caption above the field names and a couple of lines of text to the page, do this:

1. Reopen the .xsl file—CityList.xsl for this example—in Notepad.

2. Insert the following line below the `<table id="CTRL1">` element:
   ```
   <caption>Customers and Suppliers by Country and City</caption>
   ```

3. Format the caption by changing its size to 14 points and color to `darkorange`, and apply the bold attribute by adding this CSS rule after the rule for the `table` class:
   ```
   caption {font-size: 14pt; font-weight: bold; color: darkorange}
   ```

4. Insert the following three lines below the first `<tbody>` line (before the first `<tr>` element) to add the full-width table header:
   ```
   <tr>
     <th colspan="5">Northwind Traders - Confidential -
     For Internal Use Only</th>
   </tr>
   ```

5. Optionally, change the `div` CSS selector to `th` and add the `border: solid white 2px` property value. Following is the `<style>` block code:
   ```
   <style type="text/css">
     body {font-size: 11pt; color: black;
       font-family: Calibri,Tahoma,Arial,sans-serif}
     table {border: solid skyblue 2px; border-collapse: collapse}
   ```

```
caption {font-size: 14pt; font-weight: bold; color: darkorange}
th {background-color: skyblue; padding: 2px; border: solid white 2px}
td {background-color: white; border: solid skyblue 2px; padding: 2px}
</style>
```

6. If you replace `div` with `th`, replace each instance of `<div align="center"><strong>` with `<th>` and `</strong></div>` with `</th>`. Here's the `<tbody>` block:

```
<tbody>
  <tr>
    <th colspan="5">Northwind Traders - Confidential -
      For Internal Use Only</th>
  </tr>
  <tr>
    <th>Country</th>
    <th>City</th>
    <th>Company</th>
    <th>Contact</th>
    <th>Relationship</th>
  </tr>
</tbody>
```

7. Save the .xsl file, and reopen the .htm file to check your work (see Figure 24.7).

Figure 24.7
Only a few additional lines of HTML code in the .xsl file add the caption text and full-width header line shown here. A bit of extra work fixes the table header syntax and formatting.

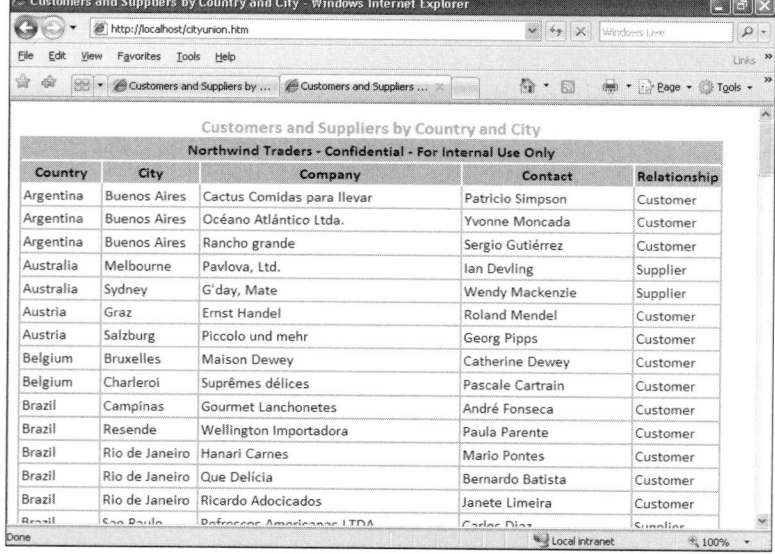

If Internet Explorer goes into an infinite loop at this point and consumes all or most of your computer's resources, see the "IE 7 Problems Rendering XML Export with Presentation" topic of the "Troubleshooting" section near the end of the chapter.

NOTE

Sample files for the preceding example—CityUnion3.xsl, CityUnion3.htm, CityUnion3.asp, and CityUnion3.html—are in the \SEUA12\Chaptr24 folder.

DEPLOYING EXPORTED XML FILE SETS TO A WEB SERVER

One advantage of exporting Access objects to static XML data documents is that their file sets are self-contained. Presentation of the data as a web page isn't dependent on an Access or SQL Server data source. Thus, you can simply copy or move the .xml, .xsl, and .htm or .asp files for any exported Access object to the default \Inetpub\wwwroot of Internet Information Server (IIS) 6+ or a virtual directory you dedicate to delivering XML-based pages. Client computers must have IE 6+ installed to render the .htm files locally; specify server-side processing with ASP to support all browsers and suppress IE's ActiveX warning messages. The .xml and .xsl files are identical for .htm and .asp pages.

It's not necessary to copy static .xml/.xsl/.htm file sets to a web server to make them accessible to others on a network. If you share the folder that holds the file set, others can open the .htm file by specifying the path and filename in IE 6+'s Open text box. Clients must have IE 6+ installed to process the .xsl file on the client. If you need interoperability with IE 5.5 or earlier, Firefox, or other browsers, use the ASP export process.

EXPORTING STATIC REPORTS AS XML AND WEB PAGES

 You can export Access reports as web pages if the report doesn't include a subreport. As an example, selecting the qryTop100Orders2006 query and clicking the Create ribbon's Report button generates a default report that you can export to an HTML document directly or as an intermediary XML/XSLT file pair. There are minor formatting differences between the two approaches. Exporting to an HTML document creates one .html file per report page and adds a set of navigation links to the files; a report based on qryTop100Orders2006 consists of three pages. Exporting to XML/XSLT files generates a single .htm web page, as shown in Figure 24.8.

You also can export to XML/XSLT file pairs reports that you import from earlier Access versions. The Invoice report is the most graphically interesting of the sample reports of Northwind.mdb and NorthwindCS.adp that don't have a subreport. Access 2007's export to XML file feature creates a remarkably accurate HTML representation of the Invoice report. Choosing the export to HTML feature omits much of the report's formatting. The Invoices report has two static bitmaps that let you test the export to XML File command's ability to include bitmaps in its HTML presentation.

The only problem with exporting the Invoice report as XML is that the resulting Invoice.xml file includes the data for all 2,155 rows of the Invoices query or view and is almost 2MB in size. The code of Invoice.xsl must process 26 elements for each of the 2,155 rows to generate the HTML to display the data. Depending on the speed of your computer, it can take more than a minute to open the resulting page in a browser.

Figure 24.8
Exporting Access 2007's default report design generates a single web page, no matter how many items the report includes.

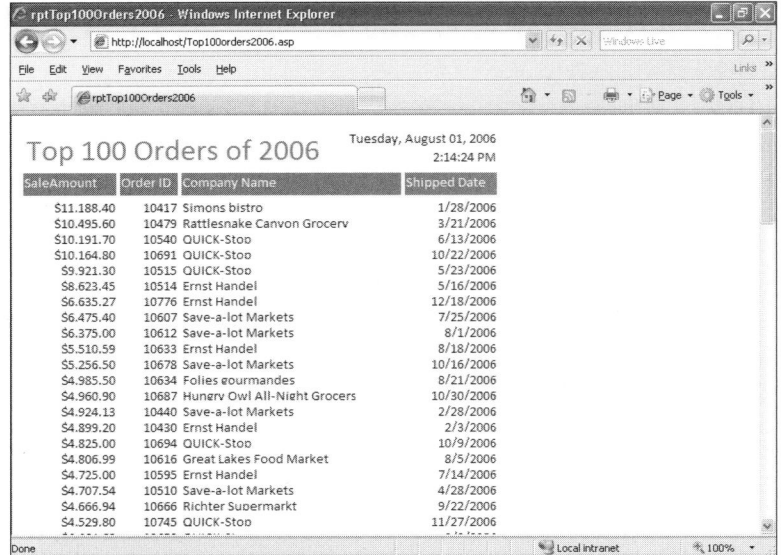

TIP

> Avoid exporting reports based on large query result sets, especially static reports. XML files are much larger than the resulting HTML files, and the entire XML file must be sent to the client for processing a static report. As mentioned earlier, processing an ASP web report on the server and sending HTML to the client is very resource intensive, so keep your ASP web reports as short as possible.

The XMLXSL24.accdb sample database includes an imported Northwind Invoice report, and Invoices and Invoice Filter queries. To create an Invoice report from a single order and export it as XML from XMLXSL24.accdb, do the following:

1. Open the Invoice report in Design View, open the Property window for the report, click the Data tab, and change the Record Source property value to Invoices Filter.

2. Add an Image subfolder to the folder in which you plan to store the files (such as \Inetpub\wwwroot), select the lighthouse image, and copy the embedded bitmap to the Clipboard. Open Windows Paint, paste the bitmap, and save the file as …\Image\ PictureLogo.bmp. Repeat the process for the name image, and store it as NameLogo.bmp.

3. Change to Report view and type a valid OrderID value in the Enter Parameter Value dialog. (**11077** is a good choice because it has many line items.) Close the report and save your changes.

4. Right-click the Invoice report item in the Navigation pane and choose <u>E</u>xport, <u>X</u>ML File to open the Export – XML File dialog.

5. Click Browse and then navigate to the folder in which to save the files. Access proposes the name of the report as the filename (Invoice.htm for this example). Click Save and OK to open the Export XML dialog.

6. Mark the Data (XML) and Presentation of Your Data (XSL) check boxes to save Invoice.xml, Invoice.xsl, and Invoice.htm in the destination folder of step 2.

7. Click the More Options button and the Presentation tab and specify Images as the folder from which to open the two small bitmaps—NameLogo.bmp and PictureLogo.bmp. Exporting a schema is optional (see Figure 24.9).

Figure 24.9
The Data, Schema, and Presentation tabs only appear if you click More Options when the Export XML dialog opens. The Images subfolder is the default location for static bitmaps to include in a report's HTML presentation.

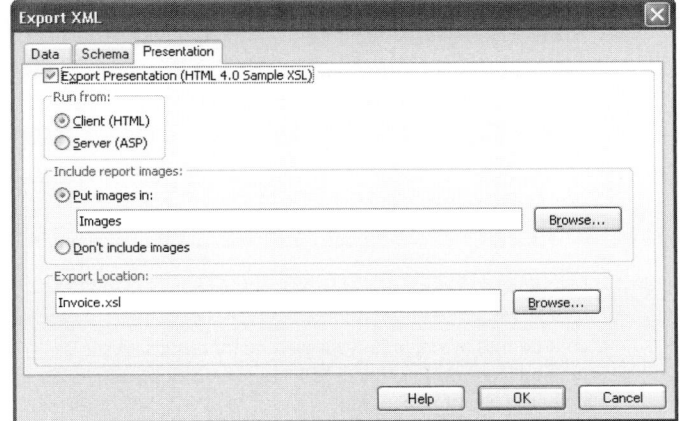

8. Click OK to close the Export XML dialog and open the Enter Parameter Value dialog. Type the OrderID value (**11077**) and click OK.

 9. Open Explorer, navigate to the destination folder, and double-click Invoice.htm to display the page in IE 6.0+ (see Figure 24.10). It takes a second or two for IE 6+ to create and modify the two DOMDocument objects.

 As suggested earlier, if IE 7 goes into an infinite loop at this point and consumes all or most of your computer's resources, see the "IE 7 Problems Rendering XML Export with Presentation" topic of the "Troubleshooting" section near the end of the chapter.

You can't export reports that contain Microsoft Graph objects; use report snapshots to display them. Reports that incorporate PivotChart or PivotTable views in subreports don't export because of the no-subreport restriction. If you try exporting these types of reports, you receive a "Microsoft Access was unable to export the data" message.

Following are some additional restrictions on exporting reports with RPT2HTML4.xsl:

- Running Sum, Can Grow, and Can Shrink properties isn't supported.
- You can't export reports that use snaking (newspaper) columns.
- SQL aggregates (SUM, AVG, and so on) that return NULL values don't evaluate correctly.

Figure 24.10
The Invoice page generated by the three files exported from the modified Invoice report is a close replica of the Access original.

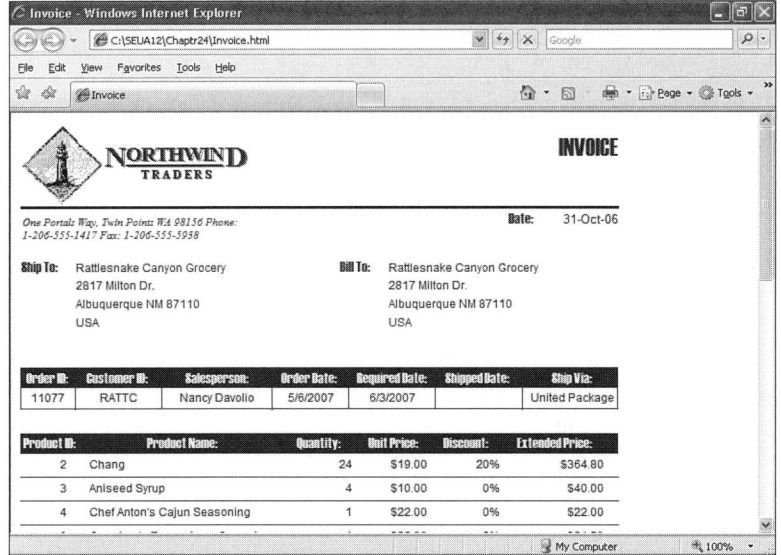

> **TIP**
>
> Make PDF files available on your website for reports whose design includes any of the preceding features. To create a PDF file, right-click the report item in the Navigation Pane and choose Export, PDF or XPS.

If you encounter an error when attempting to open the .htm file for an exported report page, see the "Problems Exporting Reports to HTML" topic of the "Troubleshooting" section near the end of the chapter.

IMPORTING XML DATA TO TABLES

Most of this chapter is devoted to exporting XML documents and XSL transforms from Access 2007. Access 2007 also can import well-formed, element-centric XML data documents to new tables or append data to existing tables. Access 2002's XML import feature was limited to XML files having elements from a single table or query. If you wanted to import order and line item data, for example, you needed an XML data document for each table. To maintain referential integrity, you had to append the orders document and then the line items document in separate operations. Access 2003 removed the single-table limitation.

Access 2007's new import XML dialog lets you import data to multiple tables from a single XML document and its XML schema. If you don't have an .xsd file for the document,

Access 2007 infers the structure of the document and can create a schema for it. Another Access 2007 XML feature is the capability to create empty related tables from an XML schema (.xsd) document. You also can transform the XML data during import with custom .xsl files.

The ability to generate tables from XML schema and import XML data to Access tables will become increasingly important as Microsoft and other software publishers, as well as many industries, move to XML as the preferred method of interchanging relational data. Most current standards for XML business documents provide XML schemas to validate instances of the documents.

IMPORTING A FLAT XML DATA DOCUMENT

 This simple example uses the Top100Orders2006.xml document file in the \SEUA12\ Chaptr24 folder. Top100Orders2006.xml doesn't have a corresponding schema.

To import the Top100Orders2006.xml document to a new table and append another set of records to the table, do this:

1. Open a database or project that doesn't have the qryTop100Orders2006 query or view. This and the following examples use a new sample database. Click the Get External Data tab.

2. Click the Import group's XML File button to open the Get External Data – XML File dialog, click Browse to open the File Open dialog, and navigate to the location where you saved the Top100Orders2006.xml file.

3. Double-click the Top100Orders2006.xml file to close the File Open dialog, and click OK to open the Import XML dialog, which displays the name of the source query as a Tables subnode. Expand the qryTop100Orders2006 node to display the view columns (see Figure 24.11).

Figure 24.11
The Import XML dialog displays the name of the source table or view from which you created the data document and its fields or columns.

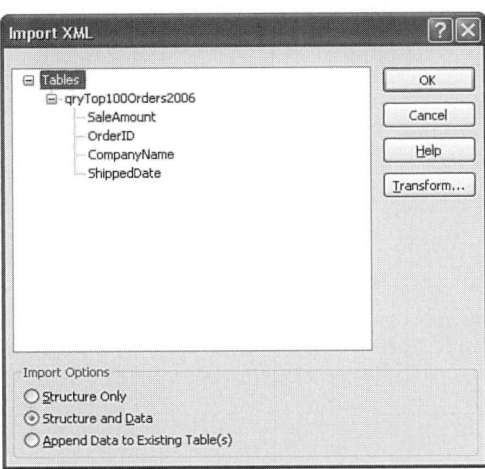

4. Accept the default Structure and Data option, and click OK to create the table with the imported values. Click OK to close the Get External Data – XML File dialog.

5. Open the new qryTop100Orders2006 table in Datasheet view, which displays Access's default Text formats for all fields, because you didn't have a schema for the XML file. Optionally, rename the table by deleting the qry prefix.

6. Change to Table Design view, and change the data type of the SaleAmount field to Currency and the OrderID field to Number, Long Integer. An Access database won't accept a change of the ShippedDate field, because Access can't handle the full ISO 8601 YYYY-MM-DDThh:mm:ss format designated by the XML Schema Part 2: Datatypes specification for the dateTime data type. You must have a schema that specifies the dateTime data type for the DateTime field to import dates successfully.

7. Access can transform the YYYY-MM-DD date-only format, so replace T00:00:00 with nothing, change to Design view, and change the ShippedDate's data type to DateTime (see Figure 24.12).

Figure 24.12
Change the field data types to those appropriate for the type of data in each column. You also can rearrange the sequence of the fields, if you want.

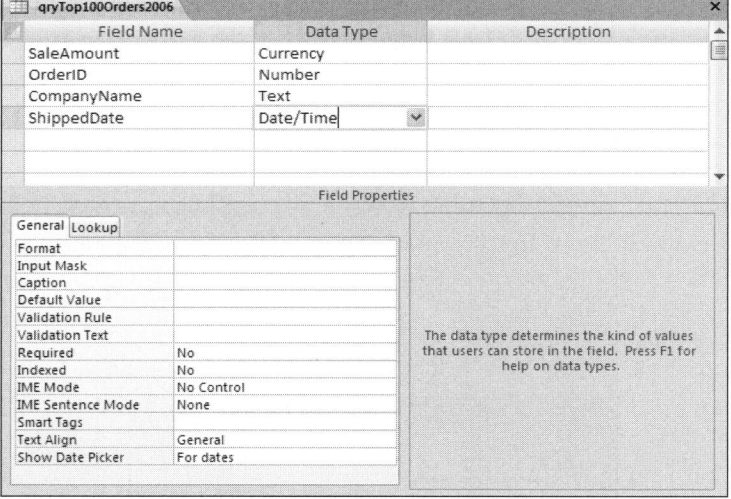

8. Return to Datasheet view and save your changes. Figure 24.13 shows the modified table in Datasheet view.

CAUTION

Don't disregard a warning message that states that rows will be lost. This message occurs when Access or SQL Server can't handle the data type change. Cancel the operation and return the data type for the field to Text or nvarchar.

Figure 24.13
Access successfully
changes the data
types of three fields;
you must remove
T00:00:00 from
ShippedDate values
to change the
ShippedDate data
type from Text to
DateTime.

SaleAmount	OrderID	CompanyName	ShippedDate
$11,188.40	10417	Simons bistro	1/28/2006
$10,495.60	10479	Rattlesnake Canyon Grocery	3/21/2006
$10,191.70	10540	QUICK-Stop	6/13/2006
$10,164.80	10691	QUICK-Stop	10/22/2006
$9,921.30	10515	QUICK-Stop	5/23/2006
$8,623.45	10514	Ernst Handel	5/16/2006
$6,635.27	10776	Ernst Handel	12/18/2006
$6,475.40	10607	Save-a-lot Markets	7/25/2006
$6,375.00	10612	Save-a-lot Markets	8/1/2006
$5,510.59	10633	Ernst Handel	8/18/2006
$5,256.50	10678	Save-a-lot Markets	10/16/2006
$4,985.90	10634	Folies gourmandes	8/21/2006
$4,960.90	10687	Hungry Owl All-Night Grocers	10/30/2006
$4,924.13	10440	Save-a-lot Markets	2/28/2006
$4,899.20	10430	Ernst Handel	2/3/2006
$4,825.00	10694	QUICK-Stop	10/9/2006
$4,806.99	10616	Great Lakes Food Market	8/5/2006
$4,725.00	10595	Ernst Handel	7/14/2006
$4,707.54	10510	Save-a-lot Markets	4/28/2006

Record: 14 1 of 100 ► ►I ► No Filter Search

qryTop100Orders2006

24

9. Test the ability of your redesigned table to accept updates from XML data documents having the same structure. Close the table, and repeat steps 2–5, except select the Append Data to Existing Table(s) option in step 4.

 10. Open the table in Datasheet view, verify that the table now has 200 rows and that the appended records (101 and greater) appear the same as the first 100.

> **NOTE**
>
> SQL Server tables imported from XML documents are read-only in datasheet view, because they lack a unique record identifier (primary key). You can edit any Access table imported from an XML document.

Importing hundreds of thousands of records as XML to populate tables isn't likely to replace Access's text import or SQL Server's bulk copy process (BCP), which uses conventional tab- or comma-delimited, or fixed-width text files. BCP data import is much faster than XML import, and conventional text files are much smaller than XML data files for the same number of records. XML import is better suited to making incremental additions to tables. Access 2007 XML import feature makes adding records to SQL Server tables considerably easier than using BCP or SQL Server 2005's Integration Services (SSIS).

IMPORTING DATA WITH AN XML SCHEMA

Access can import an XML schema in XSD format to create an empty table to which you append XML data that conforms to the schema. If the schema contains `od:AccessType=` `"datatype"` and `od:sqlSType="datatype"` attributes, the schema specifies the Access or SQL Server field data types when you create the empty table.

To export and then import the schema and then add data for the qryTop100Orders2006 table to an Access or SQL Server database, do this:

1. Right-click the qryTop100Orders2006 table and choose Export, XML File to open the Export – XML File dialog. Change the filename to **Top100Orders2006.xml**, click Browse, navigate to the folder that stores the Top100Orders2006.xml file (\SEUA12\ Chaptr24), and click Save and OK to close the dialogs.

2. In the Export XML dialog, clear the Data (XML) and mark the Schema of the Data (XSD) options. Click OK to export Top100Orders2006.xsd only, and then click OK and Close.

3. Delete the qryTop100Orders2006 table to prevent a conflict when importing the schema.

4. Click XML File in the External Data ribbon's Import group to open the Get External Data – XML File. Click Browse, double-click the Top100Orders2006.xsd item, and click OK to open the XML Import dialog.

5. Click OK to import the schema and click Close to dismiss the Get External Data – XML File dialog.

6. Open the empty table in Design view to verify that the data types are the same as those you specified in the preceding section.

7. Return to Datasheet view, and append the 100 records from the Top100Orders2006.xml data document to confirm the validity of the imported schema.

> **NOTE**
>
> Be sure to select the Append Data to Existing Table(s) option in step 7. Selecting the Structure and Data option creates a new qryTop100Orders20061 table.

Sending XML schema and data documents as email enclosures over the Internet to create and populate Access and, especially, SQL Server tables is simpler than other alternatives. Many firewalls or email applications now reject email enclosures in nontext formats such as Access .mdb and SQL Server .mdf files. XML documents are text files, so they pass through most firewalls with no problems.

EXPORTING AND IMPORTING DATA IN RELATED TABLES

Access 2007's capability to export data and schemas from multiple related tables lets you generate hierarchical XML documents. The documents contain elements from a base table, such as Orders, and child elements from corresponding records in the related tables. Access-specific schemas define the table structures and relationships. Access 2007 also lets you limit the export to a selected record or apply the current filter, and offers the option to export lookup data.

EXPORTING RELATED TABLES AND THEIR SCHEMA

To test-drive exporting related tables with a single record from the Orders table and related records from the Order Details table, do the following:

1. Open \SEUA12\Chapt24\Northwind.accdb's Orders table in Datasheet view and select the first order (10248).

2. Right-click the Orders table, choose Export, XML File to open the Export – XML File dialog, type **Order10248** in the File Name text box, click Browse, navigate to your working folder, and click Open and OK to open the Export XML dialog.

3. Accept the defaults, and click More Options to expand the Export XML dialog and display the Orders and Order Details tables. Expand the nodes to display all related lookup tables, and mark all tables for export (see Figure 24.14).

Figure 24.14
Access 2007's enhanced Export XML dialog displays the table you select for export and its directly related table, if any. Expanding Lookup Data nodes discloses other related tables.

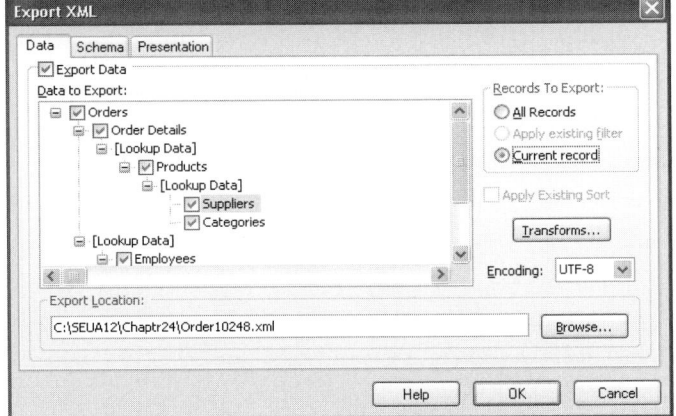

NOTE

The Order10248.xml file is 342KB and the Order10248.xsd file is 155KB. Exporting all Orders, Order Details, and lookup tables creates a 1,122KB XML file. Exporting lookup tables adds every record of the lookup tables to the end of the XML file. Bitmap images in the Categories table and Attachment images in the Employees table are stored with Base64 encoding in CDATA elements. *Base64 encoding* translates binary bytes to combinations of the 64 printable low-order ASCII text characters.

4. Click OK to export the Order10248.xml and Order10248.xsd files. If "The current record was not unique. All identical records were exported" message box opens, disregard it and click OK.

5. Open Order10248.xml in IE to verify that the three Order Details line items are present as child elements of the order.

6. Open Order10248.xsd in IE and explore the schema that defines the nine tables, indexes, and primary and foreign keys.

RE-CREATING AND POPULATING RELATED TABLES

Exporting all records of all tables in an Access database lets you import an exact image of the source database into a destination database. All table properties, including primary keys and indexes, propagate to the destination database. The schema doesn't create relationships between tables, which means that the recipient of the schema and data files must create relationships and establish referential integrity manually. Once the table structures and relationships have been created in the destination database, you can append new rows from XML data files that are exported individually.

To generate all tables from Northwind.accdb by importing Orders.xml and Orders.xsd, do the following:

1. Open the working database you created earlier in the chapter or create a new database named Orders.accdb, and click the External Data tab.

2. Click the Import group's XML File button, and open \SEUA12\Chaptr24\Orders.xml. The Import XML dialog displays Tables subnodes for the nine tables (see Figure 24.15).

Figure 24.15
The Import XML dialog displays subnodes for all tables defined by the Orders.xsd schema. Expanding the nodes shows the tables' fields.

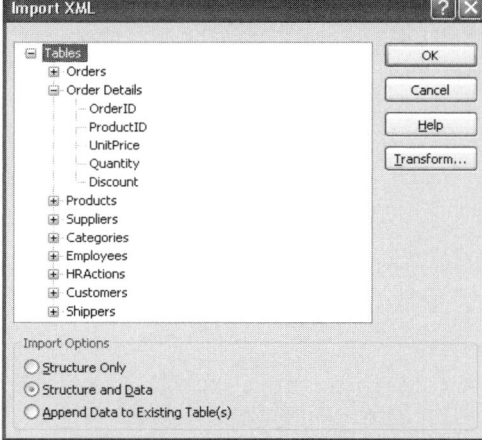

3. Click OK to import the tables, which takes a few seconds or more depending on the speed of your computer.

4. Open the imported tables in Datasheet view to confirm their resemblance to the source tables.

NOTE

> The schemas that Access 2007 generates include application-specific annotations to describe Access or SQL Server extended properties, such as captions and lookup data. Subdatasheets don't appear because the schema doesn't specify relationships. The default value of the tables' Subdatasheet Name property is [Auto], so subdatasheets appear after you establish table relationships in the Relationships window.

Appending XML data to tables with Access AutoNumber fields or SQL Server `identity` columns doesn't work. Only SQL Server or Access can update these fields. If you edit Order10248 to eliminate the values of the <OrderID> element or remove the element entirely, records in the ImportErrors table state that the table wasn't imported and data wasn't inserted.

GATHERING DATA BY EMAIL WITH INFOPATH 2007 FORMS

Microsoft Office InfoPath 2007—called XDocs during its early beta period—is a forms-based XML document generation and editing application. InfoPath's primary application is producing structured data from electronic forms based on common paper business forms, such as expense reports, employee performance reviews, vendor evaluations, time cards, and sales call reports. The structure of the data is defined by an underlying XML schema, which validates users' entries in the form's controls—text boxes, option buttons, drop-down lists, and check boxes. When you design a form from scratch, InfoPath generates the schema for you. InfoPath also can infer a schema from an existing XML document. These features mean that InfoPath form designers don't need to be XML experts to produce useful data entry and editing forms with InfoPath 2007.

InfoPath forms share many of the features of Access's forms, such as a design surface on which you place controls that are bound to an underlying data source. You review and edit data in InfoPath sections or repeating sections, which correspond to Access's bound forms and subforms. InfoPaths use VBScript or JScript event handlers to customize form behavior.

InfoPath 2007 binds to the following types of data sources:

- Access (.accdb) tables or queries
- Jet (.mdb) tables or queries
- SQL Server tables, views, table-returning functions, and stored procedures
- XML documents stored as .xml file
- Document/literal XML Web services

You can substitute InfoPath 2007 forms for HTML forms that enable Outlook 2007–based email data collection. InfoPath 2007 offers the benefits of an improved message UI, form customization, and the capability to update and add new records to a table with a single form. The downside is that all recipients must have the full InfoPath 2007 client installed; the InfoPath Web client that Microsoft Office Forms Server (MOFS) 2007 enables doesn't support updating Access data with InfoPath forms and Outlook email messages.

The basic process for gathering data with Access, InfoPath, and Outlook 2007 is almost identical to that for HTML forms. The only significant differences are the appearance of the form and minor changes to the Collect Data Through E-Mail Messages wizard's dialogs.

→ For more information about processing HTML forms, **see** "Gathering Data by Email with HTML Forms," **p. 1043**.

As mentioned in Chapter 23, you need at least two valid email addresses to test the email data gathering process. You send InfoPath form(s) to be edited and receive completed forms from your default email address. The secondary email address lets you emulate actions of the form's recipient. As was the case for HTML forms, the email addresses for the following example are oakleaf@sbcglobal.net (primary) and rogerj@sbcglobal.net (secondary, recipient). You must have Outlook address book entries for both email addresses.

CREATING AN INFOPATH FORM FOR THE SUPPLIERSUPDATE TABLE

The steps to test the email data gathering process with the SuppliersUpdate table of the sample \Seau12\Chaptr24\XMLSXSL24.accdb database are similar to those for HTML forms. The Northwind Suppliers table, which serves as the source of the SuppliersUpdate table, has an AutoNumber SupplierID primary key field to simplify adding new records.

To edit and add SuppliersUpdate records, do this:

1. Add your secondary email address to one or more of the SuppliersUpdate table's ContactEmail cells. The wizard processes only those records that have an email address.

2. Right-click the SuppliersUpdate table item in the Navigation Pane, and choose Collect and Update Data via E-mail to start the Collect Data Through E-Mail Messages Wizard and display the introductory dialog. Click Next.

3. In the Choose the Type of Data Entry Form That You Want to Send to Users dialog, select the Microsoft Office InfoPath Form option and then click Next.

4. In the Are You Collecting New Data or Updating Existing Data? dialog, select the Update Existing Information option and then click Next. The Fields to Include in E-Mail Message list includes six of the table's 13 fields because they require values.

> **NOTE**
>
> The SupplierID field doesn't appear in either field list because it's an AutoNumber field, which is read-only.

5. In the Specify the Data That You Want to Collect dialog, click the >> button to add all fields to the email message. Use the up and down arrows to rearrange the fields in their original order (see Figure 24.16).

> **NOTE**
>
> Edit the Field Properties text box's label that's seen by the recipient if you want.

6. In the Specify How You Want to Process the Replies dialog, mark the Automatically Process Replies and Add Data to CustomersUpdate. Don't mark the Only Allow Updates to Existing Data check box so an update form will be available in the message (see Figure 24.17).

Figure 24.16
Reorder the field sequence and specify the fields that recipients can edit in the third wizard dialog.

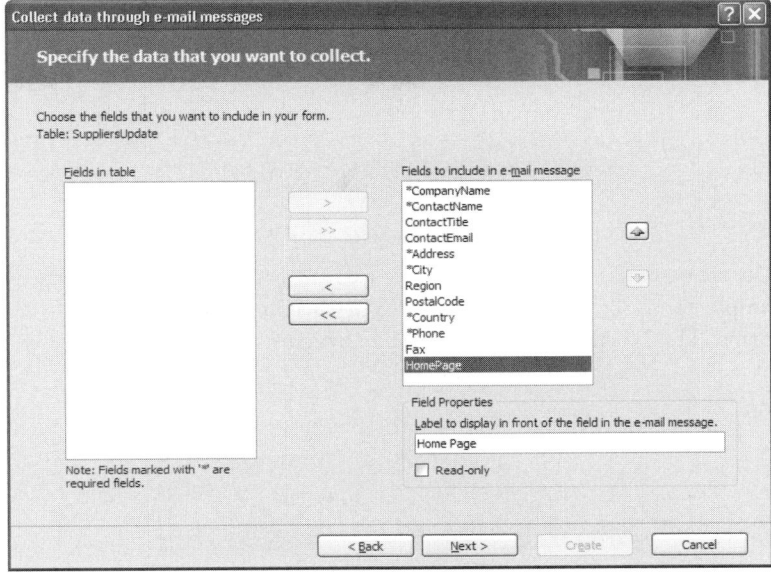

Figure 24.17
Specify if you want to process updates automatically. The Set Properties to Control the Automatic Processing of Replies link opens the Collecting Data Using E-Mail Options dialog.

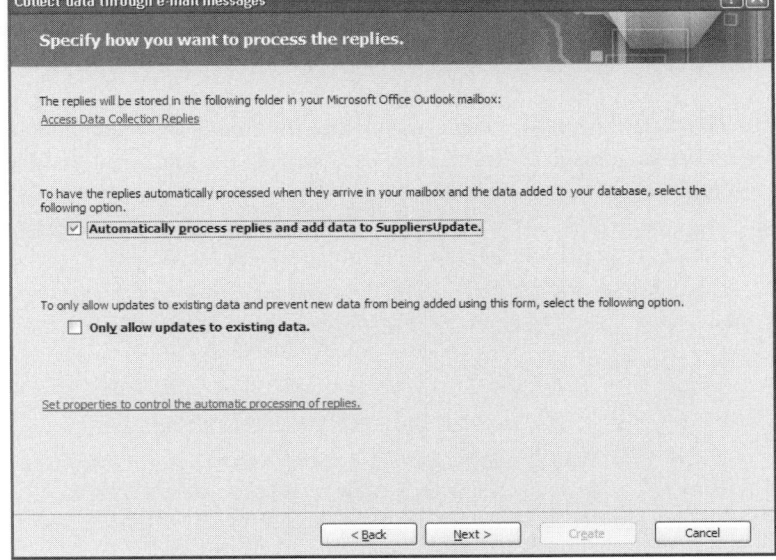

7. Click the Set Properties to Control the Automatic Processing of Replies link to open the Collecting Data Using E-Mail Options dialog. Mark the Discard Replies from Those to Whom You Did Not Send the Message and Accept Multiple Replies from Each Recipient check boxes. The latter selection allows recipients to change their minds

about edits. Set the Number of Replies to be Processed to a reasonable number (150 replies for 91 customers should be sufficient) and, if necessary, click the calendar button to select a cut-off date for responses (see Figure 24.18). Click OK to close the dialog and then click Next.

Figure 24.18
For this example, only the recipient can respond to the request. The recipient also can reply multiple times and submit multiple rows.

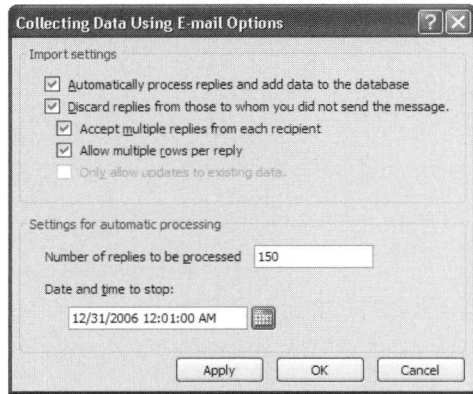

> **NOTE**
> If you have more than one row with the same email address or allow combining an edit and insert(s), you must mark the Allow Multiple Rows per Reply check box.

8. The wizard proposes to use any field in the source table that contains the word *mail*, so accept the default Current Table or Query option and ContactEmail as the field. Click Next.

9. The suggested text for the title of the email is imperious, so reword the Subject and Introduction text for politeness by adding a "Please" prefix to the Subject and Introduction text.

10. Review the Create the E-Mail Message dialog. Click Next to display a list of recipients with selection check boxes.

> **TIP**
> Make sure Outlook is running before you click send. Otherwise, the form won't be sent until you open Outlook or the email polling interval expires.

11. Click Send to send the message(s) from your default email account, close the dialog, and dismiss the wizard.

EDITING EXISTING TABLE DATA AND ADDING A NEW RECORD

The next step is to test the edit and update processing system by emulating a recipient. Do the following:

1. If it's not open, launch Outlook, click Send/Receive All, and identify the incoming message. Figure 24.19 shows a single message received from OakLeaf Systems, which contains two forms (for Exotic Liquids and New Orleans Cajun Delights).

Figure 24.19
Outlook displays the entry for an InfoPath data gathering message received by RogerJ from OakLeaf Systems. The message contains two InfoPath forms.

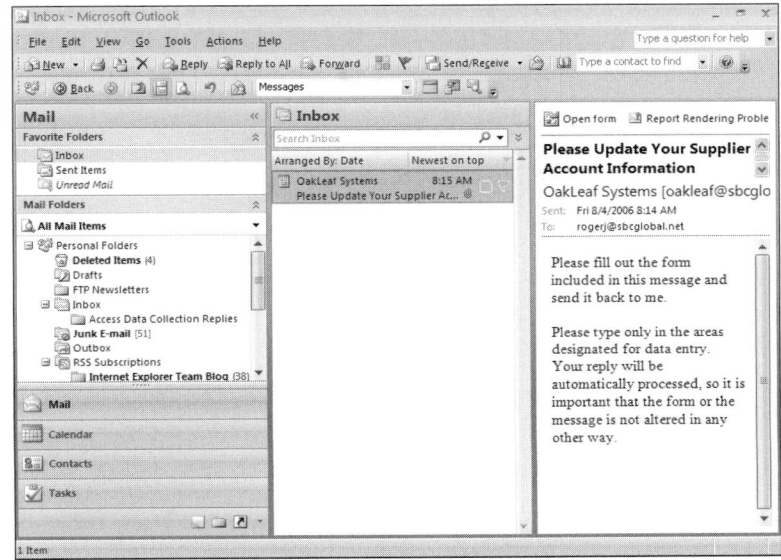

2. Click the Open Form button, click Reply, accept the default Mail Options, add optional introductory text, and make a few edits to the data (see Figure 24.20). Notice that each field displays the maximum allowable number of characters.

Figure 24.20
Introductory text has been added and edits have been made to the Company Name, Contact Name, Contact Title, and ContactEmail fields of the Exotic Liquids form.

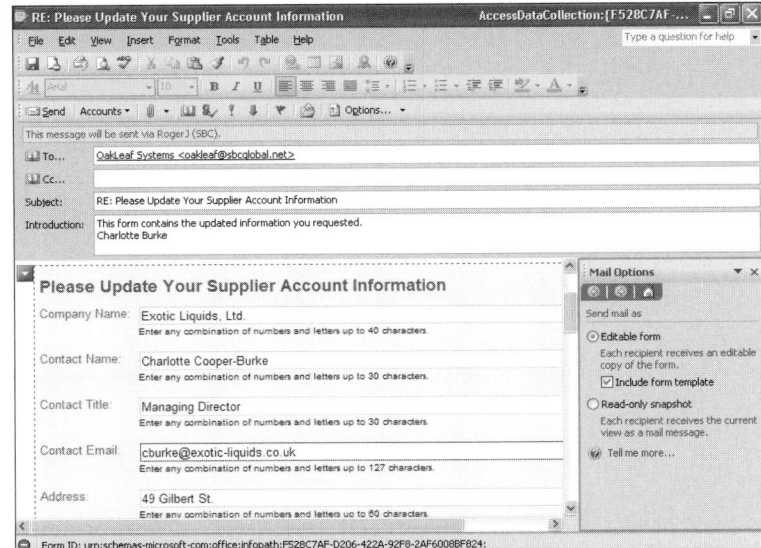

3. Click the arrow button at the top-left of the last form and choose Insert Below to create an empty form to add a new record. Alternatively, click the Insert a Row button at the bottom of the form.

4. Enter data for a new supplier account. Red asterisks indicate required fields that don't have an entry (see Figure 24.21).

Figure 24.21
Adding a new supplier account requires entries in all required fields. A red asterisk identifies required fields without data.

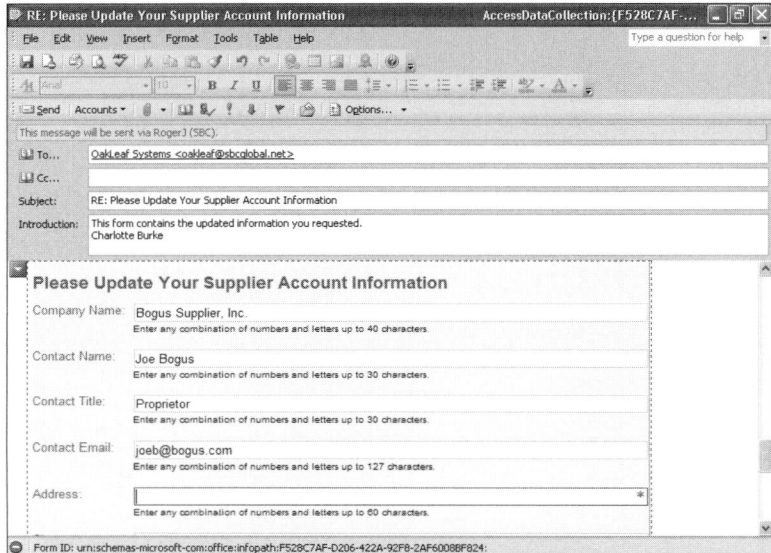

5. After completing the test entries, click the Send button to return the message with the completed forms to the originator.

CAUTION

> If you didn't click the Reply button and you click Submit at this point, the message will be sent with the originator's email address (oakleaf@sbcglobal.net) instead of the recipient's (rogerj@sbcglobal.net). Automatic updates will fail because of address mismatch and only inserts will succeed.

6. In Outlook, click Send/Receive All to receive the message with the completed forms into the Access Data Collection Replies folder.

7. Click the Access Data Collection Replies folder item to display the forms' processing status: Collecting data using e-mail was successful (see Figure 24.22).

8. Open the destination table (SuppliersUpdate for this example), press F5 to refresh the records, and verify that the table data reflects the edits you made to the forms (see Figure 24.23) and that the insert was successful.

Figure 24.22
Automatic processing applies the form edits to the table data as messages arrive. After a message is processed, the status changes to "Collecting data using e-mail was successful."

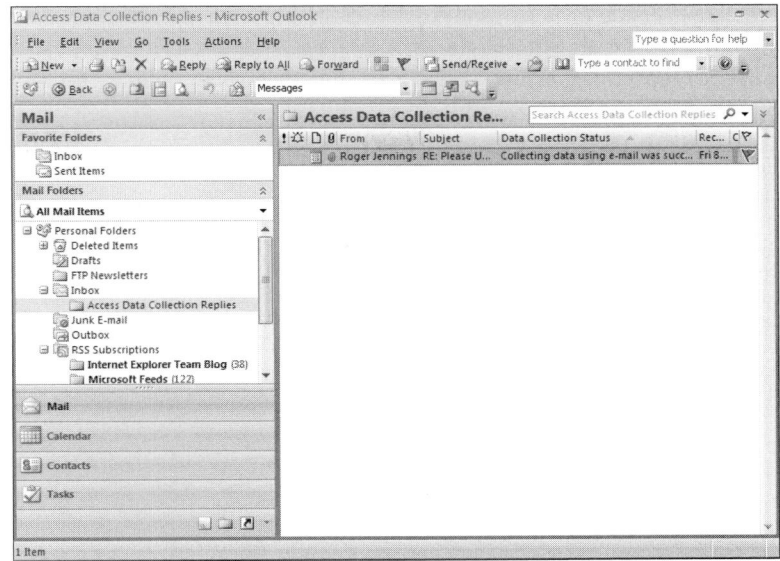

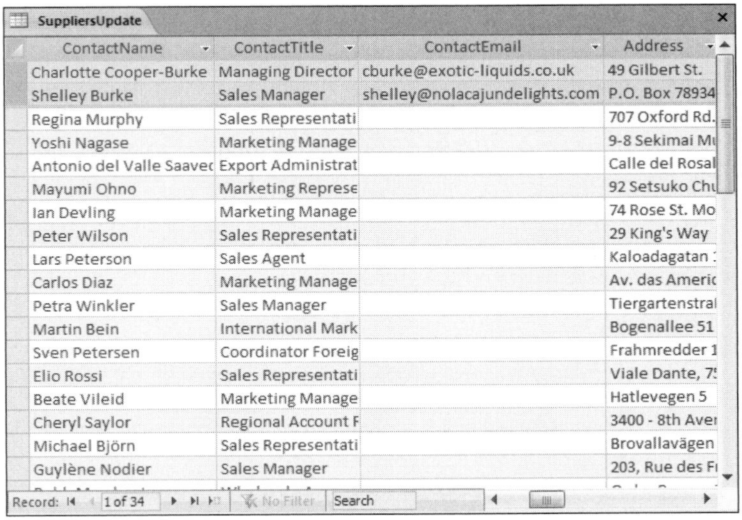

Figure 24.23
Datasheet view confirms that the edits have been applied to the SuppliersUpdate table.

TROUBLESHOOTING

PROBLEMS EXPORTING REPORTS TO HTML

My reports have missing fields, incorrect calculated values, incorrectly formatted numbers, or all three problems.

You're likely to encounter problems exporting even moderately complex reports to HTML with RPT2HTML4.xsl. For example, InventoryByCategory.htm, which you create by exporting Chapter 16's InventoryByCategory report, is missing category names, has the wrong category percentage values, and the category total value has too many decimal places. Currency formatting is missing from all dollar values (see Figure 24.24).

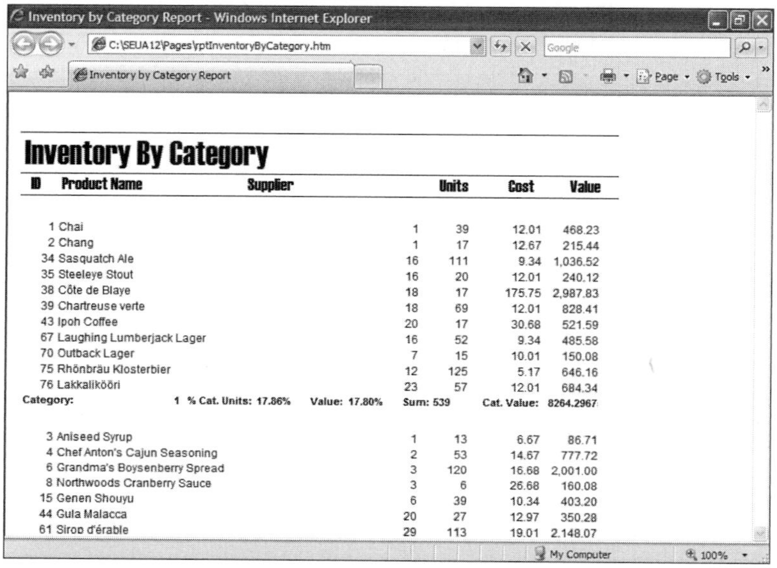

Figure 24.24
Complex reports exported to XML don't format currency data correctly and have problems with calculated field values.

This report, for example, uses Access's DLookup function to return the Category name value; Access expressions don't work in web reports. (In Access 2002, DLookup and other unsupported functions threw script errors.) You can create a modified version of the report that doesn't include problematic calculated text box values. However, the modified web report's content is less valuable than the original.

TIP

> When you design reports specifically for export to web pages, export and test the report's .htm file repeatedly as you add controls. The simpler the expression you use to populate text box controls, the more likely your report page will open without an error.

IE 7 PROBLEMS RENDERING XML EXPORT WITH PRESENTATION

When I open in IE 7 an ObjectName.htm file that generates HTML from ObjectName.xml and ObjectName.xsl files IE 7 consumes all my computer's resources but doesn't display the page.

The initial released version of IE 7 (version 7.0.5730.11, update versions 0) running under Windows XP SP2, Windows Server 2003 SP1, or Windows Server 2003 R2 has a serious problem rendering HTML generated by Access's XML and XSLT export process. If you open the .htm file with the preceding combination, IE (Iexplore.exe) enters an infinite loop and consumes all your PC's resources. If this happens to you, try to close IE 7 with the close button in its window's top right corner.

If that doesn't work, open Task Manager, click the Processes tab, select the Iexplore.exe process in the list, click End Process, and acknowledge the warning message. This problem doesn't occur with IE 7 running under Windows Vista.

> **NOTE**
>
> The \SEUA12\Chaptr24 folder contains *ObjectName*.html files created by saving the source HTML data generated by IE 7 running under Windows Vista from the ObjectName.htm file.

IN THE REAL WORLD—WHY LEARN XML?

It's unlikely to be evident to casual or even power users of Access 2007 and InfoPath 2007 how their XML features will make life easier or more productive. This is especially true for users who don't intend to import or export XML data or use InfoPath as a front end for Access databases. If you fall in that category, this and the other chapters of Part VI, "Collaborating with Access Data," might not pique your interest.

If your current or intended career involves databases, however, a full understanding of the roles of XML, XSD, XSLT, and XPath will prove to be a critical skill. The amount of web content delivered from databases will continue to increase in the future, so HTML authors and web page designers need to be conversant with—if not proficient in—XML and its derivatives. This is especially true since XHTML 1.0 has become the preferred embodiment of HTML. You should also be aware that document-literal XML web services deliver XML documents that rely on an embedded schema to describe their payload. Thus, creating and consuming XML web services requires XML and XSD skills.

Becoming proficient in data-related XML (often called XML Infosets) and, especially, XSLT coding is more challenging than becoming a journeyman VBScript, ECMAScript, VBA, or Visual Basic .NET programmer. Expect a learning curve similar to that for Java or Microsoft's C# language, but not as steep as that for C++. Books are a good starting point, but there's no substitute for working with the complex, real-world data and schemas that many XML texts avoid. Access 2007 is a great source of simple to moderately complex XML documents for gaining an understanding of XML schema language and XSLT coding.

An efficient and satisfying method for learning real-world XSLT is to start with the .xsl presentation files that RPT2HTML4.xsl generates for exported tables and queries. Once you've mastered modifying these relatively simple files, try rolling your own .xsl files to turn tables and queries into formatted HTML tables. If you're script-enabled, try adopting ReportML's approach to customizing the formatting of HTML data—including adding `<a href=http://www…>…</a>` tags to open pages having other tables that contain related data. Script is a great way to overcome XSLT's lack of variables with values you can change during the transformation process. (XSLT variables are better described as constants).

The greatest obstacle to the learning-by-writing process is the lack of production-grade debugging tools for XSLT, especially XSLT code that executes scripted functions. Opening .xsl files in IE 6+ only confirms that the XSLT is well formed. Here's hoping that Microsoft or another enterprising software vendor comes up with a combination authoring-debugging tool that's more effective than today's XSLT editors.

COLLABORATING WITH WINDOWS SHAREPOINT SERVICES

In this chapter

Windows SharePoint Services (WSS) 3.0 is a component of Windows Server 2003+ that provides an online, collaborative workspace with an ASP.NET 2.0 Web-based interface. The most common applications for WSS 3.0 are sharing documents from document libraries, managing lists, tracking tasks, handling workflows, displaying images from picture libraries, and enhancing team collaboration with calendars, blogs, wikis, discussions, and surveys.

NOTE

Widespread use of WSS is partly due to its inclusion in the very popular Windows Small Business Server 2003 R2 Standard Edition (SBS 2003 R2SE). SBS 2003 R2SE's popularity undoubtedly is due to its estimated retail price (ERP) of U.S. $599 with five client access licenses (CALs).

The Standard Edition includes Windows Server 2003 R2, WSS 2.0, Exchange Server 2003 SP2, Outlook 2003, Windows Server Update Services, and the Microsoft Shared Fax Service.

The Premium Edition adds SQL Server 2005 Workgroup Edition, the Internet and Security Acceleration Server (ISA) firewall and Internet access manager, and the Front Page 2003 website authoring tool for an additional U.S. $700.

Additional CALs for either edition are slightly less than U.S. $100 each. SBS 2003 R2 is limited to a maximum of 75 connected users or devices, but upgrades to remove the limit are available.

You can integrate WSS 3.0 and Access 2007 to improve the multiuser database experience and enable team members to collaborate in data entry and analysis or database application design. WSS 3.0 shares data from SharePoint lists, which link to Access tables. Working with an Access front end enables customized data entry with forms and sophisticated data analysis with reports. The process of setting up data security for a WSS 3.0 back end usually is simpler than securing an SQL Server database or the file share for an Access front-end/back-end application.

This chapter introduces you to WSS 3.0 and shows you how to substitute links to SharePoint lists for Access tables. This book uses the term *SharePoint* to include the WSS 3.0 and Microsoft Office SharePoint Services (MOSS) 2007 back ends, because interaction with Access is almost identical for the two products. MOSS 2007 is a set of enterprise-grade services that builds on the WSS 3.0 foundation to deliver corporate portal capabilities, content management and search facilities, advanced workflow features, business intelligence (BI) capability, records management, and business process management (BPM). MOSS 2007 replaces and upgrades Microsoft Content Management Server 2002 and SharePoint Portal Server (SPS) 2003.

TIP

Reserve substitution of SharePoint lists for Access tables to applications that involve relatively simple data structures and no more than a few hundred rows (list items). Databases created from Office Online's Access templates are good candidates for moving to SharePoint lists.

> As you'll discover in this chapter's later topic, "Moving and Publishing an Existing Database to SharePoint," SharePoint doesn't maintain referential integrity, has a limited data type repertoire, and begins to exhibit performance problems with lists of 500 items or more.

NOTE

> You can run this chapter's examples on WSS 3.0 or MOSS 2007. If you don't have Windows Server 2003 SP1 or R2, or SBS 2003 installed, you can obtain a 180-day trial version of Windows Server 2003 R2 from `http://www.microsoft.com/windowsserver2003/evaluation/trial/default.mspx`. Alternatively, you can use the "Longhorn server" beta or release version.
>
> Once you've installed and configured the appropriate Windows Server operating system with Internet Information Services (IIS) 6 or 7, download and install WSS 3.0 from the link on the page at `http://www.microsoft.com/sharepoint/`.

GETTING ACQUAINTED WITH WSS 3.0

WSS 3.0 creates and manages a collection of template-based websites in which lists are the basic data storage mechanism. Installing WSS 3.0 under Windows Server 2003 SP1 or later creates a default SharePoint site at `http://servername/` or `http://localhost/`.

WSS 3.0 stores site metadata and list data for standalone sites in a named instance (MICROSOFT##SSEE) of SQL Server 2005 Embedded Edition (SSEE). MOSS 2007 installs SQL Server 2005 Express Edition (SSX). The most important difference between SSEE and SSX is that you can't connect to SSEE with SQL Server Management Studio Standard or Express Edition. Thus, you fly *totally blind* with SSEE.

STANDARD WSS 3.0 SITE TYPES

WSS 3.0 provides built-in templates for the following collaborative site types:

- **Team sites** provide basic collaboration features; this template is the default for new WSS 3.0 sites. A Team site includes a default home page, Document Library, and empty Announcements, Calendar, Tasks, and Links lists, plus a Team Discussion Board.

- **Document Workspace sites** are a simplified version of a Team site that include a Document Library as well as Tasks and Links lists.

- **Blog sites** provide basic posting and commenting capabilities.

- **Wiki sites** let users add, edit, and link web pages quickly and easily. You can add a Wiki Library and Wiki pages to any site type.

- **Blank sites** have an empty home page and no default objects. You use a SharePoint-compatible web page designer—such as FrontPage or Windows SharePoint Designer— to add pages, lists, and other objects to the site.

This chapter's examples start with Team sites that the default template creates. Figure 25.1 shows the home page of the default initial site with its name changed from Team Site to OakLeaf Systems, the Microsoft Windows SharePoint Services logo replaced with the OakLeaf logo, and two subsites—Northwind Traders and Oakmont University—added. You add the Oakmont University subsite and customize it in the next two sections.

Figure 25.1
This initial WSS Team site has been customized with a new title, logo, and added subsites.

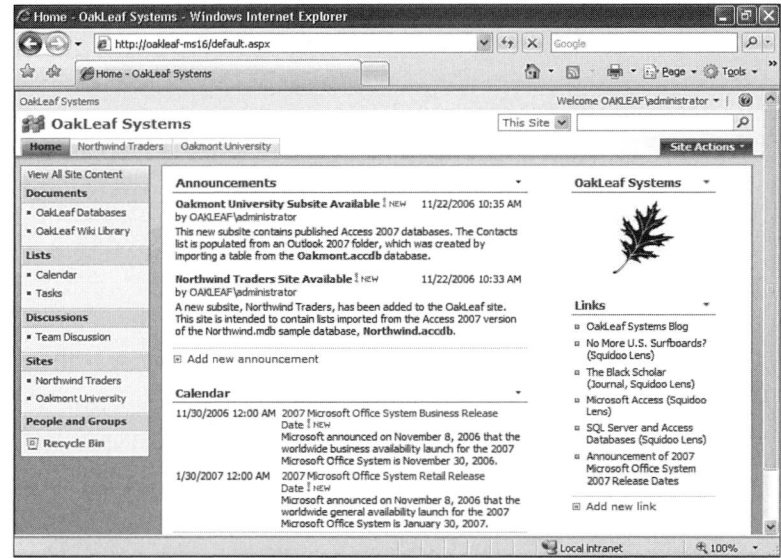

NOTE

MOSS 2007 offers a substantially wider variety of site types.

ADD A NEW WSS 3.0 SUBSITE

Microsoft designed SharePoint to make it easy for ordinary users to create, customize, and manage their own sites without the need to learn HTML or web page design and deployment techniques. Ease of use makes it practical for Access 2007 users to publish, move, link, and share their databases with SharePoint 2007.

To add a new subsite—Oakmont University for this example—to the initial (default) WSS 3.0 site, do the following:

1. On the home page of the parent site, open the Site Actions menu list and select Site Settings to open the page of the same name (see Figure 25.2).

2. In the Site Administration column, click the Sites and Workspaces link to open the eponymous page (see Figure 25.3).

Figure 25.2
Selecting Site Settings from the Site Actions menu list opens the Site Settings page, which contains links to almost all administration pages for the parent and subsites.

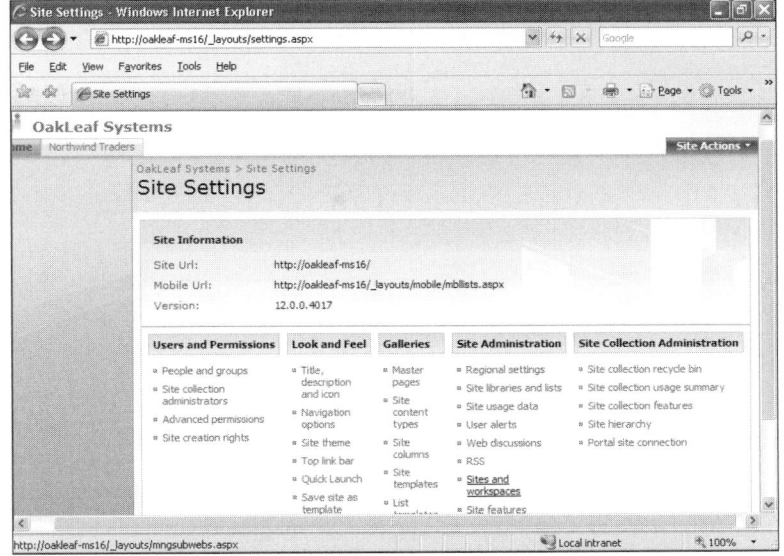

Figure 25.3
The Sites and Workspaces page lets you add a new site or workspace.

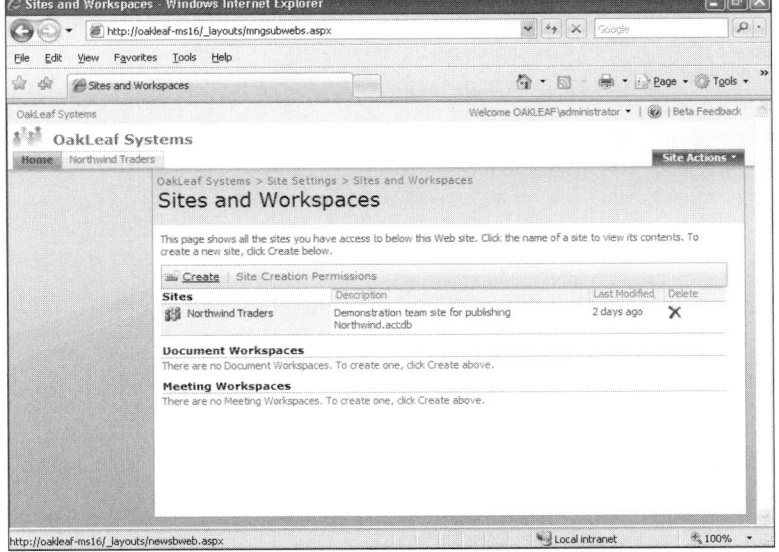

3. Click the Create link to open the New SharePoint Site page. Type the site's name in the Title text box, a brief explanation of the site's purpose in the Description text box, and the URL extension of the site (**Oakmont**) in the URL text box. Accept the default permissions, inherited from the parent site (see Figure 25.4).

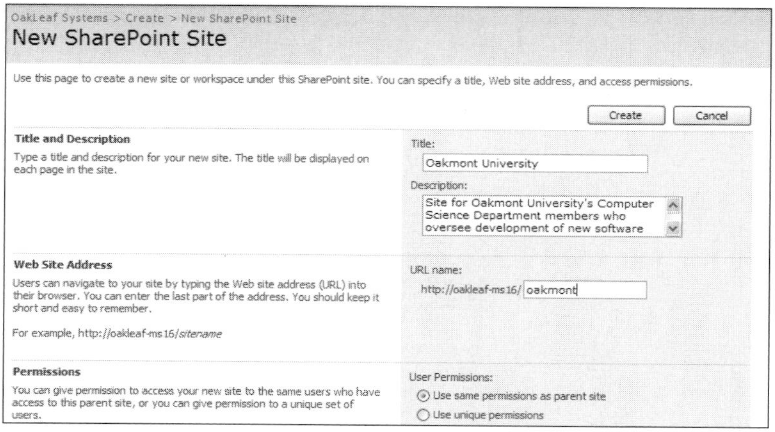

Figure 25.4
The top half of the New SharePoint Site page contains the required entries for the site.

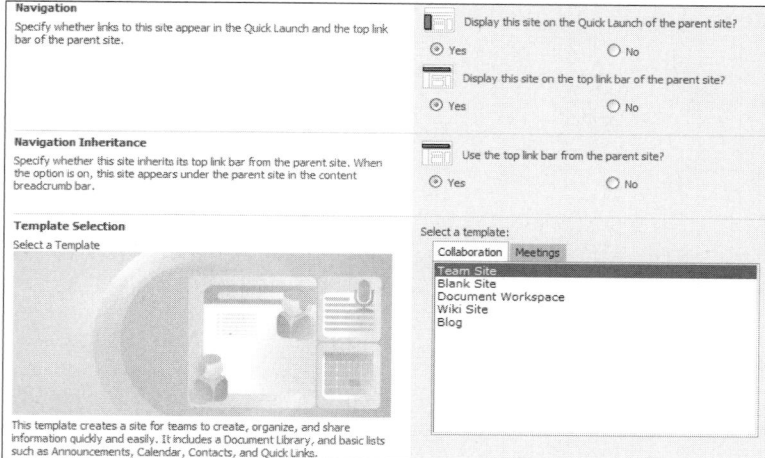

4. Accept the remaining Navigation, Navigation Inheritance, and Template Selection defaults, which add a link to the site on the parent site's Quick Launch pane and link bar, and use the Team Site template (see Figure 25.5).

Figure 25.5
For most subsites, you can accept all defaults in the New SharePoint Site page's bottom half.

25

> **NOTE**
>
> Notice the similarity between the home page's Quick Launch pane and Access 2007's Navigation Pane. Unlike the Navigation Pane, you can't change the layout of the Quick Launch pane.

5. Click the Create button at the bottom of the page to generate the new subsite's default home page whose URL is `http://computername/Oakmont/default.aspx` (see Figure 25.6).

Figure 25.6
The default subsite contains Web Parts with a substantial amount of irrelevant content.

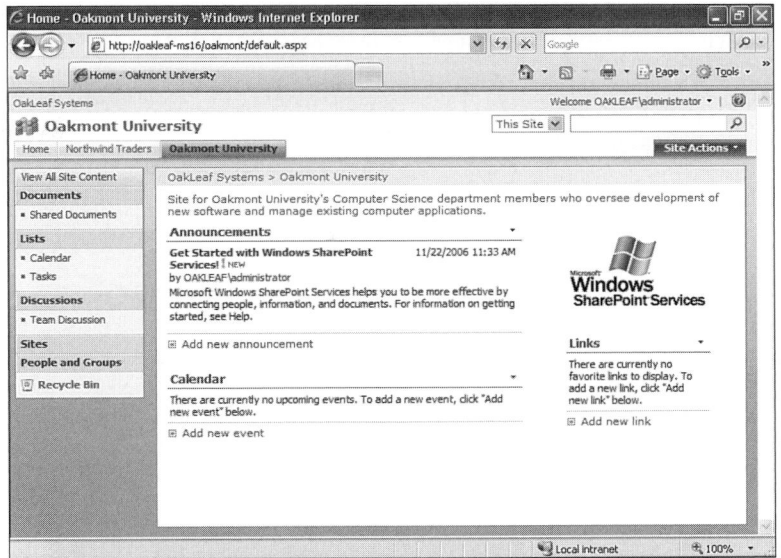

> **NOTE**
>
> The process of adding and configuring basic MOSS 2007 subsites is the same as that for WSS 3.0 subsites. The major difference is additional site type choices.

CONFIGURE THE NEW SUBSITE

The default subsite's home page—illustrated by Figure 25.6—is almost identical to that of the default parent site. It contains default SharePoint Web Parts for Announcements, Events (Calendar), Site Image (SharePoint Services logo), and Links. *SharePoint Web Parts* are ASP.NET 2.0+ web controls with SharePoint-specific properties. All default Web Parts, except Site Image, connect to lists.

This section's step-by-step procedure demonstrates methods for modifying lists, standalone Web Parts (without lists), and document libraries. These three activities are common when you create SharePoint sites that share Access 2007 databases with other users.

To start customizing the subsite by deleting the default Get Started... announcement, changing the logo in the Site Image Web Part, and renaming the Shared Documents Web Part to Oakmont Databases, do the following:

1. On the Oakmont University home page, click the Quick Launch pane's View All Site Content link to open the All Site Content page (see Figure 25.7).

2. Click the Announcements link to open the Announcements page, select the Get Started with Windows SharePoint Services! item, open the drop-down menu, and choose Delete Item (see Figure 25.8).

Figure 25.7
The All Site Content page has sections for Document Libraries, Picture Libraries, Lists, and Discussion Boards of default sites.

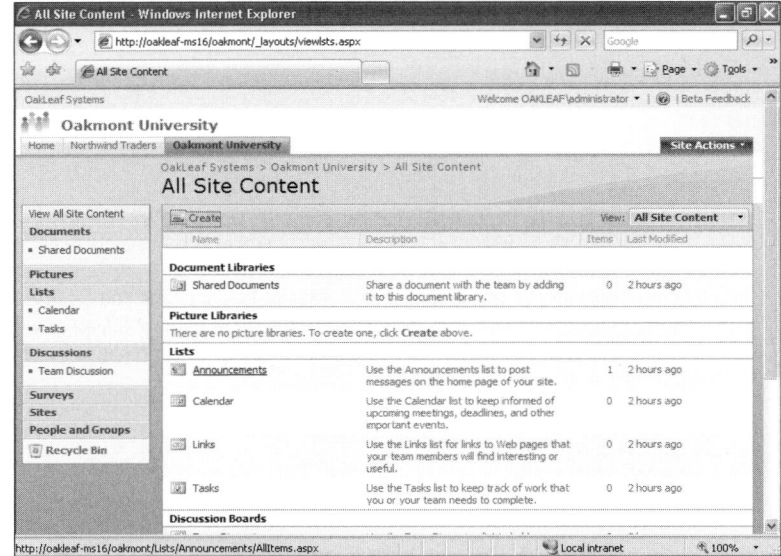

Figure 25.8
Items of lists have a drop-down menu for viewing, editing, setting permissions, deleting, and alerting users about an item.

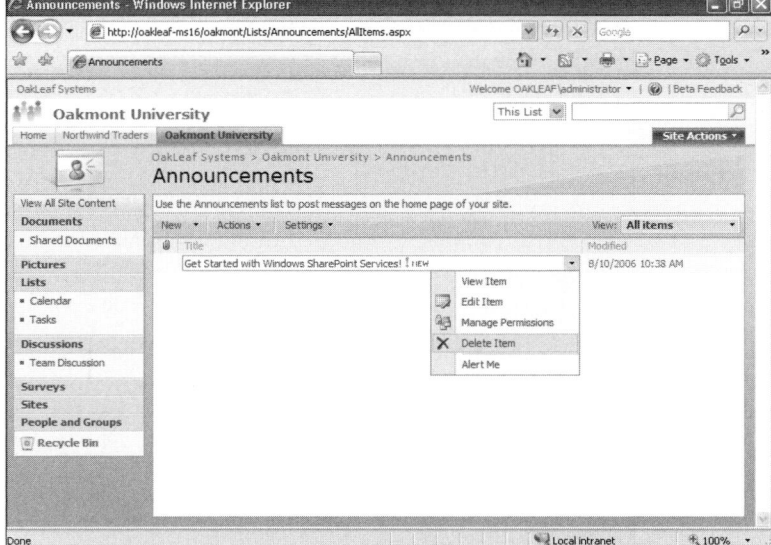

NOTE

You can add new items to lists with the home page's Web Parts, but you must open the list to edit or delete an item.

3. Click OK to send the item to the Recycle Bin, which is a new feature of SharePoint 2007.

4. Click the Oakmont University breadcrumb above the Announcements title to return to the Oakmont home page, which no longer displays an Announcement.

NOTE

The following three steps assume that you have a logo bitmap that you or someone else has copied to your \Program Files\Common Files\Microsoft Shared\Web Server Extensions\12\Templates\layouts\images folder for the default parent site. If not, copy a .gif, .jpg, or .png graphic of suitable size to that folder. You can use the copy of OakLeafSmall2.jpg in the \SEUA12\Chaptr25\Oakmont folder, or you can omit this exercise by clicking X to delete the Web Part in step 6 and then skipping to step 10.

5. Open the Site Actions list and choose Edit Page to open the home page with the Web Parts in the Left and Right column containers for editing.

6. To change the name and image of the Site Image Web Part, open the Edit menu list and choose Modify Shared Web Part (see Figure 25.9) to open the Site Image editing pane.

Figure 25.9
Web Parts have a drop-down Edit menu list with a Modify Shared Web Part choice to change Web Part property values.

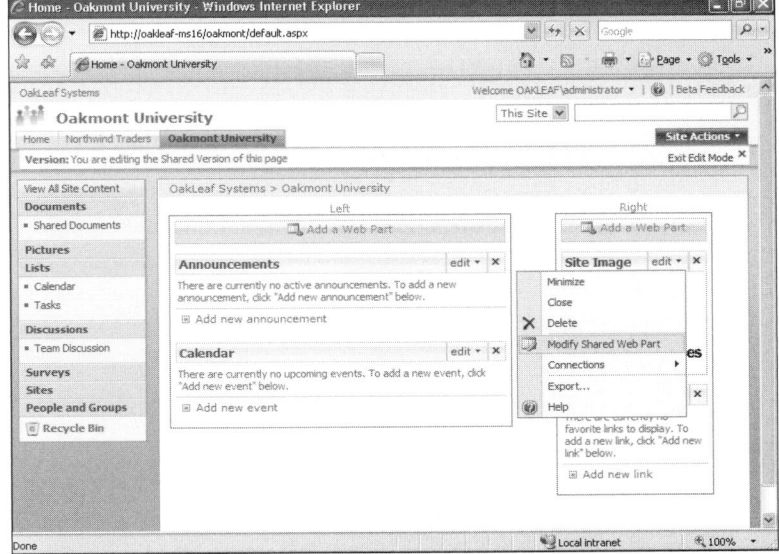

7. In the Image Link text box, replace homepage.gif with your logo's filename or **OakmontLogo.jpg**, and click Test Link to open the image in a new page.

8. Type **Oakmont University Logo** in the Alternative Text box, expand the Appearance node, and type **Oakmont University** in the Title text box (see Figure 25.10). Scroll to the Chrome Type section and select Title Only in the list box.

Figure 25.10
The editing pane for a Site Image Web Part can be used to set a substantial number of property values. The purpose of this pane is similar to Access 2007's Properties task pane/window.

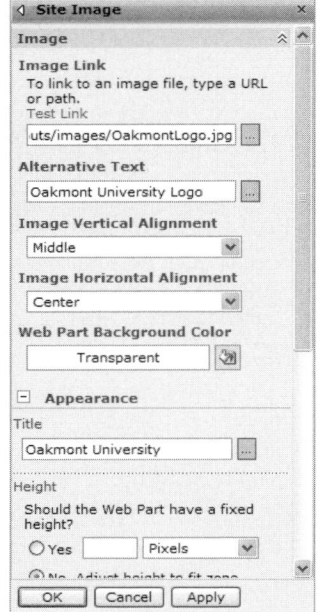

9. Click OK to save your changes, and click the Exit Edit Mode link to return to the home page with the announcement deleted and the logo image and title changed.

10. In the Quick Launch pane, click the Shared Document item to open the page of the same name. Open the Settings menu list on the toolbar and choose Document Library Settings to open the Customize Shared Documents page.

11. Click the General Settings column's General Settings link to open the Document Library General Settings: Shared Documents page. Replace Shared Documents with **Oakmont Databases** in the Name text box, and add a brief description in the Description text box (see Figure 25.11).

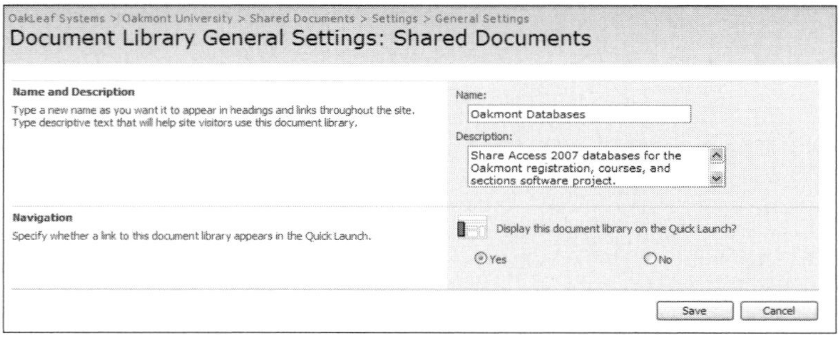

Figure 25.11
Use the Document Library General Settings: *LibraryName* page to set the library's title, description, and navigation property values.

OakLeaf Systems > Oakmont University > Shared Documents > Settings > General Settings
Document Library General Settings: Shared Documents

Name and Description
Type a new name as you want it to appear in headings and links throughout the site. Type descriptive text that will help site visitors use this document library.

Name:
Oakmont Databases

Description:
Share Access 2007 databases for the Oakmont registration, courses, and sections software project.

Navigation
Specify whether a link to this document library appears in the Quick Launch.

Display this document library on the Quick Launch?

⦿ Yes   ○ No

Save   Cancel

12. Accept the default Navigation option, and click Save to save your changes. Click the Oakmont University breadcrumb or tab to return to the home page and review your changes (see Figure 25.12).

Figure 25.12
The Oakmont University subsite's home page shows the changes made to the default Document Library title, Announcements list, and Site Image Web Part.

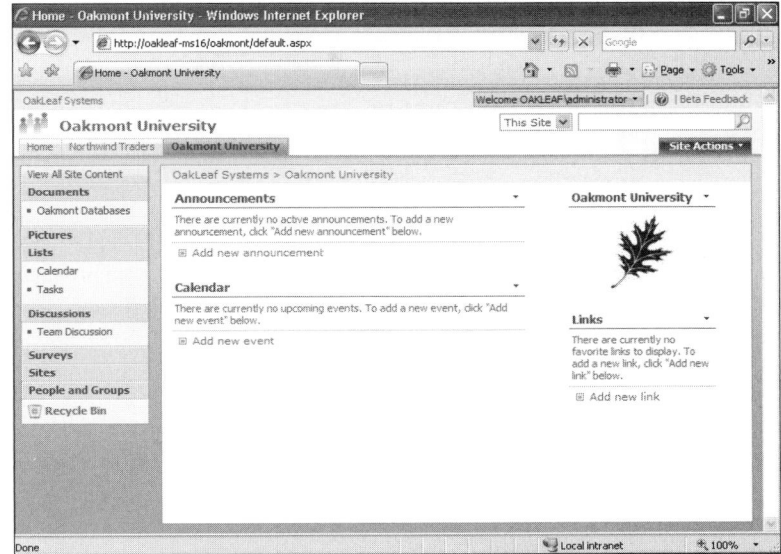

Your Oakmont University subsite is now ready to accept Access 2007 database publication in the later section "Creating a New Database from a Template and Moving It to SharePoint."

WSS 3.0 USERS AND SECURITY GROUPS

A site represents a security boundary. WSS 3.0 has a relatively simple four-level, group-based permission hierarchy for designated SharePoint users. Following are WSS 3.0's four security groups:

- **Site Collection Administrators** have full control over all SharePoint sites in the site collection. The member of the Windows Administrators group who installs WSS 3.0 becomes a Site Collection Administrators group member.

- **Site Owners** have full control permissions for the SharePoint site(s) they create. The initial Site Collection Administrator becomes an Owners group member for the default site.

- **Site Members** have read-write permissions, so they can contribute to lists, shared documents, and other site objects.

- **Site Visitors** have read-only permissions for the site.

You must be a member of the Site Collection Administrators group or the Site Owners group for a development site to complete this chapter's step-by-step examples.

Administrators add new sites; a site is a security boundary that can have its own set of users, groups, and permissions. A site contains lists and folders, and can contain a hierarchy of subsites. By default, subsites inherit user permissions assigned at the parent site level.

CREATE NEW USERS AND ASSIGN THEM TO GROUPS

To assign permissions to three fictional Windows domain user accounts—SharePoint SiteOwner, SharePoint SiteMember, and SharePoint SiteVisitor—to the OakLeaf Systems parent (default) site, do this:

1. Click the Home tab to open the initial site home page (OakLeaf Systems for this example), and click People and Groups to open the Quick Launch pane's Groups with Team Site Members (default), Team Site Visitors, and Team Site Owners items. The Team Site Owners page display the account used to install WSS 3.0 and create the default website (see Figure 25.13).

Figure 25.13
The Team Site Members page is one of three pages that display a list of users in a SharePoint group. You also add users to groups, and edit and delete users on these pages.

2. Click the New drop-down menu and choose Add Users to open the Add Users: *Initial Site* page. Select Team Site Members [Contribute] as the SharePoint group in the dropdown list. Type the full user name for the Members group—**SharePoint SiteMember**—in the Users text box.

3. Click the Check Names button to test the account. If the user name matches a local or domain account, your entry is underlined in black (see Figure 25.14). If not, a red "No exact match was found" message appears and the entry receives a wavy red underline.

Figure 25.14
Adding a user to a SharePoint group requires typing and verifying the full user name, not the user's logon ID. You can edit the user name later.

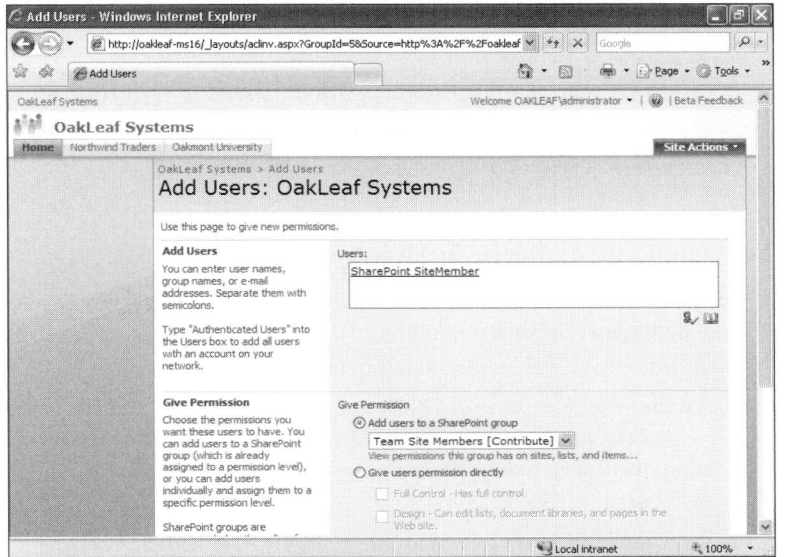

Add multiple users to a group by separating their user names with a semicolon.

25

4. Click OK to add the user to the group and return to the People and Groups: Team Site Members page, which displays the added user in the list.

5. Click the Quick Launch pane's Team Site Visitors item and repeat steps 2, 3, and 4 for the SharePoint SiteVisitor user. Do the same for the Team Site Owners group and the SharePoint SiteOwner user.

6. Test each account by logging off with your administrative account and logging on with each of the three accounts you added in the preceding steps: *DOMAIN*/SiteMember, *DOMAIN*/SiteVisitor, *DOMAIN*/SiteOwner.

NOTE

If you're not a member of an Active Directory domain or you created local user accounts, log on with those local accounts.

EDIT USER INFORMATION

You must assign user accounts by user name, but you can change the user name after you've created the account. You also can populate Picture (attachment), AboutMe (description), Job Title, and Department fields, which appear in the list's default view, plus E-Mail and SIP Address, which don't appear.

NOTE

Microsoft Office Communication Server (MOCS) 2007 uses the Session Initiation Protocol (SIP) address—also called the SIP URI (Universal Resource Identifier)—to provide presence information to clients. MOCS is one of Microsoft's Unified Communications offerings. For more about MOCS, go to http://www.microsoft.com/uc/.

To edit existing user data and add additional information about a user (SharePoint SiteOwner for this example), do the following:

1. In the People and Groups: Team Site Owners page, click the Name cell of the user whose data you want to edit. The User Information: *UserName - LogonID* page opens with only the Account and Name fields completed.

2. Click the Edit item button on the toolbar to open an editable version of the page. Change the Name field entry, if you want; this example uses one of the Oakmont Outlook contacts, Eric Arthur, you create in the later "Working Offline and Synchronizing Lists" section.

3. Complete entries for the remaining text boxes, as illustrated by Figure 25.15.

Figure 25.15
Add detailed information about and pictures of users in the User Information: - *User Name - LogonID* page.

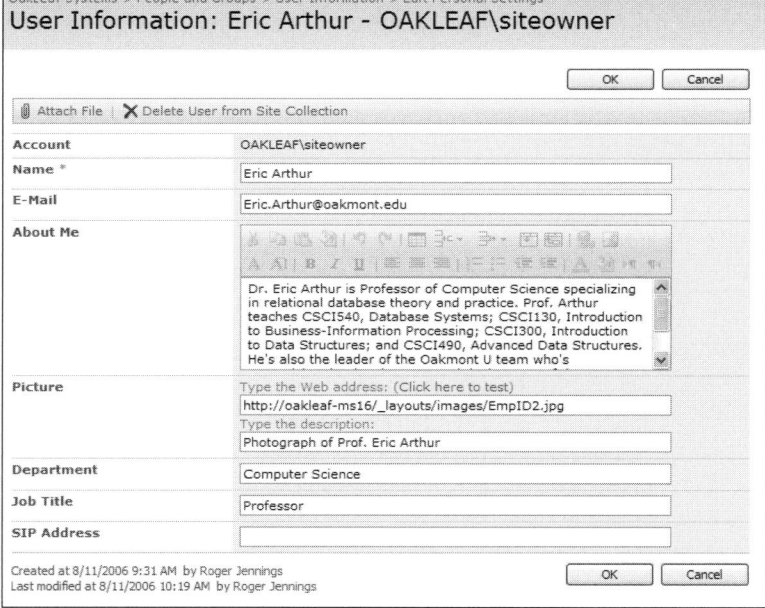

4. Click OK to return to the People and Groups: Team Site Owners page and review the user information you added (see Figure 25.16).

Figure 25.16
The People and Groups: Team Site Owners and related pages display all fields except the user's email and SIP addresses. The entry for Roger Jennings (OAKLEAF\ Administrator) appears in the Site Owners group in all People and Groups pages of the parent site and subsites.

5. Optionally, complete steps 1 through 4 for the SharePoint SiteMember (Traci Matson) and SharePoint SiteVisitor (Joanna Nordyke) users.

NOTE

> The three pages connect to the same list; each page presents a different view of the list.

MANAGING DATA WITH ACCESS AND SHAREPOINT 2007

Access 2007 enables interaction with SharePoint 2007 in the following ways:

- **Publish database to SharePoint**—Publishing an Access 2007 database to a SharePoint 2007 site stores a copy of the database in a document library on the WSS or MOSS server. Users can open a shared read-only master copy of the database or—with Site Member or Site Owner permissions—save a local read-write copy of the database to edit. Changes aren't saved to the master copy until the user republishes the local copy to the SharePoint server.

- **Move table data to SharePoint**—Moving (exporting) data to a SharePoint site creates lists that are linked as tables of your database. Access creates a new front-end application that contains the queries, forms, and reports, as well as the linked tables.

NOTE

The Move to SharePoint Site Wizard automates the process of generating SharePoint lists from Access 2007 tables and then linking new tables in an Access 2007 database to the lists. You can elect to publish the resulting database when the move is complete.

You start the Move to SharePoint Site Wizard by clicking the External Data tab and the SharePoint Lists group's Move to SharePoint button. The Wizard creates a backup copy of the source database before performing the move operation.

- **Create an Access database from a SharePoint site**—Users who want to take advantage of Access's editing and reporting capabilities can choose to open a list in a linked Access table and, if the database doesn't already exist, create a new database to hold the linked table(s) and added form(s) and report(s).

- **Export, import, or link a SharePoint list**—Access 2007 treats SharePoint lists like other data stores, such as Microsoft Excel or dBASE IV, but linked SharePoint lists are editable.

The following sections describe how to perform each of the preceding Access-related tasks.

PUBLISHING AN EXISTING ACCESS DATABASE TO A SHAREPOINT DOCUMENT LIBRARY

Sharing an existing Access 2007 database by publishing it to a SharePoint Document Library is a simple task. You don't need to link Access tables to SharePoint lists to publish the database, but linking eliminates the requirement to republish the local copy to save changes to its data. If you intend to link the tables, skip to the next section, "Moving and Publishing an Existing Database to SharePoint."

NOTE

You can use the NwindPub.accdb sample database in the \SEUA12\Chaptr25 folder to test publishing a database. The following example assumes the existence of a Northwind Traders (http://*computername*/nwind) subsite, which you can add by the process described in the earlier "Add a New WSS 3.0 Subsite" section.

If you don't want to create the subsite, you can add the sample database to the default "Shared Documents" Document Library. However, creating the Northwind Traders subsite is strongly recommended.

Do the following to publish an Access 2007 database to a WSS 3.0 Document Library:

1. Open an existing database (\SEUA12\Chaptr25\Nwind\NwindPub.accdb for this example), click the Office button, and choose Publish, Document Management Server to open the dialog of the same name. If you haven't previously published a database, a *computername* icon (oakleaf-ms16 for this example) is present, along with other default icon(s).

2. Double-click the *computername* icon to display the Document Libraries and Sites and Workspaces lists for the initial site. Continue to navigate by double-clicking icons until you reach the Document Library to store NwindPub.accdb, OakLeaf Systems/Northwind Traders/Northwind Databases for this example (see Figure 25.17).

Figure 25.17
The Publish to Web Server dialog opens to the most recently used Document Library. If you haven't published an Access database to the site, you must double-click your way down the hierarchy to the desired Document Library.

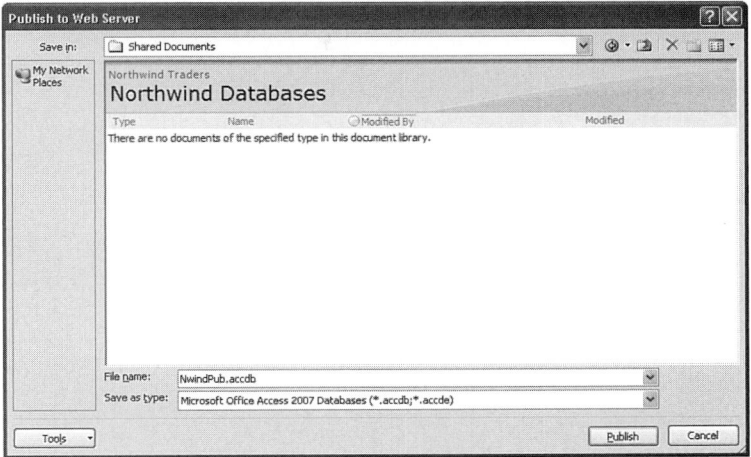

3. Click Publish to save the database in the Document Library and close the dialog.

4. Close the source version of NwindPub.accdb, open the subsite at http://localhost/nwind/, and click Northwind Databases in the Quick Launch pane's Documents section to open the Document Library, which contains a new NwindPub item.

5. Click NwindPub to open a Microsoft Internet Explorer dialog, which lets users open the database in Read-Only or Edit mode (see Figure 25.18).

> **NOTE**
> Members of the Site Visitors group see an Internet Explorer warning dialog that states, "You are opening the following file: File name: *FileName*.accdb From: *computername*."

6. If you select Read-Only mode, SharePoint opens the shared database from the Document Library (see Figure 25.19). The Document Action Bar displays a Security Alert because the Document Library isn't a trusted location and a Read-Only notice. Verify that the data is read-only, and close Access to return to the Document Library page.

7. If you select Edit mode, SharePoint opens the Save a Local Copy dialog to enable users to save a local copy of the database with a distinctive filename in a trusted location, \SEUA12\SharePoint for this example (see Figure 25.20).

Figure 25.18
Site Members, Site Owners, or Site Collection Administrators have the choice of opening a published database in Read-Only or Edit mode. Site Visitors are permitted only Read-Only access.

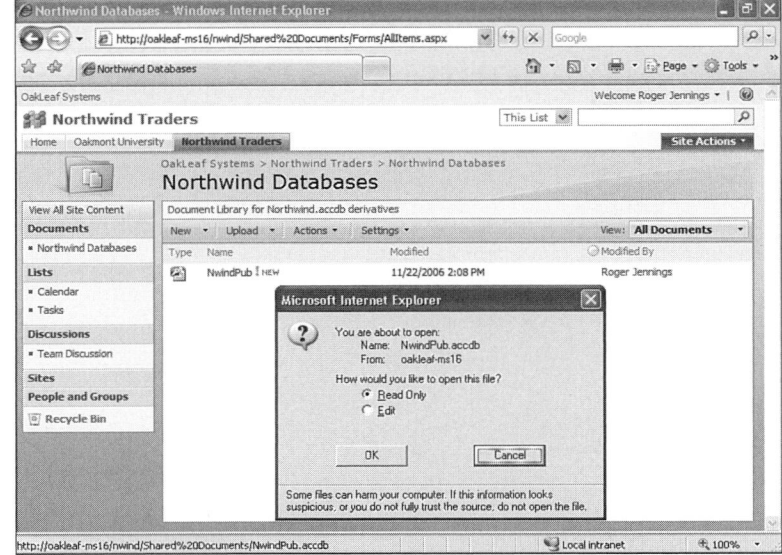

Figure 25.19
Shared databases opened in Read-Only mode from the Document Library include a Read-Only notice in the Document Action Bar.

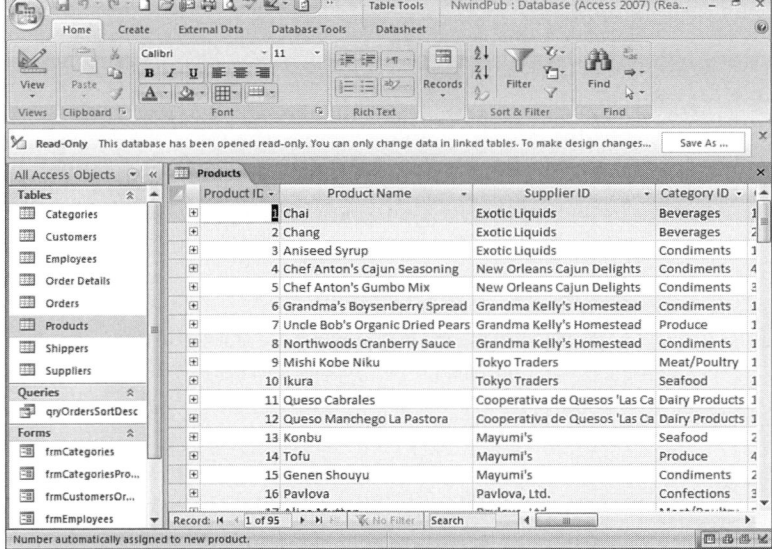

Figure 25.20
Users usually save local database copies for editing to trusted locations.

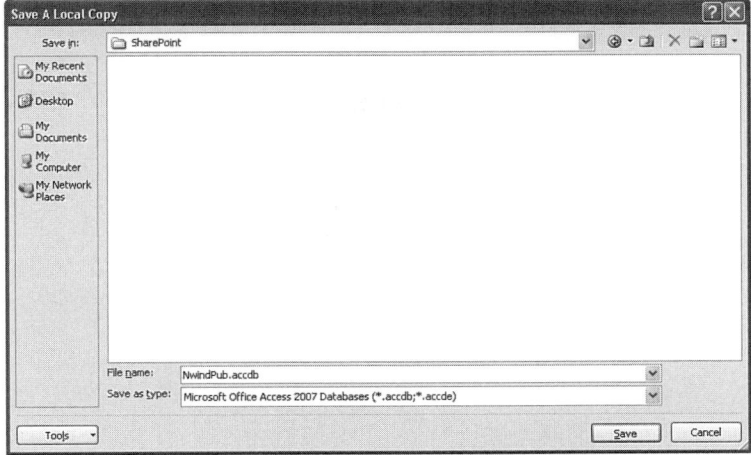

8. Click Save to create the local copy and open in Access (see Figure 25.21). The Document Action Bar displays a Publish Changes notice and a Publish to SharePoint Site button.

Figure 25.21
If the local copy is in a trusted location, the Document Action Bar displays only a Publish Changes notice and a Publish to SharePoint Site button.

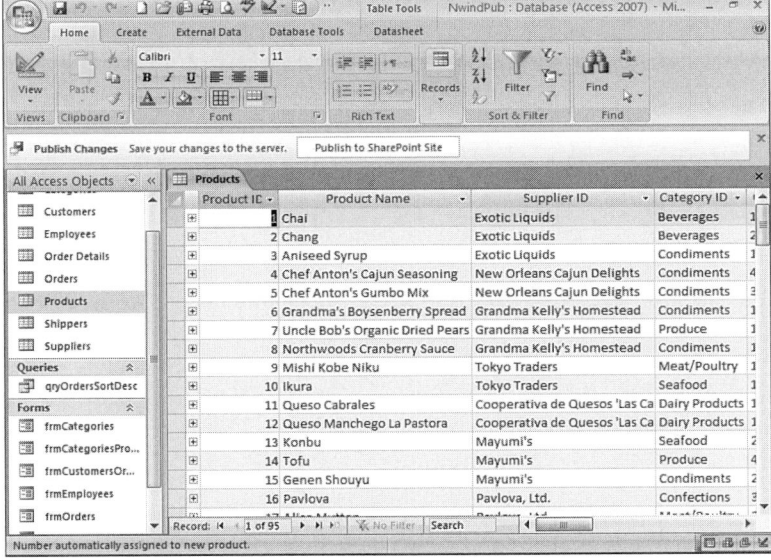

9. Click the Publish to SharePoint Site button to open the Publish to Web Server dialog (see Figure 25.22). Accept the default Document Library and filename, and click Publish to update the shared master database file, click Yes to acknowledge that you want to overwrite the file, and then close Access.

Figure 25.22
The Publish to Web Server dialog displays the default Document Library and filename for the republishing operation.

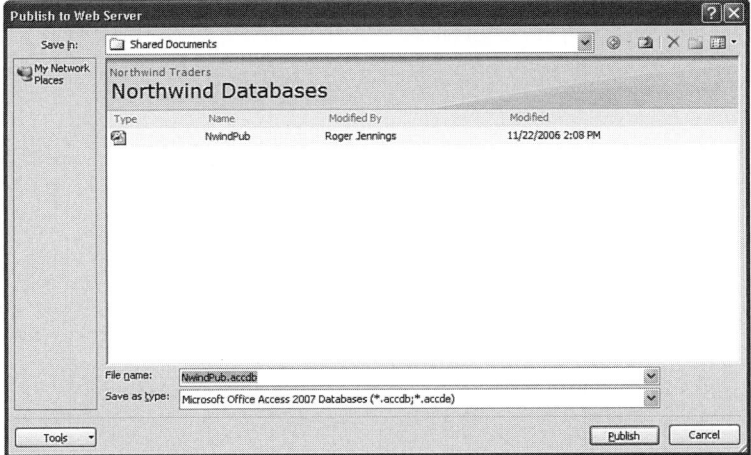

The obvious issue with the publishing and republishing scenario is the lack of concurrency protection. The last user to republish a local copy with changes overwrites any changes that other users make after the last user created the local database copy or republished changes.

NOTE

> You can add security for the source database by publishing an encrypted version of the file. Users are required to provide the password to read or create a local database copy. The local database copy is encrypted with the same password as the source database.

MOVING AND PUBLISHING AN EXISTING DATABASE TO SHAREPOINT

You can solve most data concurrency issues by moving an Access 2007 database's tables and their data to linked SharePoint lists. The process is similar to using the Database Splitter to create links to Access tables in a back-end database or upsizing Access tables to an SQL Server 2005 database. Changes to lists made by SharePoint users are reflected in Access front ends and vice-versa.

SharePoint lists exhibit few characteristics of relational tables. For example, SharePoint lists don't maintain referential integrity, support cascading updates or deletions, enable validation rules other than required entry, or handle default value expressions much more complex than =Date(). Thus, the behavior of an Access application with linked SharePoint lists differs from that of conventional Access applications with linked or self-contained tables.

SHAREPOINT LIST DATA TYPES

SharePoint lists have data types that accommodate all Access data types except OLE Object. Table 25.1 lists the SharePoint list data types and their corresponding Access data types, with limitations where applicable.

TABLE 25.1   SHAREPOINT DATA TYPES THAT CORRESPOND TO ACCESS DATA TYPES

SharePoint Data Type	Access Data Type(s)	List Limitations
Single Line of Text	Text, AutoNumber as ReplicationID	Newline (CrLf) characters in Text data type values cause a change to the Multiple Lines of Text (Memo) Data Type.
Multiple Lines of Text	Memo	This data type has an Append-Only property for revision tracking.
Number	Number (all sizes except Replication ID), AutoNumber	Lists display a maximum of nine decimal places and display as a percentage if the Access Format property value is Percentage. Access AutoNumber fields lose their AutoIncrement property.
Date or Time	Date/Time	Lists display Date Only if the Access Format value is Short Date; the Access =Date() default value corresponds to Today's Date.
Currency	Currency	Access Currency fields import as Number and require changing the data type manually.
Yes/No	Yes/No	
Hyperlink	Hyperlink	
Attachment	Attachment	Lists support only one attachment field.
Lookup	Single-valued or multi-valued Lookup fields	Other lists provide lookup data.
Choice	Single-valued or multi-valued Lookup fields	Lists display literal lookup values separated by semicolons.

NOTE

The Access AutoNumber data type becomes an ordinary SharePoint number, because all SharePoint lists have an autoincrementing ID field with a no-duplicates index. SharePoint supports only one no-duplicates index per list.

SharePoint doesn't support Access's OLE Object fields, so they aren't moved to the SharePoint lists.

When you move an Access table to a SharePoint list, the Move to SharePoint Site Wizard does a best-efforts job of matching table and list data types, transferring data from the table to the list, and regenerating Lookup or Choice field data. Access Text fields that contain newline (CrLf) characters move to Multiple Lines of Text (Memo) fields because Single Line of Text fields don't permit newline characters. Filter and Order By table properties don't propagate to the SharePoint list, and Text fields' Field Size properties don't propagate to Single Line of Text columns.

CUSTOMIZE SHAREPOINT LIST VIEWS

WSS 3.0 displays only views of SharePoint lists; the default All Items view displays all significant list columns in an Access Web Datasheet control. To display a list's default view, click the Quick Launch pane's View All Site Content item and then click the list name whose items you want to view. Figure 25.23 shows the first seven columns of the Products list created by exporting the Northwind.accdb's Products table and reordering the imported columns in the Edit Datasheet View: Products page.

Figure 25.23
This partial All Items view for the SharePoint list version of the Northwind. accdb database's Products table has the column list rearranged to resemble the field sequence of the source table.

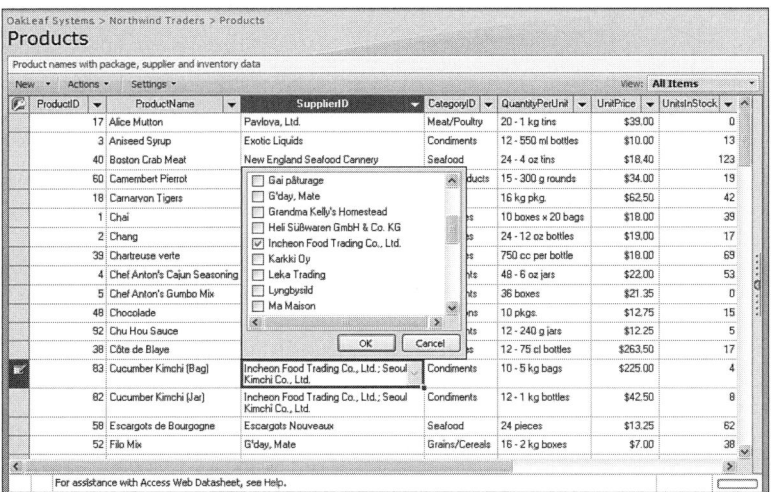

> **NOTE**
>
> The Access Web Datasheet control is a component provided by Office 2007 and isn't installed by SharePoint. SharePoint users must have Office 2007 installed to use the Access Web Datasheet control, also called the Office 2007 List Datasheet View 2007.

Editing in Datasheet view follows the Access pattern. SupplierID is a multi-valued Lookup field (MVLF), so opening this field's dropdown list displays a list with check boxes to specify multiple suppliers. Category ID is a conventional (single-valued) Lookup field with a conventional dropdown list.

Users who don't have Office 2007 display and edit lists in standard view by default. To change to standard view, open the Actions menu and choose Show in Standard View.

To edit a single item, click the Title (or its replacement, ProductName, Linked to Item with Edit Menu) cell to open the edit menu (see Figure 25.24), and choose Edit Item to open the Products: *ProductName* page (see Figure 25.25). The field sequence is that of the underlying list, not the default All Items view.

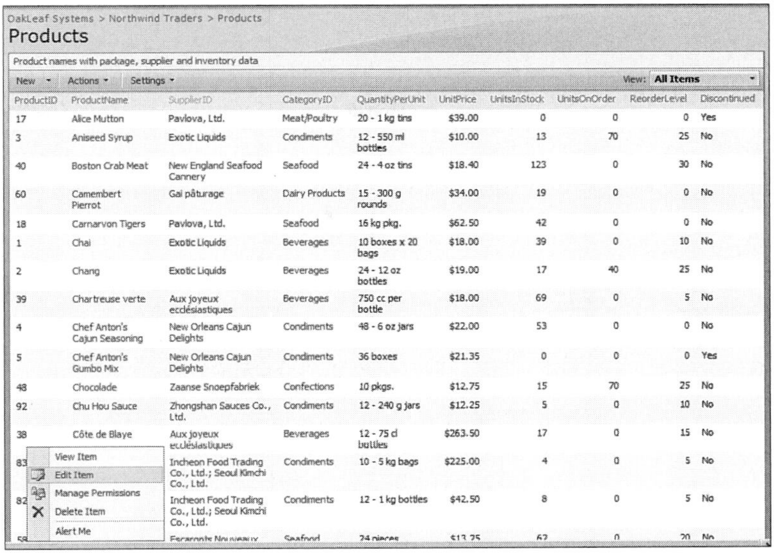

Figure 25.24
The ProductName field is linked to the edit menu. Clicking SupplierID or CategoryID opens an editing form for the selected supplier or category.

Figure 25.25
Editing an item with a multi-valued Lookup field (SupplierID) adds a pair of list boxes for selecting multiple lookup values. The single-valued Lookup field (CategoryID) has a drop-down list for selecting a single value.

To change a view's field sequence or create a new view, click the All Items button in the list header, and select Modify This View to open the Edit View: *ListName* page (see Figure 25.26). Change the list's column sequence by selecting a column's ordinal value with the associated list box. The Edit View page also lets you sort and filter the view, as well as add aggregate values (Count, Sum, Average, Maximum, Minimum, Std Deviation or Variance) for numeric columns.

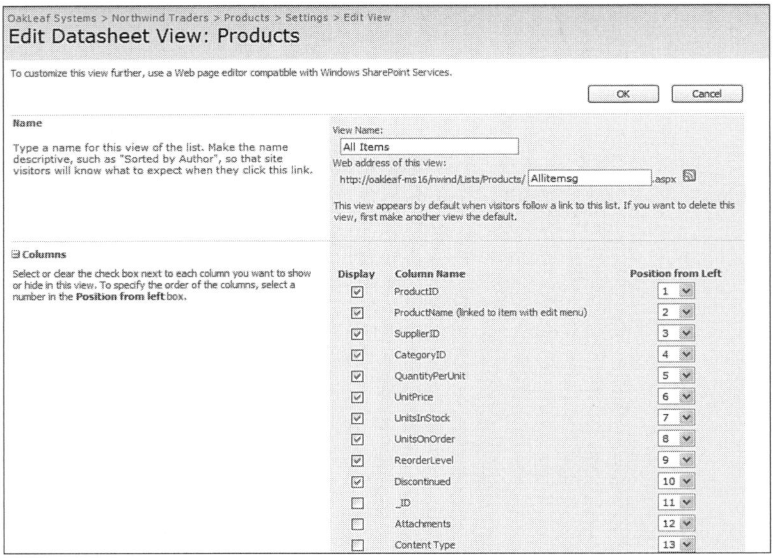

Figure 25.26
Change the view's name and column sequence in the Edit View: *ListName* page. Only the visible columns are shown here; the remaining 10 columns have cleared text boxes.

Microsoft has adopted Really Simple Syndication (RSS) 2.0 XML files as an alternative method of interacting with SharePoint lists and related content types, such as blogs. Clicking the RSS symbol to the right of the web address text box for the view opens an RSS 2.0 full-text feed for the view in IE 7 (see Figure 25.27). Clicking the green arrow to the right of the author name opens the SharePoint Products: *ProductName* page for the selected product (Boston Crab Meat for this example). You can edit or delete the item, as well as add a new item to list, manage user permissions, or request an alert when anyone edits the item. IE 7 lets users stay up to date with list data by subscribing to the view's RSS feed. The feed is compatible with all popular RSS readers.

Following is the truncated RSS document that generates the item shown in Figure 25.27:

```
<?xml version="1.0" encoding="UTF-8"?>
<!—RSS generated by Windows SharePoint Services V3 RSS Generator
  on 11/24/2006 9:47:05 AM—>
<?xml-stylesheet type="text/xsl" href="/nwind/_layouts/RssXslt.aspx?
  List=6a8d96e9-0d7a-4a1e-a2b1-9a63a895ab2c" version="1.0"?>
<rss version="2.0">
  <channel>
    <title>Northwind Traders: Products</title>
    <link>http://oakleaf-ms16/nwind/Lists/Products/Allitemsg.aspx</link>
    <description>RSS feed for the Products list.</description>
    <lastBuildDate>Fri, 24 Nov 2006 17:47:05 GMT</lastBuildDate>
    <generator>Windows SharePoint Services V3 RSS Generator</generator>
    <ttl>60</ttl>
    <image>
      <title>Northwind Traders: Products</title>
      <url>/nwind/_layouts/images/oakleaf.jpg</url>
      <link>
        http://oakleaf-ms16/nwind/Lists/Products/Allitemsg.aspx
```

```
      </link>
    </image>
    <item>
      <title>Boston Crab Meat</title>
      <link>
        http://oakleaf-ms16/nwind/Lists/Products/DispForm.aspx?ID=40
      </link>
      <description><![CDATA[<div><b>_ID:</b> 40</div>
        <div><b>QuantityPerUnit:</b> 24 - 4 oz tins</div>
        <div><b>UnitPrice:</b> $18.40</div>
        <div><b>UnitsInStock:</b> 123</div>
        <div><b>UnitsOnOrder:</b> 0</div>
        <div><b>ReorderLevel:</b> 30</div>
        <div><b>Discontinued:</b> No</div>
        <div><b>SupplierID:</b> New England Seafood Cannery</div>
        <div><b>CategoryID:</b> Seafood</div>]]>
      </description>
      <author>Roger Jennings</author>
      <pubDate>Wed, 22 Nov 2006 23:02:27 GMT</pubDate>
      <guid isPermaLink="true">http://oakleaf-
        ms16/nwind/Lists/Products/DispForm.aspx?ID=40</guid>
    </item>
  </channel>
</rss>
```

Figure 25.27
RSS 2.0 transformations of SharePoint views let users subscribe to feeds with IE 7 or third-party RSS readers. Each view is a channel that displays up to 100 items by default.

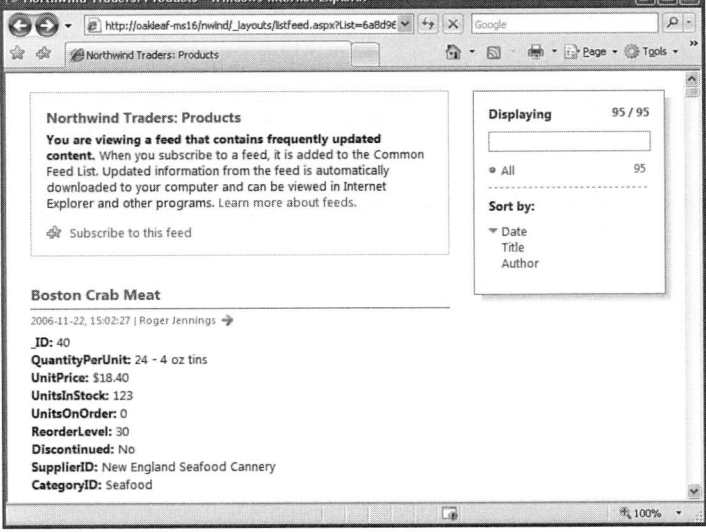

To change list data types, click the list header's Settings button and select List Settings to open the Customize *ListName* page (see Figure 25.28), which also lets you add new columns, change read-write column order, and add indexes on the underlying SQL Server 2005 fields for most columns. You also can customize feeds by clicking the Communications column's RSS 2.0 Setting link to open the Modify List RSS Settings: *ListName* page. This page lets you specify the channel's title, description, and image, as well as the fields to display, maximum number of items or days to include.

Figure 25.28
The Customize ListName page lets you modify the underlying list, rather than a view of the list. The changes you make on this page affect all the list's views.

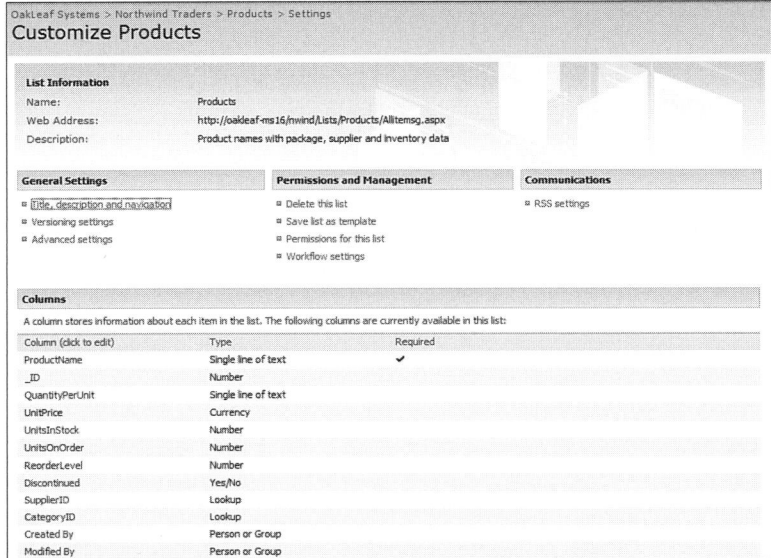

Here are a few other SharePoint list characteristics that are useful to understand before you move Access tables or entire databases to a SharePoint site:

- All SharePoint lists have default Type (icon linked to document), Attachments, Title (linked to item with edit menu), Content Type, Created, Created By, Edit (linked to edit item), ID, Modified, Modified By, Title, Title (linked to item), and Version columns.

- The All Items (default) view displays only a few default fields. You must edit the All Items view to display the fields you need in the appropriate sequence. Alternatively, you can create another named view and make it the default.

- All default fields except Attachments, Title (linked to item with edit menu), Created By, Modified By, and Title (linked to item) are read-only.

- You change list properties and field data types in the Customize *ListName* page. Change view properties in the Edit View: *ListName* page.

- When importing or moving Access tables, the first required field (Categories.CategoryName, for example) or Text-type primary key (Customers.CustomerID, for example) replaces the Title column.

- In some cases, Access AutoNumber fields, such as Orders.OrderID, moved to list columns appear as _ID values, which autoincrement.

- If a table has a multivalued field, such as Products.SupplierID, and another foreign key with a relationship specified, such as Products.CategoryID, you might be unable to export the table or move the database to SharePoint.

NOTE

> The preceding list uses Northwind.accdb tables and fields as examples because—unlike tracking databases created from Office Online templates—this database and its table structure isn't optimized for SharePoint compatibility.

MOVING AND PUBLISHING THE NORTHWIND DATABASE TO WSS 3.0

Order processing databases and related online transaction processing (OLTP) databases—such as Northwind.accdb—are much more complex than the simple Access tracking databases whose templates you download from Office Online. In the real world, you'd use SharePoint lists only for tracking very simple and infrequent transactions, such as block grants to a not-for-profit organization. However, moving a copy of Northwind.accdb to WSS 3.0 is useful to demonstrate problems with multiple relationships, multivalued fields, a large number of rows, and conflicts with Access data types such as AutoNumber.

NOTE

> The NwindMove.accdb database in the \SEUA12\Chaptr25\Nwind folder is intended for use as the source database to be moved to SharePoint in this example.

To move and publish NwindMove.accdb to the http://localhost/nwind/ WSS 3.0 site you created in the earlier "Publishing an Existing Access Database to a SharePoint Document Library" section, do the following:

1. Open NwindMove.accdb, click the External Data tab, and click the SharePoint Lists group's Move to SharePoint button to start the Move to SharePoint Site Wizard.

2. Type the site address, **http://localhost/nwind/**, in the text box and, with the "Save a copy of my database to the SharePoint Site ..." check box marked, click the Browse button (see Figure 25.29).

3. The Location dialog opens with lists of the site's Document Libraries and Sites and Workspaces, if any (see Figure 25.30).

4. Double-click the Northwind Databases item to open the Northwind Databases page (see Figure 25.31). Click OK to specify it as the Document Library to store NwindMove.accdb, close the Location dialog, and add the path to the published database, http://*computername*/nwind/Northwind Database/NwindMove.accdb, under the browse button.

Figure 25.29
Specify the site and, if applicable, subsite address in the Move to SharePoint Site Wizard's first dialog. Marking the "Save a copy of my database to the SharePoint Site …" check box specifies publishing the database to a Document Library.

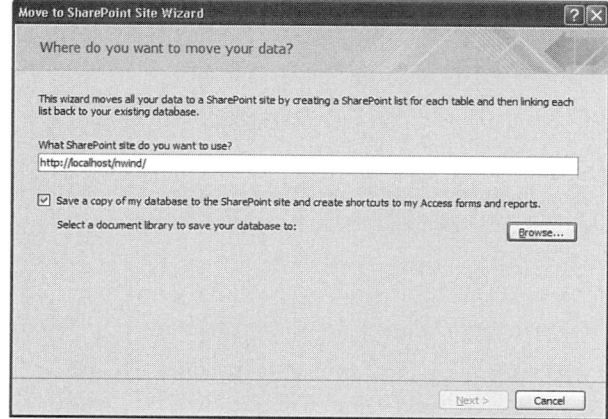

Figure 25.30
The Document Libraries group lists all libraries in the parent and selected subsite. If the Northwind subsite had subsite(s) or workspace(s), the items would appear in the Sites and Workspaces group.

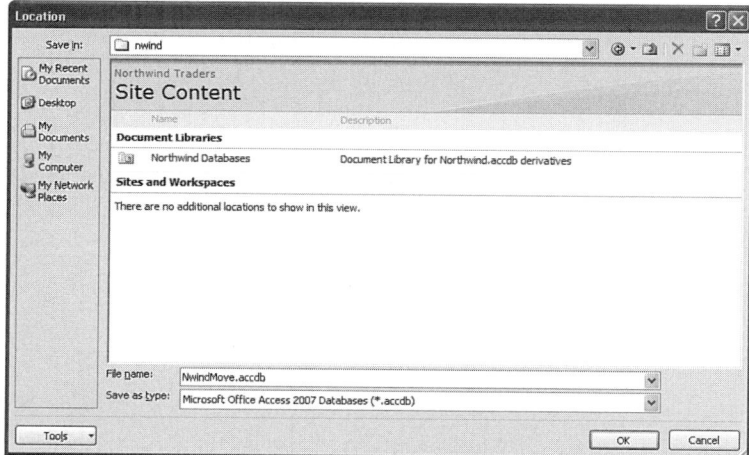

Figure 25.31
The Northwind Databases Document Library contains the NwindPub database you published to it earlier in the chapter.

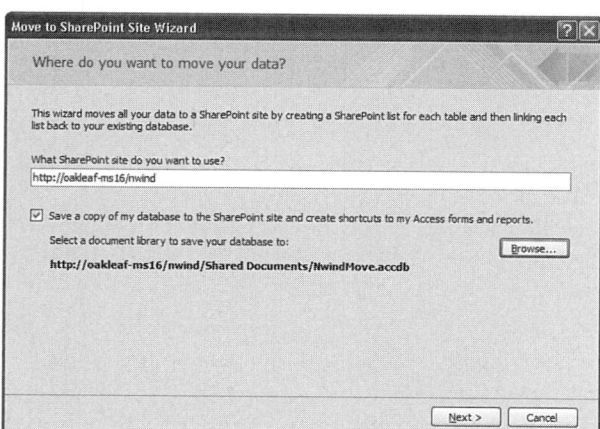

5. Click Next to start the move and publish process, which displays a progress dialog (see Figure 25.32).

Figure 25.32
The Move to SharePoint Site Wizard's second dialog displays a progress bar for the move operation, which consists of several steps for each table.

6. After a few minutes or longer, depending on your computer's CPU speed and amount of available RAM, the final Your Tables Have Been Successfully Shared dialog opens. Click the Show Details check box to display the result of the move and publish operations (see Figure 25.33).

Figure 25.33
The Details text box shows the lists created, the name and location of the backup database, and the URL for the published database.

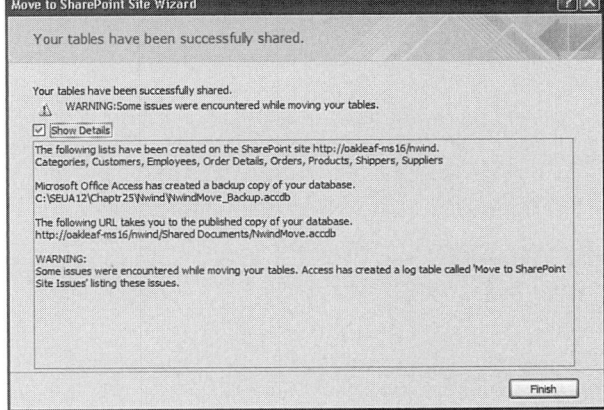

7. Click Finish to dismiss the Wizard and display the linked tables in the Navigation Pane. Access creates a backup (NwindMove_Backup.accdb for this example) of the source database.

8. Open the Navigation Pane, choose <u>O</u>bject Type and <u>A</u>ll Access Objects, and open the Move to SharePoint Site Issues table. Optionally, click the Create tab and Split Form button to display the problem descriptions in form text boxes (see Figure 25.34).

Figure 25.34
A split form makes it easier to review rows of the Move to SharePoint Site Issues table.

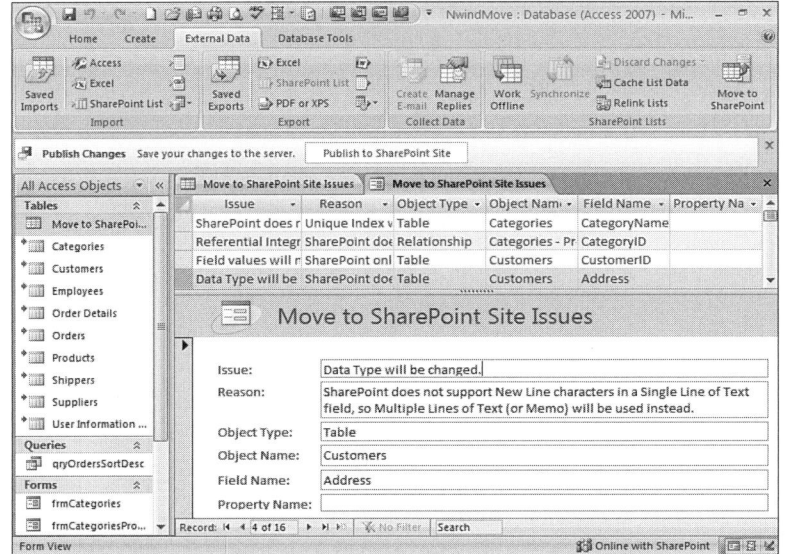

NOTE

Notice in Figure 25.34 that the SharePoint Lists group's Work Offline button is enabled, which indicates that the data is linked to the database and that users can copy the database to their computer. Users can work with the data when they can't connect to the SharePoint site and then update the site data when they reconnect. Working offline with SharePoint-hosted databases is the subject of the "Working Offline and Synchronizing Lists" section, later in this chapter.

9. Open the http://localhost/nwind subsite and click the View All Site Content to display the lists created from the Access tables (see Figure 25.35).

10. Open the default All Items view for each list and verify that it contains the content you expect and that the columns are in appropriate sequence. If not, modify the view as described in the earlier "Customize SharePoint List Views" section.

TIP

Access links to the SharePoint list, not a view of the list. Therefore, any design changes you make in the default All Items view don't propagate to the database.

11. Activate Access and browse the linked SharePoint lists. You'll find that the structure of most linked lists differ substantially from that of the original table.

The following section describes the changes to linked lists and how to work around some of the more problematic changes.

Figure 25.35
The All Site Content view displays an item for each list generated by moving an Access table to the subsite. Default lists, such as Announcements and Calendar have been deleted.

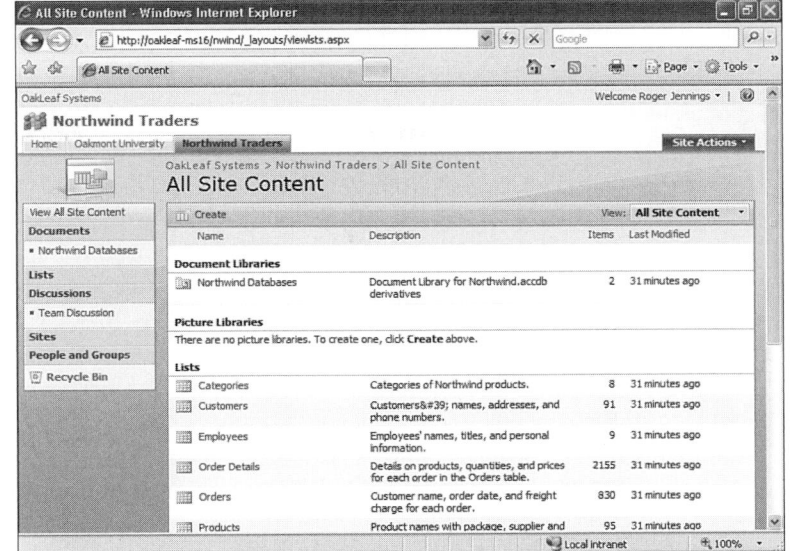

FIXING UP LISTS TO RESEMBLE SOURCE TABLES

Despite its use of an SQL Server 2005 database as its data store, SharePoint lists aren't relational tables.

Following are the most important changes to source tables made by moving tables to SharePoint lists, examples, and possible workarounds:

- AutoNumber primary key fields are renumbered and hidden, unless the original TableID field value for the first row is 1.

  For example, the OrderID field of the Orders list is the AutoNumber primary key, but its seed (initial) value is 1, not 10248, and the last record is 830, not 11077. This issue isn't so evident with tables whose AutoNumber primary key starts with 1, but the values will differ if any table rows were deleted before the move. Renumbering of rows after the deleted rows is likely to be missed by casual inspection.

- When you move a database to a SharePoint list, the original AutoNumber primary key field values appear in a hidden _ID field, which you can unhide in Access with the Unhide Columns dialog.

  For example, the Orders table's original OrderID values are in a hidden _ID field. The Categories, Employees, Products, Shippers, and Suppliers tables also have *Table*ID primary key and a hidden _ID field. These five tables export correctly because no rows have been deleted.

- You can't update fewer than all current links to a SharePoint list with the Choose the SharePoint Lists You Want to Link To dialog. If you clear check boxes to prevent re-creating the link by an import operation, the links are deleted. If you leave existing links checked, the links lose hidden primary key and _ID fields.

If you want to add a new link and retain hidden or visible primary key and _ID fields for all existing lists, you must move the table from a single-table database, and then import the link from that database.

■ Some fields lose lookup properties during the move to SharePoint list columns.

For example, the Orders table shows the Customers list's CustomerID value in a text box rather than the expected CompanyName value in a lookup combo box. You can't fix this problem in Access because linked lists are read-only in Design view (except the Caption and Lookup properties). You can add a new CompanyName Lookup field in SharePoint's Customize *ListName* page, but you can't replace the CustomerID field with it, as you'll see in the later "Replacing a Missing Lookup Field" section.

■ The length of all Single Line of Text columns is 255 characters, regardless of the Length property value set for the Access source field. You can change the maximum number of characters on the lists Change Column: *ColumnName* page.

For example, the Customers table's CustomerID field is 255, not 5 characters. In this case, the Input Mask property limits the length to 5 characters. There is no protection from duplicate CustomerID values.

■ Some lists gain unwanted/unnecessary Title fields when moved from Access tables, and all lists have Attachment fields.

The Order Details list's Title field values are missing, because Order Details has no required Text field. All linked tables have Attachments fields, unless you disable attachments on the List Advanced Settings page.

■ You can't change a column's data type from Number or Single Line of Text to Lookup.

The workaround for Single Line of Text data is to add a Lookup column to the list, and then populate the list by copying and pasting the data in SharePoint Datasheet view, as described in the "Replacing a Missing Lookup Field" section.

■ Lookup or Choice list data types alter the list's column sequence. By default, the _ID column follows the renamed Title column. You'll find Lookup or Choice columns after the last simple data type column.

For example, the Orders list's _ID column follows CustomerID, which is the renamed Title column, and EmployeeID and ShipVia columns follow ShipCountry. It's easy to change the column sequence by Datasheet view's drag-and-drop fields feature.

Figure 25.36 shows the Orders list's Datasheet view after hiding the OrderID column and changing the position of the _ID, EmployeeID, and ShipVia columns..

TIP

> If you want the column order to survive synchronization and refresh operations, you must use SharePoint's Change Field Order: *ListName* page to set the sequence. Open this page by choosing Settings, List Settings and from the list's Datasheet view open the Customize *ListName* page and click the Column Ordering link near the bottom of the page. However, you must unhide _ID columns, even if you've renamed them, after each refresh or synchronization operation.

Figure 25.36
This Orders list's Datasheet view has its OrderID and _ID columns unhidden and EmployeeID and ShipVia fields moved.

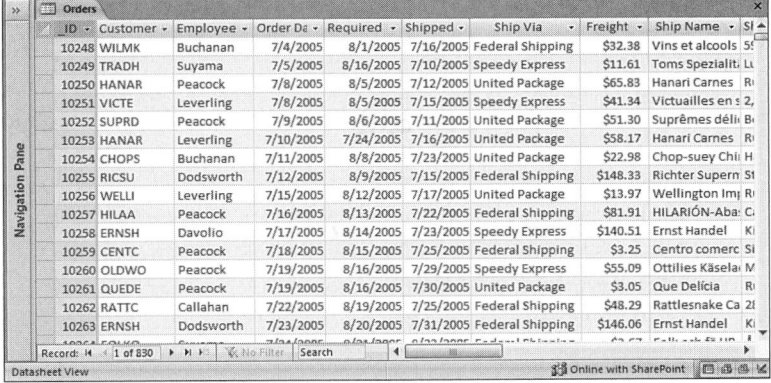

Figure 25.36's hidden _ID column has been unhidden by clicking the Home ribbon's Records button, selecting More, Unhide Columns to open the Unhide Columns dialog, and marking the _ID check box. The meaningless OrderID column is hidden (see Figure 25.37).

Figure 25.37
Use Access's Unhide Columns dialog to make the _ID field visible in Datasheet view.

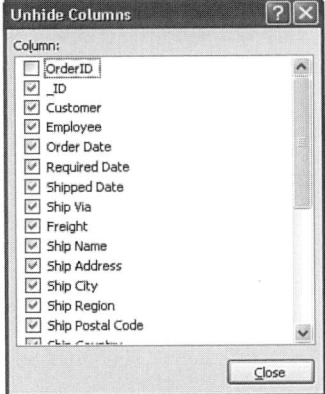

The following sections describe workarounds for most of the preceding list's issues.

CHECKING OUT AND CHECKING IN A DATABASE FROM A DOCUMENT LIBRARY

The database file that displays the newly linked lists when the move operation completes is the source database—\SEUA12\Chaptr25\Nwind\NwindMove.accdb for this example. However, users will make local copies of the source database copy in the Document Library—NwindMove in Northwind Databases. Therefore, you should make all Access database modifications to the copy in the Document Library.

SharePoint includes a version control feature that requires checking out and checking in files stored in Document Libraries. While the file is checked out to a user, no one else can edit it. By default, your \[My]Documents\SharePoint Drafts folder holds checked-out documents.

To check out a database from a Document Library, do the following:

1. Open the Document Library from the Quick Launch menu.

2. Open the menu list for the database, and choose Check Out (see Figure 25.38).

Figure 25.38
SharePoint's document version control feature requires that you check out documents for editing.

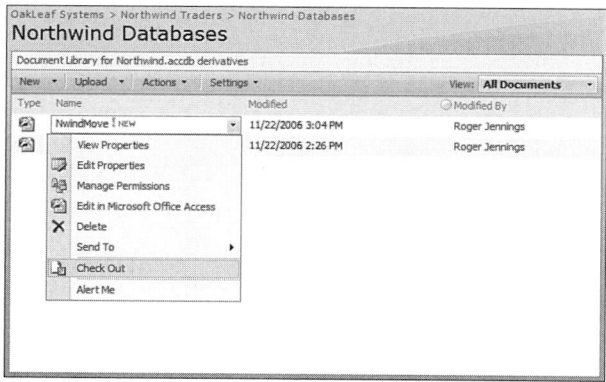

3. Accept the default Use My Local Drafts Folder option (see Figure 25.39), and click OK to create the copy in your \My Documents\SharePoint Drafts (Windows XP/2003) or \Documents\SharePoint Drafts (Windows Vista) folder.

Figure 25.39
This dialog lets you specify saving the edit copy in your \[My] Documents\ SharePoint Drafts folder.

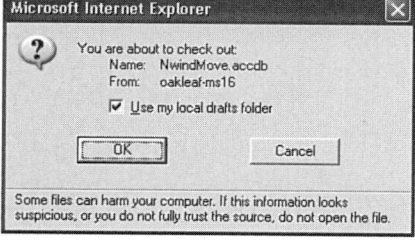

When you check out a database, the Access icon gains a green arrow symbol in its lower-right corner.

To check in the document, do this:

1. Open the Document Library from the Quick Launch menu.

2. Open the menu list for the database and choose Check In. Or, to cancel the check out operation or discard your changes, choose Discard Check Out.

3. In the Check In dialog, type a description of the changes you made in the Comments text box (see Figure 25.40), and click OK to check the database back in.

4. Click Yes when notified that you're about to upload the .accdb file to the SharePoint site name.

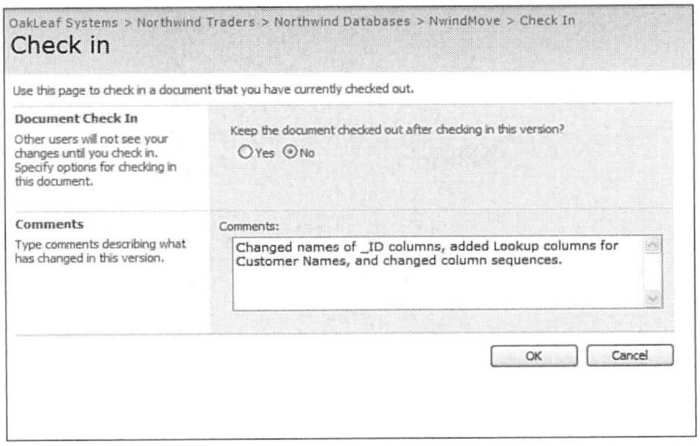

Figure 25.40
You make the changes described in the Comments text box in the next two sections.

REPLACING A MISSING LOOKUP FIELD

Lookup fields can aid in maintaining referential integrity by restricting entries in the SharePoint equivalent of foreign key columns to valid list items. For example, the NwindMove.accdb source database's Orders.CustomerID and Order Details.ProductID lookup lists prevent adding incorrect CustomerID and ProductID values to the Orders and Order Details tables.

The Access Orders table loses the lookup properties for the CustomerID field when you move or export the table to a SharePoint list. You can't change the data type of the CustomerID field from Single Line of Text to Lookup, but you can add a new Lookup column. However, populating the new Lookup column manually with 830 CustomerID values would be tedious, at best.

Fortunately, you can copy and paste in the data from the original column to a Lookup column's foreign key field, such as CustomerID, and then change the column design to show the display field, such as CompanyName. After you make this change in SharePoint, you must conform Access's Lookup properties to the SharePoint changes you made, because the Refresh Lists operation doesn't do this.

To create a CustomerID lookup list for the Orders list, do the following:

1. Open the Orders list from the All Site Content page and choose Settings, List Settings to open the Customize Orders page.
2. Click the CustomerID column to open the Change Column Orders page, and change its Column Name to Customer_ID. Click OK to return to the Customize Orders page.
3. Click the Create Column link to open the Create Column: Orders page, type **ColumnID** as the Column Name value, and select the Lookup (Information Already on This Site) option (see Figure 25.41).

Figure 25.41
Specify the CustomerID Lookup column's name and data type at the top of the Create Column: Orders page.

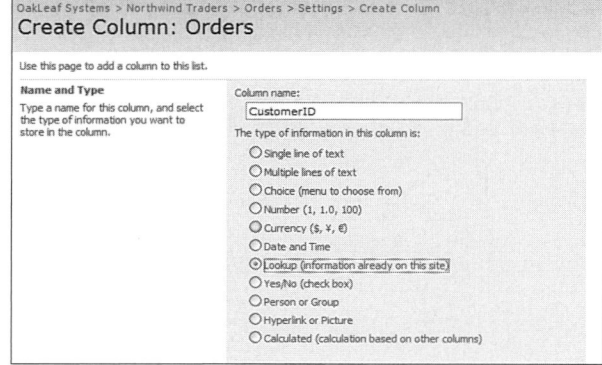

4. Scroll to the Additional Column Settings section, type an optional description, accept the No default to temporarily not require data in the column, and select Customers as the source table and, temporarily, CustomerID as the display column (see Figure 25.42). Accept the Add to Default View choice and click OK to add the column.

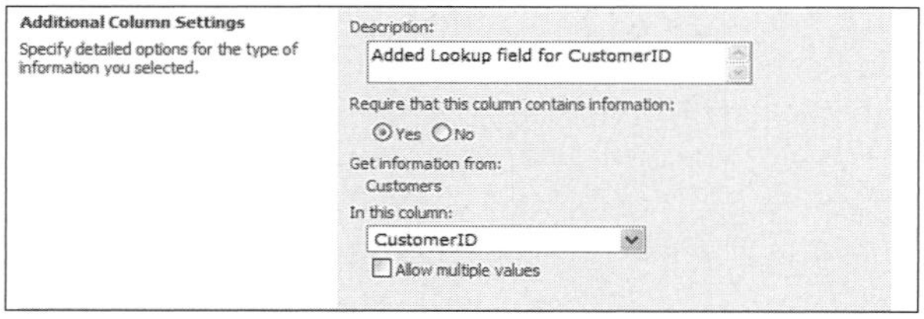

Figure 25.42
Add a description, require a value, and select the lookup source list and column in the Additional Column Settings section.

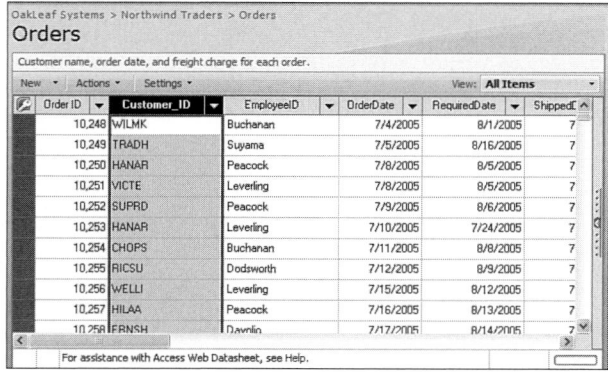

5. Click the Orders breadcrumb above the Orders caption to open the modified list in the Access Web Datasheet control. Click the Customer_ID column header to select all 830 cells (see Figure 25.43) and press Ctrl+C to copy the values to the Clipboard.

Figure 25.43
The Access Web Datasheet ActiveX grid control lets you copy and paste multiple cell values.

6. Scroll right to the last column (CustomerID), place the cursor in the first empty combo box, press Ctrl+V to copy the CustomerID values to the cells, and wait for the Pending Changes notice at the bottom of the Datasheet to disappear (see Figure 25.44). Open the combo list to verify that it behaves as expected.

Figure 25.44
The CustomerID Lookup column has values pasted from the renamed Customer_ID field.

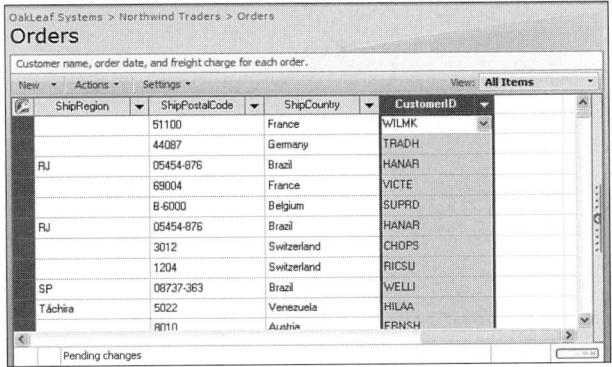

7. Choose Settings, List Settings to return to the Customize Orders page, click the CustomerID link to open the Change Column: Orders page, change the In This Column selection to CompanyName, and click OK to return to the Customize Orders page.

8. Click the Column Ordering link near the bottom of the page to open the Change Field Order: Orders page. Set the Order ID field (renamed from _ID) to 1, Customer_ID column to 15, CustomerID to 2, EmployeeID to 3, and ShipVia to 7 (see Figure 25.45). Click OK to save the new column sequence.

Figure 25.45
The Change Field Order page lets you change the order of the list's columns for new views, not existing views.

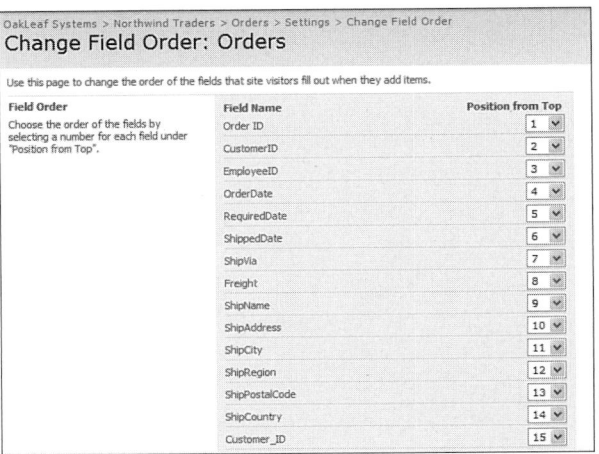

25

9. Return to the All Items view of the Orders list, and click All Items, Modify This View to open the Edit View: Orders page. Changing the list's column sequence doesn't change the All Items view's sequence.

10. Change the column sequence to match that of step 8. Optionally, change the sort order on OrderID to descending. Click OK to save the changes and verify the new All Items view (see Figure 25.46).

Figure 25.46
Here's the All Items view after making column sequence changes similar to those in Figure 25.46.

11. Open NwindMove.accdb, right-click the Orders list in the Navigation Pane, and choose SharePoint List Options, Refresh List to synchronize the linked list design with the modified SharePoint version. The Customer column opens with numbers from the Customers list's ID column.

12. Change to Design view, select the CustomerID column, and click the Lookup tab. The Display Control is a combo box, but the Row Source property value is empty.

13. Click the builder button to open the Orders : Query Builder window, drag the ID and CompanyName fields to the first two columns of the query grid (see Figure 25.47).

Figure 25.47
The key column of the Customers list is ID, which is the bound field for an Access single-valued lookup field.

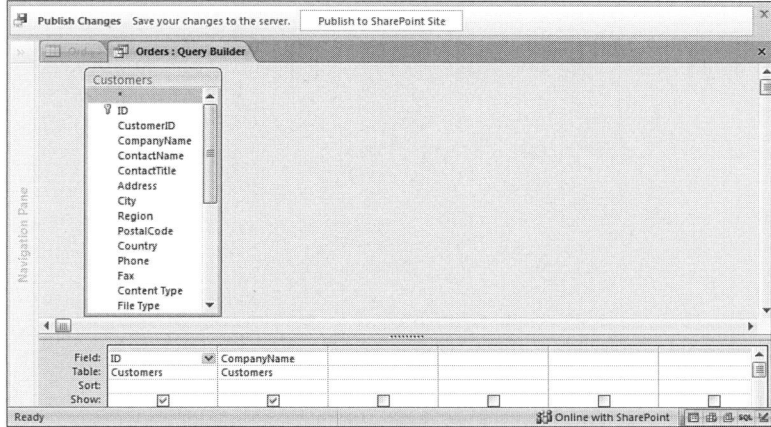

14. Close the window and save your changes to the Row Source SQL statement: SELECT Customers.ID, Customers.CompanyName FROM Customers;.

15. Change to Datasheet view, save your changes and expand the Customer column, which is aligned right because it's a Number field. Select the column and click Align Left to apply string formatting to the field.

16. Choose More, Unhide Columns from the Home ribbon's Records group, mark the Order ID check box, and close the dialog. Optionally, drag the Order_ID column from the Datasheet's far right to the right of the Customer column; alternatively, hide the Customer_ID column because it's no longer significant. Datasheet view appears as shown in Figure 25.48.

Figure 25.48
Conforming the appearance of the Orders table linked to a SharePoint list to the original Access Orders table requires a major effort.

17. Click the message pane's Publish to SharePoint Site button and click Publish to overwrite the existing NwindMove.accdb document.

Although the preceding procedure is specific to the CustomersID column of the Orders list, it works for most columns except ...ID fields, which don't appear in the Access Web Datasheet grid.

> **TIP**
>
> You can create lookup fields in Access independently of SharePoint by following steps 11 through 15 of the preceding operation, but the Row Source property's SQL Statement disappears when you publish the change to SharePoint.

USING SHAREPOINT-SPECIFIC CONTEXT MENUS AND BUTTONS

The Navigation Pane's context menu and Table Tools, Datasheet ribbon's SharePoint List group for linked SharePoint lists offer several functions that don't apply to Access tables, as shown in Figure 25.49.

Figure 25.49
Linking tables to SharePoint lists adds this SharePoint List Options submenu to the Navigation Pane's context menu and the Table Tools, Datasheet ribbon gains a SharePoint List group (inset).

Following are brief descriptions of the action taken by each SharePoint List Options command or SharePoint List group button:

- Open Default View—Opens the default SharePoint view for the selected list in Datasheet or standard view.

- Modify Columns and Settings—Opens the Customize *ListName* page.

- Alert Me—Opens the New Alert page, which configures email alerts that notify the user when there are changes to the specified item, document, list, or library.

- Modify Workflow—Opens the Change Workflow Settings: *ListName* page that lets you view or change the workflow settings for this list. Alternatively, you can add or remove workflows

- Change Permission for this List—Opens the Permissions: *ListName* page that lets you modify the list's or its parent's permissions.

- SharePoint Site Recycle Bin—Opens the Recycle Bin from which you can restore deleted lists or items.

- Relink Lists—Opens the Relink Lists dialog in which you can select another SharePoint site from which to relink corresponding links.

- Refresh List—Synchronizes the Access linked list's design and contents with the SharePoint master.

- Delete List—Deletes the selected list.

CREATING A NEW DATABASE FROM A TEMPLATE AND MOVING IT TO SHAREPOINT

Office Online's templates for simple Access databases that have one or two tables are more suited to moving to SharePoint lists than even moderately complex projects, such as NwindMove. The following sections describe how to generate a database from an Office Online template, how to move and publish it to SharePoint Issues and Contacts lists, as well as how to populate the Contacts list from your Outlook Contacts folder.

CREATING, MOVING, AND PUBLISHING THE ISSUES DATABASE

To create an Issues.accdb database from the online Issues template and publish it to a WSS 3.0 site (http://localhost/Oakmont/ for this example), do the following:

1. Launch Access, click the Office button, and choose New to open the Getting Started with Microsoft Access window.

2. Click the From Microsoft Office Online category's Business link to display icons for current Access 2007 templates in the category.

3. Click Issues for this example to add Issues.accdb to the File Name text box. Click the Browse button with the folder icon to the right of the text box to open File New Database dialog. Then navigate to your working folder (\SEUA12\Chaptr25\Oakmont for this example) and click OK.

4. Mark the Create and Link Your Database to a Windows SharePoint Services Site check box to create the database and lists on your site and link the database to the lists (see Figure 25.50).

Figure 25.50
Selecting a template from Microsoft Office Online gives you the option of creating a conventional Access database or storing the database in a SharePoint Document Library and linking its tables to SharePoint lists.

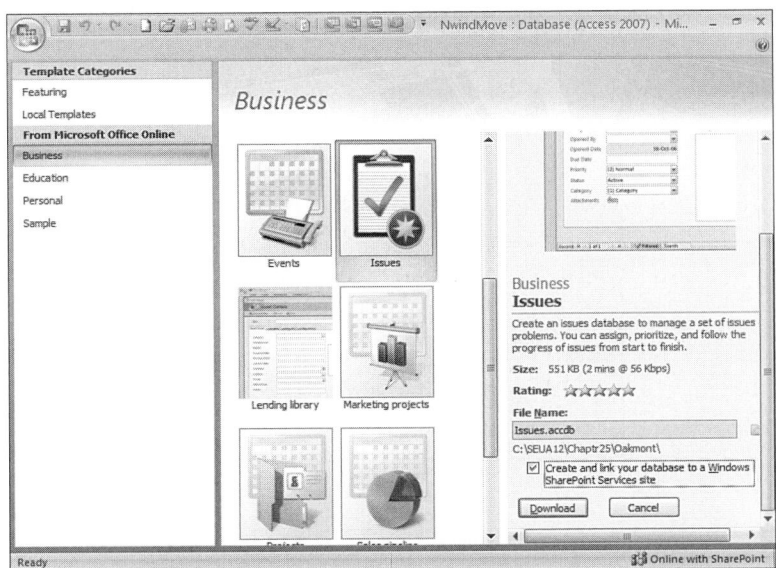

5. Close all open browser instances, and click Download to download the template and open the Create on SharePoint Site dialog. (A SharePoint site open in your browser might prevent downloading templates.) Close the Access Help dialog, if it appears.

6. Type the URL for the destination WSS site, http://*computername*/[*subsite*/], in the text box (**http://localhost/oakmont/** for this example), and accept the Save a Copy of My Database to the SharePoint Site... choice (see Figure 25.51).

Figure 25.51
Specify the URL of the SharePoint site in which to store the database and create the lists.

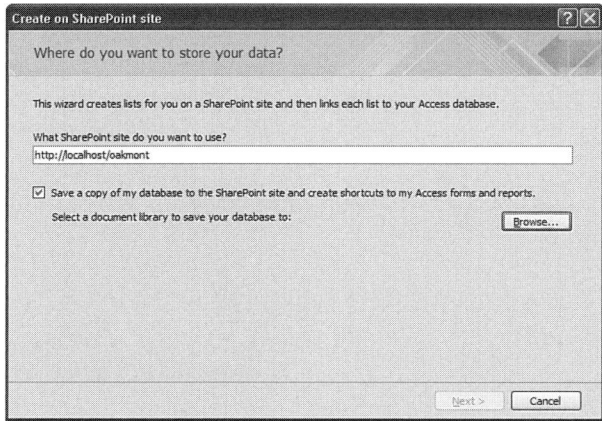

7. Click Browse to open the Location dialog with customized Document Libraries and Sites and Workspaces lists (see Figure 25.52).

Figure 25.52
The sample SharePoint site has an Oakmont Databases Document Library.

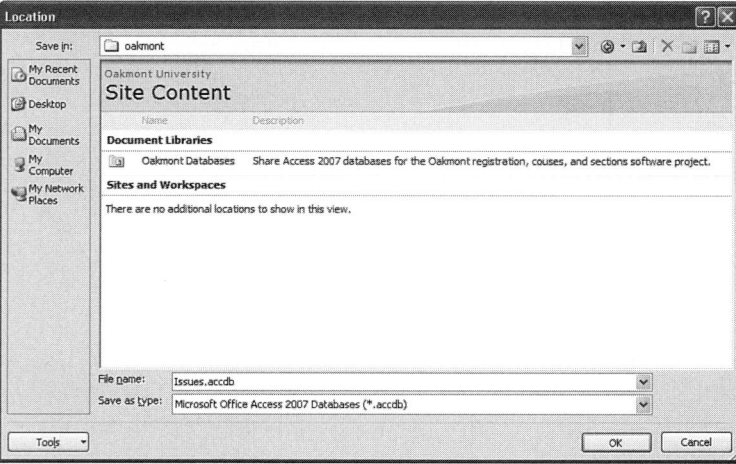

8. Double-click the Document Library in which to save the database, Oakmont Databases for this example (see Figure 25.53). Then click OK to return to the Create on SharePoint Site dialog.

Figure 25.53
The sample Oakmont Databases document library will store the Issues.accdb file.

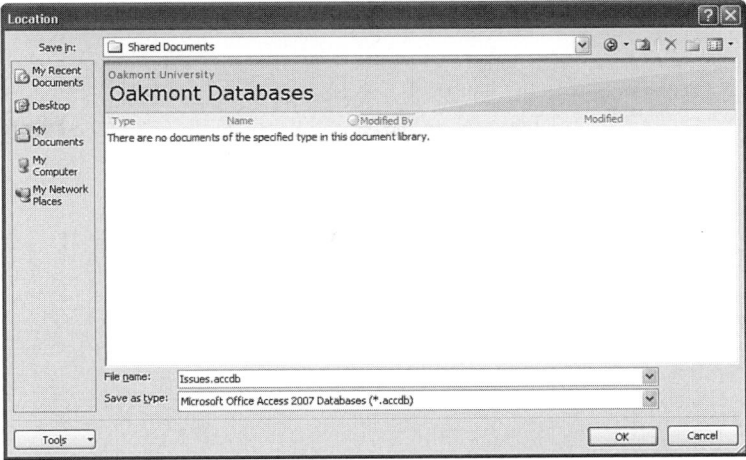

9. The Create on SharePoint Site dialog displays the URL for the database, http://*computername*/[*subsite*/]Shared Documents/*Database*.accdb. Click Next to start the database publishing process.

10. The Create on SharePoint Site dialog displays a progress bar during the list creation and database copy operation, and then opens the final "Your tables have been successfully shared" dialog. If problems were encountered during the operation, a warning message appears. Mark the Show Details check box to display status information (see Figure 25.54).

Figure 25.54
Issues commonly arise when creating SharePoint lists from Access tables. In most cases, the issues don't prevent the lists from behaving normally.

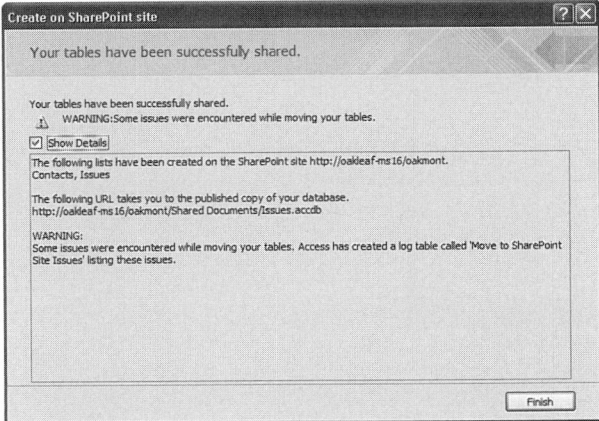

11. Click Finish to display the empty Issue List form, and then expand the Navigation pane's sections. The Category column is a value-list Choice field with three generic choices and a button to open the Edit List Items dialog (see Figure 25.55). Priority and Status also are Choice fields with supplied choices.

Figure 25.55
An empty Issue List form opens in Datasheet view when you complete the database move and publishing process for Issues.accdb. The list has Priority and Category Lookup columns with generic lists.

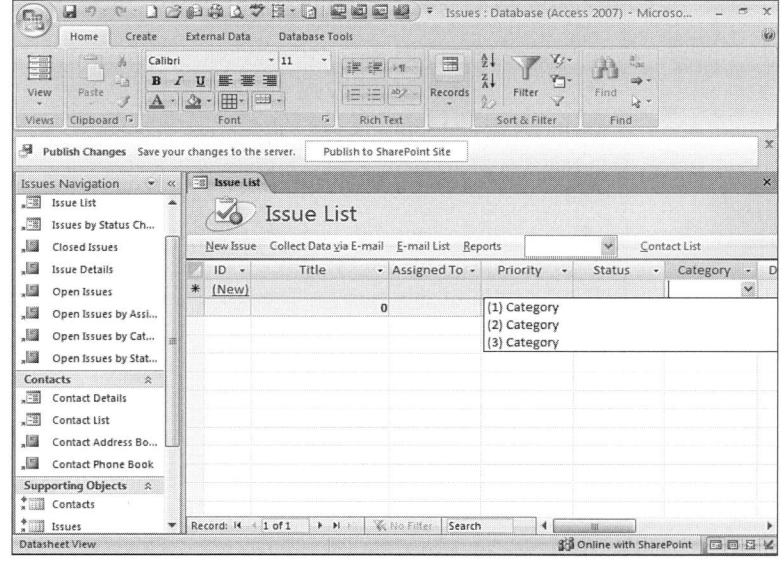

CUSTOMIZING THE ISSUES LIST

You can alter the values of some properties of the Issues list in the linked Access front end. For example, you can change the Format, Input Mask, Caption, and IME Sentence Mode, and Smart Tags property values on the General Page, and all property values on the Lookup page except Allow Multiple Values. You also can change the Default Value property of Choice fields in the Edit Values text box, despite the General page's Default Value property's "This property cannot be modified in linked tables" message.

To change a Choice column's value list and default value in the original (source) Issues.accdb database, do the following:

1. Click the button to open the Category columns' Edit List Items dialog, and replace the generic items with more appropriate category names, leaving the Default Value text box empty (see Figure 25.56). Click OK to close the dialog and save the changes to the database file.

Figure 25.56
The button below the pre-built generic Lookup column choices opens the Edit List Items dialog in which you type entries for a value list.

2. Repeat step 1 for the Priority column, except select (2) Normal in the Default Values list, and click OK to save the changes.

> **NOTE**
>
> The changes to the form's list you make in steps 1 and 2 currently affect only the source database—Issues.accdb in your \SEUA12\Chaptr25\Oakmont folder—not the copy published to the Oakmont Databases Document Library.

3. Click Publish to SharePoint Site to open the Publish to Web Server dialog, click Publish, click Yes to overwrite the current Access file version, and finally click Yes to save your changes to the Issues List form and update the SharePoint list with the changes you made in steps 1 and 2.

4. Close Issues.accdb.

WORKING OFFLINE AND SYNCHRONIZING LISTS

The capability to work with shared data while offline—that is, not connected to the network—is an increasingly important feature of desktop applications. Taking the Access database offline creates local copies of all linked SharePoint lists. If the number and size of the lists are large, the disk space occupied by the offline version of the database grows substantially. When you reconnect, Access doesn't send the changes you made while offline to SharePoint until you click the Work Online button.

To add items while disconnected from the SharePoint site to the Contacts and Issues list in the master copy of the Issues.accdb database that you open from the Document Library, do the following:

1. From SharePoint's Quick Launch menu, open the Oakmont Databases Document Library, check out the Issues.accdb file, and choose Edit in Microsoft Office Access to open it.

→ To review how to check out and check in an Access database in a Document Library, **see** "Checking Out and Checking In a Database from a Document Library," **p. 1123**.

> **NOTE**
>
> Checking out a database to your \My Documents\SharePoint Drafts folder is the equivalent of taking the file—but not the list data—offline.

2. Click the External Data tab, and then click the SharePoint List's group's Work Offline button to temporarily disconnect the tables from the SharePoint site and cache the table data locally. The Navigation Pane's linked table icons replace the linked list icons.

3. If you have some test Contacts in an Outlook folder, open the Contact List form, click the Add from Outlook button, mark the Microsoft Office Outlook dialog's Allow Access for check box, select 10 minutes, and click the Allow button to open the Select Names to Add: *FolderName* dialog.

NOTE

The \SEUA12\Chaptr25\Oakmont.pst file contains 91 Outlook contact records for Oakmont Computer Science faculty members that you can quickly import into Outlook.

4. Select a few names, click Add (see Figure 25.57), and then click OK to add the names to the Contact List form as shown in Figure 25.58).

Figure 25.57
Outlook's Select Names to Add dialog lets you add multiple names from any Contacts folder—Oakmont for this example.

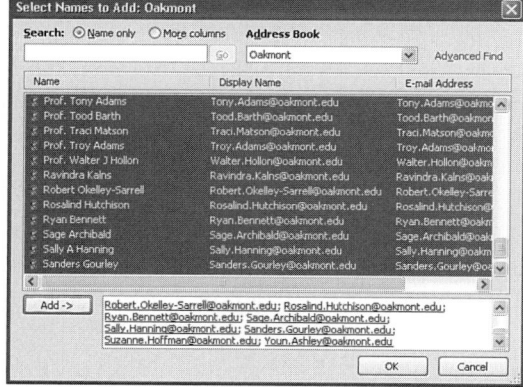

NOTE

The records in the Contact List form are sorted by last name but numbered by an arbitrary sequence of negative numbers (see Figure 25.58). Negative numbers serve as a temporary key field, which SharePoint recognizes as a set of primary key values to be replaced during synchronization.

Figure 25.58
Records added in Access to cached offline SharePoint lists have temporary negative ID (primary key) values. Synchronizing or reconnecting the database replaces the ID values with permanent positive numbers.

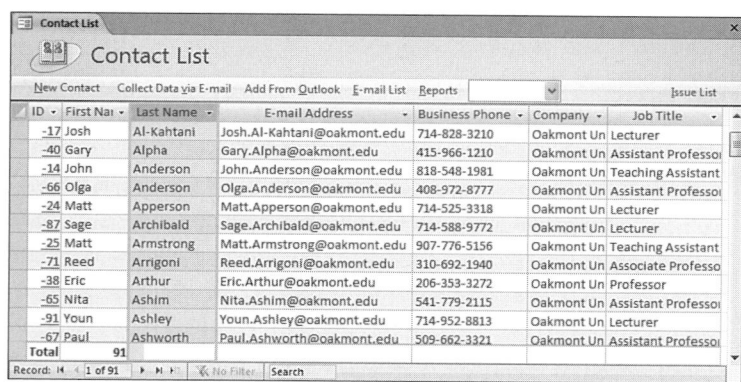

5. Open the Issue List form and add a few entries, which also uses a negative-number primary key. Notice that the lookup list sorts in first-name order and is wider than necessary (see Figure 25.59).

Figure 25.59
The Contacts lookup list is wider than necessary and sorts by first name instead of last name.

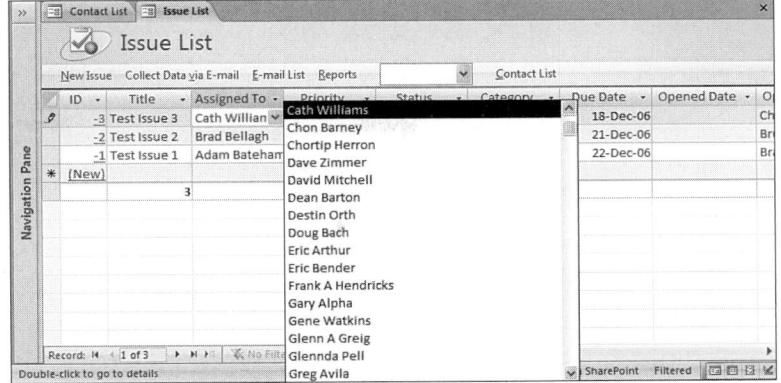

6. Optionally, fix the combo list by changing to Design view and reducing the width of the controls, replacing the Row Source property value with **SELECT [Contacts Extended].[ID], [Contacts Extended].[Contact Name], [Contacts Extended].[Last Name] FROM [Contacts Extended] ORDER BY [Contacts Extended].[Last Name];**, changing the Column Widths property value to **0";1";0"**, and saving your changes.

7. Open the SharePoint Contacts and Issues lists and verify that they're empty.

8. Return to Access, click the External Data tab, and click the SharePoint Lists group's Work Online button to reconnect to the lists and update them in SharePoint. Click Yes when asked if you want to save changes to the Issue List form.

9. Open the Issue List and Contact List datasheets and verify that the ID values are positive, which indicates that SharePoint has assigned a key value to the items.

10. Return to SharePoint and verify that the Contacts and Issues lists contain the added items.

11. Close Issues.accdb and check it into the SharePoint Document Library to save your design changes.

If you and another user edit the same record while you're offline, a Write Conflict dialog opens with a concurrency error message when you return online and attempt to update the data (see Figure 25.60). Paste the data that's copied to the Clipboard into Notepad to determine the other user's changes. The data consists of a tab-separated list of field names and a row of data.

Figure 25.60
This Write Conflict dialog opens when users have updated the same data item offline and online, and the previously offline user attempts to synchronize the data.

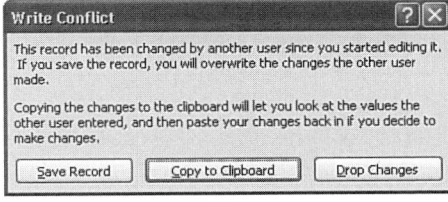

EXPORTING TABLES OR QUERIES TO A SHAREPOINT LIST

The simplest interaction with SharePoint is exporting an Access table or query as a WSS list. In this case, there is only a momentary connection between the list and your Access database. Exporting doesn't create a link between the Access table or query and SharePoint list. The most common use of Access's Export to SharePoint feature is as an intermediary for a format that SharePoint can't import directly.

To export a table—Northwind Products for this example—to the parent (OakLeaf) WSS 3.0 site, do the following:

1. Open \SEUA12\ Nwind\Northwind.accdb, right-click the Products table entry, and choose Export, SharePoint List to open the Export Data to SharePoint List dialog.

2. Complete the URL to your WSS 3.0 parent site (http://localhost/ for this example), and modify the default list name and description, if you want (see Figure 25.61).

Figure 25.61
Select or type the URL for your WSS site and give the list a name and description in the Export Data to SharePoint List dialog.

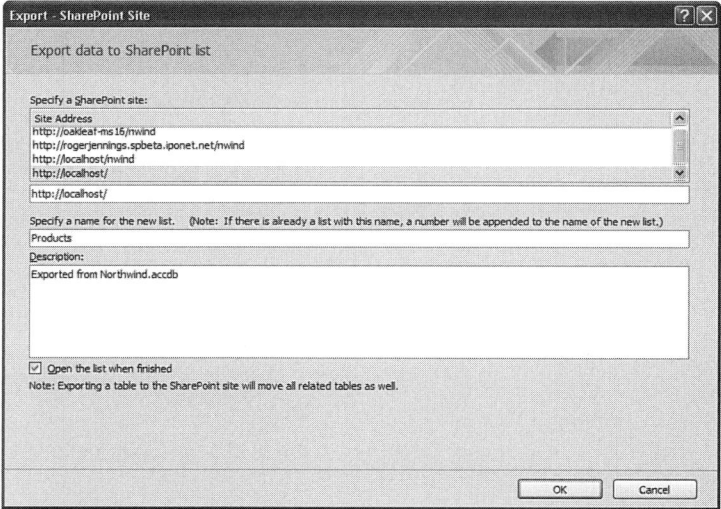

3. With the Open The List When Finished check box marked, click OK to export the list. After a minute or so, the All Items view opens (see Figure 25.62).

> **NOTE**
> The SupplierID and CategoryID columns shown in Figure 25.62 are Lookup columns based on values in the Suppliers and Categories tables. Exporting a table also exports the related tables to lists that might supply SharePoint Lookup column values.

4. Click the arrow at the right of the column name to open a column's drop-down list to sort or add a filter in datasheet view (see Figure 25.63).

Figure 25.62
The exported table opens the All Items view of the Products list in an Access Web Datasheet.

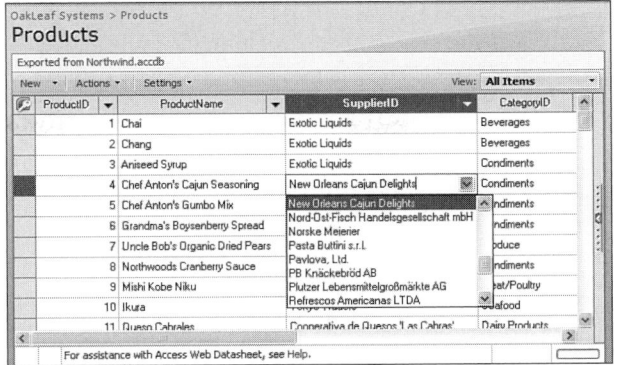

Figure 25.62
Each column's drop-down list lets you sort, filter, or both on that column.

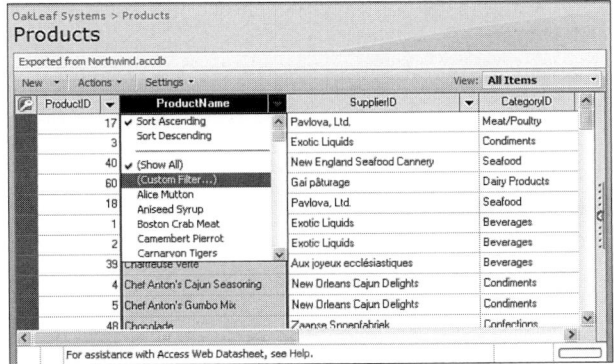

25

5. You can select Sort Ascending or Sort Descending, and then select an individual value or up to three custom filter conditions in the Custom Filter dialog (see Figure 25.64).

Figure 25.64
The Custom Filter dialog lets you apply up to three WHERE clause criteria to the list.

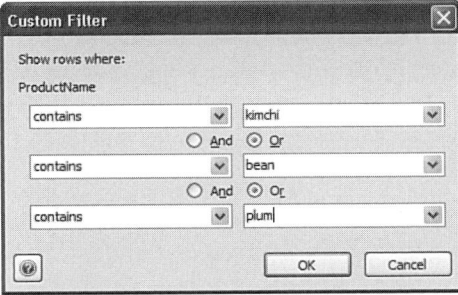

6. Open the list and select (Show All) to remove the filter. You can't remove the sort in this view; your only choice is to sort on another column, such as the key field (ProductID).

7. Click the Show Task Pane button at the right of the grid, and click the Sort link to open the Custom Sort dialog, which lets you sort the list by a sequence of up to three columns (see Figure 25.65). You can remove the sort you applied in step 5 by opening the drop-down list and selecting the empty choice for each field. You can remove all filters and sorting (except ProductID) by clicking the Remove Filter/Sort button.

Figure 25.65
The Access Web Datasheet control's task pane enables sorting on up to three column values and interaction with Access and Excel.

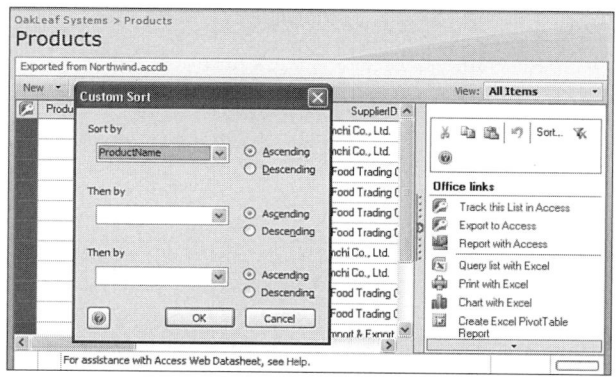

 8. Click the New menu or open it and choose New Item to move to the tentative append record at the end of the list. Like in Access, you don't add a record until you type values for at least the required fields.

 If you encounter an error when exporting your table to a WSS 3.0 list, see the "Table Column Name Conflicts with WSS Lists" topic of the "Troubleshooting" section near the end of this chapter.

LINKING A SHAREPOINT LIST TO AN ACCESS TABLE

The most common reason to export Access data to a SharePoint list is to share it with others. You export the data when you don't want to move the source database's tables to SharePoint. However, you must manually update the Access, SharePoint, or both versions to maintain current data. Linking makes edits to the SharePoint list visible in both applications, which eliminates the need for manual updates. This capability lets you establish relationships between the list and other tables, and lets you use Access forms and VBA code to maintain the list.

NOTE

You can't create a link from SharePoint to the SQL Server database of an Access Data Project. You receive a "Links can only be created between Microsoft Access database files" error message if you try.

25

LINK SHAREPOINT LISTS TO ACCESS TABLES FROM SHAREPOINT

To link new Access tables to corresponding SharePoint lists using the Products list you created in the preceding section as an example, do the following:

1. Open the Products list in the Access Web Datasheet and click the Task Pane button.

2. Click the Track This List with Access link. Select the New Database option and click OK to display the File New Database dialog.

3. Change the Database Name to ProductsTrack.accdb, and click Create to create the new database with four tables: Products, Categories, Suppliers, and User Information List (see Figure 25.66).

Figure 25.66
Tracking the Products list with Access requires lookup values from the Categories and Suppliers lists.

LINK ACCESS TABLES TO SHAREPOINT LISTS FROM ACCESS

Alternatively, you can create identical links from an Access database by doing the following:

1. Click the External Data tab and the Import group's SharePoint List button to open the Get External Data - SharePoint Site dialog (see Figure 25.67).

2. Select or type the site's address and accept the default Link to the Data Source by Creating a Linked Table option, and click Next to open a list of lists in the selected site.

3. Select the lists to link (see Figure 25.68) and click OK to generate the linked tables, which include tables related to those you chose in step 2.

Figure 25.67
Select the SharePoint site's address in the first Get External Data - SharePoint Site dialog.

Figure 25.68
Select the SharePoint lists to link in the second Get External Data - SharePoint Site dialog.

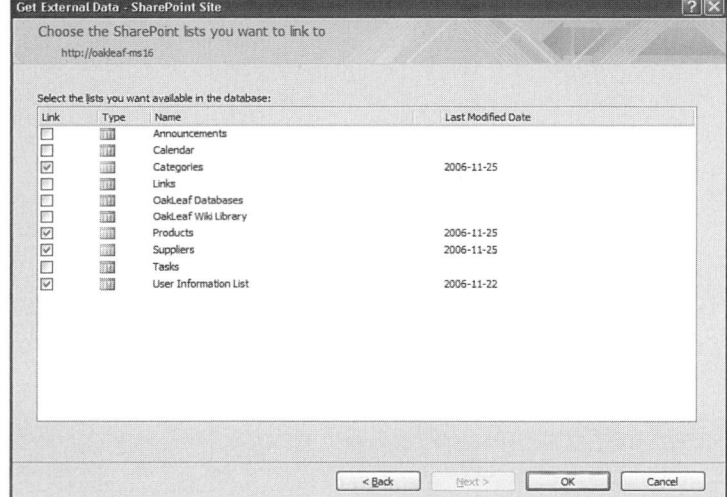

TROUBLESHOOTING

TABLE COLUMN NAME CONFLICTS WITH WSS LISTS

When I try to export an Access or SQL Server table to a WSS list, I receive an error message, the list is missing some of the table columns, or both.

WSS lists have several internal columns for list management that don't appear in datasheet or standard view. These columns are: ID, Title, Modified, Created, Created By, Modified By, Attachments, and Edit. Tables having columns with any of these names cause problems during the export process. You must rename conflicting table columns or substitute a query with column name aliases to export the table data successfully. As an example, you should rename the Employees.Title table to Employees.JobTitle or the like before moving or exporting it to a SharePoint site.

IN THE REAL WORLD—DATA-CENTRIC COLLABORATION

Collaboration is the watchword of 2007 Microsoft Office System and its members. A Google search of the Microsoft.com site returned about 15,100 instances of the word in 2003 and 94,100 in late 2006. Similarly, Bill Gates, Ray Ozzie, and Microsoft marketing folk tend to overuse buzzphrases such as "knowledge workers without limits" and "empower[ing] knowledge workers." About 864 Microsoft.com pages contain both "collaboration" and "knowledge worker." Most of this book's readers probably are knowledge workers or persons responsible for increasing knowledge workers' efficiency—such as database designers or application developers.

The role of corporate knowledge workers is to produce information that's useful to other organization members, customers, suppliers, other "business partners," or all of these groups. The usefulness of the information is related directly to the workers' knowledge and skill set. The problem is that most such information—whether generated by computer or handwritten on a business form—is unstructured or, at best, semi-structured. Some analysts suggest that more information resides in Excel worksheet files than in all the world's databases. If you add Word document files to the mix, the conclusion is undoubtedly correct. Business email contains an enormous amount of unstructured information, especially if your organization is required to archive messages for several years. Ultimately, much of this currently unstructured data will end up in the XML data type columns of SQL Server 2005 and other relational databases.

WSS 3.0, MOSS 2007, and Exchange Server are Microsoft's primary offerings for information sharing. WSS 3.0 is the logical portal candidate for small- and medium-sized organizations (SMOs) because it's easy for knowledge workers to set up and manage lists, document libraries, blogs, and wikis, and WSS client access licenses (CALs) aren't required. Access databases in Document Libraries enable those who need them to make local copies of the latest version of .accdb files. Lists make the contents of linked Access tables or queries accessible to any authorized WSS user on an intranet or via the Internet. You can control whether users have read-only, read-write, or no access to databases and lists by their WSS group membership.

NOTE

> Microsoft Office Live Collaboration is a hosted version of Windows SharePoint Services 3.0 with several prebuilt, business-oriented lists designed for small businesses with 10 or fewer employees. Microsoft Office Live Essentials combines Office Live Basics, which provides free domain-name registration, site-design tools, web hosting, website traffic reports, and Office Live Collaboration, which has a monthly service charge.

continues

continued

> You can export an Office Live Collaboration list to a static table in a new or existing Access database or link to an Office Live Collaboration list. The process is almost the same as that for a WSS 3.0 site on your intranet. You must add your Office Live site to IE 7's Trusted Sites list and specify the site as a Trusted Location in the Access Options dialog.

Consider collaboration when you design your Access databases and applications, even if SharePoint isn't on your immediate horizon. In particular, try to use the AutoNumber data type for tables' primary key field whenever possible. It won't be long until SharePoint becomes the central information source for the overwhelming majority of teams, workgroups, and departments. You'll find that adapting your table designs to conform to SharePoint's preferences will save many hours of work when the time comes to move your data to SharePoint lists and link back to Access tables.

25

PROGRAMMING AND CONVERTING ACCESS APPLICATIONS

CHAPTER **26**

Automating Access Applications with Macros 2007

In this chapter

UNDERSTANDING THE ROLE OF MACROS IN ACCESS 2007

During Access's initial development, product management believed that Access 1.0's programming language—then called *Access Basic* and sometimes *Embedded Basic*—would be difficult for new users to master and would limit sales of Microsoft's fledgling desktop database application. Word for Windows 2.0 introduced WordBasic macros in 1991 and had gained at least a year of usage history before Access 1.0's November 1992 release.

Despite the popularity of Word 2.0 and its embedded programming language derived from the Dartmouth BASIC language, the Access team decided to develop a declarative programming methodology, which they originally called *scripts* and later referred to as *macros*. *Macros* is an abbreviation for macroinstructions, a term that means a collection of individual commands that issue many other (usually hidden) commands.

Bill Gates promoted WordBasic as a macro language, so Access Basic and, later, Visual Basic for Applications (VBA) became known as macro languages also. This chapter deals almost exclusively with declarative macros, which are an alternative to using the procedural VBA language to automate Access applications. If you're not familiar with a Windows programming language, such as Visual Basic or VBA, you'll probably find defining simple declarative macros to be easier than adding programming code to a module, form, or report.

If the process you're automating is complex or involves row-by-row processing of the Recordset that serves as the Record Source for your form or report, you'll undoubtedly need to write VBA code. The next four chapters of this part primarily cover VBA topics.

WHAT ARE ACCESS MACROS?

A macro is a list of actions to take in response to an event, a process often called "attaching a macro to an event." (In macro parlance, an *action* is a synonym for *command*.) Some events are occurrences of user actions, such as clicking a command button, opening or closing a form, or typing a value in a text box. Other events are generated by Access itself, such as starting up, beginning or completing the addition of a new row, or accepting or rejecting an edited value in an existing row.

> **NOTE**
>
> Only the AutoExec (automatically executing) macro can respond to Access starting up, so almost everyone uses this macro to execute initialization code or other macro actions.

Most macro actions have easily recognizable names, such as OpenForm, OpenReport, or Beep. Almost all actions require *arguments*. Arguments specify the object to which to apply the action, as well as the how the action is to be applied. Two arguments for the OpenForm action, for example, are Form Name and View. You set these argument values to specify the name of the form to open and its view: Form, Layout, or Design. In most cases, you select the action and argument value(s) from drop-down lists in a macro datasheet (usually abbreviated *macrosheet*) that you create in Access's Macro Builder. Figure 26.1 shows the Macro Builder with a macro that executes when you click the Collect Data via E-mail button (`cmdCollectDataViaEmail`) on the Tasks with Employees application's Task List form from Chapter 2, "Building Simple Tracking Applications."

Figure 26.1
Clicking the Collect Data via E-mail button in the Task List form's header executes these three macro actions (macroinstructions) in an embedded macrosheet.

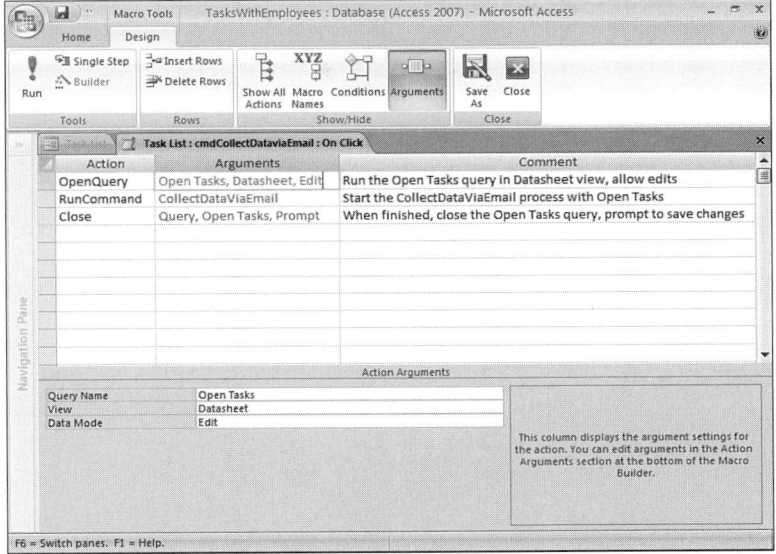

→ To review the Tasks with Employees enhanced template application, **see** "Integrating Objects from Other Template Databases," **p. 101**.

→ For an example of collecting data with an Outlook HTML form, **see** "Gathering Data by Email with HTML Forms," **p. 1043**.

26

TIP

> Online help's "Macros and Programmability, Macro Actions" topic has a complete list of all 72 macro actions with brief descriptions and a list and explanation of their arguments. This list is useful for both macro and VBA programmers because VBA executes macro actions as methods of the `Application` or `DoCmd` object.

HOW DO I VIEW A MACRO'S ACTIONS?

NEW Access 2007 introduces embedded macros, which are macros attached to forms. Embedded macros, sometimes called *macros behind forms*, correspond to VBA event-handling procedures embedded in form class modules, which often are referred to as *code behind forms* (CBF). Previous versions of Access offered standalone macros as database objects only. A standalone macro corresponds to VBA procedures in an Access module.

The Macro Builder is the same for embedded and standalone macros. To open the Macro Builder for an embedded macro, you must locate the event to which it's attached in the Property Sheet's Events page for its form or control object. For example, to open the macrosheet shown in Figure 26.1, do the following:

1. Open the Tasks with Employees.accdb database in the \SEUA12\Chaptr02 folder.
2. Open the Task List form in Layout or Design view.
3. Right-click the Collect Data via E-mail button (cmdCollectDataviaEmail) in the Form Header section, and choose Properties to open the Property Sheet for the button (see Figure 26.2).

Figure 26.2
An event with an embedded macro displays [Embedded Macro] in the event-handler list and a builder button to the right of the list.

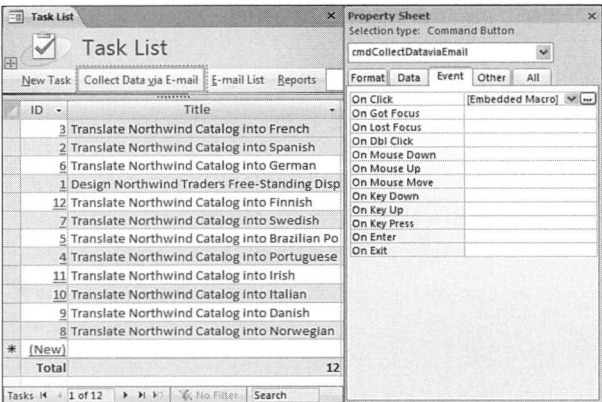

4. Click the builder button to open the Macro Builder with the macrosheet for the selected event.

> **TIP**
>
> It's quicker to right-click the control object and choose Build Event to open the Macro Builder directly. However, if the control doesn't have an event handler for its default event, the Choose Builder dialog opens.

Standalone macros, like other database objects, have names. To open the Macro Builder with a standalone macro, click its item in the Navigation Pane.

> **TIP**
>
> You'll find the description of the macro actions in the following list to be more useful if you open the builder and select each action in sequence.

The simple macro of Figure 26.1 executes the following three actions:

- `OpenQuery` executes the Open Tasks query, which is the Record Source for the Task List form in Datasheet view. You select Open Tasks from the Action Arguments pane's Query Name drop-down list of all Query objects in the application, select Datasheet as the View, and Edit as the Data Mode. This action refreshes the data behind the Task List form.

- `RunCommand`, which has a single argument (Command), performs the equivalent of clicking a ribbon's command button. In earlier Access versions, this action was called "executing a menu command." The Command drop-down list contains an entry for every native command, regardless of whether it is represented by a command button on a ribbon.

- `Close` closes the Open Tasks query by specifying Query as the Object Type, and Open Tasks as the Object Name.

The other buttons and the Reports combo box in the Form Header execute macros of similar or greater complexity. The ID and New Datasheet cells also execute macros to open the Task Details form with the data for the selected record or an empty form for adding a new Tasks record.

WHY USE MACROS INSTEAD OF VBA?

Microsoft promotes macros in online help as a "simplified programming language" and claims that "most people find it easier to build a macro than to write VBA code." Simplicity often has shortcomings, and easier doesn't necessarily mean better. However, the Access team has improved macros greatly in Access 2007. For example, embedded macros are an integral part of their containing form, so when you copy the form to the same or another database, the embedded macros copy with it. Access 2007's macros finally include error-handling with the `OnError` and `ClearMacroError` actions.

It's easier (and faster) to write macros for simple actions that don't involve complex conditional action execution. Conditional execution, controlled by VBA expressions in the Macro Builder's Conditions column, is difficult to debug. Macros are a good choice for executing a single command that has built-in error handling, such as the Next and Previous record navigation actions described in the next section.

Conditions execute VBA expressions that return **True** or **False**. If **True**, the associated action (and the following actions with ellipsis (...) in the Condition column, if any) execute. If the macro requires many actions and several conditions, it becomes difficult for anyone but the author to understand how it works or to debug it by single-stepping through the actions.

Another disadvantage of macros is their proprietary nature; proprietary to Microsoft *and Access*. As mentioned in later chapters, learning VBA lets you leverage your Office programming skills to all other members that use VBA: Word, Excel, Outlook, PowerPoint, and Visio. Gaining VBA skills also readies you for advancement to programming with Visual Basic .NET for a wider range of data-intensive desktop and web-based projects.

26

EXPLORING ACCESS 2007'S EVENT REPERTOIRE

When you interact with an Access object by using the keyboard or the mouse, you can change the object's state. The object's state is stored with the other data about the object. Access makes some of the changes in the object's state available as opportunities to interrupt normal processing. These special changes in an object's state are called *events*. An event is a change in the state of an object at which you can interrupt normal processing and define a response.

The best way to understand events is to categorize each by the type of action that causes the event to occur. There are 11 categories:

- *Mouse events* are triggered when you click form objects.
- *Keyboard events* are triggered by forms and form controls when you type or send keystrokes with the SendKeys action while the Form object has the focus.
- *Window events* are triggered by opening or closing forms or reports.
- *Focus events* are triggered when a form or form control gains or loses the focus or when a form or report becomes active or inactive.
- *Data events* are triggered by forms and form controls when you change data in controls or records, or by forms when the record pointer moves from one record to another.
- *Filter events* are triggered by forms when you apply or remove filters.
- *Print events* are triggered by reports and report sections when you print or preview a report.
- *Error events* are triggered by a form or report that has the focus when an error occurs.
- *Timing events* are triggered by forms when a specified time interval passes.
- *Class module* events fire when you open or close an instance of a VBA class. You use the With Events qualifier to intercept events from ActiveX Data Objects (ADO) and the RaiseEvent command to define custom events.
- *Reference events* fire when you add or remove a reference to an object or type library in the References collection.

Table 26.1 groups Access 2007's most commonly used events according to their source.

TABLE 26.1   EVENTS GROUPED BY CAUSE

Event Category	Source	Events
Mouse actions	The user creating mouse	Click
		DblClick
		MouseDown
		MouseUp
		MouseMove
		MouseWheel

Event Category	Source	Events
Keyboard	The user typing on the keyboard or SendKeys sending keystrokes	KeyDown KeyUp KeyPress
Window	Opening, closing, or resizing a window	Open Load Unload Close Resize
Focus	An object losing or gaining the focus, or a form or report becoming active or inactive	Enter GotFocus Exit LostFocus Activate Deactivate
Data	Making changes to a control's data, displaying records in a form, or moving the focus from one record to another in a form	Current BeforeInsert AfterInsert Delete BeforeDelConfirm AfterDelConfirm BeforeUpdate AfterUpdate Change Updated Dirty NotInList Undo
Filter	Opening or closing a filter window, or applying or removing a filter	Filter ApplyFilter
Print	Selecting or arranging data for printing	Format Print Retreat NoData Page
Error	Generating an error	Error
Timing	A specified period of time expiring	Timer
Class Module	Opening a new instance of *Class Module* or terminating an instance of *Class Module*	Initialize Terminate
Reference	Adding or removing a reference to an object or type library	ItemAdded ItemRemoved

26

The Dirty event (and Dirty property) of bound forms and their controls is one of the most useful members of Access's event repertoire. The Dirty event fires and the Dirty property is set to True when you change underlying data by typing in a bound text box or combo box, or change a page by clicking a Tab control. The Dirty event doesn't fire if you change a value with code, nor does it fire for any action on an unbound form. The Undo event is the reverse of the Dirty event; returning data in the form to its original, unmodified state fires the Undo event.

Each event that an object triggers has a corresponding event property listed in a separate category of the object's Property Sheet. Usually the corresponding event property is the event name preceded by the word *On*. For example, the Click event triggered by a command button becomes the On Click property in the button's property sheet.

Figure 26.3 shows the Event page of the Property Sheet for a bound text box displaying the 17 events that the control can trigger. Notice that all event properties—except the Before Update and After Update data event properties—follow the pattern of preceding the event name with "On". A default drop-down list, which lets you select [Event Procedure] (but not [Embedded Macro]), and a builder button appear in the first event, unless another event has been assigned a VBA or macro event handler. Clicking the builder button for an empty event opens the Choose Builder dialog, which lets you open an empty Macro Builder macrosheet, Expression Builder dialog, or Code Builder (VBA Code Editor window) when you click OK.

Figure 26.3
Text boxes fire 17 different events. Clicking the builder button for an empty event opens the Choose Builder dialog.

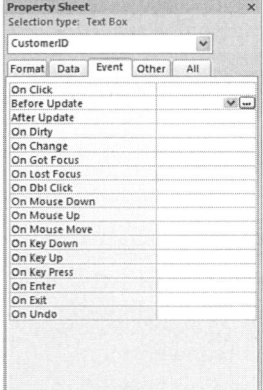 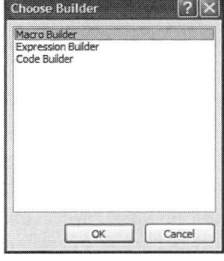

NOTE

Events are the same for embedded macros and VBA event procedures, which Access considers to be interchangeable event handlers.

GENERATING EMBEDDED MACROS WITH THE COMMAND BUTTON WIZARD

 The most common use for macros is handling the On Click event of buttons (called Command Buttons in earlier Access versions) to display objects or move the record pointer of the recordset to which the form is bound. When you add a Button control to a form with Control Wizards enabled, the Command Button Wizard's first dialog displays Categories and Actions lists. When you select a category, the most popular actions in that category appear in the Actions list.

For example, you can supplement the miniature VCR-style Navigation Buttons gadget at the bottom of the form with a set of four more-evident and easier-to-hit buttons in the form header of a split form. Figure 26.4 shows the result of adding four navigation buttons to the Details section of a split form.

Figure 26.4
Large record navigation buttons are more evident than the small VCR versions in the Navigation Buttons object. Record navigation requires error handling; for example, the macro displays the message "You can't go to the specified record" when you click the previous button when the record pointer is on the first record.

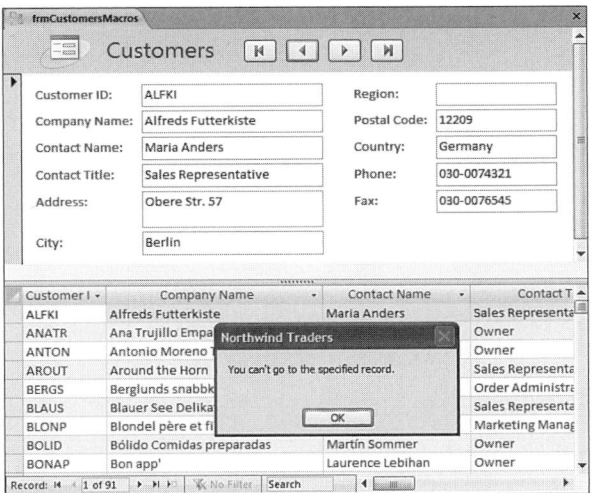

To add a Previous Record navigation button with the Command Button Wizard, do the following:

1. Create a split form based on a table, such as Customers, and change to Design view.

2. With the Use Control Wizards button of the Form Design Tools – Design ribbon activated, click the Button button and draw a button in the Header section of the form to open the first Command Button Wizard dialog.

3. With the default Record Navigation category selected, select Previous Record in the Actions list (see Figure 26.5).

Figure 26.5
Select the category and the action to perform when handling the On Click event of a button in the first Command Button Wizard dialog.

4. Click Next, accept the default Picture option, and mark the Show All Pictures check box to display a list of all bitmaps available to the Wizard (see Figure 26.6).

Figure 26.6
Select between a text caption or a bitmap icon for the action in the second Wizard dialog.

5. Click Next and replace the default control name (Command#) with a more descriptive name, such as **btnPrevious** (see Figure 26.7).

Figure 26.7
Add a descriptive name for the button, such as btnPrevious, to complete the Wizard's task.

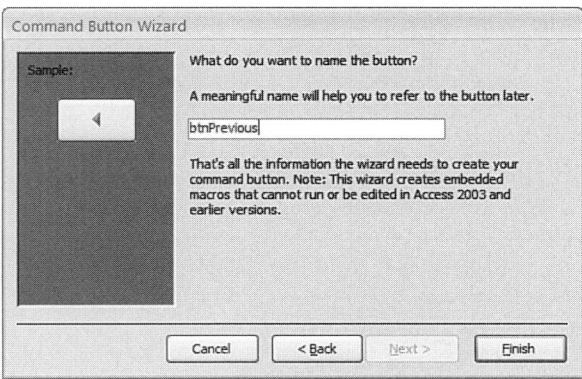

6. Click Finish to dismiss the Wizard, right-click the button you added, and choose Properties to open the Property Sheet.

7. Click the Events tab and click the On Click event's Builder button to open the Macro Builder with the Wizard-generated macrosheet (see Figure 26.8).

Figure 26.8
The Wizard generates a macro with a condition that ignores the error caused by attempting to move the record pointer before the beginning of the file (BOF).

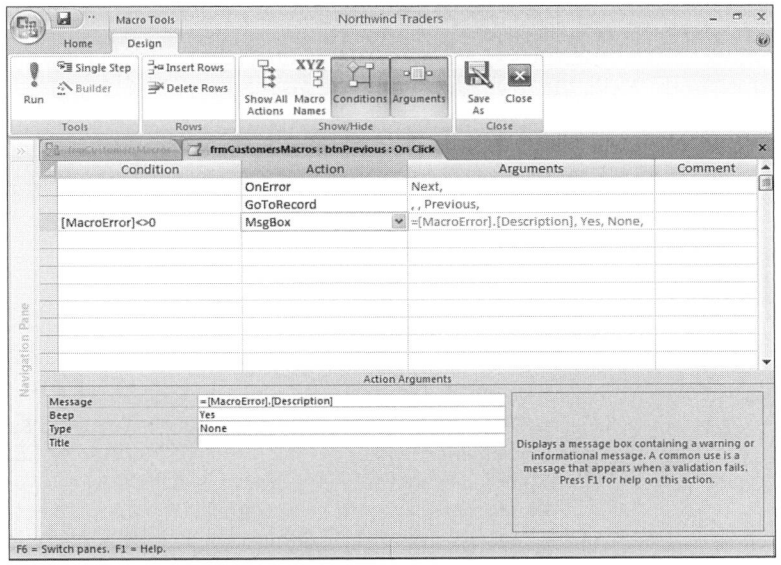

If the On Click event shows [Event Procedure] instead of [Embedded Macro], see the "Control Wizards Don't Generate Embedded Macros" topic of the "Troubleshooting" section near the end of this chapter.

26

The macrosheet for btnPrevious of Figure 26.8 demonstrates the most common method of error handling by macros:

1. Ignore errors initially by specifying OnError as the first action with Next (step) as its arguments. The other allowable argument values are Macro Name to execute a specified macro and Fail (quit with an unrecoverable error).

2. Execute the action that might generate an error; in this case, GoToRecord with , , Previous, as its argument values. The three commas are placeholders for empty Object Type, Object Name, and Offset property values.

3. Detect whether an error occurred in the preceding step(s) by the [MacroError]<>0 condition. Errors thrown by macro actions are identified by integer values. If the preceding step(s) succeed, continue. If there are no more steps, exit the macrosheet.

4. If an error occurred, display a MsgBox (message box) with =[MacroError]. [Description], Yes, None, argument values for Message, Beep, Type, and Title. If you select Warning! as the Type, and type **Previous Record Navigation Error** as the Title, the message box appears as shown in Figure 26.9.

Figure 26.9
Compare this modified message box with that shown in Figure 26.4.

Empty `Object Type` and `Object Name` arguments in an embedded macro refer to the container (in this case, the form containing the macro).

NOTE

> The actions of the preceding macrosheet correspond to the following VBA event-handling subprocedure:
>
> ```
> Private Sub btnPrevious_Click()
>     On Error Resume Next
>     DoCmd.GoToRecord , , acPrevious
>     If Err.Number > 0 Then
>         MsgBox Err.Description
>     End If
> End Sub
> ```
>
> It's clear that creating the embedded macro with the Command Button Wizard will always be faster than writing the preceding code. However, the advantage of VBA code is that all procedures are visible in a single page in the VBA Editor. Further, the VBA Editor provides IntelliSense and statement completion, which reduce errors caused by typing incorrect values for conditional statements or arguments. Finally, the ability to scroll through all code behind the form, instead of opening individual macrosheets for each event handler, aids your understanding of programming structure and makes troubleshooting much quicker.

The \SEUA12\Chaptr26\Macros26.accdb sample database's frmCustomersMacros form incorporates the preceding embedded macro.

Table 26.2 lists the Command Button Wizard's action categories and their actions.

TABLE 26.2 COMMAND BUTTON WIZARD ACTIONS GROUPED BY CATEGORIES

Category	Action
Record Navigation	Find Next
	Find Record
	Go To First Record
	Go To Last Record
	Go To Next Record
	Go To Previous Record

Category	Action
Record Operations	Add New Record
	Delete Record
	Duplicate Record
	Print Record
	Save Record
	Undo Record
Form Operations	Apply Form Filter
	Close Form
	Print a Form
	Print Current Form
	Refresh Form Data
Report Operations	Mail Report
	Open Report
	Preview Report
	Print Report
	Send Report to File
Application	Quit Application
Miscellaneous	Autodialer
	Print Table
	Run Macro
	Run Query

It's evident from the preceding table that most actions of Wizard-based buttons substitute buttons on forms for command buttons on ribbons. The primary advantage of buttons on forms over buttons on ribbons is that macro arguments can specify a particular object as the target of the action.

→ For a list of the most commonly used actions, **see** " Working with Access 2007's DoCmd Methods," **p. 1223**.

RESPONDING TO EVENTS FROM COMBO AND LIST BOXES

The most common application for combo boxes is to insert a value selected from a list into a data cell of the current record of the data source for a form. Combo boxes used to insert values in Recordsets are called "bound." An unbound combo box can pass its selected value to a macro that finds and displays a particular record or set of records. In most cases, you use the Combo Box Wizard to populate the combo box's list from a table or query.

26

CREATE A CATEGORY COMBO BOX WITH THE WIZARD

To add to a new split form an unbound combo box that ultimately selects the category of products to display, do the following:

1. In Northwind.accdb or your working database, select the Products table in the Navigation Pane, click the Create tab, and click the Split Form button to generate a split form from the Products table.

2. Change to Design view and, with the Control Wizards button active, draw a Combo Box control on to the Form Header section. When you release the mouse button, the Combo Box Wizard opens its first dialog.

3. Accept the default option (I Want the Combo Box to Look Up the Values in a Table or Query), and click Next.

4. With the default Tables option selected, select Categories in the list box and then click Next.

5. Click the >> button to add the CategoryID and CategoryName fields to the combo box's Selected Fields list, and click Next.

6. Optionally, apply an ascending sort on the CategoryID field, and click Next.

7. Double-click the right edge of the Category Name column to best-fit the column width, verify that the Hide Key Column check box is marked (see Figure 26.10), and click Next.

Figure 26.10
Setting the column width isn't important, but hiding the key field (CategoryID) prevents confusing users with more information than they need.

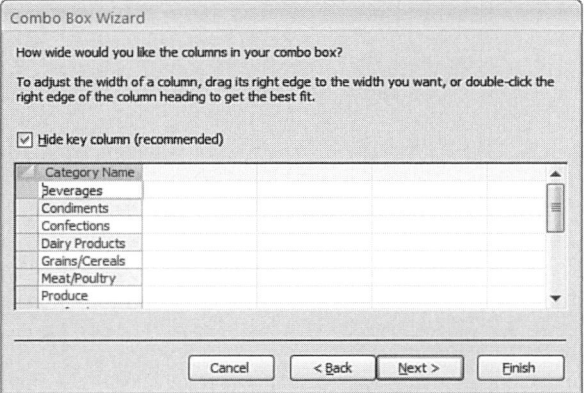

8. Accept the default option (Remember the Value for Later Use) to create an unbound combo box, and click Next.

9. Type **Select Category:** as the label name, and click Finish to dismiss the Wizard.

10. Adjust the position of the combo box and its label, and optionally change the label text's size and color.

11. Right-click the combo box, choose Properties to open the Property Sheet, click the Other tab, and change the Name property value from Combo20 (or the like) to **cboCategory**. At this point, your Products form in Design view appears similar to Figure 26.11.

Figure 26.11
Give the Wizard-created combo box a meaningful name by opening its properties sheet and clicking the Other or All tab. The cbo prefix is an abbreviation for "Combo".

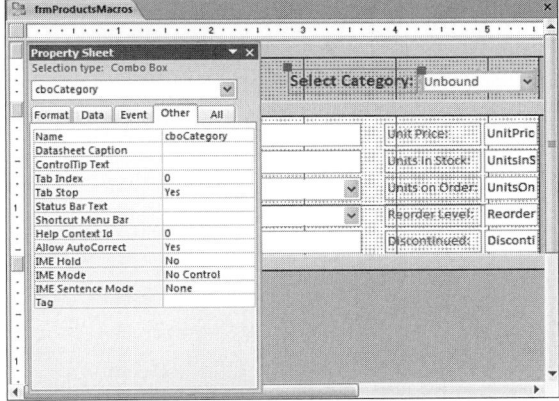

12. Save your form as **frmProductsMacros** or the like and remain in Design view with the cboCategory control's Property Sheet open.

WRITE AND TEST AN EMBEDDED APPLYFILTER MACRO

The final step is to write an embedded macro that applies an appropriate filter to a form's record source (the Products table) depending on the CategoryName value you select in the combo box. You can obtain online help with macro action syntax by typing the action name in the Search text box, pressing Enter, and clicking the *ActionName* Macro Action link. Figure 26.12 shows the online help topic for the ApplyFilter macro action.

> **NOTE**
> The help topic for the ApplyFilter macro has a note that's incorrect. Only ADPs support server filters, so the note doesn't apply to conventional .accdb database applications.

The help topic's sample macro uses Condition tests for the first letter of a company name. You can use a similar approach to generate a filter for each of the eight CategoryID values. Table 26.3 is an abbreviated list of the nine macrosheet entries.

26

Figure 26.12
Access's online help topic for the ApplyFilter macro has a sample macro at the bottom.

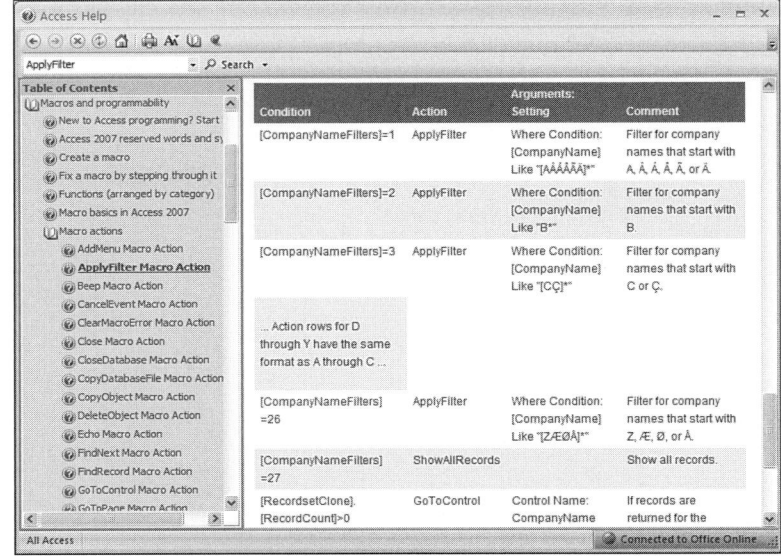

TABLE 26.3 FIVE OF THE NINE MACROSHEET ENTRIES FOR THE frmPRODUCTSMACRO SPLIT FORM

Condition	Action	Argument	Comment
(none)	ShowAllRecords	None	Clear a previous filter
[cboCategory]=1	ApplyFilter	, [CategoryID]=1,	Beverages
[cboCategory]=2	ApplyFilter	, [CategoryID]=2,	Condiments
...			
[cboCategory]=7	ApplyFilter	, [CategoryID]=7,	Produce
[cboCategory]=8	ApplyFilter	, [CategoryID]=8,	Seafood

NOTE

The preceding and trailing commas of the Arguments column entries represent unused Filter Name and Control Name argument values. This example and most ApplyFilter macros use the Where Condition argument only.

To open the macrosheet and add the nine required items, do the following:

1. Click the Property Sheet's Events tab, click the AfterUpdate builder button to open the Choose Builder dialog, select Macro Builder, and click OK to open an empty macrosheet.

2. In the first row, open the Action list and choose ShowAllRecords. This action removes the filter applied previously, if any.

3. In the second row, type **[cboCategory]=1** in the Condition column, select ApplyFilter in the Action list, and type **[CategoryID]=1** in the Where Condition text box. Optionally, type the corresponding CategoryName value in the Comments column.

4. Repeat step 3 for each of the remaining seven categories, incrementing the two CategoryID numbers by 1. Your macrosheet appears as shown in Figure 26.13 when you are done.

Figure 26.13
The completed macrosheet has a conditional ApplyFilter action for each of the eight CategoryID values.

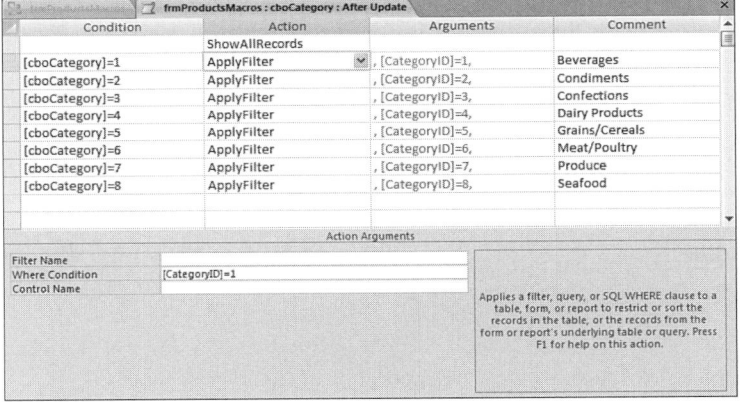

TIP
Entry will go faster if you copy [cboCategory]= to the Clipboard, paste it seven times in the Condition column, and then add the number. Similarly, copy [CategoryID]= to the Clipboard and do the same for the Where Condition text box.

5. Click the Close button to close the macrosheet and save your changes.

6. Click the Property Sheet's Data tab, change the object list from cboCategory to Form, and verify that the form's Data Source property value is Properties. If the property value is an SQL Select * From … statement, open the list and select Products.

7. Change to Form view and test the eight category choices in the combo box. Notice that the Filtered indicator is present at the bottom of the Datasheet and that you can remove and reapply the filter by clicking the Toggle Filter button (see Figure 26.14).

Figure 26.14
Selecting a category applies the appropriate filter and positions the record pointer on the first product record in the category.

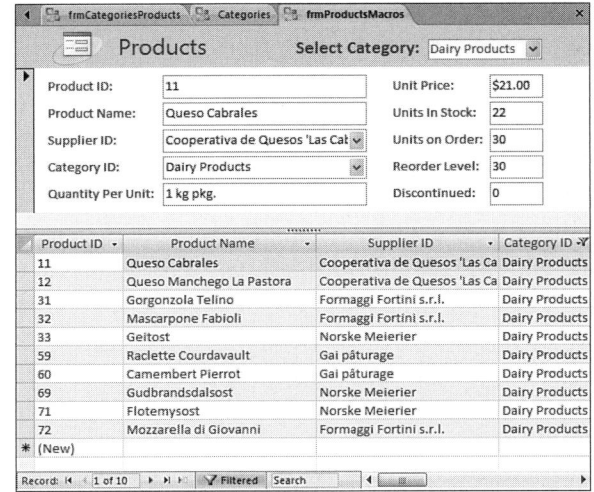

 8. Close the form, save your changes, and then reopen the form and repeat step 7.

 If you see only rows for a single category when you reopen the form and changing to another category displays no rows in the Datasheet, see the "Form Is Filtered Before Selecting a Category" topic of the "Troubleshooting" section near the end of this chapter.

The \SEUA12\Chaptr26\Macros26.accdb sample database's frmProductsMacro form incorporates the preceding embedded macro.

EXPLORING ACCESS 2007'S MACRO-BASED SWITCHBOARD MANAGER

One of the Access team's goals in moving to tabbed documents and replacing the Database Window of earlier Access versions with the Navigation Pane was to eliminate the need for switchboards. A *switchboard* usually is a hierarchical collection of relatively small forms with groups of command buttons to execute common tasks, such as opening closed forms, printing reports, or setting the focus to a form that has been overlaid by other forms, reports, or both. Figure 26.15 shows the default form (top) of a simple switchboard with buttons that open other switchboard forms (bottom)

NOTE

A custom ribbon is a much better application navigation aid than an Access switchboard, but designing custom ribbons with the declarative RibbonX XML "language" and handling callbacks—even from simple command button clicks—with VBA isn't a walk in the park.

→ For an example of adding a group and buttons to Access's ribbon UI, **see** "Customizing Applications with Ribbon Objects," **p. 1226**.

Figure 26.15
This simple switch-board created by Access's Switchboard Manager has a two-layer hierarchy. The first four buttons on the default form (top) open second-level forms that open forms and reports (bottom).

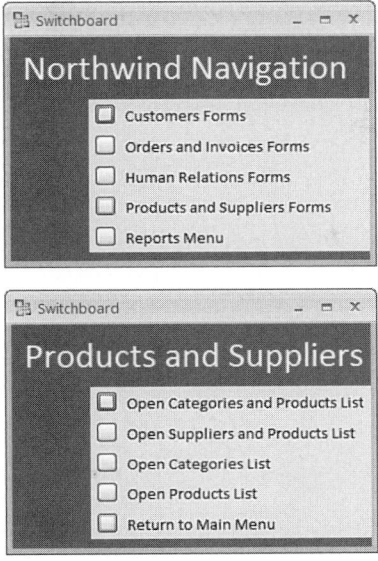

Access includes a Switchboard Manager utility for creating standardized switchboards. You create a new switchboard by clicking the Database Tools ribbon's Switchboard Manager button to open a message box that asks if you want to create a switchboard. If you answer yes, the Manager creates an empty default Switchboard form and a Switchboard Items table to hold button specifications. You can select one of the actions shown in Figure 26.16 and Table 26.4 for each button.

Figure 26.16
Switchboard buttons can initiate one of the eight actions you select from the drop-down list.

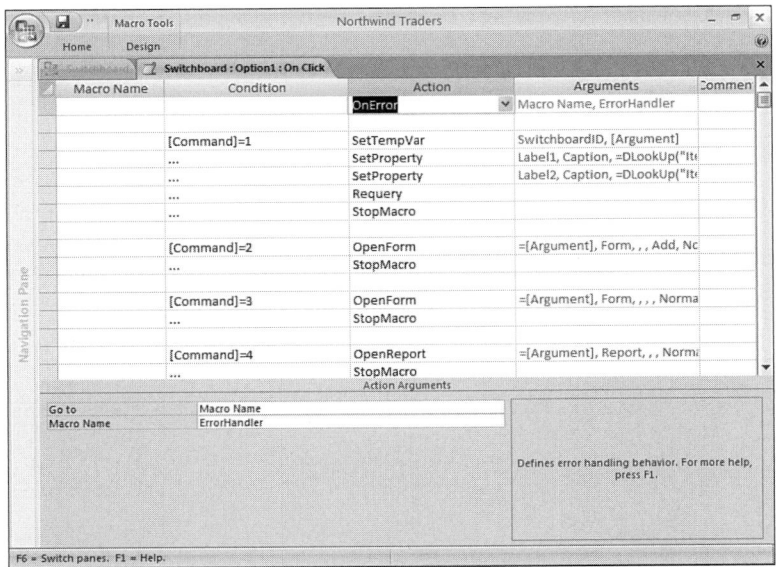

TABLE 26.4   SWITCHBOARD BUTTON ACTIONS AND ARGUMENTS

Action (Command)	Argument
1 - Go To Switchboard	Switchboard Form Name
2 - Open Form in Add Mode	Form Name
3 - Open Form in Edit Mode	Form Name
4 - Open Report	Report Name
5 - Design Application	(none, opens Switchboard Manager)
6 - Exit Application	(none)
7 - Run Macro	Macro Name (standalone)
8 - Run Code	Function Name (in module)

The original Switchboard Manager executed Access Basic or VBA event handlers in the form's class module to perform the specified actions. Apparently, the Access team believed that switchboards weren't fully obsolete, so they replaced earlier versions' VBA code with the embedded macro shown in Table 26.5.

TABLE 26.5   CONDITIONS, ACTIONS, AND ARGUMENTS FOR SWITCHBOARD MANAGER OPTIONS

Macro Name	Condition	Action	Arguments
		OnError	MacroName, ErrorHandler
Go To Switchboard	[Command]=1	SetTempVar	SwitchboardID, [Argument]
	...	Set Property	Label1, Caption, =DLookUp("ItemText", "Switchboard Items", "[SwitcboardID"))
	...	Set Property	Label2, Caption, =DLookUp("ItemText","Switchboard Items","[SwitchboardID] = " & TempVars("SwitchboardID"))
	...	Requery	
	...	Stop Macro	
Open Form (Add)	[Command]=2	OpenForm	=[Argument], Form, , , Add, Normal
	...	StopMacro	
Open Form (Edit)	[Command]=3	OpenForm	=[Argument], Form, , , Add, Normal
	...	StopMacro	

Macro Name	Condition	Action	Arguments
Open Report	[Command]=4 ...	OpenReport StopMacro	=[Argument], Report, , , Normal
Design Application	[Command]=5	RunCommand	SwitchboardManager
	...	SetTempVar	SwitchboardID, DLookUp("SwitchboardID", "Switchboard Items", "[ItemNumber] = 0 AND [Argument] = 'Default'")
	...	SetProperty	Label1, Caption, =DLookUp("ItemText","Switchboard Items", "[SwitchboardID] = " & TempVars("SwitchboardID"))
	...	SetProperty	Label2, Caption, =DLookUp("ItemText", "Switchboard Items", "[SwitchboardID] = " & TempVars("SwitchboardID"))
	...	Requery	
	...	StopMacro	
Exit Application	[Command]=6 ...	CloseDatabase StopMacro	
Run Macro	[Command]=7 ...	RunMacro StopMacro	=[Argument], ,
Run Code	[Command]=8 ...	RunCode StopMacro	=[Argument] & "()"
Unknown Option		MsgBox	Unknown option., Yes, None,
ErrorHandler		MsgBox	=[MacroError].[Description], Yes, None,

26

The \SEUA12\Chaptr26\Macros26.accdb sample database's Switchboard form incorporates the preceding embedded macro.

Macro names, other than ErrorHandler, in Table 26.5 are for reference to the actions (commands) listed in Table

NOTE

26.4. Adding the eight command names prevents the macro from executing.
[NEW] Table 26.5 provides examples of commands for common macro

operations, including domain lookup (DLookup) operations on table data to set temporary variables (TempVars), which are a new feature in Access 2007, and to deliver argument values to set Label captions.

Use the assignment operator (=) to simplify macrosheets that require only changes to argument values, not action types. For example, you can reduce the eight `ApplyFilter` actions in the macro of Table 26.3 to a single `ApplyFilter` action with =, `"[cboCategory]="` & `[cboCategory`, as the Where Condition argument.

 The \SEUA12\Chaptr26\Macros26.accdb sample database's frmProductsMacro2 form incorporates the preceding embedded macro.

TROUBLESHOOTING

CONTROL WIZARDS DON'T GENERATE EMBEDDED MACROS

Instead of [Embedded Macro], events with builder buttons in the Events page of Property Sheets display [Event Procedure].

The most likely cause of this error is that the Always Use Event Procedures check box is marked in the Access Options dialog's Object Designers page. To enforce the Access team's macros-over-VBA-code priority, marking this check box prevents the Control Wizards from generating VBA code. (The Control Wizards do generate VBA event-handling code for forms and reports in .mdb files.)

To solve this problem, do the following:

1. Click the Office Button and the Access <u>O</u>ptions link to open the Access Options dialog.
2. Click the Object Designers button and scroll to the Forms/Reports section.
3. Mark the Always Use <u>E</u>vent Procedures check box.
4. Close the dialog to return to your project.

FORM IS FILTERED BEFORE SELECTING A CATEGORY

When I open a form to which I've added a macro with ApplyFilter actions after saving it, the Datasheet or form shows a selection I didn't make. When I make another filter selection, no rows appear in the Datasheet or the form shows the tentative append record instead of a record from the selection.

When you saved the changes to the form after creating and testing the macrosheet with the ApplyFilter actions in it, the form's Data Source property value changed from the table you selected when you created the form to `Select * From TableName Where ConditionColumn=[']CriterionValue[']`. (Single quotes appear only for string criteria.) For this chapter's ApplyFilter example, the errant SQL statement is `Select * From Products Where CategoryID = 1` or another number up to 8. This persistent filter doesn't turn on the form's Filtered indicator and prevents any other selection from displaying rows.

To solve the problem, open the form in Layout or Design view and change the form's Data Source property value to the original *TableName*. If the original Data Source property value was a query, remove the column that creates the permanent filter.

IN THE REAL WORLD—MACROS REDUX?

Most professional Access 1.0, 1.1, and 2.0 developers eschewed macros in favor of Access Basic code in modules because the programming language—even in its early development stages—was much more versatile than macro actions. Macros had no means of responding to operating errors other than to quit. But you could program Access Basic to ignore them or take a specific action, such as display a message box, when an error occurred. Access 95 traded 16-bit Access Basic for 32-bit VBA and macros fell into "official" disfavor at Microsoft. Access 95 through 2003 included macro features "for backward compatibility," which implied that macros were on their way out. Adding fuel to the "no more macros" fire, Microsoft developed a Macro-to-Module converter for Access 95 and later versions to transform macros into VBA event-handling procedures with error-trapping capability.

Seasoned Access users and developers were surprised by Microsoft's reindoctrination of its customers in macro technology for Access 2007. Ostensibly, the resurrection of macros is the result of Microsoft's desire to create codeless applications that users can email as enclosures to one another and open without displaying a macro warning. It's easy to prevent Access applications containing VBA code from opening a macro warning; simply place the .accdb or .accde file in a trusted location. Emailing Access applications is a very uncommon practice, so it's more likely that the resurgence of Microsoft's interest in macros is to make Access appear "more friendly" to new users.

> **NOTE**
>
> Another reason for promoting Access macros as a substitute for VBA is to enhance competition with FileMaker, Inc.'s, FileMaker Pro. FileMaker Pro users build with the ScriptMaker feature macro-like *script steps* that execute commands, such as Perform Find, Show All Records, and Sort Records. FileMaker, Inc., which is a subsidiary of Apple, Inc., is Access's only serious competitor in the desktop database market.

26

The resurgence of Microsoft's interest in peddling macros is to be deflected by Access users and developers alike for at least four reasons:

- There's no VBA-to-macro converter. Converting a fixed set of macro actions with defined arguments to VBA isn't easy, but it's obviously doable. The reverse is impossible. This fact alone should have made the Access team reconsider their decision to renovate macros.

- Switchboards aren't compatible with tabbed documents and the Navigation Pane, which was designed specifically to replace switchboard forms.

- Customized ribbons have the potential to replace switchboards and are a much more flexible navigation aid than buttons on hierarchical forms. VBA code is required to handle callbacks from the controls you add to ribbons.

- VBA code is necessary to obtain fine-grained management of Recordsets, including row-by-row operations in loops.

The next four chapters dig deeply into VBA programming with only brief nods to macros, where appropriate. The best advice is to use macros sparingly, if at all. Bite the bullet and learn VBA.

LEARNING VISUAL BASIC FOR APPLICATIONS

In this chapter

UNDERSTANDING THE ROLE OF VBA IN ACCESS

Historically, productivity applications—such as the members of Microsoft Office—have used macros (short for macroinstructions) to automate repetitive operations. Microsoft Word and Excel, for instance, let you capture a sequence of menu choices, mouse clicks, and keyboard operations. You save the captured sequence as a macro that you subsequently execute from a menu choice or a shortcut-key combination. The macros in recent versions of Word and Excel consist of Visual Basic for Applications (VBA) code, but you don't need to understand VBA programming to create and execute Word and Excel macros. Unfortunately, the keyboard and mouse actions you use with Access applications don't translate to a usable macro. For better or worse, automation of Access applications requires programming.

> **NOTE**
>
> Access macros, the subject of Chapter 26, "Automating Access Applications with Macros 2007," were called *scripts* during Access 1.0's early development. The original Access team wanted to distinguish Access macros from event-handling procedures written in *Access Basic*, which at first was called *Embedded Basic*, and WordBASIC or Excel macros. It's unfortunate that the term *script* wasn't retained when Microsoft released Access 1.0.

Simple Access applications require you to write little or no VBA code. Most users of early versions of Access wrote Access macros, rather than various flavors of Access Basic to automate their applications. As you learned in Chapter 26, Access macros define actions, such as opening a form, that you assign to events, such as clicking a command button. Starting with Access 95, Microsoft recommended that you use VBA code instead of macros, with the clear implication that macros might not be supported in future versions of Access. The Microsoft documentation for Access 97 through 2003 states that macro support primarily is for backward compatibility. In Access 2007, you use macros to work around security issues that users might encounter with applications that contain VBA code.

This chapter describes VBA, introduces you to VBA modules and procedures that replace or augment the capabilities of Access macros, shows you how to use the new VBA editor to write and test VBA code, and helps you start writing user-defined functions. The chapter also includes examples of simple VBA programs.

> **NOTE**
>
> Version 6.0 is Microsoft's *last* upgrade to VBA and traditional Visual Basic; there have been no significant changes to VBA in Access 2000 and later. Visual Basic .NET has captured the development resources formerly devoted to VBA and VB 6.0.

GETTING ACQUAINTED WITH VBA 6.0

VBA is a real programming language, not a macro language. You create the preferred equivalent of macros with VBA functions and subprocedures. Although you can execute VBA subprocedures directly from an open code module, you more typically execute VBA subprocedures from user-initiated events, such as clicking a command button or changing the current record of a bound form. (Chapter 28, "Handling Events with VBA and Macros," explains how to use VBA subprocedures as event-handlers.) You execute VBA functions by calling them from calculated controls in forms and reports, from the Validation Rule property value of a field or table, or from within a VBA subprocedure.

WHERE YOU USE VBA CODE

Short VBA procedures using the `DoCmd` object usually are sufficient to provide the methods needed by simple applications to run queries, display forms, and print reports. The Access-specific `DoCmd` object lets you run any macro action from VBA as a method of the `DoCmd` object. For example, executing `DoCmd.OpenForm("FormName")` opens the `FormName` form.

You might want or need to use VBA code for any of the following reasons:

- To create user-defined functions (UDFs) that substitute for complex expressions you use repeatedly to validate input data, compute values for text boxes, and perform other duties. Creating a UDF that you refer to by a short name minimizes potential typing errors and lets you document the way your expressions work.

- To write query expressions that include more complex decision structures than allowed by VBA's inline `IIf` function (in an `If…Then…Else…End If` structure, for example), or to write expressions that need loops for repetitive operations.

> **NOTE**
>
> You can't incorporate VBA in T-SQL queries, so queries that include VBA user-defined functions won't upsize to SQL Server databases.

- To write and execute `SELECT` queries with `WHERE` clauses or other SQL elements whose values come from controls on forms, such as list or combo boxes.

- To execute transaction processing SQL statements with `BEGIN TRANSACTION`, `COMMIT TRANSACTION`, and `ROLLBACK TRANSACTION` keywords against Access or SQL Server databases.

- To manipulate ActiveX controls and other applications' objects with Automation code.

- To open more than one database in an Access application where attaching a table or using the Access SQL `IN` statement isn't sufficient for your application.

- To provide hard-copy documentation for your application. If you execute actions from VBA code, you can print the code to improve the documentation for your application.

 - To provide graceful error handling if something goes wrong in your application. With VBA code, you can closely control how your application responds to errors such as missing data, incorrect values entered by a user, and other problems. Error handling by the new OnError macro isn't as versatile as that provided by VBA.

27

SECURITY ISSUES WITH VBA CODE

All Office applications that support VBA macros must contend with the possibility that hackers will embed malicious VBA code in a document or database file. Any VBA code or Access function or property that can run external programs (for example, the `Shell` function) or create, alter, or delete directories or files, such as the VBA `Kill` statement or Access `ExportXML` function, is potentially malicious. Access 2000 and later define Sandbox modes that are intended to prevent execution of potentially malicious code unless specifically authorized by the user. Alternatively, you can sign your Access application with a trusted certificate to enable all VBA code and Access functions to execute, and permit Access objects to use otherwise-forbidden property values.

Signing code requires renting a code-signing certificate from a certification authority (CA), such as VeriSign or Thawte, that's included in Internet Explorer's Trusted Root Certification Authorities list. Access 2007 enables applications installed in *trusted locations* (folders) to run all VBA code and Access expressions. Access 2007 also replaces Access 2003's confusing security setting message boxes with the Office trust bar.

TYPOGRAPHIC AND NAMING CONVENTIONS USED FOR VBA

This book uses a special set of typographic conventions for references to VBA keywords and object variable names in VBA examples:

- `Monospace` type is used for all VBA code in the examples, as in `lngItemCounter`.
- **`Bold monospace`** type is used for all VBA reserved words and type-declaration symbols, as in **`Dim`** and **`%`**. (Type-declaration symbols aren't used in this book; instead, your VBA code defines the data type of each variable prior to use.) Standard function names in VBA, such as those as described in Chapter 10, "Understanding Access Operators and Expressions," also are set in bold type so that reserved words, standard function names, and reserved symbols stand out from variable names, function names, and values you assign to variables. Keywords incorporated by reference in Access, such as `DoCmd` (an Access-specific object) or `Recordset` (a data-specific object), are not set in bold type.

→ To review some of the VBA functions and their descriptions, **see** "Functions for Date and Time," **p. XXX** *(Ch 10)* and "Text Manipulation Functions," **p. XXX** *(Ch 10)*.

- *`Italic monospace`* type indicates a replaceable item, also called a placeholder, as in **`Dim`** *`DataItem`* **`As String`**. *`DataItem`* is replaced by a name that you supply.
- ***`Bold-italic monospace`*** type indicates a replaceable reserved word, such as a data type, as in **`Dim`** *`DataItem`* **`As`** ***`DataType`***; ***`DataType`*** is replaced by a VBA reserved word corresponding to the desired VBA data type, such as **`String`** or **`Object`**.
- Names of variables that refer to Jet and Access objects, such as queries, forms, or reports, use a three-letter prefix derived from the object name, as in `qryFormName`, `frmFormName`, and `rptReportName`. SQL Server objects use two-letter prefixes for views, functions, and stored procedures—`vwViewName`, `fnFunctionName`, `spProcedureName`. With a few exceptions, this book doesn't use prefixes for table or field names.

Most of the three-letter prefixes used in this book correspond to those recommended by Microsoft or the "Leszynski Naming Conventions for Access," a white paper published more than 10 years ago by Stan Leszynski, then of Kwery Corporation.

- Names of all other variables are preceded by a three-letter data type identifier, such as var*VariantVariable* (**Variant**) and int*IntegerVariable* (**Integer**). Variables representing instances of objects use an arbitrary three-letter prefix, such as cht*Object* for a PivotChart, or the obj prefix if the object type isn't an Access object.

- Optional elements appear in the text within square brackets, as in [*OptionItem*]. If you add the optional element, you don't type the brackets. Square brackets also enclose object names that contain spaces or special punctuation symbols for compatibility with Access SQL and T-SQL. In this case, your code must contain the square brackets.

- Elements that require you to choose from a set of alternatives are enclosed with French braces and separated by pipe symbols, as in **Do {While¦Until}** *Expression*…**Loop**.

- An ellipsis (…) substitutes for code that isn't shown in syntax and code examples, as in **If…Then…Else…End If**.

MODULES, FUNCTIONS, AND SUBPROCEDURES

A *module* is a container for VBA code, just as a form is a container for control objects. Access 2007 provides the following four types of modules:

- **Access modules**—You create an Access module to contain your VBA code the same way that you create any other new database object: Click the Insert tab's Advanced button in the Other group, and then choose Module. Figure 27.1 shows the IsLoaded() function of the Utility Functions module of \SEUA12\Nwind\Northwind.accdb. Access modules are also called *standard modules*.

Figure 27.1
The VBA editor displays the IsLoaded() function of the Utility Functions module.

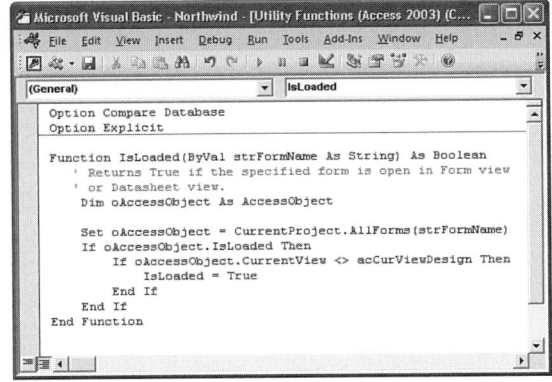

27

■ **Form modules**—Form modules contain code to respond to events triggered by forms or controls on forms. Essentially, when you add VBA code to a form object, you create a new class of object in the database. The event-handling procedures you create for the form are its new class's methods, hence the term *class module* for the code module associated with a particular form. You open a form module by clicking the View Code button of the Design tab's Tools group in Form Design view. This action opens a module that Access automatically names `Form_FormName`, where `FormName` is the name of the selected form. Forms in Access 2007 have a `HasModule` property. If this read-only property is set to Yes, then the form has a class module; otherwise, it doesn't.

TIP

Another method of opening a form module is to click the Builder button for one of the event properties for a form or a control object on a form. Selecting Code Builder from the Choose Builder dialog displays the `Form_FormName` module with a procedure stub, **Private Sub** `ObjectName_EventName()`...**End Sub**, written for you. Access 2007 adds the VBA **Private** prefix by default. Figure 27.2 shows the VBA code for the `CustomerID_AfterUpdate` and `CustomerID_BeforeUpdate` event-handling subprocedures of \SEUA12\Nwind\Northwind.accdb's Orders (Access 2007) form.

Figure 27.2
The `CustomerID_AfterUpdate` subprocedure is a typical event-handler for a combo list. The code executes when you select a CustomerID value in the Order form's Bill To combo box.

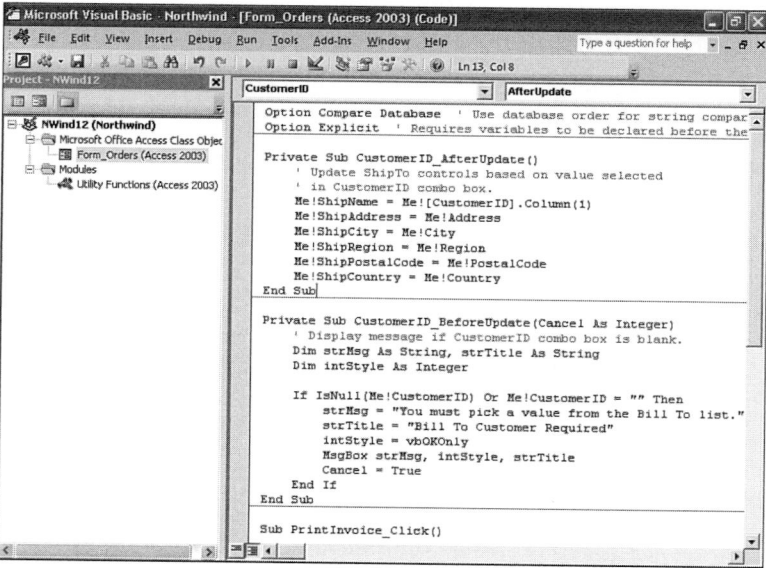

 ■ **Report modules**—Report modules contain code for responding to events triggered by reports, sections of reports, or group headers and footers. (Control objects on reports don't trigger events.) You open a report's class module the same way you open a form's class module. Report class modules are named `Report_ReportName` automatically. Like forms, if an Access 2007 report has a class module, the Has Module property value is set to Yes (`HasModule = True`).

■ **Class modules**—A class module not associated with a form or report lets you define your own custom objects, together with their properties and methods. Class Module is one of the choices of the Advanced context menu. Writing unassociated class modules is beyond the scope of this book.

ELEMENTS OF MODULES

A module consists of a Declarations section and usually one or more procedures (interchangeably called *subprocedures*) or functions. As the name suggests, the Declarations section of a module is used to declare items (usually variables and constants, the subjects of following sections) used by the procedures and functions contained in the module. You can use a module without functions or procedures to declare **Public** variables and constants that can be used by any function or procedure in any module of the database or project.

PROCEDURES

Procedures are typically defined as subprograms referred to by name in another program. Referring to a procedure by name calls or invokes the procedure; the code in the procedure executes, and then the sequence of execution returns to the program that called the procedure. Another name for a procedure is *subroutine*. Procedures are defined by beginning (**Sub**) and end (**End Sub**) reserved words with an optional **Public**, **Private**, or **Static** prefix, as in the following example:

```
Private Sub ProcName
    [Start of procedure code]
    ...
    [End of procedure code]
End Sub
```

> **TIP**
>
> You can refer to the procedure name to invoke the procedure, but VBA provides a keyword, **Call**, that explicitly invokes a procedure. Prefixing the procedure name with **Call** is good programming practice because this keyword identifies the name that follows as the name of a procedure rather than a variable.

VBA introduces another class of procedure called *property procedures* that use the {**Property Let**¦**Property Get**¦**Property Set**}…**End Property** structure to create custom properties for Access objects, such as forms or controls, or objects defined by class modules. A discussion of property procedures is beyond the scope of this book.

FUNCTIONS

Functions are a class of procedures that return values to their names, as explained in Chapter 10. C programmers would argue that procedures are a class of functions, called *void functions*, that don't return values. Regardless of how you view the difference between functions and subprocedures, keep the following points in mind:

27

- Access macros require that you write VBA functions (not subprocedures) to act in place of macro actions when using the RunCode macro action. Macros ignore the value returned by the function, if you specify a return value.

- Form and report class modules use subprocedures (not functions) to respond to events. Using form-level and report-level subprocedures for Access event-handling code mimics Visual Basic's approach for events triggered by forms, controls on forms, and other objects.

- A *custom subprocedure* is a subprocedure that isn't assigned to an event. The only way you can call a custom subprocedure in a VBA module is from a VBA function or another subprocedure. You can't directly execute a subprocedure in an Access module from any Access database object.

- Function names in Access modules are global in scope with respect to Access modules unless they are declared **Private**. Thus, you cannot have duplicate **Public** function names in any Access module in your application. However, form and report class modules can have a function with the same name as a **Public** function in a standard module because form and report function and procedure names have form-level or report-level scope. A function in a form module with the same name as a function in an Access module takes priority over the Access module version. Therefore, if you include the IsLoaded() function in a form module and call the IsLoaded() function from a procedure in the form module, the IsLoaded() function in the form module executes.

Functions are created within a structure similar to procedures, as in the following example:

```
Private Function FunctionName([Argument As DataType]) _
    As ReturnType
    [Start of function code]
    ...
    [End of function code]
    FunctionName = 123
End Function
```

In the preceding example, the FunctionName = 123 statement returns the value 123. In this case, the **ReturnType** data type must be a numeric data type, such as **Integer**. Most functions return **True** or **False** (**Boolean**), a numeric value (**Integer**, **Long**, **Single**, **Double**, or **Decimal**), or a set of characters (**String**).

To execute a VBA function in VBA code, you ordinarily use the function in an expression, such as

```
intReturnValue = FunctionName([Argument])
```

when the function returns a value. You can ignore the return value by calling the function with subprocedure syntax.

REFERENCES TO VBA AND ACCESS LIBRARIES

Access 2007 uses *references* to make Component Object Model (COM) objects available for programming by module code. A reference points to a COM dynamic link library (.dll), object library (.olb), or type library (.tlb) file installed on your computer by adding an entry to the Registry. To view the default references, open a new module in a new database, and then choose Tools, References to open the References dialog (see Figure 27.3). Current references are indicated by a mark in the adjacent check box. You add references by scrolling the list and marking the check box of each new reference. When you click OK to close the References dialog and then reopen it, the new references appear below the last of the original references.

Figure 27.3
A new database created in Access 2007 format has the four standard references shown here. The Microsoft Access 2007 Object Library enables programming of Access-specific objects, such as DoCmd.

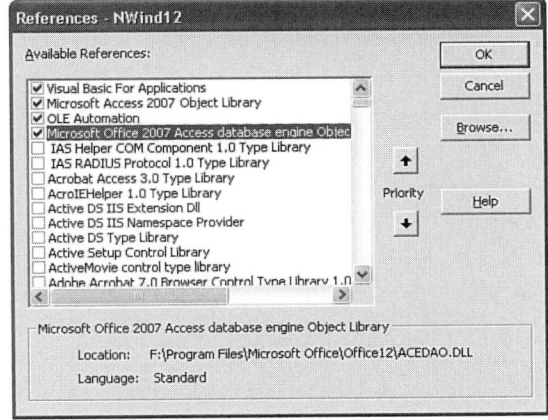

> **TIP**
>
> You can't add a reference to more than one version of the same COM object. Attempting to do this results in a "Name conflicts with existing module, project, or object library" message. For example, if the default Microsoft Office 2007 Access Database Engine Object Library is selected, you must clear its check box before adding a reference to the Microsoft DAO 3.6 Object Library.

Access 2007 resurrects the Data Access Objects (DAO) library (dao360.dll), renames it Microsoft Office 12.0 Access database engine Object Library (ACEDAO.DLL), and relocates ACEDAO.DLL to the \Program Files\Microsoft Office\OFFICE12 folder. You must use ACEDAO to take advantage of Access 2007's new database features, such as complex-type fields. Chapter 30, "Understanding Data Access Objects, OLE DB, and ADO" explains programming the ACEDAO and ADO objects with VBA.

THE OBJECT BROWSER

 Referenced objects appear in the Project/Library drop-down list of the Object Browser. To view the Object Browser, open a module and press F2, click the Object Browser button on the toolbar, or choose View, Object Browser. <All Libraries> is the default selection in the Project/Library list. Figure 27.4 shows a few of the references to Form, Report, and Module objects of Northwind.accdb in the Classes list. Only objects that can act as VBA containers appear in the Classes list; tables, queries, and macros don't qualify.

27

Figure 27.4
The Object Browser window displays classes of the object you choose in the top list (the Data Access Object, DAO, from ACEDAO.dll) in the Classes list and members of the class in the Members list. The bottom pane shows the calling syntax for the function.

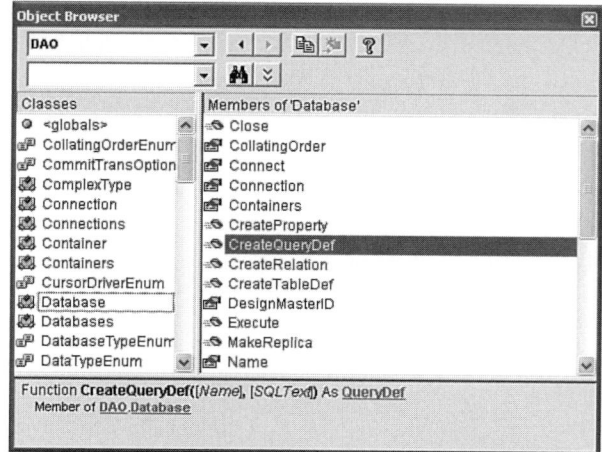

When you select a function or subprocedure name in a module, the function or subprocedure name and arguments, if any, appear in the window at the bottom of the Object Browser dialog. You can get help on Access, VBA, and other objects by clicking the help (?) button, which ignores user-defined functions and the event-handling subprocedures you write. The next chapter describes object classes and the use of the Object Browser in detail.

DATA TYPES AND DATABASE OBJECTS IN VBA

When you create Access tables, all data types that you use to assign field data types and sizes (except for OLE Object and Memo field data types) have data type counterparts in VBA. With the exception of the **Variant** and **Currency** data types, VBA data types are represented in most other dialects of BASIC, including Visual Basic .NET.

Traditional BASIC dialects use a punctuation symbol called the type-declaration character, such as **$** for the String data type, to designate the data type. The VBA data types, the type-declaration characters, the corresponding field data types, and the ranges of values are shown in the VBA Type, Symbol, Field Type, Minimum Value, and Maximum Value columns, respectively, of Table 27.1. The Field Types **Byte**, **Integer**, **Long Integer**, **Single**, and **Double** correspond to the Field Size property of the Number data type in tables, queries, forms, and reports. VBA adds the **Byte** and **Boolean** data types to support the 8-bit Byte and 1-bit Yes/No field data types.

TABLE 27.1 VBA AND CORRESPONDING FIELD DATA TYPES

VBA Type	Symbol	Field	Minimum Value	Maximum Value
Byte	None	Byte	0	255
Integer	%	Integer	−32,768	32,767

VBA Type	Symbol	Field	Minimum Value	Maximum Value
Boolean	None	Yes/No	True	False
Long	&	Long Integer, AutoNumber	–2,147,483,648	2,147,483,647
Single	!	Single	–3.402823E38 1.401298E–45	–1.401298E–45 3.402823E38
Double	#	Double	–1.7200069313486232E308 4.94065645841247E–324	4.94065645841247E–324 1.7200069313486232E308
Currency	@	Currency	–922,337,203,685, 477.5808	922,337,203,685, 477.5807
String	$	Text or Memo	0 characters	Approximately 2 billion characters
Date	None	Date/Time	January 1, 100	December 31, 9999
Variant	None	All	Any of the preceding	Any of the preceding

> **TIP**
>
> All data returned from fields of tables or queries is of the **Variant** data type by default. Variables of the **Variant** data type can hold any type of data listed in Table 27.1. If you assign the field value to a conventional data type, such as **Integer**, the data type is said to be *coerced*.

You can dispense with the type-declaration character if you explicitly declare your variables with the {**Dim**¦**Private**¦**Public**} typVarName **As** *DataType* statement, discussed later in this section. If you don't explicitly declare the variables' data type or use a symbol to define an implicit data type, VBA variables default to the **Variant** data type. Using symbols to specify data types no longer is a generally accepted programming practice.

> **TIP**
>
> Using the **Variant** data type causes VBA code to execute more slowly than when you assign variables an explicit data type with the {**Dim**¦**Private**¦**Public**} typVarName **As** *DataType* statement.

The # sign is also used to enclose values specified as dates, as in varNewYear = #1/1/2001#. In this case, bold type isn't used for the enclosing # signs because these symbols aren't intended for the purpose of the # reserved symbol that indicates the **Double** data type.

Access database objects—such as databases, tables, and queries—and application objects (forms and reports), all of which you used in prior chapters, also have corresponding object data types in VBA. These object data types are defined by the object (also called type or class) library references. The most commonly used object data types and the object library

27

that includes the objects are listed in Table 27.2. The `Database`, `QueryDef`, and `TableDef` object types are specific to Access and ACEDAO, and aren't available in ADP.

TABLE 27.2   THE MOST COMMON ACCESS DATABASE OBJECT DATA TYPES SUPPORTED BY VBA

Object Data Type	Library	Corresponding Database Object Type
`Database`	ACEDAO 12.0	Databases opened by the Access database engine when using ACEDAO
`Connection`	ADO 2.x	ADO replacement for DAO.Database object
`Form`	Access 2007	Forms, including subforms
`Report`	Access 2007	Reports, including subreports
`Control`	Access 2007	Controls on forms, subforms, reports, and subreports
`QueryDef`	ACEDAO 12.0	Access query definitions (SQL statement equivalents) when using ACEDAO
`Command`	ADO 2.x	ADO replacement for `DAO.QueryDef` object
`TableDef`	ACEDAO 12.0	Access table definitions (structure, indexes, and other table properties)
`DAO.Recordset`	ACEDAO 12.0	A virtual representation of an Access table or the result set of an Access query created by ACEDAO
`ADODB.Recordset`	ADO 2.x	ADO replacement for the `DAO.Recordset` object

N O T E

OLE DB is Microsoft's current COM-based database connectivity architecture. OLE DB is the foundation of Microsoft's Universal Data Access initiative, which is described in Chapter 30. ADO is an "Automation wrapper" over OLE DB, which makes OLE DB objects accessible to Access and all other applications that support Automation through VBA. `Recordset` is an object that's common to both DAO and ADO, so it's good programming practice to prefix `Recordset` with its source class identifier, as in `DAO.Recordset` or `ADODB.Recordset`. You must specify the prefix if you include references to ACEDAO 12.0 and ADO 2.x in your application. You can use ADO with both Access and SQL Server databases; DAO is restricted to Access databases only.

The .NET Framework 2.0's ADO.NET supplements OLE DB and ADO and currently offers an ADO.NET managed data provider for SQL Server databases. .NET adds a COM interop(erability) wrapper to ADO and OLE DB for handling connections to Access and other databases that don't have managed data providers. COM interop ensures that your Access databases won't become obsolete when Visual Studio .NET becomes the primary Windows programming environment.

VARIABLES AND NAMING CONVENTIONS

Variables are named placeholders for values of a specified data type that change when your VBA code is executed. You give variables names as you name fields, but the names of variables cannot include spaces or any other punctuation except the underscore character (_). The other restriction is that a variable cannot use a VBA keyword by itself as a name; keywords are called *reserved* words for this reason. The same rules apply to giving names to functions and procedures. Variable names in VBA typically use a combination of uppercase and lowercase letters to make them more readable.

IMPLICIT VARIABLES

You can create variables by assigning a value to a variable name, as in the following example:

```
NewVar = 1234
```

A statement of this type declares a variable, which means to create a new variable with a name you choose. The statement in the example creates a new implicit variable, NewVar, of the **Variant** data type with a value of 1234. (NewVar would be more appropriately named varNewVar.) When you don't specify a data type for an implicit variable by appending one of the type-declaration characters to the variable name, the **Variant** data type is assigned by default. The following statement uses the % type identifier to create a variable of the **Integer** data type:

```
NewVar% = 1234
```

EXPLICIT VARIABLES

It's a better programming practice to declare your variables and assign those variables a data type before you give them a value. The most common method of declaring variables is by using the **Dim** typVarName **As** *Datatype* structure, in which **As** specifies the data type. This method declares explicit variables. An example follows:

```
Dim intNewVar As Integer
```

If you don't add the **As Integer** keywords, intNewVar is assigned the **Variant** data type by default.

You can require that all variables be explicitly declared before their use by adding the statement **Option** Explicit in the Declarations section of a module. The advantage of using **Option** Explicit is that the VBA compiler detects misspelled variable names and displays an error message when misspellings are encountered. If you don't use **Option** Explicit and you misspell a variable name, the VBA interpreter creates a new implicit variable with the misspelled name. The resulting errors in your code's execution can be difficult to diagnose. The VBA editor automatically adds an **Option** Explicit statement to the Declarations section of each module if you select the Require Variable Declaration option in the VBA editor's Options dialog, which you open by choosing Tools, Options (see Figure 27.5).

27

Figure 27.5
Mark the Require Variable Declaration check box on the Editor page of the VBA editor's Options dialog. Despite many requests from Access developers, this feature isn't enabled by default.

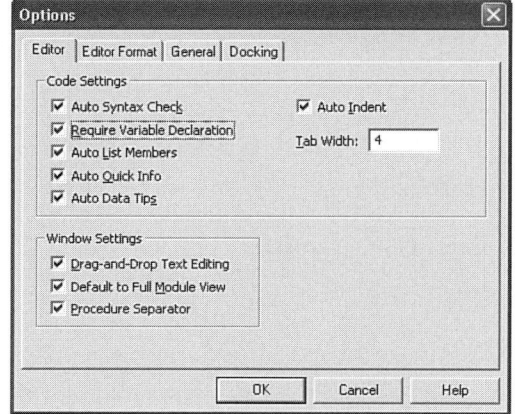

SCOPE AND DURATION OF VARIABLES

Variables have a characteristic called *scope*, which determines when the variables appear and disappear in your VBA code. Variables appear the first time you declare them and then disappear and reappear on the basis of the scope you assign to them. When a variable appears, it is said to be visible—meaning that you can assign the variable a value, change its value, and use it in expressions. Otherwise, the variable is invisible. If you use a variable's name while it's invisible, you instead create a new variable with the same name, if you haven't specified the Required Variable Declaration feature.

The following lists the four scope levels in VBA:

- **Local (procedure-level) scope**—The variable is visible only during the time when the procedure in which the variable is declared is running. Variables that you declare, with or without using **Dim** *typVarName* **As** *DataType* in a procedure or function, are local in scope.

- **Form-level and report-level scope**—The variable is visible only when the form or report in which it's declared is open. You declare form-level and report-level variables in the Declarations section of form and report modules with **Private** *typVarName* **As** *DataType*. (**Dim** *typVarName* **As** *DataType* also works, but **Private** is the preferred scope identifier.)

- **Module-level scope**—The variable is visible to all procedures and functions contained in the module in which the variable was declared. (Modules open when you open the database.) You declare variables with module scope in the Declarations section of the module with the same syntax as form-level and report-level variables.

- **Global or public scope**—The variable is visible to all procedures and functions within all modules. You declare variables with global scope in the Declarations section of a module using **Public** *typVarName* **As** *DataType*. The Public scope identifier is available only in Access modules.

The scope and visibility of variables declared in two different Access modules of the same database, both with two procedures, are illustrated by the diagram in Figure 27.6. In each procedure, variables declared with different scopes are used to assign values to variables declared within the procedure. Invalid assignment statements are shown crossed out in the figure. These assignment statements are invalid because the variable used to assign the value to the variable declared in the procedure isn't visible in the procedure.

Figure 27.6
This diagram illustrates valid and invalid assignment for variables of different scopes.

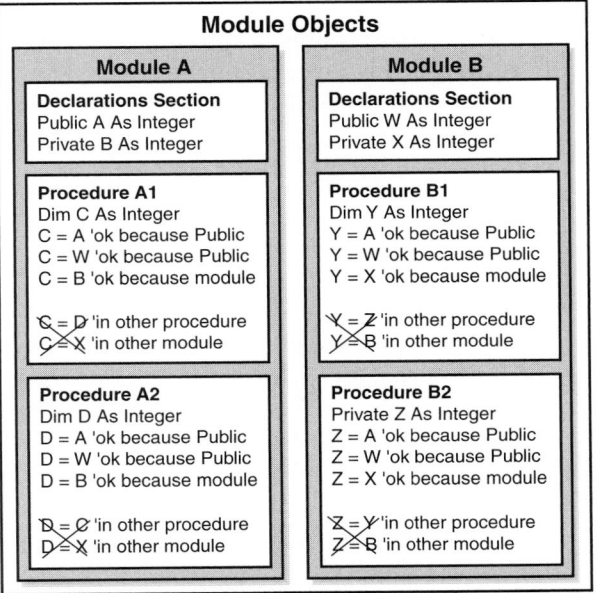

Variables also have an attribute called *duration*, or *lifetime*. The duration of a variable is your code's execution time between the first appearance of the variable (its declaration) and its disappearance. Each time a procedure or function is called, local variables declared with the `Dim typVarName As DataType` statement are set to default values—that is, 0 for numeric data types and the empty string (" ") for string variables. The duration of these local variables is usually equal to the lifetime of the function or procedure—from the time the function or procedure is called until the `End Function` or `End Sub` statement is encountered.

To preserve the values of local variables between occurrences (called *instances*) of a procedure or function, you substitute the reserved word `Static` for `Dim`. `Static` variables have a duration of your Access application, but their scope is determined by where you declare them. `Static` variables are useful when you want to count the number of occurrences of an event. You can make all variables in a function or procedure static variables by preceding `Function` or `Sub` with the `Static` keyword.

27

TIP

> Minimize the number of local variables that you declare **Static**. Local variables don't consume memory when they aren't visible. This characteristic of local variables is especially important in the case of arrays, discussed in the "VBA Arrays" section that follows shortly, because arrays are often very large.

USER-DEFINED DATA TYPES

You can create your own data type that consists of one or more Access data types. User-defined data types are discussed in this section pertaining to variables because you need to know what a variable is before you can declare a user-defined data type. You declare a user-defined data type between the **Type…End Type** keywords, as in the following example:

```
Type tagDupRec
    lngField1 As Long
    strField2 As String * 20
    sngField3 As Single
    dblField4 As Double
End Type
```

User-defined data types are particularly useful when you create a variable to hold the values of one or more records of a table that uses fields of different data types. The **String * 20** statement defines lngField2 of the user-defined data type as a fixed-length string of 20 characters, usually corresponding to the Size property of the Text field data type. String variables in user-defined data types traditionally have a fixed length, but VBA 6.0 lets you use variable-length strings. You must declare your user-defined data type (called a *record* or *structure* in other programming languages) in the Declarations section of a module.

You must explicitly declare variables to be of the user-defined type with the **Dim**, **Private**, **Public**, or **Static** keyword because no reserved symbol exists to declare a user-defined data type, as in **Dim** usrCurrentRec **As** tagDupRec. To assign a value to a field of a variable with a user-defined data type, you specify the name of the variable and the field name, separating the names with a period, as in usrCurrentRec.lngField1 = 2048.

VBA ARRAYS

Arrays are variables that consist of a collection of values (called *elements* of the array) of a single data type in a regularly ordered structure. Implicitly declared arrays aren't allowed in VBA. You declare an array with the **Dim** statement, adding the number of elements in parentheses to the variable name for the array, as in the following example:

```
Dim astrNewArray(20) As String
```

This statement creates an array of 21 elements, each of which is a conventional, variable-length string variable. You create 21 elements because the first element of an array is the 0 (zero) element, unless you specify otherwise by adding the **To** modifier, as in the following example:

```
Dim astrNewArray(1 To 20) As String
```

The preceding statement creates an array with 20 elements.

You can create multidimensional arrays by adding more values separated by commas. The statement

```
Dim alngNewArray(9, 9, 9) As Long
```

creates a three-dimensional array of 10 elements per dimension. This array, when visible, occupies 4,000 bytes of memory (10×10×10×4 bytes/long integer).

You can create a dynamic array by declaring the array using **Dim** without specifying the number of elements and then using the **ReDim** reserved word to determine the number of elements the array contains. You can **ReDim** an array as many times as you want. Each time you do so, the values stored in the array are reinitialized to their default values, determined by the data type, unless you follow **ReDim** with the reserved word, **Preserve**. The following sample statements create a dynamic array:

```
Dim alngNewArray() As Long            'In Declarations sections
ReDim Preserve alngNewArray(9, 9, 9)  'In procedure, preserves prior values
ReDim alngNewArray(9, 9, 9)           'In procedure, reinitializes all
```

Dynamic arrays are useful when you don't know how many elements an array requires when you declare it. You can **ReDim** a dynamic array to zero elements when you no longer need the values it contains; this tactic lets you recover the memory that the array consumes while it's visible. Alternatively, you can use the **Erase** reserved word followed by a dynamic array's name to remove all the array's elements from memory. (**Erase** used on an array with fixed dimensions merely reinitializes the array to its condition before you assigned any values to it.) Arrays declared with **Dim** can have up to 60 dimensions. You can only use the **ReDim** statement to alter the size of the last dimension in a multidimensional array.

Scope, duration rules, and keywords apply to arrays in the same way in which they apply to conventional variables. You can declare dynamic arrays with global and module-level scope by adding the **Public** or **Private** statement to the Declarations section of a module and then using the **ReDim** statement by itself in a procedure. If you declare an array with **Static**, rather than **Dim**, the array retains its values between instances of a procedure.

> **TIP**
>
> Don't use the **Option** Base keywords to change the default initial element of arrays from 0 to 1. **Option** Base is included in VBA for compatibility with earlier BASIC dialects. Many arrays you create from VBA objects must begin with element 0. If you're concerned about the memory occupied by an unused zero element of an array, use the **Dim** *ArrayName*(1 **To** *N*) **As** *DataType* declaration. In most cases, you can disregard the zero element.

NAMED DATABASE OBJECTS AS VARIABLES IN VBA CODE

Properties of database objects you create with Access can be treated as variables and assigned values within VBA code. For example, you can assign a new value to the text box that contains the address information for a customer by name with the following statement:

```
Forms!Customers!Address.Value = "123 Elm St."
```

The collection name `Forms` defines the type of object. The exclamation point (called the bang symbol by programmers) separates the name of the form and the name of the control object. The `!` symbol is analogous to the `\` path separator that you use when you're dealing with folder and file names. If the name of the form or the control object contains a space or other punctuation, you must enclose the name within square brackets, as in the following statement:

```
Forms!Customers![Contact Name].Value = "Joe Hill"
```

Alternatively, you can use the **Set** keyword to create your own named variable for the control object. This procedure is convenient when you need to refer to the control object several times. It's more convenient to type `txtContact` rather than the full "path" to the control object—in this case, a text box.

```
Dim txtContact As Control
Set txtContact = Forms!Customers![Contact Name]
txtContact.Value = "Joe Hill"
```

TIP

> Specifying the `Value` property when assigning a value to a control isn't required because `Value` is the default property of controls and fields of `Recordset` objects. It's good programming practice, however, to do so. Adding the `Value` property when manipulating `ADODB.Recordset` objects with VBA results in improved performance.

Another alternative is to use "dot" instead of "bang" syntax to refer to Access objects, as in this example:

```
Forms("Customers").Controls("Contact Name").Value = "Joe Hill"
```

"Dot" syntax has the advantage of enabling IntelliSense for statement completion in the VBA Editor. IntelliSense is one of the subjects of the later "Examining the Utility Functions Module" section.

You can assign any database object to a variable name by declaring the variable as the object type and using the **Set** statement to assign the object to the variable. You don't create a copy of the object in memory when you assign it a variable name; the variable refers to the object in memory. Referring to an object in memory is often called *pointing* to an object; many languages have a pointer data type that holds the address of the location in memory where the variable is stored. VBA has no direct support for pointers. The next chapter deals with creating variables that point to the Access database objects supplied by ADO 2.x.

OBJECT PROPERTIES AND THE `With…End With` STRUCTURE

VBA provides the **With…End With** structure, which offers a shorthand method of setting the values of object properties, such as the dimensions and other characteristics of a form. The **With…End With** structure also lets you set the values of fields of a user-defined data type without repeating the variable name in each instance. To use the **With…End With** structure to set object property values, you must first declare and set an object variable, as in the following example:

```
Dim frmFormName As Form
Set frmFormName = Forms!FormName
With frmFormName
    .Top = 1000
    .Left = 1000
    .Width = 5000
    .Height = 4000
End With
```

When using the **With…End With** structure with user-defined data types, you don't use the **Set** statement. Names of properties or fields within the structure are preceded by periods.

SYMBOLIC CONSTANTS

Symbolic constants are named placeholders for values of a specified data type that don't change when executing your VBA code. You precede the name of a symbolic constant with the keyword **Const**, as in **Const** sngPI **As Single** = 3.1416. You declare symbolic constants in the Declarations section of a module or within a function or procedure. Precede **Const** with the **Public** keyword if you want to create a global constant that's visible to all modules, as in **Public Const** gsngPI = 3.1416. The g prefix of the variable name is an abbreviation for **Global**, which most programmers prefer to p for **Public**. Public constants can be declared only in the Declarations section of a VBA module.

You don't need to specify a data type for constants explicitly because VBA chooses the data type that stores the data most efficiently. VBA can make this choice because it knows the value of the data when it "compiles" your code. It's a better programming practice, however, to specify the data type of constants.

NOTE

> Office's VBA is an interpreted language, so the term *compile* in a VBA context is a misnomer. When you "compile" the VBA source code that you write in a code-editing window, the VBA editor creates a tokenized, binary version of the code (called *pseudo-code*, or *p-code*) stored in an .accdb or .adp file. Only Visual Basic 6.0 compiles VBA 6.0 code to create an executable (.exe) file. Visual Basic .NET is similar to Office 2007's VBA; programs written in Visual Basic .NET create p-code that the Common Language Runtime (CLR) executes.

27

ACCESS SYSTEM-DEFINED CONSTANTS

VBA includes seven system-defined constants—**True, False**, Yes, No, On, Off, and **Null**—that are created by the VBA and Access type libraries when launched. Of these seven, you can use **True, False**, and **Null**, which are declared by the VBA library, in VBA code. The remaining four are declared by the Access type library and are valid for use with all database objects except modules. When the system-defined constants **True, False**, and **Null** are used in VBA code examples in this book, they appear in bold monospace type. This book doesn't use the Access-defined Yes, No, On, and Off constants; don't use them in the code you write.

ACCESS INTRINSIC CONSTANTS

VBA provides a number of predeclared, intrinsic, symbolic constants that are primarily for use as arguments of Access DoCmd.*ActionName* statements. These statements let you execute standard database actions in VBA (such as opening forms, printing reports, applying sorts or filters, and so on). Access 2007 intrinsic constants carry the prefix ac, as in acExportMerge. You can display the list of Access intrinsic constants in the Object Browser by selecting Access in the Project/Library list and then selecting Globals in the Classes list.

When you select a constant in the Members Of list, its numeric value appears at the bottom of the Object Browser window (see Figure 27.7). A good programming practice is to use constant names rather than their numeric values when applicable to make your code more readable. You can't use any of these intrinsic constants' names as names for constants or variables that you define.

Figure 27.7
Access has hundreds of intrinsic constants defined by the Microsoft Access 2007 Object Library. Constants with the prefix A_ are included for backward compatibility with the Access Basic language used by Access 2.0 and earlier.

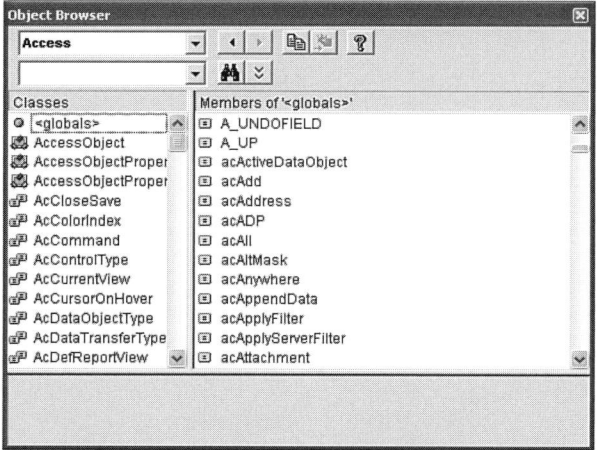

VBA INTRINSIC CONSTANTS

VBA has many of its own constants, in addition to the three mentioned in the earlier "Access System-Defined Constants" section. These constants carry a vb prefix. To see a list of the VBA constants, select VBA in the Object Browsers top combo list, accept the default <globals> class, and scroll to the vb... entries. One of the most commonly used VBA intrinsic constants is vbCrLf, which inserts a (carriage) return and line feed into a string.

VBA NAMED AND OPTIONAL ARGUMENTS

Procedures often have one or more arguments that pass values from the calling statement to the called procedure. Traditionally, you must pass all the values required by the procedure in your calling statement. As an example, if a procedure accepts four arguments, *Arg1...Arg4*, your calling statement must provide values for *Arg1...Arg4*, as in the following example:

```
Sub CallingProc()
    ...
```

```
    Call CalledProc(100000, 200000, 300000, 400000)
    ...
End Sub

Sub CalledProc(Arg1 As Long, Arg2 As Long, _
               Arg3 As Long, Arg4 As Long)
    [Subprocedure code]
End Sub
```

NOTE

> The space followed by an underscore following *Arg2* **As** **Long** in the preceding sub-procedure is called the *code-continuation character* (CCC or 3C). VBA interprets instructions on a line-by-line basis. The CCC lets you continue a statement on the next line. Using the CCC lets you format your code for easier readability.

VBA 6.0 lets you declare the arguments of the subprocedure to be **Optional**, eliminating the need to pass every parameter to the procedure. You use named arguments to pass values to specific arguments, as in the following example:

```
Sub CallingProc()
    ...
    Call CalledProc(Arg2:=200000, Arg3:=300000)
    ...
End Sub

Sub CalledProc(Optional Arg1 As Long, Optional Arg2 As Long,
               Optional Arg3 As Long, Optional Arg4 As Long)
    [Subprocedure code]
End Sub
```

The := operator specifies that the preceding element is the name of an argument; named arguments need not be entered in the order that the arguments appear in the called procedure. However, if you want to omit an argument or arguments, the corresponding argument name(s) of the called procedure must be preceded by the keyword **Optional**. Missing arguments return **Null** values to subprocedure code, but you can supply a default argument value in the subprocedure. If you omit the **As** *Datatype* modifier of an argument in the called procedure, the argument assumes the default **Variant** data type.

27

CONTROLLING PROGRAM FLOW

Useful procedures must be able to make decisions based on the values of variables and then take specified actions based on those decisions. Blocks of code, for example, might need to be repeated until a specified condition occurs. Statements used to make decisions and repeat blocks of code are the fundamental elements that control program flow in VBA and all other programming languages.

All programming languages require methods of executing different algorithms based on the results of one or more comparison operations. You can control the flow of any program in any programming language with just three types of statements: conditional execution

(**If…Then…End If**), repetition (**Do While…Loop** and related structures), and termination (**End…** and **Exit**). Additional flow control statements in VBA and other programming languages make writing code more straightforward.

BRANCHING AND LABELS

When BASIC was first developed, the only method of controlling program flow was through its GOTO *LineNumber* and GOSUB *LineNumber* statements. Every line in the program required a number that could be used as a substitute for a label. GOTO *LineNumber* caused the interpreter to skip to the designated line and continue executing the program from that point. GOSUB *LineNumber* caused the program to follow that same branch, but when the BASIC interpreter that executed the code encountered a RETURN statement, program execution jumped back to the line following the GOSUB statement and continued executing at that point.

VBA's **GoTo** *Label* statement causes your code to branch to the location named *Label*: and continue from that point. Note the colon following *Label*:, which identifies the single word you assigned as a label. However, the colon isn't required after the label name following the **GoTo**. In fact, if you add the colon, you get a "Label not found" error message.

A label name must begin in the leftmost column (1) of your code. This positioning often interferes with the orderly indenting of your code (explained in the next section), which is just one more reason, in addition to those following, for not using **GoTo**.

The **GoTo** statement is required for only one purpose in VBA: to handle errors with the **On Error GoTo** *Label* statement. Although VBA supports BASIC's ON…GOTO and ON…GOSUB statements, using those statements is not considered good programming practice. You can eliminate most GoTo statements in form and report modules by using Access's Error event and the DAO and ADO Errors collection. The Error event is described in the "Handling Runtime Errors" section later in this chapter, and the Errors collection is explained in the next chapter.

CONDITIONAL STATEMENTS

A conditional statement executes the statements between its occurrence and the terminating statement if the result of the relational operator is true. Statements that consist of or require more than one statement for completion are called structured statements, control structures, or just structures.

THE If…Then…End If STRUCTURE

The syntax of the primary conditional statement of VBA is as follows:

```
If blnCondition1 [= True] Then
   Statements to be executed if Condition1 is true
[Else[If blnCondition2[ = True] Then]]
   Optional statements to be executed if blnCondition1
   is false [and blnCondition2 is true]
End If
```

The = **True** elements of the preceding conditional statement are optional and typically not included when you write actual code. **If** blnCondition1 **Then** and **If** blnCondition1 = **True** **Then** produce the same result when blnCondition1 is **True**.

You can add a second condition with the **ElseIf** keyword. The **ElseIf** condition must be true to execute the statements that are executed if blnCondition1 is not **True** (**False**). Note that no space is used between **Else** and **If**. An **If…End If** structure that incorporates an **ElseIf** statement is the simplified equivalent of the following:

```
If blnCondition1 Then
    Statements to be executed if Expression1 is true
Else
    If blnCondition2 Then
        Statements to be executed if Condition1% is
        false and blnCondition2 is true]
    End If
End If
```

A statement is executed based on the evaluation of the immediately preceding expression. Expressions that include **If…End If** or other flow-control structures within other **If…End If** structures are said to be *nested*, as in the preceding example. The number, or depth, of **If…End If** structures that can be nested within one another is unlimited.

Note that the code between the individual keywords that make up the flow-control structure is indented. Indentation makes code within structures easier to read. You usually use the Tab key to create indentation.

To evaluate whether a character is a letter and to determine its case, you can use the following code:

```
If Asc(strChar) > 63 And Asc(strChar) < 91 Then
    strCharType = "Uppercase Letter"
ElseIf Asc(strChar) > 96 And Asc(strChar) < 123 Then
    strCharType = "Lowercase Letter"
Else
    strCharType = "Not a Letter"
End If
```

You use the **If…End If** structure more often than any other flow control statement.

> **TIP**
>
> For a list of the ASCII numeric codes for alphabetic, numeric, and special characters, type `ascii` in the Ask a Question text box of the VBA editor, and click the Character Set (0 - 127) item. Character Set (128 - 255) contains special characters.

THE Select Case…End Select CONSTRUCT

When you must choose among many alternatives, **If…End If** structures can become very complex and deeply nested. The **Select Case…End Select** construct was added to procedural BASIC to overcome this complexity. In addition to testing whether an expression evaluates to True or False, **Select Case** can evaluate variables to determine whether those variables fall within specified ranges. The generalized syntax is shown in the following example:

```
Select Case VarName
    Case Expression1[, Expressions, ...]
        (Statements executed if the value of VarName
        = Expression1 or Expressions)
    [Case Expression2 To Expression3
        (Statements executed if the value of VarName
        is in the range of Expression2 to Expression3)]
    [Case Is RelationalExpression
        (Statements executed if the value of
        VarName = RelationalExpression)]
    [Case Else
        (Statements executed if none of the
        above cases is met)]
End Select
```

Select Case evaluates *VarName*, which can be a string, a numeric variable, or an expression. It then tests each **Case** expression in sequence. **Case** expressions can take one of the following four forms:

- A single value or list of values to which to compare the value of *VarName*. Successive members of the list are separated from their predecessors by commas.

- A range of values separated by the keyword **To**. The value of the first member of the range limits must be less than the value of the second. Each string is compared by the ASCII value of its first character.

- The keyword **Is** followed by a relational operator, such as <>, <, <=, =, >=, or >, and a variable or literal value.

- The keyword **Else**. Expressions following **Case Else** are executed if no prior **Case** condition is satisfied.

The code associated with the first matching **Case** condition is executed. If no match is found and the **Case Else** statement is present, the code following the statement is executed. Program execution then continues at the line of code following the **End Select** terminating statement.

If *VarName* is a numeric type, all **Case** expressions that use *VarName* are forced to the same data type.

The following example is of **Select Case** using a numeric variable, curSales:

```
Select Case curSales
    Case 10000 To 49999.99
        intClass = 1
    Case 50000 To 100000
        intClass = 2
    Case Is < 10000
        intClass = 0
    Case Else
        intClass = 3
End Select
```

Note that because curSales is of the **Currency** type, all the comparison literals also are treated as **Currency** values for the purpose of comparison.

A more complex example that evaluates a single character follows:

```
Select Case strChar
    Case "A" To "Z"
        strCharType = "Upper Case"
    Case "a" To "z"
        strCharType = "Lower Case"
    Case "0" To "9"
        strCharType = "Number"
    Case "!", "?", ".", ",", ";"
        strCharType = "Punctuation"
    Case ""
        strCharType = "Empty String"
    Case < 32
        strCharType = "Special Character"
    Case Else
        strCharType = "Unknown Character"
End Select
```

This example demonstrates that **Select Case**, when used with strings, evaluates the ASCII value of the first character of the string—either as the variable being tested or the expressions following **Case** statements. Thus, **Case** < 32 is a valid test, although strChar is a string variable.

REPETITIVE OPERATIONS: LOOPING

In many instances, you must repeat an operation until a given condition is satisfied, whereupon the repetitions terminate. You might want to examine each character in a word, sentence, or document, or you might want to assign values to an array with many elements. Loops are used for these and many other purposes.

USING THE For...Next STATEMENT

VBA's **For...Next** statement lets you repeat a block of code for a specified number of times, as shown in the following example:

```
For intCounter = intStartValue To intEndValue [Step intIncrement]
    Statements to be executed
    [Conditional statement
    Exit For
    End of conditional statement]
Next [intCounter]
```

The block of statements between the **For** and **Next** keywords is executed (intEndValue - intStartValue + 1) / intIncrement) times. As an example, if intStartValue = 5, intEndValue = 10, and intIncrement = 1, the execution of the statement block is repeated six times. You need not add the keyword **Step** in this case—the default increment is 1. Although **Integer** data types are shown, you can use **Long** (integer) values. The use of real numbers (**Single** or **Double** data types) as values for counters and increments is possible but uncommon because decimal rounding errors can cause unexpected results.

27

The dividend of the previous expression must always be a positive number if the execution of the internal statement block is to occur. If intEndValue is less than intStartValue, intIncrement must be negative; otherwise, the **For...Next** statement is ignored by the VBA interpreter.

The optional **Exit For** statement is provided so that you can prematurely terminate the loop using a surrounding **If...Then...End If** conditional statement. Changing the value of the counter variable within the loop itself to terminate its operation is discouraged as a dangerous programming practice. You might make a change that would cause an infinite statement loop.

USING For...Next LOOPS TO ASSIGN VALUES TO ARRAY ELEMENTS

One of the most common applications of the **For...Next** loop is to assign successive values to the elements of an array. If you've declared a 26-element array named astrAlphabet, the following example assigns the capital letters A through Z to its elements:

```
For intLetter = 1 To 26
    strAlphabet(intLetter) = Chr$(intLetter + 64)
Next intLetter
```

The preceding example assigns 26 of the array's 27 elements if you used **Dim** strAlphabet(26) **As String** rather than **Dim** strAlphabet(1 **To** 26) **As String**. 64 is added to intLetter because the ASCII value of the letter A is 65, and the initial value of intLetter is 1. The VBA **Chr$()** function converts the ordinal position of intLetter in the ASCII character set to a **String** value. Using **Chr()** returns a **Variant** value that the interpreter must coerce to a **String** value.

> **TIP**
>
> VBA offers two versions of each function that returns a **String** value. It's a good practice to use the version with the **$** data type identifier when returning values to a variable declared **As String**. Complex string expressions execute much faster if the compiler doesn't need to coerce **Variant**s to **String**s.

A special case of the **For...Next** loop, **For Each** *objName* **In** *colName*...**Next** *objName*, iterates each object (*objName*) in a collection (*colName*). The following example iterates the collection of Access Form objects and lists the object names in the Immediate Window:

```
Sub ForEachExample()
    Dim objAccess As AccessObject
    For Each objAccess In CurrentProject.AllForms
        Debug.Print objAccess.Name
    Next
End Sub
```

UNDERSTANDING Do While...Loop AND Do Until...Loop

A more general form of the loop structure is **Do While...Loop**, which uses the following syntax:

```
Do While blnCondition [= True]
    Statements to be executed
    [Conditional statement
    Exit Do
    End of conditional statement]
Loop
```

This loop structure executes the intervening statements only if blnCondition equals **True** (**Not False**, a value other than 0) and continues to do so until blnCondition becomes **False** (0) or the optional **Exit Do** statement executes.

From the preceding syntax, you can duplicate the previous **For...Next** array assignment example with the following structure:

```
intLetter = 1
Do While intLetter <= 27
    astrAlphabet(intLetter) = Chr$(intLetter + 64)
    intLetter = intLetter + 1
Loop
```

Another example of a **Do** loop is the **Do Until...Loop** structure, which loops as long as the condition isn't satisfied, as in the following example:

```
Do Until {blnCondition <> True|Not blnCondition}
    Statements to be executed
    [Conditional statement
    Exit Do
    End of conditional statement]
Loop
```

The **Not** blnCondition expression is more commonly used than blnCondition **<> True**, but either is acceptable.

VBA also supports the **While...Wend** loop, which is identical to the **Do While...Loop** structure, but you can't use the **Exit Do** statement within **While...Wend**. The **While...Wend** structure is provided for compatibility with earlier versions of BASIC and should be abandoned in favor of **Do {While|Until}...Loop** in VBA.

MAKING SURE STATEMENTS IN A LOOP OCCUR AT LEAST ONCE

You might have observed that the statements within a **Do While...Loop** structure are never executed if intCondition is false when the structure is encountered in your application. You can also use a structure in which the conditional statement that causes loop termination is associated with the **Loop** statement. The syntax of this format is shown in the following example:

```
Do
    Statements to be executed
    [Conditional statement then
    Exit Do
    End of conditional statement]
Loop While intCondition[ = True]
```

A similar structure is available for the **Do Until...** Loop:

```
Do
    Statements to be executed
    [Conditional statement
```

27

```
    Exit Do
  End of conditional statement]
Loop Until intCondition[ = False]
```

These structures ensure that the loop executes at least once before the condition is tested.

HANDLING RUNTIME ERRORS

No matter how thoroughly you test and debug your code, runtime errors appear eventually. Runtime errors are errors that occur when Access executes your VBA code. Use the **On Error GoTo** instruction to control what happens in your application when a runtime error occurs. **On Error** isn't a very sophisticated instruction, but it's your only choice for error processing in Access modules. You can branch to a label or ignore the error. The general syntax of **On Error…** follows:

```
On Error GoTo LabelName
On Error Resume Next
On Error GoTo 0
```

On Error GoTo LabelName branches to that part of your code that begins with the label LabelName:. LabelName must be a label; it can't be the name of a procedure. The code following LabelName, however, can (and often does) include a procedure call to an error-handling procedure, such as ErrorProc, as in the following:

```
On Error GoTo ErrHandler
...
[RepeatCode:
(Code using ErrProc to handle errors)]
...
GoTo SkipHandler
ErrHandler:
Call ErrorProc
[GoTo RepeatCode]
SkipHandler:
...
(Additional code)
```

In this example, the **On Error GoTo** instruction causes program flow to branch to the ErrHandler label that executes the error-handling procedure ErrorProc. Ordinarily, the error-handler code is located at the end of the procedure. If you have more than one error handler or if the error handler is in the middle of a group of instructions, you must bypass it if the preceding code is error-free. Use the **GoTo** SkipHandler statement that bypasses ErrHandler: instructions. To repeat the code that generated the error after ErrorProc has completed its job, add a label such as RepeatCode: at the beginning of the repeated code, and then branch to the code in the ErrHandler: code. Alternatively, you can add the keyword **Resume** at the end of your code to resume processing at the line that created the error.

On Error Resume Next disregards the error and continues processing the succeeding instructions.

After an **On Error GoTo** statement executes, it remains in effect for all succeeding errors until execution encounters another **On Error GoTo** instruction or you turn off error processing with the **On Error GoTo 0** form of the statement.

If you don't trap errors with an **On Error GoTo** statement or if you've turned error trapping off with **On Error GoTo 0**, a runtime error message appears when an error is encountered. Clicking Debug opens the VBA Editor at the offending line. If you correct the error at this point, press F5 to continue code execution. Otherwise, your only option is to click End to halt code execution.

TIP

> Always include error-handling code in runtime applications. If you don't provide at least one error-handling routine in your VBA code for runtime Access applications you distribute with the developer toolkit for Office 2007, your application quits abruptly when the error occurs.

DETECTING THE TYPE OF ERROR WITH THE Err OBJECT

The VBA **Err** object replaces the **Err** function of earlier versions of Access. The default property, **Err.Number**, returns an integer representing the code of the last error or returns 0 if no error occurs. This property ordinarily is used within a **Select Case** structure to determine the action to take in the error handler based on the type of error incurred. Use the **Err.Description** property, which replaces the **Error** function, to return the text name of the error number specified as its argument, as in the following example:

```
strErrorName = Err.Description
Select Case Err.Number
    Case 58 To 76
        Call FileError 'procedure for handling file errors
    Case 340 To 344
        Call ArrayError 'procedure for control array errors
    Case 281 To 22000
        Call DDEError 'procedure for handling DDE errors
End Select
Err.Clear
```

TIP

> The preceding code example illustrates use of comments in VBA code. You create a comment by preceding text with an apostrophe ('). Adding explanatory comments to your code assists others in understanding the purpose of procedures and how the code within the procedures works—or is supposed to work.

27

You can substitute the actual error-processing code for the **Call** instructions shown in the preceding example, but using individual procedures for error handling is the recommended approach. **Err.Number** sets the error code to a specific integer. Use the **Err.Clear** method to reset the error code to 0 after your error handler has completed its operation, as shown in the preceding example.

The **Error** and **RaiseError** statements simulate an error so that you can test any error handlers you write. You can specify any of the valid integer error codes or create a user-defined error code by selecting an integer that's not included in the list. A user-defined error code returns "User-defined error" to **Error.Description**.

USING THE ERROR EVENT IN FORM AND REPORT MODULES

Access has an event, Error, that's triggered when an error occurs on a form or report. You can use an event-handling procedure in a form or report to process the error, or you can assign a generic error-handling function in an Access module to the Error event with an =ErrorHandler() entry to call the ErrorHandler() function.

When you invoke an error-handling function from the Error event, you must use the **Err** object to detect the error that occurred and take corrective action, as described in the preceding section.

EXPLORING THE VBA EDITOR

You write VBA functions and procedures in the VBA editor. To open the VBA editor for a module, expand the Navigation pane's Module node and then double-click the name of the module you want to open in the VBA editor. The VBA editor window incorporates a text editor, similar to Windows Notepad, in which you type your VBA code. VBA color-codes keywords and comments. By default, the VBA editor opens with all of its windows docked.

THE TOOLBAR OF THE MODULE WINDOW

Table 27.3 lists the purpose of each VBA-specific item in the toolbar of the Module window (refer to Figure 27.8) and the menu commands and key combinations that you can substitute for toolbar components.

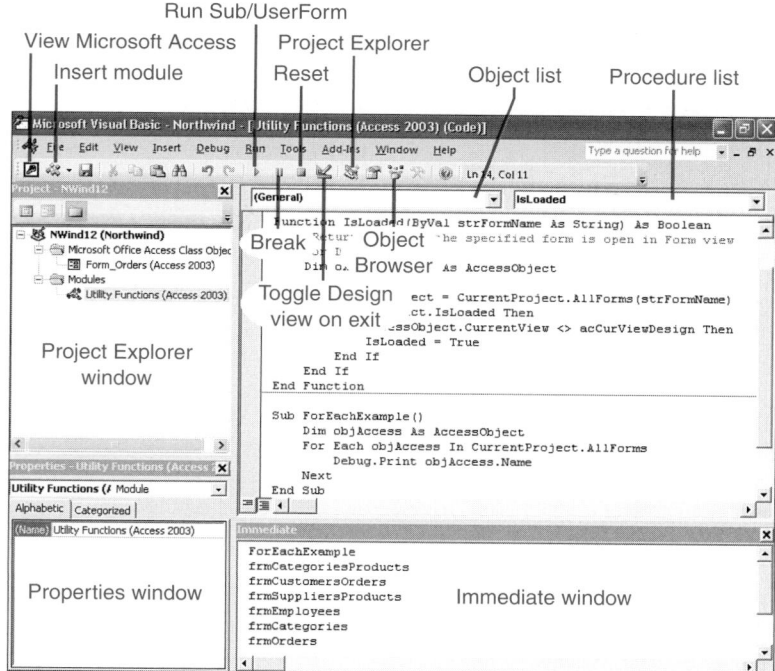

Figure 27.8
The VBA editor window opens with the Project Explorer, Properties, and Immediate windows docked, as shown here.

TABLE 27.3   VBA-SPECIFIC ELEMENTS OF THE VBA EDITOR'S TOOLBAR AND CODE-EDITING WINDOW

Button	Item	Alternative Method	Purpose
	View Micro-Access	View, Microsoft Access or press Alt+F11	Displays the Access 2007 window.
	Insert Module	Insert, Module	Creates a new, empty module. Click the down arrow next to this button to create a new class module or to insert a new procedure or function.
	Find	Edit, Find or press Ctrl+F	Similar to the Find feature used in Table or Form view; allows you to search for a specific word or phrase in a module.
	Undo	Edit, Undo or press Ctrl+Z	Rescinds the last keyboard or mouse operation performed, if possible.
	Redo	Edit, Redo	Rescinds the last undo operation, if possible.
	Run Sub/UserForm	Run, Run Sub/User/Form or press F5	Starts the execution of the current procedure, or continues executing a procedure after its execution has been halted by a break condition. If the code-editing window doesn't have the focus, this button is called Run Macro and opens the Macros dialog in which to select the macro to run, if any.
	Break	Run, Break or press Ctrl+Break	Halts execution of a procedure.
	Reset	Run, Reset or press Shift+F5	Terminates execution of a VBA procedure and reinitializes all variables to their default values.
	Design mode	Run, Design Mode	Toggles design mode for UserForms.
	Project Explorer	View, Project Explorer or press Ctrl+R	Opens the Project Explorer window.
	Properties Window	View, Properties Window or press F4	Opens the Properties window for the object selected in the Project Explorer.
	Object Browser	View, Object Browser or press F2	Opens the Object Browser window.
	Toolbox	View, Toolbox	Shows the Toolbox for adding controls to UserForms.

27

continues

TABLE 27.3 CONTINUED

Button	Item	Alternative Method	Purpose
(icon)	VBA Help	Help, Microsoft Visual Basic Help	Opens the Welcome topic of VBA online help.
N/A	Object List	None	Displays a list of objects in form or report modules. Only (General) appears for Access modules.
N/A	Procedure List	None	Displays a function or procedure in a module. Select the procedure or event name from the drop-down list. Procedures are listed in alphabetical order by name.

MODULE SHORTCUT KEYS

Additional shortcut keys and key combinations listed in Table 27.4 can help you as you write and edit VBA code. Only the most commonly used shortcut keys are listed in Table 27.4.

TABLE 27.4 PRIMARY KEY COMBINATIONS FOR ENTERING AND EDITING VBA CODE

Key Combination	Purpose
F3	Finds next occurrence of a search string
Shift+F3	Finds previous occurrence of a search string
F9	Sets or clears a breakpoint on the current line
Ctrl+Shift+F9	Clears all breakpoints
Tab	Indents single or multiple lines of code by four (default value) characters
Shift+Tab	Outdents single or multiple lines of code by four characters
Ctrl+Y	Deletes the line on which the cursor is located

You can change the default indentation of four characters per tab stop by choosing Tools, Options. Click the Editor tab and then enter the desired number of characters in the Tab Width text box.

THE VBA HELP SYSTEM

Microsoft provides an extensive, multilevel Help system to help you learn and use VBA. The majority of the help topics for VBA are supplied by a generic VBA help file that's applicable to all flavors of VBA. If you place the cursor on a keyword or select a keyword and then press the F1 key, for example, a help window for the keyword appears (see Figure 27.9). If you click the "Example" hotspot under the name of the keyword, the window displays VBA sample code (see Figure 27.10).

Figure 27.9
Placing the cursor on a keyword, such as `For Each`, and pressing F1 opens the Microsoft Visual Basic Help window with the topic for the keyword.

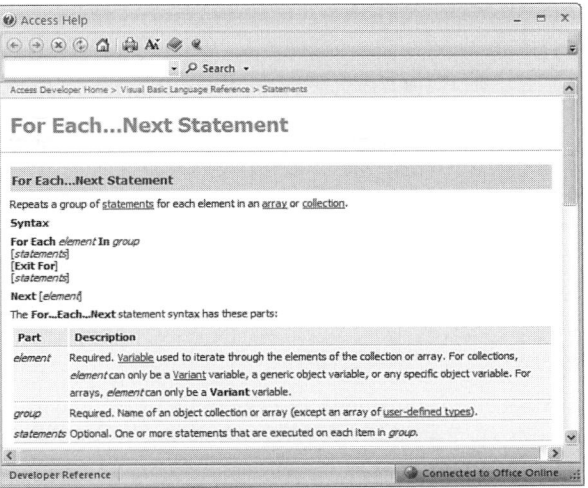

Figure 27.10
Scroll to find the VBA example code for the keyword.

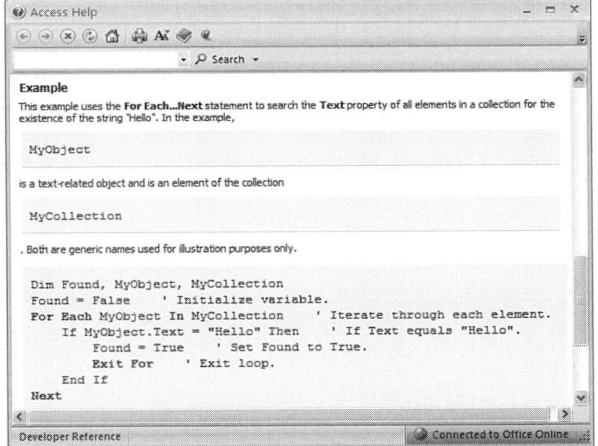

EXAMINING THE UTILITY FUNCTIONS MODULE

One recommended way to learn a new programming language is to examine simple examples of code and analyze the statements used in these examples.

The sections that follow show how to open a module, display a function in the Module window, add a breakpoint to the code, and then use the Immediate window to execute the function.

ADDING A BREAKPOINT TO THE IsLoaded() FUNCTION

When you examine the execution of VBA code written by others, and when you debug your own application, breakpoints are very useful. This section explains how to add a breakpoint to the `IsLoaded()` function so that the Suppliers form stops executing when the Suppliers form's On Current event calls the `Form_Current` event handler, which in turn calls the `IsLoaded()` function, and Access displays the code in the Module window.

TIP

> To see how form events call event handlers in a class module, change to Design view, open the Properties window, and click the Event tab. Click the Builder button of the On Current event, which has [Event Procedure] in its text box, to open the VBA editor with the corresponding event-handling subprocedure in the code window.

To add a breakpoint to the `IsLoaded()` function, follow these steps:

1. If you have the VBA editor open with Northwind as the current database, double-click Utility Functions in the Project Explorer. Otherwise, display the Database window, click the Modules shortcut, and double-click the Utility Functions module to open the VBA editor with Utility Functions active.

   Place the cursor on the line that begins with **If** `oAccessObject = …` and press F9. The breakpoint you create is indicated by changing the display of the line to reverse red and by the placement of a red dot in the margin indicator at the left of the window (see Figure 27.11, which has a line break added).

Figure 27.11
Adding a breakpoint to an instruction highlights the entire instruction and adds a red dot for each line of the instruction.

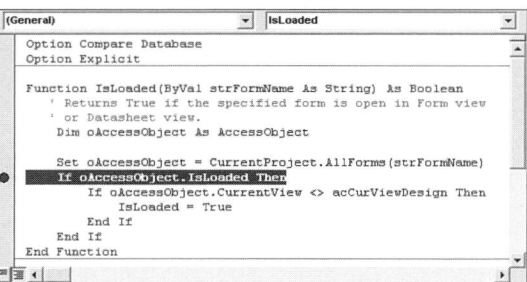

3. Click the View Microsoft Access button and open the Suppliers (Access 2003) form to execute the `Form_Current` procedure attached to the On Current event of the form. When the Suppliers form's `Form_Current` procedure calls the `IsLoaded()` function, the execution of `IsLoaded()` begins with the **Set** `oAccessObject = CurrentProject.AllForms(strFormName)` line and halts at the line with the breakpoint. When execution encounters a breakpoint, the module containing the breakpoint opens automatically. The line with the breakpoint turns yellow (see Figure 27.12).

TIP

> DataTips, which are similar in appearance to ToolTips or ScreenTips, display the name and value of variables in break mode. When you pass the mouse pointer over the `strFormName` argument, a DataTips window displays the value.

Figure 27.12
When VBA execution encounters a break-point, the interpreter stops before execut-ing the instruction. The code of the breakpoint line turns yellow. Passing the cursor over a variable displays its value in a DataTips window.

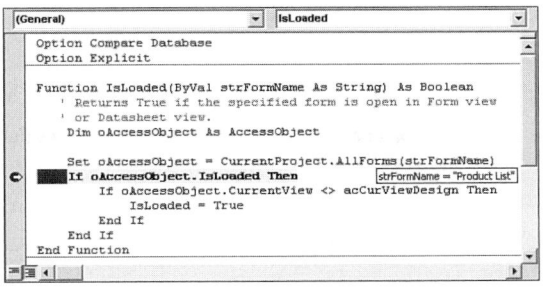

```
(General)                          IsLoaded
    Option Compare Database
    Option Explicit

    Function IsLoaded(ByVal strFormName As String) As Boolean
        ' Returns True if the specified form is open in Form view
        ' or Datasheet view.
        Dim oAccessObject As AccessObject

        Set oAccessObject = CurrentProject.AllForms(strFormName)
        If oAccessObject.IsLoaded Then        strFormName = "Product List"
            If oAccessObject.CurrentView <> acCurViewDesign Then
                IsLoaded = True
            End If
        End If
    End Function
```

4. Press F5 or click the Run Sub/UserForm button to resume execution of the VBA code. Alternatively, press F8 to step through the remaining lines of code. Access displays the Suppliers form.

5. Close the Suppliers form to execute the Form_Close procedure that's attached to the form's On Close event. When the Suppliers form's Form_Close procedure calls the IsLoaded() function, execution occurs as described in step 3, and the IsLoaded() func-tion again halts at the line with the breakpoint. In this case, IsLoaded returns **False**.

6. Place the cursor on one of the highlighted lines, and press F9 to toggle the breakpoint off.

The **Set** oAccessObject = CurrentProject.AllForms(strFormName) instruction returns a pointer to the member of the AllForms collection specified by strFormName. If strFormName isn't a member of the collection, you receive a runtime error, because the IsLoaded() func-tion doesn't include error-handling code.

PRINTING TO THE IMMEDIATE WINDOW WITH THE DEBUG OBJECT

Previous chapters of this book introduced you to the VBA editor's Immediate window and showed you how to obtain the values of variables with **?** *VarName* statements. When you want to view the values of several variables, you can use the Print method of the **Debug** object to automate printing to the Immediate window. If you add the **Debug** object to a func-tion that tests the names of each open form, you can create a list in the Immediate window of all the forms that are open.

→ For earlier examples of using the Immediate window, **see** "Using the Immediate Window," **p. 422**.

The Forms and AllForms collections contain a Form or AccessObject member for each form in the project. As shown earlier, you can use a **For** … **Next** loop with a counter to obtain the form name or a **For Each** *ObjectName* **In** *CollectionName* … **Next** loop to avoid declaring a counter variable and specify the counter value as the Item index. You must declare a Form or AccessObject variable, however, to use **For Each**.

To create a `WhatsLoaded()` function to list all open forms, follow these steps:

1. Load three or more forms. The Customers, Categories, Employees, and Main Switchboard forms are good choices because these forms load quickly.

2. In the Utility Functions module, type **Private Sub WhatsLoaded()** below the **End Function** line of the `IsLoaded()` function. The VBA interpreter adds the **End Sub** statement for you automatically.

3. Type the following code between the **Private Sub...** and **End Sub** lines:

```
Dim intCtr As Integer
For intCtr = 0 To Forms.Count - 1
    Debug.Print intCtr & " = " & Forms(intCtr).FormName
Next intCtr
```

The **For...Next** loop iterates the `Forms` collection. The **Debug.Print** statement prints the name of each open form in the Immediate window.

NOTE

> The VBA editor includes a powerful feature called IntelliSense statement autocompletion to help you write VBA code. The interpreter monitors each line of code as you type it in. When you type variable declarations, use built-in Access and VBA functions, or use object methods and properties in your code, the interpreter displays a pop-up window to help you select appropriate values.
>
> Figure 27.13 shows the pop-up list window that appears after you type the **As** keyword in the first **Dim** statement of the code you enter in step 3. For procedures, functions, and methods, the pop-up help window lists all the arguments for the procedure, function, or method, so you don't have to remember all the possible arguments. You can turn this feature on and off by choosing Tools, Options and then selecting or clearing the Auto List Members check box on the Editor tab of the Options dialog.

Figure 27.13
As you type VBA code in the editor window, an autocompletion list opens to provide a list of keywords, constants, or objects that are candidates for the following entry. As you add letters, the list displays items whose names start with those letters.

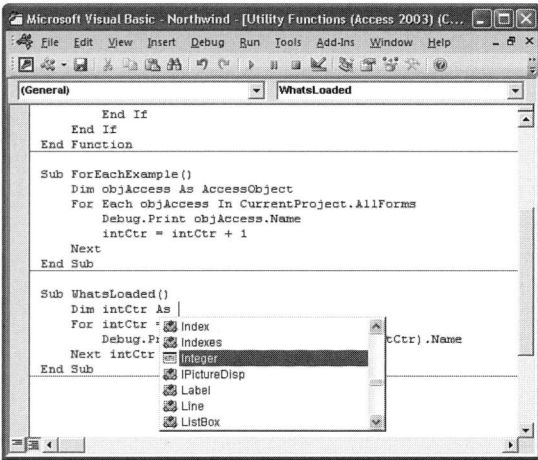

4. Place the cursor anywhere within the WhatsLoaded code you typed and press F5 or click the Run Sub/UserForm button. If the Immediate window isn't open, press Ctrl+G to open it. (The G shortcut comes from the windows prior name—Debug.) The name of each form is added to the Immediate window by the **Debug**.Print statement (see Figure 27.14).

Figure 27.14
Executing the WhatsLoaded subprocedure prints a list of the forms open in Access.

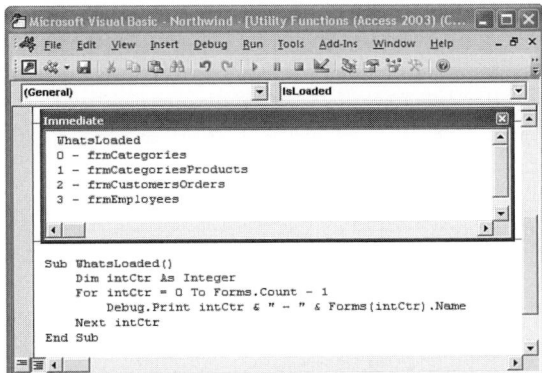

5. Close and don't save changes to the Utility Function module. Then close the other forms you opened for this example.

The **Debug**.Print statement is particularly useful for displaying the values of variables that change when you execute a loop. When you've completed the testing of your procedure, you delete the Debug statements.

To create a list of all forms and their loaded state, add the following code to the module:

```
Private Sub FormState()
    Dim accForm As AccessObject
    For Each accForm In CurrentProject.AllForms
        Debug.Print accForm.Name & _
            " Open = " & accForm.IsLoaded
    Next accForm
End Sub
```

With the cursor on a line in the subprocedure, press F5 to execute the function. The Immediate window displays a list of all forms in the current project (see Figure 27.15).

27

Figure 27.15
The `FormState` sub-procedure lists all forms in the database and indicates if the form is open.

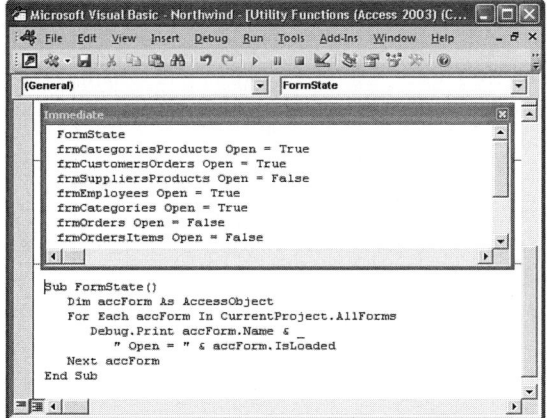

Using Text Comparison Options

Tests of text data in fields of tables, query result sets, and `Recordset` objects against **String** or **Variant** text data in modules depend on the value of the **Option Compare…** statement, which appears in the Declarations section of the Utility Functions module. To determine how text comparisons are made in the module, you can use any of the following statements:

- **Option Compare** Binary comparisons are case sensitive. Lowercase letters are not equivalent to uppercase letters. To determine the sort order of characters, Access uses the character value assigned by the Windows ANSI character set.

- **Option Compare** Text comparisons are not case sensitive. Lowercase letters are treated as the equivalent of uppercase letters. For most North American users, the sort order is the same as **Option Compare** Binary, ANSI. Unless you have a reason to specify a different comparison method, use **Option Compare** Text.

- **Option Compare** Database comparisons are case sensitive, and the sort order is that specified for the database.

Access adds **Option Compare** Database to the Declarations section when you create a new module, overriding the default. Binary and Database are keywords in VBA, but these words don't have the same meaning when used in the **Option Compare…** statement. For compatibility with changes in possible future releases of Access, you should not use Compare or Text as names of variables.

In the Real World—Macro Schizophrenia

Macros have been a common add-on to productivity applications since the early days of WordPerfect, Lotus 1-2-3, and other previously popular DOS word processing and spreadsheet applications. Each application took a different approach to automating repetitive operations, which resulted in a Tower of Macro Language Babel. WordPerfect 4.x and 5.x for

DOS, in particular, had an arcane set of macro commands and peculiar program structure that frustrated thousands of erstwhile programmers.

About 15 years ago, Bill Gates decided that all Microsoft applications using macros would share a common macro language built on BASIC. BASIC is the acronym for Beginners All-Purpose Symbolic Instruction Code, an interpreted language developed at Dartmouth College. The intended application for BASIC was programming on terminal-based (usually Teletype) time-sharing computers. Gates' choice of BASIC for a macro language isn't surprising when you consider that Microsoft Corporation was built on the foundation of Gates' BASIC interpreter that ran in the 8KB (not MB) of RAM common to the early predecessors of the PC, such as the Altair microcomputer. Gates reiterated his desire for a common macro language in an article that appeared in a late 1991 issue of the now-extinct *One-to-One with Microsoft* magazine.

NOTE

> About 10 years ago, Bill Gates gave a speech in which he mentioned a subscription model for licensing productivity software, thereby creating an "Office Annuity" for Microsoft Corporation. Microsoft abandoned the subscription model proposed for Office XP. But Microsoft's new Software Assurance terms, which most analysts and IT managers contend increases software costs substantially, is tantamount to a "Windows Annuity" for Office, operating systems, and server products.

Prior to Access 1.0, the only Microsoft application with a BASIC-like macro language was Word. WordBASIC, later Word Basic, was far more versatile, easy to understand, and useful than the competitors' pidgin-like languages. Access 1.0 offered Embedded Basic (EB)—later to become Access Basic—as its programming language. Apparently Microsoft believed that Access Basic would be incomprehensible to average Access users, so Microsoft's product team tacked on a simplified macro language. Thus, Access became saddled with the two "macro" languages mentioned early in the chapter.

Visual Basic 3.0 was the most popular Windows programming tool by the time Microsoft released Access 1.0. Visual Basic, Access, and Word each had their own Basic flavor. Microsoft touted Visual Basic as a programming language, while Access Basic and Word Basic retained the macro terminology. Excel was the next Microsoft application to gain Basic as a macro language, this time in the guise of Visual Basic, Applications Edition, also known as Visual Basic for Applications. Microsoft's goal was to unify all three Visual Basic dialects under the VBA umbrella. Microsoft finally achieved Gates' objective with the release of Visual Basic 6.0 and Office 2000. There's a common aphorism that "after a few releases, Microsoft usually gets it right." But 10 years is a long time, even by Microsoft standards.

Calling VBA a macro language is undeserved damnation by faint praise. VBA is a true programming language and, because of its integration with Microsoft Office, is undoubtedly the most widely used of all programming languages—including C/C++, COBOL, C#, Visual Basic .NET (also known as Visual Basic 2005), and Java. VBA is easier to learn than

27

Java and is an order of magnitude less difficult to master than C++ or COBOL. Although VBA doesn't qualify as a truly object-oriented (OO) programming language—it lacks inheritance and some other OO niceties—VBA is sufficiently object-enabled to handle virtually all common database-related programming chores.

After you gain experience with VBA in Access, you can leverage your programming skills in Visual Basic 6.0 or Visual Basic .NET. Unfortunately, VB 6.0 is in maintenance-mode purgatory and mastering Visual Basic .NET involves a steep learning curve for VB 6.0 pros. Even if you're an accomplished Access macro writer, use Access's Macro converter to automate the process of moving to VBA, as described in the preceding chapter.

HANDLING EVENTS WITH VBA AND MACROS

In this chapter

Introducing Event-Driven Programming

All Windows applications are event-driven, which means that an event, such as a mouse click on a command button or a change in the position of a record pointer, executes individual standalone or embedded macros, or blocks of application programming code. If you elect to use VBA, the majority of the code you write consists of event-handling subprocedures—also called *event procedures* or *event handlers*—that are contained within [{**Public**¦**Private**}] **Sub** {Form¦Report}_[ObjectName_]EventName...**End Sub** structures of class modules. *Class module* is the VBA term that describes a container for Access-specific VBA code that's embedded within a Form or Report container. As mentioned in Chapter 26, "Automating Access Applications with Macros 2007," class modules correspond to embedded macrosheets. This chapter primarily describes how to write Access VBA event-handling code in Form and Report class modules to automate your Access 2007 applications. However, it also discusses macros where appropriate.

NOTE

> This chapter, like most others, requires the Northwind.accdb sample database file to work through the exercises.

→ For more information on the Northwind.accdb file, **see** "The Accompanying CD-ROM," **p. 10**.

Understanding the Role of Class Modules

Class modules are containers for VBA code that relate to a particular class of objects. Access 2007 defines two classes (collections)—Forms and Reports—that contain VBA code for a particular instance of the class: a Form or Report object. In object-oriented programming terms, class modules *encapsulate* VBA code within a Form or Report object. Code encapsulation lets you create reusable objects. For example, when you copy a form from one Access database to another, the copy you make includes the code in the form's class module. The same is true for embedded macros.

Access's Form and Report class modules differ from conventional VBA modules in that a Form or Report object is integral to the code and contributes the object's visible properties (appearance). Conventional modules, such as Northwind.mdb's Utility Functions, appear in the Modules group of the Navigation pane. Your event-handling code creates a custom set of methods (behavior) that are applicable to the object. When you open a form or report, you create the default instance of the corresponding Form or Report object. It's the default instance of the object that appears in the Navigation Pane's forms or reports groups.

28

NOTE

> VBA also lets you create additional temporary, nondefault instances of Form and Report objects with the **New** reserved word. However, using **New** to create nondefault Form or Report instances isn't a common practice.

The **Me** self-reference specifies the current instance of the Form or Report object. You get or set form or report property values or apply methods to Form or Report objects with code such as **Me**.Width or **Me**.Recordset.MoveFirst. When you add the first event procedure to a form or report, Access creates the Form or Report class module and sets the Form.HasModule or Report.HasModule property value to True.

CREATING A SWITCHBOARD CLASS MODULE WITH THE MACRO-TO-VBA CONVERTER

 The easiest way to create a sample class module is to let an Access utility feature do it for you. As you learned in Chapter 26, Access 2007's Switchboard Manager generates macros instead of the VBA code generated by earlier Access versions. Fortunately, Access has a Macro-to-VBA Converter feature that reads each macrosheet in a standalone or embedded macro and attempts to convert the macro to a corresponding VBA event procedure. The Converter generates a VBA module from a standalone macro or a Form or Report class module from an embedded macro. The converter also changes the *EventName* property value from *MacroName* or [Embedded Macro] to [Event Procedure].

→ To review how the Switchboard Manager works, **see** "Exploring Access 2007's Macro-based Switchboard Manager," **p. 1164**.

NOTE

> The Macro-to-VBA Converter was called the *Macro To Module Converter* in earlier Access versions.

Customizing the execution of switchboard commands often justifies converting a switchboard form's embedded macro to a VBA class module. As an example, you might want to close the currently open form or report when making another switchboard selection. Doing this prevents cluttering Access's main window with an excessive number of tabs, which is likely to confuse users. Although it's possible to implement this change by editing the existing embedded macro, it's more straightforward to write VBA code to handle the task. For this example, you need to convert only the macrosheets for the Option1_Click and OptionLabel1_Click events, which are identical. Converting only the macro to customize minimizes the potential effort to debug and fix the resulting VBA code.

CAUTION

> Always run the Macro-to-VBA Converter on a copy of your Access 2007 database. Running the converter on embedded macros permanently disables subsequent VBA event-handling capability.

28

Macro conversion is a one-way, all-or-nothing process, so follow these steps to convert the macros from a copy of the database without changing any event handlers from embedded macros:

1. Open the \SEUA12\Chaptr26\Macros26.accdb database, click the Office button, and choose Manage, Back Up Database twice to create two backup copies in the same folder.

 2. Open one of the backup copies, open the Switchboard form in Design view, click the Database Tools tab, and click the Macro group's Convert Form's Macros to Visual Basic button to open the Convert Form Macros: Switchboard dialog (see Figure 28.1).

Figure 28.1
The Macro-to-VBA Converter adds error-handling code and macro comments by default.

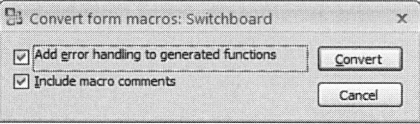

3. Accept the defaults and click OK to convert all macrosheets to VBA subprocedures and change all event handlers to [Event Procedure].

 4. Click the Visual Basic button to open the VBA Editor and double-click the Form_ Switchboard item in the Project Explorer pane, if necessary, to display the class module, which contains four procedures: Form_Current, Form_Open, Option1_Click, and OptionLabel1_Click (see Figure 28.2).

Figure 28.2
The VBA Editor displays the first two event procedures created from the embedded macro.

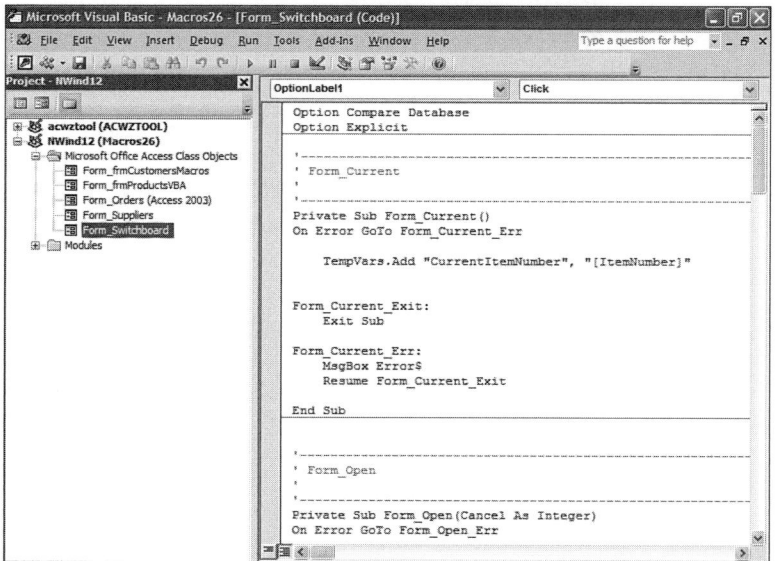

5. Click the code pane, press Ctrl+A to select all code, press Ctrl+C to copy it to the Clipboard, and close the backup copy.

 6. Reopen Macros26.accdb, open the Switchboard form in Design view, click the Form Design Tools – Design ribbon's View Code button in the Tools group to open an empty VBA Editor window, click the code window, and press Ctrl+V to paste the code to the editor.

7. Delete the duplicate **Option** Compare Database and **Option** Explicit statements, and choose <u>D</u>ebug, Compi<u>l</u>e Nwind12 to test for illegal syntax. (You can't execute code in a class module that has compile errors). The Call Argument & "()" line throws an error in two locations, so place an apostrophe (') in front of the statements temporarily.

8. Click the View Microsoft Office Access button or press Alt+F11 to return to Access, open the Property Sheet, select the Option1 button in the drop-down list, click the Events tab, open the On Click event list, and choose [Event Procedure] (see Figure 28.3).

Figure 28.3
The first step in the upgrade-to-VBA process is to assign the VBA event procedure to handle the Option1 button's On Click event.

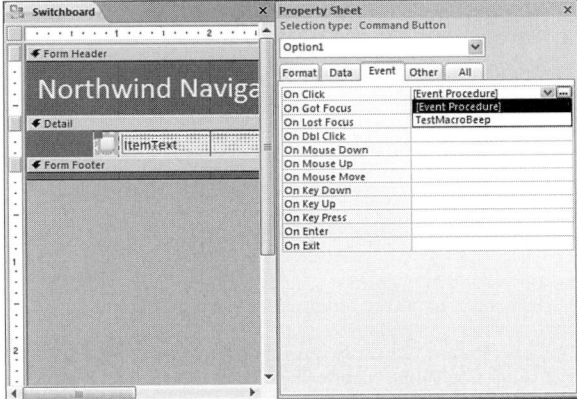

At this point, you've only assigned the Option1 button's On Click event to the Option1_Click event handler. Embedded macrosheets currently handle all other Switchboard form events.

TESTING AND FIXING CONVERTED CODE

Listing 28.1 shows the initial code of the Form_Switchboard class module's Option1_Click() procedure. All procedures have standard error-handling code consisting of **On Error GoTo** Err_Lable…Err_Lable:…**Resume** Exit_Label…**Exit Sub** statements. Adding error handling to every procedure you write is a good VBA programming practice.

→ For details on the use of the On Error statement, **see** "Handling Runtime Errors," **p. 1198**.

LISTING 28.1   EVENT-HANDLING CODE OF THE Form_Switchboard **CLASS MODULE'S**
Option1_Click() **PROCEDURE**

```
Option Compare Database
Option Explicit

Private Sub Option1_Click()
On Error GoTo Option1_Click_Err

    On Error GoTo 0
```

continues

LISTING 28.1 CONTINUED

```
      If (Command = 1) Then
         TempVars.Add "SwitchboardID", "[Argument]"
         DoCmd.SetProperty "Label1", acPropertyCaption, DLookup("ItemText", _
            "Switchboard Items", "[SwitchboardID] = " & TempVars("SwitchboardID"))
         DoCmd.SetProperty "Label2", acPropertyCaption, DLookup("ItemText", _
            "Switchboard Items", "[SwitchboardID] = " & TempVars("SwitchboardID"))
         DoCmd.Requery ""
         Exit Sub
      End If
      If (Command = 2) Then
         DoCmd.OpenForm Argument, acNormal, "", "", acAdd, acNormal
         Exit Sub
      End If
      If (Command = 3) Then
         DoCmd.OpenForm Argument, acNormal, "", "", , acNormal
         Exit Sub
      End If
      If (Command = 4) Then
         DoCmd.OpenReport Argument, acViewReport, "", "", acNormal
         Exit Sub
      End If
      If (Command = 5) Then
         DoCmd.RunCommand acCmdSwitchboardManager
         TempVars.Add "SwitchboardID", "DLookUp(""SwitchboardID"",
            ""Switchboard Items"",""[ItemNumber] = 0 AND [Argument] = 'Default'"")"
         DoCmd.SetProperty "Label1", acPropertyCaption, DLookup("ItemText", _
            "Switchboard Items", "[SwitchboardID] = " & TempVars("SwitchboardID"))
         DoCmd.SetProperty "Label2", acPropertyCaption, DLookup("ItemText", _
            "Switchboard Items", "[SwitchboardID] = " & TempVars("SwitchboardID"))
         DoCmd.Requery ""
         Exit Sub
      End If
      If (Command = 6) Then
         DoCmd.CloseDatabase
         Exit Sub
      End If
      If (Command = 7) Then
         DoCmd.RunMacro Argument, , ""
         Exit Sub
      End If
      If (Command = 8) Then
         'Call Argument & "()"
         Exit Sub
      End If
      Beep
      MsgBox "Unknown option.", vbOKOnly, ""

Option1_Click_Exit:
   Exit Sub

Option1_Click_Err:
   MsgBox Error$
   Resume Option1_Click_Exit

End Sub
```

→ To review the syntax of the DLookup() function, **see** "Using the DLookup Domain Aggregate Function for Lookups," **p. 719**.

NOTE

> Problem code and VBA reserved words in the preceding event handler are in bold type.

Following are some of the initial steps in debugging the converter's initially generated code:

1. Click the View Microsoft Office Access button or press Alt+F11 to return to Access, open the Switchboard form in Form view, and click one of the top-level menu's buttons. You receive the error message shown in Figure 28.4.

Figure 28.4
Unhandled errors open messages such as this, which indicates that an instruction returned a value of an inappropriate data type. In this case, the expected data type was **Integer** but the actual data type was **String**.

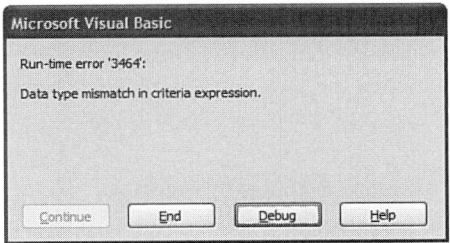

The **On Error GoTo 0** statement, which the converter appears to have added to assist debugging, overrides the **On Error GoTo** Option1_Click_Err statement and issues an unhandled error message.

2. Click Debug to close the message box and highlight the statement that caused the error (see Figure 28.5).

Figure 28.5
The VBA debugger highlights the offended statement. The preceding line is the culprit.

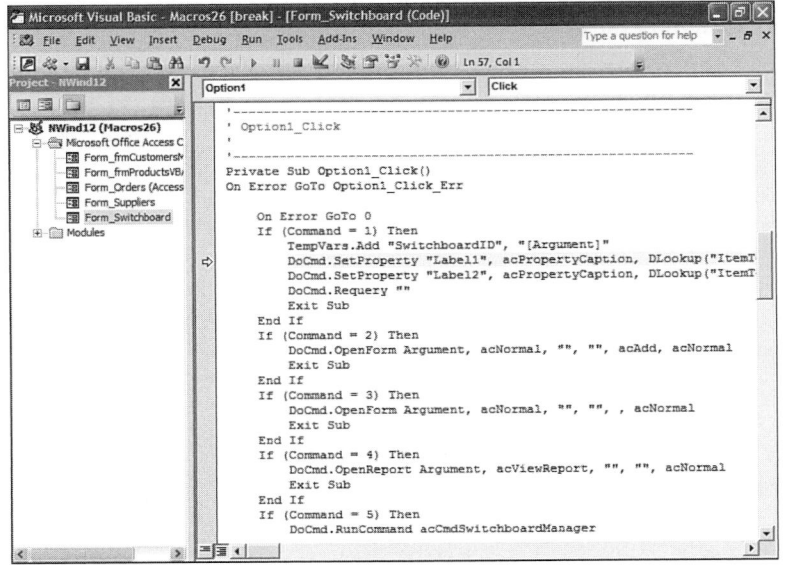

28

In this case, the "[Argument]" argument assigned itself as the value, instead of the current value of the Argument field from form's record source (the Switchboard Items table), which should be 2.

■ 3. Click the Reset button or choose Run, Reset to exit the code, and change the `TempVars.Add "SwitchboardID", "[Argument]"` statement to `TempVars.Add "SwitchboardID", Me.Recordset.Argument.Value`.

4. Press Alt+F11 to return to Access again, and click the button again. You receive another error message because error handling isn't implemented.

■ 5. Click the Reset button again, comment-out the **On Error GoTo 0** statement by prefixing it with an apostrophe (`'`), and return to Access and try again. At this point, most buttons work as expected, but if you click the Human Relations Forms button and click the Test Design Application button to open the Switchboard Manager form, and then click Close, you receive the error message shown in Figure 28.6.

Figure 28.6
This handled error message occurs because a hidden Label2 in the Form Header section isn't accessible to the code that follows the `If (Command = 5) Then` statement.

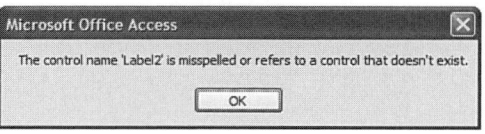

6. Comment out the `DoCmd.SetProperty "Label2", acPropertyCaption, DLookup("ItemText", "Switchboard Items", "[SwitchboardID] = " & TempVars("SwitchboardID"))` statement below the **If (Command = 5) Then** statement and retry the operation.

7. Click the top form's Reports Menu button, click Return to Main Menu, and then click the Customers Forms button. You receive the error message shown in Figure 28.7.

Figure 28.7
This handled error message occurs because the record pointer of the form's record source is at the end of the file (EOF), past the last record.

8. You can ignore this error by modifying the error handler to disregard error number 3021 with this code:

```
Option1_Click_Err:
    'MsgBox Error$
    If Err.Number = 3021 Then
        'Fix No current record error on
        'Return from submenu with no selection made
        Me.Recordset.MoveFirst
        Me.Recordset.MoveNext
        Resume Next
    Else
        MsgBox Err.Description & " Number: " & Err.Number
        Resume Option1_Click_Exit
    End If

End Sub
```

9. Finally, replace the commented 'Call Argument & "()" statement with **Eval** (Argument & "()") to invoke the TestBeep() function in the Utility Functions module.

At this point, you're ready to customize the subprocedure. The Private Sub Option1_Click procedure in the \SEUA12\Chaptr28\Events28.accdb database includes the code that closes the last-opened form or report when the user clicks a different button.

Access 2007's DoCmd object is the key to manipulating Access application objects with VBA. DoCmd lets a VBA statement execute the equivalent of an Access macro action, such as OpenForm or Quit. Application-specific reserved words, such as DoCmd, preclude a common set of VBA objects for all members of Office; thus, DoCmd is an *Access-specific object*, not a reserved word.

→ To learn more about the DoCmd object, **see** "Working with Access 2007's DoCmd Methods," **p. 1223**.

EXAMINING PROJECT CLASS MODULE MEMBERS IN OBJECT BROWSER AND PROJECT EXPLORER

Each Form and Report object in the current database that has a class module appears in the Classes list when you select the project name of the current database in the Project/Library (upper) drop-down list of Object Browser. By default, the project name for an Access database is the filename of the database without a file extension; thus, the project name for Northwind.mdb is Northwind. The default <globals> object displays all the procedures in conventional Access modules of the current database in the right-hand Members Of '<globals>' list. These procedures also appear in Members Of '*ModuleName*' entries for each module in the project.

28

TIP

To launch Object Browser, select a form or report in the Database window, click the Code button to display the class module for the form, and then press F2 or choose View, Object Browser.

When you select a Form or Report object, items representing properties of the Form or Report object and each of the control objects added to the Form or Report object appear in the Members Of '*ObjectName*' list. Each procedure also appears (in bold type) in the list. Figure 28.8 shows the list item for the Option1_Click subprocedure. Object Browser adds the **Public** prefix to functions and subprocedures that aren't declared **Private**. If you double-click a subprocedure or function item, the editor window displays its code.

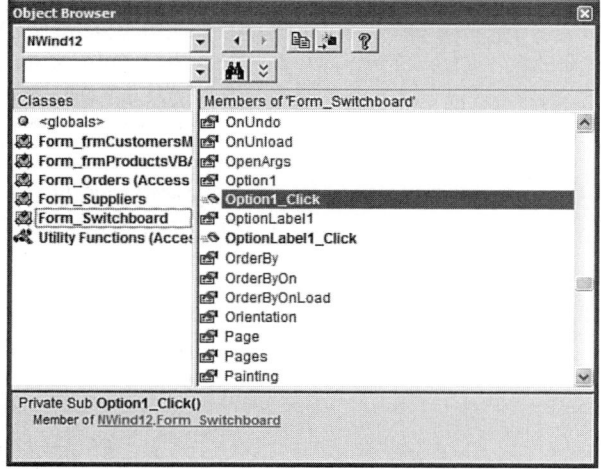

Figure 28.8
Selecting a VBA sub-procedure or function in Object Browser displays a replica of its header in the bottom pane. If the function header doesn't include a scope prefix, Object Browser adds **Public**.

The default reference to the Microsoft Access 12.0 Object library (Msacc.olb) enables programming of Access-specific objects, such as the DoCmd object described in the preceding section. To display Access-specific objects, select Access in Object Browser's Project/Library list. Scroll to and select the DoCmd object to display a list of its methods (see Figure 28.9). Object Browser's bottom pane displays the required and optional arguments of the method.

The Project Explorer window displays all Form and Report Microsoft Access Class Objects, plus modules that contain global code accessible to all class modules. Double-clicking a list item opens a new editor window. You can change the project name and add an optional project description by right-clicking the Project node and choosing *ProjectName* Properties to open the updated *ProjectName* – Project Properties window (see Figure 28.10). Independent (also called *standalone*) Class Objects have an Instancing property; Form and Report Class Objects don't have properties.

28

Figure 28.9
The Access DoCmd object has many properties. The OpenForm method probably is the most popular of DoCmd's repertoire.

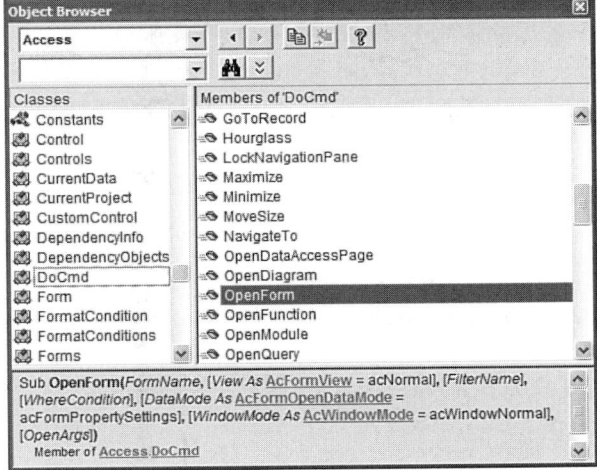

Figure 28.10
The General page of the Project Properties window lets you rename a project and add a description. The Protection page offers the option to hide your VBA code from others and password-protect the code.

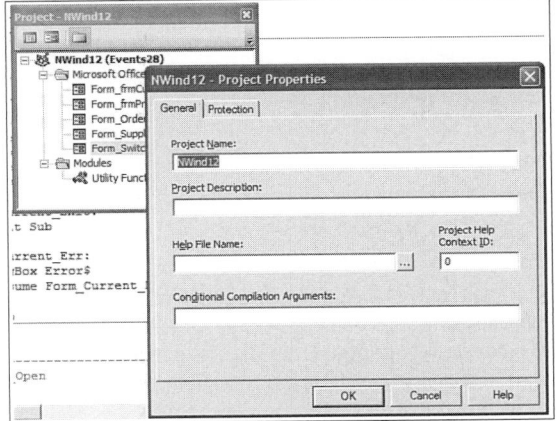

USING FUNCTIONS TO RESPOND TO EVENTS

You can create your own Main Switchboard form by adding command buttons to the form for opening other forms. It's much more efficient, however, to use a single procedure to perform a set of identical tasks in which only the name of the form changes. Minimizing the amount of code in a form speeds opening of the form and minimizes the size of your database file.

Access lets you call a function and pass one or more parameter (argument) values to the function in response to events. A function (not a subprocedure) is required, despite the fact that Access disregards the return value, if the function returns a value. You must write the function yourself before calling it from an event.

28

You can easily change code written by earlier versions of the Command Button Wizard into a general-purpose function that opens any form whose name you pass as an argument. Figure 28.11 shows a simple modification of the frmCommandWiz's cmdOpenCustomers_Click subprocedure to substitute a user-defined function for the event handler. When you replace **Sub** with **Function** in the first line, the VBA interpreter automatically changes **Exit Sub** to **Exit Function** and **End Sub** to **End Function**. You change the name of the function, add the strFormName parameter (the variable the wizard adds to identify the form), pass the value of the strFormName parameter to the OpenForm action, and eliminate code that's not needed for the function, such as **Dim** stDocName **As String**.

Figure 28.11
A few changes to the code of the cmdOpenCustomers _Click subprocedure converts it to a function that opens the form that you specify in the On Click event property value of the command button.

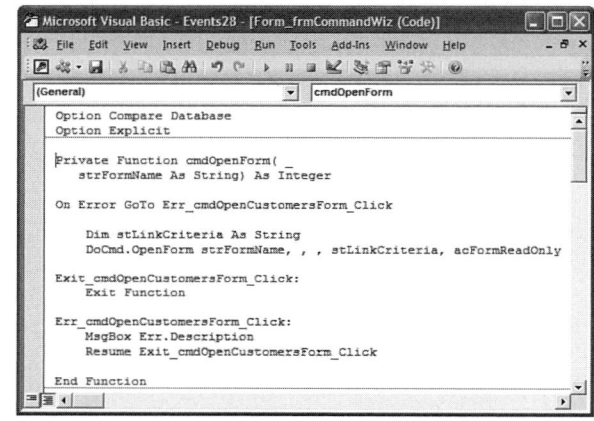

TIP

> If you don't change the name of the subprocedure or pass the cursor through the line containing the **Function** reserved word when converting from a subprocedure to a function, you receive a compile error. The VBA interpreter holds the existing subprocedure name in memory until the line is reinterpreted. Thus, creating a function of the same name results in a duplicate procedure name in the same class module if you press the Enter key when making the change. Duplicate procedure names aren't permitted within in the same module, nor are duplicate names of **Public** procedures permitted within the same project.

 If you encounter compilation errors after changing the type or name of a function or procedure, see the "Calling Procedures and Functions in Class Modules" topic of the "Troubleshooting" section near the end of this chapter.

The syntax to enter in the event text box for executing a function is as follows:

```
=FunctionName([Argument1[, Argument2[, ...]])
```

The arguments are optional, but unless you pass an argument value, such as a form name, there's no advantage to using a function call as an event handler. Arguments must be passed as literal values, such as "*FormName*" or a numeric value. Figure 28.12 shows the entry you type in the On Click text box to open the Customers form, **=cmdOpenForm("frmCustomersOrders")**. To add buttons to open other forms, copy the command button to the Clipboard, paste the copy to your form, and change the Customers caption to the name of the form you want to open.

Figure 28.12
Replacing a subproce-
dure with a function
requires the explicit
calling syntax shown
here for the On Click
event.

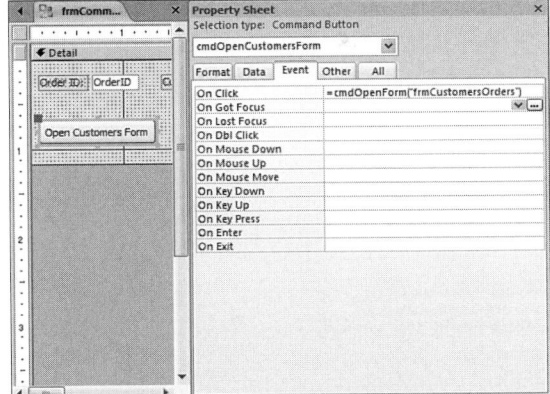

WORKING WITH ACCESS 2007'S DoCmd METHODS

Some of the DoCmd methods duplicate menu commands, such as Print, Close, and Apply Filter/Sort. Other methods substitute for mouse actions. For example, you can use the SelectObject method to select a database object in the same way that you select an open window by clicking it or to select a database object in the Navigation Pane by clicking the object's name. Other DoCmd methods provide capabilities that aren't available through menu commands, such as Beep, which emits a beep sound, or MsgBox, which displays a custom message. It's a better practice, however, to execute **Beep** and **MsgBox** directly with VBA state-ments.

DoCmd METHODS BY TASK

Table 28.1 lists commonly used DoCmd methods grouped by task.

TABLE 28.1 DoCmd METHODS GROUPED BY TASK	
Task by Category	**Method**
Manipulating	
Copy or rename a database object	CopyObject, Rename
Delete a database object	DeleteObject

continues

28

TABLE 28.1   CONTINUED

Task by Category	Method
Open a table, query, form, report, module.	OpenTable, OpenQuery, OpenForm, OpenReport, OpenModule
Open ADP objects	OpenDiagram OpenStoredProcedure OpenView
Close a database object	Close
Save a database object	Save
Print the current database object	PrintOut,
Select a database window object	SelectObject
Copy or rename an object	CopyObject, Rename
Update data or update the screen	RepaintObject, Requery, ShowAllRecords
Set the value of a field, control, or property	SetValue
Executing	
Carry out a menu command	RunCommand
Run a query	OpenQuery, RunSQL
Run a macro or a VBA procedure	RunMacro, RunCode
Run another Windows or DOS application	RunApp
Stop execution of a macro	StopMacro, StopAllMacros
Stop execution of Access	Quit
Stop execution following an event	CancelEvent
Working with Data in Forms and Reports	
Select or sort records	ApplyFilter
Find a record	FindRecord, FindNext
Move to a particular location	GoToControl, GoToRecord, GoToPage

Task by Category	Method
Importing and Exporting Data	
Output data from a table, query, exporting data form, report, or module in .xls, .rtf, or .txt formats	`OutputAs`
Include in an email message data from a table, query, form, report, or module in .xls, .rtf, or .txt format	`SendObject`
Transfer data between Access and other data formats	`TransferDatabase,` `TransferSpreadsheet,` `TransferText,` `TransferSQLDatabase,` `CopyDatabaseFile`
Miscellaneous	
Sound a beep	`Beep`
Send keystrokes to Access or a Windows application	`SendKeys`
Display an hourglass	`Hourglass`
Display or hide system information	`Echo,` `SetWarnings`
Display custom messages	`MsgBox`

→ For a related table of commonly triggered Access 2007 events, **see** "Exploring Access 2007's Event Repertoire," **p. 1152**.

ARGUMENTS OF DoCmd METHODS

Most DoCmd methods require additional information as arguments to specify how the methods work. For example, when you use the OpenForm method, you must specify the name of the form to open as the strFormName argument. Also, to specify whether you want to display the Form, Design, Print Preview, or Datasheet view, use the intView argument. To specify whether you want to allow the editing or adding of new records, use the intDataMode argument. Finally, to specify whether you want the form to be hidden, behave like a dialog, or be in normal mode, use the intWindowMode argument. You specify the values of arguments of the Integer data type by substituting Access intrinsic constants, which use the ac prefix, as in

```
DoCmd.OpenForm strFormName, acNormal, strFilterName, strCriterion, _
acEdit, acDialog, strOpenArg
```

The acNormal, acEdit, and acDialog argument values are Access intrinsic constant values for the intView, intDataMode, and intWindowMode arguments, respectively. You can also specify the numeric value of the constant, but there's no guarantee that the numeric values of Access 2007 constants will remain the same in future versions of Access. Thus, using the names of Access intrinsic constants is better programming practice than supplying numeric values for

28

method arguments. When you type DoCmd in the Visual Basic Editor, the statement autocompletion feature lists the Access constants that are applicable to each argument of the method.

The DoCmd.RunCommand method lets you execute any Access menu choice. The method requires a single acCmd*MenuChoiceName* Access command constant argument, such as acCmdApplyFilterSort, to specify the action to perform. To see the list (called an *enumeration* or *enum*) of all command-related constants, select acCommand in Object Browser's Classes list.

The OutputTo, TransferDatabase, TransferSpreadsheet, and TransferText methods deserve special attention by application developers. These bulk-transfer methods greatly simplify the data interchange between Access and other Office 2007 applications, such as Excel and Word. The more complex DoCmd methods, together with Access 2007's flexible report generation capabilities, are often the deciding factor when choosing between Visual Basic 6+ or Access 2007 for developing database front ends. Visual Basic doesn't offer equivalents of the bulk transfer Access methods.

The TransferSQLDatabase and CopyDatabaseFile methods only apply to ADP and SQL Server databases.

CUSTOMIZING APPLICATIONS WITH RIBBON OBJECTS

The CommandBars API (application programming interface) was the primary method for customizing the UI (user interface) of Access 97 through 2003. The CommandBars object model lets developers and power users add command and toggle buttons, menus, text (edit) boxes, combo boxes, and drop-down lists to the standard Access UI. The CommandBars API adhered to Windows UI standards that had been in effect since Windows 3.0.

Office 2007's new Ribbon UI is based on the RibbonX API, which lets you customize much of Access 2007's standard Ribbon UI. RibbonX is an abbreviation for *Ribbon eXtensibility*. You can hide the standard ribbons (Home, Create, External Data, and Database Tools), which Microsoft calls *tabs*, and substitute your own. Alternatively, you add custom ribbons, which contain groups and controls, or add groups with controls to the application's standard ribbons. You can hide but not delete standard ribbons; this restriction explains the use of the term *extensibility*. RibbonX adds eight new controls: dialogBoxLauncher, gallery, splitButton, label, checkBox, group, tab, and superTip.

There is no resemblance whatsoever between the CommandBar and RibbonX APIs. You create and modify CommandBar objects with VBA code in much the same way as you program any other Office application object. You define Ribbon UI objects declaratively by writing an XML document in the CustomUI namespace (http://schemas.microsoft.com/office/2006/01/customui) that conforms to (validates with) the customUI.xsd schema. RibbonX XML element and attribute values determine the properties of the ribbons, groups, and controls you add.

Customizing Access's UI requires RibbonX XML documents and event-handling code similar to that for other Office 2007 members. Access's basic Ribbon UI customization process is totally built in. Other Office 2007 members use separate COM add-in components or, for members that have Office Open XML (OOXML) file formats, add the RibbonX XML document to a Word .dotm or Excel .xltm macro-enabled template file. By default, Access stores RibbonX documents in a specially named database table. Alternatively, developers can write code to load RibbonX documents from VBA string variables, .xml files, or tables in other databases. Optionally, Access can store icons for controls as images in a table with a field of the Attachments data type.

NOTE

Microsoft Visual Studio 2005 Tools for the 2007 Microsoft Office System (VSTO or VSTO SE) includes tools for creating add-ins and customizing Ribbon UIs for Excel, InfoPath, Outlook, PowerPoint, Visio, and Word, but *not Access 2007*. The http://OpenXMLDeveloper.org website offers a Custom UI Editor for OOXML template files, but not for Access's standalone RibbonX files.

Patrick Schmid, an Office 2007 UI expert, has developed and sells RibbonCustomizer Professional V1.0, a managed .NET 2.0 add-in for customizing the UIs of Access 2007 and other Office 2007 members. You can learn more about his RibbonCustomizer add-in at http://pschmid.net/office2007/ribboncustomizer/ and download a 30-day free trial version.

CREATING NEW RIBBONX OBJECTS

Creating new ribbons or groups and controls with RibbonX is a six-step process:

1. **Write the RibbonX XML documents**—An XML document specifies whether the object replaces or augments the standard ribbon objects, defines new tabs (ribbons), groups, and controls, and specifies the names of callbacks to handle control events. In this case, *callback* is a synonym for *event handler*.

2. **Add callback code for each control**—A VBA event-handler function (not a subprocedure) in a module or a standalone named macro is required for each callback you add in step 1. It is much more common to use VBA functions than Access macros to handle callbacks.

3. **Create a USysRibbons user system table to store the RibbonX XML files**—The USysRibbons table requires two fields, RibbonName and RibbonXML, of the Text(255) and Memo data types, respectively.

4. **Populate the USysRibbons file**—Add the name and XML document for each ribbon to the USysRibbons table.

5. **Specify the initial custom ribbon for the database**—Open the Ribbon Name drop-down list in the Ribbon and Toolbar Options section of the Access Options dialog's Current Database page, and select the startup ribbon. The USysRibbons table populates the drop-down.

6. **Select custom context ribbons for individual forms and reports**—Open the Ribbon Name property's list on the Other page of the Form or Report object's Property Sheet and select the appropriate ribbon.

28

Customizing the Access UI is primarily a development activity, so the following sections provide only a brief introduction to the process with a sample application that contains a simple RibbonX replacement for Access 2007's standard ribbons.

OBTAINING RIBBONX DOCUMENTATION AND SAMPLE CODE

To write RibbonX documents that work, you need familiarity with the RibbonX XML document structure and syntax, have access to a list of names of existing Access controls, and have a source for button icons that are appropriate for your controls.

 Following is a list of the minimum documentation and reference material you need to get started with Access UI customization:

- ***Ribbon Extensibility in Access 2007***—This white paper is a tutorial and reference for customizing the UI of a MarketingProjects.accdb database created from the Marketing projects template. Open this document from http://msdn2.microsoft.com/en-us/library/bb187398.aspx.

- **Marketing projects.accdb sample database**—Download and run Marketing Projects.exe database from the link in the preceding document's "Introducing the New User Interface in Access 2007" section. Running Marketing Projects.exe installs Marketing projects.accdb in your C:\2007 Office System Developer Resources\code samples\Marketing Projects Database folder.

NOTE

> The original database (without the customized Ribbon UI) is available from the CD-ROM as \SEUA12\Chaptr02\MarketingProjects.accdb. A modified version of the customized database with macros replaced by VBA is \SEUA12\Chaptr28\CustomUI28.accdb. \SEUA12\Chaptr28\RibbonX holds copies of the database's XML documents.

- **customUI XML schema**—You need a copy of the 2007 Office System: XML Schema Reference (customUI.xsd) to provide IntelliSense for and validate the RibbonX XML documents you write. Download it from the customUI Schema link of the white paper. By default, customUI.xsd installs in your C:\2007 Office System Developer Resources\Office2007XMLSchema folder.

- **ControlID values for built-in controls**—Adding standard controls to a group or using the icons for standard controls requires you to know the ControlID string, such as ViewsDatasheetView for a toggleButton control. Download the AccessRibbonControls.xls Excel 97–2003 workbook as part of 2007OfficeControlIDsExcel2003.exe from the white paper's 2007 Office System Lists of Control IDs link (see Figure 28.13). The individual workbooks for all Office 2007 members install by default in your C:\2007 Office System Developer Resources\Documents folder.

Figure 28.13
The first few rows and columns of the Access 2007 ControlID worksheet. The ControlID is the ControlName value. Columns not shown are Group Name, Parent Control, Secondary Parent Control, Ordering (row number), and Policy ID. You use the Policy ID value to disable controls with Active Directory group policy.

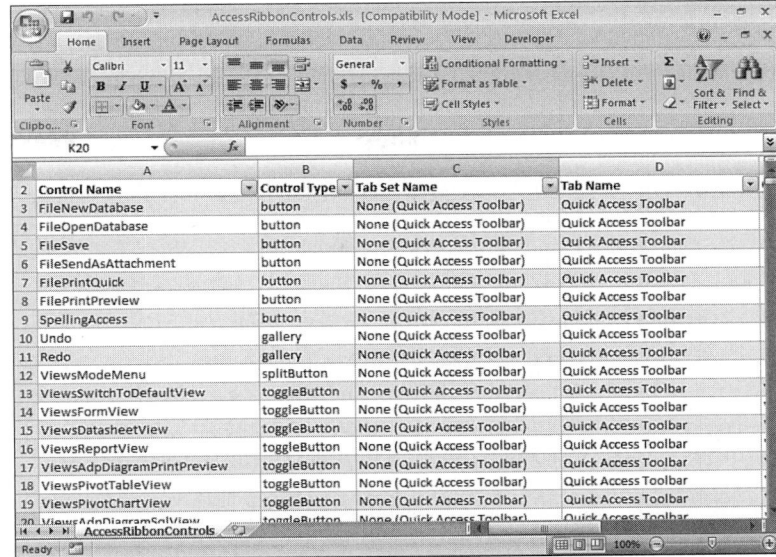

- **Icons for all Office 2007 member controls**—You can use 16×16-pixel or 32×32-pixel icons from any Office 2007 member's controls for custom controls. Download the 2007 Office Systems Icon Gallery workbook (Office2007IconsGallery.xlsm) from the white paper's link (see Figure 28.14). The workbook installs into your C:\2007 Office System Developer Resources\ Office2007IconsGallery folder by default.

Figure 28.14
The Office2007IconsGallery .xlsm workbook adds nine galleries of icons (images) from all Office 2007 members. Click an icon to open a dialog with its ControlID value and images rendered as 16×16-pixel and 32×32-pixel versions.

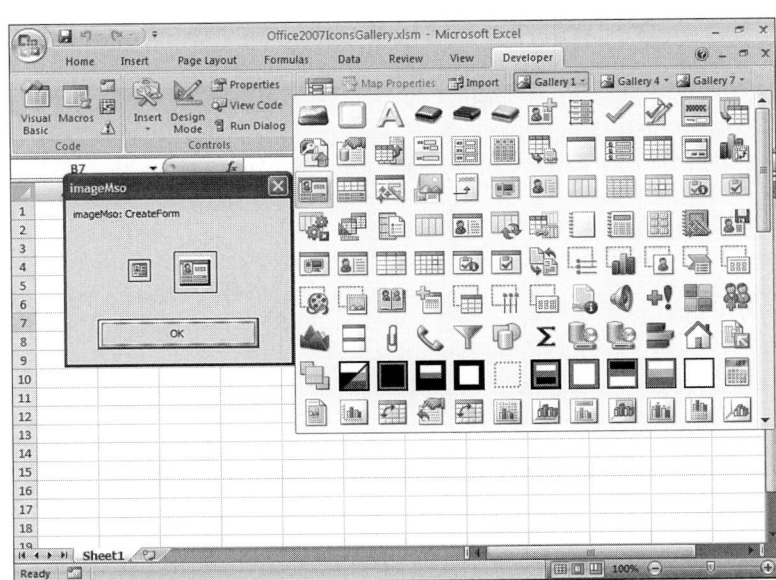

28

NOTE

> You must mark the Show Developer Tab in the Ribbon check box of the Excel Options dialog's Popular page to expose the nine Gallery # buttons. Macros must be enabled to open the imageMso dialog shown in Figure 28.14.

- ***Customizing the Office (2007) Ribbon User Interface for Developers (Part 1 of 3)***— Part 1 of this multipart tutorial and reference covers customizing the UI of all Office 2007 members that support the ribbon. A substantial part of the 40-page document covers Access 2007 customization. Open this optional article from the link on the white paper or http://msdn2.microsoft.com/en-us/library/ms406046.aspx.

- ***Customizing the Office (2007) Ribbon User Interface for Developers (Part 2 of 3)***— Part 2 contains reference tables for descriptions, attributes, and child information for RibbonX controls. Open this 11-page optional article from http://msdn2.microsoft.com/en-us/library/aa338199.aspx.

- ***Customizing the Office (2007) Ribbon User Interface for Developers (Part 3 of 3)***— Part 3 is a set of frequently asked questions (FAQs) about customizing the Ribbon UI. Open FAQs from http://msdn2.microsoft.com/en-us/library/aa722523.aspx.

The preceding documents mention editing XML with Visual Studio or XML Notepad but expect you to be familiar with the process for attaching schemas to enable IntelliSense. The following two sections provide detailed instructions.

EDITING RIBBONX DOCUMENTS WITH VISUAL STUDIO 2005

Visual Studio 2005 (VS) and Visual Basic 2005 Express Edition (VBX) or later have an XML editor that provides IntelliSense when you attach a schema to the document. All RibbonX documents require a `<customUI>` root element with a `<ribbon>` child element. Some documents extend the Office button's menu with an `<officeMenu>` group, and most documents include a `<tabs>` group with at least one `<tab>` element and `<group>` subelement. Therefore, creating a default starter XML document can save you time when starting a RibbonX document from scratch.

NOTE

> If you don't have Visual Studio 2005 Standard Edition or higher installed, you can download a free copy of Visual Basic 2005 Express Edition, which has the same XML editor, from the following MSDN page:
>
> http://msdn.microsoft.com/vstudio/express/vb/download/

28

Following is the XML content for a StarterX.xml document that you can open and edit in VS or VBX:

```
<customUI xmlns="http://schemas.microsoft.com/office/2006/01/customui">
 <ribbon startFromScratch="true" >
  <officeMenu>
  </officeMenu>
```

```
     <tabs>
      <tab id="tabName" label="Name" >
       <group id="grpName" label="Name">
        <button id="btnName" label="Name" />
       </group>
      </tab>
     </tabs>
    </ribbon>
   </customUI>
```

NOTE

Starter.xml is in the \SEUA12\Chaptr28\RibbonX folder together with the four documents
for the CustomUI28.accdb database's menus.

To open Starter.xml or one of the four .xml files from CustomUI28.accdb for editing in VS
or VBX and then attach a schema, do the following:

1. Open Windows Explorer, navigate to \SEUA12\Chaptr28\RibbonX, right-click one of
   the .xml files, and choose Open With, Microsoft Visual Studio 2005 or Microsoft
   Visual Basic 2005 Express Edition to open the file in the VS or VBX XML Editor.

2. In VS, right-click the XML Editor window and choose Properties (or in VS click the
   Properties Window button) to open the Properties pane for the document, and click
   the Schemas property's builder button to open the XSD Schemas dialog.

3. Click the XSD Schemas dialog's Add button to display the Open XSD Schema dialog.
   Navigate to the folder with the schema (the same folder as the XML document for this
   example), double-click the .xsd file, and click OK to dismiss the dialogs and add the
   schema for document validation and IntelliSense-assisted editing.

4. To prove the IntelliSense feature is operational, insert a line under a `<tab>` element and
   type a tag opening character (`<`). IntelliSense displays a list of permissible tags for the
   current location in the document hierarchy (see Figure 28.15).

5. To activate IntelliSense for an attribute name, place the cursor to the right of the last
   character of the element or an attribute value and press the spacebar.

6. Press Ctrl+S to save your changes or choose File, Save As to save the edited file with a
   different name.

EDITING RIBBONX DOCUMENTS WITH XML NOTEPAD 2007

If you prefer viewing and editing XML files in a tree view, you might prefer XML Notepad
2007 to VS or VBX. XML Notepad is a free Microsoft utility that you can download from
the XML Notepad 2007 link on MSDN's http://msdn.microsoft.com/XML/
XMLDownloads/ page. XML Notepad also supports IntelliSense if you load the document's
schema.

28

Figure 28.15
Adding a schema for the document open in the VS or VBX XML editor enables IntelliSense and document validation. This double-exposure of editing the Home.xml file shows IntelliSense for a child element of the <tab> group (left) and an attribute of the <tab> element (right).

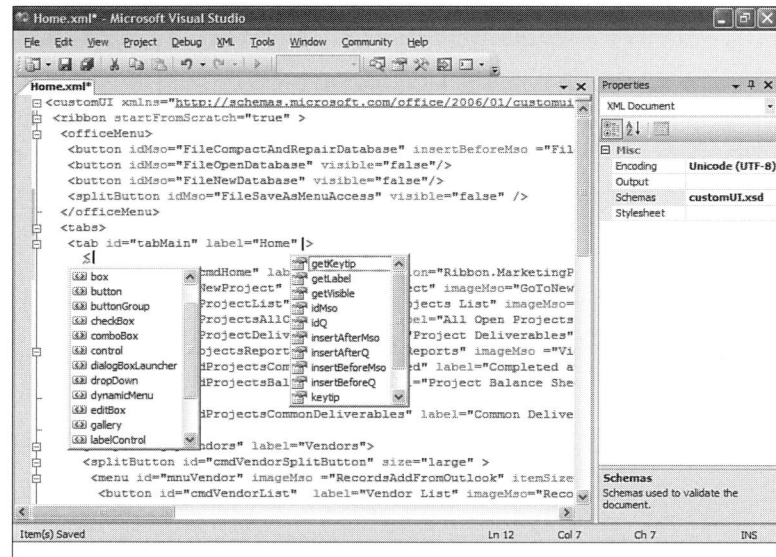

After you've downloaded and installed XML Notepad, do the following to open an RibbonX XML file and load its customUI.xsd schema:

1. Open Windows Explorer, navigate to \SEUA12\Chaptr28\RibbonX, right-click one of the .xml files, and choose Edit with XML Notepad, to open the file in XML Notepad 2007.

2. Choose View, Schemas to open the XML Schemas dialog. Click the builder button in the last column of the first (empty) row to display the Open dialog, navigate to the schema's folder, double-click the .xsd file (customUI.xsd for this example), and click OK to close the dialog.

3. Expand the tree-view nodes to display elements (yellow folder icons) and attributes (red sphere icons).

4. Test IntelliSense by double-clicking a <button> or other control element tag to display the list of available alternates (see Figure 28.16).

5. Add elements or attributes at the selected point in the hierarchy by choosing Insert, Element or Attribute, Before or After or Child.

6. Click the XSL Output tab to display the document in a color-coded, read-only document format (see Figure 28.17). Element tags are brown, attribute names are red, and attribute values are blue.

Figure 28.16
Microsoft XML
Notepad 2007 delivers a tree view of an
XML document in the
left pane. Element
and attribute text content appears in the
right list box.

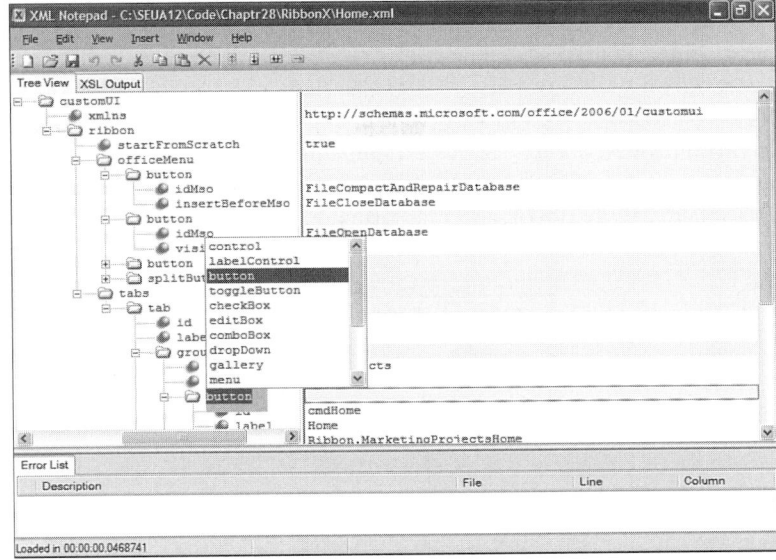

Figure 28.17
The XSL Output page
contains a read-only
rendering of the XML
content in document
format. Applying a
custom XSL transform
isn't appropriate to
this example.

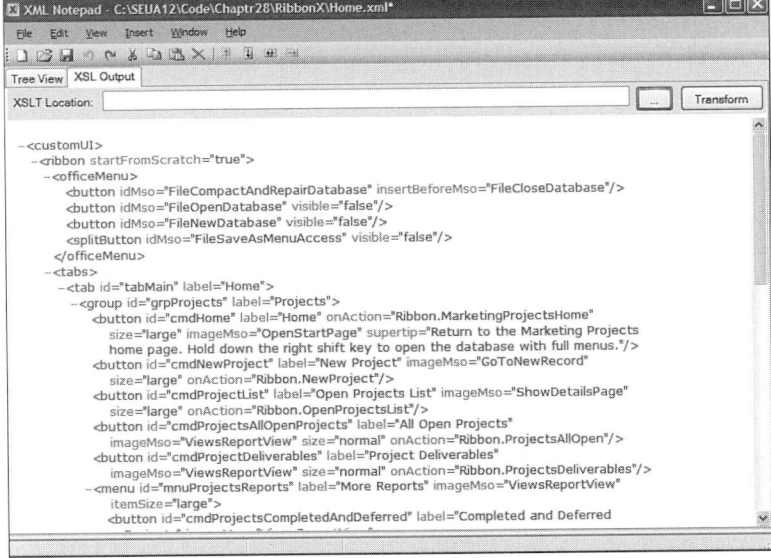

7. Choose File, Save As to save the edited XML file.

CONVERTING MACROS TO VBA CALLBACK FUNCTIONS

The downloadable Marketing projects.accdb application demonstrates replacing the standard Access ribbons (tab set) with a new Home ribbon and adding a Reports, EmployeeList, OpenProjectList, or VendorList context ribbon, depending on the user's choice of Home ribbon controls. Context ribbons contain a mix of custom groups/controls and standard Access groups, such as Clipboard, Records, Sort & Filter, and Find. Figure 28.18 shows the replacement Home ribbon and the Form and Report context ribbons.

Figure 28.18
RibbonX documents in the USysRibbons table generate the replacement Home ribbon (top) and the new Form (middle) and Report (bottom) context ribbons. The List Commands and Commands groups are custom; the remaining groups of the context ribbons are standard Access ribbon groups repurposed by RibbonX document <group> elements.

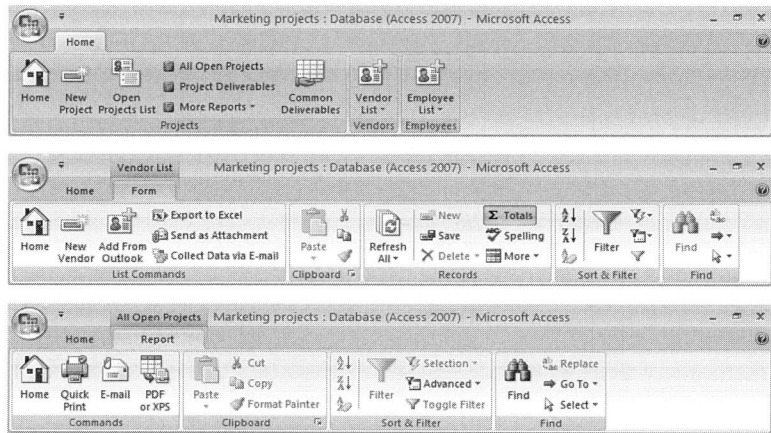

Marketing projects.accdb uses standalone Access macros in the Ribbon Macro object to handle the onAction callbacks of custom buttons; onAction corresponds to the OnClick event for buttons. Listing 28.2 is the VendorsList RibbonX document for the Vendor List – Form contextual ribbon of Figure 28.18 (middle). Macro callbacks use MacroObjectName.MacroName syntax, as in the VendorsList document's onAction="Ribbon.MarketingProjectsHome" and onAction=" Ribbon.NewVendor" attribute name/value pairs.

LISTING 28.2 THE RIBBONX XML DOCUMENT FOR THE VENDORSLIST – FORM CONTEXTUAL RIBBON CONTAINS ELEMENTS FOR NEW CUSTOM AND REPURPOSED STANDARD GROUPS AND CONTROLS

```
<customUI xmlns="http://schemas.microsoft.com/office/2006/01/customui">
 <ribbon>
  <contextualTabs>
   <tabSet idMso="TabSetFormReportExtensibility">
    <tab id="MyTab" label="Form">
     <group id="ListCommands" label="List Commands">
      <button id="cmdHome" label="Home" imageMso="OpenStartPage"
       supertip="Return to the Marketing Projects home page." size="large"
       onAction="Ribbon.MarketingProjectsHome"/>
       <button id="cmdNewVendor" label="New Vendor" imageMso="GoToNewRecord"
```

```
      size="large" onAction="Ribbon.NewVendor"/>
    <button id="cmdAddFromOutlook" label="Add From Outlook"
     imageMso="RecordsAddFromOutlook" size="large"
     onAction=" Ribbon.AddFromOutlook"/>
    <button idMso="ExportExcel" label="Export to Excel" size="normal"/>
    <button idMso="FileSendAsAttachment" label="Send as Attachment"
     size ="normal"/>
    <button id="cmdCollectDataViaEmail" label="Collect Data via E-mail"
     imageMso="CreateEmail" size="normal"
     onAction=" Ribbon.VendorsCollectDataViaEmail"/>
   </group>
   <group idMso="GroupClipboard"></group>
   <group idMso="GroupRecords"></group>
   <group idMso="GroupSortAndFilter"></group>
   <group idMso="GroupFindAccess"></group>
  </tab>
 </tabSet>
 </contextualTabs>
 </ribbon>
</customUI>
```

Macros are suited only for responding to simple callbacks, such as onAction, because macros don't support arguments or provide return values. Arguments or return values enable dynamic changes to labels and substituting custom images for standard button icons with onGetLabel and onGetImage callbacks. Therefore, most projects with custom ribbons will require VBA callback functions and must be digitally signed or run from trusted locations.

It's not a good programming practice to mix macros, with the exception of the AutoExec macro, and VBA code for handling events and callbacks. In the case of the Marketing project.accdb database, this means converting the Ribbon Macro object to a Module with Public Function *MacroName* callback handlers.

Following are the steps required to convert the 20 named macros in Marketing projects.accdb's standalone Ribbon macro to VBA callback functions:

1. Download Marketing projects.accdb as described in the earlier "Obtaining RibbonX Documentation and Sample Code" section.

2. Use the Macro-to-VBA Converter to convert the named macros in the standalone Ribbon Macro object to VBA functions in the Converted Macro-Ribbon module.

NOTE

You don't need to run the Macro-to-VBA Converter on a copy of the database when coverting standalone macros.

3. Change the name of the module to CallBacks or the like.

4. Find and replace **Function** Ribbon_*MacroName* with **Public Function** cb_*Macroname*, and Ribbon_ with cb_ to prevent potential name collisions.

NOTE

Technically, you don't need to add the `Public` prefix because VBA functions and sub-procedures in modules have public (global) scope unless prefixed with `Private`. However it's a good programming practice to declare the scope of your `Functions` and `Subs`.

5. Add the Microsoft Office 12.0 Object Library as a project reference to define the `IRibbonControl` object. Choose <u>T</u>ools, <u>R</u>eferences to open the References dialog, scroll to the Microsoft Office 12.0 Object Library item, mark its check box (see Figure 28.19), and click OK to close the dialog.

Figure 28.19
If you don't add a reference to the Microsoft Office 12.0 Object Library, VBA code that contains variables of type `IRibbonControl` won't compile.

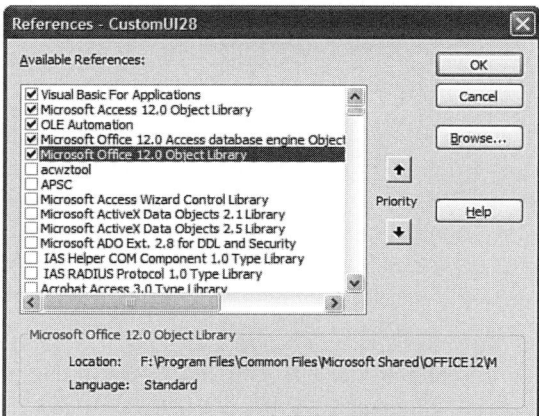

6. Find and replace `()` with `(objControl as IRibbonControl)` to accommodate the `IRibbonControl` object argument's `Context`, `Id`, and `Tag` property values. The Context value is required for the `cb_NewProject`, `cb_NewVendor`, and `cb_NewProject` functions.

NOTE

The `CodeContextObject` property returns the object in which the macro or VBA code is running. Macros use `CodeContextObject` to return the name of the form or report in which the macro is running. However, your VBA code throws runtime errors if you don't replace instances of `CodeContextObject` with `objControl.Context`, as shown in Listing 28.3.

7. Mark the Show Add-In User Interface Errors check box in the General section of the Access Options' Advanced page to prevent the application from ignoring error messages during testing.

8. Open the USysRibbons table and Notepad.

9. Select the Home ribbon's RibbonXML document, press Ctrl+X to cut it to the Clipboard, paste the document into Notepad, click Edit, Replace, replace all instances of `Ribbon.` with `cb_`, press Ctrl+A to select all text, select the empty RibbonXML cell, and press Ctrl+V to paste the modified document to the table.

10. Repeat step 9 for the VendorList, OpenProjectList, EmployeeList, and Reports contextual ribbons.

11. Close the database, save your changes, and reopen it to verify your work. Test the Home menu controls and at least the custom controls in the context menus.

LISTING 28.3 THIS TYPICAL VBA CALLBACK FUNCTION REPLACES CodeObjectContext **WITH** objControl.Context **TO SUPPLY THE NAME OF THE CALLING OBJECT**

```
Public Function cb_NewEmployee(objControl As IRibbonControl)
On Error GoTo cb_NewEmployee_Err

    With objControl.Context 'CodeContextObject
        DoCmd.OpenForm "Employee Details", acNormal, "", "", acAdd, _
            acDialog
        On Error Resume Next
        DoCmd.Requery ""
        DoCmd.SearchForRecord , "", acFirst, "[ID]=" & Nz(DMax("[ID]", _
            .Form.RecordSource), 0)
    End With


cb_NewEmployee_Exit:
    Exit Function

cb_NewEmployee_Err:
    MsgBox Error$
    Resume cb_NewEmployee_Exit

End Function
```

The \SEUA12\Chaptr28\CustomUI28.accdb database has all preceding modifications applied. You'll also find nine Northwind employees and 13 suppliers added to the Employees and Vendors tables to speed adding projects, if you are so inclined.

NOTE

> This brief section only touches the topic of customizing the Ribbon UI. Covering all Ribbon UI customization topics, including best practices, would require a book of its own. If you read the recommended documentation and perform the tutorial procedures, you'll have a good grasp of the amount of work it takes to create a usable custom Ribbon UI.

28

REFERRING TO ACCESS OBJECTS WITH VBA

One of the reasons for occasional use of the term *Access VBA* in this book is that Access defines its own set of objects and uses specialized VBA syntax to refer to many Access objects. Although Form objects are common to most Office 2000+ members as well as Visual Basic, a subform (a form embedded in a form) is unique to Access. You find Report objects and subreports only in Access. The syntax for referring to a subform or subreport and for referring to controls contained in a subform or subreport is unique to Access. Even if you're an experienced Visual Basic programmer, you must become acquainted with the object reference syntax to write VBA code and refer to objects that are unique to Access.

REFERRING TO OPEN FORMS OR REPORTS AND THEIR PROPERTIES

You can refer to a form or report only if it's open. Access uses the Forms and Reports collections to keep track of which forms and reports are open. The Forms collection is the set of open forms, and the Reports collection is the set of open reports. Because Access lets you use the same name for a form and a report, you must distinguish between the two by specifying the collection. The syntax for the reference is the collection name followed by the exclamation point operator (!), more commonly called the *bang operator*, and the name of the form or report:

```
Forms![Form Name]
Reports![Report Name]
```

Use the bang operator (!) to separate the collection name from the name of an object in the collection. You need to use the square brackets ([…]) to enclose object names that include spaces or other punctuation that's illegal in VBA statements or object names that duplicate VBA reserved words.

A Form or Report object has properties that define its characteristics. The general syntax for referring to a property is the object name followed by the dot (.) operator and the name of the property:

```
Forms![Form Name].PropertyName
Reports![Report Name].PropertyName
```

Use the dot operator to separate the object's name from the name of one of its properties. For example, Forms!frmProducts.RecordSource refers to the RecordSource property of the open frmProducts form. You can get or set the value of the RecordSource property with the following two VBA statements:

```
strSource = Forms!frmProducts.RecordSource
Forms!frmProducts.RecordSource = strSource
```

If you add the .Value qualifier to RecordSource, you receive an "Invalid Qualifier" error.

To get or set the value of a form property in the form's own *class module*, you use the **Me** self-identifier, as in:

```
strSource = Me.RecordSource
Me.RecordSource = strSource
```

28

The **Me** self-reference is valid only for the instance of the form open in Form view. Therefore, you can't use the two preceding statements in the Immediate window unless you create a breakpoint in your code, open the form in Form view, and then execute the procedure that contains the breakpoint. Figure 28.20 shows the Immediate window opened by a breakpoint and set at the first active line of code of the `ReviewProducts_Click` subprocedure of Northwind.mdb's Suppliers form from Access 2003. In Break mode, typing **?** **Me.RecordSource** returns Suppliers—the name of the table to which the Suppliers form is bound. If you press F8 repeatedly to step through the code, after you pass the `DoCmd.` `OpenForm…` statement for the Product List form, you can use the `Forms!…` syntax described in the next section to test the property values of control objects on the Product List form.

Figure 28.20
When VBA code execution reaches the breakpoint line, the VBA editor window opens in Break mode with the breakpoint instruction highlighted. Pressing F5 continues code execution and returns the focus to the currently open form.

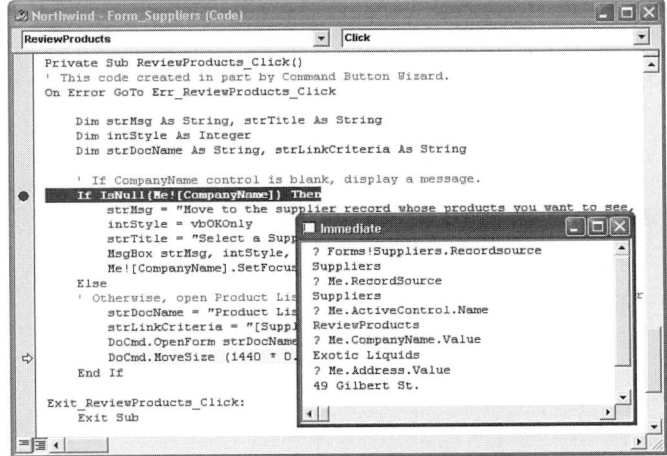

→ For detailed instructions on using breakpoints, **see** "Adding a Breakpoint to the `IsLoaded()` Function," **p. 1203**.

A form's properties window lists the form properties that you can set in Design view. Forms also have properties that you can't set in Design view and that don't appear in the property window, such as the default `Form` property. The `Form` property refers to the collection of controls on a form. Similarly, a report's default `Report` property refers to the collection of controls in a report.

REFERRING TO CONTROLS AND THEIR PROPERTIES

The following is the general syntax for referring to a control on a form or report:

```
Forms![FormName].Form![ControlName]
```

```
Reports![ReportName].Report![ControlName]
```

As before, the bang operator separates the collection name from the object name. The `Form` property is the default property that Access assumes for a form; therefore, you need not include the `Form` property explicitly in the reference.

28

The following expression is the short-form identifier syntax for a form control:

```
Forms![FormName]![ControlName]
```

Similarly, the following is the full identifier syntax for a report control:

```
Reports![ReportName]![ControlName]
```

For example, `Forms!frmProducts!ProductName` refers to the `ProductName` control on the open `frmProducts` form.

The syntax for referring to a control's property value includes the reference to the control, followed by the dot operator, and then followed by the property name:

```
Forms![FormName]![ControlName].[PropertyName]
```

```
Reports![ReportName]![ControlName].[PropertyName]
```

For example, `Forms!frmProducts!ProductName.Visible` refers to the value of the `ProductName` control's `Visible` property.

A control also has a default property. The default property of a text box is the `Text` property. To refer to the value in the `ProductName` text box control in the last example, you could use any of the following equivalent references:

```
Forms!frmProducts.Form!ProductName.Text
```

```
Forms!frmProducts!ProductName.Text
```

```
Forms!frmProducts.Form!ProductName
```

```
Forms!frmProducts!ProductName
```

NOTE

> Notice that the last two expressions refer both to the control's text value and to the control itself. The `.Text` qualifier isn't required, but adding the name of the default property is a good programming practice and complies with VBA.NET programming rules.

When you refer to a control on the active form or report, you can use a shorter version of the reference and refer to the control as follows:

```
[ControlName]
```

Likewise, you can refer to the control property as follows:

```
[ControlName].PropertyName
```

Normally, you can use either the short or full syntax to refer to a control on the active form or report. However, in some cases, you must use the short syntax. For example, the `GoToControl` action's `ControlName` argument requires the short syntax. You can explicitly refer to a control on the form of the *class module* with **Me**!ControlName statements. When you refer to a control on a form or report that's not the active object, you usually must use the full identifier syntax.

REFERRING TO CONTROLS ON A SUBFORM OR THE MAIN FORM

The key to understanding the syntax for referring to a control on a subform is to realize that the subform is a form that's bound to a subform control on the main form. The subform control has the usual attribute properties that control its display behavior, such as size and visibility, as well as linking properties that relate the records in the subform to records in the form, including the SourceObject, LinkChildFields, and LinkMasterFields properties. In addition, the subform control has the Form property. A subform control's Form property refers to the controls contained on the subform.

The following is the syntax for referring to the subform control:

```
Forms![FormName]![SubformControlName]
```

The syntax for referring to a control on a subform bound to a subform control is as follows:

```
Forms![FormName]![SubformControlName]![ControlName].PropertyName
```

When the form is active, the following short syntax refers to a control on a subform of the active form:

```
[SubformControlName]![ControlName]
```

The Form property of the subform, required in Access 95 and earlier when referring to controls on a subform, now is the subform control's default property, so you don't need to include it in the reference. Normally, you use the subform's name as the name of the subform control. For example, if sbfSuppliers is the name of a form bound to a subform control also named sbfSuppliers on the frmProducts form, the following is the full syntax for referring to the SupplierName control on the subform:

```
Forms!frmProducts!sbfSuppliers[.Form]!SupplierName
```

The short syntax is as follows:

```
sbfSuppliers[.Form]!SupplierName
```

When the focus is in a subform's control, you can refer to a control on the main form by using the control's Parent property. The Parent property refers to the collection of controls on the main form. In the previous example, to refer to the ProductName control on the main form from VBA code in the *class module* of a subform, use the following syntax:

```
Parent!ProductName
```

All the preceding syntax examples in this section apply to reports and subreports; just change Forms to Reports and Form to Report.

USING ALTERNATIVE COLLECTION SYNTAX

An alternative to the *CollectionName*!*ObjectName* syntax is to specify *CollectionName* and supply *ObjectName* as an argument value:

```
Forms("frmProducts")!sbfSuppliers!SupplierName
```

28

The advantage of the argument method is that you can substitute a `String` variable for the literal argument value:

```
Forms(strFormName)!sbfSuppliers!SupplierName
```

You also can pass a 0-based `Long` value to specify the ordinal (position) of the object in the collection:

```
Forms(2)!sbfSuppliers!SupplierName
```

Passing the ordinal value, however, isn't a safe programming practice because the ordinal position of objects in a collection change as you add or delete members.

RESPONDING TO DATA EVENTS TRIGGERED BY FORMS AND CONTROLS

`Recordsets` underlying forms and reports trigger data events when you move the record pointer or change the value in one or more cells of the `Recordset`. The two most important of these events are `BeforeUpdate` and `OnCurrent`. The following two sections illustrate the use of these two data-related events of bound forms.

VALIDATING DATA ENTRY IN A `BeforeUpdate` EVENT HANDLER

The most common use of data events is to validate updates to the `Recordset`; you add validation code to the event-handling subprocedure for the `BeforeUpdate` event. The use of code, instead of setting field-level or table-level `ValidationRule` property values, provides a much more flexible method of ensuring data consistency. Validation rules you write in VBA commonly are called business rules. Business rules often are quite complex and require access to multiple lookup tables—some of which might be located in other databases.

→ For information on enforcing business rules, see "Validating Data Entry," **p. 275**.

Listing 28.4 shows an example of a set of validation rules for postal codes in the Suppliers table of Northwind.mdb, the `Recordset` of which is bound to the Suppliers form. The `BeforeUpdate` event, which triggers before a change is made to the `Recordset`, includes a predefined `Cancel` argument. If you set `Cancel = True` in your event-handling code, the proposed update to the `Recordset` doesn't occur.

LISTING 28.4   A VBA VALIDATION SUBPROCEDURE FOR SOME INTERNATIONAL POSTAL CODES

```
Private Sub Form_BeforeUpdate(Cancel As Integer)
' If number of digits entered in PostalCode text box is
' incorrect for value in Country text box, display message
' and undo PostalCode value.

   Select Case Me!Country
      Case IsNull(Me![Country])
         Exit Sub
      Case "France", "Italy", "Spain"
```

```
            If Len(Me![PostalCode]) <> 5 Then
                MsgBox "Postal Code must be 5 characters", 0, _
                    "Postal Code Error"
                Cancel = True
                Me![PostalCode].SetFocus
            End If
        Case "Australia", "Singapore"
            If Len(Me![PostalCode]) <> 4 Then
                MsgBox "Postal Code must be 4 characters", 0, _
                    "Postal Code Error"
                Cancel = True
                Me![PostalCode].SetFocus
            End If
        Case "Canada"
            If Not Me![PostalCode] Like _
                "[A-Z][0-9][A-Z] [0-9][A-Z][0-9]" Then
                MsgBox "Postal Code not valid. " & _
                    "Example of Canadian code: H1J 1C3", _
                    0, "Postal Code Error"
                Cancel = True
                Me![PostalCode].SetFocus
            End If
    End Select
End Sub
```

USING THE ON CURRENT EVENT TO SET LINKED PIVOTCHART PROPERTIES

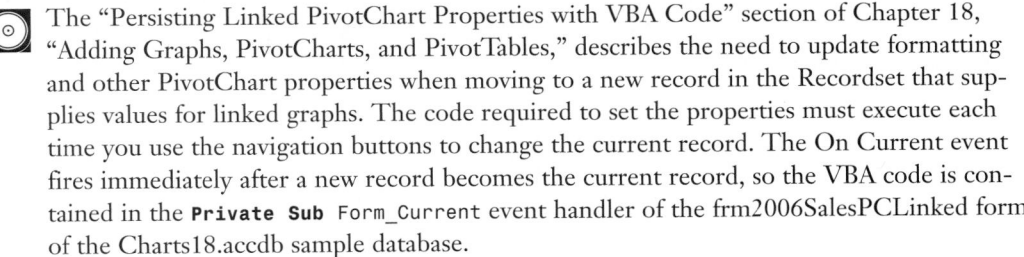 The "Persisting Linked PivotChart Properties with VBA Code" section of Chapter 18, "Adding Graphs, PivotCharts, and PivotTables," describes the need to update formatting and other PivotChart properties when moving to a new record in the Recordset that supplies values for linked graphs. The code required to set the properties must execute each time you use the navigation buttons to change the current record. The On Current event fires immediately after a new record becomes the current record, so the VBA code is contained in the **Private Sub** Form_Current event handler of the frm2006SalesPCLinked form of the Charts18.accdb sample database.

→ To review how to create linked PivotChart graphs, **see** "Working with PivotChart Forms," **p. 794**.

Form_Current's code illustrates the use of Forms!... references to objects in subforms (sbf2006SalesPCLinked for this example). The sbf2006SalesPCLinked form contains only a PivotChart and is restricted to PivotChart view. Although you can use VBA code to create a PivotChart from scratch, using the Office Web Components (OWC) design tools grafted to Access 2007's Form View toolbar is *much* easier.

ADDING A REFERENCE TO THE MICROSOFT OFFICE XP WEB CONTROLS

Microsoft no longer supports OWC, which were developed in part to supply the ActiveX components required by Access data access pages (DAP) to render forms and reports in web browsers. However, OWC provides the object model for PivotCharts and PivotTables, so it's required for programmatic access to these objects.

28

TIP

> Adding a PivotChart (or any other OWC) control to a form from the Insert Object dialog adds a reference to the individual control, so you don't need to add a reference to OWC11.dll.

To add the required reference to OWC11.dll and explore PivotChart objects in Object Browser, do the following:

1. Open the form in which you intend to write event-handling code for a PivotChart (or PivotTable) in Form Design view and click the Code button to open the VBA editor.

2. Choose Tools, References to open the References dialog, which doesn't contain a reference to any version of the Microsoft Office Web Components in the Available References list.

3. Click the Browse button to open the Add Reference dialog, navigate to the \Program Files\Microsoft Office\Office12 folder, and click to select OFFOWC.dll (see Figure 28.21).

Figure 28.21
The VBA editor's References dialog doesn't include Microsoft Office Web Components in the Available References list, so you must add the reference to OFFOWC.dll manually.

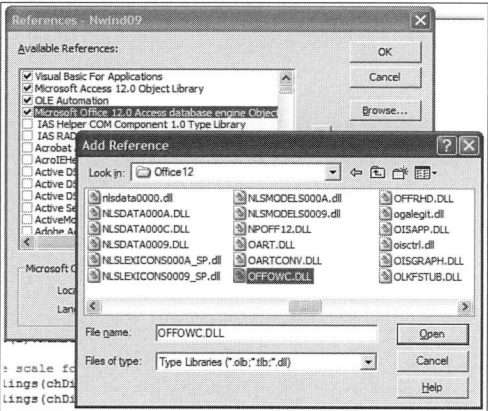

4. Click Open to add the Microsoft Office Web Components XP reference to the end of the Available References list (see Figure 28.22). Verify that the new reference's check box is marked, and click OK to close the dialog and add the reference to your VBA project.

5. Press F2 to open Object Browser, and select OWC10 in the Project/Library list. Scroll to the PivotChart objects, which have names with a Ch... prefix (see Figure 28.23).

Figure 28.22
Manually adding a reference to an object (.olb), type (.tlb), or dynamic link (.dll) library file adds the reference to the bottom of the Available References list and enables the reference.

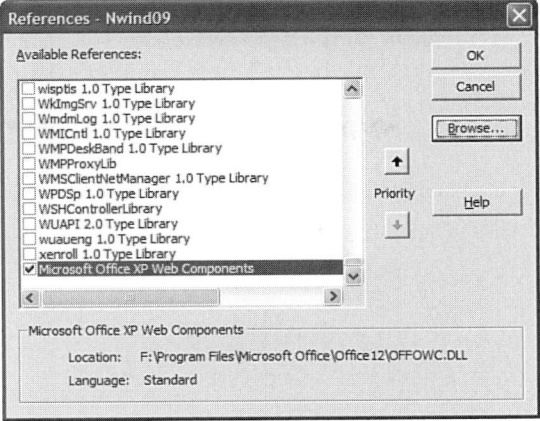

Figure 28.23
Object Browser's Classes list for the OWC11 library displays all objects exposed by OWC11.dll. PivotChart objects beginning with Ch.... PivotTable objects have a Pivot... prefix.

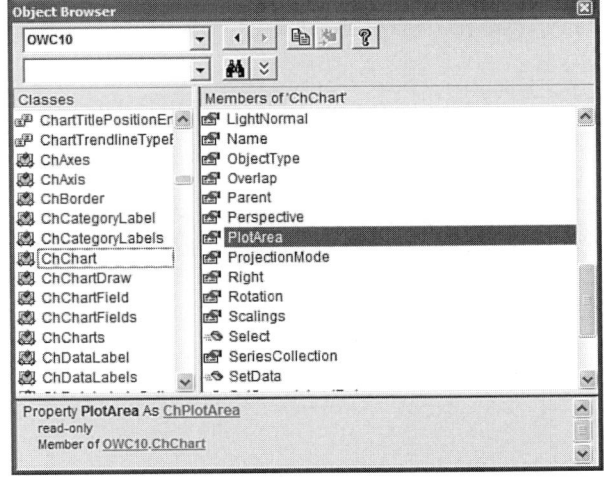

TIP

> OWC's OFFOWC implementation doesn't provide help for OWC10 objects. Clicking the ? button or pressing F1 with a object, property, or method selected returns an "Unable to Display Help" error. If you're serious about programming PivotCharts, PivotTables, or both with VBA, you're probably better off using Access 2003 or earlier.

WRITING VBA CODE TO APPLY NONPERSISTENT PROPERTY VALUES TO CHARTS

After you've created a reference to OFFOWC.dll, you declare ChartSpace (all charts or graphs), ChChart (the current graph), ChSeries (the graph's line), and, if your graph includes a trend line, ChTrendline object variables. The Form_Current event handler begins with a series of **Set** statements to create a pointer to each of these objects when you move to a new record (see Listing 28.5). The remaining Form_Current code sets custom property values of the ChChart, ChSeries, and ChTrendline objects. You can modify the code of Listing 28.5 to apply special properties to any line chart, not just linked charts. If your line chart isn't linked, change the subprocedure name to Form_Load to apply the property values when the form opens.

LISTING 28.5   VBA CODE TO SET NONPERSISTENT PROPERTIES OF LINKED PIVOTCHARTS

```vba
Option Compare Database
Option Explicit

'Declare the required OWC object variables for PivotCharts
'OFFOWC.dll provides OfficeXP (OWC10) Web Components
Private chtSpace As OWC10.ChartSpace
Private chtChart As OWC10.ChChart
Private chtSeries As OWC10.ChSeries
Private chtTrendLine As OWC10.ChTrendline

Private Sub Form_Current()
    'Update non-persistent linked PivotChart properties

    'Specify the subform's ChartSpace object
    Set chtSpace = Me.sbf2006SalesPivotChart.Form.ChartSpace
    'Specify the first (and only) chart in the Charts collection
    Set chtChart = chtSpace.Charts(0)
    'Specify the first (and only) series for the line graph
    Set chtSeries = chtChart.SeriesCollection(0)

    'Change the number format to remove the decimal digits
    chtChart.Axes(1).NumberFormat = "$#,##0"

    'Maintain the scale for all graphs
    chtChart.Scalings(chDimValues).Maximum = 25000
    chtChart.Scalings(chDimValues).Minimum = 0

    'Set the line weight to thick
    chtSeries.Line.Weight = owcLineWeightThick

    'If there are no trend lines, add one
    If chtSeries.Trendlines.Count = 0 Then
        Set chtTrendLine = chtSeries.Trendlines.Add()
    Else
        'The first graph has a trend line
        Set chtTrendLine = chtSeries.Trendlines(0)
    End If
    With chtTrendLine
        'Hide the equation and RSquared values
        .IsDisplayingEquation = False
        .IsDisplayingRSquared = False
        'Change the color and weight
        .Line.Color = "Red"
        .Line.Weight = owcLineWeightThick
    End With
End Sub
```

28

TROUBLESHOOTING

CALLING PROCEDURES AND FUNCTIONS IN CLASS MODULES

After adding test code to a form class module, I encounter a "Compile Error – Sub or Function not defined" error message when running the code from the Immediate window.

To execute subprocedures or functions in *class modules* from the Immediate window, you must preface the name of the subprocedure or function with the name of the *class module*. You also must add the class name prefix when calling with code subprocedures or functions from another *class module* or conventional module. You don't need to add the form name prefix to call public functions in conventional modules.

MISSING OBJECTS IN COLLECTIONS

"Object not found in this collection" errors occur with explicit object names or values passed as argument values.

You misspelled the object name or failed to assign a value to an argument variable. To check the names of objects, especially those with long or convoluted names, type **?** *CollectionName*(0) in the Immediate window to return the name of the first collection. If you receive an error or don't obtain the expected name, replace 0 with increasing values.

IN THE REAL WORLD—DEALING WITH EVENT-DRIVEN PROGRAMMING

Beginning programmers often find that understanding Windows event-driven programming model to be quite difficult. The same problem befalls many programmers experienced in conventional procedural languages, such as assembly, COBOL, Pascal, and xBase. With a very few exceptions, VBA code in an Access application or script in a DHTML page executes only in response to a predefined event. (The primary exceptions are variable and Windows function prototype declarations that precede VBA subprocedure and function code in modules.)

The first Office data object model that fired events was Access 97's ODBCDirect, an object wrapper over Visual Basic 4.0 Enterprise Edition's Remote Data Object (RDO) 1.0. Being able to intercept data-related events, such as when making a connection or starting and ending query execution, enables you to handle connection errors and asynchronous data operations. An asynchronous data operation is one in which control returns to your program after query execution starts. When the query completes, the corresponding event lets you write code to process the resulting `Recordset`. Your application isn't in a state of suspended animation while waiting for a "query from hell" to complete.

OLE DB and ActiveX Data Objects (ADO), however, provide a much richer (more granular) event model than ODBCDirect, as demonstrated by the event-related sections of Chapter 30, "Understanding Data Access Objects, OLE DB, and ADO." For optimum front-end VBA programming simplicity and flexibility, it's hard to beat ADO's event model. The .NET Framework's ADO.NET replacement for COM-based ADO, which emphasizes XML representation of `DataTable` and `DataSet` objects, dooms ADO and OLE DB to "legacy" status. It's unlikely that you'll see any significant upgrades to the current version, ADO 2.7, that's included in Microsoft Data Access Components (MDAC) 2.7.

The VBA code examples in this chapter cover only the basics of using VBA 6.0 for responding to events triggered by forms, controls, and Recordsets bound to forms or reports. A full course in VBA database programming exceeds both the scope and the publishing limitations of this book. Many of the examples in this chapter are drawn from the sample databases upgraded from Access 2003, created from Access 2007 templates, or downloaded from the Microsoft website. You can adapt the techniques illustrated in the event-handling subprocedures of the sample databases to custom applications you create.

The chapter touched briefly on customizing the Ribbon UI with VBA code. The use of declarative programming with XML to define UI elements is one of the characteristics of Microsoft's eXtensible Application Markup Language (XAML, pronounced *zammel*) that's part of the Windows Presentation Framework (WPF) and the Windows Workflow Foundation (WF) components of .NET Framework 3.0. XAML lets you define Windows objects with code such as the following for a button object:

```
<Button>
  <Button.Background>
    <SolidColorBrush Color="Blue"/>
  </Button.Background>
  <Button.Foreground>
    <SolidColorBrush Color="Red"/>
  </Button.Foreground>
  <Button.Content>
    This is a button
  </Button.Content>
</Button>
```

RibbonX XML syntax bears some resemblance to XAML but otherwise is unrelated. It's unfortunate that Microsoft didn't combine these two XML dialects into a single language or use XAML as the declarative language for the RibbonX UI.

To become an expert in VBA programming requires study, experimentation, and perseverance. Periodicals, books, and websites, such as those listed in the "Other Sources of Information for Access" section of the introduction to this book, are likely to satisfy the studious reader. There's no substitute, however, for experimentation. Writing and testing code is the only sure way to become proficient in Access VBA programming.

28

PROGRAMMING COMBO AND LIST BOXES

In this chapter

29

STREAMLINING DECISION SUPPORT FRONT ENDS

Decision-support applications deliver information used by executive management to analyze business trends and by line managers to analyze day-to-day performance of their business area and its staff. Most executives and line managers prefer graphs and charts to display trends, but deviations from expected results require display of detail data to pinpoint problem areas. Supervisors need more targeted data for monitoring employees' activities, such as reviewing order entry operations for accuracy and timeliness.

Decision-support applications involve read-only access to data, so you aren't limited to datasheet or form/subform views of queries. Access list boxes offer faster performance and easier multirecord navigation than forms and subforms, which are intended primarily for data entry. Combo boxes are the ideal control for letting users make ad hoc choices of the information they need to see.

NOTE

> Online-data entry applications also can take advantage of list boxes for applications such as finding a specific customer and displaying the customer's orders. The A11Oltp.accdb application described in Chapter 14, "Creating and Using Basic Access Forms," takes advantage of list boxes to display all historical customer and order data.

This chapter shows you how to combine combo boxes and list boxes with VBA code to create an interactive form for a simple decision-support application that includes a drill-down feature. You also learn how to generate Access SQL and Transact-SQL (T-SQL) queries from selections made in list and combo boxes.

CONSTRAINING QUERY CHOICES WITH COMBO BOXES

Users of decision-support applications, especially managers, aren't likely to be able to or want to use Access's graphical Query Design window. Instead, most users prefer to pick criteria (SELECT query WHERE clause elements) from one or more lists of available options. One primary advantage of offering users a set of choices to construct a query is the ability to prevent execution of ad hoc queries that return an excessive number of rows. Accidentally returning thousands of rows or—even worse—a Cartesian product of a million rows or more can bring a multiuser application or the entire network to its knees. Network and database administrators call such events "queries from hell."

TIP

> Combo boxes are the better choice for generating WHERE clause criteria because they occupy less room on forms than list boxes. Also, you can navigate quickly to a combo box item by typing the first few characters of the item in the combo box's text box element.

The following sections describe how to create an unbound form with two combo boxes that display a list of shipments to a specified country that include a particular product.

DESIGNING THE DECISION-SUPPORT QUERY

Query design is one of the most important elements of decision-support applications. One primary objective of decision-support systems is fast response time. To return selected information quickly, the query design should be as simple as possible. Include in the query only those fields needed to display necessary information, plus the foreign key fields to be selected in the combo boxes.

Follow these steps to create the minimal query for the customer-product-order information to be returned from the combo box selections:

1. Open Northwind.accdb from the \SEUA12\Nwind folder or your working copy of Northwind.accdb.

2. Create a new query in Design view and add the Customers, Orders, and Order Details tables.

3. Drag the CompanyName and Country fields of the Customers table, the OrderID and ShippedDate fields of the Orders table, and the ProductID of the Order Details table to the Query Design grid. Add a Descending sort to the OrderID column to display latest orders first (see Figure 29.1).

Figure 29.1
This query design delivers the data required to populate combo and list boxes.

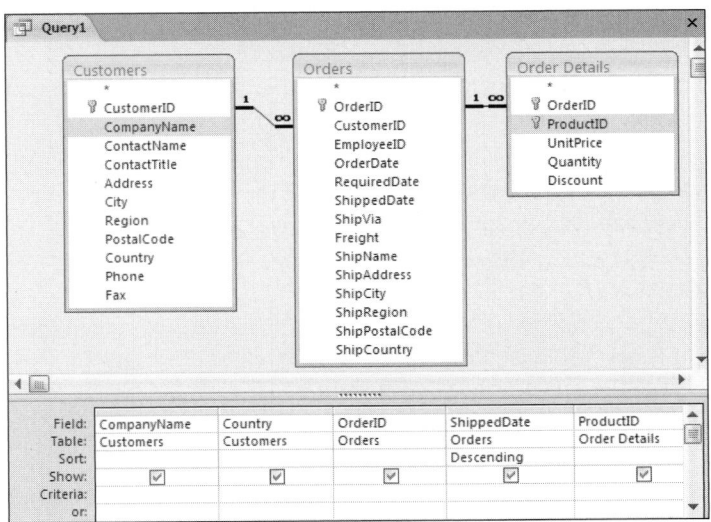

4. Click Run to test your query, and then close and save your query as **qryCombo1**.

29

CREATING THE FORM AND ADDING A LIST BOX

An Access list box is the most efficient control for displaying the read-only query result sets of decision-support applications. List boxes consume fewer computer resources than subforms, are easier for users to navigate, and have the properties and events needed to give your application drill-down capabilities. *Drill down* is the process of providing users with more detailed information about a specific item in the list. Later, the section "Drilling Down from a List Box Selection" shows you how to add drill-down capabilities to the form you create here.

→ For list and combo box basics, **see** "Adding Combo and List Boxes," **p. 660**.

To create an unbound form with a list box populated by qryCombo1, follow these steps:

1. Create a new unbound form in Design view. (Don't specify a record source for the form.) If you're running Access in multiple-document interface (MDI) mode, adjust the size of the form to about 4.5 inches wide by 2.5 inches deep.

2. Click the form selection button and then click the Property Sheet button for the form. Click the Format tab and set the Allow Datasheet View, Allow PivotTable View, and Allow PivotChart View property values to No. Set Scroll Bars to Neither, Record Selectors to No, and Navigation Buttons to No.

3. With the Control Wizards button depressed, add a list box from the Toolbox to the form. Adding the list box opens the first dialog of the List Box Wizard.

4. Select the I Want the List Box to Look Up the Values in a Table or Query option, and click Next.

5. Select the Queries option in the View frame, select qryCombo1 (created in the preceding section) from the list and then click Next.

6. Select the CompanyName field in the Available Fields list and click the > button to add the field to the Selected Fields list. Repeat the process for the OrderID and ShippedDate fields, and then click Next twice to bypass the sort dialog.

> **NOTE**
>
> You don't display the Country or Product ID in the list box because these fields are specified by combo box selection.

7. Adjust the widths of the columns to suit the list headers and data. Click Next.

8. Select OrderID as the column to uniquely identify the row. Click Next.

9. Type **Northwind Shipments by Country and Product** as the caption for the list box's label and then click Finish to add the list box to the form.

B

10. Move the label to the top of the list box, click the Bold button on the toolbar to make the label's caption more visible, and adjust the width of the label.

11. Select the list box label, open the Properties window, click the Other tab, and change the value of its Name property to **lblList**.

12. Select the list box, click the All tab, and change the Name property value of the combo box to **lstOrders**. Set Yes as the value of the Column Heads property and accept 2 (OrderID) as the Bound Column property value (see Figure 29.2).

Figure 29.2
Setting OrderID (column 2) as the Bound Column property value prepares the form for later addition of the drill-down feature.

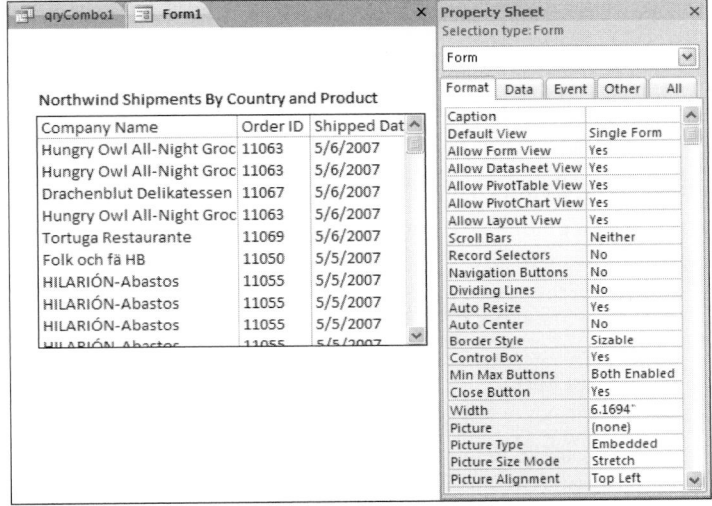

13. Click the Layout View button to check the layout of the list box. Select an AutoFormat (Verve for this example), format the font color, size, and weight to suit your taste, and adjust the column widths of the list box to accommodate the width of the text, which depends on the AutoFormat. Your form appears as shown in Figure 29.3.

Figure 29.3
The lstOrders list box displays all rows of the query at this point.

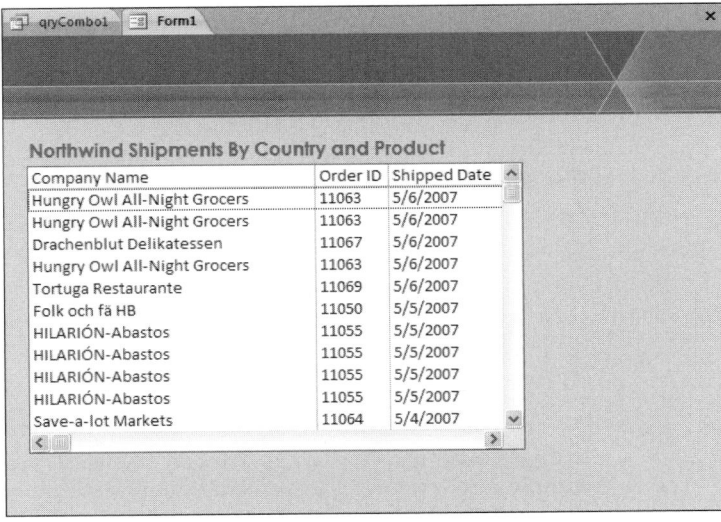

14. Press Ctrl+S to save the form, and name it **frmCombo1**.

ADDING THE QUERY COMBO BOXES TO THE FORM

You need one combo box to select the country and another to select the product. Northwind.accdb doesn't have a Countries table, so the data source for the country combo box is the Country field of the Customers table. The data source for the product combo box is the Products table.

→ For detailed combo box instructions, **see** "Using the Combo Box Wizard," **p. 660**.

To add the country and product combo boxes to the form, follow these steps:

1. Change to Design mode and add a combo box to the upper left of the form; the first dialog of the Combo Box Wizard opens.

2. Select the I Want the Combo Box to Look Up the Values in a Table or Query option and click Next.

3. With the Tables option selected, select Customers from the list and click Next.

4. Select Country in the Available Fields list and click the > button to move Country to the Selected Fields list. Click Next.

5. Open the first sort list and select Country. Click Next.

6. Adjust the width of the Country column and click Next.

7. Accept Country as the caption for the label and click Finish to add the combo box to the form.

B 8. Select the Country label, click the Bold button, and adjust the position and size of the label (look ahead to Figure 29.4).

9. Select the combo box, click the Data tab of the Properties window, and verify that the value of the Limit to List property is Yes.

10. Click the All tab of the Properties window, type **cboCountry** as the value of the Name property, and type **10** as the value of the List Rows property.

11. Repeat steps 1 and 2.

12. With the Tables option selected, select Products from the list and click Next.

13. Select ProductID in the Available Fields list and click the > button to move ProductID to the Selected Fields list. Do the same for ProductName and then click Next.

14. Select ProductName as the sort order and click Next.

15. Adjust the width of the ProductName column to accommodate long product names and then click Next.

NOTE

> The column widths you set in the wizard are valid only for the 8-point Tahoma font. If you use an AutoFormat that applies another font family and size, you must change the column widths in the Property Sheet.

16. Type **Product** as the caption for the label, and click Finish to add the combo box to the form.

B 17. Click the Bold button and adjust the position and size of the label.

18. With the text box component of the combo control selected, click the All tab of the Properties window, type **cboProduct** as the value of the Name property, and type **10** as the value of the List Rows property (see Figure 29.4).

Figure 29.4
The final form design has the two combo boxes you use to select the country and product to populate the orders list box.

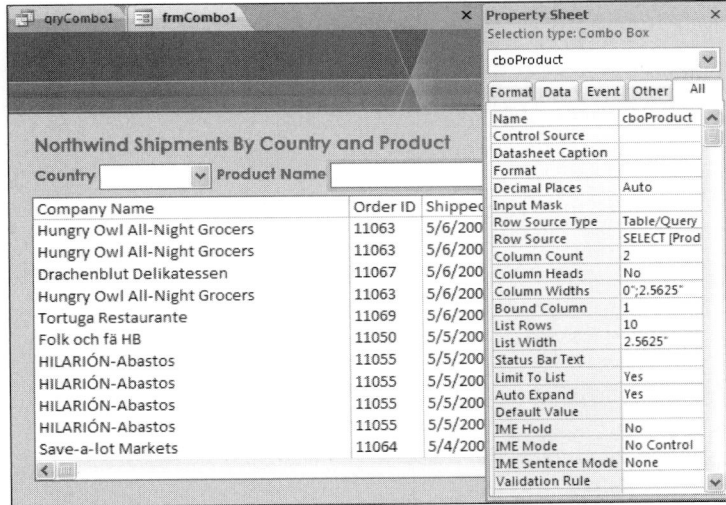

19. In Layout view, click the Control Layout group's Tab Order button to open the Tab Order dialog. Click the Auto Order button to set a cboCountry, cboProduct, lstOrders sequence. Click OK to close the dialog.

 20. Click the Form View button and test both combo boxes (see Figure 29.5).

> **NOTE**
> Figure 29.5 is a double exposure created from two display captures. You can't open both combo boxes simultaneously.

21. Press Ctrl+S to save the changes to frmCombo1.

> **TIP**
> The recommended Column Widths property value for the lstOrders list box is **2.75";0.6355";1.1"** for 11-point Calibri, which is Access 2007's default font. The recommended Width property value is **4.51"**.

Figure 29.5
At this point, the Country combo box has a row for each customer, instead of a row for each country.

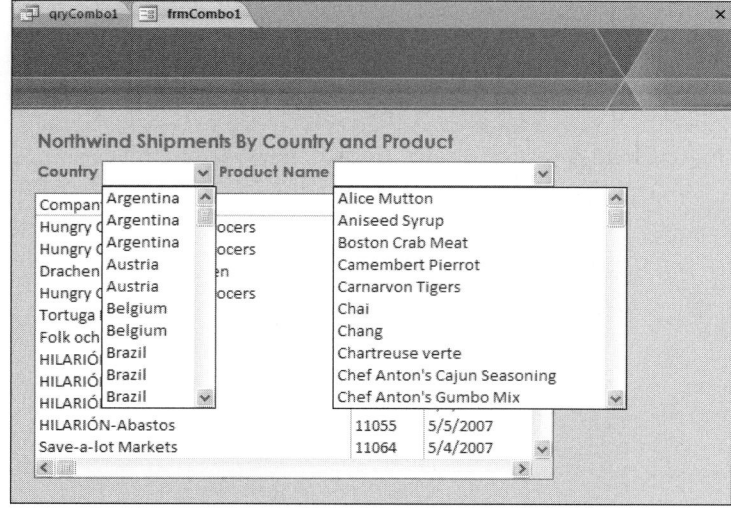

The Country combo box in Figure 29.5 has an obvious defect: multiple instances of country names. These problems arise from the SQL statement that the Combo Box Wizard creates as the value of the combo box's Row Source property:

```
SELECT Customers.CustomerID, Customers.Country
   FROM Customers ORDER BY [Country];
```

The Combo Box Wizard automatically includes the primary key field of the table (CustomerID) as the bound column, so you must remove the `Customers.CustomerID` column from the SQL statement and modify cboCountry's properties to accommodate this change. ANSI SQL's `DISTINCT` or Access SQL's `DISTINCTROW` qualifier solves the duplication problem.

→ For the differences between the two `SELECT` qualifiers, **see** "Writing `SELECT` Queries in SQL," **p. 917**.

To make the required changes to the Country combo box, do the following:

1. Select the cboCountry combo box and then click the Properties button. Access 2007 lets you change most of the properties of combo boxes in Form view.

2. Click the Data tab and then edit the value of the Row Source property to the following:
   `SELECT DISTINCT Country FROM Customers ORDER BY Country;`

   The table name prefix for field names isn't needed because the query includes just one table.

   > **NOTE**
   >
   > Make sure the Row/Source Type property value remains set to Table/Query after you make the change.

3. Click the All tab and change the value of the Column Count property from 2 to 1.

4. Remove the first 0"; element of the Column Widths property value, and set the Limit to List property value to Yes (see Figure 29.6).

Figure 29.6
Change the Row Source to a SELECT query with the DISTINCT qualifier, change the list to display a single column, and set the Limit to List property value to Yes.

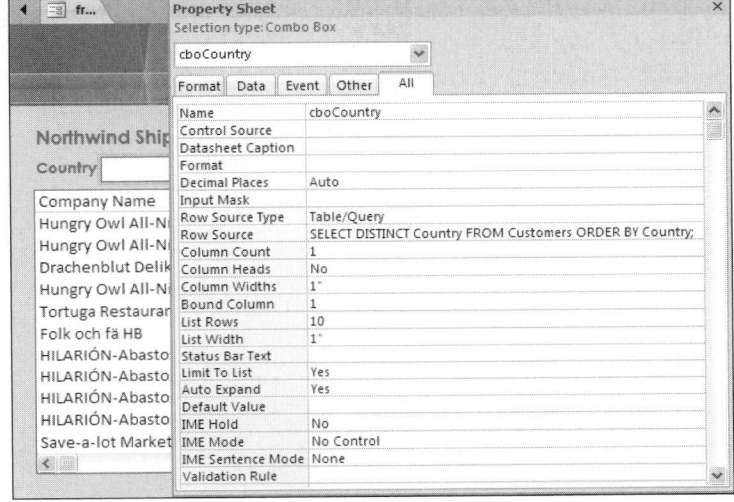

If you don't change the Column Count and Column Widths property values in steps 3 and 4, cboCountry displays an empty list.

5. Open the modified combo box. As shown in Figure 29.7, the duplicates are removed and the country names are in alphabetical order. Close the form and save your changes.

Figure 29.7
The Country list displays a single row for each country in alphabetical order.

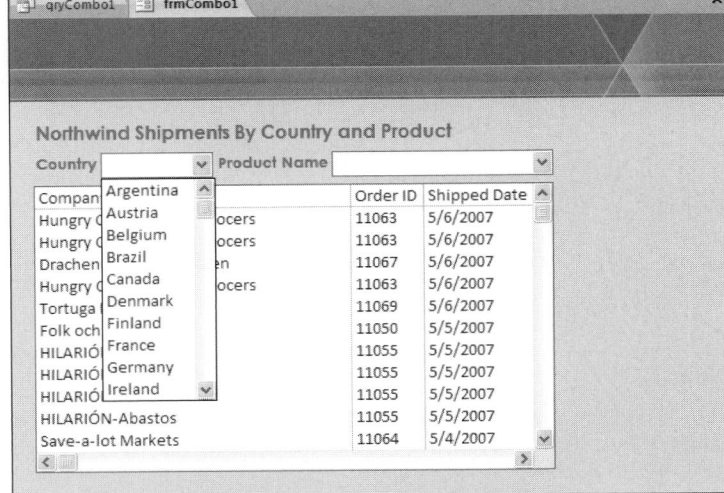

ADDING CODE TO CREATE THE QUERY'S SQL STATEMENT

Selections you make in the combo boxes return the values required for the WHERE clause criteria of the query that serves as the Row Source property of the lstOrders list box. Selecting an item in the combo list returns the value of the bound column to the combo box's Value property. The Row Source property value of the lstOrders list box created by the List Box Wizard is as follows:

```
SELECT qryCombo1.CompanyName,
    qryCombo1.OrderID, qryCombo1.ShippedDate
  FROM qryCombo1;
```

A model SQL statement that simplifies the query syntax, uses the combo box values, and sorts the rows in reverse date order (newest orders first) is this:

```
SELECT CompanyName, OrderID, ShippedDate
  FROM qryCombo1
  WHERE Country = cboCountry.Value AND
    ProductID = cboProduct.Value
  ORDER by ShippedDate DESC;
```

To write the VBA code to create the SELECT query based on combo box values and add instructions for the user, follow these steps:

1. Open frmCombo1 in Design mode, click the Form Tools, Design tab, click the Code button to display the Class Module for the frmCombo1 form in the VBA editor, and add the following constant and variable declarations for the SQL statement to the Declarations section immediately below Option Explicit:

```
Private Const strSQL1 = "SELECT CompanyName, OrderID, ShippedDate " & _
    "FROM qryCombo1 WHERE Country = ' "
Private Const strSQL2 = "' AND ProductID = "
Private Const strSQL3 = " ORDER BY ShippedDate DESC;"
Private strSQL As String
```

> **TIP**
>
> The single quotation marks (') are required to set off String values within SQL statements. Numeric values don't require quotation marks.

2. Add the following code for messages to the Declarations section:

```
Private Const strMsg1 = "Select a product from the list"
Private Const strMsg2 = "Select a country from the list"
```

3. Type **Private Sub FillList** and press Enter to create a subprocedure stub to fill the list box.

4. Add the following code to the FillList stub to create the SQL statement for the list box's RowSource property, refresh the list box by applying the Requery method, and change the caption of the list box label to display the WHERE clause criteria:

```
strSQL = strSQL1 & Me.cboCountry.Value & _
    strSQL2 & Me.cboProduct.Value & strSQL3
Me.lstOrders.RowSource = strSQL
Me.lstOrders.Requery
Me.lblList.Caption = "Shipments to " & _
Me.cboCountry.Value & " for " & _
Me.cboProduct.Column(1)
If Me.lstOrders.ListCount = 0 Then
    Me.lblList.Caption = "No " & Me.lblList.Caption
End If
```

29

NOTE

A combo box or list box's Column(*n*) property returns the value of the specified column. The first column (*n* = 0) of cboProduct is ProductID; the second (*n* = 1) is ProductName.

5. Select cboCountry from the Object list and select AfterUpdate from the Procedure list to create the **Private Sub** cboCountry_AfterUpdate() event-handler stub.

6. Add the following code to the AfterUpdate() stub to alter the caption of the list box label:

```
If Me.cboProduct.Value > 0 Then
    Call FillList
Else
    Me.lblList.Caption = strMsg1
End If
```

7. Repeat steps 5 and 6 for the cboProduct combo box, but change the code for step 6 as follows:

```
If Me.cboCountry.Value <> "" Then
    Call FillList
Else
    Me.lblList.Caption = strMsg2
End If
```

8. Select Form from the Object list and Activate from the Procedure list to create a Form_Activate event-handling stub.

9. Add the following code to Form_Activate to generate the list from persisted country and product selections:

```
If Me.cboCountry.Value <> "" And Me.cboProduct.Value > 0 Then
    Call FillList
Else
    Me.lblList.Caption = strMsg2
End If
```

10. Choose <u>D</u>ebug, Compile *ProjectName* to verify the VBA code you added. If compilation errors occur, check your code against Listing 29.1.

 11. Click the View Microsoft Access button to return to Form Design view, select the lstOrders list box, click the Data tab of the Properties window, and delete the default Row Source value so that the full result set of qryCombo1 doesn't appear when you open the form.

12. Increase the width of lblList to match the width of the list box.

13. Change to Form view to run the code. If you previously selected country and product criteria, the form displays the query result set.

Listing 29.1 contains all code added in the preceding steps. If error messages arise when compiling your code or displaying the form, compare it with this listing.

LISTING 29.1   VBA CODE FOR THE FRMCOMBO1 CLASS MODULE AS IT APPEARS IN THE EDITING WINDOW

```vba
Option Compare Database
Option Explicit

Private Const strSQL1 = "SELECT CompanyName, OrderID, ShippedDate " & _
    "FROM qryCombo1 WHERE Country = '"
Private Const strSQL2 = "' AND ProductID = "
Private Const strSQL3 = " ORDER BY ShippedDate DESC;"
Private strSQL As String

Private Const strMsg1 = "Select a product from the list"
Private Const strMsg2 = "Select a country from the list"

Private Sub cboCountry_AfterUpdate()
    If Me.cboProduct.Value > 0 Then
        Call FillList
    Else
        Me.lblList.Caption = strMsg2
    End If
End Sub

Private Sub cboProduct_AfterUpdate()
    If Me.cboCountry.Value <> "" Then
        Call FillList
    Else
        Me.lblList.Caption = strMsg1
    End If
End Sub

Private Sub FillList()
        strSQL = strSQL1 & Me.cboCountry.Value & _
            strSQL2 & Me.cboProduct.Value & strSQL3
        Me.lstOrders.RowSource = strSQL
        Me.lstOrders.Requery
        Me.lblList.Caption = "Shipments to " & _
            Me.cboCountry.Value & " for " & _
            Me.cboProduct.Column(1)
        If Me.lstOrders.ListCount = 0 Then
            Me.lblList.Caption = "No " & Me.lblList.Caption
    End If
End Sub

Private Sub Form_Activate()
    If Me.cboCountry.Value <> "" And Me.cboProduct.Value > 0 Then
        Call FillList
```

```
    Else
        Me.lblList.Caption = strMsg2
    End If
End Sub
```

Optionally add a form heading label and caption, save your form, and then test your work by selecting values from the Country and Product combo boxes to display the query result set (see Figure 29.8). You can type a few letters in the Country or Product list boxes, and then press Enter to fire the AfterUpdate event for the closest matching item.

Figure 29.8
Settings of the two combo boxes determine the contents of the orders list box.

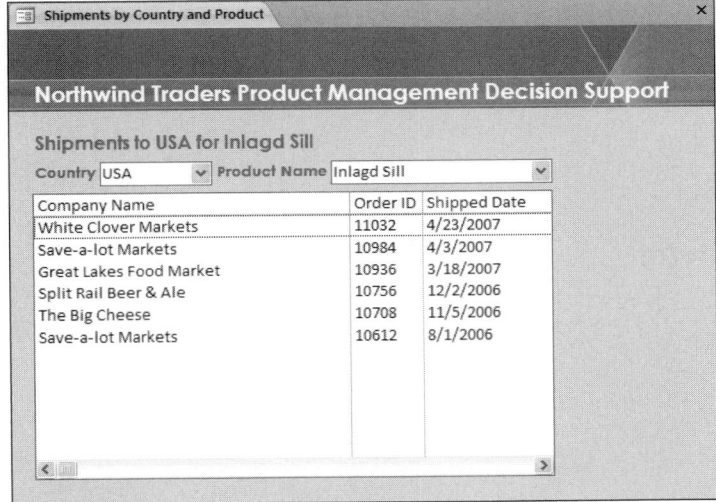

 If you encounter errors when you test your form, see the "Run-Time Error '2465'" and "Spurious Parameter Messages" topics of the "Troubleshooting" section near the end of this chapter.

 The completed frmCombo1 form is included in VBACombo.accdb, located in the \Seua11\Chaptr29 folder of the accompanying CD-ROM.

DRILLING DOWN FROM A LIST BOX SELECTION

The most common use of a drill-down form that displays a list of orders is to present the line items of a particular order. It's relatively easy to add and program a line items list box, based on the Order Details table, to the form you created in the preceding sections. An additional use of a line items list box is to verify that the cboProduct combo box correctly performs its assigned role.

CREATING THE DRILL-DOWN QUERY AND ADDING THE LIST BOX

Create the query and add the list box with the following steps:

1. Select frmCombo1in the Navigation pane, click the Office button, choose Save As to open the Save As dialog, and save fromCombo1 as **frmDrillDown**.

2. Create a new query in Design view and add the Order Details and Products tables.

3. Drag the Product Name field of the Products table and the OrderID, UnitPrice, Quantity, and Discount fields of the Order Details table to the Query Design grid. Move the OrderID field to the first column of the query. OrderID doesn't appear in the line items list box; it's used to link to the OrderID column of lstOrders.

4. Add a calculated field defined by typing the following expression in the sixth column of the Field row:

```
Extended: CCur(Format([Order Details].[UnitPrice]*
[Quantity]*(1-[Discount]),"$#,###.00"))
```

Figure 29.9 illustrates the design of the query.

Figure 29.9
The query of this design populates a list box of order line items.

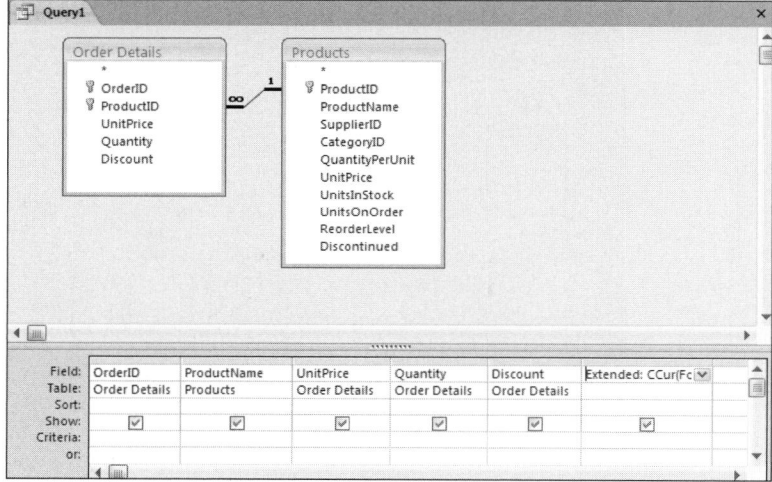

5. Run the query to verify your design, and then close it, saving it as **qryDrillDown**.

6. Open frmDrillDown in Design view, increase the height of frmDrillDown, and add a list box with the same width as lstOrders and a height of about 1 inch at the bottom of the form.

7. Select the Table or Query option in the first wizard dialog, accept the default, and click Next.

8. Select Queries and qryDrillDown and then click Next.

9. Click the >> button to add all query columns to the Selected Fields list and then select the OrderID field and click < to remove it. Click Next twice.

10. Adjust the widths of the columns to fit the size of the data in the fields. Click Next.

11. Accept the default ProductName column for the default value of the list box. Click Next.

12. Replace the default caption of the label for the combo box with **Line Items**. Click Finish.

13. Move the label to a spot above the new list box and then click the Bold button.

14. Select the new list box, click the Format tab of the Properties window, and change the value of the Column Heads property to Yes.

15. Change the Caption property value of the form to **Shipments with Line Items by Country and Product**.

16. Change to Form view to check your design (see Figure 29.10) and press Ctrl+S to save your changes.

Figure 29.10
The list box for the drill-down query in Form view displays the first few rows of the entire Order Details table.

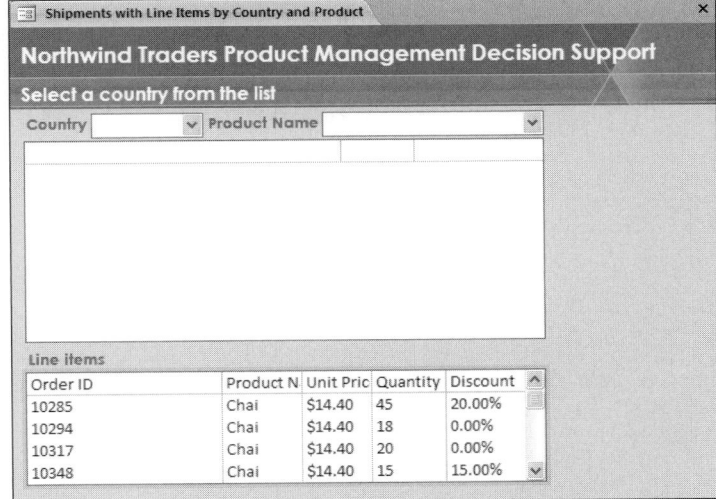

Shipments with Line Items by Country and Product					✕
Northwind Traders Product Management Decision Support					
Select a country from the list					
Country	▾	Product Name		▾	

Line items					
Order ID		Product N	Unit Pric	Quantity	Discount
10285		Chai	$14.40	45	20.00%
10294		Chai	$14.40	18	0.00%
10317		Chai	$14.40	20	0.00%
10348		Chai	$14.40	15	15.00%

TIP

The recommended Column Widths property value for the line items list box is **1.7";0.7";0.6";0.65";0.6"** for 11-point Calibri.

PROGRAMMING THE DRILL-DOWN LIST BOX

The List Box Wizard supplies the following SQL statement as the Row Source property of the new list box:

```
SELECT qryDrillDown.ProductName,
    qryDrillDown.UnitPrice, qryDrillDown.Quantity,
    qryDrillDown.Discount, qryDrillDown.Extended
  FROM qryDrillDown;
```

The simplified Access SQL statement used to populate the Line Items list box from an order selected in the lstOrders list box is as follows:

```
SELECT ProductName, UnitPrice, Quantity, Discount, Extended
   FROM qryDrillDown
   WHERE OrderID = lstOrders.Value;
```

The following steps complete the modification of the list box and add VBA code to execute the preceding query:

1. Return to Form Design view, select the drill-down list box, click the Other tab of the Properties window, and change the value of the Name property to **lstLineItems**.

2. Select the label for lstLineItems and change the value of its Name property to **lblLineItems**.

3. Click the Code button and add the following string constants to the Declarations section of the frmDrillDown Class Module:

```
Private Const strSQL4 = "SELECT ProductName, UnitPrice, Quantity, " & _
    "Discount, Extended FROM qryDrillDown WHERE OrderID = "

Private Const strMsg3 = "Double-click an order to display line items"
Private Const strMsg4 = "Line items for order "
Private Const strMsg5 = "Line items"
```

4. Select lstOrders from the Object list and DblClick from the Procedures list to add a lstOrders_DblClick subprocedure stub.

5. Add the following code to the lstOrders_DblClick stub to set the value of the RowSource property of the list box and requery the control:

```
If Me.lstOrders.Value <> "" Then
    With Me.lstLineItems
        strSQL = strSQL4 & Me.lstOrders.Value & ";"
        .RowSource = strSQL
        .Requery
    End With
    Me.lblLineItems.Caption = strMsg4 & Me.lstOrders.Value
End If
```

6. Add the following lines to the end of the Form_Activate, cboCountry_AfterUpdate, and cboProduct_AfterUpdate event handlers to clear the list box and change the label caption when opening the form or setting new query criteria:

```
With Me.lstLineItems
    .RowSource = ""
    .Requery
End With
Me.lblLineItems.Caption = strMsg5
```

7. Add the following lines to the end of the Form_Activate event handler to clear the persisted values in the lstLineItem list:

```
With Me.lstLineItems
    .RowSource = ""
    .Requery
End With
```

8. Add the following line above the **End If** line of the FillList subprocedure to change the Line Item list box label's caption:

```
Me.lblLineItems.Caption = strMsg3
```

9. Return to Access and change to Form view. Double-click one of the order items to populate lstLineItems (see Figure 29.11).

Figure 29.11
The Line Items list box displays Order Details records for the order you double-clicked in the Orders list box.

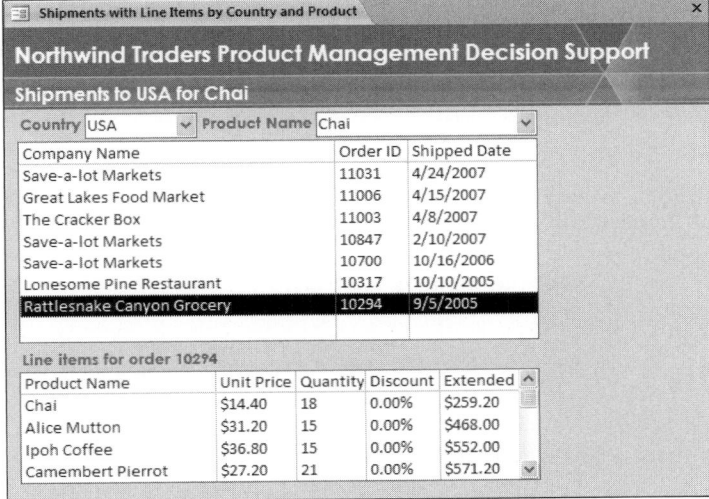

ADDING NEW FEATURES TO LIST AND COMBO BOXES

List and combo boxes offer various properties and methods that are accessible only through VBA code. The next two sections describe programming techniques that take advantage of additional list and combo box features.

ITERATING LIST BOX ITEMS AND SELECTING AN ITEM

Access list boxes share many common properties with the native ListBox control of Visual Basic 6.0 and earlier. The ListCount property returns the number of items in the list, the ItemData or Column property returns a value from the list, and the Selected property sets or returns whether the row is selected. This example emphasizes a product in the Line Items list box by automatically selecting the row corresponding to the cboProduct selection. The Column property is more versatile than the ItemData property; ItemData is restricted to values in the bound column.

Follow these steps to add the code required to automatically select a product in the lstLineItems list box:

1. Add this statement to the Declarations section of the frmDrillDown Class Module:

```
Private intCtr As Integer
```

2. Add these lines immediately above the **End If** statement of the lstOrders_DblClick event handler:

```
With Me.lstLineItems
    For intCtr = 0 To .ListCount - 1
        If .Column(0, intCtr) = Me.cboProduct.Column(1) Then
            .Selected(intCtr) = True
            Exit For
        End If
    Next intCtr
End With
```

The optional second argument of the Column property specifies the row. The **If…Then** statement determines a match between the text values of the ProductName columns of lstLineItems and cboProduct.

 3. Open the form in Form view. Double-click one of the order items to fill lstLineItems and automatically select the specified product (see Figure 29.12).

Figure 29.12
Adding a few lines of VBA code automatically highlights the Order Details record for the selected product in the Line Items list.

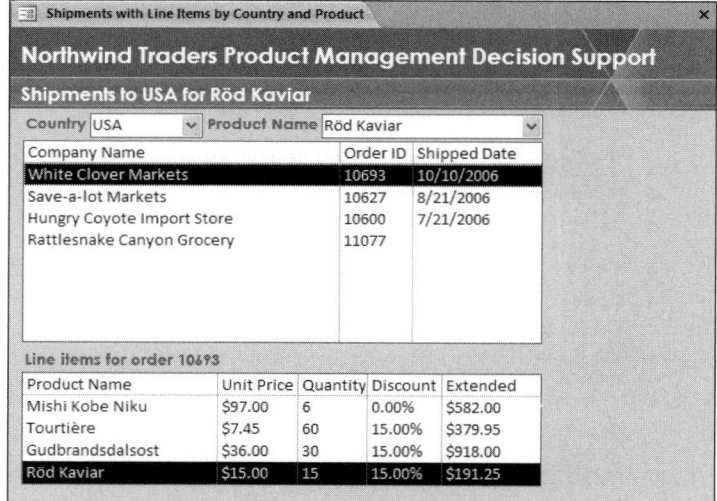

TIP

You can use code similar to what's in this example to emulate a SELECT query against the content of any list box or combo box. Selecting a list box item ensures that the item is visible in the text box, regardless of its location in the list.

ADDING AN OPTION TO SELECT ALL COUNTRIES OR PRODUCTS

It's often useful to give users the option to pick all items represented by combo box selections. In this chapter's example, selecting all countries or all products (but not both) represents an enhancement to the application. How you add an "(All)" choice to cboCountry and cboProduct and write the code for the appropriate SELECT query to fill lstOrders isn't obvious, at best.

NOTE

> Access 2002 finally added the `AddItem` method of Visual Basic list and combo boxes for populating these controls with VBA code. Unfortunately, you can't take advantage of this new feature, because you must specify Value List as the Row Source Type property of the Access list and combo boxes to use `AddItem`.

A UNION query is the most straightforward way to add custom rows to a combo or list box populated by an SQL statement. You specify your own values for each column returned by the SELECT query to which the UNION clause applies. The Access UNION query to populate cboCountry is as follows:

```
SELECT Country FROM Customers
   UNION SELECT '(All)' FROM Customers ORDER BY Country;
```

You don't need the DISTINCT modifier of the original SELECT statement because UNION queries don't return duplicate rows. The '(All)' custom item is surrounded with parentheses because the opening parenthesis character sorts before numerals and letters, making (All) the first item in the list. The Customers table has no (All) record, but all UNION queries require a FROM *TableName* clause.

→ For UNION query syntax, **see** "Using UNION Queries to Combine Multiple Result Sets," **p. 512**.

Similarly, the UNION query to fill cboProduct is as follows:

```
SELECT ProductID, ProductName FROM Products
   UNION SELECT 0, '(All)' FROM Products ORDER BY ProductName;
```

Here, you must supply a numeric value—in this case, 0—for the first column of the query (ProductID) and the '(All)' string value for the second column (ProductName). UNION queries require that both SELECT statements return the same number of columns, and all rows of each column must be of the same field data type. ProductID is an AutoNumber field, which starts with 1 unless you make the effort to begin autonumbering with a higher value.

In addition to adding the (All) item to the combo boxes, you must alter your SELECT queries to populate lstOrders when you select (All). In the all-countries case, the Access SELECT query is as follows:

```
SELECT CompanyName, OrderID, ShippedDate
   FROM qryCombo1
   WHERE ProductID = cboProduct.Value
   ORDER by ShippedDate DESC;
```

For the all-products situation, the Access query is the following:

```
SELECT CompanyName, OrderID, ShippedDate
   FROM qryCombo1
   WHERE Country = cboCountry.Value
   ORDER by ShippedDate DESC;
```

The preceding changes require you to add logic to detect when you select (All) and change the assembly of the SQL statement to suit. The following steps add the (All) selection to both combo boxes:

1. Create a copy of frmDrillDown as **frmDrillDownAll** and then open the copy in Form Design view.

2. Select cboCountry and change its Row Source property value to the following:

```
SELECT Country FROM Customers UNION SELECT '(All)'
FROM Customers ORDER BY Country;
```

3. Select cboProduct and change its Row Source property value to the following:

```
SELECT ProductID, ProductName FROM Products
UNION SELECT 0, '(All)' FROM Products ORDER BY ProductName;
```

4. Click the Code button, and add the following lines to the Declarations section to create the SQL statement that populates the lstOrder list and to prevent returning all orders:

```
Private Const strSQL5 = "SELECT Customers.CompanyName, " & _
    "Orders.OrderID, Orders.ShippedDate FROM (Customers " & _
    "INNER JOIN Orders ON Customers.CustomerID = Orders.CustomerID) " & _
    "INNER JOIN [Order Details] ON Orders.OrderID = " & _
    "[Order Details].OrderID "
Private Const strSQL6 = "WHERE Country = '"
Private Const strSQL7 = "WHERE ProductID = "

Private Const strMsg6 = "You can't select (All) countries and products"
```

5. Replace the **If...End If** code at the beginning (and before the **With**) of the cboCountry_AfterUpdate event handler as follows to indicate that you can't execute a query that returns all orders:

```
If Me.cboProduct.Value > 0 Then
    Me.lblList.Caption = strMsg1
    Call FillList
Else
    If Me.cboCountry.Value = "(All)" Then
        MsgBox strMsg6
    Else
        Me.lblList.Caption = strMsg2
        Call FillList
    End If
End If
```

6. Replace the **If...End If** code at the beginning (and before the **With**) of the cboProduct_AfterUpdate event handler to the following:

```
If Me.cboCountry.Value <> "" Then
    If Me.cboCountry.Value = "(All)" And _
        Me.cboProduct.Value = 0 Then
        MsgBox strMsg6
    Else
        Me.lblList.Caption = strMsg1
        Call FillList
    End If
Else
    Me.lblList.Caption = strMsg2
```

```
        Call FillList
    End If
```

7. Replace the first two lines of the `FillList` subprocedure (above the `Me.lstOrders.RowSource = strSQL` line) with the following:

```
If Me.cboProduct.Value = 0 Then
    strSQL = strSQL5 & strSQL6 & Me.cboCountry.Value & _
        "'" & strSQL3
ElseIf Me.cboCountry.Value = "(All)" Then
    strSQL = strSQL5 & strSQL7 & Me.cboProduct.Value & _
        strSQL3
Else
    strSQL = strSQL1 & Me.cboCountry.Value & _
        strSQL2 & Me.cboProduct.Value & strSQL3
End If
```

8. Choose <u>D</u>ebug, Compi<u>l</u>e to check your code and fix any VBA statements that won't compile.

 9. Return to Access, close the form, and reopen it in Form view. Select a product in cboProduct and (All) in cboCountry to verify your additions, and double-click lstOrders (see Figure 29.13). Reverse the process by selecting a country and then selecting (All) products.

Figure 29.13
Select a product and then (All) to display all orders shipped that include the specified product.

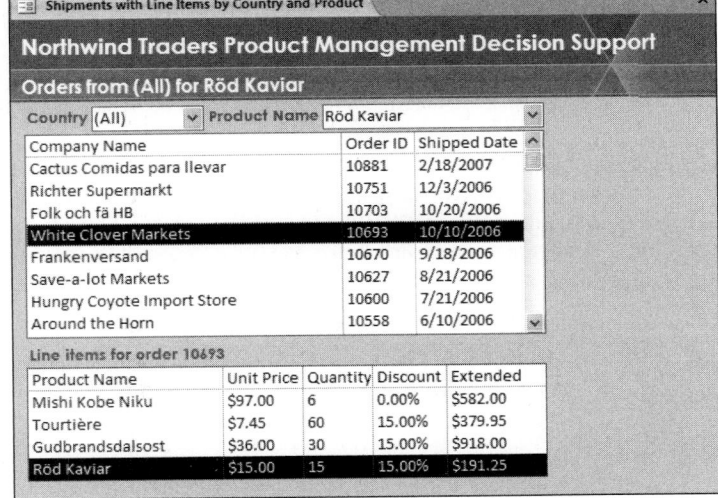

 If your orders or line items list boxes don't display the expected rows, see the "Problems with SQL Statements as Row Source Property Values" topic of the "Troubleshooting" section near the end of this chapter.

CONVERTING YOUR COMBO BOX FORM TO AN ACCESS DATA PROJECT

Access 2007's Upsizing Wizard (AUW) does a much better job of converting Access applications to Access data projects (ADP) than the Access 2000 and earlier versions. In most cases, however, the AUW can't upsize complex forms to forms that are operable in ADP. For instance, the AUW doesn't translate to Transact-SQL (T-SQL) the Access-specific SQL statements that serve as the Record Source property of bound forms and reports and the Row Source property value of controls. The forms you created in the preceding sections provide good examples of the problems you encounter when upsizing forms to ADP.

→ For an explanation of some of the limitations of the AUW, **see** "Upsizing with the Trial-and-Error Approach," **p. 949**.

Upsizing VBACombo.accdb isn't practical, so the sections that follow show you how to manually upsize forms imported to the project from VBACombo.accdb. You can't import Access queries to ADP, so you create SQL Server views based on the Access SQL of VBACombo.accdb's queries.

> **NOTE**
>
> The Northwind SQL Server database must be attached to SQL Server 2005 SP1 or 2000 SP, SQL Express, or MSDE 2000 SP4 to execute the code in the following example. If you have SQL Server 2005 SP1 or SQL Express SP1, you can attach the NorthwindSQL.mdf (and its NorthwindSQL.ldf log) file from the \SEUA12\Nwind folder. This file has more recent OrderDate, RequiredDate, and ShippedDate values than the traditional Northwind sample database for SQL Server. NorthwindSQL has a database diagram; most other versions don't have database diagrams.
>
> If you created the copy of the NorthwindSQL database as Northwind (or any other name) for use with the AddOrders.adp project described in Chapter 30, "Understanding Data Access Objects, OLE DB, and ADO," you can use AddOrders.adp to add a large number of records to the Orders and Order Details tables to test the performance of combo and list boxes with databases that are more representative of production applications.

→ To use AddOrders.adp with a copy of NorthwindSQL, **see** "Exploring the AddOrders.adp Sample Project," **p. 1328**.

IMPORTING AND TESTING THE COMBO BOX FORMS

To import the three forms you created in the preceding sections to an .adp file and test them against a local instance of SQL Server Express SP1, do the following:

1. Click the Office button to open the menu, and choose New to open the Getting Started with Microsoft Office Access Window.

2. Click the folder icon to open the File New Database dialog, navigate to the folder in which to store the file, open the Files of Type list, and select Microsoft Office Access Projects (*.adp).

3. Type **VBACombo.adp** as the File Name value, click Create to close the dialog, click Create in the Getting Started window to display a message box asking if you want to connect to an existing SQL Server database, and click Yes to open the Data Link Properties dialog.

4. Type **.\SQLEXPRESS** in the server name combo box; alternatively, open the drop-down list and select *COMPUTERNAME*\SQLEXPRESS. Select the Use Windows NT Integrated Security option.

5. Select SQLNorthwind from the drop-down database list, and click the Test Connection button to check the Data Link properties you specified (see Figure 29.14).

Figure 29.14
Establish a connection to the NorthwindSQL sample database on your machine.

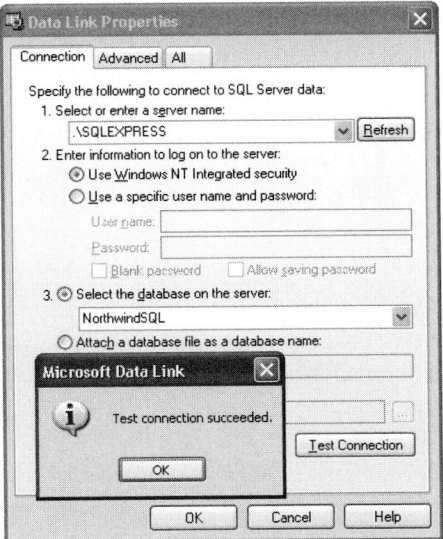

6. Click OK twice to create the connection and close the Data Link Properties dialog.

7. Click the External Data tab and click the Import group's Access button to open the Get External Data dialog. (You can import the three forms from the sample file, VBACombo.accdb or your working copy of Northwind.accdb, if you created those forms earlier.) Click Browse, navigate to the source folder, and double-click the .adddb file. Click OK to open the Import Objects dialog.

8. Click the Forms tab and click Select All if you're importing from VBACombo.accdb. If you're importing from Northwind, select the three forms—frmCombo1, frmDrillDown, and frmDrillDownAll. Then click OK to import the three forms to the project, and click Close to return to your project.

 9. Open the frmCombo1 form. The Country and Product combo boxes work, but no records appear in the Orders list box, despite the fact that combo box selections generate the correct label caption text. (Populating the Orders list box depends on the missing qryCombo1 query.).

10. Open the frmDrillDown form. You receive two error messages stating that the Access qryCombo1 and qryDrillDown queries don't exist.

REPLACING THE ACCESS qryCOMBO1 QUERY WITH AN SQL SERVER VIEW

One approach to upsizing Row Source property values from Access queries to SQL Server databases is to substitute T-SQL statements for the queries. A simpler method is to create SQL Server 2000 views that duplicate the Access queries.

To create a view to replace qryCombo1, do this:

1. Open VBACombo.accdb or Northwind.accdb (if you created the forms earlier) in another instance of Access 2007, and open qryCombo1.

2. Select SQL View to open the SQL window, select the SQL statement, and press Ctrl+C to copy the text to the Clipboard.

3. Return to the project, click the Create tab, and click the Other group's View button to open the New Query dialog. Select Design View to open the project designer.

4. Close the Add Table dialog, and click the small SQL button to open the designer's SQL pane.

5. Select the SELECT and FROM lines, press Ctrl+V to replace the lines with the qryCombo1 SQL statement, and delete the trailing semicolon.

6. Change the Orders.ShippedDate field list and WHERE clause items to **Orders.OrderDate**. (AddOrders.adp doesn't add ShippedDate values.)

7. Click the Run button, save your view as vwCombo1, and verify that the query executes correctly. Figure 29.15 shows the design of the view.

Figure 29.15
This SQL Server view replaces the Access qryCombo1 query in the three imported forms of VBACombo.adp.

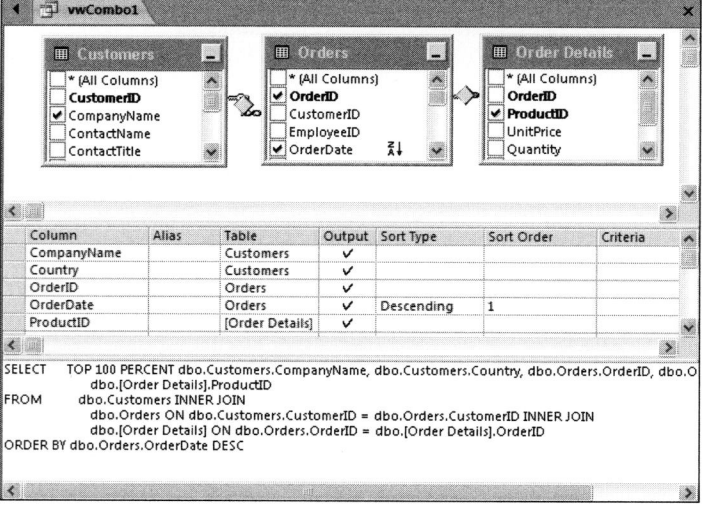

8. Open frmCombo1 in Design view and click the Code button to open the VBA editor. Replace qryCombo1 with **vwCombo1**, ShippedDate with **OrderDate** in the declaration of strSQL1, and ShippedDate with **OrderDate** in strSQL3 (see Figure 29.16).

Figure 29.16
Change qryCombo1 to vwCombo1 and ShippedDate to OrderDate in the Class Module for each form.

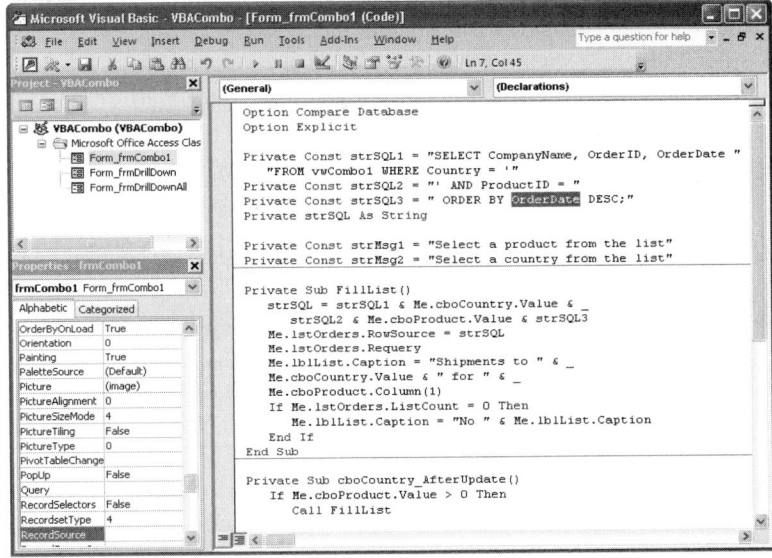

9. Change to Form view, test the form with a few combinations of Country and Product selections, close the form, and save your changes.

10. Repeat steps 8 and 9 for the frmDrillDown and frmDrillDownAll forms. In frmDrillDownAll, also change Orders.ShippedDate to **Orders.OrderDate** in the declaration of strSQL5. Acknowledge the error messages when you open frmDrillDown for testing. (The lstLineItems list isn't operable at this point.)

CONFORMING THE ACCESS SQL OF qryDrillDown TO T-SQL SYNTAX

The Access SQL statement for qryDrillDown includes the VBA **CCur** and **Format** functions that T-SQL doesn't support, and has the Percent format applied to the Discount column. Thus, you must substitute the T-SQL CONVERT function for the **CCur** and **Format** combination. The CONVERT function and an added % symbol solve the formatting problem with the Discount column.

→ For another example of using the CONVERT function, **see** "Exploring SQL Server Views," **p. 884**.

To create a view that emulates the formatting of the original Access query, do the following:

1. Copy the Access SQL statement for the qryDrillDown query to a new SQL Server view by the method described in steps 2–5 of the preceding section.

2. Click Run, save the query as **vwDrillDown**, and acknowledge the error message caused by the VBA functions in qryDrillDown's SQL statement.
3. Replace the `CCur(Format(…)) AS Extended` line with the following:

```
(dbo.[Order Details].UnitPrice * dbo.[Order Details].Quantity) *
(1 - dbo.[Order Details].Discount) AS Extended
```

4. Run the query again to check your initial changes to conform to T-SQL syntax.
5. Return to Design view, and edit the line you changed in step 3 to add the `CONVERT` function as follows:

```
CONVERT(money, (dbo.[Order Details].UnitPrice *
dbo.[Order Details].Quantity) *
(1 - dbo.[Order Details].Discount)) AS Extended
```

6. Rerun the query to check your change. The Extended column now has currency formatting.
7. If the Discount column doesn't display in percentage format, change to Design view, replace `dbo.[Order Details].Discount,` with this expression to multiply by 100, add two decimal places, convert to a string, and add the % symbol:

```
CONVERT(varchar, CONVERT(decimal(5,2), dbo.[Order Details].Discount * 100))
   + '%' AS Discount,
```

8. Run the query again to verify the format changes (see Figure 29.17). Figure 29.18 shows the query design without step 7's modification to the Discount column format.

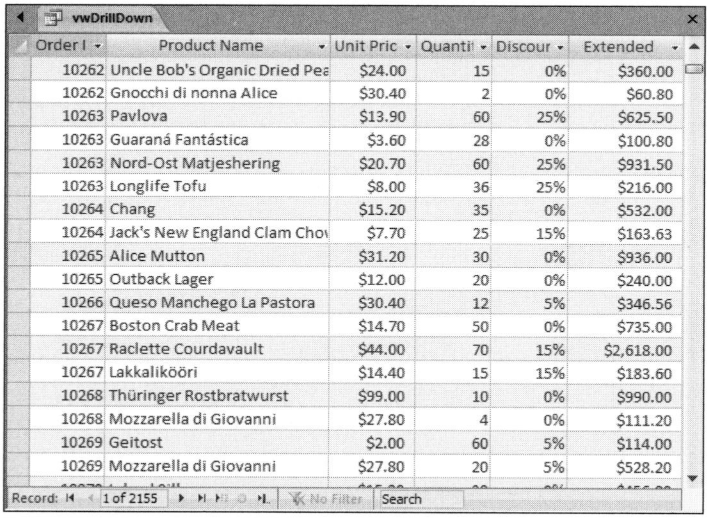

Order I	Product Name	Unit Pric	Quanti	Discour	Extended
10262	Uncle Bob's Organic Dried Pea	$24.00	15	0%	$360.00
10262	Gnocchi di nonna Alice	$30.40	2	0%	$60.80
10263	Pavlova	$13.90	60	25%	$625.50
10263	Guaraná Fantástica	$3.60	28	0%	$100.80
10263	Nord-Ost Matjeshering	$20.70	60	25%	$931.50
10263	Longlife Tofu	$8.00	36	25%	$216.00
10264	Chang	$15.20	35	0%	$532.00
10264	Jack's New England Clam Chov	$7.70	25	15%	$163.63
10265	Alice Mutton	$31.20	30	0%	$936.00
10265	Outback Lager	$12.00	20	0%	$240.00
10266	Queso Manchego La Pastora	$30.40	12	5%	$346.56
10267	Boston Crab Meat	$14.70	50	0%	$735.00
10267	Raclette Courdavault	$44.00	70	15%	$2,618.00
10267	Lakkalikööri	$14.40	15	15%	$183.60
10268	Thüringer Rostbratwurst	$99.00	10	0%	$990.00
10268	Mozzarella di Giovanni	$27.80	4	0%	$111.20
10269	Geitost	$2.00	60	5%	$114.00
10269	Mozzarella di Giovanni	$27.80	20	5%	$528.20

Figure 29.17
The result set of the modified vwDrillDown view duplicates the formatting of the Access qryDrillDown query.

9. Close the view, select frmDrillDown in the Navigation pane, and click the Code button to open the VBA editor.
10. In the Declarations section, change `qryDrillDown` to **vwDrillDown** in the declaration of `strSQL4`, and save your change.

Figure 29.18
The Design view of vwDrillDown has been modified here to improve readability of the T-SQL statements.

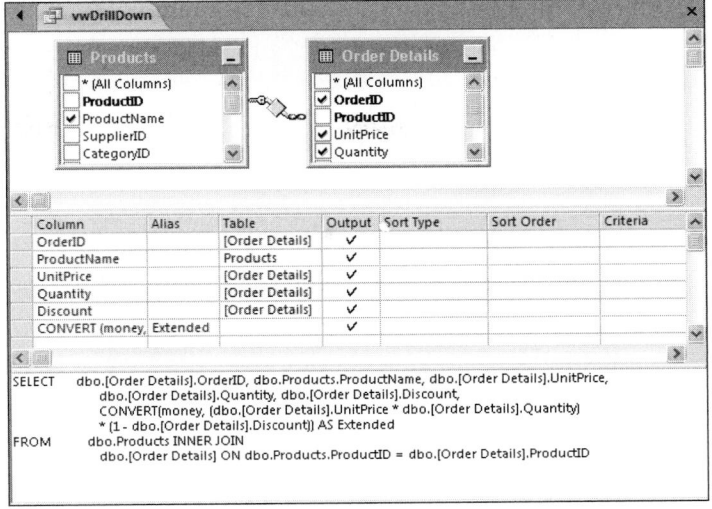

11. In Form Design view, select lstOrders, open the Properties window, click the Data tab, and delete the persisted Row Source value, if present. Select lstLineItems and delete its Row Source value.

12. Run the form and verify your changes.

13. Repeat steps 9–12 for the frmDrillDownAll form. When testing this form, verify that (All) products and (All) countries deliver the expected result.

NOTE

The VBACombo.adp sample project has two versions of each form. Form names with a (View) suffix are intended to operate with two SQL Server views that are equivalent to the queries you created in this and the preceding section. Forms without the suffix send T-SQL statements to the server, so you don't need to create the views to test these forms.

You can use Chapter 30's AddOrders.adp to add a few thousand new orders to the Orders and Order Details tables of a copy of NorthwindCS. When you connect to the copy, the time to fill lstOrders increases (as expected). The time required to retrieve the line items for an order, however, doesn't increase perceptively. Figure 29.19 shows the result of a frmDrillDownAll selection against tables with 10,830 orders and 76,380 line items. The sample forms without the suffix have two added features—when you click lstOrders, the code adds the number of orders in lstOrders to lblList's caption and adds the total amount of the order to lblLineItems' caption.

Figure 29.19
The sample frmDrillDownAll form displays a few of the 1,571 orders from the USA for a database with 10,830 orders added by the AddOrders.adp sample project.

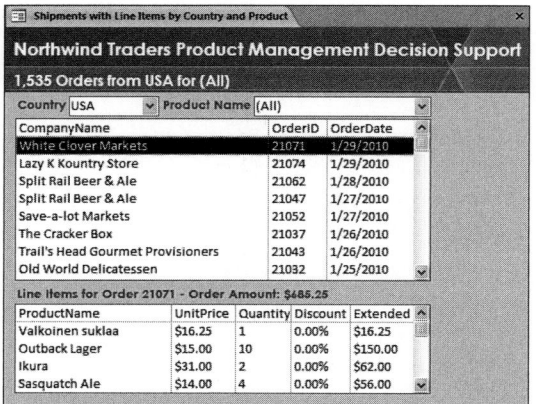

> **TIP**
>
> If your list-based application runs against tables with a large number of rows, consider adding a WHERE clause criterion to eliminate unneeded rows. For this example, you might add a date-based criterion to limit the Orders query to OrderDate values within the last year, quarter, or month. Alternatively, add a TOP 500 or TOP 25 PERCENT modifier to your SELECT statement.

TROUBLESHOOTING

RUN-TIME ERROR '2465'

I receive a "Run-Time Error '2465'" message in Form view.

The most likely cause of this error is failure to change the default Name property value of a combo box or list box to cboCountry, cboProduct, or lblList. Alternatively, you might have misspelled one of the names. Check the Object list for Combo#, Label#, or List# control names. Alternatively, select the Other page of the Property Sheet and select each control object to make sure the Name property value is correct.

SPURIOUS PARAMETER MESSAGES

A "Parameter" message appears in Form view.

One field name in your SQL statement doesn't correspond to a field name of qryCombo1. Double-check your values of the strSQL1, strSQL2, and strSQL3 constants against the field names included in qryCombo1.

PROBLEMS WITH SQL STATEMENTS AS ROW SOURCE PROPERTY VALUES

My list box doesn't display rows after I make valid selections in the Country and Product lists.

The SQL syntax for the query that populates the list box is incorrect or no orders meet your criteria. If you believe the query should return rows with the criteria you specify, set a breakpoint on the line that sets the RowSource property value of the list box. Repeat the operation that failed and, when the VBA editor opens, press Ctrl+G to open the Immediate window. Type ? and the name of the variable you use to assign the RowSource value to print the value. Break long statements by pressing Ctrl+Enter (see Figure 29.20).

Figure 29.20
Adding a breakpoint and displaying the SQL statement that provides the RowSource property of a list or combo box lets you debug the statement in the Immediate window.

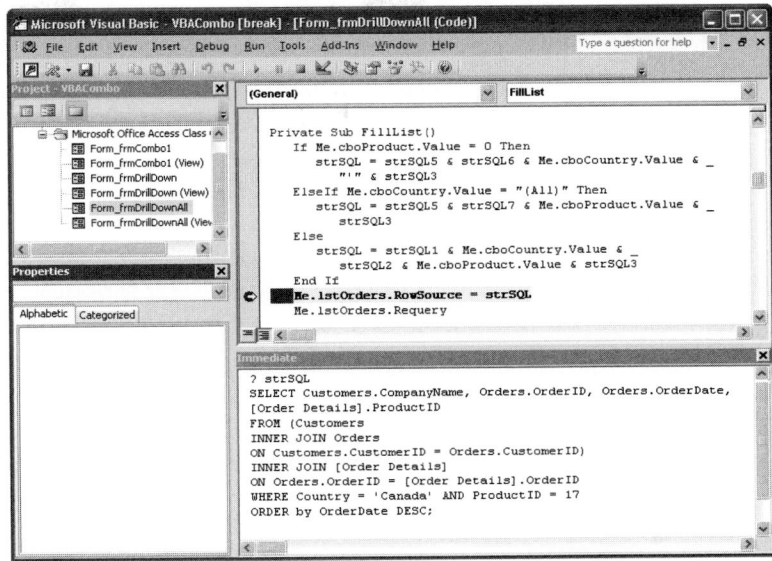

If you can't determine the source of the problem, copy the SQL statement to the Clipboard, and then paste it into the SQL window of an Access query or the SQL pane of an SQL Server view to test execution. The resulting error message *might* lead you to the source of the problem.

IN THE REAL WORLD—ACCESS COMBO AND LIST BOXES

Access's bound combo and list boxes offer many advantages over corresponding native controls available to Visual Basic 6 and .NET programmers. Automatic multifield capability in both combo and list boxes, and semi-formatted columns in Access list boxes are just two of the advantages of the Access version. When you migrate to ADP, another advantage of Access combo and list boxes becomes evident. As the frmDrillDown and frmDrillDownAll forms of the sample VBACombo.adp file demonstrate, you can populate combo and list boxes from Transact-SQL statements sent to the server as an alternative to creating SQL Server views.

The downside of sending SQL statements to SQL Server is that performance suffers because SQL Server optimizes and caches the query before execution. In many cases the changes to the query might cause cache misses. Sending long SQL statements to a remote server also contributes to list box latency. Compare the time required to first populate the Line Items list box using a connection to SQL Express's NorthwindSQL database on your

PC to that for Access's Northwind; Access is significantly faster. (The performance difference is accentuated on a slower PC or one having 256MB or less RAM.) After you run the query once, however, the performance difference is minimal because SQL Server caches the query plan in memory. When you re-execute the query, SQL Server 2000 checks to see whether the query plan's in memory; if so, it executes the copy without re-optimizing it. If you only alter WHERE clause criteria, SQL Server can use the cached version.

Views and stored procedures optimize combo and list box performance by eliminating the initial optimization step under all circumstances. The view-based examples of this chapter minimize execution time by specifying only WHERE criteria and the ORDER BY clause for each query. If your query is complex—and especially if it requires multiple joins between large tables—substitute a parameterized stored procedure to return the Recordset that populates list and combo boxes. Stored procedures return read-only Recordsets that have forward-only (Microsoft calls them *firehose*) cursors, which provide better performance than the default dynamic cursor.

Access multicolumn list boxes still have a few warts that need attention in future versions. For instance, you can't specify the alignment of individual columns; numeric values (including currency) and dates should right-align. Access 2007 combo and list boxes have an AddItem method that eliminates a very cumbersome method of adding items in Access 97 and earlier. Developers also complained about the 2KB limit on the length of the SQL statement used as the RowSource property of combo and list boxes, as well as the RecordSource property of forms in Access 2000 and earlier. The maximum length of Access 2007's RowSource and RecordSource property values is 64KB (32KB Unicode characters).

Regardless of their column format shortcomings, Access's native combo and list boxes are effective tools for both decision support and online transaction processing front ends. Consider replacing all read-only subforms with multicolumn list boxes, even if doing so requires some extra VBA code. Your customers—the users of your application—will appreciate their speedy response and space-saving format. You also gain the respect of DBAs when you substitute views and stored procedures for ad hoc queries against production databases.

UNDERSTANDING DATA ACCESS OBJECTS, OLE DB, AND ADO

In this chapter

30

GAINING A PERSPECTIVE ON MICROSOFT DATA ACCESS COMPONENTS

Integrated data management is the key to Access's success in the desktop RDBMS and client/server front-end market. Access and its wizards let you create basic data-bound forms, reports, and pages with minimal effort and little or no VBA programming. Linked tables provide dynamic access to a wide range of data sources. As your Access applications grow larger and more complex, automation with VBA code in class and public modules becomes essential. Ultimately, you'll need to write code that manipulates the Recordset objects to which your forms and, occasionally, reports are bound. Typically, you use code when you want to process a Recordset's rows sequentially instead of as a complete set. You might also need to create new Recordsets dynamically and bind them to forms or reports. At this point you must know how to program Data Access Objects (DAO), ActiveX Data Objects (ADO), or both.

DAO is the original application programming interface (API) for the Jet database engine. Microsoft's "Data Access Technologies Roadmap" white paper declared DAO to be obsolete and Jet as deprecated; deprecated components won't be upgraded with 64-bit versions. The white paper's authors told developers: "Do not use these [obsolete] technologies when you write new applications." Microsoft removed the components that supported Jet from Microsoft Data Access Components (MDAC) version 2.6 and later.

NOTE

> You can read the "Data Access Technologies Roadmap" white paper at http://msdn2.
> microsoft.com/en-us/library/ms810810.aspx.

There was much weeping, wailing, and gnashing of teeth among Access developers when Microsoft dictated the demise of DAO. Deprecating Jet in favor of SQL Server databases resulted in scores of "Jet is dead" articles in the computer press. As mentioned in earlier chapters, the SQL Server team, which owns MDAC, declared MSDE 1.0 and 2000 to be Access's strategic databases, decreed ADO to be the API of choice for Access 2000 through 2003, and made ADO 2.1 and 2.5 the default database programming references, respectively. Access data projects (ADPs) *require* an ADO reference; ADO 2.8 is the current, and probably last, version. Virtually all Microsoft investment in data access technology now is devoted to ADO.NET.

By popular demand, Access 2003 returned the default reference to "obsolete" DAO 3.6. This action proved that MSDE was more "strategic" to the SQL Server team than it was to Access users and developers. The Access team created its own copy of DAO 3.6, added support for the SharePoint-specific Attachments data type and multivalued lookup fields (complex types), and renamed the API to *Microsoft Office 12.0 Access database engine Object Library*, but kept the DAO class library abbreviation for backward compatibility. As you learned in Chapter 5, "Working with Access Databases and Tables," the Access team renamed Jet to

Access Connectivity Engine (ACE) initially, and then changed the official name to *Access Database Engine*.

> **NOTE**
>
> Access 2007's DAO implementation does not support ODBCDirect, which Access 97 introduced to enable connecting to client/server databases, such as SQL Server, without imposing the overhead of the Jet database engine. Microsoft recommends converting applications that use ODBCDirect to ADO, which is another reason for including basic ADO programming details in this book.

COMPARING DAO AND ADO OBJECTS

Access 2007's DAO version 12.0 (DAO12) library has been modified to remove objects, collections, and features that Microsoft no longer supports in .accdb databases: User and Group objects, Users and Groups collections, and replication-related elements. DAO lets you programmatically define and modify linked tables; ADO doesn't. DAO is optimized for the Jet database engine, which means that you get the same or better application performance with DAO as ADO.

> **NOTE**
>
> If you open an Access 2003 or earlier .mdb file in Access 2007, the default DAO version is 3.6, the last member of the original DAO version. DAO 3.6 supports user-level security programming and replication features, but not the new Access data types.

Figure 30.1 is a diagram that compares the basic ADO and DAO object hierarchies. The ADO object hierarchy, which can consist of nothing more than an ADODB.Connection object, is much simpler than the collection-based object hierarchy of DAO. However, the simplicity of the ADO object model is deceptive. To obtain a scrollable, updatable Recordset (Dynaset), you must open an ADODB.Recordset object on an active ADODB.Connection object.

> **NOTE**
>
> Access VBA provides a DAO shortcut, Set dbName = CurrentDB(), to bypass the first two collection layers and open the current database. ADPs offer a similar ADO shortcut, CurrentProject.Connection, which points to a default ADODB.Connection object with the Jet OLE DB Service Provider for the current database. Unlike CurrentDB(), which is optional, you must use CurrentProject.Connection as the ADODB.Connection to the currently open database. If you try to open a new ADODB.Connection to the current database, you receive a runtime error stating that the database is locked.

Figure 30.1
This diagram compares the ADO and DAO object hierarchies.

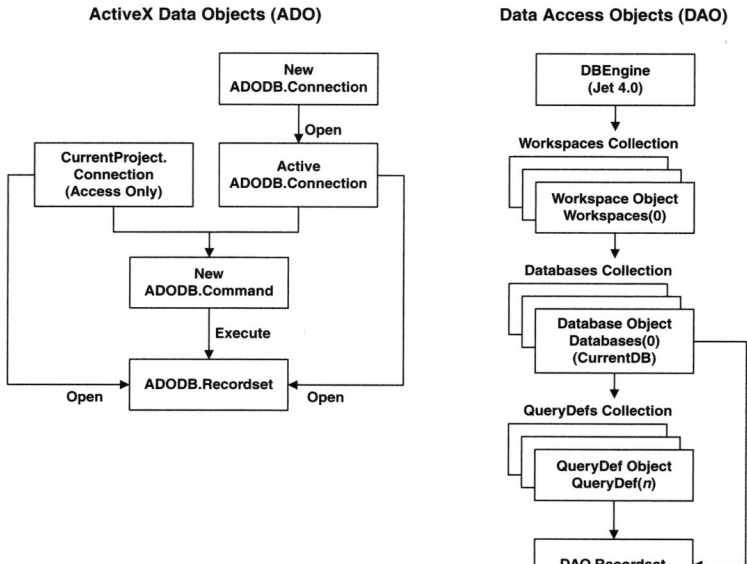

Unlike DAO objects, most of which are members of collections, you use the **New** reserved word with the **Set** instruction to create and the **Close** method, the **Set** *ObjectName* = **Nothing**, or both statements to remove instances of ADODB.Connection, ADODB.Command, and ADODB.Recordset objects independently of one another. The **Set** *ObjectName* = **Nothing** instruction releases memory consumed by the object.

Traditional DAO 3.6 supports a variety of Jet collections, such as Users and Groups, and Jet SQL Data Definition Language (DDL) operations that ADO 2.8 alone doesn't handle. Access 2007's DAO flavor provides a new Recordset2 object that has a ParentRecordset property to implement multivalued lookup fields. A Recordset2.Fields2 collection supports the Attachments data type. Except for Recordsets based on ODBC connections, the terms DAO.Recordset[.Fields] and DAO.Recordset2[.Fields2] are interchangeable in this chapter.

Microsoft ADO Extensions for DDL and Security (ADOX) 2.8 defines Jet-specific collections and objects that aren't included in ADO 2.8. The "Provider-Specific Properties and Their Values" section later in the chapter describes how to roll your own cross-reference table to aid in migrating your DAO code to ADO.

NOTE

Microsoft adds a reference to ADO 2.8 but not ADOX 2.8 to new ADPs. ADOX supports SQL Server and Jet, so Microsoft will continue to support it with a 64-bit version.

CREATING DAO.Recordset2 AND ADODB.Recordset OBJECTS

The concept of database object independence is new to Access. The best way of demonstrating this feature is to compare DAO and ADO code to create a `Recordset` object from an SQL statement. DAO and ADO let you create and manipulate Recordsets independently of forms. DAO lets you create and populate new tables (`TableDef` objects) and query definitions (`QueryDef` objects) that appear in the Navigation Pane. ADO doesn't support `TableDef` and `QueryDef` objects, but it does enable connecting to SQL Server databases and their table with OLE DB data providers.

DAO syntax uses successive instantiation of each object in the DAO hierarchy (`DBEngine`, `Workspace`, `Database`, and `Recordset`), as in the following example:

```
Dim wsName As DAO.Workspace
Dim dbName As DAO.Database
Dim rstName As DAO.Recordset2

Set wsName = DBEngine.Workspaces(0)
Set dbName = wsName.OpenDatabase ("DatabaseName.accdb")
Set rstName = dbName.OpenRecordset2 ("SQL Statement")
```

As you descend through the hierarchy, you open new child objects with methods of the parent object. However, you can skip the Workspaces collection by applying the `OpenDatabase` method to the `DBEngine` object directly.

The most common approach with ADO is to create one or more independent, reusable instances of each object in the Declarations section of a form or module:

```
Private cnnName As New ADODB.Connection
Private cmmName As New ADODB.Command
Private rstName As New ADODB.Recordset
```

> **NOTE**
>
> This book uses cnn as the object type prefix for Connection, cmm for Command, and rst for Recordset. The cmm prefix is used because the cmd prefix traditionally identifies a command button control and the com prefix identifies the MSComm ActiveX control (Microsoft Comm Control 6.0).
>
> Although you're likely to find references to DAO.Recordset and DAO.Recordset2 Dynasets and snapshots in the Access documentation, these terms don't apply to ADODB.Recordset objects. See the CursorType property of the ADODB.Recordset object in the "Recordset Properties" section later in this chapter for the CursorType equivalents of Dynasets and snapshots.

After the initial declarations, you set the properties of the new object instances and apply methods—Open for Connections and Recordsets, or Execute for Commands—to activate the object. Invoking the Open method of the ADODB.Recordset object, rather than the

OpenRecordset method of the DAO.Database object, makes ADO objects independent of one another. Object independence and batch-optimistic locking, for instance, let you close the ADODB.Recordset's ADODB.Connection object, make changes to the Recordset, and then re-open the Connection to send only the changes to the underlying tables. Minimizing the number of open database connections conserves valuable server resources.

Access 2000 introduced forms with a then-new property, Recordset, which let you assign with code a DAO.Recordset, DAO.Recordset2 or ADODB.Recordset object as the RecordSource for one or more forms. The Recordset property of a form is an important addition, because you can assign the same Recordset to multiple forms with code. All forms connected to the Recordset synchronize to the same current record. Access developers have been requesting this feature since version 1.0. Access 2002 delivered updatable ADODB.Recordsets for Jet, SQL Server, and Oracle data sources that you can assign to the Recordset property value of forms and reports. This means you can create an Access application that lets users easily select between at least three popular but fundamentally different RDBMSs.

The examples that follow demonstrate the difference in VBA code for creating and manipulating DAO.Recordset and ADODB.Recordset objects.

CREATING A DAO.Recordset2 OBJECT WITH CODE AND BINDING A FORM AND CONTROLS TO IT

Listing 30.1 shows the DAO code to create a Recordset from an external database and bind a Split Form as well as seven text boxes to the Recordset. All code examples in this chapter use DAO and ADODB prefixes to identify the objects' class and prevent conflicts with Recordset and other objects that have the same names in the two classes.

LISTING 30.1   DAO CODE TO CREATE AND BIND A FORM AND CONTROLS TO A
DAO.Recordset2 OBJECT FROM ANOTHER .ACCDB DATABASE (FRMDAO_ACCESS)

```
Private strSQL As String
Private dbNwind As DAO.Database
Private rstNwind As DAO.Recordset2

Private Sub Form_Load()
    'Open the local copy of Northwind
    Set dbNwind = DBEngine.OpenDatabase(CurrentProject.Path & _
        "\Northwind.accdb")

    'Create the Recordset
    strSQL = "SELECT * FROM Customers"
    Set rstNwind = dbNwind.OpenRecordset(strSQL)

    'Assign rstNwind as the Recordset for the form
    Set Me.Recordset = rstNwind

    'Bind controls to the Recordset's fields
    Me.txtCustomerID.ControlSource = "CustomerID"
    Me.txtCompanyName.ControlSource = "CompanyName"
    Me.txtAddress.ControlSource = "Address"
```

```
      Me.txtCity.ControlSource = "City"
      Me.txtRegion.ControlSource = "Region"
      Me.txtPostalCode.ControlSource = "PostalCode"
      Me.txtCountry.ControlSource = "Country"
End Sub

Private Sub Form_Unload(Cancel As Integer)
      'Required to prevent not found errors on opening with
      'an Access 2007 .accdb file
      Set Me.Recordset = Nothing
End Sub
```

30

> **NOTE**
>
>
>
> The preceding code and that of the other examples of these sections is in the class module of forms in \SEUA12\Chaptr30\DAO-ADOTest.accdb. The listing's caption includes the form name.

The code applies the OpenDatabase method to the DBEngine object with the path and filename of the external database, invokes the OpenRecordset method with an SQL statement on the Database object, and then sets the form's Recordset property value to the newly created DAO.Recordset. The remaining Form_Load code binds seven text boxes to specified fields of the Recordset by setting the text boxes' ControlSource property to the field name.

> **NOTE**
>
> The **Set Me.Recordset = Nothing** instruction in the Form_Unload event is to prevent firing occasional "SELECT * FROM Customers not found" errors when opening the form.

Figure 30.2 shows frmDAO_Access in Form view with VCR buttons added for Recordset navigation. Listing 30.2 contains the event-handling code for the four VCR buttons.

Figure 30.2
The four forms that demonstrate DAO and ADO Recordsets use this Split Form based on the Customers table as the data source.

LISTING 30.2 EVENT-HANDLING CODE FOR THE MoveFirst, MovePrevious, MoveNext, AND MoveLast METHODS OF THE DAO.Recordset OBJECT (FRMDAO_ACCESS)

```
Private Sub btnFirst_Click()
    rstNwind.MoveFirst
End Sub

Private Sub btnPrevious_Click()
    If Not rstNwind.BOF Then
        rstNwind.MovePrevious
    End If
End Sub

Private Sub btnNext_Click()
    If Not rstNwind.EOF Then
        rstNwind.MoveNext
    End If
End Sub

Private Sub btnLast_Click()
    rstNwind.MoveLast
End Sub
```

Invoking the *RecordsetName*.Move… methods has the identical effect as executing the corresponding GoToRecord macro action. However, the Move… methods don't have GoToRecord's built-in error-handling code. Therefore, you must test the DAO.Recordset.BOF (beginning-of-file) or EOF (end-of-file) property before invoking the MovePrevious or MoveNext method.

→ To compare the Move… methods with the GoToRecord macro action, **see** "Generating Embedded Macros with the Command Button Wizard," **p. 1155**.

CREATING THE RECORDSET FROM AN SQL SERVER EXPRESS DATABASE

DAO 3.6's ODBCDirect feature enabled using ODBC to connect to a client/server database and generate a Recordset without creating a temporary DAO.Database object. As mentioned at the beginning of this chapter, Access 2007 no longer supports the ODBCDirect feature, so you must write code to create a temporary TableDef object, link it to the client/server database, and then append it to the local database's TableDefs collection.

→ If you didn't install SSX and attach \SEUA12\Nwind\NorthwindSQL.mdf as the NorthwindSQL database previously, **see** "SQL Server 2005 Express Edition SP2 Setup," **p. 59**.

Listing 30.3 shows code for SQL Server 7 and later in the frmDAO_ODBC class module that corresponds to Listing 30.1's code for an Access 2007 database. In this case, you specify a conventional DAO.Recordset, not DAO.Recordset2, because SQL Server doesn't support the Attachment data type or multivalued lookup fields.

**LISTING 30.3 DAO CODE TO CREATE AND BIND A FORM AND CONTROLS TO A
DAO.Recordset OBJECT FROM THE NORTHWINDSQL DATABASE RUNNING ON SQL SERVER
2005 EXPRESS (FRMDAO_ODBC)**

```
Private strSQL As String
Private dbNwind As DAO.Database
Private rstNwind As DAO.Recordset
Private tdfCustomers As DAO.TableDef

Private Sub Form_Load()
    'Create a temporary linked TableDef object in the current database
    Set dbNwind = CurrentDb
    Set tdfCustomers = CurrentDb.CreateTableDef("Customers")
    With tdfCustomers
        .Connect = "ODBC;Driver={SQL Server};Server=.\SQLEXPRESS;" & _
        "Database=NorthwindSQL;Trusted_Connection=yes"
        .SourceTableName = "Customers"
    End With

    'Add the TableDef to the TableDefs, disregard error if present
    On Error Resume Next
    dbNwind.TableDefs.Append tdfCustomers
    On Error GoTo 0

    strSQL = "SELECT * FROM Customers"
    Set rstNwind = dbNwind.OpenRecordset(strSQL)

    'Assign rstNwind as the Recordset for the form
    Set Me.Recordset = rstNwind
    Me.txtCustomerID.ControlSource = "CustomerID"
    Me.txtCompanyName.ControlSource = "CompanyName"
    Me.txtAddress.ControlSource = "Address"
    Me.txtCity.ControlSource = "City"
    Me.txtRegion.ControlSource = "Region"
    Me.txtPostalCode.ControlSource = "PostalCode"
    Me.txtCountry.ControlSource = "Country"
End Sub

Private Sub Form_Unload(Cancel As Integer)
    'Prevent not found error on opening with Access 2007 .accdb file
    Set Me.Recordset = Nothing
    'Remove the TableDef, disregard if not found
    On Error Resume Next
    dbNwind.TableDefs.Delete tdfCustomers.Name
End Sub
```

The ODBC;Driver={SQL Server};Server=.\SQLEXPRESS; Database=NorthwindSQL;Trusted_
Connection=yes connection string creates a DSN-less connection to a local instance of SQL
Server 2005 Express (SSX) with integrated Windows authentication. The TableDef is temporary, so the Form_Unload event handler deletes it after freeing the memory consumed by
the Recordset.

BINDING A FORM TO ADODB.Recordset OBJECTS

Creating an ADODB.Recordset object and binding a form and controls to it isn't a remarkably different process from that for the preceding DAO.Recordset examples. The ADODB.Connection object substitutes for the DAO.Database object and defines the connection to an external .mdb database, and the ADODB.Recordset object opens on the Connection, as shown in Listing 30.4. As its name implies, Microsoft.Jet.OLEDB.4.0 is the OLE DB data provider for Jet 4.0 .mdb—but not Access .accdb—databases. The OLE DB data provider for Jet doesn't support the Attachments data type or multi-select lookup fields. You receive "Unrecognized database format '*d:\Path\Databasename*.accdb'" errors if you specify an .accdb database in the connection string.

ADO objects support events, so you declare the objects WithEvents, as shown in the declarations section, and then create instances of the objects in the Form_Load event handler with **Set** *ObjectName* = **New** *ObjectType* statements.

LISTING 30.4   ADO CODE TO CREATE AND BIND A FORM AND CONTROLS TO AN ADODB.Recordset OBJECT FROM AN EXTERNAL ACCESS 2007 DATABASE (FRMADO_JET)

```
'Enable events on the Connection and Recordset
Private WithEvents cnnNwind As ADODB.Connection
Private WithEvents rstNwind As ADODB.Recordset

Private Sub Form_Load()
    'Instantiate Connection and Recordset objects (required for WithEvents)
    Set cnnNwind = New ADODB.Connection
    Set rstNwind = New ADODB.Recordset

    'Specify the OLE DB provider and open the connection
    With cnnNwind
        .Provider = "Microsoft.Jet.OLEDB.4.0"
        .Open CurrentProject.Path & "\Northwind.mdb"
    End With

    'Set the ADODB.Recordset properties and open it
    With rstNwind
        Set .ActiveConnection = cnnNwind
        .CursorType = adOpenKeyset
        .CursorLocation = adUseClient
        .LockType = adLockOptimistic
        .Open "Customers"
    End With

    'Assign rstNwind as the Recordset for the form
    Set Me.Recordset = rstNwind
    Me.txtCustomerID.ControlSource = "CustomerID"
    Me.txtCompanyName.ControlSource = "CompanyName"
    Me.txtAddress.ControlSource = "Address"
    Me.txtCity.ControlSource = "City"
    Me.txtRegion.ControlSource = "Region"
    Me.txtPostalCode.ControlSource = "PostalCode"
    Me.txtCountry.ControlSource = "Country"
End Sub
```

```
Private Sub Form_Unload(Cancel As Integer)
    'Close the Recordset and Connection
    If Not rstNwind Is Nothing Then
        If rstNwind.State = adStateOpen Then
            rstNwind.Close
            Set rstNwind = Nothing
        End If
    End If
    If Not cnnNwind Is Nothing Then
        If cnnNwind.State = adStateOpen Then
            cnnNwind.Close
            Set cnnNwind = Nothing
        End If
    End If
End Sub
```

Listing 30.4's code substitutes a table name (Customers) for the preceding examples' SQL Statement (SELECT * FROM Customers).

→ If you didn't install SSX and attach \SEUA12\Nwind\NorthwindSQL.mdf as the NorthwindSQL database previously, **see** "SQL Server 2005 Express Edition SP2 Setup," **p. 59**.

Listing 30.5 shows the Form_Load event-handling code for a connection to the NorthwindSQL database of a local SSX instance (the Declaration section, text box binding, and Form_Unload code is identical to that of Listing 30.4). The connection uses the SQL Native Client provider (SQLNCLI) for SQL Server 2000, 2005, and SSX, which the SSX setup program installs.

LISTING 30.5   ADO CODE TO CREATE AND BIND A FORM AND CONTROLS TO AN ADODB.Recordset OBJECT FROM A LOCAL SSX INSTANCE (FRMADO_SSX)

```
Private Sub Form_Load()
    'Create the new Connection and Recordset objects (required for WithEvents)
    Set cnnNwind = New ADODB.Connection
    Set rstNwind = New ADODB.Recordset

    'Specify the OLE DB provider and open the connection
    With cnnNwind
        .Provider = "SQLNCLI" 'SQL Native Client for SQL Server 2005
        .Mode = adModeShareDenyNone
        .ConnectionString = "Data Source=.\SQLEXPRESS; " & _
            "Integrated Security = SSPI; Database=NorthwindSQL"
        .Open
    End With

    'Define the ADODB.Recordset properties
    With rstNwind
        Set .ActiveConnection = cnnNwind
        .CursorType = adOpenKeyset
        .CursorLocation = adUseClient
        .LockType = adLockOptimistic
        .Open "SELECT * FROM Customers"
```

continues

LISTING 30.5 CONTINUED

```
    End With

    'Assign rstNwind as the Recordset for the form
    Set Me.Recordset = rstNwind
    'Good practice for a single table, required for joins
    Me.UniqueTable = "Customers"
    Me.txtCustomerID.ControlSource = "CustomerID"
    Me.txtCompanyName.ControlSource = "CompanyName"
    Me.txtAddress.ControlSource = "Address"
    Me.txtCity.ControlSource = "City"
    Me.txtRegion.ControlSource = "Region"
    Me.txtPostalCode.ControlSource = "PostalCode"
    Me.txtCountry.ControlSource = "Country"
End Sub
```

The ADODB.Recordset.UniqueTable property is optional for creating an updatable Recordset unless the Recordset is based on an SQL statement having an INNER JOIN clause. In that case, the `UniqueTable` property value must be set to the name of the outermost table (also called the *most many table*) that has a primary key field.

USING THE OBJECT BROWSER TO DISPLAY DAO AND ADODB PROPERTIES, METHODS, AND EVENTS

Using Object Browser is the handiest way to find the correct syntax for programming data objects.

To use Object Browser with DAO and ADO objects, follow these steps:

1. Open in design mode one of the forms of DAO-ADOTest.accdb that you worked with in the preceding sections, and then open the VBA Editor for its code.

2. Press F2 to open Object Browser.

3. Select DAO or ADODB in the library (upper) list.

4. Select one of the top-level components, such as `Connection`, in the Classes (left) pane.

5. Select a property, event, or method, such as `Open` for ADO or `OpenRecordset` for DAO, in the Members of '*ObjectName*' (right) pane. A short-form version of the syntax for the selected method or event appears in Object Browser's lower pane (see Figure 30.3).

6. If you selected DAO in step 3, click the Help (question mark) button to open the Suggestions pane for help topics related to the selected object, property, method, or event. Figure 30.4 shows the help topic for `DAO.Connection.OpenRecordset`.

7. Click the Suggestions topic that most closely relates to the object, property, method, or event you chose in step 5 (`Connetion.OpenRecordset` for this example). Figure 30.5 shows the resulting help topic.

Figure 30.3
Object Browser displays in the status pane the syntax of the object class member you select in the Members of *'ObjectName'* pane.

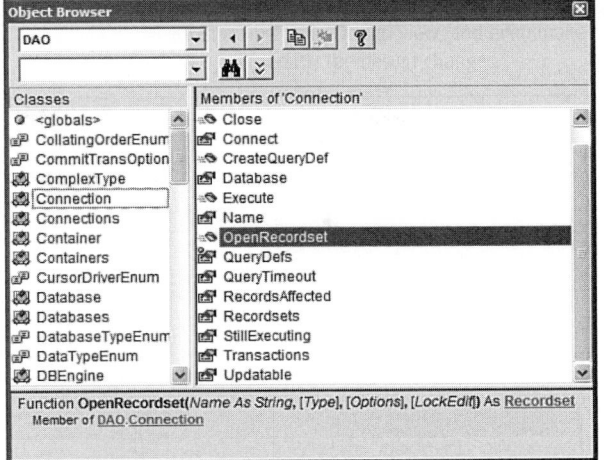

Figure 30.4
The first step in finding help for most DAO properties is the disambiguation (Suggestions) pane of the Access 2007 Developer Reference dialog. The same pane appears if you type **OpenRecordset** in the search text box, but the pane displays the first 25 of 100 hits.

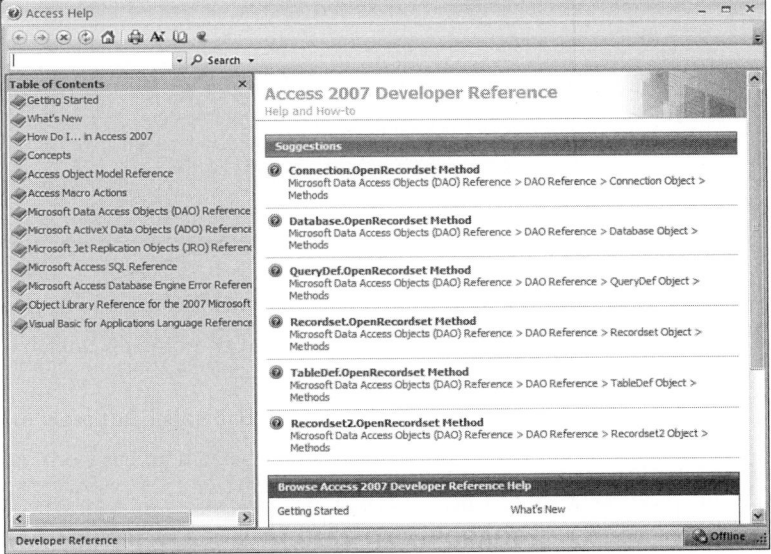

Access 2007 includes a compiled help file for ADO 2.5, which is the default reference for Access 2003 and 2007. If your project has a reference to the Microsoft ActiveX Data Objects 2.5 Library, clicking Object Browser's help button opens the Access 2007 Developer Reference's generic Browse pane. Context-sensitive (F1) help for a selected code element also opens the generic Browse pane. In this case, you can browse from the "Microsoft ActiveX Data Objects (ADO) Reference" topic in the TOC. Alternatively, type the topic in the search pane; however, searches for common data object topics usually return far too many hits to be useful.

Figure 30.5
Help topics for data objects provide complete syntax information and often include brief code samples.

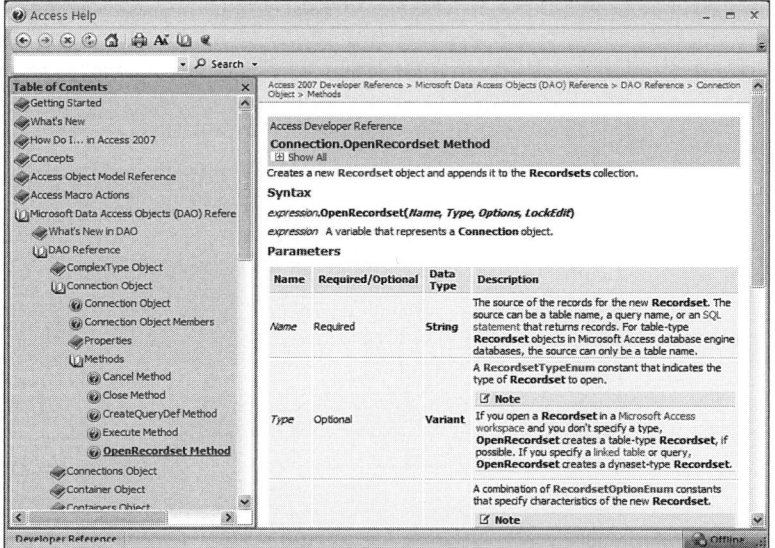

TIP

If the Browse pane shows XML document fragments or you receive an "Unable to display help" message, try changing the Connection Status (at the bottom right of the help window) from Show Content from Office Online to Show Content Only from This Computer.

You might find it easier to work directly with the compiled help file, ADO210.CHM, which you'll find in the \Program Files\Common Files\Microsoft Shared\OFFICE12\1033 folder. The file displays the traditional help window that most developers prefer (see Figure 30.6).

If you use a reference to a later ADO version, such as 2.6, 2.7, or 2.8, you receive an "Unable to display help" message instead of the Access 2007 help window's generic Browse pane when you click Object Browser's help button or choose ADODB from the Context Help dialog. However, you can select Help, Microsoft Visual Basic Help from the VBA Editor and browse the "Microsoft ActiveX Data Objects (ADO) Reference" topic.

TIP

To obtain current help files for ADO 2.8, search the Internet for "MDAC 2.8 SDK" and download the Microsoft Data Access Components (MDAC) 2.8 Software Development Kit, which installs Ado28.chm and Ado28.chi files in your \Program Files\Microsoft Data Access SDK 2.8\Docs folder.

Figure 30.6
The ADO210.CHM compiled help file opens in the traditional online help window and enhances searches for ADO-specific topics.

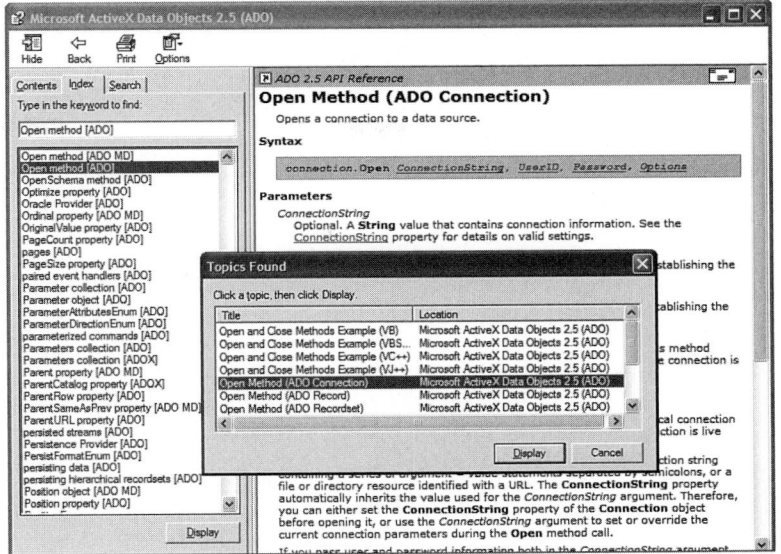

Due to Access 2007's paucity of help for ADODB objects, the following three sections provide details of the ADODB.Connection, ADODB.Command, and ADODB.Recordset objects.

WORKING WITH THE ADODB.Connection OBJECT

The Connection object is the primary top-level ADO component. You must successfully open a Connection object to a data source before you can use the associated Command or Recordset objects.

CONNECTION PROPERTIES

Table 30.1 lists the names and descriptions of the properties of the ADODB.Connection object.

TABLE 30.1 PROPERTIES OF THE ADODB.Connection OBJECT	
Property Name	**Data Type and Purpose**
Attributes	A **Long** read/write value that specifies use of retaining transactions by the sum of two constant values. The adXactCommitRetaining constant starts a new transaction when calling the CommitTrans method; adXactAbortRetaining starts a new transaction when calling the RollbackTrans method. The default value is 0 (don't use retaining transactions).
CommandTimeout	A **Long** read/write value that determines the time in seconds before terminating an Execute call against an associated Command object. The default value is 30 seconds.

continues

TABLE 30.1   CONTINUED

Property Name	Data Type and Purpose
ConnectionString	A **String** read/write variable that supplies specific information required by a data or service provider to open a connection to the data source.
ConnectionTimeout	A **Long** read/write value that determines the number of seconds before terminating an unsuccessful `Connection.Open` method call. The default value is 15 seconds.
CursorLocation	A **Long** read/write value that determines whether the client-side (`adUseClient`) or the server-side (`adUseServer`) cursor engine is used. The default is `adUseServer`.
DefaultDatabase	A **String** read/write variable that specifies the name of the database to use if not specified in the `ConnectionString`. For SQL Server examples, the value is the default Initial Catalog.
Errors	A pointer to the `Errors` collection for the connection that contains one or more `Error` objects if an error is encountered when attempting the connection. The later "Errors Collection and `Error` Objects" section describes this property.
IsolationLevel	A **Long** read/write value that determines the behavior or transactions that interact with other simultaneous transactions (see Table 30.2).
Mode	A **Long** value that determines read and write permissions for `Connection` objects (see Table 30.3).
Properties	A pointer to the OLE DB provider-specific (also called dynamic) `Properties` collection of the `Connection` object. Jet 4.0 databases have 94 `Property` objects, and SQL Server databases have 93. The next section shows you how to enumerate provider-specific properties.
Provider	A **String** read/write value that specifies the name of the OLE DB data or service provider if not specified in the `ConnectionString` value. The default value is MSDASQL, the Microsoft OLE DB Provider for ODBC. The most common providers used in the programming chapters of this book are Microsoft.Jet.OLEDB.4.0, more commonly known by its code name, "Jolt 4," and SQLOLEDB, the OLE DB provider for SQL Server.
State	A **Long** read-only value that specifies whether the connection to the database is open, closed, or in an intermediate state (see Table 30.4).
Version	A **String** read-only value that returns the ADO version number.

NOTE

Most property values identified in Table 30.1 as being read/write are writable only when the connection is in the closed state. Some provider-specific properties are read/write, but most are read-only.

PROVIDER-SPECIFIC PROPERTIES AND THEIR VALUES

The "Appendix A: DAO to ADO Quick Reference" page of Alyssa Henry's 1999 white paper, "Migrating from DAO to ADO," contained a table that translates DAO objects and properties to ADO objects, properties, and provider-specific Jet properties. The table no longer is included in the white paper, which was updated in April 2004 and renamed "Porting DAO Code to ADO with the Microsoft Jet Provider." (Search on the full name to find the MSDN archive location.) Fortunately, an archive of the table is available at http://doc.ddart.net/mssql/sql2000/html/mdacxml/htm/wpmigratingappendixa.htm.

Right-click the page in Internet Explorer 7 and choose Export to Microsoft Excel to create a worksheet from the table (see Figure 30.7). Importing the worksheet to a Jet or SQL Server table lets you view the contents in a searchable datasheet. Contents of the Microsoft website are copyrighted, so the table isn't included in this chapter's sample databases.

30

Figure 30.7

This Excel worksheet was created by importing a copy of the HTML table of the "DAO to ADO Quick Reference" page from an archive website. Property or method names with number suffixes, such as DefaultType1, refer to footnotes in the source document's web page.

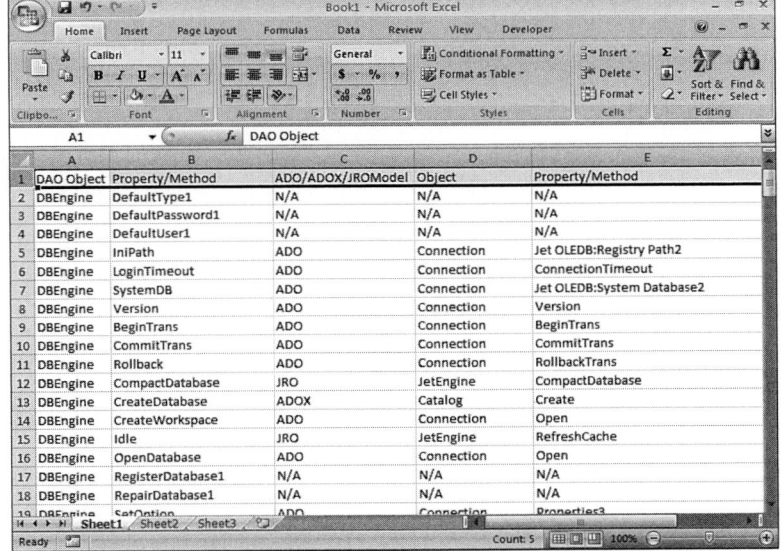

TRANSACTION ISOLATION LEVELS

The ability to specify the transaction isolation level applies only when you use the BeginTrans, CommitTrans, and RollbackTrans methods (see Table 30.6 later in this chapter) to perform a transaction on a Connection object. If multiple database users simultaneously execute transactions, your application should specify how it responds to other transactions in process. Table 30.2 lists the options for the degree of your application's isolation from other simultaneous transactions.

30

TABLE 30.2 CONSTANT ENUMERATION FOR THE `IsolationLevel` *PROPERTY*

IsolationLevelEnum	Description
adXactCursorStability	Allows reading only committed changes in other transactions (default value).
adXactBrowse	Allows reading uncommitted changes in other transactions.
adXactChaos	The transaction won't overwrite changes made to transaction(s) at a higher isolation level.
adXactIsolated	All transactions are independent of (isolated from) other transactions.
adXactReadCommitted	Same as adXactCursorStability.
adXactReadUncommitted	Same as adXactBrowse.
adXactRepeatableRead	Prohibits reading changes in other transactions.
adXactSerializable	Same as adXactIsolated.
adXactUnspecified	The transaction level of the provider can't be determined.

NOTE

Enumeration tables in this book list the default value first, followed by the remaining constants in alphabetical order. Where two members of Table 30.2 represent the same isolation level, one of the members is included for backward compatibility.

THE `Connection.Mode` PROPERTY

Unless you have a specific reason to specify a particular `ADODB.Connection.Mode` value, the default `adModeUnknown` is adequate. The Jet OLE DB provider defaults to `adModeShareDenyNone`. The Access Permissions list on the Advanced page of the Data Link properties page for SQLOLEDB is disabled, but you can set the `Mode` property with code. Table 30.3 lists all the constants for the `Mode` property.

TABLE 30.3 CONSTANT ENUMERATION FOR THE `Mode` PROPERTY

ConnectModeEnum	Description
adModeUnknown	No connection permissions have been set on the data source (default value).
adModeRead	Connect with read-only permission.
adModeReadWrite	Connect with read/write permissions.
adModeRecursive	If an adModeShareDeny… flag is specified, applies the mode to child records of a chaptered (hierarchical) Recordset object.
adoModeRecursive	Used in conjunction with the Record objects, which this chapter doesn't cover.
adModeShareDenyNone	Don't deny other users read or write access.

ConnectModeEnum	Description
adModeShareDenyRead	Deny others permission to open a read connection to the data source.
adModeShareDenyWrite	Deny others permission to open a write connection to the data source.
adModeShareExclusive	Open the data source for exclusive use.
adModeWrite	Connect with write-only permission.

30

> **TIP**
>
> You often can improve performance of client/server decision-support applications by opening the connection as read only (adModeRead). Modifying the structure of a database with SQL's DDL usually requires exclusive access to the database (adModeShareExclusive).

THE Connection.State PROPERTY

Table 30.4 lists the constants that return the state of the Connection object. These constants also are applicable to the State property of the Command and Recordset objects.

It's common to open and close connections as needed to reduce the connection load on the database. (Each open connection to a client/server database consumes a block of memory.) In many cases, you must test whether the Connection object is open or closed before applying the Close or Open method, or changing Connection property values, which are read-only when the connection is open.

TABLE 30.4 CONSTANT ENUMERATION FOR THE State PROPERTY

ObjectStateEnum	Description
adStateClosed	The Connection (or other object) is closed (default value).
adStateConnecting	A connection to the data source is in progress.
adStateExecuting	The Execute method of a Connection or Command object has been called.
adStateFetching	Rows are returning to a Recordset object.
adStateOpen	The Connection (or other object) is open (active).

Errors COLLECTION AND Error OBJECTS

Figure 30.8 illustrates the relationship between top-level ADO components and their collections. The dependent Errors collection is a property of the Connection object, and if errors are encountered with any operation on the connection, it contains one or more Error objects. The Errors collection has one property, Count, which you test to determine whether an error has occurred after executing a method call on Connection and Recordset objects. A collection is required, because it's possible for an object to generate several errors.

Figure 30.8
The `Connection`, `Command`, and `Recordset` objects have `Properties` and `Errors` collections. The `Command` object also has a `Parameters` collection, and the `Recordset` object has a `Fields` Collection. The new `Record` object isn't included in this diagram.

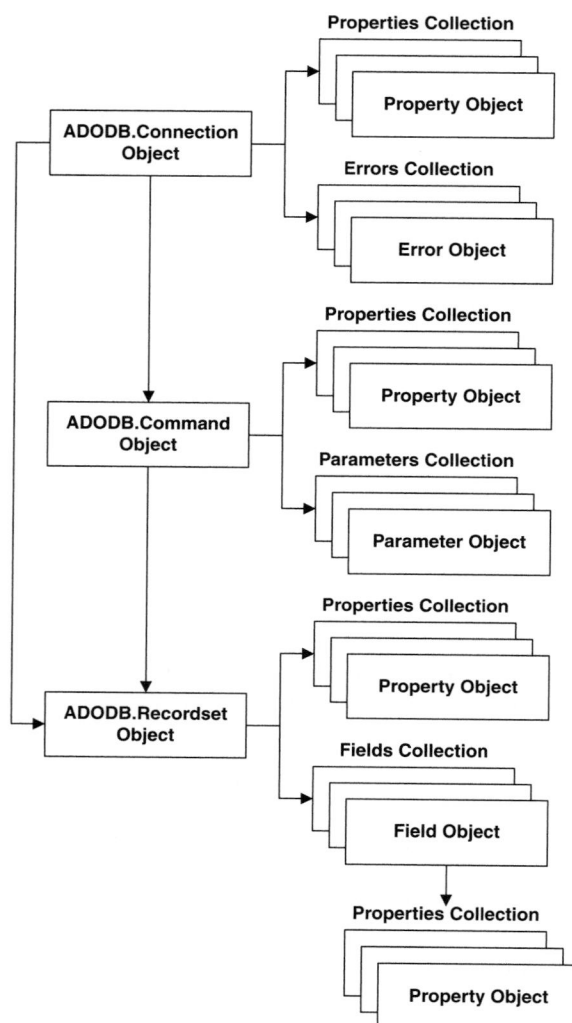

The `Errors` collection has two methods, `Clear` and `Item`. The `Clear` method deletes all current `Error` objects in the collection, resetting the value of `Count` to `0`. The `Item` method, which is the default method of the `Errors` and other collections, returns an object reference (pointer) to an `Error` object. The syntax for explicit and default use of the `Item` method is as follows:

```
Set errName = cnnName.Errors.Index({strName|intIndex})
Set errName = cnnName.Errors({strName|intIndex})
```

The `Error` object has the seven read-only properties listed in Table 30.5. `Error` objects have no methods or events. The `InfoMessage` event of the `Connection` object, described in the "Connection Events" section later in this chapter, fires when an `Error` object is added to the `Errors` collection and supplies a pointer to the newly added `Error` object.

TABLE 30.5   PROPERTY NAMES AND DESCRIPTIONS OF THE Error OBJECT

Property Name	Description
Description	A **String** value containing a brief text description of the error
HelpContext	A **Long** value specifying the error's context ID in a Windows Help file
HelpFile	A **String** value specifying the full path to and name of the Windows Help file, usually for the data provider
NativeError	A **Long** value specifying a provider-specific error code
Number	A **Long** value specifying the number assigned to the error by the provider or data source
Source	A **String** value containing the name of the object that generated the error (ADODB.*ObjectName* for ADO errors)
SQLState	A **String** value (SQLSTATE) containing a five-letter code specified by the ANSI/ISO SQL-92 standard, consisting of two characters specifying Condition, followed by three characters for Subcondition

→ For the basics of error handling in VBA, **see** "Handling Runtime Errors," **p. 1198**.

NOTE

> Unfortunately, not all RDBMS vendors implement SQLSTATE in the same way. If you test the SQLState property value, make sure to follow the vendor-specific specifications for Condition and Subcondition values.

Listing 30.6 is an example of code to open a Connection (cnnNwind) and a Recordset (rstCusts) with conventional error handling; rstCusts supplies the Recordset property of the form. The "Non-existent" table name generates a "Syntax error in FROM clause" error in the Immediate window. The **Set** *ObjectName* = **Nothing** statements in the error handler recover the memory consumed by the objects.

LISTING 30.6   VBA CODE THAT WRITES ERROR PROPERTIES TO THE IMMEDIATE WINDOW

```
Private Sub Form_Load
    Dim cnnNwind As New ADODB.Connection
    Dim rstCusts As New ADODB.Recordset

    On Error GoTo CatchErrors
    cnnNwind.Provider = "Microsoft.Jet.OLEDB.4.0"
    cnnNwind.Open CurrentProject.Path & "\Northwind.accdb", "Admin"
    With rstCusts
        Set .ActiveConnection = cnnNwind
        .CursorType = adOpenKeyset
        .LockType = adLockBatchOptimistic
        .Open "SELECT * FROM Non-existent"
    End With
```

continues

LISTING 30.6 CONTINUED

```
    Set Me.Recordset = rstCusts
    Exit Sub

CatchErrors:
    Dim colErrors As Errors
    Dim errNwind As Error
    Set colErrors = cnnNwind.Errors
    For Each errNwind In colErrors
        Debug.Print "Description:  " & errNwind.Description
        Debug.Print "Native Error: " & errNwind.NativeError; ""
        Debug.Print "SQL State:    " & errNwind.SQLState
        Debug.Print vbCrLf
    Next errNwind
    Set colErrors = Nothing
    Set errNwind = Nothing
    Set rstCusts = Nothing
    Set cnnNwind = Nothing
    Exit Sub
End Sub
```

NOTE

The frmErrors form of DAO_ADOTest.accdb and ADOTest.adp incorporates the preceding code. Open the form to execute the code, change to Design view, open the VBA editor, and press Ctrl+G to read the error message in the Immediate window.

CONNECTION METHODS

Table 30.6 lists the methods of the ADODB.Connection object. Only the Execute, Open, and OpenSchema methods accept argument values. The OpenSchema method is of interest primarily for creating database diagrams, data transformation for data warehouses and marts, and online analytical processing (OLAP) applications.

TABLE 30.6 METHODS OF THE ADODB.Connection OBJECT

Method	Description
BeginTrans	Initiates a transaction; must be followed by CommitTrans and/or RollbackTrans.
Close	Closes the connection.
CommitTrans	Commits a transaction, making changes to the data source permanent. (Requires a prior call to the BeginTrans method.)
Execute	Returns a forward-only Recordset object from a SELECT SQL statement. Also used to execute statements that don't return Recordset objects, such as INSERT, UPDATE, and DELETE queries or DDL statements. You use this method to execute T-SQL stored procedures, regardless of whether they return a Recordset.

Method	Description
Open	Opens a connection based on a connection string.
OpenSchema	Returns a Recordset object that provides information on the structure of the data source, called *metadata*.
RollbackTrans	Cancels a transaction, reversing any temporary changes made to the data source. (Requires a prior call to the BeginTrans method.)

30

THE Connection.Open AND Connection.OpenSchema METHODS

You must open a connection before you can execute a statement on it. The syntax of the Open method is

```
cnnName.Open [strConnect[, strUID[, strPwd, lngOptions]]]]
```

Alternatively, you can assign the connection string values to the Connection object's Provider and ConnectionString properties. The following example, similar to that for the Recordset object examples early in the chapter, is for a connection to Northwind.accdb in the same folder as the application .accdb or .adp file:

```
With cnnNwind
    .Provider = "Microsoft.Jet.OLEDB.4.0"
    .ConnectionString = CurrentProject.Path & "\Northwind.accdb"
    .Open
End With
```

In this case, all the information required to open a connection to Northwind.accdb is provided as property values, so the Open method needs no argument values.

If you're creating a data dictionary or designing a generic query processor for a client/server RDBMS, the OpenSchema method is likely to be of interest to you. Otherwise, you might want to skip the details of the OpenSchema method, which is included here for completeness. Schema information is called *metadata*, data that describes the structure of data.

> **TIP**
>
> ADOX 2.7+ defines a Catalog object for Jet 4.0 databases that's more useful for Jet databases than the generic OpenSchema method, which is intended primarily for use with client/server RDBMs. The Catalog object includes Groups, Users, Tables, Views, and Procedures collections.

THE Connection.Execute METHOD

The syntax of the Connection.Execute method to return a reference to a forward-only ADODB.Recordset object is

```
Set rstName = cnnName.Execute (strCommand, [lngRowsAffected[, lngOptions]])
```

Alternatively, you can use named arguments for all ADO methods. Named arguments, however, require considerably more typing than conventional comma-separated argument syntax. The named argument equivalent of the preceding **Set** statement is

```
Set rstName = cnnName.Execute (Command:=strCommand, _
    RowsAffected:=lngRowsAffected, Options:=lngOptions)
```

If strCommand doesn't return a Recordset, the syntax is

```
cnnName.Execute strCommand, [lngRowsAffected[, lngOptions]]
```

The value of strCommand can be an SQL statement, a table name, the name of a stored procedure, or an arbitrary text string acceptable to the data provider.

> **TIP**
>
> For best performance, specify a value for the lngOptions argument (see Table 30.7) so the provider doesn't need to interpret the statement to determine its type. The optional lngRowsAffected argument returns the number of rows affected by an INSERT, UPDATE, or DELETE query; these types of queries return a closed Recordset object. A SELECT query returns 0 to lngRowsAffected and an open, forward-only Recordset with 0 or more rows. The value of lngRowsAffected is 0 for T-SQL updates queries and stored procedures that include the SET NOCOUNT ON statement.

TABLE 30.7 CONSTANT ENUMERATION FOR THE lngOptions ARGUMENT OF THE Execute METHOD FOR Connection AND Command OBJECTS

CommandTypeEnum	**Description**
adCmdUnknown	The type of command isn't specified (default). The data provider determines the syntax of the command.
adCmdFile	The command is the name of a file in a format appropriate to the object type.
adCmdStoredProc	The command is the name of a stored procedure.
adCmdTable	The command is a table name, which generates an internal SELECT * FROM TableName query.
adCmdTableDirect	The command is a table name, which retrieves rows directly from the table.
adCmdText	The command is an SQL statement.

Forward-only Recordset objects, created by what's called a *firehose cursor*, provide the best performance and minimum network traffic in a client/server environment. However, forward-only Recordsets are limited to manipulation by VBA code. If you set the RecordSource property of a form to a forward-only Recordset, controls on the form don't display field values.

Connection Events

Events are useful for trapping errors, eliminating the need to poll the values of properties, such as `State`, and performing asynchronous database operations. To expose the `ADODB.Connection` events to your application, you must use the **WithEvents** reserved word (without **New**) to declare the `ADODB.Connection` object in the Declarations section of a class or form module and then use a **Set** statement with **New** to create an instance of the object, as shown in the following example:

```
Private WithEvents cnnName As ADODB.Connection

Private Sub Form_Load
   Set cnnName = New ADODB.Connection
   ...
   Code using the Connection object
   ...
   cnnName.Close
End Sub
```

The preceding syntax is required for most `Automation` objects that source (expose) events. Event-handling subprocedures for `Automation` events often are called *event sinks*. Source and sink terminology derives from the early days of transistors; the source (emitter) supplies electrons and the sink (collector) accumulates electrons.

Table 30.8 lists the events that appear in the Procedures list of the code-editing window for the `cnnName` Connection object and gives a description of when the events fire.

TABLE 30.8 EVENTS FIRED BY THE ADODB.Connection OBJECT

Event Name	When Fired
BeginTransComplete	After the BeginTrans method executes
CommitTransComplete	After the CommitTrans method executes
ConnectComplete	After a Connection to the data source succeeds
Disconnect	After a Connection is closed
ExecuteComplete	On completion of the Connection.Execute or Command.Execute method call
InfoMessage	When an Error object is added to the ADODB.Connection.Errors collection
RollbackTransComplete	After the RollbackTrans method executes
WillConnect	On calling the Connection.Open method but before the connection is made
WillExecute	On calling the Connection.Execute or Command.Execute method, just before the command executes a connection

TIP

> Take full advantage of ADO events in your VBA data-handling code. Relatively few developers currently use event-handling code in ordinary database front ends. ADO's event model will be of primary interest to developers migrating from Access 97's RDO to ADO. Developers of data warehousing and OLAP applications, which often involve very long-running queries, are most likely to use events in conjunction with asynchronous query operations.

USING THE ADODB.Command OBJECT

The primary purpose of the Command object is to execute parameterized stored procedures, either in the form of the default temporary prepared statements or persistent, precompiled T-SQL statements in SQL Server databases. MSDE and SQL Server create temporary prepared statements that exist only for the lifetime of the current client connection. Precompiled SQL statements are procedures stored in the database file; their more common name is *stored procedure*. When creating Recordset objects from ad hoc SQL statements, the more efficient approach is to bypass the Command object and use the Recordset.Open method.

Command PROPERTIES

The Command object has relatively few properties, many of which duplicate those of the Connection object. Table 30.9 lists the names and descriptions of the Command object's properties. Like the Connection object, the Command object has its own provider-specific Properties collection, which you can print to the Immediate window using statements similar to those for Command objects described in the earlier "Provider-Specific Properties and Their Values" section.

TABLE 30.9 PROPERTIES OF THE Command OBJECT

Property Name	Description
ActiveConnection	A pointer to the Connection object associated with the Command. Use **Set** cmm*Name*.ActiveConnection = cnn*Name* for an existing open Connection. Alternatively, you can use a valid connection string to create a new connection without associating a named Connection object. The default value is **Null**.
CommandStream	A **Variant** read/write value that contains the input stream used to specify the output stream.
CommandText	A **String** read/write value that specifies an SQL statement, table name, stored procedure name, or an arbitrary string acceptable to the provider of the ActiveConnection. The value of the CommandType property determines the format of the CommandText value. The default value is an empty string, " ". CommandText and CommandStream are mutually exclusive. You can't specify a CommandStream and a CommandText value for the same Command object.
CommandTimeout	A **Long** read/write value that determines the time in seconds before terminating a Command.Execute call. This value overrides the Connection.CommandTimeout setting. The default value is **30** seconds.

Property Name	Description
CommandType	A **Long** read/write value that specifies how the data provider interprets the value of the CommandText property. (CommandType is the equivalent of the optional lng*CommandType* argument of the Connection.Execute method, described earlier in the chapter [refer to Table 30.7]). The default value is adCmdUnknown.
Dialect	A **String** read/write value that accepts one of four globally unique ID (GUID) values specifying the type of CommandStream object. Valid settings are DBGUID_DEFAULT (the provider decides how to handle the CommandStream value), DBGUID_SQL (an SQL statement), DBGUID_MSSQLXML (an SQL Server XML AUTO query), and DBGUID_XPATH (an SQL Server XPath query).
Name	A **String** read/write value specifying the name of the command, such as cmmNwind.
NamedParameters	A **Boolean** read/write value that, when set to **True**, specifies that the names of members of the Parameters collection be used, rather than their sequence, when passing parameter values to and from SQL Server functions and stored procedures, or accepting return or output values from stored procedures.
Prepared	A **Boolean** read/write value that determines whether the data source compiles the CommandText SQL statement as a prepared statement (a temporary stored procedure). The prepared statement exists only for the lifetime of the Command object's ActiveConnection. Many client/server RDBMSs, including Microsoft SQL Server, support prepared statements. If the data source doesn't support prepared statements, setting Prepared to **True** results in a trappable error.
Properties	Same as the Properties collection of the Connection object.
State	A **Long** read/write value specifying the status of the Command. Refer to Table 30.4 for ObjectStateEnum constant values.

30

TIP

> Always set the CommandType property to the appropriate adCmd... constant value. If you accept the default adCmdUnknown value, the data provider must test the value of CommandText to determine whether it is the name of a stored procedure, a table, or an SQL statement before executing the query. If the targeted database contains a large number of objects, testing the CommandText value for each Command object you execute can significantly reduce performance.
>
> The initial execution of a prepared statement often is slower than for a conventional SQL query because some data sources must compile, rather than interpret, the statement. Therefore, you should limit use of prepared statements to parameterized queries in which the query is executed multiple times with differing parameter values.

Parameters COLLECTION

To supply and accept parameter values, the Command object uses the Parameters collection, which is similar to the DAO and ODBCDirect Parameters collections. ADODB.Parameters is independent of its parent, ADODB.Command, but you must associate the Parameters collection with a Command object before defining or using Parameter objects.

The Parameters collection has a read-only **Long** property, Count, an Item property that returns a Parameter object, and the methods listed in Table 30.10. The syntax for the Count and Item properties property is

```
lngNumParms = cmmName.Parameters.Count
prmParamName = cmmName.Parameters.Item(lngIndex)
```

TABLE 30.10   METHOD NAMES, DESCRIPTIONS, AND CALLING SYNTAX FOR THE Parameters COLLECTION

Method Name	Description and VBA Calling Syntax
Append	Appends a Parameter object created by the cmmName.CreateParameter method, described in the "Command Methods" section, to the collection. The calling syntax is Parameters.Append prmName.
Delete	Deletes a Parameter object from the collection. The calling syntax is cmmName.Parameters.Delete {strName¦intIndex}, where strName is the name of the Parameter or intIndex is the 0-based ordinal position (index) of the Parameter in the collection.
Refresh	Retrieves the properties of the current set of parameters for the stored procedure or query specified as the value of the CommandText property. The calling syntax is cmmName.Parameters.Refresh. If you don't specify your own members of the Parameters collection with the CreateParameter method, accessing any member of the Parameters collection automatically calls the Refresh method. If you apply the Refresh method to a data source that doesn't support stored procedures, prepared statements, or parameterized queries, the Parameters collection is empty (cmmName.Parameters.Count = 0).

You gain a performance improvement for the initial execution of your stored procedure or query if you use the cmmName.CreateParameter method to predefine the required Parameter objects. The Refresh method makes a round-trip to the server to retrieve the properties of each Parameter.

Parameter OBJECT

One Parameter object must exist in the Parameters collection for each parameter of the stored procedure, prepared statement, or parameterized query. Table 30.11 lists the property names and descriptions of the Parameter object. The syntax for getting and setting Parameter property values is

```
typPropValue = cmmName.Parameters({strName¦lngIndex}).PropertyName
cmmName.Parameters({strName¦lngIndex}).PropertyName = typPropValue
```

You don't need to use the `Index` property of the Parameters collection; `Index` is the default property of `Parameters`.

TABLE 30.11   PROPERTY NAMES AND DESCRIPTIONS FOR Parameter OBJECTS

Property Name	Description
Attributes	A **Long** read/write value representing the sum of the `adParam...` constants listed in Table 30.12.
Direction	A **Long** read/write value representing one of the `adParam...` constants listed in Table 30.13.
Name	A **String** read/write value containing the name of the `Parameter` object, such as `prmStartDate`. The name of the `Parameter` object need not (and usually does not) correspond to the name of the corresponding parameter variable of the stored procedure. After the `Parameter` is appended to the `Parameters` collection, the `Name` property value is read-only.
NumericScale	A **Byte** read/write value specifying the number of decimal places for numeric values.
Precision	A **Byte** read/write value specifying the total number of digits (including decimal digits) for numeric values.
Size	A **Long** read/write value specifying the maximum length of variable-length data types supplied as the `Value` property. You must set the `Size` property value before setting the `Value` property to variable-length data.
Type	A **Long** read/write value representing a valid OLE DB 2+ data type, the most common of which are listed in Table 30.14.
Value	The value of the parameter having a data type corresponding to the value of the `Type` property.

TABLE 30.12   CONSTANT VALUES FOR THE Attributes PROPERTY OF THE Parameter OBJECT

ParameterAttributesEnum	Description
adParamSigned	The `Parameter` accepts signed values (default).
adParamNullable	The `Parameter` accepts **Null** values.
adParamLong	The `Parameter` accepts long binary data.

30

TABLE 30.13 CONSTANT VALUES FOR THE Direction PROPERTY OF THE Parameter OBJECT

ParameterDirectionEnum	Description
adParamInput	Specifies an input parameter (default).
adParamOutput	Specifies an output parameter.
adParamInputOutput	Specifies an input/output parameter.
adParamReturnValue	Specifies the return value of a stored procedure.
adParamUnknown	The parameter direction is unknown.

The Type property has the largest collection of constants of any ADO enumeration; you can review the entire list of data types by selecting the DataTypeEnum class in Object Browser. Most of the data types aren't available to VBA programmers, so Table 30.14 shows only the most commonly used DataTypeEnum constants. In most cases, you only need to choose among adChar (for **String** values), adInteger (for **Long** values), and adCurrency (for **Currency** values). You use the adDate data type to pass Date/Time parameter values to Jet databases, but not to most stored procedures. Stored procedures generally accept datetime parameter values as the adChar data type, with a format, such as mm/dd/yyyy, acceptable to the RDBMS.

TABLE 30.14 COMMON CONSTANT VALUES FOR THE Type PROPERTY OF THE Parameter AND Field OBJECTS

DataTypeEnum	Description of Data Type
adBinary	**Binary** value.
adBoolean	**Boolean** value.
adChar	**String** value.
adCurrency	**Currency** values are fixed-point numbers with four decimal digits stored in an 8-byte, signed integer, which is scaled (divided) by 10,000.
adDate	**Date** values are stored as a **Double** value, the integer part being the number of days since December 30, 1899, and the decimal part being the fraction of a day.
adDecimal	Exact numeric value with a specified precision and scale.
adDouble	**Double**-precision floating-point value.
adInteger	A 4-byte signed **Long** integer.
adLongVarBinary	Long binary value (Parameter objects only).
adLongVarChar	**String** value greater than 225 characters (Parameter objects only).
adNumeric	Exact numeric value with a specified precision and scale.
adSingle	**Single**-precision floating-point value.

DataTypeEnum	**Description of Data Type**
adSmallInt	A 2-byte signed **Integer**.
adTinyInt	**Byte** (1-byte signed integer).
adVarBinary	Binary value for Jet OLE Object and SQL Server image fields (Parameter objects only).
adVarChar	**String** value for Jet Memo and SQL Server text fields (Parameter objects only).

30

NOTE

The values for the Type property in the preceding table are valid for the Type property of the Field object, discussed later in the chapter, except for those data types in which "Parameter objects only" appears in the Description of Data Type column. The members of DataTypeEnum are designed to accommodate the widest possible range of desktop and client/server RDBMSs, but the ad... constant names are closely related to those for the field data types of Microsoft SQL Server 2000 and MSDE, which support Unicode strings.

For a complete list with descriptions of DataTypeEnum constants, go to http://msdn.microsoft.com/library/en-us/ado270/htm/mdcstdatatypeenum.asp.

The Parameter object has a single method, AppendChunk, which you use to append long text (adLongText) or long binary (adLongVarBinary) **Variant** data as a parameter value. The syntax of the AppendChunk method call is

```
cmmName.Parameters({strName|lngIndex}).AppendChunk = varChunk
```

The adParamLong flag of the prmName.Attributes property must be set to apply the AppendChunk method. If you call AppendChunk more than once on a single Parameter, the second and later calls append the current value of varChunk to the parameter value.

Command METHODS

Command objects have only three methods: Cancel, CreateParameter and Execute. Executing Command.Cancel terminates an asynchronous command opened with the adAsyncConnect, adAsyncExecute, or adAsyncFetch option.

You must declare an ADODB.Parameter object, prmName, prior to executing CreateParameter. The syntax of the CreateParameter method call is

```
Set prmName = cmmName.CreateParameter [strName[, lngType[, _
   lngDirection[, lngSize[, varValue]]]]]
cmmName.Parameters.Append prmName
```

The arguments of `CreateParameter` are optional only if you subsequently set the required `Parameter` property values before executing the `Command`. For example, if you supply only the *strName* argument, you must set the remaining properties, as in the following example:

```
Set prmName = cmmName.CreateParameter strName
cmmName.Parameters.Append prmName
With prmName
    .Type = adChar
    .Direction = adParamInput
    .Size = Len(varValue)
    .Value = varValue
End With
```

The syntax of the `Command.Execute` method is similar to that for the `Connection.Execute` method except for the argument list. The following syntax is for `Command` objects that return `Recordset` objects:

```
Set rstName = cmmName.Execute([lngRowsAffected[, _
    avarParameters[, lngOptions]]])
```

For `Command` objects that don't return rows, use this form:

```
cmmName.Execute [lngRowsAffected[, avarParameters[, lngOptions]]]
```

All the arguments of the `Execute` method are optional if you set the required `Command` property values before applying the `Execute` method. Listing 30.7 later in this chapter gives an example of the use of the `Command.Execute` method without arguments.

TIP

> Presetting all property values of the `Command` object, rather than supplying argument values to the `Execute` method, makes your VBA code easier for others to comprehend.

Like the `Connection.Execute` method, the returned value of *lngRowsAffected* is 0 for `SELECT` and DDL queries and the number of rows modified by execution of `INSERT`, `UPDATE`, and `DELETE` queries. (For SQL Server, *lngRowsAffected* is 0 if the SQL statement includes `SET NOCOUNT ON`.) The *avarParameters* argument is an optional **Variant** array of parameter values. Using the `Parameters` collection is a better practice than using the *avarParameters* argument because output parameters don't return correct values to the array. For *lngOptions* constant values, refer to Table 30.7.

Code to Pass Parameter Values to a Stored Procedure

Most stored procedures that return `Recordset` objects require input parameters to supply values to `WHERE` clause criteria to limit the number of rows returned. The code of Listing 30.7 executes a simple SQL Server 2000 stored procedure with a `Command` object. The Sales by Year stored procedure of the NorthwindCS project has two `datetime` input parameters, `@Beginning_Date` and `@Ending_Date`, the values for which are supplied by `strBegDate` and `strEndDate`, respectively. The stored procedure, whose SQL statement follows, returns the ShippedDate and OrderID columns of the Orders table, the Subtotal column of the Order

Subtotals view, and a calculated Year value. The stored procedure returns rows for values of the OrderDate field between `strBegDate` and `strEndDate`.

```
ALTER PROCEDURE "Sales by Year"
  @Beginning_Date datetime,
  @Ending_Date datetime
  AS SELECT Orders.ShippedDate, Orders.OrderID,
     "Order Subtotals".Subtotal,
     DATENAME(yy,ShippedDate) AS Year
  FROM Orders INNER JOIN "Order Subtotals"
     ON Orders.OrderID = "Order Subtotals".OrderID
  WHERE Orders.ShippedDate Between @Beginning_Date And @Ending_Date
```

30

LISTING 30.7   CODE USING A Command OBJECT TO EXECUTE A PARAMETERIZED STORED PROCEDURE

```
Option Explicit
Option Compare Database

Private cnnOrders As New ADODB.Connection
Private cmmOrders As New ADODB.Command
Private prmBegDate As New ADODB.Parameter
Private prmEndDate As New ADODB.Parameter
Private rstOrders As New ADODB.Recordset

Private Sub Form_Load()
    Dim strBegDate As String
    Dim strEndDate As String
    Dim strFile As String

    strBegDate = "1/1/1997"
    strEndDate = "12/31/1997"
    strFile = CurrentProject.Path & "Orders.rst"

    'Specify the OLE DB provider and open the connection
    With cnnOrders
        .Provider = "SQLOLEDB.1"
        On Error Resume Next
        .Open "Data Source=(local);" & _
           "UID=sa;PWD=;Initial Catalog=NorthwindCS"
        If Err.Number Then
            .Open "Data Source=(local);" & _
                "Integrated Security=SSPI;Initial Catalog=NorthwindCS"
        End if
        On Error GoTo 0
    End With

    With cmmOrders
        'Create and append the BeginningDate parameter
        Set prmBegDate = .CreateParameter("BegDate", adChar, _
           adParamInput, Len(strBegDate), strBegDate)
        .Parameters.Append prmBegDate
        'Create and append the endingDate parameter
        Set prmEndDate = .CreateParameter("EndDate", adChar, _
```

continues

LISTING 30.7 CONTINUED

```
        adParamInput, Len(strEndDate), strEndDate)
    .Parameters.Append prmEndDate

    Set .ActiveConnection = cnnOrders
    'Specify a stored procedure
    .CommandType = adCmdStoredProc
    'Brackets must surround stored procedure names with spaces
    .CommandText = "[Sales By Year]"
    'Receive the Recordset
    Set rstOrders = .Execute   'returns a "firehose" Recordset
End With

With rstOrders
    'Save (persist) the forward-only Recordset to a file
    On Error Resume Next
    'Delete the file, if it exists
    Kill strFile
    On Error GoTo 0
    .Save strFile
    .Close
    .Open strFile, "Provider=MSPersist", , , adCmdFile
End With

'Assign rstOrders to the Recordset of the form
Set Me.Recordset = rstOrders

Me.txtShippedDate.ControlSource = "ShippedDate"
Me.txtOrderID.ControlSource = "OrderID"
Me.txtSubtotal.ControlSource = "Subtotal"
Me.txtYear.ControlSource = "Year"
End Sub
```

CAUTION

When used in ADO code, names of stored procedures and views having spaces must be enclosed with square brackets. Including spaces in database object names, especially in client/server environments, isn't a recommended practice. Microsoft's Access developers often add spaces in names of views and stored procedures, perhaps because SQL Server 2000 and 2005 support this dubious feature. Use underscores to make object names more readable if necessary.

NOTE

The code of Listing 30.7 uses an ADO 2.5+ feature, persisted (saved) Recordset objects. Stored procedures return forward-only ("firehose") Recordset objects, which you can't assign to the Recordset property of a form. To create a Recordset with a cursor acceptable to Access forms, you must persist the Recordset as a file and then close and reopen the Recordset with the MSPersist OLE DB provider as the ActiveConnection property value. The "Recordset Methods" section, later in the chapter, provides the complete syntax for the Save and Open methods of the Recordset object.

Figure 30.9 shows the result of executing the code of Listing 30.2. The frmParams form that contains the code is included in the DAO-ADOTest.accdb and ADOTest.adp files described earlier in the chapter. The AddOrders.adp project, described in the "Exploring the AddOrders.adp Sample Project" section near the end of the chapter, also includes code for setting stored procedure parameter values.

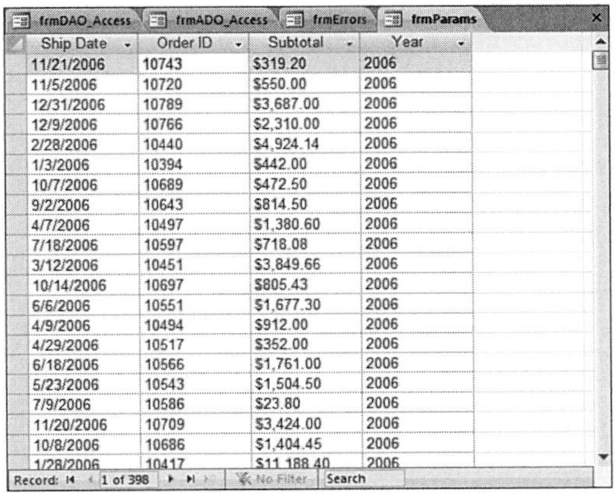

Figure 30.9
This Datasheet view of the read-only Recordset returned by the Sales By Year stored procedure displays the value of each order received in 2006.

Ship Date	Order ID	Subtotal	Year
11/21/2006	10743	$319.20	2006
11/5/2006	10720	$550.00	2006
12/31/2006	10789	$3,687.00	2006
12/9/2006	10766	$2,310.00	2006
2/28/2006	10440	$4,924.14	2006
1/3/2006	10394	$442.00	2006
10/7/2006	10689	$472.50	2006
9/2/2006	10643	$814.50	2006
4/7/2006	10497	$1,380.60	2006
7/18/2006	10597	$718.08	2006
3/12/2006	10451	$3,849.66	2006
10/14/2006	10697	$805.43	2006
6/6/2006	10551	$1,677.30	2006
4/9/2006	10494	$912.00	2006
4/29/2006	10517	$352.00	2006
6/18/2006	10566	$1,761.00	2006
5/23/2006	10543	$1,504.50	2006
7/9/2006	10586	$23.80	2006
11/20/2006	10709	$3,424.00	2006
10/8/2006	10686	$1,404.45	2006
1/28/2006	10417	$11,188.40	2006

Record: 1 of 398   No Filter   Search

UNDERSTANDING THE ADODB.Recordset OBJECT

Creating, viewing, and updating Recordset objects is the ultimate objective of most Access database front ends. Opening an independent ADODB.Recordset object offers a myriad of cursor, locking, and other options. You must explicitly open a Recordset with a scrollable cursor if you want to use code to create the Recordset for assignment to the Form.Recordset property. Unlike Jet and ODBCDirect Recordset objects, ADODB.Recordset objects expose a number of events that are especially useful for validating Recordset updates.

Recordset PROPERTIES

Microsoft attempted to make ADODB.Recordset objects backward compatible with DAO.Recordset objects to minimize the amount of code you must change to migrate existing applications from DAO to ADO. Unfortunately, the attempt at backward compatibility for code-intensive database applications didn't fully succeed. You must make substantial changes in DAO code to accommodate ADO's updated Recordset object. Therefore, most Access developers choose ADO for new Access front-end applications and stick with DAO when maintaining existing Jet projects.

Table 30.15 lists the names and descriptions of the standard property set of ADODB.Recordset objects. ADODB.Recordset objects have substantially fewer properties than DAO.Recordset objects have. The standard properties of ADODB.Recordset objects are those that are supported by the most common OLE DB data providers for relational databases.

TABLE 30.15 PROPERTY NAMES AND DESCRIPTIONS FOR ADODB.Recordset OBJECTS

Property Name	Description
AbsolutePage	A **Long** read/write value that sets or returns the number of the page in which the current record is located or one of the constant values of **PositionEnum** (see Table 30.16). You must set the PageSize property value before getting or setting the value of AbsolutePage. AbsolutePage is 1 based; if the current record is in the first page, AbsolutePage returns 1. Setting the value of AbsolutePage causes the current record to be set to the first record of the specified page.
AbsolutePosition	A **Long** read/write value (1 based) that sets or returns the position of the current record. The maximum value of AbsolutePosition is the value of the RecordCount property.
ActiveCommand	A **Variant** read-only value specifying the name of a previously opened Command object with which the Recordset is associated.
ActiveConnection	A pointer to a previously opened Connection object with which the Recordset is associated or a fully qualified ConnectionString value.
BOF	A **Boolean** read-only value that, when True, indicates that the record pointer is positioned before the first row of the Recordset and there is no current record.
Bookmark	A **Variant** read/write value that returns a reference to a specific record or uses a Bookmark value to set the record pointer to a specific record.
CacheSize	A **Long** read/write value that specifies the number of records stored in local (cache) memory. The minimum (default) value is 1. Increasing the value of CacheSize minimizes round trips to the server to obtain additional rows when scrolling through Recordset objects.
CursorLocation	A **Long** read/write value that specifies the location of a scrollable cursor, subject to the availability of the specified CursorType on the client or server (see Table 30.17). The default is to use a cursor supplied by the OLE DB data source (called a *server-side* cursor).
CursorType	A **Long** read/write value that specifies the type of Recordset cursor (see Table 30.18). The default is a forward-only (firehose) cursor.
DataMember	Returns a pointer to an associated Command object created by Visual Basic's Data Environment Designer.
DataSource	Returns a pointer to an associated Connection object.
EditMode	A **Long** read-only value that returns the status of editing of the current record (see Table 30.19).
EOF	A **Boolean** read-only value that, when True, indicates that the record pointer is beyond the last row of the Recordset and there is no current record.
Fields	A pointer to the Fields collection of Field objects of the Recordset.

Property Name	Description
Filter	A **Variant** read/write value that can be a criteria string (a valid SQL WHERE clause without the WHERE reserved word), an array of Bookmark values specifying a particular set of records, or a constant value from FilterGroupEnum (see Table 30.20).
Index	A **String** read/write value that sets or returns the name of an existing index on the base table of the Recordset. The Recordset must be closed to set the Index value to the name of an index. The Index property is used primarily in conjunction with the Recordset.Seek method.
LockType	A **Long** read/write value that specifies the record-locking method employed when opening the Recordset (see Table 30.21). The default is read-only, corresponding to the read-only characteristic of forward-only cursors.
MarshalOptions	A **Long** read/write value that specifies which set of records is returned to the server after client-side modification. The MarshallOptions property applies only to the lightweight ADOR.Recordset object, a member of RDS.
MaxRecords	A **Long** read/write value that specifies the maximum number of records to be returned by a SELECT query or stored procedure. The default value is 0, all records.
PageCount	A **Long** read-only value that returns the number of pages in a Recordset. You must set the PageSize value to cause PageCount to return a meaningful value. If the Recordset doesn't support the PageCount property, the value is -1.
PageSize	A **Long** read/write value that sets or returns the number of records in a logical page. You use logical pages to break large Recordsets into easily manageable chunks. PageSize isn't related to the size of table pages used for locking in Jet (2KB) or SQL Server (2KB in version 6.5 and earlier, 8KB in version 7+) databases.
PersistFormat	A **Long** read/write value that sets or returns the format of Recordset files created by calling the Save method. The two constant values of PersistFormatEnum are adPersistADTG (the default format, Advanced Data TableGram or ADTG) and adPersistXML, which saves the Recordset as almost-readable XML. The XML schema, rowset, is a variation of the XML Data Reduced (XDR) schema, a Microsoft-only attribute-centric namespace that isn't compatible with Access's XSD (XML Schema) format.
Properties	A pointer to the Properties collection of provider-specific Property values of the Recordset.
RecordCount	A **Long** read-only value that returns the number of records in Recordset objects with scrollable cursors if the Recordset supports approximate positioning or Bookmarks. (See the Recordset.Supports method later in this chapter.) If not, you must apply the MoveLast method to obtain an accurate RecordCount value, which retrieves and counts all records. If a forward-only Recordset has one or more records, RecordCount returns -1 (**True**). An empty Recordset of any type returns 0 (**False**).

30

continues

TABLE 30.15 CONTINUED

Property Name	Description
Sort	A **String** read/write value, consisting of a valid SQL ORDER BY clause without the ORDER BY reserved words, which specifies the sort order of the Recordset.
Source	A **String** read/write value that can be an SQL statement, a table name, a stored procedure name, or the name of an associated Command object. If you supply the name of a Command object, the Source property returns the value of the Command.CommandText property as text. Use the lngOptions argument of the Open method to specify the type of the value supplied to the Source property.
State	A **Long** read/write value representing one of the constant values of ObjectStateEnum (refer to Table 30.4).
Status	A **Long** read-only value that indicates the status of batch operations or other multiple-record (bulk) operations on the Recordset (see Table 30.22).
StayInSync	A **Boolean** read/write value, which, if set to **True**, updates references to child (chapter) rows when the parent row changes. StayInSync applies only to hierarchical Recordset objects.

The most obvious omission in the preceding table is the DAO.Recordset's NoMatch property value used to test whether applying one of the DAO.Recordset.Find… methods or the DAO.Recordset.Seek method succeeds. The new ADODB.Recordset.Find method, listed in the "Recordset Methods" section later in this chapter, substitutes for DAO's FindFirst, FindNext, FindPrevious, and FindLast methods. The Find method uses the EOF property value for testing the existence of one or more records matching the Find criteria.

Another omission in the ADODB.Recordset object's preceding property list is the PercentPosition property. The workaround, however, is easy:

```
rstName.AbsolutePostion = Int(intPercentPosition * rstName.RecordCount / 100)
```

Tables 30.16 through 30.22 enumerate the valid constant values for the AbsolutePage, CursorLocation, CursorType, EditMode, Filter, LockType, and Status properties. Default values appear first, if defined; the list of remaining enumeration members is ordered by frequency of use in Access applications.

TABLE 30.16 CONSTANT VALUES FOR THE AbsolutePage PROPERTY

AbsolutePageEnum	Description
adPosUnknown	The data provider doesn't support pages, the Recordset is empty, or the data provider can't determine the page number.
adPosBOF	The record pointer is positioned at the beginning of the file. (The BOF property is **True**.)
adPosEOF	The record pointer is positioned at the end of the file. (The EOF property is **True**.)

TABLE 30.17 CONSTANT VALUES FOR THE CursorLocation PROPERTY

CursorLocationEnum	Description
adUseClient	Use cursor(s) provided by a cursor library located on the client. The ADOR.Recordset (RDS) requires a client-side cursor.
adUseServer	Use cursor(s) supplied by the data source, usually (but not necessarily) located on a server (default value).

TABLE 30.18 CONSTANT VALUES FOR THE CursorType PROPERTY

CursorTypeEnum	Description
adOpenForwardOnly	Provides only unidirectional cursor movement and a read-only Recordset (default value).
adOpenDynamic	Provides a scrollable cursor that displays all changes, including new records, which other users make to the Recordset.
adOpenKeyset	Provides a scrollable cursor that hides only records added or deleted by other users; similar to a DAO.Recordset of the Dynaset type.
adOpenStatic	Provides a scrollable cursor over a static copy of the Recordset. Similar to a DAO.Recordset of the snapshot type, but the Recordset is up-datable.

TABLE 30.19 CONSTANT VALUES FOR THE EditMode PROPERTY

EditModeEnum	Description
adEditNone	No editing operation is in progress (default value).
adEditAdd	A tentative append record has been added, but not saved to the database table(s).
adEditDelete	The current record has been deleted.
adEditInProgress	Data in the current record has been modified, but not saved to the database table(s).

TABLE 30.20 CONSTANT VALUES FOR THE Filter PROPERTY

FilterGroupEnum	Description
adFilterNone	Removes an existing filter and exposes all records of the Recordset (equivalent to setting the Filter property to an empty string, the default value).
adFilterAffectedRecords	View only records affected by the last execution of the CancelBatch, Delete, Resync, or UpdateBatch method.

continues

30

30

TABLE 30.20 CONTINUED

FilterGroupEnum	Description
adFilterFetchedRecords	View only records in the current cache. The number of records is set by the `CacheSize` property.
adFilterConflictingRecords	View only records that failed to update during the last batch update operation.
adFilterPendingRecords	View only records that have been modified but not yet processed by the data source (for Batch Update mode only).

TABLE 30.21 CONSTANT VALUES FOR THE `LockType` PROPERTY

LockTypeEnum	Description
adLockReadOnly	Specifies read-only access (default value).
adLockBatchOptimistic	Use Batch Update mode instead of the default Immediate Update mode.
adLockOptimistic	Use optimistic locking (lock the record or page only during the table update process).
adLockPessimistic	Use pessimistic locking (lock the record or page during editing and the updated process).
adLockUnspecified	No lock type specified. (Use this constant only for `Recordset` clones.)

TABLE 30.22 CONSTANT VALUES FOR THE `Status` PROPERTY (APPLIES TO BATCH OR BULK `Recordset` OPERATIONS ONLY)

RecordStatusEnum	Description of Record Status
adRecOK	Updated successfully.
adRecNew	Added successfully.
adRecModified	Modified successfully.
adRecDeleted	Deleted successfully.
adRecUnmodified	Not modified.
adRecInvalid	Not saved; the Bookmark property is invalid.
adRecMultipleChanges	Not saved; saving would affect other records.
adRecPendingChanges	Not saved; the record refers to a pending insert operation.
adRecCanceled	Not saved; the operation was canceled.
adRecCantRelease	Not saved; existing record locks prevented saving.
adRecConcurrencyViolation	Not saved; an optimistic concurrency locking problem occurred.
adRecIntegrityViolation	Not saved; the operation would violate integrity constraints.

RecordStatusEnum	**Description of Record Status**
adRecMaxChangesExceeded	Not saved; an excessive number of pending changes exist.
adRecObjectOpen	Not saved; a conflict with an open storage object occurred.
adRecOutOfMemory	Not saved; the machine is out of memory.
adRecPermissionDenied	Not saved; the user doesn't have required permissions.
adRecSchemaViolation	Not saved; the record structure doesn't match the database schema.
adRecDBDeleted	Not saved or deleted; the record was previously deleted.

Fields COLLECTION AND Field OBJECTS

Like DAO's Fields collection, ADO's dependent Fields collection is a property of the Recordset object, making the columns of the Recordset accessible to VBA code and bound controls. The Fields collection has one property, Count, and only two methods, Item and Refresh. You can't append new Field objects to the Fields collection, unless you're creating a persisted Recordset from scratch or you use ADOX's ALTER TABLE DDL command to add a new field.

All but one (Value) of the property values of Field objects are read-only, because the values of the Field properties are derived from the database schema. The Value property is read-only in forward-only Recordsets and Recordsets opened with read-only locking. Table 30.23 gives the names and descriptions of the properties of the Field object.

TABLE 30.23   PROPERTY NAMES AND DESCRIPTIONS OF THE Field OBJECT

Field **Property**	**Description**
ActualSize	A **Long** read-only value representing the length of the Field's value by character count.
Attributes	A **Long** read-only value that represents the sum of the constants (flags) included in FieldAttributeEnum (see Table 30.24).
DefinedSize	A **Long** read-only value specifying the maximum length of the Field's value by character count.
Name	A **String** read-only value that returns the field (column) name.
NumericScale	A **Byte** read-only value specifying the number of decimal places for numeric values.
OriginalValue	A **Variant** read-only value that represents the Value property of the field before applying the Update method to the Recordset. (The CancelUpdate method uses OriginalValue to replace a changed Value property.)
Precision	A **Byte** read-only value specifying the total number of digits (including decimal digits) for numeric values.

continues

30

TABLE 30.23 CONTINUED

Field Property	Description
Properties	A collection of provider-specific `Property` objects. SQL Server 2000's extended properties are sample `Properties` collection members for the SQL Server OLE DB provider.
Status	An undocumented **Long** read-only value.
Type	A **Long** read-only value specifying the data type of the field. Refer to Table 30.14 for `Type` constant values.
UnderlyingValue	A **Variant** read-only value representing the current value of the field in the database table(s). You can compare the values of `OriginalValue` and `UnderlyingValue` to determine whether a persistent change has been made to the database, perhaps by another user.
Value	A **Variant** read/write value of a subtype appropriate to the value of the `Type` property for the field. If the `Recordset` isn't updatable, the `Value` property is read-only.

`Value` is the default property of the `Field` object, but it's a good programming practice to set and return field values by explicit use of the `Value` property name in VBA code. In most cases, using var*Name* = rstName.Fields(*n*).Value instead of var*Name* = rstName.Fields(*n*) results in a slight performance improvement.

TABLE 30.24 CONSTANT VALUES AND DESCRIPTIONS FOR THE ATTRIBUTES PROPERTY OF THE Field OBJECT

FieldAttributeEnum	Description
adFldCacheDeferred	The provider caches field values. Multiple reads are made on the cached value, not the database table.
adFieldDefaultStream	The field contains a stream of bytes. For example, the field might contain the HTML stream from a web page specified by a field whose `adFldIsRowURL` attribute is **True**.
adFldFixed	The field contains fixed-length data with the length determined by the data type or field specification.
adFldIsChapter	The field is a member of a chaptered recordset and contains a child recordset of this field.
adFldIsCollection	The field contains a reference to a collection of resources, rather than a single resource.
adFldIsNullable	The field accepts **Null** values.
adFldIsRowURL	The field contains a URL for a resource such as a web page.
adFldKeyColumn	The field is the primary key field of a table.

FieldAttributeEnum	Description
adFldLong	The field has a long binary data type, which permits the use of the AppendChunk and GetChunk methods.
adFldMayBeNull	The field can return **Null** values.
adFldMayDefer	The field is deferrable, meaning that Values are retrieved from the data source only when explicitly requested.
adFldNegativeScale	The field contains data from a column that supports negative Scale values.
adFldRowID	The field is a row identifier (typically an identity, AutoIncrement, or GUID data type).
adFldRowVersion	The field contains a timestamp or similar value for determining the time of the last update.
adFldUpdatable	The field is read/write (updatable).
adFldUnknownUpdatable	The data provider can't determine whether the field is updatable. Your only recourse is to attempt an update and trap the error that occurs if the field isn't updatable.

The Field object has two methods, AppendChunk and GetChunk, which are applicable only to fields of various long binary data types, indicated by an adFldLong flag in the Attributes property of the field. The AppendChunk method is discussed in the "Parameter Object" section earlier in this chapter. The syntax for the AppendChunk method call, which writes **Variant** data to a long binary field (fldName), is

```
fldName.AppendChunk varData
```

> **NOTE**
>
> ADO 2.x doesn't support the Access OLE Object field data type, which adds a proprietary object wrapper around the data (such as a bitmap) to identify the OLE server that created the object (for bitmaps, usually Windows Paint).

The GetChunk method enables you to read long binary data in blocks of the size you specify. Following is the syntax for the GetChunk method:

```
varName = fldName.GetChunk(lngSize)
```

A common practice is to place AppendChunk and GetChunk method calls within **Do Until…Loop** structures to break up the long binary value into chunks of manageable size. In the case of the **GetChunk** method, if you set the value of lngSize to less than the value of the field's ActualSize property, the first GetChunk call retrieves lngSize bytes. Successive GetChunk calls retrieve lngSize bytes beginning at the next byte after the end of the preceding call. If the remaining number of bytes is less than lngSize, only the remaining bytes appear in varName. After you retrieve the field's bytes, or if the field is empty, GetChunk returns **Null**.

NOTE

Changing the position of the record pointer of the field's `Recordset` resets `GetChunk's` byte pointer. Accessing a different `Recordset` and moving its record pointer doesn't affect the other `Recordset's` `GetChunk` record pointer.

Recordset METHODS

`ADODB.Recordset` methods are an amalgam of the `DAO.Recordset` and `rdoResultset` methods. Table 30.25 gives the names, descriptions, and calling syntax for `Recordset` methods. OLE DB data providers aren't required to support all the methods of the `Recordset` object. If you don't know which methods the data provider supports, you must use the `Supports` method with the appropriate constant from `CursorOptionEnum`, listed in Table 30.28 later in this chapter, to test for support of methods that are provider dependent. Provider-dependent methods are indicated by an asterisk after the method name in Table 30.25.

TABLE 30.25   NAMES AND DESCRIPTIONS OF METHODS OF THE Recordset OBJECT

Method Name	Description and Calling Syntax
AddNew	Adds a new record to an updatable `Recordset`. The calling syntax is `rstName.AddNew [{varField¦avarFields}, {varValue¦avarValues}]`, where `varField` is a single field name, `avarFields` is an array of field names, `varValue` is single value, and `avarValues` is an array of values for the columns defined by the members of `avarFields`. Calling the `Update` method adds the new record to the database table(s). If you add a new record to a `Recordset` having a primary key field that isn't the first field of the `Recordset`, you must supply the name and value of the primary key field in the `AddNew` statement.
Cancel	Cancels execution of an asynchronous query and terminates creation of multiple `Recordsets` from stored procedures or compound SQL statements. The calling syntax is `rstName.Cancel`.
CancelBatch	Cancels a pending batch update operation on a `Recordset` whose `LockEdits` property value is `adBatchOptimistic`. The calling syntax is `rstName.CancelBatch [lngAffectRecords]`. The optional `lngAffectRecords` argument is one of the constants of `AffectEnum` (see Table 30.26).
CancelUpdate	Cancels a pending change to the table(s) underlying the `Recordset` before applying the `Update` method. The calling syntax is `rstName.CancelUpdate`.
Clone	Creates a duplicate `Recordset` object with an independent record pointer. The calling syntax is **Set** `rstDupe = rstName.Clone()`.
Close	Closes a `Recordset` object, allowing reuse of the `Recordset` variable by setting new `Recordset` property values and applying the `Open` method. The calling syntax is `rstName.Close`.

Method Name	Description and Calling Syntax
CompareBookmarks	Returns the relative value of two bookmarks in the same Recordset or a Recordset and its clone. The calling syntax is lng*Result* = rst*Name*.CompareBookmarks(var*Bookmark1*, var*Bookmark2*).
Delete	Deletes the current record immediately from the Recordset and the underlying tables, unless the LockEdits property value of the Recordset is set to adLockBatchOptimistic. The calling syntax is rst*Name*.Delete.
Find	Searches for a record based on criteria you supply. The calling syntax is rst*Name*.Find str*Criteria*[, lng*SkipRecords*, lng*SearchDirection*[, lng*Start*]], where str*Criteria* is a valid SQL WHERE clause without the WHERE keyword, the optional lng*SkipRecords* value is the number of records to skip before applying Find, lng*SearchDirection* specifies the search direction (adSearchForward, the default, or adSearchBackward), and the optional var*Start* value specifies the Bookmark value of the record at which to start the search or one of the members of BookmarkEnum (see Table 30.27). If Find succeeds, the EOF property returns **False**; otherwise, EOF returns **True**.
GetRows	Returns a two-dimensional (row, column) **Variant** array of records. The calling syntax is avar*Name* = rst*Name*.GetRows(lng*Rows*[, var*Start*[, {str*FieldName*¦lng*FieldIndex*¦avar*FieldNames*¦avar*FieldIndexes*}]]), where lng*Rows* is the number of rows to return, var*Start* specifies a Bookmark value of the record at which to start the search or one of the members of BookmarkEnum (see Table 30.27), and the third optional argument is the name or index of a single column, or a **Variant** array of column names or indexes. If you don't specify a value of the third argument, GetRows returns all columns of the Recordset.
GetString	By default, returns a tab-separated **String** value for a specified number of records, with records separated by return codes. The calling syntax is str*Clip* = rst*Name*.GetString (lng*Rows*[, str*ColumnDelimiter*[, str*RowDelimiter*, [str*NullExpr*]]]), where lng*Rows* is the number of rows to return, str*ColumnDelimiter* is an optional column-separation character (vbTab is the default), str*RowDelimiter* is an optional row-separation character (vbCR is the default), and str*NullExpr* is an optional value to substitute when encountering **Null** values (an empty string, " ", is the default value).
Move	Moves the record pointer from the current record. The calling syntax is rst*Name*.Move lngNum*Records*[, var*Start*], where lngNum*Records* is the number of records by which to move the record pointer and the optional var*Start* value specifies the Bookmark of the record at which to start the search or one of the members of BookmarkEnum (see Table 30.27).
MoveFirst	Moves the record pointer to the first record. The calling syntax is rst*Name*.MoveFirst.

30

continues

30

TABLE 30.25   CONTINUED

Method Name	Description and Calling Syntax
MoveLast	Moves the record pointer to the last record. The calling syntax is rst*Name*.MoveLast.
MoveNext	Moves the record pointer to the next record. The calling syntax is rst*Name*.MoveNext. The MoveNext method is the only Move… method that you can apply to a forward-only Recordset.
MovePrevious	Moves the record pointer to the previous record. The calling syntax is rst*Name*.MovePrevious.
NextRecordset	Returns additional Recordset objects generated by a compound Jet SQL statement, such as SELECT * FROM Orders; SELECT * FROM Customers, or a T-SQL stored procedure that returns multiple Recordsets. The calling syntax is rst*Next* = rst*Name*.NextRecordset[(lng*RecordsAffected*)], where lng*RecordsAffected* is an optional return value that specifies the number of records in rst*Next*, if SET NOCOUNT ON isn't included in the SQL statement or stored procedure code. If no additional Recordset exists, rst*Next* is set to **Nothing**.
Open	Opens a Recordset on an active Command or Connection object. The calling syntax is rst*Name*.Open [var*Source*[, var*ActiveConnection*[, lng*CursorType*[, lng*LockType*[, lng*Options*]]]]]. The Open arguments are optional if you set the equivalent Recordset property values, which is the practice recommended in this book. For valid values, refer to the Source, ActiveConnection, CursorType, and LockType properties in Table 30.15 earlier in this chapter and to the CommandTypeEnum values listed in Table 30.7 earlier in this chapter for the lng*Options* property.
Requery	Refreshes the content of the Recordset from the underlying table(s), the equivalent of calling Close and then Open. Requery is a very resource-intensive operation. The calling syntax is rst*Name*.Requery.
Resync	Refreshes a specified subset of the Recordset from the underlying table(s). The calling syntax is rst*Name*.Resync [lng*AffectRecords*], where lng*AffectRecords* is one of the members of AffectEnum (see Table 30.26). If you select adAffectCurrent or adAffectGroup as the value of lng*AffectRecords*, you reduce the required resources in comparison with adAffectAll (the default).
Save	Creates a file containing a persistent copy of the Recordset. The calling syntax is rst*Name*.Save str*FileName*, where str*FileName* is the path to and the name of the file. You open a Recordset from a file with a rst*Name*.Open str*FileName*, Options:=adCmdFile statement. This book uses .rst as the extension for persistent Recordsets in the ADTG format and .xml for XML formats.

Method Name	Description and Calling Syntax
Seek	Performs a high-speed search on the field whose index name is specified as the value of the Recordset.Index property. The calling syntax is rstName.Seek avarKeyValues[, lngOption], where avarKeyValues is a **Variant** array of search values for each field of the index. The optional lngOption argument is one of the members of the SeekEnum (see Table 30.29) constant enumeration; the default value is adSeekFirstEQ (find the first equal value). You can't specify adUseClient as the CursorLocation property value when applying the Seek method; Seek requires a server-side (adUseServer) cursor.
Supports	Returns **True** if the Recordset's data provider supports a specified cursor-dependent method; otherwise, Supports returns **False**. The calling syntax is blnSupported = rstName.Supports(lngCursorOptions). Table 30.28 lists the names and descriptions of the CursorOptionEnum values.
Update	Applies the result of modifications to the Recordset to the underlying table(s) of the data source. For batch operations, Update applies the modifications only to the local (cached) Recordset. The calling syntax is rstName.Update.
UpdateBatch	Applies the result of all modifications made to a batch-type Recordset (LockType property set to adBatchOptimistic, CursorType property set to adOpenKeyset or adOpenStatic, and CursorLocation property set to adUseClient) to the underlying table(s) of the data source. The calling syntax is rstName.UpdateBatch [lngAffectRecords], where lngAffectRecords is a member of AffectEnum (see Table 30.26).

The "Code to Pass Parameter Values to a Stored Procedure" section, earlier in the chapter, illustrates the use of the Save and Open methods with persisted Recordsets of the ADTG type.

TIP

> The Edit method of DAO.Recordset objects is missing from Table 30.25. To change the value of one or more fields of the current record of an ADODB.Recordset object, execute rstName.Fields(n).Value = varValue for each field whose value you want to change and then execute rstName.Update. ADODB.Recordset objects don't support the Edit method.
>
> To improve the performance of Recordset objects opened on Connection objects, set the required property values of the Recordset object and then use a named argument to specify the intOptions value of the Open method, as in rstName.Open Options:=adCmdText. This syntax is easier to read and less prone to error than the alternative, rstName.Open , , , , adCmdText.

TABLE 30.26   NAMES AND DESCRIPTIONS OF CONSTANTS FOR THE `CancelBatch` METHOD'S `lngAffectRecords` ARGUMENT

AffectEnum	Description
adAffectAll	Include all records in the `Recordset` object, including any records hidden by the `Filter` property value (the default).
adAffectAllChapters	Include all chapter fields in a chaptered recordset, including any records hidden by the `Filter` property value.
adAffectCurrent	Include only the current record.
adAffectGroup	Include only those records that meet the current `Filter` criteria.

TABLE 30.27   NAMES AND DESCRIPTIONS OF `Bookmark` CONSTANTS FOR THE `Find` METHOD'S `varStart` ARGUMENT

BookmarkEnum	Description
adBookmarkCurrent	Start at the current record (the default value).
adBookmarkFirst	Start at the first record.
adBookmarkLast	Start at the last record.

TABLE 30.28   NAMES AND DESCRIPTIONS OF CONSTANTS FOR THE `Supports` METHOD

CursorOptionEnum	Permits
adAddNew	Applying the `AddNew` method
adApproxPosition	Setting and getting `AbsolutePosition` and `AbsolutePage` property values
adBookmark	Setting and getting the `Bookmark` property value
adDelete	Applying the `Delete` method
adFind	Applying the `Find` method
adHoldRecords	Retrieving additional records or changing the retrieval record pointer position without committing pending changes
adIndex	Use of the `Index` property
adMovePrevious	Applying the `GetRows`, `Move`, `MoveFirst`, and `MovePrevious` methods (indicates a bidirectional scrollable cursor)
adNotify	Use of `Recordset` events
adResync	Applying the `Resync` method
adSeek	Applying the `Seek` method
adUpdate	Applying the `Update` method
adUpdateBatch	Applying the `UpdateBatch` and `CancelBatch` methods

Table 30.29 lists the SeekEnum constants for the optional lngSeekOptions argument of the Seek method. Unfortunately, the syntax for the ADODB.Recordset.Seek method isn't even close to being backward-compatible with the DAO.Recordset.Seek method.

TABLE 30.29   NAMES AND DESCRIPTIONS OF CONSTANTS FOR THE Seek METHOD'S lngSeekOptions ARGUMENT

SeekEnum	Finds
adSeekFirstEQ	The first equal value (the default value)
adSeekAfterEQ	The first equal value or the next record after which a match would have occurred (logical equivalent of >=)
adSeekAfter	The first record after which an equal match would have occurred (logical equivalent of >)
adSeekBeforeEQ	The first equal value or the previous record before which a match would have occurred (logical equivalent of <=)
adSeekBefore	The first record previous to where an equal match would have occurred (logical equivalent of <)
adSeekLastEQ	The last record having an equal value

TIP

> Use the Find method for searches unless you are working with a table having an extremely large number of records. Find takes advantage of index(es), if present, but Find's search algorithm isn't quite as efficient as Seek's. You'll probably encounter the threshold for considering substituting Seek for Find in the range of 500,000 to 1,000,000 records. Tests on a large version the Oakmont.accdb Access and Oakmont SQL Server Students table (50,000) rows show imperceptible performance differences between Seek and Find operations.

Recordset EVENTS

Recordset events are new to users of DAO. Table 30.30 names the Recordset events and gives the condition under which the events fire.

TABLE 30.30   NAMES AND OCCURRENCE OF RECORDSET EVENTS

Event Name	When Fired
EndOfRecordset	When the record pointer attempts to move beyond the last record
FetchComplete	When all records have been retrieved asynchronously
FetchProgress	During asynchronous retrieval, periodically reports the number of records returned
FieldChangeComplete	After a change to the value of a field

continues

TABLE 30.30   CONTINUED

Event Name	When Fired
MoveComplete	After execution of the Move or Move... methods
RecordChangeComplete	After an edit to a single record
RecordsetChangeComplete	After cached changes are applied to the underlying tables
WillChangeField	Before a change to a field value
WillChangeRecord	Before an edit to a single record
WillChangeRecordset	Before cached changes are applied to the underlying tables
WillMove	Before execution of the Move or Move... methods

EXPLORING THE ADDORDERS.ADP SAMPLE PROJECT

 The AddOrders.adp sample project in the \SEUA12\Chaptr30 folder of the accompanying CD-ROM demonstrates practical application for this chapter's example of the programming of ADO objects, methods, and properties. The primary purpose of the AddOrders project is to add a large number of records to the Orders and Order Details tables of a copy of the NorthwindSQL SQL Server database. Working with test tables having a large number of rows lets you debug online transaction processing (OLTP) applications with real-world data. The code uses random record numbers to specify the CustomerID for each added order and the ProductID for order line items.

The AddOrders project also lets you compare the performance difference between sending SQL statements to the server and using stored procedures to add, edit, and delete Orders and Order Details records. Code in the frmAddNorthwindOrders Class Module creates the required stored procedures.

To give the AddOrders.adp project a test drive, do the following:

1. If you haven't done so already, attach \SEUA12\Nwind\NorthwindSQL.mdf to your local SSX instance.

→ If you didn't install SSX and attach \SEUA12\Nwind\NorthwindSQL.mdf as the NorthwindSQL database previously, **see** "SQL Server 2005 Express Edition SP2 Setup" **p. 59**.

2. Open AddOrders.adp, choose File, Connection, and specify the server (usually .\SQLEXPRESS), Windows NT Integrated Security, and NorthwindSQL as the database. When you add a connection to AddOrders.adp, you have the option of using the project's connection or specifying a connection to another server or database.

3. Click Connect and click Yes when the message box asks if you want to use the current connection to the new database. If you specified SQL Server security, type your login ID and password in the two text boxes. You receive the message about the OrderID field's Identity attribute shown in Figure 30.10.

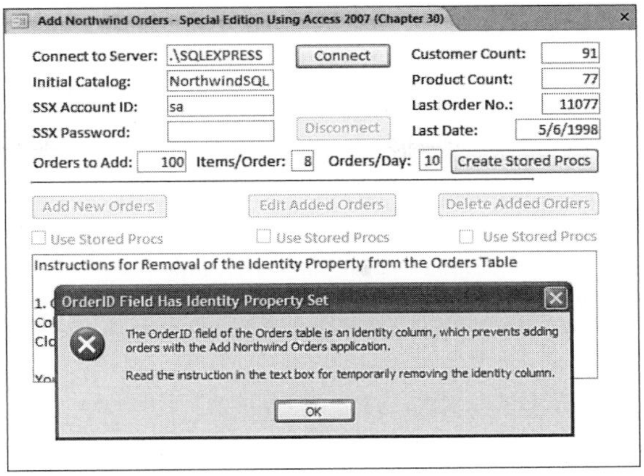

Figure 30.10
Opening
NorthwindSQL for
bulk record addition
with OrderID as an
identity (autonumber)
field displays the
warning message
shown here.

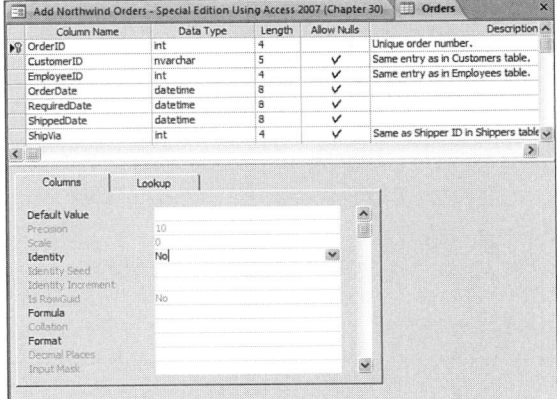

NOTE

The `Identity` attribute must be removed from the Orders table to permit deleting added records and then adding new records with numbers that are consecutive with the original OrderID numbers (10248–11077).

4. Acknowledge the message, open the Orders table in Design view, and select the OrderID column. In the Columns property page, select Identity and change the value from Yes to No (see Figure 30.11). Close the table and save the changes.

Figure 30.11
Set the `Identity`
attribute of the
OrderID field of the
Orders table to No in
the da Vinci table
designer.

TIP

You also can change the design in SQL Server Enterprise Manager, but using Access's Table Design view is easier.

30

5. In the form, click the Clear Report Text button, click Connect to open the connection to the database, and click the Create Stored Procs button to add three stored procedures to the database. Adding the procedures enables the three Use Stored Procs check boxes.

6. Change the Orders to Add, Items/Order, and Orders/Day values, if you want, and click Add New Orders. The number of Orders and Order Details records added and the time required for addition appears in the text box.

7. Mark the Use Stored Procs check box under the Add New Orders button to compare the speed of order addition with a stored procedure. It's unlikely that you'll see any significant change in performance by moving to stored procedures (see Figure 30.12).

Figure 30.12
Adding, editing, or deleting records adds the number of records affected and timing data to the text box.

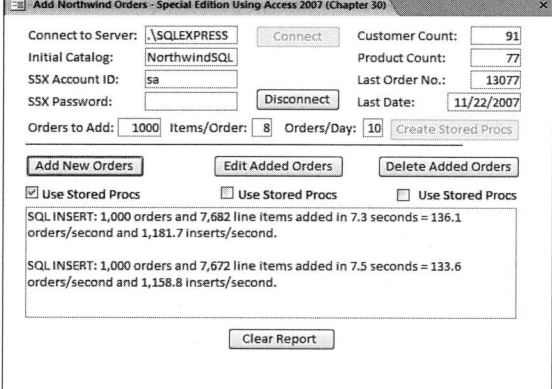

8. Repeat steps 6 and 7, but click the Edit Added Orders button to change the Quantity values of all Order Details records you've added.

9. Click the Delete Added Orders button to restore the tables to their original number of records. A message box lets you choose between bulk and individual order deletion.

NOTE

> The code in the form's Class Module originated in a Visual Basic 6.0 program for testing SQL Server 7.0 and 2000 OLTP performance in a variety of server hardware configurations. Only a few code changes were necessary to the Visual Basic 6.0 code that was copied to the Access form.

TROUBLESHOOTING

SPACES IN ADO OBJECT NAMES

When I attempt to open a Command object on the views, functions, or stored procedures of NorthwindCS, I receive a "Syntax error or access violation" message.

SQL Server 7.0+ (unfortunately) supports spaces in object names, such as views and stored procedures. However, SQL Server wants these names enclosed within double quotes. Sending double quotes in an object name string is a pain in VBA, but surrounding the object name with square brackets also solves the problem. For example, cnn*Name*.CommandText = "Sales By Year" fails but cnn*Name*.CommandText = "[Sales By Year]" works. Using square brackets for otherwise-illegal object identifiers is the better programming practice.

IN THE REAL WORLD—WHY LEARN ADO PROGRAMMING?

As observed in Chapter 4, "Exploring Relational Database Theory and Practice," "Everything has to be somewhere" is a popular corollary of the Law of Conservation of Matter. So just about everything you need to know to start programming data objects with DAO and ADO is concentrated in this chapter. The problem with this "laundry list" approach to describing a set of data-related objects is that readers are likely to doze off in mid-chapter. If you've gotten this far (and have at least scanned the intervening code and tables), you probably surmised that ADO is more than just a replacement for DAO—it's an expansive approach to database connectivity with Access and client/server RDBMSs.

Microsoft designed ADO expressly for data-intensive web-based applications. You can use VBScript or JScript (Microsoft's variant of ECMAScript) to open and manipulate ADO Connection, Command, and Recordset objects on web pages. Web compatibility was an important feature for Access developers when Access supported data access pages (DAP). Now that Access 2007 has abandoned DAP in favor of SharePoint for intranet deployment, ADO loses much of its raison d'etre in automating simple Access projects.

NOTE

> A side effect of Access diverging from Jet databases is lack of .accdb connectivity to .NET projects. ADO.NET currently uses the Jet 4.0 OLE DB data provider to connect to .mdb files. There's no indication that Microsoft will update this data provider to support the Attachment data type or multi-select lookup fields.

An incentive for becoming ADO-proficient is migrating from Jet 4.0 to ADP and SQL Server back ends. When SQL Server marketing honchos say that SQL Server is Microsoft's "strategic database direction," believe them. Jet still isn't dead, but the handwriting is on the wall; ultimately SQL Server or SQL Server Compact Edition (SSCE) will replace Jet in all but ancient Windows database applications. The ADO 2.7 documentation on MSDN stated that "Microsoft has deprecated the Microsoft Jet Engine, and plans no new releases or service packs for this component."

NOTE

Microsoft's intention might have been to release no new service packs (SPs) for Jet 4.0, but Access 2003 required a new Jet 4.0 SP7 (build 4.0.7320.0) to support macro security and "sandbox" mode. Microsoft released SP8 (4.0.8015.0) in October 2003, and there have been two updates (4.0.8618.0 with Windows XP SP2, and 4.0.9025 with Windows Server 2003 SP1) since then.

Obviously the SQL Server and MDAC folks didn't anticipate that the Access team would decide to roll their own version of deprecated Jet, add an obsolete DAO dependency, recommend replacing VBA with macros, remove user-level security, and promote SharePoint as the "strategic" approach to multiuser table and application sharing for Access 2007. Seasoned Access developers were surprised, even shocked, at the transformation between versions 2003 and 2007.

The jury's still out on the issue of whether a significant percentage of Access users will sacrifice relational tables for SharePoint's flat file model. It's clear that the populating, searching, and sorting performance of SharePoint lists with thousands of rows doesn't come close to that of similar native Access or SQL Server tables.

SQL Server 2005 is setting sales records and has become a major contributor to the Microsoft Server and Tools segment's year-after-year revenue and earnings increases. SSX is a robust, reliable replacement for .mdb and .accdb databases at the group, department, and even division level. The new Navigation Pane and tabbed documents will make Access ADP front ends to networked SSX instances very attractive for important but budget-constrained projects.

If your intention is to design and implement highly reliable and very secure multiuser database applications for your employer or clients, ADP and ADO is the way to go. Learning ADO also will give you a head start when you finally migrate your largest projects to the .NET Framework, Visual Studio, and ADO.NET.

Casual databases that you create from templates and have only a few trusted users probably can rely on macros and DAO for their limited programming requirements.

UPGRADING 200X APPLICATIONS TO ACCESS 2007

In this chapter

UNDERSTANDING THE .MDB FILE UPGRADE PROCESS

Access 2007's new .accdb format marks an abrupt departure from the Jet juggernaut that Access 1.0 spawned by the introduction of the .mdb database file in November 1992. Each version of Jet-based Access—1.0, 1.1, 2.0, 95, 97, 2000, 2002, and 2003—had a different database file structure at the binary (byte) level. The differences between 16-bit .mdb files created with versions 1.0 and 1.1 were relatively minor; thus, you could use the Compact feature of Access to convert version 1.0 .mdb files to version 1.1, or vice versa. The file formats of later versions of Jet databases are sufficiently different to require, with the exception of the Access 2000 and 2002 formats, one-way conversion during the upgrade process. Access 2007 can open some Access 97 files and all Access 200x files. Access 2007 treats 2000 and 2002 .mdb files as a single version.

31

NOTE

> As mentioned in Chapter 1, "Access 2007 for Access 200x Users: What's New," Microsoft's "Data Access Technologies Roadmap" (http://msdn.microsoft.com/library/en-us/dnmdac/html/data_mdacroadmap.asp) designates Jet as a *deprecated* technology and Access's Data Access Objects (DAO) as *obsolete*. Thus, the Access team has created a new version of Jet, originally called *ACE* (for *Access Compatibility Engine*) and now officially named the *Access database engine*. Similarly, Microsoft Office 2007 Access database engine Objects (ACCDAO.dll) replaces DAO (DAO360.dll).
>
> This chapter uses the term *Access 200x* to refer to Access versions that use Jet 4.0–2000, 2002, and 2003. Although you can open some Access 97 files in Access 2007, Microsoft recommends upgrading Access 97 files to Access 2000, and then upgrading the 2000 .mdb versions to Access 2007 .accdb files.

Access 2000–2007 save ordinary forms, reports, and modules in compound document files (DocFiles), which are stored within application .mdb files. This change supports Access Data Projects (ADP), which save application objects in .adp DocFiles, not in .mdb or .accdb files. Access 2007 uses 200x .adp files without upgrading. The "Moving from MSDE to the SQL Server 2005 Express Edition" section later in this chapter covers issues you encounter when upgrading from MSDE 1.0 or 2000 to the new SQL Server 2005 Express edition (SQL Express or SQLX) client/server database.

REVIEWING UPGRADE PROS AND CONS

The primary incentive for upgrading Access databases is to take advantage of new features that aren't available by opening Access 200x files in Access 2007. The most significant new features are:

- The Attachments data type with compressed storage for images (not available for Access data projects)
- Multivalued lookup fields (not available for Access data projects)

- Layout view for forms and reports (not available for Access data projects)
- Password-protected databases with secure encryption
- Email .accdb files as attachments
- Append-only memo fields for earlier version retention (not available for Access data projects)
- Embedded macros for forms and reports
- Increased integration with SharePoint (not applicable to Access data projects)

If all or even a few of the preceding features are important to your Access application and its users, and all potential database users have or will upgrade to Office 2007 Professional or higher, the application is a good candidate for upgrading.

CAUTION

> The Access 2007 .accdb and .accde file formats don't support user-level security and disregards all permissions you assign to Access groups or users. All users gain the equivalent of Admins permission to all application and data objects. Your only choice for securing the design of application and data objects is to make and distribute .accde (.mde-like) versions of your .accdb file(s). Alternatively, you can edit the file extension to create a read-only .accdr file without the ribbon UI or Navigation pane but, users can just as easily change the .accdr extension back to .accdb.

CONVERTING UNSECURED FILES FROM ACCESS 9X TO 200X

The definition of an unsecured Access 9x file is an .mdb file containing data objects, application objects, or both, that you or others created with Access's default Admin account, with or without Access 97's database-level password protection. In this case, the Admin account has Administrator privileges and is the owner of all objects in the .mdb file(s).

TIP

> If you're upgrading from Access 2000, 2002, or 2003 to Access 2007, skip to the later "Upgrading Access 200x Files to Access 2007" section.

NOTE

> The following sections don't apply to .mdb files you create as the Admin user with password protection for the Admin account. If the Admin user has a password stored in a workgroup (System.mdw) file, the .mdb file is considered secure. The later "Converting Secure Access 9x Files to 200x" section covers conversion of files with an Admin password.

CAUTION

> Don't upgrade shared data (back-end) .mdb files or workgroup .mdw files to Jet 4.0 format until all users who connect to these files have upgraded their application .mdb (front-end) files to Jet 4.0. Access 9x front ends can't link to Jet 4.0 tables; you receive an "Unrecognized data format" error message if you attempt to link an Access 9x front end to Jet 4.0 .mdb or .mdw files.

UPGRADING ON FIRST OPENING THE FILE IN ACCESS 200X

Access 97 was a very robust and bug-free release, so a substantial percentage of production Access applications remain in that decade-old format. Conversion of unsecured Access 9x (95 or 97) .mdb files to Jet 4.0 is straightforward. If you're opening the Access 9x .mdb file for the first time in Access 200x, do the following:

1. Make sure you have sufficient disk space to accommodate the new .mdb file. The size of the Access 200x version will be about 10% to 15% larger than the Access 9x version.

2. If the Access 9x .mdb file contains VBA code, open the code editor window and compile the code in Access 9x. Compiling all code in the source .mdb file minimizes the likelihood of errors during the upgrade process.

3. Compact and repair the file in Access 9x. Compacting the file immediately before conversion often speeds the conversion process and ensures against problems during conversion.

4. Close the Access 9x .mdb file if it's open. You must have exclusive access to the file for conversion to proceed.

5. Open the Access 9x .mdb file in Access 200x, which displays the Convert/Open Database dialog (see Figure 31.1). By default, the conversion is to Access 2000 format. If the database is password-protected, you must type the password to open the .mdb file.

Figure 31.1
The Convert/Open Database dialog appears when you open an Access 9x .mdb file in Access 2003.

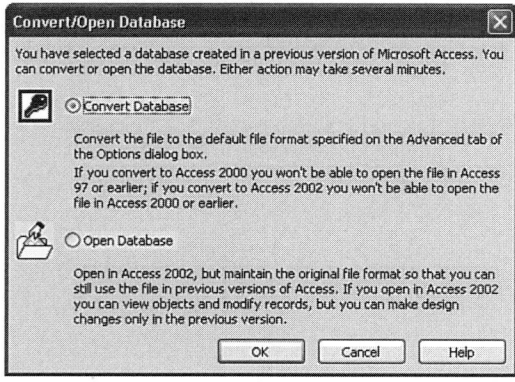

6. Accept the default Convert Database option and click OK to open the Convert Database Into dialog.

7. Replace the default db1.mdb with a new filename for the converted file (see Figure 31.2). Unlike the compact/repair process, you can't use the original filename and overwrite the Access 9x file. If you want to use the same filename, create a new folder in which to save the file.

Figure 31.2
You must specify a different location or filename when converting an .mdb file from Access 9x to Jet 4.0.

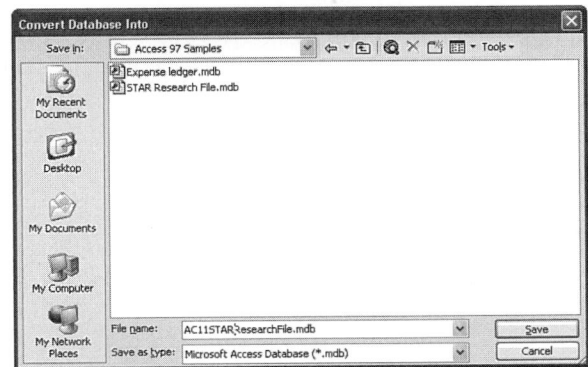

31

> **TIP**
>
> Keep a backup copy of your Access 9x .mdb files after conversion in a different folder or on removable media. You might find it necessary to restore your backup in the event you discover unexpected changes in your application caused by conversion artifacts. After you move the Access 9x file(s) to a new location, you can rename the converted file(s) to the original name(s).

8. Click Save to close the dialog and perform the conversion. After a few seconds—or minutes, if the file is large—the message shown in Figure 31.3 appears. Click OK to open your newly converted file in the Database window.

Figure 31.3
You receive this message after converting an Access 9x .mdb to Access 200x format.

TIP

> You don't need to convert the existing default workgroup information file, System.mdw, which Access 9x installs in the \Windows\System32. If your application is secure, however, you must first compact the Access 97 workgroup file in Access 200x, and then use Workgroup Administrator to join the workgroup defined by your Access 9x System.mdw. (You can't compact the Access 9x workgroup file if a user is connected to it.) Compacting the workgroup information file in Access 200x doesn't change its version.

You can't open or convert Access 97 .mde files in Access 200x. When you attempt to open an .mde file, the terse message shown in Figure 31.4 appears. This restriction makes it impossible to run demonstration versions of commercial Access 97 applications under Access 2003. If you don't have Access 97 installed, you must wait for the upgraded version from the publisher.

Figure 31.4
You receive this message if you attempt to open an Access 9x .mde file in Access 200x.

UPGRADING AFTER OPENING THE FILE IN ACCESS 200X

When you elect to open an unsecured Access 9x file in Access 200x, you can't change the design of any Access objects. If you've previously opened an Access 9x file in Access 2003 and selected the Open Database option in the Convert/Open Database dialog, the Convert/Open Database dialog doesn't appear on successive open operations. You receive the message shown in Figure 31.5 the first time you open an Access 9x database in Access 200x.

Figure 31.5
When you open an Access 9x .mdb file in Access 200x, you receive this message.

You can't save changes to the design of any object in an Access 9x database opened in Access 200x; you receive the message shown in Figure 31.5 when you open an object in Design view.

NOTE

> You can open Access 9x objects in Design view, and even make changes to the design. However, you can't save (persist) the design changes.

Do the following to convert a previously opened database to the Jet 4.0 format:

1. Compile the VBA code and compact the file to be converted in Access 9x.

2. For this example, launch Access 200x without opening a current database.

3. Choose Tools, Database Utilities, Convert Database, To Access 2000 File Format to open the Database to Convert From dialog.

4. Navigate to and select the Access 9x database to convert (see Figure 31.6).

Figure 31.6
When you convert an Access 9x database without opening it in Access 200x, select the source .mdb file in the Database to Convert From dialog.

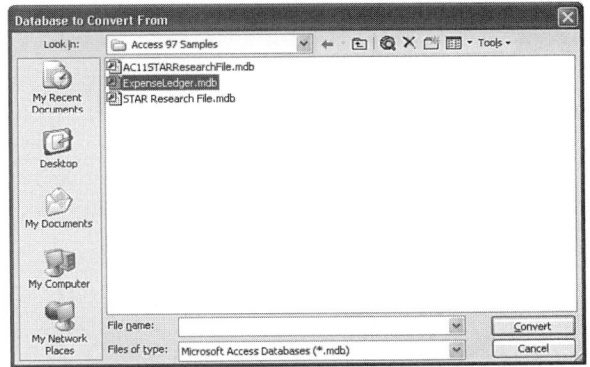

5. Click Convert to open the Convert Database Into dialog.

6. Replace the default db1.mdb with a new filename for the converted file (refer to Figure 31.2).

7. Click Save to close the dialog and save the file in Access 2000 format.

8. Acknowledge the warning message, and then open the file in Access 200x.

FIXING MISSING VBA REFERENCES IN ACCESS 9X UPGRADES

Access 9x installs a Microsoft DAO 2.5/3.0 Compatibility Library reference to Dao2532.tlb, which supports the 16-bit VBA of Access 2.0 and earlier, as well as VBA syntax obsoleted by 32-bit Access 9x VBA. If you don't have this file on the machine used to upgrade the Access 9x .mdb file(s), you receive the two error messages shown in Figure 31.7 when opening the file, the error message of Figure 31.8 when you run any VBA procedure, or both.

Figure 31.7

These two error messages appear when you open an Access 9x .mdb file without having the Dao2532.tlb type library file on your computer.

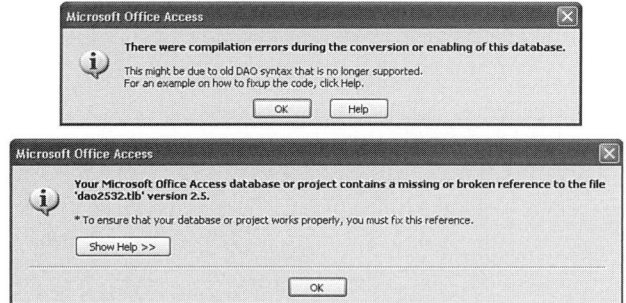

Figure 31.8

This error message opens when you attempt to run a VBA procedure in an Access 9x .mdb file without the Da02532.tlb type library present.

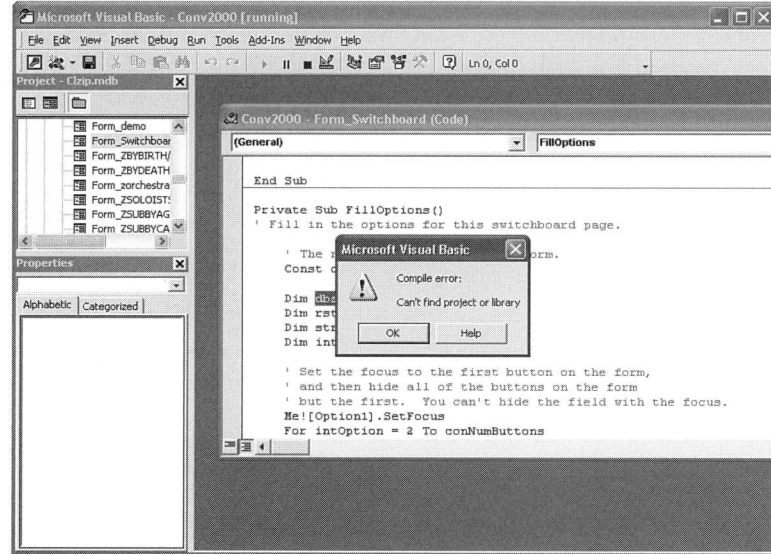

To correct the error, clear the check box(es) for the MISSING: Microsoft DAO 2.5/3.0 Compatibility Library reference and the MISSING: utility.mda reference, if present, and add a reference to Microsoft DAO 3.6 Object Library (DAO360.dll) if the machine on which you're upgrading doesn't have Access 2007 installed, or Microsoft Office Access 2007 database engine Object Library (ACCDAO.dll) if it does (see Figure 31.9).

Compile the VBA code to verify the new references. Upgrading to Access 2007 will replace DAO360.dll with ACCDAO.dll.

Figure 31.9
Replace the missing Microsoft DAO 25/30 Object Library with Microsoft Office Access 2007 database engine Object Library (ACCDAO.dll), if present; otherwise, use Microsoft DAO 3.6 Object Library (DAO360.dll).

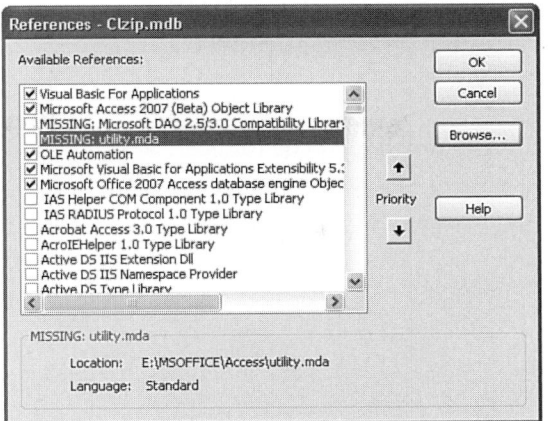

CONVERTING SECURE ACCESS 9X FILES TO 200X

Converting secure Access 9x files to Access 200x is a complex process that requires advance planning. Multiuser networked applications are the most common environment for secure Access files. To upgrade either the front-end or back-end .mdb file(s), you must open the files exclusively under an account that has Modify Design or Administer permissions for all objects in the .mdb file. Alternatively, you must be the owner (creator) of all the database's objects. All users must close their front-end applications for you to obtain exclusive-open access to the back-end .mdb file.

TIP

> VBA code in secured forms and modules becomes unsecured when converting to Jet 4.0 because the change to the VBA Integrated Design Environment results in a different storage mechanism for your code. After you convert secured front-end .mdbs containing any VBA code, leave the VBA code unprotected until you make the final conversion to Access 2007.

UPGRADING IN A MIXED ACCESS 97 AND 200X ENVIRONMENT

If you have many database users or several shared databases in operation, it's unlikely that you can upgrade all database users at one time without incurring excessive downtime. In this case, you must perform the following sequence of operations:

1. Make a backup copy of your Access 9x System.mdw file.

2. Launch Access 200x and choose Tools, Database Utilities, Compact and Repair Database to open the Database to Compact From dialog. Choose Workgroup Files (*.mdw) in the Files of Type list and navigate to and select the shared workgroup file, usually System.mdw, and compact it with the same name. Click Cancel to close the Convert/Open Database dialog.

3. Open the Access 97 version of the front-end .mdb file in Access 97 to verify that the compacted System.mdw file opens with your Admins account and that you have design permissions for front-end objects. Verify that members of groups other than Admins don't have design permissions.

4. Choose Tools, Security, Workgroup Administrator, and join the workgroup you updated in step 2. Close and reopen Access 200x.

5. Open and convert the secure front-end .mdb file to Access 2000 format.

6. Thoroughly test the Jet 4.0 version of the secure application .mdb file with the existing Access 97 data .mdb file(s) and the compacted Access 97 System.mdw file.

7. Upgrade the front-end .mdb file to Access 2007 and distribute it to users who have Office 2007 installed.

UPGRADING THE BACK-END DATABASE AND WORKGROUP FILE

After you've upgraded all your client .mdb files, you can upgrade the back-end (data) .mdb file when all users have moved to Access 2007. Access front ends can connect to Access or Jet back ends of an equal or lower version number.

You can retain user-level security for linked Access tables by upgrading the back-end database to Access 200x so you can modify table designs in Access 2007. In this case, Access 2007 users must log in when opening the front-end .accdb file to provide their credentials to the back-end .mdb file. If you don't convert the back end to the .accdb format, you can't use the new Attachments, multivalued lookup, and append-only Memo data types.

If you decide to upgrade the back-end database and (optionally) the workgroup file, complete the upgrade process as follows:

1. Compact the shared data .mdb file with a new name so that you can convert the file to a new version with the same name as the old version.

2. Upgrade the data .mdb file to Jet 4.0.

CAUTION

> Don't delete the original .mdb file. You might need to revert to the original files in case you encounter conversion problems.

3. Create a local copy of the existing shared workgroup file and join the local workgroup so you can compact the original workgroup file.

4. Compact the shared workgroup file with a new name and then convert it to Jet 4.0 with the original name.

CAUTION

> Don't delete the original .mdw file. You might need it as conversion insurance.

5. After testing the new configuration, upgrade the back-end .mdb file to an Access 2007 .accdb file if you're willing to give up user-level security on the back end.

UPGRADING ACCESS 200X FILES TO ACCESS 2007

Upgrading unsecured Access 200x .mdb files to Access 2007 .accdb files is simple, but secured .mdb files complicate the process, if you want to move from security based on workgroup files to password protection and encryption.

UPGRADING UNSECURED ACCESS 200X FILES

To upgrade an Access 200x file to Access 2007, do the following:

1. Open the .mdb file in Access 2007, which displays the file type, such as Access 2000 File Format, in the window header. Access 2007 disregards the database password, if specified.

2. If the file is encrypted, click the Database Tools tab and click the Encode/Decode button to decrypt the .mdb file. You receive an error message if you attempt to upgrade an encrypted .mdb file.

3. Click the Office button, choose Manage, Backup Database, and save the backup copy with its date suffix.

4. Click the Office button again, choose Convert, accept the default or change the filename, and save the file with the new .accdb extension.

5. Acknowledge the message box that warns you that you can't open the .accdb file in earlier Access versions (see Figure 31.10).

Figure 31.10
You receive this message when Access upgrades an .mdb file to an Access 2007 .accdb file.

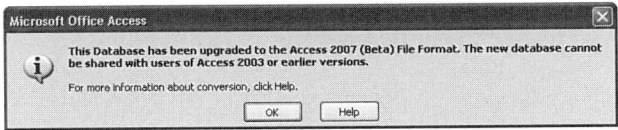

6. Close the .mdb file, open the .accdb file, and compile the VBA file to verify that references are correct.

UPGRADING SECURED ACCESS 200X FILES

The default Access 2007 workgroup file is Application Data\Microsoft\Access\System1. mdw, which is shorthand for the full path and filename: *d*:\Documents and Settings\ *AdminUser.Domain*\Application Data\Microsoft\Access\System1.mdw. *AdminUser* is the user with administrative privileges who installed Office 2007; *Domain* is the Active Directory domain or the computer name.

The Registry key that specifies the default workgroup file is `HKEY_CURRENT_USER\Software\Microsoft\Office\12.0\Access\Access Connectivity Engine\Engines\SystemDB`. Editing the Registry manually is a bit chancy, but there's no UI component to open the Workgroup Administrator. However, you can open the Workgroup Administrator with the VBA `DoCmd.RunCommand acCmdWorkgroupAdministrator` instruction, as described shortly.

CREATING A SHORTCUT FOR AN ACCESS 2007 FRONT END WITH AN ACCESS 200X BACK END

If you want to specify a nondefault workgroup file to preserve user-level security on an Access 2007 application with an Access 200x back-end database, the best approach is to retain Access 2007's default System1.mdw workgroup file and open the secure front end from a shortcut that uses the following syntax:

"Path to Access 2007 Msaccess.exe" "Path to *FrontEnd*.accdb " /wrkgrp "Path to workgroup *Security*.mdw"

Here's a sample Target expression for front-end, back-end, and workgroup files in the C:\SEUA12\Chaptr31 folder:

"C:\Program Files\Microsoft Office\Office12\MSACCESS.EXE"
"C:\SEUA12\Chaptr31\Nwind2007.accdb" /WRKGRP
"C:\SEUA12\Chaptr31\Secured.mdw"

Figure 31.11 shows the Shortcut page of a new shortcut with the workgroup file specified by the value of the /WRKGRP command-line argument. Create an additional shortcut with the source .mdb path and filename to enable opening it in Access 2007 for conversion.

Figure 31.11
This is a shortcut for an application with an Access 2007 Nwind2007.accdb front-end file and an Access 200x NwindData.mdb back-end file.

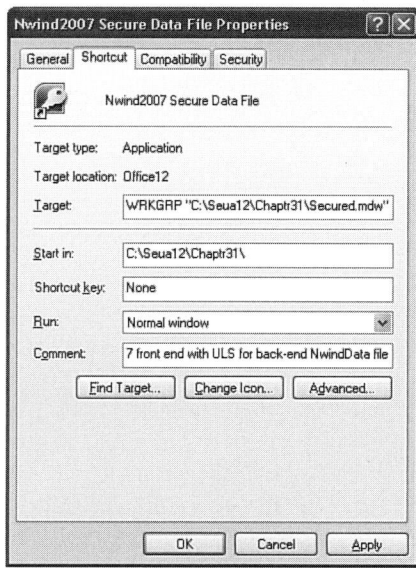

Click the appropriate shortcut to open the secure front-end file and convert it to an unsecure .accdb file by the process described in the earlier "Upgrading Unsecured Access 200x Files" section.

If you decide to convert the back-end .mdb file to an unsecured .accdb file, repeat the process with the appropriate .mdb shortcut.

Use the appropriate .accdb shortcut to open the front-end .accdb file.

SPECIFYING A NEW DEFAULT WORKGROUP FILE FOR AN ACCESS 2007 FRONT END WITH AN ACCESS 200X BACK END

If you want to specify a different default workgroup file with Access 2007's Workgroup Administrator to secure the back-end database file, do the following:

1. Open any Access 2007 database on the machine.
2. Press Ctrl+G to open the Visual Basic editor and the Immediate Window.
3. Type **DoCmd.RunCommand acCmdWorkgroupAdministrator** in the Immediate Window and press Enter to open the Access 2007 Workgroup Administrator.
4. Click Join to open the Workgroup Information File dialog. Then type or browse for the path and filename of the new default workgroup file (see Figure 31.12).

31

Figure 31.12
Access 2007's Workgroup Administrator is built into MSACCESS.EXE, not a separate Wrkgadm.exe executable file.

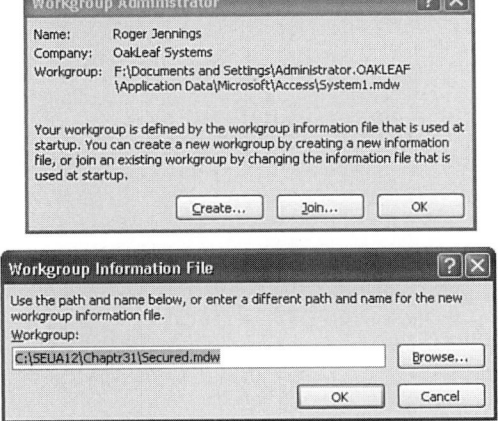

5. Click OK twice to close both dialogs and establish the new default workgroup file, and close Access.

Alternatively, you can execute the following instruction in the Immediate Window:

```
Application.SetDefaultWorkgroupFile "C:\SEUA12\Chaptr31\Secure.mdw"
```

The new default workgroup file supports opening the .mdb and converted .accdb file.

REMOVING THE USERNAME/PASSWORD REQUIREMENT FROM .ACCDB FILES

If you've converted both the front-end .mdb and back-end .mdb files to the .accdb format and changed the default workgroup, your database is password protected but not secure because Access 2007 ignores user-level security but not the *Secure*.mdw file. At this point, you can revert the default workgroup file to …\System1.mdw with the Workgroup Administrator or SetDefaultWorkgroupFile method.

You can add some security to the front end by opening the database in Exclusive mode and then clicking the Database Tools tab and Encrypt with Password button. Type and retype to verify the password, and click OK to set the database password, which is stored in the database, not the workgroup file.

MOVING FROM MSDE TO THE SQL SERVER 2005 EXPRESS EDITION

When you upgrade from Office 2000, 2002, or 2003 to 2007, your existing MSDE installation remains intact, and your existing ADP, DAP, and linked Jet databases continue to connect to the local instance of MSDE installed from the Office 2000 CD-ROM (MSDE 1.0, SQL Server 7.0) or the Office 2002 or 2003 CD-ROM (MSDE 2000, SQL Server 2000), or the remote server specified by the front-end application's ODBC or OLE DB/ADO connection string.

You can continue to use MSDE 1.0 with Access 2007, but doing so prevents you from taking advantage of the many new and important features of SQL Server 2005 Express (SSX) Service Pack 2, including SQL Server Management Studio Express (SSMSX), full support for declarative referential integrity (DRI), linked servers, and extended properties that support Access 2002 and later features—such as lookup fields, subdatasheets, and input masks. If you intend to update your Access 2000 ADP files to Access 2007, upgrading from MSDE 1.0 to SSX is essential.

NOTE
> As mentioned in Chapter 1, SSX SP2 is required to run SQL Server 2005 Express under Windows Vista. The full name of the product to install is SQL Server 2005 Express Edition with Advanced Services Service Pack 2, which includes SSMS.

UPGRADING FROM MSDE 1.0 TO SQL SERVER 2005

By default, MSDE 1.0 and 2000 install with the default SQL Server instance name, which is the computer name. SSX installs a named instance, *ComputerName*\SQLEXPRESS by default, so SSX installs side by side with MSDE.

Unlike MSDE, the Office 2007 installation disks don't include setup files for SSX and its accessories. You must download and install SQL Server 2005 Express Edition with

Advanced Features to obtain SSX with the Full-Text Search feature and SQL Server Reporting Services, plus SSMSX.

→ To review the installation process for a new SSX instance, **see** "SQL Server 2005 Express Edition SP2 Setup," **p. 59**.

REMOVING MSDE AND INSTALLING SQL SERVER 2000

If you decide to migrate your ADP or linked client/server applications to Access 2007 and SQL Server 2005, do the following before removing MSDE:

1. Stop MSDE and back up your data (.mdf) and log (.ldf) files, plus at least master.mdf, mastlog.ldf, msdbdata.mdf, and msdblog.ldf. Removing MSDE 1.0 doesn't delete production .mdf and .ldf files, but it does delete the existing master, msdb, model, and tempdb database and log files. Loss of the model and tempdb databases isn't important.

2. If you've added custom settings for MSDE features, such as publish/subscribe replication, server roles, SQL Server logins, and the like, make sure you document them thoroughly. You must manually reestablish your server-wide MSDE settings in SSX.

Removing MSDE isn't as simple as the "Install and Configure SQL Server Desktop Engine" online Help topic suggests. Do the following to remove MSDE and all its components, including SQL Service Manager from your computer:

1. Open SQL Server Service Manager and clear the Auto-start Service when OS Starts check box for MSSQLServer and SQLServerAgent.

2. Delete the shortcut to Service Manager in your …\Start Menu\Programs\Startup folder(s). The location of the Service Manager shortcut depends on your operating system. Use Search to search for **service manager**, and delete *all* Service Manager shortcuts you find.

3. Reboot your computer and verify that the Service Manager icon no longer appears in the tray.

4. Choose Start, Programs, MSDE, Uninstall MSDE to start the uninstall process. Click Yes to confirm you want to continue with removal, click OK when uninstallation completes, and then reboot your computer.

5. Perform a new installation of SSX as described in the "Downloading and Installing SSX" section of Chapter 1.

6. Reboot your computer when Setup completes.

Removing MSDE 1.0 deletes the Programs, MSDE menu; MSDE 2000 doesn't add a menu. Other SQL Server 200x editions and SSX add a Microsoft SQL Server menu to replace the MSDE menu.

ATTACHING AND UPGRADING MSDE DATABASES

ADP and ODBC-linked Jet front ends lose their connections to existing MSDE databases when you migrate to SSX, so you must reattach the database files to the new SSX instance

31

and fix the server connections for your front-end applications. When you attach the MSDE.mdf file, SQL Server upgrades the database to the SQL Server 2005 version. This process is not reversible; the upgraded database files no longer are operable with MSDE 1.0 or 2000.

ACCESS DATA PROJECTS

To reattach and upgrade the MSDE files for ADP, do this:

1. Open the .adp file in Access 2003. The project displays "Disconnected" in the Database window's title bar.

2. Choose File, Connection to open the Data Link Properties dialog.

3. Accept (local) or select the server name in the Select or Enter a Server Name list.

4. Select the Attach a Database File as a Database Name option, and type the database name for your project in the first text box.

5. Click the Browse button to open the Select SQL Server Database File dialog and navigate to the folder that holds the MSDE .mdf file for the database. The default location of MSDE 1.0 .mdf and .ldf files is C:\MSSQL7\Data; MSDE 2000 ordinarily uses C:\Program Files\Microsoft SQL Server\MSSQL\Data. Select the file and click Open to add the filename to the Using the Filename text box (see Figure 31.13).

Figure 31.13
Specify the database name and .mdf file to upgrade MSDE databases to SSX and attach them to ADP.

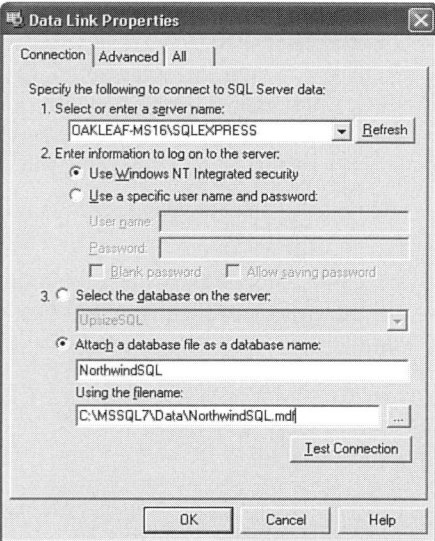

6. Click Test Connection to upgrade the attached file, which takes a few seconds or more, depending on the size of the database.

7. Click OK to close the Data Link Properties dialog, and verify that your project works correctly with the upgraded database.

8. Repeat steps 1 through 7 for each project that has an upgraded database.

NOTE

> Attaching the files moves the .mdf and .ldf files from their original location (normally \MSSQL7\Data) to the standard location for SQL Server 2005 files (\Program Files\Microsoft SQL Server\MSSQL.1\MSSQL\Data).

After you've attached the upgraded tables, they appear in the Select the Database on the Server List. If you maintained the original database name and security option, you don't need to modify the Data Link Properties entries for other front ends that connect to the upgraded database.

Jet Front Ends Linked with ODBC

ODBC DSNs that link Jet front ends to MSDE databases fail after migrating to SSX. If the Jet front ends share SSX databases you've upgraded for ADP, the upgrade process of the preceding section makes the DSNs operable. You must attach and upgrade other MSDE databases to enable connectivity with existing ODBC DSNs.

If you installed SQL Server Management Studio Express with SSX, you can attach and upgrade the MSDE files by doing this:

1. Open SSMS, and expand the COMPUTERNAME\SQLEXPRESS node to display the object types list.

2. Right-click the Databases node of the migrated server, and choose <u>A</u>ttach to open the Attach Databases dialog.

3. Click the Add button to open the Locate Database Files – *ServerName* dialog, navigate to and select the .mdf file to attach, and click OK.

4. Accept or change the database name in the Attach As text box (see Figure 31.14). Note that you can't change the database's owner in SSMSX in this dialog; you can in the full version.

5. Click OK to attach the database, and click OK again to acknowledge the "success" message.

If you don't have SSMS, you can attach and upgrade MSDE files by creating a temporary project—typically Adp1.adp—and performing the steps in the preceding "Access Data Projects" section for each database you need to upgrade.

Figure 31.14
Use Enterprise Manager's Attach Database tool to reattach and upgrade MSDE databases you connect to Jet front ends with ODBC.

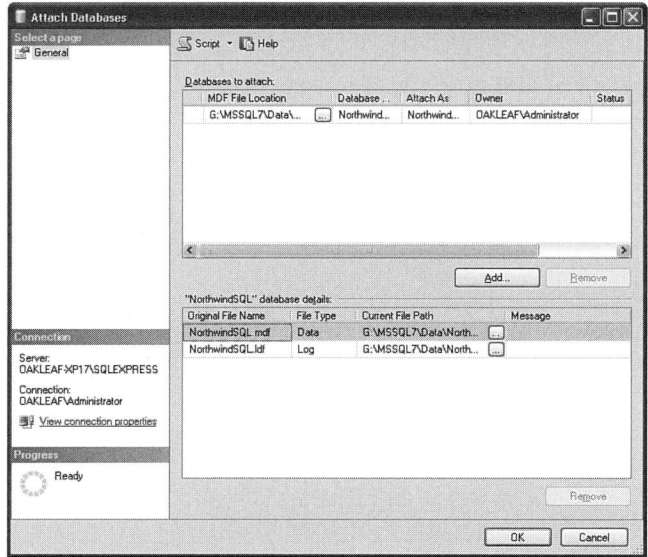

CHANGING THE DATABASE OWNER AND SETTING DATABASE COMPATIBILITY LEVEL

SQL Server Management Studio Express's Properties dialog has several pages that you can use to set property values for SSX databases. As an example, to change the database owner from the Windows logon account to the traditional sa (system administrator account), do the following:

1. Open SSMS, right-click the database name in the Databases list, and choose Properties to open the Properties – *DatabaseName* dialog.

2. Select the Files page, and click the builder button to open the Select Database Owner dialog. Type **sa** in the text box, click Check Names to add brackets around sa (see Figure 31.15), and click OK to change the database owner to sa.

3. Click OK to close the Properties window if you're finished making changes.

Changing the database owner to sa lets you maintain a single owner for all the instance's databases.

SQL Server 2005 supports three database compatibility levels: SQL Server 7.0 (70) or MSDE 1.0, SQL Server 2000 (80) or MSDE 2000, and SQL Server 2005 (90) or SSX. Database compatibility levels affect the behavior of many SQL Server features. You must specify SQL Server 2005 (90) compatibility to take advantage of new SQL Server 2005 data types, such as varchar(max), nvarchar(max), varbinary(max), and xml. When upgrading MSDE databases to SSX, you should set the database compatibility level to SQL Server 2005 (90) by doing the following:

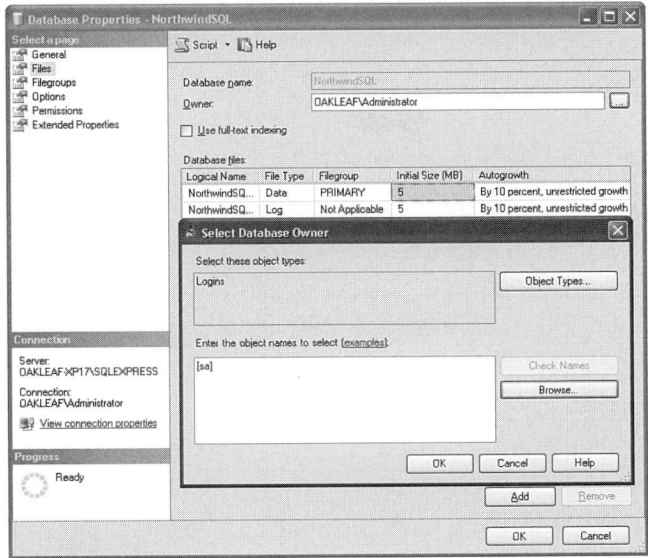

Figure 31.15
Use SSMSX's Files page of the Properties dialog to change the database owner to sa.

31

1. Open SSMS, right-click the database name in the Databases list, and choose Properties to open the Properties – *DatabaseName* dialog.

2. Select the Options page, open the Compatibility Level list, and select SQL Server 2005 (90), as shown in Figure 31.16.

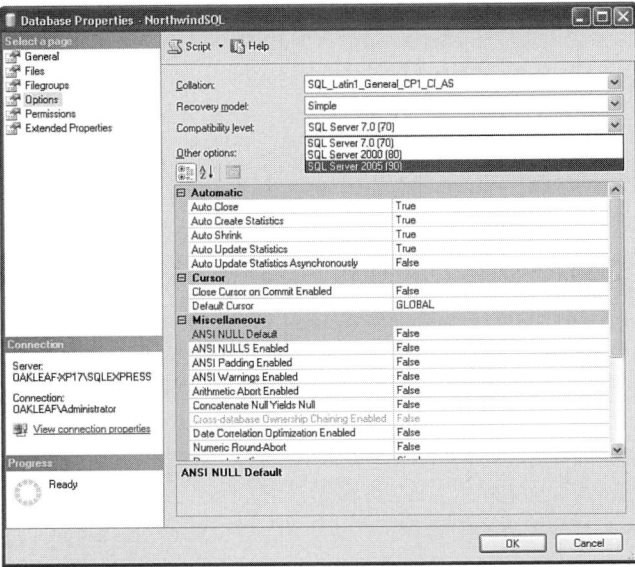

Figure 31.16
Use the SSMSX Properties dialog's Options page to change the upgraded database's compatibility level to SQL Server 2005 (90).

TROUBLESHOOTING

MISSING LIBRARY OR PROJECT MESSAGE

I get a "The expression EventName you entered as the event property setting produced the following error: Can't find project or library" message when attempting to open or convert an Access 97 application .mdb.

The most common cause of this error message results from use of Access 97's Microsoft DAO 2.5/3.5 Compatibility Library, which permits compiling code with the remnants of Access 2.0's VBA code conventions that are incompatible with DAO 3.5+. You must update the code to DAO 3.5x standards in Access 97, and then convert the Access 97 version to Jet 4.0. In Access 97, substitute a reference to the Microsoft DAO 3.51 Object Library for the Microsoft DAO 2.5/3.5 Compatibility Library. Correct the unsupported syntax by repeatedly compiling the code until all modules compile and the application runs properly. Then convert the .mdb file to Access 2000 format with DAO 3.6.

IN THE REAL WORLD—THE ACCESS UPGRADE BLUES

Previous upgrades to Access (except the 1.0 to 1.1 transition) undoubtedly increased the market for mood-altering substances—both legal and illegal—among Access developers. Migrating from Access 97 or 200x to Access 2007 isn't a piece of cake. The larger and more complex your Access application, the more taxing the process.

Owners and users of production database applications resist changes; their watchwords are "If it isn't broke, don't fix it." Thus, database applications have a tendency to be upgraded far less often than other desktop productivity software, such as word processing and spreadsheet applications. Access Basic detritus from version 2.0 or earlier plagues the conversion of mature Access applications. (Many developers didn't upgrade Access 2.0 applications to Access 95 because of performance issues. Some Access 2.0 accounting applications remain in use today.) Thus, the more history behind your code, the greater the chance that it breaks when upgrading.

The obvious temptation is not to upgrade any Access 9x application to Access 2005. This approach is viable only for applications you distribute as self-contained runtime versions generated by the Office 9x Developer Edition's Setup Wizard, because Access 9x is only available from online auction shops, such as eBay. Access 97 runtime versions install roughly 50MB of Access 97, Jet 3.51, DAO 3.51, and other obsolete dependency files on Office 2003 users' PCs. The Access 97 runtime baggage probably won't be a problem for today's desktop PCs, but road warriors' older laptops often have much less available disk space than modern desktops.

If you avoid temptation and bite the upgrade bullet, take the opportunity to optimize your VBA code. Make sure that the first line in every module is **Option** Explicit, substitute variable declarations for explicit references to objects used more than once in your code, and minimize the use of the **Variant** data type. Add .Value instead of using the default property value of Access and Jet objects. Search for all instances of `CreateObject`, which results in late binding, and replace the call with a referenced object variable declaration, such as **Private** `objName` **As** `ObjectLibrary.ObjectName`, for a class member to force early binding. When you complete the optimization process, your Access 2007 application *might* execute as quickly as its 16-bit Access 2.0 predecessor. (But don't count on it.)

After you've converted your application to Jet 4.0 and DAO 3.6, and then gone through an exhaustive testing process, your next decision is whether to move from DAO to ADO 2.6 and ADOX 2.8. OLE DB and ADO are Microsoft's current recommendations for database connectivity, but surfing the current ADO/ADOX versions demonstrates no significant performance improvement or other benefits that justify the time and effort required for conversion. ADO/ADOX don't offer full parity with ACCDAO, Access 2007's DAO 3.6 replacement for Jet databases. You can't use VBA code to program Access 2007's new Attachments data type or multivalued lookup fields, and many workarounds for missing DAO/ACCDAO features are inelegant, at best.

Finally, make the transition from Access/Jet databases to SQL Server 2005 and its successors. The inherent limitations of Jet 4.0 are here to stay in ACCDAO. SQL Server 2005 delivers industrial-strength reliability and scalability to your Access 2007 applications.

31

APPENDIX

GLOSSARY

.NET   Microsoft's strategy, announced in June 2000, to reorient its operating systems, developer tools, and productivity applications from the Component Object Model (COM) to the .NET Framework and its Common Language Runtime (CLR). The CLR supports multiple programming languages, such as Microsoft's Visual C#, Visual Basic .NET, and Visual J#. Much of Microsoft's marketing campaign for the .NET Framework and Visual Studio .NET focuses on support for Internet-enabled XML web services. Microsoft Office 2003 installs version 1.1 of the .NET Framework to support Excel 2003 and Word 2003. The .NET Framework is a reincarnation of *Next Generation Windows Services* (*NGWS*), the follow-up to Microsoft's earlier *Distributed iNternet Architecture* (*Windows DNA*). See also *CLR, COM, SOAP,* and *XML web services*.

Access Data Project   See *ADP*.

Access SQL   Former name of Jet SQL, a dialect of ANSI SQL-92 resurrected by Access 2007, which no longer uses the Jet database. See also *ANSI, Jet SQL, SQL,* and *Transact-SQL*.

Active Server Pages   See *ASP*.

ActiveX   A Microsoft trademark for a collection of technologies based on the Common Object Model (COM) and Distributed Common Object Model (DCOM). See also *COM, COM+,* and *DCOM*.

ActiveX components   A replacement term for OLE Automation mini-servers and in-process servers, also called Automation servers. See also *Automation*.

ActiveX controls   Insertable objects supplied in the form of .ocx files that, in addition to offering a collection of properties and methods, also fire events. ActiveX controls are lightweight versions of earlier OLE controls that also use the .ocx file extension.

ActiveX Data Objects   See *ADO*.

ActiveX Data Object Extensions   See *ADOX*.

ActiveX documents   Files such as those created by Microsoft Excel 7+ and Word 7+ that can be displayed in their native format in Internet Explorer 3+. ActiveX documents originally were called Document Objects or DocObjects.

ActiveX scripting   Another name for Visual Basic, Scripting Edition (VBScript), a simplified version of VBA designed for client- and server-side automation of web pages.

add-in   Wizards and other programming aids, usually in the form of Access libraries, that help Access programmers create and deploy applications. You use Access's Add-In Manager to install Microsoft and third-party add-ins. COM add-ins are a class of add-in objects introduced in Office 2000. See also *COM* and *Builder*.

ADO   An abbreviation for ActiveX Data Objects, which are similar in concept to the Data Access Object (DAO) and Remote Data Object (RDO). ADO uses Microsoft's OLE Database (OLE DB) technology to access data from various data sources, including text files and mainframe databases. ADO is a member of the Microsoft Data Access Components (MDAC.) ADO 2.x was the preferred database connectivity method for Access 2000 through 2003. Access 2007 requires DAO to take advantage of new Access data types, such as Attachment and multivalued fields (MVF). See also *DAO, MDAC, MSDE, MVF, OLE DB*, and *SSX*.

ADO MD   An abbreviation for ADO Multidimensional (Expressions), the Automation library that provides access to CubeDef and Cellset objects created with the PivotTable Service or Microsoft SQL Server Analysis Services (formerly Microsoft Decision Support Services, MSDSS, and OLAP Services). See also *Cellset, CubeDef, MDX, OLAP*, and *PivotTable Service*.

ADODB   An abbreviation and object library name for ADO 2.x. ADODB is used as an object prefix to specify the source of an ADO data object, as in `ADODB.Recordset`.

ADOX   An abbreviation for ActiveX Data Object Extensions, a set of extensions to ADO 2.1+ that support Jet 4.0's SQL Data Definition Language reserved words, such as `CREATE GROUP` and `ALTER USER`. See also *data definition*.

ADP   An abbreviation for Access data projects, an alternative to conventional Access client/server applications that store application objects (forms and reports) in Access .accdb files. ADP requires an ADO 2.1+ connection to one of the five editions of SQL Server 7.0, 2000 (Desktop or MSDE, Personal, Developer, Standard, Enterprise, or DataCenter editions), or 2005 (Express, Developer, Workgroup, Standard, or Enterprise). ADP stores application objects in OLE docfiles having an .adp or .ade (encrypted) extension. See also *ADO, application object, docfile, MSDE*, and *SSX*.

ADTG   An abbreviation for Advanced Data TableGram, a Microsoft-proprietary MIME format used by ADO `Recordset`s saved to files. See also *ADO* and *MIME*.

aggregate functions   The ANSI SQL functions `AVG()`, `SUM()`, `MIN()`, `MAX()`, and `COUNT()`, and Jet SQL functions `StDev()`, `Var()`, `First()`, and `Last()`. Aggregate functions calculate summary values from a group of values in a specified column and are usually associated with `GROUP BY` and `HAVING` clauses. See also *domain aggregate functions*.

alias   A temporary name assigned to a table in a self-join, to a column of a query, or to rename a table, implemented by the `AS` reserved word in ANSI SQL. You can use `AS` to rename any field or table with Jet SQL or SQL Server's Transact-SQL. `Alias` is also an embedded keyword option for the VBA `Declare` statement. The `Alias` keyword is used to register prototypes of DLL functions so that the function can be called from programs by another name. Aliasing the ANSI versions of 32-bit Windows API functions to function names without the A suffix is common when converting Access 97 and earlier applications to Access 2007, which uses Unicode for text data.

ANSI   An acronym for the American National Standards Institute. ANSI in the Windows context refers to the ANSI character set that Microsoft decided to use for Windows (rather than the IBM PC character set that includes special characters such as those used for line drawing, called the OEM character set). The most common character set is ASCII (American Standard Code for Information Interchange), which for English alphabetic and numeric characters is the same as ANSI. ANSI also is the standards body responsible for the definition of SQL. The latest ANSI standard is SQL-99 (also called SQL:1999 and SQL3); most of today's RDBMSs support the previous version, SQL-92. See also *ASCII*, *SQL*, and *Unicode*.

application object   Any object in a database application that doesn't contain or define data (data objects). Access forms, reports, macros, and modules are examples of application objects. Production Access applications usually store application objects separately from data objects. See also *data object*.

argument   A piece of data supplied to a function that the function uses or acts on to perform its task. Arguments are enclosed in parentheses. Additional arguments, if any, are separated by commas. Arguments passed to procedures usually are called parameters.

array   An ordered sequence of values (elements) stored within a single named variable, accessed by referring to the variable name with the number of the element (index or subscript) in parentheses, as in `strValue = strArray(3)`. VBA arrays can have more than one dimension, in which case access to the value includes indexes for each dimension, as in `strValue = strArray(3,3)`.

ASCII   An acronym for the American Standard Code for Information Interchange. A set of standard numerical values for printable, control, and special characters used by PCs and most other computers. Other commonly used codes for character sets are ANSI (used by Windows 3.1+), Unicode (used by Windows 98 and Windows NT), and EBCDIC (Extended Binary-Coded Decimal Interchange Code, used by IBM for mainframe computers). See also *ANSI* and *Unicode*.

ASP   An acronym for Active Server Pages, Microsoft's server-side technology for dynamically creating standard HTML (Internet) web pages. Conventional ASP uses VBScript or ECMAScript to manipulate ASP objects. Access 2007 lets you export tables, queries, and forms in ASP format for web deployment. Exported .asp files send data in HTML tables to client browsers. ASP.NET is the successor to ASP. See also *ECMAScript*.

ASP.NET   An .NET upgrade to ASP that supports the Simple Object Access Protocol (SOAP), managed code compiled by the Common Language Runtime (CLR) and Web Forms, a new methodology for designing interactive HTML forms. ASP.NET also supports the creation of XML web services. See also *.NET*, *CLR*, *SOAP*, and *XML web services*.

assign   To give a value to a named variable.

asynchronous   A process that can occur at any time, regardless of the status of the operating system or running applications.

attached table   A table that's not stored in the currently open Jet database (a native table), but which you can manipulate as though the table were a native table. In Jet 3+ terminology, an attached table is a linked table. See also *linked table*.

Attachment   A new Access data type that's compatible with Windows SharePoint Services (WSS) 3.0 and Microsoft Office SharePoint Services (MOSS) 2007 and can replace the OLE Object field type, which WSS and MOSS don't support. The Attachment field can hold multiple images (.bmp, .jpg, .gif, or .png) or documents that have supported MIME types. Attachments are compressed to minimize storage space requirements. See also *MIME*, *MOSS*, and *WSS*.

authentication   The process of verifying a user's identity, most commonly by a login ID and password.

Automation   An ActiveX and OLE 2+ term that refers to a means of manipulating another application's objects.

Automation client   An ActiveX- or OLE 2–compliant Windows application with an application programming (macro) language, such as VBA, that can reference and manipulate objects exposed by (OLE) Automation servers.

Automation server   Technically, any COM-compliant Windows application that supports Automation operations by exposing a set of objects for manipulation by Automation client applications. This book restricts the term *Automation server* to applications that expose application objects, but aren't ActiveX full servers. The members of Office 2003 are examples of full Automation servers.

AutoNumber   A Jet 3+ replacement for the Counter field data type of Jet 2.0, Access 1.x, and Access 2.0. AutoNumber fields can be of the Increment or Random type. Fields of the Increment AutoNumber field data type usually are used to create primary keys when a unique primary key can't be created easily from data in the table.

back end   In a split Access data base, the .accdb or .mdb file, or ODBC-linked database that contains the tables for an Access application. In an upsized Access database, the SQL Server 7.0, 2000, or 2005 database that usually contains all the application's tables. In an Access Data Project (ADP), the SQL Server 7.0, 2000, or 2005 database that contains all tables, views, functions, and stored procedures, and processes ad-hoc SQL queries for the project. See *split database*, *ODBC*, *front end*, and *ADP*.

base date   A date used as a reference from which other date values are calculated. In the case of VBA and SQL Server, the base date is 12/30/1899, 12:00 a.m. Dates earlier than the base date are negative.

base tables   The permanent tables from which a query is created, usually acting as the one side of a one-to-many relationship. Jet documentation also uses the term *base table* to refer to a table in the current database in contrast to a linked (attached) table. See also *linked table*.

batch   A group of statements or database operations processed as an entity. Execution of DOS batch files, such as AUTOEXEC.BAT, and SQL statements are examples of batch processes.

batch update   A process in which multiple update operations on a Recordset are conducted on a locally cached copy of the Recordset. When all updates are completed, calling the UpdateBatch method attempts to make permanent (persist) all changes to the underlying tables in a single operation. Access 2007's ADP supports batch updates without the need to write VBA code. See also *ADP*.

binary string   A string consisting of binary, not text, data that contains bytes outside the range of ANSI or ASCII values for printable characters or those that don't correspond to Unicode characters. Access 2007 requires that you store binary strings as arrays of the Byte data type to avoid problems with Unicode/ANSI conversion.

binding   The process of connecting one object to another through interfaces. In Access 2007, local object binding is accomplished by COM interfaces and remote object binding by DCOM interfaces. See also *COM, COM+, DCOM,* and *data binding*.

bitwise   A process that evaluates each bit of a combination, such as a byte or word, rather than process the combination as a single element. Logical operations and masks use bitwise procedures.

Boolean   A type of arithmetic in which all digits are bits—that is, the numbers can have only two states: on (true or 1) or off (false or 0). Widely used in set theory and computer programming, Boolean, named after the mathematician George Boole, also is used to describe a VBA data type that can have only two states: true or false. In VBA, true is represented by `&HFF` (all bits of an 8-bit byte set to 1) and false by `&H0` (all bits set to 0). **Boolean** is a VBA data type.

bound   A term commonly used in Access applications to identify form, report, and control objects that are connected to and can receive values from data objects. See also *binding*.

breakpoint   A designated statement that causes VBA program execution to halt after the statement preceding it is executed. To toggle breakpoints on or off, press F9 on the line of code in Access's VBA editor before which you want execution to halt.

Builder   A component that provides assistance in defining new objects, writing SQL statements, or creating expressions. Buttons with an ellipsis symbol commonly open Access Builders.

built-in functions   Functions that are included in a computer language and don't need to be created by the programmer as user-defined functions. VBA has hundreds of built-in functions, many of which you can use in Jet queries.

business rules   A set of rules for adding or altering data in a database that are specific to an enterprise's method of conducting its operations. Business rules are in addition to rules for maintaining the domain and referential integrity of tables in a database. Business rules most commonly are implemented in the middle tier of a three-tier client/server database environment. See also *middle tier* and *three-tier*.

cache   A block of memory reserved for temporary storage. Caches usually store data from disk files in memory to speed access to the data. Access Recordset objects, which store in memory an image of data in tables or data returned by queries, are typical cached objects.

CAL   An acronym for Client Access License, which is required for client PCs connecting to Microsoft server products, such as Windows 2000+/NT/Longhorn, SQL Server 2000+, and Exchange 2000+. With the exception of bundled server products, such as Small Business Server 2000+ and BackOffice 2000+, separate CALs are required for each server product. CALs aren't required for a local installation of or connections to MSDE, which is covered by an Office XP license. You do, however, require a CAL if a local copy of MSDE connects to SQL Server 2000 or SSX connects to SQL Server 2005, such as occurs with SQL Server merge replication. See *MSDE* and *SSX*.

Cartesian product   Named for René Descartes, a French mathematician. The term describes JOIN operations that return all possible combinations of rows and columns from each table in a database. The number of rows in a Cartesian product is equal to the number of rows in table 1 times that in table 2 times that in table 3, and so on. Cartesian rows that don't satisfy the JOIN condition are disregarded.

cascading deletion   A process that deletes data from one table based on a deletion from another table to maintain referential integrity. Triggers and declarative referential integrity (DRI) are two means of implementing cascading deletions. DRI or triggers generally are used to delete detail data (such as invoice items) when the master record (invoice) is deleted. All Access releases, Jet 2+, and SQL Server 7.0+ provide cascading deletion as an optional element of its referential integrity features. See also *DRI* and *referential integrity*.

cascading update   A process that automatically changes foreign key values to correspond to altered values of a primary key. DRI or triggers implement cascading updates, which are another optional referential integrity element.

Cellset   The multidimensional equivalent of an ADO Recordset. See also *ADO MD*, *CubeDef*, *OLAP*, and *PivotTable Service*.

chaptered Recordset   See *hierarchical Recordset*.

child   In Access, a reference to the table or query that serves as the record source for a subform, subreport, or subdatasheet. Also used in computer programming in general to describe an object that's related to but lower in hierarchical level than a parent object.

class identifier   See *CLSID*.

clause   The portion of an SQL statement beginning with a keyword that names a basic operation to be performed.

client   The device or application that receives data from or manipulates a server device or application. The data might be in the form of a file received from a network file server, an object from an ActiveX component or Automation server, or values from a DDE server assigned to client variables. See also *Automation client*.

A

client tier   A logical entity that represents a networked computer where an Access application interacts with a client/server database or a browser displays a web page from a remote data source. The client tier often is called the *presentation tier*. See also *middle tier* and *data source tier*.

CLR   The abbreviation for Common Language Runtime, the unifying components of the .NET Framework to support intercommunication of components written in different programming languages, such as Visual Basic .NET, managed Visual C++, and Visual C#. Excel 2007 and Word 2007 support the CLR as a macro language, in addition to VBA; Microsoft chose not to support CLR programming for Access 2007 and Outlook 2007.

CLSID   An identification tag that's associated with an Automation object created by a specific server. CLSID values appear in the Registry and must be unique for each ActiveX component or Automation server and for each type of object that the server can create. See also *Registry*.

clustered index   An index in which the physical record order and index order of a table are the same. SQL Server offers the option of using a clustered (recommended) or nonclustered index on the primary key of a table.

coercion   The process of forcing a change from one data type to another, such as `Integer` to `String`. VBA supports type coercion; Visual Basic .NET coerces data types unless explicitly instructed not to by adding an `Option` `Strict` `On` instruction prior to the first line of code.

collection   A group of objects of the same class that are contained within another object. Collections are named as the plural of their object class—for example, the `Parameters` collection is a group of `Parameter` objects contained in a `Command` object.

COM   An acronym for Component Object Model, the name of Microsoft's design strategy to implement ActiveX. Distributed COM (DCOM) allows networked and cross-platform implementation of ActiveX and Automation. See also *DCOM*.

COM+   A feature of Windows 2000 and later Windows server operating systems that integrates COM, DCOM, and elements of MSMQ into the operating system. COM+ adds event services, load balancing, asynchronous queuing services with MSMQ, and an in-memory database for the MTS catalog. See also *COM, DCOM, MSMQ,* and *MTS*.

comment   Explanatory material within source code not designed to be interpreted or compiled into the final application. In VBA, comments are usually preceded by an apostrophe (`'`) but can also be created by preceding them with the `Rem` keyword.

common dialog   A standardized dialog, provided by Windows, that can be created by a Windows API function call to functions contained in Cmdlg32.dll and its successors. Common dialogs include File Open, File Save, Print and Printer Setup, ColorPalette, Font, and Search and Replace. Access 2003 provides the `Application.FileDialog` object as a simpler alternative to the File Open and File Save common dialogs.

comparison operators   See *operator*.

compile To create an executable or object (machine-language) file from source (readable) code. In Access, *compile* means to create pseudocode (tokenized code), not native code, from the VBA source code you write in the code-editing window. The .NET Framework's CLR compiles source code to an intermediate language (IL), which executes on a specified processor class, such as Intel's x86 or Itanium processors.

Component Object Model See *COM*.

composite key or index A key or index based on the values in two or more columns. See also *index* and *key or key field*.

compound In computer programming, a set of instructions or statements that requires more than one keyword or group of related keywords to complete. `Select Case…Case…End Select` is an example of a compound statement in VBA.

concatenation Combining two expressions, usually strings, to form a longer expression. The concatenation operator is `&` in Jet SQL and VBA, although VBA also permits and Transact-SQL requires the + symbol to be used to concatenate strings.

concurrency The condition when more than one user has access to a specific set of records or files at the same time. Also used to describe the capability of a database management system to handle simultaneous and potentially conflicting update queries against a single set of tables.

container An object or application that can create or manipulate compound documents or host ActiveX controls.

CORBA An acronym for Common Object Request Broker Architecture, the primary competitor to Microsoft's COM- and DCOM-based technologies. See also *COM*, *COM+*, and *DCOM*.

correlated subquery A subquery that can't be evaluated independently. Subqueries depend on an outer query for their result. See also *subquery* and *nested query*.

counter A special field data type of Access 1.x and 2.0 and Jet 2.0 tables that numbers each new record consecutively; called an AutoNumber field in Access 95+ and Jet 3+. See also *AutoNumber*.

CubeDef An ADO MD object that provides the metadata for multidimensional data, such as that provided by Microsoft SQL Server Analysis or PivotTable Services. See also *ADO MD*, *Cellset*, *OLAP*, and *PivotTable Service*.

current database The database opened in Access by choosing <u>F</u>ile, <u>O</u>pen Database (or the equivalent) that contains the objects of an Access application.

current record The record in a `Recordset` object whose values are available to bound forms, reports, and controls. The current record supplies values of the record's data cells to control objects that are bound to the table's fields. The current record is specified by a record pointer.

[NEW] DAO The abbreviation for Data Access Objects, the original object library for all database objects in Access. The top member of the DAO hierarchy is the DBEngine object, which contains Workspace, User, and Group objects in collections. Database objects are contained in Workspace objects. ADO was the preferred alternative to DAO in Access 2000 to 2003, although ADO 2.1–2.6 are supported for backward compatibility. DAO is the preferred object library for Access 2007 because it supports the Attachment and MVF data type. See also *ADO*, *Attachment*, and *MVF*.

[NEW] DAP An abbreviation for data access pages, a Web-based technology introduced in Access 2000 for generating data-bound Dynamic HTML pages for use on intranets. DAP uses the Data Source Control (DSC) for data binding and uses other ActiveX controls, such as the Office Web Components (OWC), for displaying and manipulating data. See also *DHTML*, *DSC*, and *OWC*. DAP and OWC are technologies that Microsoft has deprecated in favor of SharePoint; Access 2007 doesn't support creating or editing DAP. See also *MOSS* and *WSS*.

Data Access Object see *DAO*.

Data access pages See *DAP*.

data binding Connecting two or more data-related objects, usually a data consumer to a data provider, to pass a Recordset or other data object between objects. Access 2007 has the capability to bind a variety of OLE DB data providers to OLE DB data consumers via ADO. Alternatively, Access 2007 uses DAO and ODBC for data binding. See also *ADO*, *data consumer*, *DAO*, *data object*, *data provider*, and *ODBC*.

data consumer An OLE DB term for an object that presents and/or manipulates data. All Access 2003 data-bound controls are capable of being OLE DB or ODBC data consumers.

data definition The process of describing databases and database objects such as tables, indexes, views, procedures, rules, default values, triggers, and other characteristics. SQL's Data Definition Language (DDL) defines the components of SQL-compliant databases.

data dictionary The result of the data definition process. Also used to describe a set of database system tables that contain the data definitions of database objects, often called *metadata*.

data element The value contained in a data cell, also called a *data item* or simply an *element*. A piece of data that describes a single property of a data entity, such as a person's first name, last name, age, sex, or hair color. In this case, the person is the data entity.

data entity A distinguishable set of objects that is the subject of a data table and usually has at least one unique data element. A data entity might be a person (unique Social Security number), an invoice (unique invoice number), or a vehicle (unique vehicle ID number, because license plates aren't necessarily unique across state lines).

data integrity The maintenance of rules that prevent inadvertent or intentional modifications to the content of a database that would compromise its accuracy or reliability. See also *domain integrity* and *referential integrity*.

data object   A component of a database. Data objects include tables, views, indexes, stored procedures, columns, rules, triggers, database diagrams, and defaults. See also *application object*.

data provider   An OLE DB term for an object that connects to a database or other source of persistent data and supplies data to a data consumer. The SQLOLEDB OLE DB data provider for SQL Server is an example of a native OLE DB provider. MSDASQL, the OLE DB data provider for ODBC, is a nonnative (indirect) data provider. The preferred native data provider for SQL Server 2005 [Express Edition] is the SQL Native Client, which supports both OLE DB and ODBC connections. See also *ODBC, OLE DB*, and *SQL Native Client*.

data shaping   The process of creating a hierarchical (also called *chaptered*) `Recordset` object using SHAPE syntax. See also *hierarchical Recordset* and *SHAPE statements*.

data sharing   The feature that allows more than one user to access information stored in a database from the same or a different application. Multiuser Access applications that use Jet databases employ data sharing.

data source   A database or other form of persistent (file) data storage. Data source commonly is used to describe an ODBC data source name (DSN). In Access 2003, a data source is a named OLE DB data provider or service provider.

Data Source Control   See *DSC*.

data source tier   A logical entity that represents a server running a client/server RDBMS, such as SQL Server, also called the *data services tier*. See also *client tier, middle tier*, and *three-tier*.

data type   The description of how the computer is to interpret a particular item of data. Data types are generally divided into three families: strings that usually have text or readable content, numeric data, and objects. The types of numeric data supported vary with the compiler or interpreter. Most programming languages support a user-defined record or structure data type that can contain multiple data types within it. Field data types, which define the data types of values in Jet and SQL Server database tables, are distinguished from VBA data types in this book.

database   A set of related data tables and other database objects, such as a data dictionary or database diagram, that are organized as a group.

database administrator   The individual(s) responsible for the administrative functions of client/server databases. The database administrator (DBA) has privileges (permissions) for all commands that might be executed by the RDBMS and is ordinarily responsible, directly or indirectly, for maintaining system security, including access by users to the RDBMS itself and performing backup and restoration functions.

database developer   A person responsible for the design and implementation of the table structure, user interface elements and programming code that make up a database application.

database device   A file in which databases and related information, such as transaction logs, are stored. Database devices usually have physical names (such as a filename) and a logical name (the parameter of the USE statement). In SQL Server 6.5 and earlier, database devices use the .dat file extension. SQL Server 7.0+ dispenses with database devices and stores databases and logs in conventional operating system files with .mdf and .ldf extensions, respectively.

database owner   The user who originally created a database. The database owner has control over all the objects in the database but can delegate control to other users. Access calls the database owner the creator. The database owner is identified by the prefix dbo in SQL Server.

date function   A function that provides date and time information or manipulates date and time values.

DCOM   An acronym for Distributed Common Object Model. Allows communication and manipulation of objects over a network connection. Windows NT 4.0 was the first Microsoft operating system to support DCOM (formerly called NetworkOLE). Microsoft's goal for its .NET technologies is to replace DCOM with XML web services and remoting. See also *COM, COM+*, and *XML web services*.

DDE   An abbreviation for dynamic data exchange. DDE is a method that early versions of Windows and OS/2 used to transfer data between different applications. Automation implemented by ActiveX components provides a more robust method for communication between applications or components of applications. DDE is obsolete.

deadlock   A condition that occurs when two users with a lock on one data item attempt to lock the other's data item. Most RDBMSs detect this condition, prevent its occurrence, and advise both users of the potential deadlock situation.

debug   The act of removing errors in the source code for an application.

declaration   A statement that creates a user-defined data type, names a variable, creates a symbolic constant, or registers the prototypes of functions incorporated within dynamic link libraries.

declarations section   A section of a VBA module reserved for statements containing declarations, such as **Public** or **Private** variables.

declarative referential integrity   See *DRI*.

declare   In text and not as a keyword, to create a user-defined data holder for a variable or constant. As a VBA keyword, to register a function contained in a dynamic link library in the declarations section of a module.

default   A value assigned or an option chosen when no value is specified by the user or assigned by a program statement.

default database   The logical name of the database assigned to a user when logging in to the database application.

dependent   A condition in which master data in a table (such as invoices) is associated with detail data in a subsidiary table (invoice items). In this case, invoice items are dependent on invoices.

design-master replica   The member of a Jet replica set that allows changes in the design of objects, such as tables. The design-master replica usually (but not necessarily) is the .mdb file that is updated by briefcase replicas of the file.

Design View   One of three modes of operation of Access, also called design time or Design mode. Design View lets you create and modify database objects and write VBA code. Layout View is new in Access 2007 and enables altering the layout of forms and reports with live data visible in controls. The other views or modes are Layout View and Run mode, also called runtime (when the application is executing). Run mode has object-specific views— Datasheet View, Form View, and Report View. See also *Layout View*.

DHTML   An abbreviation for Dynamic HTML, an extension of HTML 4.0 that permits client-side scripting to modify the appearance and/or content of a web page without requiring repeated roundtrips to the web server. Early web browsers implemented DHTML differently, so DHTML was suitable only for intranets on which all clients run a single browser. Most current browsers have very similar DHTML interpreters, which makes DHTML practical for Internet use.

disconnected Recordset   A Recordset object that is cached on the client and doesn't have an active connection to its source database. After editing the data in an updatable disconnected Recordset, reconnecting to the server updates the database. Use of disconnected Recordsets, which requires VBA code, minimizes the number of simultaneous connections to the database. Access 2007's ADP supports disconnected Recordsets. See also *Recordset*.

distributed database   A database, usually of the client/server type, that's located on more than one database server, often at widely separated locations. Synchronization of data contained in distributed databases is most commonly accomplished by the two-phase commit or replication methods. See also *replication* and *two-phase commit*.

Distributed Transaction Coordinator   See *DTC*.

DLL   An abbreviation for dynamic link library, a file containing a collection of Windows functions designed to perform a specific class of operations. Most DLLs carry the .dll extension, but some Windows DLLs, such as Gdi32.exe, use the .exe extension. Applications call (invoke) functions within DLLs, as necessary, to perform the desired operation.

docfile   The file format for creating persistent OLE objects, now called ActiveX documents. ADP uses docfiles to store application objects. Docfiles include file property values derived from the File menu's Properties command. See also *ActiveX documents* and *ADP*.

domain aggregate functions   A set of functions, identical to the SQL aggregate functions, such as Sum or Max that you can incorporate within Access queries. See also *aggregate functions*.

A

domain integrity   The process of ensuring that values added to fields of a table comply with a set of rules for reasonableness and other constraints. For example, domain integrity is violated if you enter a ship date value that's earlier than an order date. Access maintains domain integrity by field-level and table-level validation rules. See also *business rules*.

DRI   An abbreviation for declarative referential integrity, a set of SQL-92 SQL keywords, including CONSTRAINT, FOREIGN KEY, REFERENCES, and CASCADE, which, when included in the CREATE TABLE statement, enforce referential integrity rules for the table. Jet enforces referential integrity by an internal programming mechanism. SQL Server 7.0+ supports DRI; earlier versions used triggers to handle referential integrity violations. See also *referential integrity* and *trigger*.

DSC   An abbreviation for Data Source Control, one of the four Office Web Components (OWC). The DSC provides data binding for Data access pages. Office 2007 doesn't install OWC, which Microsoft has deprecated in favor of MOSS 2007's Excel Services. See also *DAP* and *OWC*.

DTC   An abbreviation for Microsoft's Distributed Transaction Coordinator, a feature of SQL Server required to support distributed transactions and Microsoft Transaction Server (MTS). See also *distributed database* and *MTS*.

dynamic data exchange   See *DDE*.

dynamic link library   See *DLL*.

dynaset   A set of rows and columns in your computer's memory that represent the values in an attached table, a table with a filter applied, or a query result set. You can update the values of the fields of the underlying table(s) by changing the values of the data cells of an updatable dynaset object. In Access 95+ and Jet 2+, Dynaset is a type of Recordset object. See also *Recordset*.

ECMAScript   The official name for Netscape's JavaScript, now that standardization of JavaScript is under the aegis of the European Computer Manufacturers Association (ECMA). Microsoft's version of ECMAScript is JScript.

empty   A condition of a VBA **Variant** variable that has been declared but hasn't been assigned a value. Empty is not the same as the **Null** value, nor is it equal to the empty or zero-length string (" "). Assigning an empty **Variant** to a **String** variable, however, results in a zero-length string.

enabled   The capability of a control object to respond to user actions such as a mouse click, expressed as the **True** or **False** value of the Enabled property of the control.

equi-join   A JOIN in which the values in the columns being joined are compared for equality. Only those rows with matching column values appear in the query result set. Access queries default to equi-joins—also called *inner joins*. See also *outer join* and *self-join*.

A

error trapping   A procedure by which errors generated during the execution of an application are rerouted to a designated group of code lines (called an *error handler*) that performs a predefined operation, such as ignoring the error. If errors aren't trapped in VBA, the standard modal message dialog with the text message for the error that occurred appears.

event   The occurrence of an action taken by the user and recognized by one of the object's event properties, such as VBA's `Click` and `DblClick` event handlers for most controls. Events are usually related to mouse movements and keyboard actions; however, events also can be generated by code with the Timer control object and during manipulation of database objects. ADO `Connection`, `Command`, and `Recordset` objects trigger many data-related events.

exclusive lock   A lock that prevents others from locking data items until the exclusive lock is cleared. Exclusive locks are placed on data items by update operations, such as SQL's `INSERT`, `UPDATE`, and `DELETE`. Jet and SQL Server 6.5 use page locking. SQL Server 6.5 provides row locking for `INSERT` operations, and SQL Server 7.0+ provides both `INSERT` and `UPDATE` row locking.

exponent   The second element of a number expressed in scientific notation, the power of 10 by which the first element, the mantissa, is multiplied to obtain the actual number. For +1.23E3, the exponent is 3, so you multiply 1.23 by 1,000 (10 to the third power) to obtain the result 1,230.

expression   A combination of variable names, values, functions, and operators that return a result, usually assigned to a variable name. *Result* = 1 + 1 is an expression that returns 2 to the variable named *Result*. *DiffVar* = *LargeVar-SmallVar* returns the difference between the two variables to *DiffVar*. Functions can be used in expressions, and the expression can return the value determined by the function to the same variable as that of the argument. `strVar` = `Mid$`(`strVar`, 2, 3) replaces the value of `strVar` with three of its characters, starting at the second character.

extended properties   A feature of SQL Server 2000 and 2005 that supports properties previously restricted to Access and Jet databases, such as lookup fields, subdatasheets, master-child table relationships, text for data validation messages, data entry masks, and column formatting.

facts table   The table of a multidimensional database, also called a *measures table*, that stores numeric data (metrics). The facts table is related to the dimension tables. See also *ADO MD*, *metrics*, *PivotTable Service*, *star schema*, and *snowflake schema*.

field   Synonym for a column that contains attribute values. Also, a single item of information in a record or row.

fifth normal form   The rule for relational databases requiring that a table that has been divided into multiple tables must be capable of being reconstructed to its exact original structure by one or more `JOIN` statements.

A

first normal form   The rule for relational databases which dictates that tables must be flat. Flat tables can contain only one data value set per row. Members of the data value set, called data cells, are contained in one column of the row and must have only one value.

flag   A variable, usually **Boolean** (**True/False**), that is used to determine the status of a particular condition within an application. The term *set* is often used to indicate turning a flag from **False** to **True**, and *reset* for the reverse.

flow control   In general usage, conditional expressions that control the execution sequence of instructions or statements in the source code of an application. **If…Then…End If** is a flow control statement.

foreign key   A column or combination of columns whose value matches the primary key in a record of another table allowing both records to be joined as related data. Foreign keys need not be unique for each record or row. See also *primary key*.

form   In this book, an Access Form object contains the control objects that appear on its surface and the code associated with the events, methods, and properties applicable to the form and its control objects.

form level   Variables that are declared in the Declarations section of an Access form. These variables are said to have form-level scope and aren't visible to procedures outside the Form object in which the variables are declared.

fourth normal form   The rule for relational databases which requires that only related data entities be included in a single table and that tables cannot contain data related to more than one data entity when many-to-one relationships exist among the entities.

front end   When used with database management systems, an application used to access and view database records, as well as add to, edit, or delete them. An Access front end consists of an .accdb, .accde, .mdb, or .mde file containing all application objects (queries, forms, reports, macros, and modules) or an .adp or .ade Access Data Project file that contains forms, reports, macros, and modules. See *back end*, *split database*, and *ADP*.

function   A subprogram called from within an expression in which a value is computed and returned to the program that called it through its name. Functions are classified as internal to the application language when their names are keywords. You can create your own user-defined functions in VBA by adding code between **Function** *FunctionName*…**End Function** statements.

function (SQL Server)   An SQL Server 2000+ feature that substitutes for views and stored procedures that return a single Recordset. Unlike with views, you can specify the name of a user-defined function as the data source for a **SELECT** query. Functions enable ADP to execute the equivalent of nested Jet queries (a query against a **SELECT** query's Recordset). Functions also can return numeric and character (scalar) values.

global   Pertaining to the program as a whole. Global variables and constants are accessible to, and global variables can be modified by, code at the form, module, and procedure level. VBA uses the reserved word **Public** to create or refer to global variables.

globally unique identifier See *GUID*.

group In reports, one or more records that are collected into a single category, usually for the purpose of totaling. Database security systems use the term *group* to identify a collection of database users with common permissions. See also *permissions*.

GUID An acronym for globally unique identifier, pronounced *goo-id*. GUIDs consist of 32 hexadecimal characters surrounded by French braces, as in {00000535-0000-0010-8000-00AA006D2EA4}, which the operating system creates from a combination of numeric values, including PC-specific values. COM makes extensive use of GUIDs to identify objects, interfaces, and other COM elements. Jet 4.0 and SQL Server 7.0+ have a GUID data type, primarily used to uniquely identify rows in a table for replication purposes.

handle An unsigned `Long` integer assigned by Windows to uniquely identify an instance (occurrence) of a module (application, `hModule`), task (`hTask`), window (`hWnd`), or device context (`hDC`) of a graphic object. Handles in 32-bit Windows applications are 32-bit unsigned long integers (dw, or double words). Also used to identify the sizing elements of control objects in Design mode. See also *sizing handle*.

hierarchical Recordset A Recordset that contains detail records in the form of a `Variant` array. Hierarchical Recordsets are more efficient than conventional Recordsets for displaying one-to-many query result sets, because cells of the one side aren't repeated. The PivotTable component is capable of displaying hierarchical Recordsets in Access's PivotTable view and DAP. See also *Cellset*, *CubeDef*, *MDX*, *OLAP*, and *PivotTable Service*.

host Any computer on a network running an Internet Protocol (IP). See also *IP* and *IP address*.

HTTP An abbreviation for Hypertext Transport Protocol, the transport protocol used by the World Wide Web and private intranets.

identifier A synonym for name or symbol, usually applied to variable and constant names.

index For arrays, the position of the particular element with respect to others, usually beginning with 0 as the first element. In the context of database files or tables, index refers to a lookup table, usually in the form of a file or component of a file, that relates the value of a field in the indexed file to its record or page number and location in the page (if pages are used).

InfoPath A new Microsoft form design and development tool—codenamed XDocs during its early beta period—for displaying and manipulating XML data. InfoPath uses XML schemas to validate data entry and XSLT to create form-based views of the data. The primary data sources for InfoPath forms are XML document files and XML web services. Alternatively, InfoPath can use ADO to connect to Jet and SQL Server databases directly. The official name of InfoPath 2.0 is Microsoft Office InfoPath 2007. Access 2007 offers InfoPath forms as an option for Outlook-based email data collection. See also *ADP*, *ADO*, *XML Schema*, *XML web services*, and *XSLT*.

A

initialize In programming, setting all variables to their default values and resetting the point of execution to the first executable line of code. Initialization is accomplished automatically in VBA when you start an application.

inner query Synonym for subquery. See also *subquery*.

in-process A term applied to Automation servers, also called *ActiveX DLLs*, that operate within the same process space (memory allocation) of the Automation client. In-process servers commonly are called *InProc servers*.

instance (SQL Server) A named SQL Server running on a Windows 2000+ server. The default instance is the server's computer name. All versions of SQL Server 2000 except MSDE and the Personal Edition permit running multiple, independent instances of SQL Server on a single server. Instances other than the default instance are called *named instances*.

integer A whole number. In most programming languages, an integer is a data type that occupies two bytes (16 bits). Integers can have signs (as in the VBA **Integer** data type), taking on values from –32,768 to +32,767, or be unsigned. In the latter case, integers can represent numbers up to 65,535. SQL Server's integer data type is a 32-bit bit value, which corresponds to VBA's **Long** data type.

intersection The group of data elements included in both tables that participate in a JOIN operation.

intranet A private network that uses Internet protocols and common Internet applications (such as web browsers) to emulate the public Internet. Intranets on LANs and high-speed WANs provide increased privacy and improved performance compared with today's Internet.

invoke To cause execution of a block of code, particularly a procedure or subprocedure. Invoke also indicates application of a method to an object.

IP An abbreviation for Internet Protocol, the basic network transmission protocol of the Internet.

IP address The 32-bit hexadecimal address of a host, gateway, or router on an IP network. For convenience, IP addresses are specified as the decimal value of the four address bytes, separated by periods, as in 124.33.15.1. An address is classified as type A, B, or C, depending on the subnet mask applied. See also *subnet mask*.

JDBC An abbreviation for Java Database Connector, despite Sun Microsystems' insistence that JDBC "doesn't stand for anything." JDBC is Java's purportedly platform-agnostic version of ODBC, which it closely resembles.

Jet Microsoft's name for the database engine native to Access and Visual Basic. The name *Jet* came from the acronym for Joint Engine Technology, an early predecessor of Jet 4.0, which was used by Access 2003. Access 2007 uses its own version of Jet and thus has abandoned references to Jet in documentation and online help.

Jet SQL   The dialect of ANSI SQL used by the Data Access Object and by all versions of Microsoft Access. For the most part, Access SQL complies with ANSI SQL-92. Jet SQL offers additional features, such as the capability to include user-defined functions within queries. The politically correct name for Access 2007 is *Access SQL*. See also *Transact-SQL*.

join   A basic operation, initiated by the SQL JOIN statement, that links the rows or records of two or more tables by one or more columns in each table. See also *equi-join, outer join, self-join, primary key*, and *foreign key*.

key or key field   A field that identifies a record by its value, also called a *primary key* [field], or is used to join a record to a related record, called a foreign key [field]. Access automatically creates an index on primary key fields, which must consist of unique values. See also *primary key* and *foreign key*.

key value   A value of a key field included in an index.

keyword   A word that has specific meaning to the interpreter or compiler in use and causes predefined events to occur when encountered in source code. Keywords and reserved words are not exactly the same. You can use keywords as variable, procedure, or function names, but you can't use reserved words as variable or constant names. Using keywords for this purpose, however, isn't a good programming practice.

label   In VBA programming, a name given to a target line in the source code at which execution results on the prior execution of a **GoTo** *LabelName* instruction. A label also is an Access control object that displays, but can't update, character values.

LAN   An acronym for local area network, a system comprising multiple computers that are physically interconnected through network adapter cards and cabling. LANs allow one computer to share specified resources, such as disk drives, printers, and modems, with other computers on the LAN.

Layout View—A new view in Access 2007 that enables altering the layout of forms and reports with live data visible in controls. The presence of typical data in controls makes it easier to specify the correct size of text box, combo box, image, and other data-bound controls without the need for repeated cycling between Run mode and Design View. See *Design View*.

leaf level   The lowest level of an index. Indexes derive the names of their elements from the objects found on trees, such as trunks, limbs, and leaves.

library   A collection of functions, compiled as a group and accessible to applications by calling the function name and any required arguments. DLLs are one type of library; those used by compilers to provide built-in functions are another type.

library database   An Access database that's automatically attached to Access when you launch it. Access library databases usually have the extension .accda (formerly .mda); compiled libraries, which hide the original source code, use the extension .accde (formerly .mde). Attachment of library databases to Access is controlled by Registry entries.

linked table   A table that's not stored in the currently open Access database (native table), but which you can manipulate as though it were a native table. Linked tables were called *attached tables* in Access 1.x and 2.0 and Jet 2.0.

livelock   A request for an exclusive lock on a data item that's repeatedly denied because of shared locks imposed by other users.

local   The scope of a variable declared within a procedure, rather than at the form, module, or global level. Local variables are visible (defined) only within the procedure in which they were declared. VBA uses the prefix `Private` to define functions, subprocedures, and variables of local scope.

local area network   See *LAN*.

lock   A restriction of access to a table, portion of a table, or data item imposed to maintain data integrity of a database. Locks can be shared, in which case more than one user can access the locked element(s), or exclusive, in which the user with the exclusive lock prevents other users from creating simultaneous shared or exclusive locks on the element(s). Jet classifies locks as optimistic (a lock applied only when physically changing table data) and pessimistic (a lock applied for the duration of the user's editing operation). Access 2007 uses page locks (8KB of the .accdb, formerly .mdb, file), which can lock several adjacent records unless you specify row locking in the Advanced Page of the Access Options dialog; earlier versions of Access used 2KB pages. Some RDBMSs provide row locks that lock only a single record. SQL Server 6.5 uses row locking for `INSERT` operations and page locking for `UPDATE` and `DELETE` operations. SQL Server 7.0+ offers row locking for all three operations.

logical   A synonym for Boolean, a data type that can have a true or false value only. Logical is also used to define a class of operators whose result is only True or False. VBA includes a `Boolean` data type.

loop   A compound program flow-control structure that causes statements contained between the instructions that designate the beginning and end of the structure to be repeatedly executed until a given condition is satisfied. When the condition is satisfied, program execution continues at the source code line after the loop termination statement.

mantissa   The first element of a number expressed in scientific notation that's multiplied by the power of 10 given in the exponent to obtain the actual number. For +1.23E3, the exponent is 3, so you multiply the mantissa, 1.23, by 1,000 (10 to the third power) to obtain the result: 1,230.

master database   A database that controls user access to other databases, usually in a client/server system.

master table   A table containing data on which detail data in another table depends. Master tables have a primary key that's matched to a foreign key in a detail table and often have a one-to-many relationship with detail tables. Master tables usually are called *base tables*.

MDAC   An abbreviation for Microsoft Data Access Components, a collection of the files required to implement Microsoft's Universal Data Access strategy. MDAC includes ActiveX Data Objects (ADO), Remote Data Services (RDS), OLE DB, and ODBC. Windows XP SP2, 2003 SP1, and Vista install MDAC version 2.8 SP1, plus support for Jet databases. See also *ADO, ODBC, OLE DB*, and *Universal Data Access*.

MDX   An acronym for Multidimensional Expressions, MDX is an SQL-like language for creating and manipulating multidimensional data (cubes) created by Microsoft SQL Server Analytical Services. See also *ADO MD, Cellset, CubeDef, OLAP*, and *PivotTable Service*.

Memo   An Access or Jet field data type that can store text with a length of up to about 64,000 bytes. (The length of Jet's Text field data type is limited to 255 bytes.)

metadata   Data that describes the structure, organization, and/or location of data. Metadata commonly is called "data about data."

method   One characteristic of an object and a classification of keywords in VBA. Methods are the procedures that apply to an Access object. Methods that apply to a class of objects are inherited by other objects of the same class.

metrics   Numeric data, also called *measures*, contained within a facts table of a multidimensional database. See also *facts table*.

Microsoft Data Engine   The desktop version of SQL Server 7.0 included with Access 2000, often called MSDE 1.0. SQL Server 2005 Express Edition (SSX) supersedes MSDE 1.0 and 2000. See *MSDE* and *SSX*.

Microsoft Office SharePoint Services   See *MOSS*.

Microsoft SQL Server 2005 Express Edition   See *SSX*.

Microsoft SQL Server Desktop Edition   See *MSDE*.

Microsoft Transaction Server   See *MTS*.

middle tier   A logical entity that connects a data source tier to a client tier and implements business rules or performs other data-related services. See also *business rules, client tier, data source tier*, and *three-tier*.

MIME   An acronym for Multipurpose Internet Mail Extensions, an Internet standard that lets binary data be published and read on the Internet or intranets. The header of a file containing binary data exposes the MIME type of the data. Recordsets transported by RDS use a special MIME data type called the Advanced Data TableGram protocol (ADTG). See also *ADTG*.

mission critical   A cliché used in software and hardware advertising to describe the need to use the promoted product if you want to create a reliable database system.

MOD   An acronym for Microsoft Office Developer Edition, which includes a royalty-free license to distribute Msaccess.exe for runtime use, the runtime version of Microsoft Chart, additional ActiveX controls, and other distributable components of Access 2007. MOD also includes the Setup Wizard, which you use to create images of the distribution disks for your application. Microsoft apparently has decided not to release MOD 2003. Instead, Microsoft committed to provide an Office 2007 add-on product for distributing runtime Access 2007 applications that will ship "shortly after the release of Microsoft Office System 2007."

modal   A window or dialog that must be closed before users can take further action within the application. *Modal dialog* is a standard Access form style.

modeless   A window or dialog that users can close or minimize without taking any other action; the opposite of modal.

module   A block of code, consisting of one or more procedures, for which the source code is stored in a single location (a form or report class module, or public `Module` object in Access). In a compiled language, a code module is compiled to a single object file.

module level   Variables and constants that are declared in the Declarations section of a VBA module, such as an Access `Module` object. These variables have module-level scope and are visible (defined) to all procedures contained within the module, unless declared **Public**, in which case the variables are visible to all procedures.

MOSS   The abbreviation for Microsoft Office SharePoint Services (or Servers) 2007, which replaces Microsoft SharePoint Portal Server (SPS). MOSS builds on Windows SharePoint Services (WSS) 3.0 technology to provide the following (quoting Microsoft): "features enhancements and new functionality in six major areas: Individual Impact, Enterprise Content Lifecycle, Collaboration, Knowledge Discovery and Insight, Information Worker Solutions, and Fundamentals. New technologies to support these areas include the Business Data Catalog, Document Management functionality, Web Content Management functionality, Excel Services, Infopath Forms Services, and enhancements to Search, User Profiles, Audience Targeting, and Single Sign-on." See also *WSS*.

MSDE   An acronym for Microsoft [SQL Server] Desktop Edition, a special version of Microsoft SQL Server 2000 that was included with Office 2003 but not installed by default. SQL Server 2005 Express Edition (SSX) supersedes MSDE 2000, but isn't included with the Microsoft Office 2007 setup files. ADP uses SSX, MSDE, or other SQL Server versions as the only data source; DAP offers the option of connecting to MSDE. See also *ADP*, *DAP*, *SSMSX*, and *SSX*.

MSMQ   An acronym for Microsoft Message Queue Server, a middle-tier component (similar to Microsoft Transaction Server) that uses messaging techniques to permit execution of transactions over unreliable network connections. See also *middle tier*.

MTS   An acronym for Microsoft Transaction Server, a component-based transaction monitor (TM) and object request broker (ORB) for developing, deploying, and managing the middle tier of component-based applications. Access 2003 applications can connect to MTS objects using VBA code. MTS is an integral component of COM+. See also *COM+*, *middle tier*, *ORB*, *three-tier*, and *TM*.

Multidimensional Expressions   See *MDX*.

NEW **multiple-items form**   An Access 2007 form template that auto-generates an access form from a table or query and displays a row for each record in the table or query. See also *split form*.

multiuser   Concurrent use of a single computer by more than one user, usually by way of remote terminals or an application that multiple persons can use simultaneously. UNIX is inherently a multiuser operating system. Jet uses the term *multiuser* to refer to split database applications that share a common back-end .mdb file on a network file server. Each user ordinarily has a local copy of the front end. See *back end*, *front end*, and *split database*.

NEW **Multivalued field**   See *MVF*.

NEW **MVF**   An abbreviation for multivalued field, which is a new Access 2007 field data type that emulates a many-to-many relationship with a hidden relation table. MVFs support lookup fields with multiple values and are compatible with a similar SharePoint Lookup column data type.

Named Pipes   A method of interprocess communication, originally developed for OS/2, that provides a secure channel for network communication. Named Pipes is one of the methods of connecting to an SQL Server database, but TCP/IP connections are more common.

natural join   An SQL `JOIN` operation in which the values of the columns engaged in the join are compared, with all columns of each table in the join that don't duplicate other columns being included in the result. Same as an equi-join except that the joined columns aren't duplicated in the result. See also *equi-join*.

nested query   An SQL `SELECT` statement that contains subqueries. See also *subquery*. An Access query that uses one or more queries—rather than tables—as its data source is called a nested query also.

newline pair   A combination of a carriage return, the Enter key (CR or `Chr(13)`), and line feed (LF or `Chr(10)`) used to terminate a line of text onscreen or within a text file. Other characters or combinations can be substituted for the CR/LF pair to indicate the type of newline character (soft, hard, deletable, and so on). The VBA newline constant is `vbCrLf`.

nonclustered index   An index that stores key values and pointers to data based on these values. In this case, the leaf level points to data pages rather than to the data itself, as is the case for a clustered index. Equivalent to `SET INDEX TO field_name` in xBase. See also *clustered index*.

normal forms   A set of five rules (the first three originally defined by Dr. E. F. Cobb) used to design relational databases. Five normal forms are generally accepted in the creation of relational databases. See also *first normal form*, *second normal form*, *third normal form*, *fourth normal form*, and *fifth normal form*.

normalization   Creation of a database according to the five generally accepted rules of normal forms. See also *normal forms*.

not-equal join   A JOIN statement that specifies that the columns engaged in the join don't equal one another. In Access, you must specify a not-equal join by using the SQL WHERE `field1 <> field2` clause.

null   A variable of no value or of unknown value. The default values—0 for numeric variables and an empty string ("") for string variables—aren't the same as the **Null** value. The NULL value in SQL statements specifies a data cell with no value assigned to the cell.

object   In programming, elements that combine data (properties) and behavior (methods) in a single container of code are called objects. Objects inherit their properties and methods from the classes above them in the hierarchy and can modify the properties and methods to suit their own purposes. The code container can be part of the language itself, or you can define your own objects in source code.

object library   A file with the extension .olb that contains information on the objects, properties, and methods exposed by an .exe or .dll file of the same filename that supports Automation. See also *type library*.

object permissions   Permissions granted by the database administrator for others to view and modify the values of database objects, including data in tables.

object request broker   See *ORB*.

ODBC   An abbreviation for the Microsoft Open Database Connectivity API, a set of functions that provide access to client/server RDBMSs, desktop database files, text files, and Excel worksheet files through ODBC drivers. ODBC most commonly is used to connect to client/server databases, such as Microsoft SQL Server, Sybase, IBM DB2/Informix, and Oracle. Microsoft intends for OLE DB to replace ODBC and won't provide significant enhancements for ODBC. The SQL Native Client data provider provides OLE DB and ODBC support for SQL Server 2005 (Express edition). See *ADO*, *OLE DB*, and *SQL Native Client*.

offset   The number of bytes from a reference point, usually the beginning of a file, to the particular byte of interest. The first byte in a file, when offset is used to specify location, is always 0.

Office Web Components   See *OWC*.

OLAP An acronym for *online analytical processing*, a technology that operates on nonrelational, multidimensional databases (data cubes). Microsoft SQL Server Analytical Services, a component of SQL Server 2000, enables the creation, manipulation, and distribution of multidimensional data. Analytical Services were called OLAP Services in SQL Server 7.0. See also *ADO MD*, *PivotTable Service*, *snowflake schema*, and *star schema*.

OLE DB A Microsoft framework for providing a uniform interface to data from various sources, including text files and mainframe databases. OLE DB replaces ODBC as a means of database access, but includes an ODBC provider that takes the place of the ODBC driver manager. ADO is an Automation wrapper for OLE DB. See also *ADO* and *ODBC*.

OLTP An abbreviation for *online transaction processing*. OLTP most commonly refers to database applications that update multiple tables, such as order entry and reservation systems, which use transaction processing to ensure data integrity. See also *transaction*.

online analytical processing See *OLAP*.

operand One variable or constant on which an operator acts. In 1 + 2 = 3, 1 and 2 are operands, + and = are the operators. See also *operator*.

operator A keyword or reserved symbol that, in its unary form, acts on a single variable, or otherwise acts on two variables, to give a result. Operators can be of the conventional mathematic types, such as + (add), – (subtract), / (divide), and * (multiply), as well as logical, such as **And** and **Not**. The unary minus (-), when applied to a single variable in a statement such as intVar = -intVar, inverts the sign of intVar from - to + or from + to -.

optimistic locking A method of locking a record or page of a table that makes the assumption that the probability of other users locking the same record or page is low. With optimistic locking, the record or page is locked only when the data is updated, not during the editing process (LockType property set to adLockOptimistic). See also *pessimistic locking*.

ORB An acronym for *object request broker*, a server-based application that provides a means for client applications to locate and instantiate middle-tier objects in three-tier applications. See also *middle tier*, *MTS*, and *three-tier*.

outer join An SQL JOIN operation in which all rows of the joined tables are returned, whether or not a match is made between columns. SQL database managers that don't support the OUTER JOIN reserved words use the *= (LEFT JOIN) operator to return all the rows in the first table and the =* (RIGHT JOIN) to return all the rows in the second table.

outer query A synonym for the primary query in a statement that includes a subquery. See also *subquery*.

A

OWC   The abbreviation for Microsoft Office Web Components, which consist of the following four ActiveX Controls: Data Source (DSC), PivotChart, PivotTable, and Spreadsheet. The DSC is used only with DAP; the remaining three controls can be embedded in forms. Office 2003 installs OWC versions 10 and 11; upgrading ADP created in Access 2000 (OWC 9.0) and 2002 (OWC 10.0) changes the version to 11.0. OWC has special licensing restrictions for users of Access 2003 runtime applications who don't have Office 2003 licenses. Office 2007 doesn't install OWC, which Microsoft has deprecated in favor of MOSS 2007's Excel Services. See also *DAP, DSC, PivotChart, PivotTable,* and *Spreadsheet Control.*

page   In tables of client/server RDBMSs, such as Microsoft SQL Server 7.0+, Access, and Jet 3.6+ databases, a page is an 8KB block that contains records of tables. Client/server and Jet databases lock pages, whereas other desktop databases usually lock individual records. Most RDBMSs require page locking when variable-length records are used in tables.

parameter   The equivalent of an argument, but associated with the procedure that receives the value of an argument from the calling function. The terms *parameter* and *argument,* however, are often used interchangeably. An ADO `Parameter` object provides or returns a value to or from a query or a stored procedure.

permissions   Authority given by the system administrator, database administrator, or database owner to perform operations on a network or on data objects in a database. Permissions also are called *user rights.*

persistent   An object that's stored in the form of a file or an element of a file, rather than only in memory. Jet `Table` and `QueryDef` objects are persistent because they're stored in .mdb files. `Recordset` objects, on the other hand, usually are stored in memory. Such objects are called *temporal* or *impersistent* objects. ADO 2.x lets you persist `Recordset` objects as files.

pessimistic locking   A method of locking a record or page of a table that makes the assumption that the probability of other users locking the same record or page is high. With pessimistic locking, the record or page is locked during the editing and updating process (`LockType` property set to `adLockPessimistic`). See also *optimistic locking.*

PivotChart   An ActiveX Control that displays charts or graphs derived from data displayed by a PivotTable control. Access 2003 adds a new PivotChart view for tables, queries, and forms. The PivotChart control is a member of the Office Web Components (OWC). Office 2007 doesn't install OWC, which Microsoft has deprecated in favor of MOSS 2007's Excel Services. See also *OWC* and *MOSS.*

PivotTable   An ActiveX Control that displays data in spreadsheet format in which the user can expand or contract the level of detail displayed and interchange the axes of the data presentation. Access 2007 offers a PivotTable view of tables, queries, and forms that doesn't depend on the PivotTable Control. The PivotTable Control is a member of the Office Web Components (OWC). Office 2007 doesn't install OWC, which Microsoft has deprecated in favor of MOSS 2007's Excel Services. See also *OWC* and *MOSS.*

A

PivotTable Service   A Microsoft-trademarked desktop OLAP implementation that used ADO MD to operate on persistent (file-based) multidimensional data cubes created by a subset of Microsoft SQL Server Analytical Services. The PivotTable service delivers hierarchical Recordsets to PivotTables. See also *ADO MD*, *Cellset*, *CubeDef*, *hierarchical Recordsets*, and *OLAP*.

point   In typography, the unit of measurement of the vertical dimension of a font, about 1/72 of an inch. The point is also a unit of measurement in Windows, where it represents exactly 1/72 of a logical inch, or 20 twips. Unless otherwise specified, all distance measurements in VBA are in twips.

precedence   The sequence of execution of operators in statements that contain more than one operator.

primary key   The column or columns whose individual or combined values (in the case of a composite primary key) uniquely identify a row in a table.

procedure   A self-contained collection of source code statements, executable as an entity. All VBA procedures begin with the reserved word `Sub` or `Function` (which can be preceded by the `Public`, `Private`, `Static`, or `Property` reserved words) and terminate with `End Sub` or `End Function`.

programmable object   An object exposed by an Automation server with a set of properties and methods applicable to the object. The application programming language of an Automation client application can manipulate the exposed object.

projection   A projection identifies the desired subset of the columns contained in a table. You create a projection with a query that defines the fields of the table you want to display but without criteria that limit the records that are displayed.

property   One of two principal characteristics of objects (the other is the method). Properties define the manifestation of the object—for example, its appearance. Properties might be defined for an object or for the class of objects to which the particular object belongs, in which case they are said to be *inherited*.

proxy   An object that supplies parameter marshaling and communication methods required by a client to instantiate an Automation component running in another execution environment, such as on a server. The proxy is located on the client PC and communicates with a corresponding stub on the server. The Office Web Services Toolkit's Web Service Reference tool automatically creates client proxies for XML web services. See also *three-tier*, *WSR*, and *XML web services*.

qualification   A search condition that data values must meet to be included in the result of the search.

qualified   To precede the name of a database object with the name of the database and the object's owner, or to precede the name of a file with its drive designator and the path to the directory in which the file is stored. The terms *well-qualified path* and *well-formed path* to a file appear often in documentation.

A

query   A request to retrieve data from a database with the SQL SELECT instruction (select query) or to modify data in the database, called an *action query* by Access.

QueryDef   A persistent Access or Jet object that stores the Access or Jet SQL statements that define a query. QueryDef objects are optimized, when applicable, by the Access or Jet database engine's query optimizer and stored in a special format in the .accdb (formerly .mdb) file.

RDBMS   An abbreviation for *relational database management system*. An RDBMS is an application that can create, organize, and edit databases; display data through user-selected views; and, in some cases, print formatted reports. Most RDBMSs include at least a macro language, and most provide a system programming language. Access, dBASE, Paradox, and FoxPro are desktop RDBMSs. SQL Server and Oracle are typical client/server RDBMSs.

record   A single element of a relational database table that contains a cell for each field defined for the table. A record is the logical equivalent of a row of a spreadsheet. This book uses *record* when referring to table data and *row* for query result sets.

Recordset   A temporary local image of a table or a query result set stored in the PC's memory or virtual memory. Recordset objects are the primary means for manipulating data with VBA.

reference   In VBA, the incorporation of pointers to specific sets of programmable objects exposed by Automation servers in a type library and manipulated by VBA code in the Automation client. You create a VBA reference to a set of objects exposed by an Automation component in the References dialog that's accessible by choosing Tools, References when a code module is the active Access object. After you declare a reference to the set of objects, the VBA interpreter checks the syntax of your code against the syntax specified for the referenced object. You also can use predefined intrinsic constants for the referenced objects in your VBA code. See also *type library*.

referential integrity   Rules governing the relationships between primary keys and foreign keys of tables within a relational database that determine data consistency. Referential integrity requires the values of every foreign key in every table be matched by the value of a primary key in another table. Jet 2+ includes features for maintaining referential integrity, such as cascading updates and cascading deletions. SQL Server 7.0+ uses triggers or SQL's declarative referential integrity (DRI) keywords to maintain referential integrity. See also *DRI* and *trigger*.

refresh   To redisplay records in Access's Datasheet views or in a form or report so as to reflect changes others in a multiuser environment have made to the records.

Registry   A database that contains information required for the operation of 32-bit Windows. The Registry also includes user information, such as user IDs, encrypted passwords, and permissions. Windows XP/2003+/Vista include Regedit.exe for editing the Registry. ActiveX components add entries to the Registry to specify the location of their .exe files. Automation servers add Registry entries for each object they expose.

relation Synonym for a table or a data table in an RDBMS.

relational database See *RDBMS*.

relational operators Operators such as >, <, <>, and = that compare the values of two operands and return **True** or **False** depending on the values compared. They are sometimes called *comparison operators*.

replication The process of duplicating database objects (usually tables) in more than one location, including a method of periodically rationalizing (synchronizing) updates to the objects. Database replication is an alternative to the two-phase commit process. Microsoft SQL Server 7.0+ supports replication of databases across multiple Windows 2000+ servers. See also *two-phase commit*.

ReportML Microsoft's XML representation of the design of Access forms and reports that is used as an intermediary when saving Access 2007 forms and reports as XML files.

reserved word A word that's reserved for specific use by the programming language. You can't assign a reserved word as the name of a constant, variable, function, or subprocedure. Although the terms *reserved word* and *keyword* often are used interchangeably, they don't describe an identical set of words. VBA reserved words are set in **bold monospace type** in this book. See also *keyword*.

restriction A query statement that defines a subset of the rows of a table based on the value of one or more of its columns. A restriction more commonly is called a *criterion*.

Ribbon An Office 2007 user interface (UI) component that substitutes for menus a tabbed region with related command buttons above the application's window. Groups contain related command buttons. Whether users will find the Ribbon UI an improvement over menus remains to be seen.

RibbonX The application programming interface (API) for Office 2007 ribbons, which uses XML files to define ribbons, groups, and buttons and the action performed when the user clicks a button.

rollback In transaction processing, the cancellation of a proposed transaction that modifies one or more tables and undoes changes, if any, made by the transaction before a COMMIT or COMMIT TRANSACTION SQL statement.

routine A synonym for *procedure*.

row A set of related columns that describe a specific data entity. Row is a synonym for record. This book uses *row* when referring to query result sets and *record* for data in tables.

row aggregation functions See *aggregate functions*.

rowset An OLE DB term for a set of rows returned by a fetch with a block cursor. ADO creates Recordsets from rowsets.

rule A specification that determines the data type and data value that can be entered in a column of a table. Rules are classified as validation rules and business rules. See also *business rules*.

Run mode The mode when Access 2007 is executing your application. Run mode is called *runtime* by Microsoft; however, the term *runtime* normally is used to describe the distributable version of Access (*runtime Access*) applications.

scope In programming, the extent of visibility (definition) of a variable. VBA has the following types of scope: global (**Public**, visible to all objects and procedures in the application), form/report (**Private**, visible to all objects and procedures within a single form or report), module (visible to all procedures in a single module file), and local (**Dim**, visible only within the procedure in which declared). The scope of a variable depends on where it's declared. See also *form level*, *global*, *local*, and *module level*.

second normal form The rule for relational databases requiring that columns that aren't key fields each be related to the key field—that is, a row might not contain values in data cells that don't pertain to the value of the key field. In an invoice item table, for instance, the columns of each row must pertain solely to the value of the invoice number key field.

seek To locate a specific byte, record, or chunk within a disk file. The Seek method of Access VBA can be used only with DAO Recordset objects of the column(s) type and requires that the table be indexed. ADO 2.1+ has a Seek method; previous versions of ADO didn't offer Seek.

select list The list of column names, separated by commas, that specify the columns to be included in the result of a SELECT statement.

self-join An SQL JOIN operation used to compare values within the columns of one table. Self-joins join a table with itself, requiring that the table be assigned two different names, one of which must be an alias.

separator A reserved symbol used to distinguish one item from another, as exemplified by the use of the exclamation point (!, bang character) in Access to separate the name of an object class from a specific object of the class, and an object contained within a specified object. The period separator (., dot) separates the names of objects and their methods or properties.

sequential access file A file in which one record follows another in the sequence applicable to the application. Text files, for the most part, are sequential.

service provider An OLE DB term for an object that is both a data consumer and a data provider to another data consumer. OLE DB service providers include query engines and other intermediaries.

session In DAO, an instance of the Jet database engine for a single user represented by the `Workspace` object. You can establish multiple sessions that become members of the `Workspaces` collection. With ADO, a `Connection` object represents a session. In RDBMS terminology, a session is the period between the time that a user opens a connection to a database and the time that the connection to the database is closed.

SHAPE statements An SQL-like language for defining parent-child relationships within hierarchical Recordsets. See also *hierarchical Recordsets*.

shared lock A lock created by read-only operations that doesn't allow the user who creates the shared lock to modify the data. Other users can place shared locks on data so they can read it, but none can apply an exclusive lock on the data while any shared locks are in effect.

SID An acronym for security ID, a numeric value that identifies a logged-in user who has been authenticated by Windows NT or a user group. Access workgroup files use SIDs to authenticate users of secured Jet databases.

single-stepping A debugging process by which the source code is executed one line at a time to allow you to inspect the value of variables, find infinite loops, or remove other types of bugs.

sizing handle The small rectangles on the perimeter of control objects that appear on the surface of the form or report in Design mode when the object is selected. You drag the handles of the rectangles to shrink or enlarge the size of control objects.

snowflake schema An alternative to the star schema for multidimensional data. Snowflake schema store dimension definitions in a set of hierarchical tables, rather than the star schema's individual tables. See also *ADO MD*, *facts table*, *PivotTable Service*, and *star schema*.

 SOAP Originally an acronym for Simple Object Access Protocol. SOAP is an XML-based messaging protocol for exchanging information between applications, usually over a network. SOAP is one of the primary enablers of XML web services. SOAP has three parts: an envelope that describes and incorporates the message's content; rules for encoding and decoding the content; and methods for processing XML messages or to represent remote procedure calls (RPCs) and responses to RPCs. Office 2007 members and SQL Server 2005 support SOAP 1.2, which is a W3C standard. The May 8, 2000, SOAP 1.1 note is at http://www.w3.org/TR/2000/NOTE-SOAP-20000508/. The latest version of the W3C's SOAP 1.2 standard is at http://www.w3.org/TR/soap12-part0/. See also *WSDL* and *XML web services*.

SOAP toolkit A set of components or libraries designed to simplify the process of encoding conventional data or objects as SOAP messages. The Microsoft SOAP Toolkit 3.0 enables writing VBA code that consumes XML web services. SOAP Toolkit 3.0 also provides the Internet Services API (ISAPI) extensions needed to host (provide) web services and filters to listen for incoming SOAP messages. See also *VSTO* and *XML web services*.

A

split database   An Access database in which the tables (back end) and application objects (front end) are contained in separate files, which are usually created by running Access's Database Splitter utility. See *back end* and *front end*.

NEW Split Form   An Access 2007 standard form template that horizontally divides a form based on a table or query into two sections. The default configuration is a Datasheet View in the top section and a Details View in the bottom section of the record selected in Datasheet View. See also *multiple-items form*.

Spreadsheet Control   An ActiveX Control that emulates an Excel worksheet. The Office 2003 (last) version of the control can be bound to data. The Spreadsheet Control is one of the Office Web Components (OWC). Office 2007 doesn't install OWC, which Microsoft has deprecated in favor of MOSS 2007 Excel Services. See also *OWC* and *MOSS*.

SQL   An acronym, pronounced *S-Q-L*, for Structured Query Language, a language developed by IBM Corporation for processing data contained in mainframe computer databases. (Sequel is the name of a language, similar to SQL, developed by IBM but no longer in use.) SQL has now been institutionalized by the creation of an ANSI standard for the language.

SQL aggregate functions   See *aggregate functions*.

NEW SQL Native Client   The preferred OLE DB and ODBC data provider for all SQL Server 2005 editions because it supports new SQL Server 2005 data types, such as `xml`, `varchar(max)`, `nvarchar(max)`, and `varbinary(max)`. SQL Native Client is one of the ODBC driver choices for linking SQL Server 2005 tables to Access databases—use it.

NEW SQL Server 2005 Express Edition   See *SSX*.

NEW SQL Server Management Studio Express   See *SSMSX*.

NEW SSMSX   The abbreviation for SQL Server Management Studio Express, a management tool for SSX. SSMSX is a stripped-down version of SQL Server Management Studio (SSMS) that's a component of SQL Server 2005 Developer, Workgroup, Standard, and Enterprise editions. Microsoft didn't provide management tools for MSDE 1.0 and 2000. See *MSDE* and *SSX*.

NEW SSX   The most common abbreviation for SQL Server 2005 Express Edition, the freely distributable version of SQL Server 2005. Unlike the earlier MSDE 1.0 and MSDE 2000 versions, SSX doesn't have a limit of five concurrent queries (called a *throttle*, but better described as a "choke.") See also *MSDE* and *SSMSX*.

star schema   The most common schema (database design) for multidimensional data. Multiple base tables storing dimension definitions form the points of a star. The body of the star is the dependent facts table. See also *ADO MD*, *facts table*, *PivotTable Service*, and *snowflake schema*.

statement   A syntactically acceptable (to the interpreter or compiler of the chosen language) combination of instructions or keywords and symbols, constants, and variables. A VBA statement must appear on a single line or use the line-continuation pair (a space followed by an underscore) to permit multiple-line statements.

A

static   When referring to a variable, *static* indicates a variable that retains its last value until another is assigned, even though the procedure in which it is defined has completed execution. All global variables are static. VBA variables declared as **Static** are similar to global variables, but their visibility is limited to their declared scope. The term is also used to distinguish between statically linked (conventional) executable files and those that use DLLs.

stored procedure   A set of SQL statements (and with those RDBMSs that support them, flow-control statements) that are stored under a procedure name so that the statements can be executed as a group by the database server.

string   A data type used to contain textual material, such as alphabetic characters and punctuation symbols. Numbers can be included in or constitute the value of string variables, but can't be manipulated by mathematical operators.

structure   Two or more keywords used together to create an instruction, which is usually conditional in nature. In C, C#, and C++ programming, a structure is a user-defined data type. See also *compound*.

Structured Query Language   See *SQL*.

stub   A procedure or user-defined function that, in VBA, consists only of `Sub` *SubName*…`End Sub` or `Function` *FnName*…`End Function` lines with no intervening code. Access automatically creates stubs for subprocedures for event-handling code stored in `Form` and `Report` objects. Stubs block out the procedures required by the application that can be called by the main program. The intervening code statements are filled in during the programming process.

subform   An Access form contained within another form, which commonly has a link to the data source for the parent form.

subnet mask   A local bit mask (set of flags) that specifies which bits of the IP address specify a particular IP network or a host within a subnetwork. An IP address of `128.66.12.1` with a subnet mask of `255.255.255.0` specifies host 1 on subnet `128.66.12.0`. The subnet mask determines the maximum number of hosts on a subnetwork.

subprocedure   A procedure called by a procedure other than the main procedure (`WinMain` in Windows). In Access, all procedures except functions are subprocedures because Msaccess.exe implements the `WinMain` function.

subquery   An SQL `SELECT` statement that's included (nested) within another `SELECT`, `INSERT`, `UPDATE`, or `DELETE` statement or nested within another subquery.

subreport   An Access report contained within another report.

syntax   The set of rules governing the expression of a language, often called *grammar*. As with English, Spanish, Esperanto, or Swahili, programming languages each have their own syntax. Some languages allow much more latitude (irregular forms) in their syntax. VBA has a relatively rigid syntax, whereas C provides more flexibility at the expense of complexity. The syntax of SQL is defined by ANSI, but most RDBMS vendors add proprietary extensions to SQL. See also *ANSI*.

system administrator The individual(s) responsible for the administrative functions for all applications on a LAN or users of a UNIX cluster or network, usually including supervision of all databases on servers attached to the LAN. If the system administrator's (sa's) responsibility is limited to databases, the term *database administrator (DBA)* is ordinarily assigned.

system databases Databases that control access to databases on a server or across a LAN. Microsoft SQL Server has four system databases: the master database (which controls user databases), tempdb (which holds temporary tables), msdbdata (for data relating to management tasks), and model (which is used as the skeleton to create new user databases). Any database that's not a user database is a system database.

system function Functions that return data about the database (metadata) rather than from the content of the database.

system object An object defined by Access rather than by the user. Examples of Access system objects are the `Application`, **`Screen`**, and **`Debug`** objects.

system table A data dictionary table that maintains information on users of the database manager and each database under the control by the system. Access system tables carry the prefix MSys and are hidden.

tab order The order in which the focus is assigned to multiple control objects within a form or dialog with successive pressings of the Tab key.

table A database object consisting of a group of records (rows) divided into fields (columns) that contain data or Null values. A table, which also is called a *relation*, is treated as a database object.

text file A disk file containing characters with values ordinarily ranging from `Chr(1)` through `Chr(127)` in which lines of text are separated from one another with newline pairs (`Chr(13)` **&** `Chr(10)`).

theta join An SQL `JOIN` operation that uses comparison or relational operators in the `JOIN` statement. See also *operator*.

third normal form The rule for relational databases which imposes the requirement that a column that's not a key column can't depend on another column that's not a key column. The third normal form is generally considered the most important because it's the first in the series that isn't intuitive.

three-tier The architecture of a database application, usually involving a client/server RDBMS, where the front-end application is separated from the back-end RDBMS by a middle-tier application. In Access applications, the middle tier usually is implemented as an ActiveX (Automation) component, which implements the database connection, enforces business rules, and handles transfer of data to and from databases of the RDBMS. See also *business rules*.

time stamp The date and time data attributes applied to a disk file when created or edited. SQL Server supports the `timestamp` field data type to resolve concurrency issues when updating tables.

timer   A native Access form property that's invisible in Run mode and used to trigger a `Timer` event at preselected intervals.

TM   An abbreviation for *transaction monitor*, an application that manages database transactions, usually between more than one database, to ensure data consistency during `INSERT` and `UPDATE` operations. See also *MTS*.

toggle   A property of an object, such as a check box, that alternates its state when repeatedly clicked or activated by a shortcut key combination.

transaction   A group of processing steps that are treated as a single activity to perform a desired result. A transaction might entail all the steps necessary to modify the values in or add records to each table involved when a new invoice is created. RDBMSs that can process transactions must include the capability to cancel a transaction by a rollback instruction or to cause it to become a permanent part of the tables with the `COMMIT` or `COMMIT TRANSACTION` statement. See also *rollback*.

transaction monitor   A synonym for *transaction manager*. See also *TM*.

Transact-SQL   A superset of ANSI SQL-92 used by Microsoft SQL Server. Transact-SQL (T-SQL) includes flow-control instructions and the capability to define and use stored procedures that include conditional execution and looping.

trigger   A stored procedure that executes automatically when a user or query executes an instruction that might affect the referential integrity of a database. Triggers usually occur before the execution of `INSERT`, `DELETE`, or `UPDATE` statements so that the effect of the statement on referential integrity can be examined by a stored procedure before execution. See also *stored procedure*.

twip   The smallest unit of measurement in Windows and the default unit of measurement of VBA. The twip is 1/20 of a point, or 1/1440 of a logical inch.

two-phase commit   A process applicable to updates to multiple (distributed) databases that prevents a transaction from completing until all the distributed databases acknowledge that the transaction can be completed. The replication process has supplanted two-phase commit in most of today's distributed client/server RDBMSs. See also *replication*.

type   See *data type*.

type library   A file with the extension .tlb that provides information about the types of objects exposed by an ActiveX component or Automation server. See also *object library*.

unary   See *operator*.

UNC   An abbreviation for Uniform Naming Convention, the method of identifying the location of files on a remote server. UNC names begin with \\ and take the form *ServerName**ShareName**FolderName**FileName.Ext*. All 32-bit Windows applications support UNC.

A

Unicode   A replacement for the 7- or 8-bit ASCII and ANSI representations of characters with a 16-bit model that allows a wider variety of characters to be used. Windows Me/98 and Windows XP/2000+/NT support Unicode. Access 95 and later support Unicode data.

unique index   An index in which no two key fields or combinations of key fields on which the index is created can have the same value.

Universal Data Access   Microsoft's all-encompassing database strategy based on COM, DCOM, OLE DB, ADO, MTS, Internet Information Services, ASP, and other proprietary Windows technologies. Data Access Objects (DAO) are *not* members of the Universal Data Access technology. See also *ADO*, *ASP*, *COM*, *DAO*, *DCOM*, *MTS*, and *OLE DB*.

update   A permanent change to data values in one or more data tables. An update occurs when the `INSERT`, `DELETE`, `UPDATE`, or `TRUNCATE TABLE` SQL commands are executed.

user defined   A data type, also called a *record*, that's specified in your VBA source code by a `Type…End Type` declaration statement in the Declarations section of a module. The elements of the user-defined record type can be any data type valid for the language and can include other user-defined types.

user-defined transaction   A group of instructions combined under a single name and executed as a block when the name is invoked in a statement executed by the user.

validation   The process of determining whether an update to a value in a table's data cell is within a preestablished range or is a member of a set of allowable values. Validation rules establish the range or set of allowable values. Access 2+ supports validation rules at the field and table levels.

variable   The name given to a symbol that represents or substitutes for a number (numeric), letter, or combination of letters (string).

VBA   An abbreviation for Visual Basic for Applications, the official name of which is Visual Basic, Applications Edition. VBA is Microsoft's common application programming (macro) language for members of Microsoft Office and Visual Basic 6.0. Each application has its own "flavor" of VBA as a result of automatically created references to the application's object hierarchy in VBA code.

VDT   An abbreviation for Visual Data Tools, which comprises the Query Designer and Database Designer for SQL Server. VDT (commonly called the *da Vinci toolset*) lets you create views, modify data structures, and add tables to Microsoft SQL Server databases. Access Data Projects use a subset of the VDT to create new tables, modify table structure, and add data to tables.

view   The method by which data is presented for review by users, usually onscreen, or supplied to intermediary applications. Views can be created from subsets of columns from one or more tables by implementing the SQL `CREATE VIEW` instruction. An Access or Jet select query is equivalent to an SQL Server view.

Visual Basic for Applications   See *VBA*.

Visual Data Tools   See *VDT*.

Visual Studio Tools for Office   See *VSTO.*

VSTO   An abbreviation for Visual Studio Tools for Office 2005, which enables substituting .NET code (primarily Visual Basic .NET or Visual C#) in .NET assemblies for embedded VBA code in Excel, Word, Outlook, and InfoPath 2003. The next version of VSTO (code-named *v3* when this book was written) will support the new ribbon UI and add-ins for Access, Excel, SharePoint Designer, InfoPath, Outlook, PowerPoint, Project, Publisher, Visio, and Word 2007. VSTO v3 will require the next version of Visual Studio (code-named *Orcas*), which will release about 6 to 9 months after Office 2007.

 W3C   An abbreviation for the World Wide Web Consortium, which "develops interoperable technologies (specifications, guidelines, software, and tools) to lead the Web to its full potential." W3C's home page is at http://www.w3.org/.

 Web Services Interoperability Organization   A vendor-supported consortium (WS-I.org) dedicated to developing recommendations to make web services created by different SOAP toolkits and hosted by common application servers interoperate with one another. Go to http://www.ws-i.org for additional information about WS-I's activities.

Web services   See *XML web services.*

Web Services Reference   See *WSR.*

wildcard   A character that substitutes for and allows a match by any character or set of characters in its place. The DOS ? and * wildcards are used in Jet expressions; SQL uses _ and % as wildcards.

Windows SharePoint Services   See *WSS.*

 WSDL   An acronym (pronounced *wizdle*) for Web Service Description Language, an XML dialect that describes the capabilities, data structure, and location of an XML web service. Like SOAP 1.1, WSDL 1.1 isn't a W3C standard; the WSDL 1.1 W3C Note of March 15, 2001, is at http://www.w3.org/TR/wsdl. The current version of the W3C specification for WSDL 1.2 is at http://www.w3.org/TR/wsdl12/.

WSR   An abbreviation for the Web Services Reference 2.0 tool, a COM add-in for the VBA Editor that's installed by the Office Web Services Toolkit. WSR uses an XML web service's WSDL 1.1 file to generate the VBA code for an XML web service proxy. WSR simplifies the VBA code for enabling an Access application to consume an XML web service. See *SOAP toolkit, WSR,* and *XML web services.*

WSS   An abbreviation for Windows SharePoint Services, a browser-based collaboration application that's a component of Windows Server 2003 but is delivered separately as a web-based download. WSS is the foundation for Microsoft Office SharePoint Server 2007. WSS usually runs on an organization's intranet, but is the engine that runs the Microsoft Office Live Collaboration service. When this book was written, WSS 3.0 was the current version; WSS 3.0 requires .NET Framework versions 2.0 and 3.0 and the Windows Workflow Foundation for installation. Access 2007 can import, export, or link to WSS Lists, and share .accdb or .accde files from WSS document libraries. See also *MOSS.*

xBase   Any language interpreter or compiler or a database manager built on the dBASE III+ model and incorporating all dBASE III+ commands and functions. Microsoft's Visual FoxPro and Computer Associates' CA-Clipper are xBase dialects.

XDocs   The codename for Microsoft InfoPath during its beta period. See *InfoPath*.

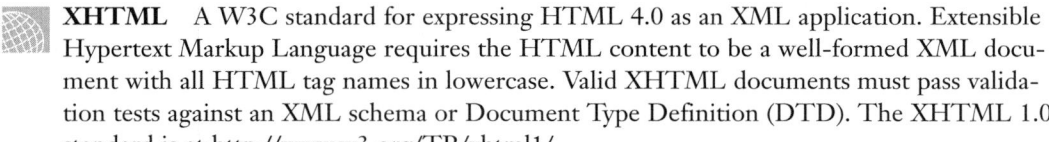 **XHTML**   A W3C standard for expressing HTML 4.0 as an XML application. Extensible Hypertext Markup Language requires the HTML content to be a well-formed XML document with all HTML tag names in lowercase. Valid XHTML documents must pass validation tests against an XML schema or Document Type Definition (DTD). The XHTML 1.0 standard is at http://www.w3.org/TR/xhtml1/.

XML Infoset   A W3C standard for XML Information Set, a set of definitions for 11 different types of information items—and their properties—that can make up a conforming XML document. All but three information items (Document, Element, and Namespace) are optional. Adherence to XML Infoset definitions is especially important for authoring data-related XML documents that interoperate with multiple XML parsers and schema validators. XML documents exported by Access conform to the XML Infoset definitions. W3C's XML Information Set recommendation is at http://www.w3.org/TR/xml-infoset/.

 XML   An abbreviation for Extensible Markup Language, a derivative of SGML (Standardized General Markup Language) that permits definition of custom markup tags. XML is especially useful for displaying and manipulating data when using the Internet HTTP protocol. XML documents carry an .xml extension. Data-related variations of XML include XML Query and XML Schema. The World Wide Web Consortium (W3C, http://www.w3.org/) maintains the XML standards, called recommendations. The second edition of the XML 1.0 standard (October 6, 2000) is at http://www.w3.org/TR/REC-xml.

 **XML Schema**   A standardized XML document type (xsd XML namespace) for describing the structure of documents and data. Most XML schema documents have an .xsd extension. XML Schema was a W3C candidate recommendation when this books was written. Access 2003's XML import/export features use the XSD namespace; some SQL Server 2000 XML features use XDR. A primer for XML Schema, which uses a purchase order as the model, is available at http://www.w3.org/TR/xmlschema-0/.

XML web services   Software components that reside on web servers and use SOAP as the protocol and XML as the message format to communicate with one another—usually by HTTP or secure HTTP (HTTPS)—through corporate and personal firewalls. Microsoft uses the XML prefix to distinguish SOAP-based web services from conventional web-based services, such as search engines, portals, and e-commerce. W3C's Web Services Activity (http://www.w3.org/2002/ws/) coordinates development of basic XML web services specifications. See also *SOAP*, *WSDL*, and *XML*.

 XSL   An abbreviation for Extensible Stylesheet Language, which specifies how the contents of an XML document are formatted for presentation to the user with XML Formatting Objects. XSL documents use the .xsl extension. The October 15, 2001, XSL 1.0 recommendation is at http://www.w3.org/TR/xsl/.

XSLT   An abbreviation for XSL Transformations, part of the XSL standard but maintained by a different W3C working group (WG). XSLT is a language for transforming an XML document into other XML documents or XHTML pages. XSLT documents also use the .xsl extension. Access 2003 makes extensive use of XSLT in conjunction with the use of ReportML for exporting Access application objects to XML/XSL files and DAP. The W3C recommendation for XSLT 1.0 (November 16, 1999) is at http://www.w3.org/TR/xslt/. A working draft of XSLT 1.1 and a requirements document for XSLT 2.0 also are available from the W3C website. See also *ReportML*.

Yes/No field   A field of a table whose allowable values are Yes (True) or No (False). Yes/No fields were called logical or Boolean fields by Access 95 and earlier.

A

INDEX

How can we make this index more useful? Email us at indexes@quepublishing.com

testing, 283-285

troubleshooting, 285

data verification, data validation versus, 287

data visualization, PivotTables and PivotCharts, 547-548

data-centric collaboration, 1143-1144

data-related XML, advantages of learning, 1089-1090

data-type conversion functions, 421, 432-433

database compatibility levels, changing, 1350-1351

database connectivity, upgrades and, 1353

Database Design for Mere Mortals (Hernandez), 199

database diagrams, 873, 901-902

Database Diagrams page (Database window), 873

Database Documenter, 259-262

database engine. *See* Access database engine

Database object, 73, 1182

database objects

pointing to, 1188

properties

as variables, 1187-1189

With…End With structure, 1188-1189

renaming, 245

VBA data types, 1181-1182

database owner

changing, 1350-1351

defined, 198

database roles, 853-854

Database Splitter, 163, 813-816

Database to Convert From dialog, 1339

Database Tools ribbon, 27-28

Database Utilities (Tools menu), 162-163

Backup SQL Database, 902, 904

Compact and Repair Database, 163

Convert Database, 164

Copy Database File, 907

Make ADE File, 909

Make MDE File, 164-165, 863

Restore SQL Database, 904-905

Transfer Database, 840

Database window for ADP, 873-874

databases. *See also* Access databases; applications; Jet databases; RDBMSs; SQL Server databases

.accde files, creating, 164-165

.accdr files, creating, 165

add-ins, 204

backing up, 902-905

compacting, 163-164, 170

connections

remote SQL Server databases, 907-908

troubleshooting, 909

converting, 164

to Access 2002 format, 164

compile errors, 170

secured Access 9x files, 1341-1342

troubleshooting, 170

unsecured Access 9x files, 1335-1339

corrupted databases, 164

creating, 204-206

from Office Online templates, 1131-1137

from SharePoint 2007, 1106

current database, 516

default location, 120

designing, importance of customer input, 263

distributed databases, 177

documentation, creating data dictionaries, 259-262

external databases

defined, 516

queries against, 516-518

hierarchical databases, 177

history of, 177-180

legacy databases

converting fields to Access data types, 356-358

images in, 354-356

importing, 345-350

linking with ODBC, 350-354

troubleshooting importing, 371-372

linking, 180

network databases, 177

Northwind sample database, 225

adding tables, 230-233

designing tables, 226-230

preparing to add tables, 225-226

opening, 118-120

publishing to SharePoint 2007, 1105-1110, 1131-1134

customizing SharePoint lists, 1134-1135

synchronizing SharePoint lists, 1135-1137

record-locking information files, 203

relational databases, 178. *See also* data validation; entity integrity; normalization; primary keys; referential integrity; transactions

books for more information, 199

structure of, 181-185

remote SQL Server databases, connecting to, 907-909

repairing, 164

spreadsheets versus, 176

tables, modifying in other databases, 940, 942

E

E-mail command button (Office gallery), 39

E-Mail List macro, 77

EB (Embedded Basic), 1209

Echo method, 1225

Edit method (Recordset object), 1325

Edit Relationships dialog, 239, 457-458

editing. *See also* **customizing; updating**
fields, 244-245
changing data types, 246-247
rearranging fields, 245-246
form controls, disabling, 620
graph design, 778-780
mailing labels, 738-741
queries in PivotTables, 528-530
relationships, 244-248
report controls, 719-722
RibbonX documents
with Visual Studio 2005, 1230-1231
with XMLNotepad 2007, 1231-1233
tables with InfoPath forms, 1084-1087
text, keyboard operations for, 270
text controls, 606-607
user information (WSS 3.0), 1103-1105

Editing group (Advanced page), 150

EditMode property (Recordset object), 1314, 1317

element-centric XML documents, 1059

elements (XML), 1057
adding to exported tables/queries, 1069-1070

email attachments, reports as, 765-766

email data collection
with HTML forms, 101, 1043-1050
with InfoPath forms, 1081-1082
creating forms, 1082-1084
editing table data, 1084-1087

email messages, creating with SendObject macro, 96-100

Embedded Basic (EB), 1209

embedded macros. *See* **macros**

embedding
charts, 321
image files, linking versus, 356

Employees table (Northwind sample database), 225-226

empty subtype, Null subtype versus, 425

enabling
object dependencies, 248-250
SSX connections through Windows Firewall, 67-68
unsafe macros, 42

encapsulating VBA code, 1212-1213

End Sub reserved words, 1177

EndOfRecordset event (Recordset object), 1327

Enter Parameter Value dialog, 404, 945
troubleshooting, 518

entering data. *See* **data entry**

entities, replacing illegal characters with, 1066

entity integrity, 193. *See also* **data validation**

***Envisioning Information* (Tufte), 548**

EOF property (Recordset object), 1314

equal sign (=)
assignment operator, 415
equal to operator, 416

equal to operator, 416

equi-joins. *See* **inner joins**

Err object, 1199

Error Checking group (Object Designers page), 149

error checking smart tags, 651-652

error correction (forms), 651-652

Error event, 1200

error events, 1152-1153

error handling. *See also* **troubleshooting**
macros, 56, 1157-1158
runtime errors (VBA)
Err object, 1199
Error event, 1200
On Error... statement, 1198-1199

error messages, upsizing process, 953. *See also* **troubleshooting**

Error objects, 1297-1300

error prevention. See **data validation; entity integrity; referential integrity; transactions**

Error statement, 1199

Errors collection, 1297-1300

errors in Upsizing Wizard, correcting, 957-959

Errors property (Connection object), 1294

Esc key, 143

escape characters, 224

ETC (evil type coercion), 424

group sections (reports), 702, 746-747
by alphabetic code characters, 749
by date/time, 751
by numeric value, 748-749
preventing widowed records, 733-734
by ranges of values, 750-751
sorting, 709, 751-752
by using subgroups, 749

Group, Sort, and Total pane, 746-749

GROUPBY clause (SQL), 385
aggregate functions, 924-925

grouped reports, creating with Report Wizard, 704-712

grouping form/report controls, 55

groups of records, blocks of cells versus, 275

groups/totals reports, 703

GUIDs (Globally Unique Identifiers), 182, 217

H

harmful code, 40

Harris, Jensen, 171

hashing, 318

HasModule property, 1176

HAVING clause (SQL), 442
aggregate functions, 924-925

headers
creating forms with, 643-644
defined, 345
form headers
adding, 694-695
background colors, 600-601
labels, adding, 644-646
properties, 635
sizing, 636

group headers, 702
adding, 762
deleting, 762-763
page breaks, 763
HTML table headers, 1069-1070
page headers, 702
adding, 762
deleting, 762-763
printing, 763
report headers, 702
adding, 762
deleting, 762-763
disabling printing, 731
XML document headers, 1057

heads-down data entry. *See* data entry
Datasheet view versus, 286
defined, 194

Help system. *See also* online help
Help task pane, 158
for macros, 1149
for VBA, 422-424, 1202-1203

HelpContext property (Error object), 1299

HelpFile property (Error object), 1299

hidden indexes, 243

hidden tables, Upsizing Wizard and, 829

hiding
fields, 314
prebuilt categories (Navigation pane), 46

hierarchical databases, 177

history
of computer-based sorting and searching, 317
of databases, 177-180
of Microsoft support for HTML, 1051-1053
of Microsoft support for XML, 1052-1053
of programming languages for macros, 1208-1210

Hobson's choice, 807

Hollerith, Herman, 177

Home Inventory template, 78

Home ribbon, 25-26, 127-128
command buttons, 128-131

host variables, 919

Hour function, 427

Hourglass method, 1225

HRActions table (Northwind sample database)
adding, 230-233
designing, 226-227
assigning field names, 228-229
assigning field properties, 229-230
information to include, 227-228
importing, 267
records, adding, 281-283

.htm files, default location, 120

HTML (Hypertext Markup Language), 1006
creating by exporting tables/queries as XML, 1060-1067
dynamic tables, displaying with ASP, 1037-1043
exporting
reports to, troubleshooting, 1087-1088
tables to, 1024-1026, 1060-1062
formatting tables, 1067-1070
forms
creating, 1043-1050
in Outlook, 101
history of Microsoft support for, 1051-1053
Internet Explorer 7 (IE 7), troubleshooting, 1088
lists, importing, 1017-1020
standards, 1006
templates, 1029-1031

master/child forms, 584-585
Tab Order dialog, 590
reports, 53-54, 712
Report Layout Tools – Arrange ribbon, 714-715
Report Layout Tools – Format ribbon, 712-713
Report Layout Tools – Page Setup ribbon, 714

LCase function, 429

.ldb files, 203

Left function, 429

left outer joins, 928
creating, 484-486

legacy database files
importing, 345-348
converting fields to Access data types, 356-358
images, 354-356
ISAM tables, 348-350
troubleshooting, 371-372
linking with ODBC, 350-354

legal issues, importing HTML tables, 1006

legends
in PivotCharts, 541
reversing with x-axis, 807

Len function, 429

Lending Library template, 77

Length property (Table Design window), 876

less than operator (<), 416

less than or equal to operator (<=), 416

Leszynski Naming Conventions for Access, 1175

level of detail in PivotTable fields, increasing, 533-534

libraries. See also add-ins
missing libraries, troubleshooting, 1352
references, 1178-1179

licensing
Microsoft Small Business Server (SBS), 911
MSDE, 870
Software Assurance and Licensing terms, 1209
SQL Server, 870-871

lifetime of VBA variables, 1185. See also duration

Like expressions, date constraints in, 949

Like operator, 418-419

line graphs, 770
adding to reports, 784-787
changing graph type, 780, 782, 784
creating
with Chart Wizard, 773-778
from crosstab queries, 788-792, 794
modifying design, 778-780
query data source
Chart Wizard, 770-773
crosstab queries, 788, 790

line graphs. See graphs

line spacing in report sections, 729-731

line-item sources, 770

Link Child Fields table property, 208

link connection string, changing, 840-842

link expression errors, troubleshooting reports, 766

Link Master Fields table property, 209

Link Spreadsheet Wizard, 330

Link Tables dialog, 352

linked charts in static tables, 985-986

linked graphs, 788
assigning crosstab queries, 790
creating from crosstab queries, 788-794
defined, 773

designing crosstab queries, 788-789
linking to records, 790-792, 794

linked PivotCharts
cloning, 801-803
creating, 801
formatting, 803-804
persisting properties in, 804-805

linked servers, 868

Linked Table Manager, 162, 358-359, 839

linked tables, troubleshooting queries with, 518

linking
charts, 321
client/server databases manually, 843
attaching exported tables, 847-849
creating ODBC data source, 843-846
exporting table data to RDBMS, 846-847
databases, 180
HTML documents to CSS files, 1036
to HTML tables, 1017
image files, embedding versus, 356
importance of, 320
ISAM tables, 348-350
legacy databases
converting fields to Access data types, 356-358
images in, 354-356
Outlook 2007 files to Access tables, 335-337
PivotCharts, 801
cloning linked forms/subforms, 801-803
persisting linked properties, 804-805
setting linked properties, 1243-1246
SharePoint 2007 lists, 1106, 1140-1141

For...Next statement, 1195-1196

While...Wend loop, 1197

Lotus 1-2-3, importing Lotus spreadsheet files, 96

LTrim function, 429

M

Macro Builder, 1149

macro commands, 72

Macro-to-VBA Converter, class modules

creating, 1213-1215

debugging, 1217-1219

testing, 1215-1219

macros, 57, 72, 117-118, 1208-1209

actions

Close, 1151

definition of, 1148

OpenQuery, 1151

RunCommand, 1151

viewing, 1149-1151

advantages/disadvantages, 1151, 1169

ApplyFilter, 1161, 1163-1164

arguments, 1148-1149

AutoExec, 1148

compared to VBA, 1151

converting to VBA callback functions, 1234-1237

definition of, 1148

embedded macros, 72

in templates, 77

error handling, 1157-1158

events

data events, 1153

Dirty, 1154

error events, 1153

event properties, 1154

filter events, 1153

focus events, 1153

keyboard events, 1153

mouse events, 1152

print events, 1153

reference events, 1153

responding from combo and list boxes, 1159-1161

timing events, 1153

types of, 1152

window events, 1153

generating with Command Button Wizard, 1155, 1157-1159

application actions, 1159

form operations actions, 1159

Previous Record button, 1155-1157

record navigation actions, 1158

record operations actions, 1159

report operations actions, 1159

history of programming languages for, 1208-1210

Macro Builder, 1149

macros behind forms, 1149

macrosheets, 1149

new features, 23, 56-57

online help, 1149

opening forms/reports, 91-93

role of, 1148

SendObject macro, creating e-mail messages, 96-100

Switchboard Manager, 1164-1168

in templates, 77

troubleshooting, 1168

unsafe macros, enabling, 42

VBA versus, 1172

macrosheets, 1149

Mail Merge Recipients dialog, 363

Mail Merge Wizard, 359-360

form letters

creating, 360-365

merging with different data sources, 365-367

mailing labels, 703

creating with Label Wizard, 734-737

editing, 738-741

printing multicolumn reports as, 734-741

mainframe computers, 177

Make MDE File command, 163, 165, 863

Make Table dialog, 402, 553

make-table queries, 401, 551. *See also* action queries

converting SELECT queries to, 553-555

creating, 402-404

defined, 550

designing SELECT query for, 551-553

final steps in example, 556-557

parameters, adding, 404-405

primary-key fields, adding, 895

relationships, establishing, 555-556

syntax, 936

make-table stored procedures, 894-896

Manage command button (Office gallery), 38

management tools, Access versus SQL Server, 910-911

manually linking client/server databases, 843

attaching exported tables, 847-849

creating ODBC data source, 843-846

exporting table data to RDBMS, 846-847

many-to-many relationships, 183

with lookup fields, 104-106

queries, creating from, 459-463

Map Custom Fields dialog, 333

margins

for form/report controls, 56

reports, 731-732

Marketing Projects template, 76

markup tags (HTML)

defined, 1006

for lists, 1017

for tables, 1007-1008

N

Y